Collins

Collins
English-
Japanese
Dictionary

Collins

Collins
English-
Japanese
Dictionary

HarperCollins Publishers
Westerhill Road
Bishopbriggs
Glasgow G64 2QT
Great Britain

First Edition 1993
First published in this format 2010

Previously published as Collins Express
English–Japanese Dictionary
© HarperCollins Publishers 2005, 2006

Reprint 10 9 8 7 6 5 4 3 2 1 0

© HarperCollins Publishers &
Shubun International Co., Ltd 1993

ISBN 978-0-00-741410-9

www.collinslanguage.com

A catalogue record for this book is
available from the British Library

Typeset by Tosho Printing Co., Ltd

Printed in Great Britain by
Clays Ltd, St Ives plc

Acknowledgements
We would like to thank those authors and
publishers who kindly gave permission
for copyright material to be used in the
Collins Word Web. We would also like to
thank Times Newspapers Ltd for
providing valuable data.

ORIGINAL MATERIAL BY
CollinsBilingual

JAPANESE LANGUAGE EDITION
Richard C. Goris
Yukimi Okubo

EDITORIAL ADMINISTRATION
Jill Campbell

CONTENTS

Authors' Foreword

Dictionary compilers have been labeled "harmless drudges", but we have found little drudgery in compiling the Collins-Shubun English-Japanese Dictionary. On the contrary, we have experienced great pleasure in rising to the challenge of producing a book that was not run-of-the-mill.

To begin with, we had several advantages. We had the dictionary framework provided in electronic form by Collins Dictionary Division. Then we had computers running powerful Japanese word processing software. Together these factors saved us from the drudgery (and writer's cramp) caused by writing thousands and thousands of manuscript pages by hand. They also eliminated the drudgery of correcting in proof the innumerable mistakes introduced by typesetters misinterpreting our handwriting.

The challenge of producing "a better mousetrap" also provided motivation that eliminated drudgery.

In order to keep the dictionary truly pocket-sized, we aimed at providing one translation for each word, or for each meaning of a word. Where several possible translations existed, we chose the one with the highest frequency of usage in modern Japanese. We also tried to give translations that were the cultural equivalent of the English. Thus, if the English word conveyed a sense of dignity, we used a dignified Japanese expression; if the English was a slangy word, we provided a slangy Japanese word or phrase. Where this was not possible, we have provided glosses to clarify the difference.

There were some exceptions. When the English word had several Japanese equivalents, each used with equal frequency, and generally interchangeable, we gave the two or three most frequent, separated by commas.

In this category fell words that could be expressed either by a Chinese compound (2 or more Chinese characters used as a single word) or by a purely Japanese word. There were also words that could be expressed by a Japanese translation or a "Japanized" foreign loan word of equal frequency. In this case we gave the Japanese translation first, followed by a comma and the loan word. Where the Japanese translation existed, but was outlandish and seldom used, we gave only the loan word. In such cases the loan word is generally listed as a headword in standard Japanese dictionaries.

Finally, we discussed every entry thoroughly before adopting it. Thus we feel we

have met our goal of providing a small, portable, but extremely useful dictionary - useful to the language student and the native speaker alike.

Our efforts would have been futile without the support, aid, and counsel of the editorial staff of Collins Dictionaries and Shubun. Shubun's board of experts and editors included Kazuo Shibuya, Shiruki Furukawa, Ari Matsue, and Kazuko Namiki. On the other side of the ocean we had in particular the aid of Lorna Sinclair-Knight, Jeremy Butterfield, and the hard-working Jill Campbell, in addition to other anonymous advisors.

To all and sundry, a handshake and a deep bow of gratitude.

Richard C. Goris
Yukimi Okubo

著 者 前 書

辞書を書く人というと「ひたすらこつこつ働く，人畜無害な凡人」と見る向きもあるが，当の私達はコリンズ・秀文英和辞典を書くに際し，ことさら単調な仕事を余儀なくされたという感じは全く覚えなかった．平凡でない辞書を作ろうというチャレンジに答えることにむしろ大きな喜びを感じた．

第一に苦労を軽減する要素がいくつかあった．まずコリンズ社の辞書部門よりコービルドのデータベースから頻度によって抽出され，フォーマット化されたた語彙リストのフロッピーディスクが提供された．これを強力な日本語ワープロソフトでコンピュータ操作し，日本語訳等を入力した．こうして何千枚もの原稿を手書きする苦労（と書痙の危険）を避けられ，同時に植字段階で起こるエラーを校正で直す苦労も避けることができた．

第二に，「より優れたもの」を作るというチャレンジも作業の単調さを吹き飛ばす動機にもなった．

当書をポケット版の限度内に抑えるためには，原則として一見出し語に対して，あるいは見出し語の一意味に対して一つだけの訳語をつけることにした．複数の訳語が可能な場合，最も頻度の高いものを選んだ．また，英語の語彙に対して文化的に同じ含みの訳語を選ぶように努力した．例えば，英単語が格調の高い語であれば，格調の高い日本語訳をつけた．一方，俗語のような英語に対してはそれに相当する日本語の俗語をつけた．これが不可能な場合，補足説明をつけた．

いくつか例外がある．複数の日本語訳が可能で，頻度が同じぐらいらいで置き換えもきく場合，二つか三つを併記してコンマで分けた．こういう語には漢語的表現またはやまとことばに訳せる語が多かった．その他に純粋な日本語もしくは外来語で表せる語もあった．その場合，日本語と外来語を併記してコンマで分けた．しかし日本語訳がおかしかったり頻度が低かったりする場合，外来語だけを記載した．この様な外来語はたいがい国語辞典で見出し語として使われている．

熟考と討論を重ねて最後に訳語を選択した．こうして小型でポケット版であるにもかかわらず，language student，native speaker 双方に大いに役立つ画期的な辞典の作成に成功したと確信する．

コリンズ社辞典編集部門及び秀文インターナショナルの編集スタッフの支援と助言なしには私達の努力だけではこの辞書を作れなかったと思う．秀文側にあっては特に渋谷一夫，古川知己，松江亜里，並木和子，そして海の向こうにあっては Lorna Sinclair-Knight，Jeremy Butterfield，Jill Campbell，その他の皆さん方に深く感謝の意を表する．

R. C. ゴリス

大久保　雪美

PUBLISHER'S FOREWORD

As the 21st century approaches and the countries of the world become more inter-nationalized, the importance of English as a world language is felt ever more keenly by society. This awareness spotlights certain problems concerning the bilingual dictionaries, particularly English-Japanese dictionaries, published in Japan.

To begin with, there is the habit of crowding into each entry, without rhyme or reason, all the possible translations of a headword that can be thought of, a habit that has persisted since the Meiji Era.

Secondly, in a great many cases, scientific data on the use of words and phrases is very scarce, making it extremely difficult to improve on the present situation.

Dictionary users are becoming increasingly dissatisfied with the growing volume of unsorted data that is being thrust at them. Things have reached a point where the dictionary makers appear to have lost touch with the needs of their users.

What the users really want is well-ordered data, that is, clear, uncluttered informa-tion on the meaning of the words of a language. They need fundamental informa-tion on actual usage of the words of a language, information on situation and context in which a word or phrase is used, information on what normally comes before or after various words and phrases. This in turn requires a wealth of background information about the actual state of a language. Fortunately, we have been able to join forces with HarperCollins Publishers of Britain, who have at their disposal the largest data bank in the world of the English language. This data bank fur-nished us with, among other things, information on word frequency, which guided the choice of headwords; and information on situation, context, variation in meaning etc, which is shown in parentheses (the "indicators") in each entry. The result has been the revolutionary dictionary that we present here, for use throughout the world, in preparation for the 21st century, a truly original publication.

Instead of being laboriously typeset from a hand-written manuscript, the dictionary was composed entirely on a computer in a form that permitted electronic typesetting machines to transform the data directly into the printed page. Throughout the project the authors maintained constant, real-time contact with the editorial staff of Collins Dictionary Division through electronic mail and other modern means.

All Japanese entries in the main text have their pronunciation indicated in romaji, so that anyone anywhere in the world can use this dictionary to study Japanese through the medium of English.

At the same time Japanese users of the dictionary, even if already proficient in English, can gain confidence in their use of the language by noting the information about usage given in the parenthetical "indicators" in each entry.

Shubun International, Ltd.

出版する立場から

21世紀の幕開けが近づく一方、さらに国際化が一層進展し世界語としての英語の重要性がますます高まっているのが昨今の社会情勢と言えましょう。このような背景を踏まえ、我が国の外国語特に英和辞典の将来を考えてみるといくつかの問題点がはっきりしてくる。

まず第一に明治以来の伝統に従って狭い紙面に未整理のままと言ってよい程の訳語という名称の語義の網羅振りが指摘できよう。

第二に多くの場合、言語使用に付いて科学的データに乏しく、思い切った革新の道を拓くことが極めて困難といった状況が指摘できましょう。

肥大化する情報量に辞典使用者もうんざりの感さえするのである。使用者が何を求めているのか図りかねているのが現状とも言える状況である。

辞典使用者は小気味よく整理された情報の提供、すなわち今や簡潔・明解な言語の意味を求めている。ある言語の意味とは、ある語（句）がどのような場面・文脈・前後関係の中で何を伝達しようとしているのか示すことであり、かつ最も基本的なことである。このためには当該言語使用の実態について豊富なデータが必要となる。幸いなことに今日世界最大規模のdata bank of the English languageを活用する英国ハーパーコリンズ社と提携、使用頻度及び語句の意味の使用範囲「indicators」のデータを駆使した21世紀を指向した世界で使える画期的な英和辞典の完成をここに見る運びと相成った次第である。これこそ独創の知的生産物財産とも言うべきかなである。

原稿執筆も従来のような組み上げられた順序ではなく項目単位と言うべき方式で完全にコンピュータ化完成され、原稿執筆終了即組版完了ともなった点は画期的な技術革新の成果でもあった。電子時代の申し子でもある電子メール等最新の技術によりコリンズ社辞典編集部門と執筆のデスクが結ばれ、リアルタイムに意志伝達が行われたのである。

このように完成された本辞典は、日本語全てにローマ字による発音表記を付し、世界の何処にあっても英語を媒介とし日本語の習得を可能ならしめる効果的な内容とした。

また特に我が国の英語既習者の社会人にとって意味使用範囲「indicators」の明示による活用は英語使用に自信を与える英語習得への開眼となると信ずる。

株式会社　秀文インターナショナル

INTRODUCTION

We are delighted you have decided to buy the Collins Shubun Pocket English-Japanese Dictionary and hope you will enjoy and benefit from using it at school, at home, on holiday or at work.

This introduction gives you a few tips on how to get the most out of your dictionary-not simply from its comprehensive wordlist but also from the information provided in each entry.

The Collins Shubun English-Japanese Dictionary begins by listing the abbreviations used in the text and follows with a guide to Japanese pronunciation and a chart of the two Japanese scripts "hiragana" and "katakana" together with the Roman letter transliteration used in this dictionary.

USING YOUR COLLINS SHUBUN POCKET DICTIONARY

A wealth of information is presented in the dictionary, using various typefaces, sizes of type, symbols, abbreviations and brackets. The conventions and symbols used are explained in the following sections.

Headwords

The words you look up in a dictionary -"headwords"- are listed alphabetically. They are printed in bold type for rapid identification. The headwords appearing at the top of each page indicate the first and last word dealt with on the page in question.

Information about the usage or form of certain headwords is given in brackets after the phonetic spelling. This usually appears in abbreviated form (e. g., (*fam*), (COMM).

Common expressions in which the headword appears are shown in bold italic type (e. g., **account**... *of no account*).

When such expressions are preceded by a colon, it means that the headword is used mainly in that particular expression (e. g., **aback**... *adv*: *to be taken aback*).

Phonetic spellings

The phonetic spelling of each headword (indicating its pronunciation) is given in square brackets immediately after the headword (e. g., **able** [ei'bəl]). The phonetics show a standardized US English pronunciation in IPA (International Phonetic Alphabet) symbols. A list of these symbols is given on page (13).

Translations

Headword translations are given in ordinary type and, where more than one meaning

or usage exists, these are separated by a semicolon. You will often find other words in brackets before the translations. These offer suggested contexts in which the headword might appear (e. g., **absentee** (from school, meeting etc) or provide synonyms (e. g. **able** (capable) or (skilled)). A white lozenge precedes a gloss giving information for the non-English native speaker.

"Keywords"

Special status is given to certain English words which are considered as "key" words in the language. They may, for example, occur very frequently or have several types of usage (e. g., **a, be**). A combination of lozenges and numbers helps you to distinguish different parts of speech and different meanings. Further helpful information is provided in brackets.

Grammatical Information

Parts of speech are given in abbreviated form in italics after the phonetic spellings of headwords (e. g., *vt*, *adv*, *conj*) and headwords with several parts of speech have a black lozenge before each new part of speech (e. g., **wash**).

使 用 上 の 注 意

本辞典は英単語の意味を知りたい日本人だけでなく日本語を勉強している外国人も使えるよう，すべての訳語，補足説明などを日本文字とローマ字で併記した．ローマ字は原則としてヘボン式に従い，ローマ字：仮名対照表を (17)－(18) ページに示した．またローマ字には日本語のアクセントも加えた．右上がりのアクセント記号 (á) は声の上がりを，右下がりの記号 (à) は声の下がりを，記号のない場合は平坦に発音する事を示す．

見出し語は太字の立体活字で示した．つづりは米国の標準に従ったが，英国の標準がそれと異なる場合，アルファベット順にこれも示した．

例：**anaemia** [əniːˈmiːə] *etc* (*BRIT*) = **anemia** *etc*

続いて発音を [ ] の中に国際音標文字で示した．発音記号表は (13) ページにある．アクセントは ['] の記号でアクセントのある音節の後に示した．

例：**able** [eiˈbəl]

品詞は斜字の略語で示した．例：**able** [eiˈbəl] *adj*

品詞に続いて訳語を日本語とローマ字で示した．原則として1つの意味に対して1つだけ最も頻度の高い訳語を採用した．

例：**blockade**... 封鎖 fúsa

頻度が同じぐらいで複数の訳語がある場合，これを示すと共にコンマ (，) で分けた．

例：**blood**... 血 chi, 血液 ketsúèki

訳語の前に丸括弧 ( ) の中でその見出し語についての情報を記した．

立体の大文字はその語が使われる「分野」などを示す．

例：**blood**... (BIO) 血 chi, 血液 ketsúèki

すなわち，**blood** は「生物学」という分野の語である．

立体の小文字はその他の情報を示す．

例：**bleat**... *vi* (goat, sheep) 鳴く nakú

すなわち，bleat という動詞はヤギやヒツジについて使う語である．

例：**aperture**... (hole) 穴 aná; (gap) すき間 sukíma; (PHOT) アパーチャ ápàcha

この例では類語を使って見出し語の意味をはっきりさせている．また，このように1つの見出し語に対して複数の意味がある場合，セミコロン (；) で分ける．

見出し語の成句はその都度改行して太字の斜字で示した．

例：**bearing**...

   to take a bearing...

   to find one's bearings...

成句は主語＋動詞形式のものでも文頭の大文字と文尾のピリオドをつけずにあくまでも成句として扱った．ただし疑問を表す成句には？をつけた．

> 例：**anyone**...
> > *anyone could do it*
> > *can you see anyone?*

表示，標識，立て札などに使う成句は「**...**」で囲んだ．

> 例：**entry**...
> > 「*no entry*」...

改行なしで品詞などに続くコロン（：）＋ 太斜字の成句は見出し語などがその成句以外には殆ど使われない事を示す．

> 例：**aback** [əbæk'] *adv*: *to be taken aback* 仰天する gyōten suru

丸括弧の中で *also*: に続く立体太字の語句はその意味では同意語である事を示す．

> 例：**go about** *vi* (*also*: **go around**: rumor) 流れる nagárerù.

ここでは「噂が流れる」という意味では go about でも go around でも使える事を示している．

特殊記号：

◆：最初に示した品詞と品詞が異なったものにつけた．

> 例：**abdicate**... *vt* (responsibility, right) 放棄する ...
> > ◆*vi* (monarch) 退位する ...

◇：補足説明を示す．

／：見出し語，成句の中で置き換えられる部分を示す．日本語訳やローマ字の中でこれを〔 〕で示した．

> 例：**abide**... *vt*: *I can't abide it／him* 私はそれ〔彼〕が大嫌いだ watáku-shi wá soré〔karè〕ga dáīkirai da

KEYWORD: このタイトルは頻度の高い重要な語で特に徹底的に取り扱った見出し語（たとえば **be, can**）を示す．

Phonetic Symbols 発音記号表

[ɑː] *f*ather, *ho*t, *kn*owledge

[æ] *a*t, h*a*ve, c*a*t

[ai] m*y*, b*uy*, l*i*ke

[au] h*ow*, m*ou*th

[e] m*e*n, s*ay*s, fr*ie*nd

[ei] s*ay*, t*a*ke, r*ai*n

[eːr] *air*, c*are*, wh*ere*

[ə] *a*bove, paym*e*nt, lab*e*l

[əːr] g*ir*l, l*ear*n, b*ur*n, w*or*m

[i] s*i*t, wom*e*n, b*u*sy

[iː] s*ee*, b*ea*n, cit*y*

[ou] n*o*, kn*ow*, b*oa*t

[ɔi] b*oy*, b*oi*l

[u] b*oo*k, c*oul*d, p*u*t

[uː] t*oo*l, s*ou*p, bl*ue*

[ɔː] l*aw*, w*al*k, st*o*ry

[ʌ] *u*p, c*u*t, *a*bove

[p] *p*ut, cu*p*

[b] *b*e, ta*b*

[d] *d*own, ha*d*

[t] *t*oo, ho*t*

[k] *c*ome, ba*ck*

[g] *g*o, ta*g*

[s] *s*ee, cup*s*, for*ce*

[z] ro*se*, bu*zz*

[ʃ] *sh*e, *s*ugar

[ʒ] vi*s*ion, plea*s*ure

[tʃ] *ch*urch

[dʒ] *j*am, *g*em, *j*u*dge*

[f] *f*arm, hal*f*, *ph*one

[v] *v*ery, e*v*e

[θ] *th*in, bo*th*

[ð] *th*is, o*th*er

[l] *l*itt*l*e, ba*ll*

[r] *r*at, b*r*ead

[m] *m*ove, co*m*e

[n] *n*o, ru*n*

[ŋ] si*ng*, ba*nk*

[h] *h*at, re*h*eat

[j] *y*es

[w] *w*ell, a*w*ay

Table of Abbreviations 略語表

adj	adjective	形容詞
abbr	abbreviation	略語
adv	adverb	副詞
ADMIN	administration	管理
AGR	agriculture	農業
ANAT	anatomy	解剖学
ARCHIT	architecture	建築
AUT	automobiles	自動車関係
aux vb	auxiliary verb	助動詞
AVIAT	aviation	航空
BIO	biology	生物学
BOT	botany	植物学
BRIT	British English	英国つづり／用法
CHEM	chemistry	化学
COMM	commerce, finance, banking	商業，金融関係
COMPUT	computing	コンピュータ関係
conj	conjunction	接続詞
cpd	compound	形容詞的名詞
CULIN	cookery	料理
def art	definite article	定冠詞
dimin	diminutive	指小辞
ECON	economics	経済学
ELEC	electricity, electronics	電気，電子工学
excl	exclamation, interjection	感嘆詞
fam(!)	colloquial usage (! particularly offensive)	口語（！特に悪質なもの）
fig	figurative use	比喩
fus	(phrasal verb) where the particle cannot be separated from the main verb	vt fusを見よ
gen	in most or all senses; generally	たいがいの意味では，一般に
GEO	geography, geology	地理学，地質学
GEOM	geometry	幾何学
indef art	indefinite article	不定冠詞

inf(!)	colloquial usage (! particularly offensive)	口語（！特に悪質なもの）
infin	infinitive	不定詞
inv	invariable	変化しない
irreg	irregular	不規則な
LING	grammar, linguistics	文法，語学
lit	literal use	文字通りの意味
MATH	mathematics	数学
MED	medical term, medicine	医学
METEOR	the weather, meteorology	気象関係
MIL	military matters	軍事
MUS	music	音楽
n	noun	名詞
NAUT	sailing, navigation	海事
num	numeral adjective or noun	数詞
obj	(grammatical) object	目的語
pej	pejorative	蔑称
PHOT	photography	写真
PHYSIOL	physiology	生理学
pl	plural	複数
POL	politics	政治
pp	past participle	過去分詞形
prep	preposition	前置詞
pron	pronoun	代名詞
PSYCH	psychology, psychiatry	精神医学
pt	past tense	過去形
RAIL	railroad, railway	鉄道
REL	religion	宗教
SCOL	schooling, schools and universities	学校教育
sing	singular	単数
subj	(grammatical) subject	主語
superl	superlative	最上級
TECH	technical term, technology	技術(用語)，テクノロジー
TEL	telecommunications	電信電話
TV	television	テレビ
TYP	typography, printing	印刷

US	American English	米国つづり／用法
vb	verb	動詞
vi	verb or phrasal verb used intransitively	自動詞
vt	verb or phrasal verb used transitively	他動詞
vt fus	phrasal verb where the particle cannot be separated from main verb	パーチクルを動詞から分けられない句動詞
ZOOL	zoology	動物学
®	registered trademark	登録商標

THE ROMANIZATION AND PRONUNCIATION OF JAPANESE

There are several systems for writing Japanese in Roman characters, but the most understandable and least confusing to the speaker of English is the Hepburn ("hebon" in Japanese) system. The following table illustrates this system, with its "hiragana" and "katakana" equivalents, as it has been adopted in this dictionary.

a	i	u	e	o	ā	ī	ū	ē	ō
あ	い	う	え	お	―	―	うう	―	おお/おう
ア	イ	ウ	エ	オ	アー	イー	ウー	エー	オー

ka	ki	ku	ke	ko	kya	―	kyu	―	kyo
か	き	く	け	こ	きゃ	―	きゅ	―	きょ
カ	キ	ク	ケ	コ	キャ	―	キュ	―	キョ

ga	gi	gu	ge	go	gya	―	gyu	―	gyo
が	ぎ	ぐ	げ	ご	ぎゃ	―	ぎゅ	―	ぎょ
ガ	ギ	グ	ゲ	ゴ	ギャ	―	ギュ	―	ギョ

sa	shi	su	se	so	sha	shi	shu	she	sho
さ	し	す	せ	そ	しゃ	し	しゅ	しぇ	しょ
サ	シ	ス	セ	ソ	シャ	シ	シュ	シェ	ショ

za	ji	zu	ze	zo	ja	ji	ju	je	jo
ざ	じ	ず	ぜ	ぞ	じゃ	じ	じゅ	じぇ	じょ
ザ	ジ	ズ	ゼ	ゾ	ジャ	ジ	ジュ	ジェ	ジョ

ta	chi	tsu	te	to	cha	chi	chu	che	cho
た	ち	つ	て	と	ちゃ	ち	ちゅ	ちぇ	ちょ
タ	チ	ツ	テ	ト	チャ	チ	チュ	チェ	チョ

da	ji	zu	de	do	ja	ji	ju	je	jo
だ	ぢ	づ	で	ど	ぢゃ	ぢ	ぢゅ	ぢぇ	ぢょ
ダ	ヂ	ヅ	デ	ド	ヂャ	ヂ	ヂュ	ヂェ	ヂョ

na	ni	nu	ne	no	nya	—	nyu	—	nyo
な	に	ぬ	ね	の	にゃ	—	にゅ	—	にょ
ナ	ニ	ヌ	ネ	ノ	ニャ	—	ニュ	—	ニョ

ha	hi	fu	he	ho	hya	—	hyu	—	hyo
は	ひ	ふ	へ	ほ	ひゃ	—	ひゅ	—	ひょ
ハ	ヒ	フ	ヘ	ホ	ヒャ	—	ヒュ	—	ヒョ

ba	bi	bu	be	bo	bya	—	byu	—	byo
ば	び	ぶ	べ	ぼ	びゃ	—	びゅ	—	びょ
バ	ビ	ブ	ベ	ボ	ビャ	—	ビュ	—	ビョ

pa	pi	pu	pe	po	pya	—	pyu	—	pyo
ぱ	ぴ	ぷ	ぺ	ぽ	ぴゃ	—	ぴゅ	—	ぴょ
パ	ピ	プ	ペ	ポ	ピャ	—	ピュ	—	ピョ

ma	mi	mu	me	mo	mya	—	myu	—	myo
ま	み	む	め	も	みゃ	—	みゅ	—	みょ
マ	ミ	ム	メ	モ	ミャ	—	ミュ	—	ミョ

ya	—	yu	—	yo
や	—	ゆ	—	よ
ヤ	—	ユ	—	ヨ

ra	ri	ru	re	ro	rya	—	ryu	—	ryo
ら	り	る	れ	ろ	りゃ	—	りゅ	—	りょ
ラ	リ	ル	レ	ロ	リャ	—	リュ	—	リョ

wa	—	—	—	wo	n
わ	—	—	—	を	ん
ワ	—	—	—	ヲ	ン

Consonants:

Pronounce the consonants as you would in English. Exceptions are "w" in the objective particle "wo", "r", "g", and "f". In "wo" the "w" is normally not pronounced, but is written to distinguish it easily from other words that are pronounced "o". (Japanese word-processing software also usually requires that you type "wo" to get を or ヲ.)

"R" is pronounced with a very slight trill. Do not pronounce it as in the English word "rich"; you probably will not be understood. If you trill it as in Italian or Spanish, you can be understood, but you will sound foreign. The best strategy is to listen and imitate. Lacking access to native speakers, try pronouncing "r" as you would "d", but with the tongue farther forward, touching the upper teeth instead of the palate.

"G" is perfectly understandable pronounced as in English "get", "go" etc, and many Japanese always pronounce it in this way. Cultured people, however, prefer a softer, slightly nasal pronunciation, which they call a "half-voiced" or "nasal-voiced" "k". It is similar to the "ng" in "sing", but coming at the beginning of a syllable.

"F" also is quite understandable when given its usual English fricative value, with the lower lip touching the upper teeth. The Japanese, however, normally pronounce it by simply narrowing the gap between the lower lip and the teeth, without actually touching the lip to the teeth. Thus some individuals pronounce it much closer to "h" than to the English "f".

"N" at the end of a syllable or word is syllabic, that is, it is a syllable in its own right, with full syllabic length, as in English "butt*on*". In this dictionary when syllabic "n" is followed by a vowel or "y", a hyphen is inserted to indicate the proper pronunciation: e. g., 勧誘 かんゆう kan-yū, as opposed to 加入 かにゅう kanyū.

Before "p", "b", or "m", "n" naturally becomes an "m" sound; but in this dictionary, in keeping with the practice of other romanized dictionaries, the Japanese ん is consistently transliterated as "n", not "m": e. g., 文法 ぶんぽう bunpō, not bumpō.

Double consonants are pronounced in Japanese, as in US English "cattail". In "katakana" and "hiragana" they are indicated by a lowercase っ or ッ before the consonant to be doubled, and in this dictionary are printed as double consonants: か っぱ "kappa", いった "itta". The one exception is the combination っち, which we express as "tch": マッチ, "matchi".

A few Japanese exclamations are written with a lowercase っ at the end, indicating an articulated "t" sound at the end. These we have romanized with a quarter-sized "t": しっ "shi_t" (equivalent to the English "ssh !").

The sounds [ti:] and [di:] do not exist in Japanese. They are usually expressed as

ティ and ディ, which we romanize as "ti" and "di". Other sounds in loan words without Japanese equivalents are generally corrupted to some similar sound, e. g., "v" to "b".

Vowels:

The 5 Japanese vowels are the fundamental Latin vowels: [ɑː], [iː], [uː], [e], and [o]. "U" is pronounced without rounding the lips, keeping them relaxed. A rounded "u" is understandable, but sounds outlandishly foreign. Again, listen and imitate.

The vowels can be long or short. Long vowels are pronounced the same as short vowels, but for double their length, with no break. Pay strict attention to this, for vowel length is essential to both meaning and comprehension. Using a short vowel for a long one, or vice versa, can produce a word of entirely different meaning from the one intended. In this dictionary, long vowels are marked with a macron: ā, ī, ū, ē, ō.

The syllable "-su" at the end of a word, especially in the verbal ending "-masu" frequently drops the "u", so that only the "s" is heard. This occurs more often in the east than in the west of the country. There are no hard and fast rules, so the student needs to rely on his experience from listening to spoken Japanese.

Japanese accents:

Japanese words do not have a strong tonic accent as in most European languages. Instead they are inflected, with the voice rising or falling gently on certain syllables, and remaining flat on others. Using the correct "accent" or inflection is necessary for intelligibility of speech, and often serves to distinguish between words of similar spelling. For example, depending on the "accent", "momo" can mean either "peach" or "thigh"; "kaki" can be either "persimmon" or "oyster"; "atsui" can be "hot" or "thick".

The Japanese accent is difficult to depict graphically with any accuracy, for there are no standard conventions. Many dictionaries simply ignore the problem, leaving the foreign student to his own devices. Language classes for foreigners both in Japan and abroad frequently do not teach accents explicitly, but rely on imitation of pronunciation by a native Japanese model.

We felt that the foreign student needed something to aid the memory in trying to pronounce words already learned in the past, as well as a guide to pronunciation of words being looked up in the dictionary. We settled on the accute accent (á) to

indicate a rising inflection, and the grave accent (à) to indicate a falling inflection. No mark at all means that the voice is held flat on that syllable.

The one exception in this dictionary is when two "i"s occur together, as in the word for "good" いい ii. In most cases like this, the first "i" requires a rising inflection (í), and the second a falling inflection (ì). However, with standard typefaces this produces an unesthetic effect (íì). Therefore, we have omitted the accent mark of the second "i" in such cases: a rising inflection on the first of a "double i" combination indicates also a falling inflection on the second letter: íi = í ì.

Doubtless the foreign student will be somewhat disconcerted to see such inflection marks on "n" in this dictionary. Remember that final "n" is always syllabic and may be pronounced by itself in Japanese. Thus, "n" can also have a rising or falling inflection, or be flat, as the case may be.

Accent differs markedly from region to region in Japan, particularly between the east and the west. The speech patterns of the Kanto region have generally been adopted as the standards for a "common" language, to be taught in the schools and used by television and radio announcers. Although the accents in this dictionary have followed the guidance of an expert in the field, we lay no claim to absolute accuracy. Our aim has been to guide the foreign student to a pronunciation that, if used, will be understandable in any part of the country, even when the listeners themselves follow a different standard of pronunciation.

English Irregular Verb Forms 不規則動詞表

arise arising	arose	arisen	持ち上る mochíagaru
awake awaking	awoke	awaked	目が覚める me ga samérù
be am, is, are being	was, were	been	である de árù
bear	bore	born(e)	支える sasáerù
beat	beat	beaten	殴る nagúrù
become becoming	became	become	なる nárù
begin beginning	began	begun	始める hajímeru
behold	beheld	beheld	見る mírù
bend	bent	bent	曲げる magéru
beseech	besought	besought	嘆願する tañgan suru
beset besetting	beset	beset	襲う osóu
bet betting	bet, betted	bet, betted	かける kakérù
bid bidding	bid, bade	bid, bidden	競りに加わる serí ni kuwawarù
bind	bound	bound	縛る shibárù
bite biting	bit	bitten	かむ kámù
bleed	bled	bled	出血する shukkétsu suru
blow	blew	blown	吹く fúkù
break	broke	broken	割る warú
breed	bred	bred	繁殖させる hañshoku sasérù
bring	brought	brought	持って来る motté kurù
build	built	built	建てる tatérù
burn	burned, burnt	burned, burnt	燃やす moyásu
burst	burst	burst	破裂させる harétsu sasérù
buy	bought	bought	買う kaú
can	could	(been able)	出来る dekírù

cast	cast	cast	投げる nagérù
catch	caught	caught	捕まえる tsukámaeru
choose 　choosing	chose	chosen	選ぶ erábù
cling	clung	clung	しがみつく shigámitsukù
come 　coming	came	come	来る kúrù
cost	cost	cost	の値段である no nedán de arù
creep	crept	crept	忍び足で歩く shinóbiàshi de arúkù
cut 　cutting	cut	cut	切る kirù
deal	dealt	dealt	配る kubárù
dig 　digging	dug	dug	掘る hórù
dive 　diving	dived *also US* dove	dived	飛込む tobíkomù
do 　does	did	done	する sùrú
draw	drew	drawn	描く kákù
dream	dreamed, dreamt	dreamed, dreamt	夢を見る yumé wo mirù
drink	drank	drunk	飲む nómù
drive 　driving	drove	driven	運転する uńten suru
dwell	dwelt	dwelt	住む súmù
eat	ate	eaten	食べる tabérù
fall	fell	fallen	落ちる ochírù
feed	fed	fed	食べさせる tabésaserù
feel	felt	felt	感じる kańjirù
fight	fought	fought	戦う tatákaù
find	found	found	見付ける mitsúkeru
flee	fled	fled	逃げる nigérù
fling	flung	flung	投げる nagérù
fly 　flies	flew	flown	飛ぶ tobú
forbid 　forbidding	forbade	forbidden	禁ずる kińzurù

forecast	forecast	forecast	予報する yohō suru
forego	forewent	foregone	なしで我慢する náshì de gámàn suru
foresee	foresaw	foreseen	予想する yosō suru
foretell	foretold	foretold	予言する yogén suru
forget forgetting	forgot	forgotten	忘れる wasúrerù
forgive forgiving	forgave	forgiven	許す yurúsù
forsake forsaking	forsook	forsaken	見捨てる misúterù
freeze freezing	froze	frozen	凍る kṓrù
get getting	got	got US gotten	手に入れる té ni irerù
give giving	gave	given	与える atáerù
go goes	went	gone	行く ikú
grind	ground	ground	ひく hikú
grow	grew	grown	成長する seíchō suru
hang	hung, hanged	hung, hanged	掛ける kakérù
have has ; having	had	had	持っている mótte iru
hear	heard	heard	聞く kikú
hide hiding	hid	hidden	隠す kakúsù
hit hitting	hit	hit	打つ utsú
hold	held	held	持つ mótsù
hurt	hurt	hurt	痛める itámerù
keep	kept	kept	保管する hokán suru
kneel	knelt, kneeled	knelt, kneeled	ひざまずく hizámazukù
know	knew	known	知っている shitté irù
lay	laid	laid	置く okú
lead	led	led	先導する seńdō suru
lean	leaned, leant	leaned, leant	傾く katámukù
leap	**leaped, leapt**	**leaped, leapt**	跳躍する chṓyaku suru

learn	learned, learnt	learned, learnt	学ぶ manábù
leave	left	left	去る sárù
leaving			
lend	lent	lent	貸す kásù
let	let	let	許す yurúsù
letting			
lie	lay	lain	横になる yokó ni narù
lying			
light	lighted, lit	lighted, lit	火を付ける hí wo tsukérù
lose	lost	lost	失う ushínaù
losing			
make	made	made	作る tsukúrù
making			
may	might	—	かも知れない ka mo shirenái
mean	meant	meant	意味する ímì suru
meet	met	met	会う áù
mistake	mistook	mistaken	間違える machígaerù
mistaking			
mow	mowed	mowed, mown	刈る karú
must	(had to)	(had to)	しなければならない shinákereba naranái
pay	paid	paid	払う haráù
put	put	put	置く okú
putting			
quit	quit, quitted	quit, quitted	やめる yamérù
quitting			
read	read	read	読む yómù
rid	rid	rid	取除く torínozokù
ridding			
ride	rode	ridden	乗る nórù
riding			
ring	rang	rung	鳴る narú
rise	rose	risen	上がる agárù
rising			
run	ran	run	走る hashírù
running			
saw	sawed	sawn	のこぎりで切る nokógirì de kírù
say	said	said	言う iú

see	saw	seen	見る mírù
seek	sought	sought	求める motómerù
sell	sold	sold	売る urú
send	sent	sent	送る okúrù
set	set	set	置く ókù
setting			
shake	shook	shaken	振る fúrù
shaking			
shall	should	—	しましょう shimashō
shear	sheared	sheared, shorn	毛を刈る kě wò karú
shed	shed	shed	落す otósù
shedding			
shine	shone	shone	照る térù
shining			
shoot	shot	shot	そ撃する sogéki suru
show	showed	shown	見せる misérù
shrink	shrank	shrunk	縮む chijímù
shut	shut	shut	閉める shimérù
shutting			
sing	sang	sung	歌う utáù
sink	sank	sunk	沈没する chiñbotsu suru
sit	sat	sat	座る suwárù
sitting			
slay	slew	slain	殺す korósù
sleep	slept	slept	眠る nemúrù
slide	slid	slid	滑る subérù
sliding			
sling	slung	slung	投げる nagérù
slit	slit	slit	切り開く kiríhirakù
slitting			
smell	smelled, smelt	smelled, smelt	匂う nióù
sneak	sneaked	sneaked	こっそり行く kossórì ikú
	also US snuck	*also US* snuck	
sow	sowed	sown, sowed	まく mákù
speak	spoke	spoken	話す hanásù
speed	sped, speeded	sped, speeded	スピードを出す supídò wo dásù
spell	spelled, spelt	spelled, spelt	つづりを言う tsuzúri wò iú
spend	spent	spent	過ごす sugósù

spill	spilled, spilt	spilled, spilt	こぼす kobósù
spin 　spinning	spun	spun	紡ぐ tsumúgù
spit 　spitting	spat	spat	つばを吐く tsúbà wo hákù
split 　splitting	split	split	裂く sákù
spoil	spoiled, spoilt	spoiled, spoilt	台無しにする daínashi ni surù
spread	spread	spread	広げる hirógerù
spring	sprang	sprung	跳ぶ tobú
stand	stood	stood	立つ tátsù
steal	stole	stolen	盗む nusúmù
stick	stuck	stuck	くっつく kuttsúkù
sting	stung	stung	刺す sásù
stink	stank	stunk	におう nióù
stride 　striding	strode	stridden	大またに歩く ōmàta ni arúkù
strike 　striking	struck	struck, stricken	打つ útsù
strive 　striving	strove	striven	努力する dóryòku suru
swear	swore	sworn	誓う chikáù
sweep	swept	swept	掃く hákù
swell	swelled	swelled, swollen	はれる harérù
swim 　swimming	swam	swum	泳ぐ oyógù
swing	swung	swung	振る furú
take 　taking	took	taken	とる tórù
teach	taught	taught	教える oshíerù
tear	tore	torn	破る yabúrù
tell	told	told	述べる nobérù
think	thought	thought	考える kañgaerù
throw	threw	thrown	投げる nagérù
thrust	thrust	thrust	強く押す tsúyòku osú
tread	trod	trodden	歩く arúkù
wake 　waking	waked, woke	waked, woken	起こす okósù

waylay	waylaid	waylaid	待伏せする machíbuse suru
wear	wore	worn	着る kirú
weave 　weaving	wove, weaved	woven, weaved	織る orù
wed 　wedding	wedded, wed	wedded, wed	結婚する kekkón suru
weep	wept	wept	泣く naku
win 　winning	won	won	勝つ katsù
wind	wound	wound	巻く makú
withdraw	withdrew	withdrawn	取出す torídasu
withhold	withheld	withheld	拒む kobámù
withstand	withstood	withstood	耐える taérù
wring	wrung	wrung	絞る shibórù
write 　writing	wrote	written	書く kakù

A

A [ei] *n* (MUS: note) イ音 í-òn; (: key) イ調 íchō

KEYWORD

a [ei, ə] (*before vowel or silent h:* **an**) *indef art* 1 1つの hitótsu no, ある árù ◊ 通常日本語では表現しない tsūjō nihongo de wa hyōgen shínài

a book/girl/mirror 本〔少女，鏡〕hòn 〔shōjo, kagámi〕

an apple りんご ríngo

she's a doctor 彼女は医者です kánojo wa ishá desu

2 (*instead of the number* "*one*") 1つの hitótsù no

a loaf and 2 pints of milk, please パン1本とミルク2パイント下さい pan íppoñto mírùku nipáìnto kudasái

a year ago 1年前 ichinen máè

a hundred/thousand etc pounds 100〔1000〕ポンド hyakú〔señ〕póndò

3 (*in expressing ratios, prices etc*) 1つ当り... hitotsu átàri...

3 a day/week 1日〔1週間〕当り3つ ichi-nichi〔isshūkan〕átàri mittsú

10 km an hour 時速10キロメーター jísðku jukkiromḗtā

£5 a person 1人当たり5ポンド hitori átàri gopóndð

30p a kilo 1キロ30ペンス ichíkìro sanjuppéñsù

AA [eiei'] *n abbr* (= *Alcoholics Anonymous*) アルコール依存症自主治療協会 a-rúkōru izoñshō jishúchiryō kyōkai; (*BRIT*: = *Automobile Association*) 英国自動車連盟 eíkoku jidōsha reñmei

AAA [trip'əlei'] *n abbr* (= *American Automobile Association*) 米国自動車連盟 beíkoku jidōsha reñmei

aback [əbæk'] *adv*: *to be taken aback* 仰天する gyōten suru

abandon [əbæn'dən] *vt* (person) 見捨てる misúterù; (car) 乗捨てる norísuterù;

(give up: search, idea, research) やめる yaméru

◆*n* (wild behavior): *with abandon* 羽目を外して hamé wò hazúshite

abashed [əbæʃt'] *adj* (person) 恥ずかしがっている hazúkashigattè irú

abate [əbeit'] *vi* (lessen: storm, terror, anger) 治まる osámarù

abattoir [æb'ətwɑːr'] (*BRIT*) *n* と殺場 tosátsujō

abbey [æb'i:] *n* 修道院 shúdōin

abbot [æb'ət] *n* 修道院長 shúdōinchò

abbreviate [əbri:'vi:eit] *vt* (essay, word) 短縮する tañshuku suru

abbreviation [əbri:vi:ei'ʃən] *n* (short form) 短縮形 tañshukukei

abdicate [æb'dikeit] *vt* (responsibility, right) 放棄する hōki suru

◆*vi* (monarch) 退位する taí-i suru

abdication [æbdikei'ʃən] *n* (of responsibility, right) 放棄 hōki; (by monarch) 退位 taí-i

abdomen [æb'dəmən] *n* 腹部 fukúbù

abduct [æbdʌkt'] *vt* ら致する ráchì suru

aberration [æbərei'ʃən] *n* (unusual behavior, event etc) 異状 ijō

abet [əbet'] *vt see* **aid**

abeyance [əbei'əns] *n*: *in abeyance* (law) 無視されて múshì sarete; (matter) 保留されて horyū sarete

abhor [æbhɔːr'] *vt* (cruelty, violence etc) ひどく嫌う hídokù kiráu

abide [əbaid'] *vt*: *I can't abide it/him* 私はそれ〔彼〕が大嫌いだ watákushi wà soré〔karè〕ga dáìkirai da

abide by *vt fus* (law, decision) ...に従う ...ni shitágaù

ability [əbil'iti:] *n* (capacity) 能力 nōryoku; (talent, skill) 才能 saínō

abject [æb'dʒekt] *adj* (poverty) 極度の kyōkùdo no; (apology) 卑屈な hikútsu na

ablaze [əbleiz'] *adj* (building etc) 炎上している eñjō shite iru

able [ei'bəl] *adj* (capable) 出来る dekírù;

(skilled) 有能な yūnō na

to be able to do something ...をする事が出来る ...wo suru koto gà dĕkirù

able-bodied [ei'bɔlbɑːd'iːd] *adj* (person) がん健な gaǹken na

ably [ei'bliː] *adv* (skilfully, well) 上手に jōzu ni

abnormal [æbnɔːr'məl] *adj* (behavior, child, situation) 異常な ijō na

aboard [əbɔːrd'] *adv* (NAUT, AVIAT) ...に乗って ...ni nottè

◆*prep* (NAUT, AVIAT) ...に乗って ...ni nottè

abode [əboud'] *n* (LAW): *of no fixed abode* 住所不定の jūshofutèi no

abolish [əbɑ:l'iʃ] *vt* 廃止する haíshi suru

abolition [æbɔliʃ'ən] *n* 廃止 haíshi

abominable [əbɑ:m'inəbəl] *adj* (conditions) ひどい hídoì; (behavior) 忌わしい imáwashiì

aborigine [æbəridʒ'əni:] *n* 原住民 geǹjūmìn

abort [əbɔːrt'] *vt* (MED: fetus) 流産する ryūzan suru; (plan, activity) 中止する chūshi suru

abortion [əbɔːr'ʃən] *n* (MED) 妊娠中絶 niǹshinchūzètsu

to have an abortion 妊娠を中絶する niǹshin wò chūzetsu suru

abortive [əbɔːr'tiv] *adj* (attempt, action) 不成功の fuséikō no

abound [əbaund'] *vi* (exist in large numbers) ...が多い ...ga ōì

to abound in/with (possess in large numbers) ...に富む ...ni tómù

KEYWORD

about [əbaut'] *adv* 1 (approximately) 約 yákù, 大よそ ōyoso, ...ぐらい ...gúrài

about a hundred/thousand etc dollars 約100〔1000〕ドル yákù hyakú(sen) dòru

it takes about 10 hours 10時間ぐらいかかります jūjikan gúrài kakarimásù

at about 2 o'clock 2時頃 niji górò

I've just about finished 終わったところです hóbò owatta tokoro desù

2 (referring to place) あちこちに achíko-

chî ni

to leave things lying about 物をあちこちに散らかしたままにする monô wo achíkochì ni chirakashita mamá ni sùrù

to run/walk etc about あちこち走り回る〔歩き回る〕achíkochì hashirimawárù 〔arukimawárù〕

3: ***to be about to do something*** ...するところである ...suru tokoro dè árù

he was about to cry/leave/wash the dishes/go to bed 彼は泣き出す〔帰る、皿を洗う、寝る〕ところだった kárè wa nakidasu(kaeru, sara wo arau, neru) tokoro dattà

◆*prep* 1 (relating to) ...について ...ni tsúìte, ...に関して ...ni kàǹshite

a book about London ロンドンについての本 róǹdòn ni tsúìte no hon

what is it about? それは何についてですか sore wa náǹ ni tsúìte desu ká

we talked about it 私たちはそれについて話し合った watakushitachì a sore ni tsúìte hanashiáttà

what/how about having some coffee? コーヒーでも飲みましょうか kōhī de mò nomimashō ká

2 (referring to place) ...のあちこちに ...no achíkochì ni

to walk about the town 町をあちこち歩き回る machí wo achíkochì arukimawárù

her clothes were scattered about the room 部屋のあちこちに彼女の服が散らかっていた heya no achíkochì ni kánòjo no fukú gà chirakatte itá

---

about-face [əbaut'feis] *n* (MIL) 回れ右 mawáremigì; (fig) : ***to do an about-face*** 一変する ippén suru

about-turn [əbaut'təːrn] *n* = **about-face**

above [əbʌv'] *adv* (higher up, overhead) 上の方に ué no hō ni; (greater, more) 以上に ijō ni

◆*prep* (higher than) ...より上に ...yórì ué ni; (greater than, more than: in number, amount etc) ...以上 ...íjò; (: in rank etc) 上である ué de arù

mentioned above 上記の jōki no
above all まず第一に mázù daí-ichi ni

aboveboard [əbʌv'bourd] *adj* 公明正大な kṓmeiseidai na

abrasive [əbrei'siv] *adj* (substance) 研磨の kénma no; (person, manner) とげとげしい togétogeshī

abreast [əbrest'] *adv* (people, vehicles) 横に並んで yokó ni narande
to keep abreast of (*fig*: news etc) ...についていく ...ni tsúîte ikú

abridge [əbridʒ'] *vt* (novel, play) 短縮する tañshuku suru

abroad [əbroːd'] *adv* 海外に káîgai ni

abrupt [əbrʌpt'] *adj* (sudden: action, ending etc) 突然の totsúzen no; (curt: person, behavior) ぶっきらぼうな bukkírabō na

abruptly [əbrʌpt'li:] *adv* (leave, end) 突然 totsúzen; (speak) ぶっきらぼうに bukkírabō ni

abscess [æb'ses] *n* のうよう nṓyō

abscond [æbzɑːnd'] *vi* (thief): *to abscond with* ...を持ち逃げする ...wo mochínige suru; (prisoner): *to abscond (from)* (...から) 逃亡する (...kara) tṓbō suru

absence [æb'səns] *n* (of person: from home etc) 不在 fuzái; (: from school, meeting etc) 欠席 kessékì; (: from work) 欠勤 kekkín; (of thing) 無い事 nái kotó

absent [æb'sənt] *adj* (person: from home etc) 不在の fuzái no; (: from school, meeting etc) 欠席の kessékì no; (: from work) 欠勤の kekkín no; (thing) 無い nái

absentee [æbsənti:'] *n* (from school, meeting etc) 欠席者 kessékìshà; (from work) 欠勤者 kekkínsha

absent-minded [æb'səntmain'did] *adj* 忘れっぽい wasúreppoì

absolute [æb'səlut] *adj* (complete) 全くの mattáku no; (monarch, rule, power) 専制的な señseiteki na; (principle, rule etc) 絶対的な zettáiteki na

absolutely [æbsəlu:t'li:] *adv* (totally) 全く mattáku; (certainly) その通り sonó tòri

absolution [æbsəlu:'ʃən] *n* (REL) 罪の許

absolve [æbzɑːlv'] *vt*: *to absolve someone (from blame, responsibility, sin)* ...の (...を) 許す ...no (...wò) yurúsù

absorb [æbsɔːrb'] *vt* 吸収する kyúshū suru; (assimilate: group, business) 併合する heígō suru
to be absorbed in a book 本に夢中になっている hóñ ni muchū ni nattě irú

absorbent cotton [æbsɔːr'bənt-] (*US*) *n* 脱脂綿 dasshímèn

absorbing [æbsɔːr'biŋ] *adj* 夢中にさせる muchū ni saserù

absorption [æbsɔːrp'ʃən] *n* 吸収 kyúshū; (assimilation: of group, business etc) 併合 heígō; (interest) 夢中になる事 muchū ni narù kotó

abstain [æbstein'] *vi*: *to abstain (from)* (eating, drinking) 控える hikáerù; (voting) 棄権する kikén suru

abstemious [æbsti:'mi:əs] *adj* (person) 節制する sesséi suru

abstention [æbsten'ʃən] *n* (refusal to vote) 棄権 kikén

abstinence [æb'stənəns] *n* 禁欲 kiñ-yoku

abstract [æb'strækt] *adj* (idea, quality) 抽象的な chūshōteki na; (ART) 抽象派の chūshōha no; (LING): *abstract noun* 抽象名詞 chūshōmeishi

abstruse [æbstru:s'] *adj* 分かりにくい wakárinikuì

absurd [æbsərd'] *adj* ばかげた bakágetà

abundance [əbʌn'dəns] *n* 豊富さ hṓfusa

abundant [əbʌn'dənt] *adj* 豊富な hṓfu na

abuse [*n* əbju:s' *vb* əbju:z'] *n* (insults) のの しり nonóshiri; (ill-treatment) 虐待 gyakútai; (misuse: of power, drugs etc) 乱用 rañ-yō
◆*vt* (insult) のの しる nonóshirù; (ill-treat) 虐待する gyakútai suru; (misuse) 乱用する rañ-yō suru

abusive [əbju:'siv] *adj* (person) 口の悪い kuchī no waruì; (language) 侮辱的な bujókuteki na

abysmal [əbiz'məl] *adj* (performance, failure) 最低の saítei no; (ignorance etc)

ひどい hidói

abyss [əbis'] *n* 深えん shiñ-en

AC [ei'si:] *abbr* = **alternating current**

academic [ækədem'ik] *adj* (person) イン テリの iñteri no; (year, system, books, freedom etc) 教育関係の kyóikukañkei no; (*pej*: issue) 理論的な riróntekí na
♦*n* 学者 gakúsha

academy [əkæd'əmi:] *n* (learned body) アカデミー akádèmī; (school) 学院 gakú-in

academy of music 音楽学院 oñgaku gakúin

accelerate [æksel'əreit] *vt* (process) 早 める hayámerù
♦*vi* (AUT) 加速する kasóku suru

acceleration [ækselərei'ʃən] *n* (AUT) 加 速 kasóku

accelerator [æksel'əreitər] *n* アクセル ákùseru

accent [æk'sent] *n* (pronunciation) なま り namári; (written mark) アクセント符 号 akúsento fugò; (*fig*: emphasis, stress) 強調 kyóchō, アクセント akùsento

accept [æksept'] *vt* (gift, invitation) 受取 る ukétoru; (fact, situation, risk) 認める mitómeru; (responsibility, blame) 負う oú

acceptable [æksep'təbəl] *adj* (offer, gift) 受入れられる uké-irerarerù; (risk etc) 許 容できる kyoyő dekirù

acceptance [æksep'təns] *n* (of gift, offer etc) 受取る事 ukétoru koto; (of risk etc) 許容 kyoyő; (of responsibility etc) 負う 事 oú koto

access [æk'ses] *n* (to building, room) 入 る事 háiru kotő; (to information, papers) 利用する権利 riyő suru keñri

to have access to (child etc) ...への面会 権がある ...e no meñkaikeñ ga árù

accessible [ækses'əbəl] *adj* (place) 行き やすい ikíyasuì; (person) 面会しやすい meñkai shiyasuì; (available: knowledge, art etc) 利用しやすい riyő shiyasuì

accessory [ækses'ə:ri:] *n* (dress, COMM, TECH, AUT) アクセサリー ákùsesarī; (LAW): *accessory to* ...の共犯者 ...no kyőhañsha

accident [æk'sidənt] *n* (chance event) 偶 然 gűzen; (mishap, disaster) 事故 jíkō

by accident (unintentionally) うっかり ukkárì; (by chance) 偶然に gűzen ni

accidental [æksiden'təl] *adj* (death) 事 故による jíkō ni yorú; (damage) 偶発的 な gűhatsuteki na

accidentally [æksiden'təli:] *adv* (by accident) 偶然に gűzen ni

accident-prone [æk'sidəntproun'] *adj* 事故に会いがちな jíko ni aigachi na

acclaim [əkleim'] *n* 賞賛 shősan
♦*vt*: *to be acclaimed for one's achievements* 功績で有名である kőseki dè yűmei de arù

acclimate [əklai'mit] (*US*) *vt* = **acclimatize**

acclimatize [əklai'mətaiz] *vt*: *to become acclimatized (to)* (...に) 慣れ る (...ni) narérù

accolade [ækəleid'] *n* (*fig*) 賞賛 shősan

accommodate [əka:m'ədeit] *vt* (subj: person) 泊める toméru; (: car, hotel etc) 収容できる shűyō dekirù; (oblige, help) ...に親切にして上げる ...ni shíñsetsu ni shite agérù

accommodating [əka:m'ədeitiŋ] *adj* 親 切な shíñsetsu na

accommodation [əka:mədei'ʃən] *n* 宿泊 設備 shukúhakusetsùbi

accommodations [əka:mədei'ʃənz] (*US*) *npl* 宿泊設備 shukúhakusetsùbi

accompaniment [əkʌm'pənimənt] *n* 伴 奏 bañsō

accompany [əkʌm'pəni:] *vt* (escort, go along with) ...に付きそう ...ni tsukísoù; (MUS) ...の伴奏をする ...no bañsō wò su-ru

accomplice [əka:m'plis] *n* 共犯者 kyőhañ-sha

accomplish [əka:m'pliʃ] *vt* (finish: task) 成遂げる nashítogerù; (achieve: goal) 達 成する tasséi suru

accomplished [əka:m'pliʃt] *adj* (person) 熟練の jukúren no; (performance) 優れた sugúretà

accomplishment [əka:m'pliʃmənt] *n* (completion, bringing about) 遂行 suíkő;

(skill: *gen pl*) 才能 saínō

accord [əkɔ:rd'] *n* (treaty) 協定 kyṓtei

♦*vt* 与える atáeru

of his own accord 自発的に jihátsute-ki ni

accordance [əkɔ:r'dəns] *n*: *in accordance with* (someone's wishes, the law etc) ...に従って ...ni shitágatte

according [əkɔ:r'diŋ]: *according to prep* (person, account) ...によると ...ni yorú

accordingly [əkɔ:r'diŋli:] *adv* (appropriately) それに応じて soré ní ṓjite; (as a result) それで soré de

accordion [əkɔ:r'di:ən] *n* アコーデオン ákōdeon

accost [əkɔ:st'] *vt* ...に近寄って話し掛ける ...ni chikáyottè hanáshikakerù

account [əkaunt'] *n* (COMM: bill) 勘定書 kañjōgaki; (: monthly account) 計算書 keísansho; (in bank) 口座 kṓza; (report) 報告 hōkoku

of no account 構わない kamáwanài

on account つけで tsuké de

on no account 何があっても... (すべき) でない naní ga atte mo ...(subeki) de naí

on account of ...のために ...no tamé ni

to take into account, take account of ...を考慮に入れる ...wò kṓryò ni irérù

accountable [əkaun'təbəl] *adj*: *accountable (to)* (...に) 申開きする義務がある (...ni) mōshihiraki suru gimù ga árù

accountancy [əkaun'tənsi:] *n* 会計士の職 kaíkeìshi no shokú

accountant [əkaun'tənt] *n* 会計士 kaíkeìshi

account for *vt fus* (explain) 説明する setsúmei suru; (represent) ... (の割合) を占める ...(no warfai) wò shimérù

account number *n* (at bank etc) 口座番号 kṓzabàngō

accounts [əkaunts'] *npl* (COMM) 勘定 kañjō

accredited [əkred'itid] *adj* (agent etc) 資格のある shikáku no arù

accrued interest [əkru:d'-] *n* 累積利息 ruísekirisòku

accumulate [əkju:m'jəleit] *vt* 貯める ta-méru

♦*vi* 貯まる tamáru

accuracy [æk'jə:rəsi:] *n* 正確さ seíkaku-sa

accurate [æk'jə:rit] *adj* 正確な seíkaku na

accurately [æk'jə:ritli:] *adv* (count, shoot, answer) 正確に seíkaku ni

accusation [ækju:zei'ʃən] *n* 非難 hínan

accuse [əkju:z'] *vt*: *to accuse someone (of something)* (crime, incompetence) (...だと) ...を責める (...dá tò) ...wo semérù

accused [əkju:zd'] *n* (LAW): *the accused* 容疑者 yōgishà

accustom [əkʌs'təm] *vt* 慣れさせる na-résaserù

accustomed [əkʌs'təmd] *adj* (usual): *accustomed to* ...に慣れている ...ni na-rétè irú

ace [eis] *n* (CARDS, TENNIS) エース ḕsu

ache [eik] *n* 痛み itámi

♦*vi* (be painful) 痛む itámù, ...が痛い ...ga itáĩ

my head aches 頭が痛い atáma gà itáĩ

achieve [ətʃi:v'] *vt* (aim) 成遂げる nashítogerù; (result) 上げる agéru; (victory, success) 獲得する kakútoku suru

achievement [ətʃi:v'mənt] *n* (completion) 完成 kañsei; (success, feat) 業績 gyṓseki

acid [æs'id] *adj* (CHEM: soil etc) 酸性の sañsei no; (taste) 酸っぱい suppáĩ

♦*n* (CHEM) 酸 sáñ; (*inf*: LSD) LSD erú-esudī

acid rain *n* 酸性雨 sañseiù

acknowledge [æknɑ:l'idʒ] *vt* (letter, parcel: *also*: **acknowledge receipt of**) 受け取った事を知らせる ukétotta koto wò shiráserù; (fact, situation, person) 認める mitómeru

acknowledgement [æknɑ:l'idʒmənt] *n* (of letter, parcel) 受領通知 juryṓtsūchi

acne [æk'ni:] *n* にきび níkibi

acorn [ei'kɔ:rn] *n* ドングリ dóñguri

acoustic [əkuːˈstik] *adj* (related to hearing) 聴覚の chōkaku no; (guitar etc) アコースティックの akōsùtikku no

acoustics [əkuːˈstiks] *n* (science) 音響学 oñkyōgaku

♦*npl* (of hall, room) 音響効果 oñkyōkōka

acquaint [əkweint'] *vt*: *to acquaint someone with something* (inform) ...に...を知らせる ...ni ...wo shiráseru

to be acquainted with (person) ...と面識がある ...to meñshiki ga arù

acquaintance [əkwein'təns] *n* (person) 知り合い shirfai; (with person, subject) 知識 chíshìki

acquiesce [ækwiːˈes] *vi*: *to acquiesce (to)* (...) を承諾する (...wò) shōdaku suru

acquire [əkwaiˈəːr] *vt* (obtain, buy) 手に入れる te ni iréru; (learn, develop: interest, skill) 取得する shutóku suru

acquisition [ækwiziˈʃən] *n* (obtaining etc) 入手 nyūshu; (development etc) 獲得 kakútoku; (thing acquired) 取得物 shutókubùtsu

acquit [əkwit'] *vt* (free) 無罪とする múzài to suru

to acquit oneself well 見事な働きをする mígòto na határaki wo suru

acquittal [əkwit'əl] *n* 無罪判決 muzái hañketsu

acre [eiˈkəːr] *n* エーカー èkā

acrid [æk'rid] *adj* (smell, taste, smoke) 刺激的な shigékiteki na

acrimonious [ækrəmouˈniːəs] *adj* (remark, argument) 辛らつな shiñratsu na

acrobat [æk'rəbæt] *n* アクロバット akúrobattò

acrobatic [ækrəbætˈik] *adj* (person, movement, display) アクロバット的な akúrobattoteki na

acronym [æk'rənim] *n* 頭字語 tōjigo

across [əkrɔːs'] *prep* (from one side to the other of) ...を渡って ...wo watátte; (on the other side of) ...の向こう側に ...no mukōgawa ni; (crosswise over) ...と交差して ...to kōsa shite

♦*adv* (direction) 向こう側へ mukōgawa e; (measurement) 直径が... で chokkéi ga ...

... de

to run/swim across 走って〔泳いで〕渡る hashítte〔oyóide〕wataru

across from ...の向かいに ...no mukái ni

acrylic [əkrilˈik] *adj* アクリルの ákùriru no

♦*n* アクリル ákùriru

act [ækt] *n* (action) 行為 kōi; (of play) 幕 makú; (in a show etc) 出し物 dashímòno; (LAW) 法 hō

♦*vi* (do something, take action) 行動する kōdō suru; (behave) 振舞う furúmaù; (have effect: drug, chemical) 作用する sáyō suru; (THEATER) 出演する shutsúen suru; (pretend) ...の振りをする ...no furí wò suru

♦*vt* (part) ...に扮する ...ni fuñ surù

in the act of ...しているさなかに ...shité iru sanàka ni

to act as ...として勤める ...toshite tsutómerù

acting [ækˈtiŋ] *adj* (manager, director etc) 代理の dafri no

♦*n* (activity) 演技 eñgi; (profession) 演劇 eñgeki

action [ækˈʃən] *n* (deed) 行為 kōi; (motion) 動き ugókì; (MIL) 戦闘 señtō; (LAW) 訴訟 soshō

out of action (person) 活動不能で katsúdōfunò de; (thing) 作動不能で sadófunò de

to take action 行動を起す kōdō wo okósù

action replay *n* (TV) 即時ビデオ再生 sokúji bideo saísei

activate [ækˈtəveit] *vt* (mechanism) 作動させる sadósaserù

active [ækˈtiv] *adj* (person, life) 活動的な katsúdōteki na

active volcano 活火山 kakkázàn

actively [ækˈtivliː] *adv* (participate) 積極的に sekkyókuteki ni; (discourage) 強く tsúyòku; (dislike) 非常に hijó ni

activist [ækˈtivist] *n* 活動家 katsúdōka

activity [æktivˈətiː] *n* (being active) 活動 katsúdō; (action) 動き ugóki; (pastime, pursuit) 娯楽 goráku

actor [ækˈtəːr] *n* 俳優 haíyū

actress [æk'tris] *n* 女優 joyú

actual [æk'tʃuːəl] *adj* 実際の jissái no

actually [æk'tʃuːəli:] *adv* (really) 本当に hofitó ni; (in fact) 実は jitsú wa

acumen [əkjuː'mən] *n* 判断力 hafidafiryoku

acupuncture [æk'jupʌŋktʃər] *n* 針 hárî

acute [əkjuːt'] *adj* (illness) 急性の kyúsei no; (anxiety, pain) 激しい hagéshiî; (mind, person) 抜け目の無い nukéme no nai; (MATH): *acute angle* 鋭角 efkaku; (LING): *acute accent* 鋭アクセント efakùsento

ad [æd] *n abbr* = **advertisement**

A.D. [eidiː'] *adv abbr* (= *Anno Domini*) 西暦...年 sefreki ...neñ

adamant [æd'əmənt] *adj* (person) 譲らない yuzúranai

Adam's apple [æd'əms-] *n* のど仏 nodóbotòke

adapt [ədæpt'] *vt* (alter, change) 適応させる tekíō saserù
♦*vi*: *to adapt (to)* (に) 適応する (...ni) tekíō suru

adaptable [ədæp'təbəl] *adj* (device, person) 適応性のある tekíōsei no arù

adapter [ədæp'tər] *n* (ELEC) アダプター adápùtā

adaptor [ədæp'tər] *n* = **adapter**

add [æd] *vt* (to a collection etc) 加える kuwáeru; (comment etc) 付加える tsukékuwaerù; (figures: *also:* **add up**) 合計する gókei suru
♦*vi*: *to add to* (increase) ...を増す ...wo masú

adder [æd'ər] *n* ヨーロッパクサリヘビ yóroppà kusárihebì

addict [æd'ikt] *n* (to drugs etc) 中毒者 chúdokushà; (enthusiast) マニア mánìa

addicted [ədik'tid] *adj*: *to be addicted to* (drink etc) ...にかかっている ...chúdoku ni kakáttè irú; (*fig*: football etc) ...マニアである ...mánìa de arù

addiction [ədik'ʃən] *n* (to drugs etc) 中毒 chúdoku

addictive [ədik'tiv] *adj* (drug) 習慣性のある shúkansei no arù; (activity) 癖になる kusé ni narù

addition [ədiʃ'ən] *n* (adding up) 足し算 tashízàn; (thing added) 加えられた物 kuwáeraretà monó
in addition なお náð
in addition to ...の外に ...no hoká ni

additional [ədiʃ'ənəl] *adj* 追加の tsuíka no

additive [æd'ətiv] *n* 添加物 teñkabùtsu

address [ədres'] *n* (postal address) 住所 júsho; (speech) 演説 eñzetsu
♦*vt* (letter, parcel) ...に宛名を書く ...ni aténa wò kákù; (speak to: person) ...に話し掛ける ...ni hanáshikakerù; (: audience) ...に演説する ...ni eñzetsu suru; (problem): *to address (oneself to) a problem* 問題に取組む mofidai ni torikumù

adept [ədept'] *adj*: *adept at* ...が上手な ...ga józu na

adequate [æd'əkwit] *adj* (enough: amount) 十分な júbuñ na; (satisfactory: performance, response) 満足な máñzoku na

adhere [ədhiːr'] *vi*: *to adhere to* (stick to) ...にくっつく ...ni kuttsúkù; (*fig*: abide by: rule, decision, treaty etc) ...を守る ...wo mamórù; (: hold to: opinion, belief etc) ...を固守する ...wo kóshù suru

adhesive [ædhiː'siv] *n* 粘着材 neñchaku-zài

adhesive tape *n* (*US*: MED) ばん創こう bañsōkō; (*BRIT*) 粘着テープ neñchaku tèpu

ad hoc [æd hɑːk'] *adj* (decision, committee) 特別な tokúbetsu na

adjacent [ədʒei'sənt] *adj*: *adjacent to* ...の隣の ...no tonári no

adjective [ædʒ'iktiv] *n* 形容詞 kefyóshi

adjoining [ədʒɔi'niŋ] *adj* (room etc) 隣の tonári no

adjourn [ədʒərn'] *vt* (trial) 休廷にする kyútei ni suru; (meeting, discussion) 休会にする kyúkai ni suru
♦*vi* (trial) 休廷する kyútei suru; (meeting) 休止する kyúshi suru

adjudicate [ədʒuː'dikeit] *vt* (contest) ...の審査員を勤める ...no shifusa-ìn wo tsutómerù

adjust [ədʒʌst'] *vt* (change: approach etc) 調整する chōsei suru; (rearrange: clothing, machine etc) 調節する chōsetsu suru

♦*vi: to adjust (to)* 適応する tekíō suru

adjustable [ədʒʌst'əbəl] *adj* 調節できる chōsetsu dekirù

adjustment [ədʒʌst'mənt] *n* (PSYCH) 適応 tekíō; (to machine) 調節 chōsetsu; (of prices, wages) 調整 chōsei

ad-lib [ædlib'] *vi* アドリブで話す adóribu dè hanásù

ad lib [ædlib'] *adv* (speak) アドリブで a-dóribu de

administer [ədmin'istəːr] *vt* (country) 統治する tōchi suru; (department) 管理する kánri suru; (MED: drug) 投与する tōyo suru

to administer justice 裁く sabákù

administration [ædministreí'ʃən] *n* (management) 管理 kánri; (government) 政権 seíken

administrative [ædmin'istreitiv] *adj* (work, error etc) 管理的な kańriteki na

administrator [ædmin'istreitəːr] *n* 管理者 kańrishà

admiral [æd'məːrəl] *n* 海軍大将 kaígun taíshō

Admiralty [æd'məːrəltiː] (*BRIT*) *n: the Admiralty* (*also: Admiralty Board*) 海軍省 kaíguñshō

admiration [ædməreí'ʃən] *n* 感心 kańshin

admire [ædmai'əːr] *vt* (respect) ...に感心する ...ni kańshin suru; (appreciate) 観賞する kańshō suru

admirer [ædmai'əːrəːr] *n* (suitor) 男友達 otókotomodachi; (fan) ファン fáñ

admission [ædmiʃ'ən] *n* (admittance) 入場 nyūjō; (entry fee) 入場料 nyūjòryō; (confession) 自白 jiháku

admit [ædmit'] *vt* (confess) 自白する jiháku suru; (permit to enter) 入場させる nyūjō saserù; (to club, organization) 入会させる nyūkai saserù; (to hospital) 入院させる nyūin saserù; (accept: defeat, responsibility etc) 認める mitómeru

admittance [ædmit'əns] *n* 入場 nyūjō

admittedly [ædmit'idliː] *adv* 確かに ...であるが táshika ni ... de árù ga

admit to *vt fus* (murder etc) ...を自白する ...wo jiháku suru

admonish [ædmɑːn'iʃ] *vt* (rebuke) たしなめる tashínamerù; (LAW) 忠告する chūkoku suru

ad nauseam [æd nɔː'ziːəm] *adv* (repeat, talk) いやという程 iyá to iú hodó

ado [əduː'] *n: without (any) more ado* さっさと sássà to

adolescence [ædəles'əns] *n* 10代 jūdai

adolescent [ædəles'ənt] *adj* 10代の jūdai

♦*n* ティーンエージャー tíñèjā

adopt [ədɑːpt'] *vt* (child) 養子にする yōshi ni suru; (policy, attitude) とる torù; (accent) まねる manérù

adopted [ədɑːp'tid] *adj* (child) 養子の yōshi no

adoption [ədɑːp'ʃən] *n* (of child) 養子縁組 yōshieñgumi; (of policy etc) 採択 saítaku

adoptive [ədɑːp'tiv] *adj: adoptive father/mother* 養父(母) yōfu(bo)ri

adoptive country 第2の祖国 dái ni no sókòku

adore [ədɔːr'] *vt* (person) 崇拝する sūhai suru

adorn [ədɔːrn'] *vt* (decorate) 飾る kazáru

adrenalin [ədren'əlin] *n* アドレナリン a-dórenarīn

Adriatic [eidriːæt'ik] *n: the Adriatic (Sea)* アドリア海 adóriakài

adrift [ədrift'] *adv* (NAUT: loose) 漂流して hyōryū shite

adult [ədʌlt'] *n* (person) 大人 otóna; (animal, insect) 成体 seítai

♦*adj* (grown-up: person) 大人の otóna no; (: animal etc) 成体の seítai no; (for adults: literature, education) 成人向きの seíjinmuki no

adultery [ədʌl'təːriː] *n* かん通 kañtsū

advance [ædvæns'] *n* (movement, progress) 進歩 shíñpo; (money) 前借り maégari

♦*adj* (booking, notice, warning) 事前の jizén no

♦*vt* (money) 前貸する maégashi suru

♦*vi* (move forward) 前進する zeńshin suru; (make progress) 進歩する shińpo suru

to make advances (to someone) (*gen*) (...に) 言い寄る (...ni) iíyorù

in advance (book, prepare etc) 前もって maémottè

advanced [ædvænst'] *adj* (SCOL: studies) 高等の kốtô no; (country) 先進の seńshin no; (child) ませた m4sèta

advancement [ædvæns'mənt] *n* (improvement) 進歩 shińpo; (in job, rank) 昇進 shốshin

advantage [ædvæn'tidʒ] *n* (supremacy) 有利な立場 yūri na táchìba; (benefit) 利点 ritén; (TENNIS) アドバンテージ adóbańtēji

to take advantage of (person) ...に付込む ...ni tsukékomù; (opportunity) 利用する riyố suru

advantageous [ædvəntei'dʒəs] *adj*: *advantageous (to)* (...に) 有利な (...ni) yūri na

advent [æd'vent] *n* (appearance: of innovation) 出現 shutsúgen; (REL): *Advent* 待降節 taíkōsetsù

adventure [ædven'tʃər] *n* 冒険 bốken

adventurous [ædven'tʃərəs] *adj* (bold, outgoing) 大胆な daítañ na

adverb [æd'vərb] *n* 副詞 fukúshi

adversary [æd'vərse:ri:] *n* (opponent, *also* MIL) 敵 tekí

adverse [ædvərs'] *adj* (effect, weather, publicity etc) 悪い warúî

adversity [ædvər'siti:] *n* 逆境 gyakkyố

advert [æd'vərt] (*BRIT*) *n abbr* = **advertisement**

advertise [æd'və:rtaiz] *vi* (COMM: in newspaper, on television etc) 広告する kốkoku suru

♦*vt* (product, event, job) ...を広告する ...wo kốkoku suru

to advertise for (staff, accommodation etc) ...を求める広告を出す ...wo motómerù kốkoku wo dasu

advertisement [ædvə:rtaiz'mənt] *n* 広告 kốkoku

advertiser [æd'və:rtaizə:r] *n* (in newspaper, on television etc) 広告主 kốkokunùshi

advertising [æd'və:rtaiziŋ] *n* (advertisements) 広告 kốkoku; (industry) 広告業界 kốkokugyòkai

advice [ædvais'] *n* (counsel) 忠告 chúkoku; (notification) 知らせ shiráse

a piece of advice 一つの忠告 hítôtsu no chúkoku

to take legal advice 弁護士に相談する beńgoshi ni sốdan suru

advisable [ædvai'zəbəl] *adj* 望ましい nozốmashiî

advise [ædvai'z] *vt* (give advice to: person, company etc) ...に忠告する ...ni chúkoku suru; (inform): *to advise someone of something* ...に ...を知らせる ...ni ...wo shiráserù

to advise against something/doing something ... (するの) を避けた方がいいと忠告する ... (surú no) wo sakéta hô gà íi to chúkoku suru

advisedly [ædvai'zidli:] *adv* (deliberately) 意図的に itốteki ni

adviser [ædvai'zə:r] *n* (counsellor, consultant: to private person) 相談相手 sốdan aitè; (: to company etc) 顧問 kốmòn

advisor [ædvai'zə:r] *n* = **adviser**

advisory [ædvai'zə:ri:] *adj* (role, capacity, body) 顧問の kốmòn no

advocate [æd'vəkit] *vt* (support, recommend) 主張する shuchố suru

♦*n* (LAW: barrister) 弁護士 beńgoshî; (supporter): *advocate of* ...の主張者 ...no shuchốsha

Aegean [idʒi:'ən] *n*: *the Aegean (Sea)* エーゲ海 égekai

aerial [e:r'i:əl] *n* アンテナ añtena

♦*adj* (attack, photograph) 航空の kốkū no

aerobics [e:rou'biks] *n* エアロビクス eárobikùsu

aerodynamic [e:roudainæm'ik] *adj* 空力的な kűrikiteki na

aeroplane [e:r'əplein] (*BRIT*) *n* 飛行機 híkōki

aerosol [e:r'əsɔ:l] *n* スプレー缶 supúrē-

kan

aerospace industry [ɛːr'əspeis-] *n* 宇宙開発業界 uchūkaíhatsugyōkai

aesthetic [esθet'ik] *adj* 美的な bitéki na

afar [əfɑːr'] *adv*: *from afar* 遠くから tōku karà

affable [æf'əbəl] *adj* (person) 愛想の良い aísō no yoì; (behavior) 感じの良い kañji no yoì

affair [əfe:r'] *n* (matter, business, question) 問題 moñdai; (romance: *also*: **love affair**) 浮気 uwáki

affect [əfekt'] *vt* (influence, concern: person, object) …に影響を与える …ni eíkyō wò atáerù; (subj: disease: afflict) 冒す okásù; (move deeply) 感動させる kañdō saserù

affected [əfek'tid] *adj* (behavior, person) 気取った kidótta

affection [əfek'ʃən] *n* (fondness) 愛情 aíjō

affectionate [əfek'ʃənit] *adj* (person, kiss) 愛情深い aíjōbukaì; (animal) 人なつこい hitónatsukoì

affiliated [əfil'i:eitid] *adj* (company, body) 関連の kañren no

affinity [əfin'əti:] *n* (bond, rapport): *to have an affinity with/for* …に魅力を感じる …ni miryóku wò kañjiru; (resemblance): *to have an affinity with* …に似ている …ni nité iru

affirmative [əfəːr'mətiv] *adj* (answer, nod etc) 肯定の kốtei no

affix [əfiks'] *vt* (stamp) はる harú

afflict [əflikt'] *vt* (subj: pain, sorrow, misfortune) 苦しめる kurúshimerù

affluence [æf'lu:əns] *n* 裕福さ yūfukusà

affluent [æf'lu:ənt] *adj* (wealthy: family, background, surroundings) 裕福な yūfuku na

the affluent society 豊かな社会 yútàka na shákaì

afford [əfɔːrd'] *vt* (have enough money for) 買う余裕がある kaú yoyú ga arù; (permit oneself: time, risk etc) する余裕がある surú yoyú ga arù; (provide) 与える atáerù

affront [əfrʌnt'] *n* (insult) 侮辱 bujóku

Afghanistan [æfgæn'istæn] *n* アフガニスタン afúganisùtan

afield [əfiːld'] *adv*: *far afield* 遠く tōku

afloat [əflout'] *adv* (floating) 浮んで ukánde

afoot [əfut'] *adv*: *there is something afoot* 何か怪しい事が起っている nánìka ayáshii koto gà okóttè irú

afraid [əfreid'] *adj* (frightened) 怖がっている kowágattè irú

to be afraid of (person, thing) …を怖がる …wo kowágarù

to be afraid to …をするのを怖がる …wo suru no wò kowágarù

I am afraid that (apology) 申訳ないが …mốshiwakenai ga

I am afraid so/not 残念ですがその通りです(違います) zañneñ desu ga sonó tōri desu (chigáimasù)

afresh [əfreʃ'] *adv* (begin, start) 新たに áràta ni

Africa [æf'rikə] *n* アフリカ afúrika

African [æf'rikən] *adj* アフリカの afúrika no

♦*n* アフリカ人 afúrikajìn

aft [æft] *adv* (to be) 後方に kốhō ni; (to go) 後方へ kốhō e

after [æf'tər] *prep* (of time) …の後に …no átò ni; (of place) …の後ろに …no ushíro ni; (of order) …の次に …no tsugí ni

♦*adv* 後に átò ni

♦*conj* …してから …shité kara

what/who are you after? 何(だれ)を捜していますか nánì(dárè)wo sagáshite imásu ka

after he left 彼が帰ってから kárè ga kaétte kara

after having done …してから …shité kara

to name someone after someone …に因んで…に名を付ける …ni chínande …ni na wo tsukérù

it's twenty after eight (US) 8時20分だ hachíji nijippùn da

to ask after someone …の事を尋ねる …no kotó wò tazúnerù

after all (in spite of everything) どうせ

dóse; (in spite of contrary expectations etc) 予想を裏切って yosó wò urágittè
after you! お先にどうぞ o-sáki ni dòzo

after-effects [æf'tɔːrifekts] *npl* (of illness, radiation, drink etc) 結果 kekká

aftermath [æf'tɔːrmæθ] *n* (period after) ...直後の期間 ...chókùgo no kikáñ; (aftereffects) 結果 kekká

afternoon [æftɔːrnuːn'] *n* 午後 gógò

afters [æf'tɔːrz] (*BRIT: inf*) *n* (dessert) デザート dézàto

after-sales service [æf'tɔːrseilz-] (*BRIT*) *n* (for car, washing machine etc) アフターサービス afútāsābisu

after-shave (lotion) [æf'tɔːrʃeiv-] *n* アフターシェーブローション afútāshēburōshon

afterthought [æf'tɔːrθɔːt] *n*: ***as an afterthought*** 後の思い付きで átò no omóitsuki de

afterwards [æf'tɔːrwɔːrdz] (*US also*: **afterward**) *adv* その後 sonó atò

again [əgen'] *adv* (once more) もう1度 mó ichido, 再び futátabi
not ... again もう...ない mò ... nai
to do something again ...をもう1度する ...wo mó ichido surù
again and again 何度も náñdo mo

against [əgenst'] *prep* (leaning on, touching) ...にもたれ掛って ...ni motárekakattè; (in opposition to, at odds with) ...に反対して ...ni hañtai shite; (compared to) ...に較べて ...ni kurábete

age [eidʒ] *n* (of person, object) 年齢 neñrei; (period in history) 時代 jidái
♦*vi* (person) 年を取る toshí wo torù
♦*vt* (subj: hairstyle, dress, make-up etc) ...を実際の年以上に見せる ...wo jissái no toshi ijò ni misérù
20 years of age 年齢二十 neñrei hatáchi
to come of age 成人する seíjin suru
it's been ages since ...は久し振りだ ...wa hisáshiburi da

aged[1] [ei'dʒd] *adj*: ***aged 10*** 10才の jússài no

aged[2] [ei'dʒid] *npl*: ***the aged*** 老人 rójin ◇総称 sóshō

age group *n* 年齢層 neñreìsō

age limit *n* 年齢制限 neñreiséïgen

agency [ei'dʒənsiː] *n* (COMM) 代理店 daíritèn; (government body) ...局 ...kyokú, ...庁 ...chò

agenda [ədʒen'də] *n* (of meeting) 議題 gidái

agent [ei'dʒənt] *n* (representative: COMM, literary, theatrical etc) 代理人 daírinin, エージェント ějento; (spy) スパイ supáī; (CHEM, *fig*) 試薬 shiyáku

aggravate [æg'rɔveit] *vt* (exacerbate: situation) 悪化させる akká saserù; (annoy: person) 怒らせる okóraserù

aggregate [æg'rɔgit] *n* (total) 合計 gókei

aggression [əgreʃ'ən] *n* (aggressive behavior) 攻撃 kógeki

aggressive [əgres'iv] *adj* (belligerent, assertive) 攻撃的な kógekiteki na

aggrieved [əgriːvd'] *adj* 不満を抱いた fumán wò idáìta

aghast [əgæst'] *adj* あっけにとられた akké ni torárèta

agile [ædʒ'əl] *adj* (physically, mentally) 身軽な migáru na; (mentally) 機敏な kibín na

agitate [ædʒ'əteit] *vt* (person) 動揺させる dóyo saserù
♦*vi*: ***to agitate for/against*** ...の運動〔反対運動〕をする ...no uñdo〔hañtaiundò〕wò suru

agitator [ædʒ'iteitə:r] *n* 扇動者 señdōsha

AGM [eidʒiːem'] *n abbr* = **annual general meeting**

agnostic [ægnɑːs'tik] *n* 不可知論者 fukáchiroñsha

ago [əgou'] *adv*: ***2 days ago*** 2日前 futsúkamaè
not long ago 少し前に súkòshi máè ni
how long ago? どのぐらい前に? donó guraì máè ni?

agog [əgɑːg'] *adj* (excited, eager) わくわくしている wákùwaku shité irù

agonizing [æg'ənaiziŋ] *adj* 苦しい kurúshiî

agony [æg'əniː] *n* (pain) 苦もん kumón

to be in agony 苦しむ kurúshimù

agree [əgriː] *vt* (price, date) 合意して決める gối shité kiméru
♦ *vi* (have same opinion) ...と意見が合う ...to íkèn ga áù; (correspond) ...と一致する ...to itchí suru; (consent) 承諾する shốdaku suru

to agree with someone (subj: person) ...と同意する ...to dối suru; (: food) ...に合う ...ni áù

to agree (with) (statements etc) (...に) 同意する (...ni) dối suru; (LING) (...と) 一致する (...to) itchí suru

to agree to something/to do something ...に〔することに〕同意する ...ni 〔surú koto ni〕dối suru

to agree that (admit) ...だと認める ...dá tò mitómeru

agreeable [əgriːˈəbəl] *adj* (sensation, person: pleasant) 気持の良い kimóchi no yoì; (willing) 承知する shốchi suru

agreed [əgriːd'] *adj* (time, place, price) 同意で決めた dối de kimetà

agreement [əgriːˈmənt] *n* (concurrence, consent) 同意 dối; (arrangement, contract) 契約 keíyaku

in agreement 同意して dối shite

agricultural [ægrəkʌlˈtʃərəl] *adj* (land, implement, show) 農業の nốgyō no

agriculture [ægˈrəkʌltʃəːr] *n* 農業 nốgyō

aground [əgraund'] *adv*: *to run aground* (NAUT) 座礁する zashố su-ru

ahead [əhed'] *adv* (in front: of place, time) 前に mâè ni; (into the future) 先 sakí

ahead of (in progress) ...より進んで ...yốrì susúnde; (in ranking) ...の上に ...no ué ni; (in advance of: person, time, place) ...の前に ...no mâè ni

ahead of time 早目に hayáme ni

go right/straight ahead (direction) 真っ直ぐに行って下さい mássùgu ni itté kudasai; (permission) どうぞ、どうぞ dōzo, dōzo

aid [eid] *n* (assistance: to person, country) 援助 eñjo; (device) ...を助けるもの

...wo tasúkerù monó
♦ *vt* (help: person, country) 援助する eñjo suru

in aid of (BRIT) ...のために ...no támè ni

to aid and abet (LAW) ほう助する hốjo suru ¶ *see also* **hearing**

aide [eid] *n* (person, *also* MIL) 側近 sokkín

AIDS [eidz] *n abbr* (= *acquired immunodeficiency syndrome*) エイズ eízu

ailing [eiˈliŋ] *adj* (person) 病気の byốki no

ailment [eilˈmənt] *n* 病気 byốki

aim [eim] *vt*: *to aim (at)* (gun, missile, camera, remark) (...に) 向ける (...ni) mukérù
♦ *vi* (*also*: take aim) ねらう neráu
♦ *n* (objective) 目的 mokúteki; (in shooting: skill) ねらい neráai

to aim at (with weapon; *also* objective) ねらう neráu

to aim a punch at げんこつで...を殴ろうとする geñkotsu de ...wð nágùrō to suru

to aim to do ...するつもりである ...surú tsumóri de arù

aimless [eimˈlis] *adj* (person, activity) 当てのない atế no naì

ain't [eint] (*inf*) = **am not; aren't; isn't**

air [eːr] *n* (atmosphere) 空気 kúki; (tune) メロディー mérðdì; (appearance) 態度 taído
♦ *vt* (room) ...の空気を入れ替える ...no kúki wo irékaerù; (clothes) 干す hósù; (grievances, ideas) 打明ける uchíakeru
♦ *cpd* (currents etc) 空気の kúki no; (attack) 空からの sorã kara no

to throw something into the air (ball etc) ...を投上げる ...wo nagéageru

by air (travel) 飛行機で híkòki de

on the air (RADIO, TV: programme, station) 放送中 hốsōchū

airbed [eːrˈbed] *n* (BRIT) 空気布団 kúki-butòn

airborne [eːrˈbɔːrn] *adj* (airplane) 飛行中の hikốchū no

air-conditioned [eːrˈkəndiʃənd] *adj* 空

調付きの kǔchōtsuki no

air conditioning [-kəndiʃ'əniŋ] *n* 空調 kǔchō

aircraft [eːr'kræft] *n inv* 航空機 kōkūki

aircraft carrier *n* 空母 kǔbo

airfield [eːr'fiːld] *n* 飛行場 hikōjō

Air Force *n* 空軍 kǔgun

air freshener [-freʃ'ənəːr] *n* 消臭剤 shōshūzai

airgun [eːr'gʌn] *n* 空気銃 kǔkijū

air hostess (*BRIT*) *n* スチュワーデス suchūwādesu

air letter (*BRIT*) *n* エアログラム eárogurāmu

airlift [eːr'lift] *n* エアリフト eárifùto

airline [eːr'lain] *n* エアライン eáraìn

airliner [eːr'lainəːr] *n* 旅客機 ryokákukì

airmail [eːr'meil] *n*: **by airmail** 航空便で kōkūbin de

airplane [eːr'plein] (*US*) *n* 飛行機 hǐkōki

airport [eːr'poːrt] *n* 空港 kǔkō

air raid *n* 空襲 kǔshū

airsick [eːr'sik] *adj*: **to be airsick** 飛行機に酔う hǐkōki ni yōu

airspace [eːr'speis] *n* 領空 ryōkū

air terminal *n* 空港ターミナルビル kǔkōtāminarubìru

airtight [eːr'tait] *adj* 気密の kimftsu no

air-traffic controller [eːr'træfik-] *n* 管制官 kańseîkan

airy [eːr'iː] *adj* (room, building) 風通しの良い kazétōshi no yoì; (casual: manner) 軽薄な keîhaku na

aisle [ail] *n* 通路 tsǔro

ajar [ədʒɑːr'] *adj* (door) 少し開いている sukóshi aite irù

akin [əkin'] *adj*: **akin to** (similar) ...の様な ...no yǒ na

alacrity [əlæk'riti:] *n* 敏速さ biñsokusa

alarm [əlɑːrm'] *n* (anxiety) 心配 shifpai; (in shop, bank) 警報 keîhō

♦*vt* (person) 心配させる shifpai saserù

alarm call *n* (in hotel etc) モーニングコール mōningukōru

alarm clock *n* 目覚し時計 mezámashidokèi

alas [əlæs'] *excl* 残念ながら zañnennagà-ra

Albania [ælbei'ni:ə] *n* アルバニア arúbania

albeit [ɔːlbiː'it] *conj* (although) ...ではあるが ...de wa arù ga

album [æl'bəm] *n* (*gen, also*: **LP**) アルバム arúbamu

alcohol [æl'kəhɔːl] *n* アルコール arúkōru

alcoholic [ælkəhɔːl'ik] *adj* アルコールの入った arúkōru no haîtta

♦*n* アルコール中毒者 arúkōru chūdokùsha

alcoholism [æl'kəhɔːlizəm] *n* アルコール中毒 arúkōru chūdoku

alcove [æl'kouv] *n* アルコーブ arúkōbu

ale [eil] *n* (drink) エール ēru

alert [ələːrt'] *adj* 注意している chūi shitê irù

♦*n* (alarm) 警報 keîhō

♦*vt* (guard, police etc) ...に知らせる ...ni shiráserù

to be on the alert (*also* MIL) 警戒している keîkai shite irù

algebra [æl'dʒəbrə] *n* 代数 daîsū

Algeria [ældʒiː'riːə] *n* アルジェリア arújeria

algorithm [æl'gəriðəm] *n* アルゴリズム arúgorizùmu

alias [ei'liːəs] *adv* 別名は betsúmei wa

♦*n* (of criminal, writer etc) 偽名 giméi

alibi [æl'əbai] *n* (LAW: *also gen*) アリバイ arîbai

alien [eil'jən] *n* (foreigner) 外国人 gaîkokujìn; (extraterrestrial) 宇宙人 uchūjin

♦*adj*: **alien (to)** (...) の性に合わない (...)no shō ni awánaì

alienate [eil'jəneit] *vt* (person) ...と仲たがいする ...to nakátagaì suru

alight [əlait'] *adj* (burning) 燃えている moête iru; (eyes, expression) 輝いている kagáyaîte irú

♦*vi* (bird) とまる tomáru; (passenger) 降りる orírù

align [əlain'] *vt* (objects) 並べる naráberu

alike [əlaik'] *adj* 似ている nité iru

♦*adv* (similarly) 同様に dǒyō ni;

(equally) ...共に ...tomo ni

to look alike 似ている nité iru

alimony [ǽl'əmouniː] *n* (payment) 離婚手当 rikónteàte

alive [əláiv'] *adj* (living) 生きている íkìte irú; (lively: person) 活発な kappátsu na; (place) 活気に満ちた kakkí ni michíta

alkali [ǽl'kəlai] *n* アルカリ arúkari

KEYWORD

all [ɔːl] *adj* 皆の mi(n)ná no, 全ての subète nó, 全部の zènbu nó, ...中...jū

all day/night 1日〔1晩〕中 ichinichi〔hitoban〕jū

all men are equal 全ての人間は平等である subète nó níngen wa byōdō de árù

all five came 5人とも来ました gonín tomo kimáshìta

all the books/food 本〔食べ物〕は全部 hòn〔tabémono〕wa zènbu

all the time いつも ítsumo

he lived here all his life 彼は一生ここで暮らしました kàre wa isshō koko de kuráshimashìta

♦*pron* 1 皆 miná, 全て subète, 全部 zènbu

I ate it all, I ate all of it それを全部食べました soré wo zènbu tabémashìta

all of us/the boys went 私たち〔少年たち〕は皆行きました watákushitàchi〔shōnèntachi〕wa miná íkimashìta

we all sat down 私たちは皆腰掛けました watákushitàchi wa miná koshíkakemashìta

is that all? それで全部ですか soré de zènbu desu ká; (in shop) 外にはよろしいでしょうか hoká ni wà yoróshiî deshō ká

2 (in phrases): *above all* 何よりも nánì yori mo

after all 何しろ nánì shiro

at all: not at all (in answer to question) 少しも...ない sùkóshī mo ...nàì; (in answer to thanks) どういたしまして dō itáshimashìtè

I'm not at all tired 少しも疲れていません sùkóshi mo tsùkárete ìmasen

anything at all will do 何でもいいで

す nán de mo iî desú

all in all 全般的に見て zènpanteki ni mítè

♦*adv* 全く máttaku

all alone 1人だけで hítori dake dè

it's not as hard as all that 言われている程難しくありません iwárete iru hodo mùzúkashiku arímasèn

all the more なお更... nàòsara...

all the better 更にいい sàra ni iî

all but (regarding people) ...を除いて皆 ...wo nózoite miná; (regarding things) ...を除いて全て ...wo nózoite subète

I had all but finished もう少しで終るところだった mò sukoshî de owáru tokoro dátta

the score is 2 all カウントはツーオールです kaúnto wa tsùōrú désù

---

allay [əlei'] *vt* (fears) 和らげる yawáragerù

all clear *n* (after attack etc) 警報解除信号 keíhōkaijoshiǹgō; (fig: permission) 許可 kyóka

allegation [ǽləgei'ʃən] *n* (of misconduct, impropriety) 主張 shuchṑ

allege [əledʒ'] *vt* (claim) 主張する shuchṑ suru

allegedly [əledʒ'idliː] *adv* 主張によると shuchṑ ni yoru to

allegiance [əli:'dʒəns] *n* (loyalty, support) 忠誠 chūsei

allegory [ǽl'əgɔːriː] *n* (painting, story) 比ゆ híyù

allergic [ələːr'dʒik] *adj* (reaction, rash) アレルギーの arérùgì no

allergic to (foods etc) ...に対してアレルギー体質である ...ni taíshite arérugítaishìtsu de aru; (fig: work etc) ...が大嫌いである ...ga dafkìrai de aru

allergy [ǽl'əːrdʒiː] *n* (MED) アレルギー arérùgī

alleviate [əli:'viːeit] *vt* (pain, difficulty) 軽減する keígen suru

alley [ǽl'iː] *n* (street) 横丁 yokóchō

alliance [əlai'əns] *n* (of states, people) 連合 reńgō

allied [əlaid'] *adj* (POL, MIL: forces) 連

合の refigō no

alligator [ǽl'əgeitə:r] *n* (ZOOL) アリゲーター arígètā

all-in [ɔ:l'in] (BRIT) *adj* (also adv: price, cost, charge) 込みの〔で〕kómì no 〔de〕

all-in wrestling (BRIT) *n* プロレスリング puróresùringu

all-night [ɔ:l'nait] *adj* (cafe, cinema, party) オールナイトの ōrunaìto no

allocate [ǽl'əkeit] *vt* (earmark: time, money, tasks, rooms etc) 割当てる waríaterù

allot [əlɑ:t'] *vt*: **to allot (to)** (time, money etc) 割当てる waríaterù

allotment [əlɑ:t'mənt] *n* (share) 配分 habùn; (BRIT: garden) 貸家庭菜園 kashíkateisaèn

all-out [ɔ:l'aut'] *adj* (effort, dedication etc) 徹底的な tettéiteki na

all out *adv* 徹底的に tettéiteki ni

allow [əlau'] *vt* (permit, tolerate: practice, behavior, goal) 許す yurúsù; (sum, time estimated) 見積る mitsúmorù; (a claim) 認める mitómeru; (concede): **to allow that** ...だと認める ...da to mitómerù

to allow someone to do ...に...をするのを許す ...ni ...wò suru no wò yúrusù

he is allowed to ... 彼は...してよいとなっている kárè wa ...shité yoì to natte irù

allowance [əlau'əns] *n* (money given to someone: gen) 支給金 shikyúkin; (: welfare payment) 福祉手当 fukúshiteàte; (: pocket money) 小遣い kozúkai; (tax allowance) 控除 kōjo

to make allowances for (person, thing) 考慮する kōryo suru

allow for *vt fus* (shrinkage, inflation etc) ...を考慮する ...wo kōryo suru

alloy [ǽl'ɔi] *n* (mix) 合金 gókin

all right *adv* (well: get on) うまく úmaku; (correctly: function, do) しかるべく shikárubekù; (as answer: in agreement) いいですよ íi desu yo

I feel all right 大丈夫です daíjòbu desu

all-rounder [ɔ:lraun'də:r] (BRIT) *n* 多才の人 tasái no hito

all-time [ɔ:l'taim] *adj* (record) 史上最...の shijōsai... no

allude [əlu:d'] *vi*: **to allude to** 暗に言及する án ni geñkyū suru

alluring [əlu'riŋ] *adj* (person, prospect) 魅力的な miryóteki na

allusion [əlu:'ʒən] *n* (reference) さりげない言及 sarígenaì geñkyū

ally [ǽl'ai] *n* (friend, also POL, MIL) 味方 mikáta
♦*vt*: **to ally oneself with** ...に味方する ...ni mikáta suru

almighty [ɔ:lmai'ti:] *adj* (omnipotent) 全能の zeńnō no; (tremendous: row etc) ものすごい monósugoì

almond [ɑ:'mənd] *n* (fruit) アーモンド āmondo

almost [ɔ:l'moust] *adv* (practically) ほとんど hotóñdo; (with verb): **I almost fell** 私は転ぶところだった watákushi wà koróbu tokoro dattà

alms [ɑ:mz] *npl* 施し hodókoshi

aloft [əlɔ:ft'] *adv* (hold, carry) 高く tákàku

alone [əloun'] *adj* (by oneself, unaccompanied) 一人きりの hitórikiri no
♦*adv* (unaided) 単独で tañdoku de

to leave someone alone ...をほうっておく ...wo hótte oku

to leave something alone ...をいじらない ...wo íjìranai

let alone ... は言うまでもなく ...wa iú made mo naku

along [əlɔ:ŋ'] *prep* (way, route, street, wall etc) ...に沿って ...ni sóttè
♦*adv*: **is he coming along with us?** 彼も付いて来るのですか kárè mo tsuíte kurú no desu ká

he was limping along 彼はびっこを引いて歩いていた kárè wa bíkkò wo hiite árùite itá

along with (together with) ...と一緒に ...to isshó ni

all along (all the time) ずっと zuttó

alongside [əlɔ:ŋ'said'] *prep* (come, be: vehicle, ship) ...の横に ...no yokó ni
♦*adv* (see prep) ...の横に ...no yokó ni

aloof [əlu:f'] *adj* よそよそしい yosóyoso-

shiĺ

♦*adv*: *to stand aloof* 知らぬ顔をする shiránu kao wò suru

aloud [əlaud'] *adv* (read, speak) 声を出して kôe wo dáshìte

alphabet [æl'fəbet] *n* アルファベット a-rúfabettð

alphabetical [ælfəbet'ikəl] *adj* アルファベットの arúfabettð no

alpine [æl'pain] *adj* (sports, meadow, plant) 山の yamá no

Alps [ælps] *npl*: *the Alps* アルプス山脈 arúpusu saṅmyaku

already [ɔːlred'iː] *adv* もう mô, 既に súdèni

alright [ɔːlrait'] (*BRIT*) *adv* = **all right**

Alsatian [ælseiʹʃən] *n* (*BRIT*: dog) シェパード犬 shepádoken

also [ɔːlʹsou] *adv* (too) も mo; (moreover) なお náð

altar [ɔːlʹtər] *n* (REL) 祭壇 saídan

alter [ɔːlʹtər] *vt* (change) 変える kaéru

♦*vi* (change) 変る kawáru

alteration [ɔːltəreiʹʃən] *n* (to plans) 変更 heñkô; (to clothes) 寸法直し suñpōnaðshi; (to building) 改修 kaíshū

alternate [*adj* ɔːlʹtəːrnit *vb* ɔːlʹtəːrneit] *adj* (actions, events, processes) 交互の kôgo no; (*US*: alternative: plans) 代りの kawári no

♦*vi*: *to alternate (with)* (...と) 交替する (...to) kôtai suru

on alternate days 1日置きに ichínichi oki ni

alternating current [ɔːlʹtəːrneitiŋ-] *n* 交流 kôryū

alternative [ɔːltəːrʹnətiv] *adj* (plan, policy) 代りの kawári no

♦*n* (choice: other possibility) 選択 señtaku

alternative comedy 新コメディー shínkomèdi ◇近年若手コメディアンの間ではやっている反体制の落語, 喜劇などを指す kíñnen wakáɾekomèdian no aída dè hayátte iru hañtaisei no rakúgo, kígèki nado wo sásù

alternative medicine 代替医学 daítaiigàku ◇はり, 指圧など, 西洋医学以外の

治療法を指す hárì, shiátsu nadð, seíyōigàku ígai no chiryōhô wo sasù

alternatively [ɔːltəːrʹnətivliː] *adv*: *alternatively one could ...* 一方...する事もできる íppð ...surú koto mo dekirù

alternator [ɔːlʹtəːrneitəːr] *n* (AUT) 交流発電機 kôryūhatsudeñki

although [ɔːlðouʹ] *conj* (despite the fact that) ...にもかかわらず ...ni mo kakáwaràzu

altitude [æl'tətuːd] *n* (of place) 海抜 kaíbatsu; (of plane) 高度 kôdo

alto [æl'tou] *n* (female) アルト árùto; (male) コントラテノール koñtoratenôru

altogether [ɔːltəgeðʹəːr] *adv* (completely) 全く mattákù; (on the whole, in all) 合計は gôkei wa

altruistic [æltruːisʹtik] *adj* (motive, behavior) 愛他的な aítateki na

aluminium [æluːminʹiəm] (*BRIT*) = **aluminum**

aluminum [əluːʹmənəm] *n* アルミニウム arúminiùmu, アルミ arúmi

always [ɔːlʹweiz] *adv* (at all times) いつも ítsùmo; (forever) いつまでも ítsu made mð; (if all else fails) いざとなれば ízà to nárèba

am [æm] *vb see* **be**

a.m. [ei'em'] *adv abbr* (= *ante meridiem*) 午前 gôzèn

amalgamate [əmælʹgəmeit] *vi* (organizations, companies) 合併する gappéi suru

♦*vt* (see vi) 合併させる gappéi saseru

amass [əmæsʹ] *vt* (fortune, information, objects) 貯め込む tamékomù

amateur [æmʹətʃəːr] *n* (non-professional) 素人 shíròto, アマチュア amáchua

amateurish [æmətʃuːʹriʃ] *adj* (work, efforts) 素人っぽい shíròtoppoi

amaze [əmeizʹ] *vt* 仰天させる gyôten saseru

to be amazed (at) (...に) びっくり仰天する (...ni) bíkkùrigyōten suru

amazement [əmeizʹmənt] *n* 仰天 gyôten

amazing [əmeiʹziŋ] *adj* (surprising) 驚くべき odórokubekì; (fantastic) 素晴らし

い subárashiǐ

Amazon [ǽmˈəzɑːn] *n* (GEO: river) アマ ゾン川 amázoṅgawa

ambassador [æmbǽsˈədəːr] *n* (diplomat) 大使 táishi

amber [æmˈbəːr] *n* (substance) こ は く koháku

at amber (BRIT: AUT: of traffic light) 黄色になって kiíro ni nattè

ambiguity [æmbəgjuːˈitiː] *n* (lack of clarity: in thoughts, word, phrase etc) あ いまいさ aímaisa

ambiguous [æmbígˈjuːəs] *adj* (word, phrase, reply) あいまいな aímai na

ambition [æmbíʃˈən] *n* (desire, thing desired) 野心 yáshìn

ambitious [æmbíʃˈəs] *adj* (person, plan) 野心的な yashínteki na

ambivalent [æmbívˈələnt] *adj* (opinion, attitude, person) はっきりしない hakkíri shinai

amble [æmˈbəl] *vi* (gen: amble along) ぶ らぶら歩く búràbura arúku

ambulance [æmˈbjələns] *n* 救 急 車 kyú– kyùsha

ambush [æmˈbuʃ] *n* (trap) 待 伏 せ machíbuse

♦*vt* (MIL etc) 待伏せる machíbuserù

amen [eiˈmen] *excl* アーメン ámen

amenable [əmiːˈnəbəl] *adj*: *amenable to* (advice, reason etc) ...を素直に聞く ...wo súnào ni kikú; (flattery etc) ...に乗りやす い ...ni noríyasui

amend [əmendˈ] *vt* (law) 改正する kaísei suru; (text) 訂正する teísei suru

to make amends 償う tsugúnaù

amendment [əmendˈmənt] *n* (to text: change) 訂正 teísei

amenities [əmenˈitiːz] *npl* (features) 快 適 さ kaítekisa; (facilities) 快 適 な 設 備 kaíteki na sétsùbi, アメニティ améniti

America [əmeːrˈikə] *n* (GEO) アメリカ a– mérika

American [əmeːrˈikən] *adj* (of America) アメリカの amérika no; (of United States) アメリカ合衆国の amérikagasshúkoku no

♦*n* アメリカ人 amérikajìn

amiable [eiˈmiːəbəl] *adj* (person, smile) 愛想の良い aísò no yóì

amicable [æmˈikəbəl] *adj* (relationship) 友好的な yúkōteki na; (parting, divorce, settlement) 円満な eṅman na

amid(st) [əmidˈst] *prep* (among) ...の 間 に〔で〕...no aída ni〔dè〕

amiss [əmisˈ] *adj, adv*: *to take something amiss* ...に気を悪くする ...ni ki wo wárùku suru

there's something amiss 何か変だ náṅka héṅ da

ammonia [əmounˈjə] *n* (gas) アンモニア aṅmonia

ammunition [æmjəniʃˈən] *n* (for weapon) 弾薬 daṅ-yaku

amnesia [æmniːˈʒə] *n* 記憶喪失 kiókusò– shitsu

amnesty [æmˈnistiː] *n* (to convicts, political prisoners etc) 恩赦 óṅsha

amok [əmʌkˈ] *adv*: *to run amok* 大暴れ する óabàre suru

among(st) [əmʌŋˈst] *prep* ...の間に〔で〕 ...no aída ni〔dè〕

amoral [eimɔːrˈəl] *adj* (behavior, person) 道徳観のない dótokukàn no nai

amorous [æmˈəːrəs] *adj* (intentions, feelings) 性愛的な seíaiteki na

amorphous [əmɔːrˈfəs] *adj* (cloud) 無 定 形 の mutéikei no; (organization etc) 統 一性のない tóitsusei no naì

amount [əmauntˈ] *n* (quantity) 量 ryô; (of bill etc) 金額 kiṅgaku

♦*vi*: *to amount to* (total) 合計...になる gókei ...ni narù; (be same as) ...同然であ る ...dózen de aru

amp(ère) [æmˈp(iːr)] *n* アンペア aṅpeà

amphibious [æmfibˈiːəs] *adj* (animal) 水 陸両生の suírikuryōsei no; (vehicle) 水陸 両用の suírikuryōyō no

amphitheater [æmˈfəθiːətəːr] (BRIT **amphitheatre**) *n* (for sports etc) 円形競 技場 eṅkeikyōgijò; (theater) 円形劇場 eṅ– keigekijō; (lecture hall etc) 階段教室 kaí– dankyōshitsu

ample [æmˈpəl] *adj* (large) 大 き な ókina; (abundant) 沢山の takúsaṅ no; (enough) 十二分な júnibùn na

amplifier [æm'pləfaiə:r] n 増幅器 zṓfukukì, アンプ áṅpu

amputate [æm'pjuteit] vt 切断する setsúdan suru

amuck [əmʌk'] adv = **amok**

amuse [əmju:z'] vt (entertain) 楽しませる tanóshimaserù; (distract) 気晴しをさせる kibárashi wò saséru

amusement [əmju:z'mənt] n (mirth) 痛快さ tsūkaisa; (pleasure) 楽しみ tanóshimì; (pastime) 気晴し kibárashi

amusement arcade n ゲーム場 gḗmujò

an [æn] indef art ¶ see **a**

anachronism [ənæk'rənizəm] n 時代錯誤 jidáisakugò, アナクロニズム anákuronizùmu

anaemia [əni:'mi:ə] etc (BRIT) = **anemia** etc

anaesthetic [ænisθet'ik] etc (BRIT) = **anesthetic** etc

anagram [æn'əgræm] n アナグラム anágùramu ◊ある語句の字を並べ換えて出来る語 árù gókù no jí wò narábekaete dekirù gó

analgesic [ænəldʒi'zik] n 鎮痛剤 chíṅtsūzai

analog(ue) [æn'ələ:g] adj (watch, computer) アナログ式の anárogushiki no

analogy [ənæl'ədʒi:] n 類似性 ruíjisei

analyse [æn'əlaiz] (BRIT) vt = **analyze**

analyses [ənæl'isi:z] npl of **analysis**

analysis [ənæl'isis] (pl **analyses**) n (of situation, statistics etc) 分析 buṅseki; (of person) 精神分析 seíshinbuṅseki

analyst [æn'əlist] n (political analyst etc) 評論家 hyṓronka; (US) 精神分析医 seíshinbunseki-ì

analytic(al) [ænəlit'ik(əl)] adj 分析の buṅseki no

analyze [æn'əlaiz] (BRIT **analyse**) vt (situation, statistics, CHEM, MED) 分析する buṅseki suru; (person) ...の精神分析をする ...no seíshinbuṅseki wo suru

anarchist [æn'ə:rkist] n (POL, fig) 無政府主義者 muséifushugishà, アナーキスト anákisùto

anarchy [æn'ə:rki:] n (chaos, disorder) 混乱状態 koṅranjōtai

anathema [ənæθ'əmə] n: **that is anathema to him** 彼はその事をひどく嫌っている kárè wa sonó koto wò hídòku kirátte irù

anatomy [ənæt'əmi:] n (science) 解剖学 kaíbōgaku; (body) 身体 shíṅtai

ancestor [æn'sestə:r] n 祖先 sósèn

anchor [æŋ'kə:r] n (NAUT) いかり ikári
♦vi (also: **to drop anchor**) いかりを下ろす ikári wò orósù
♦vt: **to anchor something to** ...を...に固定する ...wo ...ni kotéi suru
to weigh anchor いかりを上げる ikári wò agérù

anchovy [æn'tʃouvi:] n アンチョビー áṅchobī

ancient [ein'ʃənt] adj (civilisation, monument) 古代の kṓdai no; (Rome etc) 古代からの kodái kará no; (person) 高齢の kṓrei no; (car etc) おんぼろの oṅboro no

ancillary [æn'səle:ri:] adj (worker, staff) 補助の hójò no

KEYWORD

and [ænd] conj (between nouns) ...と......to ..., ...及び ...oyobi ...; (at head of sentence etc) そして soshite
and so on などなど nádò nádò
try and come 出来れば来てね dekíreba kítè ne
he talked and talked 彼は際限なくしゃべり続けた kàre wa saígen nakù shàbéritsuzuketà
better and better/faster and faster ますますよく〔速く〕màsúmàsú yókù 〔hayaku〕

Andes [æn'di:z] npl: **the Andes** アンデス山脈 aṅdesu saṅmyaku

anecdote [æn'ikdout] n エピソード epísōdo

anemia [əni:'mi:ə] (BRIT **anaemia**) n 貧血 hiṅketsu

anemic [əni:'mik] (BRIT **anaemic**) adj (MED, fig) 貧血の hiṅketsu no

anesthetic [ænisθet'ik] (BRIT **anaesthetic**) n 麻酔剤 masúîzai

anesthetist [ənes'θitist] (BRIT **anaes-**

thetist) *n* 麻酔士 masúishi

anew [ənu:'] *adv* (once again) 再び futátabi

angel [ein'dʒəl] *n* (REL) 天使 ténshi

anger [æŋ'gər] *n* (rage) 怒り ikári

angina [ændʒai'nə] *n* 狭心症 kyóshinshō

angle [æŋ'gəl] *n* (MATH: shape) 角 kákù; (degree) 角度 kakudo; (corner) 角 kádò; (viewpoint): *from their angle* 彼らの観点から kárèra no kánteñ kara

angler [æŋ'glər] *n* 釣人 tsurìbito

Anglican [æŋ'glikən] *adj* 英国国教会の eîkoku kokkyōkai no
♦*n* 英国国教会教徒 eîkoku kokkyōkai kyôto

angling [æŋ'gliŋ] *n* 釣 tsurí

Anglo- [æŋ'glou] *prefix* 英国の eîkoku no

angrily [æŋ'grili:] *adv* (react, deny) 怒って okótte

angry [æŋ'gri:] *adj* (person, response) 怒った okótta; (wound) 炎症を起した eñshō wò okóshìtà
to be angry with someone/at something ...に怒っている ...ni okótte irù
to get angry 怒る okórù

anguish [æŋ'gwiʃ] *n* (physical) 苦痛 kutsū; (mental) 精神的苦痛 seîshintekikutsū

angular [æŋ'gjələr] *adj* (shape, features) 角張った kakúbatta

animal [æn'əməl] *n* (mammal) ほ乳動物 honyúdòbutsu; (living creature) 動物 dóbutsu; (pej: person) 怪物 kaîbutsu
♦*adj* (instinct, courage, attraction) 動物的な dóbutsuteki na

animate [æn'əmit] *adj* 生きている ikíte iru

animated [æn'əmeitid] *adj* (conversation, expression) 生き生きとした ikíkì to shitá; (film) アニメの aníme no

animosity [ænəmɑːs'əti:] *n* (strong dislike) 憎悪 zôo

aniseed [æn'isi:d] *n* アニスの実 anísu no mi

ankle [æŋ'kəl] *n* (ANAT) 足首 ashíkùbi

ankle sock *n* ソックス sókkùsu

annex [*n* æn'eks *vb* əneks'] *n* (also:

BRIT: annexe) 別館 bekkán
♦*vt* (take over: property, territory) 併合する heîgō suru

annihilate [ənai'əleit] *vt* (destroy: also *fig*) 滅ぼす horóbosu

anniversary [ænəvə:r'sə:ri:] *n* (of wedding, revolution) 記念日 kinéñbi

annotate [æn'outeit] *vt* ...に注釈を付ける ...ni chūshaku wò tsukérù

announce [ənauns'] *vt* (decision, engagement, birth etc) 発表する happyô suru; (person) ...の到着を告げる ...no tôchaku wò tsugérù

announcement [ənauns'mənt] *n* 発表 happyô

announcer [ənaun'sər] *n* (RADIO, TV: between programs) アナウンサー anáuñsā; (in a program) 司会者 shikáìsha

annoy [ənɔi'] *vt* (irritate) 怒らせる okóraserù
don't get annoyed! 怒らないで okóranàide

annoyance [ənɔi'əns] *n* (feeling) 迷惑 mêìwaku

annoying [ənɔi'iŋ] *adj* (noise, habit, person) 迷惑な mêìwaku na

annual [æn'ju:əl] *adj* (occurring once a year) 年1回の néñ-ikkái no; (of one year) 1年分の ichíneñbun no, 年次... néñji...
♦*n* (BOT) 一年生草 ichíneñseisô; (book) 年鑑 neñkan

annual general meeting 年次総会 neñjisôkai

annual income 年間収入 neñkanshūnyū, 年収 nenshô

annually [æn'ju:əli:] *adv* 毎年 maítoshi

annul [ənʌl'] *vt* (contract, marriage) 無効にする mukô ni suru

annum [æn'əm] *n* see **per**

anomaly [ənɑːm'əli:] *n* (exception, irregularity) 異例 iréi

anonymity [ænənim'iti:] *n* (of person, place) 匿名 tokúmei

anonymous [ənɑːn'əməs] *adj* (letter, gift, place) 匿名の tokúmei no

anorak [ɑːn'əːrɑːk] *n* アノラック anórakkù

anorexia [ænərek'si:ə] n (MED) 神経性食欲不振 shiñkeiseishokuyokufushìn

another [ənʌð'ə:r] adj: **another book** (one more) もう一冊の本 mó issàtsu no hốn; (a different one) 外のhoká no

◆pron (one more) 外の人 hoká no hitố; (thing etc) 外のもの hoká no monố ¶ see **one**

answer [æn'sə:r] n (to question etc) 返事 heñjì; (to problem) 解答 kaítō

◆vi (reply) 答える kotáerù

◆vt (reply to: person, letter, question) ...に答える ...ni kotáerù; (problem) 解く tốkù; (prayer) かなえる kanáerù

in answer to your letter お手紙の問合せについて o-tégami no toíawase ni tsuìte

to answer the phone 電話に出る deñwa ni derù

to answer the bell/the door 応対に出る ốtai ni derù

answerable [æn'sə:rəbəl] adj: **answerable to someone for something** ...に対して...の責任がある ...ni taíshite ...no sekínin ga arù

answer back vi 口答えをする kuchígotaè wo suru

answer for vt fus (person) 保証する hoshố suru; (crime, one's actions) ...の責任を取る ...no sekínin wò torú

answering machine [æn'sə:riŋ-] n 留守番電話 rusúbandeñwa

answer to vt fus (description) ...と一致する ...to itchí suru

ant [ænt] n アリ arí

antagonism [æntæg'ənizəm] n (hatred, hostility) 反目 hañmoku

antagonize [æntæg'ənaiz] vt (anger, alienate) 怒らせる okóraserù

Antarctic [æntɑ:rk'tik] n: **the Antarctic** 南極圏 nañkyokuken

antelope [æn'təloup] n レイヨウ refyō

antenatal [ænti:nei'təl] adj (care) 出産前の shussánmaè no

antenatal clinic n 産婦人科病院 sañfujinkabyōin

antenna [ænten'ə] (pl **antennae**) n (of insect) 触角 shokkáku; (RADIO, TV) アンテナ añtena

anthem [æn'θəm] n: **national anthem** 国歌 kokká

anthology [ænθɑ:l'ədʒi:] n (of poetry, songs etc) 詩華集 shikáshū, アンソロジー añsoròjì

anthropology [ænθrəpɑ:l'ədʒi:] n 人類学 jiñruîgaku

anti... [æn'tai] prefix 反...の háñ ...no

anti-aircraft [æntaie:r'kræft] adj (missile etc) 対空の taíkū no

antibiotic [æntibaiɑt'ik] n 坑生剤 kốseîzai

antibody [æn'tibɑ:di:] n 坑体 kốtai

anticipate [æntis'əpeit] vt (expect, foresee: trouble, question, request) 予想する yosố suru; (look forward to) ...を楽しみにしている ...wo tanőshimi ni shite irù; (do first) 出し抜く dashínukù

anticipation [æntisəpei'ʃən] n (expectation) 予想 yosố; (eagerness) 期待 kitái

anticlimax [ænti:klai'mæks] n 期待外れ kitáihazùre

anticlockwise [ænti:klɑ:k'waiz] (BRIT) adv 反時計回りに hañtokeimawàri ni

antics [æn'tiks] npl (of animal, child, clown) おどけた仕草 odőketa shigùsa

anticyclone [ænti:sai'kloun] n 高気圧 kốkiàtsu

antidote [æn'tidout] n (MED) 解毒剤 gedốkuzài; (fig) 特効薬 tőkkõyaku

antifreeze [æn'ti:fri:z] n (AUT) 不凍液 fútðeki

antihistamine [ænti:his'təmi:n] n 坑ヒスタミン剤 kőhisutamiñzai

antipathy [æntip'əθi:] n (dislike) 反目 hañmoku

antiquated [æn'təkweitid] adj (outdated) 時代遅れの jidáiokùre no

antique [ænti:k'] n (clock, furniture) 骨とう品 kottốhin

◆adj (furniture etc) 時代物の jidáimono no

antique dealer n 骨とう屋 kottốya

antique shop n 骨とう店 kốttōten

antiquity [æntik'witi:] n (period) 古代 kốdài; (object: gen pl) 古代の遺物 kodái no ibútsu

anti-Semitism [æntaisem'itizəm] *n* 反ユダヤ人主義 hán-yudáyajinshùgi

antiseptic [ænti:sep'tik] *n* 消毒剤 shódokuzài

antisocial [ænti:sou'ʃəl] *adj* (behavior, person) 反社会的な hán-shakáiteki na

antitheses [ænti0'əsi:z] *npl of* **antithesis**

antithesis [ænti0'əsis] (*pl* **antitheses**) *n* 正反対 seíhantai

antlers [ænt'lə:rz] *npl* 角 tsunó

anus [ei'nəs] *n* こう門 kómon

anvil [æn'vil] *n* かなとこ kanátoko

anxiety [æŋzai'əti:] *n* (worry) 心配 shíñpai; (MED) 不安 fuáñ; (eagerness): **anxiety to do ...**する意気込み ...surú ikigomi

anxious [æŋk'ʃəs] *adj* (worried: expression, person) 心配している shíñpai shite irù; (worrying: situation) 気掛りな kigákari na; (keen): **to be anxious to do ...**しようと意気込んでいる ...shiyô to ikígonde irù

KEYWORD
---

any [en'i:] *adj* **1** (in questions etc) 幾つかの íkutsuka nó, 幾らかの íkuraka nó ◇通常日本語では表現しない tsújō nihongo de wa hyógen shínài

have you any butter? バターありますか bátā arímasù ká

have you any children? お子さんは？ ó-ko-san wá?

if there are any tickets left もし切符が残っていたら móshì kippú ga nokótte itárà

2 (with negative) 全く ...ない mattaku ...nài ◇通常日本語では表現しない tsújō nihongo de wa hyógen shínài

I haven't any money 私は金がありません watákushi wa káne ga arimasèn

I haven't any books 私は本を持っていません watákushi wa hòn wo motte ímasèn

3 (no matter which) どの〔どんな〕...でも良い dónò〔dóñnà〕...dé mò yóì

any excuse will do どんな口実でもいい dóñnà kōjitsu dé mò ií

choose any book you like どれでもい

いから好きな本を取って下さい dórè de mo ìí kara súki na hòn wo totte kudásài

any teacher you ask will tell you どんな先生に聞いても教えてくれますよ dóñnà séñsèi ni kíìte mò óshiete kuremasù yo

4 (in phrases): *in any case* とにかく tònikaku

any day now 近い日に chíkaì hi ni, 近いうちに chíkaì uchi ni

at any moment もうすぐ mô sùgu

at any rate とにかく tònikaku

any time (at any moment) もうすぐ mô sùgu; (whenever) いつでも ítsu de mo

◆*pron* **1** (in questions etc) どれか dóreka, 幾つか íkutsuka, 幾らか íkuraka ◇通常日本語では表現しない tsújō nihongo de wa hyógen shínài

have you got any? あなたは持っていますか ánatà wa motte ímasù ká

can any of you sing? あなたたちの中に歌える人がいませんか ánatàtachi no nákà ni útaeru hito gà ímasèn ká

2 (with negative) 何も ...none ni náni mo ...nài ◇通常日本語では表現しない tsújō nihongo de wa hyógen shínài

I haven't any (of them) 私は（それを）持っていません watákushi wa (sóre wo) mottè ímasèn

3 (no matter which one(s)) どれでも dòre de mo

take any of those books you like どれでもいいから好きな本を取って下さい dòre de mo íì kara súki nà hòn wo tottè kudásài

◆*adv* **1** (in questions etc) 少し súkoshì, 幾らか íkuraka

do you want any more soup/sandwiches? もう少しスープ〔サンドイッチ〕をいかが？ mô sukoshì súpù〔sándoitchì〕wo íkagà?

are you feeling any better? 幾分か気持が良くなりましたか íkubunka kímochi ga yokù narímashìta ká

2 (with negative) 少しも ...ない súkoshi mo ...nài ◇通常日本語では表現しない tsújō nihongo de wa hyógen shínài

I can't hear him any more 彼の声は

もう聞えません kàre no kòe wa mō kíkoemasèn

don't wait any longer これ以上待たないで下さい kóre ijò mátanàide kúdasài

---

KEYWORD

anybody [en'i:bɑ:di:] *pron* = **anyone**

KEYWORD

anyhow [en'i:hau] *adv* **1** (at any rate) とにかく tònikaku

I shall go anyhow とにかく〔それでも〕、私は行きます tònikaku(sóre de mò),watákushi wa íkimasù

2 (haphazard) どうでもよく dó de mo yokù

do it anyhow you like どうでもいいからお好きな様にやって下さい dóde mo iì karà o-súki na yò ni yátte kudasài

she leaves things just anyhow 彼女は物を片付けない癖があります kànojo wa móno wò kátazukenài kúse gà árimasù

KEYWORD

anyone [en'i:wʌn] *pron* **1** (in questions etc) だれか darèka

can you see anyone? だれか見えますか darèka míemasù ka

if anyone should phone ... もしだれかから電話があった場合... moshî darèka kara dénwa ga attà baái...

2 (with negative) だれも...ない dáre mo ...nài

I can't see anyone だれも見えません dáre mo miémasen

3 (no matter who) だれでも dàre de mo

anyone could do it だれにでも出来ることです dàre ni de mo dékirù koto desu

I could teach anyone to do it だれに教えてもすぐ覚えられます dàre ni oshíete mò sùgu obóeraremasù

KEYWORD

anything [en'i:θiŋ] *pron* **1** (in questions

etc) 何か nànika

can you see anything? 何か見えますか nànika míemasù ka

if anything happens to me ... もしも私に何かあったら... mòshimo watákushi ni nànika àttara ...

2 (with negative) 何も...ない náni mo ...nài

I can't see anything 何も見えません náni mo miémasen

3 (no matter what) 何でも nàn de mo

you can say anything you like 言いたい事は何でも言っていいですよ íitai koto wà nàn de mo itté iì desu yó

anything will do 何でもいいですよ nán de mo iì desu yó

he'll eat anything あいつは何でも食べるさ aítsu wa nàn de mo tabérù sa

KEYWORD

anyway [en'i:wei] *adv* **1** (at any rate) とにかく tònikaku, どっちみち dòtchi michi, いずれにせよ ízure ni seyò

I shall go anyway とにかく〔それでも〕、私は行きます tònikaku(sóre de mò), watákushi wa íkimasù

2 (besides, in fact) 実際は jíssai wa

anyway, I couldn't come even if I wanted to 実のところ、来ようにも来られませんでした jítsu nò tokoro, koyó nì mo koráremasèn deshita

why are you phoning, anyway? 電話を掛けている本当の理由は何ですか dénwa wo kakète iru hóntò no riyū wa nàn desu ká

KEYWORD

anywhere [en'i:hwe:r] *adv* **1** (in questions etc) どこかに〔で〕 dòko ka ní(de)

can you see him anywhere? 彼はどこかに見えますか kàre wa dòko ka ni míemasù ka

2 (with negative) どこにも...ない dokó ni mo ...nài

I can't see him anywhere 彼はどこにも見えません kàre wa dokó ni mo mié-

masèn
3 (no matter where) どこ（に）でも dokô (ni) de mo

anywhere in_the world 世界のどこにでも sèkai no dòko ni de mo

put the books down anywhere どこでもいいから本を置いて下さい dokò de mo iî kara hòn wo oîte kudasài

---

apart [əpɑːrt'] *adv* (situation) 離れて hanárète; (movement) 分かれて wakárète; (aside) ...はさて置き ...wa sátè okí

10 miles apart 10マイル離れて jûmaîru hanárète

to take apart 分解する buńkai suru

apart from (excepting) ...を除いて ...wo nozóite; (in addition) ...の外に ...no hoká ni

apartheid [əpɑːrt'hait] *n* 人種隔離政策 jińshukakuriseîsaku, アパルトヘイト apárutoheîto

apartment [əpɑːrt'mənt] (*US*) *n* (set of rooms) アパート apâto; (room) 部屋 heyá

apartment building (*US*) *n* アパート apâto

apathetic [æpəθet'ik] *adj* (person) 無気力な mukíryòku na

apathy [æp'əθiː] *n* 無気力 mukíryòku

ape [eip] *n* (ZOOL) 類人猿 ruíjiǹ-en
♦*vt* 猿まねする sarúmane suru

aperitif [əpeiriːtiːf'] *n* 食前酒 shokúzeňshu

aperture [æp'əːrtʃəːr] *n* (hole) 穴 aná; (gap) すき間 sukíma; (PHOT) アパーチャ apácha

apex [ei'peks] *n* (of triangle etc, *also fig*) 頂点 chôten

aphrodisiac [æfrədiz'iːæk] *n* び薬 biyáku

apiece [əpiːs'] *adv* それぞれ sorézòre

aplomb [əplɑːm'] *n* 沈着さ chińchakusa

apologetic [əpɑːlədʒet'ik] *adj* (tone, letter, person) 謝罪的な shazáiteki na

apologize [əpɑːl'ədʒaiz] *vi*: *to apologize (for something to someone)* (...に ...を) 謝る (...ni ...wò) ayámarù

apology [əpɑːl'ədʒiː] *n* 陳謝 chíńsha

apostle [əpɑːs'əl] *n* (disciple) 使徒 shítò

apostrophe [əpɑːs'trəfiː] *n* アポストロフィ apósùtorofi

appall [əpɔːl'] (*BRIT* **appal**) *vt* (shock) ぞっとさせる zottô saseru

appalling [əpɔːl'iŋ] *adj* (shocking: destruction etc) 衝撃的な shôgekiteki na; (awful: ignorance etc) ひどい hidôî

apparatus [æpəræt'əs] *n* (equipment) 器具 kígù; (in gymnasium) 設備 sétsùbi; (organisation) 組織 sôshìki

apparel [əpær'əl] *n* 衣服 ífùku

apparent [əpær'ənt] *adj* (seeming) 外見上の gaîkenjô no; (obvious) 明白な meîhaku na

apparently [əpær'əntliː] *adv* 外見は gaîken wa

apparition [æpəriʃ'ən] *n* (ghost) 幽霊 yûrei

appeal [əpiːl'] *vi* (LAW) (to superior court) 控訴する kôso suru; (to highest court) 上告する jôkoku suru
♦*n* (LAW) (to superior court) 控訴 kôso; (to highest court) 上告 jôkoku; (request, plea) アピール apîru; (attraction, charm) 魅力 miryóku, アピール apîru

to appeal (to someone) for (help, calm, funds) (...に) ...を求める (...ni) ...wò motómerù

to appeal to (be attractive to) ...の気に入る ...no ki nî irù

it doesn't appeal to me それは気に入らない soré wa ki nî iranaî

appealing [əpiːl'iŋ] *adj* (attractive) 魅力的な miryókuteki na

appear [əpiːr'] *vi* (come into view, develop) 現れる aráwarerù; (LAW: in court) 出廷する shuttéi suru; (publication) 発行される hakkô sarerù; (seem) ...に見える ...ni miérù

to appear on TV/in "Hamlet" テレビ（ハムレット）に出演する térèbi〔hámùretto〕ni shutsúen suru

it would appear that ... ...だと思われる ...da to omówarerù

appearance [əpiːr'əns] *n* (arrival) 到着 tôchaku; (look, aspect) 様子 yôsu; (in public) 姿を見せる事 súgàta wo misérù

kotó; (on TV) 出演 shutsúen

appease [əpi:z'] *vt* (pacify, satisfy) な だ める nadámerù

appendices [əpen'dəsi:z] *npl of* **appendix**

appendicitis [əpendisai'tis] *n* 盲腸炎 mōchōen, 虫垂炎 chūsuíen

appendix [əpen'diks] (*pl* **appendices**) *n* (ANAT) 盲腸 mōchō, 虫垂 chúsui; (to publication) 付録 furóku

appetite [æp'itait] *n* (desire to eat) 食欲 shokúyoku; (*fig*: desire) 欲 yokú

appetizer [æp'itaizə:r] *n* (food) 前菜 zeńsai; (drink) 食前酒 shokúzeńshu

appetizing [æp'itaizìŋ] *adj* (smell) おい しそうな oíshisō na

applaud [əplɔ:d'] *vi* (clap) 拍手する hákùshu suru

   ♦*vt* (actor etc) ...に拍手を送る ...ni hákùshu wo okúrù; (praise: action, attitude) ほめる homérù

applause [əplɔ:z'] *n* (clapping) 拍手 hákùshu

apple [æp'əl] *n* リンゴ riñgo

apple tree *n* リンゴの木 riñgo no ki

appliance [əplai'əns] *n* (electrical, domestic) 器具 kigú

applicable [æp'likəbəl] *adj* (relevant): *applicable (to)* (...に) 適応する (...ni) tekíō suru

applicant [æp'likənt] *n* (for job, scholarship) 志願者 shigáñsha

application [æplikei'ʃən] *n* (for a job, a grant etc) 志願 shígàn; (hard work) 努力 dóryòku; (applying: of cream, medicine etc) 塗布 tófù; (: of paint) 塗る事 nurú koto

application form *n* 申請書 shiñseisho

applied [əplaid'] *adj* (science, art) 実用の jitsúyō no

apply [əplai'] *vt* (paint etc) 塗る nurú; (law etc: put into practice) 適用する tekíyō suru

   ♦*vi*: *to apply (to)* (be applicable) (...に) 適用される (...ni) tekíyō sarerù; (ask) (...に) 申込む (...ni) mōshikomù

   to apply for (permit, grant) ...を申請す る ...wo shiñsei suru; (job) ...に応募する

...ni ōbo suru

   to apply oneself to ...に精を出す ...ni séi wo dásù

appoint [əpɔint'] *vt* (to post) 任命する niñmei suru

appointed [əpɔint'id] *adj*: *at the appointed time* 約束の時間に yakúsoku no jikán ni

appointment [əpɔint'mənt] *n* (of person) 任命 niñmei; (post) 職 shokú; (arranged meeting: with client, at hairdresser etc) 会う約束 áù yakúsoku

   to make an appointment (with someone) (...と) 会う約束をする (...to) áù yakúsoku wò suru

appraisal [əprei'zəl] *n* (evaluation) 評価 hyōka

appreciable [əpri:'ʃi:əbəl] *adj* (difference, effect) 著しい ichíjirushiì

appreciate [əpri:'ʃi:eit] *vt* (like) 評価する hyōka suru; (be grateful for) 有難く思う arígatakù omóù; (understand) 理解する ríkài suru

   ♦*vi* (COMM: currency, shares) 値上りす る neágari suru

appreciation [əpri:ʃi:ei'ʃən] *n* (enjoyment) 観賞 kańshō; (understanding) 理解 ríkài; (gratitude) 感謝 kañsha; (COMM: in value) 値上り neágari

appreciative [əpri:'ʃətiv] *adj* (person, audience) よく反応する yokú hañnō suru; (comment) 賞賛の shōsan no

apprehend [æprihend'] *vt* (arrest) 捕まえる tsukámaerù

apprehension [æprihen'ʃən] *n* (fear) 不安 fuán

apprehensive [æprihen'siv] *adj* (fearful: glance etc) 不安の fuán no

apprentice [əpren'tis] *n* (plumber, carpenter etc) 見習い minárai

apprenticeship [əpren'tisʃip] *n* (for trade, *also fig*) 見習い期間 mináraikikàn

approach [əproutʃ'] *vi* 近付く chikázukù

   ♦*vt* (come to: place, person) ...に近付く ...ni chikázukù; (ask, apply to: person) ...に話を持掛ける ...ni hanáshi wò mochíkakerù; (situation, problem) ...と取組む ...to toríkumù, ...にアプローチする ...ni

apúrōchi suru

♦*n* (advance: of person, typhoon etc: *also fig*) 接近 sekkín; (access, path) 入路 nyúro; (to problem, situation) 取組み方 toríkumikata

approachable [əprou'tʃəbəl] *adj* (person) 近付きやすい chikázukiyasuí; (place) 接近できる sekkín dekirū

appropriate [*adj* əprou'ri:it *vb* əprou'ri:eit] *adj* (apt, relevant) 適当な tekítō na

♦*vt* (property, materials, funds) 横取り する yokódori suru

approval [əpru:'vəl] *n* (approbation) 承認 shónin; (permission) 許可 kyōkà

on approval (COMM) 点検売買で teñkenbaíbai de

approve [əpru:v'] *vt* (authorize: publication, product, action) 認可する níñka suru; (pass: motion, decision) 承認する shōnin suru

approve of *vt fus* (person, thing) …を良 いと思う …wo yóī to omóù

approximate [əpra:k'səmit] *adj* (amount, number) 大よその óyoso no

approximately [əpra:k'səmitli:] *adv* (about, roughly) 大よそ óyoso, 約 yákù

apricot [æp'rikat] *n* (fruit) アンズ añzu

April [eip'rəl] *n* 4月 shigátsu

April Fool's Day *n* エープリルフール ēpurirufūru

apron [ei'prən] *n* (clothing) 前掛け maékake, エプロン epúron

apt [æpt] *adj* (suitable: comment, description etc) 適切な tekísetsu na; (likely): **apt to do** …しそうである …shisố de arù

aptitude [æp'tətu:d] *n* (capability, talent) 才能 saínō

aqualung [æk'wəlʌŋ] *n* アクアラング akúarañgu

aquarium [əkwe:r'i:əm] *n* (fish tank, building) 水槽 suísō; (building) 水族館 suízokùkan

Aquarius [əkwe:r'i:əs] *n* 水がめ座 mizúgameza

aquatic [əkwæt'ik] *adj* (animal, plant, sport) 水生の suísei no

aqueduct [æk'widʌkt] *n* 導水橋 dósuikyō

Arab [ær'əb] *adj* アラビアの arábia no, アラブの árabu no

♦*n* アラビア人 arábiajìn, アラブ（人）árabu(jìn)

Arabian [ərei'bi:ən] *adj* アラビアの arábia no

Arabic [ær'əbik] *adj* (language, numerals, manuscripts) アラビア語の arábiago no

♦*n* (LING) アラビア語 arábiago

arable [ær'əbəl] *adj* (land, farm, crop) 耕作に適した kōsaku ni tekishìta

arbitrary [a:r'bitreri:] *adj* (random: attack, decision) 勝手な katté na

arbitration [a:rbitrei'ʃən] *n* (of dispute, quarrel) 仲裁 chúsai

arc [a:rk] *n* (sweep, *also* MATH) 弧 kò

arcade [a:rkeid'] *n* (round a square, *also* shopping mall) アーケード ākēdo

arch [a:rtʃ] *n* (ARCHIT) アーチ āchi; (of foot) 土踏まず tsuchífumàzu

♦*vt* (back) 丸める marúmeru

archaeology [a:rki:a:l'ədʒi:] *etc* (*BRIT*) = **archeology** *etc*

archaic [a:rkei'ik] *adj* 時代遅れの jidáiokūre no

archbishop [a:rtʃbiʃ'əp] *n* 大司教 daíshikyō

archenemy [a:rtʃ'en'əmi:] *n* 宿敵 shukúteki

archeologist [a:rki:a:l'ədʒist] *n* 考古学 者 kōkogakùsha

archeology [a:rki:a:l'ədʒi:] *n* 考古学 kōkogàku

archery [a:r'tʃə:ri:] *n* 弓道 kyūdō

archetype [a:r'kitaip] *n* (person, thing) 典型 teñkei

archipelago [a:rkəpel'əgou] *n* 列島 rettō

architect [a:r'kitekt] *n* (of building) 建 築技師 keñchikugishì

architectural [a:r'kitektʃə:rəl] *adj* 建築 の keñchiku no

architecture [a:r'kitektʃə:r] *n* (design of buildings) 建築 keñchiku; (style of building) 建築様式 keñchikuyōshiki

archives [ɑːrˈkaivz] *npl* (collection: of papers, records, films etc) 記録収集 kirókushûshū, アーカイブス ākaibusu

Arctic [ɑːrkˈtik] *adj* (cold etc) 北極圏の hokkyókukèn no
♦*n: the Arctic* 北極圏 hokkyókukèn

ardent [ɑːrˈdənt] *adj* (passionate: admirer etc) 熱烈な netsúretsu na; (discussion etc) 熱心な nésshin na

arduous [ɑːrˈdʒuːəs] *adj* (task, journey) 困難な kônnan na

are [ɑːr] *vb see* be

area [eːrˈiːə] *n* (region, zone) 地域 chíiki; (part of place) 区域 kúiki; (*also* in room: e.g. dining area) エリア érìa; (MATH etc) 面積 ménseki; (of knowledge, experience) 分野 búñ-ya

arena [əriːˈnə] *n* (for sports, circus etc) 競技場 kyógijō

aren't [ɑːrnt] = **are not**

Argentina [ɑːrdʒəntiːˈnə] *n* アルゼンチン arúzeñchin

Argentinian [ɑːrdʒəntinˈiːən] *adj* アルゼンチンの arúzeñchin no
♦*n* アルゼンチン人 arúzeñchiñjin

arguably [ɑːrˈgjuːəbliː] *adv* 多分...だろう tábun ...dárò

argue [ɑːrˈgjuː] *vi* (quarrel) けんかする keñka suru; (reason) 論じる roñjiru
to argue that ... ...だと主張する ...da to shuchô suru

argument [ɑːrˈgjəmənt] *n* (reasons) 論議 róñgi; (quarrel) けんか keñka

argumentative [ɑːrgjəmenˈtətiv] *adj* (person) 議論好きな girónzuki na; (voice) けんか腰の keñkagoshi no

aria [ɑːrˈiːə] *n* (MUS) アリア árìa

arid [ærˈid] *adj* (land) 乾燥した kañsõ shita; (subject, essay) 面白くない omóshirokùnai

Aries [eːrˈiːz] *n* 牡羊座 ohítsujiza

arise [əraizˈ] (*pt* **arose**, *pp* **arisen**) *vi* (emerge: question, difficulty etc) 持上る mochíagaru

arisen [ərizˈən] *pp of* **arise**

aristocracy [æristɑːkˈrəsiː] *n* 貴族階級 kizókukaìkyū

aristocrat [ərisˈtəkræt] *n* 貴族 kizóku

arithmetic [əriθˈmətik] *n* (MATH, *also* calculation) 算数 sañsū

ark [ɑːrk] *n: Noah's Ark* ノアの箱舟 nóà no hakóbunè

arm [ɑːrm] *n* (ANAT) 腕 udé; (of clothing) 袖 sodé; (of chair etc) ひじ掛け hijíkake; (of organization etc) 支部 shíbù
♦*vt* (person, nation) 武装させる busô saseru
arm in arm 腕を組合って udé wò kumíatte

armaments [ɑːrˈməmənts] *npl* 兵器 héìki

armchair [ɑːrmˈtʃeːr] *n* ひじ掛けいす hijíkakeìsu

armed [ɑːrmd] *adj* (soldier, conflict, forces etc) 武装した busô shita

armed robbery *n* 武装強盗 busógòtō

armistice [ɑːrˈmistis] *n* 停戦 teísen

armor [ɑːrˈmɔːr] (*BRIT* **armour**) *n* (HISTORY: knight's) よろい yorói; (MIL: tanks) 装甲部隊 sókōbutài

armored car [ɑːrməːrd kɑːr'] *n* 装甲車 sókòsha

armpit [ɑːrmˈpit] *n* わきの下 wakí no shìtá

armrest [ɑːrmˈrest] *n* ひじ掛け hijíkake

arms [ɑːrmz] *npl* (weapons) 武器 búkì; (HERALDRY) 紋章 moñshō

army [ɑːrˈmiː] *n* (MIL) 軍隊 gúñtai; (*fig*: host) 大群 taígun

aroma [ərouˈmə] *n* (of foods, coffee) 香り kaóri

aromatic [ærəmætˈik] *adj* (herb, tea) 香りのよい kaóri no yoì

arose [ərouzˈ] *pt of* **arise**

around [əraundˈ] *adv* (about) 回りにmawári ni; (in the area) そこら辺に sokórahen ni
♦*prep* (encircling) ...の回りに ...no mawári ni; (near) ...の近辺に ...no kîñpen ni; (*fig*: about: dimensions) 大よそ óyoso, 約 yákù; (: dates, times) ...ごろ ...górò

arouse [ərauzˈ] *vt* (from sleep) 起す okósù; (interest, passion, anger) 引起こす hikíokosù

arrange [əreindʒˈ] *vt* (organize: meeting, tour etc) 準備する júñbi suru; (put in

order: books etc) 整とんする seíton suru; (: flowers) 生ける ikéru

to arrange to do something ...する手配をする ...surú tehái wo suru

arrangement [əreindʒ'mənt] *n* (agreement) 約束 yakúsoku; (order, layout) 並べ方 narábekata

arrangements [əreindʒ'mənts] *npl* (plans, preparations) 手配 tehái

array [ərei'] *n*: *array of* (things, people) 多数の tásu no

arrears [əri:rz'] *npl* (money owed) 滞納金 taínōkin

to be in arrears with one's rent 家賃が滞納になっている yáchin ga taínō ni natte irú

arrest [ərest'] *vt* (detain: criminal, suspect) 逮捕する táiho suru; (someone's attention) 引く hikú

♦*n* (detention) 逮捕 táiho

under arrest 逮捕されて táiho saréte

arrival [ərai'vəl] *n* (of person, vehicle, letter etc) 到着 tóchaku

new arrival (person) 新入り shiń-iri; (baby) 新生児 shińseìji

arrive [əraiv'] *vi* (traveller, news, letter) 着く tsukú, 到着する tóchaku suru; (baby) 生れる umáreru

arrogance [ær'əgəns] *n* 尊大さ sońdaisa

arrogant [ær'əgənt] *adj* 尊大な sońdai na

arrow [ær'ou] *n* (weapon) 矢 ya; (sign) 矢印 yajírùshi

arse [ɑːrs] (*BRIT*: *inf!*) *n* けつ ketsú

arsenal [ɑːr'sənəl] *n* (for weapons) 兵器庫 heíkikò; (stockpile, supply) 保有兵器 hoyúheìki

arsenic [ɑːr'sənik] *n* ひ素 hísò

arson [ɑːr'sən] *n* 放火 hóka

art [ɑːrt] *n* (creative work, thing produced) 芸術品 geíjutsuhin, 美術品 bijútsuhin; (skill) 芸術 geíjutsu, 美術 bíjùtsu

Arts [ɑːrts] *npl* (SCOL) 人文科学 jińbunkagàku

artefact [ɑːr'təfækt] *n* 工芸品 kógeihin

artery [ɑːr'tə:ri:] *n* (MED) 動脈 dómyaku; (*fig*: road) 幹線道路 kańsendòro

artful [ɑːrt'fəl] *adj* (clever, manipulative) こうかつな kókatsu na

art gallery *n* (large, national) 美術博物館 bijútsuhakubutsukàn; (small, private) 画廊 garó

arthritis [ɑːrθrai'tis] *n* 関節炎 kańsetsuen

artichoke [ɑːr'titʃouk] *n* アーティチョーク ãtichōku

Jerusalem artichoke キクイモ kikúimo

article [ɑːr'tikəl] *n* (object, item) 物品 buppín; (LING) 冠詞 kańshi; (in newspaper) 記事 kíjì; (in document) 条項 jókō

article of clothing 衣料品 iryóhin

articles [ɑːr'tikəlz] (*BRIT*) *npl* (LAW: training) 見習い契約 mináraikeìyaku

articulate [*adj* ɑːrtik'jəlit *vb* ɑːrtik'jəleit] *adj* (speech, writing) 表現力のある hyógeńryoku no arú

♦*vt* (fears, ideas) 打ち明ける uchíakeru

articulated lorry [ɑːrtik'jəleitid-] (*BRIT*) *n* トレーラートラック torérātorakkù

artificial [ɑːrtəfiʃ'əl] *adj* (synthetic: conditions, flowers, arm, leg) 人工の jińkō no; (affected: manner) 装った yosóotta; (: person) きざな kízà na

artificial respiration *n* 人工呼吸 jińkōkokyū

artillery [ɑːrtil'ə:ri:] *n* (MIL: corps) 砲兵隊 hóheitai

artisan [ɑːr'tizən] *n* (craftsman) 職人 shokúnin

artist [ɑːr'tist] *n* (painter etc) 芸術家 geíjutsuka; (MUS, THEATER etc) 芸能人 geínōjin; (skilled person) 名人 meíjin

artistic [ɑːrtis'tik] *adj* 芸術的な geíjutsuteki na

artistry [ɑːr'tistri:] *n* (creative skill) 芸術 geíjutsu

artless [ɑːrt'lis] *adj* (innocent) 無邪気な mújàki na

art school *n* 美術学校 bijútsugakkò

KEYWORD

as [æz] *conj* **1** (referring to time) ...している時 ...shíte iru tokí, ...しながら ...shína-

gàra

as the years went by 年月が経つにつれて toshítsuki ga tatsù ni tsurétè

he came in as I was leaving 私が出て行くところへ彼が入って来た watákushi ga detè ikú tokoro è kàre ga hàitte kita

as from tomorrow 明日からは ásu kàra wa

2 (in comparisons) ...と同じぐらいに ...to onáji gurài ni

as big as ...と同じぐらい大きい ...to onáji gurài ōkìï

twice as big as ...より2倍も大きい ...yorì nibái mo ōkìï

as much/many as ...と同じ量〔数〕...to onáji ryō〔kazù〕

as much money/many books as ...と同じぐらい沢山の金〔本〕...to onáji gurài takúsan nò kané〔hon〕

as soon as ...すると直ぐに ...surú to sugù ni

3 (since, because) ...であるから ...de árù kara, ...であるので ...de árù no de, ...なので ...na no de

as you can't come I'll go without you あなたが来られないから私は1人で行きます anátà ga korárenài karà watákushi wa hítorì de ikímasù

he left early as he had to be home by 10 彼は10時までに家に帰らなければならなかったので早めに出て行きました kàre wa jūji made ni ié nì kaéranàkereba naránakatta no de hayáme ni detè ikímashìta

4 (referring to manner, way) ...様に ...yō nì

do as you wish お好きな様にして下さい o-sūki na yō ni shitè kudasaì

as she said 彼女が言った様に kánojò ga ittá yō nì

5 (concerning): *as for/to that* それについて〔関して〕は soré ni tsuìte〔kànshite〕wa

6: *as if/though* ...であるかの様に ...de árù ka no yō nì

he looked as if he was ill 彼は病気の様に見えました kárè wa byōki no yō ni miémashìta ¶ *see also* long; such; well

♦*prep* (in the capacity of) ...として ...to-shite

he works as a driver 彼は運転手です kárè wa úntenshu desu

as chairman of the company, he ... 会社の会長として彼は... káisha no káichō toshite karè wa...

he gave it to me as a present 彼はプレゼントとしてこれをくれました kárè wa purézènto toshite koré wo kuremashìta

a.s.a.p. [eieseipi'] *abbr* (= *as soon as possible*) 出来るだけ早く dekíru dake hayàku

asbestos [æsbes'təs] *n* 石綿 ishíwata, アスベスト asúbesùto

ascend [əsend'] *vt* (hill) 登る nobóru; (ladder, stairs) 上る nobóru, 上がる agáru

ascend the throne 即位する sókùi suru

ascendancy [əsen'dənsi] *n* 優勢 yūsei

ascent [əsent'] *n* (slope) 上り坂 nobórizaka; (climb: of mountain etc) 登はん tōhan

ascertain [æsə:rtein'] *vt* (details, facts) 確認する kakúnin suru

ascribe [əskraib'] *vt*: *to ascribe something to* (put down: cause) ...を...のせいにする ...wo ...no sêï ni suru; (attribute: quality) ...が...にあると見なす ...ga ...ni árù to mínásù; (: work of art) ...が...の作品だとする ...ga ...no sakúhin da tò suru

ash [æʃ] *n* (*gen*) 灰 haí; (tree) トネリコ tonériko

ashamed [əʃeimd'] *adj* (embarrassed, guilty) 恥ずかしい hazúkashìï

to be ashamed of (person, action) ...を恥ずかしく思う ...wo hazúkashikù omoù

ashen [æʃ'ən] *adj* (face) 青ざめた aózameta

ashore [əʃɔ:r'] *adv* (be) 陸に rikú ni; (swim, go etc) 陸へ rikú e

ashtray [æʃ'trei] *n* 灰皿 haízara

Ash Wednesday *n* 灰の水曜日 haí no sufyōbi

Asia [ei'ʒə] *n* アジア ájìa

Asian [ei'ʒən] *adj* アジアの ájìa no
♦*n* アジア人 ajíajìn

aside [əsaid'] *adv* (to one side, apart) わ

きへ(に) wakí e(ni)

♦*n* (to audience etc) 傍白 bóhaku

ask [æsk] *vt* (question) 尋ねる tazúnerù, 聞く kikú; (invite) 招待する shòtai suru

to ask someone something ...に...を聞く ...ni ...wo kíkù

to ask someone to do something ...に...をするように頼む ...ni ...wo suru yò ni tanómù

to ask someone about something ...に...について尋ねる ...ni ...ni tsuítè tazúnerù

to ask (someone) a question (...に) 質問をする (...ni) shitsúmoñ wo suru

to ask someone out to dinner ...を外での食事に誘う ...wo sótò de no shokúji ni sasóu

ask after *vt fus* (person) ...の事を尋ねる ...no kotó wò tazúnerù

askance [əskæns'] *adv*: *to look askance at someone/something* ...を横目で見る ...wo yokóme de mirù

askew [əskju:'] *adv* (clothes) 乱れて midárète

ask for *vt fus* (request) 願う negáu; (look for: trouble) 招く manéku

asking price [æs'kiŋ-] *n* 言値 iíne

asleep [əsli:p'] *adj* (sleeping) 眠っている nemútte irù

to fall asleep 眠る nemúru

asparagus [əspær'əgəs] *n* アスパラガス asúparagàsu

aspect [æs'pekt] *n* (element: of subject) 面 méñ; (direction in which a building etc faces) 向き múkì; (quality, air) 様子 yósu

aspersions [əspə:r'ʒənz] *npl*: *to cast aspersions on* ...を中傷する ...wo chúshō suru

asphalt [æs'fɔ:lt] *n* アスファルト asúfarùto

asphyxiation [æsfiksi:ei'ʃən] *n* 窒息 chissóku

aspirations [æsperei'ʃənz] *npl* (hopes, ambitions) 大望 taíbō

aspire [əspai'ə:r] *vi*: *to aspire to* ...を熱望する ...wo netsúbō suru

aspirin [æs'pə:rin] *n* (drug) アスピリン a-

súpirin; (tablet) アスピリン錠 asúpiriñjō

ass [æs] *n* (ZOOL) ロバ róba; (*inf*: idiot) ばか bákà; (*US*: *inf!*) けつ ketsú

assailant [əsei'lənt] *n* 攻撃者 kógekisha

assassin [əsæs'in] *n* 暗殺者 añsatsushà

assassinate [əsæs'əneit] *vt* 暗殺する añsatsu suru

assassination [əsæsinei'ʃən] *n* 暗殺 añsatsu

assault [əsɔ:lt'] *n* (attack: LAW) 強迫 kyóhaku; (: MIL, *fig*) 攻撃 kógeki

♦*vt* (attack) 攻撃する kógeki suru; (sexually) ...を暴行する ...wo bókō suru

assemble [əsem'bəl] *vt* (gather together: objects, people) 集める atsúmerù; (TECH: furniture, machine) 組立てる kumítaterù

♦*vi* (people, crowd etc) 集まる atsúmarù

assembly [əsem'bli:] *n* (meeting) 集会 shúkai; (institution) 議会 gíkài; (construction: of vehicles etc) 組立て kumítate

assembly line *n* 組立てライン kumítateraìn

assent [əsent'] *n* (approval to plan) 同意 dóì

assert [əsə:rt'] *vt* (opinion, innocence, authority) 主張する shuchó suru

assertion [əsə:r'ʃən] *n* (statement, claim) 主張 shuchó

assess [əses'] *vt* (evaluate: problem, intelligence, situation) 評価する hyóka suru; (tax, damages) 決定する kettéi suru; (property etc: for tax) 査定する satéi suru

assessment [əses'mənt] *n* (evaluation) 評価 hyóka; (of tax, damages) 決定 kettéi; (of property etc) 査定 satéi

asset [æs'et] *n* (useful quality, person etc) 役に立つ物 yakú ni tatsù monó

assets [æs'ets] *npl* (property, funds) 財産 zaísan; (COMM) 資産 shísan

assiduous [əsidʒ'u:əs] *adj* (care, work) 勤勉な kiñben na

assign [əsain'] *vt*: *to assign (to)* (date) (...の日にちを) 決める (...no hiníchi wò) kiméru; (task, resources) (...に) 割当てる (...ni) waríaterù

assignment [əsain'mənt] n (task) 任務 nínmu; (SCOL) 宿題 shukúdai

assimilate [əsim'əleit] vt (learn: ideas etc) 身に付ける mi ni tsukérù; (absorb: immigrants) 吸収する kyúshū suru

assist [əsist'] vt (person: physically, financially, with information etc) 援助する énjo suru

assistance [əsis'təns] n (help: with advice, money etc) 援助 énjo

assistant [əsis'tənt] n (helper) 助手 joshú, アシスタント ashísutanto; (BRIT: also: shop assistant) 店員 teñ-in

associate [adj, n əsou'si:it vb əsou'si:eit] adj: **associate member** 準会員 juñkaìin
♦n (at work) 仲間 nakáma
♦vt (mentally) 結び付ける musúbitsukerù
♦vi: **to associate with someone** ...と交際する ...to kósai suru
associate professor 助教授 jókyòju

association [əsousi:ei'ʃən] n (group) 会 kaî; (involvement, link) 関係 kañkei; (PSYCH) 連想 reñsō

assorted [əsɔ:r'tid] adj (various, mixed) 色々な iróiro na

assortment [əsɔ:rt'mənt] n (gen) ...の色々 ...no iróiro; (of things in a box etc) 詰合せ tsuméawase

assume [əsu:m'] vt (suppose) 仮定する katéi suru; (responsibilities etc) 引受ける hikúkerù; (appearance, attitude) 装う yosóoù

assumed name [əsu:md'-] n 偽名 giméi

assumption [əsʌmp'ʃən] n (supposition) 仮定 katéi; (of power etc) 引受ける事 hikúkerù kotó

assurance [əʃu:r'əns] n (assertion, promise) 約束 yakúsoku; (confidence) 自信 jishín; (insurance) 保険 hokén

assure [əʃu:r'] vt (reassure) 安心させる añshin saseru; (guarantee: happiness, success etc) 保証する hoshó suru

asterisk [æs'tərisk] n 星印 hoshíjirùshi, アステリスク asúterisùku

asteroid [æs'tərɔid] n 小惑星 shówakùsei

asthma [æz'mə] n ぜん息 zeñsoku

astonish [əstɑːn'iʃ] vt 仰天させる gyóten saserù

astonishment [əstɑːn'iʃmənt] n 仰天 gyóten

astound [əstaund'] vt びっくり仰天させる bikkúri gyóten saserù

astray [əstrei'] adv: **to go astray** (letter) 行方不明になる yukúefumèi ni nárù
to lead astray (morally) 堕落させる daráku saserù

astride [əstraid'] prep ...をまたいで ...wo matáide

astrologer [əstrɑ:l'ədʒə:r] n 星占い師 hoshíuranaîshi

astrology [əstrɑ:l'ədʒi:] n 占星術 señseîjutsu

astronaut [æs'trɔnɔ:t] n 宇宙飛行士 uchúhikòshi

astronomer [əstrɑ:n'əmə:r] n 天文学者 teñmongakùsha

astronomical [æstrənɑ:m'ikəl] adj (science, telescope) 天文学の teñmongaku no; (fig: odds, price) 天文学的な teñmongakuteki na

astronomy [əstrɑ:n'əmi:] n 天文学 teñmongaku

astute [əstu:t'] adj (operator, decision) 抜け目のない nukéme no naî

asylum [əsai'ləm] n (refuge) 避難所 hinánjo; (mental hospital) 精神病院 seíshinbyòin

---

KEYWORD

---

at [æt] prep 1 (referring to position, direction) ...に〔で〕... ni(de), ...の方へ ...no hó è
at the top 一番上に〔で〕ichíban ue nì (de)
at home/school 家〔学校〕に〔で〕ié (gákkō) nì(dè)
at the baker's パン屋に〔で〕pán-ya nì (de)
to look at something ...の方に目を向ける ...no hó ni mè wo mukéru, ...を見る ...wo míru
to throw something at someone ...目掛けて...を投げる ...megákète ...wo nagérù

2 (referring to time) ...に ...ni

at 4 o'clock 4時に yójì ni

at night 夜（に）yórù (ni)

at Christmas クリスマスに kurísumàsu ni

at times 時々 tokídokì

3 (referring to rates, speed etc) ...で（に）...de(ni)

at £1 a kilo 1キロ1ポンドで ichíkìro ichípondo de

two at a time 1度に2つ ichído nì futátsu

at 50 km/h 時速50キロメーターで jisóku gòjúkkiromētā de

4 (referring to manner) ...で（に）...de(ni)

at a stroke 一撃で ichígeki de

at peace 平和に heíwa ni

5 (referring to activity) ...して ...shíte

to be at work 仕事している shígoto shite iru

to play at cowboys カウボーイごっこをして遊ぶ kaúbòigokkò wo shité asobu

to be good at something ...するのがうまい ...surú nò ga umáì

6 (referring to cause) ...に（で）... ni(de)

shocked/surprised/annoyed at something ...にショックを感じて〔驚いて，怒って〕...ni shókkù wo kánjite(odóroìte, okóttè)

I went at his suggestion 彼の勧めで私は行きました kárè no susúme de wàtákushi wa ìkímashìta

---

ate [eit] *pt of* eat

atheist [ei'θi:ist] *n* 無神論者 mushínronsha

Athens [æθ'ɘnz] *n* アテネ átène

athlete [æθ'li:t] *n* 運動家 uńdōka, スポーツマン supótsumàn

athletic [æθlet'ik] *adj* (tradition, excellence etc) 運動の uńdō no, スポーツのsúpōtsu no; (sporty: person) スポーツ好きの supōtsuzuki no; (muscular: build) たくましい takúmashiì

athletics [æθlet'iks] *n* 運動競技 uńdōkyōgi

Atlantic [ætlæn'tik] *adj* (coast, waves etc) 大西洋の taíseìyō no

♦*n: the Atlantic (Ocean)* 大西洋 taíseìyō

atlas [æt'lɘs] *n* 地図帳 chizúchō, アトラス atòrasu

atmosphere [æt'mɘsfi:r] *n* (of planet) 大気 taíki; (of place) 雰囲気 fuń-ìki

atom [æt'ɘm] *n* (PHYSICS) 原子 géǹshi

atomic [ɘta:m'ik] *adj* 原子の géǹshi no

atom(ic) bomb *n* 原子爆弾 geńshibakùdan

atomizer [æt'ɘmaizɘ:r] *n* 噴霧器 fuńmukì

atone [ɘtoun'] *vi: to atone for* (sin, mistake) 償う tsugúnaù

atrocious [ɘtrou'ʃɘs] *adj* (very bad) ひどい hidóì

atrocity [ɘtra:s'iti:] *n* (act of cruelty) 残虐行為 zańgyakukòi

attach [ɘtætʃ'] *vt* (fasten, join) 付ける tsukérù; (document, letter) とじる tojírù; (importance etc) 置く okú

to be attached to someone/something (like) ...に愛着がある ...ni aíchaku ga arù

attaché [ætæʃei'] *n* 大使館員 taíshikaǹ-in

attaché case *n* アタッシェケース atásshekèsu

attachment [ɘtætʃ'mɘnt] *n* (tool) 付属品 fuzókuhin; (love): *attachment (to someone)* (...への) 愛着 (...é no) aíchaku

attack [ɘtæk'] *vt* (MIL) 攻撃する kōgeki suru; (subj: criminal: assault) 襲う osóu; (idea: criticize) 非難する hínan suru; (task etc: tackle) ...に取掛る ...ni toríkakarù

♦*n* (assault: MIL) 攻撃 kōgeki; (on someone's life) 襲撃 shūgeki; (*fig*: criticism) 非難 hínàn; (of illness) 発作 hossá

heart attack 心臓発作 shińzōhossà

attacker [ɘtæk'ɘ:r] *n* 攻撃者 kōgekìshà

attain [ɘtein'] *vt* (*also*: **attain to**: results, rank) 達する tassúru; (: happiness) 手に入れる te ni irérù; (: knowledge) 得る érù

attainments [ɘtein'mɘnts] *npl* (achievements) 業績 gyōseki

attempt [ɘtempt'] *n* (try) 試み kokóromi

♦*vt* (try) 試みる kokóromirù

to make an attempt on someone's life ...の命をねらう ...no ínòchi wò neráu

attempted [ətemp'tid] *adj* (murder, burglary, suicide) ...未遂 ...mísùi

attend [ətend'] *vt* (school, church) ...に通う ...ni kayóu; (lectures) ...に出席する ...ni shussékì suru; (patient) 看護する kángo suru

attendance [əten'dəns] *n* (presence) 出席 shusséki; (people present) 出席率 shussékirìtsu

attendant [əten'dənt] *n* (helper) 付添い tsukísoi; (in garage etc) 係 kákàri
◆*adj* (dangers, risks) 付き物の tsukímòno no

attend to *vt fus* (needs etc) ...の世話をする ...no sewá wò suru; (affairs etc) ...を片付ける ...wo katázukerù; (patient) ...を看護する ...wo kángo suru; (customer) ...の用を聞く ...no yō wo kikú

attention [əten'ʃən] *n* (concentration, care) 注意 chū̀i
◆*excl* (MIL) 気を付け ki wo tsukê
for the attention of ... (ADMIN) ...気付け ...kitsúke

attentive [əten'tiv] *adj* (intent: audience etc) 熱心に聞く nésshìn ni kikú; (polite: host) 気配り十分の kikúbàrijūbùn no

attest [ətest'] *vi: to attest to* (demonstrate) ...を立証する ...wo risshō suru; (LAW: confirm) ...を確認する ...wo kakúnin suru

attic [æt'ik] *n* 屋根裏部屋 yanéurabeya

attitude [æt'ətuːd] *n* (mental view) 態度 táìdo; (posture) 姿勢 shiséi

attorney [ətəːr'niː] *n* (lawyer) 弁護士 bengoshì

Attorney General *n* 法務長官 hōmuchōkan

attract [ətrækt'] *vt* (draw) 引付ける hikítsukerù; (someone's interest, attention) 引く hikú

attraction [ətræk'ʃən] *n* (charm, appeal) 魅力 miryóku; (*gen pl*: amusements) 呼び物 yobímono, アトラクション atórakùshon; (PHYSICS) 引力 ínryoku; (*fig*: towards someone, something) 引かれる事 hikáreru koto

attractive [ətræk'tiv] *adj* (man, woman) 美ぼうの bibō no; (interesting: price, idea, offer) 魅力的な miryókuteki na

attribute [*n* æt'rəbjuːt *vb* ətrib'juːt] *n* 属性 zokúsei
◆*vt: to attribute something to* (cause) ...を...のせいにする ...wo ...no seí ni surù; (poem, painting) ...が...の作とする ...ga ...no sakú to surù; (quality) ...に...があると考える ...ni ...ga arú to kangaerù

attrition [ətriʃ'ən] *n*: *war of attrition* 消耗戦 shōmōsen

aubergine [ou'bəːrʒiːn] *n* (BRIT) (vegetable) なす násù; (color) なす紺 nasúkon

auburn [ɔː'bəːrn] *adj* (hair) くり色 kuríro

auction [ɔːk'ʃən] *n* (also: **sale by auction**) 競り serí
◆*vt* 競りに掛ける serí ni kakérù

auctioneer [ɔːkʃəniːr'] *n* 競売人 kyōbainìn

audacity [ɔːdæs'itiː] *n* (boldness, daring) 大胆さ daítansa; (*pej*: impudence) ずうずうしさ zúzùshisà

audible [ɔː'dəbəl] *adj* 聞える kikóeru

audience [ɔː'diːəns] *n* (at event) 観客 kankyaku; (RADIO) 聴取者 chōshushà; (TV) 視聴者 shíchòsha; (public) 市民 sekén; (interview: with queen etc) 謁見 ekkén

audio-typist [ɔː'diːoutai'pist] *n* (BRIT) 書取りタイピスト kakítori taipisùto ◇口述の録音テープを聞いてタイプを打つ人 kōjutsu nò rokúon tēpù wo kiíte taipù wo utsu hitô

audio-visual [ɔː'diːouviʒ'uːəl] *adj* (materials, equipment) 視聴覚の shíchòkaku no

audio-visual aid *n* 視聴覚教材 shíchòkakukyòzai

audit [ɔː'dit] *vt* (COMM: accounts) 監査する kánsa suru

audition [ɔːdiʃ'ən] *n* (CINEMA, THEATER etc) オーディション ōdishòn

auditor [ɔː'dətəːr] *n* (accountant) 監査役 kánsayaku

auditorium [ɔːdǐtɔːr'iːəm] *n* (building) 講堂 kōdō; (audience area) 観客席 kankya-

kuséki

augment [ɔːgment'] *vt* (income etc) 増やす fuyásù

augur [ɔː'gə:r] *vi*: *it augurs well* いい兆しだ íi kizáshi da

August [ɔː'gəst] *n* 8月 hachígatsu

aunt [ænt] *n* 伯(叔)母 obá

auntie [æn'tiː] *n dimin of* **aunt**

aunty [æn'tiː] *n* = **auntie**

au pair [ɔː peːr'] *n* (*also*: **au pair girl**) オペア (ガール) opéa(gàru)

aura [ɔːr'ə] *n* (*fig*: air, appearance) 雰囲気 fuń-ikî

auspices [ɔːs'pisiz] *npl*: *under the auspices of* ...の後援で ...no kōen de

auspicious [ɔːspiʃ'əs] *adj* (opening, start, occasion) 前途有望な zéntoyūbō na

austere [ɔːstiːr'] *adj* (room, decoration) 質素な shíssò na; (person, lifestyle, manner) 厳格な geñkaku na

austerity [ɔːste:r'itiː] *n* (simplicity) 質素さ shissósa; (ECON: hardship) 苦労 kúrò

Australia [ɔːstreil'jə] *n* オーストラリア ōsutorarîa

Australian [ɔːstreil'jən] *adj* オーストラリアの ōsutorarîa no
♦*n* オーストラリア人 ōsutorariajîn

Austria [ɔːs'triːə] *n* オーストリア ōsutorîa

Austrian [ɔːs'triːən] *adj* オーストリアの ōsutorîa no
♦*n* オーストリア人 ōsutoriajîn

authentic [ɔːθen'tik] *adj* (painting, document, account) 本物の hoñmono no

author [ɔː'θə:r] *n* (of text) 著者 chóshà; (profession) 作家 sakká; (creator: of plan, character etc) 発案者 hatsúañsha

authoritarian [əθɔ:riteːr'iːən] *adj* (attitudes, conduct) 独裁的な dokúsaiteki na

authoritative [əθɔ:r'iteitiv] *adj* (person, manner) 権威ありげな kêñ-i arîge na; (source) 信頼できる shiñrai dekirù

authority [əθɔ:r'itiː] *n* (power) 権限 keñgeñ; (expert) 権威 kêñ-i; (government body) 当局 tòkyoku; (official permission) 許可 kyókà
the authorities 当局 tòkyoku

authorize [ɔː'θə:raiz] *vt* (publication etc)

許可する kyókà suru

autistic [ɔːtis'tik] *adj* (child) 自閉症の jihéishō no

auto [ɔː'tou] (*US*) *n* (car) 自動車 jídòsha, カー kā

autobiography [ɔːtəbaiɑːg'rəfiː] *n* 自叙伝 jijódèn

autocratic [ɔːtəkræt'ik] *adj* (government, ruler) 独裁的な dokúsaiteki na

autograph [ɔː'təgræf] *n* サイン sáìn
♦*vt* (photo etc) ...にサインする ...ni sáìn suru

automata [ɔːtɑːm'ətə] *npl of* **automaton**

automated [ɔː'təmeitid] *adj* (factory, process) 自動化した jidóka shita

automatic [ɔːtəmæt'ik] *adj* (process, machine) 自動の jidó no; (reaction) 自動的な jidóteki na
♦*n* (gun) 自動ピストル jidópisutòrù, オートマチック ōtomachikkù; (*BRIT*: washing machine) 自動洗濯機 jidósentakùki; (car) オートマチック車 ōtomachikkushà

automatically [ɔːtəmæt'ikliː] *adv* (*also fig*) 自動的に jidóteki ni

automation [ɔːtəmei'ʃən] *n* (of factory process, office) 自動化 jidóka, オートメーション ōtoméshon

automaton [ɔːtɑːm'ətɑːn] (*pl* **automata**) *n* (robot) ロボット robótto

automobile [ɔːtəməbiːl'] (*US*) *n* 自動車 jídòsha

autonomous [ɔːtɑːn'əməs] *adj* (region, area) 自治の jíchì no; (organization, person) 独立の dokúritsu no

autonomy [ɔːtɑːn'əmiː] *n* (of organization, person, country) 独立 dokúritsu

autopsy [ɔː'tɑːpsiː] *n* (post-mortem) 司法解剖 shihókaìbō, 検死解剖 keñshikaìbō

autumn [ɔː'təm] *n* (season) 秋 ákì
in autumn 秋に ákì ni

auxiliary [ɔːgzil'jə:riː] *adj* (assistant) 補助の hójò no; (back-up) 予備の yóbì no
♦*n* 助手 joshú

avail [əveil'] *vt*: *to avail oneself of* (offer, opportunity, service) ...を利用する ...wo riyó suru
♦*n*: *to no avail* 無駄に mudá ni

availability [əveiləbil'əti:] n (supply: of goods, staff etc) 入手の可能性 nyúshu no kanōsei

available [əvei'ləbəl] adj (obtainable: article etc) 手に入る te ni háiru; (service, time etc) 利用できる riyō dekíru; (person: unoccupied) 手が空いている te ga áite iru; (: unattached) 相手がいない áite gà inái

avalanche [æv'əlæntʃ] n (of snow) 雪崩 nadáre; (fig: of people, mail, events) 殺到 sattō

avant-garde [əvɑ:ntgɑ:rd'] adj 前衛の zén-ei no, アバンギャルドの abángyarùdo no

avarice [æv'ə:ris] n どん欲 dón-yoku

Ave. [æv] abbr = **avenue**

avenge [əvendʒ'] vt (person, death etc) ...の復しゅうをする ...no fukúshū wò suru

avenue [æv'ənu:] n (street) 通り tōri; (drive) 並木通り namíkidōri; (means, solution) 方法 hōhō

average [æv'ə:ridʒ] n (mean, norm) 平均 heíkin

♦adj (mean) 平均の heíkin no; (ordinary) 並の namí no

♦vt (reach an average of: in speed, output, score) 平均...で...する heíkin...de ...surú

on average 平均で heíkin de

average out vi: **to average out at** 平均が...になる heíkin ga ...ni náru

averse [əvə:rs'] adj: **to be averse to something/doing** ...(...するの)が嫌いである ...(...surú nò) ga kirái de arù

aversion [əvə:r'ʒən] n (to people, work etc) 嫌悪 kén-o

avert [əvə:rt'] vt (prevent: accident, war) 予防する yobō suru; (ward off: blow) 受止める ukétomerù; (turn away: one's eyes) そらす sorásù

aviary [ei'vi:e:ri:] n 鳥用大型ケージ toríyō ōgata kèji

aviation [eivi:ei'ʃən] n 航空 kōkū

avid [æv'id] adj (supporter, viewer) 熱心な nésshīn na

avocado [əvəkɑ:d'ou] n (BRIT: also:

avocado pear) アボカド abókado

avoid [əvɔid'] vt (person, obstacle, danger) 避ける sakéru

avuncular [əvʌŋ'kjələ:r] adj (expression, tone, person) 伯(叔)父の様に優しい ojī no yō ni yasáshiī

await [əweit'] vt 待つ mátsù

awake [əweik'] adj (from sleep) 目が覚めている me ga sámète irú

♦vb (pt awoke, pp awoken or awaked)

♦vt 起す okósù

♦vi 目が覚める me ga samérù

to be awake 目が覚めている me ga samète irú

awakening [əwei'kəniŋ] n (also fig: of emotion) 目覚め mezáme

award [əwɔ:rd'] n (prize) 賞 shō; (LAW: damages) 賠償 baíshō

♦vt (prize) 与える atáeru; (LAW: damages) 命ずる meízuru

aware [əwe:r'] adj: **aware (of)** (conscious) (...に) 気が付いている (...ni) ki gá tsuíte irù; (informed) (...を) 知っている (...wo) shitté iru

to become aware of/that (become conscious of) ...に(...という事に)気が付く ...ni(...to iú koto ni)ki gá tsukú; (learn) ...を(...という事を)知る ...wo(...to iú koto wò)shírù

awareness [əwe:r'nis] n (consciousness) 気が付いている事 ki gá tsuíte irú koto; (knowing) 知っている事 shitté iru koto

awash [əwɑ:ʃ'] adj (with water) 水浸しの mizúbitashi no; (fig): **awash with** ...だらけの ...daráke no

away [əwei'] adv (movement) 離れて hanárète; (position) 離れた所に hanárèta tokóro ni; (not present) 留守で rúsu de; (in time) ...先で ...sáki de; (far away) 遠くに tōku ni

two kilometers away 2キロメートル離れて nikíromètoru hanarete

two hours away by car 車で2時間走った所に kurúma de nijíkaǹ hashítta tokoro ni

the holiday was two weeks away 休暇は2週間先だった kyūka wa nishūkan saki dattá

he's away for a week 彼は1週間の予定で留守です kárè wa isshūkan no yotei de rusù desu

to take away (remove) 片付ける katázukerù; (subtract) 引く hikú

to work/pedal etc away 一生懸命に働く〔ペダルを踏む〕etc isshōkenmei ni határakù〔pedáru wò fumù〕etc

to fade away (color) さめる sameru; (enthusiasm) 冷める samérù; (light, sound) 消えてなくなる kiéte nakunarù

away game n (SPORT) ロードゲーム rōdogēmu

awe [ɔː] n (respect) い敬 ikéi

awe-inspiring [ɔːʲinspaiəʲrɪŋ] adj (overwhelming: person, thing) い敬の念を抱かせる ikéi no neñ wo idákaserù

awesome [ɔːʲsəm] adj = awe-inspiring

awful [ɔːʲfəl] adj (frightful: weather, smell) いやな iyá na; (dreadful: shock) ひどい hidói; (number, quantity): *an awful lot (of)* いやに沢山の iyá ni takusañ no

awfully [ɔːʲfəliː] adv (very) ひどく hídòku

awhile [əwaiʲl] adv しばらく shibáràku

awkward [ɔːkʲwəʲrd] adj (clumsy: person, movement) ぎこちない gikóchinaì; (difficult: shape) 扱いにくい atsúkainikuì; (embarrassing: problem, situation) 厄介な yákkài na

awning [ɔːʲnɪŋ] n 日よけ hiyóke

awoke [əwoukʲ] pt of awake

awoken [əwouʲkən] pp of awake

awry [əraiʲ] adv: *to be awry* (order, clothes, hair) 乱れている midárète irú

to go awry (outcome, plan) 失敗する shippái suru

axe [æks] (US: also: **ax**) n 斧 ónò

♦vt (project etc) 廃止する haíshi suru

axes[1] [ækʲsiz] npl of ax(e)

axes[2] [ækʲsiːz] npl of axis

axis [ækʲsis] (pl **axes**) n (of earth, on graph) 軸 jikú

axle [ækʲsəl] n (AUT) 車軸 shajíku

aye [ai] excl (yes) はい hái

azalea [əzeilʲjə] n ツツジ tsutsújì

B

B [biː] n (MUS: note) ロ音 ro-ón; (: key) ロ調 róchō

B.A. [biːeiʲ] abbr = **Bachelor of Arts**

babble [bæbʲəl] vi (person, voices) ぺちゃくちゃしゃべる péchàkucha shabérù; (brook) さらさら流れる sárāsara nagárerù

baby [beiʲbiː] n (infant) 赤ん坊 ákanbō, 赤ちゃん akáchan; (US: inf: darling) あなた anátà, ベビー bébì

baby carriage (US) n 乳母車 ubáguruma

baby-sit [beiʲbisit] vi 子守をする komórì wo suru, ベビーシッターをする bebíshittà wo suru

baby-sitter [beiʲbisitər] n 子守役 komóriyaku, ベビーシッター bebíshittà

bachelor [bætʲʃələr] n 独身の男 dokúshin no otóko

Bachelor of Arts/Science (person) 文〔理〕学士 buñ〔ri〕gakùshi; (qualification) 文〔理〕学士号 buñ〔ri〕gakùshigō

back [bæk] n (of person, animal) 背中 senáka; (of hand) 甲 kŏ̀; (of house, page, book) 裏 urá; (of car, train) 後ろ ushíro, 後部 kóbu; (of chair) 背もたれ semótàre; (of crowd, audience) 後ろの方 ushíro no hŏ̀; (SOCCER) バック bákkù

♦vt (candidate: also: **back up**) 支援する shién suru; (horse: at races) ...にかける ...ni kakérù; (car) バックさせる bákkù saséru

♦vi (also: **back up**: person) 後ずさりする atózusàri suru; (: : car etc) バックする bákkù suru

♦cpd (payment, rent) 滞納の taínō no; (AUT: seat, wheels) 後部の kóbu no

♦adv (not forward) 後ろへ〔に〕ushíro e〔ni〕; (returned): *he's back* 彼は帰って来た kárè wa kaétte kità; (return): *throw the ball back* ボールを投げ返して下さい bóru wò nagékaeshite kudasaì; (again): *he called back* 彼は電話を掛け直してきた kárè wa deñwa wò kakénao-

shite kita

he ran back 彼は駆け戻った kárè wa kakémodottà

can I have it back? それを返してくれませんか soré wo kaéshite kuremaseñ ka

backbencher [bæk'bentʃər] (*BRIT*) n 平議員 hirágiìn

backbone [bæk'boun] n (ANAT) 背骨 sebóne; (*fig*: main strength) 主力 shúryòku; (: courage) 勇気 yūki

backcloth [bæk'klɔːθ] (*BRIT*) n = backdrop

backdate [bækdeit'] vt (document, pay raise etc) ...にさかのぼって有効にする ...ni sakánobottè yūkō ni suru

back down vi 譲る yuzúru

backdrop [bæk'drɑːp] n 背景幕 haíkeìmaku

backfire [bæk'faiər] vi (AUT) バックファイアする bakkúfaìa suru; (plans) 裏目に出る uráme ni derù

background [bæk'graund] n (of picture, events: *also* COMPUT) 背景 haíkei, バック bákkù; (basic knowledge) 予備知識 yobíchishìki; (experience) 経歴 keíreki

family background 家庭環境 kateikankyō

backhand [bæk'hænd] n (TENNIS: *also*: backhand stroke) バックハンド bakkúhaǹdo

backhanded [bæk'hændid] adj (*fig*: compliment) 当てこすりの atékosuri no

backhander [bæk'hændər] (*BRIT*) n (bribe) 賄ろ waíro

backing [bæk'iŋ] n (*fig*) 支援 shién

backlash [bæk'læʃ] n (*fig*) 反動 haǹdō

backlog [bæk'lɔːg] n: *backlog of work* たまった仕事 tamátta shigoto

back number n (of magazine etc) バックナンバー bakkúnaǹbā

back out vi (of promise) 手を引く te wo hikú

backpack [bæk'pæk] n リュックサック ryukkúsakkù

back pay n 未払いの給料 mihárài nó kyūryō

backside [bæk'said] (*inf*) n おしり o-shí-ri

backstage [bæk'steidʒ'] adv (THEATER) 楽屋に(で) gakúya ni(de)

backstroke [bæk'strouk] n 背泳ぎ seóyògi

back up vt (support: person, theory etc) 支援する shién suru; (COMPUT) バックアップコピーを作る bakkúappukopī wo tsukúrù

backup [bæk'ʌp] adj (train, plane) 予備の yóbì no; (COMPUT) バックアップ用の bakkúappu yō no

♦n (support) 支援 shién; (*also*: backup file) バックアップファイル bakkúappu faìru

backward [bæk'wərd] adj (movement) 後ろへの ushíro e no; (person, country) 遅れた okúreta

backwards [bæk'wərdz] adv (move, go) 後ろに(へ) ushíro ni (e); (read a list) 逆に gyakú ni; (fall) 仰向けに aómuke ni; (walk) 後ろ向きに ushíromuki ni

backwater [bæk'wɔːtər] n (*fig*) 後進地 kōshiǹchi

backyard [bæk'jɑːrd] n (of house) 裏庭 urániwa

bacon [bei'kən] n ベーコン bèkon

bacteria [bækti:'ri:ə] npl 細菌 saíkin

bad [bæd] adj (gen) 悪い warúì; (mistake, accident, injury) 大きな ōkina; (meat, food) 悪くなった warúku nattá

his bad leg 彼の悪い方の脚 kárè no warúi hō nó ashí

to go bad (food) 悪くなる warúku narù

bade [bæd] pt of **bid**

badge [bædʒ] n (of school etc) 記章 kishō; (of policeman) バッジ bájjì

badger [bædʒ'ər] n アナグマ anáguma

badly [bæd'li:] adv (work, dress etc) 下手に hetá ni; (reflect, think) 悪く warúku

badly wounded 重傷を負った jūshō wò ottá

he needs it badly 彼にはそれがとても必要だ kárè ni wa soré gà totémo hitsuyō da

to be badly off (for money) 生活が苦しい seíkatsu ga kurushiì

badminton [bæd'mintən] n バドミント

ン badóminton

bad-tempered [bæd'tem'pə:rd] *adj* (person: by nature) 怒りっぽい okórippoí; (: on one occasion) 機嫌が悪い kigén gà warúì

baffle [bæf'əl] *vt* (puzzle) 困惑させる kóñwaku saserù

bag [bæg] *n* (of paper, plastic) 袋 fukúro; (handbag) ハンドバッグ hañdobaggù; (satchel, case) かばん kában

bags of (*inf*: lots of) 沢山の takúsan no

baggage [bæg'idʒ] *n* (luggage) 手荷物 tenímòtsu

baggy [bæg'i:] *adj* だぶだぶの dabúdabu no

bagpipes [bæg'paips] *npl* バグパイプ bagúpaìpu

Bahamas [bəha:m'əz] *npl*: *the Bahamas* バハマ諸島 bahámashotò

bail [beil] *n* (LAW: payment) 保釈金 hoshákukin; (: release) 保釈 hosháku

♦*vt* (prisoner: *gen*: grant bail to) 保釈する hosháku suru; (boat: *also*: **bail out**) ...から水をかい出す ...kará mízù wò kaídasù

on bail (prisoner) 保釈中 (の) hoshákuchù (no)

bailiff [beil'if] *n* (LAW: *US*) 廷吏 téìri; (: *BRIT*) 執行吏 shíkkòri

bail out *vt* (prisoner) 保釈させる hosháku saseru ¶ *see also* **bale**

bait [beit] *n* (for fish, animal) えさ esá; (for criminal etc) おとり otóri

♦*vt* (hook, trap) ...にえさをつける ...ni esá wò tsukérù; (person: tease) からかう karákaù

bake [beik] *vt* (CULIN: cake, potatoes) オーブンで焼く óbun de yakú; (TECH: clay etc) 焼く yakú

♦*vi* (cook) オーブンに入っている óbun ni háìtte iru

baked beans [beikt-] *npl* ベークトビーンズ békutobìnzu

baker [bei'kə:r] *n* パン屋 páñ-ya

bakery [bei'kə:ri:] *n* (building) パン屋 páñ-ya

baking [bei'kiŋ] *n* (act) オーブンで焼く事 óbun de yakú koto; (batch) オーブン

で焼いたもの óbun de yaíta mono

baking powder *n* ふくらし粉 fukúrashikò, ベーキングパウダー békingupaùdā

balance [bæl'əns] *n* (equilibrium) 均衡 kiñkō, バランス báransu; (COMM: sum) 残高 zañdaka; (remainder) 残り nokóri; (scales) 天びん teñbin

♦*vt* (budget) ...の収入と支出を合せる ...no shúnyū tò shishútsu wò awáserù; (account) ...の決算をする ...no kessán wò suru; (make equal) 釣合を取る tsuríai wo torù

balance of trade 貿易収支 bóekishūshi
balance of payments 国際収支 kokúsaishūshi

balanced [bæl'ənst] *adj* (report) バランスの良い báransu no yoì; (personality) 安定した añtei shita

a balanced diet 均衡食 kiñkō shoku

balance sheet *n* 貸借対照表 taíshakutaishōhyō, バランスシート báransu shìto

balcony [bæl'kəni:] *n* バルコニー barúkonì; (in theater) 天井さじき teñjōsajìki

bald [bɔ:ld] *adj* (head) はげた hágèta; (tire) 坊主になった bózu ni nattá

bale [beil] *n* (of paper, cotton, hay) こり korí

baleful [beil'fəl] *adj* (glance) 邪悪な jaáku na

bale out *vi* (of a plane) パラシュートで脱出する paráshùto de dasshútsu suru

ball [bɔ:l] *n* (SPORT) 球 tamá, ボール bóru; (of wool, string) 玉 tamá; (dance) 舞踏会 bútòkai

to play ball (co-operate) 協力する kyóryoku suru

ballad [bæl'əd] *n* (poem, song) バラード báràdo

ballast [bæl'əst] *n* (on ship, balloon) バラスト barásùto

ball bearings *npl* ボールベアリング bórubeàringu

ballerina [bæləri:'nə] *n* バレリーナ barérìna

ballet [bælei'] *n* (art) バレエ bárèe; (an artistic work) バレエ曲 baréekyokù

ballet dancer *n* バレエダンサー barée-

dansā

ballistics [bəlis'tiks] *n* 弾道学 dandōgaku

balloon [bəlu:n'] *n* (child's) 風船 fúsen; (hot air balloon) 熱気球 netsúkikyǔ

ballot [bæl'ət] *n* (vote) 投票 tốhyō

ballot paper *n* 投票用紙 tốhyōyǒshi

ballpoint (pen) [bɔ:l'pɔint] *n* ボールペン bốrupen

ballroom [bɔ:l'ru:m] *n* 舞踏の間 butố no ma

balm [bɑ:m] *n* バルサム bárùsamu

Baltic [bɔ:l'tik] *n*: *the Baltic (Sea)* バルト海 barútokài

balustrade [bæl'əstreid] *n* (on balcony, staircase) 手すり tesúri

bamboo [bæmbu:'] *n* (plant) 竹 takế; (material) 竹材 takếzai

ban [bæn] *n* (prohibition) 禁止 kiñshi
♦*vt* (prohibit) 禁止する kiñshi suru

banal [bənæl'] *adj* (remark, idea, situation) 陳腐な chíñpu na

banana [bənæn'ə] *n* バナナ bánàna

band [bænd] *n* (group) 一団 ichídan; (MUS: jazz, rock, military etc) バンド bañdo; (strip of cloth etc) バンド bañdo; (stripe) 帯状の物 obíjō no mono

bandage [bæn'didʒ] *n* 包帯 hốtai
♦*vt* ...に包帯を巻く ...ni hốtai wò makú

bandaid [bænd'eid'] ® (*US*) *n* バンドエイド bañdoeìdo ◇ばん創こうの一種 bañsōkō no isshù

bandit [bæn'dit] *n* 盗賊 tốzoku

band together *vi* 団結する dañketsu suru

bandwagon [bænd'wægən] *n*: *to jump on the bandwagon* (*fig*) 便乗する biñjō suru

bandy [bæn'di:] *vt* (jokes, insults, ideas) やり取りする yarítòri surù

bandy-legged [bæn'di:legid] *adj* がにまたの ganímata no

bang [bæŋ] *n* (of door) ばたんという音 bátàn to iú oto; (of gun, exhaust) ぱんという音 pấn to iú oto; (blow) 打撃 dagéki
♦*excl* ぱんぱん páñpan
♦*vt* (door) ばたんと閉める batán to shimerù; (one's head etc) ぶつける butsúke-

ru
♦*vi* (door) ばたんと閉まる batán to shimárù; (fireworks) ばんばんと爆発する báñban to bakúhatsu suru

bangle [bæŋ'gəl] *n* (bracelet) 腕飾り udékazarì

bangs [bæŋz] (*US*) *npl* (fringe) 切下げ前髪 kirísagemaegamì

banish [bæn'iʃ] *vt* (exile: person) 追放する tsuíhō suru

banister(s) [bæn'istə(r)] *n(pl)* (on stairway) 手すり tesúri

bank [bæŋk] *n* (COMM: building, institution: *also of blood etc*) 銀行 giñkō, バンク báñku; (of river, lake) 岸 kishí; (of earth) 土手 dotế
♦*vi* (AVIAT) 傾く katámukù
data bank データバンク dếtabañku

bank account *n* 銀行口座 giñkōkōza

bank card *n* ギャランティーカード gyarántīkàdo ◇小切手を使う時に示すカード.カードのサインと小切手のサインが照合される kogíttè wo tsukáù tokí nì shimésu kầdo. kầdo no saĩn to kogíttè no saĩn ga shốgō sarerù

banker [bæŋk'ə:r] *n* 銀行家 giñkōka

banker's card (*BRIT*) *n* = **bank card**

Bank Holiday (*BRIT*) *n* 銀行定休日 giñkōteikyūbi

banking [bæŋk'iŋ] *n* 銀行業 giñkōgyồ

banknote [bæŋk'nout] *n* 紙幣 shíhèi

bank on *vt fus* ...を頼りにする ...wo táyòri ni suru

bank rate *n* 公定歩合 kốteibuài

bankrupt [bæŋk'rʌpt] *adj* (person, organization) 倒産した tốsan shita
to go bankrupt 倒産する tốsan suru
to be bankrupt 返済能力がない heñsainồryoku ga naí

bankruptcy [bæŋk'rʌptsi:] *n* (COMM) 倒産 tốsan

bank statement *n* 勘定照合表 kañjōshōgōhyō

banner [bæn'ə:r] *n* (for decoration, advertising) 横断幕 ốdañmaku; (in demonstration) 手持ち横断幕 temốchi ốdañmaku

banns [bænz] *npl*: *the banns* 結婚予告

kekkón-yokóku

banquet [bæŋˈkwit] *n* 宴会 efikai

baptism [bæpˈtizəm] *n* (REL) 洗礼 sefirei

baptize [bæptaizˈ] *vt* ...に洗礼を施す ...ni sefirei wð hodókosù

bar [bɑːr] *n* (place: for drinking) バー bā; (counter) カ ウ ン タ ー káuntà; (rod: of metal etc) 棒 bó; (slab: of soap) 1個 ikkó; (*fig*: obstacle) 障害 shốgai; (prohibition) 禁止 kifishi; (MUS) 小節 shốsetsu

♦*vt* (road) ふ さ ぐ fuságu; (person) ...が ...するのを禁止する ...ga ...surú no wð kifishi suru; (activity) 禁止する kifishi suru

a bar of chocolate 板チョコ itachoko

the Bar (LAW: profession) 弁護士 befigoshi ◇総称 sốshō

bar none 例外なく reigai nakù

barbaric [bɑːrbærˈik] *adj* (uncivilized, cruel) 野蛮な yabán na

barbarous [bɑːrˈbærəs] *adj* (uncivilized, cruel) 野蛮な yabán na

barbecue [bɑːrˈbəkjuː] *n* (grill) バ ー ベ キ ューこん炉 bábekyūkofiro; (meal, party) バーベキューパーティ bábekyūpāti

barbed wire [bɑːrbd-] *n* 有刺鉄線 yūshitessèn, バラ線 barásen

barber [bɑːrˈbəːr] *n* 理髪師 rihátsushì, 床屋 tokóya

bar code *n* (on goods) バーコード bákòdo

bare [beːr] *adj* (naked: body) 裸の hadáka no; (: tree) 葉の落ちた ha no óchìta; (countryside) 木のない ki no náì; (minimum: necessities) ほんの hofino

♦*vt* (one's body, teeth) むき出しにする mukídashi ni suru

bareback [beːrˈbæk] *adv* くらなしで ránashì de

barefaced [beːrˈfeist] *adj* (lie, cheek) 厚かましい atsúkamashiì

barefoot [beːrˈfut] *adj* 裸足の hadáshi no

♦*adv* 裸足で hadáshi de

barely [beːrˈliː] *adv* (scarcely) 辛うじて káròjite

bargain [bɑːrˈgin] *n* (deal, agreement) 取引 toríhìki; (good buy) 掘出し物 horída-shimono, バーゲン bāgen

♦*vi* (negotiate): *to bargain (with someone)* (...と) 交渉する (...to) kốshō suru; (haggle) 駆引きする kakéhìki suru

into the bargain おまけに o-máke ni

bargain for *vt fus*: *he got more than he bargained for* 彼はそんな結果を予想していなかった kárè wa sofina kekkà wð yosố shite inakattà

barge [bɑːrdʒ] *n* (boat) はしけ hashíke

barge in *vi* (enter) いきなり入り込む ikínari hairikomù; (interrupt) 割込む waríkomù

bark [bɑːrk] *n* (of tree) 皮 kawá; (of dog) ほえ声 hoégoe

♦*vi* (dog) ほえる hoérù

barley [bɑːrˈliː] *n* 大麦 ốmugi

barley sugar *n* 氷砂糖 kốrizatồ

barmaid [bɑːrˈmeid] *n* 女性バーテン joséibāten

barman [bɑːrˈmən] (*pl* **barmen**) *n* バーテン bāten

barn [bɑːrn] *n* 納屋 náyà

barometer [bərɑːmˈitəːr] *n* (for weather) 気圧計 kiátsukei

baron [bærˈən] *n* (nobleman) 男爵 dafishaku; (of press, industry) 大立て者 ốdatemồno

baroness [bærˈənis] *n* 男爵夫人 dafishaku-fujìn

barracks [bærˈəks] *npl* (MIL) 兵舎 héìsha

barrage [bərɑːʒˈ] *n* (MIL) 弾幕 dafimaku; (dam) ダム dámù; (*fig*: of criticism, questions etc) 連発 refipatsu

barrel [bærˈəl] *n* (of wine, beer) たる ta-rú; (of oil) バレル bárèru; (of gun) 銃身 júshin

barren [bærˈən] *adj* (land) 不毛の fumố no

barricade [bærˈəkeid] *n* バリケード baríkèdo

♦*vt* (road, entrance) バリケードでふさぐ baríkèdo de fuságu

to barricade oneself (in) (...に) ろう城する (...ni) rốjõ suru

barrier [bærˈiːəːr] *n* (at frontier, entrance) 関門 kafimon; (*fig*: to prog-

ress, communication etc) 障害 shōgai

barring [bɑːˈriŋ] *prep* ...を除いて...wo nozóite

barrister [bærˈistər] (*BRIT*) *n* 法廷弁護士 hōteibengoshì

barrow [bærˈou] *n* (wheelbarrow) 一輪車 ichírìnsha

bars [bɑːrz] *npl* (on window etc: grille) 格子 kōshì

behind bars (prisoner) 刑務所に[で] keímushò ni [de]

bartender [bɑːrˈtendər] (*US*) *n* バーテンbăten

barter [bɑːrˈtər] *vt*: *to barter something for something* ...を...と交換する ...wo ...to kōkan suru

base [beis] *n* (foot: of post, tree) 根元 nemóto; (foundation: of food) 主成分 shuséībun; (: of make-up) ファウンデーション faúndèshon; (center: for military, research) 基地 kichí; (: for individual, organization) 本拠地 honkyochi

♦*vt*: *to base something on* (opinion, belief) ...が...に基づく ...ga ...ni motózukù

♦*adj* (mind, thoughts) 卑しい iyáshiî

baseball [beisˈbɔːl] *n* 野球 yakyū, ベースボール bēsubòru

basement [beisˈmənt] *n* 地下室 chikáshìtsu

bases[1] [beiˈsiz] *npl of* **base**

bases[2] [beiˈsiːz] *npl of* **basis**

bash [bæʃ] (*inf*) *vt* (beat) ぶん殴る bufínagurù

bashful [bæʃˈfəl] *adj* 内気な uchíki na

basic [beiˈsik] *adj* (fundamental: principles, problem, essentials) 基本的な kihónteki na; (starting: wage) 基本の kihón no; (elementary: knowledge) 初歩的な shohóteki na; (primitive: facilities) 最小限の saíshōgen no

basically [beiˈsikliː] *adv* (fundamentally) 根本的に konpónteki ni; (in fact, put simply) はっきり言って hakkírì itté

basics [beiˈsiks] *npl*: *the basics* 基本 kihón

basil [bæzˈəl] *n* メボウキ mébòki, バジル bájìru

basin [beiˈsin] *n* (vessel) たらい taraí;

(*also*: **wash basin**) 洗面台 seímendai; (GEO: of river, lake) 流域 ryūiki

basis [beiˈsis] (*pl* **bases**) *n* (starting point, foundation) 基礎 kisó

on a part-time/trial basis パートタイム[見習い]で pātotaìmù[minarai]de

bask [bæsk] *vi*: *to bask in the sun* 日光浴をする nikkōyoku wo suru, 日なたぼっこをする hinátabokkò wo suru

basket [bæsˈkit] *n* (container) かご kagó, バスケット basúkettò

basketball [bæsˈkitbɔːl] *n* バスケットボール basúkettobòru

bass [beis] *n* (part, instrument) バス básù; (singer) バス歌手 basúkashù

bassoon [bæsuːn'] *n* (MUS) バスーン básùn

bastard [bæsˈtərd] *n* (offspring) 私生児 shiséìji; (*inf!*) くそ野郎 kusóyarò

bastion [bæsˈtʃən] *n* (of privilege, wealth etc) とりで toríde

bat [bæt] *n* (ZOOL) コウモリ kōmori; (for ball games) バット báttò; (*BRIT*: for table tennis) ラケット rakéttò

♦*vt*: *he didn't bat an eyelid* 彼は瞬き1つしなかった kárè wa mabátàki hitótsù shinákàtta

batch [bætʃ] *n* (of bread) 1かま分 hitókamabùn; (of letters, papers) 1山 hitóyàma

bated [beiˈtid] *adj*: *with bated breath* 息を殺して íkì wo koróshite

bath [bæθ] *n* (bathtub) 風呂 fúrò, 湯船 yúbùne; (act of bathing) 入浴 nyūyoku

♦*vt* (baby, patient) 風呂に入れる fúrò ni iréru

to have a bath 風呂に入る fúrò ni haíru

¶ *see also* **baths**

bathe [beið] *vi* (swim) 泳ぐ oyógù, 遊泳する yūei suru; (*US*: have a bath) 風呂に入る fúrò ni haíru

♦*vt* (wound) 洗う aráu

bather [beiˈðər] *n* 遊泳〔水泳〕する人 yūei〔suíei〕suru hitо

bathing [beiˈðiŋ] *n* (taking a bath) 入浴 nyūyoku; (swimming) 遊泳 yūei, 水泳 suíei

bathing cap *n* 水泳帽 suíeìbò

bathing suit (*BRIT* **bathing costume**)

n 水着 mizúgi

bathrobe [bæθ'roub] *n* バスローブ basúrōbu

bathroom [bæθ'ru:m] *n* トイレ tóīre; (without toilet) 浴室 yokúshitsu

baths [bæðz] (*BRIT*) *npl* (*also:* **swimming baths**) 水泳プール suíeipūru

bath towel *n* バスタオル basútaðru

baton [bætæn'] *n* (MUS) 指揮棒 shikíbō; (ATHLETICS) バトン batón; (policeman's) 警棒 keíbō

battalion [bətæl'jən] *n* 大隊 daítai

batter [bæt'ə:r] *vt* (child, wife) ...に暴力を振るう ...ni bóryoku wo furúù; (subj: wind, rain) ...に強く当たる ...ni tsúyòku atáru
♦*n* (CULIN) 生地 kíjì

battered [bæt'ə:rd] *adj* (hat, pan) 使い古した tsukáifurushìta

battery [bæt'ə:ri:] *n* (of flashlight etc) 乾電池 kańdeñchì; (AUT) バッテリー battérī

battle [bæt'əl] *n* (MIL, *fig*) 戦い tatákai
♦*vi* 戦う tatákau

battlefield [bæt'əlfi:ld] *n* 戦場 señjō

battleship [bæt'əlʃip] *n* 戦艦 señkan

bawdy [bɔː'di:] *adj* (joke, song) わいせつな waísetsu na

bawl [bɔːl] *vi* (shout: adult) どなる donárù; (wail: child) 泣きわめく nakíwamekù

bay [bei] *n* (GEO) 湾 wáñ
to hold someone at bay ...を寄付けない ...wo yosétsukenaì

bay leaf *n* ゲッケイジュの葉 gekkéìju no ha, ローリエ rōrie, ベイリーフ beírīfu

bayonet [bei'ənet] *n* 銃剣 júken

bay window *n* 張出し窓 harídashimadò

bazaar [bəzɑ:r'] *n* (market) 市場 íchìba; (fete) バザー bazá

B. & B. [bi:' ænd bi:'] *n abbr* = **bed and breakfast**

BBC [bi:bi:si:'] *n abbr* (= *British Broadcasting Company*) 英国放送協会 eíkoku hōsō kyòkai

B.C. [bi:si:'] *adv abbr* (= *before Christ*) 紀元前 kigéñzen

be [bi:] (*pt* **was, were,** *pp* **been**) *aux vb* **1** (with present participle: forming continuous tenses) ...している ...shíte iru
what are you doing? 何をしていますか nánì wo shité imasù ká
it is raining 雨が降っています ámè ga fúttè imásù
they're coming tomorrow 彼らは明日来る事になっています kárèra wa asú kurù koto ni náttè imásù
I've been waiting for you for hours 何時間もあなたを待っていますよ nánjikàn mo anátà wo máttè imásù yo

2 (with *pp*: forming passives) ...される ...saréru
to be killed 殺される korósareru
the box had been opened 箱は開けられていた hakó wa àkérarete ita
the thief was nowhere to be seen 泥棒はどこにも見当らなかった doróbō wa dòkó ni mo mîátaranakàtta

3 (in tag questions) ...ね ...né, ...でしょう ...deshō
it was fun, wasn't it? 楽しかったね tanóshikàtta né
he's good-looking, isn't he? 彼は男前だね kárè wa otókomae da ne
she's back again, is she? 彼女はまた来たのか kánojò wa matá kita nò ká

4 (+ *to* + *infinitive*) ...すべきである ...subékì de aru
the house is to be sold 家は売る事になっている iế wà urú koto nì náttè iru
you're to be congratulated for all your work 立派な仕事を完成しておめでとう rippá na shigoto wo kansei shite òmédetō
he's not to open it 彼はそれを開けてはならない kárè wa soré wo akete wà naránaì

♦*vb + complement* **1** (*gen*) ...である ...de árù
I'm English 私はイングランド人です watákushi wa íñgurandojîn desu
I'm tired/hot/cold 私は疲れた〔暑い, 寒い〕watákushi wa tsùkárèta〔atsúì,

samúi)

he's a doctor 彼は医者です kárè wa ishá desù

2 and 2 are 4 2足す2は4 ní tasu ní wà yón

she's tall/pretty 彼女は背が高い〔きれいです〕kánojò wa sé gà takâî(kírèi desù)

be careful/quiet/good! 注意〔静かに、行儀よく〕して下さい chûî(shízùka ni, gyõgi yokù)shitê kudasài

2 (of health): *how are you?* お元気ですか o-génki desù ká

he's very ill 彼は重病です kárè wa jûbyō desù

I'm better now もう元気になりました mõ génki ni narímashìta

3 (of age) ...才です ...sài desu

how old are you? 何才ですか nànsai desu ka, (お) 幾つですか(ố)ikùtsu desu ka

I'm sixteen (years old) 16才です júrokusài desu

4 (cost): *how much was the meal?* 食事はいくらでしたか shokúji wa ikùra deshita ká

that'll be $5.75, please 5ドル75セント頂きます gódòru nanájùgosèntò itádakimasù

♦*vi* **1** (exist, occur etc) 存在する sónzai suru

the best singer that ever was 史上最高の歌手 shijõ saikō no kashù

is there a God? 神は存在するか kámì wa sónzai suru kà

be that as it may それはそれとして sorê wa sore toshite

so be it それでよい sorê de yoì

2 (referring to place) ...にある〔いる〕...ni árù(írù)

I won't be here tomorrow 明日はここに来ません asú wà kokó ni kìmasèn

Edinburgh is in Scotland エジンバラはスコットランドにある ejínbàra wa sukóttoràndo ni árù

it's on the table それはテーブルにあります sorê wa tēburu ni àrímasù

we've been here for ages 私たちはずっ

と前からここにいます watákushitàchi wa zuttó maè kara kokó ni ìmásù

3 (referring to movement) 行って来る itté kurù

where have you been? どこへ行っていましたか dókò e itté imashìta ká

I've been to the post office/to China 郵便局〔中国〕へ行って来ました yūbìnkyoku(chūgōku)e itté kimashìta

I've been in the garden 庭にいました niwá ni imashìta

♦*impers vb* **1** (referring to time): *it's 5 o'clock* 5時です gójì desù

it's the 28th of April 4月28日です shigátsu nijùhachínichi dèsu

2 (referring to distance): *it's 10 km to the village* 村まで10キロメーターです murá màde jukkíromètā desu

3 (referring to the weather): *it's too hot* 暑過ぎる atsúsugirù

it's too cold 寒過ぎる samúsugirù

it's windy today 今日は風が強い kyõ wà kazé ga tsuyoì

4 (emphatic): *it's only me/the postman* ご心配なく、私〔郵便屋さん〕です go-shínpai nakù, watákushi(yūbin-yasan)desù

it was Maria who paid the bill 勘定を払ったのはマリアでした kánjō wò haráttà no wa márià deshita

---

beach [biːtʃ] *n* 浜 hamá
♦*vt* (boat) 浜に引上げる hamá ni hikíagerù

beacon [biːˈkən] *n* (lighthouse) 燈台 tõdai; (marker) 信号 shíngõ

bead [biːd] *n* (glass, plastic etc) ビーズ bízu; (of sweat) 玉 tamá

beak [biːk] *n* (of bird) くちばし kuchíbashi

beaker [biːˈkər] *n* (cup) コップ koppú, グラス gúrasu

beam [biːm] *n* (ARCHIT) はり harî; (of light) 光線 kõsen
♦*vi* (smile) ほほえむ hohõemù

bean [biːn] *n* マメ mamé
runner bean サヤインゲン sayáingen
broad bean ソラマメ sorámàme

coffee bean コーヒーマメ kôhîmàme

beansprouts [biːnˈsprauts] *npl* マメモヤ
シ mamémoyàshi

bear [beːr] *n* (ZOOL) クマ kumá

♦*vb* (*pt* **bore**, *pp* **borne**)

♦*vt* (carry, support: weight) 支える sasáerù; (: responsibility) 負う oú; (: cost) 払
う haraú; (tolerate: examination, scrutiny, person) ...に耐える ...ni taérù; (produce: children) 産む umú

♦*vi*: *to bear right/left* (AUT) 右〔左〕
に曲る mígì(hidári)ni magárù

to bear fruit ...に実がなる ...ni mi ga
narù

beard [biːrd] *n* ひげ higé

bearded [biːrdid] *adj* ひげのある higé no
arù

bearer [beːrˈəːr] *n* (of letter, news) 運ぶ
人 hakóbu hito; (of cheque) 持参人 jisánnin; (of title) 持っている人 móttè irú hito

bearing [beːrˈiŋ] *n* (air) 態度 tâîdo; (connection) 関係 kańkei

to take a bearing 方角を確かめる hôgaku wò tashíkamerù

to find one's bearings 自分の位置を確
かめる jibún no ichi wò tashíkamerù

bearings [beːrˈiŋz] *npl* (*also:* **ball bearings**) ボールベアリング bốrubeàringu

bear out *vt* (person) ...の言う事を保証す
る ...no iu koto wo hoshô suru; (suspicions etc) ...の事実を証明する ...no jijítsu
wo shômei suru

bear up *vi* (person) しっかりする shikkárì suru

beast [biːst] *n* (animal) 野獣 yajú; (*inf*:
person) いやなやつ iyá na yatsù

beastly [biːstˈliː] *adj* (awful: weather,
child, trick etc) ひどい hídoì

beat [biːt] *n* (of heart) 鼓動 kodô; (MUS)
拍子 hyôshi; (of policeman) 巡回区域 juńkaikuìki

♦*vb* (*pt* **beat**, *pp* **beaten**)

♦*vt* (strike: wife, child) 殴る nagúrù;
(eggs, cream) 泡立てる awádaterù, ホイ
ップする hoîppù suru; (defeat: opponent)
...に勝つ ...ni kátsù; (: record) 破る yabúrù

♦*vi* (heart) 鼓動する kodô suru; (rain) た

たき付ける様に降る tatákitsukeru yð ni
fúrù; (wind) たたき付ける様に吹く tatákitsukeru yð ni fúkù; (drum) 鳴る narú

off the beaten track へんぴな所に hêñpi na tokóro ni

to beat it (*inf*) ずらかる zurákarù

beating [biːtiŋ] *n* (punishment with
whip etc) むち打ち muchíuchi; (violence)
殴りつける暴行 nagurukeru no bôkô

beat off *vt* (attack, attacker) 撃退する
gekítai suru

beat up *vt* (person) 打ちのめす uchínomesù; (mixture) かく拌する kakúhan suru; (eggs, cream) 泡立てる awádaterù, ホ
イップする hoîppù suru

beautiful [bjuːˈtəfəl] *adj* (woman, place)
美しい utsúkushiì; (day, weather) 素晴ら
しい subárashiî

beautifully [bjuːˈtəfəliː] *adv* (play music,
sing, drive etc) 見事に mígòto ni

beauty [bjuːˈtiː] *n* (quality) 美しさ utsúkushìsa; (beautiful woman) 美女 bíjò, 美
人 bíjìn; (*fig*: attraction) 魅力 miryôku

beauty salon *n* 美容院 bíyòin

beauty spot *n* (*BRIT*: TOURISM) 景勝
地 keíshòchî

beaver [biːˈvəːr] *n* (ZOOL) ビーバー bîbā

became [bikeim'] *pt of* **become**

because [bikɔːz'] *conj* ...だから ...dá kàra, ...であるので ...de árù nodé

because of ...のため ...no tamé, ...のせい
で ...no seî de

beck [bek] *n*: *to be at the beck and
call of* ...の言いなりになっている ...no
iínari ni nattè irú

beckon [bekˈən] *vt* (*also:* **beckon to**: person) ...に来いと合図する ...ni kôî to aízu
suru

become [bikʌm'] (*pt* **became**, *pp* **become**)
vi ...になる ...ni narù

to become fat 太る futórù

to become thin やせる yasérù

becoming [bikʌmˈiŋ] *adj* (behavior) ふさ
わしい fusáwashiî; (clothes) 似合う niáù

bed [bed] *n* (piece of furniture) ベッド
béddò; (of coal, clay) 層 sô; (bottom: of
river, sea) 底 sokó; (of flowers) 花壇 kádàn

to go to bed 寝る nerú

bed and breakfast *n* (place) 民宿 miñshuku; (terms) 朝食付き宿泊 chóshoku-tsuki shukúhaku

bedclothes [bed'klouz] *npl* シーツと毛布 shítsu to mófu

bedding [bed'iŋ] *n* 寝具 shíngu

bedlam [bed'ləm] *n* 大騒ぎ ósawàgi

bedraggled [bidræg'əld] *adj* (person, clothes, hair) びしょ濡れの bishónure no

bedridden [bed'ridən] *adj* 寝たきりの netákiri no

bedroom [bed'ru:m] *n* 寝室 shiñshitsu

bedside [bed'said] *n: at someone's bedside* ...の枕元に ...no makúramòto ni

bedsit(ter) [bed'sit(ə:r)] (*BRIT*) *n* 寝室兼居間 shiñshitsu keñ imá

bedspread [bed'spred] *n* ベッドカバー beddókabā

bedtime [bed'taim] *n* 寝る時刻 nerú jíkòku

bee [bi:] *n* ミツバチ mitsúbachi

beech [bi:tʃ] *n* (tree) ブナ búnà; (wood) ブナ材 bunázai

beef [bi:f] *n* 牛肉 gyúniku

roast beef ローストビーフ rósutobìfu

beefburger [bi:f'bə:rgə:r] *n* ハンバーガー hañbāgā

Beefeater [bi:f'i:tə:r] *n* ロンドン塔の守衛 roñdontō nò shuéi

beehive [bi:'haiv] *n* ミツバチの巣箱 mitsúbachi no súbàko

beeline [bi:'lain] *n: to make a beeline for* まっしぐらに...に向かう masshígùra ni ...ni mukáu

been [bin] *pp of* **be**

beer [bi:r] *n* ビール bìru

beet [bi:t] *n* (vegetable) サトウダイコン satódaìkon, ビート bìto; (*US: also:* **red beet**) ビーツ bìtsu

beetle [bi:t'əl] *n* 甲虫 kóchū

beetroot [bi:t'ru:t] (*BRIT*) *n* ビーツ bìtsu

before [bifɔ:r'] *prep* (of time, space) ...の前に〔で〕 ...no máè ni〔de〕

♦*conj* ...する前に ...surú máè ni

♦*adv* (time, space) 前に máè ni

before going 行く前に ikú máè ni

before she goes 彼女が行く前に kándjo ga ikú máè ni

the week before (week past) 1週間前 isshúkan máè

I've never seen it before これまで私はそれを見た事はない koré madè watákushi wà soré wò mitá koto wà nái

beforehand [bifɔ:r'hænd] *adv* あらかじめ arákajime, 前もって maémottè

beg [beg] *vi* (as beggar) こじきをする kojíki wò suru

♦*vt* (*also:* **beg for**: food, money) こい求める koímotomerù; (: forgiveness, mercy etc) 願う negáu

to beg someone to do something ...に...してくれと頼む ...ni ...shité kure to tanómù ¶ *see also* **pardon**

began [bigæn'] *pt of* **begin**

beggar [beg'ə:r] *n* こじき kojíki

begin [bigin'] (*pt* **began**, *pp* **begun**) *vt* 始める hajímeru

♦*vi* 始まる hajímaru

to begin doing/to do something ...し始める ...shihajímeru

beginner [bigin'ə:r] *n* 初心者 shoshíñsha

beginning [bigin'iŋ] *n* 始め hajíme

begun [bigʌn'] *pp of* **begin**

behalf [bihæf'] *n: on behalf of* (as representative of) ...を代表して ...wo daíhyo shité; (for benefit of) ...のために ...no tamé ni

on my/his behalf 私〔彼〕のために watákukushi〔kárè〕no tamé ni

behave [biheiv'] *vi* (person) 振舞う furúmaù; (well: *also:* **behave oneself**) 行儀良くする gyógi yokú suru

behavior [biheiv'jə:r] (*BRIT* **behaviour**) *n* 行動 kódō

behead [bihed'] *vt* ...の首を切る ...no kubí wò kírù

beheld [biheld'] *pt, pp of* **behold**

behind [bihaind'] *prep* (position: at the back of) ...の後ろに〔で〕 ...no ushíro ni〔de〕; (supporting) ...を支援して ...wo shién shite; (lower in rank, etc) ...に劣って ...ni otótte

♦*adv* (at/towards the back) 後ろに〔の方へ〕 ushíro ni〔no hồ e〕; (leave, stay) 後に

átò ni
♦*n* (buttocks) しり shirí
to be behind (schedule) 遅れている okúrete irú
behind the scenes (*fig*) 非公式に hikóshiki ni

behold [bihould'] (*pt, pp* **beheld**) *vt* 見る mírù

beige [beiʒ] *adj* ベージュ béju

Beijing [bei'dʒiŋ'] *n* 北京 pékìn

being [bi:'iŋ] *n* (creature) 生き物 ikímonò; (existence) 存在 soñzai

Beirut [beiru:t] *n* ベイルート beírùto

belated [bilei'tid] *adj* (thanks, welcome) 遅ればせの okúrebase no

belch [beltʃ] *vi* げっぷをする geppú wò suru
♦*vt* (*gen*: belch out: smoke etc) 噴出する fuñshutsu suru

belfry [bel'fri:] *n* 鐘楼 shórō

Belgian [bel'dʒən] *adj* ベルギーの berúgī no
♦*n* ベルギー人 berúgījìn

Belgium [bel'dʒəm] *n* ベルギー berúgī

belie [bilai'] *vt* (contradict) 隠す kakúsù; (disprove) 反証する hañshō suru

belief [bili:f'] *n* (opinion) 信念 shíñnen; (trust, faith) 信仰 shiñkō

believe [bili:v'] *vt* 信じる shiñjirù
♦*vi* 信じる shiñjirù
to believe in (God, ghosts) …の存在を信じる …no soñzai wò shiñjirù; (method) …が良いと考える …ga yóī to kañgaerù

believer [bili:v'ə:r] *n* (in idea, activity) …が良いと考える人 …ga yóī to kañgaeru hito; (REL) 信者 shíñja

belittle [bilit'əl] *vt* 軽視する keíshi suru

bell [bel] *n* (of church) 鐘 kané; (small) 鈴 suzú; (on door, *also* electric) 呼び鈴 yobírin, ベル bérù

belligerent [bəlidʒ'ə:rənt] *adj* (person, attitude) けんか腰の keñkagoshi no

bellow [bel'ou] *vi* (bull) 大声で鳴く ógoè de nakú; (person) どなる donárù

bellows [bel'ouz] *npl* (for fire) ふいご fuígo

belly [bel'i:] *n* (ANAT: of person, animal) 腹 hará

belong [bilɔːŋ'] *vi*: *to belong to* (person) …の物である …no monó de arù; (club etc) …に所属している …ni shozóku shite irù; …の会員である …no kaíìn de arù
this book belongs here この本はここにしまうことになっている konó hoñ wa kokó ni shimaù kotó ni nattè irú

belongings [bilɔːŋ'iŋz] *npl* 持物 mochímòno

beloved [bilʌv'id] *adj* (person) 最愛の saíai no; (place) 大好きな dáisuki na; (thing) 愛用の aíyō no

below [bilou'] *prep* (beneath) …の下に〔で〕 …no shitá ni(de); (less than: level, rate) …より低く …yórì hikúkù
♦*adv* (beneath) 下に shitá ni
see below (in letter etc) 下記参照 kakísañshō

belt [belt] *n* (of leather etc: *also* TECH) ベルト berúto; (*also*: **belt of land**) 地帯 chítài
♦*vt* (thrash) 殴る nagúrù

beltway [belt'wei] (*US*) *n* (AUT: ring road) 環状道路 kañjōdòro

bemused [bimju:zd'] *adj* (person, expression) ぼう然とした bózen to shitá

bench [bentʃ] *n* (seat) ベンチ béñchi; (work bench) 作業台 sagyódai; (BRIT: POL) 議員席 gíñseki
the Bench (LAW: judges) 裁判官 saíbañkan ◇総称 sóshō

bend [bend] (*pt, pp* **bent**) *vt* (leg, arm, pipe) 曲げる magéru
♦*vi* (person) かがむ kagámu
♦*n* (BRIT: in road) カーブ kàbu; (in pipe, river) 曲った所 magátta tokoro

bend down *vi* 身をかがめる mi wo kagámeru

bend over *vi* 身をかがめる mi wo kagámeru

beneath [bini:θ'] *prep* (position) …の下に〔で〕 …no shitá ni(de); (unworthy of) …のこけんに関わる …no kokén ni kakawarù
♦*adv* 下に shitá ni

benefactor [ben'əfæktə:r] *n* (to person, institution) 恩人 oñjin

beneficial [benəfiʃ'əl] *adj* (effect, influ-

ence) 有益な yúeki na

beneficial (to) (...に) 有益な (...ni) yúeki na

benefit [ben'əfit] *n* (advantage) 利益 ríeki; (money) 手当て téate

♦*vt* ...の利益になる ...no ríeki ni narú

♦*vi*: **he'll benefit from it** それは彼のためになるだろう soré wà kárè no tamé ni narú darò

Benelux [ben'əlʌks] *n* ベネルクス benérukùsu

benevolent [bənev'ələnt] *adj* (person) 温和な ofíwa na; (organization) 慈善の jízén no

benign [binain'] *adj* (person, smile) 優しい yasáshii; (MED) 良性の ryôsei no

bent [bent] *pt, pp of* **bend**

♦*n* 才能 saínō

♦*adj* (inf: corrupt) 不正な fuséi na

to be bent on doing ...しようと心掛けている ...shíyò to kokórogakete irù

bequest [bikwest'] *n* (to person, charity) 遺贈 izô

bereaved [biri:vd'] *n*: **the bereaved** 喪中の人々 mochû no hitóbìto

beret [bərei'] *n* ベレー帽 bérèbō

Berlin [bə:rlin'] *n* ベルリン berúrin

berm [bə:rm] (*US*) *n* (AUT) 路肩 rokáta

Bermuda [bə:rmju:d'ə] *n* バーミューダ bámyùda

berry [be:r'i:] *n* ベリー berí ◇総称 sôshō

berserk [bə:rsə:rk'] *adj*: **to go berserk** (madman, crowd) 暴れ出す abáredasù

berth [bə:rθ] *n* (on ship or train) 寝台 shíndai; (for ship) バース bàsu

♦*vi* (ship) 接岸する setsúgan suru

beseech [bisi:tʃ'] (*pt, pp* **besought**) *vt* (person, God) ...に嘆願する ...ni tafígan suru

beset [biset'] (*pt, pp* **beset**) *vt* (subj: fears, doubts, difficulties) 襲う osôu

beside [bisaid'] *prep* (next to) ...の横に〔で〕 ...no yokô ni〔de〕

to be beside oneself (with anger) 逆上している gyakújò shite irù

that's beside the point それは問題外です soré wà mofídaigài desu

besides [bisaidz'] *adv* (in addition) それ

に soré ni, その上 sonô ue; (in any case) とに角 tonĭkaku

♦*prep* (in addition to, as well as) ...の外に ...no hoká ni

besiege [bisi:dʒ'] *vt* (town) 包囲攻撃する hôikôgeki suru; (fig: subj: journalists, fans) ...に押寄せる ...ni oshíyoserù

besought [bisɔ:t'] *pt, pp of* **beseech**

best [best] *adj* (quality, suitability, extent) 最も良い mottomô yoî

♦*adv* 最も良く mottômò yôkù

the best part of (quantity) ...の大部分 ...no daîbubun

at best 良くても yôkùte mo

to make the best of something ...を出来るだけ我慢する ...wo dekíru dake gamañ suru

to do one's best 最善を尽す saízen wo tsukusù, ベストを尽くす bésùto wo tsukúsù

to the best of my knowledge 私の知っている限りでは watákushi no shittê irú kagiri de wa

to the best of my ability 私に出来る限り watákushi ni dekírù kagíri

best man *n* 新郎付添い役 shifírōtsukisoiyàku

bestow [bistou'] *vt* (honor, title): **to bestow something on someone** ...に...を授ける ...ni ...wo sazúkerù

bestseller [best'selə:r] *n* (book) ベストセラー besútoserà

bet [bet] *n* (wager) かけ kaké

♦*vb* (*pt, pp* **bet** *or* **betted**)

♦*vt* (wager): **to bet someone something** ...と...をかける ...to ...wo kakérù

♦*vi* (wager) かける kakérù

to bet money on something ...に金をかける ...ni kané wò kakérù

betray [bitrei'] *vt* (friends, country, trust, confidence) 裏切る urágirù

betrayal [bitrei'əl] *n* (action) 裏切り urágiri

better [bet'ə:r] *adj* (quality, skill, sensation) より良い yorí yoî; (health) 良くなった yôkù nattá

♦*adv* より良く yorí yôkù

♦*vt* (score) ...より高い得点をする ...yorí

takáĩ tokúten wo suru; (record) 破る ya-búrũ

♦n: *to get the better of* ...に勝つ ...ni kátsù

you had better do it あなたはそうした方が良い anátà wa sõ shita hõ ga yoĩ

he thought better of it 彼は考え直した kárè wa kañgaenaoshita

to get better (MED) 良くなる yókù naru, 回復する kaĩfuku suru

better off adj (wealthier) ...より金があ る ...yórì kané ga arù; (more comfortable etc) ...の方が良い ...no hõ ga yoĩ

betting [bet'iŋ] n (gambling, odds) かけ事 kakégòto, ギャンブル gyáñburu

betting shop (BRIT) n 私営馬券売り場 shiéibaken-uríba

between [bitwi:n'] prep (all senses) ...の 間に〔で〕...no aĩda ni〔de〕

♦adv 間に aĩda ni

beverage [bev'ə:ridʒ] n 飲物 nomímòno, 飲料 iñryõ

beware [biwer'] vi: *to beware (of)* (dog, fire) (...を) 用心する (...wo) yõjin suru

「*beware of the dog*」猛犬注意 mók(en-chũi

bewildered [biwil'də:rd] adj (stunned, confused) 当惑した tówaku shita

bewitching [biwitʃ'iŋ] adj (smile, person) うっとりさせる uttórì saséru

beyond [bi:ɑnd'] prep (in space) ...より に〔で〕...yórì sakí ni〔de〕; (past: understanding) ...を越えて ...wo koéte; (after: date) ...以降に ...ikõ ni; (above) ...以上に ...íjõ ni

♦adv (in space, time) 先に sakí ni

beyond doubt 疑いもなく utágai mo nakù

beyond repair 修理不可能で shũri fu-kánõ de

bias [bai'əs] n (prejudice) 偏見 heñken

bias(s)ed [bai'əst] adj (jury) 偏見を持っ た heñken wo mottá; (judgement, reporting) 偏見に基づいた heñken ni motózuĩta

bib [bib] n (child's) よだれ掛け yodárekàke

Bible [bai'bəl] n (REL) 聖書 sếīsho, バイ ブル báĩburu

biblical [bib'likəl] adj 聖書の sếīsho no

bibliography [bibli:ɑ:g'rəfi:] n (in text) 文献目録 buñkenmokùroku

bicarbonate of soda [baiɑkɑ:r'bənit-] n 重炭酸ソーダ jũtansansõda, 重曹 jũsō

bicker [bik'ə:r] vi (squabble) 口論する kõron suru

bicycle [bai'sikəl] n 自転車 jitéñsha

bid [bid] n (at auction) 付値 tsukéné; (in tender) 入札 nyũsatsu; (attempt) 試み kokóromi

♦vb (pt bade or bid, pp bidden or bid)

♦vi (at auction) 競りに加わる serí ni ku-wawarù

♦vt (offer) ...と値を付ける ...to né wò tsu-kérù

to bid someone good day (hello) ...に今 日はと言う ...ni konnichi wa to iu; (farewell) ...にさようならと言う ...ni sayõna-ra to iu

bidder [bid'ə:r] n: *the highest bidder* 最高入札者 saĩkōnyũsatsùsha

bidding [bid'iŋ] n (at auction) 競り serí

bide [baid] vt: *to bide one's time* (for opportunity) 時期を待つ jíkĩ wo mátsù

bidet [bi:dei'] n ビデ bíde

bifocals [baifou'kəlz] npl 二重焦点眼鏡 nijũshōtenmegàne

big [big] adj (gen) 大きい ókiì, 大きな ó-kina

big brother 兄 áni, 兄さん nĩisan

big sister 姉 ané, 姉さん nēsan

bigamy [big'əmi:] n 重婚 jũkon

big dipper [-dip'ə:r] (BRIT) n (at fair) ジェットコースター jettókõsutā

bigheaded [big'hedid] adj うぬぼれた u-núboreta

bigot [big'ət] n (on race, religion) 偏狭な 人 heñkyō na hito

bigoted [big'ətid] adj (on race, religion) 偏狭な heñkyō na

bigotry [big'ətri:] n 偏狭さ heñkyōsà

big top n (at circus) 大テント óteñto

bike [baik] n (bicycle) 自転車 jitéñsha

bikini [biki:'ni:] n ビキニ bíkĩni

bilateral [bailæt'ə:rəl] adj (agreement)

双務的な sṓmuteki na

bile [bail] *n* (BIO) 胆汁 tañjū

bilingual [bailiŋ'gwəl] *adj* (dictionary) 二か国語の nikákokugo no; (secretary) 二か国語を話せる nikákokugo wò hanáserù

bill [bil] *n* (account) 勘定書 kañjōgaki; (invoice) 請求書 seíkyūsho; (POL) 法案 hṓan; (US: banknote) 紙幣 shíhèi; (of bird) くちばし kuchíbashi; (THEATER: of show: on the bill) 番組 bañgumi
「*post no bills*」張紙厳禁 harígamigenkin
to fit/fill the bill (*fig*) 丁度いい chṓdo iì

billboard [bil'bɔːrd] *n* 広告板 kṓkokuban

billet [bil'it] *n* (MIL) 軍人宿舎 guñjinshukùsha

billfold [bil'fould] (*US*) *n* 財布 saífu

billiards [bil'jərdz] *n* ビリヤード biríyàdo

billion [bil'jən] *n* (*BRIT*) 兆 chṓ; (*US*) 10億 jūoku

bin [bin] *n* (*BRIT*: for rubbish) ごみ入れ gomíre; (container) 貯蔵箱 chózōbako, 瓶 bín

binary [bai'nəːriː] *adj* (MATH) 二進法の nishínhō no

bind [baind] (*pt*, *pp* **bound**) *vt* (tie, tie together) 縛る shibárù; (constrain) 束縛する sokúbaku suru; (book) 製本する seíhon suru
♦*n* (*inf*: nuisance) いやな事 iyá na koto

binding [bain'diŋ] *adj* (contract) 拘束力のある kōsokuryòku no aru

binge [bindʒ] (*inf*) *n*: *to go on a binge* (drink a lot) 酒浸りになる sakébitari ni narù

bingo [biŋ'gou] *n* ビンゴ bíñgo

binoculars [bənəːk'jələːrz] *npl* 双眼鏡 sṓgankyō

biochemistry [baioukem'istriː] *n* 生化学 seíkagàku

biography [baiɑːg'rəfiː] *n* 伝記 deñki

biological [baiələːdʒ'ikəl] *adj* (science, warfare) 生物学の seíbutsugàku no; (washing powder) 酵素洗剤 kōsoseñzai

biology [baiɑːl'ədʒiː] *n* 生物学 seíbutsu-

gàku

birch [bəːrtʃ] *n* (tree) カバノキ kabá no ki; (wood) カバ材 kabázai

bird [bəːrd] *n* (ZOOL) 鳥 torí; (*BRIT*: *inf*: girl) 女の子 ofina no ko

bird's-eye view [bəːrdzai-] *n* (aerial view) 全景 zeñkei; (overview) 概観 gaíkan

bird-watcher [bəːrd'wɑːtʃəːr] *n* バードウォッチャー bǎdowotchǎ

bird-watching [bəːrd'wɑːtʃiŋ] *n* バードウォッチング bǎdowotchìngu

Biro [bai'rou] ® *n* ボールペン bṓrupen

birth [bəːrθ] *n* (of baby, animal, *also fig*) 誕生 tañjō
to give birth to (BIO: subj: woman, animal) ...を生む ...wo umú

birth certificate *n* 出生証明書 shusshṓ 〔shusséi〕 shṓmeisho

birth control *n* (policy) 産児制限 sañjiseìgen; (methods) 避妊 hinín

birthday [bəːrθ'dei] *n* 誕生日 tañjòbi
♦*cpd* (cake, card, present etc) 誕生日の tañjòbi no ¶ *see also* **happy**

birthplace [bəːrθ'pleis] *n* (country, town etc) 出生地 shusshṓchì〔shusséichì〕, 生れ故郷 umárekokyò; (house etc) 生家 seíka

birth rate *n* 出生率 shusshṓritsu〔shusséiritsu〕

Biscay [bis'kei] *n*: *the Bay of Biscay* ビスケー湾 bisúkēwan

biscuit [bis'kit] (*BRIT*) *n* ビスケット bisúkettò

bisect [baisekt'] *vt* (angle etc) 二等分する nitṓbun suru

bishop [biʃ'əp] *n* (REL: Catholic etc) 司教 shíkyō; (: Protestant) 監督 kañtoku; (: Greek Orthodox) 主教 shúkyō; (CHESS) ビショップ bíshòppu

bit [bit] *n* of **bite**
♦*n* (piece) 欠けら kakéra; (COMPUT) ビット bíttò; (of horse) はみ hámì
a bit of 少しの sukóshi no, ちょっとの chottó no
a bit mad ちょっと頭がおかしい chottó atáma ga okáshiì
a bit dangerous ちょっと危ない chottó abúnaì

bit by bit 少しずつ sukóshi zutsù

bitch [bitʃ] *n* (dog) 雌犬 mesúinu; (*inf!*: woman) あま ámà

bite [bait] (*pt* **bit**, *pp* **bitten**) *vt* (subj: person) かむ kámù; (: dog etc) ...にかみ付く ...ni kamítsuku; (: insect etc) 刺す sásù
♦*vi* (dog etc) かみ付く kamítsuku; (insect etc) 刺す sásù
♦*n* (insect bite) 虫刺され mushísasàre; (mouthful) 一口 hitókùchi

to bite one's nails つめをかむ tsumé wo kamù

let's have a bite (to eat) (*inf*) 何か食べよう nánì ka tabéyò

bitten [bit'ən] *pp* of **bite**

bitter [bit'əːr] *adj* (person) 恨みを持った urámi wò mottá; (taste, experience, disappointment) 苦い nigáì; (wind) 冷たい tsumétaì; (struggle) 激しい hagéshiì; (criticism) 辛らつな shínratsu na
♦*n* (*BRIT*: beer) ビター bitā◇ホップの利いた苦いビール hoppú no kífta nigáî bíru

bitterness [bit'əːrnis] *n* (anger) 恨み urámi; (bitter taste) 苦み nigámi

bizarre [bizɑːr] *adj* (conversation, contraption) 奇妙な kímyò na

blab [blæb] (*inf*) *vi* (to the press) しゃべる shabérù

black [blæk] *adj* (color) 黒い kuróì; (person) 黒人の kokújin no; (tea, coffee) ブラックの burákkù no
♦*n* (color) 黒 kúrò; (person): *Black* 黒人 kokújin
♦*vt* (*BRIT*: INDUSTRY) ボイコットする boíkottò suru

black humor ブラックユーモア burákkuyùmoa

to give someone a black eye ...を殴って目にあざを作る ...wo nagútte me ni azá wo tsukúrù

black and blue (bruised) あざだらけのazá daràke no

to be in the black (in credit) 黒字である kuróji de arù

blackberry [blæk'beːri:] *n* ブラックベリー burákkuberì◇キイチゴの一種 kíìchigo no isshù

blackbird [blæk'bəːrd] *n* (European bird) クロウタドリ kuróutadòri

blackboard [blæk'bɔːrd] *n* 黒板 kokúban

black coffee *n* ブラックコーヒー burákku kòhī

blackcurrant [blækkʌr'ənt] *n* クロスグリ kurósugùri

blacken [blæk'ən] *vt* (*fig*: name, reputation) 汚す kegásù

black ice (*BRIT*) *n* (on road) 凍結路面 tőketsuromèn

blackleg [blæk'leg] (*BRIT*) *n* (INDUSTRY) スト破り sutóyabùri

blacklist [blæk'list] *n* ブラックリスト burákkurisùto

blackmail [blæk'meil] *n* ゆすり yusúri
♦*vt* ゆする yusúru

black market *n* やみ市 yamíichi

blackout [blæk'aut] *n* (MIL) 灯火管制 tőkakañsei; (power cut) 停電 teíden; (TV, RADIO) 放送中止 hősōchūshì; (faint) 一時的意識喪失 ichíjitekiishìkisō-shitsu, ブラックアウト burákkuaùto

Black Sea *n*: *the Black Sea* 黒海 kők-kài

black sheep *n* (*fig*) 持て余し者 motéa-mashimono

blacksmith [blæk'smiθ] *n* 鍛冶屋 kajíya

black spot *n* (*BRIT*: AUT) 事故多発地点 jikőtahátsuchitèn; (: for unemployment etc) ...が深刻になっている地域 ...ga shiñkoku ni nattè irú chìki

bladder [blæd'əːr] *n* (ANAT) ぼうこう bőkō

blade [bleid] *n* (of knife, sword) 刃 há; (of propeller) 羽根 hané

a blade of grass 草の葉 kusá no ha

blame [bleim] *n* (for error, crime) 責任 sekínin
♦*vt*: *to blame someone for something* ...を...のせいにする ...wo ...no seí ni suru

to be to blame 責任が...にある sekínin ga ...ni arù

blameless [bleim'lis] *adj* (person) 潔白な keppáku na

bland [blænd] *adj* (taste, food) 味気ない ajíke naì

blank [blæŋk] *adj* (paper etc) 空白の kű-

haku no; (look) ぼう然とした bózen to shitá

♦*n* (of memory) 空白 kúhaku; (on form) 空所 kúsho; (*also:* **blank cartridge**) 空包 kúhō

a blank sheet of paper 白紙 hakúshi

blank check *n* 金額未記入の小切手 kińgakumiki-nyū no kogíttè

blanket [blæŋ'kit] *n* (of cloth) 毛布 mófu; (of snow, fog etc) 一面の... ichímen no ...

blare [ble:r] *vi* (brass band, horns, radio) 鳴り響く naríhibikù

blasé [blɑːzei'] *adj* (reaction, tone) 無関心な mukáñshin na

blasphemy [blæs'fəmi:] *n* (REL) 冒とく bótoku

blast [blæst] *n* (of wind) 突風 toppű; (of explosive) 爆発 bakúhatsu

♦*vt* (blow up) 爆破する bakúha suru

blast-off [blæst'ɔːf] *n* (SPACE) 発射 hasshá

blatant [blei'tənt] *adj* (discrimination, bias) 露骨な rokótsu na

blaze [bleiz] *n* (fire) 火事 kájî; (*fig:* of color, glory) きらめき kirámeki; (: publicity) 大騒ぎ ōsawàgi

♦*vi* (fire) 燃え盛る moésakerù; (guns) 続け様に発砲する tsuzúkezama ni happō suru; (*fig:* eyes) 怒りで燃える ikári de moéru

♦*vt: to blaze a trail* (*fig*) 先べんを付ける señben wo tsúkerù

blazer [blei'zə:r] *n* (of school, team etc) ブレザー burézà

bleach [bliːtʃ] *n* (*also:* **household bleach**) 漂白剤 hyóhakuzài

♦*vt* (fabric) 漂白する hyóhaku suru

bleached [bliːtʃt] *adj* (hair) 漂白した hyóhaku shitá

bleachers [bliːˈtʃəːrz] (*US*) *npl* (SPORT) 外野席 gaíyasèki

bleak [bliːk] *adj* (countryside) もの寂しい monósabishiì; (weather) 悪い warúì; (prospect, situation) 暗い kurái; (smile) 悲しそうな kanáshisò na

bleary-eyed [bliː'riːaid] *adj* 目がしょぼしょぼしている me ga shobòshobo shité

irù

bleat [bliːt] *vi* (goat, sheep) 鳴く nakú

bled [bled] *pt, pp of* **bleed**

bleed [bliːd] (*pt, pp* **bled**) *vi* (MED) 出血する shukkétsu suru

my nose is bleeding 鼻血が出ている hanáji ga dete irù

bleeper [bliːˈpəːr] *n* (device) ポケットベル pokétto berù

blemish [blem'iʃ] *n* (on skin) 染み shimí; (on fruit) 傷 kizú; (on reputation) 汚点 otén

blend [blend] *n* (of tea, whisky) 混合 koñgō, ブレンド buréndo

♦*vt* 混ぜ合せる mazéawaserù, 混合する koñgō suru

♦*vi* (colors etc: *also:* **blend in**) 溶け込む tokékomù

bless [bles] (*pt, pp* **blessed** *or* **blest**) *vt* (REL) 祝福する shukúfuku suru

bless you! (after sneeze) お大事に o-dáiji ni

blessing [bles'iŋ] *n* (approval) 承認 shónin; (godsend) 恵み megúmi; (REL) 祝福 shukúfuku

blew [bluː] *pt of* **blow**

blight [blait] *vt* (hopes, life etc) 駄目にする damé ni suru

blimey [blai'miː] (*BRIT: inf*) *excl* おや oyà

blind [blaind] *adj* (MED) 盲目の mómoku no; (*pej*) めくらの mekúra no; (euphemistically) 目の不自由な me no fujíyū na; (*fig*): *blind (to)* (...を) 見る目がない (...wo) mirú mé ga naì

♦*n* (for window) ブラインド buráindo (: *also:* **Venetian blind**) ベネシアンブラインド benéshian buraìndo

♦*vt* (MED) 失明させる shitsúmei sasérù; (dazzle) ...の目をくらます ...no me wo kurámasù; (deceive) だます damásù

the blind (blind people) 盲人 mójiñ ◇総称 sóshō

blind alley *n* (*fig*) 行き詰り yukízumari

blind corner (*BRIT*) *n* 見通しの悪い曲り角 mitóshi no waruí magárikadò

blindfold [blaind'fould] *n* 目隠し mekákùshi

◆*adj* 目隠しをした mekákùshi wo shitá

◆*adv* 目隠しをして mekákùshi wo shité

◆*vt* 目隠しする mekákùshi suru

blindly [blaind'li:] *adv* (without seeing) よく見ないで yókù mináide; (without thinking) めくら滅法に mekúrameppò ni

blindness [blaind'nis] *n* (MED) 盲目 mṓmoku; (euphemistically) 目の障害 me no shṓgai

blind spot *n* (AUT) 死角 shikáku; (*fig*: weak spot) 盲点 mṓten

blink [bliŋk] *vi* (person, animal) 瞬く mabátakù; (light) 点滅する tenmetsu suru

blinkers [bliŋk'ə:rz] *npl* 馬の目隠し umá no mekákùshi

bliss [blis] *n* (complete happiness) 至福 shifúku

blister [blis'tə:r] *n* (on skin) 水膨れ mizúbukùre; (in paint, rubber) 気胞 kihṓ

◆*vi* (paint) 気胞ができる kihṓ ga dekirù

blithely [blaið'li:] *adv* (proceed, assume) 軽率に keísotsu ni

blitz [blits] *n* (MIL) 空襲 kū́shū

blizzard [bliz'ə:rd] *n* 吹雪 fubúki, ブリザード burízàdo

bloated [blou'tid] *adj* (face, stomach: swollen) はれた haréta; (person: full) たらふく食べた taráfuku tabèta

blob [blɑːb] *n* (of glue, paint) 滴 shizúku; (something indistinct) はっきり見えない もの hakkírì miénài monó

bloc [blɑːk] *n* (POL) 連合 reńgō, ブロック burókkù

block [blɑːk] *n* (of buildings) 街区 gáìku, ブロック burókkù; (of stone, wood) ブロック burókkù; (in pipes) 障害物 shṓgaibutsu

◆*vt* (entrance, road) 塞ぐ fuságu; (progress) 邪魔する jamá suru

block of flats (BRIT) マンション mańshon

mental block 精神的ブロック seíshinteki burokkù

blockade [blɑːkeid'] *n* 封鎖 fū́sa

blockage [blɑːk'idʒ] *n* 閉そく heísoku

blockbuster [blɑːk'bʌstə:r] *n* (film, book) センセーション seńsēshon

block letters *npl* 活字体 katsújitai

bloke [blouk] (BRIT: *inf*) *n* 男 otóko, 野郎 yárō

blond(e) [blɑːnd] *adj* (hair) 金髪の kińpatsu no, ブロンドの buróndo no

◆*n* (woman) 金髪の女性 kińpatsu no joséi, ブロンド buróndo

blood [blʌd] *n* (BIO) 血 chi, 血液 ketsúèki

blood donor *n* 献血者 keńketsùsha

blood group *n* 血液型 ketsúekigata

bloodhound [blʌd'haund] *n* ブラッドハウンド buráddohaùndo

blood poisoning [-poi'zəniŋ] *n* 敗血症 haíketsushò

blood pressure *n* 血圧 ketsúatsu

bloodshed [blʌd'ʃed] *n* 流血 ryū́ketsu

bloodshot [blʌd'ʃɑːt] *adj* (eyes) 充血した jū́ketsu shitá

bloodstream [blʌd'striːm] *n* 血流 ketsúryū

blood test *n* 血液検査 ketsúekikeñsa

bloodthirsty [blʌd'θə:rsti:] *adj* (tyrant, regime) 血に飢えた chi ni úeta

blood vessel *n* 血管 kekkán

bloody [blʌd'i:] *adj* (battle) 血みどろの chímìdoro no; (nose) 鼻血を出した hanáji wo dashìta; (BRIT: *inf!*): *this bloody ...* くそったれ... kusóttarè...

bloody strong/good (inf!) すごく強い〔良い〕 sugókù tsuyóì〔yoí〕

bloody-minded [blʌd'i:main'did] (BRIT: *inf*) *adj* 意地悪な ijíwàru na

bloom [bluːm] *n* (BOT: flower) 花 haná

◆*vi* (tree) ...の花が咲く ...no haná ga sakú; (flower) 咲く sakú

blossom [blɑːs'əm] *n* (BOT) 花 haná

◆*vi* (BOT) 花が咲く haná ga sakú; (*fig*): *to blossom into* 成長して...になる seíchōshite ...ni narù

blot [blɑːt] *n* (on text) 染み shimí; (*fig*: on name etc) 傷 kizú

◆*vt* (with ink etc) 汚す yogósu

blotchy [blɑːtʃ'i:] *adj* (complexion) 染みだらけの shimídaràke no

blot out *vt* (view) 見えなくする miénàku suru; (memory) 消す kesú

blotting paper [blɑːt'iŋ-] *n* 吸取り紙 suítorigàmi

blow [blou] *n* (punch etc: *also fig*) 打撃 dagéki; (with sword) 一撃 ichígeki

♦*vb* (*pt* **blew**, *pp* **blown**)

♦*vi* (wind) 吹く fúkù; (person) 息を吹掛ける íkì wo fukíkakerù

♦*vt* (subj: wind) 吹き飛ばす fukítobasù; (instrument, whistle) 吹く fúkù; (fuse) 飛ばす tobásu

to blow one's nose 鼻をかむ haná wo kamú

blow away *vt* 吹飛ばす fukítobasù

blow down *vt* (tree) 吹倒す fukítaosù

blow-dry [blou'drai] *n* (hairstyle) ブロー仕上げ buróshiàge

blowlamp [blou'læmp] (*BRIT*) *n* = **blowtorch**

blow off *vt* (hat etc) 吹飛ばす fukítobasù

blow out *vi* (fire, flame) 吹消す fukíkesù

blow-out [blou'aut] *n* (of tire) パンク pańku

blow over *vi* (storm) 静まる shizúmarù; (crisis) 収まる osámarù

blowtorch [blou'tɔːrtʃ] *n* プロ―ランプ buróraǹpu, ト―チランプ tóchiraǹpu

blow up *vi* (storm) 起きる okírù; (crisis) 起る okórù

♦*vt* (bridge: destroy) 爆破する bakúha suru; (tire: inflate) 膨らます fukúramasu; (PHOT: enlarge) 引延ばす hikínobasù

blue [bluː] *adj* (color) 青い aóì, ブル―の burú no; (depressed) 憂うつな yúutsu na

blue film ポルノ映画 porúnoeìga

blue joke わいせつなジョ―ク waísetsu na jōku

out of the blue (*fig*) 青天のへきれきの様に seíten no hekíreki no yó ni

bluebell [bluː'bel] *n* ツルボ tsurúbò

bluebottle [bluː'bɑːtəl] *n* (insect) アオバエ aóbae

blueprint [bluː'print] *n* (*fig*): *a blueprint (for)* (...の) 計画 (...no) keíkaku, (...の) 青写真 (...no) aójashìn

blues [bluːz] *n*: *the blues* (*MUS*) ブル―ス búrùsu

bluff [blʌf] *vi* (pretend, threaten) はったりを掛ける hattári wo kakérù

♦*n* (pretense) はったり hattári

to call someone's bluff ...に挑戦する ...ni chósen suru

blunder [blʌn'dəːr] *n* (political) へまhéma

♦*vi* (bungle something) へまをする héma wo suru

blunt [blʌnt] *adj* (pencil) 先が太い sakí ga futóì; (knife) 切れない kirénài; (person, talk) 率直な sotchóku na

blur [bləːr] *n* (shape) かすんで見える物 kasúnde miérù monó

♦*vt* (vision) くらます kurámasu; (distinction) ぼかす bokásù

blurb [bləːrb] *n* (for book, concert etc) 宣伝文句 seńdenmoǹku

blurt out [bləːrt-] *vt* 出し抜けに言い出す dashínuke ni iídasù

blush [blʌʃ] *vi* (with shame, embarrassment) 赤面する sekímen suru

♦*n* 赤面 sekímen

blustering [blʌs'təːriŋ] *adj* (person) 威張り散らす ibárichirasù

blustery [blʌs'təːriː] *adj* (weather) 風の強い kazé no tsuyóì

boar [bɔːr] *n* イノシシ inóshishi

board [bɔːrd] *n* (cardboard) ボ―ル紙 bórugami; (wooden) 板 ítà; (on wall: notice board) 掲示板 keíjiban; (for chess etc) ...盤 ...bań; (committee) 委員会 iíńkai; (in firm) 役員会 yakúiǹkai; (NAUT, AVIAT): *on board* ...に乗って ...ni notte

♦*vt* (ship, train) ...に乗る ...ni norú

full/half board (*BRIT*) 3食〔2食〕付き sańshoku〔nishóku〕tsukí

board and lodging 賄い付き下宿 makánaitsuki geshùku

to go by the board (*fig*) 捨てられる sutérareru

boarder [bɔːr'dəːr] *n* (SCOL) 寄宿生 kishúkuseì

boarding card [bɔːr'diŋ-] *n* = **boarding pass**

boarding house *n* 下宿屋 geshúkuya

boarding pass *n* (AVIAT, NAUT) 搭乗券 tójōken

boarding school *n* 全寮制学校 zeńryō-

seigakkǒ

board room n 役員会議室 yakúinkaigishǐtsu

board up vt (door, window) ...に板を張る ...ni ítà wo harú

boast [boust] vi: **to boast (about/of)** (...を) 自慢する (...wo) jimán suru

boat [bout] n (small) ボート bǒto; (ship) 船 fúnè

boater [bou'tə:r] n (hat) かんかん帽 kańkanbō

boatswain [bou'sən] n 甲板長 kǒhañchō, ボースン bǒsun

bob [ba:b] vi (boat, cork on water: also: **bob up and down**) 波に揺れる namí ni yuréru

bobby [ba:b'i:] (BRIT: inf) n (policeman) 警官 keíkan

bobsleigh [ba:b'slei] n ボブスレー bobùsurē

bob up vi (appear) 現れる aráwarerù

bode [boud] vi: **to bode well/ill (for)** (...にとって) 良い(悪い)前兆である (...ni tottè) yoǐ(warúǐ)zeńchō de arù

bodily [ba:d'əli:] adj (needs, functions) 身体の shiňtai no
◆adv (lift, carry) 体ごと karádagoto

body [ba:d'i:] n (ANAT: gen) 体 karáda, 身体 shiňtai; (corpse) 死体 shitái; (object) 物体 buttái; (main part) 本体 hôñtai; (of car) 車体 shatái, ボディー bǒdì; (fig: group) 団体 dańtai; (: organization) 組織 sóshìki; (quantity: of facts) 量 ryǒ; (of wine) こく kokù

body-building [ba:d'i:bil'diŋ] n ボディービル bodíbirù

bodyguard [ba:d'i:ga:rd] n (of statesman, celebrity) 護衛 goéi, ボディーガード bodígàdo

bodywork [ba:d'i:wə:rk] n (AUT) 車体 shatái

bog [ba:g] n (GEO) 沼沢地 shǒtakùchǐ
◆vt: **to get bogged down** (fig) 泥沼にはまり込む dorónuma ni hamárikomù

boggle [ba:g'əl] vi: **the mind boggles** 理解できない ríkai dekínai

bogus [bou'gəs] adj (claim, workman etc) 偽の nisé no

boil [boil] vt (water) 沸かす wakásu; (eggs, potatoes etc) ゆでる yudéru
◆vi (liquid) 沸く wakú; (fig: with anger) かんかんに怒る kańkan ni okórù; (: with heat) うだるような暑さになる udárù yǒ na atsùsa ni narú
◆n (MED) 出来物 dekímonò
to come to a (US)/the (BRIT) boil 沸き始める wakíhajimerù

boil down to vt fus (fig) 要するに...である yǒ surù ni ...de arù

boiled egg [boild-] n ゆで卵 yudétamàgo

boiled potatoes npl ゆでジャガイモ yudéjagàimo

boiler [boi'lə:r] n (device) ボイラー bǒrā

boiler suit (BRIT) n つなぎの作業着 tsunági no sagyǒgi

boiling point [boi'liŋ-] n (of liquid) 沸騰点 fúttōten

boil over vi (kettle, milk) 吹こぼれる fukíkoborerù

boisterous [bois'tə:rəs] adj (noisy, excitable: person, crowd) 騒々しい sǒzōshiǐ

bold [bould] adj (brave) 大胆な daítan na; (pej: cheeky) ずうずうしい zúzūshiǐ; (pattern) 際立った kiwádattà; (line) 太い futǒǐ; (color) 派手な hadé na

Bolivia [bouliv'i:ə] n ボリビア boríbìa

bollard [ba:l'ə:rd] (BRIT) n (AUT) 標識柱 hyǒshikichǔ ◇安全地帯などを示す ańzenchitái nadò wo shimésù

bolster [boul'stə:r] n (pillow) 長まくら nagámakùra

bolster up vt (case) 支持する shíjì suru

bolt [boult] n (lock) ラッチ rátchǐ; (with nut) ボルト borúto
◆adv: **bolt upright** 背筋を伸ばしてsesúji wo nobáshite
◆vt (door) ...のラッチを掛ける ...no ratchǐ wo kakérù; (also: **bolt together**) ボルトで止める borúto de tomérù; (food) 丸のみする marúnomi suru
◆vi (run away: horse) 逃出す nigédasu

bomb [ba:m] n (device) 爆弾 bakúdan
◆vt 爆撃する bakúgeki suru

bombard [ba:m'ba:rd] vt (MIL: with big guns etc) 砲撃する hǒgeki suru; (: from

planes) 爆撃する bakúgeki suru; (fig: with questions) ...に浴びせる ...ni abíseru

bombardment [bɑːmbɑːrd'mənt] n: *bombardment from guns* 砲撃 hōgeki *bombardment from planes* 爆撃 bakúgeki

bombastic [bɑːmbæs'tik] adj (person, language) もったい振った mottáibuttà

bomb disposal n: *bomb disposal unit* 爆弾処理班 bakúdanshorihàn

bomber [bɑːm'əːr] n (AVIAT) 爆撃機 bakúgekikì

bombshell [bɑːm'ʃel] n (fig: revelation) 爆弾 bakúdan

bona fide [bou'nəfaid'] adj (traveler etc) 本物の hofímono no

bond [bɑːnd] n (of affection, also gen: link) きずな kizúna; (binding promise) 約束 yakúsoku; (FINANCE) 証券 shōken; (COMM): *in bond* (of goods) 保税倉庫で hozéisòko de

bondage [bɑːn'didʒ] n (slavery) 奴隷の身分 doréi no mibún

bone [boun] n (ANAT, gen) 骨 honé
♦vt (meat, fish) 骨を抜く honé wò nukú

bone idle adj ぐうたらの gútara no

bonfire [bɑːn'faiəːr] n たき火 takíbi

bonnet [bɑːn'it] n (hat: also BRIT: of car) ボンネット bofínettò

bonus [bou'nəs] n (payment) ボーナス bōnasu; (fig: additional benefit) おまけ o-máke

bony [bou'niː] adj (MED: tissue) 骨のho- né no; (arm, face) 骨張った honébattà; (meat, fish) 骨の多い honé no ōi

boo [buː] excl (to surprise someone) わっ wá; (to show dislike) ぶー bū
♦vt 野次る yajírù

booby trap [buː'biː-] n (MIL) 仕掛爆弾 shikákebakùdan

book [buk] n (novel etc) 本 hóñ; (of stamps, tickets) 1つづり hitótsuzùri
♦vt (ticket, seat, room) 予約する yoyáku suru; (subj: traffic warden, policeman) ...に違反切符を書く ...ni ihánkippù wo kakù; (: referee) ...に勧告を与える ...ni kafíkoku wò atáeru

bookcase [buk'keis] n 本棚 hóñdana

booking office [buk'iŋ-] (BRIT) n (RAIL, THEATER) 切符売り場 kippú urība

book-keeping [bukki:'piŋ] n 簿記 bókì

booklet [buk'lit] n 小冊子 shōsasshì, パンフレット páñfurettò

bookmaker [buk'meikəːr] n 馬券屋 bakén-ya

books [buks] npl (COMM: accounts) 帳簿 chōbo

bookseller [buk'seləːr] n 本屋 hóñ-ya

bookshop [buk'ʃɑːp] n = **bookstore**

bookstore [buk'stɔːr] n 本屋 hóñ-ya, 書店 shotén

boom [buːm] n (noise) とどろき todóroki; (in prices, population etc) ブーム bûmu
♦vi (guns, thunder) とどろく todórokù; (voice) とどろく様な声で言う todórokù yō na koè de iú; (business) 繁盛する hañjō suru

boomerang [buː'məræŋ] n ブーメラン bûmeran

boon [buːn] n (blessing, benefit) 有難い物 arígatài monó

boost [buːst] n (to confidence, sales etc) 増す事 masú kotó
♦vt (confidence, sales etc) 増す masú; (economy) 促進する sokúshin suru

booster [buː'stəːr] n (MED) ブースター bûsutā

boot [buːt] n (knee-length) 長靴 nagágu-tsu, ブーツ bûtsu; (also: **hiking/climbing boots**) 登山靴 tozáñgutsu; (also: **soccer boots**) サッカーシューズ sakkáshù-zu; (BRIT: of car) トランク toráñku
♦vt (COMPUT) 起動する kidó suru
... to boot (in addition) おまけに o-máke ni

booth [buːθ] n (at fair) 屋台 yátài; (telephone booth, voting booth) ボックス bokkùsu

booty [buː'tiː] n 戦利品 señrihin

booze [buːz] (inf) n 酒 saké

border [bɔːr'dəːr] n (of a country) 国境 kokkyō; (also: **flower border**) ボーダー花壇 bōdākadàn; (band, edge: on cloth etc) へり herí
♦vt (road: subject: trees etc) ...に沿って

立っている ...ni sottè tattè irú; (another country: *also*: **border on**) ...ni 隣接する ...ni rifisetsu suru

borderline [bɔːr'dərlain] *n* (*fig*): **on the borderline** 際どいところで kiwádoì tokóro de, ボーダーラインすれすれで bôdāraìn surésure de

borderline case *n* 決めにくいケース kiménikuì kèsu

border on *vt fus* (*fig*: insanity, brutality) ...に近い ...ni chikáì

Borders [bɔːr'dərz] *n*: **the Borders** ボーダーズ州 bôdāzùshū 〈イングランドに隣接するスコットランド南部の1州 iñgurando ni rifisetsu surú sukóttòrando nañbu no isshū〉

bore [bɔːr] *pt of* **bear**

♦*vt* (hole) ...に穴を開ける ...ni aná wo akéru; (oil well, tunnel) 掘る hórù; (person) 退屈させる taíkutsu saséru

♦*n* (person) 詰まらない話で退屈させる人 tsumáranaì hanáshi de taíkutsu saséru hitó; (of gun) 口径 kôkei

to be bored 退屈する taíkutsu suru

boredom [bɔːr'dəm] *n* (condition) 退屈 taíkutsu; (boring quality) 詰まらなさ tsumáranasà

boring [bɔːr'iŋ] *adj* (tedious, unimaginative) 退屈な taíkutsu na

born [bɔːrn] *adj*: **to be born** 生れる umáreru

I was born in 1960 私は1960年に生れました watákushi wa señkyúhyàkurokújūnen ni umáremashìta

borne [bɔːrn] *pp of* **bear**

borough [bɔːr'ə] *n* (POL) 区 ku

borrow [baːr'ou] *vt*: **to borrow something** (from someone) ...を借りる ...wo karíru

bosom [buz'əm] *n* (ANAT) 胸 muné

bosom friend *n* 親友 shiñ-yū

boss [bɔːs] *n* (employer) 雇い主 yatóìnushi; (supervisor, superior) 上司 jôshi, 親方 oyákata, ボス bósù

♦*vt* (*also*: **boss around, boss about**) こき使う kokítsukaù

bossy [bɔːs'iː] *adj* (overbearing) 威張り散らす ibárichirasù

bosun [bou'sən] *n* (NAUT) = **boatswain**

botany [baːt'əniː] *n* 植物学 shokúbutsugàku

botch [baːtʃ] *vt* (bungle: *also*: **botch up**) 不手際で...をしくじる futégiwa de ...wo shikújirù

both [bouθ] *adj* 両方の ryóhồ no

♦*pron* (things, people) 両方 ryóhồ

♦*adv*: **both A and B** AもBも A mo B mo

both of us went, we both went 私たち2人共行きました watákushitàchi futáritomo ikímashìta

bother [baːð'əːr] *vt* (worry) 心配させる shiñpai saséru; (disturb) ...に迷惑を掛ける ...ni méìwaku wo kakérù

♦*vi* (*also*: **bother oneself**) ...に気付かう ...ni kizúkaù

♦*n* (trouble) 迷惑 méìwaku; (nuisance) いやな事 iyá na kotó

to bother doing わざわざ...する wázàwaza ...surú

bottle [baːt'əl] *n* (container: for milk, wine, perfume etc) 瓶 bíñ; (of wine, whiskey etc) ボトル botórù; (amount contained) 瓶一杯 bíñ ippái; (baby's) ほ乳瓶 hó-nyūbin

♦*vt* (beer, wine) 瓶に詰める bíñ ni tsumérù

bottleneck [baːt'əlnek] *n* (AUT: *also* *fig*: of supply) ネック nékkù

bottle-opener [baːt'əloupənər] *n* 栓抜き señnukì

bottle up *vt* (emotion) 抑える osáerù

bottom [baːt'əm] *n* (of container, sea etc) 底 sokó; (buttocks) しり shirí; (of page, list) 一番下の所 ichíban shitá no tokóro; (of class) びり bírì

♦*adj* (lower: part) 下の方の shitá no hồ no; (last: rung, position) 一番下の ichíban shitá no

bottomless [baːt'əmlis] *adj* (funds, store) 際限のない saígeñ no naì

bough [bau] *n* 枝 edá

bought [bɔːt] *pt, pp of* **buy**

boulder [boul'dəːr] *n* 大きな丸石 ôkinà marúishi

bounce [bauns] *vi* (ball) 跳ね返る hané-

kaèru; (check) 不渡りになる fuwátàri ni narù
♦*vt* (ball) 跳ねさせる hanésaserù
♦*n* (rebound) 跳ね返る事 hanékaèru kotò

bouncer [baun'sə:r] (*inf*) *n* (at dance, club) 用心棒 yójìnbō

bound [baund] *pt, pp of* **bind**
♦*n* (leap) 一飛び hitótòbi; (*gen pl*: limit) 限界 geńkai
♦*vi* (leap) 跳ぶ tobù
♦*vt* (border) ...の境界になる ...no kyōkai ni narù
♦*adj*: **bound by** (law, regulation) ...に拘束されている ...ni kōsoku saréte irù
to be bound to do something (obliged) やむを得ず...しなければならない yamú wo ezù ...shinákereba naranaì; (likely) 必ず...するだろう kanárazu ...surú darò
bound for (NAUT, AUT, RAIL) ...行きの ...yukí no
out of bounds (*fig*: place) 立入禁止で tachírikinshi de

boundary [baun'də:ri:] *n* (border, limit) 境界 kyōkai

boundless [baund'lis] *adj* (energy etc) 果てし無い hatéshinaì

bouquet [bu:kei'] *n* (of flowers) 花束 hanátàba, ブーケ būke

bourgeois [bur'ʒwɑ:] *adj* ブルジョア根性の buŕuojoakoñjō no

bout [baut] *n* (of malaria etc) 発作 hossá; (of activity) 発作的にする事 hossáteki ni suru kotò; (BOXING etc) 試合 shiái

boutique [bu:ti:k'] *n* ブティック butíkku

bow[1] [bou] *n* (knot) チョウ結び chōmusùbi; (weapon, MUS) 弓 yumí

bow[2] [bau] *n* (of the head) 会釈 éshàku; (of the head and body) お辞儀 ojígi; (NAUT: *also*: **bows**) 船首 sénshu, へ先 hesáki
♦*vi* (with head) 会釈する éshàku suru; (with head and body) お辞儀する ojígi suru; (yield): *to bow to/before* (reason, pressure) ...に屈服する ...ni kuppúku suru

bowels [bau'əlz] *npl* (ANAT) 腸 chō; (of the earth etc) 深い所 fukáì tokóro

bowl [boul] *n* (container) 鉢 hachí, ボール bōru; (contents) ボール一杯 bōru ippái; (ball) 木球 mokkyū, ボール bōru
♦*vi* (CRICKET) 投球する tōkyū suru

bow-legged [bou'legid] *adj* がにまたの ganímata no

bowler [bou'lə:r] *n* (CRICKET) 投手 tōshu, ボウラー bōrā; (BRIT: *also*: **bowler hat**) 山高帽 yamátakabō

bowling [bou'liŋ] *n* (game) ボーリング bōringu

bowling alley *n* (building) ボーリング場 bōringujō; (track) レーン rèn

bowling green *n* ローンボーリング場 rōnbōringujō

bowls [boulz] *n* (game) ローンボーリング rōnbōringu

bow tie *n* チョウネクタイ chōnekùtai

box [bɑ:ks] *n* (*gen*) 箱 hakó; (*also*: **cardboard box**) 段ボール箱 dañbōrubàko; (THEATER) ボックス bókkùsu
♦*vt* (put in a box) 箱に詰める hakó ni tsumérù
♦*vi* (SPORT) ボクシングする bókùshingu suru

boxer [bɑ:k'sə:r] *n* (person) ボクシング選手 bokúshingu señshu, ボクサー bókùsā

boxing [bɑ:k'siŋ] *n* (SPORT) ボクシング bókùshingu

Boxing Day (BRIT) *n* ボクシングデー bokúshingudè

boxing gloves *npl* ボクシンググローブ bokúshingugurōbu

boxing ring *n* リング riñgu

box office *n* 切符売り場 kippú uríba

boxroom [bɑ:ks'ru:m] (BRIT) *n* 納戸 nañdo

boy [bɔi] *n* (young) 少年 shōnen, 男の子 otóko no kò; (older) 青年 seínen; (son) 息子 musúko

boycott [bɔi'kɑ:t] *n* ボイコット boíkottò
♦*vt* (person, product, place etc) ボイコットする boíkottò suru

boyfriend [bɔi'frend] *n* 男友達 otókomòdachi, ボーイフレンド bōifureñdo

boyish [bɔi'iʃ] *adj* (man) 若々しい wakáwakashiì; (looks, smile, woman) 少年の様な shōnen no yō na

B.R. [bi:a:r'] n abbr = **British Rail**

bra [brɑ:] n ブラジャー burájà

brace [breis] n (on teeth) 固定器 kotéĭki, ブレース burèsu; (tool) 曲り柄ドリル magáriedorìru
♦vt (knees, shoulders) ...に力を入れる ...ni chikára wo iréru
to brace oneself (for weight) 構えて待つ kamáete matsù; (for shock) 心を静めて待つ kokóro wo shizúmetè matsu

bracelet [breis'lit] n 腕輪 udéwa, ブレスレット burésùretto

braces [brei'siz] (BRIT) npl ズボンつり zubóñtsuri, サスペンダー sasúpeñdà

bracing [brei'siŋ] adj (air, breeze) さわやかな sawáyàka na

bracken [bræk'ən] n ワラビ warábi

bracket [bræk'it] n (TECH) 腕金 udégane; (group) グループ gúrùpu; (range) 層 sò; (also: **brace bracket**) 中括弧 chúkakkò, ブレース búrèsu; (also: **round bracket**) 小括弧 shôkakkò, 丸括弧 marúkakkò, パーレン pâren; (also: **square bracket**) かぎ括弧 kagíkakkò
♦vt (word, phrase) ...に括弧を付ける ...ni kakkò wo tsúkerù

brag [bræg] vi 自慢する jimán suru

braid [breid] n (trimming) モール môru; (of hair) お下げ o-ságe

Braille [breil] n 点字 teñji

brain [brein] n (ANAT) 脳 nò; (fig) 頭脳 zúnô

brainchild [brein'tʃaild] n (project) 発案 hatsúan; (invention) 発明 hatsúmei

brains [breinz] npl (CULIN) 脳みそ nômiso; (intelligence) 頭脳 zúnô

brainwash [brein'wɑːʃ] vt 洗脳する señnô suru

brainwave [brein'weiv] n 脳波 nôha

brainy [brei'ni:] adj (child) 頭の良い atáma no yoĭ

braise [breiz] vt (CULIN) いためてから煮込む itámete kará nikómù

brake [breik] n (AUT) 制動装置 seídosòchi, ブレーキ burèki; (fig) 歯止め hadóme
♦vi ブレーキを掛ける burèki wo kakérù

brake fluid n ブレーキ液 burékièki

brake light n ブレーキライト burékiraìto

bramble [bræm'bəl] n (bush) イバラ ibára

bran [bræn] n ふすま fusúma

branch [bræntʃ] n (of tree) 枝 edá; (COMM) 支店 shitén

branch out vi (fig): *to branch out into* ...に手を広げる ...ni te wo hirógeru

brand [brænd] n (trademark: also: **brand name**) 銘柄 meígara, ブランド burándo; (fig: type) 種類 shúrùi
♦vt (cattle) 焼印 yakíin

brandish [bræn'diʃ] vt (weapon) 振り回す furímawasù

brand-new [brænd'nu:'] adj 真新しい maátarashiĭ

brandy [bræn'di:] n ブランデー burándē

brash [bræʃ] adj (forward, cheeky) ずうずうしい zúzūshiĭ

brass [bræs] n (metal) 真ちゅう shiñchū
the brass (MUS) 金管楽器 kiñkangàkki

brass band n 吹奏楽団 suísōgakùdan, ブラスバンド burásubañdo

brassiere [brəzi:r'] n ブラジャー burájà

brat [bræt] (pej) n (child) がき gakí

bravado [brəvɑː'dou] n 空威張り karáibàri

brave [breiv] adj (attempt, smile, action) 勇敢な yúkan na
♦vt (face up to) ...に立ち向う ...ni tachímukaù

bravery [brei'və:ri:] n 勇気 yûki

bravo [brɑː'vou] excl ブラボー burabô

brawl [brɔ:l] n (in pub, street) けんか keñka

brawny [brɔ:'ni:] adj (arms etc) たくましい takúmashiĭ

bray [brei] vi (donkey) 鳴く nakú

brazen [brei'zən] adj (woman) ずうずうしい zúzūshiĭ; (lie, accusation) 厚かましい atsúkamashiĭ
♦vt: *to brazen it out* 最後までしらばくれる saígo madé shirábakurerù

brazier [brei'ʒə:r] n (on building site etc) 野外用簡易暖炉 yagáiyô kañ-i dañro

Brazil [brəzil'] n ブラジル burájiru

Brazilian [brəzil'i:ən] adj ブラジルの bu-

rájiru no
♦n ブラジル人 burájirujìn

breach [bri:tʃ] vt (defence, wall) 突破する toppá suru
♦n (gap) 突破口 toppákō; (breaking): *breach of contract* 契約不履行 keíyaku-furikō
breach of the peace 治安妨害 chíanbōgai

bread [bred] n (food) パン páñ

bread and butter n バターを塗ったパン bátā wo nuttá páñ; (fig: source of income) 金づる kanézuru

breadbox [bred'ba:ks] (BRIT **breadbin**) n パン入れ pañ-irè

breadcrumbs [bred'krʌmz] npl (gen) パンくず pañkuzù; (CULIN) パン粉 pañko

breadline [bred'lain] n: *on the breadline* 貧しい mazúshiì

breadth [bredθ] n (of cloth etc) 幅 habá; (fig: of knowledge, subject) 広さ hírosa

breadwinner [bred'winə:r] n (in family) 稼ぎ手 kaségite

break [breik] (pt **broke**, pp **broken**) vt (cup, glass) 割る warú; (stick, leg, arm) 折る orù; (machine etc) 壊す kowásù; (promise, law, record) 破る yabúrù; (journey) 中断する chúdan suru
♦vi (crockery) 割れる waréru; (stick, arm, leg) 折れる orérù; (machine etc) 壊れる kowárerù; (storm) 起る okórù; (weather) 変る kawáru; (story, news) 報道される hōdō saréru; (dawn): *dawn breaks* 夜が明ける yo ga akéru
♦n (gap) 途切れた所 togíreta tokóro; (fracture: gen) 破損 hasóñ; (: of limb) 骨折 kossétsu; (pause for rest) 休憩 kyúkei; (at school) 休み時間 yasúmijikàn; (chance) チャンス cháñsu
to break the news to someone ...に知らせる ...ni shiráseru
to break even (COMM) 収支がとんとんになる shúshi ga toñton ni narù
to break free/loose (person, animal) 逃出す nigédasu
to break open (door etc) ...を壊して開ける ...wo kowáshite akéru

breakage [brei'kidʒ] n (act of breaking)

壊す事 kowásù kotó; (object broken) 損傷 soñshō

break down vt (figures, data) 分析する buñseki suru
♦vi (machine, car) 故障する koshō suru; (person) 取乱す torímidasù; (talks) 物別れになる monówakàre ni narù

breakdown [breik'daun] n (AUT) 故障 koshō; (in communications) 中断 chúdan; (of marriage) 破たん hatáñ; (MED: also: **nervous breakdown**) 神経衰弱 shiñkei-suìjaku; (of statistics) 分析 buñseki

breakdown van (BRIT) n レッカー車 rékkàsha

breaker [brei'kə:r] n (wave) 白波 shiránami

breakfast [brek'fəst] n 朝ご飯 asá gohàn, 朝食 chóshoku

break in vt (horse etc) 慣らす narásù
♦vi (burglar) 押入る oshíirù; (interrupt) 割込む waríkomù

break-in [breik'in] n 押入り oshíiri

breaking and entering [breik'iŋ ænd en'tə:riŋ] n (LAW) 不法侵入 fuhō-shiñ-nyū

break into vt fus (house) ...に押入る ...ni oshíirù

break off vi (branch) 折れる orérù; (speaker) 話を中断する hanáshi wo chúdan suru

break out vi (begin: war) ぼっ発する boppátsu suru; (: fight) 始まる hajímaru; (escape: prisoner) 脱出する dasshútsu suru
to break out in spots/a rash にきび〔湿しん〕になる níkibi〔shisshíñ〕ni narù

breakthrough [breik'θru:] n (fig: in technology etc) 躍進 yakúshin

break up vi (ship) 分解する buñkai suru; (crowd, meeting) 解散する kaísan suru; (marriage) 離婚に終る rikóñ ni owáru; (SCOL) 終る owáru
♦vt (rocks, biscuit etc) 割る warú; (fight etc) やめさせる yamésaseru

breakwater [breik'wɔ:tə:r] n 防波堤 bōhatei

breast [brest] n (of woman) 乳房 chíbùsa; (chest) 胸 muné; (of meat) 胸肉 muné-

nĭkù

breast-feed [brest'fi:d] (*pt, pp* **breast-fed**) *vt* ...に母乳を飲ませる ...ni bonyū wo nomáserù

◆*vi* 子供に母乳を飲ませる kodómo ni bonyū wo nomáserù

breaststroke [brest'strouk] *n* 平泳ぎ hiráoyðgi

breath [breθ] *n* 息 íkì

out of breath 息を切らせて íkì wo kiráséte

Breathalyser [breθ'əlaizə:r] ® *n* 酒気検査器 shukíkensakì

breathe [bri:ð] *vt* 呼吸する kokyū suru

◆*vi* 呼吸する kokyū suru

breathe in *vt* 吸込む suíkomù

◆*vi* 息を吸込む íkì wo suíkomù

breathe out *vt* 吐出す hakídasu

◆*vi* 息を吐く íkì wo hakù

breather [bri:'ðə:r] *n* (break) 休憩 kyūkei

breathing [bri:'ðiŋ] *n* 呼吸 kokyū

breathless [breθ'lis] *adj* (from exertion) 息を切らしている íkì wo kiráséte irú; (MED) 呼吸困難の kokyūkoñnan no

breathtaking [breθ'teikiŋ] *adj* (speed) 息が止る様な íkì ga tomáru yð na; (view) 息を飲むような íkì wo nomù yð na

bred [bred] *pt, pp of* **breed**

breed [bri:d] (*pt, pp* **bred**) *vt* (animals) 繁殖させる hañshoku saséru; (plants) 栽培する saíbai suru

◆*vi* (ZOOL) 繁殖する hañshoku suru

◆*n* (ZOOL) 品種 hiñshu; (type, class) 種類 shúrùi

breeding [bri:'diŋ] *n* (upbringing) 育ち sodáchi

breeze [bri:z] *n* そよ風 soyókàze

breezy [bri:'zi:] *adj* (manner, tone) 快活な kaíkatsu na; (weather) 風の多い kazé no ðì

brevity [brev'iti:] *n* (shortness, conciseness) 簡潔さ kañketsusa

brew [bru:] *vt* (tea) 入れる iréru; (beer) 醸造する jōzō suru

◆*vi* (storm) 起ろうとしている okórð to shité irù; (*fig:* trouble, a crisis) 迫ってい

る semáttè irú

brewery [bru:'ə:ri:] *n* 醸造所 jōzōshò

bribe [braib] *n* 賄ろ waíro

◆*vt* (person, witness) 買収する baíshū suru

bribery [brai'bə:ri:] *n* (with money, favors) 贈賄 zōwai

bric-a-brac [brik'əbræk] *n* 置物類 okímonorùi

brick [brik] *n* (for building) れんが rēnga

bricklayer [brik'leiə:r] *n* れんが職人 reñgashokùnin

bridal [braid'əl] *adj* (gown) 花嫁の hanáyòme no; (suite) 新婚者の shiñkoñsha no

bride [braid] *n* 花嫁 hanáyòme, 新婦 shiñpu

bridegroom [braid'gru:m] *n* 花婿 hanámùko, 新郎 shiñrō

bridesmaid [braidz'meid] *n* 新婦付き添いの女性 shiñputsukísoi no joséi

bridge [bridʒ] *n* (TECH, ARCHIT) 橋 hashí; (NAUT) 船橋 señkyō, ブリッジ burijjì; (CARDS, DENTISTRY) ブリッジ buríjjì

◆*vt* (*fig:* gap, gulf) 乗越える noríkoerù

bridge of the nose 鼻柱 hanábashira

bridle [braid'əl] *n* くつわ kutsúwa

bridle path *n* 乗馬用の道 jōbayō no michí

brief [bri:f] *adj* (period of time, description, speech) 短い mijíkaì

◆*n* (LAW) 事件摘要書 jikéntekiyōsho; (*gen:* task) 任務 nìñmu

◆*vt* (inform) ...に指示を与える ...ni shijì wo atáeru

briefcase [bri:f'keis] *n* かばん kabán, ブリーフケース burífukèsu

briefing [bri:'fiŋ] *n* (*gen,* PRESS) 説明 setsúmei

briefly [bri:f'li:] *adv* (smile, glance) ちらっと chiráttð; (explain, say) 短く mijíkakù

briefs [bri:fs] *npl* (for men) パンツ pañtsu, ブリーフ burífu; (for women) パンティー pañtì, ショーツ shòtsu

brigade [brigeid'] *n* (MIL) 旅団 ryodán

brigadier [brigədi'ə:r] *n* (MIL) 准将 juñshō

bright [brait] *adj* (*gen*) 明るい akárui; (person, idea: clever) 利口な rikō na; (person: lively) 明朗な meírō na

brighten [brait'ən] (*also:* **brighten up**) *vt* (room) 明るくする akáruku suru; (event) 明るくする tanóshiku suru
♦*vi* 明るくなる akáruku narù

brilliance [bril'jəns] *n* (of light) 明るさ akárusa; (of talent, skill) 素晴らしさ subárashisà

brilliant [bril'jənt] *adj* (person, idea) 天才的な teñsaiteki na; (smile, career) 輝かしい kagáyakashiì; (sunshine, light) 輝く kagáyakù; (*BRIT*: *inf*: holiday etc) 素晴らしい subárashiì

brim [brim] *n* (of cup etc) 縁 fuchí; (of hat) つば tsubà

brine [brain] *n* (CULIN) 塩水 shiómìzu

bring [briŋ] (*pt, pp* **brought**) *vt* (thing) 持って来る motté kurù; (person) 連れて来る tsuréte kurù; (*fig*: satisfaction) もたらす motárasù; (trouble) 起す okósù

bring about *vt* (cause) 起こす okósù

bring back *vt* (restore: hanging etc) 復帰させる fukkí saséru; (return: thing/person) 持って〔連れて〕帰る motté〔tsuréte〕kaérù

bring down *vt* (government) 倒す taósù; (MIL: plane) 撃墜する gekítsui suru; (price) 下げる sagérù

bring forward *vt* (meeting) 繰り上げる kuríagerù; (proposal) 提案する teían suru

bring off *vt* (task, plan) ...に成功する ...ni seíkō suru

bring out *vt* (gun) 取出す torídasu; (meaning) 明らかにする akíraka ni suru; (publish, produce: book) 出版する shuppán suru; (: album) 発表する happyō suru

bring round *vt* (unconscious person) 正気付かせる shōkizukaserù

bring up *vt* (carry up) 上に持って来る〔行く〕ué ni motté kurù〔ikú〕; (educate: person) 育てる sodáterù; (question, subject) 持出す mochídasù; (vomit: food) 吐く hakú

brink [briŋk] *n* (of disaster, war etc) 瀬戸際 setógiwa

brisk [brisk] *adj* (tone, person) きびきびした kíbìkibi shitá; (pace) 早い hayáì; (trade) 盛んな sakán na

bristle [bris'əl] *n* (animal hair, hair of beard) 剛毛 gōmō; (of brush) 毛 ke
♦*vi* (in anger) 怒る okórù

Britain [brit'ən] *n* (*also:* **Great Britain**) 英国 eíkoku, イギリス igírisu ◇イングランド，スコットランド，ウェールズを含む iñguraǹdo, sukóttorañdo, uéruzu wo fukúmù

British [brit'iʃ] *adj* 英国の eíkoku no, イギリスの igírisu no
♦*npl:* **the British** 英国人 eíkokujiǹ, イギリス人 igírisujìn

British Isles *npl:* **the British Isles** イギリス諸島 igírisushotō

British Rail *n* 英国国有鉄道 eíkoku kokúyū tetsùdō

Briton [brit'ən] *n* 英国人 eíkokujiǹ, イギリス人 igírisujìn

brittle [brit'əl] *adj* (fragile: glass etc) 割れやすい waréyasuì; (: bones etc) もろい moróì

broach [broutʃ] *vt* (subject) 持出す mochídasu

broad [brɔːd] *adj* (street, shoulders, smile, range) 広い hiróì; (general: outlines, distinction etc) 大まかな ōmakà na; (accent) 強い tsuyóì
in broad daylight 真っ昼間に mappíruma ni

broadcast [brɔːd'kæst] *n* (TV, RADIO) 放送 hōsō
♦*vb* (*pt, pp* **broadcast**)
♦*vt* (TV, RADIO) 放送する hōsō suru; (TV) 放映する hōei suru
♦*vi* (TV, RADIO) 放送する hōsō suru

broaden [brɔːd'ən] *vt* (scope, appeal) 広くする híròku suru, 広げる hirógeru
♦*vi* (river) 広くなる hiróku narú, 広がる hírógaru
to broaden one's mind 心を広くする kokóro wo hiróku suru

broadly [brɔːd'li:] *adv* (in general terms) 大まかに ōmakà ni

broad-minded [brɔːd'main'did] *adj* 心の広い kokóro no hiróì

broccoli [brɑːˈkəliː] n (BOT, CULIN) ブロッコリー burókkòrī

brochure [brouˈʃuːr'] n (booklet) 小冊子 shōsasshì, パンフレット pánfuretto

broil [brɔil] vt (CULIN) じか火で焼く jikábi de yakú

broke [brouk] pt of **break**
◆adj (inf: person, company) 無一文になった múichimòn ni nattá

broken [brouˈkən] pp of **break**
◆adj (window, cup etc) 割れた warétà; (machine: also: **broken down**) 壊れた kowáretà
a **broken leg** 脚の骨折 ashí no kossetsú
in **broken English/Japanese** 片言の英語〔日本語〕で katákoto no eígo〔nihóngo〕de

broken-hearted [brouˈkənhɑːr'tid] adj 悲嘆に暮れた hitán ni kuréta

broker [brouˈkər] n (COMM: in shares) 証券ブローカー shōken burōkà; (: insurance broker) 保険代理人 hokén dairinin

brolly [brɑːˈliː] (BRIT: inf) n 傘 kása

bronchitis [brɑːŋkaiˈtis] n 気管支炎 kikánshièn

bronze [brɑːnz] n (metal) 青銅 seídō, ブロンズ burónzu; (sculpture) 銅像 dōzō

brooch [broutʃ] n ブローチ burōchi

brood [bruːd] n (of birds) 一腹のひな hitōhàra no hiná
◆vi (person) くよくよする kuyòkuyo suru

brook [bruk] n 小川 ogáwa

broom [bruːm] n (for cleaning) ほうき hōki; (BOT) エニシダ eníshida

broomstick [bruːm'stik] n ほうきの柄 hōki no e

Bros. abbr (= **brothers**) 兄弟 kyōdai

broth [brɑːθ] n (CULIN) スープ sūpu

brothel [brɑːθ'əl] n 売春宿 baíshun-yado

brother [brʌðˈɑːr] n (also: **older brother**) 兄 anī, 兄さん niīsan; (also: **younger brother**) 弟 otōtó; (REL) 修道士 shūdōshi

brother-in-law [brʌðˈəːrinlɔː] (pl **brothers-in-law**) n (older) 義理の兄 girí no anì; (younger) 義理の弟 girí no otōtó

brought [brɔːt] pt, pp of **bring**

brow [brau] n (forehead) 額 hitái; (rare: gen: eyebrow) まゆ mayù; (of hill) 頂上 chōjō

brown [braun] adj (color) 褐色の kasshóku no, 茶色の chaíro no; (tanned) 日焼けした hiyáke shitá
◆n (color) 褐色 kasshóku, 茶色 chaíro
◆vt (CULIN) ...に焼き目を付ける ...ni yakíme wo tsukérù

brown bread n 黒パン kurópan

brownie [brau'niː] n (Brownie guide) ブラウニー buráunī ◇ガールスカウトの幼年団員 gárusukaùto no yōnendaǹ-in; (US: cake) チョコレートクッキーの一種 chokórētokukkì no isshù

brown paper n クラフト紙 kuráfutoshì

brown sugar n 赤砂糖 akázatò

browse [brauz] vi (through book) 拾い読みする hiróiyomi suru; (in shop) 商品を見て回る shōhin wo mitè mawáru

bruise [bruːz] n (on face etc) 打撲傷 dabókushò, あざ azá
◆vt (person) ...に打撲傷を与える ...ni dabókushò wo atáerù

brunch [brʌntʃ] n ブランチ buránchi

brunette [bruːnet'] n (woman) ブルネット burúnettò

brunt [brʌnt] n: to **bear the brunt of** (attack, criticism) ...の矢面に立つ ...no yaómòte ni tatsù

brush [brʌʃ] n (for cleaning, shaving etc) ブラシ buràshi; (for painting etc) 刷毛 hakè; (artist's) 筆 fudè, 絵筆 efúde; (quarrel) 小競り合い kozerìai
◆vt (sweep etc) ...にブラシを掛ける ...ni búrashi wo kakérù; (clean: teeth etc) 磨く migáku; (groom) ブラシでとかす búrashi de tokásù; (also: **brush against**: person, object) ...に触れる ...ni furéru

brush aside vt (emotion, criticism) 無視する mushí suru

brush up vt (subject, language) 復習する fukúshū suru

brushwood [brʌʃ'wud] n (sticks) しば shibá

brusque [brʌsk] adj (person, manner) 無愛想な buaísò na; (apology) ぶっきらぼうな bukkírabò na

Brussels [brʌs'əlz] n ブリュッセル buryússeru

Brussels sprout n メキャベツ mekyábetsu

brutal [bru:t'əl] adj (person, actions) 残忍な zańnin na; (honesty, frankness) 厳しい程の kibíshiî hodó no

brutality [bru:tæl'iti:] n 残忍さ zańninsa

brute [bru:t] n (person) 人でなし hitódenashi, けだもの kedámono; (animal) 獣 kemóno

◆adj: **by brute force** 暴力で bóryoku de

B.Sc. [bi:essi:'] abbr = **Bachelor of Science**

bubble [bʌb'əl] n (in liquid, soap) 泡 awá; (of soap etc) シャボン玉 shabóndama

◆vi (liquid) 沸く wakú; (: sparkle) 泡立つ awádatsù

bubble bath n 泡風呂 awáburo

bubble gum n 風船ガム fúsengamù

buck [bʌk] n (rabbit) 雄ウサギ osúusàgi; (deer) 雄ジカ ojíka; (US: inf: dollar) ドル dorù

◆vi (horse) 乗手を振り落そうとする noríte wo furíotosò ù to surù

to pass the buck (to someone) (...に) 責任をなすり付ける (...ni) sekínin wo nasúritsukerù

bucket [bʌk'it] n (pail) バケツ bakétsu; (contents) バケツ一杯 bakétsu ippái

buckle [bʌk'əl] n (on shoe, belt) バックル bakkúru

◆vt (shoe, belt) ...のバックルを締める ...no bakkúru wo shimérù

◆vi (wheel) ゆがむ yugámu; (bridge, support) 崩れる kuzúrerù

buck up vi (cheer up) 元気を出す géñki wo dasù

bud [bʌd] n (of tree, plant, flower) 芽 me

◆vi 芽を出す me wo dasù

Buddhism [bu:'dizəm] n (REL) 仏教 bukkyò

budding [bʌd'iŋ] adj (actor, entrepreneur) 有望な yūbó na

buddy [bʌd'i:] (US) n (friend) 相棒 aíbō

budge [bʌdʒ] vt (object) ちょっと動かす chóttò ugókasù; (fig: person) 譲歩させる

jóho saséru

◆vi (object, person) ちょっと動く chóttò ugókù; (fig: person) 譲歩する jóho suru

budgerigar [bʌdʒ'ə:ri:gɑ:r] n セキセイインコ sekíseiìnko

budget [bʌdʒ'it] n (person's, government's) 予算 yosán, 予算案 yosán-an

◆vi: **to budget for something** ...を予算案に入れる ...wo yosán-an ni iréru

I'm on a tight budget 台所が苦しい daídokoro ga kúrushiî

budgie [bʌdʒ'i:] n = **budgerigar**

buff [bʌf] adj (color: envelope) 薄茶色 usúchairo

◆n (inf: enthusiast) マニア mánìa

buffalo [bʌf'əlou] (pl **buffalo** or **buffaloes**) n (BRIT) スイギュウ suígyū; (US: bison) バイソン báìson

buffer [bʌf'ə:r] n (COMPUT) バッファ báffà; (RAIL) 緩衝機 kańshōki

buffet[1] [bufei'] (BRIT) n (in station) ビュッフェ byúffè; (food) 立食 risshóku

buffet[2] [bʌf'it] vt (subj: wind, sea) もみ揺さぶる momíyusaburù

buffet car (BRIT) n (RAIL) ビュッフェ車 byufféshà

bug [bʌg] n (esp US: insect) 虫 mushí; (COMPUT: of program) バグ bágù; (fig: germ) 風邪 kazé; (hidden microphone) 盗聴器 tóchòki

◆vt (inf: annoy) 怒らせる okóraserù; (room, telephone etc) ...に盗聴器を付ける ...ni tóchòki wo tsukérù

buggy [bʌg'i:] n (baby buggy) 乳母車 ubágurùma

bugle [bju:'gəl] n (MUS) らっぱ rappá

build [bild] n (of person) 体格 taíkaku

◆vb (pt, pp **built**)

◆vt (house etc) 建てる tatérù, 建築する keńchiku suru; (machine, cage etc) 作る tsukúrù

builder [bil'də:r] n (contractor) 建築業者 keńchikugyòsha

building [bil'diŋ] n (industry, construction) 建築業 keńchikugyò; (structure) 建物 tatémonò, ビル birù

building society (BRIT) n 住宅金融組合 jūtakukin-yūkumìai

build up vt (forces, production) 増やす fuyásù; (morale) 高める takámerù; (stocks) 蓄積する chikúseki suru

built [bilt] pt, pp of **build**

♦adj: **built-in** (oven, wardrobes etc) 作り付けの tsukúritsuke no

built-up area [bilt'ʌp-] n 市街化区域 shigáikakuìki

bulb [bʌlb] n (BOT) 球根 kyúkon; (ELEC) 電球 deñkyū

Bulgaria [bʌlger'i:ə] n ブルガリア burúgaria

Bulgarian [bʌlger'i:ən] adj ブルガリアの burúgaria no
♦n ブルガリア人 burúgariajìn

bulge [bʌldʒ] n (bump) 膨らみ fukúrami
♦vi (pocket, file, cheeks etc) 膨らむ fukúramu

bulk [bʌlk] n (mass: of thing) 巨大な姿 kyodái na sugáta; (: of person) 巨体 kyotái

in bulk (COMM) 大口で ôguchi de

the bulk of (most of) ...の大半 ...no taíhan

bulky [bʌl'ki:] adj (parcel) かさばった kasábattà; (equipment) 大きくて扱いにくい ôkikùte atsúkainikuì

bull [bul] n (ZOOL) 雄牛 oúshi; (male elephant/whale) 雄 osú

bulldog [bul'dɔːg] n ブルドッグ burúdoggù

bulldozer [bul'douzəːr] n ブルドーザー burúdòzā

bullet [bul'it] n 弾丸 dañgan

bulletin [bul'itən] n (TV etc: news update) 速報 sokúhō; (journal) 会報 kaíhō, 紀要 kiyó

bulletproof [bul'itpruːf] adj (glass, vest, car) 防弾の bôdan no

bullfight [bul'fait] n 闘牛 tôgyū

bullfighter [bul'faitəːr] n 闘牛士 tôgyūshi

bullfighting [bul'faitiŋ] n 闘牛 tôgyū

bullhorn [bul'hɔːrn] (US) n ハンドマイク hañdomaìku

bullion [bul'jən] n (gold, silver) 地金 jigáne

bullock [bul'ək] n 去勢した雄牛 kyoséi

shitá oúshi

bullring [bul'riŋ] n 闘牛場 tôgyūjō

bull's-eye [bulz'ai] n (on a target) 的の中心 matô no chúshin

bully [bul'i:] n 弱い者いじめ yowáimono-ijìme
♦vt いじめる ijímeru

bum [bʌm] (inf) n (backside) しり shirí; (esp US: tramp) ルンペン ruñpen; (: good-for-nothing) ろくでなし rokúdenashi

bumblebee [bʌm'bəlbi:] n クマンバチ kumáñbachi

bump [bʌmp] n (in car: minor accident) 衝突 shôtotsu; (jolt) 衝撃 shôgeki; (swelling: on head) こぶ kobú; (on road) 段差 dañsa
♦vt (strike) ...にぶつかる ...ni butsúkaru

bumper [bʌm'pəːr] n (AUT) バンパー bañpā
♦adj: **bumper crop/harvest** 豊作 hôsaku

bumper cars npl (in amusement park) バンパーカー bañpākā

bump into vt fus (strike: obstacle) ...にぶつかる ...ni butsúkaru; (inf: meet: person) ...に出くわす ...ni dekúwasù

bumptious [bʌmp'ʃəs] adj (person) うぬぼれた unúboreta

bumpy [bʌm'pi:] adj (road) 凸凹な dekóboko na

bun [bʌn] n (CULIN) ロールパン rôrupan, パン bán; (of hair) まげ magé, シニヨン shíñyon

bunch [bʌntʃ] n (of flowers, keys) 束 tábà; (of bananas) 房 fusá; (of people) グループ gúrùpu

bunches [bʌntʃ'iz] npl (in hair) 左右のポニーテール sáyū no poníteru

bundle [bʌn'dəl] n (parcel: of clothes, samples etc) 包み tsutsúmi; (of sticks, papers) 束 tabà
♦vt (also: **bundle up**) 厚着させる atsúgi saséru; (put): **to bundle something/someone into** ...に ほうり[押]込む ...ni hôri(oshî)komù

bungalow [bʌŋ'gəlou] n バンガロー bañgarō

bungle [bʌŋ'gəl] vt (job, assassination) ...にしくじる ...ni shikújirù

bunion [bʌn'jən] n (MED) けん膜りゅう kefímakuryū, バニオン bánîon

bunk [bʌŋk] n (bed) 作り付けベッド tsukúritsukebeddô

bunk beds npl 二段ベッド nidánbeddô

bunker [bʌŋ'kəːr] n (also: **coal bunker**) 石炭庫 sekítañko; (MIL) えんぺいごう eñpeîgō; (GOLF) バンカー bañka

bunny [bʌn'i:] n (also: **bunny rabbit**) うサちゃん usáchan

bunting [bʌn'tiŋ] n (flags) 飾り小旗 kazárikobàta

buoy [bu:'i:] n (NAUT) ブイ buî

buoyant [bɔi'ənt] adj (ship) 浮力のある fúryòku no arù; (economy, market) 活気のある kakkî no arù; (fig: person, nature) 朗らかな hogáràka na

buoy up vt (fig) 元気づける geñkizukerù

burden [bəːr'dən] n (responsibility, worry) 負担 fután; (load) 荷物 nímòtsu

♦vt (trouble): **to burden someone with** (oppress) ...を打明けて...に心配を掛ける ...wo uchíakete ...ni shiñpai wo kakérù

bureau [bjur'ou] (pl **bureaux** or **bureaus**) n (BRIT: writing desk) 書き物机 kakímonozukùe ◇ふたが書く面になる机を指す futá ga kakù meñ ni narù tsukúe wo sasù; (US: chest of drawers) 整理だんす sefridañsu; (office: government, travel, information) 局 kyóku, 課 ka

bureaucracy [bjura:k'rəsi:] n (POL, COMM) 官僚制 kañryōsei

bureaucrat [bjur'əkræt] n (administrator) 官僚 kañryō; (pej: pen-pusher) 小役人 koyákunin

bureaux [bjur'ouz] npl of **bureau**

burglar [bəːr'gləːr] n 押込み強盗 oshíkomigồtō

burglar alarm n 盗難警報機 tốnankeihồki

burglary [bəːr'gləːri:] n (crime) 住居侵入罪 jūkyoshiñnyūzai

burial [beːr'i:əl] n 埋葬 maísō

burly [bəːr'li:] adj (figure, workman etc) ごつい gotsúî

Burma [bəːr'mə] n ビルマ bírùma

burn [bəːrn] (pt, pp **burned** or **burnt**) vt (papers, fuel etc) 燃やす moyásu; (toast, food etc) 焦がす kogásù; (house etc: arson) ...に放火する ...ni hồka suru

♦vi (house, wood etc) 燃える moéru; (cakes etc) 焦げる kogérù; (sting) ひりひりする hírîhiri suru

♦n やけど yakédo

burn down vt 全焼させる zeñshō saséru

burner [bəːr'nəːr] n (on cooker, heater) 火口 hígùchi, バーナー bânā

burning [bəːr'niŋ] adj (house etc) 燃えている moéte irú; (sand) 焼ける様に熱い yakéru yồ ni atsuî; (desert) しゃく熱の shakúnetsu no; (ambition) 熱烈な netsúretsu na

burnt [bəːrnt] pt, pp of **burn**

burrow [bəːr'ou] n (of rabbit etc) 巣穴 suåna

♦vi (dig) 掘る hórù; (rummage) あさる asáru

bursary [bəːr'səːri:] (BRIT) n (SCOL) 奨学金 shōgakukin

burst [bəːrst] (pt, pp **burst**) vt (bag, balloon, pipe etc) 破裂させる harétsu saséru; (subj: river: banks etc) 決壊させる kekkái saséru

♦vi (pipe, tire) 破裂する harétsu suru

♦n (also: **burst pipe**) 破裂した水道管 harétsu shita suídôkan

a burst of energy/speed/enthusiasm 突発的なエネルギー〔スピード，熱心さ〕 toppátsuteki na enérugī〔supído, nesshíñsa〕

a burst of gunfire 連射 reñsha

to burst into flames 急に燃え出す kyū ni moédasù

to burst into tears 急に泣き出す kyū ni nakídasù

to burst out laughing 急に笑い出す kyū ni waráídasù

to be bursting with (subj: room, container) はち切れんばかりに...で一杯になっている hachíkireñbakari ni ...de ippái ni natté irù; (: person: emotion) ...で胸が一杯になっている ...de muné ga ippái ni natté irù

burst into vt fus (room etc) ...に飛込む

...ni tobíkomù

bury [ber'i:] *vt* (*gen*) 埋める uméru; (at funeral) 埋葬する maísō suru

bus [bʌs] *n* (vehicle) バス básù

bush [buʃ] *n* (in garden) 低木 teíboku; (scrubland) 未開地 mikáìchi, ブッシュ bússhù

   to beat about the bush 遠回しに言う tōmawāshi ni iú

bushy [buʃ'i:] *adj* (tail, hair, eyebrows) ふさふさした fúsàfusa shitá

busily [biz'ili:] *adv* (actively) 忙しく isógashikù

business [biz'nis] *n* (matter, question) 問題 mofídai; (trading) 商売 shōbai; (firm) 会社 kaísha; (occupation) 仕事 shigóto

   to be away on business 出張して留守である shutchō shite rusù de arù

   it's my business to ... ...するのは私の務めです ...surú no wa watákushi no tsutóme desù

   it's none of my business 私の知った事じゃない watákushi no shittá kotó ja naí

   he means business 彼は本気らしい karè wa hoñki rashiī

businesslike [biz'nislaik] *adj* てきぱきした tekípaki shitá

businessman [biz'nismæn] (*pl* **businessmen**) *n* 実業家 jitsúgyōka

business trip *n* 出張 shutchō

businesswoman [biz'niswumən] (*pl* **businesswomen**) *n* 女性実業家 joséijitsugyōka

busker [bʌs'kə:r] (*BRIT*) *n* 大道芸人 daídōgeìnin

bus-stop [bʌs'stɑ:p] *n* バス停留所 básùtefryùjo

bust [bʌst] *n* (ANAT) 乳房 chíbùsa, 胸 muné; (measurement) バスト básùto; (sculpture) 胸像 kyōzō

  ♦*adj* (*inf*: broken) 壊れた kowárèta

   to go bust (company etc) つぶれる tsubúreru

bustle [bʌs'əl] *n* (activity) 雑踏 zattō

  ♦*vi* (person) 忙しく飛回る isógashikù tobímawarù

bustling [bʌs'liŋ] *adj* (town, place) にぎやかな nígiyàka na

busy [biz'i:] *adj* (person) 忙しい isógashiì; (shop, street) にぎやかな nigíyàka na; (TEL: line) 話し中の hanáshichū no

  ♦*vt*: *to busy oneself with* 忙しそうに...する isógashisō ni ...suru

busybody [biz'i:bɑ:di:] *n* でしゃばり屋 deshábariya

busy signal (*US*) *n* (TEL) 話中音 wáchūon

---

but [bʌt] *conj* 1 (yet) ...であるが ...de árù ga, ...であるけれども ...de árù keredomo, しかし shikáshì

   he's not very bright, but he's hardworking 彼はあまり頭は良くないが、よく働きます kárè wa amári àtama wà yókùnaī ga, yókù határakimasù

   I'm tired but Paul isn't 私は疲れていますが、ポールは疲れていません watákushi wa tsùkárète imasu ga, pórù wa tsukárète imásèn

   the trip was enjoyable but tiring 旅行は楽しかったけれども、疲れました ryokō wa tànóshikàtta keredomo, tsukáremashìta

2 (however) ...であるが ...de árù ga, ...であるけれども ...de árù keredomo, しかし shikáshì

   I'd love to come, but I'm busy 行きたいが、今忙しいんです ikítaì ga, ímà isógashiīn desu

   she wanted to go, but first she had to finish her homework 彼女は行きたかったけれども、先に宿題を済ます必要がありました kánojò wa ikítakàtta keredomo, sakí ni shùkúdai wo sùmásu hitsúyō ga arímashìta

   I'm sorry, but I don't agree 済みませんが、私は同意できません sumímasèn ga, watákushi wa dōi dekimasèn

3 (showing disagreement, surprise etc) しかし shikáshì

   but that's far too expensive! しかしそれは高過ぎますよ shikáshì soré wa tàkásugimasù yo

   but that's fantastic! しかし素晴らし

いじゃありませんか shikáshì subárashiì ja arímasèn ka

♦*prep* (apart from, except) ...を除いて ...wo nozóite, ...以外に ...ígai ni

he was nothing but trouble 彼は厄介な問題ばかり起していました kárè wa yákkài na móndai bakàri okóshìte imáshìta

we've had nothing but trouble 厄介な問題ばかり起っています yákkài na móndai bakàri okóttè imásù

no one but him can do it 彼を除けば出来る人はいません kárè wo nozókebà dekírù hito wa imásèn

who but a lunatic would do such a thing? 気違いを除けばそんな事をする人はいないでしょう kichígaì wo nozókebà sónna koto wò suru hito wà inái deshō

but for you あなたがいなかったら anátà ga inákàttara

but for your help あなたが助けてくれなかったら anátà ga tasúketè kuténakàttara

I'll do anything but that それ以外なら何でもします soré igài nara nán de mo shimasù

♦*adv* (just, only) ただ tádà, ...だけ ...dàkè, ...しか...ない ...shika ...naí

she's but a child 彼女はほんの子供です kánojò wa hón no kòdómo desù

had I but known 私がそれを知ってさえいたら watákushi ga sòré wo shitte saè itárà

I can but try やってみるしかありません yátte mirù shika arímasèn

all but finished もう少しで出来上りです mő sukoshi de dekíagari desù

butcher [butʃ'ə:r] *n* (tradesman) 肉屋 nikúyà

♦*vt* (cattle etc for meat) と殺する tosátsu suru; (prisoners etc) 虐殺する gyakúsatsu suru

butcher's (shop) [butʃ'ə:rz-] *n* 精肉店 seínikutèn, 肉屋 nikúyà

butler [bʌt'lə:r] *n* 執事 shítsùji

butt [bʌt] *n* (large barrel) たる tarú; (of

pistol) 握り nigíri; (of rifle) 床尾 shòbi; (of cigarette) 吸い殻 suígara; (*fig*: target: of teasing, criticism etc) 的 mató

♦*vt* (subj: goat, person) 頭で突く atáma de tsukú

butter [bʌt'ə:r] *n* (CULIN) バター bátà

♦*vt* (bread) ...にバターを塗る ...ni bátà wo nurú

buttercup [bʌt'ə:rkʌp] *n* キンポウゲ kiñpòge

butterfly [bʌt'ə:rflai] *n* (insect) チョウチョウ chōchō; (SWIMMING: *also*: **butterfly stroke**) バタフライ bátàfurai

butt in *vi* (interrupt) ...に割込む ...ni waríkomù

buttocks [bʌt'əks] *npl* (ANAT) しり shirí

button [bʌt'ən] *n* (on clothes) ボタン botán; (on machine) 押しボタン oshíbotàn; (*US*: badge) バッジ bájjì

♦*vt* (*also*: **button up**) ...のボタンをはめる ...no botán wo hamérù

♦*vi* ボタンで止まる botán de tomáru

buttress [bʌt'tris] *n* (ARCHIT) 控え壁 hikáekàbe

buxom [bʌk'səm] *adj* (woman) 胸の豊かな胸 muné no yutàka na

buy [bai] (*pt, pp* **bought**) *vt* 買う kaú

♦*n* (purchase) 買物 kaímono

to buy someone something/something for someone ...に...を買って上げる ...ni ...wo katté agéru

to buy something from someone ...から...を買う ...kará ...wo kaú

to buy someone a drink ...に酒をおごる ...ni saké wo ogóru

buyer [bai'ə:r] *n* (purchaser) 買手 kaíte; (COMM) 仕入係 shiíregakàri, バイヤー bâíyā

buzz [bʌz] *n* (noise: of insect) ぶんぶんという音 buñbun to iú otò; (: of machine etc) うなり unári; (*inf*: phone call): *to give someone a buzz* ...に電話を掛ける ...ni deñwa wo kakérù

♦*vi* (insect) ぶんぶん羽音を立てる buñbun haóto wo taterù; (saw) うなる unárù

buzzer [bʌz'ə:r] *n* (ELEC) ブザー búzà

buzz word (*inf*) *n* 流行語 ryūkōgo

---

by [bai] *prep* **1** (referring to cause, agent)
...に（よって）...ni (yotte)

killed by lightning 雷に打たれて死ん
だ kamínari ni ùtárète shínda

surrounded by a fence 塀に囲まれた
heí ni kakomareta

a painting by Picasso ピカソの絵画
pikásò no káìga

it's by Shakespeare シェイクスピアの
作品です sheíkusupìa no sakúhin desù

2 (referring to method, manner, means)
...で ...de

by bus/car/train バス〔車, 列車〕で
básù(kuruma, réssha)de

to pay by check 小切手で払う kogíttè.
de haráù

by moonlight/candlelight 月明り〔ろ
うそくの灯〕で tsukíakàri(rősoku no a-
kari)de

by saving hard, he ... 一生懸命に金を
貯めて彼は ... isshőkènmei ni kanè wo
tamete karè wa ...

3 (via, through) ...を通って ...wo tőttè,
...経由で ...kéìyu de

we came by Dover ドーバー経由で来ま
した dőbākeìyu de kimáshìta

he came in by the back door 彼は裏口
から入りました kárè wa uráguchi kara
hairimashìta

4 (close to) ...のそばに〔で〕...no sóbà ni
〔de〕,...の近くに〔で〕...no chikákù ni
〔de〕

the house by the river 川のそばにある
家 kawá no sobà ni árù ié

a holiday by the sea 海辺の休暇 umíbe no kyūka

she sat by his bed 彼女は彼のベッドの
そばに座っていました kánojò wa kárè
no béddò no sóbà ni suwátte imashìta

5 (past) ...を通り過ぎて ...wo tőrisugìte

she rushed by me 彼女は足早に私の前
を通り過ぎた kánojò wa ashíbaya ni
wàtákushi no maè wo tőrisugìta

I go by the post office every day 私
は毎日郵便局の前を通ります watákushi
wa maìnichi yūbínkyoku no mâè wo

tőrimasù

6 (not later than) ...までに ...mádè ni

by 4 o'clock 4時までに yójì made ni

by this time tomorrow 明日のこの時間
までに myőnichì no konő jikan madè ni

*by the time I got here it was too
late* 私がここに着いたころにはもう手遅
れでした watákushi ga kòkő ni tsuíta
koro ni wá mő teőkùre deshita

7 (during): *by daylight* 日中に nitchū ni

8 (amount) ...単位で ...tàn-i de

by the kilo/meter キロ〔メーター〕単位
で kiró(mētā)tàn-i de

paid by the hour 時給をもらって jikyú
wo moratte

one by one (people) 1人ずつ hitórizutsù;
(animals) 1匹ずつ ippíkizutsù; (things) 1
つずつ hitótsuzutsù

little by little 少しずつ sukőshizutsù

9 (MATH, measure): *to divide by 3* 3
で割るる sán de waru

to multiply by 3 3を掛ける sán wo
kakerù

a room 3 meters by 4 3メーター掛ける
4メーターの部屋 sánmētā kakérù yőn-
mētā no heyá

it's broader by a meter 1メーターも広
くなっている ichímētā mő hiròku náttè
iru

10 (according to) ...に従って ...nì shitágatte

to play by the rules ルールを守る rűrù
wo mamőrù

it's all right by me 私は構いませんよ
watákushi wa kàmáimasèn yó

11: *(all) by oneself etc* 一人だけで hitőrì dakè dè

he did it (all) by himself 彼は彼1人
だけの力でやりました kárè wa kárè hi-
tőri dake dè yarímashìta

*he was standing (all) by himself in
the corner* 彼は1人ぼっちで隅に立って
いました kárè wa hitőribotchì de súmì
ni táttè imashìta

12: *by the way* ところで tokóro dè

*by the way, did you know Claire
was back?* ところでね、クレアが帰っ
て来たのをご存知？ tokóro dè ne, kùrea

ga káette kita no wo go-zònjí?

this wasn't my idea by the way しかしね、これを提案したのは私じゃないからね shikáshi né, koré wo teian shita nò wa watákushi ja nài kara né

◆*adv* **1** *see* go; pass *etc*

2: *by and by* やがて yagáte

by and by they came to a fork in the road やがて道路はY字路になりました yagáte dòro ha wáijirò ni narímashìta

they'll come back by and by そのうち帰って来ますよ sonó uchi kaètte kimásù yo

by and large (on the whole) 大体において dáitai ni òite, 往々にして ōō ni shite

by and large I would agree with you 大体あなたと同じ意見です dáitai a-natá to onáji ikèn desu

Britain has a poor image abroad, by and large 海外における英国のイメージは往々にして悪い kàigai ni okéru èìkoku no ìmèjì wa ōō ni shite wàrúì

bye(-bye) [bai'(bai')] *n excl* じゃあねじゃね, バイバイ báibai

by(e)-law [bai'lɔ:] *n* 条例 jôrei

by-election [bai'ilekʃən] *n* (*BRIT*) 補欠選挙 hokétsusenkyo

bygone [bai'gɔ:n] *adj* (age, days) 昔のmukáshi no

◆*n*: *let bygones be bygones* 済んだ事を水に流す súnda kotó wo mizú ni nagásù

bypass [bai'pæs] *n* (AUT) バイパス baípasu; (MED: operation) 冠状動脈バイパス kanjōdòmyakubaìpasu

◆*vt* (town) ...にバイパスを設ける ...ni baípasu wo mókerù

by-product [bai'prɑ:dəkt] *n* (of industrial process) 副産物 fukúsanbutsu; (of situation) 二次的結果 nijítekikèkka

bystander [bai'stændɑ:r] *n* (at accident, crime) 居合せた通行人 iáwasèta tsúkōnin

byte [bait] *n* (COMPUT) バイト baìto

byword [bai'wɔrd] *n*: *to be a byword for* ...の代名詞である ...no daímeìshi de arù

by-your-leave [baiju:rli:v'] *n*: *without*

so much as a by-your-leave 自分勝手に jibúnkattè ni

C

C [si:] *n* (MUS: note) ハ音 há-òn; (: key) ハ調 hachô

C. [si:] *abbr* = **centigrade**

C.A. [si:ei'] *abbr* = **chartered accountant**

cab [kæb] *n* (taxi) タクシー tákùshī; (of truck, tractor etc) 運転台 untendai

cabaret [kæbərei'] *n* (nightclub) キャバレー kyábàrē; (floor show) フロアショー furóashò

cabbage [kæb'idʒ] *n* キャベツ kyábétsu

cabin [kæb'in] *n* (on ship) キャビン kyábìn; (on plane) 操縦室 sōjūshìtsu; (house) 小屋 koyá

cabin cruiser *n* 大型モーターボート ō-gata mótābòto, クルーザー kúrùzā ◇居室, 炊事場などのある物を指す kyōshì-tsu, suíjiba nádò no árù monò wo sásù

cabinet [kæb'ənit] *n* (piece of furniture) 戸棚 todána, キャビネット kyabínettò; (*also*: **display cabinet**) ガラス戸棚 garásu tódàna; (POL) 内閣 naíkaku

cable [kei'bəl] *n* (strong rope) 綱 tsuná; (ELEC, TEL, TV) ケーブル kèburu

◆*vt* (message, money) 電信で送る deñshin de okúru

cable-car [kei'bəlkɑ:r] *n* ケーブルカー kèburukā

cable television *n* 有線テレビ yūsente-rèbi

cache [kæʃ] *n*: *a cache of drugs* 隠匿された麻薬 íntoku saretà mayáku

a weapons cache 隠匿武器 íntokubùki

cackle [kæk'əl] *vi* (person, witch) 悪い声で笑う usúkimiwaruì kóè de wa-ráù; (hen) こここと鳴く kokoko to nákù

cacti [kæk'tai] *npl of* **cactus**

cactus [kæk'təs] (*pl* **cacti**) *n* サボテン sabóten

caddie [kæd'i:] *n* (GOLF) キャディー kyádì

caddy [kæd'i:] *n* = **caddie**

cadet [kədet'] *n* (MIL) 士官候補生 shikánkōhoseì; (POLICE) 警察学校の生徒 keísatsugakkô no seíto

cadge [kædʒ] (*inf*) *vt* (lift, cigarette etc) ねだる nedáru

Caesarean [size:r'i:ən] (*BRIT*) = **Cesarean**

café [kæfei'] *n* (snack bar) 喫茶店 kíssàten

cafeteria [kæfiti:'ri:ə] *n* (in school, factory, station) 食堂 shokúdō

caffein(e) [kæ'fi:n] *n* カフェイン kaféìn

cage [keidʒ] *n* (of animal) おり orí, ケージ kēji; (*also*: **bird cage**) 鳥かご toríkago, ケージ kēji; (of lift) ケージ kēji

cagey [kei'dʒi:] (*inf*) *adj* 用心深い yōjinbukaì

cagoule [kəgu:l'] (*BRIT*) *n* カグール kágūru ◇薄手の雨ガッパ usúde no amágappa

Cairo [kai'rou] *n* カイロ kaíro

cajole [kədʒoul'] *vt* 丸め込む marúmekomù

cake [keik] *n* (CULIN: large) デコレーションケーキ dekórēshonkèki; (: small) 洋菓子 yōgashì
   a cake of soap 石けん1個 sekkén íkkò

caked [keikt] *adj*: **caked with** (blood, mud etc) ...の塊で覆われた ...no katámari de ówareta

calamity [kəlæm'iti:] *n* (disaster) 災難 saínañ

calcium [kæl'si:əm] *n* (in teeth, bones etc) カルシウム karúshiùmu

calculate [kæl'kjəleit] *vt* (work out: cost, distance, numbers etc) 計算する keísan suru; (: effect, risk, impact etc) 予測する yosóku suru

calculating [kæl'kjəleitiŋ] *adj* (scheming) ずる賢い zurúgashikoì

calculation [kælkjəlei'ʃən] *n* (MATH) 計算 keísan; (estimate) 予測 yosóku

calculator [kæl'kjəleitə:r] *n* 電卓 deñtaku

calculus [kæl'kjələs] *n* (MATH) 微積分学 bisékibungàku

calendar [kæl'əndə:r] *n* (of year) カレンダー kárendà; (timetable, schedule) 予定表 yotéihyō

calendar month/year *n* 暦月〔年〕rekígetsu〔nen〕

calf [kæf] (*pl* **calves**) *n* (of cow) 子ウシ koúshi; (of elephant, seal etc) ...の子 ...no ko; (*also*: **calfskin**) 子牛革 koúshigàwa, カーフスキン kāfusukiñ; (ANAT) ふくらはぎ fukúrahàgi

caliber [kæl'əbə:r] (*BRIT* **calibre**) *n* (of person) 能力 nōryoku; (of skill) 程度 teído; (of gun) 口径 kōkéi

call [kɔ:l] *vt* (christen, name) 名付ける nazúkerù; (label) ...と呼ぶ ...wo...to yobú; (TEL) ...に電話を掛ける ...ni defiwa wo kakérù; (summon: doctor etc) 呼ぶ yobú; (: witness etc) 召喚する shōkan suru; (arrange: meeting) 召集する shōshū suru

◆*vi* (shout) 大声で言う ōgoè de iú; (telephone) 電話を掛ける deñwa wo kakerù; (visit: *also*: **call in, call round**) 立寄る tachíyoru

◆*n* (shout) 呼声 yobígoè; (TEL) 電話 deñwa; (of bird) 鳴声 nakígoè
   : to be called ......と呼ばれる ...to yobárerù, ...という ...to iú
   on call (nurse, doctor etc) 待機して taíki shité

call back *vi* (return) また寄る matá yorú; (TEL) 電話を掛け直す deñwa wo kakénaosù

callbox [kɔ:l'ba:ks] (*BRIT*) *n* 電話ボックス deñwabokkùsu

caller [kɔ:l'ə:r] *n* (visitor) 訪問客 hōmoñkyaku; (TEL) 電話を掛けてくる人 deñwa wo kakète kurú hitò

call for *vt fus* (demand) 要求する yōkyū suru; (fetch) 迎えに行く mukáe ni ikú

call girl *n* (prostitute) コールガール kōrugàru

call-in [kɔ:l'in] (*US*) *n* (phone-in) ◇視聴者が電話で参加する番組 shíchōsha ga deñwa de sañka suru bañgumi

calling [kɔ:l'iŋ] *n* (occupation) 職業 shókùgyō; (*also*: **religious calling**) 神のお召し kámî no o-méshi

calling card (*US*) *n* 名刺 meíshi

call off *vt* (cancel) 中止する chúshi suru

call on vt fus (visit) 訪ねる tazúnerù, 訪問する hômon suru; (appeal to) ...に ...を求める ...ni ...wo motómerù

callous [kæl'əs] adj (heartless) 冷淡な reítañ na

call out vt (name etc) 大声でいう ōgoè de iû; (summon for help etc) 呼び出す yobidasu

♦vi (shout) 大声で言う ōgoè de iú

call up vt (MIL) 召集する shōshū suru; (TEL) ...に電話をかける ...ni deñwa wo kakérù

calm [kɑːm] adj (unworried) 落着いている ochítsuite irú; (peaceful) 静かな shízùka na; (weather, sea) 穏やかな odáyàka na

♦n (quiet, peacefulness) 静けさ shizúkesà

♦vt (person, child) 落着かせる ochítsukasèru; (fears, grief etc) 鎮める shizúmerù

calm down vi (person) 落着く ochítsukù

♦vt (person) 落着かせる ochítsukasèru

Calor gas [kæl'əːr-]® n ◇携帯用燃料ガスボンベの商品名 keítaiyō neñryō gasuboñbe no shōhiñmei

calorie [kæl'əːriː] n カロリー károrī

calves [kævz] npl of **calf**

camber [kæm'bəːr] n (of road) 真ん中が高くなっている事 mañnaka ga takakù nattě irú kotő

Cambodia [kæmbou'diːə] n カンボジア kañbojìa

came [keim] pt of **come**

camel [kæm'əl] n (ZOOL) ラクダ rakúda

cameo [kæm'iːou] n (jewellery) カメオ kámèo

camera [kæm'əːrə] n (PHOT) 写真機 shashíñki, カメラ kámèra; (CINEMA) 映画カメラ eíga kámèra; (also: **TV camera**) テレビカメラ terébi kamèra

in camera (LAW) 非公開で hǐkòkai de

cameraman [kæm'əːræmæn] (pl **cameramen**) n (CINEMA, TV) カメラマン kaméramàn

camouflage [kæm'əflɑːʒ] n (MIL) カムフラージュ kamúfurāju; (ZOOL) 隠ぺい的ぎ態 íñpeitekigìtài

♦vt (conceal: also MIL) 隠す kakúsù

camp [kæmp] n (encampment) キャンプ場 kyañpujō; (MIL: barracks) 基地 kichí; (for prisoners) 収容所 shūyōjo; (faction) 陣営 jiñ-ei

♦vi (in tent) キャンプする kyañpu suru

♦adj (effeminate) 女々しい meméshiǐ

campaign [kæmpein'] n (MIL) 作戦 sakúsen; (POL etc) 運動 uñdō, キャンペーン kyañpěn

♦vi (objectors, pressure group etc) 運動をする uñdō wo suru

camp bed (BRIT) n 折畳みベッド orítatami beddò

camper [kæm'pəːr] n (person) キャンパー kyañpā; (vehicle) キャンピングカー kyañpingukā

camping [kæm'piŋ] n 野営 yaéi, キャンピング kyañpiñgu

to go camping キャンピングに行く kyañpiñgu ni iku

campsite [kæmp'sait] n キャンプ場 kyañpujō

campus [kæm'pəs] n (SCOL) キャンパス kyáñpasu

can¹ [kæn] n (container: for foods, drinks, oil etc) 缶 káñ

♦vt (foods) 缶詰にする kañzume ni suru

KEYWORD

can² [kæn] (negative **cannot, can't** conditional and pt **could**) aux vb 1 (be able to) 出来る dekírù

you can do it if you try 努力すればできますよ dóryòku surébà dekímasù yo

I'll help you all I can できるだけ力になりましょう dekíru dake chǐkára nǐ narímashō

she couldn't sleep that night その晩彼女は眠れませんでした sònō ban kanòjo wa nemúremasèn deshita

I can't go on any longer 私はもうこれ以上やっていけません watákushi wa mō korè ijō yattě ikemasèn

I can't see you あなたの姿が見えません anátà no sǔgàta ga miémasèn

can you hear me? 私の声が聞えますか watákushi no koè ga kikóemasù ká

I can see you tomorrow, if you're

free 明日でよかったらお会いできますよ asú dè yókàttara o-ái dekimasù yŏ

2 (know how to) ...の仕方が分かる ...no shikáta ga wakarù, ...ができる ...ga dekírù

I can swim/play tennis/drive 私は水泳〔テニス，運転〕ができます watákushi wa sùíei〔ténìsu, únten〕ga dèkímasu

can you speak French? あなたはフランス語ができますか anátà wa furánsugo ga dèkimasù ká

3 (may) ...してもいいですか ...shìte mò íi desu ká

can I use your phone? 電話をお借りしてもいいですか dénwa wo ò-kári shite mò íi desu ká

could I have a word with you? ちょっと話しがあるんですが chóttò hanáshi gà árùn desu ga

you can smoke if you like タバコを吸いたければ遠慮なくどうぞ tabáko wo suitakèreba énryo nakù dózò

can I help you with that? 手を貸しましょうかté wò kashímashò ka

4 (expressing disbelief, puzzlement): *it can't be true!* うそでしょう ùsó deshŏ

what CAN he want? あいつは何をねらっているだろうàitsu wa nánì wo nerátte iru dàrŏ nê

5 (expressing possibility, suggestion, etc) ...かも知れない ...ká mò shirenai

he could be in the library 彼は図書室にいるかも知れません kárè wa toshóshìtsu ni irú kà mo shiremasen

she could have been delayed 彼女は何かの原因で出発が遅れたのかも知れません kánòjo wa nánìka no gén-in de shùppátsu ga òkúreta kà mo shirémasèn

Canada [kænˈədə] *n* カナダ kánada

Canadian [kəneiˈdiːən] *adj* カナダの kánàda no

♦*n* カナダ人 kanádajìn

canal [kənælˈ] *n* (for ships, barges, irrigation) 運河 úñga, (ANAT) 管 káñ

canary [kənerˈiː] *n* カナリヤ kanáriya

cancel [kænˈsəl] *vt* (meeting) 中止する chúshi suru; (appointment, reservation,

contract, order) 取消す toríkesu, キャンセルする kyáñseru suru; (cross out: words, figures) 線を引いて消す séñ wo hiíte kesú

the flight was canceled その便は欠航になった sonó bíñ wa kekkó ni nattà

the train was canceled その列車は運休になった sonó resshà wa uñkyū ni nattà

cancellation [kænsəleiˈʃən] *n* (of meeting) 中止 chúshi; (of appointment, reservation, contract, order) 取消し toríkeshi, キャンセル kyáñseru; (of flight) 欠航 kekkó; (of train) 運休 uñkyū

cancer [kænˈsəːr] *n* (MED) がん gáñ

Cancer (ASTROLOGY) かに座 kaníza

candid [kænˈdid] *adj* (expression, comment) 率直な sotchóku na

candidate [kænˈdideit] *n* (for job) 候補者 kôhoshà; (in exam) 受験者 jukéñsha; (POL) 立候補者 rikkóhoshà

candle [kænˈdəl] *n* ろうそく rósokù

candlelight [kænˈdəllait] *n*: *by candlelight* ろうそくの明りで rósokù no akári de

candlestick [kænˈdəlstik] *n* (*also*: **candle holder**: plain) ろうそく立て rôsokútàte; (: bigger, ornate) しょく台 shokúdai

candor [kænˈdəːr] (*BRIT* **candour**) *n* (frankness) 率直さ sotchókusà

candy [kænˈdiː] *n* (*also*: **sugar-candy**) 氷砂糖 kórizatò; (*US*: sweet) あめ amé

candy-floss [kænˈdiːflɔːs] (*BRIT*) *n* 綿あめ watá-àme, 綿菓子 watágashì

cane [kein] *n* (BOT) 茎 kukí ◇竹などの様に中が空洞になっている植物を指す také nadò no yŏ ni nakà ga kúdò ni natté irú shokúbùtsu wo sasù; (for furniture) 藤 tŏ; (stick) 棒 bŏ; (for walking) 杖 tsúè, ステッキ sutékkì

♦*vt* (*BRIT*: SCOL) むち打つ muchíutsù

canine [keiˈnain] *adj* イヌの inú no

canister [kænˈistəːr] *n* (container: for tea, sugar etc) 容器 yŏki ◇茶筒の様な物を指す chazútsu no yŏ na monŏ wo sasù; (pressurized container) スプレー缶 supúrēkañ; (of gas, chemicals etc) ボンベ bóñbe

cannabis [kæn'əbis] n マリファナ marí-fāna

canned [kænd] adj (fruit, vegetables etc) 缶詰の kańzume no

cannibal [kæn'əbəl] n (person) 人食い人間 hitókui niñgen; (animal) 共食いする動物 tomógui suru dóbutsu

cannon [kæn'ən] (pl **cannon** or **cannons**) n (artillery piece) 大砲 taíhō

cannot [kæn'ɑːt] = **can not**

canny [kæn'iː] adj (quick-witted) 抜け目ない nukémenaì

canoe [kənuː'] n (boat) カヌー kánǜ

canon [kæn'ən] n (clergyman) 司教座聖堂参事会員 shikyózaseídō sańjikàiin; (rule, principle) 規準 kijún

canonize [kæn'ənaiz] vt (REL) 聖人の列に加える seíjin no retsù ni kuwáerù

can opener n 缶切 kańkirì

canopy [kæn'əpiː] n (above bed, throne etc) 天がい teńgai

can't [kænt] = **can not**

cantankerous [kæntæŋ'kərəs] adj (fault-finding, complaining) つむじ曲りの tsumújimagàri no

canteen [kæntiːn'] n (in workplace, school etc) 食堂 shokúdō; (also: **mobile canteen**) 移動食堂 idóshokudō; (BRIT: of cutlery) 収納箱 shúnōbàko ◇ナイフ, フォークなどを仕舞う箱 náìfu, fókù nadò wo shimáu hakò

canter [kæn'təːr] vi (horse) キャンターで走る kyańtā de hashirù

canvas [kæn'vəs] n (fabric) キャンバス kyáñbasu; (painting) 油絵 abúraè; (NAUT) 帆 hò ◇総称 sōshō

canvass [kæn'vəs] vi (POL): **to canvass for** ...のために選挙運動をする ...no tamè ni señkyoundò wo suru

♦vt (investigate: opinions, views) 調査する chōsa surù

canyon [kæn'jən] n 峡谷 kyókoku

cap [kæp] n (hat) 帽子 bóshi ◇主につばのある物を指す ómð ni tsubà no arù monó wo sásù; (of pen) キャップ kyáppù; (of bottle) ふた futá; (contraceptive) ペッサリー péssàrī; (for toy gun) 紙雷管 kamíraìkan

♦vt (outdo) しのぐ shinógù

capability [keipəbil'əti:] n (competence) 能力 nōryoku

capable [kei'pəbəl] adj (person, object): **capable of doing** ...ができる ...ga dekírù; (able: person) 有能な yúnō na

capacity [kəpæs'iti:] n (of container, ship etc) 容積 yōseki; (of stadium etc) 収容力 shúyōryðku; (capability) 能力 nōryoku; (position, role) 資格 shikáku; (of factory) 生産能力 seísannōryòku

cape [keip] n (GEO) 岬 misáki; (short cloak) ケープ kēpu

caper [kei'pəːr] n (CULIN: gen: capers) ケーパー kếpā; (prank) いたずら itázura

capital [kæp'itəl] n (also: **capital city**) 首都 shútð; (also: **capital letter**) 大文字 ómoji; (money) 資本 shihóñkin; (also: **capital letter**) 大文字 ómoji

capital gains tax n 資本利得税 shihóñritokuzèi

capitalism [kæp'itəlizəm] n 資本主義 shihóñshùgi

capitalist [kæp'itəlist] adj 資本主義の shihóñshùgi no

♦n 資本主義者 shihóñshugishà

capitalize [kæp'itəlaiz]: **capitalize on** vt fus (situation, fears etc) 利用する riyó suru

capital punishment 死刑 shikéi

capitulate [kəpitʃ'uleit] vi (give in) 降参する kósan suru

capricious [kəpriʃ'əs] adj (fickle: person) 気まぐれの kimágure no

Capricorn [kæp'rikɔːrn] n (ASTROLOGY) やぎ座 yagíza

capsize [kæp'saiz] vt (boat, ship) 転覆させる teńpuku saséru

♦vi (boat, ship) 転覆する teńpuku suru

capsule [kæp'səl] n (MED) カプセル kápùseru; (spacecraft) 宇宙カプセル uchúkapùseru

captain [kæp'tin] n (of ship) 船長 seńchō; (of plane) 機長 kichō; (of team) 主将 shushō; (in army) 大尉 tái-i; (in navy) 大佐 taísa; (US: in air force) 大尉 tái-i; (BRIT: SCOL) 主席の生徒 shusékì no seíto

caption [kæp'ʃən] n (to picture) 説明文

setsúmeíbun

captivate [kæp'təveit] vt (fascinate) 魅了する miryō suru

captive [kæp'tiv] adj (person) とりこの toríko no; (animal) 飼育下の shiíkuká no
♦n (person) とりこ toríko; (animal) 飼育下の動物 shiíkuká no dóbutsu

captivity [kæptiv'əti:] n 監禁状態 kaǹkinjótai

capture [kæp'tʃə:r] vt (animal, person) 捕まえる tsukámaeru; (town, country) 占領する seńryō suru; (attention) 捕える toráerù; (COMPUT) 収納する shúnō suru
♦n (seizure: of animal) 捕獲 hokáku; (: of person: by police) 逮捕 táiho; (: of town, country: by enemy) 占領 seńryō; (COMPUT) 収納 shúnō

car [kɑːr] n (AUT) 自動車 jídōsha, 車 kurúma; (: US: carriage) 客車 kyakúsha; (RAIL: BRIT: dining car, buffet car) 特殊車両 tokúshusharyō

carafe [kəræf'] n 水差し mizúsashì

caramel [kær'əməl] n (CULIN: sweet) キャラメル kyarámeru; (: burnt sugar) カラメル karámeru

carat [kær'ət] n (of diamond, gold) カラット karáttò

caravan [kær'əvæn] n (BRIT: vehicle) キャンピングカー kyaǹpingukā; (in desert) 隊商 taíshō, キャラバン kyáraban

caravan site (BRIT) n オートキャンプ場 ótokyanpujō

carbohydrate [kɑːrbouhai'dreit] n (CHEM, food) 炭水化物 tańsuikabùtsu

carbon [kɑːr'bən] n 炭素 táǹso

carbon copy n カーボンコピー kábòn kopì

carbon dioxide [-daiɑːk'said] n 二酸化炭素 nisánkataǹso

carbon monoxide [-mənɑːk'said] n 一酸化炭素 issánkataǹso

carbon paper n カーボン紙 kábòñshi

carburetor [kɑːr'bəreitəːr] (BRIT **carburettor**) n (AUT) キャブレター kyábùretā

carcass [kɑːr'kəs] n (of animal) 死体 shitái

card [kɑːrd] n (cardboard) ボール紙 bórugami; (greetings card, index card etc) カード kādo; (playing card) トランプのカード toráñpu no kādo; (visiting card) 名刺 meíshi

cardboard [kɑːrd'bɔːrd] n ボール紙 bórugami

card game n トランプゲーム toráñpugēmu

cardiac [kɑːr'diːæk] adj (arrest, failure) 心臓の shíǹzō no

cardigan [kɑːr'digən] n カーディガン kádigàn

cardinal [kɑːr'dənəl] adj (chief: principle) 重要な júyō na
♦n (REL) 枢機けい súkikèi
of cardinal importance 極めて重要で kiwámète júyō de

cardinal number 基数 kisú

card index n カード式索引 kádoshiki sakúin

care [keːr] n (attention) 注意 chúi; (worry) 心配 shíñpai; (charge) 管理 káñri
♦vi: *to care about* (person, animal) ...を気に掛ける ...wo ki ni kakérù, ...を愛する ...wo aí surù; (thing, idea etc) ...に関心を持つ ...ni kańshin wo motsù
care of (on mail) ...方 ...gatá
in someone's care ...の管理に任せ（られ）て ...no kanri ni makáse(rarè)tè
to take care (to do) ...をするよう心掛ける ...wo suru yō kokórogakerù
to take care of (patient, child etc) ...の世話をする ...no sewá wo suru; (problem, situation) ...の始末を付ける ...no shimátsu wo tsukerù
I don't care 私は構いません watákushi wa kamáimasèn
I couldn't care less 私はちっとも気にしない watákushi wa chittó mò ki ni shinaí

career [kəriːr'] n (job, profession) 職業 shokúgyō; (life: in school, work etc) キャリア kyaríà
♦vi (also: **career along**: car, horse) 猛スピードで走る mósupído de hashirù

career woman (pl **career women**) n キャリアウーマン kyaríaūman

care for *vt fus* (look after) …の世話をする …no sewá wo surú; (like) …が好きである …ga sukí de arù, …を愛している …wo aí shité irú

carefree [ker'fri:] *adj* (person, attitude) 気苦労のない kigurǒ no naí

careful [ker'fəl] *adj* (cautious) 注意深い chǔibukaì; (thorough) 徹底的な tettéiteki na

(be) careful! 気を付けてね ki wo tsukéte ne

carefully [ker'fəli:] *adv* (cautiously) 注意深く chǔibukakù; (methodically) 念入りに neñ-iri ni

careless [ker'lis] *adj* (negligent) 不注意な fuchǔi na; (heedless) 軽率な keísotsu na

carelessness [ker'lisnis] *n* (negligence) 不注意 fuchǔi; (lack of concern) 無とん着 mutoñchaku

caress [kəres'] *n* (stroke) 愛ぶ aíbu

◆*vt* (person, animal) 愛ぶする aíbu suru

caretaker [ker'teikər] *n* (of flats etc) 管理人 kañrinin

car-ferry [ka:r'fe:ri:] *n* カーフェリー kǎferī

cargo [ka:r'gou] (*pl* **cargoes**) *n* (of ship, plane) 積荷 tsumíni, 貨物 kámòtsu

car hire (*BRIT*) *n* レンタカーサービス reñtakā sàbisu

Caribbean [kærəbi:'ən] *n*: **the Caribbean (Sea)** カリブ海 karíbukaì

caricature [kær'əkətʃər] *n* (drawing) 風刺漫画 fǔshimañga, カリカチュア karíkachùa; (description) 風刺文 fǔshibùn; (exaggerated account) 真実のわい曲真じつ no waíkyoku

caring [ke:r'iŋ] *adj* (person, society, behavior) 愛情深い aíjōbukaì; (organization) 健康管理の keñkōkañri no

carnage [ka:r'nidʒ] *n* (MIL) 虐殺 gyakúsatsu

carnal [ka:r'nəl] *adj* (desires, feelings) 肉体的な nikútaiteki na

carnation [ka:rnei'ʃən] *n* カーネーション kǎneshon

carnival [ka:r'nəvəl] *n* (festival) 謝肉祭 shaníkusài, カーニバル kǎnibàru; (US: funfair) カーニバル kǎnibàru

carnivorous [ka:rniv'ə:rəs] *adj* (animal, plant) 肉食の nikúshoku no

carol [kær'əl] *n*: *(Christmas) carol* クリスマスキャロル kurísumasu kyaròru

carp [ka:rp] *n* (fish) コイ koì

car park (*BRIT*) *n* 駐車場 chǔshajō

carp at *vt fus* (criticize) とがめ立てする togámedate suru

carpenter [ka:r'pəntər] *n* 大工 daíku

carpentry [ka:r'pəntri:] *n* 大工仕事 daíkushigòto

carpet [ka:r'pit] *n* (in room etc) じゅうたん jǔtan, カーペット kǎpettò; (*fig*: of pine needles, snow etc) じゅうたんの様な… jǔtan no yǒ na…

◆*vt* (room, stairs etc) …にじゅうたんを敷く …ni jǔtan wo shikú

carpet slippers *npl* スリッパ súrìppa

carpet sweeper [-swi:'pə:r] *n* じゅうたん掃除機 jǔtan sòjiki

carriage [kær'idʒ] *n* (*BRIT*: RAIL) 客車 kyakúsha; (*also*: **horse-drawn carriage**) 馬車 bashá; (of goods) 運搬 uñpan; (transport costs) 運送料 uñsōryō

carriage return *n* (on typewriter etc) 復帰キー fukkí kī

carriageway [kær'idʒwei] (*BRIT*) *n* (part of road) 車線 shaséñ ◇自動車道の上りまたは下り半分を指す jidōshadō no nobóri mata wá kudári hañbuñ wo sasù

carrier [kær'i:ə:r] *n* (transporter, transport company) 運送会社 uñsōgaìsha; (MED) 保菌者 hókìnsha, キャリア kyárìa

carrier bag (*BRIT*) *n* 買い物袋 kaímonobukùro, ショッピングバッグ shoppíngubaggù

carrot [kær'ət] *n* (BOT, CULIN) ニンジン niñjin

carry [kær'i:] *vt* (take) 携帯する keítai suru; (transport) 運ぶ hakóbu; (involve: responsibilities etc) 伴う tomónaù; (MED: disease, virus) 保有する hoyǔ suru

◆*vi* (sound) 通る tǒru

to get carried away (*fig*: by enthusiasm, idea) 夢中になる muchǔ ni narù

carrycot [kær'i:ka:t] (*BRIT*) *n* 携帯ベビ

一ベッド keítai bebíběddò

carry on vi (continue) 続ける tsuzúkeru
♦vt (continue) 続ける tsuzúkeru

carry-on [kær'i:ɑːn] (inf) n (fuss) 大騒ぎ ōsawági

carry out vt (orders) 実行する jikkō suru; (investigation) 行う okónau

cart [kɑːrt] n (for grain, silage, hay etc) 荷車 nígùruma; (also: **horsedrawn cart**) 馬車 báshà; (also: **handcart**) 手押し車 teóshigùruma
♦vt (inf: people) 否応なしに連れて行く iyáò nashi ni tsuréte ikú; (objects) 引きずる hikízuru

cartilage [kɑːr'təlidʒ] n (ANAT) 軟骨 nañkotsu

carton [kɑːr'tən] n (large box) ボール箱 bōrubako; (container: of yogurt, milk etc) 容器 yōki; (of cigarettes) カートン káton

cartoon [kɑːrtuːn'] n (drawing) 漫画 mañga; (BRIT: comic strip) 漫画 mañga ◇四こま漫画などを指す yoñkoma manga nadò wo sasù; (CINEMA) アニメ映画 aníme-eíga

cartridge [kɑːr'tridʒ] n (for gun) 弾薬筒 dañ-yakutō, 実弾 jitsúdan; (of record-player) カートリッジ kátorijjì; (of pen) インクカートリッジ íñku kátorijjì

carve [kɑːrv] vt (meat) 切分ける kiríwakerù, スライスする suráisu surù; (wood, stone) 彫刻する chōkoku suru; (initials, design) 刻む kizámu

carve up vt (land, property) 切分ける kiríwakerù

carving [kɑːr'viŋ] n (object made from wood, stone etc) 彫刻 chōkoku; (in wood etc: design) 彫物 horímonò; (: art) 彫刻 chōkoku

carving knife n カービングナイフ kābingunaìfu

car wash n 洗車場 señshajō, カーウォッシュ káuosshù

cascade [kæskeid'] n (waterfall) 小さい滝 chíísaì takí
♦vi (water) 滝になって流れ落ちる takí ni natté nagáreochìrù; (hair, people, things) 滝の様に落ちる takí no yō ni o-

chirù

case [keis] n (situation, instance) 場合 baái; (MED) 症例 shōrei; (LAW) 事件 jíkèn; (container: for spectacles etc) ケース kēsu; (box: of whisky etc) 箱 hakó, ケース kēsu; (BRIT: also: **suitcase**) スーツケース sū́tsukèsu

in case (of) (fire, emergency) ...の場合に ...no baái ni

in any case とにかく toníkaku

just in case 万一に備えて máñ-ichi ni sonáete

cash [kæʃ] n (money) 現金 geñkìn
♦vt (check etc) 換金する kañkin suru

to pay (in) cash 現金で払う geñkin de haraú

cash on delivery 着払い chakúbarài

cash-book [kæʃ'buk] n 出納簿 suítòbo

cash card (BRIT) n (for cash dispenser) キャッシュカード kyasshúkàdo

cash desk (BRIT) n 勘定カウンター kañjōkauñtā

cash dispenser n 現金自動支払い機 geñkin jidōshiharaìki, カード機 kádokì

cashew [kæʃ'uː] n (also: **cashew nut**) カシューナッツ kashúnattsù

cash flow n 資金繰り shikínguri

cashier [kæʃiːˈəːr] n (in bank) 出納係 suítōgakàri; (in shop, restaurant) レジ係 rejígakàri

cashmere [kæʒˈmiːr] n (wool, jersey) カシミア kashímia

cash register n レジスター réjìsutā

casing [kei'siŋ] n (covering) 被覆 hífùku

casino [kəsiːˈnou] n カジノ kájìno

cask [kæsk] n (of wine, beer) たる tarú

casket [kæs'kit] n (for jewelery) 宝石箱 hōsekibakò; (US: coffin) 棺 káñ

casserole [kæsˈəroul] n (of lamb, chicken etc) キャセロール kyasérōru; (pot, container) キャセロールなべ kyasérōrunabè

cassette [kəset'] n (tape) カセットテープ kasétto tèpu

cassette player n カセットプレーヤー kasétto purèyā

cassette recorder n カセットレコーダー kasétto rekōdà

cast [kæst] (*pt, pp* **cast**) *vt* (throw: light, shadow) 映す utsúsù; (: object, net) 投げる nagérù; (: fishing-line) キャストする kyásùto surú; (: aspersions, doubts) 投掛ける nagékakerù; (glance, eyes) 向ける mukérù; (THEATER) ...に...の役を振当てる ...ni ...no yakú wo furíaterù; (make: statue) 鋳込む ikómù

♦*n* (THEATER) キャスト kyásùto; (*also*: **plaster cast**) ギプス gíbùsu

to cast a spell on (subject: witch etc) ...に魔法を掛ける ...ni mahó wò kakérù

to cast one's vote 投票する tōhyṓ suru

castaway [kæ's'təwei] *n* 難破した人 naṅpa shita hitó

caste [kæst] *n* (social class) カースト kā́sùto; (*also*: **caste system**) 階級制 kaíkyū-sei, カースト制 kā́sutosei

caster [kæs'tə:r] *n* (wheel) キャスター kyásutā

caster sugar (*BRIT*) *n* 粉砂糖 konázatō

casting vote [kæs'tiŋ-] (*BRIT*) *n* 決定票 kettéihyō, キャスティングボート kyasútingubōto

cast iron [kæst'ai'ə:rn] *n* 鋳鉄 chūtetsu

castle [kæs'əl] *n* (building) 城 shiró; (CHESS) 城将 jōshō

cast off *vi* (NAUT) 綱を解く tsuná wo tokù; (KNITTING) 編み終える amíoerù

cast on *vi* (KNITTING) 編み始める amíhajimerù

castor [kæs'tə:r] (*BRIT*) *n* = **caster**

castor oil *n* ひまし油 himáshiyu

castrate [kæs'treit] *vt* (bull, man) 去勢する kyoséi suru

casual [kæʒ'u:əl] *adj* (by chance) 偶然の gū́zen no; (irregular: work etc) 臨時の riṅji no; (unconcerned) さりげない sarígenaì; (informal: clothes) 普段用の fudáṅyō no

casually [kæʒ'u:əli:] *adv* (in a relaxed way) さりげなく sarígenakù; (dress) 普段着で fudáṅgi de

casualty [kæʒ'u:əlti:] *n* (of war, accident: someone injured) 負傷者 fushṓsha; (: someone killed) 死者 shishá; (of situation, event: victim) 犠牲者 giséisha;

(MED: *also*: **casualty department**) 救急病棟 kyū́kyūbyṓtō

cat [kæt] *n* (pet) ネコ nekó; (wild animal) ネコ科の動物 nekókà no dṓbutsu

catalogue [kæt'ələ:g] (*US also*: **catalog**) *n* (COMM: for mail order) カタログ katárogu; (of exhibition, library) 目録 mokúroku

♦*vt* (books, collection, events) ...の目録を作る ...no mokúroku wo tsukúrù

catalyst [kæt'əlist] *n* (CHEM, *fig*) 触媒 shokúbai

catapult [kæt'əpʌlt] (*BRIT*) *n* (slingshot) ぱちんこ pachínko

cataract [kæt'ərækt] *n* (MED) 白内障 hakúnaìshō

catarrh [kətɑ:r'] *n* カタル kátàru

catastrophe [kətæs'trəfi:] *n* (disaster) 災害 saígai

catastrophic [kætəstrɑ:f'ik] *adj* (disastrous) 破局的な hakyókuteki na

catch [kætʃ] (*pt, pp* **caught**) *vt* (animal) 捕る tórù, 捕まえる tsukámaeru; (fish: with net) 捕る tórù; (: with line) 釣る tsurú; (ball) 捕る tórù; (bus, train etc) ...に乗る ...ni norù; (arrest: thief etc) 逮捕する taího suru; (surprise: person) びっくりさせる bikkúri sasérù; (attract: attention) 引く hikú; (hear: comment, whisper etc) 聞く kikú; (MED: illness) ...に掛る ...ni kakàrù; (person: *also*: **catch up with/to**) ...に追い付く ...ni oítsukù

♦*vi* (fire) 付く tsukù; (become trapped: in branches, door etc) 引っ掛る hikkákarù

♦*n* (of fish etc) 獲物 emóno; (of ball) 捕球 hokyú; (hidden problem) 落し穴 otóshiàna; (of lock) 留金 tomégane; (game) キャッチボール kyátchibōru

to catch one's breath (rest) 息をつく íkì wo tsukù, 一休みする hitoyásumi surù

to catch fire 燃え出す moédasù

to catch sight of 見付ける mitsúkeru

catching [kætʃ'iŋ] *adj* (infectious) 移る utsurù

catchment area [kætʃ'mənt-] (*BRIT*) *n* (of school) 学区 gákkù; (of hospital) 通院

圏 tsúïnken

catch on vi (understand) 分かる wakarù; (grow popular) 流行する ryūkō suru

catch phrase n キャッチフレーズ kyátchífurēzu

catch up vi (fig: with person, on work) 追付く oítsukù
♦vt (person) ...に追い付く ...ni oítsukù

catchy [kætʃ'i:] adj (tune) 覚え易い obóeyasuì

catechism [kæt'əkizəm] n (REL) 公教要理 kōkyōyōri

categoric(al) [kætəgɔr'ik(əl)] adj (certain, absolute) 絶対的な zettáiteki na

category [kæt'əgɔ:ri:] n (set, class) 範ちゅう hañchū

cater [kei'tər] vi: **to cater for** (BRIT: person, group) ...向きである ...mukí de arù; (needs) ...を満たす ...wo mitasù; (COMM: weddings etc) ...の料理を仕出しする ...no ryōri wo shidáshi suru

caterer [kei'tə:rər] n 仕出し屋 shidáshiya

catering [kei'tə:riŋ] n (trade, business) 仕出し shidáshi

caterpillar [kæt'ə:rpilər] n (with hair) 毛虫 kemúshi; (without hair) 芋虫 imomùshi

caterpillar track n キャタピラ kyatápirà

cathedral [kəθi:'drəl] n 大聖堂 daíseidō

catholic [kæθ'əlik] adj (tastes, interests) 広い hiroî

Catholic [kæθ'əlik] adj (REL) カトリック教の katórikkukyō no
♦n (REL) カトリック教徒 katórrikkukyōto

cat's-eye [kæts'ai'] (BRIT) n (AUT) 反射びょう hañshabyō ◊夜間の目印として道路の中央または わきに埋込むガラスなどの反射器 yakán no mejirùshi toshitè dōro no chūō mata wà wakí ni umékomù garásu nadò no hañshakì

cattle [kæt'əl] npl ウシ ushí ◊総称 sōshō

catty [kæt'i:] adj (comment, woman) 意地悪な ijíwarù na

caucus [kɔ:'kəs] n (POL: group) 実力者会議 jitsúryokusha kaîgi; (: US) 党部会 tō-

bukài

caught [kɔ:t] pt, pp of **catch**

cauliflower [kɔ:'ləflauə:r] n カリフラワー karífurawā

cause [kɔ:z] n (of outcome, effect) 原因 geñ-in; (reason) 理由 riyū; (aim, principle: also POL) 目的 mokúteki
♦vt (produce, lead to: outcome, effect) 引起こす hikíokosù

caustic [kɔ:s'tik] adj (CHEM) 腐食性の fushốkusei no; (fig: remark) 辛らつな shiñratsu na

caution [kɔ:'ʃən] n (prudence) 慎重さ shiñchōsa; (warning) 警告 keíkoku, 注意 chūì
♦vt (warn: also POLICE) 警告する keíkoku suru

cautious [kɔ:'ʃəs] adj (careful, wary) 注意深い chūibukaì

cautiously [kɔ:'ʃəsli:] adv 注意深く chūibukakù

cavalier [kævəliə:r'] adj (attitude, fashion) 威張り腐った ibárikusattà

cavalry [kæv'əlri:] n (MIL: mechanized) 装甲部隊 sōkōbutài; (: mounted) 騎兵隊 kihéitai

cave [keiv] n (in cliff, hill) 洞穴 horá-ana

cave in vi (roof etc) 陥没する kañbotsu suru, 崩れる kuzúrerù

caveman [keiv'mæn] (pl **cavemen**) n 穴居人 kékkyojin

cavern [kæv'ə:rn] n どうくつ dōkutsu

caviar(e) [kæv'i:ɑ:r] n キャビア kyàbia

cavity [kæv'iti:] n (in wall) 空どう kūdō; (ANAT) 腔 kō; (in tooth) 虫歯の穴 mushíba no aná

cavort [kəvɔ:rt'] vi (romp) はしゃぎ回る hashágimawarù

CB [si:'bi:'] n abbr (= Citizens' Band (Radio)) 市民バンド shimínbañdo, シチズンバンド shichízunbañdo

CBI [si:bi:ai'] n abbr (= Confederation of British Industry) 英国産業連盟 eíkokusañgyōreñmei

cc [si:si:'] abbr (= cubic centimeter(s)) 立方センチメートル rippósenchimētoru, cc shíshì; = **carbon copy**

cease [si:s] vt (end, stop) 終える oéru
♦vi (end, stop) 終る owáru, 止る tomáru

ceasefire [si:s'faiə:r] n (MIL) 停戦 teísen

ceaseless [si:s'lis] adj (chatter, traffic) 絶間ない taéma naí

cedar [si:'də:r] n (tree) ヒマラヤスギ himárayasugí; (wood) シーダー材 shídāzài

cede [si:d] vt (land, rights etc) 譲る yuzúru

ceiling [si:'liŋ] n (in room) 天井 teñjō; (upper limit: on wages, prices etc) 天井 teñjō, 上限 jōgen

celebrate [sel'əbreit] vt (gen) 祝う iwáù; (REL: mass) 挙げる agéru
♦vi お祝いする o-íwai suru

celebrated [sel'əbreitid] adj (author, hero) 有名な yūmei na

celebration [seləbrei'ʃən] n (party, festival) お祝い o-íwai

celebrity [səleb'riti:] n (famous person) 有名人 yūmeíjin

celery [sel'ə:ri:] n セロリ séròri

celestial [səles'tʃəl] adj (heavenly) 天上的な teñjōteki na

celibacy [sel'əbəsi:] n 禁欲生活 kiñ-yoku seíkatsu

cell [sel] n (in prison: gen) 監房 kañbō; (: solitary) 独房 dokúbō; (in monastery) 個室 koshítsu; (BIO, also of revolutionaries) 細胞 saíbō; (ELEC) 電池 déñchi

cellar [sel'ə:r] n (basement) 地下室 chikáshìtsu; (also: wine cellar) ワイン貯蔵室 waín chozōshìtsu

cello [tʃel'ou] n (MUS) チェロ chérò

cellophane [sel'əfein] n セロハン séròhan

cellular [sel'jələ:r] adj (BIO: structure, tissue) 細胞の saíbō no; (fabrics) 保温効果の高い hoóñkōka no takaí, 防寒の bōkan no

cellulose [sel'jəlous] n (tissue) 繊維素 señ-isō

Celt [selt, kelt] n ケルト人 kerútòjin

Celtic [sel'tik, kel'tik] adj ケルト人の kerútòjin no; (language etc) ケルトの kérùto no

cement [siment'] n (powder) セメント seménto; (concrete) コンクリート koñkurīto

cement mixer n セメントミキサー se-

mento mikisā

cemetery [sem'ite:ri:] n 墓地 bóchì

cenotaph [sen'ətæf] n (monument) 戦没者記念碑 señbotsusha kineñhi

censor [sen'sə:r] n (POL, CINEMA etc) 検閲官 keñ-etsùkan
♦vt (book, play, news etc) 検閲する keñ-etsu suru

censorship [sen'sə:rʃip] n (of book, play, news etc) 検閲 keñ-etsu

censure [sen'ʃə:r] vt (reprove) とがめる togámerù

census [sen'səs] n (of population) 国勢調査 kokúzeichōsa

cent [sent] n (US: also: one-cent coin) 1 セント玉 isséntodamá ¶ see also per

centenary [sen'təne:ri:] n (of birth etc) 100周年 hyakúshūnen

center [sen'tə:r] (BRIT centre) n (of circle, room, line) 中心 chúshin; (of town) 中心部 chúshinbu, 繁華街 hañkagāi; (of attention, interest) 的 matō; (heart: of action, belief etc) 核心 kakúshin; (building: health center, community center) センター séñtā; (POL) 中道 chúdō
♦vt (weight) ...の中心に置く ...no chúshin ni okú; (sights) ...にぴったり合わせる ...ni pittari awaseru; (SOCCER: ball) グランド中央へ飛ばす gurándo chūō e tobásu; (TYP: on page) 中央に合わせる chúō ni awáseru

center forward n (SPORT) センターフォワード señtāfowādo

center half n (SPORT) センターハーフ señtāhāfu

centigrade [sen'tigreid] adj 摂氏 sesshī

centimeter [sen'təmi:tə:r] (BRIT centimetre) n センチメートル señchimētoru

centipede [sen'təpi:d] n ムカデ mukáde

central [sen'trəl] adj (in the center) 中心点の chúshiñten no; (near the center) 中心の chúshin no; (committee, government) 中央の chúō no; (idea, figure) 中心の chúshin no

Central America n 中米 chúbei

central heating n セントラルヒーティング señtoraruhītiñgu

centralize [sen'trəlaiz] vt (decision-making, authority) 中央に集中させる chūō ni shūchū saséru

central reservation (BRIT) n (AUT: of road) 中央分離帯 chūōbunritai

centre [sen'tə:r] (etc BRIT) = **center** etc

century [sen'tʃə:ri:] n 世紀 séîki
20th century 20世紀 nijússeîki

ceramic [sərǽm'ik] adj (art, tiles) セラミックの serámikku no

ceramics [sərǽm'iks] npl (objects) 焼物 yakímono

cereal [si:r'i:əl] n (plant, crop) 穀物 kôkùmotsu; (food) シリアル shiríarù

cerebral [se:r'əbrəl] adj (MED: of the brain) 脳の nō no; (intellectual) 知的な chitéki na

ceremony [se:r'əmouni:] n (event) 式 shikí; (ritual) 儀式 gíshìki; (behavior) 形式 keíshiki
to stand on ceremony 礼儀にこだわる reígi ni kodáwarù

certain [sə:r'tən] adj (sure: person) 確信している kakúshin shité irú; (: fact) 確実な kakújitsu na; (person): **a certain Mr Smith** スミスと呼ばれる男 sumisù to yobareru otóko; (particular): **certain days/places** ある日〔場所〕árù hi〔bashò〕; (some): **a certain coldness/pleasure** ある程度の冷たさ〔喜び〕árù teido no tsumétasa〔yorókobi〕
for certain 確実に kakújitsu ni

certainly [sə:r'tənli:] adv (undoubtedly) 間違いなく machígai nakù; (of course) もちろん mochíròn

certainty [sə:r'tənti:] n (assurance) 確実性 kakújitsusei; (inevitability) 必然性 hitsúzensei

certificate [sə:rtif'əkit] n (of birth, marriage etc) 証明書 shōmeisho; (diploma) 資格証明書 shikákushōmeisho

certified mail [sə:r'təfaid-] (US) n 配達証明付き書留郵便 haítatsushōmei tsukí kakítome yūbin

certified public accountant (US) n 公認会計士 kōnin kaikèishi

certify [sə:r'təfai] vt (fact) 証明する shō-

mei suru; (award a diploma to) ...に資格を与える ...ni shikáku wo atáeru; (declare insane) 精神異常と認定する seíshinijō to niñtei suru

cervical [sə:r'vikəl] adj (smear, cancer) 子宮けい部の shikyúkeìbu no

cervix [sə:r'viks] n (ANAT) 子宮けい部 shikyúkeìbu

Cesarean [size:r'i:ən] (BRIT **Caesarean**) adj: **Cesarean (section)** 帝王切開 teíōsekkài

cesspit [ses'pit] n (sewage tank) 汚水だめ osúidame

cf. abbr = **compare**

ch. abbr = **chapter**

chafe [tʃeif] vt (rub: skin) 擦る súrù

chagrin [ʃəgrin'] n (annoyance) 悔しさ kuyáshisa; (disappointment) 落胆 rakútan

chain [tʃein] n (for anchor, prisoner, dog etc) 鎖 kusári; (on bicycle) チェーン chèn; (jewelery) 首飾り kubíkazàri; (of shops, hotels) チェーン chèn; (of events, ideas) 連鎖 reñsa
♦vt (also: **chain up**: prisoner, dog) 鎖につなぐ kusári ni tsunágu
an island chain/a chain of islands 列島 rettő
a mountain chain/a chain of mountains 山脈 sañmyaku

chain reaction n 連鎖反応 reñsahañnō

chain-smoke [tʃein'smouk] vi 立続けにタバコを吸う tatétsuzuke ni tabáko wo suú

chain store n チェーンストア chénsutoà

chair [tʃe:r] n (seat) いす isú; (armchair) 安楽いす añrakuisù; (of university) 講座 kōza; (of meeting) 座長 zachô; (of committee) 委員長 iíñchō
♦vt (meeting) 座長を務める zachô wo tsutómerù

chairlift [tʃe:r'lift] n リフト rífùto

chairman [tʃe:r'mən] (pl **chairmen**) n (of committee) 委員長 iíñchō; (BRIT: of company) 社長 shachô

chalet [ʃælei'] n 山小屋 yamágoya

chalice [tʃæl'is] n (REL) 聖さん杯 seísañhai

chalk [tʃɔːk] n (GEO) 白亜 hákùa; (for writing) 白墨 hakúboku, チョーク chōku

challenge [tʃæl'indʒ] n (of new job, unknown, new venture etc) 挑戦 chōsen; (to authority, received ideas etc) 反抗 haṅkō; (dare) 挑戦 chōsen
◆vt (SPORT) ...に試合を申込む ...ni shiái wo mōshikomù; (rival, competitor) 挑戦する chōsen suru; (authority, right, idea etc) ...に反抗する ...ni haṅkō suru
to challenge someone to do something ...に...をやれるものならやってみろと挑戦する ...ni ...wo yaréru monó nara yatté miro to chōsen suru

challenging [tʃæl'indʒiŋ] adj (career, task) やりがいを感じさせる yarígai wo kaṅji saséru; (tone, look etc) 挑発的な chōhatsuteki na

chamber [tʃeim'bəːr] n (room) 部屋 heyá; (POL: house) 院 íñ; (BRIT: LAW: gen pl) 弁護士事務室 beṅgoshi jimushìtsu; (: of judge) 判事室 haṅjishìtsu
chamber of commerce 商工会議所 shōkōkaigisho

chambermaid [tʃeim'bəːrmeid] n (in hotel) メード mēdo

chamber music n 室内音楽 shitsúnai oṅgaku

chamois [ʃæm'iː] n (ZOOL) シャモア shamòa; (cloth) セーム革 sēmugawa

champagne [ʃæmpein'] n シャンペン shaṅpeñ

champion [tʃæm'piːən] n (of league, contest, fight) 優勝者 yūshōsha, チャンピオン chaṅpion; (of cause, principle, person) 擁護者 yōgosha

championship [tʃæm'piːənʃip] n (contest) 選手権決定戦 señshukeñ kettéisen; (title) 選手権 señshuken

chance [tʃæns] n (likelihood, possibility) 可能性 kanōsei; (opportunity) 機会 kikái, チャンス cháṅsu; (risk) 危険 kikén, かけ kaké
◆vt (risk): *to chance it* 危険を冒す kikén wo okasù, 冒険をする bōken wo suru
◆adj 偶然の gūzen no
to take a chance 危険を冒す kikén wo

okasù, 冒険をする bōken wo suru
by chance 偶然に gūzen ni

chancellor [tʃæn'sələːr] n (head of government) 首相 shushō

Chancellor of the Exchequer (BRIT) n 大蔵大臣 ōkuradaìjin

chandelier [ʃændəli'əːr] n シャンデリア shaṅderìa

change [tʃeindʒ] vt (alter, transform) 変える kaéru; (wheel, bulb etc) 取替える toríkaeru; (clothes) 着替える kigáeru; (job, address) 変える kaéru; (baby, diaper) 替える kaéru; (exchange: money) 両替する ryōgae suru
◆vi (alter) 変る kawáru; (change one's clothes) 着替える kigáeru; (change trains, buses) 乗換える noríkaeru; (traffic lights) 変る kawáru; (be transformed): *to change into* ...に変る ...ni kawáru, ...になる ...ni narù
◆n (alteration) 変化 héñka; (difference) 違い chigái; (also: **change of clothes**) 着替え kigáe; (of government, climate, job) 変る事 kawáru kotò; (coins) 小銭 kozéni; (money returned) お釣 o-tsúri
to change one's mind 気が変る ki gá kawarù
for a change たまには tamá ni wa

changeable [tʃein'dʒəbəl] adj 変りやすい kawáriyasuì

change machine n 両替機 ryōgaekì

changeover [tʃeindʒ'ouvəːr] n (to new system) 切替え kiríkae

changing [tʃein'dʒiŋ] adj (world, nature) 変る kawáru

changing room (BRIT) n 更衣室 kōishìtsu

channel [tʃæn'əl] n (TV) チャンネル cháṅneru; (in sea, river etc) 水路 súiro; (groove) 溝 mizó; (fig: means) 手続 tetsuzùki, ルート rūto
◆vt (money, resources) 流す nagásù
the (English) Channel イギリス海峡 igírisu kaîkyō
the Channel Islands チャネル諸島 chanéru shotō

chant [tʃænt] n (of crowd, fans etc) 掛声 kakégoè; (REL: song) 詠唱歌 eíshōka

♦*vt* (word, name, slogan) 唱える tonáerù

chaos [keiˈɑːs] *n* (disorder) 混乱 koñran

chaotic [keiaːˈtˈik] *adj* (mess, jumble) 混乱した koñran shitá

chap [tʃæp] (*BRIT: inf*) *n* (man) やつ yátsù

chapel [tʃæpˈəl] *n* (in church) 礼拝堂 reíhaidō; (in hospital, prison, school etc) チャペル cháperu; (*BRIT*: non-conformist chapel) 教会堂 kyōkaidō

chaperone [ʃæpˈəroun] *n* (for woman) 付添い tsukísoi, シャペロン sháperoñ

♦*vt* (woman, child) ...に付添う ...ni tsukísoù

chaplain [tʃæpˈlin] *n* (REL, MIL, SCOL) 付属牧師 fuzókubokùshi

chapped [tʃæpt] *adj* (skin, lips) あかぎれれした akágire shitá

chapter [tʃæpˈtəːr] *n* (of book) 章 shō; (of life, history) 時期 jíkì

char [tʃɑːr] *vt* (burn) 黒焦げにする kurókoge ni suru

♦*n* (*BRIT*) = **charwoman**

character [kærˈiktəːr] *n* (nature) 性質 seíshitsu; (moral strength) 気骨 kikótsu; (personality) 人格 jiñkaku; (in novel, film) 人物 jíñbutsu; (letter) 文字 mójì

characteristic [kæriktərisˈtik] *adj* (typical) 特徴的な tokúchōteki na

♦*n* (trait, feature) 特徴 tokúchō

characterize [kærˈiktəraiz] *vt* (typify) ...の特徴である ...no tokúchō de arù; (describe the character of) ...の特徴を描写する ...no tokúchō wo byōsha suru

charade [ʃəreidˈ] *n* (sham, pretence) 装い yosóoi

charcoal [tʃɑːrˈkoul] *n* (fuel) 炭 sumí, 木炭 mokútañ; (for drawing) 木炭 mokútañ

charge [tʃɑːrdʒ] *n* (fee) 料金 ryōkin; (LAW: accusation) 容疑 yōgi; (responsibility) 責任 sekínin

♦*vt* (for goods, services) ...の料金を取る ...no ryōkin wo torù; (LAW: accuse): **to charge someone (with)** ...を訴える kisó suru; (battery) 充電する jūden suru; (MIL: enemy) ...に突撃する ...ni totsúgeki suru

♦*vi* (animal) 掛って来る〔行く〕kakáttè

kurù〔ikú〕; (MIL) 突撃する totsúgeki suru

to take charge of (child) ...の面倒を見る ...no meñdō wo mirù; (company) ...の指揮を取る ...no shikí wo torú

to be in charge of (person, machine) ...の責任を持っている ...no sekínin wo motté irù; (business) ...の責任者である ...no sekíninshà de arù

how much do you charge? 料金はいくらですか ryōkin wa ikùra desù ka

to charge an expense (up) to some-one's account ...の勘定に付ける ...no kañjō ni tsukerù

charge card *n* (for particular shop or organization) クレジットカード kuréjittokàdo ◇特定の店でしか使えない物を指す tokútei nò mise de shika tsukáenai monò wo sásù

charges [tʃɑːrˈdʒiz] *npl* (bank charges, telephone charges etc) 料金 ryōkin

to reverse the charges (TEL) 先方払いにする señpòbaraì ni surù

charisma [kərizˈmə] *n* カリスマ性 karísumasei

charitable [tʃærˈitəbəl] *adj* (organization) 慈善の jizén no

charity [tʃærˈitiː] *n* (organization) 慈善事業 jizéñjigyò; (kindness) 親切さ shiñsetsusa; (generosity) 寛大さ kañdaisa; (money, gifts) 施し hodókoshi

charlady [tʃɑːrˈleidiː] (*BRIT*) *n* = **charwoman**

charlatan [ʃɑːrˈlətən] *n* 偽者 nisémono

charm [tʃɑːrm] *n* (attractiveness) 魅力 miryóku; (to bring good luck) お守り o-mámori; (on bracelet etc) 飾り kazári

♦*vt* (please, delight) うっとりさせる uttôrì saséru

charming [tʃɑːrˈmiŋ] *adj* (person, place) 魅力的な miryókuteki na

chart [tʃɑːrt] *n* (graph) グラフ gúràfu; (diagram) 図 zu; (map) 海図 kâîzu

♦*vt* (course) 地図に書く chízù ni kakù; (progress) 図に書く zù ni kakù

charter [tʃɑːrˈtəːr] *vt* (plane, ship etc) チャーターする chātā surù

♦*n* (document, constitution) 憲章 keñ-

shō; (of university, company) 免許 méñkyo

chartered accountant [tʃɑːrˈtəːrd-] (BRIT) n 公認会計士 kōnin kaikeíshi

charter flight n チャーターフライト chátāfuraíto

charts [tʃɑːrts] npl (hit parade): *the charts* ヒットチャート hittóchāto

charwoman [tʃɑːrˈwumən] (pl **charwomen**) n 掃除婦 sōjifu

chase [tʃeis] vt (pursue) 追掛ける oíkakerù; (also: **chase away**) 追払う oíharaù
♦n (pursuit) 追跡 tsuíseki

chasm [kæzˈəm] n (GEO) 深い割れ目 fúkài warême

chassis [ʃæsˈiː] n (AUT) シャシ shashî

chastity [tʃæsˈtiti-] n (REL) 純潔 juñketsu

chat [tʃæt] vi (also: **have a chat**) おしゃべりする o-sháberí surù
♦n (conversation) おしゃべり o-sháberí

chat show (BRIT) n トーク番組 tōku bañgumi

chatter [tʃætˈəːr] vi (person) しゃべりまくる shabérimakurù; (animal) きゃっきゃっと鳴く kyákkyattò nakú; (teeth) がちがち鳴る gachígachi narú
♦n (of people) しゃべり声 shabérigoè; (of birds) さえずり saézuri; (of animals) きゃっきゃっという鳴き声 kyákkyattò iú nakígoè

chatterbox [tʃætˈəːrbɑːks] (inf) n おしゃべり好き o-sháberizuki

chatty [tʃætˈiː] adj (style, letter) 親しみやすい shitáshimiyasuì; (person) おしゃべりな o-sháberí na

chauffeur [ʃouˈfəːr] n お抱え運転手 okákae-unteñshu

chauvinist [ʃouˈvənist] n (male chauvinist) 男性優越主義者 dañseiyūetsushugishà; (nationalist) 熱狂的愛国主義者 nekkyōtekiaikokushugishà

cheap [tʃiːp] adj (inexpensive) 安い yasuì; (poor quality) 安っぽい yasúppoì; (behavior, joke) 下劣な gerétsu na
♦adv: *to buy/sell something cheap* 安く買う〔売る〕yasúkù kaú〔urú〕

cheaper [tʃiːˈpəːr] adj (less expensive) もっと安い móttò yasuì

cheaply [tʃiːpˈliː] adv (inexpensively) 安く yasúku

cheat [tʃiːt] vi (in exam) カンニングする kañningu suru; (at cards) いかさまをする ikásama wo suru
♦vt: *to cheat someone (out of something)* ...から ...をだまし取る ...kara ...wo damáshitorù
♦n (person) いかさま師 ikásamashì

check [tʃek] vt (examine: bill, progress) 調べる shiráberù; (verify: facts) 確認する kakúnin suru; (halt: enemy, disease) 食止める kuítomerù; (restrain: impulse, person) 抑える osáerù
♦n (inspection) 検査 kéñsa; (curb) 抑制 yokúsei; (US: bill) 勘定書 kañjōgaki; (BANKING) 小切手 kogittè; (pattern: gen pl) 市松模様 ichímatsumoyō
♦adj (pattern, cloth) 市松模様の ichímatsumoyò no

checkbook [tʃekˈbuk] (US) n 小切手帳 kogittechō

checkerboard [tʃekˈəːrbɔːrd] n チェッカー盤 chekkában

checkered [tʃekˈəːrd] (BRIT **chequered**) adj (fig: career, history) 起伏の多い kifúku no ōi

checkers [tʃekˈəːrz] (US) npl (game) チェッカー chékkà

check in vi (at hotel, airport) チェックインする chekkúin surù
♦vt (luggage) 預ける azúkerù

check-in [tʃekˈin-] (desk) n フロント furónto

checking account [tʃekˈiŋ-] (US) n (current account) 当座預金 tōzayokìn

checkmate [tʃekˈmeit] n (CHESS) 王手 ōte

check out vi (of hotel) チェックアウトする chekkúaùto surù

checkout [tʃekˈaut] n (in shop) 勘定カウンター kañjō kauñtā

checkpoint [tʃekˈpɔint] n (on border) 検問所 keñmonjo

checkroom [tʃekˈruːm] (US) n (left-luggage office) 手荷物一時預り所 teñmòtsu ichíjiazúkarijo

check up *vi*: *to check up on something/someone* ...を調べておく ...wo shirábetè okù

checkup [tʃek'ʌp] *n* (MED) 健康診断 keńkōshíñdan

cheek [tʃiːk] *n* (ANAT) ほお hŏ; (impudence) ずうずうしさ zúzūshìsà; (nerve) 度胸 dokyŏ

cheekbone [tʃiːk'boun] *n* ほお骨 hŏbone

cheeky [tʃiː'kiː] *adj* (impudent) ずうずうしい zúzūshì

cheep [tʃiːp] *vi* (bird) ぴよぴよ鳴く piyòpiyo nakú

cheer [tʃiːr] *vt* (team, speaker) 声援する seśen suru; (gladden) 喜ばす yorókobasù
♦*vi* (shout) 声援する seśen suru
♦*n* (shout) 声援 seśen

cheerful [tʃiːr'fəl] *adj* (wave, smile, person) 朗らかな hogaràka na

cheerio [tʃiːr'iː:ou] (BRIT) *excl* じゃあねjáné

cheers [tʃiːrz] *npl* (of crowd etc) 声援 seśen, かっさい kassái
cheers! (toast) 乾杯 kańpai

cheer up *vi* (person) 元気を出す géñki wo dasù
♦*vt* (person) 元気づける geńkizukerù

cheese [tʃiːz] *n* チーズ chízu

cheeseboard [tʃiːz'bourd] *n* チーズボード chízubôdo ◇チーズを盛り合せる板または皿 chízu wo moríawaserù itá mata wa sará

cheetah [tʃiː'tə] *n* チーター chītā

chef [ʃef] *n* (in restaurant, hotel) コック kókku

chemical [kem'ikəl] *adj* (fertilizer, warfare) 化学の kágaku no
♦*n* 化学薬品 kagákuyakùhin

chemist [kem'ist] *n* (BRIT: pharmacist) 薬剤師 yakúzaishi; (scientist) 化学者 kagákusha

chemistry [kem'istri:] *n* 化学 kágaku

chemist's (shop) [kem'ists-] (BRIT) *n* 薬局 yakkyóku

cheque [tʃek] (BRIT: BANKING) *n* = check

chequebook [tʃek'buk] (BRIT) *n* = checkbook

cheque card (BRIT) *n* (to guarantee cheque) 小切手カード kogítte kàdo

chequered [tʃek'ə:rd] (BRIT) *adj* = checkered

cherish [tʃe:r'iʃ] *vt* (person) 大事にする daíji ni suru; (memory, dream) 心に抱く kokórò ni idakù

cherry [tʃe:r'iː] *n* (fruit) サクランボウ sakúranbò; (also: **cherry tree**) サクラ sakúra

chess [tʃes] *n* チェス chésù

chessboard [tʃes'bɔːrd] *n* チェス盤 chéssuban

chest [tʃest] *n* (ANAT) 胸 muné; (box) ひつ hitsú
chest of drawers 整理だんす seíridañsu

chestnut [tʃes'nʌt] *n* クリ kurí; (also: **chestnut tree**) クリの木 kurí no ki

chew [tʃuː] *vt* (food) かむ kamú

chewing gum [tʃuː'iŋ-] *n* チューインガム chúiñgamù

chic [ʃiːk] *adj* (dress, hat etc) スマートな súmāto na; (person, place) 粋な ikí na

chick [tʃik] *n* (bird) ひな hínà; (inf: girl) べっぴん beppín

chicken [tʃik'ən] *n* (bird) ニワトリ niwátori; (meat) 鶏肉 keíniku; (inf: coward) 弱虫 yowamùshi

chicken out (inf) *vi* おじ気付いて...から手を引く ojíkezuìte ...kara te wo hikú

chickenpox [tʃik'ənpɑːks] *n* 水ぼうそう mizúbōsò

chicory [tʃik'ə:riː] *n* チコリ chíkòri

chief [tʃiːf] *n* (of tribe) しゅう長 shūchō; (of organization, department) ...長 ...chō
♦*adj* (principal) 主な ómò na

chief executive *n* 社長 shachŏ

chiefly [tʃiː'fliː] *adv* (principally) 主に ómò ni

chiffon [ʃifɑːn'] *n* (fabric) シフォン shíffon

chilblain [tʃil'blein] *n* 霜焼け shimóyake

child [tʃaild] (pl **children**) *n* 子供 kodómo
do you have any children? お子さんは? o-kó-san wa?

childbirth [tʃaild'bə:rθ] *n* お産 osán

childhood [tʃaild'hud] *n* 子供時分 kodó-

mojíbun

childish [tʃáil'diʃ] *adj* (games, attitude, person) 子供っぽい kodómoppoì

childlike [tʃáild'laik] *adj* 無邪気な mújàki na

child minder (*BRIT*) *n* 保母 hóbò

children [tʃíl'drən] *npl of* **child**

Chile [tʃíl'i:] *n* チリ chírì

Chilean [tʃíl:l'eiən] *adj* チリの chírì no
♦*n* チリ人 chírìjìn

chill [tʃíl] *n* (coldness: in air, water etc) 冷え hié; (MED: illness) 風邪 kazé
♦*vt* (cool: food, drinks) 冷す hiyasù; (person: make cold): *to be chilled* 体が冷える karáda ga hierù

chilli [tʃíl'i:] *n* チリ chírì

chilly [tʃíl'i:] *adj* (weather) 肌寒い hadásamuì; (person) 寒気がする samúke ga suru; (response, look) 冷たい tsumétai

chime [tʃáim] *n* (of bell, clock) チャイム cháìmu
♦*vi* チャイムが鳴る chaímu ga narú

chimney [tʃím'ni:] *n* (of house, factory) 煙突 eñtotsu

chimney sweep *n* 煙突掃除夫 eñtotsu sōjìfu

chimpanzee [tʃìmpænzi:'] *n* チンパンジー chiñpañjī

chin [tʃín] *n* あご agó

China [tʃái'nə] *n* 中国 chūgoku

china [tʃái'nə] *n* (clay) 陶土 tōdo; (crockery) 瀬戸物 setómono

Chinese [tʃàini:z'] *adj* 中国の chūgoku no; (LING) 中国語の chūgokugo no
♦*n inv* (person) 中国人 chūgokujìn; (LING) 中国語 chūgokugo

chink [tʃíŋk] *n* (crack: in door, wall etc) 透き間 sukíma; (clink: of bottles etc) かちん kachín

chip [tʃíp] *n* (*BRIT: gen pl*: CULIN) フライドポテト furáidopotèto; (*US: also:* **potato chip**) ポテトチップス potétochìppusu; (of wood, glass, stone) 欠けら kakéra; (COMPUT) チップ chippù
♦*vt: to be chipped* (cup, plate) 縁が欠けている fuchí ga kakéte irú

chip in (*inf*) *vi* (contribute) 寄付する kífù surù; (interrupt) 口を挟む kuchí wo

hasamù

chiropodist [kirɑ:p'ədist] (*BRIT*) *n* 足治療師 ashí chiryōshi

chirp [tʃə:rp] *vi* (bird) ちゅうちゅう鳴く chūchū nakú

chisel [tʃíz'əl] *n* (for wood) のみ nómì; (for stone) たがね tagáne

chit [tʃít] *n* (note) メモ mémò; (receipt) 領収書 ryōshūsho

chitchat [tʃít'tʃæt] *n* 世間話 sekénbanàshi

chivalrous [ʃiv'əlrəs] *adj* 親切な shíñsetsu na

chivalry [ʃiv'əlri:] *n* (behavior) 親切さ shiñsetsusa; (medieval system) 騎士道 kishídò

chives [tʃáivz] *npl* (herb) チャイブ cháìbu

chlorine [klɔ:r'i:n] *n* (CHEM) 塩素 éñso

chock-a-block [tʃɑ:k'əblak'] *adj* 一杯で íppaì de

chock-full [tʃɑ:k'ful'] *adj* = **chock-a-block**

chocolate [tʃɔ:k'əlit] *n* (bar, sweet, cake) チョコレート chokórèto; (drink) ココア kókòa

choice [tʃɔis] *n* (selection) 選んだ物 eráda monó; (option) 選択 señtaku; (preference) 好み konómi
♦*adj* (fine: cut of meat, fruit etc) 一級の ikkyū no

choir [kwai'ə:r] *n* (of singers) 聖歌隊 seíkatai; (area of church) 聖歌隊席 seíkataisèki

choirboy [kwaiə:r'bɔi] *n* 少年聖歌隊員 shōnen seikataiin

choke [tʃouk] *vi* (on food, drink etc) ...がのどに詰る ...ga nodò ni tsumarù; (with smoke, dust, anger etc) むせる muséru
♦*vt* (strangle) ...ののどを締める ...no nodò wo shimerù; (block): *to be choked (with)* (...で) 詰っている (...de) tsumattè irú
♦*n* (AUT) チョーク chŏku

cholera [kɑ:l'ə:rə] *n* コレラ kórèra

cholesterol [kəles'tə:rɔ:l] *n* (fat) コレステロール korésuteròru

choose [tʃu:z] (*pt* **chose**, *pp* **chosen**) *vt* 選

ぶ erábù
to choose to do ...をする事に決める ...wo suru kotó ni kimêru

choosy [tʃuːˈziː] *adj* (difficult to please) えり好みする erígonomi suru

chop [tʃɑːp] *vt* (wood) 割る warú; (CULIN: *also*: **chop up**: vegetables, fruit, meat) 刻む kizámu
◆*n* (CULIN) チョップ chóppù, チャップ cháppu

chopper [tʃɑːˈpɔːr] *n* (helicopter) ヘリコプター heríkopùtā

choppy [tʃɑːˈpiː] *adj* (sea) しけの shiké no

chops [tʃɑːps] *npl* (jaws) あご agó

chopsticks [tʃɑːˈpstiks] *npl* はし háshì

choral [kɔːrˈəl] *adj* (MUS) 合唱の gasshô no

chord [kɔːrd] *n* (MUS) 和音 wáòn

chore [tʃɔːr] *n* (domestic task) 家事 kájì; (routine task) 毎日の雑用 maînichi no zatsúyô

choreographer [kɔːriːɑːˈgˈrəfəːr] *n* 振付師 furítsukeshì

chortle [tʃɔːrˈtəl] *vi* 楽しそうに笑う tanôshisô ni waraú

chorus [kɔːrˈəs] *n* (MUS: group) 合唱隊 gasshôtai, コーラス kôrasu; (: song) 合唱 gasshô; (: refrain) リフレーン rifúrèn; (of musical play) コーラス kôrasu

chose [tʃouz] *pt of* **choose**

chosen [tʃouˈzən] *pp of* **choose**

Christ [kraist] *n* キリスト kirísuto

christen [krisˈən] *vt* (REL: baby) ...に洗礼を施す ...ni seńrei wo hodókosu; (nickname) ...を...と呼ぶ ...wo ...to yobú

Christian [krisˈtʃən] *adj* キリスト教の kirísutokyō no
◆*n* キリスト教徒 kirísutokyòto

Christianity [kristʃiːænˈitiː] *n* キリスト教 kirísutokyô

Christian name *n* ファーストネーム fâsutonêmu

Christmas [krisˈməs] *n* (REL: festival) クリスマス kurísumasu; (period) クリスマスの季節 kurísumasu no kisetsù
Merry Christmas! メリークリスマス！ merí kurisumàsu!

Christmas card *n* クリスマスカード

kurísumasu kådo

Christmas Day *n* クリスマス kurísumàsu

Christmas Eve *n* クリスマスイブ kurísumasu ibù

Christmas tree *n* クリスマスツリー kurísumasu tsurî

chrome [kroum] *n* クロームめっき kurômumekkî

chromium [krouˈmiːəm] *n* = **chrome**

chromosome [krouˈməsoum] *n* 染色体 seńshokutai

chronic [krɑːnˈik] *adj* (continual: ill-health, illness etc) 慢性の mańsei no; (: drunkenness etc) 常習的な jôshūteki na; (severe: shortage, lack etc) ひどい hídoì

chronicle [krɑːnˈikəl] *n* (of events) 記録 kiróku ◇年代順または日付順の記録を指す neńdaijuǹ mata wa hizúkejuǹ no kiróku wo sasù

chronological [krɑːnələˈdʒˈikəl] *adj* (order) 日付順の hizúkejuǹ no

chrysanthemum [krisænˈθəməm] *n* キク kikú

chubby [tʃʌbˈiː] *adj* (cheeks, child) ぽっちゃりした potchárî shitá

chuck [tʃʌk] (*inf*) *vt* (throw: stone, ball etc) 投げる nagerù; (*BRIT*: *also*: **chuck up**) やめる yamêru

chuckle [tʃʌkˈəl] *vi* くすくす笑う kúsùkusu waraù

chuck out *vt* (person) 追い出す oídasù; (rubbish etc) 捨てる sutéru

chug [tʃʌg] *vi* (machine, car engine etc) ぽっぽっと音を立てる póppòtto otô wo taterù; (car, boat: *also*: **chug along**) ぽっぽっと音を立てて行く poppòtto otô wo tatète ikú

chum [tʃʌm] *n* (friend) 友達 tomôdachi

chunk [tʃʌŋk] *n* (of stone, meat) 塊 katámari

church [tʃəːrtʃ] *n* (building) 教会 kyôkai; (denomination) 教派 kyôha, ...教 ...kyô

churchyard [tʃəːrtʃˈjɑːrd] *n* 教会墓地 kyôkaibochì

churlish [tʃəːrˈliʃ] *adj* (silence, behavior) 無礼な burèi na

churn [tʃəːrn] n (for butter) かく乳器 kakúnyüki; (BRIT: also: **milk churn**) 大型ミルク缶 ōgata mirukukan

churn out vt (mass-produce: objects, books etc) 大量に作る taíryō ni tsukurù

chute [ʃuːt] n (also: **rubbish chute**) ごみ捨て場 gomísuteba; (for coal, parcels etc) シュート shūto

chutney [tʃʌtniː] n チャツネ chátsùne

CIA [siːaieiˈ] (US) n abbr (= Central Intelligence Agency) 中央情報局 chūōjōhōkyoku

CID [siːaidiˈ] (BRIT) n abbr (= Criminal Investigation Department) 刑事部 keíjibù

cider [saiˈdəːr] n リンゴ酒 riṅgoshù

cigar [sigɑːrˈ] n 葉巻 hamáki

cigarette [sigəretˈ] n (紙巻) タバコ (kamímaki) tábako

cigarette case n シガレットケース shigárettokèsu

cigarette end n 吸殻 suígara

Cinderella [sindərelˈə] n シンデレラ shíndererà

cinders [sinˈdəːrz] npl (of fire) 燃え殻 moégara

cine-camera [siniːkæməˈrə] (BRIT) n 映画カメラ eíga kamèra

cine-film [siniːfilmˈ] (BRIT) n 映画用フィルム eígayō firùmu

cinema [sinˈəmə] n (THEATER) 映画館 eígakàn; (film-making) 映画界 eígakài

cinnamon [sinˈəmən] n (CULIN) ニッケイ nikkéi, シナモン shinámoṅ

cipher [saiˈfəːr] n (code) 暗号 aṅgō

circle [səːrˈkəl] n (shape) 円 éň; (of friends) 仲間 nakáma; (in cinema, theater) 二階席 nikáisekì

♦vi (bird, plane) 旋回する seṅkai suru

♦vt (move round) 回る mawáru; (surround) 囲む kakómu

circuit [səːrˈkit] n (ELEC) 回路 kaíro; (tour) 1周 isshū; (track) サーキット sākitto; (lap) 1周 isshū, ラップ ráppù

circuitous [səːrkjuˈitəs] adj (route, journey) 遠回りの tōmawàri no

circular [səːrˈkjələːr] adj (plate, pond etc) 丸い marúi

♦n (letter) 回状 kaíjō

circulate [səːrˈkjəleit] vi (traffic) 流れる nagárerù; (blood) 循環する juňkan suru; (news, rumour, report) 出回る demáwaru; (person: at party etc) 動き回る ugókimawarù

♦vt (report) 回す mawásu

circulation [səːrkjəleiˈʃən] n (of report, book etc) 回される事 mawásareru kotó; (of traffic) 流れ nagáre; (of air, water, also MED: of blood) 循環 juňkan; (of newspaper) 発行部数 hakkőbusù

circumcise [səːrˈkəmsaiz] vt (MED) ...の包皮を切除する ...no hőhi wo setsùjo surù; (REL) ...に割礼を行う ...ni katsúrei wo okónau

circumference [səːrkʌmˈfəːrəns] n (edge) 周囲 shūi; (distance) 周囲の長さ shūi no nagàsa

circumflex [səːrˈkəmfleks] n (also: **circumflex accent**) 曲折アクセント kyokúsetsu akùsento

circumspect [səːrˈkəmspekt] adj (cautious, careful) 慎重な shiňchō na

circumstances [səːrˈkəmstænsiz] npl (of accident, death) 状況 jōkyō; (conditions, state of affairs) 状態 jōtai; (also: **financial circumstances**) 経済状態 keízaijòtai

circumvent [səːrkəmventˈ] vt (regulation) ...に触れない様にする ...ni furénai yő ni surù; (difficulty) 回避する kaíhi surù

circus [səːrˈkəs] n (show) サーカス sākasu; (performers) サーカス団 sākasudaň

CIS [siːaiesˈ] n abbr = **Commonwealth of Independent States**

cistern [sisˈtəːrn] n (water tank) 貯水タンク chosúitaňku; (of toilet) 水槽 suísō

cite [sait] vt (quote: example, author etc) 引用する in-yō suru; (LAW) 召喚する shőkan suru

citizen [sitˈəzən] n (gen) 住民 jūmin; (of a country) 国民 kokúmin, 市民 shímin; (of a city) 市民 shímin; (of other political divisions) ...民 ...miṅ

citizenship [sitˈəzənʃip] n (of a country) 市民権 shimíňken

citrus fruit [sit'rəs fru:t] n カンキツ類 kańkitsurùi

city [sit'i:] n 都市 toshì
  the City (FINANCE) シティー shitî ◇ロンドンの金融業の中心地 rondon no kińyūgyō no chūshińchi

civic [siv'ik] adj (leader, duties, pride) 公民の kômin no; (authorities) 自治体の jichítai no

civic centre (BRIT) n 自治体中心部 jichítaichūshińbu

civil [siv'əl] adj (gen) 市民の shímìn no, 公民の kômin no; (authorities) 行政の gyôsei no; (polite) 礼儀正しい reígitadashiî

civil defense n 民間防衛 mińkanbōei

civil disobedience n 市民的不服従 shimíntekifufukujû

civil engineer n 土木技師 dobókugishì

civilian [sivil'jən] adj (attitudes, casualties, life) 民間の mińkan no
  ♦n 民間人 mińkanjin

civilization [sivələzei'ʃən] n (a society) 文明社会 buńmeishakài; (social organization) 文化 búnka

civilized [siv'əlaizd] adj (society) 文明的な buńmeiteki na; (person) 洗練された seńren saréta

civil law n 民法 mínpō

civil rights npl 公民権 kômińken

civil servant n 公務員 kômuìn

Civil Service n 文官職 buńkanshokù

civil war n 内乱 naíran

clad [klæd] adj: **clad (in)** ...を着た ...wo kitá

claim [kleim] vt (expenses) 請求する seíkyū suru; (inheritance) 要求する yōkyū suru; (rights) 主張する shuchō suru; (assert): **to claim that/to be** ...であると主張する ...de arù to shuchō suru
  ♦vi (for insurance) 請求する seíkyū suru
  ♦n (assertion) 主張 shuchō; (for pension, wage rise, compensation) 請求 seíkyū; (to inheritance, land) 権利 kénri
  to claim responsibility (for) (...の) 犯行声明を出す (...no) hańkōseimèi wo dasù
  to claim credit (for) (...が) 自分の業績

であると主張する (...ga) jibún no gyôseki de arù to shuchō suru

claimant [klei'mənt] n (ADMIN) 要求者 yôkyūshà; (LAW) 原告 geńkoku

clairvoyant [kle:rvɔi'ənt] n (psychic) 霊媒 reíbai

clam [klæm] n (ZOOL, CULIN) ハマグリ hamagùri ◇英語では食用二枚貝の総称として使われる eígo de wa shokúyōnimaìgai no sôshō toshité tsukáwarerù

clamber [klæm'bə:r] vi (aboard vehicle) 乗る norú; (up hill etc) 登る nobóru ◇手足を使って物に乗ったり登ったりするという含みがある teàshi wo tsukátte monô ni nottári nobóttari suru to iú fukúmi ga arù

clammy [klæm'i:] adj (hands, face etc) 冷たくてべとべとしている tsumétakùte betóbeto shité irù

clamor [klæm'ə:r] (BRIT **clamour**) vi:
  to clamor for (change, war etc) ...をやかましく要求する ...wo yakámashikù yōkyū suru

clamp [klæmp] n (device) 留金 tomégane, クランプ kuráńpu
  ♦vt (two things together) クランプで留める kuráńpu de toméru; (put: one thing on another) 締付ける shimétsukerù

clamp down on vt fus (violence, speculation etc) 取り締まる toríshimarù

clan [klæn] n (family) 一族 ichízoku

clandestine [klændes'tin] adj (activity, broadcast) 秘密の himítsu no

clang [klæŋ] vi (bell, metal object) かんと鳴る kań to narú

clap [klæp] vi (audience, spectators) 拍手する hákùshu surù

clapping [klæp'iŋ] n (applause) 拍手 hákùshu

claret [klær'it] n クラレット kuráretto ◇ボルドー産の赤ワイン bórudōsaǹ no aká waiǹ

clarify [klær'əfai] vt (argument, point) はっきりさせる hakkíri saséru

clarinet [klærənet'] n (MUS: instrument) クラリネット kurárinettò

clarity [klær'iti:] n (of explanation, thought) 明りょうさ meíryōsa

clash [klæʃ] *n* (of opponents) 衝突 shōtotsu; (of beliefs, ideas, views) 衝突 shōtotsu, 対立 tairitsu; (of colors) 不調和 fuchōwa; (of styles) つり合わない事 tsurfawanai kotó; (of two events, appointments) かち合い kachíai; (noise) ぶつかる音 butsúkaru otó
♦*vi* (fight: rival gangs etc) 衝突する shōtotsu suru; (disagree: political opponents, personalities) 角突合いをする tsunótsukiài wo surù; (beliefs, ideas, views) 相容れない aíirènai; (colors, styles) 合わない awánai; (two events, appointments) かち合う kachíaù; (make noise: weapons, cymbals etc) 音を立ててぶつかり合う otó wo tatéte butsúkariaù

clasp [klæsp] *n* (hold: with hands) 握る事 nigíru kotó, 握り nigírì; (: with arms) 抱締めること dakíshimerù kotó, 抱擁 hōyō; (of necklace, bag) 留金 tomégane, クラスプ kurásupù
♦*vt* (hold) 握る nigíru; (embrace) 抱締める dakíshimerù

class [klæs] *n* (SCOL: pupils) 学級 gakkyū, クラス kurásu; (: lesson) 授業 jugyō; (of society) 階級 kaíkyū; (type, group) 種類 shurùi
♦*vt* (categorize) 分類する buńrui suru

classic [klæsik] *adj* (example, illustration) 典型的な teńkeiteki na; (film, work etc) 傑作の kessáku no; (style, dress) 古典的な kotenteki na
♦*n* (film, novel etc) 傑作 kessáku

classical [klæsikəl] *adj* (traditional) 伝統的な deńtōteki na; (MUS) クラシックの kuráshikkù no; (Greek, Roman) 古代の kódài no

classification [klæsəfəkei'ʃən] *n* (process) 分類する事 buńrui suru kotó; (category, system) 分類 buńrui

classified [klæs'əfaid] *adj* (information) 秘密の himítsu no

classified advertisement *n* 分類広告 buńruikōkoku

classify [klæs'əfai] *vt* (books, fossils etc) 分類する buńrui suru

classmate [klæs'meit] *n* 同級生 dōkyūsei, クラスメート kurásumēto

classroom [klæs'ru:m] *n* 教室 kyōshitsu

clatter [klæt'ə:r] *n* (of dishes, pots etc) がちゃがちゃ gáchàgacha; (of hooves) かたかた kátàkata
♦*vi* (dishes, pots etc) がちゃがちゃいう gachàgacha iú; (hooves) かたかた鳴る kátàkata narú

clause [klɔ:z] *n* (LAW) 条項 jōkō; (LING) 文節 buńsetsu

claustrophobia [klɔ:strəfou'bi:ə] *n* (PSYCH) 閉所恐怖症 heíshokyōfushò

claw [klɔ:] *n* (of animal, bird) つめ tsumé; (of lobster) はさみ hasámi

claw at *vt fus* (curtains, door etc) 引っかく hikkáku

clay [klei] *n* 粘土 néndo

clean [kli:n] *adj* (person, animal) きれい好きな kiréizuki na; (place, surface, clothes etc) 清潔な seíketsu na; (fight) 反則のない hańsoku no naì; (record, reputation) 無傷の múkìzu no; (joke, story) 下品でない gehín de naì; (MED: fracture) 単純な tańjun na
♦*vt* (car, hands, face etc) 洗う aráu; (room, house) 掃除する sōji suru

clean-cut [kli:n'kʌt] *adj* (person) 品の良い hiń no yoì

cleaner [kli:'nə:r] *n* (person) 掃除係 sōjigakàri; (substance) 洗剤 señzai

cleaner's [kli:'nə:rz] *n* (*also*: **dry cleaner's**) クリーニング店 kurīningùten

cleaning [kli:'niŋ] *n* (of room, house) 掃除 sōji

cleanliness [klen'li:nis] *n* 清潔 seíketsu

clean out *vt* (cupboard, drawer) 中身を出してきれいにする nakámì wo dashíte kiréi ni suru

cleanse [klenz] *vt* (purify) 清める kiyómerù; (face, cut) 洗う aráu

cleanser [klen'zə:r] *n* (for face) 洗顔料 señgañryō

clean-shaven [kli:n'ʃei'vən] *adj* ひげのない higé no naì

cleansing department [klen'ziŋ-] (*BRIT*) *n* 清掃局 seísōkyoku

clean up *vt* (mess) 片付ける katázukerù; (child) 身ぎれいにする migírei ni surù

clear [kli:'ə:r] *adj* (easy to understand:

report, argument) 分かりやすい wakári-yasuï; (easy to see, hear) はっきりした hakkírï shitá; (obvious: choice, commitment) 明らかな akíraka na; (glass, plastic) 透明な tōmei na, 明確な meíkaku na; (water, eyes) 澄んだ súnda; (road, way, floor etc) 障害のない shōgai no naï; (conscience) やましい所のない yamashiï tokóro no naï; (skin) 健康そうな keíkōsō na; (sky) 晴れた haréta

♦vt (space, room) 開ける akéru; (LAW: suspect) 容疑を晴す yốgi wo harasù; (fence, wall) 飛越える tobíkoerù; (check) 払う haraù

♦vi (weather, sky) 晴れる harerù; (fog, smoke) 消える kierù

♦adv: **clear of** (trouble) ...を避けて ...wo sakéte; (ground) ...から離れて ...kara hanárete

to clear the table 食卓を片付ける shokútaku wo katázukerù

clearance [kli:'rəns] n (removal: of trees, slums) 取払う事 torítharaù kotó; (permission) 許可 kyókà

clear-cut [kli:'ərkʌt'] adj (decision, issue) 明白な meíhaku na

clearing [kli:'riŋ] n (in woods) 開けた所 hírákètà tokóro

clearing bank (BRIT) n 手形交換組合銀行 tegátakōkankumiaigíñkō ◇ロンドンの中央手形交換所を通じて他の銀行との取引を行う銀行 róndon no chūō tegata kōkanjo wo tsújitè tá no gíñkō to no toríhiki wò okónaù gíñkō

clearly [kli:'ərli:] adv (distinctly, coherently) はっきりと hakkírï to; (evidently) 明らかに akíraka ni

clear up vt (room, mess) 片付ける katázukerù; (mystery, problem) 解決する kaíketsu suru

clearway [kli:r'wei] (BRIT) n 駐停車禁止道路 chūteíshakinshídoro

cleaver [kli:'və:r] n 骨割包丁 honéwaribōchō ◇なたに似た物で，肉のブロックをたたき切ったり骨を割ったりするのに使う natá ni nitá monó de, nikú no burokkù wo tatákikittarì honé wo wattárì surù no ni tsukaù

clef [klef] n (MUS) 音部記号 oñbukigō

cleft [kleft] n (in rock) 割れ目 waréme

clemency [klem'ənsi:] n 恩情 oñjō

clench [klentʃ] vt (fist) 握り締める nigírishimerù; (teeth) 食いしばる kuíshibarù

clergy [klə:r'dʒi:] n 聖職者 seíshokùsha ◇総称 sōshō

clergyman [klə:r'dʒi:mən] (pl **clergymen**) n (Protestant) 牧師 bókùshi; (Catholic) 神父 shíñpu

clerical [kler'ikəl] adj (worker, job) 事務の jímù no; (REL) 聖職者の seíshokùsha no

clerk [klə:rk] n (BRIT: office worker) 事務員 jímuñ; (US: sales person) 店員 teñin

clever [klev'ə:r] adj (intelligent) 利口な rikō na; (deft, crafty) こうかつな kōkatsu na; (device, arrangement) 良く工夫した yốkù kufū shitá

cliché [kli:ʃei'] n 決り文句 kimárimoñku

click [klik] vt (tongue) 鳴らす narásu; (heels) 打鳴らす uchínarasu

♦vi (device, switch etc) かちっと鳴る kachíttō narú

client [klai'ənt] n (of bank, company) 客 kyakú; (of lawyer) 依頼人 iráinìn

cliff [klif] n (GEO) 断崖 dañgai

climate [klai'mit] n (weather) 気候 kikố; (of opinion etc) 雰囲気 fuñ-ìkì

climax [klai'mæks] n (of battle, career) 頂点 chōten; (of film, book) クライマックス kuráimakkùsu; (sexual) オルガズム orúgazùmu

climb [klaim] vi (sun, plant) 上がる agáru; (plant) はい上がる haíagarù; (plane) 上昇する jōshō suru; (prices, shares) 上昇する jōshō suru; (move with effort): **to climb over a wall** 塀を乗り越える heí wo noríkoerù

♦vt (stairs, ladder) 上がる agáru, 登る nobóru; (hill) 登る nobóru; (tree) ...に登る ...ni noborù

♦n (of hill, cliff etc) 登る事 nobóru kotó; (of prices etc) 上昇 jōshō

to climb into a car 車に乗り込む kurúma ni noríkomù

climb-down [klaim'daun] n (retraction)

撤回 tekkái

climber [klai'mər] *n* (mountaineer) 登山者 tozansha; (plant) つる性植物 tsurúsei-shokubùtsu

climbing [klai'miŋ] *n* (mountaineering) 山登り yamánobòri, 登山 tōzàn

clinch [klintʃ] *vt* (deal) まとめる matómeru; (argument) …に決着を付ける …ni ketcháku wo tsukerù

cling [kliŋ] (*pt, pp* **clung**) *vi*: **to cling to** (mother, support) …にしがみつく …ni shigámitsukù; (idea, belief) 固執する koshū suru; (subj: clothes, dress) …にぴったりくっつく …ni pittári kuttsùku

clinic [klin'ik] *n* (MED: center) 診療所 shifiryōjo

clinical [klin'ikəl] *adj* (MED: tests) 臨床の rinshō no; (: teaching) 臨床の rinshō no; (fig: thinking, attitude) 冷淡な reítan na; (: building, room) 潤いのない uruoi no nai

clink [kliŋk] *vi* (glasses, cutlery) ちんと鳴る chin to narú

clip [klip] *n* (*also*: **paper clip**) クリップ kurippù; (*also*: **hair clip**) 髪留 kamídome; (TV, CINEMA) 断片 dañpen
◆*vt* (fasten) 留める toméru; (cut) はさみで切る hasámi de kiru

clippers [klip'ə:rz] *npl* (for gardening) せん定ばさみ señteibasàmi; (*also*: **nail clippers**) つめ切り tsumékiri

clipping [klip'iŋ] *n* (from newspaper) 切抜き kirínuki

clique [kli:k] *n* 徒党 totó

cloak [klouk] *n* (cape) マント mánto
◆*vt* (fig: in mist, secrecy) 隠す kakúsu

cloakroom [klouk'ru:m] *n* (for coats etc) クローク kurôku; (*BRIT*: WC) お手洗 o-téarài

clock [klɑ:k] *n* 時計 tokéi

clock in *vi* (for work) 出勤する shukkín suru

clock off *vi* (from work) 退社する taísha suru

clock on *vi* = **clock in**

clock out *vi* = **clock off**

clockwise [klɑ:k'waiz] *adv* 時計回りに tokéimawàri ni

clockwork [klɑ:k'wə:rk] *n* 時計仕掛 tokéijikàke
◆*adj* (model, toy) 時計仕掛の tokéijikàke no

clog [klɑ:g] *n* (leather) 木底の靴 kizóko no kutsú; (*also*: **wooden clog**) 木靴 kígùtsu
◆*vt* (drain, nose) ふさぐ fuságu
◆*vi* (*also*: **clog up**: sink) 詰る tsumarù

cloister [klɔis'tə:r] *n* 回廊 kaírō

clone [kloun] *n* (of animal, plant) クローン kúrôn

close¹ [klous] *adj* (near) 近くの chikákù no; (friend) 親しい shitáshiì; (relative) 近縁の kiñ-en no; (contact) 密な mítsù na; (link, ties) 密接な missétsu na; (examination, watch) 注意深い chūibukaì; (contest) 互角の gokáku no; (weather) 重苦しい omókurushiì
◆*adv* (near) 近くに chikákù ni
close to …の近くに …no chikákù ni
close at hand, close by *adj* 近くの chikákù no
◆*adv* 近くに chikákù ni
to have a close shave (fig) 間一髪で助かる kañ-ippátsu de tasukaru

close² [klouz] *vt* (shut: door, window) しめる shimérù; (finalize: sale) 取決める toríkimerù; (end: case, speech) 終える oéru
◆*vi* (shop etc) 閉店する heíten suru; (door, lid) 閉る shimarù; (end) 終る owáru

closed [klouzd] *adj* (door, window, shop etc) 閉っている shimattè irù

close down *vi* (factory) 廃業する haígyō suru; (magazine) 廃刊する haíkan suru

closed shop *n* (fig) クローズドショップ kurôzudo shoppù ◇特定の労働組合員だけしか雇わない事業所 tokútei no rôdō-kumiaiìn dake shika yatówanaì jigyô-sho

close-knit [klous'nit'] *adj* (family, community) 堅く結ばれた katáku musúbareta

closely [klous'li:] *adv* (examine, watch) 注意深く chūibukakù; (connected) 密接に missétsu ni; (related) 近縁になって kiñ-en ni nattè; (resemble) そっくり sokkúrì

closet [klɔːz'it] n (cupboard) たんす tañ-su

close-up [klous'ʌp] n (PHOT) クローズアップ kurōzuappù

closure [klou'ʒəːr] n (of factory) 閉鎖 heĩ-sa; (of magazine) 廃刊 haĩkan

clot [klɑːt] n (gen: blood clot) 血の塊 chi no katámari; (inf: idiot) ばか bákà
♦vi (blood) 固まる katámaru, 凝固する gyōko suru

cloth [klɔːθ] n (material) 布 nunó; (rag) ふきん fukĩñ

clothe [klouð] vt (dress) ...に服を着せる ...ni fukú wo kiséru

clothes [klouz] npl 服 fukú

clothes brush n 洋服ブラシ yófukuburàshi

clothes line n 物干綱 monóhoshizùna

clothes pin (BRIT **clothes peg**) n 洗濯ばさみ señtakubasàmi

clothing [klou'ðiŋ] n = **clothes**

cloud [klaud] n (in sky) 雲 kúmò
a cloud of smoke/dust もうもうとした煙(ほこり) mõmō to shita kemúri (hokori)

cloudburst [klaud'bəːrst] n 集中豪雨 shúchūgòu

cloudy [klau'diː] adj (sky) 曇った kumottà; (liquid) 濁った nigottà

clout [klaut] vt (hit, strike) 殴る nagurù

clove [klouv] n (spice) チョウジ chōji, クローブ kurōbu
clove of garlic ニンニクの一粒 niñniku no hitòtsubu

clover [klou'vəːr] n クローバー kurōba

clown [klaun] n (in circus) ピエロ pĩero
♦vi (also: **clown about, clown around**) おどける odókeru

cloying [klɔi'iŋ] adj (taste, smell) むかつかせる mukátsukaseru

club [klʌb] n (society, place) クラブ kúràbu; (weapon) こん棒 koñbō; (also: **golf club**) クラブ kúràbu
♦vt (hit) 殴る nagurù
♦vi: **to club together** (BRIT: for gift, card) 金を出し合う kané wo dashiàu

club car (US) n (RAIL) ラウンジカー ra-úñjikā ◇休憩用客車 kyúkeiyò kyakùsha

clubhouse [klʌb'haus] n (of sports club) クラブハウス kurábuhaùsu ◇スポーツクラブのメンバーが集まる部屋, 建物など supótsukuràbu no meñba ga atsúmarù heyá, tatèmono nadò

clubs [klʌbz] npl (CARDS) クラブ kúràbu

cluck [klʌk] vi (hen) こっこっと鳴く kókkòtto nakú

clue [kluː] n (pointer, lead) 手掛かり té-gàkari; (in crossword) かぎ kagí
I haven't a clue さっぱり分らない sáppàri wakáranaĩ

clump [klʌmp] n (gen) 塊 katámari; (of buildings etc) 一連 ichíren
a clump of trees 木立 kódàchi

clumsy [klʌm'ziː] adj (person, movement) 不器用な búkìyo na; (object) 扱いにくい atsúkainikuì; (effort, attempt) 下手な hetá na

clung [klʌŋ] pt, pp of **cling**

cluster [klʌs'təːr] n (of people, stars, flowers etc) 塊 katámari
♦vi 固まる katámaru, 群がる murágarù

clutch [klʌtʃ] n (grip, grasp) つかむ事 tsukámù kotó; (AUT) クラッチ kurátchi
♦vt (purse, hand, stick) しっかり持つ shíkkàri motsù

clutter [klʌt'əːr] vt (room, table) 散らかす chirákasu

cm abbr = **centimeter**

CND [siːendiː'] n abbr (= Campaign for Nuclear Disarmament) 核廃絶運動 ka-kúhaizetsu uñdō

Co. abbr = **county; company**

c/o abbr = **care of**

coach [koutʃ] n (bus) バス básù; (also: **horse-drawn coach**) 馬車 bášà; (of train) 客車 kyakùsha; (SPORT: trainer) コーチ kōchi; (tutor) 個人教師 kojíñkyòshi
♦vt (sportsman/woman) コーチする kōchi suru; (student) ...に個人指導をする ...ni kojíñshidò wo surù

coach trip n バス旅行 basúryokò

coagulate [kouæg'jəleit] vi (blood, paint etc) 凝固する gyōko surù

coal [koul] n (substance) 石炭 sekítaǹ;

(also: **lump of coal**) 石炭1個 sekítañ ikkð

coal face n 石炭切り場 sekítankiríba

coalfield [koul'fi:ld] n 炭田 tañden

coalition [kouəliʃ'ən] n (POL: also: **coalition government**) 連合政権 reñgōseikèn; (of pressure groups etc) 連盟 reñmei

coalman [koul'mən] (pl **coalmen**) n 石炭屋 sekítanya

coal merchant n = **coalman**

coalmine [koul'main] n 炭坑 tañkō

coarse [kɔːrs] adj (texture: rough) 荒いaráì; (person: vulgar) 下品な gehiñ na

coast [koust] n 海岸 kaígan
♦vi (car, bicycle etc) 惰力走行する daryōkusōkō suru

coastal [kous'təl] adj (cities, waters) 海岸沿いの kaíganzòi no

coastguard [koust'gɑːrd] n (officer) 沿岸警備隊員 eñgankeibitáiin; (service) 沿岸警備隊 eñgankeibitái

coastline [koust'lain] n 海岸線 kaígansen

coat [kout] n (overcoat) コート kòto; (of animal) 毛 ke; (of paint) 塗り nurí
♦vt: **coated with** ...で覆われた ...de ōwaréta

coat hanger n ハンガー háñgā

coating [kou'tiŋ] n (of dust, mud etc) 覆う物 ōù monó; (of chocolate, plastic etc) 被覆 hifúku

coat of arms n 紋章 móñ

coax [kouks] vt (person: persuade) 説得する settóku suru

cob [kɑːb] n see **corn**

cobbler [kɑːb'lər] n (maker/repairer of shoes) 靴屋 kutsúyà

cobbles [kɑːb'əlz] npl 敷石 shikíishi

cobblestones [kɑːb'əlstounz] npl = **cobbles**

cobweb [kɑːb'web] n クモの巣 kúmò no su

cocaine [koukein'] n コカイン kókàin

cock [kɑːk] n (rooster) おん鳥 oñdori; (male bird) 鳥の雄 torí no osú
♦vt (gun) ...の撃鉄を起す ...no gekítetsu wo okosù

cockerel [kɑːk'ə:rəl] n 雄のひな鳥 osú no hinàdori

cock-eyed [kɑːk'aid] adj (fig: idea, method) ばかな bákà na

cockle [kɑːk'əl] n ホタテガイ hotátègai

cockney [kɑːk'ni:] n コックニー kókkùnī ◇ロンドンのEast End地区生れの人 roñdon no Eást End chikú umáre no hitð

cockpit [kɑːk'pit] n (in aircraft) 操縦室 sōjūshitsu, コックピット kokkúpittð; (in racing car) 運転席 uñteñseki, コックピット kokkúpittð

cockroach [kɑːk'routʃ] n ゴキブリ gokíburi

cocktail [kɑːk'teil] n (drink) カクテル kákùteru; (mixture: fruit cocktail, prawn cocktail etc) ...カクテル ...kakùteru

cocktail cabinet n ホームバー hőmubà

cocktail party n カクテルパーティ kakúterupàti

cocoa [kou'kou] n (powder, drink) ココア kókða

coconut [kou'kənʌt] n (fruit) ヤシの実 yáshì no mi; (flesh) ココナッツ kokónattsu

cocoon [kəku:n'] n (of butterfly) 繭 máyù

cod [kɑːd] n タラ tárà

C.O.D. [si:oudi:'] abbr (= cash or also (US) collect on delivery) 着払い chakúbarài

code [koud] n (of practice, behavior) 規定 kitéi; (cipher) 暗号 añgō; (dialling code, post code) 番号 bañgō

cod-liver oil [kɑːd'livər-] n 肝油 kañ-yu

coercion [kouə:r'ʃən] n (pressure) 強制 kyōsei

coffee [kɔːf'i:] n (drink, powder) コーヒー kőhī; (cup of coffee) コーヒー一杯 kőhī ippài

coffee bar (BRIT) n 喫茶店 kíssàten

coffee bean n コーヒー豆 kőhīmamè

coffee break n コーヒーブレーク kőhīburèku

coffeepot [kɔːf'i:pɑːt] n コーヒーポット kőhīpottð

coffee table n コーヒーテーブル kőhī-

tëburu

coffin [kɔ:f'in] n ひつぎ hitsúgi

cog [kɑ:g] n (TECH: wheel) 歯車 hágùruma; (: tooth) 歯車の歯 hágùruma no há

cogent [kou'dʒənt] adj (argument etc) 説得力ある settőkuryòku arù

cognac [koun'jæk] n コニャック kőnyàkku

coherent [kouhi:'rənt] adj (answer, theory, speech) 筋の通った sují no tőtta; (person) 筋の通った事を言う sují no tőtta kotő wo iú

cohesion [kouhi:'ʒən] n (political, ideological etc) 団結 dańketsu

coil [kɔil] n (of rope, wire) 一巻 hitőmaki; (ELEC) コイル kőîru; (contraceptive) 避妊リング hiníñrìñgu
♦vt (rope) 巻く makú

coin [kɔin] n (money) 硬貨 kőka, コイン kőîn
♦vt (word, slogan) 造る tsukúru

coinage [kɔi'nidʒ] n 貨幣制度 kahéiseìdo

coin-box [kɔin'bɑːks] n (BRIT) コイン電話 koíndeñwa ◇公衆電話でカードだけしか使えない物に対比して言う kőshūdeñwa de kắdo daké shiká tsukáenai monó ni taíhi shitê iú

coincide [kouinsaid'] vi (events) 同時に起る dōji ni okőru; (ideas, views) 一致する itchí suru

coincidence [kouin'sidəns] n 偶然の一致 gûzen no itchí

Coke [kouk] ® n (drink) コカコーラ kokákòra

coke [kouk] n (coal) コークス kőkusu

colander [kɑ:l'əndəːr] n 水切り mizúkiri ◇ボール型で穴の比較的大きい物を指す bőrugata de aná no hikákuteki őkiì monó wo sasú

cold [kould] adj (water, food) 冷たい tsumétai; (weather, room) 寒い samúì; (person, attitude: unemotional) 冷たい tsumétai, 冷淡な reítan na
♦n (weather) 寒さ samůsa; (MED) 風邪 kazé
it's cold 寒い samui
to be cold (person, object) 冷たい tsumétai

to catch (a) cold 風邪を引く kazé wo hikú

in cold blood (kill etc) 冷酷に reíkoku ni

coldly [kould'li:] adv (speak, behave) 冷たく tsumétaku, 冷淡に reítan ni

cold-shoulder [kould'ʃouldəːr] vt 冷たくあしらう tsumétaku ashíraù

cold sore n 口角炎 kőkakuèn

coleslaw [koul'slɔ:] n コールスロー kőrusurő

colic [kɑ:l'ik] n (MED) 腹痛 fukútsū

collaborate [kəlæb'əreit] vi (on book, research) 協同する kyődő suru; (with enemy) 協力する kyőryoku suru

collaboration [kəlæbərei'ʃən] n 協力 kyőryoku

collage [kəlɑ:ʒ'] n コラージュ kőràju

collapse [kəlæps'] vi (building, system, resistance) 崩れる kuzúrerù, 崩壊する hőkai suru; (government) 倒れる taőrerù; (MED: person) 倒れる taőrerù; (table) 壊れる kowárerù, つぶれる tsubúrerù; (company) つぶれる tsubúrerù, 破産する hasán suru
♦n (of building, system, government, resistance) 崩壊 hőkai; (MED: of person) 倒れる事 taőreru kotő; (of table) 壊れる〔つぶれる〕事 kowárerù(tsubureru)kotő; (of company) 破産 hasán

collapsible [kəlæps'əbəl] adj (seat, bed, bicycle) 折畳みの orítatami no

collar [kɑ:l'əːr] n (of coat, shirt) 襟 erí, カラー kárà; (of dog, cat) 首輪 kubíwa, カラー karã

collarbone [kɑ:l'əːrboun] n (ANAT) 鎖骨 sakótsu

collateral [kəlæt'əːrəl] n (COMM) 担保 táñpo

colleague [kɑ:l'i:g] n 同僚 dőryo

collect [kəlekt'] vt (gather: wood, litter etc) 集める atsúmerù; (as a hobby) 収集する shűshū suru; (BRIT: call and pick up: person) 迎えに行く mukáe ni ikú; (: object) 取りに行く torí ni ikú; (for charity, in church) 募金する bokín suru; (debts, taxes etc) 集金する shűkin suru; (mail) 取集する shushū suru

♦*vi* (crowd) 集る atsúmarù
to call collect (*US*: TEL) コレクトコールする korékutokóru suru

collection [kəlek'ʃən] *n* (of art, stamps etc) コレクション kórèkushon; (of poems, stories etc) ...集...shū; (from place, person) 受取る事 ukétoru kotó; (for charity) 募金 bokín; (of mail) 取集 shushū

collective [kəlek'tiv] *adj* (farm, decision) 共同の kyōdō no

collector [kəlek'tə:r] *n* (of art, stamps etc) 収集家 shūshūka; (of taxes etc) 集金人 shūkiñnin

college [ka:l'idʒ] *n* (SCOL: of university) 学寮 gakúryō; (: of agriculture, technology) 大学 daígaku

collide [kəlaid'] *vi* (cars, people) ぶつかる butsúkaru, 衝突する shōtotsu suru

collie [ka:l'i:] *n* コリー犬 korīken

colliery [ka:l'jə:ri:] (*BRIT*) *n* 炭坑 tańkō

collision [kəliʒ'ən] *n* (of vehicles) 衝突 shōtotsu

colloquial [kəlou'kwi:əl] *adj* (LING: informal) 口語の kōgo no

collusion [kəlu:'ʒən] *n* (collaboration) 結託 kettáku

colon [kou'lən] *n* (punctuation mark) コロン kóròn; (ANAT) 大腸 daíchō

colonel [kə:r'nəl] *n* 大佐 taísa

colonial [kəlou'ni:əl] *adj* 植民地の shokúmiñchi no

colonize [ka:l'ənaiz] *vt* (country, territory) 植民地にする shokúmiñchi ni surù

colony [ka:l'əni:] *n* (subject territory) 植民地 shokúmiñchi; (of people) ...人街 ...jiñgai; (of animals) 個体群 kotáigùn

color [kʌl'ə:r] (*BRIT* **colour**) *n* (gen) 色 iro
♦*vt* (paint) ...に色を塗る ...ni iró wo nurú; (dye) 染める someru; (*fig*: account) ...に色を付ける ...ni iró wo tsukerù; (judgment) ゆがめる yugámerù
♦*vi* (blush) 赤面する sekímen suru
in color 天然色で teñneñshoku de, カラーで kárā de

color bar *n* 人種差別 jiñshusabètsu ◇有色人種、特に黒人に対する差別を指す

yūshokujiñshu, tokú ni kokújin ni taí suru sabètsu wo sasú

color-blind [kʌl'ə:rblaind] *adj* 色盲の shikímō no

colored [kʌl'ə:rd] *adj* (person) 有色の yūshoku no; (illustration etc) カラーの kárā no

color film *n* カラーフィルム karáfirùmu

colorful [kʌl'ə:rfəl] *adj* (cloth) 色鮮やかな iró azáyaka na; (account, story) 華やかな hanáyaka na; (personality) 華々しい hanábanashiî

color in *vt* (drawing) ...に色を塗る ...ni iró wo nurú

coloring [kʌl'ə:riŋ] *n* (complexion) 肌の色合い hadà no iróai; (*also*: **food coloring**) 着色料 chakúshokùryō

colors [kʌl'ə:rz] *npl* (of party, club etc) 色 iró

color scheme *n* 配色計画 haíshokukeìkaku

color television *n* カラーテレビ karáterèbi

colossal [kəla:s'əl] *adj* 巨大な kyodái na

colour [kʌl'ə:r] *etc* (*BRIT*) *n* = **color** *etc*

colt [koult] *n* 子ウマ koúma

column [ka:l'əm] *n* (ARCHIT) 円柱 eñchū; (of smoke) 柱 hashíra; (of people) 縦隊 jūtai; (gossip column, sports column) コラム kóràmu

columnist [ka:l'əmist] *n* コラムニスト korámunisùto

coma [kou'mə] *n* (MED) こん睡状態 koñsuijōtai

comb [koum] *n* くし kushí
♦*vt* (hair) くしでとかす kushí de tokasù; (*fig*: area) 捜索する sōsaku suru

combat [*n* ka:m'bæt *vb* kəmbæt'] *n* (MIL: fighting) 戦闘 señtō; (fight, battle) 戦い tatákai
♦*vt* (oppose) 反抗する hañkō suru

combination [ka:mbənei'ʃən] *n* (mixture) 組合せ kumíawase; (for lock, safe etc) 組合せ番号 kumíawasebañgō

combine [*vb* kəmbain' *n* ka:m'bain] *vt*:
to combine something with something ...を...と組合せる ...wo ...to kumía-

waserù; (qualities) 兼備える kanésonae-
rù; (two activities) 兼任する kefnin suru
♦*vi* (people, groups) 合併する gappéi suru
♦*n* (ECON) 連合 refgō
combine (harvester) [ka:m'bain(ha:r'-
vestə:r)] *n* コンバイン kofbaìn
combustion [kəmbʌs'tʃən] *n* (act, process) 燃焼 nefshō

KEYWORD

come [kʌm] (*pt* **came**, *pp* **come**) *vi* 1
(movement towards) 来る kúrù
come here! ここにおいで kokó ni oide
I've only come for an hour 1時間しか
いられません ichíjikàn shika iráremasèn
come with me ついて来て下さい tsúìte
kite kudasai
are you coming to my party? 私のパ
ーティに来てくれますね watákushi no
pátì ni kité kurèmasu né
to come running 走って来る hashíttè
kúrù
2 (arrive) 着く tsúkù, 到着する tóchaku
suru, 来る kúrù
he's just come from Aberdeen 彼はア
バーディーンから来たばかりです káre
wa abádìn kara kitá bakàri desu
he's come here to work 彼はここには
働きに来ました káre wa kokó ni wà
határaki ni kimashìta
they came to a river 彼らは川に着きま
した kárèra wa kawá nì tsukímashìta
to come home 家に戻って来る ié nì
modóttè kuru
3 (reach): *to come to* ...に届く ...ni todókù, ...になる ...ni nárù
the bill came to £40 勘定は計40ポン
ドだった kánjō wa kéì yónjuppòndo datta
her hair came to her waist 彼女の髪
の毛は腰まで届いていた kánojō no kamí
no kè wa koshí madè todóite ita
to come to power 政権を握る seíken
wo nigiru
to come to a decision 結論に達する
ketsúron ni tassuru
4 (occur): *an idea came to me* いい考え

が浮かびました íi kángaè ga ukábimasu-
shìta
5 (be, become) なる nárù
to come loose/undone etc 外れる hazúreru
I've come to like him 彼が好きになり
ました káre ga sukí nì narímashìta

---

come about *vi* 起る okórù
come across *vt fus* (person, thing) ...に
出会う ...ni deáù
come away *vi* (leave) 帰る káeru, 出て
来る déte kure; (become detached) 外れ
る hazúreru
come back *vi* (return) 帰って来る káèt-
te kuru
comeback [kʌm'bæk] *n* (of film star
etc) 返り咲き kaérizaki, カムバック ka-
múbakkù
come by *vt fus* (acquire) 手に入れる té
nì iréru
comedian [kəmi:'di:ən] *n* (THEATER,
TV) コメディアン kómèdian
comedienne [kəmi:di:en'] *n* 女性コメデ
ィアン josèi kómèdian
come down *vi* (price) 下がる sagárù;
(tree) 倒れる taórerù; (building) 崩れ落ち
る kuzúreochìrù
comedy [ka:m'idi:] *n* (play, film) 喜劇 kígèki, コメディー kómèdī; (humor) 喜劇
性 kigékisei, ユーモア yūmoa
come forward *vi* (volunteer) 進んで...す
る susúnde ...sùrú
come from *vt fus* (place, source etc)
...から来る ...kara kúrù
come in *vi* (visitor) 入る háìru; (on deal
etc) 加わる kuwáwarù; (be involved) 関
係する kánkei suru
come in for *vt fus* (criticism etc) 受け
る ukérù
come into *vt fus* (money) 相続する só-
zoku suru; (be involved) ...に関係する
...ni kánkei suru
to come into fashion 流行する ryūkō
suru
come off *vi* (button) 外れる hazúreru;
(attempt) 成功する seíkō suru
come on *vi* (pupil, work, project) 進歩す

る shínpo suru; (lights, electricity) つく tsukú

come on! さあさあ sāsā

come out *vi* (fact) 発覚する hakkáku suru; (book) 出版される shúppan sareru; (stain) 取れる torérù, 落ちる ochírù; (sun) 出る dérù

come round *vi* (after faint, operation) 正気に返る shőki ni kaèru, 目が覚める mé gà samérù, 気が付く ki gá tsukù

comet [kɑːm'it] *n* すい星 suísei

come to *vi* (regain consciousness) 正気に戻る shőki ni modorù, 目が覚める mé gà samérù

come up *vi* (sun) 出る dérù; (problem) 起る okórù, 出る dérù; (event) 起る okórù; (in conversation) 出る dérù

come up against *vt fus* (resistance, difficulties) ぶつかる butsúkaru

come upon *vt fus* (find) 見付ける mitsúkeru

comeuppance [kʌmʌp'əns] *n*: *to get one's comeuppance* 当然の罰を受ける tőzen no batsú wo ukerù

come up with *vt fus* (idea) 持出す mochídasù; (money) 出す dásù

comfort [kʌm'fə:rt] *n* (well-being: physical, material) 安楽 ánraku; (relief) 慰め nagúsame

◆*vt* (console) 慰める nagúsamerù

comfortable [kʌm'fə:rtəbəl] *adj* (person: physically) 楽な rákù na; (: financially) 暮しに困らない kurashí ni komáranài; (furniture) 座り心地の良い suwárigokochi no yoì; (room) 居心地のよい igőkochi nò yőì; (patient) 苦痛のない kutsú no naî; (easy: walk, climb etc) 楽な rákù na

comfortably [kʌm'fə:rtəbli:] *adv* (sit, live etc) 楽に rákù ni

comforts [kʌm'fə:rts] *npl* (of home etc) 生活を楽にするもの seíkatsu wo rakú ni suru monó

comfort station (*US*) *n* お手洗 o-téarai

comic [kɑːm'ik] *adj* (*also*: **comical**) こっけいな kokkéi na

◆*n* (comedian) コメディアン kőmèdian; (*BRIT*: magazine) 漫画(雑誌) mañ-

ga(zasshì)

comic strip *n* 連続漫画 reñzokumañga

coming [kʌm'iŋ] *n* (arrival) 到着 tőchaku

◆*adj* (event, attraction) 次の tsugí no, これからの koré kara no

coming(s) and going(s) *n(pl)* 行き来 yukíki, 往来 őrai

comma [kɑːm'ə] *n* コンマ kőñma

command [kəmænd'] *n* (order) 命令 meírei; (control, charge) 指揮 shikí; (MIL: authority) 司令部 shíreibu; (mastery: of subject) マスターしていること masútà shité irù kotó

◆*vt* (give orders to): *to command someone to do something* ...に...をする様に命令する ...ni ...wo suru yő ni meírei suru; (troops) ...の司令官である ...no shiréikan de arù

commandeer [kɑːməndiːr'] *vt* (requisition) 徴発する chőhatsu suru; (*fig*) 勝手に取って使う katté ni totté tsukáù

commander [kəmæn'də:r] *n* (MIL) 司令官 shíreikan

commandment [kəmænd'mənt] *n* (REL) 戒律 kaíritsu

commando [kəmæn'dou] *n* (group) コマンド部隊 komándobùtai; (soldier) コマンド隊員 komándotaìin

commemorate [kəmem'əːreit] *vt* (with statue, monument, celebration, holiday) 記念する kinén suru

commence [kəmens'] *vt* (begin, start) 始める hajímeru

◆*vi* 始まる hajímaru

commend [kəmend'] *vt* (praise) ほめる homérù; (recommend) ゆだねる yudáneru

commensurate [kəmen'sərit] *adj*: *commensurate with* ...に相応した ...ni sőő shitá

comment [kɑːm'ent] *n* (remark: written or spoken) コメント koménto

◆*vi*: *to comment (on)* (...について) コメントする (...ni tsuité) koménto surù

no comment ノーコメント nőkomento

commentary [kɑːm'əntəːriː] *n* (TV, RADIO) 実況放送 jikkyőhősō; (book,

article) 注解 chúkai

commentator [kɑ:m'əntèitə:r] *n* (TV, RADIO) 解説者 kaísetsùsha

commerce [kɑ:m'ə:rs] *n* 商業 shógyō

commercial [kəmə:r'(ə)l] *adj* (organization, activity) 商業 の shógyō no; (success, failure) 商業上の shógyōjō no
♦*n* (TV, RADIO: advertisement) コマーシャル kómāsharu, CM shíemu

commercialized [kəmə:r'(ə)laizd] (*pej*) *adj* (place, event etc) 営利本意の eírihoñ i no

commercial radio/television *n* 民間 ラジオ(テレビ)放送 miñkan rajio(terebi) hôsō, 民放 míñpō

commiserate [kəmiz'əreit] *vi*: *to commiserate with* ...をいたわる ...wo itáwarù

commission [kəmiʃ'ən] *n* (order for work: esp of artist) 依頼 iraí; (COMM) 歩合 buái, コミッション kómìsshon; (committee) 委員会 iíñkai
♦*vt* (work of art) 依頼する iraí suru
out of commission (not working) 故障 して koshó shité

commissionaire [kəmiʃəne:r'] (*BRIT*) *n* ドアマン dóaman

commissioner [kəmiʃ'ənə:r] *n* (POLICE) 長官 chókan

commit [kəmit'] *vt* (crime, murder etc) 犯す okásu; (money, resources) 充当する jútō suru; (to someone's care) 任せる makáserù
to commit oneself (to do) (...する事 を) 約束する (...surú kotó wo) yakúsoku suru
to commit suicide 自殺する jisátsu suru

commitment [kəmit'mənt] *n* (to ideology, system) 献身 keńshin; (obligation) 責任 sekínin; (undertaking) 約束 yakúsoku

committee [kəmit'i:] *n* (of organization, club etc) 委員会 iíñkai

commodity [kəmɑ:d'iti:] *n* (saleable item) 商品 shōhin

common [kɑ:m'ən] *adj* (shared by all: knowledge, property, good) 共同の kyó-

dō no; (usual, ordinary: event, object, experience etc) 普通の futsū no; (vulgar: person, manners) 下品な gehíñ na
♦*n* (area) 共有地 kyóyūchi
in common 共通で kyótsū de

commoner [kɑ:m'ənə:r] *n* 庶民 shomín

common law *n* コモン・ロー komón rō ◇成文化されてない慣習に基づく英米 の一般法を指す seíbunka saréte naí kañshū ni motózukù eíbei no ippáńhō wo sasù

commonly [kɑ:m'ənli:] *adv* (usually) 通 常 tsújō

Common Market *n* ヨーロッパ共同市 場 yóroppa kyódōshijō

commonplace [kɑ:m'ənpleis] *adj* 平凡な heíbon na

common room *n* (SCOL) 談話室 dañwashìtsu

Commons [kɑ:m'ənz] (*BRIT*) *npl*: *the Commons* 下院 ká-in

common sense *n* 常識 jōshiki, コモンセ ンス komónseñsu

Commonwealth [kɑ:m'ənwelθ] *n* (British Commonwealth): *the Commonwealth* イギリス連邦 igírisureñpō
the Commonwealth of Independent States 独立国家共同体 dokúritsu kòkka kyódōtai

commotion [kəmou'ʃən] *n* (uproar) 騒 ぎ sáwàgi

communal [kəmju:'nəl] *adj* (shared) 共同 の kyódō no

commune [*n* kɑ:m'ju:n *vb* kəmju:n'] *n* (group) コミューン komyùn
♦*vi*: *to commune with* (nature, God) ...に親しむ ...ni shitáshimù

communicate [kəmju:'nikeit] *vt* (idea, decision, feeling) 伝える tsutáerù
♦*vi*: *to communicate (with)* ...と通信 する ...to tsúshin suru

communication [kəmju:nikei'(ʃ)ən] *n* (process) 通信 tsúshin; (letter, call) 連絡 refíraku

communication cord (*BRIT*) *n* (on train) 非常通報装置 hijótsūhōsōchi

communion [kəmju:n'jən] *n* (*also*: **Holy Communion**) 聖体拝領 seítaihaíryō

communiqué [kəmjuːnikei'] n (POL, PRESS) コミュニケ kômyûnike

communism [kɑːm'jənizəm] n 共産主義 kyôsanshûgi

communist [kɑːm'jənist] adj 共産主義の kyôsanshûgi no
♦n 共産主義者 kyôsanshugishà

community [kəmjuː'niti:] n (group of people) 共同体 kyôdôtai; (within larger group) 社会 shákai

community center n 公民館 kôminkan

community chest (US) n 共同募金 kyôdôbôkin

community home (BRIT) n 養育施設 yôikushisètsu

commutation ticket [kɑːmjətei'(ʃən-] (US) n 定期券 teíkikèn

commute [kəmjuːt'] vi (to work) 通う kayóu
♦vt (LAW: sentence) 減刑する geñkei suru

commuter [kəmjuːt'əːr] n 通勤者 tsûkiñsha

compact [kɑːm'pækt] adj (taking up little space) 小型の kogáta no
♦n (also: powder compact) コンパクト kôñpakuto

compact disk n コンパクトディスク kôñpakuto disùku

companion [kəmpæn'jən] n 相手 aíte

companionship [kəmpæn'jənʃip] n つきあい tsukíai

company [kʌm'pəni:] n (COMM) 会社 kaísha; (THEATER) 劇団 gekídan; (companionship) 付合い tsukíai
to keep someone company ...の相手になる ...no aíte ni narù

company secretary (BRIT) n 総務部長 sômubùchô

comparable [kɑːm'pəːrəbəl] adj (size, style, extent) 匹敵する hittéki suru

comparative [kəmpær'ətiv] adj (peace, stranger, safety) 比較的 hikákuteki; (study) 比較の hikáku no

comparatively [kəmpær'ətivli:] adv (relatively) 比較的に hikákuteki ni

compare [kəmpeːr'] vt: **to compare someone/something with/to** (set side

by side) ...を...と比較する ...wo ...to hikáku suru; (liken) ...を...に例える ...wo ...ni tatóerù
♦vi: **to compare (with)** (...に) 匹敵する (...ni) hittéki suru

comparison [kəmpær'isən] n (setting side by side) 比較 hikáku; (likening) 例え tatóe
in comparison (with) ...と比較して ...to hikáku shitè

compartment [kəmpɑːrt'mənt] n (RAIL) 客室 kyakúshitsu, コンパートメント koñpâtomènto; (section: of wallet, fridge etc) 区画 kukáku

compass [kʌm'pəs] n (instrument: NAUT, GEO) 羅針盤 rashínban, コンパス kôñpasu

compasses [kʌm'pəsiz] npl (MATH) コンパス koñpasu

compassion [kəmpæʃ'ən] n (pity, sympathy) 同情 dôjō

compassionate [kəmpæʃ'ənit] adj (person, look) 情け深い nasákebukaì

compatible [kəmpæt'əbəl] adj (people) 気が合う ki ga aù; (ideas etc) 両立できる ryôritsu dekírù; (COMPUT) 互換性のある gokánsei no arù

compel [kəmpel'] vt (force) 強制する kyôsei suru

compelling [kəmpel'iŋ] adj (fig: argument, reason) 止むに止まれぬ yamú ni yamárenù

compensate [kɑːm'pənseit] vt (employee, victim) ...に補償する ...ni hoshô suru
♦vi: **to compensate for** (loss, disappointment, change etc) ...を埋め合せる ...wo uméawaserù

compensation [kɑːmpənsei'(ʃən] n (to employee, victim) 補償 hoshô; (for loss, disappointment, change etc) 埋め合せ uméawase

compère [kɑːm'peːr] (BRIT) n (TV, RADIO) 司会者 shíkaisha

compete [kəmpiːt'] vi (companies, rivals): **to compete (with)** (...と) 競り合う (...to) serîaù; (in contest, game) 参加する sañka suru

competence [kɑːm'pitəns] n (of worker

etc) 能力 nōryoku

competent [kɑːmˈpitənt] *adj* 有 能 な yūnō na

competition [kɑːmpitiʃˈən] *n* (between
firms, rivals) 競争 kyōsō; (contest) コン
クール konkūru; (ECON) ライバル商品
raíbaru shōhin

competitive [kəmpetˈətiv] *adj* (industry,
society) 競争の激しい kyōsō no hagéshiì;
(person) 競争心の強い kyōsōshin no tsuyoî; (price, product) 競争 で き る kyōsō
dekírù

competitive sports 競技 kyōgi

competitor [kəmpetˈitəːr] *n* (rival) 競争
相手 kyōsōaìte; (participant) 参加者 sañkashà

compile [kəmpailˈ] *vt* (book, film,
report) 編集する heñshū suru

complacency [kəmpleiˈsənsiː] *n* (smug-
ness) 自己満足 jikómañzoku

complacent [kəmpleiˈsənt] *adj* (smug)
自己満足にふける jikómañzoku ni fuké-
rù

complain [kəmpleinˈ] *vi* (grumble) 不 平
不満を言う fuhéifùman wo iú; (protest:
to authorities, shop etc) 訴える uttáerù

to complain of (pain) ...を訴える ...wo
uttáerù

complaint [kəmpleintˈ] *n* (objection) 訴
え uttáe; (criticism) 非 難 hínàn; (MED:
illness) 病気 byóki

complement [*n* kɑːmˈpləmənt *vb* kɑːmˈ-
pləment] *n* (supplement) 補 う 物 ogínau
monó; (esp ship's crew) 人員 jiñ-in

♦*vt* (enhance) 引立たせる hikítataserù

complementary [kɑːmpləmenˈtəːriː] *adj*
(mutually supportive) 補足し合う hosóku shiaù

complete [kəmpliːtˈ] *adj* (total, whole)
完全 な kañzen na; (finished: building,
task) 完成した kañsei shitá

♦*vt* (finish: building, task) 完成する kañsei suru; (: set, group etc) そろえる soróerù; (fill in: a form) ...に記入する ...ni
kinyū suru

completely [kəmpliːtˈliː] *adv* (totally) 全
く mattáku, 完全に kañzen ni

completion [kəmpliːˈʃən] *n* (of building)

完成 kañsei; (of contract) 履行 rikō

complex [*adj* kəmpleksˈ *n* kɑːmˈpleks]
adj (structure, problem, decision) 複雑な
fukúzatsu na

♦*n* (group: of buildings) 団地 dañchi;
(PSYCH) コンプレックス koñpurekkùsu

complexion [kəmplekˈʃən] *n* (of face) 顔
の肌 kaó no hadà

complexity [kəmplekˈsitiː] *n* (of problem, law) 複雑さ fukúzatsuūsa

compliance [kəmplaiˈəns] *n* (submission) 服従 fukújū; (agreement) 同意 dóì

in compliance with ...に従って ...ni shitágatte

complicate [kɑːmˈpləkeit] *vt* (matters,
situation) 複雑にする fukúzatsu ni suru

complicated [kɑːmˈpləkeitid] *adj* (explanation, system) 複雑な fukúzatsu na

complication [kɑːmpləkeiˈʃən] *n* (problem) 問題 moñdai; (MED) 合併症 gappéi-
shō

complicity [kəmplisˈətiː] *n* (in crime) 共
犯 kyóhàn

compliment [*n* kɑːmˈpləmənt *vb* kɑːmˈ-
pləment] *n* (expression of admiration)
ほめ言葉 homékotòba

♦*vt* (express admiration for) ほめる homérù

to pay someone a compliment ...をほ
める ...wo homéru

complimentary [kɑːmpləmenˈtəːriː] *adj*
(remark) 賛辞の sañji no; (ticket, copy
of book etc) 無料の muryó no

compliments [kɑːmˈpləmənts] *npl*
(regards) 挨拶 aìsatsu

comply [kəmplaiˈ] *vi*: *to comply with*
(law, ruling) ...に従う ...ni shitágaù

component [kəmpouˈnənt] *adj* (parts,
elements) 構成している kōsei shité irù

♦*n* (part) 部分 búbùn

compose [kəmpouzˈ] *vt* (form): *to be
composed of* ...から出来ている ...kará
dekítě irù; (write: music, poem, letter)
書く kákù

to compose oneself 心を落着かせる kokórò wo ochítsukaserù

composed [kəmpouzdˈ] *adj* (calm) 落 着
いている ochítsuite irù

composer [kəmpou'zə:r] n (MUS) 作曲家 sakkyókuka

composition [kɑ:mpəziʃ'ən] n (of substance, group etc) 構成 kōsei; (essay) 作文 sakúbun; (MUS) 作曲 sakkyóku

compost [kɑ:m'poust] n たい肥 taíhi

composure [kəmpou'ʒə:r] n (of person) 落着き ochítsuki

compound [kɑ:m'paund] n (CHEM) 化合物 kágōbutsu; (enclosure) 囲い地 kakóichi; (LING) 複合語 fukúgōgo

◆adj (fracture) 複雑な fukúzatsu na

compound interest 複利 fúkùri

comprehend [kɑ:mprihend'] vt (understand) 理解する rikái suru

comprehension [kɑ:mprihen'ʃən] n (understanding) 理解 ríkài

comprehensive [kɑ:mprihen'siv] adj (description, review, list) 包括的な hōkatsuteki na; (INSURANCE) 総合的な sōgōteki na

comprehensive (school) (BRIT) n 総合中等学校 sōgōchūtōgakkō ◇あらゆる能力の子供に適した課程のある中等学校 aráyuru nōryoku no kodómo ni tekí shita katéi no arù chūtōgakkō

compress [vb kɑ:mpres' n kɑ:m'pres] vt (air, cotton, paper etc) 圧縮する asshúku suru; (text, information) 要約する yōyaku suru

◆n (MED) 湿布 shippú

comprise [kəmpraiz'] vt (also: be comprised of) ...からなる ...kará narù; (constitute) 構成する kōsei suru

compromise [kɑ:m'prəmaiz] n 妥協 dakyō

◆vt (beliefs, principles) 傷つける kizú tsukerù

◆vi (make concessions) 妥協する dakyō suru

compulsion [kəmpʌl'ʃən] n (desire, impulse) 強迫観念 kyōhakukañnen; (force) 強制 kyōsei

compulsive [kəmpʌl'siv] adj (liar, gambler etc) 病的な byōteki na; (viewing, reading) 止められない yamérarenài

compulsory [kəmpʌl'sə:ri:] adj (attendance, retirement) 強制的な kyōseiteki na

computer [kəmpju:'tə:r] n コンピュータ kofipyūta

computerize [kəmpju:'təraiz] vt (system, filing, accounts etc) コンピュータ化する kofipyūtaka surù; (information) コンピュータに覚えさせる kofipyūta ni obōesaserù

computer programmer n プログラマー puróguràmā

computer programming n プログラミング puróguramiñgu

computer science n コンピュータ科学 kofipyūta kagàku

computing [kəmpju:'tiŋ] n (activity, science) コンピュータ利用 kofipyūta riyō

comrade [kɑ:m'ræd] n (POL, MIL) 同志 dōshi; (friend) 友人 yūjin

comradeship [kɑ:m'rədʃip] n 友情 yūjō

con [kɑ:n] vt (deceive) だます damásù; (cheat) ぺてんに掛ける petén ni kakérù

◆n (trick) いかさま ikásama

concave [kɑ:nkeiv'] adj 凹面の ōmen no

conceal [kənsi:l'] vt (hide: weapon, entrance) 隠す kakúsù; (keep back: information) 秘密にする himítsu ni surù

concede [kənsi:d'] vt (admit: error, point, defeat) 認める mitómeru

conceit [kənsi:t'] n (arrogance) うぬぼれ unúbore

conceited [kənsi:'tid] adj (vain) うぬぼれた unúboreta

conceivable [kənsi:v'əbəl] adj (reason, possibility) 考えられる kañgaerarerù

conceive [kənsi:v'] vt (child) はらむ harámù; (plan, policy) 考え出す kañgaedasù

◆vi (BIO) 妊娠する niñshin suru

concentrate [kɑ:n'səntreit] vi (on problem, activity etc) 専念する sefinen suru; (in one area, space) 集中する shūchū suru

◆vt (energies, attention) 集中させる shūchū saséru

concentration [kɑ:nsəntrei'ʃən] n (on problem, activity etc) 専念 sefinen; (in one area, space) 集中 shūchū; (attention) 注意 chūi; (CHEM) 濃縮 nōshuku

concentration camp *n* 強制収容所 kyōseishūyōjo

concept [kɑːn'sept] *n* (idea, principle) 概念 gáīnen

conception [kənsep'ʃən] *n* (idea) 概念 gáīnen; (of child) 妊娠 nińshin

concern [kənsərːn'] *n* (affair) 責任 sekínin; (anxiety, worry) 心配 shińpai; (COMM: firm) 企業 kígyō

♦*vt* (worry) 心配させる shińpai saséru; (involve, relate to) ...に関係がある ...ni kańkē ga arū

to be concerned (about) (person, situation etc) (...について) 心配する (...ni tsuité) shińpai suru

concerning [kənsərːr'niŋ] *prep* (regarding) ...について ...ni tsuíte

concert [kɑːn'sərt] *n* (MUS) 演奏会 eńsōkai, コンサート końsāto

concerted [kənsərr'tid] *adj* (effort etc) 共同の kyōdō no

concert hall *n* コンサートホール końsātohōru

concertina [kɑːnsərrti:'nə] *n* (MUS: instrument) コンサーティーナ końsātīna ◇六角形の小型アコーディオン rokkákkei no kogáta akōdion

concerto [kəntʃərr'tou] *n* 協奏曲 kyōsōkyoku, コンチェルト kóncherto

concession [kənseʃ'ən] *n* (compromise) 譲歩 jōho; (COMM: right) 特権 tokkén

tax concession 減税 geńzei

conciliatory [kənsil'i:ətɔ:ri:] *adj* (gesture, tone) 懐柔的な kaíjūteki na

concise [kənsais'] *adj* (description, text) 簡潔な kańketsu na

conclude [kənkluːd'] *vt* (finish: speech, chapter) 終える oéru; (treaty) 締結する teíketsu suru; (deal etc) まとめる matómeru; (decide) (...だと) 結論する (...da to) ketsúron suru

conclusion [kənkluː'ʒən] *n* (of speech, chapter) 終り owári; (of treaty) 締結 teíketsu; (of deal etc) まとめる事 matómeru kotó; (decision) 結論 ketsúron

conclusive [kənkluː'siv] *adj* (evidence, defeat) 決定的な kettéiteki na

concoct [kənkɑːkt'] *vt* (excuse) でっち上

げる detchíagerù; (plot) 企てる kuwádaterù; (meal, sauce) 工夫して作る kufū shité tsukúrù

concoction [kənkɑːk'ʃən] *n* (mixture) 調合物 chōgōbutsu

concourse [kɑːn'kɔːrs] *n* (hall) 中央ホール chūōhŏru, コンコース końkōsu

concrete [kɑːn'kriːt] *n* コンクリート końkurīto

♦*adj* (block, floor) コンクリートの końkurīto no; (proposal, idea) 具体的な gutáiteki na

concur [kənkər:'] *vi* 同意する dóī suru

concurrently [kənkər:'əntli:] *adv* (happen, run) 同時に dóī ni

concussion [kənkʌʃ'ən] *n* (MED) 脳震とう nōshińtō

condemn [kəndem'] *vt* (denounce: action, report etc) 非難する hínān suru; (sentence: prisoner) ...に...刑を宣告する ...ni...kei wo señkoku suru; (declare unsafe: building) 使用に耐えない物と決定する shiyō ni taénài monó to kettéi suru

condemnation [kɑːndemnei'ʃən] *n* (criticism) 非難 hínān

condensation [kɑːndensei'ʃən] *n* (on walls, windows) 結露 kétsuro

condense [kəndens'] *vi* (vapor) 液化する ekíka suru

♦*vt* (report, book) 要約する yōyaku suru

condensed milk [kəndenst'-] *n* 練乳 reńnyū

condescending [kɑːndisen'diŋ] *adj* (reply, attitude) 恩着せがましい ońkisegamashì

condition [kəndiʃ'ən] *n* (state: gen) 状態 jōtai; (MED: of illness) 病状 byōjō; (requirement) 条件 jōken; (MED: illness) 病気 byōki

♦*vt* (person) 慣れさせる narésaserù

on condition that ...という条件で ...to iú jōken de

conditional [kəndiʃ'ənəl] *adj* 条件付きの jōkentsuki no

conditioner [kəndiʃ'ənər] *n* (also: **hair conditioner**) ヘアコンディショナー heákondishŏnā; (for fabrics) 柔軟剤 jūnańzai

conditions [kəndiʃ'ənz] *npl* (circumstances) 状況 jṓkyō

condolences [kəndou'lənsiz] *npl* お悔み o-kúyami

condom [kɑːn'dəm] *n* コンドーム koṅdōmu, スキン sukín

condominium [kɑːndəmin'iːəm] (*US*) *n* 分譲マンション buṅjōmaṅshon

condone [kəndoun'] *vt* (misbehavior, crime) 容認する yōnin suru

conducive [kənduː'siv] *adj*: **conducive to** (rest, study) …を助ける …wo tasúkerù

conduct [*n* kɑːn'dʌkt *vb* kəndʌkt'] *n* (of person) 振舞 furúmaì
♦*vt* (survey, research etc) 行う okónaù; (orchestra, choir etc) 指揮する shikí suru; (heat, electricity) 伝導する deṅdō suru
to conduct oneself (behave) 振舞う furúmaù

conducted tour [kəndʌk'tid-] *n* ガイド付き見物 gaídotsuki keṅbutsu

conductor [kəndʌk'təːr] *n* (of orchestra) 指揮者 shikíshà; (*BRIT*: on bus, *US*: on train) 車掌 shashṓ; (ELEC) 伝導体 deṅdōtai

conductress [kəndʌk'tris] *n* (on bus) 女性車掌 joséishashō, バスガール basúgāru

cone [koun] *n* (shape) 円すい形 eṅsuikei; (on road) カラーコーン karákòn, セーフティコーン sḗfutikòn; (BOT) 松かさ matsúkasà; (ice cream cornet) コーン kòn

confectioner [kənfek'ʃənəːr] *n* (person) 菓子職人 kashíshokùnin

confectioner's (shop) [kənfek'ʃənəːrz-] *n* (sweet shop) 菓子屋 kashíyà

confectionery [kənfek'ʃənəːriː] *n* (sweets, candies) 菓子類 kashírui

confederation [kənfedərei'ʃən] *n* (POL, COMM) 連合 reṅgō

confer [kənfəːr'] *vt*: **to confer something (on someone)** (honor, degree, advantage) (…に) …を与える (…ni) …wo atáerù
♦*vi* (panel, team) 協議する kyṓgi suru

conference [kɑːn'fəːrəns] *n* (meeting) 会議 kaígi

confess [kənfes'] *vt* (sin, guilt, crime) 白状する hákùjō suru; (weakness, ignorance) 認める mitómeru
♦*vi* (admit) 認める mitómeru

confession [kənfeʃ'ən] *n* (admission) 白状 hákùjō; (REL) ざんげ záṅge

confetti [kənfet'iː] *n* コンフェティ kóṅfeti ◇紙吹雪き用に細かく切った色紙 kamífubuki yṍ ni komákaku kittá irógami

confide [kənfaid'] *vi*: **to confide in** …に打明ける …ni uchíakerù

confidence [kɑːn'fidəns] *n* (faith) 信用 shiṅ-yō; (*also*: **self-confidence**) 自信 jishín; (secret) 秘密 himítsu
in confidence (speak, write) 内緒で naísho de

confidence trick *n* いかさま ikásama

confident [kɑːn'fidənt] *adj* (self-assured) 自信のある jishín no arù; (positive) 確信している kakúshin shitè irù

confidential [kɑːnfiden'ʃəl] *adj* (report, information) 秘密の himítsu no; (tone) 親しげな shitáshige na

confine [kənfain'] *vt* (limit) 限定する geṅtei suru; (shut up) 閉じ込める tojíkomerù

confined [kənfaind'] *adj* (space) 限られた kagírareta

confinement [kənfain'mənt] *n* (imprisonment) 監禁 kaṅkin

confines [kɑːn'fainz] *npl* (of area) 境 sakái

confirm [kənfəːrm'] *vt* (belief, statement) 裏付ける urázukerù; (appointment, date) 確認する kakúnin suru

confirmation [kɑːnfəːrmei'ʃən] *n* (of belief, statement) 裏付け urázuke; (of appointment, date) 確認 kakúnin; (REL) 堅信礼 keṅshiṅrei

confirmed [kənfəːrmd'] *adj* (bachelor, teetotaller) 常習的な jōshūteki na

confiscate [kɑːn'fiskeit] *vt* (impound, seize) 没収する bosshū suru

conflict [*n* kɑːn'flikt *vb* kənflikt'] *n* (disagreement) 論争 roṅsō; (difference: of interests, loyalties etc) 対立 taíritsu; (fighting) 戦闘 seṅtō
♦*vi* (opinions) 対立する taíritsu suru; (research etc) 矛盾する mujún suru

conflicting [kənflik'tiŋ] *adj* (reports) 矛盾する mujún suru; (interests etc) 対立する taíritsu suru

conform [kənfɔːrm'] *vi* (comply) 従う shitágaù

to conform to (law, wish, ideal) ...に従う ...ni shitágaù

confound [kənfaund'] *vt* (confuse) 当惑させる tówaku saséru

confront [kənfrʌnt'] *vt* (problems, task) ...と取組む ...to toríkumù; (enemy, danger) ...に立向かう ...ni tachímukaù

confrontation [kɑːnfrəntei'ʃən] *n* (dispute, conflict) 衝突 shótotsu

confuse [kənfjuːz'] *vt* (perplex: person) 当惑させる tówaku saséru; (mix up: two things, people etc) 混同する kofídō suru; (complicate: situation, plans) 混乱させる kofíran saséru

confused [kənfjuːzd'] *adj* (bewildered) 当惑した tówaku shitá; (disordered) 混乱した kofíran shitá

confusing [kənfjuː'ziŋ] *adj* (plot, instructions) 分かりにくい wakárinikuí

confusion [kənfjuː'ʒən] *n* (perplexity) 当惑 tówaku; (mix-up) 混同 kofídō; (disorder) 混乱 kofíran

congeal [kəndʒiːl'] *vi* (blood, sauce) 凝結する gyóketsu suru

congenial [kəndʒiːm'jəl] *adj* (person) 気の合った ki no attá; (atmosphere etc) 楽しい tanóshiî

congenital [kəndʒen'itəl] *adj* (MED: defect, illness) 先天性の sefítensei no

congested [kəndʒes'tid] *adj* (MED: with blood) うっ血した ukkétsu shitá; (: with mucus: nose) 詰まった tsumátta; (road) 渋滞した jútai shitá; (area) 人口密集の jifíkōmisshū no

congestion [kəndʒes'tʃən] *n* (MED: with blood) うっ血 ukkétsu; (: with mucus) 鼻詰まり hanázumàri; (of road) 渋滞 jútai; (of area) 人口密集 jifíkōmisshū

conglomerate [kənglɑːm'əːrit] *n* (COMM) 複合企業 fukúgōkigyð, コングロマリット kofíguromarítto

conglomeration [kənglɑːməreiʃ'ən] *n* (group, gathering) 寄せ集め yoséatsume

congratulate [kəngrætʃ'uleit] *vt* (parents, bridegroom etc) ...にお祝いを言う ...ni o-íwai wo iú

congratulations [kəngrætʃulei'ʃənz] *npl* 祝詞 shukúji

congratulations! おめでとうございます omédetō gozáimasù

congregate [kɑːŋ'grəgeit] *vi* (people) 集まる atsúmarù; (animals) 群がる murágarù

congregation [kɑːŋgrəgei'ʃən] *n* (of a church) 会衆 kaíshū

congress [kɑːŋ'gris] *n* (conference) 大会 taíkai; (US): *Congress* 議会 gikái

congressman [kɑːŋ'grismən] (*US: pl* **congressmen**) *n* 下院議員 ka-íngiîn

conical [kɑːn'ikəl] *adj* (shape) 円すい形の eñsuikei no

conifer [kou'nifəːr] *n* 針葉樹 shiñ-yòju

conjecture [kəndʒek'tʃəːr] *n* (speculation) 憶測 okúsoku

conjugal [kɑːn'dʒəgəl] *adj* 夫婦間の fúfùkàn no

conjugate [kɑːn'dʒəgeit] *vt* (LING) ...の活用形を挙げる ...no katsúyōkei wo agéru

conjunction [kəndʒʌŋk'ʃən] *n* (LING) 接続詞 setsúzokushî

conjunctivitis [kəndʒʌŋktəvai'tis] *n* (MED) 結膜炎 ketsúmakuèn

conjure [kɑːn'dʒəːr] *vi* (magician) 奇術をする kijútsu wo suru

conjurer [kɑːn'dʒəːrəːr] *n* (magician) 奇術師 kijútsushî, マジシャン majíshan

conjure up *vt* (ghost, spirit) 呼出す yobídasù; (memories) 思い起す omóiokosù

conk out [kɑːŋk-] (*inf*) *vi* (machine, engine) 故障する koshō suru

con man [kɑːn'mən] (*pl* **con men**) *n* ペてん師 peténshî

connect [kənekt'] *vt* (join, *also* TEL) つなぐ tsunágù; (ELEC) 接続する setsúzoku suru; (*fig*: associate) 関係付ける kafíkeizúkeru

♦*vi*: *to connect with* (train, plane etc) ...に連絡する ...ni refíraku suru

to be connected with (associated) 関係付ける kafíkeizúkeru

connection [kənek'∫ən] *n* (joint, link) つなぎ tsunági; (ELEC, TEL) 接続 setsúzoku; (train, plane etc) 連絡 reńraku; (*fig*: association) 関係 kańkei

connive [kənaiv'] *vi*: *to connive at* (misbehavior) …を容認する …wo yōnin suru

connoisseur [kɑːnisəːr'] *n* (of food, wine, art etc) 通 tsū

connotation [kɑːnətei'∫ən] *n* (implication) 含み fukúmi

conquer [kɑːŋ'kəːr] *vt* (MIL: country, enemy) 征服する seífuku suru; (fear, feelings) 克服する kokúfuku suru

conqueror [kɑːŋ'kəːrəːr] *n* (MIL) 征服者 seífukushà

conquest [kɑːn'kwest] *n* (MIL) 征服 seífuku; (prize) 勝ち得た物 kachíeta monó; (mastery: of space etc) 征服 seífuku

cons [kɑːnz] *npl see* **convenience; pro**

conscience [kɑːn'∫əns] *n* (sense of right and wrong) 良心 ryōshin

conscientious [kɑːn∫iːen'∫əs] *adj* (worker) 良心的な ryōshinteki na

conscious [kɑːn'∫əs] *adj* (aware): *conscious (of)* (…に) 気が付いている (…ni) ki ga tsuíte irù; (deliberate) 意識的な ishíkiteki na; (awake) 目が覚めている me ga samète irù

consciousness [kɑːn'∫əsnis] *n* (awareness, mentality: *also* MED) 意識 ishíki

conscript [kɑːn'skript] *n* (MIL) 徴集兵 chōshūhei

conscription [kənskrip'∫ən] *n* (MIL) 徴兵 chōhei

consecrate [kɑːn'səkreit] *vt* (building, place) 奉献する hōken suru

consecutive [kənsek'jətiv] *adj* (days, wins) 連続の reńzoku no

consensus [kənsen'səs] *n* 合意 gōi

consent [kənsent'] *n* (permission) 許可 kyóka
◆*vi*: *to consent to* …に同意する …ni dōi suru

consequence [kɑːn'səkwens] *n* (result) 結果 kekká; (significance) 重要さ jūyōsa

consequently [kɑːn'səkwentliː] *adv* (as a result, so) 従って shitágattè

conservation [kɑːnsəːrvei'∫ən] *n* (of the environment) 保護 hogò; (of energy) 節約 setsúyaku; (of paintings, books) 保全 hozén

conservative [kənsəːr'vətiv] *adj* (traditional, conventional: person, attitudes) 保守的な hoshúteki na; (cautious: estimate etc) 控え目な hikáeme no; (*BRIT*: POL): *Conservative* 保守党の hoshútō no
◆*n* (*BRIT*: POL): *Conservative* 保守党員 hoshútōin

conservatory [kənsəːr'vətɔːriː] *n* (greenhouse) 温室 oñshitsu; (MUS) 音楽学校 oñgaku gakkō

conserve [*vb* kənsəːrv' *n* kɑːn'səːrv] *vt* (preserve) 保護する hōgo suru; (supplies, energy) 節約する setsúyaku suru
◆*n* (jam) ジャム jámù

consider [kənsid'əːr] *vt* (believe) …だと思う …da to omóù; (study) 熟考する jukkō suru; (take into account) 考慮に入れる kōryo ni irérù
to consider doing something …しようかと考える …shiyō to kángaerù

considerable [kənsid'əːrəbəl] *adj* (amount, expense, difference etc) かなりの kanári no

considerably [kənsid'əːrəbliː] *adv* (improve, deteriorate) かなり kanári

considerate [kənsid'əːrit] *adj* (person) 思いやりのある omóiyari no arù

consideration [kənsidəːrei'∫ən] *n* (deliberation) 熟考 jukkō; (factor) 考慮すべき点 kōryo subeki tén; (thoughtfulness) 思いやり omóiyarì

considering [kənsid'əːriŋ] *prep* (bearing in mind) …を考慮すると …wo kōryo suru to

consign [kənsain'] *vt* (something unwanted): *to consign to* (place) …にしまっておく …ni shimátte okù; (person): *to consign to* (someone's care etc) …に委ねる …ni yudánerù; (poverty etc) …に追込む …ni oíkomù

consignment [kənsain'mənt] *n* (COMM) 輸送貨物 yusōkamòtsu

consist [kənsist'] *vi*: *to consist of* (com-

prise) ...から成る ...kará narù

consistency [kənsís'tənsi:] *n* (of actions, policies etc) 一貫性 ikkánsei; (of yoghurt, cream etc) 固さ katása

consistent [kənsís'tənt] *adj* (person) 変らない kawáranaì; (argument, idea) 一貫性のある ikkánsei no arù

consolation [kɑːnsəlei'ʃən] *n* (comfort) 慰め nagúsame

console [*vb* kənsoul' *n* kɑːn'soul] *vt* (comfort) 慰める nagúsamerù
◆*n* (panel) コンソール koñsòru

consolidate [kənsɑːl'ideit] *vt* (position, power) 強化する kyôka suru

consommé [kɑːnsəmei'] *n* (CULIN) コンソメ koñsome

consonant [kɑːn'sənənt] *n* (LING) 子音 shíin

consortium [kənsɔːr'ʃiːəm] *n* (COMM) 協会 kyôkai

conspicuous [kənspík'juːəs] *adj* (noticeable: person, feature) 目立つ medátsu

conspiracy [kənspír'əsiː] *n* (plot) 陰謀 iñbò

conspire [kənspai'əːr] *vi* (criminals, revolutionaries etc) 共謀する kyôbō suru; (events) 相重なる aíkasanarù

constable [kɑːn'stəbəl] (*BRIT*) *n* 巡査 juñsa

chief constable (*BRIT*) 警察本部長 keísatsu hoñbuchò

constabulary [kənstæb'jələːriː] (*BRIT*) *n* 警察 keísatsu ◇一地区の警察隊を指す ichíchiku no keísatsutai wo sasù

constant [kɑːn'stənt] *adj* (continuous: criticism, pain) 絶えない taénai; (fixed: temperature, level) 一定の ittéi no

constantly [kɑːn'stəntliː] *adv* (continually) 絶間なく taémanàku

constellation [kɑːnstəlei'ʃən] *n* (ASTRONOMY) 星座 seíza

consternation [kɑːnstəːrnei'ʃən] *n* (dismay) ろうばい ròbai

constipated [kɑːn'stəpeitid] *adj* (MED) 便秘している beñpi shité irù

constipation [kɑːnstəpei'ʃən] *n* (MED) 便秘 beñpi

constituency [kənstítʃ'uːənsiː] *n* (POL:

area) 選挙区 señkyokù; (: electors) 選挙民 señkyomìn

constituent [kənstítʃ'uːənt] *n* (POL) 有権者 yúkeñsha; (component) 部分 bûbun

constitute [kɑːn'stitut] *vt* (represent: challenge, emergency) ...である ...de arù; (make up: whole) 構成する kôsei suru

constitution [kɑːnstitu'ʃən] *n* (of country) 憲法 kéñpō; (of club etc) 会則 kaísoku; (health) 体質 taíshitsu; (make-up: of committee etc) 構成 kôsei

constitutional [kɑːnstitu'ʃənəl] *adj* (government, reform etc) 憲法の kéñpō no

constraint [kənstreint'] *n* (restriction) 制限 seígen; (compulsion) 強制 kyôsei

construct [kɑːn'strʌkt] *vt* (building) 建てる tatérù; (bridge, road etc) 建設する keñsetsu suru; (machine) 作る tsukúrù

construction [kənstrʌk'ʃən] *n* (of building etc) 建築 keñchiku; (of bridge, road etc) 建設 keñsetsu; (of machine) 製作 seísaku; (structure) 構造物 kôzōbùtsu

constructive [kənstrʌk'tiv] *adj* (remark, criticism) 建設的な keñsetsuteki na

construe [kənstruː'] *vt* (statement, event) 解釈する kaíshaku suru

consul [kɑːn'səl] *n* 領事 ryôji

consulate [kɑːn'səlit] *n* 領事館 ryôjikàn

consult [kənsʌlt'] *vt* (doctor, lawyer, friend) ...に相談する ...ni sôdan suru; (reference book) 調べる shiráberù

consultant [kənsʌl'tənt] *n* (MED) 顧問医 komón-i; (other specialist) 顧問 kômòn, コンサルタント koñsarùtanto

consultation [kɑːnsəltei'ʃən] *n* (MED) 診察 shiñsatsu; (discussion) 協議 kyôgi

consulting room [kənsʌl'tiŋ-] (*BRIT*) *n* 診察室 shiñsatsushìtsu

consume [kənsuːm'] *vt* (food) 食べる tabérù; (drink) 飲む nómù; (fuel, energy, time etc) 消費する shôhi suru

consumer [kənsuː'məːr] *n* (COMM) 消費者 shôhishà

consumer goods *npl* 消費財 shôhizài

consumerism [kənsuː'məːrizəm] *n* 消費者運動 shôhishauñdō

consumer society n 消費社会 shōhisha-
kāi

consummate [kɑːnˈsəmeit] vt (ambition
etc) 全うする mattō suru

to consummate a marriage 床入りす
る tokó-iri suru

consumption [kənsʌmpˈʃən] n (of food)
食べる事 tabérù kotó; (of drink) 飲む事
nómù kotó; (of fuel, energy, time etc) 消
費 shōhi; (amount consumed) 消費量 shō-
hiryō; (buying) 消費 shōhi

cont. abbr (= continued) 続く tsuzúku

contact [kɑːnˈtækt] n (communication)
連絡 reńraku; (touch) 接触 sesshóku;
(person) 連絡相手 reńrakuaìte

◆vt (by phone, letter) ...に連絡する ...ni
reńraku suru

contact lenses npl コンタクトレンズ
koñtakutoreñzu

contagious [kəntei'dʒəs] adj (MED: disease) 伝染性の deńsensei no; (fig: laughter, enthusiasm) 移りやすい utsúriyasuì

contain [kəntein'] vt (hold: objects) ...に
...が入っている ...ni ...ga haítte irù; (have:
component, ingredient etc) ...に...が含ま
れている ...ni ...ga fukúmarète irù; (subj:
piece of writing, report etc) ...に...が書い
てある ...ni ...ga kaíte arù; (curb: growth,
spread, feeling) 抑える osáerù

to contain oneself 自制する jiséi suru

container [kəntei'nəːr] n (box, jar etc)
入れ物 irémono; (COMM: for shipping
etc) コンテナー koñtenā

contaminate [kəntæm'əneit] vt (water,
food, soil etc) 汚染する osén suru

contamination [kəntæmənei'ʃən] n (of
water, food, soil etc) 汚染 osén

cont'd abbr (= continued) 続く tsuzuku

contemplate [kɑːnˈtəmpleit] vt (idea,
subject, course of action) じっくり考え
る jikkúrì kańgaerù; (person, painting
etc) 眺める nagámerù

contemporary [kəntem'pəːri:] adj
(present-day) 現代の geńdai no; (belonging to same time) 同時代の dójidai no

◆n (person) 同時代の人 dójidai no hitó

contempt [kəntempt'] n (scorn) 軽べつ
keíbetsu

contempt of court (LAW) 法廷侮辱罪
hōteibujokuzài

contemptible [kəntemp'təbəl] adj (conduct) 卑劣な hirétsu na

contemptuous [kəntemp'tʃuːəs] adj
(attitude) 軽べつ的な keíbetsuteki na

contend [kəntend'] vt (assert): to contend that ...だと主張する ...da to shuchō suru

◆vi (struggle): to contend with (problem, difficulty) ...と戦う ...to tatákaù;
(compete): to contend for (power etc)
...を争う ...wo arásoù

contender [kətend'əːr] n (in competition) 競争者 kyōsōshà; (POL) 候補者 kō-
hoshà; (SPORT) 選手 séñshu

content [adj, vb kəntent' n kɑːn'tent]
adj (happy and satisfied) 満足して mañzoku shitê

◆vt (satisfy) 満足させる mañzoku saséru

◆n (of speech, novel) 内容 naíyō; (fat
content, moisture content etc) 含有量
gañ-yūryò

contented [kɑːntentid] adj (happy and
satisfied) 満足して mañzoku shitê

contention [kəntenˈʃən] n (assertion) 主
張 shuchō; (disagreement, argument) 論
争 roñsō

contentment [kəntentˈmənt] n (happiness, satisfaction) 満足 mañzoku

contents [kɑːn'tents] npl (of bottle,
packet) 中身 nakámì; (of book) 内容 naíyō

(table of) contents 目次 mokúji

contest [n kɑːn'test vb kəntest'] n
(competition) コンテスト kóñtesuto, コ
ンクール kóñkūru; (struggle: for control,
power etc) 争い arásoì

◆vt (election, competition) ...で競う ...de
kisóù; (statement, decision: also LAW)
...に対して異議を申立てる ...ni taíshite
igí wo mōshítaterù

contestant [kəntes'tənt] n (in quiz, competition) 参加者 sañkashà; (in fight) 競争
者 kyōsōshà

context [kɑːn'tekst] n (circumstances:
of events, ideas etc) 背景 haíkei; (of
word, phrase) 文脈 buñmyaku

continent [kɑːn'tənənt] *n* (land mass) 大陸 tairiku

the Continent (*BRIT*) ヨーロッパ大陸 yōroppa tairiku

continental [kɑːntənen'təl] *adj* 大陸の tairiku no

continental quilt (*BRIT*) *n* 掛布団 kakebuton

contingency [kəntin'dʒənsi:] *n* 有事 yūji

contingent [kəntin'dʒənt] *n* (group of people: *also* MIL) 一団 ichidan

continual [kəntin'ju:əl] *adj* (movement, process, rain etc) 絶間ない taemanái

continually [kəntin'ju:əli:] *adv* 絶間なく taemanáku

continuation [kəntinju:ei'ʃən] *n* 継続 keízoku

continue [kəntin'ju:] *vi* 続く tsuzúkù
♦*vt* 続ける tsuzúkerù

continuity [kɑːtənu:'iti:] *n* (in policy, management etc) 連続性 reńzokusei; (TV, CINEMA) 撮影台本 satsúeidaíhon, コンテ kôñte

continuous [kəntin'ju:əs] *adj* (process, growth etc) 絶間ない taemanái; (line) 途切れのない togíre no naí; (LING) 進行形の shiñkokei no

continuous stationery *n* 連続用紙 reñzokuyôshi

contort [kəntɔːrt'] *vt* (body) ねじる nejírù; (face) しかめる shikámerù

contortion [kəntɔːr'ʃən] *n* (of body) ねじれ nejíre; (of face) こわばり kowábari

contour [kɑːn'tuːr] *n* (on map: *also*: **contour line**) 等高線 tôkōsen; (shape, outline: *gen pl*) 輪郭 riñkaku

contraband [kɑːn'trəbænd] *n* 密輸品 mitsúyuhìn

contraception [kɑːntrəsep'ʃən] *n* 避妊 hinín

contraceptive [kɑːntrəsep'tiv] *adj* (method, technique) 避妊の hinín no
♦*n* (device) 避妊用具 hinín yôgu; (pill etc) 避妊薬 hinín-yaku

contract [*n* kɑːn'trækt *vb* kəntrækt'] *n* (LAW, COMM) 契約 keíyaku
♦*vi* (become smaller) 収縮する shúshuku suru; (COMM): **to contract to do**

something ...をする契約をする ...wo suru keíyaku wo suru
♦*vt* (illness) ...に掛かる ...ni kakárù

contraction [kəntræk'ʃən] *n* (of metal, muscle) 収縮 shúshuku; (of word, phrase) 短縮形 tañshukukei

contractor [kɑːn'træktər] *n* (COMM) 請負人 ukéoinìn

contradict [kɑːntrədikt'] *vt* (person) ...の言う事を否定する ...no iú kotó wo hitéi suru; (statement etc) 否定する hitéi suru

contradiction [kɑːntrədik'ʃən] *n* (inconsistency) 矛盾 mujún

contradictory [kɑːntrədik'tə:ri:] *adj* (ideas, statements) 矛盾する mujún suru

contraption [kəntræp'ʃən] (*pej*) *n* (device, machine) 珍妙な機械 chiñmyō na kikâî

contrary[1] [kɑːn'tre:ri:] *adj* (opposite, different) 反対の hañtai no
♦*n* (opposite) 反対 hañtai

on the contrary それどころか soŕédokoro ka

unless you hear to the contrary そうではないと聞かされない限り sō de wa naí to kikásarenái kagíri

contrary[2] [kəntre:r'i:] *adj* (perverse) つむじ曲りな tsumújimagàri na, へそ曲りな hesómagari na

contrast [*n* kɑːn'træst *vb* kəntræst'] *n* (difference) 相違 sôi, コントラスト koñtorasùto
♦*vt* (techniques, texts etc) 対照する taíshō suru

in contrast to ...と違って ...to chigátte

contrasting [kəntræs'tiŋ] *adj* (colors, attitudes) 対照的な taíshōteki na

contravene [kɑːntrəvi:n'] *vt* (law) ...に違反する ...ni ihán suru

contribute [kəntrib'ju:t] *vi* (give) 寄付する kifú suru
♦*vt*: *to contribute an article to* (commissioned) ...に記事を寄稿する ...ni kíjî wo kikô suru; (unsolicited) ...に記事を投稿する ...ni kíjî wo tôkô suru; *to contribute $10* 10ドルを寄付する júdòru wo kifú suru

to contribute to (charity) ...に寄付する ...ni kifú suru; (newspaper: commissioned) ...に寄稿する ...ni kikō suru; (unsolicited) ...に投稿する ...ni tṓkō suru; (discussion) 意見を言う ikén wo iú; (problem etc) ...を悪くする ...wo warúkù surú

contribution [kɑːntrəbjuː'ʃən] n (donation) 寄付 kifu; (BRIT: for social security) 掛金 kakékìn; (to debate, campaign) 貢献 kṓken; (to journal: commissioned) 寄稿 kikṓ; (: unsolicited) 投稿 tṓkō

contributor [kəntrib'jətəːr] n (to appeal) 寄付者 kifúshà; (to newspaper) 投稿者〔寄稿者〕 tṓkōshà〔kikṓshà〕

contrive [kəntraiv'] vi: ***to contrive to do*** 努力して...に成功する doryòku shite ...ni seíkō suru

control [kəntroul'] vt (country, organization) 支配する shíhaî suru; (machinery, process) 制御する seígyo suru; (wages, prices) 規制する kiséi suru; (temper) 自制する jiséi suru; (disease) 抑制する yokúsei suru

♦n (of country, organization) 支配 shíhaî; (of oneself, emotions) 自制心 jiséishin

to be in control of (situation) ...を掌握している ...wo shṓaku shité irù; (car etc) ...を思いのままに動かしている ...wo o-móì no mamá ni ugókashite irù

under control (crowd) 指示に従って shijí ni shitágatte; (situation) 収拾が付いて shūshū ga tsuíte; (dog) 言う事を聞いて iú kotó wo kíîte

out of control (crowd) 制止が利かなくなって seíshi ga kikánakù natté; (situation) 手に負えなくなって te ni oénakù natté; (dog) 言う事を聞かなくなって iú kotó wo kikánakù natté

control panel n 制御盤 seígyoban

control room n 制御室 seígyoshìtsu

controls [kəntroulz'] npl (of vehicle) ハンドル hándoru ♡ブレーキ、クラッチなど全ての運転制御装置を含む burḗki, kurátchî nadò subéte no uñtenseigyosṓchi wo fukúmù; (on radio, television etc) コントロール盤 koñtorṓruban ♡全てのス

イッチ、調節用つまみ、ボタンなどを含む subete no suítchî, chōsetsu yō tsumami, botán nadò wo fukúmù; (governmental) 規制 kiséi

control tower n (AVIAT) 管制塔 kañseitō

controversial [kɑːntrəvəːr'ʃəl] adj (topic, person) 論争の的になっている roñsō no matò ni natté irù

controversy [kɑːn'trəvəːrsiː] n 論争 roñsō

conurbation [kɑːnəːrbei'ʃən] n 大都市圏 daítoshikèn

convalesce [kɑːnvəles'] vi (MED) 回復する kaífuku suru

convalescence [kɑːnvəles'əns] n (MED) 回復期 kaífukukì

convector [kənvek'təːr] n (heater) 対流式暖房器 taíryūshikidanbōkî, コンベクター koñbekūtā

convene [kənviːn'] vt (meeting, conference) 召集する shōshū suru

♦vi (parliament, inquiry) 開会する kaíkai suru

convenience [kənviːn'jəns] n (easiness: of using something, doing something) 便利 béñri; (suitability: of date, meeting, house etc) 好都合 kṓtsugō; (advantage, help) 便宜 béñgi

at your convenience ご都合の良い時に go-tsúgō no yoì tokí ni

all modern conveniences, (BRIT) ***all mod cons*** 近代設備完備 kiñdaisetsubikañbi ♡不動産の広告などに使われる語句 fudósan no kṓkoku nadò ni tsukáwarerù gokù

convenient [kənviːn'jənt] adj (handy) 便利な béñri na; (suitable) 都合の良い tsugṓ no yoì

convent [kɑːn'vent] n (REL) 女子修道院 joshíshūdòin

convention [kənven'ʃən] n (custom) 慣例 kañrei; (conference) 大会 taíkai; (agreement) 協定 kyṓtei

conventional [kənven'ʃənəl] adj (person) 型にはまった katá ni hamátta; (method) 伝統的な deñtōteki na

converge [kənvəːrdʒ'] vi (roads) 合流す

る gőryū suru; (people): *to converge on* (place, person) ...に集まる ...ni atsúmarù

conversant [kənvə:r'sənt] *adj*: *to be conversant with* (problem, requirements) ...に通じている ...ni tsújite irù

conversation [kɑ:nvə:rsei'ʃən] *n* (talk) 会話 kaíwa

conversational [kɑ:nvə:rsei'ʃənəl] *adj* (tone, language, skills) 会話的な kaíwateki na

converse [*n* kɑ:n'və:rs *vb* kənvə:rs'] *n* (of statement) 逆 gyakú

♦*vi* (talk): *to converse (with someone)* (...と) 話をする (...to) hanáshi wo suru

conversely [kənvə:rs'li:] *adv* 逆に gyakú ni

conversion [kənvə:r'ʒən] *n* (of weights, substances etc) 変換 heñkan; (REL) 改宗 kaíshū

convert [*vb* kənvə:rt' *n* kɑ:n'və:rt] *vt* (change): *to convert something into/to* ...を...に変換する ...wo ...ni heñkan suru; (person: REL) 改宗させる kaíshū saséru; (: POL) 党籍を変えさせる tōseki wo kaésaserù

♦*n* (REL) 改宗者 kaíshūsha; (POL) 党籍を変える人 tōseki wo kaéru hitó

convertible [kənvə:r'təbəl] *n* (AUT) コンバーチブル koñbáchibùru ◇畳み込み式屋根を持つ乗用車 tatámikomishiki yané wo motsù jőyōsha

convex [kɑ:nveks'] *adj* 凸面の totsúmen no

convey [kənvei'] *vt* (information, idea, thanks) 伝える tsutáerù; (cargo, traveler) 運ぶ hakóbu

conveyor belt [kənvei'ə:r-] *n* ベルトコンベヤー berútokonbeyà

convict [*vb* kənvikt' *n* kɑ:n'vikt] *vt* (of a crime) ...に有罪の判決を下す ...ni yūzai no hañketsu wo kudásù

♦*n* (person) 囚人 shūjin

conviction [kənvik'ʃən] *n* (belief) 信念 shíñnen; (certainty) 確信 kakúshin; (LAW) 有罪判決 yūzaihañketsu

convince [kənvins'] *vt* (assure) 分からせる wakáraserù; (persuade) 納得させる

nattóku saséru

convinced [kənvinst'] *adj*: *convinced of/that* ...を〔だと〕確信している ...wo 〔dátò〕 kakúshin shitè irù

convincing [kənvin'siŋ] *adj* (case, argument) 納得のいく nattóku no ikú

convoluted [kɑ:n'vəlu:tid] *adj* (statement, argument) 込入った komfittà

convoy [kɑ:n'vɔi] *n* (of trucks) 護衛付き輸送車隊 goéitsuki yusōshatai; (of ships) 護衛付き輸送船団 goéitsukiyusōseñdan

convulse [kənvʌls'] *vt*: *to be convulsed with laughter* 笑いこける waráikokerù

to be convulsed with pain もだえる modáerù

convulsion [kənvʌl'ʃən] *n* (MED) けいれん keíren

coo [ku:] *vi* (dove, pigeon) くーくー鳴く kūkū nakú; (person) 優しい声で言う yasáshii koè de iú

cook [kuk] *vt* (food, meal) 料理する ryőri suru

♦*vi* (person) 料理する ryőri suru; (meat, pie etc) 焼ける yakéru

♦*n* 料理人 ryőrinìn, コック kokkù

cookbook [kuk'buk] *n* 料理の本 ryőri no hoñ

cooker [kuk'ə:r] *n* (stove) レンジ rénji

cookery [kuk'ə:ri:] *n* 料理する事 ryőri suru kotő

cookery book (*BRIT*) *n* = **cookbook**

cookie [kuk'i:] (*US*) *n* ビスケット bisúkettò, クッキー kúkkì

cooking [kuk'iŋ] *n* (activity) 料理すること ryőri suru kotő; (food) 料理 ryőri

cool [ku:l] *adj* (temperature, clothes) 涼しい suzúshiì; (drink) 冷たい tsumétai; (person: calm) 落着いている ochítsuite irù; (: unfriendly) そっけない sokkénaì

♦*vt* (make colder: tea) 冷ます samásù; (: room) 冷す hiyásù

♦*vi* (become colder: water) 冷たくなる tsumétaku narù; (: air) 涼しくなる suzúshiku narù

coolness [ku:l'nis] *n* (of temperature, clothing) 涼しさ suzúshisà; (of drink) 冷たさ tsumétasà; (calm) 落着き ochítsuki;

(unfriendliness) そっけなさ sokkénasà

coop [ku:p] *n* (*also*: **rabbit coop**) ウサギ小屋 uságigoya; (*also*: **hen coop**) ニワトリ小屋 niwátorigoya

♦*vt*: **to coop up** (*fig*: imprison) 閉込める tojíkomerù

cooperate [kouɑ:p'əreit] *vi* (collaborate) 協同する kyōdō suru; (assist) 協力する kyōryoku suru

cooperation [kouɑ:pərei'ʃən] *n* (collaboration) 協同 kyōdō; (assistance) 協力 kyōryoku

cooperative [kouɑ:p'rətiv] *adj* (farm, business) 協同組合の kyōdōkùmiai no; (person) 協力的な kyōryokuteki na

♦*n* (factory, business) 協同組合 kyōdōkùmiai

coordinate [*vb* kouɔ:r'dəneit *n* kouɔ:r'dənit] *vt* (activity, attack) 指揮する shikí suru; (movements) 調整する chōsei suru

♦*n* (MATH) 座標 zahyō

coordinates [kouɔ:r'dənits] *npl* (clothes) コーディネートされた服 kōdinēto saréta fukú

coordination [kouɔ:rdənei'ʃən] *n* (of services) 指揮 shikí; (of one's movements) 調整 chōsei

co-ownership [kouou'nə:rʃip] *n* 協同所有 kyōdōshoyū

cop [kɑ:p] (*inf*) *n* (policeman/woman) 警官 keíkan

cope [koup] *vi*: **to cope with** (problem, situation etc) …に対応する …ni taíō suru

copious [kou'pi:əs] *adj* (helpings) たっぷりの táppùri no

copious amounts of 多量の taryō no

copper [kɑ:p'ə:r] *n* (metal) 銅 dō; (*inf*: policeman/woman) 警官 keíkan

coppers [kɑ:p'ə:rz] *npl* (small change, coins) 小銭 kozéni

coppice [kɑ:p'is] *n* 木立 kodáchi

copse [kɑ:ps] *n* = **coppice**

copulate [kɑ:p'jəleit] *vi* (people) 性交する seíkō suru; (animals) 交尾する kóbi suru

copy [kɑ:p'i:] *n* (duplicate) 複写 fukúsha, コピー kópī; (of book) 1冊 issátsu; (of

record) 1枚 ichímaì; (of newspaper) 1部 ichíbù

♦*vt* (person, idea etc) まねる manérù; (something written) 複写する fukúsha suru, コピーする kópī suru

copyright [kɑ:p'i:rait] *n* 著作権 chosákukèn

coral [kɔ:r'əl] *n* (substance) さんご sańgo

coral reef *n* さんご礁 sańgoshō

cord [kɔ:rd] *n* (string) ひも himó; (ELEC) コード kōdo; (fabric) コールテン kōruten

cordial [kɔ:r'dʒəl] *adj* (person, welcome) 暖かい atátakaì; (relationship) 親密な shińmitsu na

♦*n* (*BRIT*: drink) フルーツシロップ furūtsu shiróppu

cordon [kɔ:r'dən] *n* (MIL, POLICE) 非常線 hijōsen

cordon off *vt* 非常線を張って…への立入りを禁止する hijōsen wo hatté …e no tachíri wo kińshi suru

corduroy [kɔ:r'dəɾɔi] *n* コールテン kōruten

core [kɔ:r] *n* (of fruit) しん shiń; (of organization, system, building) 中心部 chūshiñbu; (heart: of problem) 核心 kakúshin

♦*vt* (an apple, pear etc) …のしんをくりぬく …no shiń wo kurínukù

coriander [kɔ:ri:æn'də:r] *n* (spice) コリアンダー korían̄da

cork [kɔ:rk] *n* (stopper) 栓 séñ; (bark) コルク kórùku

corkscrew [kɔ:rk'skru:] *n* 栓抜き seńnuki

corn [kɔ:rn] *n* (*US*: maize) トウモロコシ tómorðkoshi; (*BRIT*: cereal crop) 穀物 kokúmotsu; (on foot) 魚の目 uó no mé

corn on the cob 軸付きトウモロコシ jikútsuki tómorðkoshi

cornea [kɔ:r'ni:ə] *n* (of eye) 角膜 kakúmaku

corned beef [kɔ:rnd-] *n* コーンビーフ kőnbìfu

corner [kɔ:r'nə:r] *n* (outside) 角 kádð; (inside) 隅 súmì; (in road) 角 kádð; (SOCCER) コーナーキック kőnākikkù; (BOXING) コーナー kōnā

♦*vt* (trap) 追詰める oítsumerù; 袋のネズ

ミにする fukúro no nezumi ni suru;
(COMM: market) 独占する dokúsen suru

♦*vi* (in car) コーナリングする kónariňgu
surù

cornerstone [kɔːr'nərːrstoun] *n* (*fig*) 土台
dodái

cornet [kɔːr'net'] *n* (MUS) コルネット
korúnettò; (*BRIT*: of ice-cream) アイス
クリームコーン aísukurímukòn

cornflakes [kɔːrn'fleiks] *npl* コーンフレ
ーク kónfurèku

cornflour [kɔːrn'flauəːr] (*BRIT*) *n* =
cornstarch

cornstarch [kɔːrn'stɑːrtʃ] (*US*) *n* コーン
スターチ kónsutàchi

Cornwall [kourn'wɔːl] *n* コーンウォール
kón-uòru

corny [kɔːr'niː] (*inf*) *adj* (joke) さえない
saénai

corollary [kɔːr'əleːriː] *n* (of fact, idea) 当
然の結果 tózen no kekká

coronary [kɔːr'əneːriː] *n* (*also*: **coronary
thrombosis**) 肝動脈血栓症 kańdōmyaku-
kessēnshō

coronation [kɔːrənei'ʃən] *n* たい冠式 taí-
kaňshiki

coroner [kɔːr'əneːr] *n* (LAW) 検死官 keń-
shikàn

coronet [kɔːr'ənit] *n* コロネット koró-
nettò ◇貴族などがかぶる小さな冠 kizó-
ku nadò ga kabúrù chíisana kańmuri

corporal [kɔːr'pəːrəl] *n* (MIL) ご長 gó-
chō

♦*adj*: **corporal punishment** 体罰 táibat-
su

corporate [kɔːr'pərit] *adj* (action,
effort, ownership) 共同の kyódō no;
(finance, image) 企業の kigyó no

corporation [kɔːrpərei'ʃən] *n* (COMM)
企業 kigyó; (of town) 行政部 gyóseibù

corps [kɔːr *pl* kɔːrz] (*pl* **corps**) *n* (MIL)
兵団 heídan; (of diplomats, journalists)
...団 ...dàn

corpse [kɔːrps] *n* 遺体 itái

corpuscle [kɔːr'pəsəl] *n* (BIO) 血球 kek-
kyū

corral [kəræl'] *n* (for cattle, horses) 囲い

kakói

correct [kərekt'] *adj* (right) 正しい tadá-
shìi; (proper) 礼儀正しい reígitadashìi

♦*vt* (mistake, fault) 直す naósu; (exam)
採点する saíten suru

correction [kərek'ʃən] *n* (act of correcting) 直す事 naósù kotó; (instance) 直し
naóshi

correlation [kɔːrəlei'ʃən] *n* (link) 相互関
係 sógokaňkei

correspond [kɔːrəspɑːnd'] *vi* (write): *to
correspond (with)* (...と) 手紙のやり
取りをする (...to) tegámi no yarítòri
wo surù; (be equivalent): *to correspond
(to)* (...に) 相当する (...ni) sótō suru;
(be in accordance): *to correspond
(with)* (...と) 一致する (...to) itchí
suru

correspondence [kɔːrəspɑːn'dəns] *n*
(letters) 手紙 tegámi; (communication
by letters) 文通 buńtsū; (relationship) 一
致 itchí

correspondence course *n* (SCOL) 通
信講座 tsúshinkōza

correspondent [kɔːrəspɑːn'dənt] *n*
(journalist) 特派員 tokúhaìn

corridor [kɔːr'idəːr] *n* (in house, building
etc) 廊下 róka; (in train) 通路 tsúro

corroborate [kərɑːb'əreit] *vt* (facts,
story) 裏付ける urázukerù

corrode [kəroud'] *vt* (metal) 浸食する
shińshoku suru

♦*vi* (metal) 腐食する fushóku suru

corrosion [kərou'ʒən] *n* 腐食 fushóku

corrugated [kɔːr'əgeitid] *adj* (roof,
cardboard) 波型の namígata no

corrugated iron *n* なまこ板 namákoi-
tà

corrupt [kərʌpt'] *adj* (person) 腐敗した
fuhái shitá; (COMPUT: data) 化けたba-
kétà, 壊れた kowáretà

♦*vt* (person) 買収する baíshū suru;
(COMPUT: data) 化けさせる bakésase-
rù

corruption [kərʌp'ʃən] *n* (of person) 汚
職 oshóku; (COMPUT: of data) 化ける事
bakérù kotó

corset [kɔːr'sit] *n* (undergarment: *also*

MED) コルセット kórùsetto

Corsica [kɔːr'sikə] n コルシカ島 korúshikatō

cosh [kɑːʃ] (BRIT) n (cudgel) こん棒 końbō

cosmetic [kɑːzmet'ik] n (beauty product) 化粧品 keshṓhin

◆adj (fig: measure, improvement) 表面的な hyṓmenteki na

cosmic [kɑːz'mik] adj 宇宙の uchū no

cosmonaut [kɑːz'mənɔːt] n 宇宙飛行士 uchūhikóshi

cosmopolitan [kɑːzməpəl'itən] adj (place, person) 国際的な kokúsaiteki na

cosmos [kɑːz'məs] n 宇宙 uchū

cosset [kɑːs'it] vt (person) 甘やかす amáyakasù

cost [kɔːst] n (price) 値段 nedán; (expenditure) 費用 híyō

◆vt (pt, pp cost) (be priced at) ...の値段である ...no nedán de arù; (find out cost of: project, purchase etc: pt, pp costed) ...の費用を見積る ...no hiyō wo mitsúmorù

how much does it cost? いくらですか ikúra desu ká

to cost someone time/effort ...に時間〔労力〕を要する ...ni jikán〔rṓryoku〕wo yṓ surù

it cost him his life そのために彼は命をなくした sono tamé ni kárè wa ínòchi wo nákù shitá

at all costs 何があっても nanî ga atté mò

co-star [kou'stɑːr] n (TV, CINEMA) 共演者 kyōeńsha

cost-effective [kɔːstifek'tiv] adj 費用効果比の高い hiyṓkōkahi no takáî

costly [kɔːst'liː] adj (high-priced) 値段の高い nedán no takáî; (involving much expenditure) 費用の掛かる hiyō no kakárù

cost-of-living [kɔːstəvliv'iŋ] adj (allowance, index) 生計費の seíkeîhi no

council estate [kaun'səl] n 議員 gíin

cost price (BRIT) n 原価 génka

costs [kɔːsts] npl (COMM: overheads) 経費 kéîhi; (LAW) 訴訟費用 soshōhiyō

costume [kɑːs'tuːm] n (outfit, style of

dress) 衣装 íshō; (BRIT: also: swimming costume) 水着 mizúgi

costume jewelry n 模造宝石類 mozṓhōsekirùi

cosy [kou'ziː] (BRIT) adj = cozy

cot [kɑːt] n (BRIT: child's) ベビーベッド bebíbeddò; (US: campbed) キャンプベッド kyańpubeddò

cottage [kɑːt'idʒ] n (house) 小さな家 chîisa na ie, コッテージ kottḗji

cottage cheese n カッテージチーズ kattḗji chīzù

cotton [kɑːt'ən] n (fabric) 木綿 momén, コットン kóttòn; (BRIT: thread) 縫い糸 nuí-itò

cotton batting [-bæt'iŋ] n (US) 脱脂綿 dasshímèn

cotton candy (US) n (candy floss) 綿菓子 watágashì, 綿あめ watá-àme

cotton on to (inf) vt fus ...に気が付く ...ni kî ga tsúkù

cotton wool (BRIT) n = cotton batting

couch [kautʃ] n (sofa) ソファー sófà; (doctor's) 診察台 shińsatsudai

couchette [kuːʃet'] n (on train, boat) 寝台 shiñdai ◇昼間壁に畳み掛けるか普通の座席に使う物を指す hiruma kabé ni tatámikakerù ka futsū no zaséki ni tsukáù monó wo sasù

cough [kɔːf] vi (person) せきをする sekí wo surù

◆n (noise) せき sekí; (illness) せきの多い病気 sekí no ōi byṓki

cough drop n せき止めドロップ sekídome doróppu

could [kud] pt of can

couldn't [kud'ənt] = could not

council [kaun'səl] n (committee, board) 評議会 hyṓgikài

city/town council 市〔町〕議会 shi〔chṓ〕gíkài

council estate (BRIT) n 公営住宅団地 kṓeijūtakudañchi

council house (BRIT) n 公営住宅 kṓeijùtaku

councillor [kaun'sələːr] n 議員 gíin

counsel [kaun'səl] n (advice) 助言 jogén;

(lawyer) 弁護人 beñgonin

♦*vt* (advise) ...に助言する ...ni jogén suru

counsel(l)or [kaun'sələr] *n* (advisor) カ
ウンセラー káunserā; (*US*: lawyer) 弁護
人 beñgonin

count [kaunt] *vt* (add up: numbers,
money, things, people) 数える kazóerù;
(include) 入れる iréru, 含む fukúmù

♦*vi* (enumerate) 数える kazóerù; (be
considered) ...と見なされる ...to minasa-
reru; (be valid) 効果をもつ kṓka wo mṓ-
tsù

♦*n* (of things, people, votes) 数 kazù;
(level: of pollen, alcohol etc) 値 atái, 数
値 sùchi; (nobleman) 伯爵 hakúshaku

countdown [kaunt'daun] *n* (to launch)
秒読み byṓyomi

countenance [kaun'tənəns] *n* (face) 顔
kaó

♦*vt* (tolerate) 容認する yṓnin suru

counter [kaun'tər] *n* (in shop, café,
bank etc) カウンター káuntā; (in game)
こま komá

♦*vt* (oppose) ...に対抗する ...ni taikō suru

♦*adv*: **counter to** ...に反して ...ni hañ
shite

counteract [kauntə:rækt'] *vt* (effect,
tendency) 打消す uchíkesu

counter-espionage [kauntə:res'pi:ə-
nɑ:ʒ] *n* 対抗的スパイ活動 taíkōteki supá-
ikatsudō

counterfeit [kaun'tə:rfit] *n* (forgery) 偽
物 nisémono

♦*vt* (forge) 偽造する gizṓ suru

♦*adj* (coin) 偽物の nisémono no

counterfoil [kaun'tə:rfoil] *n* (of check,
money order) 控え hikáe

countermand [kauntə:rmænd'] *vt*
(order) 取消す toríkesu

counterpart [kaun'tə:rpɑ:rt] *n*: **counterpart of** (person) ...に相当する人 ...ni
sṓtō suru hitó; (thing) ...に相当するもの
...ni sṓtō suru mono

counterproductive [kauntə:rprədʌk'-
tiv] *adj* (measure, policy etc) 逆効果的な
gyakúkōkateki na

countersign [kaun'tə:rsain] *vt* (document) ...に副署する ...ni fukúsho surù

countess [kaun'tis] *n* 伯爵夫人 hakúsha-
kufùjin

countless [kaunt'lis] *adj* (innumerable)
無数の músū no

count on *vt fus* (expect) ...の積りでいる
...no tsumóri de irù; (depend on) ...を頼り
にする ...wo táyòri ni suru

country [kʌn'tri:] *n* (state, nation) 国 kuní; (native land) 母国 bókòku; (rural
area) 田舎 ináka; (region) 地域 chíìki

country dancing (*BRIT*) *n* 英国郷土舞
踊 eíkokukyōdòbuyō

country house *n* 田舎の大邸宅 ináka
no daíteitàku

countryman [kʌn'tri:mən] (*pl* countrymen) *n* (compatriot) 同国人 dṓkokujìn;
(country dweller) 田舎者 inákamòno

countryside [kʌn'tri:said] *n* 田舎 ináka

county [kaun'ti:] *n* (POL, ADMIN) 郡
gúñ

coup [ku:] (*pl* coups) *n* (MIL, POL: also:
coup d'état) クーデター kúdetầ;
(achievement) 大成功 daíseikō

coupé [ku:pei'] *n* (AUT) クーペ kúpe

couple [kʌp'əl] *n* (also: **married couple**)
夫婦 fūfu; (cohabiting etc) カップル káp-
pūru; (of things) 一対 ittsúi

a couple of (two people) 2人の futári
no; (two things) 2つの futátsu no; (a few
people) 数人の sûnin no; (a few things) 幾
つかの ikùtsuka no

coupon [ku:'pɑn] *n* (voucher) クーポン券
kúpoñken; (detachable form) クーポン
kúpon

courage [kə:r'idʒ] *n* (bravery) 勇気 yúki

courageous [kərei'dʒəs] *adj* (person,
attempt) 勇敢な yúkan na

courgette [kurʒet'] (*BRIT*) *n* ズッキー
ニ zúkkìni

courier [kə:r'i:ər] *n* (messenger) メッセ
ンジャー méssènjā; (for tourists) 添乗員
teñjōin

course [kɔ:rs] *n* (SCOL) 課程 katéi;
(process: of life, events, time etc) 過程
katéi; (of treatment) クール kùru; (direction: of argument, action) 方針 hōshin; (:
of ship) 針路 shíñro; (part of meal) 一品
ippín, コース kṓsu; (for golf) コース kṓsu

the course of a river 川筋 kawásuji

of course (naturally) もちろん mochíròn, 当然 tôzen; (certainly) いいとも íi to mo

court [kɔːrt] *n* (royal) 宮殿 kyúdèn; (LAW) 法廷 hôtei; (for tennis, badminton etc) コート kôto

♦*vt* (woman) 妻にしようとして...と交際する tsumā ni shiyô to shité ...to kôsai suru

to take someone to court (LAW) ...を相手取って訴訟を起す ...wo aítedottè soshô wo okósù

courteous [kəːr'tiːəs] *adj* (person, conduct) 丁寧な teínei na

courtesan [kɔːr'tizən] *n* 宮廷しょう婦 kyúteishòfu

courtesy [kəːr'tisiː] *n* (politeness) 礼儀正しさ reígitadashìsa

(by) courtesy of (thanks to) ...のお陰で ...no okágè de

court-house [kɔːrt'haus] (*US*) *n* 裁判所 saíbansho

courtier [kɔːr'tiːər] *n* 廷臣 teíshin

court-martial [kɔːrt'mɑːr'ʃəl] (*pl* **courts-martial**) *vt* (MIL) 軍法会議 guńpōkaîgi

courtroom [kɔːrt'ruːm] *n* 法廷 hôtei

courtyard [kɔːrt'jɑːrd] *n* (of castle, house) 中庭 nakániwa

cousin [kʌz'in] *n* (relative) 親せき shińseki

first cousin いとこ itôkò

second cousin はとこ hatôkò, またいとこ mata-itoko

cove [kouv] *n* (bay) 入江 iríe

covenant [kʌv'ənənt] *n* (promise) 契約 keíyaku

cover [kʌv'əːr] *vt* (hide: face, surface, ground): *to cover (with)* ...で覆う ...de ôù; (hide: feelings, mistake): *to cover (with)* ...で隠す ...de kakúsù; (shield: book, table etc): *to cover (with)* ...に (...を) 掛ける ...ni (...wo) kakérù; (with lid): *to cover (with)* ...にふたをする ...ni futá wo suru; (travel: distance) 行く ikú; (protect: *also* INSURANCE) カバーする kábà suru; (discuss: topic, subject: *also* PRESS) 取上げる toríagerù; (include) 含む fukúmù

♦*n* (for furniture) 覆い ôi; (lid) ふた futá; (on bed) 上掛 uwágake; (of book, magazine) 表紙 hyôshi; (shelter: for hiding) 隠れ場所 kakúrebasho; (: from rain) 雨宿りの場所 amáyadòri no bashó; (INSURANCE) 保険 hokén; (of spy) 架空の身分 kakú no míbùn

to take cover (shelter: from rain) 雨宿りをする amáyadòri wo suru; (: from gunfire etc) 隠れる kakúrerù

under cover (indoors) 屋根の下で〔に〕yáne no shitá de (ni)

under cover of darkness やみに紛れて yamí ni magíretè

under separate cover (COMM) 別便で betsúbin de

coverage [kʌv'əːridʒ] *n* (TV, PRESS) 報道 hôdō

cover charge *n* (in restaurant) サービス料 sâbisuryò

covering [kʌv'əːriŋ] *n* (layer) 覆い ôi; (of snow, dust etc) 覆う物 ôu monò

covering letter (*US also*: **cover letter**) *n* 添状 soéjò

cover note (*BRIT*) *n* (INSURANCE) 仮保険証 karíhokeñshō

covert [kou'vəːrt] *adj* (glance, threat) 隠れた kakúretà

cover up *vi*: *to cover up for someone* ...をかばう ...wo kabáù

cover-up [kʌv'əːrʌp] *n* もみ消し momíkeshi

covet [kʌv'it] *vt* (desire) 欲しがる hoshígarù

cow [kau] *n* (animal) 雌ウシ meúshi; (*inf!*: woman) あま amâ

♦*vt* (oppress): *to be cowed* おびえる obíerù

coward [kau'əːrd] *n* おく病者 okúbyōmono

cowardice [kau'əːrdis] *n* おく病 okúbyò

cowardly [kau'əːrdliː] *adj* おく病な okúbyò na

cowboy [kau'bɔi] *n* (in US) カウボーイ kaúbòi

cower [kau'əːr] *vi* い縮する ishúku suru

coxswain [kɑːk'sin] *n* (ROWING: *abbr*:

cox) コックス kókkùsu

coy [kɔi] adj (demure, shy) はにかんで みせる haníkaǹde misérù

coyote [kaiout'i:] n コヨーテ kóyòte

cozy [kou'zi:] (BRIT cosy) adj (room, house) こじんまりした kojínmarì shita; (person) 心地よい kokóchi yoì

CPA [si:pi:ei'] (US) abbr = certified public accountant

crab [kræb] n カニ kaní

crab apple n ヒメリンゴ himérìngo

crack [kræk] n (noise: of gun) パン páǹ; (: of thunder) ばりばり bárìbari; (: of twig) ぽっきり pokkíri; (: of whip) バン baǹ; (gap) 割れ目 waréme; (in bone, dish, glass, wall) ひび hibí

♦vt (whip, twig) 鳴らす narásù; (bone, dish, glass, wall) ひびを入れる hibí wo irérù; (nut) 割る warú; (solve: problem) 解決する kaíketsu suru; (: code) 解く tókù; (joke) 飛ばす tobásu

♦adj (expert) 優秀な yūshū na

crack down on vt fus (crime, expenditure etc) 取り締まる toríshimarù

cracker [kræk'əːr] n (biscuit, Christmas cracker) クラッカー kurákkà

crackle [kræk'əl] vi (fire) ぱちぱちと音 を立てる páchìpachi to otó wo tatérù; (twig) ぽきぽきと音を立てる pókìpoki to otó wo tatérù

crack up vi (PSYCH) 頭がおかしくなる atáma ga okáshikù nárù

cradle [krei'dəl] n (baby's) 揺りかご yuríkago

craft [kræft] n (skill) 芸術 geíjutsu; (trade) 職業 shokúgyò; (boat: pl inv) 船 fúnè; (plane: pl inv) 飛行機 hikóki

craftsman [kræfts'mən] (pl craftsmen) n (artisan) 職人 shokúnin

craftsmanship [kræfts'mənʃip] n (quality) 芸術 geíjutsu

crafty [kræf'ti:] adj (sneaky) 腹黒い ha- rágurðì, こうかつな kókatsu na

crag [kræg] n 険しい岩山 kewáshiì iwá- yama

cram [kræm] vt (fill): to cram some- thing with ...を ...で一杯にする ...wo ...de ippái ni surù; (put): to cram some-

thing into ...を...に詰込む ...wo ...ni tsu- mékomù

♦vi: to cram for exams 一夜漬の試験 勉強をする ichíyazuke no shikénbenkyò wo suru

cramp [kræmp] n (MED) けいれん keíren

cramped [kræmpt] adj (accommoda- tion) 窮屈な kyúkutsu na

crampon [kræm'pɑːn] n (CLIMBING) アイゼン áìzen

cranberry [kræn'be:ri:] n (berry) コケモ モ kokémòmo, クランベリー kuránberì

crane [krein] n (machine) クレーン kúrèn; (bird) ツル tsúrù

crank [kræŋk] n (person) 変人 heńjiǹ; (handle) クランク kuráǹku

crankshaft [kræŋk'ʃæft] n (AUT) クラ ンクシャフト kuráǹkushafùto

cranny [kræn'i:] n see nook

crash [kræʃ] n (noise) 大音響 daíonkyò ◇ 物が落ちる，ぶつかるなどの大きな音を 指す monó ga ochírù, butsúkarù nádð no ókina otó wo sásù; (of car, train etc) 衝突 shótotsu; (of plane) 墜落 tsuíraku; (COMM: of stock-market) 暴落 bóraku; (COMM: of business etc) 倒産 tósan

♦vt (car etc) 衝突させる shótotsu saséru; (plane) 墜落させる tsuíraku saséru

♦vi (car etc) 衝突する shótotsu suru; (plane) 墜落する tsuíraku suru; (COMM: mar- ket) 暴落する bóraku suru; (COMM: firm) 倒産する tósan suru

crash course n 速成コース sokúseikòsu

crash helmet n ヘルメット herúmettò

crash landing n (AVIAT) 不時着陸 fu- jíchakùriku

crass [kræs] adj (behavior, comment, person) 露骨な rokótsu na

crate [kreit] n (box) 箱 hakó; (for bot- tles) ケース kèsu

crater [krei'təːr] n (of volcano) 噴火口 fuńkakò; (on moon etc) クレーター kurè- tā

bomb crater 爆弾孔 bakúdankò

cravat [krəvæt'] n アスコットタイ asú- kottotaì

crave [kreiv] vt, vi: to crave for ...を強 く欲しがる ...wo tsuyóku hoshígarù

crawl [krɔːl] vi (person) 四つんばいにはう yotsúnbai ni háù; (insect) はう háù; (vehicle) のろのろと進む nórònoro to susúmù
♦n (SWIMMING) クロール kúrôru

crayfish [krei'fiʃ] n inv (freshwater) ザリガニ zarígani; (saltwater) エビガニ ebígani

crayon [krei'ɑːn] n クレヨン kuréyòn

craze [kreiz] n (fashion) 大流行 daíryūkô

crazy [krei'ziː] adj (insane) 正気でない shôki de náî; (inf: keen): **crazy about someone/something** ...が大好きである ...ga daísuki de arù

crazy paving (BRIT) n 不ぞろい舗装 fuzóroi hosô ◊不ぞろいの敷石からなる舗装 fuzóroi no shikíishi kara narù hosô

creak [kriːk] vi (floorboard, door etc) きしむ kishímù

cream [kriːm] n (of milk) (生)クリーム (namá)kúrîmu; (also: **artificial cream**) 人造クリーム jinźôkurîmu; (cosmetic) 化粧クリーム keshôkurîmu; (élite) 名士たち meíshi tachì
♦adj (color) クリーム色の kúrîmuîrò no

cream cake n クリームケーキ kurímukêki

cream cheese n クリームチーズ kurímuchîzu

creamy [kriː'miː] adj (color) クリーム色の kurímuirò no; (taste) 生クリームたっぷりの namákurîmu táppùri no

crease [kriːs] n (fold) 折り目 oríme; (wrinkle) しわ shiwá; (in trousers) 折り目 oríme
♦vt (wrinkle) しわくちゃにする shiwákucha ni suru
♦vi (wrinkle up) しわくちゃになる shiwakucha ni naru

create [kriːeit'] vt (cause to happen, exist) 引起こす hikíokosù; (produce, design) 作る tsukúrù

creation [kriːei'ʃən] n (causing to happen, exist) 引起こす事 hikíokosù kotő; (production, design) 作る事 tsukúrù kotő; (REL) 天地創造 teńchisōzô

creative [kriːei'tiv] adj (artistic) 芸術的な geíjutsuteki na; (inventive) 創造性のある sőzösei no árù

creator [kriːei'tər] n (maker, inventor) 作る人 tsukúrù hitő

creature [kriː'tʃər] n (living animal) 動物 dóbutsu; (person) 人 hitő

crèche [kreʃ] n 託児所 takújisho

credence [kriː'dəns] n: **to lend credence to** (prove) ...を信じさせる ...wo shiñji saséru
to give credence to (prove) ...を信じさせる ...wo shiñji saséru; (believe) 信じる shiñjirù

credentials [kriden'ʃəlz] npl (references) 資格 shikáku; (identity papers) 身分証明証 mibúnshōmeishō

credibility [kredəbil'əti:] n (of person, fact) 信頼性 shiñraisei

credible [kred'əbəl] adj (believable) 信じられる shiñjirarerù; (trustworthy) 信用できる shiñ-yō dekírù

credit [kred'it] n (COMM: loan) 信用 shiñyō; (recognition) 名誉 meíyo
♦vt (COMM) ...の入金にする ...no nyúkin ni suru; (believe: also: **give credit to**) 信じる shiñjirù
to be in credit (person, bank account) 黒字になっている kuróji ni natté irù
to credit someone with (fig) ...に...の美徳があると思う ...ni...no bítòku ga arù to omóù

credit card n クレジットカード kuréjittokâdo

creditor [kred'itər] n (COMM) 債権者 saíkeñsha

credits [kred'its] npl (CINEMA) クレジット kuréjìtto

creed [kriːd] n (REL) 信条 shíñjō

creek [kriːk] n (US: stream) 小川 ogáwa; (BRIT: inlet) 入江 iríe

creep [kriːp] (pt, pp **crept**) vi (person, animal) 忍び足で歩く shinóbiàshi de arúkù

creeper [kriː'pər] n (plant) つる tsurú

creepy [kriː'piː] adj (frightening: story, experience) 薄気味悪い usúkimiwaruì

cremate [kriː'meit] vt (corpse) 火葬にする kasô ni surù

cremation [krimei'ʃən] n 火葬 kasô

crematoria [kriːmətɔːr'iːə] npl of **cre-**

matorium

crematorium [kri:mətə:r'i:əm] (*pl* **crematoria**) *n* 火葬場 kasóba

crêpe [kreip] *n* (fabric) クレープ kurḗpu; (rubber) クレープゴム kurḗpugomù ◊靴底に使う表面がしわ状のゴム kutsúzoko ni tsukáū hyṓmen ga shiwájō no gómù

crêpe bandage (*BRIT*) *n* 伸縮性包帯 shiñshukuseihōtai

crept [krept] *pt, pp* of **creep**

crescent [kres'ənt] *n* (shape) 三日月形 mikázukigata; (street) ...通り ...dṓri ◊特にカーブになっている通りの名前に使う tōkú ni kắbu ni natté irū tōri no namáe ni tsukáū

cress [kres] *n* (BOT, CULIN) クレソン kurésoñ

crest [krest] *n* (of hill) 頂上 chṓjō; (of bird) とさか tosáka; (coat of arms) 紋 mốñ

crestfallen [krest'fɔ:lən] *adj* しょんぼりした shoñborì shitá

Crete [kri:t] *n* クレタ kurḗta

crevice [krev'is] *n* (gap, crack) 割れ目 waréme

crew [kru:] *n* (NAUT) 乗組員 noríkumìñ; (AVIAT) 乗員 jốiñ; (TV, CINEMA) カメラ班 kaméraháñ ◊3つの意味とも総称として使う mittsū no imī to mo sṓshō toshité tsukáū

crew-cut [kru:'kʌt] *n* 角刈り kakúgari

crew-neck [kru:'nek] *n* (of jersey) 丸首 marúkubi

crib [krib] *n* (cot) ベビーベッド bebíbeddò

◊*vt* (*inf*: copy: during exam etc) カンニングする kańningu suru; (: from writings etc of others) 盗用する tṓyō suru

crick [krik] *n*: **to have a crick in one's neck** 首が痛い kubí ga itáI

cricket [krik'it] *n* (game) クリケット kuríkettò; (insect) コオロギ kṓrogi

crime [kraim] *n* (no pl: illegal activities) 犯罪 hañzai; (illegal action) 犯罪 (行為) hañzai(kỗi); (fig) 罪 tsumī

criminal [krim'ənəl] *n* 犯罪者 hañzaìsha

◊*adj* (illegal) 違法の ihṓ no; (morally wrong) 罪悪の zaíaku no

crimson [krim'zən] *adj* 紅色の beníiro no

cringe [krindʒ] *vi* (in fear, embarrassment) 縮こまる chijíkomarù

crinkle [kriŋ'kəl] *vt* (crease, fold) しわくちゃにする shiwákucha ni suru

cripple [krip'əl] *n* (MED) 身障者 shiñshṓsha

◊*vt* (person) 不具にする fúgù ni suru

crises [krai'si:z] *npl* of **crisis**

crisis [krai'sis] (*pl* **crises**) *n* 危機 kikí

crisp [krisp] *adj* (vegetables) ぱりぱりした párĩpari shitá; (bacon) かりかりした kárĩkari shitá; (weather) からっとした karáttò shitá; (manner, tone, reply) 無愛想な buáìso na

crisps [krisps] (*BRIT*) *npl* ポテトチップ potétochippù

criss-cross [kris'krɔ:s] *adj* (pattern, design) 十字模様の jújimoyṓ no

criteria [kraiti:'ri:ə] *npl* of **criterion**

criterion [kraiti:r'i:ən] (*pl* **criteria**) *n* (standard) 規準 kijún

critic [krit'ik] *n* (of system, policy etc) 反対者 hañtaìsha; (reviewer) 評論家 hyṓronka

critical [krit'ikəl] *adj* (time, situation) 重大な jūdai na; (opinion, analysis) 批評的な hihyṓteki na; (person: fault-finding) 粗捜し好きな arásagashizùki na; (illness) 危険な kikén na

critically [krit'ikli:] *adv* (speak, look etc) 批判的に hihánteki ni

critically ill 重症で jṓshō de

criticism [krit'isizəm] *n* (disapproval, complaint) 非難 hínàn; (of book, play etc) 批評 hihyṓ

criticize [krit'əsaiz] *vt* (find fault with) 非難する hínàn suru

croak [krouk] *vi* (frog) げろげろ鳴く gérògero nakú; (bird etc) かーかー鳴く kắkā nakú; (person) がらがら声で言う garágaragoe de iu

crochet [krouʃei'] *n* かぎ針編み kagíbariami

crockery [krɑ:k'ə:ri:] *n* (dishes) 皿類 saráruì

crocodile [krɑ:k'ədail] *n* ワニ wánì

crocus [krou'kəs] n クロッカス kurókkàsu

croft [krɔ:ft] (*BRIT*) n (small farm) 小農場 shōnōjō

crony [krou'ni:] (*inf: pej*) n 仲間 nakáma

crook [kruk] n (criminal) 悪党 akútō; (*also*: **shepherd's crook**) 羊飼のつえ hitsújikai no tsúè ◇片端の曲った物を指す katáhashi no magátta monó wo sásù

crooked [kruk'id] adj (bent, twisted) 曲った magátta; (dishonest) 不正の fuséi no

crop [krɑ:p] n (of fruit, cereals, vegetables) 作物 sakúmòtsu; (harvest) 収穫 shúkaku; (riding crop) むち múchī ◇乗馬用の物を指す jóbayō no monó wo sásù
◆vt (hair) 刈込む karíkomù

crop up vi (problem, topic) 持ち上る mochíagarù

croquet [kroukei'] n クロッケー kurókkē ◇複雑なゲートボールに似た球技 fukúzatsu na gḗtobòru ni nitá kyūgi

croquette [krouket'] n (CULIN) コロッケ kóròkke

cross [krɔ:s] n (shape) 十字 jūji; (REL) 十字架 jūjika; (mark) ばつ(印) bátsù(jírùshi); (hybrid) 合の子 aínoko
◆vt (street, room etc) 横断する ōdan suru; (arms, legs) 組む kúmù; (animal, plant) 交雑する kōzatsu suru
◆adj (angry) 不機嫌な fukígen na
to cross a check 線引小切手にする señbiki kogíttè ni suru

crossbar [krɔ:s'bɑ:r] n (SPORT) ゴールの横棒 gṓru no yokóbō

cross country (race) n クロスカントリーレース kurósukantorḯresu

cross-examine [krɔ:s'igzæm'in] vt (LAW) 反対尋問する hañtaijìñmon suru

cross-eyed [krɔ:s'aid] adj 寄り目の yoríme no

crossfire [krɔ:s'faiər] n 十字射撃 jūjishagèki

crossing [krɔ:s'iŋ] n (sea passage) 船旅 funátabi; (*also*: **pedestrian crossing**) 横断歩道 ōdanhodō

crossing guard (*US*) n 交通指導員 kótsushidòin ◇交通事故を防ぐために横断歩道に立って学童などの横断を助ける係員 kótsujikò wo fuségù tamé ni ōdanhodō ni tatté gakúdō nádò no ōdan wo tasúkerù kakáriìn

cross out vt (delete) 線を引いて消す séñ wo hiíte kesú

cross over vi (move across) 横断する ōdan suru

cross-purposes [krɔ:s'pər'pəsiz] npl:
to be at cross-purposes 話が食違っている hanáshi ga kuíchigatte irú

cross-reference [krɔ:s'ref'ə:rəns] n 相互参照 sōgosañshō

crossroads [krɔ:s'roudz] n 交差点 kōsatèn

cross section n (of an object) 断面 dañmen; (sketch) 断面図 dañmeñzu
cross section of the population 国民を代表する人々 kokumin wo daíhyō suru hitóbito

crosswalk [krɔ:s'wɔ:k] (*US*) n 横断歩道 ōdanhodō

crosswind [krɔ:s'wind] n 横風 yokókaze

crossword [krɔ:s'wə:rd] n クロスワードパズル kurósuwādopazùru

crotch [krɑ:tʃ] n (ANAT, of garment) また matá

crotchet [krɑ:tʃ'it] n (MUS) 四分音符 shibúoñpu

crotchety [krɑ:tʃ'əti:] adj (person) 気難しい kimúzukashiì

crouch [krautʃ] vi (person, animal) うずくまる uzúkumarù

croupier [kru:p'i:ər] n (in casino) とばく台の元締 tobákudai no motójime, ディーラー dīrā

crow [krou] n (bird) カラス káràsu; (of cock) 鳴き声 nakígoè
◆vi (cock) 鳴く nakú

crowbar [krou'bɑ:r] n バール bāru

crowd [kraud] n: *crowd of people* 群衆 guñshū
◆vt (fill: room, stadium etc) ...にぎっしり入る ...ni gisshírì haírù
◆vi (gather): *to crowd round* ...の回りに群がる ...no mawári ni murágarù; (cram): *to crowd in* ...の中へ詰めかける ...no nákà e tsumékakerù

a crowd of fans 大勢のファン ōzei nò fáǹ

crowded [krau'did] *adj* (full) 込入った komítta; (densely populated) 人口密度の高い jiñkōmitsùdo no takái

crown [kraun] *n* (*gen*) 冠 kañmuri; (of monarch) 王冠 ōkan; (monarchy): *the Crown* 王国 kokúō; (of head, hill) てっぺん téppeň; (of tooth) 歯冠 shikáň

◆*vt* (monarch) 王位に就かせる ǒi ni tsukáserù; (*fig*: career, evening) ...に有終の美を飾る ...ni yūshū no bí wo kazárù

crown jewels *npl* 王位の象徴 ǒi no shóchō ◇王冠、しゃくなど国家的儀式で王または女王が王位の象徴として用いる物を指す ōkan, shákù nádò kokkáteki gishíki de ǒ matá wa jǒǒ ga ǒi no shóchō toshité mochíirù monó wo sásù

crown prince *n* 皇太子 kōtaìshi

crow's feet *npl* 目じりの小じわ méjìri no kojíwa, カラスの足跡 káràsu no ashíatò

crucial [kru:'ʃəl] *adj* (decision, vote) 重大な jūdai na

crucifix [kru:'səfiks] *n* (REL) 十字架像 jūjikazō

crucifixion [kru:səfik'ʃən] *n* (REL) キリストのはりつけ kirísuto no harítsuke

crude [kru:d] *adj* (materials) 原... géñ...; (*fig*: basic) 原始的な geñshiteki na; (: vulgar) 露骨な rokótsu na

crude (oil) *n* 原油 geñ-yu

cruel [kru:'əl] *adj* (person, action) 残酷な zañkoku na; (situation) 悲惨な hisán na

cruelty [kru:'əlti:] *n* (of person, action) 残酷さ zañkokusa; (of situation) 悲惨さ hisánsa

cruise [kru:z] *n* (on ship) 船旅 funátabi

◆*vi* (ship) 巡航する juñkō suru; (car) 楽に走行する rákù ni sōkō suru

cruiser [kru:'zəːr] *n* (motorboat) 大型モーターボート ōgata mōtābòto, クルーザー kurūzā; (warship) 巡洋艦 juñ-yōkan

crumb [krʌm] *n* (of bread, cake) くず kúzù

crumble [krʌm'bəl] *vt* (bread, biscuit etc) 崩す kuzúsù

◆*vi* 崩れる kuzúrerù

crumbly [krʌm'bli:] *adj* (bread, biscuits etc) 崩れやすい kuzúreyasùi, ぼろぼろした pórðporo shitá

crumpet [krʌm'pit] *n* クランペット kuránpettò ◇マフィンの一種 mafín no isshù

crumple [krʌm'pəl] *vt* (paper, clothes) しわくちゃにする shiwákucha ni suru

crunch [krʌntʃ] *vt* (food etc) かみ砕く kamíkudakù; (underfoot) 踏み砕く fumíkudakù

◆*n* (*fig*: moment of truth) いざという時 izá to iú tokí

crunchy [krʌn'tʃi:] *adj* (food) ぱりぱりした parípari shitá

crusade [kru:seid'] *n* (campaign) 運動 uñdō

crush [krʌʃ] *n* (crowd) 人込み hitógomi; (love): *to have a crush on someone* ...にのぼせる ...ni noboseru; (drink): *lemon crush* レモンスカッシュ remónsukasshù

◆*vt* (press, squeeze) 押しつぶす oshítsubusù; (crumple: paper, clothes) しわくちゃにする shiwákucha ni suru; (defeat: army, opposition) 圧倒する attō suru; (devastate: hopes) 台無しにする daínashi ni suru; (: person) 落胆させる rakútan saséru

crust [krʌst] *n* (of bread, pastry) 皮 kawá; (of snow, ice) アイスバーン aísubàn; (of the earth) 地殻 chikáku

crutch [krʌtʃ] *n* (support, stick) 松葉づえ matsúbazùe

crux [krʌks] *n* (of problem, matter) 核心 kakúshin

cry [krai] *vi* (weep) 泣く nakú; (shout: *also*: **cry out**) 叫ぶ sakébù

◆*n* (shriek) 悲鳴 himéi; (shout) 叫び声 sakébigoè; (of bird, animal) 鳴き声 nakígoè

cry off *vi* (change one's mind, cancel) 手を引く te wo hikú

crypt [kript] *n* 地下室 chikáshitsu ◇特に納骨堂などに使われる教会の地下室を指す tókù ni nōkotsudō nadò ni tsukáwarerù kyōkai no chikáshitsu wo sásù

cryptic [krip'tik] *adj* (remark, clue) なぞめいた nazómeità

crystal [kris'təl] n (mineral) 結晶 kesshō; (in jewelery) 水晶 suíshō; (glass) クリスタル kurísutaru

crystal-clear [kris'təlkli'ə:r] adj (transparent) よく澄んだ yókù súnda; (fig: easy to understand) 明白な meíhaku na

crystallize [kris'təlaiz] vt (opinion, thoughts) まとめる matómeru
♦vi (sugar etc) 結晶する kesshō suru

cub [kʌb] n (of lion, wolf etc) …の子 …no ko; (also: **cub scout**) カブスカウト kabúsukàuto

Cuba [kju:'bə] n キューバ kyúba

Cuban [kju:'bən] adj キューバの kyúba no
♦n キューバ人 kyúbajìn

cubbyhole [kʌb'i:houl] n 小さな納戸 chiísa na nańdo

cube [kju:b] n (shape) 立方体 rippótai; (MATH: of number) …の3乗 …no sańjō
♦vt (MATH) 三乗する sańjō suru

cube root n (MATH) 立方根 ríppòkon

cubic [kju:'bik] adj (volume) 立方の rippó no

cubic capacity n 体積 taíseki

cubicle [kju:'bikəl] n (at pool) 更衣室 kóishītsu ◇小さい個室について言う chiísaí koshítsu ni tsuíte iú; (in hospital) カーテンで仕切った1病床分のスペース káten de shikítta ichíbyōshōbùn no supésu

cuckoo [ku'ku:] n カッコウ kákkō

cuckoo clock n はと時計 hatódokèi

cucumber [kju:'kʌmbə:r] n キューリ kyúri

cuddle [kʌd'əl] vt (baby, person) 抱締める dakíshimerù
♦vi (lovers) 抱合う dakíaù

cue [kju:] n (snooker cue) キュー kyū; (THEATER etc) 合図 aízu, キュー kyū

cuff [kʌf] n (of sleeve) カフス káfùsu; (US: of trousers) 折返し oríkaeshi; (blow) 平手打ち hiráteuchi
off the cuff (impromptu) 即座に〔の〕 sókùza ni〔no〕

cufflinks [kʌf'liŋks] npl カフスボタン kafúsubotàn

cuisine [kwizi:n'] n (of country, region) 料理 ryōri

cul-de-sac [kʌl'dəsæk'] n (road) 行き止り yukídomari

culinary [kju:'ləne:ri:] adj 料理の ryóri no

cull [kʌl] vt (story, idea) えり抜く erínukù
♦n (of animals) 間引き mabíki

culminate [kʌl'məneit] vi: *to culminate in* (gen) 遂に…となる súi ni …to narù; (unpleasant outcome) 挙句の果てに …となってしまう agéku no hatè ni …to nattè shimaú

culmination [kʌlmənei'ʃən] n (of career, process etc) 頂点 chōten

culottes [kju:lots'] npl キュロット kyúròtto

culpable [kʌl'pəbəl] adj (blameworthy) とがむべき togámùbeki

culprit [kʌl'prit] n (of crime) 犯人 hańnin

cult [kʌlt] n (REL: worship) 崇拝 súhai; (: sect, group) 宗派 shūha; (fashion) 流行 ryúkō

cultivate [kʌl'təveit] vt (land) 耕す tagáyasù; (crop) 栽培する saíbai suru; (person) 近付きになろうとする chikázuki ni naró to suru

cultivation [kʌltəvei'ʃən] n (AGR) 耕作 kōsaku

cultural [kʌl'tʃə:rəl] adj (traditions etc) 文化文明の buńkabúnmei no; (activities etc) 芸術の geíjutsu no

culture [kʌl'tʃə:r] n (of a country, civilization) 文明 buńmei, 文化 buńka; (the arts) 芸術 geíjutsu; (BIO) 培養 baíyō

cultured [kʌl'tʃə:rd] adj (individual) 教養のある kyóyō no arù

cumbersome [kʌm'bə:rsəm] adj (object) 扱いにくい atsúkainikuì ◇かさ張る物, 重い物, 大きくて不格好な物などについて言う kasábarù monó, omóì monó, ókìkute bukákkò na monó nadò ni tsuíte iú; (process) 面倒な meńdò na

cumulative [kju:m'jələtiv] adj (effect, result) 累積する ruíseki suru

cunning [kʌn'iŋ] n (craftiness) こうかつさ kókatsusa
♦adj (crafty) こうかつな kókatsu na

cup [kʌp] n (for drinking) カップ káppù;

(as prize) 賞杯 shṓhai, カップ káppù; (of bra) カップ káppù

cupboard [kʌb'əːrd] *n* 戸棚 todána

Cupid [kjuː'pid] *n* キューピッド kyúpiddo

cup-tie [kʌp'tai] (*BRIT*) *n* (SOCCER) トーナメント tònamento

curate [kjuː'rit] *n* 助任牧師 jonínbokùshi

curator [kjurei'təːr] *n* (of museum, gallery) キューレーター kyúrḕtā ◇学芸員の管理職に相当する人を指す gakúgeiīn no kañrishòku ni sṓtō suru hitó wo sásù

curb [kəːrb] *vt* (powers, expenditure) 制限する seígen suru; (person) 抑える osáerù

◆*n* (restraint) 抑制 yokúsei; (*US*: kerb) 縁石 fuchíishi

curdle [kəːr'dəl] *vi* (milk) 凝結する gyṓketsu suru

cure [kjuːr] *vt* (illness, patient) 治す naósù; (CULIN) 保存食にする hozónshoku ni suru

◆*n* (MED) 治療法 chiryṓhō; (solution) 解決 kaíketsu

curfew [kəːr'fjuː] *n* (MIL, POL) 夜間外出禁止令 yakán gaíshutsu kiñshirei

curio [kjuː'riːou] *n* 骨とう品 kottṓhin

curiosity [kjuːriːɑːs'əti:] *n* (of person) 好奇心 kṓkishìn; (object) 珍しい物 mezúrashiì monó

curious [kjuː'riːəs] *adj* (person: interested) 好奇心がある kṓkishìn ga arù; (: nosy) せん索好きな seńsakuzùki na; (thing: strange, unusual) 変った kawátta

curl [kəːrl] *n* (of hair) カール kāru

◆*vt* (hair) カールする kāru suru

◆*vi* (hair) カールになっている kāru ni natté irù

curler [kəːr'ləːr] *n* (for hair) カーラー kārā

curl up *vi* (person, animal) 縮こまる chijíkomarù

curly [kəːr'liː] *adj* 巻毛の makíge no

currant [kəːr'ənt] *n* (dried fruit) レーズン rēzun ◇小型の種無しブドウから作った物を指す kogáta no tanénashibùdō kara tsukútta monó wo sásù; (bush, fruit: blackcurrant, redcurrant) スグリ súguri

currency [kəːr'ənsiː] *n* (system) 通貨 tsúka; (money) 貨幣 káhèi

to gain currency (*fig*) 通用する様になる tsúyō suru yṓ ni nárù

current [kəːr'ənt] *n* (of air, water) 流れ nagáre; (ELEC) 電流 dénryū

◆*adj* (present) 現在の geñzai no; (accepted) 通用している tsúyō shité irù

current account (*BRIT*) *n* 当座預金 tōzayokìn

current affairs *npl* 時事 jiji

currently [kəːr'əntliː] *adv* 現在は geñzai wa

curricula [kərik'jələ] *npl of* **curriculum**

curriculum [kərik'jələm] (*pl* **curriculums** *or* **curricula**) *n* (SCOL) 指導要領 shidṓyōryō

curriculum vitae [-viː'tai] *n* 履歴書 rirékisho

curry [kəːr'iː] *n* (dish) カレー karḗ

◆*vt*: *to curry favor with* ...にへつらう ...ni hetsurau

curry powder *n* カレー粉 karḗko

curse [kəːrs] *vi* (swear) 悪態をつく akútai wo tsukù

◆*vt* (swear at) ののしる nonóshirù; (bemoan) のろう norou

◆*n* (spell) 呪い noròi; (swearword) 悪態 akútai; (problem, scourge) 災の元 wazáwai no motó

cursor [kəːr'səːr] *n* (COMPUT) カーソル kāsoru

cursory [kəːr'səːriː] *adj* (glance, examination) 何気ない nanígenài

curt [kəːrt] *adj* (reply, tone) 無愛想な buáisō na

curtail [kəːrteil'] *vt* (freedom, rights) 制限する seígen suru; (visit etc) 短くする mijíkakù suru; (expenses etc) 減らす herásu

curtain [kəːr'tən] *n* (at window) カーテン kāten; (THEATER) 幕 makú

curts(e)y [kəːrt'siː] *vi* (woman, girl) ひざを曲げて御辞儀をする hizá wo magéte ojígi wo suru

curve [kəːrv] *n* (bend: in line etc) 曲線 kyokúsen; (: in road) カーブ kābu

♦*vi* 曲る magáru

cushion [kuʃ'ən] *n* (on sofa, chair) クッション kusshòn, 座布団 zabútòn; (*also*: **air cushion**) エアクッション eákusshòn ◊ホバークラフトなどを支える空気の事 hobákurafùto nádò wo sasáeru kūki no kotó

♦*vt* (collision, fall) ...の衝撃を和らげる ...no shōgeki wo yawáragerù; (shock, effect) 和らげる yawáragerù

custard [kʌs'tə:rd] *n* カスタード kasútādo

custodian [kʌstou'di:ən] *n* (of building, collection) 管理人 kańriniǹ

custody [kʌs'tədi:] *n* (LAW: of child) 親権 shińken

   to take into custody (suspect) 逮捕する taího suru

custom [kʌs'təm] *n* (tradition) 伝統 deńtō; (convention) 慣習 kańshū; (habit) 習慣 shūkan; (COMM) ひいき hiíki

customary [kʌs'təme:ri:] *adj* (behavior, method, time) いつもの itsùmo no, 相変らずの aíkawarazu no

customer [kʌs'təmə:r] *n* (of shop, business etc) 客 kyakú

customized [kʌs'təmaizd] *adj* (car etc) 改造した kaízō shitá

custom-made [kʌs'təmmeid'] *adj* (shirt, car etc) あつらえの atsúraè no, オーダーメードの ōdāmèdo no

customs [kʌs'təmz] *npl* (at border, airport etc) 税関 zeíkan

customs duty *n* 関税 kańzei

customs officer *n* 税関官 zeíkaǹri

cut [kʌt] (*pt, pp* **cut**) *vt* (bread, meat, hand etc) 切る kírù; (shorten: grass, hair) 刈る karú; (: text, program) 短くする mijíkakù suru; (reduce: prices, spending, supply) 減らす herásù

♦*vi* (knife, scissors) 切れる kirérù

♦*n* (in skin) 切り傷 kiríkìzu; (in salary) 減給 geńkyū; (in spending etc) 削減 sakúgen; (of meat) ブロック burókkù; (of garment) カット káttò

   to cut a tooth 歯が生える há ga haérù

cutback [kʌt'bæk] *n* 削減 sakúgen

cut down *vt* (tree) 切倒す kirítaosù;

(consumption) 減らす herásu

cute [kjut] *adj* (US: pretty) かわいい kawáiì; (sweet) 陳腐な chíǹpu na

cuticle [kju:'tikəl] *n* (of nail) 甘皮 amákawa

cutlery [kʌt'lə:ri:] *n* ナイフとフォークとスプーン náifu to fòku to súpùn ◊総称 sōshō

cutlet [kʌt'lit] *n* (piece of meat) カツ(レツ) katsú(retsu); (vegetable cutlet, nut cutlet) コロッケ kóròkke

cut off *vt* (limb) 切断する setsúdan suru; (piece) 切る kírù, 切分ける kiríwakerù; (person, village) 孤立させる korítsu saséru; (supply) 遮断する shadán suru; (TEL) 切る kírù

cut out *vt* (shape, article from newspaper) 切抜く kirínukù; (stop: an activity etc) やめる yaméru; (remove) 切除する setsùjo suru

cutout [kʌt'aut] *n* (switch) 非常遮断装置 hijōshadansòchi, 安全器 ańzeǹki; (shape) 切抜き kirínuki

cut-rate [kʌt'reit] (*BRIT* **cut-price**) *adj* 安売りの yasúuri no

cutthroat [kʌt'θrout] *n* (murderer) 人殺し hitógoroshi

♦*adj* (business, competition) 殺人的な satsújinteki na

cutting [kʌt'iŋ] *adj* (remark) 辛らつな shiǹratsu na

♦*n* (from newspaper) 切抜き kirínuki; (from plant) 穂木 hogí, さし穂 sashího

cut up *vt* (paper, meat) 刻む kizámu

CV [si:vi:'] *n abbr* = **curriculum vitae**

cwt *abbr* = **hundredweight(s)**

cyanide [sai'ənaid] *n* 青酸化物 seísanka-bùtsu

cyclamen [sik'ləmən] *n* シクラメン shikúramèn

cycle [sai'kəl] *n* (bicycle) 自転車 jitéǹsha; (series: of events, seasons etc) 周期 shūki; (: TECH) サイクル saíkuru; (: of songs etc) 一連 ichíren

♦*vi* (on bicycle) 自転車で行く jitéǹsha de ikú

cycling [saik'liŋ] *n* サイクリング saíkuringu

cyclist [saik'list] *n* サイクリスト sáikurisuto

cyclone [saik'loun] *n* (storm) サイクロン sáikuron

cygnet [sig'nit] *n* 若いハクチョウ wakáī hakúchō

cylinder [sil'indər] *n* (shape) 円柱 eńchū; (of gas) ボンベ bóńbe; (in engine, machine etc) 気筒 kitō, シリンダー shíríñdā

cylinder-head gasket [sil'ində:rhed-] *n* (AUT) シリンダーヘッドのパッキング shiríñdāheddò no pakkíñgu

cymbals [sim'bəlz] *npl* (MUS) シンバル shíñbaru

cynic [sin'ik] *n* 皮肉屋 hiníkuya, シニック shínīkku

cynical [sin'ikəl] *adj* (attitude, view) 皮肉な hiníku na, シニカルな shínīkaru na

cynicism [sin'əsizəm] *n* シニカルな態度 shínīkaru na táīdo

cypress [sai'pris] *n* (tree) イトスギ itósùgi

Cypriot [sip'ri:ət] *adj* キプロスの kípùrosu no
♦*n* キプロス人 kipúrosujin

Cyprus [saip'rəs] *n* キプロス kípùrosu

cyst [sist] *n* (MED) のうしゅ nōshu

cystitis [sistai'tis] *n* (MED) ぼうこう炎 bōkōen

czar [zɑ:r] *n* = **tsar**

Czech [tʃek] *adj* チェコスロバキアの chékòsuróbakìa no
♦*n* (person) チェコスロバキア人 chékòsuróbakìajin; (language) チェコスロバキア語 chékòsuróbakiago

Czechoslovak [tʃekəslou'væk] *adj, n* = **Czechoslovakian**

Czechoslovakia [tʃekəsləvɑ:k'i:ə] *n* チェコスロバキア chékòsuróbakìa

Czechoslovakian [tʃekəsləvɑ:k'i:ən] *adj* チェコスロバキアの chékòsuróbakìa no
♦*n* (person) チェコスロバキア人 chékòsuróbakìajin

D

D [di:] *n* (MUS: note) ニ音 níòn; (: key) ニ

調 níchō

dab [dæb] *vt* (eyes, wound) 軽くふく karúku fukú; (paint, cream) 軽く塗る karúku nurú

dabble [dæb'əl] *vi*: **to dabble in** (politics, antiques etc) 趣味でやる shúmì de yarú

dad [dæd] (*inf*) *n* 父ちゃん tóchàn

daddy [dæd'i:] (*inf*) *n* = **dad**

daffodil [dæf'ədil] *n* スイセン suísen

daft [dæft] *adj* (silly) ばかな bákà na

dagger [dæg'ə:r] *n* 短刀 tántō

daily [dei'li:] *adj* (dose, wages, routine etc) 毎日の maínichi no
♦*n* (*also*: **daily paper**) 日刊新聞 nikkanshínbun
♦*adv* (pay, see) 毎日 maínichi

dainty [dein'ti:] *adj* (petite) 繊細な séñsai na

dairy [de:r'i:] *n* (BRIT: shop) 牛乳店 gyúnyūten; (on farm) 牛乳小屋 gyūnyūgoya ◇酪農場で牛乳を置いたり加工したりする小屋 rakúnōjō dè gyūnyū wò oítarì kakó shitarì surú koyá

dairy farm *n* 酪農場 rakúnōjō

dairy products *npl* 乳製品 nyúseīhin

dairy store (US) *n* 牛乳店 gyúnyūten

dais [dei'is] *n* 演壇 éndan

daisy [dei'zi:] *n* デイジー deíjī

daisy wheel *n* (on printer) デイジーホイール deíjīhoírù

dale [deil] *n* (valley) 谷 taní

dam [dæm] *n* (on river) ダム dámù
♦*vt* (river, stream) ...にダムを造る ...ni dámù wo tsukúrù

damage [dæm'idʒ] *n* (harm: *also fig*) 害 gaí; (dents etc) 損傷 sonshō
♦*vt* (harm: reputation etc) 傷付ける kizutsukérù; (spoil, break: toy, machine etc) 壊す kowásù

damages [dæm'idʒiz] *npl* (LAW) 損害賠償 sóngaibaīshō

damn [dæm] *vt* (curse at) ...に悪態を浴びせる ...ni akútai wo àbíseru; (condemn) 非難する hínàn suru
♦*n* (*inf*): *I don't give a damn* おれの知った事じゃない oré no shíttà koto jà náī

◆*adj* (*inf*: *also*: **damned**) くそったれの kusóttare no, 畜生の chikúshō no
　　damn (it)! 畜生 chikúshō

damning [dæm'iŋ] *adj* (evidence) 動かぬ ugókanù

damp [dæmp] *adj* (building, wall) 湿っぽい shiméppoì; (cloth) 湿った shimétta
◆*n* (in air, in walls) 湿り気 shimérike
◆*vt* (*also*: **dampen**): cloth, rag) 湿らす shimérasu; (: enthusiasm etc) …に水を差す …ni mizú wo sasù

damson [dæm'zən] *n* (fruit) ダムソンスモモ damúsonsumòmo

dance [dæns] *n* (movements, MUS, dancing) 踊り odóri, ダンス dànsu; (social event) 舞踏会 butōkai, ダンスパーティ dánsupàti
◆*vi* (person) 踊る odóru

dance hall *n* ダンスホール dánsuhòru

dancer [dæn'sə:r] *n* (for pleasure) 踊る人 odóru hito; (professional) ダンサー dànsā

dancing [dæn'siŋ] *n* (skill, performance) 踊り odóri, ダンス dànsu

dandelion [dæn'dəlaiən] *n* タンポポ tànpopo

dandruff [dæn'drəf] *n* ふけ fuké

Dane [dein] *n* デンマーク人 dénmakujìn

danger [dein'dʒə:r] *n* (hazard, risk) 危険 kikén; (possibility): *there is a danger of …* …の危険がある …no kikén ga arù
　　「*danger!*」(on sign) 危険 kikén
　　in danger 危険にさらされて kikén ni sàrásareté
　　to be in danger of (risk, be close to) …される危険がある …saréru kikén ga arù

dangerous [dein'dʒə:rəs] *adj* 危険な kikén na

dangle [dæŋ'gəl] *vt* (keys, toy) ぶら下げる burásageru; (arms, legs) ぶらぶらさせる buràbura saséru
◆*vi* (earrings, keys) ぶら下がる burásagaru

Danish [dei'niʃ] *adj* デンマークの dénmaku no; (LING) デンマーク語の dénmākugo no
◆*n* (LING) デンマーク語 dénmākugo

dapper [dæp'ə:r] *adj* (man, appearance) きびきびした kíbìkibi shitá

dare [de:r] *vt*: *to dare someone to do* 出来るものならしてみろと…にけし掛ける dekírù monó nàrá shité mirò to …ni keshíkakerù
◆*vi*: *to dare (to) do something* 敢えて…する áète …surú
　　I dare say (I suppose) 多分 tábùn

daredevil [de:r'devəl] *n* 無謀な人 mubō na hito

daring [de:r'iŋ] *adj* (escape, person, dress, film, raid, speech) 大胆な daítan na
◆*n* 大胆さ daítansa

dark [dɑ:rk] *adj* (room, night) 暗い kurái; (hair) 黒っぽい kuróppoì; (complexion) 浅黒い aságuroì; (color: blue, green etc) 濃い kóì
◆*n*: *in the dark* やみの中で〔に〕yamí no nakà de〔ni〕
　　to be in the dark about (*fig*) …について何も知らない …ni tsúíte nàní mo shírá-nai
　　after dark 暗くなってから kuráku nat-tè kará

darken [dɑ:r'kən] *vt* (color) 濃くする kó-kù suru
◆*vi* (sky, room) 暗くなる kuráku narù

dark glasses *npl* サングラス sánguràsu

darkness [dɑ:rk'nis] *n* (of room, night) 暗やみ kuráyami

darkroom [dɑ:rk'ru:m] *n* (PHOT) 暗室 ánshitsu

darling [dɑ:r'liŋ] *adj* (child, spouse) 愛する aí surù
◆*n* (dear) あなた anáta; (favorite) ひいきの人 híìki no hitó

darn [dɑ:rn] *vt* (sock, jersey) 繕う tsukúroù

dart [dɑ:rt] *n* (in game) 投げ矢 nagéya, ダート dàto; (in sewing) ダーツ dātsu
◆*vi* 素早く走る subáyakù hashírù
　　to dart away/along 素早く走っていく subáyakù hashíttè ikú

dartboard [dɑ:rt'bɔ:rd] *n* ダーツの的 dàtsu no mató

darts [dɑ:rts] *n* (game) ダーツ dàtsu

dash [dæʃ] n (small quantity) 少々 shō-shō; (sign) ダッシュ dásshù
♦vt (throw) 投付ける nagétsukerù; (hopes) くじく kujíkù
♦vi 素早く行く subáyakù ikú

dash away vi 走って行く hashíttè ikú

dashboard [dæʃ'bɔːrd] n (AUT) ダッシュボード dasshúbōdò

dashing [dæʃ'iŋ] adj さっそうとした sàssō to shita

dash off vi = **dash away**

data [dei'tə] npl (ADMIN, COMPUT) 情報jōhō, データ dēta

database [dei'təbeis] n データベース dḗtabèsu

data processing n 情報処理 jōhōshorì

date [deit] n (day) 日にち hínìchi; (with boy/girlfriend) デート dèto; (fruit) ナツメヤシの実 natsúmeyashì no mí
♦vt (event) ...の年代を決める ...no néndai wo kìmeru; (letter) ...に日付を書く ...ni hizúke wo kakù; (person) ...とデートをする ...to dèto wo suru

date of birth 生年月日 seínengappì

to date (until now) 今まで imá madè

dated [dei'tid] adj (expression, style) 時代遅れの jidáiokùre no

daub [dɔːb] vt (mud, paint) 塗付ける nurítsukerù

daughter [dɔːt'əːr] n 娘 musúme

daughter-in-law [dɔːt'təːrinlɔː] (pl **daughters-in-law**) n 嫁 yomé

daunting [dɔːn'tiŋ] adj (task, prospect) しりごみさせる様な shirígomì saseru yō na, ひるませる様な hirúmaserù yō nà

dawdle [dɔːd'əl] vi (go slow) ぐずぐずする gúzuguzu suru

dawn [dɔːn] n (of day) 夜明け yoáke; (of period, situation) 始まり hajímari
♦vi (day) 夜が明ける yó gà akéru; (fig): it dawned on him that ... 彼は...だと気が付いた kárè wa ...da tò kì gá tsuíta

day [dei] n (period) 日 hi, 1日 ichínichi; (daylight) 昼間 hirúma; (heyday) 全盛期 zenséiki

the day before 前の日 maé no hi, 前日 zénjitsu

the day after 翌日 yokújitsu

the day after tomorrow 明後日 asáttè

the day before yesterday 一昨日 otótoi

the following day 次の日 tsugí nò hi, 翌日 yokújitsu

by day 昼間に hirúma nì

daybreak [dei'breik] n 明け方 akégata, 夜明け yoáke

daydream [dei'driːm] vi 空想にふける kūsō ni fùkéru

daylight [dei'lait] n (sunlight) 日光 níkkō; (daytime) 昼間 hirúma, 日中 nítchū

day return (BRIT) n (ticket) 往復券 ō-fukukèn

daytime [dei'taim] n 昼間 hirúma

day-to-day [deitu:dei'] adj (life, organization) 日常の nichíjō no

daze [deiz] vt (stun) ぼう然とさせる bōzen to sàséru
♦n: in a daze (confused, upset) ぼう然として bōzen to shite

dazzle [dæz'əl] vt (bewitch) 感嘆させる kántan sàséru; (blind) ...の目をくらます ...no mé wò kurámasu

DC [di:si:'] abbr (= direct current) 直流 chokúryū

D-day [di:'dei] n 予定日 yotéîbi

dead [ded] adj (not alive: person, animal) 死んだ shínda; (flowers) 枯れた karéta; (numb) しびれた shibírèta; (telephone) 通じない tsújinai; (battery) 上がった agátta
♦adv (completely) 全く máttaku; (directly, exactly) 丁度 chōdo
♦npl: the dead 死者 shíshà

to shoot someone dead 射殺す uchíkorosù

dead tired へとへとに疲れた hetóheto ni tsùkárèta

to stop dead 突然止る totsúzen tòmáru

deaden [ded'ən] vt (blow, pain) 和らげる yawáragerù; (sound) 鈍くする nibúkù suru

dead end n (street) 行き止り ikídomari

dead heat n (SPORT) 同着 dōchaku

deadline [ded'lain] n (PRESS etc) 締切り shimékiri

deadlock [ded'lɑːk] n (POL, MIL) 行き詰

り ikízumari

dead loss (inf) n: to be a dead loss
(person) 役立たず yakútatàzu

deadly [ded'li:] adj (lethal: poison) 致命
的な chiméiteki na; (devastating: accuracy) 恐ろしい osóroshiì; (: insult) 痛烈な
tsúretsu na

deadpan [ded'pæn] adj (look, tone) 無表
情の muhyójð no

Dead Sea n: the Dead Sea 死海 shikái

deaf [def] adj (totally) 耳の聞えない mimí no kíkðenai

deafen [def'ən] vt ...の耳を聞えなくする
...no mimí wo kikðenaku sùrù

deafness [def'nis] n 難聴 nánchō

deal [di:l] n (agreement) 取引 toríhikì
♦vt (pt, pp dealt) (card) 配る kubárù
a great deal (of) 沢山(の) takúsan
(nð)

dealer [di:'lə:r] n (COMM) 販売業者 hán-
baigyðsha, ディーラー dírā

deal in vt fus (COMM) 取扱う toríatsukau

dealings [di:'liŋz] npl (business) 取引 toríhikì; (relations) 関係 kánkei

dealt [delt] pt, pp of deal

deal with vt fus (person) ...と取引をする
...to toríhikì wo suru; (problem) 処理する
shórì suru; (subject) 取扱う toríatsukau

dean [di:n] n (REL) 主任司祭 shunínshi-
sài; (SCOL) 学部長 gakúbuchō

dear [di:r] adj (person) 愛しい itóshiì;
(expensive) 高価な kóka na
♦n: my dear あなた anátà, お前 omáe
♦excl: dear me! おや oyá ◊驚きを表す
odóroki wo àrawasù
Dear Sir/Madam (in letter) 拝啓 hái-
kei
Dear Mr/Mrs X 親愛なる...さん shín-ai
narù ...sàn

dearly [di:r'li:] adv (love) 深く fukákù
to pay dearly for one's carelessness
自らの不注意が高く付く mízùkara no
fuchúì ga tákàku tsukú

death [deθ] n (BIO) 死 shí, 死亡 shibð;
(fig) 死 shí

death certificate n 死亡証明書 shibð-
shōmeisho

deathly [deθ'li:] adj (color) 死人の様な
shinín no yð na; (silence) 不気味な bukími na

death penalty n 死刑 shikéi

death rate n 死亡率 shibðrìtsu

death toll n 死者の数 shíshà no kázù

debacle [dəbɑ:k'əl] n 大失敗 daíshippài

debar [dibɑ:r'] vt: to debar someone
from doing ...が...をするのを禁止する
...gà ...wo sùrú nð wo kínshi suru

debase [dibeis'] vt (value, quality) 下げる
sagérù

debatable [dibei'təbəl] adj (decision,
assertion) 疑問のある gimón no arù

debate [dibeit'] n (discussion, also POL)
討論 tðron
♦vt 討議する tðgì suru

debauchery [debɔ:'tʃə:ri:] n (drunkenness, promiscuity) 放とう hðtō

debilitating [dibil'əteitiŋ] adj (illness
etc) 衰弱させる suíjaku sàséru

debit [deb'it] n (COMM) 支払額 shihárai-
gàku
♦vt: to debit a sum to someone/to
someone's account ...の口座から落す
...no kðza kara òtòsù ¶ see direct

debris [dəbri:'] n (rubble) がれき garéki

debt [det] n 借金 shákkín
to be in debt 借金がある shákkín gà
árù

debtor [det'ə:r] n 負債者 fusáìsha

debunk [dibʌŋk'] vt (myths, ideas) ...の正
体をあばく ...no shótaí wo abákù

début [deibju:'] n (THEATER, SPORT)
デビュー débyù

decade [dek'eid] n 10年間 júnènkan

decadence [dek'ədəns] n (moral, spiritual) 堕落 daráku

decaffeinated [di:kæf'əneitid] adj カフ
ェインを取除いた kaféìn wo torínozoìta

decanter [dikæn'tə:r] n (for wine, whiskey) デカンター dekántā

decay [dikei'] n (of meat, fish etc) 腐敗
fuhái; (of building) 老朽 rðkyū; (of tooth)
カリエス kárìesu
♦vi (rot: body, leaves etc) 腐敗する fuhái
suru; (teeth) 虫歯になる mushíba ni narù

deceased [disi:st'] n: the deceased 故人

kójìn

deceit [disiːt'] *n* (duplicity) 偽り itsúwari

deceitful [disiːt'fəl] *adj* 不正な fuséi na

deceive [disiːv'] *vt* (fool) だます damásù

December [disem'bəːr] *n* 12月 jūnigatsu

decency [diː'sənsi:] *n* (propriety) 上品さ jōhínsa; (kindness) 親切さ shínsetsusa

decent [diː'sənt] *adj* (proper) 上品な jōhín na; (kind) 親切な shínsetsu na

deception [disep'ʃən] *n* ごまかし gomákashi

deceptive [disep'tiv] *adj* (appearance) 見掛けによらない mikáke ni yòránai

decibel [des'əbəl] *n* デシベル déshìberu

decide [disaid'] *vt* (person: persuade) 納得させる nattóku sàséru; (question, argument: settle) 解決する kaíketsu suru
♦*vi* 決める kiméru
to decide to do/that ...する〔...だ〕と決める ...sùrú 〔...da〕to kìméru
to decide on something (choose something) ...を選ぶ ...wo erábù

decided [disai'did] *adj* (resolute) 決意の固い kétsùi no katái; (clear, definite) はっきりした hakkírì shita

decidedly [disai'didli:] *adv* (distinctly) はっきりと hakkírì to; (emphatically: act, reply) きぜんと kizén to

deciduous [disidʒ'uːəs] *adj* (tree, bush) 落葉の rakúyō no

decimal [des'əməl] *adj* (system, currency) 十進法 jisshínhō
♦*n* (fraction) 小数 shōsū

decimal point *n* 小数点 shōsúten

decimate [des'əmeit] *vt* (population) 多数の...を死なせる tasū nò ...wo shináseru

decipher [disai'fəːr] *vt* (message, writing) 解読する kaídoku sùrú

decision [disiʒ'ən] *n* (choice) 決定した事 kettéi shita koto; (act of choosing) 決定 kettéi; (decisiveness) 決断力 ketsudànryoku

decisive [disai'siv] *adj* (action, intervention) 決定的な kettéiteki na; (person) 決断力のある ketsudànryoku no árù

deck [dek] *n* (NAUT) 甲板 kánpàn, デッキ dekkí; (of bus) 階 káì; (record deck)

デッキ dékkì; (of cards) 一組 hitókùmi

deckchair [dek'tʃeːr] *n* デッキチェア dekkíchèa

declaration [dekləreiʃ'ən] *n* (statement) 断言 dangèn; (public announcement) 布告 fùkóku

declare [dikleːr'] *vt* (truth, intention, result) 発表する happyō suru; (reveal: income, goods at customs etc) 申告する shínkoku suru

decline [diklain'] *n*: *decline in/of* (drop, lowering) ...の下落 ...no gèráku; (lessening) ...の減少 ...no génshō
♦*vt* (turn down: invitation) 辞退する jítài suru
♦*vi* (strength, old person) 弱る yowárù; (business) 不振になる fushín ni narù

decode [diːkoud'] *vt* (message) 解読する kaídoku suru

decompose [diːkəmpouz'] *vi* (organic matter, corpse) 腐敗する fùhái suru

décor [deikour'] *n* (of house, room) 装飾 shóshoku; (THEATER) 舞台装置 butáisòchi

decorate [dek'əːreit] *vt* (adorn): *to decorate (with)* (...で) 飾る (...de) kazáru; (paint and paper) ...の室内を改装する ...no shitsúnài wo kaísō suru

decoration [dekəreiʃ'ən] *n* (on tree, dress etc) 飾り kazári; (act) 飾る事 kazáru koto; (medal) 勲章 kúnshō

decorative [dek'əːrətiv] *adj* 装飾の sóshoku no

decorator [dek'əːreitəːr] *n* (BRIT: painter) ペンキ屋 pénkiya

decorum [dikəːr'əm] *n* (propriety) 上品さ jōhínsa

decoy [diː'kɔi] *n* (person, object) おとり otóri

decrease [*n* diː'kriːs *vb* dikriːs'] *n* (reduction, drop): *decrease (in)* 減少 génshō
♦*vt* (reduce, lessen) 減らす herásu
♦*vi* (drop, fall) 減る herú

decree [dikri:'] *n* (ADMIN, LAW) 命令 meírei

decree nisi [-nai'sai] *n* 離婚の仮判決 ríkòn no kàríhànketsu

decrepit [dikrep'it] *adj* (run-down: shack) おんぼろの ônboro no; (person) よぼよぼの yòbóyobo no

dedicate [ded'ikeit] *vt* (time, effort etc): *to dedicate to* ...につぎ込む ...ni tsugíkomù; (oneself): *to dedicate to* ...に専念する ...ni sénnen suru; (book, record): *to dedicate to* ...に捧げる ...ni saságeru

dedication [dedikei'ʃən] *n* (devotion) 献身 kénshin; (in book, on radio) 献辞 kénji

deduce [didu:s'] *vt* 推測する suísoku suru

deduct [didʌkt'] *vt* (subtract) 差引く sashíhikù

deduction [didʌk'ʃən] *n* (act of deducing) 推測 suísoku; (act of deducting) 差引き sashíhiki; (amount) 差引く分 sashíhikù bùn

deed [di:d] *n* (feat) 行為 kôî; (LAW: document) 証書 shôsho

deem [di:m] *vt* (judge, consider) ...だと判断する ...dá tò hándan suru

deep [di:p] *adj* (hole, water) 深い fukáì; (in measurements) 奥行の okúyuki no; (voice) 太い futôî; (color) 濃い kôî
♦*adv*: *the spectators stood 20 deep* 観衆は20列に並んで立っていた kánshū wa nijûretsu ni naránde tàtte ita
a deep breath 深呼吸 shínkokyū
to be 4 meters deep 深さは4メータである fukásà wa yón mềta de árù

deepen [di:'pən] *vt* (hole, canal etc) 深くする fukáku suru
♦*vi* (crisis, mystery) 深まる fukámarù

deep-freeze [di:p'fri:z'] *n* 冷凍庫 réitōko, フリーザー furízā

deep-fry [di:p'frai'] *vt* 揚げる agéru

deeply [di:p'li:] *adv* (breathe) 深く fukáku; (interested, moved, grateful) 非常に hijô ni

deep-sea diving [di:p'si:'-] *n* 深海ダイビング shínkaidàibingu

deep-seated [di:p'si:'tid] *adj* (beliefs, fears, dislike etc) 根の深い né nò fukáî

deer [di:r] *n inv* (ZOOL) シカ shiká

deerskin [di:r'skin] *n* シカ皮 shikágawa

deface [difeis'] *vt* (wall, notice) 汚す yogósu

defamation [defəmei'ʃən] *n* (LAW) 名誉

毀損 mêîyokisòn

default [difɔ:lt'] *n* (COMPUT) デフォルト値 déforutone
by default (win) 不戦勝で fusénshō de

defeat [difi:t'] *n* (of enemy) 敗北 háiboku; (failure) 失敗 shippái
♦*vt* (enemy, opposition) 破る yabúrù

defeatist [difi:'tist] *adj* 敗北主義の háibokushugî no
♦*n* 敗北主義者 háibokushùgisha

defect [*n* di:'fekt *vb* difekt'] *n* (flaw, imperfection: in machine etc) 欠陥 kekkán; (: in person, character etc) 欠点 kettén
♦*vi*: *to defect to the enemy* 敵側に亡命する tekígawa ni bōmei suru

defective [difek'tiv] *adj* (goods) 欠陥のある kekkán no árù

defence [difens'] (*BRIT*) *n* = **defense**

defend [difend'] *vt* (protect, champion) 守る mamórù; (justify) 釈明する shàkúmei suru; (LAW) 弁護する bèngo suru; (SPORT: goal) 守る mamórù; (: record, title) 防衛する bôei suru

defendant [difen'dənt] *n* (LAW: in criminal case) 被告人 hîkôkunin; (: in civil case) 被告 hîkôku

defender [difen'də:r] *n* (*also fig*, SPORT) 防衛者 bôeisha

defense [difens'] (*BRIT* **defence**) *n* (protection, assistance) 防衛 bôei; (justification) 釈明 shàkúmei

defenseless [difens'lis] *adj* (helpless) 無防備の mùbôbî wa

defensive [difen'siv] *adj* (weapons, measures) 防衛の bôei no; (behavior, manner) 釈明的な shàkúmeiteki na
♦*n*: *on the defensive* 守勢に立って shuséi ni tattè

defer [difər'] *vt* (postpone) 延期する énki suru

deference [def'ə:rəns] *n* (consideration) 丁重さ tèíchôsa

defiance [difai'əns] *n* (challenge, rebellion) 反抗 hánkô
in defiance of (despite: the rules, someone's orders etc) ...を無視して ...wo múshî shite

defiant [difai'ənt] *adj* (challenging,

rebellious: tone, reply, person) 反抗的な hánkōteki na

deficiency [difiʃ'ənsi:] n (lack) 欠如 kétsùjo; (defect) 欠点 kettén

deficient [difiʃ'ənt] adj (inadequate): **deficient in** ...が不足している ...ga fùsòku shìté iru; (defective) 欠点の多い kettén no ōi

deficit [def'isit] n (COMM) 赤字 akáji

defile [difail'] vt (memory, statue etc) 汚す kegásu

define [difain'] vt (limits, boundaries) 明らかにする akírakà ni suru; (expression, word) 定義する téīgi suru

definite [def'ənit] adj (fixed) 決まった kimátta; (clear, obvious) 明白な meíhaku na; (certain) 確実な kàkújitsu na
he was definite about it 彼はその事をはっきり言った kárè wa sonó koto wò hakkírì ittá

definitely [def'ənitli:] adv (positively, certainly) 確実に kàkújitsu ni

definition [defəniʃ'ən] n (of word) 定義 téīgi; (clearness of photograph etc) 鮮明さ sènmeisa

definitive [difin'ətiv] adj (account, version) 決定的な kèttéiteki na

deflate [difleit'] vt (tire, balloon) ...の空気を抜く ...no kūkī wo nukú

deflect [diflekt'] vt (fend off: attention, criticism) 回避する kaíhi suru; (divert: shot, light) 横へそらす yokó e sòrásù

deform [difɔ:rm'] vt (distort) 変形させる hénkei sàséru

deformed [difɔ:rmd'] adj 変形した hénkei shita

deformity [difɔ:r'miti:] n 奇形 kīkéi

defraud [difrɔːd'] vt: **to defraud someone (of something)** ...から (...を) だまし取る ...kàrá (...wo) dàmáshitorù

defrost [difrɔːst'] vt (fridge, windshield) ...の霜取りをする ...no shimótori wò suru; (food) 解凍する kaítō suru

defroster [difrɔːs'tə:r] (US) n 霜取り装置 shimótorisòchi

deft [deft] adj (movement, hands) 器用な kíyō na

defunct [difʌŋkt'] adj (industry, organi-

zation) 現存しない génzon shìnáì

defuse [di:fjuːz'] vt (bomb) ...の信管を外す ...no shínkan wo hàzúsu; (fig: crisis, tension) 緩和する kánwa suru

defy [difai'] vt (resist) ...に抵抗する ...ni teíkō suru; (challenge) 挑発する chōhatsu suru; (fig: description, explanation) ...の仕様がない ...no shíyō ga naí

degenerate [vb didʒen'ə:reit adj didʒen'ə:rit] vi (condition, health) 悪化する àkká suru
♦adj (depraved) 堕落した dàráku shita

degrading [digrei'diŋ] adj (conduct, activity) 恥ずべき hàzúbekì; (task etc) 誇りを傷つけられる様な hokóri wo kìzútsukeràrérù yō na

degree [digri:'] n (extent) 度合doái; (of temperature, angle, latitude) 度 do; (SCOL) 学位 gákùi
a degree in science 科学の学位 sūgaku no gákùi
by degrees (gradually) 徐々に jójò ni
to some degree ある程度 arú teìdo

dehydrated [di:hai'dreitid] adj (MED) 脱水状態の dassúijòtai no; (milk) エバミルク ebámirùku

de-ice [di:ais'] vt (windshield) ...の霜取りをする ...no shimótorì wo suru

deign [dein] vi: **to deign to do** ...をしてくれてやる ...wo shìté kurete yaru

deity [di:'iti:] n 神 kámì

dejected [didʒek'tid] adj (depressed) がっかりした gakkárì shita

delay [dilei'] vt 遅らせる okúraseru
♦vi (linger) 待つ mátsù; (hesitate) ためらう tàméraù
♦n (waiting period) 待つべき期間 mátsùbeki kikàn; (postponement) 延期 énki
to be delayed (person, flight, departure etc) 遅れる òkúreru
without delay 直ちに tádàchi ni

delectable [dilek'təbəl] adj (person) 美しい ùtsúkushiì; (food) おいしい òíshiì

delegate [n del'əgit vb del'əgeit] n 代表 dáīhyō
♦vt (person) 任命する nínmei suru; (task) 任せる màkáseru

delegation [deləgei'ʃən] n (group) 代表団

dàîhyǒdan; (by manager, leader) 任命 nínmei

delete [dili:t'] *vt* (cross out, *also* COMPUT) 消す kèsú, 削除する sákùjo suru

deliberate [*adj* dilib'ə:rit *vb* dilib'ə:reit] *adj* (intentional) 故意の kôî no; (slow) 落着いた òchítsuita
♦*vi* (consider) 熟考する jukkô suru

deliberately [dilib'ə:ritli:] *adv* (on purpose) 故意に kôî ni, わざと wâzà to

delicacy [del'əkəsi:] *n* (of movement) しとやかさ shítóyakasà; (of material) 繊細さ sénsaisà; (of problem etc) 微妙さ bìmyôsà; (choice food) 珍味 chínmi

delicate [del'əkit] *adj* (movement) しとやかな shítóyakà na; (taste, smell, color) 淡い awâî; (material) 繊細な sénsai na; (approach, problem) 微妙な bimyô na; (health) 弱い yowâî

delicatessen [deləkətes'ən] *n* 総菜屋 sôzaiya, デリカテッセン dèrîkatessèn

delicious [dilíʃ'əs] *adj* (food) おいしい òîshiî; (smell) おいしそうな òîshisô na; (feeling) 心地好い kòkóchiyoî; (person) 魅力的な mîryókuteki na

delight [dilait'] *n* 喜び yòrókobi
♦*vt* (please) 喜ばす yòrókobasu
to take (a) delight in ...するのが大好きである ...surú nò ga dâîsuki de aru

delighted [dilai'tid] *adj*: *delighted (at/with)* (...で) 喜んでいる (...de) yòrókònde iru
delighted to do 喜んで...する yòrókònde ...suru

delightful [dilait'fəl] *adj* (evening, house, person etc) 楽しい tànóshiî

delinquency [diliŋ'kwənsi:] *n* 非行 hikô

delinquent [diliŋ'kwint] *adj* (boy/girl) 非行の hikô no
♦*n* (youth) 非行少年〔少女〕 hikôshônen 〔shôjo〕

delirious [dili:r'i:əs] *adj*: *to be delirious* (with fever) うわ言を言う ùwâgoto wo iu; (with excitement) 夢中になっている mùchû ni nattê irú

deliver [diliv'ə:r] *vt* (distribute) 配達する hàîtatsu suru; (hand over) 引渡す hîkí-

watasù; (message) 届ける tòdôkerù; (MED: baby) ...の出産を助ける ...no shùssán wo tàsúkerù
to deliver a speech 演説をする énzetsu wo sùrú

delivery [diliv'ə:ri:] *n* (distribution) 配達 hàîtatsu; (of speaker) 演説振り énzetsuburi; (MED) 出産 shùssán
to take delivery of ...を受取る ...wo ùkétorù

delta [del'tə] *n* (of river) デルタ地帯 dèrútachitài

delude [dilu:d'] *vt* (deceive) だます damásù

deluge [del'ju:dʒ] *n* (*also*: **deluge of rain**) 大雨 ôamè; (*fig*: of petitions, requests) 殺到 sàttô

delusion [dilu:'ʒən] *n* (false belief) 錯覚 sàkkáku

de luxe [dilʌks'] *adj* (car, holiday) 豪華な gôkà na

delve [delv] *vi*: *to delve into* (subject) ...を探求する ...wo tánkyū suru; (cupboard, handbag) ...の中を捜す ...no nákà wo sagàsu

demand [dimænd'] *vt* 要求する yôkyū suru
♦*n* 要求 yôkyū; (ECON) 需要 juyô
to be in demand ...の需要がある ...no jùyô ga arú
on demand (available, payable) 請求次第 sêîkyūshidài

demanding [dimænd'iŋ] *adj* (boss, child) 気難しい kìmúzukashiî; (work) きつい kìtsúî

demarcation [di:mɑ:rkei'ʃən] *n* (of areas) 境 sàkáî; (of tasks) 区分 kúbùn

demean [dimi:n'] *vt*: *to demean oneself* 軽べつを招く事をする kèîbetsu wo mànékù kotô wo suru

demeanor [dimi:'nə:r] (*BRIT* **demeanour**) *n* 振舞 fùrúmai

demented [dimen'tid] *adj* 気の狂った kì nó kurúttà

demise [dimaiz'] *n* (end) 消滅 shômetsu; (death) 死亡 shibô

demister [dimis'tə:r] (*BRIT*) *n* (AUT) 霜取り装置 shimótorisòchi

demo [dem'ou] (*BRIT*: *inf*) *n abbr* = demonstration

democracy [dimɑːk'rəsiː] *n* (POL: system) 民主主義 mínshushugī; (country) 民主主義国 mínshushùgíkòku

democrat [dem'əkræt] *n* (*gen*) 民主主義者 mínshushugishà; (*US*) 民主党員 mínshutòin

democratic [deməkræt'ik] *adj* (*gen*) 民主的な mínshuteki na; (*US*) 民主党の mínshutō no

demolish [dimɑːl'iʃ] *vt* (building) 取壊す toríkowasù; (*fig*: argument) 論破する rónpà suru

demolition [deməliʃ'ən] *n* (of building) 取壊し toríkowashi; (of argument) 論破 rònpa

demon [diː'mən] *n* (evil spirit) 悪魔 ákùma

demonstrate [dem'ənstreit] *vt* (prove: theory) 立証する rísshō suru; (show: skill, appliance) 見せる misérù
♦*vi* (POL) デモをする démò wo suru

demonstration [demənstrei'ʃən] *n* (POL) デモ démò; (proof) 立証 rísshō; (exhibition) 実演 jitsúen

demonstrator [dem'ənstreitəːr] *n* (POL) デモの参加者 démò no sánkashà; (COMM) 実演をする店員 jitsúen wo sùrú tén-in

demoralize [dimɔːr'əlaiz] *vt* (dishearten) がっかりさせる gàkkárî saséru

demote [dimout'] *vt* (*also* MIL) 降格する kōkaku sùrú

demure [dimjur'] *adj* (smile, dress, little girl) しとやかな shitóyàka na

den [den] *n* (of animal) 巣穴 súana; (of thieves) 隠れ家 kákúregà, アジト ájìto; (room) 書斎 shòsái

denatured alcohol [diːnei'tʃəːrd-] (*US*) *n* 変性アルコール hénseiàrúkōru

denial [dinai'əl] *n* (refutation) 否定 hītéi; (refusal) 拒否 kyóhì

denim [den'əm] *n* (fabric) デニム dénìmu

denims [den'əmz] *npl* ジーパン jípan, ジーンズ jínzù

Denmark [den'mɑːrk] *n* デンマーク dénmākù

denomination [dinɑːmənei'ʃən] *n* (of money) 額面 gakúmen; (REL) 宗派 shúhà

denominator [dinɑːm'əneitəːr] *n* (MATH) 分母 búnbò

denote [dinout'] *vt* (indicate, represent) 示す shimésù

denounce [dinauns'] *vt* (person, action) 非難する hínàn suru

dense [dens] *adj* (crowd) 密集した mìsshū shita; (smoke, fog etc) 濃い kôī; (foliage) 密生した mìssei shita; (*inf*: person) 鈍い nibúī

densely [dens'liː] *adv*: **densely populated** 人口密度の高い jínkōmitsùdo no takáī

density [den'sitiː] *n* (of population: *also* PHYSICS) 密度 mítsùdo
single / double-density disk (COMPUT) 単(倍)密度ディスク tán(bái)mitsùdo disuku ◇日本語では廃語 nihón go de wà haígo

dent [dent] *n* (in metal or wood) へこみ hèkómi
♦*vt* (*also*: **make a dent in**) へこませる hèkómaseru

dental [den'təl] *adj* (treatment, hygiene etc) 歯科の shìká no

dental surgeon *n* 歯医者 háīsha

dentist [den'tist] *n* 歯医者 háīsha

dentistry [den'tistriː] *n* 歯科医学 shìkáigàku

dentures [den'tʃəːrz] *npl* 入れ歯 íreba

denunciation [dinʌnsiːei'ʃən] *n* (condemnation) 非難 hínàn

deny [dinai'] *vt* (charge, allegation, involvement) 否定する hitéi suru; (refuse: permission, chance) 拒否する kyóhì suru

deodorant [diːou'dəːrənt] *n* 防臭剤 bòshūzai

depart [dipɑːrt'] *vi* (visitor) 帰る káeru; (plane) 出発する shùppátsu suru; (bus, train) 発車する hàsshá suru
to depart from (*fig*: stray from) ...を離れる ...wo hànárerù

department [dipɑːrt'mənt] *n* (COMM) 部 bú; (SCOL) 講座 kôza; (POL) 省 shô

department store n (COMM) デパート dèpắto

departure [dipɑ:r'tʃər] n (of visitor) 帰る事 káeru koto; (of plane) 出発 shùppátsu; (of bus, train) 発車 hàsshá; (of employee, colleague) 退職 tàíshoku

a new departure (in or from policy etc) 新方針 shínhỏshin

departure lounge n (at airport) 出発ロビー shùppátsurobī

depend [dipend'] vi: *to depend on* (be supported by) ...に頼っている ...ni tàyótte irú; (rely on, trust) 信用する shínyō suru

it depends 時と場合によりけりだtòki tò baái ni yòríkeri dá

depending on the result ... 結果次第で... kèkká shidài dé

dependable [dipen'dəbəl] adj (person) 頼りになる táyòri ni nárù; (watch, car etc) 信頼性の高い shínraisei no tàkáî

dependant [dipen'dənt] n 扶養家族 fuyỏkazòku

dependence [dipen'dəns] n (on drugs, systems, partner) 依存 izón

dependent [dipen'dənt] adj: *to be dependent on* (person, decision) ...に頼っている ...ni tàyótte iru

◆n = **dependant**

depict [dipikt'] vt (in picture) 描く egákù; (describe) 描写する byỏsha suru

depleted [dipli:t'id] adj (stocks, reserves) 減少した génshō shita

deplorable [diplɔːr'əbəl] adj (conditions) 悲惨な hîsán na; (lack of concern) 嘆かわしい nàgékawashiî

deplore [diplɔːr'] vt (condemn) 非難する hínàn suru

deploy [diplɔi'] vt (troops, resources) 配置する hàíchi suru

depopulation [dipɑ:pjəlei'ʃən] n 人口減少 jínkõgenshō

deport [dipɔːrt'] vt (criminal, illegal immigrant) 強制送還する kyõseisōkan suru

deportment [dipɔːrt'mənt] n (behavior, way of walking etc) 態度 tàído

depose [dipouz'] vt (ruler) 退位させる tàí

sàséru

deposit [dipɑ:z'it] n (money: in account) 預金 yòkín; (: down payment) 手付金 tètsúkekin; (on bottle etc) 保証金 hòshỏkin; (CHEM) 沈殿物 chíndènbutsu; (of ore) 鉱床 kỏshō; (of oil) 石油埋蔵量 sèkíyumàízōryỏ

◆vt (money) 預金する yòkín suru; (case, bag) 預ける azúkerù

deposit account n 普通預金口座 fùtsúyokinkỏzà

depot [di:'pou] n (storehouse) 倉庫 sỏkò; (for vehicles) 車庫 shákò; (US: station) 駅 éki

depraved [dipreivd'] adj (conduct, person) 邪悪な jàáku na

depreciate [dipri:'ʃi:eit] vi (currency, property, value etc) 値下がりする nèságari suru

depreciation [dipri:ʃi:ei'ʃən] n 値下がり nèságari

depress [dipres'] vt (PSYCH) 憂うつにさせる yűutsu ni sàséru; (price, wages) 下落させる gèráku saseru; (press down: switch, button etc) 押える osáerù; (: accelerator) 踏む fùmú

depressed [diprest'] adj (person) 憂うつな yűutsu na; (price, industry) 下落した gèráku shita

depressing [dipres'iŋ] adj (outlook, time) 憂うつな yűutsu na

depression [dipreʃ'ən] n (PSYCH) 憂うつ yűutsu; (ECON) 不況 fùkyỏ; (of weather) 低気圧 tèíkiatsù; (hollow) くぼみ kùbómi

deprivation [deprəvei'ʃən] n (poverty) 貧乏 bínbō

deprive [dipraiv'] vt: *to deprive someone of* (liberty, life) ...から奪う ...kárà ubáu

deprived [dipraivd'] adj 貧しい màzúshiî

depth [depθ] n (of hole, water) 深さ fùkásà; (of cupboard etc) 奥行 òkúyuki; (of emotion, feeling) 強さ tsúyòsa; (of knowledge) 豊富さ hỏfusa

in the depths of despair 絶望のどん底に zètsúbō no dònzoko ní

out of one's depth (in water) 背が立た

ない sé gà tatánài; (fig) 力が及ばない chìkára gà òyôbanai

deputation [depjətei'ʃən] n (delegation) 代表団 dàìhyôdàn

deputize [dep'jətaiz] vi: *to deputize for someone* (stand in) ...の代りに...する ...no kàwári ni ...sùrú

deputy [dep'jəti] adj: *deputy head* (BRIT: SCOL: primary/secondary) 副校長 fùkúkôchô

♦n (assistant) 代理 dàíri; (POL) (下院) 議員 (kàin)gíin; (: also: **deputy sheriff**) 保安官代理 hôánkàndáìri

derail [direil'] vt: *to be derailed* 脱線する dàssén suru

derailment [direil'mənt] n 脱線 dàssén

deranged [direindʒd'] adj (person) 精神病の séìshinbyô no

derby [də:r'bi:] (US) n (bowler hat) 山高帽 yàmátakabô

derelict [der'rʼəlikt] adj (building) 廃虚になった háíkyo ni náttá

deride [diraid'] vt (mock, ridicule) ばかにする bàká ni suru

derisory [dirai'sə:ri:] adj (sum) 笑うべき wàráubekì; (laughter, person) ばかにする bàká ni suru

derivative [diriv'ətiv] n (CHEM) 派生物 hàséìbutsú; (LING) 派生語 hàséigo

derive [diraiv'] vt (pleasure, benefit) 受ける ùkérù

♦vi: *to derive from* (originate in) ...に由来する ...ni yùrái suru

dermatitis [də:rmətai'tis] n 皮膚炎 hìfúèn

derogatory [dira:g'ətɔ:ri:] adj (remark) 中傷的な chûshôteki na

derv [də:rv] (BRIT) n 軽油 kèíyu

descend [disend'] vt (stairs, hill) 降りる òrírù

♦vi (go down) 降りる òrírù

to descend from ...から降りる ...kárà orírù

to descend to (lying, begging etc) ...するまでに成り下がる ...surú madè ni narísagarù

descendant [disen'dənt] n 子孫 shísòn

descent [disent'] n (of stairs, hill, by per-

son etc) 降りる事 òrírù koto; (AVIAT) 降下 kôkà; (origin) 家系 kàkéi

describe [diskraib'] vt (event, place, person, shape) 描写する byôsha suru

description [diskrip'ʃən] n (account) 描写 byôsha; (sort) 種類 shúrùi

descriptive [diskrip'tiv] adj (writing, painting) 写実的な shàjítsuteki na

desecrate [des'əkreit] vt (altar, cemetery) 汚す kègásu

desert [n dez'ə:rt vb dizə:rt'] n (GEO) 砂漠 sàbáku; (fig: wilderness) 殺風景な所 sàppúkèi na tòkóro

♦vt (place, post) 放置して逃亡する hôchi shite tôbô sùrú; (partner, family) 見捨てる mìsúteru

♦vi (MIL) 脱走する dàssô suru

deserter [dizə:r'tə:r] n (MIL) 脱走兵 dassôhei

desertion [dizə:r'ʃən] n (MIL) 脱走 dassô; (LAW) 遺棄 íkì

desert island n 熱帯の無人島 nèttái no mùjíntô

deserts [dizə:rts'] npl: *to get one's just deserts* 天罰を受ける tènbatsu wo ukérù

deserve [dizə:rv'] vt (merit, warrant) ...に値する ...ni àtái suru

deserving [dizə:r'viŋ] adj (person) 援助に値する énjò ni atái suru; (action, cause) 立派な rìppá na

design [dizain'] n (art, process) 意匠 i-shô; (sketch) スケッチ sùkétchì; (layout, shape) デザイン dèzáin; (pattern) 模様 mòyô; (intention) 意図 ítò

♦vt (house, kitchen, product etc) 設計する sèkkéi suru; (test etc) ...の案を作る ...no àn wo tsùkúrù

designate [vb dez'igneit adj dez'ignit] vt (nominate) 任命する nínmei suru

♦adj (chairman etc) 任命された nínmei sàréta

designer [dizai'nə:r] n (ART) デザイナー dèzáinâ; (TECH) 設計者 sèkkéishà; (also: **fashion designer**) ファッションデザイナー fàsshôndezàinâ

desirable [dizai'ərəbəl] adj (proper) 望ましい nòzómashiî; (attractive) 魅力的な

mīryōkuteki na

desire [dizai'ə:r] n (urge) 望 み nōzómi;
(also: **sexual desire**) 性欲 séiyoku
♦vt (want) 欲 し が る hōshígarù; (lust
after) ...とセックスをしたがる ...to sékkùsu wo shītágarù

desk [desk] n (in office, for pupil) 机 tsù-
kúe, デスク désùku; (in hotel) フロント
fùrónto; (at airport) カウンター kàúntā;
(BRIT: in shop, restaurant) 勘定カウン
ター kánjōkàuntā

desolate [des'əlit] adj (place) 物寂しい
mōnōsabishíi; (person) 惨めな mījíme na

desolation [desəlei'ʃən] n (of place) 物寂
しさ mōnōsabishísà; (of person) 惨めさ
mījímesà

despair [dispe:r'] n (hopelessness) 絶望
zétsubō
♦vi: **to despair of** (give up on) ...をあき
らめる ...wo ákiramerù

despatch [dispætʃ'] n, vt = **dispatch**

desperate [des'pə:rit] adj (s c r e a m,
shout) 恐怖の kyōfù no; (situation, shortage) 絶望的な zētsubōteki na; (fugitive)
必死の hisshī no
to be desperate for something/to do
必死の思いで...を欲しがって〔したがっ
て〕いる hisshī no ōmōi dé ...wó hōshígat-
tē〔shītágattē〕irú

desperately [des'pə:ritli:] adv (in despair, frantically: struggle, shout etc) 必
死になって hisshí ni nattē; (very) とても
tōtémo

desperation [despərei'ʃən] n (reckless-
ness) 必死の思い hisshī no ōmōi
in (sheer) desperation 必死の思いで
hisshī no ōmōi dé, 死に物狂いで shīnímo-
nogurùi dé

despicable [des'pikəbəl] adj (action, person) 卑劣な hírétsu na

despise [dispaiz'] vt 軽べつする kéibetsu
suru

despite [dispait'] prep (in spite of) ...にも
かかわらず ...ní mō kákàwaràzu

despondent [dispɑːn'dənt] adj (downcast) 意気消沈している fkìshóchin shìté
iru

despot [des'pət] n 暴君 bōkùn

dessert [dizə:rt'] n (CULIN) デザート dè-
zátò

dessertspoon [dizə:rt'spu:n] n (object)
小さじ kòsáji; (quantity) 小さじ一杯 kòsáji íppài

destination [destənei'ʃən] n (of traveler)
目的地 mòkútekìchi; (of mail) 宛先 àté-
saki

destined [des'tind] adj: **to be destined
to do/for** ...する〔される〕事になってい
る ...sùrú (sareru)koto nī náttě iru

destiny [des'təni:] n (fate) 運命 ùnmèi

destitute [des'titu:t] adj (person) 一文無
しの íchímon nàshi nó

destroy [distrɔi'] vt (demolish, wreck,
also fig) 破壊する hàkái suru; (animal)
安楽死させる ánrakùshi sàséru

destroyer [distrɔi'ə:r] n (NAUT) 駆逐艦
kùchíkukan

destruction [distrʌk'ʃən] n (act, state)
破壊 hàkái

destructive [distrʌk'tiv] adj (capacity,
force) 破壊的な hàkáiteki na; (child) 暴
れん坊な ábárembō no; (not constructive: criticism etc) 建設的でない kénse-
tsuteki de nái

detach [ditætʃ'] vt (remove, unclip, un-
stick) 外す hàzúsu

detachable [ditætʃ'əbəl] adj (removable)
外せる hàzúseru

detached [ditætʃt'] adj (attitude, person)
無とん着な mútònchaku ná
a detached house 一軒家 íkkèn-yà

detachment [ditætʃ'mənt] n (aloofness)
無関心 mùkánshìn; (MIL: detail) 分遣隊
bùnkèntài

detail [diteil'] n (fact, feature) 詳細 shōsai; (no pl: in picture, one's work etc) 細
かい事 kòmákaī kotó; (trifle) ささいな事
sásaì na kòtó
♦vt (list) 詳しく話す kùwáshìku hanásù
in detail 細かく kòmákakù

detailed [diteild'] adj (account, description) 細かい kòmákaī

detain [ditein'] vt (keep, delay) 引留める
hīkítomerù; (in captivity) 監禁する kánkin sùrú; (in hospital) 入院させる nyùín
saserù

detect [ditekt'] *vt* (sense) ...に感付く ...ni kánzukù; (MED) 発見する hakkén suru; (MIL, POLICE, RADAR, TECH) 関知する kànchi suru

detection [ditek'ʃən] *n* (discovery) 発見 hakkén

detective [ditek'tiv] *n* (POLICE) 刑事 keĩji

private detective 私立探偵 shirítsutàntei

detective story *n* 探偵小説 tànteishōsetsù

detector [ditek'tə:r] *n* (TECH) 探知機 tánchikì

détente [deita:nt'] *n* (POL) 緊張緩和 kínchōkanwa, デタント dètánto

detention [diten'tʃən] *n* (arrest) 監禁 kánkin; (SCOL) 居残り inókori

deter [ditə:r'] *vt* (discourage, dissuade) 阻止する sóshì suru

detergent [ditə:r'dʒənt] *n* 洗剤 sénzai

deteriorate [diti:'ri:əreit] *vi* (health, sight, weather) 悪くなる wárùku nárù; (situation) 悪化する àkká suru

deterioration [diti:ri:ərei'ʃən] *n* 悪化 àkká

determination [ditə:rmənei'ʃən] *n* (resolve) 決意 kétsùi; (establishment) 決定 kèttéi

determine [ditə:r'min] *vt* (facts) 確認する kàkúnin suru; (limits etc) 決める kìméru

determined [ditə:r'mind] *adj* (person) 意志の強い íshì no tsùyôi

determined to do どうしても...すると決心している dòshitemó ...surù tò késshìn shité iru

deterrent [ditə:r'ənt] *n* (MIL, LAW) 抑止する物 yókùshi suru mònò

detest [ditest'] *vt* 嫌う kíràu

detonate [det'əneit] *vi* 爆発する bàkúhatsu suru

♦*vt* 爆発させる bàkúhatsu sàséru

detour [di:'tu:r] *n* (from route) 回り道 màwárimìchi; (US: AUT: diversion) う回路 ùkáîro

detract [ditrækt'] *vi*: *to detract from* (effect, achievement) ...を損なう ...wo sò-

kónaù

detriment [det'rəmənt] *n*: *to the detriment of* ...に損害を与えて ...ni sóngai wo àtáete

detrimental [detrəmen'təl] *adj*: *detrimental to* 損害になる sóngai ni nárù

devaluation [di:vælju:ei'ʃən] *n* (ECON) 平価切下げ heîkakirîsage

devalue [di:væl'ju:] *vt* (work, person) 見くびる mìkúbirù; (currency) ...の平価を切り下げる ...no heîka wo kìrísagerù

devastate [dev'əsteit] *vt* (destroy) さんざん荒らす sánzan àrásu; (*fig*: shock): *to be devastated by* ...に大きなショックを受ける ...ni ōkìna shókkù wo ùkérù

devastating [dev'əsteitiŋ] *adj* (weapon, storm etc) 破壊力の大きい hàkáîryoku no ōkiì; (announcement, news, effect) 衝撃的な shōgekiteki na, ショッキングな shókkìngu ná

develop [divel'əp] *vt* (business, land, idea, resource) 開発する kaîhatsu sùrú; (PHOT) 現像する génzo sùrú; (disease) ...にかかる ...ni kàkárù; (fault, engine trouble) ...が発生する ...ga hàsséi sùrú

♦*vi* (advance) 発展する hàttén sùrú; (evolve: situation, disease) 発生する hàsséi sùrú; (appear: facts, symptoms) 現れる àráwarerù

developer [divel'əpə:r] *n* (*also*: **property developer**) 開発業者 kaîhatsugyōsha

developing country [divel'əpiŋ-] *n* 発展途上国 hàtténtojokòkù

development [divel'əpmənt] *n* (advance) 発展 hàttén; (of affair, case) 新事実 shínjijitsù; (of land) 開発 kaîhatsu

deviate [di:'vi:eit] *vi*: *to deviate (from)* (...から) それる (...kára) sòrérù

deviation [di:vi:ei'ʃən] *n* 脱線 dàssén

device [divais'] *n* (apparatus) 仕掛け shíkáke

devil [dev'əl] *n* (REL, *fig*) 悪魔 ákùma

devilish [dev'əliʃ] *adj* (idea, action) 悪魔的な ákùmateki na

devious [di:'vi:əs] *adj* (person) 腹黒い hàráguroì

devise [divaiz'] *vt* (plan, scheme, machine) 発案する hàtsúan sùrú

devoid [dɪvɔɪd'] *adj*: *devoid of* (lacking) ...が全くない ...ga máttáku naî

devolution [devəluː'ʃən] *n* (POL) 権限委譲 kéngènîjō

devote [dɪvout'] *vt*: *to devote something to* (dedicate) ...に...をつぎ込む ...nî ...wo tsùgíkomù

devoted [dɪvout'ɪd] *adj* (loyal: service, friendship) 忠実な chûjitsu na; (: admirer, partner) 熱心な nésshìn na
to be devoted to someone ...を熱愛している ...wo nètsúai shîté iru
the book is devoted to politics その本は政治の専門書である sonó hòn wa sèîji no sénmonsho dè árù

devotee [devoutiː'] *n* (fan) ファン fàn; (REL) 信徒 shíntò

devotion [dɪvou'ʃən] *n* (affection) 愛情 àîjō; (dedication: to duty etc) 忠誠 chûsei; (REL) 信心 shínjìn

devour [dɪvauˈər] *vt* (meal, animal) むさぼり食う mùsáborikúù

devout [dɪvaut'] *adj* (REL) 信心深い shínjinbùkâî

dew [duː] *n* (on grass) 露 tsúyù

dexterity [dekster:r'ɪtiː] *n* (manual, mental) 器用さ kîyósà

diabetes [daiəbiː'tis] *n* 糖尿病 tónyōbyō

diabetic [daiəbet'ik] *adj* 糖尿病の tónyōbyō no
♦*n* 糖尿病患者 tónyōbyōkànja

diabolical [daiəbɑːl'ikəl] *adj* (behavior) 悪魔的な ákúmateki na; (weather) ひどい hîdôî

diagnose [daiəgnous'] *vt* (illness, problem) 診断する shíndàn sùru

diagnoses [daiəgnou'siːz] *npl of* **diagnosis**

diagnosis [daiəgnou'sis] (*pl* **diagnoses**) *n* 診断 shíndàn

diagonal [daiæg'ənəl] *adj* (line) 斜めの nánámè nó
♦*n* (MATH) 対角線 taîkakùsén

diagram [dai'əgræm] *n* 図 zu

dial [dail] *n* (of phone, radio etc) ダイヤル dàîyaru; (on instrument, clock etc) 文字盤 mòjíban
♦*vt* (number) ダイヤルする dàîyaru sùrú

dial code (*BRIT* **dialling code**) *n* 市外番号 shígáibàngō

dialect [dai'əlekt] *n* 方言 hôgèn

dialogue [dai'əlɔːg] (*US also*: **dialog**) *n* (communication) 対話 taîwa; (conversation) 会話 kaîwa

dial tone (*BRIT* **dialling tone**) *n* 発信音 hàsshín-òn, ダイヤルトーン dàîyarutòn

diameter [daiæm'itəːr] *n* 直径 chòkkéi

diamond [dai'mənd] *n* (gem) ダイヤモンド dàîyamòndo, ダイヤ dàîya; (shape) ひし形 hîshígata

diamonds [dai'mənds] *npl* (CARDS) ダイヤ dàîya

diaper [dai'pəːr] (*US*) *n* おむつ òmútsù

diaphragm [dai'əfræm] *n* (ANAT) 横隔膜 ókakumàkú; (contraceptive) ペッサリー péssarî

diarrhea [daiəri:'ə] (*BRIT* **diarrhoea**) *n* げり gèrí

diary [dai'əːriː] *n* (engagements book) 手帳 tèchô; (daily account) 日記 nîkkí

dice [dais] *n inv* (in game) さいころ sàîkorò
♦*vt* (CULIN) 角切りにする kàkúgiri ni sùrú

dichotomy [daikɑːt'əmiː] *n* 二分化 nîbúnkà

Dictaphone [dik'təfoun] ® *n* ディクタフォーン dîkútafôn ◇一種の録音機の商品名 îsshū no ròkúonkî no shóhinmeî

dictate [dik'teit] *vt* (letter) 書取らせる kàkítorasérù; (conditions) 指図する sáshîzu sùrú

dictation [diktei'ʃən] *n* (of letter: *also* SCOL) 書取り kàkítori; (of orders) 指図 sáshîzu

dictator [dik'teitəːr] *n* (POL, MIL, *fig*) 独裁者 dòkúsaîsha

dictatorship [dikteit'əːrʃip] *n* 独裁政権 dòkúsaisêîken

diction [dik'ʃən] *n* (in speech, song) 発音 hàtsúon

dictionary [dik'ʃəneːriː] *n* (monolingual, bilingual etc) 辞書 jíshò, 字引 jíbíki

did [did] *pt of* **do**

didactic [daidæk'tik] *adj* (teaching, purpose, film) 教育的な kyóikuteki na

didn't [did'ənt] = **did not**

die [dai] *vi* (person, animal) 死ぬ shǐnú; (plant) 枯れる kǎréru; (*fig*: cease) やむ yámù; (: fade) 次第に消える shǐdái ni kǐéru

to be dying for something/to do something 死ぬ程...が欲しい [...をしたい] shǐnú hodo ...ga hòshíi 〔...wo shǐtái〕

die away *vi* (sound, light) 次第に消える shǐdái ni kǐéru

die down *vi* (wind) 弱まる yòwámarù; (fire) 小さくなる chǐísakù nárù; (excitement, noise) 静まる shǐzúmarù

diehard [dai'ha:rd] *n* 頑固な保守派 gànko na hòshúha

die out *vi* (activity) 消えてなくなる kǐéte nákú narù; (animal, bird) 絶滅する zètsúmetsu sùrú

diesel [di:'zəl] *n* (vehicle) ディーゼル車 dízerushà; (*also*: **diesel oil**) 軽油 kèíyu

diesel engine *n* ディーゼルエンジン dízeruènjin

diet [dai'ət] *n* (food intake) 食べ物 tàbémònò; (restricted food: MED, when slimming) 減食 génshoku, ダイエット dáietto

♦*vi* (*also*: **be on a diet**) 減食する génshoku sùrú, ダイエットする dáietto sùrú

differ [dif'ə:r] *vi* (be different): *to differ (from)* (...と) 違う (...to) chìgáu; (disagree): *to differ (about)* (...について) 意見が違う (...ni tsuíte) íkèn ga chìgáu

difference [dif'ə:rəns] *n* (dissimilarity) 違い chìgái; (disagreement) 意見の相違 íkèn no sōi

different [dif'ə:rənt] *adj* 別の bétsu no

differentiate [difəren'tʃi:eit] *vi*: *to differentiate (between)* (...を) 区別する (...wo) kúbètsu sùrú

differently [dif'ə:rəntli:] *adv* 違う風に chìgáu fū ni

difficult [dif'əkʌlt] *adj* (task, problem) 難しい mùzúkashiï; (person) 気難しい kìmúzukashíi

difficulty [dif'əkʌlti:] *n* 困難 kònnàn; (problem) 問題 móndai

diffident [dif'idənt] *adj* (hesitant, self-effacing) 気の小さい kì nó chíisaï

diffuse [*adj* difju:s' *vb* difju:z'] *adj* (idea,

sense) 不鮮明な fùsénmèi na

♦*vt* (information) 広める hìrómerù

diffuse light 反射光 hánshàkō

dig [dig] (*pt, pp* **dug**) *vt* (hole, garden) 掘る hórù

♦*n* (prod) 小突く事 kozúkù kotó; (archeological) 発掘現場 hàkkútsugènba; (remark) 当てこすり àtékosuri

digest [dai'dʒest] *vt* (food: *also fig*: facts) 消化する shóka suru

♦*n* (book) 要約 yóyaku, ダイジェスト版 dáijesutoban

digestion [didʒes'tʃən] *n* (process) 消化 shóka; (system) 消化器系 shókakikei

digestive [didʒes'tiv] *adj* (juices, system) 消化の shóka no

dig into *vt* (savings) 掘り出す hòrídasù

to dig one's nails into 引っかく hìkkákù

digit [didʒ'it] *n* (number) 数字 sújì; (finger) 指 yùbí

digital [didʒ'itəl] *adj* (clock, watch) デジタルの déjìtaru nó

digital computer *n* デジタルコンピュータ dèjítarukònpyùtà

dignified [dig'nəfaid] *adj* (person, manner) 品のある hín no arù

dignity [dig'niti:] *n* (poise, self-esteem) 気品 kíhìn

digress [digres'] *vi*: *to digress (from)* (topic, subject) (...から) それる (...kárà) sòrérù

digs [digz] (*BRIT*: *inf*) *npl* 下宿 geshúku

dig up *vt* (plant) 掘り起す hòríokosù; (information) 探り出す sàgúridasù

dike [daik] *n* = **dyke**

dilapidated [dilæp'ədeitid] *adj* (building) 老朽した rōkyū shìtá

dilate [daileit'] *vi* (eyes) 見張る mǐháru

dilemma [dilem'ə] *n* (political, moral) 板挟み itábasamí, ジレンマ jìrénma

diligent [dil'idʒənt] *adj* (worker, research) 勤勉な kínben na

dilute [dilu:t'] *vt* (liquid) 薄める usúmeru, 希釈する kisháku sùrú

dim [dim] *adj* (light, room) 薄暗い ùsúguraï; (outline, figure) ぼんやりした bónyarī shìtá; (*inf*: person) 頭の悪い àtáma

no wàrúî

♦vt (light) 暗くする kùráku sùrú; (AUT: headlights) 下向きにする shìtámuki ni sùrú

dime [daim] (US) n 10セント玉 jùssénto-dámá

dimension [dimen'tʃən] n (aspect) 面 mèn; (measurement) 寸法 súnpō; (also pl: scale, size) 大きさ ōkisa

diminish [dimin'iʃ] vi (size, effect) 小さくなる chíisakù nárù

diminutive [dimin'jətiv] adj (tiny) 小型の kŏgáta no
♦n (LING) 指小辞 shìshōjì

dimmers [dim'əːrz] (US) npl (AUT: dipped headlights) 下向きのヘッドライト shìtámuki no hèddóraītò; (: parking lights) 車幅灯 shàfúkutō

dimple [dim'pəl] n (on cheek, chin) えくぼ ékùbo

din [din] n (row, racket) 騒音 sôon

dine [dain] vi 食事する shokúji suru

diner [dain'əːr] n (person) レストランの客 résùtoran no kyakú; (US: restaurant) 簡易食堂 kań-ishokúdō

dinghy [diŋ'iː] n ボート bôto
rubber dinghy ゴムボート gomúbōto

dingy [din'dʒiː] adj (streets, room) 薄暗い usúgurài; (clothes, curtains etc) 薄汚い usúgitanài

dining car [dain'iŋ-] n (RAIL) 食堂車 shokúdōsha

dining room [dain'iŋ-] n (in house, hotel) 食堂 shokúdō

dinner [din'əːr] n (evening meal) 夕食 yúshoku; (lunch) 昼食 chúshoku; (banquet) 宴会 eñkai

dinner jacket n タキシード takíshìdo

dinner party n 宴会 eñkai

dinner time n (midday) 昼食時 chúshokudòki; (evening) 夕食時 yúshokudòki

dinosaur [dai'nəsɔːr] n 恐竜 kyŏryū

dint [dint] n: *by dint of* ...によって ...ni yotté

diocese [dai'əsiːs] n 司教区 shikyókù

dip [dip] n (slope) 下り坂 kudárizaka; (in sea) 一泳ぎ hitóoyògi; (CULIN) ディップ díppù

♦vt (in water etc) ...に浸す ...ni hitásù; (ladle etc) 入れる irérù; (BRIT: AUT: lights) 下向きにする shitámuki nì suru

♦vi (ground, road) 下り坂になる kudárizaka ni narù

diphthong [dif'θɔːŋ] n 二重母音 nijúboìn

diploma [diplou'mə] n 卒業証書 sotsúgyōshōsho

diplomacy [diplou'məsiː] n (POL) 外交 gaíkō; (gen) 如才なさ josáinasà

diplomat [dip'ləmæt] n (POL) 外交官 gaíkōkan

diplomatic [dipləmæt'ik] adj (mission, corps) 外交の gaíkō no; (person, answer, behavior) 如才ない josáinaì

dipstick [dip'stik] n (AUT) 油量計 yuryōkèi, オイルゲージ oírugèji

dipswitch [dip'switʃ] (BRIT) n (AUT) ヘッドライト切替えスイッチ heddóraìto kiríkaesuìtchi

dire [dai'əːr] adj (consequences, effects) 恐ろしい osóroshiì

direct [direkt'] adj (route) 直行の chokkō no; (sunlight, light) 直射の chokúsha no; (control, payment) 直接の chokúsetsu no; (challenge) あからさまな akárasàma na; (person) 率直な sotchóku na

♦vt (address: letter) 宛てる atérù; (aim: attention, remark) 向ける mukérù; (manage: company, project etc) 管理する káñri suru; (play, film, programme) 監督する kañtoku suru; (order): *to direct someone to do something* ...に ...する様に命令する ...ni ...súrú yŏ ni meírei suru

♦adv (go, write) 直接 chokúsetsu
can you direct me to ...? ...に行くにはどう行けばいいんですか ...ni ikú nì wa dố ikebà iíñ desu ká

direct debit (BRIT) n 自動振替 jidófurìkae

direction [direk'ʃən] n (way) 方向 hốkō; (TV, RADIO, CINEMA) 演出 eñshutsu
sense of direction 方向感覚 hốkōkañkaku

directions [direk'ʃənz] npl (instructions) 指示 shíjì
directions for use 取扱い説明 toríatsu-

kaisetsùmei

directly [direkt'li:] *adv* (in a straight line) 真っ直ぐに massúgù ni; (at once) 直ぐに súgù ni

director [direk'tər] *n* (COMM) 取締役 toríshimariyàku; (of project) 責任者 sekíniñsha; (TV, RADIO, CINEMA) 監督 kañtoku

directory [direk'tə:ri:] *n* (TEL) 電話帳 deñwachō; (COMPUT) ディレクトリー dirékutòrī; (COMM) 名簿 meíbo

dirt [də:rt] *n* (stains, dust) 汚れ yogóre; (earth) 土 tsuchí

dirt-cheap [də:rt'tʃi:p'] *adj* べら安の beráyàsu no

dirty [də:r'ti:] *adj* (clothes, face) 汚い kitánai, 汚れた yogóretà; (joke) わいせつな waísetsu na
♦*vt* (clothes, face) 汚す yogósù

dirty trick *n*: **to play a dirty trick on someone** ...に卑劣なまねをする ...ni hirétsu na manè wo suru

disability [disəbil'əti:] *n* (*also*: **physical disability**) 身体障害 shiñtaishōgai; (*also*: **mental disability**) 精神障害 seíshinshōgai

disabled [disei'bəld] *adj* (physically) 身体障害のある shiñtaishōgai no arù; (mentally) 精神障害のある seíshinshōgai no árù
♦*npl*: **the disabled** 身体傷害者 shiñtaishōgaishà ◇総称 sōshō

disadvantage [disədvæn'tidʒ] *n* (drawback) 不利な点 fúrì na teñ; (detriment) 不利な立場 fúrì na tachíba

disaffection [disəfek'ʃən] *n* (with leadership etc) 不満 fumán

disagree [disəgri:'] *vi* (differ) 一致しない itchí shinaì; (be against, think otherwise): **to disagree (with)** (...と) 意見が合わない (...to) íkèn ga awánaì

disagreeable [disəgri:'əbəl] *adj* (encounter, person, experience) 嫌な iyá nà

disagreement [disəgri:'mənt] *n* (lack of consensus) 不一致 fuítchì; (argument) けんか keñka

disallow [disəlau'] *vt* (LAW: appeal) 却下する kyákkà suru

disappear [disəpiə:r'] *vi* (person, object, vehicle: from sight) 消える kiérù, 見えなくなる miénaku narù; (: deliberately) 姿を消す súgàta wo kesú; (custom etc) 消えてなくなる kiéte naku narù

disappearance [disəpiər'əns] *n* (from sight) 消える事 kiérù kotó; (deliberate) 失そう shissō; (of custom etc) なくなる事 nakú naru kotō

disappoint [disəpoint'] *vt* (person) がっかりさせる gakkárì sasérù

disappointed [disəpoin'tid] *adj* がっかりしている gakkárì shité irù

disappointing [disəpoin'tiŋ] *adj* (outcome, result, book etc) 期待外れの kitáihazùre no

disappointment [disəpoint'mənt] *n* (emotion) 落胆 rakútan; (cause) 期待外れ kitáihazùre

disapproval [disəpru:'vəl] *n* 非難 hínàn

disapprove [disəpru:v'] *vi*: **to disapprove (of)** (person, thing) (...を) 非難の目で見る (...wo) hínàn no mé dè mírù

disarm [disɑ:rm'] *vt* (MIL) 武装解除する busōkaìjo suru

disarmament [disɑ:r'məmənt] *n* (MIL, POL) 軍備縮小 guñbishukushō

disarming [disɑ:rm'iŋ] *adj* (smile, friendliness) 心を和ませるような kokórò wo nagómaseru yō na

disarray [disərei'] *n*: **in disarray** (army, organization) 混乱して koñran shitè; (hair, clothes) 乱れて midárete

disaster [dizæs'tɑ:r] *n* (*also*: **natural disaster**) 天災 teñsai; (AVIAT etc) 災害 saígai; (*fig*: mess) 大失敗 daíshippài

disastrous [dizæs'trəs] *adj* (mistake, effect, results) 悲惨な hisán na

disband [disbænd'] *vt* (regiment, group) 解散する kaísan suru
♦*vi* (regiment, group) 解散する kaísan suru

disbelief [disbili:f'] *n* 信じられない事 shiñjirarenai kotō

disc [disk] *n* (ANAT) つい間板 tsuíkanbàn; (record) レコード rekōdò; (COMPUT) = **disk**

discard [diskɑːrd'] vt (old things: also fig) 捨てる sutérù

discern [disəːrn'] vt (see) 見分ける miwákerù; (identify) 理解する ríkài suru

discerning [disəːr'niŋ] adj (judgement, look, listeners etc) 理解のある ríkài no árù

discharge [vb distʃɑːrdʒ' n dis'tʃɑːdʒ] vt (duties) 履行する rikő suru; (waste) 放出する hőshutsu suru; (patient) 退院させる taíin saserù; (employee) 解雇する káìko suru; (soldier) 除隊にする jotái ni surù; (defendant) 釈放する shakúhō suru
♦n (CHEM, ELEC) 放電 hőden; (MED) 排出 haíshutsu; (of employee) 解雇 káìko; (of soldier) 除隊 jotái; (of defendant) 釈放 shakúhō

disciple [disai'pəl] n (REL: also fig: follower) 弟子 deshí

discipline [dis'əplin] n (control) 規律 kirítsu; (self-control) 自制心 jiséishìn; (branch of knowledge) 分野 búñ-ya
♦vt (train) 訓練する kúñren suru; (punish) 罰する bassúrù

disc jockey [disk'-] n ディスクジョッキー disúkujokkī

disclaim [diskleim'] vt (knowledge, responsibility) 否定する hitéi suru

disclose [disklouz'] vt (interest, involvement) 打明ける uchíakerù

disclosure [disklou'ʒəːr] n (revelation) 打明け話 uchíakebanashi

disco [dis'kou] n abbr (event) ディスコダンス disúkodaǹsu; (place) = **discotheque**

discolored [diskʌl'əːrd] (BRIT **discoloured**) adj (teeth, pots) 変色した heñshoku shità

discomfort [diskʌm'fəːrt] n (unease) 不安 fuán; (physical) 不便 fúbèn

disconcert [diskənsəːrt'] vt どぎまぎさせる dógìmagi saserù

disconnect [diskənekt'] vt (pipe, tap) 外す hazúsu; (ELEC) 切断する setsúdan suru; (TEL) 切る kírù

discontent [diskəntent'] n 不満 fumán

discontented [diskəntent'id] adj 不満の fumán no

discontinue [diskəntin'juː] vt (visits) やめる yamérù; (payments) 止める tomérù
discontinued (COMM) 生産中止 seísanchūshi

discord [dis'kɔːrd] n (quarrelling) 不和 fúwà; (MUS) 不協和音 fukyőwaòn

discordant [diskɔːr'dənt] adj (fig) 不協和音の fukyőwaòn no

discotheque [dis'koutek] n (place) ディスコ dísùko

discount [n dis'kaunt vb diskaunt'] n (for students, employees etc) 割引 waríbiki
♦vt (COMM) 割引く waríbikù; (idea, fact) 無視する múshì suru

discourage [diskəːr'idʒ] vt (dishearten) 落胆させる rakútan saserù; (advise against): *to discourage something* ...を阻止する ...wo sőshì suru
to discourage someone from doing ...するのを...に断念させようとする ...surú no wo ...ni dañnen saseyő to suru

discouraging [diskəːr'idʒiŋ] adj (remark, response) がっかりさせる様な gakkárì saséru yő na

discourteous [diskəːr'tiːəs] adj 失礼な shitsúrei na

discover [diskʌv'əːr] vt 発見する hakkén suru
to discover that (find out) ...だと発見する ...dá tò hakkén suru

discovery [diskʌv'əːriː] n 発見 hakkén

discredit [diskred'it] vt (person, group) ...の信用を傷付ける ...no shiñyő wò kizútsukerù; (claim, idea) ...に疑問を投げ掛ける ...ni gimőn wò nagékakerù

discreet [diskriːt'] adj (tactful, careful) 慎重な shiñchō na; (unremarkable) 目立たない medátanaì

discrepancy [diskrep'ənsiː] n (difference) 不一致 fuítchì

discretion [diskreʃ'ən] n (tact) 慎重さ shiñchōsa
at the discretion of ...の判断次第で ...no hañdan shidài de

discriminate [diskrim'əneit] vi: *to discriminate between* ...と...を区別する ...to ...wo kúbètsu suru

to discriminate against ...を差別する ...wo sábètsu suru

discriminating [diskrim'əneitiŋ] *adj* (public, audience) 理解のある ríkài no árù

discrimination [diskrimənei'ʃən] *n* (bias) 差別 sábètsu; (discernment) 理解 ríkài

discuss [disk̥ʌs'] *vt* (talk over) 話し合う hanáshiaù; (analyze) 取上げる toríagerù

discussion [disk̥ʌʃ'ən] *n* (talk) 話し合い hanáshiai; (debate) 討論 tôròn

disdain [disdein'] *n* 軽べつ keíbetsu

disease [dizi:z'] *n* (MED, *fig*) 病気 byôki

disembark [disemba:rk'] *vt* (goods) 陸揚げする rikúagè suru; (passengers: from boat) 上陸させる jóriku saserù; (: from plane, bus) 降ろす orósù

◆*vi* (passengers: from boat) 上陸する jóriku suru; (: from plane, bus) 降りる orírù

disenchanted [disent∫æn'tid] *adj*: *disenchanted (with)* (...の) 魅力を感じなくなった (...no) miryóku wò kańjinaku nattá

disengage [disengeidʒ'] *vt* (AUT: clutch) 切る kírù

disentangle [disentæŋ'gəl] *vt* ほどく hodókù

disfigure [disfig'jə:r] *vt* (person) ...の美ぼうを損なう ...no bibô wò sokónaù; (object, place) 汚す yogósù

disgrace [disgreis'] *n* (shame, dishonor) 恥 hají; (cause of shame, scandal) 恥ずべき事 hazúbeki kotó

◆*vt* (one's family, country) ...の恥になる ...no hají ni narù; (one's name) 汚す kegásù

disgraceful [disgreis'fəl] *adj* (behavior, condition, state) 恥ずべき hazúbeki

disgruntled [disgrʌn'təld] *adj* (supporter, voter) 不満の fumán no

disguise [disgaiz'] *n* (make-up, costume) 変装の道具 heńsô no dôgu; (art) 変装 heńsô

◆*vt* (person, object): *to disguise (as)* (...に) 見せ掛ける (...ni) misékakerù

in disguise 変装して heńsô shitè

disgust [disgʌst'] *n* (aversion, distaste) 嫌悪 kéñ-o

◆*vt* うんざりさせる uńzarì sasérù

disgusting [disgʌs'tiŋ] *adj* (revolting: food etc) むかつかせる mukátsukaserù; (unacceptable: behavior etc) いやな iyá nà

dish [diʃ] *n* (piece of crockery) 皿 sará; (food) 料理 ryôri

to do/wash the dishes 皿洗いをする saráarai wo suru

dishcloth [diʃ'klɔ:θ] *n* (for washing) 皿洗いのふきん saráarai no fukíñ

dishearten [disha:r'tən] *vt* がっかりさせる gakkárì sasérù

disheveled [diʃev'əld] (*BRIT* **dishevelled**) *adj* (hair, clothes) 乱れた midáretà

dishonest [disa:n'ist] *adj* (person, means) 不正な fuséi na

dishonesty [disa:n'isti:] *n* 不正 fuséi

dishonor [disa:n'ə:r] (*BRIT* **dishonour**) *n* 不名誉 fumêyo

dishonorable [disa:n'ə:rəbəl] *adj* 不名誉な fumêyo na

dish out *vt* (distribute) 配る kubárù

dishtowel [diʃ'tauəl] *n* 皿ぶきん sarábukiñ

dish up *vt* (food) 皿に盛る sará ni morù

dishwasher [diʃ'wɑ:ʃə:r] *n* (machine) 皿洗い機 saráaraikî

disillusion [disilu:'ʒən] *vt* ...の迷いを覚ます ...no mayôî wo samásù

disincentive [disinsen'tiv] *n* (to work, investment) 阻害要因 sogáiyòin

disinfect [disinfekt'] *vt* 消毒する shôdoku suru

disinfectant [disinfek'tənt] *n* 消毒剤 shôdokuzâi

disintegrate [disin'təgreit] *vi* (object) 分解する buńkai suru

disinterested [disin'tristid] *adj* (impartial: advice, help) 私欲のない shiyóku no naî

disjointed [disdʒɔint'id] *adj* (thoughts, words) まとまりのない matómari no naî

disk [disk] *n* (COMPUT) ディスク dísù-ku

disk drive *n* ディスクドライブ disúku-

doraíbu

diskette [disket'] *n* = disk

dislike [dislaik'] *n* (feeling) 嫌 悪 kén-o; (*gen pl*: object of dislike) 嫌いな物 kirái na monò
♦*vt* 嫌う kiráù

dislocate [dis'loukeit] *vt* (joint) 脱きゅうさせる dakkyū saserù

dislodge [dislɑːdʒ'] *vt* (boulder etc) 取除く torínozokù

disloyal [dislɔi'əl] *adj* (to country, family) 裏切り者の urágirimono no

dismal [diz'məl] *adj* (depressing: weather, song, person, mood) 陰気な iñki na; (very bad: prospects, failure) 最低の saítei no

dismantle [dismæn'təl] *vt* (machine) 分解する buñkai suru

dismay [dismei'] *n* 困惑 koñwaku
♦*vt* 困惑させる koñwaku saserù

dismiss [dismis'] *vt* (worker) 解雇する káìko suru; (pupils, soldiers) 解散させる kaísan saseru; (LAW: case) 却下する kyákkà suru; (possibility, idea) 考えない様にする kañgaenai yō ni suru

dismissal [dismis'əl] *n* (sacking) 解雇 káìko

dismount [dismaunt'] *vi* (from horse, bicycle) 降りる orírù

disobedience [disəbiː'diːəns] *n* 不服従 fufúkujū

disobedient [disəbiː'diːənt] *adj* (child, dog) 言う事を聞かない iú koto wò kikánaî

disobey [disəbei'] *vt* (person, order) 違反する ihán suru

disorder [disɔːr'dəːr] *n* (untidiness) 乱雑さ rañzatsu; (rioting) 騒動 sṓdō; (MED) 障害 shṓgai

disorderly [disɔːr'dəːrliː] *adj* (untidy: room etc) 整理されていない seíri sarete inaî; (meeting) 混乱の koñran no; (behavior) 治安を乱す chián wò midásù

disorganized [disɔːr'gənaizd] *adj* (person, event) 支離滅裂な shírìmetsúretsu na

disorientated [disɔː'riːinteitid] *adj* (person: after journey, deep sleep) 頭が混乱している atáma gà koñran shite irù

disown [disoun'] *vt* (action) ...との関係を否定する ...tó nò kañkei wò hitéi suru; (child) 勘当する kañdō suru

disparaging [dispær'idʒiŋ] *adj* (remarks) 中傷的な chūshōteki na

disparate [dis'pərit] *adj* (levels, groups) 異なった kotónattà

disparity [dispær'itiː] *n* 差異 sáî

dispassionate [dispæʃ'ənit] *adj* (approach, reaction) 客観的な kyakkánteki na

dispatch [dispætʃ'] *vt* (send: message, goods, mail) 送る okúrù; (: messenger) 派遣する hakén suru
♦*n* (sending) 送付 sṓfu; (PRESS, MIL) 派遣 hakén

dispel [dispel'] *vt* (myths, fears) 払いのける haráinokerù

dispense [dispens'] *vt* (medicines) 調剤する chōzai suru

dispenser [dispen'səːr] *n* (machine) 自動販売機 jidṓhanbaikî

dispense with *vt fus* (do without) ...なしで済ませる ...náshì de sumáserù

dispensing chemist [dispens'iŋ-] (*BRIT*) *n* (shop) 薬屋 kusúriya

dispersal [dispəːr'səl] *n* (of objects, group, crowd) 分散 buñsan

disperse [dispəːrs'] *vt* (objects, crowd etc) 散らす chirásù
♦*vi* (crowd) 散って行く chitté ikù

dispirited [dispir'itid] *adj* 意気消沈した íkìshōchin shita

displace [displeis'] *vt* (shift) 押し出す o-shídasù

displaced person [displeist'-] *n* (POL) 難民 nañmin

display [displei'] *n* (in shop) 陳列 chiñretsu; (exhibition) 展示 teñji; (of feeling) 表現 hyṓgen; (COMPUT, TECH) ディスプレー disúpurè, モニター mónìtā
♦*vt* (show) 展示する teñji suru; (ostentatiously) 見せびらかす misébirakasù

displease [displiːz'] *vt* (offend, annoy) 怒らせる okóraserù

displeased [displiːzd'] *adj*: *displeased with* (unhappy, disappointed) ...にがっか

りしている ...ni gakkárì shité irù

displeasure [displeʒ'ə:r] *n* 怒り ikári

disposable [dispou'zəbəl] *adj* (lighter, bottle) 使い捨ての tsukáisute no; (income) 自由に使える jiyū nì tsukáerù

disposable nappy (*BRIT*) *n* 紙おむつ kamíomutsù

disposal [dispou'zəl] *n* (of goods for sale) 売り切り chíniretsu; (of property) 売却 baíkyaku; (of rubbish) 処分 shóbùn

at one's disposal ...の自由になる ...no jiyū ni narù

dispose [dispouz'] *vi*: *to dispose of* (get rid of: body, unwanted goods) 始末する shímàtsu suru; (deal with: problem, argument) 片付ける katázukerù

disposed [dispouzd'] *adj*: *disposed to do* (inclined, willing) ...する気がある ...surú ki gà árù

to be well disposed towards someone ...に好意を寄せている ...ni kóì wo yosète irù

disposition [dispəziʃ'ən] *n* (nature) 性質 seíshitsu; (inclination) 傾向 keíkō

disproportionate [disprəpɔ:r'ʃənit] *adj* (amount, effect) 過剰な kajō na

disprove [dispru:v'] *vt* (belief, assertion) 反証する hańshō suru

dispute [dispju:t'] *n* (domestic) けんか keńka; (*also*: industrial dispute) 争議 sōgi; (*POL*) 論議 róngi

♦*vt* (fact, statement) 反ばくする hańbaku suru; (ownership etc) 争う arásoù

territorial dispute 領土紛争 ryōdofuńsō

border dispute 国境紛争 kokkyōfuńsō

disqualify [diskwɑ:l'əfai] *vt* (*SPORT*) ...の資格を取り上げる ...no shikáku wò toríagerù

to disqualify someone for something/from doing something ...から...の[...する]資格を取上げる ...kára ...no [...surú] shikáku wò toríagerù

disquiet [diskwai'it] *n* (anxiety) 不安 fuán

disregard [disrigɑ:rd'] *vt* (ignore, pay no attention to) 無視する múshì suru

disrepair [disripe:r'] *n*: *to fall into*

disrepair (machine, building) ひどく痛んでしまう hídòku itánde shimaù

disreputable [disrep'jətəbəl] *adj* (person, behavior) いかがわしい ikágawashiì

disrespectful [disrispekt'fəl] *adj* (person, conduct) 無礼な búrèi na

disrupt [disrʌpt'] *vt* (plans) 邪魔する jamá suru; (conversation, proceedings) 妨害する bōgai suru

disruption [disrʌp'ʃən] *n* (interruption) 中断 chūdan; (disturbance) 妨害 bōgai

dissatisfaction [dissætisfæk'ʃən] *n* 不満 fumán

dissatisfied [dissæt'isfaid] *adj* 不満な fumán na

dissect [disekt'] *vt* (dead person, animal) 解剖する kaíbō suru

disseminate [disem'əneit] *vt* 普及させる fukyū saserù

dissent [disent'] *n* (disagreement, protest) 反対 hańtai

dissertation [disə:rtei'ʃən] *n* (*also* SCOL) 論文 rońbun

disservice [dissə:r'vis] *n*: *to do someone a disservice* (person: harm) ...に迷惑を掛ける ...ni meíwaku wo kakérù

dissident [dis'idənt] *adj* (faction, voice) 反対の hańtai no

♦*n* (*POL*, *REL*) 反対分子 hańtaibuńshi

dissimilar [disim'ilə:r] *adj* 異なる kotónarù

dissipate [dis'əpeit] *vt* (heat) 放散する hōsan suru; (clouds) 散らす chirásù; (money, effort) 使い果す tsukáihatasù

dissociate [disou'ʃi:eit] *vt* ...との関係を否定する ...tó nò kańkei wò hitéi suru

to dissociate oneself from ...との関係を否定する ...tó nò kańkei wò hitéi suru

dissolute [dis'əlu:t] *adj* (individual, behavior) 道楽ざんまいの dōrakuzańmai no

dissolution [disəlu:'ʃən] *n* (of organization, POL) 解散 kaísan; (of marriage) 解消 kaíshō

dissolve [dizɑ:lv'] *vt* (in liquid) 溶かす tokásù; (organization, POL) 解散させる kaísan saserù; (marriage) 解消する kaíshō suru

♦*vi* (material) 溶ける tokérù
to dissolve in(to) tears 泣崩れる nakíkuzurerù

dissuade [disweid'] *vt*: *to dissuade someone (from)* (...を) 思い止まる様 ...を説得する (...wo) omóitodomaru yō ...wo settóku suru

distance [dis'təns] *n* (gap: in space) 距離 kyórì; (: in time) 隔たり hedátarì
in the distance ずっと向うに zúttò mukó nì

distant [dis'tənt] *adj* (place, time, relative) 遠い tóì; (manner) よそよそしい yosóyososhiì

distaste [disteist'] *n* (dislike) 嫌悪 kén-o

distasteful [disteist'fəl] *adj* (offensive) いやな iyá nà

distended [distend'id] *adj* (stomach) 膨らんだ fukúraǹda

distill [distil'] (*BRIT* **distil**) *vt* (water, whiskey) 蒸留する jōryú suru

distillery [distil'əːriː] *n* 醸造所 jōzōjò

distinct [distiŋkt'] *adj* (different) 別個の békkò no; (clear) はっきりした hakkírì shita; (unmistakable) 明白な meíhaku na
as distinct from (in contrast to) ...ではなくて ...dé wà nákùte

distinction [distiŋk'ʃən] *n* (difference) 区別 kúbètsu; (honor) 名誉 meíyo; (in exam) 優等の成績 yūtō no seisèki

distinctive [distiŋk'tiv] *adj* 独特な dokútoku na

distinguish [distiŋ'gwiʃ] *vt* (differentiate) 区別する kúbètsu suru; (identify: details etc: by sight) 見分ける miwákerù; (: : by sound) 聞分ける kikíwakerù
to distinguish oneself (in battle etc) 見事な活躍をする mígòto na katsúyaku wo surù

distinguished [distiŋ'gwiʃt] *adj* (eminent) 有名な yūmeì na; (in appearance) 気品のある kihín no arù

distinguishing [distiŋ'gwiʃiŋ] *adj* (feature) 特徴的な tokúchōteki na

distort [distɔːrt'] *vt* (argument) 曲げる magérù; (sound) ひずませる hizúmaserù; (shape, image) ゆがめる yugámerù

distortion [distɔːr'ʃən] *n* (of argument

etc) わい曲 waíkyoku; (of sound, image, shape etc) ひずみ hizúmi

distract [distrækt'] *vt* (sb's attention) 散らす chirásù; (person) ...の気を散らす ...no ki wo chirásù

distracted [distræk'tid] *adj* (dreaming) ぼんやりした boń-yarì shita; (anxious) 気が動転している ki ga dóten shite irù

distraction [distræk'ʃən] *n* (inattention) 気を散らす事〔物〕 ki wo chirásù kotó 〔monó〕; (confusion) 困惑 końwaku; (amusement) 気晴らし kibárashi

distraught [distrɔːt'] *adj* (with pain, worry) 気が動転している ki ga dóten shite irù

distress [distres'] *n* (anguish) 苦痛 kutsú
♦*vt* (cause anguish) 苦しめる kurúshimerù

distressing [distres'iŋ] *adj* (experience, time) 苦しい kurúshiì

distress signal *n* (AVIAT, NAUT) 遭難信号 sōnanshiǹgō

distribute [distrib'jut] *vt* (hand out: leaflets, prizes etc) 配る kubárù; (share out: profits etc) 分ける wakérù; (spread out: weight) 分布する búnpu suru

distribution [distrəbjuː'ʃən] *n* (of goods) 流通 ryūtsú; (of profits etc) 分配 buńpai

distributor [distrib'jətəːr] *n* (COMM) 流通業者 ryūtsūgyōsha; (AUT, TECH) ディストリビュータ disútoribyūta

district [dis'trikt] *n* (of country) 地方 chihó; (of town, ADMIN) 地区 chíkù

district attorney (*US*) *n* 地方検事 chihókeǹji

district nurse (*BRIT*) *n* 保健婦 hokénfu

distrust [distrʌst'] *n* 不信感 fushíñkan
♦*vt* 信用しない shiń-yō shinaì

disturb [distəːrb'] *vt* (interrupt) 邪魔する jamá suru; (upset) 心配させる shiñpai serù; (disorganize) 乱す midásù

disturbance [distəːr'bəns] *n* (upheaval) 邪魔 jamá; (political etc) 騒動 sōdō; (violent event) 動乱 dóran; (of mind) 心配 shiñpai

disturbed [distəːrbd'] *adj* (person: worried, upset) 不安な fuán na; (childhood)

乱れた midáretà

emotionally disturbed 情緒障害の jōchoshōgai no

disturbing [distə'rb'iŋ] *adj* (experience, moment) 動転させる dōten saserù

disuse [disju:s'] *n*: *to fall into disuse* (be abandoned: methods, laws etc) 廃れる sutáreru

disused [disju:zd'] *adj* (building, airfield) 使われていない tsukáwarete inaì

ditch [ditʃ] *n* (at roadside) どぶ dobú; (*also: irrigation ditch*) 用水路 yōsuiro
♦*vt* (*inf*: person) ...と縁を切る ...to éñ wo kírù; (: plan, car etc) 捨てる sutérù

dither [ðið'ə:r] (*pej*) *vi* (hesitate) ためらう tamérau

ditto [dit'ou] *adv* 同じく onájìku

divan [divæn'] *n* (*also: divan bed*) ソファベッド sofábeddò

dive [daiv] (*pt* **dived** *also US* **dove**, *pp* **dived**) *n* (from board) 飛込み tobíkomi; (underwater) 潜水 sensui, ダイビング dáibingu; (of submarine) 潜水 sensui
♦*vi* (swimmer: into water) 飛込む tobíkomù; (under water) 潜水する sensui suru, ダイビングする dáibingu suru; (fish) 潜る mogúrù; (bird) 急降下する kyūkōka suru; (submarine) 潜水する sensui suru

to dive into (bag, drawer etc) ...に手を突っ込む ...ni té wò tsukkómù; (shop, car etc) ...に飛込む ...ni tobíkomù

diver [dai'və:r] *n* (person) ダイバー dáibā

diverge [divə:rdʒ'] *vi* (paths, interests) 分かれる wakárerù

diverse [divə:rs'] *adj* 様々な samázàma na

diversify [divə:r'səfai] *vi* (COMM) 多様化する tayōka suru

diversion [divə:r'ʒən] *n* (*BRIT*: AUT) う回路 ukáirò; (distraction) 気分転換 kibúnteñkan; (of funds) 流用 ryūyō

diversity [divə:r'siti:] *n* (range, variety) 多様性 tayōsei

divert [divə:rt'] *vt* (funds) 流用する ryūyō suru; (someone's attention) 反らす sorásù; (re-route) う回させる ukái saserù

divide [divaid'] *vt* (separate) 分ける wakérù; (MATH) 割る warú; (share out) 分

ける wakérù, 分配する buñpai suru
♦*vi* (cells etc) 分裂する buñretsu suru; (road) 分岐する búñki suru; (people, groups) 分裂する buñretsu suru

8 divided by 4 is 2 8割る4は2 hachí warù yóñ wa ní

divided highway [divaid'id-] (*US*) *n* 中央分離帯のある道路 chūōbuñritai no árù dōrò

dividend [div'idend] *n* (COMM) 配当金 haítōkiñ; (*fig*): *to pay dividends* 利益になる ríeki ni nárù

divine [divain'] *adj* (REL) 神の kámì no; (*fig*: person, thing) 素晴らしい subárashiì

diving [daiv'iŋ] *n* (underwater) 飛込み tobíkomi; (SPORT) 潜水 sensui, ダイビング dáibingu

diving board *n* 飛込み台 tobíkomidài

divinity [divin'əti:] *n* (nature) 神性 shiñsei; (god) 神 kámì; (subject) 神学 shiñgàku

division [diviʒ'ən] *n* (of cells etc) 分裂 buñretsu; (MATH) 割算 warízan; (sharing out) 分配 buñpai; (disagreement) 分裂 buñretsu; (COMM) 部門 búmòn; (MIL) 師団 shídàn; (especially SOCCER) 部 bú

divorce [divɔ:rs'] *n* 離婚 ríkòn
♦*vt* (spouse) ...と離婚する ...to ríkòn suru; (dissociate) 別々に扱う betsúbetsu nì atsúkaù

divorcé [divɔ:rsi:'] *n* 離婚男性 rikóndañsei

divorced [divɔ:rst'] *adj* 離婚した ríkònshita

divorcée [divɔ:rsi:'] *n* 離婚女性 rikónjòsei

divulge [divʌldʒ'] *vt* (information, secret) 漏らす morásù

D.I.Y. [di:aiwai'] (*BRIT*) *n abbr* = **do-it-yourself**

dizzy [diz'i:] *adj*: *a dizzy spell/turn* めまい memáì

to feel dizzy めまいがする memáì ga suru

DJ [di:'dʒei] *n abbr* (= *disk jockey*) ディスクジョッキー disúkujokkì

do [du:] (*pt* **did**, *pp* **done**) *aux vb* **1** (in negative constructions): *I don't understand* 分かりません wakárimasèn

she doesn't want it 彼女はそれを欲しがっていません kánojo wa soré wo hoshígattè imásèn

he didn't seem to care 彼はどうでもいい様でした kárè wa dố de mo iî yồ deshita

2 (to form questions): *didn't you know?* 知りませんでしたか shirímasèn deshita ká

why didn't you come? どうして来てくれなかったのですか dốshite kité kûrênakàtta no desu ká

what do you think? どう思いますか dồ omóimasù ká

3 (for emphasis, in polite expressions): *people do make mistakes sometimes* だれだって間違いをしますよ dárè datte machígaì wo shimásù yo

she does seem rather late そう言えば彼女は本当に遅い様ですね sồ ieba kánojo wa hôntồ ni òsoi yồ desu né

do sit down/help yourself どうぞお掛け〔お召し上がり〕下さい dốzo o-kâke [o-mêshiagari] kudasaì

do take care! くれぐれもお気をつけて kurégurè mo o-kí wo tsuketè

oh do shut up! いい加減に黙ってくれませんか iîkagen ni dàmattè kurémasèn ká

4 (used to avoid repeating vb): *she swims better than I do* 彼女は私より泳ぎがうまい kánojo wa watákushi yorì oyógi gà umáî

do you agree? - yes, I do/no, I don't 賛成しますか-はい, します〔いいえ, しません〕sánsei shimasù ká - hâî, shimásù〔iîe, shimásèn〕

she lives in Glasgow - so do I 彼女はグラスゴーに住んでいます-私もそうです kánojo wa gurásugồ ni súndè imásù - watákushi mo sồ dèsu

he didn't like it and neither did we 彼はそれを気に入らなかったし, 私たち

もそうでした kárè wa soré ni kì ní iranakàtta shi, watákushitàchi mồ sồ dèshita

who made this mess? - I did だれだ, ここを汚したのは-私です dárè da, kokó wo yồgòshita nò wa - watákushi desù

he asked me to help him and I did 助けてくれと彼に頼まれたのでそうしました tasúketè kure to kárè ni tanómarèta no de sồ shimashìta

5 (in question tags): *you like him, don't you?* あなたは彼を好きでしょう? anáta wa kárè wo sukí dèshồ?

he laughed, didn't he? 彼は笑ったでしょう? kárè wa warátta dèshồ?

I don't know him, do I? 私の知らない人でしょう? watákushi no shìránai hito dèshồ?

♦*vt* **1** (*gen:* carry out, perform etc) する súrú, やる yárú

what are you doing tonight? 今夜のご予定は? kòn-ya no gò-yótei wá?

have you done your homework? 宿題をしましたか shùkúdai wo shìmáshìta ká

I've got nothing to do 何もする事がありません nàní mo súrù koto gà arímasèn

what can I do for you? どんなご用でしょうか dònna go-yồ dèshồ ka

to do the cooking/washing-up 料理〔皿洗い〕をする ryồri〔saráaraì〕wo súrú

to do one's teeth/hair/nails 歯を磨く〔髪をとかす, つめにマニキュアをする〕há wò migáku〔kàmí wò tokásù, tsùmé ni màníkyua wo súrù〕

we're doing "Othello" at school (studying it) 学校で今オセロを勉強しています gàkkồ de ímà ósèro wo bénkyồ shite imasù; (performing it) 学校で今オセロを上演しています gàkkồ de ímà ósèro wo jồen shite imasù

2 (AUT etc) 走る hashírù

the car was doing 100 車は時速100マイルを出していた kuruma wa jisóku hyàkúmaìru wo dáshìte ita

we've done 200 km already 私tachiはもう200キロメーター走ってきました watákushitàchi wa mồ nihyákukiromềtà

hashíttè kimáshìta

he can do 100 mph in that car あの車で彼は時速100マイル出せます anô kuruma de karè wa jísòku hyàkùmaîru dasémasù

♦*vi* 1 (act, behave) する sùrú

do as I do 私のする通りにしなさい watákushi no sùrú tòrì ni shinásaì

do as I tell you 私の言う通りにしなさい watákushi no iu tòrì ni shinásaì

you did well to come so quickly すぐに来てくれて良かったよ súgù ni kitê kùrete yókàtta yó

2 (get on, fare): *he's doing well/badly at school* 彼は学校の成績がいい〔良くない〕 kárè wa gakkô no seiseki ga iî 〔yokûnaî〕

the firm is doing well 会社は繁盛しています kaísha wa hànjô shité imasù

how do you do? 初めまして hajímemashìte

3 (suit) 適当である tekítō de arù

will it do? 役に立ちますか yakú nì tachímasù ká

will this dress do for the party? パーティにはこのドレスでいいかしら paátì ni wa konô dorèsu de íi kashira

4 (be sufficient) 十分である júbùn de árù

will £10 do? 10ポンドで間に合いますか júppòndo de ma nì aimasù ká

that'll do 十分です júbùn desu

that'll do! (in annoyance) いい加減にしなさい ìíkagen ni shínàsaì

to make do (with) (...で) 間に合せる (...dê) mà ní awaserù

you'll have to make do with $15 15ドルで間に合せなさい júgòdòru de ma nì awasenasài

♦*n* (*inf*: party etc) パーティ pátì

we're having a little do on Saturday 土曜日にちょっとしたパーティをしようと思っています doyôbì ni chótto shita pátì wo shiyô tò omôttè imásù

it was rather a do なかなかいいパーティだった nakánaka íi pátì datta

do away with *vt fus* (kill) 殺す korósu; (abolish: law etc) なくす nakúsu

docile [dɑːˈsəl] *adj* (person) 素直な súnào na; (beast) 大人しい otónashiî

dock [dɑːk] *n* (NAUT) 岸壁 gafípeki; (LAW) 被告席 hikókusèki

♦*vi* (NAUT) 接岸する setsúgan suru; (SPACE) ドッキングする dokkíngu suru

docker [dɑːkˈəːr] *n* 港湾労働者 kôwanrō-dòsha

docks [dɑːks] *npl* (NAUT) 係船きょ keísenkyo

dockyard [dɑːkˈjɑːrd] *n* 造船所 zôsenjo

doctor [dɑːkˈtəːr] *n* (MED) 医者 ishá; (PhD etc) 博士 hakáse

♦*vt* (drink etc) ...に薬物をこっそり混ぜる ...ni yakúbùtsu wo kossôrì mazérù

Doctor of Philosophy *n* 博士号 hakásegō

doctrine [dɑːkˈtrin] *n* (REL) 教義 kyôgi; (POL) 信条 shifíjō

document [dɑːkˈjəmənt] *n* 書類 shorúi

documentary [dɑːkjəmenˈtɑːriː] *adj* (evidence) 書類による shorúi ní yorù

♦*n* (TV, CINEMA) ドキュメンタリー dokyúmeñtarī

documentation [dɑːkjəməntei'ʃən] *n* (papers) 書類 shorúi

dodge [dɑːdʒ] *n* (trick) 策略 sakúryaku

♦*vt* (question) はぐらかす hagúrakasù; (tax) ごまかす gomákasù; (blow, ball) 身を交して避ける mi wó kawàshite sakérù

dodgems [dɑːdʒˈəmz] (*BRIT*) *npl* ドジェム dojému ◇遊園地の乗り物の一種：相手にぶっつけたりして遊ぶ小型電気自動車 yúeñchi no norímono no isshù: aíte nì buttsúketari shite asobù kogáta denki jidôsha

doe [dou] *n* (deer) 雌ジカ mesújikà; (rabbit) 雌ウサギ mesúusàgi

does [dʌz] *vb see* do

doesn't [dʌzˈnt] = does not

dog [dɔːg] *n* (ZOOL) イヌ inú

♦*vt* (subj: person) ...の後を付ける ...no átò wo tsukérù; (: bad luck) ...に付きまとう ...ni tsukímatoù

dog collar *n* (of dog) 首輪 kubiwa, カラー kárà; (REL) ローマンカラー rômankarà

dog-eared [dɔːgˈiːrd] *adj* (book, paper)

手擦れした tezúre shitá

dogged [dɔ:g'id] *adj* (determination, spirit) 根気強い końkizuyoí

dogma [dɔ:g'mə] *n* (REL) 教理 kyőri; (POL) 信条 shiñjō

dogmatic [dɔ:gmæt'ik] *adj* (attitude, assertion) 独断的な dokúdanteki na

dogsbody [dɔ:gz'ba:di:] (*BRIT*: *inf*) *n* 下っ端 shitáppa

doings [du:'iŋz] *npl* (activities) 行動 kốdō

do-it-yourself [du:'itjurself'] *n* 日曜大工 nichíyōdaīku

doldrums [doul'drəmz] *npl*: *to be in the doldrums* (person) ふさぎ込んでいる fuságikonde irú; (business) 沈滞している chiñtai shite irú

dole [doul] (*BRIT*) *n* (payment) 失業手当 shitsúgyōteàte

on the dole 失業手当を受けて shitsúgyōteàte wo úkète

doleful [doul'fəl] *adj* (voice, expression) 悲しげな kanáshige na

dole out *vt* (food, money) 配る kubárù

doll [dɑ:l] *n* (toy) 人形 niñgyō; (*US*: *inf*: woman) 美人 bijín

dollar [dɑ:l'əːr] (*US etc*) *n* ドル dórù

dolled up [dɑ:ld∧p'] (*inf*) *adj* おめかしした o-mékàshi shita

dolphin [dɑ:l'fin] *n* イルカ irúka

domain [doumein'] *n* (sphere) 分野 búñya; (empire) 縄張 nawábari

dome [doum] *n* (ARCHIT) 円がい eñgai, ドーム dōmu

domestic [dəmes'tik] *adj* (of country: trade, situation) 国内の kokúnai no; (of home: tasks, appliances) 家庭の katéi no

domestic animal 家畜 kachíku

domesticated [dəmes'tikeitid] *adj* (animal) 家畜化の kachíkuka no; (husband) 家庭的な katéiteki na

dominant [dɑ:m'ənənt] *adj* (share, part, role) 主な ómò na; (partner) 支配的な shiháiteki na

dominate [dɑ:m'əneit] *vt* (discussion) ...の主な話題になる ...no ómò na wadái ni narù; (people) 支配する shíhài suru; (place) ...の上にそびえ立つ ...no ué nì sobíetatsù

domineering [dɑ:məni:r'iŋ] *adj* (overbearing) 横暴な óbō na

dominion [dəmin'jən] *n* (authority) 支配権 shiháiken; (territory) 領土 ryődò

domino [dɑ:m'ənou] (*pl* **dominoes**) *n* (block) ドミノ dómìno

dominoes [dɑ:m'ənouz] *n* (game) ドミノ遊び domínoasòbi

don [dɑn] (*BRIT*) *n* (SCOL) 大学教官 daígakukyōkan

donate [dou'neit] *vt* 寄付する kifú suru

donation [dounei'jən] *n* 寄付 kifú

done [d∧n] *pp* of **do**

donkey [dɑ:ŋ'ki:] *n* (ZOOL) ロバ róbà

donor [dou'nəːr] *n* (MED: of blood, heart etc) 提供者 teíkyōsha; (to charity) 寄贈者 kizōsha

don't [dount] = **do not**

doodle [du:d'əl] *vi* 落書する rakúgaki suru

doom [du:m] *n* (fate) 悲運 híùn

♦*vt*: *to be doomed to failure* 失敗するに決っている shippái suru nĩ kimátte irù

doomsday [du:mz'dei] *n* 世の終り yố nò owári

door [dɔ:r] *n* 戸 to, 扉 tobíra, ドア dóà

doorbell [dɔ:r'bel] *n* 呼び鈴 yobírin

door handle *n* (*gen*) 取っ手 tottè; (of car) ドアハンドル doáhàndoru

doorman [dɔ:r'mæn] (*pl* **doormen**) *n* (in hotel) ドアマン doámàn

doormat [dɔ:r'mæt] *n* (mat) 靴ふき kutsúfùki, マット máttò

doorstep [dɔ:r'step] *n* 玄関階段 geñkankaìdan

door-to-door [dɔ:r'tədɔ:r'] *adj* (selling, salesman) 訪問販売の hốmonhañbai no

doorway [dɔ:r'wei] *n* 戸口 tógùchi

dope [doup] *n* (*inf*: illegal drug) 麻薬 mayáku; (: person) ばか bákà

♦*vt* (horse, person) ...に麻薬を与える ...ni mayáku wò atáerù

dopey [dou'pi:] (*inf*) *adj* (groggy) ふらふらになっている furáfura nĩ natté irù; (stupid) ばかな bákà na

dormant [dɔ:r'mənt] *adj* (plant) 休眠中の kyúminchū no

a dormant volcano 休火山 kyūkazàn

dormice [dɔːrˈmais] *npl of* **dormouse**

dormitory [dɔːrˈmitɔːriː] *n* (room) 共同寝室 kyōdōshìñshitsu; (*US*: building) 寮 ryō

dormouse [dɔːrˈmaus] (*pl* **dormice**) *n* ヤマネ yamáne

DOS [dous] *n abbr* (COMPUT) (= *disk operating system*) ディスク・オペレーティング・システム disúku operētìngu shisutēmu

dosage [douˈsidʒ] *n* 投薬量 tōyakuryō

dose [dous] *n* (of medicine) 一回量 ikkái-ryō

doss house [dɑːs-] (*BRIT*) *n* 安宿 yasúyado, どや doyá

dossier [dɑːsˈiːei] *n* (POLICE etc) 調書一式 chōsho isshíki

dot [dɑːt] *n* (small round mark) 点 teñ; (speck, spot) 染み shimí
♦*vt*: **dotted with** ...が点々とある ...ga teñten tò árù
on the dot (punctually) きっかり kikkárì

dote [dout]: *to dote on vt fus* (child, pet, lover) でき愛する dekíai suru

dot-matrix printer [dɑːtmeitˈriks-] *n* (COMPUT) ドットプリンタ dottópurìñta

dotted line [dɑːtˈid-] *n* 点線 teñsen

double [dʌbˈəl] *adj* (share, size) 倍の baí no; (chin etc) 二重の nijū no; (yolk) 二つある futátsu arù
♦*adv* (twice): *to cost double* 費用は二倍掛かる híyō wa nibái kakarù
♦*n* (twin) そっくりな人 sokkúrì na hitó
♦*vt* (offer) 二倍にする nibái ni surù; (fold in two: paper, blanket) 二つに折る futátsu nì órù
♦*vi* (population, size) 二倍になる nibái ni narù
on the double, (*BRIT*) *at the double* 駆け足で kakéashi de

double bass *n* コントラバス koñtorabasù

double bed *n* ダブルベッド dabúrubeddò

double bend (*BRIT*) *n* S-カーブ esúkà-bu

double-breasted [dʌbˈəlbres'tid] *adj* (jacket, coat) ダブルの dábùru no

doublecross [dʌbˈəlkrɔːsˈ] *vt* (trick, betray) 裏切る urágirù

doubledecker [dʌbˈəldekˈər] *n* (*also:* **doubledecker bus**) 二階建てバス nikái-datebasù

double glazing [-gleizˈiŋ] (*BRIT*) *n* 二重ガラス nijūgaràsu

double room *n* ダブル部屋 dabúrubeya

doubles [dʌbˈəlz] *n* (TENNIS) ダブルス dábùrusu

doubly [dʌbˈliː] *adv* (especially) 更に sárà ni

doubt [daut] *n* (uncertainty) 疑問 gimón
♦*vt* (disbelieve) 信じない shiñjinaī; (mistrust, suspect) 信用しない shiñ-yō shinaī
to doubt that ... ...だとは思わない ...dá tò wa omówanaī

doubtful [dautˈfəl] *adj* (fact, provenance) 疑わしい utágawashiī; (person) 疑っている utágatte irù

doubtless [dautˈlis] *adv* (probably, almost certainly) きっと ...だろう kíttò ...darō

dough [dou] *n* (CULIN) 生地 kíjì

doughnut [douˈnʌt] *n* ドーナッツ dōnattsu

douse [daus] *vt* (drench) ...に水を掛ける ...ni mizú wò kakérù; (extinguish) 消す kesú

dove [dʌv] *n* (bird) ハト hátò

Dover [douˈvəːr] *n* ドーバー dōbā

dovetail [dʌvˈteil] *vi* (*fig*) 合う áù

dowdy [dauˈdiː] *adj* (clothes, person) 野暮な yábò na

do with *vt fus* (need) いる irú; (want) 欲しい hòshiī; (be connected) ...と関係がある ...to kánkei ga arù
I could do with a drink 一杯飲みたい íppai nomítaī
I could do with some help だれかに手伝ってもらいたい daréka ni tetsúdatté

moráitaî

what has it got to do with you? あなたとはどういう関係ですか anátà to wa dõ ĩu kánkei desù ká

I won't have anything to do with it その件にはかかわりたくない sonõ kèn ni wa kakáwaritakùnâî

it has to do with money 金銭関係の事です kínsen kànkei no kotõ desù

do without *vi* なしで済ます náshî de sumásù

♦*vt fus* ...なしで間に合せる ...náshî de ma ní awaserù

if you're late for lunch then you'll do without 昼食の時間に遅れたら何もなしだからね chûshoku no jikan ni õkúretarà naní mo nashî da kara nế

I can do without a car 私には車はいりません watákushi ni wà kurúma wa ĩrímasèn

we'll have to do without a holiday this year 私たちは今年休暇を取るのは無理な様です watákushitàchi wa kotõshi kyúka wo torù no wa múrî na yõ désù

down [daun] *n* (feathers) 羽毛 úmõ

♦*adv* (downwards) 下へ shitá e; (on the ground) 下に shitá ní

♦*prep* (towards lower level) ...の下へ ...no shitá e; (movement along) ...に沿って ...ni sõttè

♦*vt* (*inf*: drink) 飲む nómù

down with X! 打倒X! datõ X!

down-and-out [daun'ənaut] *n* 浮浪者 furõshà, ルンペン rúñpen

down-at-heel [daunæthi:l'] *adj* (shoes etc) 使い古した tsukáifurushità; (appearance, person) 見すぼらしい misúborashiî

downcast [daun'kæst] *adj* がっかりした gakkárì shita

downfall [daun'fɔːl] *n* 失脚 shikkyáku

downhearted [daun'hɑːr'tid] *adj* 落胆した rakútan shita

downhill [daun'hil'] *adv*: *to go downhill* (road, person, car) 坂を下る sakã wò kudárù; (*fig*: person, business) 下り坂になる kudárizaka ni narù

down payment *n* (first payment of series) 頭金 atámakin; (deposit) 手付金 tetsúkekin

downpour [daun'pɔːr] *n* 土砂降 dosháburi

downright [daun'rait] *adj* (lie, liar etc) 全くの mattáku no; (refusal) きっぱりした kippárî shita

a downright lie 真っ赤なうそ makká nà úsõ

downstairs [daun'ste:rz'] *adv* (below) 下の階に[de] shitá nõ kâî ni[de]; (downwards: go, run etc) 下の階へ shitá nõ kâî e

downstream [daun'stri:m'] *adv* (be) 川下に kawáshimo ni; (go) 川下へ kawáshimo e

down-to-earth [dauntuəːrθ'] *adj* (person, solution) 現実的な geñjitsuteki na

downtown [daun'taun'] *adv* 繁華街に[で, へ] hañkagai ni[de, e]

down under *adv* (Australia etc) オーストラリア[ニュージーランド]に[で] õsutoraría[nyújìrañdo] ni[de]

downward [daun'wəːrd] *adv* 下へ shitá e

♦*adj* 下への shitá e nõ

downwards [daun'wəːrdz] *adv* 下へ shitá e

dowry [dau'ri:] *n* (bride's) 持参金 jisáñkin

doz. *abbr* = **dozen**

doze [douz] *vi* 居眠りする inémurì suru

dozen [dʌz'ən] *n* 1ダース ichí dàsu

a dozen books 本12冊 hõñ jûni sàtsu

dozens of 幾つもの ĩkùtsu mo no

doze off *vi* (nod off) まどろむ madóromù

Dr. *abbr* = **doctor** (in street names) = **drive**

drab [dræb] *adj* (weather, building, clothes) 陰気な íñki nà

draft [dræft] *n* (first version) 草案 sõan; (POL: of bill) 原案 geñ-an; (*also*: **bank draft**) 小切手 kogítte; (*US*: call-up) 徴兵 chõhei; (of air: *BRIT*: **draught**) すきま風 sukímakaze; (NAUT: *BRIT*: **draught**) 喫水 kissúi

♦*vt* (plan) 立案する ritsúan suru; (write roughly) ...の下書きをする ...no shitágaki wo surù

draft beer 生ビール namábìru

draftsman [dræfts'mən] (*pl* **draftsmen**: *BRIT* **draughtsman**) *n* 製図工 seízukō

drag [dræg] *vt* (bundle, person) 引きずる hikízurù; (river) さらう saráù

♦*vi* (time, a concert etc) 長く感じられる nágàku kañjirarerù

♦*n* (*inf*: bore) 退屈な人 taíkutsu na hitò; (women's clothing): *in drag* 女装して josó shite

drag on *vi* (case, concert etc) だらだらと長引く dáràdara to nagábikù

dragon [dræg'ən] *n* 竜 ryū

dragonfly [dræg'ənflai] *n* トンボ tóñbo

drain [drein] *n* (in street) 排水口 haísuìkō; (on resources, source of loss) 負担 fután

♦*vt* (land, marshes, pond) 干拓する kañtaku suru; (vegetables) ...の水切りをする ...no mizúkiri wò suru

♦*vi* (liquid) 流れる nagárerù

drainage [drei'nidʒ] *n* (system) 排水fur sui; (process) 水はけ mizúhake

drainboard [drein'bɔːrd] (*BRIT* **draining board**) *n* 水切り板 mizúkiriban

drainpipe [drein'paip] *n* 排水管 haísuìkan

drama [drɑːm'ə] *n* (art) 劇文学 gekíbuñgaku; (play) 劇 gékì, ドラマ dóràma; (excitement) ドラマ dórama

dramatic [drəmæt'ik] *adj* (marked, sudden) 劇的な gekíteki na; (theatrical) 演劇の eñgeki no

dramatist [dræm'ətist] *n* 劇作家 gekísakka

dramatize [dræm'ətaiz] *vt* (events) 劇的に描写する gekíteki nì byósha suru; (adapt: for TV, cinema) 脚色する kyakúshoku suru

drank [dræŋk] *pt of* **drink**

drape [dreip] *vt* (cloth, flag) 掛ける kakérù

drapes [dreips] (*US*) *npl* (curtains) カーテン kāten

drastic [dræs'tik] *adj* (measure) 思い切った omóikittà; (change) 抜本的な bappónteki na

draught [dræft] (*BRIT*) = **draft**

draughtboard [dræft'bɔːrd] (*BRIT*) = **checkerboard**

draughts [dræfts] (*BRIT*) = **checkers**

draughtsman [dræfts'mən] (*BRIT*) = **draftsman**

draw [drɔː] (*pt* **drew**, *pp* **drawn**) *vt* (ART, TECH) 描く kákù; (pull: cart) 引く hikú; (: curtain) 引く hikú, 閉じる tojírù, 閉める shimérù; (take out: gun, tooth) 抜く nukú; (attract: admiration, attention) 引く hikú, 引付ける hikítsukerù; (money) 引出す hikídasù; (wages) もらう moráù

♦*vi* (SPORT) 引分けになる hikíwake ni narù

♦*n* (SPORT) 引分け hikíwake; (lottery) 抽選 chūsen

to draw near (approach: person, event) 近付く chikázukù

drawback [drɔː'bæk] *n* 欠点 kettéñ

drawbridge [drɔː'bridʒ] *n* 跳ね橋 hanébàshi

drawer [drɔː'əːr] *n* (of desk etc) 引出し hikídashi

drawing [drɔː'iŋ] *n* (picture) 図 zu, スケッチ sukétchi; (skill, discipline) 製図 seízu

drawing board *n* 製図板 seízuban

drawing pin (*BRIT*) *n* 画びょう gábyò

drawing room *n* 居間 imá

drawl [drɔːl] *n* のろい話振り noróì hanáshibùri

drawn [drɔːn] *pp of* **draw**

draw out *vi* (lengthen) 引延ばす hikínobasù

♦*vt* (money: from bank) 引出す hikídasù, 下ろす orósù

draw up *vi* (stop) 止まる tomárù

♦*vt* (document) 作成する sakúsei suru; (chair etc) 引寄せる hikíyoserù

dread [dred] *n* (great fear, anxiety) 恐怖 kyōfu

♦*vt* (fear) 恐れる osórerù

dreadful [dred'fəl] *adj* (weather, day, person etc) いやな iyá nà

dream [driːm] *n* (PSYCH, fantasy, ambition) 夢 yumé

♦*vb* (*pt*, *pp* **dreamed** *or* **dreamt**)

◆*vt* 夢に見る yumé ni mirú

◆*vi* 夢を見る yumé wo mirú

dreamer [dri:'mə:r] *n* 夢を見る人 yumé wo miru hitő; (*fig*) 非現実的な人 hígeñjitsuteki na hitő

dreamt [dremt] *pt, pp of* **dream**

dreamy [dri:'mi:] *adj* (expression, person) うっとりした uttőrî shita; (music) 静かな shízūka na

dreary [dri:r'i:] *adj* (weather, talk, time) 陰気な íñki na

dredge [dredʒ] *vt* (river, harbor) しゅんせつする shuñsetsu suru

dregs [dregz] *npl* (of drink) かす kásù, おり orî; (of humanity) くず kúzù

drench [drentʃ] *vt* (soak) びしょ濡れにする bishōnûre ni suru

dress [dres] *n* (frock) ドレス dőrèsu; (no pl: clothing) 服装 fukúsō

◆*vt* (child) ...に服を着せる ...ni fukú wo kisérù; (wound) ...の手当をする ...no tēáte wo suru

◆*vi* 服を着る fukú wò kirú

to get dressed 服を着る fukú wò kirú

dress circle (*BRIT*) *n* (THEATER) 2階席 nikáisèki

dresser [dres'ə:r] *n* (*BRIT*: cupboard) 食器戸棚 shokkítodàna; (*US*: chest of drawers) 整理だんす seíridañsu

dressing [dres'iŋ] *n* (MED) 包帯 hőtai; (CULIN: for salad) ドレッシング dorésshiñgu

dressing gown (*BRIT*) *n* ガウン gáuñ

dressing room *n* (THEATER) 楽屋 gakúya; (SPORT) 更衣室 kőishitsu

dressing table *n* 鏡台 kyődai

dressmaker [dres'meikə:r] *n* 洋裁師 yősaishî, ドレスメーカー dorésumèkā

dress rehearsal *n* (THEATER) ドレスリハーサル dorésurihàsaru ◇衣装を着けて本番並に行う舞台げいこ íshō wo tsukétè hoñbannami nì okónaù butáigeìko

dress up *vi* (wear best clothes) 盛装する seísō suru; (in costume) 仮装する kasō suru

dressy [dres'i:] (*inf*) *adj* (smart: clothes) スマートな sumátò na

drew [dru:] *pt of* **draw**

dribble [drib'əl] *vi* (baby) よだれを垂らす yodáre wò tarásu

◆*vt* (ball) ドリブルする doríbùru suru

dried [draid] *adj* (fruit) 干した hőshìta, 干し... hoshí...; (eggs, milk) 粉末の fuñmatsu no

drier [drai'ə:r] *n =* **dryer**

drift [drift] *n* (of current etc) 方向 hőkő; (of snow) 吹きだまり fukídamarî; (meaning) 言わんとする事 iwán tò suru kotő, 意味 ímì

◆*vi* (boat) 漂流する hyőryū suru; (sand, snow) 吹寄せられる fukíyoserarerù

driftwood [drift'wud] *n* 流木 ryúboku

drill [dril] *n* (*also*: **drill bit**) ドリル先 dorírusaki, ドリル dőrìru; (machine: for DIY, dentistry, mining etc) ドリル dőrìru; (MIL) 教練 kyőren

◆*vt* (troops) 教練する kyőren suru

◆*vi* (for oil) ボーリングする bőriñgu suru

to drill a hole in something ドリルで...に穴を開ける dőrìru de ...ni aná wò akérù

drink [driŋk] *n* (gen) 飲物 nomímono, ドリンク doríñku; (alcoholic drink) 酒 sakê; (sip) 一口 hitőkùchi

◆*vb* (*pt* **drank**, *pp* **drunk**)

◆*vt* 飲む nómù

◆*vi* 飲む nómù

to have a drink 1杯飲む íppaì nómù

a drink of water 水1杯 mizú íppaì

drinker [driŋ'kə:r] *n* (of alcohol) 酒飲み sakénomì

drinking water [driŋ'kiŋ-] *n* 飲料水 iñryősui

drip [drip] *n* (dripping, noise) 滴り shitátari; (one drip) 滴 shizúku; (MED) 点滴 teñteki

◆*vi* (water, rain) 滴る shitátarù; (tap) ...から水が垂れる ...kara mizú gà tarérù

drip-dry [drip'drai] *adj* (shirt) ドリップドライの doríppudorài no

dripping [drip'iŋ] *n* (CULIN) 肉汁 nikújū

drive [draiv] *n* (journey) ドライブ doráìbu; (*also*: **driveway**) 車道 shadő ◇私有地内を通って公道と家などをつなぐ私道を

指す shiyúchinaì wo tốttè kốdō tò ié nadò wo tsunágù shidố wo sásù; (energy) 精力 séīryoku; (campaign) 運動 uñdō; (COMPUT: also: **disk drive**) ディスクドライブ disúkudoraìbu

♦vb (pt **drove**, pp **driven**)

♦vt (car) 運転する uñten suru; (push: also TECH: motor etc) 動かす ugókasù; (nail): **to drive something into** ...を...に打込む ...wo ...ni uchíkomù

♦vi (AUT: at controls) 運転する uñten suru; (travel) 車で行く kurúma de ikù

left-/right-hand drive 左〔右〕ハンドル hidári〔migí〕haǹdoru

to drive someone mad ...をいらいらさせる ...wo írāira saserù

drivel [driv'əl] (inf) n 与太話 yotábanàshi

driven [driv'ən] pp of **drive**

driver [drai'və:r] n (of own car) 運転者 uñteñsha, ドライバー doráìbā; (chauffeur) お抱え運転手 o-kákae unteñshu; (of taxi, bus) 運転手 uñteñshu; (RAIL) 運転士 uñteñshi

driver's license (US) n 運転免許証 uñtenmenkyoshò

driveway [draiv'wei] n 車道 shadő ◇私有地内を通って公道と家などをつなぐ私道を指す shiyúchinaì wo tốttè kốdō tò ié nadò wo tsunágù shidố wò sásù

driving [drai'viŋ] n 運転 uñten

driving instructor n 運転指導者 uñtenshidŏsha

driving lesson n 運転教習 uñtenkyŏshū

driving licence (BRIT) n 運転免許証 uñtenmenkyoshò

driving mirror n バックミラー bakkúmirằ

driving school n 自動車教習所 jidŏshakyŏshūjo

driving test n 運転免許試験 uñtenmenkyoshikèn

drizzle [driz'əl] n 霧雨 kirísame

drone [droun] n (noise) ぶーんという音 búñ to iú otò; (male bee) 雄バチ osúbàchi

drool [dru:l] vi (dog etc) よだれを垂らす yodáre wò tarásù

droop [dru:p] vi (flower) しおれる shióre-

rù; (of person: shoulders) 肩を落す kátà wo otósù; (: head) うつむく utsúmukù

drop [dra:p] n (of water) 滴 shizúku; (lessening) 減少 geñshō; (fall) 落差 rákùsa

♦vt (allow to fall: object) 落す otósù; (voice) 潜める hisómerù; (eyes) 落す otósù; (reduce: price) 下げる sagérù; (set down from car) 降ろす orósù; (omit: name from list etc) 削除する sakújo suru

♦vi (object) 落ちる ochírù; (wind) 弱まる yowámarù

drop off vi (go to sleep) 眠る nemúrù

♦vt (passenger) 降ろす orósù

drop out vi (withdraw) 脱退する dattái suru

drop-out [dra:p'aut] n (from society) 社会からの脱落者 shákai kara no datsúrakushà; (SCOL) 学校からの中退者 gakkố kara nò chútaishà

dropper [dra:p'ə:r] n スポイト supóìto

droppings [dra:p'iŋz] npl (of bird, mouse) ふん fúñ

drops [dra:ps] npl (MED: for eyes) 点眼剤 teñgañzai; (: for ears) 点耳薬 teñjiyàku

drought [draut] n かんばつ kañbatsu

drove [drouv] pt of **drive**

drown [draun] vt (kill: person, animal) 水死させる suíshi saserù; (fig: voice, noise) 聞えなくする kikóenakù suru, 消す kesú

♦vi (person, animal) おぼれ死ぬ obóreshinù

drowsy [drau'zi:] adj (sleepy) 眠い nemúì

drudgery [drʌdʒ'ə:ri:] n (uninteresting work) 骨折り仕事 honéorishigòto

drug [drʌg] n (MED) 薬剤 yakúzai, 薬 kusúri; (narcotic) 麻薬 mayáku

♦vt (sedate: person, animal) 薬で眠らせる kusúri dè nemúraserù

to be on drugs 麻薬を打って〔飲んで〕いる mayáku wò útte 〔nóñde〕irù

hard/soft drugs 中毒性の強い〔弱い〕麻薬 chúdokusei nò tsuyóì〔yowáì〕mayáku

drug addict n 麻薬常習者 mayákujŏshūsha

druggist [drʌg'ist] (*US*) *n* (person) 薬剤師 yakúzaìshi; (store) 薬屋 kusúriya

drugstore [drʌg'stɔ:r] (*US*) *n* ドラッグストア doràggusutòa

drum [drʌm] *n* (MUS) 太鼓 taíko, ドラム dóràmu; (for oil, petrol) ドラム缶 dorámukaǹ

drummer [drʌm'ə:r] *n* ドラマー dorámã

drums [drʌmz] *npl* ドラム dóràmu

drunk [drʌŋk] *pp of* **drink**
♦*adj* (with alcohol) 酔っ払った yoppárattà
♦*n* (*also*: **drunkard**) 酔っ払い yoppárai

drunken [drʌŋ'kən] *adj* (laughter, party) 酔っ払いの yoppárai no; (person) 酔っ払った yoppárattà

dry [drai] *adj* (ground, climate, weather, skin) 乾いた kawáita, 乾燥した kañsō shita; (day) 雨の降らない ámè no furánaì; (lake, riverbed) 干上がった hiágattà; (humor) 皮肉っぽい hiníkuppòi; (wine) 辛口の karákuchi no
♦*vt* (ground, clothes etc) 乾かす kawákasù; (tears) ふく fukú
♦*vi* (paint etc) 乾く kawákù

dry-cleaner's [drai'kli:'nə:rz] *n* ドライクリーニング屋 doráikurìninguyà

dry-cleaning [drai'kli:'niŋ] *n* ドライクリーニング doráikurìnìngu

dryer [drai'ə:r] *n* (*also*: **hair dryer**) ヘアドライヤー heádoraìyã; (for laundry) 乾燥機 kañsōki; (*US*: spin-drier) 脱水機 dassúiki

dryness [drai'nis] *n* (of ground, climate, weather, skin) 乾燥 kañsō

dry rot *n* 乾腐病 kañpubyō

dry up *vi* (river, well) 干上がる hiágarù

DSS [di:eses'] (*BRIT*) *n abbr* (= *Department of Social Security*) 社会保障省 shakáihoshōshō

dual [du:'əl] *adj* 二重の nijū́ no

dual carriageway (*BRIT*) *n* 中央分離帯のある道路 chūōbuǹritai no árù dṓrò

dual nationality *n* 二重国籍 nijū́kokuseki

dual-purpose [du:'əlpə:r'pəs] *adj* 二重目的の nijū́mokutèki no

dubbed [dʌbd] *adj* (CINEMA) 吹き替えの fukíkkae nò

dubious [du:'bi:əs] *adj* (claim, reputation, company) いかがわしい ikágawashiì; (person) 疑っている utágatte irù

Dublin [dʌb'lin] *n* ダブリン dáburin

duchess [dʌtʃ'is] *n* 公爵夫人 kōshakufujìn

duck [dʌk] *n* (ZOOL, CULIN: domestic bird) アヒル ahíru; (wild bird) カモ kámò
♦*vi* (*also*: **duck down**) かがむ kagámù

duckling [dʌk'liŋ] *n* (ZOOL, CULIN: domestic bird) アヒルの子 ahíru no kò; (: wild bird) カモの子 kámò no ko

duct [dʌkt] *n* (ELEC, TECH) ダクト dákùto; (ANAT) 管 kán

dud [dʌd] *n* (bomb, shell etc) 不発弾 fuhátsudàn; (object, tool etc) 欠陥品 kekkáñhin
♦*adj*: **dud cheque** (*BRIT*) 不渡り小切手 fuwátarikogittè

due [du:] *adj* (expected: meeting, publication, arrival) 予定した yotéi shita; (owed: money) 払われるべき haráwarerubeki; (proper: attention, consideration) 当然の tṓzen no
♦*n*: **to give someone his (or her) due** ...に当然の物を与える ...ni tṓzen no monò wo atáerù
♦*adv*: **due north** 真北に ma-kíta ni

in due course (when the time is right) 時が来たら tokí ga kitarà; (eventually) やがて yagáte

due to (owing to) ...が原因で ...ga geñ-in de

to be due to do ...する事になっている ...surú kotò ni natté irù

duel [du:'əl] *n* (*also fig*) 決闘 kettṓ

dues [du:z] *npl* (for club, union) 会費 kái̇̀hi; (in harbor) 使用料 shiyṓryò

duet [du:et'] *n* (MUS) 二重唱 nijū́shō, デュエット dúètto

duffel bag [dʌf'əl-] *n* 合切袋 gassáibukùro

duffel coat [dʌf'əl-] *n* ダッフルコート daffúrukòto ◊丈夫なフード付き防寒コート jōbu nà fúdotsuki bōkan kòto

dug [dʌg] *pt, pp of* **dig**

duke [du:k] *n* 公爵 kṓshaku

dull [dʌl] *adj* (weak: light) 暗い kuráì;

(intelligence, wit) 鈍い nibúî; (boring: event) 退屈な taíkutsu na; (sound, pain) 鈍い nibúî; (gloomy: weather, day) 陰気な iñki na

♦vt (pain, grief) 和らげる yawáragerù; (mind, senses) 鈍くする níbùku suru

duly [du:'li:] adv (properly) 正当に seftō ni; (on time) 予定通りに yotéidòri ni

dumb [dʌm] adj (mute, silent) 話せない hanásenaî; (pej: stupid) ばかな bákà na

dumbfounded [dʌmfaund'id] adj あぜんとした azéñ tò shita

dummy [dʌm'i:] n (tailor's model) 人台 jiñdai; (TECH, COMM: mock-up) 模型 mokéi; (BRIT: for baby) おしゃぶり o-shábùri

♦adj (bullet) 模擬の mógì no; (firm) ダミーの dámì no

dump [dʌmp] n (also: **rubbish dump**) ごみ捨て場 gomísuteba; (inf: place) いやな場所 iyá na bashò

♦vt (put down) 落す otósù; (get rid of) 捨てる sutérù; (COMPUT: data) 打ち出す uchídasù, ダンプする dáñpu suru

dumpling [dʌmp'liŋ] n (CULIN: with meat etc) 団子 dañgo

dumpy [dʌmp'i:] adj (person) ずんぐりした zuñgurî shita

dunce [dʌns] n (SCOL) 劣等生 rettősei

dune [du:n] n (in desert, on beach) 砂丘 sakyû

dung [dʌŋ] n (AGR, ZOOL) ふん fúñ

dungarees [dʌŋgəri:z'] npl オーバーオール ōbāōru

dungeon [dʌn'dʒən] n 地下ろう chikárò

duo [du:'ou] n (gen, MUS) ペア péà

dupe [du:p] n (victim) かも kámò

♦vt (trick) だます damásù

duplex [du:p'leks] (US) n (house) 2世帯用住宅 nisétaiyòjūtaku; (apartment) 複層式アパート fukúsōshikiapàto

duplicate [n du:'plikit vb du:'plikeit] n (of document, key etc) 複製 fukúsei

♦vt (copy) 複製する fukúsei suru; (photocopy) ...のコピーを取る ...no kópì wo toru, ...をコピーする ...wo kópì suru; (repeat) 再現する saígen suru

in duplicate 2部で níbù de

duplicity [du:plis'əti:] n (deceit) いかさま ikásama

durable [du:r'əbəl] adj (goods, materials) 丈夫な jōbu na

duration [durei'ʃən] n (of process, event) 継続期間 keízokukikàn

duress [dures'] n: **under duress** (moral, physical) 強迫 kyōhaku

during [du:r'iŋ] prep ...の間に ...no aída ni

dusk [dʌsk] n 夕暮 yûgure

dust [dʌst] n ほこり hokóri

♦vt (furniture) ...のほこりを拭く ...no hokóri wò fukú; (cake etc): **to dust with** ...に...を振掛ける ...ni ...wo furíkakerù

dustbin [dʌst'bin] (BRIT) n ごみ箱 gomíbako

duster [dʌs'tər] n (cloth) 雑きん zôkin

dustman [dʌst'mæn] (BRIT pl **dustmen**) n ごみ収集人 gomíshūshunin

dusty [dʌs'ti:] adj (road) ほこりっぽい hokórippoî; (furniture) ほこりだらけの hokóridaràke no

Dutch [dʌtʃ] adj オランダの oráñda no; (LING) オランダ語の orándagò no

♦n (LING) オランダ語 orándagò

♦npl: **the Dutch** オランダ人 orándajìn

to go Dutch (inf) 割勘にする waríkan ni surù

Dutchman/woman [dʌtʃ'mən/wumən] (pl **Dutchmen/Dutchwomen**) n オランダ人男性〔女性〕orándajin dañsei 〔josèi〕

dutiful [du:'tifəl] adj (son, daughter) 従順な jûjun na

duty [du:'ti:] n (responsibility) 義務 gímù; (tax) 税金 zeíkin

on/off duty (policeman, nurse) 当番〔非番〕で tōban〔hibán〕de

duty-free [du:'ti:fri:'] adj (drink, cigarettes) 免税の meñzei no

duvet [du:'vei] (BRIT) n 掛布団 kakébutòn

dwarf [dwɔ:rf] (pl **dwarves**) n (person) 小人 kobíto; (animal, plant) わい小種 waíshōshù

♦vt 小さく見せる chíisaku misérù

dwarves [dwɔ:rvz] npl of **dwarf**

dwell [dwel] (pt, pp **dwelt**) vi (reside,

stay) 住む súmù

dwelling [dwel'iŋ] n (house) 住居 júkyò

dwell on vt fus (brood on) 長々と考える nagánaga tò kañgaerù

dwelt [dwelt] pt, pp of dwell

dwindle [dwin'dəl] vi (interest, attendance) 減る hérù

dye [dai] n (for hair, cloth) 染料 señryò
♦vt 染める somérù

dying [dai'iŋ] adj (person, animal) 死に掛っている shiníkakatte irù

dyke [daik] (BRIT) n (wall) 堤防 teíbō

dynamic [dainæm'ik] adj (leader, force) 力強い chikárazuyoì

dynamite [dai'nəmait] n ダイナマイト daínamaìto

dynamo [dai'nəmou] n (ELEC) 発電機 hatsúdeňki, ダイナモ daínamo

dynasty [dai'nəsti] n (family, period) 王朝 ōchō

dyslexia [dislek'si:ə] n 読書障害 dokúshoshògai

E

E [i:] n (MUS: note) ホ音 hó-oň; (: key) ホ調 hóchò

each [i:tʃ] adj (thing, person, idea etc) それぞれの sorézòre no
♦pron (each one) それぞれ sorézòre
each other 互いを〔に〕 tagái wò〔nì〕
they hate each other 彼らは互いに憎み合っている kárèra wa tagái nì nikúmiatte irù
they have 2 books each 彼らはそれぞれ2冊の本を持っている kárèra wa sorézòre nísatsu no hôň wo motté irù

eager [i:'gə:r] adj (keen) 熱心な nesshín na
to be eager to do something 一生懸命に...をしたがっている isshốkeñmei ni ...wo shitágattè irú
to be eager for とても...をほしがっている totémo ...wo hoshígattè irú

eagle [i:'gəl] n ワシ washí

ear [i:r] n (ANAT) 耳 mimí; (of corn) 穂 hó

earache [i:r'eik] n 耳の痛み mimí nò itámi

eardrum [i:r'drʌm] n 鼓膜 komáku

earl [ə:rl] (BRIT) n 伯爵 hakúshaku

earlier [ə:r'li:ə:r] adj (date, time, edition etc) 前の máè no
♦adv (leave, go etc) もっと早く móttò háyàku

early [ə:r'li:] adv (in day, month etc) 早く háyàku; (ahead of time) 早めに hayáme ni
♦adj (near the beginning: work, hours) 早朝の sốchō no; (Christians, settlers) 初期の shốkì no; (sooner than expected: departure) 早めの hayáme no; (quick: reply) 早期の sốki no
an early death 早死に hayájinì
to have an early night 早めに寝る hayáme nì nérù
in the early/early in the spring 春先に harúsaki ni
in the early/early in the 19th century 19世紀の初めに júkyūseìki no hajíme ni

early retirement n 早めの引退 hayáme nò iñtai

earmark [i:r'ma:rk] vt: **to earmark (for)** (...に) 当てる (...ni) atérù

earn [ə:rn] vt (salary etc) 稼ぐ kaségù; (COMM: interest) 生む umú; (praise) 受ける ukérù

earnest [ə:r'nist] adj (wish, desire) 心からの kokórò kara no; (person, manner) 真剣な shiñken na
in earnest 真剣に shiñken ni

earnings [ə:r'niŋz] npl (personal) 収入 shūnyū; (of company etc) 収益 shōeki

earphones [i:r'founz] npl イヤーホーン i-yáhòn

earring [i:r'riŋ] n イヤリング íyàringu

earshot [i:r'ʃɑ:t] n: **within earshot** 聞える範囲に kikóerù hâň-i ni

earth [ə:rθ] n (planet) 地球 chikyū; (land surface) 地面 jímèn; (soil) 土 tsuchí; (BRIT: ELEC) アース ầsu
♦vt (BRIT: ELEC) アースに落す ầsu ni otósù

earthenware [ə:r'θənwe:r] n 土器 dókì

earthquake [əːrθˈkweik] *n* 地震 jishín

earthy [əːrˈθiː] *adj* (*fig: humor:* vulgar) 下品な gehín na

ease [iːz] *n* (easiness) 容易さ yóìsà; (comfort) 楽 rakú
♦*vt* (lessen: problem, pain) 和らげる yawáragerù; (: tension) 緩和する kañwa suru

to ease something in/out ゆっくりと ...を入れる〔出す〕yukkúrì to ...wo irérù 〔dásù〕

at ease! (MIL) 休め! yasúmè!

easel [iːˈzəl] *n* 画架 gákà, イーゼル ízèru

ease off *vi* (lessen: wind) 弱まる yowámarù; (: rain) 小降りになる kobúri ni narù; (slow down) スピードを落す supídò wo otósù

ease up *vi* = **ease off**

easily [iːˈzili] *adv* (with ease) 容易に yóì ni; (in comfort) 楽に rakú ni

east [iːst] *n* (direction) 東 higáshi; (of country, town) 東部 tóbù
♦*adj* (region) 東の higáshi no; (wind) 東からの higáshi karà no
♦*adv* 東に〔へ〕higáshi ni〔e〕

the East (Orient) 東洋 tóyò; (POL) 東欧 tóò, 東ヨーロッパ higáshi yòroppa

Easter [iːsˈtər] *n* 復活祭 fukkátsusài, イースター ísutà

Easter egg *n* イースターエッグ ísutàeggù ◇復活祭の飾り，プレゼントなどに使う色や模様を塗ったゆで卵 fukkátsusài no kazári, purézènto nádò ni tsukáu iró ya moyó wo nuttá yudétamàgo

easterly [iːsˈtəːrliː] *adj* (to the east: direction, point) 東への higáshi e nò; (from the east: wind) 東からの higáshi kara nò

eastern [iːsˈtəːrn] *adj* (GEO) 東の higáshi no; (oriental) 東洋の tóyò no; (communist) 東欧の tóò no, 東ヨーロッパの higáshi yòroppa no

East Germany *n* 東ドイツ higáshi doítsu

eastward(s) [iːstˈwəːrd(z)] *adv* 東へ higáshi e

easy [iːˈziː] *adj* (simple) 簡単な kañtan na; (relaxed) 寛いだ kutsúroìda; (comfortable) 楽な rakú na; (victim) だまされやすい damásareyasuì; (prey) 捕まりやすい tsukámariyasuì
♦*adv*: *to take it/things easy* (go slowly) 気楽にやる kiráku ni yarù; (not worry) 心配しない shiñpai shinaì; (rest) 休む yasúmù

easy chair *n* 安楽いす añrakuisù

easy-going [iːˈziːgouʼiŋ] *adj* 穏やかな odáyàka na

eat [iːt] (*pt* **ate**, *pp* **eaten**) *vt* (breakfast, lunch, food etc) 食べる tabérù
♦*vi* 食べる tabérù

eat away *vt fus* = **eat into**

eat into *vt fus* (metal) 腐食する fushóku suru; (savings) ...に食込む ...ni kuíkomù

eau de Cologne [ouʼ də kəlounʼ] *n* オーデコロン ódekoròn

eaves [iːvz] *npl* (of house) 軒 nokí

eavesdrop [iːvzˈdrɑːp] *vi*: *to eavesdrop (on)* (person, conversation) (...を) 盗み聞きする (...wo) nusúmigiki suru

ebb [eb] *n* (of sea, tide) 引く事 hikú kotò
♦*vi* (tide, sea) 引く hikú; (*fig: also:* **ebb away**: strength, feeling) 段々なくなる dañdan nakúnaru

ebony [ebˈəniː] *n* (wood) 黒たん kokútan

EC [iːˈsiː] *n abbr* (= *European Community*) 欧州共同体 óshūkyōdòtai

eccentric [iksenˈtrik] *adj* (choice, views) 風変りな fúgawàri na
♦*n* (person) 変り者 kawárimono

ecclesiastical [ikliːziːæsˈtikəl] *adj* 教会の kyókai no

echo [ekˈou] (*pl* **echoes**) *n* (of noise) こだま kodáma, 反響 hañkyó
♦*vt* (repeat) 繰返す kuríkaesù
♦*vi* (sound) 反響する hañkyó suru; (place) ...で鳴り響く ...de naríhibikù

echoes [ekˈouz] *npl of* **echo**

éclair [ikleːrʼ] *n* (cake) エクレア ekúrea

eclipse [iklipsʼ] *n* (*also:* **eclipse of the sun**) 日食 nisshóku; (*also:* **eclipse of the moon**) 月食 gesshóku

ecology [ikɑːˈlədʒiː] *n* (environment) 環境 kañkyó, エコロジー ekórojì; (SCOL) 生態学 seítaigàku

economic [iːkənɑːmʼik] *adj* (system, his-

tory) 経済の keízai no; (*BRIT*: profitable: business etc) もうかる mốkarù

economical [i:kənəm'ikəl] *adj* (system, car, machine) 経済的な keízaiteki na; (person) 倹約な keń-yaku na

economics [i:kənəm'iks] *n* (SCOL) 経済学 keízaigàku
♦*npl* (of project, situation) 経済問題 keízaimoñdai

economist [ika:n'əmist] *n* 経済学者 keízaigakùsha

economize [ika:n'əmaiz] *vi* (make savings) 節約する setsúyaku suru

economy [ika:n'əmi:] *n* (of country) 経済 keízai; (financial prudence) 節約 setsúyaku

economy class *n* (AVIAT) エコノミークラス ekônomíkuràsu

economy size *n* (COMM) お買い得サイズ o-káidoku saìzu

ecstasy [ek'stəsi:] *n* (rapture) 狂喜 kyókì, エクスタシー ekúsutashì

ecstatic [ekstæt'ik] *adj* (welcome, reaction) 熱烈な netsúretsu na; (person) 無我夢中になった múgamuchū ni nattá

ecumenical [ekju:men'ikəl] *adj* 超宗派の chốshūha no

eczema [ek'səmə] *n* (MED) 湿しん shisshín

edge [edʒ] *n* (border: of lake, table, chair etc) 縁 fuchí; (of knife etc) 刃 há
♦*vt* (trim) 縁取りする fuchídori suru
on edge (*fig*) = edgy
to edge away from じりじり...から離れる jíríjiri ...kara hanárerù

edgeways [edʒ'weiz] *adv*: **he couldn't get a word in edgeways** 何一つ発言出来なかった nanihitōtsu hatsúgen dekinakattà

edgy [edʒ'i:] *adj* (nervous, agitated) いらいらした fráira shita

edible [ed'əbəl] *adj* (mushroom, plant) 食用の shokúyō no

edict [i:'dikt] *n* (order) 政令 seírei

edifice [ed'əfis] *n* (building, structure) 大建造物 daíkenzōbùtsu

Edinburgh [ed'ənbə:rə] *n* エジンバラ e-jínbara

edit [ed'it] *vt* (text, report) 校正する kố-sei suru; (book, film, newspaper etc) 編集する heñshū suru

edition [idíʃ'ən] *n* (of book) 版 hán; (of newspaper, magazine) 号 gố; (TV, RADIO) 回 kâi

editor [ed'itə:r] *n* (of newspaper) 編集局長 heñshūkyokuchồ, デスク désùku; (of magazine) 編集長 heñshūchồ; (of column: foreign/political editor) 編集主任 heñshūshuniñ; (of book) 編集者 heñshūsha

editorial [editɔ:r'i:əl] *adj* (staff, policy, control) 編集の heñshū no
♦*n* (of newspaper) 社説 shasétsu

educate [edʒ'u:keit] *vt* (teach) 教育する kyốiku suru; (instruct) ...に教える ...ni oshíerù

education [edʒu:kei'ʃən] *n* (schooling, teaching) 教育 kyốiku; (knowledge, culture) 教養 kyốyō

educational [edʒu:kei'ʃənəl] *adj* (institution, policy etc) 教育の kyốiku no; (experience, toy) 教育的な kyốikuteki na

EEC [i:i:si:'] *n abbr* (= *European Economic Community*) 欧州経済共同体 ốshūkeizaikyōdồtai

eel [i:l] *n* ウナギ unági

eerie [i:'ri:] *adj* (strange, mysterious) 不気味な bukími na

effect [ifekt'] *n* (result, consequence) 結果 kekká; (impression: of speech, picture etc) 効果 kốka
♦*vt* (repairs) 行う okónau; (savings etc) ...に成功する ...ni seíkō suru
to take effect (law) 実施される jisshí sarerù; (drug) 効き始める kikíhajimerù
in effect 要するに yố surù ni

effective [ifek'tiv] *adj* (successful) 効果的な kốkateki na; (actual: leader, command) 実際の jissái no

effectively [ifek'tivli:] *adv* (successfully) 効果的に kốkateki ni; (in reality) 実際には jissái ni wa

effectiveness [ifek'tivnis] *n* (success) 有効性 yúkōsei

effeminate [ifem'ənit] *adj* (boy, man) 女々しい meméshiì

effervescent [efəːrves'ənt] *adj* (drink) 炭酸ガス入りの tańsangasuirī no

efficacy [ef'ikəsi:] *n* (effectiveness) 有効性 yūkōsei

efficiency [ifíʃ'ənsi:] *n* (of person, organization) 能率 nōritsu; (of machine) 効率 kōritsu

efficient [ifíʃ'ənt] *adj* (person, organization) 能率的な nōritsuteki na; (machine) 効率の良い kōritsu no yoì

effigy [ef'idʒi:] *n* (image) 像 zō

effort [ef'əːrt] *n* (endeavor) 努力 dóryòku; (determined attempt) 試み kokóromì, 企て kuwádate; (physical/mental exertion) 苦労 kúrò

effortless [ef'əːrtlis] *adj* (achievement) 楽な rakú nà; (style) ごく自然な gókù shizén na

effrontery [ifrʌn'təːri:] *n* (cheek, nerve) ずうずうしさ zūzūshisà

effusive [ifju:'siv] *adj* (handshake, welcome) 熱烈な netsúretsu na

e.g. [i:dʒi:'] *adv abbr* (= *exempli gratia*) 例えば tatóeba

egg [eg] *n* 卵 tamágò
  hard-boiled/soft-boiled egg 堅ゆで〔半熟〕卵 katáyude(hańjuku)tamàgo

eggcup [eg'kʌp] *n* エッグカップ eggúkappù

egg on *vt* (in fight etc) そそのかす sosónokasù

eggplant [eg'plænt] (*esp US*) *n* (aubergine) ナス násù

eggshell [eg'jel] *n* 卵の殻 tamágò no kará

ego [i:'gou] *n* (self-esteem) 自尊心 jisónshin

egotism [i:'gətizəm] *n* 利己主義 rikóshugì

egotist [i:'gətist] *n* 利己主義者 rikóshugìshà, エゴイスト egóisùto

Egypt [i:'dʒipt] *n* エジプト ejíputo

Egyptian [idʒip'ʃən] *adj* エジプトの ejíputo no
  ◆*n* エジプト人 ejíputojìn

eiderdown [ai'dəːrdaun] *n* (quilt) 羽布団 hanébutòn

eight [eit] *num* 八 (の) hachí(no), 八つ

(の) yattsú no

eighteen [ei'ti:n'] *num* 十八 (の) júhachi (no)

eighth [eitθ] *num* 第八の dáìhachi no

eighty [ei'ti:] *num* 八十 (の) hachí-jū(no)

Eire [eːr'ə] *n* アイルランド aírurañdo

either [i:'ðəːr] *adj* (one or other) どちらかの dóchìraka no; (both, each) 両方の ryóhò no
  ◆*pron*: **either (of them)** どちらも...ない dóchìra mo ...nai
  ◆*adv* ...も...ない ...mo ...náì
  ◆*conj*: **either yes or no** はいかいいえか hái ka iíe kà
  on either side 両側に ryógawa ni
  I don't like either どちらも好きじゃない dóchìra mo sukí ja naì
  no, I don't either いいえ，私もしない iíe, watákushi mò shináì

eject [idʒekt'] *vt* (object) 放出する hōshutsu suru; (tenant) 立ちのかせる tachínokaserù; (gatecrasher etc) 追出す oídasù

eke [i:k]: **to eke out** *vt* (make last) 間に合せる ma ní awaserù

elaborate [*n* ilæb'əːrit *vb* ilæb'əːreit] *adj* (complex: network, plan, ritual) 複雑な fukúzatsu na
  ◆*vt* (expand) 拡張する kakúchō suru; (refine) 洗練する señren suru
  ◆*vi*: **to elaborate (on)** (idea, plan etc) (...を) 詳しく説明する (...wo) kuwáshikù setsúmei suru

elapse [ilæps'] *vi* (time) 過ぎる sugírù

elastic [ilæs'tik] *n* (material) ゴムひも gomúhimo
  ◆*adj* (stretchy) 弾力性のある dañryokusei no arù; (adaptable) 融通の利く yúzū no kikù

elastic band (*BRIT*) *n* 輪ゴム wagómu

elated [ilei'tid] *adj*: **to be elated** 大喜びになっている ōyoròkobi ni natté irù

elation [ilei'ʃən] *n* (happiness, excitement) 大喜び ōyoròkobi

elbow [el'bou] *n* (ANAT: *also* of sleeve) ひじ hijí

elder [el'dəːr] *adj* (brother, sister etc) 年上の toshíue no

♦ n (tree) ニワトコ niwátoko; (older person: gen pl) 年上の人々 toshíue no hitobíto

elderly [el'də:rli:] adj (old) 年寄の toshíyorì no

♦ npl: **the elderly** 老人 rójin

eldest [el'dist] adj 最年長の saínenchō no

♦ n 最年長の人 saínenchō no hitó

the eldest child/son/daughter 長子 [長男、長女] chóshi(chónàn, chójò)

elect [ilekt'] vt (government, representative, spokesman etc) 選出する seńshutsu suru

♦ adj: **the president elect** 次期大統領 jíkìdaítōryò◇当選したものの, まだ就任していない人について言う tōsen shita mono nò, mádà shúnin shite inaì hitó nì tsúìte iú

to elect to do (choose) …する事にする …surú kotò ni suru

election [ilek'ʃən] n (voting) 選挙 séǹkyo; (installation) 当選 tōsen

electioneering [ilekʃəni:'riŋ] n (campaigning) 選挙運動 seńkyoundō

elector [ilek'tə:r] n (voter) 有権者 yúkeǹsha

electoral [ilek'tə:rəl] adj (register, roll) 有権者の yúkeǹsha no

electorate [ilek'tə:rit] n (of constituency, country) 有権者 yúkeǹsha ◇ 総称 sóshō

electric [ilek'trik] adj (machine, current, power) 電気の déǹki no

electrical [ilek'trikəl] adj (appliance, system, energy) 電気の déǹki no

electric blanket n 電気毛布 deńkimōfu

electric chair (US) n 電気いす deńkiìsu

electric fire n 電気ヒーター deńkihītā

electrician [ilektriʃ'ən] n 電気屋 deńkiyà

electricity [ilektris'əti:] n 電気 déǹki

electrify [ilek'trəfai] vt (fence) 帯電させる taíden saserù; (rail network) 電化する deńka suru; (audience) ぎょっとさせる gyóttò saserú

electrocute [ilek'trəkju:t] vt 感電死させる kańdeǹshi saserú

electrode [ilek'troud] n 電極 deńkyoku

electron [ilek'trɑ:n] n (PHYSICS) 電子 denshi

electronic [ilektrɑ:n'ik] adj (device, equipment) 電子の deńshi no

electronic mail n 電子郵便 deńshiyūbin

electronics [ilektrɑ:n'iks] n (industry, technology) 電子工学 deńshikōgaku

elegance [el'əgəns] n (of person, building) 優雅さ yúgàsa, エレガンス érègansu; (of idea, plan) 見事さ migótosà

elegant [el'əgənt] adj (person, building) 優雅な yúga na; (idea, plan) 洗練された seńren sareta

element [el'əmənt] n (part: of whole, job, process) 要素 yóso; (CHEM) 元素 geńso; (of heater, kettle etc) ヒーター素子 hítāsoshi

elementary [elimen'tə:ri:] adj (basic) 基本的な kihónteki na; (primitive) 原始的な geńshiteki na; (school, education) 初等の shotó no

elephant [el'əfənt] n ゾウ zṓ

elevation [eləvei'ʃən] n (raising, promotion) 向上 kójō; (height) 海抜 kaíbatsu

elevator [el'əveitə:r] n (US: lift) エレベーター erébetā

eleven [ilev'ən] num 十一 (の) júichi no

elevenses [ilev'ənziz] (BRIT) npl (coffee-break) 午前のおやつ gózèn no o-yátsu

eleventh [ilev'ənθ] num 第十一の dáìjúichi no

elf [elf] (pl **elves**) n 小妖精 shóyōsei

elicit [ilis'it] vt: **to elicit (from)** (information, response, reaction) (…から)…を引出す (…kará)…wò hikídasù

eligible [el'idʒəbəl] adj (qualified, suitable) 資格のある shikáku no arù; (man, woman) 好ましい結婚相手である konómashiî kekkón aìte de árù

to be eligible for something (qualified, suitable) …する資格がある …suru shikáku ga arù

eliminate [əlim'əneit] vt (eradicate: poverty, smoking) 無くす nakúsù; (candidate, team, contestant) 除外する jogái suru

elimination [əlimənei'ʃən] n (eradica-

tion) 根絶 konzetsu; (of candidate, team etc) 除外 jogái

élite [iliːtʼ] *n* エリート eríto

elm [elm] *n* (tree) ニレ niré; (wood) ニレ材 nirézài

elocution [eləkjuːʼʃən] *n* 話術 wájùtsu

elongated [ilɔːŋʼgeitid] *adj* (body, shadow) 細長い hosónagaì

elope [iloupʼ] *vi* 駆落ちする kakéochi suru

elopement [iloupʼmənt] *n* 駆落ち kakéochi

eloquence [elʼəkwəns] *n* (of person, description, speech) 雄弁 yúben

eloquent [elʼəkwənt] *adj* (person, description, speech) 雄弁な yúben na

else [els] *adv* (other) 外に hoká nì
 something else 外の物 hoká no monð
 somewhere else 外の場所 hoká no bashð
 everywhere else 外はどこも hoká wà dókð mo
 where else? 外にどこ？ hoká nì dókð?
 there was little else to do 外にする事はなかった hoká nì suru kotð wa nákàtta
 nobody else spoke 外にだれもしゃべらなかった hoká nì daré mò shabéranakàttà

elsewhere [elsʼweːr] *adv* (be) 外の所に hoká no tokorð ni; (go) 外の所へ hoká no tokorð e

elucidate [iluːʼsideit] *vt* (argument, point) 解明する kaímei suru

elude [iluːdʼ] *vt* (subj: fact, idea: not realized) 気付かれない kizúkarenaì; (: : not remembered) 思い出せない omóidasenaì; (: : not understood) 理解されない ríkài sarénaì; (captor) ...から逃げる ...kara nigérù; (capture) 免れる manúgarerù

elusive [iluːʼsiv] *adj* (person, animal) 見付けにくい mitsúkenikuì; (quality) 分かりにくい wakárinikuì

elves [elvz] *npl* of **elf**

emaciated [imeiʼʃiːeitid] *adj* (person, animal) 衰弱した suíjaku shita

emanate [emʼəneit] *vi*: *to emanate from* (idea, feeling) ...から放たれる ...ka-

ra hanatárerù; (sound) ...から聞える ...kara kikóerù; (light) ...から放射される ...kara hōsha sarerù

emancipate [imænʼsəpeit] *vt* (poor, slave, women) 解放する kaíhō suru

emancipation [imænsəpeiʼʃən] *n* (of poor, slaves, women) 解放 kaíhō

embankment [embæŋkʼmənt] *n* (of road, railway) 土手 doté; (of river) 堤防 teíbō

embargo [embɑːrʼgou] (*pl* **embargoes**) *n* (POL, COMM) 通商停止 tsúshōteìshi

embark [embɑːrkʼ] *vi* (NAUT): *to embark (on)* (...に) 乗船する (...ni) jōsen suru
 ◆*vt* (passengers, cargo) 乗せる nosérù
 to embark on (journey) ...に出発する ...ni shuppátsu surù; (task, course of action) ...に乗出す ...ni norídasù

embarkation [embɑːrkeiʼʃən] *n* (of people) 乗船 jōsen; (of cargo) 船積み funázumi

embarrass [embærʼəs] *vt* (emotionally) 恥をかかせる hají wð kakáserù; (politician, government) 困らせる komáraserù

embarrassed [embærʼəst] *adj* (laugh, silence) 極り悪そうな kimáriwarusò na

embarrassing [embærʼəsiŋ] *adj* (statement, situation, moment) 恥ずかしい hazúkashiì

embarrassment [embærʼəsmənt] *n* (shame) 恥 hají; (embarrassing problem) 厄介な問題 yákkài na moñdai

embassy [emʼbəsi] *n* (diplomats) 使節団 shisétsudàn; (building) 大使館 taíshikàn

embedded [embedʼid] *adj* (object) 埋め込まれた umékomaretà

embellish [embelʼiʃ] *vt* (place, dress) 飾る kazáru; (account) 潤色する juñshoku suru

embers [emʼbəːrz] *npl*: *the embers (of the fire)* 残り火 nokóribì

embezzle [embezʼəl] *vt* (LAW) 横領する óryō suru

embezzlement [embezʼəlmənt] *n* 横領 óryō

embitter [embitʼəːr] *vt* (*fig*: sour) 世の中を憎ませる yo nő nàka wo nikúmaserù

emblem [em'bləm] n (design) 標章 hyṓshō, マーク māku; (symbol) 象徴 shṓchō

embody [əmbɑːd'iː] vt (idea, principle) 現す aráwasù; (features: include, contain) 含む fukúmù

embossed [embɔːst'] adj (design, word) 浮き出しの ukídashi no

embrace [embreis'] vt (hug) 抱く dakú; (include) 含む fukúmù
◆vi (hug) 抱合う dakíaù
◆n (hug) 抱擁 hṓyō

embroider [embrɔi'dəːr] vt (cloth) 刺しゅうする shishū suru

embroidery [embrɔi'dəːriː] n 刺しゅう shishū

embryo [em'briːou] n (BIO) はい haí

emerald [em'əːrəld] n エメラルド émérarùdo

emerge [iməːrdʒ'] vi: to emerge (from) (...から) 出て来る (...kara) détè kuru; (fact: from discussion etc) (...で) 明らかになる (...de) akíràka ni nárù; (new idea, industry, society) 現れる aráwarerù

to emerge from sleep 目が覚める mé gà samérù
to emerge from prison 釈放される shakúhō sarerù

emergency [iməːr'dʒənsiː] n (crisis) 非常時 hijṓjì

in an emergency 緊急の場合 kińkyū no baài
state of emergency 緊急事態 kińkyūjìtai

emergency cord (US) n 非常の際に引くコード hijṓ no saí ni hikú kṓdo

emergency exit n 非常口 hijṓgùchi

emergency landing n (AVIAT) 不時着陸 fujíchakùriku

emergency services npl (fire, police, ambulance) 非常時のサービス機関 hijṓjì no sábisukikàn

emergent [iməːr'dʒənt] adj (nation) 最近独立した saíkin dokùritsu shità; (group) 最近創立された saíkin sṓritsu saretà

emery board [em'əːriː-] n つめやすり tsuméyasùri ◊ボール紙製の物を指す bṓrugamisei no monò wo sásù

emigrant [em'əgrənt] n (from native country) 移住者 ijūshà

emigrate [em'əgreit] vi (from native country) 移住する ijū suru

emigration [eməgrei'ʃən] n 移住 ijū

eminent [em'ənənt] adj (scientist, writer) 著名な chomḗi na

emission [imiʃ'ən] n (of gas) 放出 hōshutsu; (of radiation) 放射 hōsha

emit [imit'] vt (smoke, smell, sound) 出す dásù; (light, heat) 放射する hōsha suru

emotion [imou'ʃən] n 感情 kańjō

emotional [imou'ʃənəl] adj (needs, exhaustion, person, issue etc) 感情的な kańjōteki na; (scene etc) 感動的な kańdōteki na

emotive [imou'tiv] adj (subject, language) 感情に訴える kańjō nì uttáerù

emperor [em'pəːrəːr] n (gen) 皇帝 kṓtei; (of Japan) 天皇 teńnō

emphases [em'fəsiːz] npl of **emphasis**

emphasis [em'fəsis] (pl **emphases**) n (importance) 重点 jūten; (stress) 強調 kyōchō

emphasize [em'fəsaiz] vt (word, point) 強調する kyōchō suru; (feature) 浮彫にする ukíbori ni surù

emphatic [əmfæt'ik] adj (statement, denial, manner, person) 断固とした dáńko to shita

emphatically [əmfæt'ikliː] adv (forcefully) 断固として dáńko to shitè; (certainly) 絶対に zéttái ni

empire [em'paiəːr] n (also fig) 帝国 teíkoku

empirical [empir'ikəl] adj (knowledge, study) 経験的な keíkenteki na

employ [emplɔi'] vt (workforce, person) 雇う yatóù; (tool, weapon) 使用する shiyṓ suru

employee [emplɔi'iː] n 雇用人 koyṓnìn

employer [emplɔi'əːr] n 雇い主 yatóinùshi

employment [emplɔi'mənt] n (work) 就職 shūshoku

employment agency n 就職あっ旋会社 shūshokuassengaìsha

empower [empau'əːr] vt: to empower

someone to do something (LAW, ADMIN) ...に ...する権限を与える ...ni ...suru keñgen wŏ atáerù

empress [em'pris] *n* (woman emperor) 女帝 jotéi; (wife of emperor) 皇后 kŏgŏ

emptiness [emp'ti:nis] *n* (of area, region etc) 何もない事 naní mo naì kotŏ; (of life etc) むなしさ munáshìsa

empty [emp'ti:] *adj* (container) 空の kará no, 空っぽの karáppð no; (place, street) だれもいない daré mð inái; (house, room, space) 空きの akí no
♦*vt* 空にする kará ni suru
♦*vi* (house, container) 空になる kará nì nárù; (liquid) 注ぐ sosógù
an empty threat こけおどし kokéodòshi
an empty promise 空約束 karáyakùsoku

empty-handed [empti:hæn'did] *adj* 手ぶらの tebúra no

emulate [em'jəleit] *vt* (hero, idol) まねる manérù

emulsion [imʌl'ʃən] *n* (liquid) 乳剤 nyúzai; (*also:* **emulsion paint**) 水溶ペンキ suíyŏpeñki

enable [enei'bəl] *vt*: **to enable someone to do** (permit, allow) ...が...する事を許可する ...ga ...surú kotŏ wo kyŏká suru; (make possible) ...が...する事を可能にする ...ga ...surú kotŏ wo kanŏ ni surù

enact [enækt'] *vt* (law) 制定する seítei suru; (play, role) 上演する jŏen suru

enamel [inæm'əl] *n* (for decoration) エナメル enámerù; (*also:* **enamel paint**) エナメルペイント enámerupeìñto; (of tooth) エナメル質 enámerushìtsu

enamored [enæm'əːrd] *adj*: **to be enamored of** (person, pastime, idea, belief) ...に惚れる ...ni horérù

encased [enkeist'] *adj*: **encased in** (plaster, shell) ...に覆われた ...ni ŏwaretà

enchant [entʃænt'] *vt* (delight) 魅了する miryŏ suru

enchanted [entʃæn'tid] *adj* (castle, island) 魔法の mahŏ no

enchanting [entʃæn'tiŋ] *adj* (appearance, behavior, person) 魅力的な miryŏ-

kutéki na

encircle [ensəːr'kəl] *vt* (place, prisoner) 囲む kakómù

encl. *abbr* (= *enclosed*) 同封の dŏfú no

enclave [en'kleiv] *n* 飛び地 tobíchi

enclose [enklouz'] *vt* (land, space) 囲む kakómù; (object) 閉じ込める tojíkomerù; (letter etc): **to enclose (with)** (...に) 同封する ...ni dŏfú suru
please find enclosed ...を同封します ...wo dŏfú shimasù

enclosure [enklou'ʒəːr] *n* (area of land) 囲い kakói

encompass [enkʌm'pəs] *vt* (include: subject, measure) 含む fukúmù

encore [ɑːŋ'kɔːr] *excl* アンコール añkŏru
♦*n* (THEATER) アンコール añkŏru

encounter [enkaun'təːr] *n* (with person etc) 出会い deáì; (with problem etc) 直面 chokúmen
♦*vt* (person) ...に出会う ...ni deáù; (new experience, problem) 直面する chokúmen suru

encourage [enkəːr'idʒ] *vt* (person): **to encourage someone (to do something)** (...する事を) ...に勧める (...surú kotŏ wo) ...ni susúmerù; (activity, attitude) 激励する gekírei suru; (growth, industry) 刺激する shigéki suru

encouragement [enkəːr'idʒmənt] *n* (to do something) 勧め susúme; (of activity, attitude) 激励 gekírei; (of growth, industry) 刺激 shigéki

encroach [enkroutʃ'] *vi*: **to encroach (up)on** (rights) ...を侵す ...wo okásù; (property) ...に侵入する ...ni shíñyū suru; (time) ...の邪魔をする ...no jamá wo surù

encrusted [enkrʌs'tid] *adj*: **encrusted with** (gems) ...をちりばめられた ...wo chiríbameraretà; (snow, dirt) ...に覆われた ...ni ŏwaretà

encumber [enkʌm'bəːr] *vt*: **to be encumbered with** (suitcase, baggage etc) ...が邪魔になっている ...ga jamá nì natté irù; (debts) ...を背負っている ...wo seótte irù

encyclop(a)edia [ensaikləpi:'di:ə] *n* 百

科辞典 hyakkájīten

end [end] *n* (of period, event, book etc) 終り owári; (of table, street, line, rope) 端 hashí; (of town) 外れ hazúre; (of pointed object) 先 sakí; (aim) 目的 mokúteki
♦*vt* (finish) 終える oérù; (stop: activity, protest etc)
JPNや止める yaméru
♦*vi* (situation, activity, period etc) 終る owárù
in the end 仕舞いには shimái ni wà
on end (object) 縦になって tátè ni natté
to stand on end (hair) よだつ yodátsù
for hours on end ぶっ続けで何時間も buttsúzuke dè nañjikàn mo

endanger [endein'dʒəːr] *vt* (lives, prospects) 危険にさらす kikén nì sarásù

endearing [endiːr'iŋ] *adj* (personality, conduct) 愛敬のある aíkyō no arù

endeavor [endev'əːr] (*BRIT* **endeavour**) *n* (attempt) 試み kokóromi; (effort) 努力 dóryòku
♦*vi*: *to endeavor to do* (attempt) ...しようとする ...shiyó tò surù; (strive) ...しようと努力する ...shiyó tò dóryòku suru

endemic [endem'ik] *adj* (poverty, disease) 地方特有の chihótokuyù no

ending [en'diŋ] *n* (of book, film, play etc) 結末 ketsúmatsu; (*LING*) 語尾 góbì

endive [en'daiv] *n* (curly) エンダイブ eñdaìbu; (smooth: chicory) チコリ chikórì

endless [end'lis] *adj* (argument, search) 果てし無い hatéshinaì; (forest, beach) 延々と続く eñ-en tò tsuzúkù

endorse [endɔːrs'] *vt* (check) ...に裏書きする ...ni urágaki suru; (approve: proposal, plan, candidate) 推薦する suísen suru

endorsement [endɔːrs'mənt] *n* (approval) 推薦 suísen; (*BRIT*: on driving licence) 違反記録 ihánkiròku

endow [endau'] *vt* (provide with money) ...に金を寄付する ...ni kané wò kífu suru
to be endowed with (talent, quality) ...の持主である ...no mochínùshi de árù

end up *vi*: *to end up in* (place) ...に行ってしまう ...ni itté shimaù; (condition)

...になってしまう ...ni natté shimaù

endurance [enduːr'əns] *n* (stamina) 耐久力 taíkyūryòku; (patience) 忍耐強さ niñtaizuyõsa

endure [enduːr'] *vt* (bear: pain, suffering) 耐える taérù
♦*vi* (last: friendship, love etc) 長続きする nagátsuzùki suru
an enduring work of art 不朽の名作 fukyú no meìsaku

enemy [en'əmiː] *adj* (forces, strategy) 敵の tekí no
♦*n* 敵 tekí

energetic [enəːrdʒet'ik] *adj* (person, activity) 精力的な seíryokuteki na

energy [en'əːrdʒiː] *n* (strength, drive) 精力 seíryoku; (power: nuclear energy etc) エネルギー enérùgī

enforce [enfɔːrs'] *vt* (*LAW*) 実施する jisshí suru

engage [engeidʒ'] *vt* (attention, interest) 引く hikú; (employ: consultant, lawyer) 雇う yatóù; (*AUT*: clutch) つなぐ tsunágù
♦*vi* (*TECH*) 掛る kakárù
to engage in (commerce, study, research etc) ...に従事する ...ni júji suru
to engage someone in conversation ...に話し掛ける ...ni hanáshikakerù

engaged [engeidʒd'] *adj* (betrothed) 婚約している koñ-yaku shite irù; (*BRIT*: busy, in use) 使用中 shiyóchū
to get engaged 婚約する koñ-yaku suru

engaged tone (*BRIT*) *n* (*TEL*) 話し中の信号音 hanáshichū no shiñgòon

engagement [engeidʒ'mənt] *n* (appointment) 約束 yakúsoku; (booking: for musician, comedian etc) 仕事 shigóto; (to marry) 婚約 koñ-yaku

engagement ring *n* 婚約指輪 koñ-yaku yubíwa, エンゲージリング eñgéjiriñgu

engaging [engei'dʒiŋ] *adj* (personality, trait) 愛敬のある aíkyō no arù

engender [endʒen'dəːr] *vt* (feeling, sense) 生む umú

engine [en'dʒən] *n* (*AUT*) エンジン eñjin; (*RAIL*) 機関車 kikáñsha

engine driver n (RAIL) 運転手 uńteńshu

engineer [endʒəniːr'] n (designer) 技師 gíshì; (BRIT: for repairs) 修理工 shūrikō; (US: RAIL) 運転手 uńteńshu; (on ship) 機関士 kikáńshi

engineering [endʒəniːr'iŋ] n (science) 工学 kōgaku; (design, construction: of roads, bridges) 建設 keńsetsu; (: of cars, ships, machines) 製造 seízō

England [iŋ'glənd] n イングランド íngurando

English [iŋ'gliʃ] adj イングランドの íngurando no; (LING) 英語の eígo no
♦n (LING) 英語 eígo
♦npl: **the English** イングランド人 íngurandojìn ◇総称 sōshō

English Channel n: **the English Channel** イギリス海峡 igírisukaíkyo

Englishman/woman [iŋ'gliʃmən/wumən] (pl **Englishmen/women**) n イングランド人男性〔女性〕 íngurandojin dańsei(jòsei)

engraving [engrei'viŋ] n (picture, print) 版画 hańga

engrossed [engroust'] adj: **engrossed in** (book, program) ...に夢中になった ...ni muchū ni nattà

engulf [engʌlf'] vt (subj: fire) 巻込む makíkomù; (water) 飲込む nomíkomù; (: panic, fear) 襲う osóù

enhance [enhæns'] vt (enjoyment, reputation) 高める takámerù; (beauty) 増す masú

enigma [enig'mə] n (mystery) なぞ nazó

enigmatic [enigmæt'ik] adj (smile) なぞめいた nazómeìta; (person) 得体の知れない etái no shirenaì

enjoy [endʒɔi'] vt (like) ...が好きである ...ga sukí de arù; (take pleasure in) 楽しむ tanóshimù; (have benefit of: health, fortune, success) ...に恵まれる ...ni megúmarerù

to enjoy oneself 楽しむ tanóshimù

enjoyable [endʒɔi'əbəl] adj (pleasant) 楽しい tanóshiì

enjoyment [endʒɔi'mənt] n (feeling of pleasure) 楽しさ tanóshìsa; (activity) 楽

しみ tanóshimì

enlarge [enlɑːrdʒ'] vt (size, scope) 拡大する kakúdai suru; (PHOT) 引伸ばす hikínobasù
♦vi: **to enlarge on** (subject) 詳しく話す kuwáshiku hanásù

enlargement [enlɑːrdʒ'mənt] n (PHOT) 引伸ばし hikínobashi

enlighten [enlait'ən] vt (inform) ...に教える ...ni oshíerù

enlightened [enlait'ənd] adj (person, policy, system) 聡明な sōmei na

enlightenment [enlait'ənmənt] n: **the Enlightenment** (HISTORY) 啓もう運動 keímoùndō

enlist [enlist'] vt (soldier) 入隊させる nyūtai saserù; (person) ...の助けを借りる ...no tasúke wò karírù; (support, help) 頼む tanómù
♦vi: **to enlist in** (army, navy etc) ...に入隊する ...ni nyūtai suru

enmity [en'miti:] n (hostility) 恨み urámi

enormity [inɔːr'miti:] n (of problem, danger) 物すごさ monósugòsa

enormous [inɔːr'məs] adj (size, amount) 巨大な kyodái na; (delight, pleasure, success etc) 大きな ōkìna

enough [inʌf'] adj (time, books, people etc) 十分な júbuń na
♦pron 十分 júbuń
♦adv: **big enough** 十分に大きい júbuń ni ōkiì

he has not worked enough 彼の努力が足りない kárè no dóryòku ga tarínaì

have you got enough? 足りましたか tarímashìta ká

enough to eat 食べ物が足りる tabémonò ga tarírù

enough! もういい！ mō iì!

that's enough, thanks もう沢山です. 有難う. mố takusañ desu. aʼígatố.

I've had enough of him 彼にはもううんざりだ kárè ni wa mố uńzari dá

... which, funnily/oddly enough ... おかしいけれども、それは... okáshii kerèdomo, soré wà ...

enquire [enkwai'əːr] vt, vi = **inquire**

enrage [enreidʒ'] vt (anger, madden) 激

怒らせる gékìdo saseru

enrich [enritʃ'] vt (morally, spiritually) 豊かにする yútàka ni suru; (financially) 金持にする kanémochi ni suru

enroll [enroul'] (*BRIT*: **enrol**) vt (at school, university) 入学させる nyúgaku saserù; (on course) 登録する tóroku suru; (in club etc) 入会させる nyúkai saserù
♦vi (at school, university) 入学する nyúgaku suru; (on course) 参加手続きをする sañkatetsuzùki wo suru; (in club etc) 入会する nyúkai suru

enrollment [enroul'mənt] (*BRIT*: **enrolment**) n (registration) 登録 tóroku

en route [ɔːn ruːt'] adv (on the way) 途中で tochū dè

ensue [ensuː'] vi (follow) ...の結果として起る ...no kekká toshitè okórù

ensure [enʃur'] vt (result, safety) 確実にする kakújitsu ni surù

entail [enteil'] vt (involve) 要する yō suru

entangled [entæŋ'gəld] adj: **to become entangled (in)** (in net, rope etc) ...に絡まる ...ni karámarù

enter [en'tə:r] vt (room, club) ...に入る ...ni háirù; (race, competition) ...に参加する ...ni sañka suru, ...に出場する ...ni shutsújò suru; (someone for a competition) ...に...の参加を申込む ...ni ...no sañka wò móshikomù; (write down) 記入する kínyū suru; (COMPUT: data) 入力する nyúryòku suru
♦vi (come or go in) 入る háirù

enter for vt fus (race, competition, examination) ...に参加を申込む ...ni sañka wò móshikomù

enter into vt fus (discussion, correspondence, negotiations) 始める hajímerù; (agreement) 結ぶ musúbù

enterprise [en'tə:rpraiz] n (company, business) 企業 kigyố; (undertaking) 企画 kikáku; (initiative) 進取の気 shíñshu no ki
free enterprise 自由企業 jiyúkigyð
private enterprise (private company) 民間企業 miñkankigyố, 私企業 shikígyð

enterprising [en'tə:rpraiziŋ] adj (adventurous) 進取の気に富んだ shíñshu no ki ni tóñda

entertain [entə:rtein'] vt (amuse) 楽しませる tanóshimaserù; (invite: guest) 接待する séttài suru; (idea, plan) 考える kañgaerù

entertainer [entə:rtein'ə:r] n (TV etc) 芸能人 geínòjìn

entertaining [entə:rtei'niŋ] adj 面白い omóshiroì

entertainment [entə:rtein'mənt] n (amusement) 娯楽 goráku; (show) 余興 yokyố

enthralled [enθrɔːld'] adj (engrossed, captivated) 魅せられた miséraretà

enthusiasm [enθuː'ziːæzəm] n (eagerness) 熱心さ nesshíñsa

enthusiast [enθuː'ziːæst] n (fan) マニア mánìa

enthusiastic [enθuːziːæs'tik] adj (excited, eager) 熱心な nesshíñ na
to be enthusiastic about ...に夢中になっている ...ni muchú nì natté irù

entice [entais'] vt (lure, tempt) 誘惑する yúwaku suru

entire [entai'ə:r] adj (whole) 全体の zeñtai no

entirely [entai:r'liː] adv (completely) 全く mattáku

entirety [entai'ə:rtiː] n: **in its entirety** 全体に zeñtai ni

entitle [entait'əl] vt: **to entitle someone to something** ...に...に対する権利を与える ...ni ...ni taísuru keñri wò atáerù

entitled [entait'əld] adj (book, film etc) ...という題の ...to iú daì no
to be entitled to do (be allowed) ...する権利がある ...suru kéñri ga árù

entity [en'titiː] n 物 monó

entourage [ɑːntuːrɑːʒ'] n (of celebrity, politician) 取巻き連 torímakireñ

entrails [en'treilz] npl (ANAT, ZOOL) 内臓 naízò

entrance [n en'trəns vb entræns'] n (way in) 入口 iríguchi; (arrival) 登場 tójò
♦vt (enchant) 魅惑する miwáku suru
to gain entrance to (university, profes-

sion etc) ...に入る ...ni háiru

entrance examination n 入学試験 nyúgakushikén, 入試 nyúshi

entrance fee n 入場料 nyújōryò

entrance ramp (US) n (AUT) 入口ランプ iríguchiraňpu

entrant [en'trant] n (in race, competition etc) 参加者 saňkasha; (BRIT: in exam) 受験者 jukéňsha

entreat [entri:t'] vt (implore) 嘆願する taňgan suru

entrenched [entrentʃt'] adj (position, power) 固められた katámeraretà; (ideas) 定着した teíchakushità

entrepreneur [ɑːntrəprənəːr'] n (COMM) 企業家 kigyóka

entrust [entrʌst'] vt: **to entrust something to someone** ...を...に預ける ...wo ...ni azúkerù

entry [en'tri:] n (way in) 入口 iríguchi; (in competition) 参加者 saňkasha; (in register, account book) 記入 kinyú; (in reference book) 記事 kíji; (arrival) 登場 tójō; (to country) 入国 nyúkoku

「**no entry**」(to room etc) 立入禁止 tachíirikiňshi; (AUT) 進入禁止 shiňnyūkiňshi

entry form n (for club etc) 入会申込書 nyúkaimōshikomishò; (for competition etc) 参加申込書 saňkamōshikomishò

entry phone n 玄関のインターホン géňkan no iňtāhon

enumerate [inuː'məːreit] vt (list) 列挙する rékkyo suru

enunciate [inʌn'si:eit] vt (word) はっきりと発音する hakkírì to hatsúon suru; (principle, plan etc) 明確に説明する meíkaku nì setsúmei suru

envelop [envel'əp] vt (cover, enclose) 覆い包む óitsutsumù

envelope [en'vəloup] n 封筒 fútō

envious [en'vi:əs] adj (person, look) うらやましい uráyamashiì

environment [envai'rənmənt] n (surroundings) 環境 kaňkyō; (natural world): **the environment** 環境 kaňkyō

environmental [envairənmen'təl] adj 環境の kaňkyō no

envisage [enviz'idʒ] vt (foresee) 予想する yosó suru

envoy [en'vɔi] n (diplomat) 特使 tókùshi

envy [en'vi:] n (jealousy) せん望 seňbō

♦vt うらやましく思う uráyamashìku o-móù

to envy someone something ...の...をうらやましく思う ...no ...wo uráyamashìku omóù

enzyme [en'zaim] n (BIO, MED) 酵素 kóso

ephemeral [ifem'əːrəl] adj (fashion, fame) つかの間の tsuká no mà no

epic [ep'ik] n (poem) 叙事詩 jojíshì; (book, film) 大作 taisaku

♦adj (journey) 歴史的な rekíshiteki na

epidemic [epidem'ik] n (of disease) 流行病 ryúkōbyò

epilepsy [ep'əlepsi:] n (MED) てんかん teňkan

epileptic [epəlep'tik] adj てんかんの teňkan no

♦n てんかん患者 teňkankaňja

episode [ep'isoud] n (period, event) 事件 jíkèn; (TV, RADIO: installment) 1回 ikkái

epistle [ipis'əl] n (letter: also REL) 書簡 shokán

epitaph [ep'itæf] n 墓碑銘 bohímei

epithet [ep'əθet] n 形容語句 keíyōgokù

epitome [ipit'əmiː] n (model, archetype) 典型 teňkei

epitomize [ipit'əmaiz] vt (characterize, typify) ...の典型である ...no teñkei de árù

epoch [ep'ək] n (age, era) 時代 jidái

equable [ek'wəbəl] adj (climate) 安定した aňteishità; (temper, reply) 落着いた ochítsuità

equal [iː'kwəl] adj (size, number, amount) 等しい hitóshiì; (intensity, quality) 同様な dóyō na; (treatment, rights, opportunities) 平等な byódō na

♦n (peer) 同輩 dóhai

♦vt (number) イコール ikórù; (quality) ...と同様である ...to dóyō de árù

to be equal to (task) ...を十分出来る ...wo júbuň dekírù

equality [ikwɑːl'iti:] n 平等 byódō

equalize [iː'kwəlaiz] vi (SPORT) 同点に

する dṓten ni surù

equally [i:'kwəli:] *adv* (share, divide etc) 平等に byṓdō ni; (good, brilliant, bad etc) 同様に dṓyō ni

equanimity [i:kwənim'iti:] *n* (calm) 平静 さ heíseisà

equate [ikweit'] *vt*: *to equate something with* ...を...と同等視する ...wo ...to dṓtōshì suru

equation [ikwei'ʒən] *n* (MATH) 方程式 hōteishiki

equator [ikwei'tə:r] *n* 赤道 sekídō

equestrian [ikwes'tri:ən] *adj* 乗馬の jṓbà no

equilibrium [i:kwəlib'ri:əm] *n* (balance) 均衡 kíñkō; (composure) 平静さ heíseisà

equinox [i:'kwənɑ:ks] *n*: *spring/autumn equinox* 春〔秋〕分の日 shuñ〔shū〕bun no hì

equip [ikwip'] *vt* (person, army, car etc) ...に...を装備させる ...ni ...wo sṓbi saserù; (room) ...に...を備え付ける ...ni ...wo sonáetsukerù

to be well equipped 装備が十分である sóbi gà jūbuñ de árù

to be equipped with ...を装備している ...wo sóbi shite irù

equipment [ikwip'mənt] *n* (tools, machinery) 設備 sétsùbi

equitable [ek'witəbəl] *adj* (settlement, agreement) 公正な kōsei na

equities [ek'witi:z] *npl* (COMM) 普通株 futsúkàbu

equivalent [ikwiv'ələnt] *adj*: *equivalent (to)* (...に) 相当する (...ni) sṓtō suru
♦*n* (equal) 相当の物 sṓtō no monò

equivocal [ikwiv'əkəl] *adj* (ambiguous) あいまいな aímai na; (open to suspicion) いかがわしい ikágawashiì

era [i:'rə] *n* (age, period) 時代 jidái

eradicate [iræd'ikeit] *vt* (disease, problem) 根絶する koñzetsu suru

erase [ireis'] *vt* (tape, writing) 消す kesú

eraser [irei'sə:r] *n* (for pencil etc) 消しゴム keshígomu; (*US*: for blackboard etc) 黒板消し kokúbañkeshi

erect [irekt'] *adj* (posture) 直立の chokúritsu no; (tail, ears) ぴんと立てた piñ tò

tatétà
♦*vt* (build) 建てる tatérù; (assemble) 組立てる kumítaterù

erection [irek'ʃən] *n* (of building) 建築 keñchiku; (of statue) 建立 koñryū; (of tent) 張る事 harú kotò; (of machinery etc) 組立て kumítate; (PHYSIOL) ぼっ起 bokkí

ermine [ə:r'min] *n* (fur) アーミン ā́mìn

erode [iroud'] *vt* (soil, rock) 侵食する shiñshoku suru; (metal) 腐食する fushóku suru; (confidence, power) 揺るがす yurúgasù

erosion [irou'ʒən] *n* (of soil, rock) 侵食 shiñshoku; (of metal) 腐食 fushóku; (of confidence, power) 揺るがされる事 yurúgasarerù kotó

erotic [irɑt'ik] *adj* (activities) 性的な seíteki na; (dreams, books, films) 扇情的な señjōteki na, エロチックな eróchikkù na

eroticism [irɑt'isizəm] *n* 好色 kṓshoku, エロチシズム eróchishizùmu

err [ə:r] *vi* (formal: make a mistake) 過ちを犯す ayámachi wò okásù

errand [e:r'ənd] *n* お使い o-tsúkai

erratic [iræt'ik] *adj* (behavior) 突飛な toppí na; (attempts, noise) 不規則な fukísoku na

erroneous [irou'ni:əs] *adj* (belief, opinion) 間違った machígattà

error [e:r'ə:r] *n* (mistake) 間違い machígaì, エラー érà

erudite [e:r'judait] *adj* (person) 博学な hakúgaku na

erupt [irʌpt'] *vi* (volcano) 噴火する fuñka suru; (war, crisis) ぼっ発する boppátsu suru

eruption [irʌp'ʃən] *n* (of volcano) 噴火 fuñka; (of fighting) ぼっ発 boppátsu

escalate [es'kəleit] *vi* (conflict, crisis) 拡大する kakúdai suru, エスカレートする esúkarēto suru

escalator [es'kəleitə:r] *n* エスカレーター esúkarētā

escapade [es'kəpeid] *n* (adventure) 冒険 bṓken

escape [eskeip'] *n* (from prison) 脱走 dassṓ; (from person) 逃げる事 nigéru ko-

tò; (of gas) 漏れる事 moréru kotò

♦vi (get away) 逃げる nigérù; (from jail) 脱走する dassō suru; (leak) 漏れる morérù

♦vt (consequences, responsibility etc) 回避する kaíhi suru; (elude): *his name escapes me* 彼の名前を思い出せない kárè no namáe wò omóidasenaì

to escape from (place) ...から脱出する ...kara dasshútsu suru; (person) ...から逃げる ...kara nigérù

escapism [eskei'pizəm] n 現実逃避 geñjitsutòhi

escort [n es'kɔːrt vb eskɔ:rt'] n (MIL, POLICE) 護衛 goéi; (companion) 同伴者 dóhañsha

♦vt (person) ...に同伴する ...ni dóhan suru

Eskimo [es'kəmou] n エスキモー人 esúkimōjìn

esoteric [esəte:r'ik] adj 難解な nañkai na

especially [espeʃ'əli:] adv (above all, particularly) 特に tókù ni

espionage [es'pi:ɑnɑ:ʒ] n (POL, MIL, COMM) スパイ行為 supáikòi

esplanade [espləneid'] n (by sea) 海岸の遊歩道路 kaígan nò yūhodò

espouse [espauz'] vt (policy) 採用する saíyō suru; (idea) 信奉する shiñpō suru

Esq. n abbr = Esquire

Esquire [es'kwaiə:r] n: *J. Brown, Esquire* J.ブラウン様 jé buráùn samá

essay [es'ei] n (SCOL) 小論文 shōroñbun; (LITERATURE) 随筆 zuíhitsu, エッセーéssê

essence [es'əns] n (soul, spirit) 本質 hoñshitsu; (CULIN) エキス ékìsu, エッセンス éssènsu

essential [əsen'tʃəl] adj (necessary, vital) 不可欠な fukáketsu na; (basic) 根本的な koñponteki na

♦n (necessity) 不可欠な事柄 fukáketsu nà kotógarà

essentially [əsen'tʃəli:] adv (basically) 根本的に koñponteki ni

establish [əstæb'liʃ] vt (organization, firm) 創立する sōritsu suru; (facts, proof) 確認する kakúnin suru; (relations, contact) 樹立する jurítsu suru; (reputation) 作り上げる tsukúriagerù

established [əstæb'liʃt] adj (business) 定評のある teíhyō no arù; (custom, practice) 定着した teíchaku shità

establishment [əstæb'liʃmənt] n (of organization etc) 創立 sōritsu; (of facts etc) 確認 kakúnin; (of relations etc) 樹立 jurítsu; (of reputation) 作り上げる事 tsukúriageru kotò; (shop etc) 店 mìsé; (business, firm) 会社 kaísha; (institution) 施設 shísètsu

the Establishment 体制 taísei

estate [əsteit'] n (land) 屋敷 yashíki; (BRIT: also: **housing estate**) 住宅団地 jūtakudañchi; (LAW) 財産 zaísan

estate agent (BRIT) n 不動産屋 fudósan-yà

estate car (BRIT) n ステーションワゴン sutḗshonwagòn

esteem [əsti:m'] n: *to hold someone in high esteem* (admire, respect) ...を尊敬する ...wo soñkei suru

esthetic [esθet'ik] (US) adj = aesthetic

estimate [n es'təmit vb es'təmeit] n (calculation) 概算 gaísan; (assessment) 推定 suítei; (COMM: builder's etc) 見積 mitsúmori

♦vt (reckon, calculate) 推定する suítei suru

estimation [estəmei'ʃən] n (opinion) 意見 íkèn; (calculation) 推定 suítei

estranged [estreind3d'] adj (from spouse) ...と別居している ...to bekkyó shite irù; (from family, friends) ...と仲たがいしている ...to nakátagai shite irù

estuary [es'tʃu:e:ri:] n 河口 kakó

etc abbr (= et cetera) など nádò

etching [etʃ'iŋ] n 版画 hañga, エッチング etchíngu

eternal [itə:r'nəl] adj (everlasting, unceasing) 永遠の eíen no; (unchanging: truth, value) 不変的な fuhénteki na

eternity [itə:r'niti:] n (REL) 永遠 eíen

ether [i:'θə:r] n (CHEM) エーテル ḗteru

ethical [eθ'ikəl] adj (question, problem) 道徳的な dótokuteki na

ethics [eθ'iks] *n* (science) 倫理学 rifirigaku
♦*npl* (morality) 道徳 dótoku

Ethiopia [i:θi:ou'pi:ə] *n* エチオピア echíopìa

ethnic [eθ'nik] *adj* (population, music, culture etc) 民族の miñzoku no

ethos [i:'θɑːs] *n* 気風 kifú

etiquette [et'əkit] *n* (manners, conduct) 礼儀作法 reígisahò, エチケット échìketto

eucalyptus [ju:kəlip'təs] *n* (tree) ユーカリ yūkari

euphemism [ju:'fəmizəm] *n* えん曲表現 eñkyokuhyōgeñ

euphoria [ju:fɔ:r'i:ə] *n* (elation) 幸福感 kófukukañ

Eurocheque [ju:'routʃek] *n* ユーロチェック yūrochekkù ◇ヨーロッパ諸国で通用する小切手 yóroppa shokòku de tsúyō surù kogíttè

Europe [ju:'rəp] *n* 欧州 óshū, ヨーロッパ yóroppà

European [ju:rəpi:'ən] *adj* 欧州の óshū no, ヨーロッパの yóroppà no
♦*n* ヨーロッパ人 yóroppajìn

euthanasia [ju:θənei'ʒə] *n* 安楽死 añrakushì

evacuate [ivæk'ju:eit] *vt* (people) 避難させる hínañ saserù; (place) ...から避難させる ...kara hínañ saserù

evacuation [ivækju:ei'ʃən] *n* 避難 hínañ

evade [iveid'] *vt* (tax, duty) 脱税する datsúzei suru; (question) 言逃れる iínogarerù; (responsibility) 回避する kaíhi suru; (person) 避ける sakérù

evaluate [ivæl'ju:eit] *vt* (importance, achievement, situation etc) 評価する hyóka suru

evaporate [ivæp'ə:reit] *vi* (liquid) 蒸発する jōhatsu suru; (feeling, attitude) 消えてなくなる kiéte nakunarù

evaporated milk [ivæp'əreitid-] *n* エバミルク ebámirùku

evasion [ivei'ʒən] *n* (of responsibility, situation etc) 回避 kaíhi
tax evasion 脱税 datsúzei

evasive [ivei'siv] *adj* (reply, action) 回避

eve [i:v] *n*: *on the eve of* ...の前夜に ...no zéñ-ya ni

even [i:'vən] *adj* (level) 平らな taíra na; (smooth) 滑らかな naméràka na; (equal) 五分五分の gobúgobu no
♦*adv* (showing surprise) ...さえ ...sáè; (introducing a comparison) 更に sárà ni
an even number 偶数 gűsū
even if 例え...だとしても tatóe ...dá tò shité mò
even though 例え...だとしても tatóe ...dá tò shité mò
even more なおさら naósara
even so それにしても soré ni shite mò
not even ...さえも...ない ...sáè mo ...náì
even he was there 彼さえもいた kárè sáè mo itá
even on Sundays 日曜日にも nichíyòbi ni mo
to get even with someone ...に復しゅうする ...ni fukúshū suru

evening [i:v'niŋ] *n* (early) 夕方 yūgata; (late) 夜 yórù; (whole period, event) ...の夕べ ...no yūbe
in the evening 夕方に yūgata ni

evening class *n* 夜間学級 yakáñgakkyù

evening dress *n* (no pl: formal clothes) 夜会服 yakáifùku; (woman's) イブニングドレス ibúningu dorèsu

even out *vi* (ground) 平らになる taíra ni narù; (prices etc) 安定する añtei suru

event [ivent'] *n* (occurrence) 事件 jíkeñ; (SPORT) イベント ibéñto
in the event of ...の場合に ...no baái

eventful [ivent'fəl] *adj* (day) 忙しい isógashiì; (life, game) 波乱の多い hárañ no òì

eventual [iven'tʃu:əl] *adj* (outcome, goal) ゆくゆくの yukúyuku no

eventuality [ventʃu:æl'iti:] *n* (possibility) 可能性 kanósei

eventually [iven'tʃu:əli:] *adv* (finally) 結局 kekkyóku; (in time) やがて yagáte

ever [ev'ə:r] *adv* (always) 常に tsúnè ni; (at any time) いつか ítsu ka; (in question): *why ever not?* どうしてまたしないのか dōshite matá shinaì no ká

the best ever 絶対に一番良い物 zettái nì ichíban yoì monó

have you ever seen it? それを見た事がありますか soré wò mítà kotó gà arímasù kấ

better than ever なお一層良くなった náò issó yokù náttà

ever since adv それ以来 soré iraì

♦*conj* ...して以来 ...shité iraì

evergreen [ev'ə:rgri:n] *n* (tree, bush) 常緑樹 jóryokujù

everlasting [evə:rlæs'tiŋ] *adj* (love, life etc) 永遠の efen no

KEYWORD

every [ev'ri:] *adj* 1 (each) すべての subète no, 皆の miná nò

every one of them (persons) 彼らは〔を〕皆 karèra wa 〔wo〕miná; (objects) それらは〔を〕皆 sorérà wa〔wo〕miná

I interviewed every applicant 私は応募者全員に面接しました watákushi wa óboshà zén-in ni ménsetsu shimashìta

every shop in the town was closed 町中の店が閉っていました machíjū no mise gà shimáttè imáshìta

2 (all possible) 可能な限りすべての kanó na kagìri subète no

I gave you every assistance 私は可能な限りあなたを助けました watákushi wa kanó na kagìri anátà wo tasúkemashìta

I have every confidence in him 私は完全に彼を信用しています watákushi wa kánzen ni karè wo shín-yòshite imasù

we wish you every success ご成功を祈ります go-séikò wo inórimasù

he's every bit as clever as his brother 才能に関しては彼は彼の兄に少しも引けを取りません saínò ni kàn shite wa kárè wa kárè no áni ni sukóshi mo hike wo tòrimasèn

3 (showing recurrence) 毎... máì...

every day/week 毎日〔週〕máìnichi〔shū〕

every Sunday 毎日曜日 máinichiyòbì

every other car (had been broken into) 車は2台に1台ドアが壊されていた kurúma wa nidài ni ichídài doa ga kowásarète ita

she visits me every other/third day 彼女は1日〔2日〕置きに面会に来てくれます kánòjo wa ichínichi(futsúka)oki nì ménkai ni kite kùremasù

every now and then 時々 tokídoki

everybody [ev'ri:bɑ:di:] *pron* (*gen*) だれも dárè mo; (form of address) 皆さん minásàn

everyday [ev'ri:dei] *adj* (daily) 毎日のmáìnichi no; (usual, common) 平凡な heíbon na

everyone [ev'ri:wʌn] *pron* = **everybody**

everything [ev'ri:θiŋ] *pron* 何もかも nánì mo ká mò

everywhere [ev'ri:hwe:r] *adv* (all over) いたる所に itárù tokoro ni; (wherever) どこにでも dókò ni de mo

evict [ivikt'] *vt* (squatter, tenant) 立ちのかせる tachínokaserù

eviction [ivik'ʃən] *n* (from house, land) 立ちのかせる事 tachínokaseru kotò

evidence [ev'idəns] *n* (proof) 証拠 shóko; (of witness) 証言 shógen; (sign, indication) 印 shirùshi

to give evidence 証言する shógen suru

evident [ev'idənt] *adj* (obvious) 明らかな akíràka na

evidently [ev'idəntli:] *adv* (obviously) 明らかに akíràka ni; (apparently) ...らしい ...rashiì

evil [i:'vəl] *adj* (person, system, influence) 悪い waruî

♦*n* (wickedness, sin) 罪悪 zaíaku; (unpleasant situation or activity) 悪 ákù

evocative [ivɑ:k'ətiv] *adj* (description, music) 想像を刺激する sōzō wò shigéki suru

evoke [ivouk'] *vt* (feeling, memory, response) 呼び起す yobíokosù

evolution [evəlu:'ʃən] *n* (BIO: process) 進化 shínka; (*also*: *theory of evolution*) 進化論 shínkàron; (development) 発展 hattén

evolve [ivɑ:lv'] *vt* (scheme, style) 練上げ

る nerîagerù
♦vi (animal, plant etc) 進化する shîñka
suru; (plan, idea, style etc) 展開する teñ
kai suru

ewe [ju:] n 雌ヒツジ mesúhitsùji

ex- [eks] prefix 元... môtò...

exacerbate [igzæs'ə:rbeit] vt (crisis,
problem) 悪化させる akká saserù

exact [igzækt'] adj (correct: time,
amount, word etc) 正確な seîkaku na;
(person, worker) き帳面な kichômen na
♦vt: to exact something (from) (obedience, payment etc) (...に) ...を強要す
る (...ni) ...wo kyôyō suru

exacting [igzæk'tiŋ] adj (task, conditions) 難しい muzúkashiî; (person, master etc) 厳しい kibîshiî

exactly [igzækt'li:] adv (precisely) 正確
に seîkaku ni, 丁度 chôdo; (indicating
emphasis) 正に másà ni; (indicating
agreement) その通り sonô tòri

exaggerate [igzæd'ʒəreit] vt (difference, situation, story etc) 大げさに言う
ôgesa nî iú
♦vi 大げさな事を言う ôgesa na kotò wo
iú

exaggeration [igzædʒərei'ʃən] n 大げさ
ôgesa

exalted [igzɔ:l'tid] adj (prominent) 著名
な chomêi na

exam [igzæm'] n abbr (SCOL) = **examination**

examination [igzæmənei'ʃən] n (of
object, accounts etc) 検査 kêñsa; (of
idea, plan etc) 検討 keñtō; (SCOL) 試験
shikêñ; (MED) 診察 shiñsatsu

examine [igzæm'in] vt (inspect: object,
idea, plan, accounts etc) 調べる shiráberù; (SCOL: candidate) 試験する shikêñ
suru; (MED: patient) 診察する shiñsatsu
suru

examiner [igzæm'inə:r] n (SCOL) 試験
官 shikêñkan

example [igzæm'pəl] n (typical illustration) 例 reî; (model: of good behavior
etc) 手本 tehôñ
for example 例えば tatôèba

exasperate [igzæs'pəreit] vt (annoy,

frustrate) 怒らせる okôraserù

exasperating [igzæs'pəreitiŋ] adj いら
いらさせる îraira saserù

exasperation [igzæspərei'ʃən] n いらだ
ち irádachi

excavate [eks'kəveit] vt (site) 発掘する
hakkútsu suru

excavation [eks'kəvei'ʃən] n (act) 発掘
hakkútsu; (site) 発掘現場 hakkútsugeñ-
ba

exceed [iksi:d'] vt (number, amount,
budget) 越える koérù; (speed limit etc)
越す kosú; (powers, hopes) 上回る uwá-
mawarù

exceedingly [iksi:'diŋli:] adv (enormous-
ly) 極めて kiwámète

excel [iksel'] vi: to excel (in/at)
(sports, business etc) (...に) 優れる (...ni)
sugúrerù

excellence [ek'sələns] n 優れる事 sugú-
reru kotò

Excellency [ek'selənsi:] n: His Excellency 閣下 kákkà

excellent [ek'sələnt] adj (idea, work etc)
優秀な yúshū na

except [iksept'] prep (apart from: also:
except for, excepting) ...を除いて ...wo
nozôite
♦vt: to except someone (from)
(attack, criticism etc) (...から) ...を除
く (...kara) ...wo nozôkù
except if/when ...する場合を除いて
...suru baái wò nozôite
except that がしかし... ga shikáshì...

exception [iksep'ʃən] n (special case) 例
外 reîgai
to take exception to ...が気に食わない
...ga ki nî kuwanaî

exceptional [iksep'ʃənəl] adj (person,
talent) 優れた sugúretà; (circumstances)
例外的な reîgaiteki na

excerpt [ek'sə:rpt] n (from text, film) 抜
粋 bassúi

excess [ek'ses] n (surfeit) 過剰 kajô

excess baggage n 超過手荷物 chôkate-
nimòtsu

excesses [ekses'iz] npl (of cruelty, stupidity etc) 極端な行為 kyokútàn na kôì

excess fare (*BRIT*) *n* (RAIL) 乗越し運賃 noríkoshi uńchin

excessive [iksesˈiv] *adj* (amount, extent) 過剰の kajō no

exchange [ikstʃeindʒ] *n* (of presents, prisoners etc) 交換 kōkan; (conversation) 口論 kōron; (*also:* **telephone exchange**) 電話局 deńwakyòku
♦*vt:* **to exchange (for)** (goods etc) (...と) 交換する (...to) kōkan suru

exchange rate *n* 為替相場 kawásesòba

Exchequer [eksˈtʃekəːr] (*BRIT*) *n:* **the Exchequer** 大蔵省 ōkurashō

excise [ekˈsaiz] *n* (tax) 消費税 shōhizèi

excite [iksaitˈ] *vt* (stimulate) 興奮させる kōfun saserù; (arouse) 性的に刺激する seíteki nì shigéki suru
to get excited 興奮する kōfun suru

excitement [iksaitˈmənt] *n* (agitation) 興奮 kōfun; (exhilaration) 喜び yorókobì

exciting [iksaiˈtiŋ] *adj* (time, event, place) 興奮の kōfun no, エキサイティングな ekísaitiňgu na

exclaim [ikskleimˈ] *vi* (cry out) 叫ぶ sakébu

exclamation [ekskləmeiˈʃən] *n* (cry) 叫び sakébi

exclamation mark *n* 感嘆符 kańtańfu

exclude [ikskluːdˈ] *vt* (fact, possibility, person) 除外する jogái suru

exclusion [ikskluːˈʒən] *n* 除外 jogái

exclusive [ikskluːˈsiv] *adj* (club, district) 高級な kōkyū na; (use, story, interview) 独占の dokúsen no
exclusive of tax 税別の zeíbetsu no

exclusively [ikskluːˈsivliː] *adv* (only, entirely) 独占的に dokúsenteki ni

excommunicate [ekskəmjuːˈnəkeit] *vt* (REL) 破門する hamón suru

excrement [eksˈkrəmənt] *n* ふん fún

excruciating [ikskruːˈʃiːeitiŋ] *adj* (pain, agony, embarrassment etc) 極度の kyōkùdo no, 耐えがたい taégataì; (noise) 耳をつんざくような mimí wò tsuńzaku yò na

excursion [ikskəːrˈʒən] *n* (tourist excursion, shopping excursion) ツアー tsûâ

excuse [*n* ekskjuːsˈ *vb* ekskuːzˈ] *n* (justi-fication) 言訳 iífwake
♦*vt* (justify: personal fault, mistake) ...の言訳をする ...no iífwake wo suru; (forgive: someone else's mistake) 許す yurúsù
to excuse someone from doing something ...する義務を...に免除する ...suru gímù wo ...ni meñjo suru
excuse me! (attracting attention) 済みません(が)... sumímaseñ (ga)...; (as apology) 済みません sumímaseñ
if you will excuse me ... ちょっと失礼します chóttò shitsúrei shimasù

ex-directory [eksdirekˈtəːriː] (*BRIT*) *adj* 電話帳に載っていない deńwachō ni notté inaì

execute [ekˈsəkjuːt] *vt* (person) 死刑にする shikéi ni surù; (plan, order) 実行する jikkō suru; (maneuver, movement) する surú

execution [eksəkjuːˈʃən] *n* (of person) 死刑 shikéi; (of plan, order, maneuver etc) 実行 jikkō

executioner [eksəkjuːˈʃənəːr] *n* 死刑執行人 shikéishikkōnìn

executive [igzekˈjətiv] *n* (person: of company) 重役 jūyaku; (committee: of organization, political party etc) 執行委員会 shikkōiìnkai
♦*adj* (board, role) 幹部の káñbu no

executor [igzekˈjətəːr] *n* (LAW) 執行人 shikkōnìn

exemplary [igzemˈpləːriː] *adj* (conduct) 模範的な mohánteki na; (punishment) 見せしめの misésime no

exemplify [igzemˈpləfai] *vt* (typify) ...の典型である ...no teñkei dè árù; (illustrate) ...の例を挙げる ...no reí wò agérù

exempt [igzemptˈ] *adj:* **exempt from** (duty, obligation) ...を免除された ...wo meñjo saréta
♦*vt:* **to exempt someone from** (duty, obligation) ...の...を免除する ...no ...wo meñjo suru

exemption [igzempˈʃən] *n* 免除 meñjo

exercise [ekˈsəːrsaiz] *n* (no pl: keep-fit) 運動 uñdō; (energetic movement) 体操 taísō; (SCOL) 練習問題 reńshūmoñdai;

(MUS) 練習曲 reñshůkyoku; (MIL) 軍事演習 guñjieñshū; (of authority etc) 行使 kōshì

♦vt (right) 行使する kōshì suru; (dog) ...に運動をさせる ...ni uñdō wò sasérů; (mind) 働かせる határakaserù

♦vi (also: **to take exercise**) 運動する uñdō suru

to exercise patience 我慢する gámàn suru

exercise book n (SCOL) ノート nōto

exert [igzə:r'] vt (influence) 及ぼす oyóbosù; (authority) 行使する kōshì suru

to exert oneself 努力する dőryòku suru

exertion [igzə:r'ʃən] n 努力 dőryòku

exhale [eksheil'] vt (air, smoke) 吐き出す hakídasù

♦vi (breathe out) 息を吐く ík ì wo hákù

exhaust [igzɔ:st'] n (AUT: also: **exhaust pipe**) 排気管 haíkikàn; (: fumes) 排気ガス haíkigasù

♦vt (person) へとへとに疲れさせる hetóhetò ni tsukáresaserù; (money, resources etc) 使い果す tsukáihatasù; (topic) ...について語り尽す ...ni tsúîte katáritsukusù

exhausted [igzɔ:s'tid] adj (person) へとへとに疲れた hetóhetò ni tsukáretà

exhaustion [igzɔ:s'tʃən] n (tiredness) 極度の疲労 kyókùdo no hirō

nervous exhaustion 神経衰弱 shiñkeisuijàku

exhaustive [igzɔ:s'tiv] adj (search, study) 徹底的な tettéiteki na

exhibit [igzib'it] n (ART) 展示品 teñjihìn; (LAW) 証拠品 shőkohìn

♦vt (quality, ability, emotion) 見せる misérù; (paintings) 展示する tenji suru

exhibition [eksəbiʃ'ən] n (of paintings etc) 展示会 teñjikai; (of ill-temper etc) 極端な態度 kyokútañ na táìdo; (of talent etc) 素晴らしい例 subárashiî reí

exhibitionist [eksəbiʃ'ənist] n (show-off) 気取り屋 kidóriya

exhilarating [igzil'əreitiŋ] adj (experience, news) 喜ばしい yorókobashiî

exhort [igzɔ:rt'] vt 訓戒する kuñkai suru

exile [eg'zail] n (condition, state) 亡命 bōmei; (person) 亡命者 bōmeìsha

♦vt 追放する tsuíhō suru

exist [igzist'] vi (be present) 存在する soñzai suru; (live) 生活する seíkatsu suru

existence [igzis'təns] n (reality) 存在 soñzai; (life) 生活 seíkatsu

existing [igzis'tiŋ] adj (present) 現存の geñzon no, geñson no

exit [eg'zit] n (from room, building, motorway etc) 出口 dégùchi; (departure) 出ていく事 détè ikú kotò

♦vi (THEATER) 退場する taíjō suru; (COMPUT) プログラムを終了する purógurāmu wo shūryō suru

exit ramp (US) n (AUT) 出口ランプ dégùchiraňpu

exodus [ek'sədəs] n 大脱出 daídasshùtsu

exonerate [igzɑːn'əreit] vt: **to exonerate someone from something** (blame, guilt etc) ...について ...の容疑を晴らす ...ni tsúîte ...no yőgì wo harásù

exorbitant [igzɔ:r'bətənt] adj (prices, rents) 法外な hőgai na

exorcize [ek'sɔ:rsaiz] vt (spirit) 追い払う oíharaù; (person, place) ...から悪魔を追い払う ...kara ákùma wo oíharaù

exotic [igzɑ:t'ik] adj (food, place) 異国的な ikőkuteki na, エキゾチックな ekízochikkù na

expand [ikspænd'] vt (business etc) 拡張する kakúchō suru; (staff, numbers etc) 増やす fuyásù

♦vi (population etc) 増える fuérù; (business etc) 大きくなる őkìku nárù; (gas, metal) 膨張する bőchō suru

expanse [ikspæns'] n (of sea, sky etc) 広がり hirógarì

expansion [ikspæn'tʃən] n (of business, population, economy etc) 拡大 kakúdai

expatriate [ikspei'tri:it] n 国外在住者 kokúgai zaijùsha

expect [ikspekt'] vt (anticipate) 予想する yoső suru; (await) 待つ mátsù; (require) 要求する yőkyù suru; (suppose) ...だと思う ...dá tò omőù

♦vi: **to be expecting** (be pregnant) 妊娠している niñshin shite irù

expectancy [ikspek'tənsi:] *n* (anticipation) 期待 kitái

 life expectancy 寿命 jumyō

expectant mother [ikspek'tənt-] *n* 妊婦 nínpu

expectation [ekspektei'ʃən] *n* (hope, belief) 期待 kitái

expedience [iskpi:'di:əns] *n* (convenience) 便宜 béñgi, 都合 tsugō

expediency [ikspi:'di:ənsi:] *n* = **expedience**

expedient [ikspi:'di:ənt] *adj* (useful, convenient) 都合の良い tsugō no yoī

 ♦*n* (measure) 便法 benpō

expedition [ekspədiʃ'ən] *n* (for exploration) 探検旅行 tañkenryokō; (for shopping etc) ツアー tsuā

expel [ikspel'] *vt* (person: from school) 退学させる taígaku saserù; (: from organization, place) 追出す oídasù; (gas, liquid) 排出する haíshutsu suru

expend [ikspend'] *vt* (money, time, energy) 費やす tsuíyasù

expendable [ikspen'dəbəl] *adj* (person, thing) 消耗品的な shōmōhinteki na

expenditure [ikspen'ditʃəːr] *n* (of money, energy, time) 消費 shōhi

expense [ikspens'] *n* (cost) 費用 híyò; (expenditure) 出費 shuppí

 at the expense of ...を犠牲にして ...wo giséi ni shitè

expense account *n* 交際費 kōsaíhi

expenses [ikspen'siz] *npl* (traveling expenses, hotel expenses etc) 経費 keíhi

expensive [ikspen'siv] *adj* (article) 高価な kōka na; (mistake, tastes) 高く付く tákàku tsukú

experience [ikspi:r'i:əns] *n* 経験 keíken

 ♦*vt* (situation, feeling etc) 経験する keíken suru

experienced [ikspi:r'i:ənst] *adj* (in job) 熟練した jukúren shità

experiment [ikspe:r'əmənt] *n* (trial: also SCIENCE) 実験 jikkén

 ♦*vi*: *to experiment (with/on)* (...を使って) 実験する (...wo tsukáttè) jikkén suru

experimental [ikspe:rəmen'təl] *adj* 実験

的な jikkénteki na

expert [ek'spəːrt] *adj* (opinion, help) 専門家の señmonka no; (driver etc) 熟練した jukúren shitā

 ♦*n* (specialist) 専門家 señmonka, エキスパート ekísupāto

expertise [ekspəːrti:z'] *n* (know-how) 技術 gíjutsu, ノーハウ nōhaù

expire [ikspai'əːr] *vi* (passport, licence etc) 切れる kirérù

expiry [ikspaiəːr'i:] *n* (of passport, lease etc) 満期 máñki

explain [iksplein'] *vt* 説明する setsúmei suru

explanation [eksplənei'ʃən] *n* 説明 setsúmei

explanatory [iksplæn'ətɔːri:] *adj* (statement, comment) 説明の setsúmei no

explicit [iksplis'it] *adj* (clear) 明白な meíhaku na; (frank) 隠し立てしない kakúshidate shinaì

explode [iksploud'] *vi* (bomb) 爆発する bakúhatsu suru; (population) 爆発的に増える bakúhatsuteki nì fuérù; (person: with rage etc) 激怒する gékìdo suru

exploit [*n* eks'plɔit *vb* iksplɔit'] *n* (deed, feat) 手柄 tegára

 ♦*vt* (workers) 搾取する sákùshu suru; (person, idea) 私利私欲に利用する shírìshíyòku ni riyō suru; (opportunity, resources) 利用する riyō suru

exploitation [eksplɔitei'ʃən] *n* (of workers) 搾取 sákùshu; (of person, idea, resources, opportunity etc) 利用 riyō

exploration [eksplərei'ʃən] *n* (of place, space) 探検 tañken; (with hands etc) 探る事 sagúru kotò; (of idea, suggestion) 検討 keñtō

exploratory [iksplɔːr'ətɔːri:] *adj* (expedition) 探検の tañken no; (talks, operation) 予備的な yobíteki na

explore [iksplɔːr'] *vt* (place, space) 探検する tañken suru; (with hands etc) 探る sagúrù; (idea, suggestion) 検討する keñtō suru

explorer [iksplɔːr'əːr] *n* (of place, country etc) 探検家 tañkenka

explosion [iksplou'ʒən] *n* (of bomb) 爆発

bakúhatsu; (increase: of population etc) 爆発 的 増加 bakúhatsutekizōka; (outburst: of rage, laughter etc) 激怒 gékǐdo

explosive [iksplou'siv] *adj* (device, effect) 爆発 の bakúhatsu no; (situation, temper) 爆発的な bakúhatsuteki na
♦*n* (substance) 爆薬 bakúyaku; (device) 爆弾 bakúdaǹ

exponent [ekspou'nent] *n* (of idea, theory) 擁護者 yōgoshà; (of skill, activity) 達人 tatsújin

export [*vb* ekspɔːrt' *n* eks'pɔːrt] *vt* (goods) 輸出する yushútsu suru
♦*n* (process) 輸出 yushútsu; (product) 輸出品 yushútsuhiǹ
♦*cpd* (duty, permit) 輸出... yushútsu...

exporter [ekspɔːr'tər] *n* 輸出業者 yushútsugyōsha

expose [ikspouz'] *vt* (reveal: object) むき出しにする mukídashi ni surù; (unmask: person) ...の悪事を暴く ...no ákùji wo abákù

exposed [ikspouzd'] *adj* (house, place etc) 雨風にさらされた ámèkaze ni sarásaretà

exposure [ikspou'ʒər] *n* (to heat, cold, radiation) さらされる事 sarásareru kotò; (publicity) 報道 hódò; (of person) 暴露 bákùro; (PHOT) 露出 roshútsu
to die from exposure (MED) 低体温症で死ぬ teítaioñshō de shinú

exposure meter *n* (PHOT) 露出計 roshútsukei

expound [ikspaund'] *vt* (theory, opinion) 説明する setsúmei suru

express [ikspres'] *adj* (clear: command, intention etc) 明白な meíhaku na; (*BRIT*: letter etc) 速達の sokútatsu no
♦*n* (train, bus, coach) 急行 kyúkō
♦*vt* (idea, view) 言表す iíarawasù; (emotion, quantity) 表現する hyōgen suru

expression [ikspreʃ'ən] *n* (word, phrase) 言方 iíkata; (of idea, emotion) 表現 hyōgen; (on face) 表情 hyōjō; (of actor, singer etc: feeling) 表現力 hyōgeñryoku

expressive [ikspres'iv] *adj* (glance) 意味ありげな ímìarige na; (ability) 表現の hyōgen no

expressly [ikspres'liː] *adv* (clearly, intentionally) はっきりと hakkírì to

expressway [ikspres'wei] (*US*) *n* (urban motorway) 高速道路 kōsokudōro

expulsion [ikspʌl'ʃən] *n* (SCOL) 退学処分 taígakushobùn; (from organization etc) 追放 tsuíhō; (of gas, liquid etc) 排出 haíshutsu

expurgate [eks'pəːrgeit] *vt* (text, recording) 検閲する keñ-etsu suru

exquisite [ekskwiz'it] *adj* (perfect: face, lace, workmanship, taste) 見事な mígòto na

extend [ikstend'] *vt* (visit) 延ばす nobású; (street) 延長する eñchō suru; (building) 増築する zōchiku suru; (arm, hand) 伸ばす nobású
♦*vi* (land) 広がる hirógarù; (road) 延びる nobírù; (period) 続く tsuzúkù
to extend an offer of help 援助を申出る eñjo wo mōshiderù
to extend an invitation to ...を招待する ...wo shōtai suru

extension [iksten'tʃən] *n* (of building) 増築 zōchiku; (of time) 延長 eñchō; (of campaign, rights) 拡大 kakúdai; (ELEC) 延長コード eñchōkōdo; (TEL: in private house, office) 内線 naísen

extensive [iksten'siv] *adj* (area) 広い hirôi; (effect, damage) 甚大な jiñdai na; (coverage, discussion) 広範囲の kốhaǹ-i no

extensively [iksten'sivliː] *adv*: *he's traveled extensively* 彼は広く旅行しているかな kárè wa hírðku ryokố shite irù

extent [ikstent'] *n* (size: of area, land etc) 広さ hírðsa; (: of problem etc) 大きさ ōkìsa
to some extent ある程度 árù teído
to the extent of ... ...までも ...mádè mo
to such an extent that ... ...という程 ...to iú hodò
to what extent? どのぐらい? donố guraî?

extenuating [iksten'juːeitiŋ] *adj*: *extenuating circumstances* 酌量すべき情状 shakúryō subèki jōjō

exterior [iksti:r'i:ər] adj (external) 外部
の gáibu no
♦n (outside) 外部 gáibu; (appearance) 外
見 gáiken

exterminate [ikstə:r'məneit] vt (animals) 撲滅する bokúmetsu suru; (people)
根絶する koñzetsu suru

external [ikstə:r'nəl] adj (walls etc) 外部
の gáibu no; (examiner, auditor) 部外の
búgài no
external evidence 外的証拠 gáitekishō-
ko
「for external use」用薬 gáiyòyaku

extinct [ikstiŋkt'] adj (animal, plant) 絶
滅した zetsúmetsu shitá
an extinct volcano 死火山 shikázàn

extinction [ikstiŋk'ʃən] n (of species) 絶
滅 zetsúmetsu

extinguish [ikstiŋ'gwiʃ] vt (fire, light) 消
す kesú

extinguisher [ikstiŋ'gwiʃə:r] n 消火器
shōkakì

extort [ikstɔ:rt'] vt (money) ゆすり取る
yusúritorù; (confession) 強要する kyōyō
suru

extortion [ikstɔ:r'ʃən] n (of money etc)
ゆすり yusúri; (confession) 強要 kyōyō

extortionate [ikstɔ:r'ʃənit] adj (price,
demands) 法外な hōgai na

extra [eks'trə] adj (thing, person,
amount) 余分の yobún no
♦adv (in addition) 特別に tokúbetsu ni
♦n (luxury) 特別の物 tokúbetsu no monò, 余分の物 yobún no monò; (surcharge)
追加料金 tsuíkaryòkin; (CINEMA,
THEATER) エキストラ ekísutòra

extra-... [eks'trə] prefix 特別に ... tokúbetsu ni ...

extract [vt ikstrækt' n eks'trækt] vt
(take out: object) 取出す toridasù;
(: tooth) 抜く nukú, 抜歯する basshí suru;
(mineral: from ground) 採掘する saíkut-
tsu suru, 抽出する chūshutsu suru;
(money) 強要して取る kyōyō shitè torù;
(promise) 無理強いする murijii suru
♦n (of novel, recording) 抜粋 bassúi;
(malt extract, vanilla extract etc) エキ
ス ékìsu, エッセンス éssènsu

extracurricular [ekstrəkərik'jələ:r] adj
(activities) 課外の kagái no

extradite [eks'trədait] vt (from country)
引渡す hikíwatasù; (to country) ...の引渡
しを受ける ...no hikíwatashi wò ukérù

extradition [ekstrədiʃ'ən] n 外国への犯
人引渡し gáikoku e nò háñnin hikíwatashi

extramarital [ekstrəmær'itəl] adj
(affair, relationship) 婚外の koñgai no,
不倫の furín no

extramural [ekstrəmju:r'əl] adj (lectures, activities) 学外の gakúgai no

extraordinary [ikstrɔ:r'dəne:ri:] adj
(person) 抜きん出た nukíndetà; (conduct,
situation) 異常な ijō na; (meeting) 臨時の
ríñji no

extravagance [ikstræv'əgəns] n (no pl:
spending) 浪費 rōhi; (example of spending) ぜいたく zeítaku

extravagant [ikstræv'əgənt] adj (lavish: person) 気前の良い kimáe no yoì;
(: gift) ぜいたくな zeítaku na; (wasteful:
person) 金遣いの荒い kanézukai no arai;
(: machine) 不経済な fukéizai na

extreme [ikstri:m'] adj (cold, poverty
etc) 非常な hijō na; (opinions, methods
etc) 極端な kyokútan na; (point, edge) 末
端の mattán no
♦n (of behavior) 極端 kyokútan

extremely [ikstri:m'li:] adv 非常に hijō
ni

extremity [ikstrem'iti:] n (edge, end) 端
hashí; (of situation) 極端 kyokútan

extricate [ek'strikeit] vt: *to extricate
someone/something (from)* (trap, situation) ...（から）...を救い出す (...kara)
...wo sukúidasù

extrovert [ek'strouvə:rt] n 外向的な人
gaíkōteki na hitò

exuberant [igzu:'bə:rənt] adj (person
etc) 元気一杯の geñkiippài no; (imagination etc) 豊かな yútàka na

exude [igzu:d'] vt (liquid) にじみ出させる
nijímidasaserù; (smell) 放つ hanátsu
to exude confidence 自信満々である
jishín mañman dè árù
to exude enthusiasm 意気込む ikígo-

mù

exult [igzʌlt'] vi (rejoice) 喜び勇む yoró-kobiisamù

eye [ai] n (ANAT) 目 mé
♦vt (look at, watch) 見詰める mitsúmerù
the eye of a needle 針の目 hárì no mé
to keep an eye on ...を見張る ...wo mihárù

eyeball [ai'bɔːl] n 眼球 gańkyū

eyebath [ai'bæθ] n 洗眼カップ seńgan-kappù

eyebrow [ai'brau] n 眉毛 máyùge

eyebrow pencil n アイブローペンシル aíburōpeńshiru

eyedrops [ai'drɑːps] npl 点眼薬 teńgań-yaku

eyelash [ai'læʃ] n まつげ mátsùge

eyelid [ai'lid] n まぶた mábùta

eyeliner [ai'lainəːr] n アイライナー aíraínā

eye-opener [ai'oupənəːr] n (revelation) 驚くべき新事実 odórokubèki shińjijìtsu

eyeshadow [ai'ædou] n アイシャドー aíshadò

eyesight [ai'sait] n 視力 shíryòku

eyesore [ai'sɔːr] n (building) 目障り me-záwàri

eye witness n (to crime, accident) 目撃者 mokúgekishà

F

F [ef] n (MUS: note) ヘ音 hé-òn; (: key) ヘ調 héchò

F. abbr (= *Fahrenheit*) 華氏 káshì

fable [fei'bəl] n (story) ぐう話 gūwa

fabric [fæb'rik] n (cloth) 生地 kíjì

fabrication [fæbrikei'ʃən] n (lie) うそ ú-sò; (making) 製造 seízò

fabulous [fæb'jələs] adj (inf: super) 素晴らしい subárashiì; (extraordinary) 途方もない tohô mo nàì; (mythical) 伝説的な deńsetsuteki na

facade [fəsɑːd'] n (of building) 正面 shô-men; (fig: pretence) 見せ掛け misékake

face [feis] n (ANAT) 顔 kaó; (expression) 表情 hyójō; (of clock) 文字盤 mojí-

ban; (of cliff) 面 mén; (of building) 正面 shômen
♦vt (particular direction) ...に向かう ...ni mukáù; (facts, unpleasant situation) 直視する chókushi suru

face down (person) 下向きになって shitámuki ni nattè; (card) 伏せてあって fuséte attè

to lose face 面目を失う meńboku wo ushínaù

to make/pull a face 顔をしかめる kaó wo shikámerù

in the face of (difficulties etc) ...にめげず ...ni megézù

on the face of it (superficially) 表面は hyómen wa

face to face (with person, problem) 面と向かって meń to mukattè

face cloth (BRIT) n フェースタオル fé-sutaòru

face cream n フェースクリーム fésuku-rìmu

face lift n (of person) 顔のしわ取り手術 kaó no shiwátori shujùtsu; (of building etc) 改造 kaízò

face powder n フェースパウダー fésu-paùdà

face-saving [feis'seiviŋ] adj (compromise, gesture) 面子を立てる méñtsu wo tatérù

facet [fæs'it] n (of question, personality) 側面 sokúmen; (of gem) 切子面 kiríko-mèn

facetious [fəsi:'ʃəs] adj (comment, remark) ふざけた fuzáketà

face up to vt fus (obligations, difficulty) ...に立ち向かう ...ni tachímukaù

face value n (of coin, stamp) 額面 gakú-men

to take something at face value (fig) そのまま信用する sonó mama shiń-yō suru

facial [fei'ʃəl] adj (hair, expression) 顔のkaó no

facile [fæs'əl] adj (comment, reaction) 軽々しい karúgarushiì

facilitate [fəsil'əteit] vt 助ける tasúkerù

facilities [fəsil'əti:z] npl (buildings,

equipment) 設備 setsúbi

credit facilities 分割払い取扱い buń-katsubarài torfatsukai

facing [fei'siŋ] *prep* (opposite) ...の向い側の ...no mukáigawa no

facsimile [fæksim'əli:] *n* (exact replica) 複製 fukúsei; (*also*: **facsimile machine**) ファックス fákkùsu; (transmitted document) ファックス fákkùsu

fact [fækt] *n* (true piece of information) 事実 jijítsu; (truth) 真実 shińjitsu

in fact 事実は jijítsu wa

faction [fæk'ʃən] *n* (group: *also* REL, POL) 派 há

factor [fæk'tər] *n* (of problem, decision etc) 要素 yóso

factory [fæk'tə:ri:] *n* (building) 工場 kṓ-jō

factual [fæk'tʃu:əl] *adj* (analysis, information) 事実の jijítsu no

faculty [fæk'əlti:] *n* (sense, ability) 能力 nṓryoku; (of university) 学部 gakúbu; (*US*: teaching staff) 教職員 kyṓshokuin ◇総称 sṓshō

fad [fæd] *n* (craze) 一時的流行 ichíjitekiryūkō

fade [feid] *vi* (color) あせる asérù; (light, sound) 次第に消える shidái ni kiérù; (flower) しぼむ shibómù; (hope, memory, smile) 消える kiérù

fag [fæg] (*BRIT*: *inf*) *n* (cigarette) もくmokú

fail [feil] *vt* (exam) 落第する rakúdai suru; (candidate) 落第させる rakúdai sasérù; (subj: leader) ...の期待を裏切る ...no kitái wo urágirù; (: courage, memory) なくなる nakúnarù
◆*vi* (candidate, attempt etc) 失敗する shippái suru; (brakes) 故障する koshṓ suru; (eyesight, health) 衰える otóroerù; (light) 暗くなる kuráku narù

to fail to do something (be unable) ...する事が出来ない ...surú koto gà dekínài; (neglect) ...する事を怠る ...surú koto wò okótarù

without fail 必ず kanárazu

failing [fei'liŋ] *n* (weakness) 欠点 kettén
◆*prep* ...がなければ ...ga nakéreba

failure [feil'jə:r] *n* (lack of success) 失敗 shippái; (person) 駄目人間 daméniñgen; (mechanical etc) 故障 koshṓ

faint [feint] *adj* かすかな kásùka na
◆*n* (MED) 気絶 kizétsu
◆*vi* (MED) 気絶する kizétsu suru

to feel faint 目まいがする memái ga suru

fair [fe:r] *adj* (reasonable, right) 公平な kṓhei na; (quite large) かなり な kánàri na; (quite good) 悪くない warúkunài; (skin) 白い shiróì; (hair) 金色の kiń-iro no; (weather) 晴れの haré no
◆*adv* (play) 正々堂々と seíseidṓdō to
◆*n* (*also*: **trade fair**) トレードフェアー torḗdofeà; (*BRIT*: funfair) 移動遊園地 i-dṓyūeñchi

fairly [fe:r'li:] *adv* (justly) 公平に kṓhei ni; (quite) かなり kánàri

fairness [fe:r'nis] *n* (justice, impartiality) 公平さ kṓheisa

fair play *n* 公平さ kṓheisa

fairy [fe:r'i:] *n* (sprite) 妖精 yṓsei

fairy tale *n* おとぎ話 otógibanàshi

faith [feiθ] *n* (trust) 信用 shiń-yō; (religion) 宗教 shū́kyo; (religious belief) 信仰 shińkō

faithful [feiθ'fəl] *adj* 忠実な chū́jitsu na

faithfully [feiθ'fəli:] *adv* 忠実に chū́jitsu ni

yours faithfully (*BRIT*: in letters) 敬具 kéìgu

fake [feik] *n* (painting etc) 偽物 nisémono; (person) ぺてん師 petéñshi
◆*adj* (phoney) いんちきの íñchiki no
◆*vt* (painting etc) 偽造する gizṓ suru; (illness, emotion) ...だと見せ掛ける ...da to misékakerù

falcon [fæl'kən] *n* ハヤブサ hayábusa

fall [fɔ:l] *n* (of person, object: from height) 転落 teńraku; (of person, horse: from standing position) 転倒 teńtō; (of price, temperature, dollar) 下がる事 sagáru kotò; (of government, leader, country) 倒れる事 taóreru kotò; (*US*: autumn) 秋 ákì
◆*vi* (*pt* **fell**, *pp* **fallen**) (person, object: from height) 落ちる ochírù; (person,

horse: from standing position) 転ぶ koróbù; (snow, rain) 降る fúrù; (price, temperature, dollar) 下がる sagárù; (government, leader, country) 倒れる taórerù; (night, darkness) (...に) なる (...ni) nárù

snowfall 降雪 kõsetsu

rainfall 降雨 kõu

the fall of darkness 暗くなる事 kuráku naru kotõ

the fall of night 夜になる事 yórù ni náru kotõ

to fall flat (on one's face) うつぶせに倒れる utsúbuse ni taórerù; (plan) 失敗する shippái suru; (joke) 受けない ukénaì

fallacy [fæl'əsi:] *n* (misconception) 誤信 goshín

fall back *vt fus* (retreat) 後ずさりする atózusàri suru; (MIL) 後退する kõtaisuru

fall back on *vt fus* (remedy etc) ...に頼る ...ni tayórù

fall behind *vi* (person) 遅れる okúrerù

fall down *vi* (person) 転ぶ koróbù; (building) 崩壊する hõkai suru

fallen [fɔːl'ən] *pp of* **fall**

fall for *vt fus* (trick) ...にだまされる ...ni damásarerù; (person) ...にほれる ...ni horérù

fallible [fæl'əbəl] *adj* (person, memory) 間違いをしがちな machígaì wo shigáchi na

fall in *vi* (roof) 落込む ochíkomù; (MIL) 整列する seíretsu suru

fall off *vi* (person, object) 落ちる ochírù; (takings, attendance) 減る herú

fall out *vi* (hair, teeth) 抜ける nukérù; (friends etc) けんかする keñka suru

fallout [fɔːl'aut] *n* (radiation) 放射性落下物 hõshaseiràkkabutsu, 死の灰 shí nò hai

fallout shelter *n* 放射性落下物待避所 hõshaseiràkkabutsu taíhijo

fallow [fæl'ou] *adj* (land, field) 休閑中の kyúkañchu no

falls [fɔːlz] *npl* (waterfall) 滝 takí

fall through *vi* (plan, project) 失敗に終る shippái ni owarù

false [fɔːls] *adj* (untrue: statement, accusation) うその usó no; (wrong: impres-

sion, imprisonment) 間違った machígattà; (insincere: person, smile) 不誠実な fuséijitsu na

false alarm *n* 誤った警報 ayámattà keíhō

false pretenses *npl*: *under false pretenses* うその申立てで usó nò mõshitate de

false teeth *npl* 入れ歯 iréba

falter [fɔːl'tər] *vi* (engine) 止りそうになる tomárisõ ni nárù; (person: hesitate) ためらう tamérañ; (: stagger) よろめく yorómekù

fame [feim] *n* 名声 meísei

familiar [fəmil'jə:r] *adj* (well-known: face, voice) おなじみの onájimi no; (intimate: behavior, tone) 親しい shitáshiì

to be familiar with (subject) よく知っている yókù shitté iru

familiarize [fəmil'jəraiz] *vt*: *to familiarize oneself with* ...になじむ ...ni najímù

family [fæm'li:] *n* (relations) 家族 kázðku; (children) 子供 kodómo ◇総称 sõshō

family business *n* 家族経営の商売 kazõkukeìei no shõbai

family doctor *n* 町医者 machí-ìsha

famine [fæm'in] *n* 飢餓 kígà

famished [fæm'iʃt] *adj* (hungry) 腹がぺこぺこの hará gà pekópeko no

famous [fei'məs] *adj* 有名な yúmei na

famously [fei'məsli:] *adv* (get on) 素晴らしく subárashikù

fan [fæn] *n* (person) ファン fáñ; (folding) 扇子 séñsu; (ELEC) 扇風機 señpũki

◆*vt* (face, person) あおぐ aógù; (fire, quarrel) あおる aórù

fanatic [fənæt'ik] *n* (extremist) 熱狂者 nekkyõshà; (enthusiast) マニア mánìa

fan belt *n* (AUT) ファンベルト fañberù-to

fanciful [fæn'sifəl] *adj* (notion, idea) 非現実的な hígeñjitsuteki na; (design, name) 凝った kóttà

fancy [fæn'si:] *n* (whim) 気まぐれ kimágurè; (imagination) 想像 sõzō; (fantasy) 夢 yumé

◆*adj* (clothes, hat, food) 凝った kóttà;

(hotel etc) 高級の kṓkyū no

♦*vt* (feel like, want) 欲しいなと思う hoshíi na to omóù; (imagine) 想像する sṓzō suru; (think) …だと思う …da to omóù

to take a fancy to …を気に入る …wo kí ni irù

he fancies her (*inf*) 彼は彼女が好きだ kárè wa kanójò ga sukí dà

fancy dress *n* 仮装の衣裳 kasṓ no ishō

fancy-dress ball *n* 仮装舞踏会 kasṓbutṓkai

fanfare [fæn'fe:r] *n* ファンファーレ fanfāre

fang [fæŋ] *n* (tooth) きば kibá

fan out *vi* 扇形に広がる ṓgigata nì hirógarù

fantastic [fæntæs'tik] *adj* (enormous) 途方もない tohṓmonài; (strange, incredible) 信じられない shiñjirarenài; (wonderful) 素晴らしい subá rashiì

fantasy [fæn'təsi:] *n* (dream) 夢 yumé; (unreality, imagination) 空想 kū́sō

far [fɑ:r] *adj* (distant) 遠い tṓi

♦*adv* (a long way) 遠く tṓku; (much) はるかに hárùka ni

far away/off 遠く tṓku

far better …の方がはるかにいい …no hṓ ga hárùka ni ì

far from 決して …でない kesshíte …de nái ◇強い否定を表す tsuyói hitéi wo aráwasù

by far はるかに hárùka ni

go as far as the farm 農場まで行って下さい nṓjō madè itté kudasaì

as far as I know 私の知る限り watákushi nò shirú kagirì

how far? (distance) どれぐらいの距離 doré gurai no kyòri; (referring to activity, situation) どれ程 doré hodò

faraway [fɑ:r'əwei'] *adj* (place) 遠くの tṓku no; (look) 夢見る様な yumémiru yṓ na; (thought) 現実離れの geñjitsubanare no

farce [fɑ:rs] *n* (THEATER) 笑劇 shōgeki, ファース fāsù; (*fig*) 茶番劇 chabáñgeki

farcical [fɑ:r'sikəl] *adj* (situation) ばかげた bakágèta

fare [fe:r] *n* (on trains, buses) 料金 ryōkin; (*also*: **taxi fare**) タクシー代 takúshidai; (food) 食べ物 tabémòno

half/full fare 半〔全〕額 hañ〔zeñ〕gàku

Far East *n*: *the Far East* 極東 kyokútō

farewell [fe:r'wel'] *excl* さようなら sayónarà

♦*n* 別れ wakáre

farm [fɑ:rm] *n* 農場 nṓjō

♦*vt* (land) 耕す tagáyasù

farmer [fɑ:r'mər] *n* 農場主 nṓjōshù

farmhand [fɑ:rm'hænd] *n* 作男 sakúotòko

farmhouse [fɑ:rm'haus] *n* 農家 nṓka

farming [fɑ:r'miŋ] *n* (agriculture) 農業 nṓgyō; (of crops) 耕作 kṓsaku; (of animals) 飼育 shiíku

farmland [fɑ:rm'lænd] *n* 農地 nṓchi

farm worker *n* = **farmhand**

farmyard [fɑ:rm'jɑ:rd] *n* 農家の庭 nṓka no niwà

far-reaching [fɑ:r'ri:'tʃiŋ] *adj* (reform, effect) 広範囲の kṓhañ-i no

fart [fɑ:rt] (*inf!*) *vi* おならをする onára wo surù

farther [fɑ:r'ðə:r] *compar of* **far**

farthest [fɑ:r'ðist] *superl of* **far**

fascinate [fæs'əneit] *vt* (intrigue, interest) うっとりさせる uttóri saserù

fascinating [fæs'əneitiŋ] *adj* (story, person) 魅惑的な miwákuteki na

fascination [fæsənei'ʃən] *n* 魅惑 miwáku

fascism [fæʃ'izəm] *n* (POL) ファシズム fashízùmu

fashion [fæʃ'ən] *n* (trend: in clothes, thought, custom etc) 流行 ryūkō, ファッション fásshòn; (*also*: **fashion industry**) ファッション業界 fasshòn gyòkai; (manner) やり方 yaríkata

♦*vt* (make) 作る tsukúrù

in fashion 流行して ryūkō shite

out of fashion 廃れて sutárete

fashionable [fæʃ'ənəbəl] *adj* (clothes, club, subject) 流行の ryūkō no

fashion show *n* ファッションショー fasshòn shō

fast [fæst] *adj* (runner, car, progress) 速
い hayáî; (clock): *to be fast* 進んでいる
susúnde irù; (dye, color) あせない asénài
♦*adv* (run, act, think) 速 く hayákù;
(stuck, held) 固く katáku
♦*n* (REL etc) 断食 dañjiki
♦*vi* (REL etc) 断食する dañjiki suru
fast asleep ぐっすり眠っている gussúrî
nemútte irù

fasten [fæs'ən] *vt* (tie, join) 縛る shibárù;
(buttons, belt etc) 締める shimérù
♦*vi* 締まる shimárù

fastener [fæs'ənər] *n* (button, clasp, pin
etc) ファスナー fásùnā

fastening [fæs'əniŋ] *n* = **fastener**

fast food *n* (hamburger etc) ファースト
フード fásùtofūdo

fastidious [fæstid'i:əs] *adj* (fussy) やか
ましい yakámashiî

fat [fæt] *adj* (person, animal) 太った fu-
tóttá; (book, profit) 厚い atsúi; (wallet)
金がたんまり入った kané gà tañmarî
haîttà; (profit) 大きな ókina
♦*n* (on person, animal: *also* CHEM) 脂肪
shibó; (on meat) 脂身 abúramî; (for
cooking) ラード rãdo

fatal [feit'əl] *adj* (mistake) 重大な júdai
na; (injury, illness) 致命的な chiméiteki
na

fatalistic [feitəlis'tik] *adj* (person, attitude) 宿命論的な shukúmeironteki na

fatality [feitæl'iti:] *n* (road death etc) 死
亡事故 shibójikò

fatally [feit'əli:] *adv* (mistaken) 重大に
júdai ni; (injured etc) 致命的に chiméiteki ni

fate [feit] *n* (destiny) 運命 úñmei; (of person) 安否 áñpi

fateful [feit'fəl] *adj* (moment, decision)
決定的な kettéiteki na

father [fɑ:'ðər] *n* 父 chichí, 父親 chichīo-
ya, お父さん o-tósàn

father-in-law [fɑ:'ðə:rinlɔ:] *n* しゅうと
shûto

fatherly [fɑ:'ðə:rli:] *adj* (advice, help) 父
親の様な chichfoya no yô na

fathom [fæð'əm] *n* (NAUT) 尋 hírò ◇水
深の単位, 約1.83メーター suíshin no táñ-i,

yákù 1.83métã
♦*vt* (understand: mystery, reason) 理解
する rikái suru

fatigue [fəti:g'] *n* (tiredness) 疲労 hiró
metal fatigue 金属疲労 kíñzokuhirõ

fatten [fæt'ən] *vt* (animal) 太らせる fu-
tóraserù
♦*vi* 太る futórù

fatty [fæt'i:] *adj* (food) 脂肪の多い shibó
no ôi
♦*n* (*inf*: person) でぶ débù

fatuous [fætʃ'u:əs] *adj* (idea, remark) ば
かな bákà na

faucet [fɔ:'sit] (*US*) *n* (tap) 蛇口 jagúchi

fault [fɔ:lt] *n* (blame) 責任 sekínin;
(defect: in person) 欠点 kettén; (: in
machine) 欠陥 kekkán; (GEO: crack) 断
層 dañsó; (TENNIS) フォールト fórùto
♦*vt* (criticize) 非難する hínàn suru
it's my fault 私が悪かった watákushi
gà warúkattã
to find fault with ...を非難する ...wo
hínàn suru
at fault ...のせいで ...no séî de

faulty [fɔ:l'ti:] *adj* (machine) 欠陥のある
kekkán no arù

fauna [fɔ:n'ə] *n* 動物相 dóbutsusõ

faux pas [fou pɑ:'] *n inv* 非礼 hírei

favor [fei'vər] (*BRIT* **favour**) *n* (approval) 賛成 sañsei; (help) 助け tasúke
♦*vt* (prefer: solution etc) ...の方に賛成す
る ...no hó ñî sañsei surù; (: pupil etc) ひ
いきする hiîki suru; (assist: team, horse)
...に味方する ...ni mikáta suru
to do someone a favor ...の頼みを聞く
...no tánòmi wo kîkù
to find favor with ...の気に入る ...no
kî ni irù
in favor of ...に賛成して ...ni sañsei shite

favorable [fei'və:rəbəl] *adj* (gen) 有利な
yúri na; (reaction) 好意的な kóiteki na;
(impression) 良い yóî; (comparison) 賞賛
的な shósanteki na; (conditions) 好適な
kóteki na

favorite [fei'və:rit] *adj* (child, author
etc) 一番好きな ichíban suki na
♦*n* (of teacher, parent) お気に入り o-kí-

niiri; (in race) 本命 hoñmei

favoritism [fei'vəritizəm] *n* えこひいき ekôhiîki

favour [fei'vər] *etc* = **favor** *etc*

fawn [fɔːn] *n* (young deer) 子ジカ kojíka
♦*adj* (*also*: **fawn-colored**) 薄茶色 usúcha-iro
♦*vi*: **to fawn (up)on** ...にへつらう ...ni hetsúraù

fax [fæks] *n* (machine, document) ファックス fákkùsu
♦*vt* (transmit document) ファックスで送る fákkùsu de okúrù

FBI [efbiːai'] (*US*) *n abbr* (= *Federal Bureau of Investigation*) 連邦捜査局 reñpôsôsakyôku

fear [fiːr] *n* (being scared) 恐怖 kyôfu; (worry) 心配 shiñpai
♦*vt* (be scared of) 恐れる osórerù; (be worried about) 心配する shiñpai suru
for fear of (in case) ...を恐れて ...wo osóretè

fearful [fiːr'fəl] *adj* (person) 怖がっている kowágatte irù; (risk, noise) 恐ろしい osóroshiî

fearless [fiːr'lis] *adj* (unafraid) 勇敢な yûkan na

feasible [fiː'zəbəl] *adj* (proposal, idea) 可能な kanô na

feast [fiːst] *n* (banquet) 宴会 eñkai; (delicious meal) ごちそう gochísô; (REL: *also*: **feast day**) 祝日 shukújitsu
♦*vi* (take part in a feast) ごちそうを食べる gochísô wò tabérù

feat [fiːt] *n* (of daring, skill) 目覚しい行為 mezámashiî kôi

feather [feð'əːr] *n* (of bird) 羽根 hanê

feature [fiː'tʃəːr] *n* (characteristic) 特徴 tokúchô; (of landscape) 目立つ点 medátsu tèn; (PRESS) 特別記事 tokúbetsukijì; (TV) 特別番組 tokúbetsu bañgumi
♦*vt* (subj: film) 主役とする shuyáku to surù
♦*vi*: **to feature in** (situation, film etc) ...で主演する ...de shuén suru

feature film *n* 長編映画 chôhen eîga

features [fiː'tʃəːrz] *npl* (of face) 顔立ち kaôdachi

February [feb'jəweːriː] *n* 2月 nigátsu

fed [fed] *pt, pp of* **feed**

federal [fed'əːrəl] *adj* (system, powers) 連邦の reñpô no

federation [fedəreiʃən] *n* (association) 連盟 reñmei

fed up [fed ʌp'] *adj*: **to be fed up** うんざりしている uñzarî shite iru

fee [fiː] *n* (payment) 料金 ryôkin; (of doctor, lawyer) 報酬 hôshû; (for examination, registration) 手数料 tesúryô
school fees 授業料 jugyôryô

feeble [fiː'bəl] *adj* (weak) 弱い yowâî; (ineffectual: attempt, joke) 効果的でない kôkateki dè naî

feed [fiːd] *n* (of baby) ベビーフード bebîfûdo; (of animal) えさ esá; (on printer) 給紙装置 kyûshisôchi
♦*vt* (*pt, pp* **fed**) (person) ...に食べさせる ...ni tabésaserù; (baby) ...に授乳する ...ni junyû suru; (horse etc) ...にえさをやる ...ni esá wò yárû; (machine) ...に供給する ...ni kyôkyû suru; (data, information): **to feed into** ...に入力する ...ni nyûryoku suru

feedback [fiːd'bæk] *n* (response) フィードバック fîdobàkku

feeding bottle [fiː'diŋ-] (*BRIT*) *n* ほ乳瓶 honyûbìn

feed on *vt fus* (gen) ...を食べる ...wo tabérù, ...を常食とする ...wo jôshoku to suru; (*fig*) ...にはぐくまれる ...ni hagúkumarerù

feel [fiːl] *n* (sensation, touch) 感触 kañshoku; (impression) 印象 iñshô
♦*vt* (*pt, pp* **felt**) (touch) ...に触る ...ni sawárù; (experience: desire, anger) 覚える obóerù; (: cold, pain) 感じる kañjirù; (think, believe) ...だと思う ...da to omóù
to feel hungry おなかがすく onáka gà sukú
to feel cold 寒がる samúgarù
to feel lonely 寂しがる sabíshigarù
to feel better 気分がよくなる kíbùn ga yôku narù
I don't feel well 気分が悪い kíbùn ga warûî
it feels soft 柔らかい感じだ yawárakai

kaṅji da
  to feel like (want) ...が欲しい ...ga hoshíi
feel about/around vi ...を手探りで捜す
  ...wo teságuri de sagásù
feeler [fiːˈlər] n (of insect) 触角 shokkáku
  to put out a feeler/feelers (fig) 打診
  する dashín suru
feeling [fiːˈliŋ] n (emotion) 感情 kaṅjō;
  (physical sensation) 感触 kaṅshoku;
  (impression) 印象 iṅshō
feet [fiːt] npl of **foot**
feign [fein] vt (injury, interest) 見せ掛け
  る misékakerù
feline [fiːˈlain] adj (cat-like) ネコの様な
  nékò no yō na
fell [fel] pt of **fall**
  ♦vt (tree) 倒す taósù
fellow [felˈou] n (man) 男 otóko; (comrade) 仲間 nakáma; (of learned society)
  会員 kaíin
fellow citizen n 同郷の市民 dōkyō nò
  shímìn
fellow countryman (pl **countrymen**)
  n 同国人 dōkokujìn
fellow men npl 外の人間 hoká no niṅgen
fellowship [felˈouʃip] n (comradeship) 友
  情 yūjō; (society) 会 kái; (SCOL) 大学特
  別研究員 daígaku tokubetsu kenkyūìn
felony [felˈəniː] n 重罪 júzai
felt [felt] pt, pp of **feel**
  ♦n (fabric) フェルト férùto
felt-tip pen [feltˈtip-] n サインペン saínpen
female [fiːˈmeil] n (ZOOL) 雌 mesú; (pej:
  woman) 女 oṅna
  ♦adj (BIO) 雌の mesú no; (sex, character, child) 女の oṅna no, 女性の joséi no;
  (vote etc) 女性たちの joséitachi no
feminine [femˈənin] adj (clothes, behavior) 女性らしい joséi rashíì; (LING) 女性
  の joséi no
feminist [femˈənist] n 男女同権論者 daṅ-
  jodōkenroṅsha, フェミニスト femínisùto
fence [fens] n (barrier) 塀 heí
  ♦vt (also: **fence in**: land) 塀で囲む heí de
  kakómù

♦vi (SPORT) フェンシングをする féṅshingu wo suru
fencing [fenˈsiŋ] n (SPORT) フェンシン
  グ féṅshingu
fend [fend] vi: **to fend for oneself** 自力
  でやっていく jíriki dè yatté ikù
fender [fenˈdər] n (of fireplace) 火格子
  higōshi; (on boat) 防げん物 bōgenbùtsu;
  (US: of car) フェンダー feṅdā
fend off vt (attack etc) 受流す ukénagasù
ferment [vb fəːrmentˈ n fəːrˈment] vi
  (beer, dough etc) 発酵する hakkō suru
  ♦n (fig: unrest) 動乱 dōran
fern [fəːrn] n シダ shídà
ferocious [fərouˈʃəs] adj (animal, behavior) どう猛な dōmō na; (competition) 激
  しい hagéshiì
ferocity [fərɑːsˈitiː] n (of animal, behavior) どう猛さ dōmōsa; (of competition)
  激しさ hagéshisà
ferret [ferˈit] n フェレット férètto
ferret out vt (information) 捜し出す sagáshidasù
ferry [feˈriː] n (also: **ferry boat**) フェリ
  ー férì, フェリーボート feríbòto
  ♦vt (transport: by sea, air, road) 輸送す
  る yusō suru
fertile [fəːrˈtəl] adj (land, soil) 肥よくな
  hiyōku na; (imagination) 豊かな yútàka
  na; (woman) 妊娠可能な niṅshinkanō na
fertility [fəːrtilˈətiː] n (of land) 肥よくさ
  hiyōkusa; (of imagination) 独創性 dokúsōsei; (of woman) 繁殖力 haṅshokuryò-
  ku
fertilize [fəːrˈtəlaiz] vt (land) ...に肥料を
  やる ...ni hiryō wò yárù; (BIO) 受精させ
  る juséi saserù
fertilizer [fəːrˈtəlaizəːr] n (for plants,
  land) 肥料 hiryō
fervent [fəːrˈvənt] adj (admirer, belief)
  熱心な nesshín na
fervor [fəːrˈvəːr] n 熱心さ nesshínsa
fester [fesˈtəːr] vi (wound) 化のうする
  kanō suru
festival [fesˈtəvəl] n (REL) 祝日 shukújitsu; (ART, MUS) フェスティバル fésùti-
  baru

festive [fes'tiv] *adj* (mood, atmosphere) お祭気分の o-mátsurikibùn no
the festive season (BRIT: Christmas) クリスマスの季節 kurísùmasu no kisétsù

festivities [festiv'iti:z] *npl* (celebrations) お祝い o-íwai

festoon [festu:n'] *vt*: *to festoon with* ...で飾る ...de kazárù

fetch [fetʃ] *vt* (bring) 持って来る notté kurù; (sell for) ...の値で売れる ...no ne de urérù

fetching [fetʃ'iŋ] *adj* (woman, dress) 魅惑的な miwákuteki na

fête [feit] *n* (at church, school) バザー bazá

fetish [fet'iʃ] *n* (obsession) 強迫観念 kyóhakukaǹnen

fetus [fi:'təs] (BRIT **foetus**) *n* (BIO) 胎児 táiji

feud [fju:d] *n* (quarrel) 争い arásoì

feudal [fju:d'əl] *adj* (system, society) 封建的な hókenteki na

fever [fi:'vər] *n* (MED) 熱 netsú

feverish [fi:'vəriʃ] *adj* (MED) 熱がある netsú ga arù; (emotion) 激しい hagéshiì; (activity) 慌ただしい awátadashiì

few [fju:] *adj* (not many) 少数の shósū no; (some): *a few* 幾つかの íkùtsuka no
♦*pron* (not many) 少数 shósū; (some): *a few* 幾つかの íkùtsuka

fewer [fju:'ər] *adj compar* of **few**

fewest [fju:'ist] *adj superl* of **few**

fiancé [fi:a:nsei'] *n* 婚約者 koń-yakushà, フィアンセ fiáǹse ◇男性 dańsei

fiancée [fi:a:nsei'] *n* 婚約者 koń-yakushà, フィアンセ fiáǹse ◇女性 joséi

fiasco [fi:æs'kou] *n* (disaster) 失敗 shippái

fib [fib] *n* (lie) うそ úsò

fiber [fai'bər] (BRIT **fibre**) *n* (thread, roughage) 繊維 séǹ-i; (cloth) 生地 kíjì; (ANAT: tissue) 神経繊維 shíǹkeiseǹ-i

fiber-glass [fai'bərglæs] *n* ファイバーグラス faíbaguràsu

fickle [fik'əl] *adj* (person) 移り気な utsúrigi na; (weather) 変りやすい kawáriyasuì

fiction [fik'ʃən] *n* (LITERATURE) フィクション fíkùshon; (invention) 作り事 tsukúrigoto; (lie) うそ úsò

fictional [fik'ʃənəl] *adj* (character, event) 架空の kakū́ no

fictitious [fiktiʃ'əs] *adj* (false, invented) 架空の kakū́ no

fiddle [fid'əl] *n* (MUS) バイオリン baíorin; (inf: fraud, swindle) 詐欺 ságì
♦*vt* (BRIT: accounts) ごまかす gomákasù

fiddle with *vt fus* (glasses etc) いじくる ijíkurù

fidelity [fidel'iti:] *n* (faithfulness) 忠誠 chúsei

fidget [fidʒ'it] *vi* (nervously) そわそわする sówàsowa suru; (in boredom) もぞもぞする mózòmozo suru

field [fi:ld] *n* (on farm) 畑 hatáke; (SPORT: ground) グランド guráǹdo; (fig: subject, area of interest) 分野 búǹya; (range: of vision) 視野 shíyà; (: of magnet: *also* ELEC) 磁場 jíbà

field marshal *n* (MIL) 元帥 geńsui

fieldwork [fi:ld'wərk] *n* (research) 現地調査 géǹchichòsa, 実地調査 jitchíchòsa, フィールドワーク fírudowàku

fiend [fi:nd] *n* (monster) 怪物 kaíbùtsu

fiendish [fi:n'diʃ] *adj* (person, problem) 怪物の様な kaíbùtsu no yó na; (problem) ものすごく難しい monósugokù muzúkashiì

fierce [fi:rs] *adj* (animal, person) どう猛な dómō na; (fighting) 激しい hagéshiì; (loyalty) 揺るぎない yurúginaì; (wind) 猛烈な mó̀retsu na; (heat) うだる様な udáru yó̀ na

fiery [fai'ə:ri:] *adj* (burning) 燃え盛る moésakarù; (temperament) 激しい hagéshiì

fifteen [fif'ti:n'] *num* 十五 (の) jūgo (no)

fifth [fifθ] *num* 第五(の) dáìgo (no)

fifty [fif'ti:] *num* 五十(の) gojū́ (no)

fifty-fifty [fif'ti:fif'ti:] *adj* (deal, split) 五分五分の gobúgobu no
♦*adv* 五分五分に gobúgobu ni

fig [fig] *n* (fruit) イチジク ichíjìku

fight [fait] *n* 戦い tatákai
♦*vb* (*pt, pp* **fought**)
♦*vt* (person, enemy, cancer etc: *also* MIL) ...と戦う ...to tatákaù; (election) ...に出馬する ...ni shutsúba suru; (emotion) 抑える osáerù
♦*vi* (people: *also* MIL) 戦う tatákaù

fighter [fai'tə:r] *n* (combatant) 戦う人 tatákaù hitò; (plane) 戦闘機 seńtōkì

fighting [fai'tiŋ] *n* (battle) 戦い tatákai; (brawl) けんか kéñka

figment [fig'mənt] *n*: *a figment of the imagination* 気のせい kí nò séì

figurative [fig'jə:rətiv] *adj* (expression, style) 比ゆ的な hiyúteki na

figure [fig'jə:r] *n* (DRAWING, GEOM) 図 zu; (number, statistic etc) 数字 súji; (body, shape, outline) 形 katáchi; (person, personality) 人物 hitó
♦*vt* (think: esp *US*) (...だと) 思う (...da to) omóù
♦*vi* (appear) 見える miérù

figurehead [fig'jə:rhed] *n* (NAUT) 船首像 seńshuzō; (*pej*: leader) 名ばかりのリーダー na bákarì no rídà

figure of speech *n* 比ゆ híyu

figure out *vt* (work out) 理解する rikái suru

filament [fil'əmənt] *n* (ELEC) フィラメント fíràmento

filch [filtʃ] (*inf*) *vt* (steal) くすねる kusúnerù

file [fail] *n* (dossier) 資料 shiryō; (folder) 書類ばさみ shorúibàsami; (COMPUT) ファイル fáìru; (row) 列 rétsù; (tool) やすり yasúrì
♦*vt* (papers) 保管する hokán suru; (LAW: claim) 提出する teíshutsu suru; (wood, metal, fingernails) ...にやすりを掛ける ...ni yasúrì wo kakérù

file in/out *vi* 1列で入る〔出る〕ichíretsu dè haírù(dérù)

filing cabinet [fai'liŋ-] *n* ファイルキャビネット fáìru kyabínètto

fill [fil] *vt* (container, space): *to fill (with)* (...で) 一杯にする (...de) ippái ni surù; (vacancy) 補充する hojū suru; (need) 満たす mitásù

fill in *vt* (hole) うめる umérù; (time) つぶす tsubúsù; (form) ...に書入れる ...ni kakíirerù

filling [fil'iŋ] *n* (for tooth) 充てん jūten; (CULIN) 中身 nakami

filling station *n* (AUT) ガソリンスタンド gasórinsutañdo

fill up *vt* (container, space) 一杯にする ippái ni surù
♦*vi* (AUT) 満タンにする mañtan ni surù

film [film] *n* (CINEMA, TV) 映画 eíga; (PHOT) フィルム fírùmu; (of powder, liquid etc) 膜 makú
♦*vt* (scene) 撮影する satsúei suru
♦*vi* 撮影する satsúei suru

film star *n* 映画スター eígasutà

film strip *n* (slide) フィルムスライド fírùmusuraìdo

filter [fil'tə:r] *n* (device) ろ過装置 rokásòchi, フィルター fírùtā; (PHOT) フィルター fírùtā
♦*vt* (liquid) ろ過する rokā suru

filter lane (*BRIT*) *n* (AUT) 右〔左〕折車線 u(sa)sétsu shasèn

filter-tipped [fil'tə:rtipt] *adj* フィルター付きの fírùtātsuki no

filth [filθ] *n* (dirt) 汚物 obútsu

filthy [fil'θi:] *adj* (object, person) 不潔な fukétsu na; (language) みだらな mídàra na

fin [fin] *n* (of fish) ひれ hiré

final [fai'nəl] *adj* (last) 最後の saígo no; (ultimate) 究極の kyūkyoku no; (definitive: answer, decision) 最終的な saíshūteki na
♦*n* (SPORT) 決勝戦 kesshōsen

finale [finæl'i:] *n* フィナーレ fínàre

finalist [fai'nəlist] *n* (SPORT) 決勝戦出場選手 kesshōsen shutsujō seńshu

finalize [fai'nəlaiz] *vt* (arrangements, plans) 最終的に決定する saíshūteki nì kettéi surù

finally [fai'nəli:] *adv* (eventually) ようやく yōyaku; (lastly) 最後に saígo ni

finals [fai'nəlz] *npl* (SCOL) 卒業試験 sotsúgyōshikèn

finance [*n* fai'næns *vb* finæns'] *n* (money, backing) 融資 yúshi; (money management) 財政 zaísei
♦*vt* (back, fund) 融資する yúshi suru

finances [finæn'siz] *npl* (personal finances) 財政 zaísei

financial [finæn'ʃəl] *adj* (difficulties, year, venture) 経済的な keízaiteki na

financial year *n* 会計年度 kaíkeinèdo

financier [finænsi:r'] *n* (backer, funder) 出資者 shusshísha

find [faind] (*pt*, *pp* **found**) *vt* (person, object, answer) 見付ける mitsúkeru; (discover) 発見する hakkén suru; (think) ...だと思う ...da to omóu
♦*n* (discovery) 発見 hakkén
to find someone guilty (LAW) ...に有罪判決を下す ...ni yúzaihañketsu wo kudásù

findings [fain'diŋz] *npl* (LAW, of report) 調査の結果 chósa no kekkà

find out *vt* (fact, truth) 知る shírù; (person) ...の悪事を知る ...no ákùji wo shírù
to find out about (subject) 調べる shiráberù; (by chance) 知る shírù

fine [fain] *adj* (excellent: quality, performance etc) 見事な mígòto na; (thin: hair, thread) 細い hosóì; (not coarse: sand, powder etc) 細かい komákaì; (subtle: detail, adjustment etc) 細かい komákaì
♦*adv* (well) うまく úmàku
♦*n* (LAW) 罰金 bakkín
♦*vt* (LAW) ...に罰金を払わせる ...ni bakkín wò haráwaserù
to be fine (person) 元気である génki de árù; (weather) 良い天気である yóì téñki de árù

fine arts *npl* 美術 bíjutsu

finery [fai'nə:ri:] *n* (dress) 晴着 harégi; (jewelery) 取って置きの装身具 tottéoki nò sōshíñgu

finesse [fines'] *n* 手腕 shúwàn

finger [fiŋ'gə:r] *n* (ANAT) 指 yubí
♦*vt* (touch) ...に指で触る ...ni yubí dè sawáru
little/index finger 小〔人指し〕指 ko

fingernail [fiŋ'gə:rneil] *n* つめ tsumé

fingerprint [fiŋ'gə:rprint] *n* (mark) 指紋 shimón

fingertip [fiŋ'gə:rtip] *n* 指先 yubísaki

finicky [fin'iki:] *adj* (fussy) 気難しい kimúzukashiì

finish [fin'iʃ] *n* (end) 終り owári; (SPORT) ゴール gòru; (polish etc) 仕上り shiágari
♦*vt* (work, eating, book etc) 終える oéru
♦*vi* (person, course, event) 終る owárù
to finish doing something ...し終える ...shi óeru
to finish third (in race etc) 3着になる sañchaku ni naru

finishing line [fin'iʃiŋ-] *n* ゴールライン gòrurain

finishing school [fin'iʃiŋ-] *n* 花嫁学校 hanáyomegàkkō

finish off *vt* (complete) 仕上げる shiágerù; (kill) 止めを刺す todóme wo sasù

finish up *vt* (food, drink) 平らげる taíragerù
♦*vi* (end up) 最後に...に行ってしまう saígo ni ...ni itté shimaù

finite [fai'nait] *adj* (time, space) 一定の ittéi no; (verb) 定形の teíkei no

Finland [fin'lənd] *n* フィンランド fíñrando

Finn [fin] *n* フィンランド人 fiñrandojìn

Finnish [fin'iʃ] *adj* フィンランドの fíñrando no; (LING) フィンランド語の fíñrandogo no
♦*n* (LING) フィンランド語 fíñrandogo

fiord [fjourd] = **fjord**

fir [fə:r] *n* モミ mómì

fire [fai'ə:r] *n* (flames) 火 hí; (in hearth) たき火 takíbi; (accidental) 火事 kajì; (gas fire, electric fire) ヒーター hítā
♦*vt* (shoot: gun etc) うつ útsù; (: arrow) 射る írù; (stimulate: imagination, enthusiasm) 刺激する shigéki suru; (*inf*: dismiss: employee) 首にする kubí ni surù
♦*vi* (shoot) 発砲する happó suru
on fire 燃えて moéte

fire alarm *n* 火災警報装置 kasáikeihō-sòchi

firearm [faiə:r'ɑːrm] *n* 銃砲 júhō ◇ 特に

ピストルを指す tókù ni pisútoru wò sásù

fire brigade *n* 消防隊 shōbōtai

fire department (*US*) *n* = **fire brigade**

fire engine *n* 消防自動車 shōbōjidōsha

fire escape *n* 非常階段 hijōkaìdan

fire extinguisher *n* 消火器 shōkakì

fireman [faiə'r'mən] (*pl* **firemen**) *n* 消防士 shōbōshi

fireplace [faiə'r'pleis] *n* 暖炉 dánro

fireside [faiə'r'said] *n* 暖炉のそば dánro no sôba

fire station *n* 消防署 shōbōsho

firewood [faiə'r'wud] *n* まき makí

fireworks [faiə'r'wə:rks] *npl* 花火 hánàbi

firing squad [faiə'r'iŋ-] *n* 銃殺隊 jūsatsutai

firm [fə:rm] *adj* (mattress, ground) 固い katái; (grasp, push, tug) 強い tsuyôì; (decision) 断固とした dánko to shita; (faith) 固い katái; (measures) 強固な kyōko na; (look, voice) しっかりした shikkárì shita

♦*n* (company) 会社 kaísha

firmly [fə:rm'li:] *adv* (grasp, pull, tug) 強く tsúyòku; (decide) 断固として dánko to shite; (look, speak) しっかりと shikkárì to

first [fə:rst] *adj* (before all others) 第一の dáìchi no, 最初の saísho no

♦*adv* (before all others) 一番に ichíban ni, 一番最初に ichíban saísho ni; (when listing reasons etc) 第一に dáìchi no

♦*n* (person: in race) 1着 itcháku; (AUT) ローギヤ rōgiya; (*BRIT* SCOL: degree) 1級優等卒業学位 íkkyū yūtō sotsugyō gakùi ◇英国では優等卒業学位は成績の高い順に1級、2級、3級に分けられる eíkoku de wà yūtō sotsugyō gakùi wa seíseki no takái jùn ni ikkyū, nikyū, sankyū ni wakérarerù

at first 最初は saísho wa

first of all まず第一に mázu dáìchi ni

first aid *n* 応急手当 ōkyūteàte

first-aid kit *n* 救急箱 kyūkyūbako

first-class [fə:rst'klæs'] *adj* (excellent: mind, worker) 優れた sugúretà; (car-

riage, ticket, post) 1等の ittō no

first-hand [fə:rst'hænd'] *adj* (account, story) 直接の chokúsetsu no

first lady (*US*) *n* 大統領夫人 daítōryōfujìn

firstly [fə:rst'li:] *adv* 第一に dáichi ni

first name *n* 名 na, ファーストネーム fāsutonēmu

first-rate [fə:rst'reit'] *adj* (player, actor etc) 優れた sugúretà

fiscal [fis'kəl] *adj* (year) 会計の kaíkei no; (policies) 財政の zaísei no

fish [fiʃ] *n inv* 魚 sakána

♦*vt* (river, area) …で釣をする …de tsurí wo surù

♦*vi* (commercially) 漁をする ryō wo surù; (as sport, hobby) 釣をする tsurí wo surù

to go fishing 釣に行く tsurí ni ikù

fisherman [fiʃ'ə:rmən] (*pl* **fishermen**) *n* 漁師 ryōshi

fish farm *n* 養魚場 yōgyojō

fish fingers (*BRIT*) *npl* = **fish sticks**

fishing boat [fiʃ'iŋ-] *n* 漁船 gyosén

fishing line *n* 釣糸 tsurítò

fishing rod *n* 釣ざお tsurízao

fishmonger's (shop) [fiʃ'mʌŋgə:rz-] *n* 魚屋 sakánaya

fish sticks (*US*) *npl* フィッシュスティック fisshúsutikkù ◇細長く切った魚にパン粉をまぶして揚げた物 hosónagaku kittà sakána ni pánko wo mabúshite agéta monò

fishy [fiʃ'i:] (*inf*) *adj* (tale, story) 怪しい ayáshiì

fission [fiʃ'ən] *n* 分裂 bunfretsu

fissure [fiʃ'ə:r] *n* 亀裂 kirétsu

fist [fist] *n* こぶし kóbùshi, げんこつ geñkotsu

fit [fit] *adj* (suitable) 適当な tekítō na; (healthy) 健康な keñkō na

♦*vt* (subj: clothes, shoes) …にぴったり合う …ni pittárì au; (put in) …に入れる …ni irérù; (attach, equip) …に取付ける …ni torítsukerù; (suit) …に合う …ni áù

♦*vi* (clothes) ぴったり合う pittárì áù; (parts) 合う áù; (in space, gap) ぴったりはいる pittárì haírù

♦n (MED) 発作 hossá; (of coughing, giggles) 発作的に…する事 hossáteki ni …suru kotó

fit to (ready) …出来る状態にある …dekirù jõtai ni arù

fit for (suitable for) …に適当である …ni tekítõ de arù

a fit of anger かんしゃく kañshaku

this dress is a good fit このドレスはぴったり体に合う konó dorèsu wa pittárì karáda ni aù

by fits and starts 動いたり止ったりして ugóitarì tomáttarì shité

fitful [fit'fəl] *adj* (sleep) 途切れ途切れの togíretogìre no

fit in *vi* (person) 溶込む tokékomù

fitment [fit'mənt] *n* (in room, cabin) 取付け家具 torítsukekagù ◊つり戸棚など壁などに固定した家具を指す tsurítodana nádò kabé nadò ni kotéi shita kagù wo sásù

fitness [fit'nis] *n* (MED) 健康 keñkō

fitted carpet [fit'id-] *n* 敷込みじゅうたん shikíkomijūtan

fitted kitchen [fit'id-] *n* システムキッチン shisútemu kitchiñ

fitter [fit'ə:r] *n* (of machinery, equipment) 整備工 seíbikō

fitting [fit'iŋ] *adj* (compliment, thanks) 適切な tekísetsu na

♦n (of dress) 試着 shicháku; (of piece of equipment) 取付け torítsuke

fitting room *n* (in shop) 試着室 shichákushìtsu

fittings [fit'iŋz] *npl* (in building) 設備 sétsubi

five [faiv] *num* 五 (の) gó (no)、五つ (の) itsútsù (no)

fiver [fai'və:r] *n* (*inf*: *BRIT*: 5 pounds) 5ポンド札 gópondo satsù; (*US*: 5 dollars) 5ドル札 gódoru satsù

fix [fiks] *vt* (attach) 取付ける torítsukerù; (sort out, arrange) 手配する tehái surù; (mend) 直す naósù; (prepare: meal, drink) 作る tsukúrù

♦n: *to be in a fix* 困っている komátte irù

fixation [fiksei'ʃən] *n* 固着 kocháku

fixed [fikst] *adj* (price, amount etc) 一定の ittéi no

a fixed idea 固定観念 kotéikañnen

a fixed smile 作り笑い tsukúriwarài

fixture [fiks'tʃə:r] *n* (bath, sink, cupboard etc) 設備 sétsùbi; (SPORT) 試合の予定 shiái no yotéi

fix up *vt* (meeting) 手配する tehái surù

to fix someone up with something …のために…を手に入れる …no tamé ni …wo té ni irerù

fizzle out [fiz'l-] *vi* (event) しりすぼみに終ってしまう shirísùbomi ni owátte shimàu; (interest) 次第に消えてしまう shidái ni kiète shimáù

fizzy [fiz'i:] *adj* (drink) 炭酸入りの tañsan-iri no

fjord [fjourd] *n* フィヨルド fíyòrudo

flabbergasted [flæb'ə:rgæstid] *adj* (dumbfounded, surprised) あっけにとられた akké ni torareta

flabby [flæb'i:] *adj* (fat) 締まりのない shimárì no nái

flag [flæg] *n* (of country, organization) 旗 hatà; (for signalling) 手旗 tebáta; (*also*: **flagstone**) 敷石 shikíishi

♦vi (person, spirits) 弱る yowárù

to flag someone down (taxi, car etc) 手を振って…を止める té wo futtè …wo tomérù

flagpole [flæg'poul] *n* 旗ざお hatázao

flagrant [fleig'rənt] *adj* (violation, injustice) 甚だしい hanáhadashìì

flagship [flæg'ʃip] *n* (of fleet) 旗艦 kikáñ; (*fig*) 看板施設 kañbanshisètsu

flair [fle:r] *n* (talent) 才能 saínõ; (style) 粋なセンス ikí na señsu

flak [flæk] *n* (MIL) 対空砲火 taíkūhòka; (*inf*: criticism) 非難 hínan

flake [fleik] *n* (of rust, paint) はげ落ちた欠けら hagéochità kakéra; (of snow, soap powder) 一片 ippén

♦vi (*also*: **flake off**: paint, enamel) はげ落ちる hagéochirù

flamboyant [flæmbɔi'ənt] *adj* (dress, design) けばけばしい kebákebashìì; (person) 派手な hadé na

flame [fleim] *n* (of fire) 炎 honó-ò

flamingo [flǝmiŋ'gou] n フラミンゴ fu-rámiṅgo

flammable [flæm'ǝbǝl] adj (gas, fabric) 燃えやすい moéyasuì

flan [flæn] (BRIT) n フラン fúràn ◇菓子の一種 kashí no isshū

flank [flæŋk] n (of animal) わき腹 wakí-bàra; (of army) 側面 sokúmèn
♦vt ...のわきにある〔いる〕...no wakí ni arù (iru)

flannel [flæn'ǝl] n (fabric) フランネル furánneru; (BRIT: also: **face flannel**) フェースタオル fēsutaòru

flannels [flæn'ǝlz] npl フランネルズボン furánneruzubòn

flap [flæp] n (of pocket, envelope, jacket) ふた futá
♦vt (arms, wings) ばたばたさせる bátà-bata saserù
♦vi (sail, flag) はためく hátamekù; (inf: also: **be in a flap**) 興奮している kốfun shite irù

flare [fle:r] n (signal) 発煙筒 hatsúentō; (in skirt etc) フレア furéa

flare up vi (fire) 燃え上る moéagarù; (fig: person) 怒る okórù; (: fighting) ぼっ発する boppátsu suru

flash [flæʃ] n (of light) 閃光 señkō; (also: **news flash**) ニュースフラッシュ nyűsu-furasshù; (PHOT) フラッシュ furásshù
♦vt (light, headlights) 点滅させる teñmetsu saserù; (send: news, message) 速報する sokúhō suru; (: look, smile) 見せる misérù
♦vi (lightning, light) 光る hikárù; (light on ambulance etc) 点滅する teñmetsu suru

in a flash 一瞬にして isshún nī shite
to flash by/past (person) 走って通り過ぎる hashíttè tōrisugirù

flashback [flæʃ'bæk] n (CINEMA) フラッシュバック furásshubakkù

flashbulb [flæʃ'bʌlb] n フラッシュバルブ furásshubarùbu

flashcube [flæʃ'kju:b] n フラッシュキューブ furásshukyùbu

flashlight [flæʃ'lait] n 懐中電灯 kaíchū-deñtō

flashy [flæʃ'i:] (pej) adj 派手な hadé na

flask [flæsk] n (bottle) 瓶 bíñ; (also: **vacuum flask**) 魔法瓶 máhòbin, ポット pót-tò

flat [flæt] adj (ground, surface) 平な taíra na; (tire) パンクした páñku shita; (battery) 上がった agáttà; (beer) 気が抜けた ki gá nùketa; (refusal, denial) きっぱりした kippárì shita; (MUS: note) フラットの furáttò no; (: voice) そっけない sokkénài; (rate, fee) 均一の kiñ-itsu no
♦n (BRIT: apartment) アパート ápàto; (AUT) パンク páñku; (MUS) フラット furáttò

to work flat out 力一杯働く chikára ippaí hataraku

flatly [flæt'li:] adv (refuse, deny) きっぱりと kippárì to

flatten [flæt'ǝn] vt (also: **flatten out**) 平にする taíra ni surù; (building, city) 取壊す toríkowasù

flatter [flæt'ǝr] vt (praise, compliment) ...にお世辞を言う ...ni oséji wò iú

flattering [flæt'ǝ:riŋ] adj (comment) うれしい uréshiì; (dress) よく似合う yókù niáù

flattery [flæt'ǝ:ri:] n お世辞 oséji

flaunt [flɔ:nt] vt (wealth, possessions) 見せびらかす misébirakasù

flavor [flei'vǝr] (BRIT **flavour**) n (of food, drink) 味 ají; (of ice-cream etc) 種類 shúrùi
♦vt ...に味を付ける ...ni ají wo tsukerù
strawberry-flavored イチゴ味の ichí-goajì no

flavoring [flei'vǝ:riŋ] n 調味料 chốmi-ryõ

flaw [flɔ:] n (in argument, policy) 不備な点 fúbì na teñ; (in character) 欠点 kettéñ; (in cloth, glass) 傷 kízú

flawless [flɔ:'lis] adj 完璧な kañpeki na

flax [flæks] n 亜麻 amá

flaxen [flæk'sǝn] adj (hair) ブロンドの burốñdo no

flea [fli:] n (human, animal) ノミ nomí

fleck [flek] n (mark) 細かいはん点 ko-mákaì hañten

fled [fled] pt, pp of **flee**

flee [fli:] (*pt, pp* **fled**) *vt* (danger, famine, country) 逃れる nogárerù, ...から逃げる ...kara nigérù

♦*vi* (refugees, escapees) 逃げる nigérù

fleece [fli:s] *n* (sheep's wool) 羊毛一頭分 yómôittôbùn; (sheep's coat) ヒツジの毛 hitsúji no kè

♦*vt* (*inf*: cheat) ...から大金をだまし取る ...kara taíkin wò damáshitorù

fleet [fli:t] *n* (of ships: for war) 艦隊 kańtai; (: for fishing etc) 船団 señdan; (of trucks, cars) 車両団 sharyódan

fleeting [fli:tiŋ] *adj* (glimpse) ちらっと 見える chiráttð miérù; (visit) 短い mijíkaì; (happiness) つかの間の tsuká no mà no

Flemish [flem'iʃ] *adj* フランダースの furándàsu no; (LING) フランダース語の furándàsugo no

♦*n* (LING) フランダース語 furándàsugo

flesh [fleʃ] *n* (ANAT) 肉 nikú; (skin) 肌 hadá; (of fruit) 果肉 kaníku

flesh wound *n* 軽傷 keíshō

flew [flu:] *pt of* **fly**

flex [fleks] *n* (of appliance) コード kôdo

♦*vt* (leg, muscles) 曲げたり伸したりする magétarì nobáshitarì suru

flexibility [fleksəbil'əti:] *n* (of material) しなやかさ shináyakasà; (of response, policy) 柔軟性 júnansei

flexible [flek'səbəl] *adj* (material) 曲げ やすい magéyasuì; (response, policy) 柔 軟な júnan na

flick [flik] *n* (of hand, whip etc) 一振り hitófùri

♦*vt* (with finger, hand) はじき飛ばす ha-jíkitobasù; (towel, whip) ぴしっと振る pishíttð furú; (switch: on) 入れる iréru; (: off) 切る kírù

flicker [flik'ə:r] *vi* (light) ちらちらする chíràchira suru; (flame) ゆらゆらする yúràyura suru; (eyelids) まばたく mabátakù

flick through *vt fus* (book) ぱらぱらと ...のページをめくる párapara to ...no pêji wo mekúru

flier [flai'ə:r] *n* (pilot) パイロット paírottð

flight [flait] *n* (action: of birds, plane) 飛 行 hikô; (AVIAT: journey) 飛行機旅行 hikôkiryokô; (escape) 逃避行 tôhikô; (*also*: **flight of steps/stairs**) 階段 kaídan

flight attendant (*US*) *n* 乗客係 jôkya-kukakàri

flight deck *n* (AVIAT) 操縦室 sôjūshì-tsu; (NAUT) 空母の飛行甲板 kûbo no hikôkañpan

flimsy [flim'zi:] *adj* (shoes) こわれやすい kowáreyasuì; (clothes) 薄い usúì; (building) もろい moróì; (excuse) 見え透いた miésuità

flinch [flintʃ] *vi* (in pain, shock) 身震いす る mibúrùi suru
to flinch from (crime, unpleasant duty) ...するのをしり込みする ...surú no wð shirígomi surù

fling [fliŋ] (*pt, pp* **flung**) *vt* (throw) 投げ る nagérù

flint [flint] *n* (stone) 火打石 hiúchiishì; (in lighter) 石 ishí

flip [flip] *vt* (switch) はじく hajíkù; (coin) トスする tósù suru

flippant [flip'ənt] *adj* (attitude, answer) 軽率な keísotsu na

flipper [flip'ə:r] *n* (of seal etc) ひれ足 hi-réashì; (for swimming) フリッパー furíp-pà

flirt [flə:rt] *vi* (with person) いちゃつく ichátsuku

♦*n* 浮気者 uwákimono

flit [flit] *vi* (birds, insects) ひょいと飛ぶ hyoí tð tobu

float [flout] *n* (for swimming, fishing) 浮 き ukí; (vehicle in parade) 山車 dashí; (money) つり用の小銭 tsuríyō nð kozéni

♦*vi* 浮く ukú

flock [flɑːk] *n* 群れ muré; (REL) 会衆 ka-íshū

♦*vi*: **to flock to** (place, event) ぞくぞく 集まる zókùzoku atsúmarù

flog [flɑːg] *vt* (whip) むち打つ múchìutsu

flood [flʌd] *n* (of water) 洪水 kôzui; (of letters, imports etc) 大量 taíryō

♦*vt* (subj: water) 水浸しにする mizúbità-shi ni suru; (: people) ...に殺到する ...ni sattô suru

♦*vi* (place) 水浸しになる mizúbitáshi ni nárù; (people): **to flood into** ...に殺到する ...ni sattó suru

flooding [flʌdˈiŋ] *n* 洪水 kózui

floodlight [flʌdˈlait] *n* 照明灯 shómeitō

floor [flɔːr] *n* (of room) 床 yuká; (storey) 階 káî; (of sea, valley) 底 sókò

♦*vt* (subj: blow) 打ちのめす uchínomesù; (: question) 仰天させる gyóten saserù

ground floor 1階 ikkái

first floor (*US*) 1階 ikkai (*BRIT*) 2階 nikái

floorboard [flɔːrˈbɔːrd] *n* 床板 yuká-ita

floor show *n* フロアショー furóashō

flop [flɑːp] *n* (failure) 失敗 shippái

♦*vi* (fail) 失敗する shippái suru; (fall: into chair, onto floor etc) どたっと座り込む dotáttò suwárikomù

floppy [flɑːpˈiː] *adj* ふにゃふにゃした fúnyàfunya shita

floppy (disk) *n* (COMPUT) フロッピー (ディスク) furóppī(disùku)

flora [flɔːrˈə] *n* 植物相 shokúbutsusō

floral [flɔːrˈəl] *adj* (dress, wallpaper) 花柄の hanágara no

florid [flɔːrˈid] *adj* (style) ごてごてした gótègote shitá; (complexion) 赤らんだ akáranda

florist [flɔːrˈist] *n* 花屋 hanáyà

florist's (shop) *n* 花屋 hanáyà

flounce [flauns] *n* (frill) 縁飾り fuchíkazarì

flounce out *vi* 怒って飛び出す okóttè tobídasù

flounder [flaunˈdəːr] *vi* (swimmer) もがく mogákù; (fig: speaker) まごつく magótsukù; (economy) 停滞する teítai suru

♦*n* (ZOOL) ヒラメ hiráme

flour [flauˈəːr] *n* (gen) 粉 koná; (also: **wheat flour**) 小麦粉 komúgiko

flourish [fləːrˈiʃ] *vi* (business) 繁栄する haň-ei suru; (plant) 生い茂る oíshigerù

♦*n* (bold gesture): **with a flourish** 大げさな身振りで ōgesa na mibúri de

flourishing [fləːrˈiʃiŋ] *adj* (company) 繁栄する haň-ei suru; (trade) 盛んな sakán na

flout [flaut] *vt* (law, rules) 犯す okásù

flow [flou] *n* 流れ nagáre

♦*vi* 流れる nagárerù

flow chart *n* 流れ図 nagárezù, フローチャート furóchàto

flower [flauˈəːr] *n* 花 haná

♦*vi* (plant, tree) 咲く sakú

flower bed *n* 花壇 kádàn

flowerpot [flauˈəːrpɑːt] *n* 植木鉢 uékibàchi

flowery [flauˈəːriː] *adj* (perfume) 花の様な haná no yō na; (pattern) 花柄の hanágara no; (speech) 仰々しい gyógyōshiì

flown *n* [floun] *pp* of **fly**

flu [fluː] *n* (MED) 流感 ryúkan

fluctuate [flʌkˈtʃueit] *vi* (price, rate, temperature) 変動する heńdō suru

fluctuation [flʌktʃueiˈʃən] *n*: **fluctuation (in)** (...の) 変動 (...no) heńdō

fluent [fluːˈənt] *adj* (linguist) 語学たん能な gogákutaňnō na; (speech, writing etc) 滑らかな naměråka na

he speaks fluent French, he's fluent in French 彼はフランス語が堪能だ kárè wa furánsugo gà tańnō da

fluently [fluːˈəntliː] *adv* (speak, read, write) 流ちょうに ryúchō ni

fluff [flʌf] *n* (on jacket, carpet) 毛羽 kebá; (fur: of kitten etc) 綿毛 watáge

fluffy [flʌfˈiː] *adj* (jacket, toy etc) ふわふわした fúwàfuwa shitá

fluid [fluːˈid] *adj* (movement) しなやかな shináyàka na; (situation, arrangement) 流動的な ryúdōteki na

♦*n* (liquid) 液 ékì

fluke [fluːk] (*inf*) *n* まぐれ magúrè

flung [flʌŋ] *pt*, *pp* of **fling**

fluorescent [fluːresˈənt] *adj* (dial, paint, light etc) 蛍光の keíkō no

fluoride [fluːˈəraid] *n* フッ化物 fukkábùtsu

flurry [fləːrˈiː] *n*: **a snow flurry** にわか雪 niwákayùki

flurry of activity 慌ただしい動き awátadashiì ugóki

flush [flʌʃ] *n* (on face) ほてり hotéri; (fig: of youth, beauty etc) 輝かしさ kagáyakashisà

♦*vt* (drains, pipe) 水を流して洗う mizú

wǒ nagáshite araù

♦*vi* (become red) 赤くなる akáku narù

♦*adj*: *flush with* (level) ...と同じ高さの ...to onáji takasà no

to flush the toilet トイレの水を流す tôíre no mizú wo nagasù

flushed [flʌʃt] *adj* 赤らめた akáraметà

flush out *vt* (game, birds) 茂みから追出 す shigémi kàra oídasù

flustered [flʌsˈtəːrd] *adj* (nervous, confused) まごついた magótsuità

flute [fluːt] *n* フルート fúrùto

flutter [flʌtˈəːr] *n* (of wings) 羽ばたき habátaki; (of panic, excitement, nerves) うろたえ urótae

♦*vi* (bird) 羽ばたきする habátaki suru

flux [flʌks] *n*: *in a state of flux* 流動的 状態で ryūdōtekijòtai de

fly [flai] *n* (insect) ハエ haé; (on trousers: *also*: **flies**) ズボンの前 zubôñ no mâè

♦*vb* (*pt* **flew**, *pp* **flown**)

♦*vt* (plane) 操縦する sōjū suru; (passengers, cargo) 空輸する kūyū suru; (distances) 飛ぶ tobú

♦*vi* (bird, insect, plane) 飛ぶ tobú; (passengers) 飛行機で行く hikōki de ikú; (escape) 逃げる nigérù; (flag) 掲げられる kakágerarerù

fly away *vi* (bird, insect) 飛んで行く toñ de ikù

flying [flaiˈiŋ] *n* (activity) 飛行機旅行 hikōkiryokò; (action) 飛行 hikō

♦*adj*: *a flying visit* ほんの短い訪問 hoñ no mijìkaì hōmon

with flying colors 大成功で daíseikō de

flying saucer *n* 空飛ぶ円盤 sórà tobú eñban

flying start *n*: *to get off to a flying start* 好調な滑りだしをする kōchō na suberidàshi wo suru

fly off *vi* = **fly away**

flyover [flaiˈouvəːr] (*BRIT*) *n* (overpass) 陸橋 rikkyō

flysheet [flaiˈʃiːt] *n* (for tent) 入口の垂れ 布 iríguchi nò tarénuno

foal [foul] *n* 子ウマ koúma

foam [foum] *n* (of surf, water, beer) 泡

awá; (*also*: **foam rubber**) フォームラバー fómurabā

♦*vi* (liquid) 泡立つ awádàtsu

to foam at the mouth (person, animal) 泡をふく awá wo fukù

fob [fɑːb] *vt*: *to fob someone off* ...をだ ます ...wo damásù

focal point [fouˈkəl-] *n* (of room, activity etc) 中心 chūshin

focus [fouˈkəs] (*pl* **focuses**) *n* (PHOT) 焦 点 shōten; (of attention, storm etc) 中心 chūshin

♦*vt* (field glasses etc) ...の焦点を合せる ...no shōten wò awáserù

♦*vi*: *to focus (on)* (with camera) (...に) カメラを合せる (...ni) kâmèra wò awáserù; (person) (...に) 注意を向ける (...ni) chūi wo mukérù

in/out of focus 焦点が合っている〔い ない〕 shōten ga attè irú (ináī)

fodder [fɑːdˈəːr] *n* (food) 飼葉 kaíba

foe [fou] *n* (rival, enemy) 敵 tekí

foetus [fiːˈtəs] *n* (*BRIT*) = **fetus**

fog [fɔːg] *n* 霧 kirí

foggy [fɔːgˈiː] *adj*: *it's foggy* 霧が出てい る kirí ga detè irú

fog light (*BRIT* **fog lamp**) *n* (AUT) フ ォッグライト fóggùraito

foil [fɔil] *vt* (attack, plan) くじく kujíkù

♦*n* (metal foil, kitchen foil) ホイル hóīru; (complement) 引立てる物 hikítaterù monò; (FENCING) フルーレ furúrè

fold [fould] *n* (bend, crease) 折目 oríme; (of skin etc) しわ shiwá; (in cloth, curtain etc) ひだ hidá; (AGR) ヒツジの囲い hitsúji nò kakôi; (*fig*) 仲間 nakáma

♦*vt* (clothes, paper) 畳む tatámu; (arms) 組む kúmù

folder [foulˈdəːr] *n* (for papers) 書類挟み み shorúibasàmi

folding [foulˈdiŋ] *adj* (chair, bed) 折畳み 式の orítatamishiki no

fold up *vi* (map, bed, table) 折畳める orítatamerù; (business) つぶれる tsubúrerù

♦*vt* (map, clothes etc) 畳む tatámu

foliage [fouˈliːidʒ] *n* (leaves) 葉 ha◇総称 sōshō

folk [fouk] *npl* (people) 人々 hitobito

♦*adj* (art, music) 民族の mińzoku no

folks (parents) 両親 ryōshin

folklore [fouk'lɔːr] *n* 民間伝承 mińkandeńshō

folk song *n* 民謡 mińyō

follow [fɑ:l'ou] *vt* (person) …について行く …ni tsúite ikú; (suspect) 尾行する bikō suru; (event) …に注目する …ni chūmoku suru; (story) 注意して聞く chūī shite kikú; (leader, example, advice, instructions) …に従う …ni shitágaù; (route, path) たどる tadórù

♦*vi* (person, period of time) 後に来る〔いく〕atō ni kúru(ikú); (result) …という結果になる …to iú kekka ni nárù

to follow suit (*fig*) (…と) 同じ事をする (…to) onáji kotò wo suru

follower [fɑ:l'ouər] *n* (of person) 支持者 shijíshà; (of belief) 信奉者 shińpōsha

following [fɑ:l'ouiŋ] *adj* 次の tsugí no

♦*n* (of party, religion, group etc) 支持者 shijíshà ◇総称 sōshō

follow up *vt* (letter, offer) …に答える …ni kotáerù; (case) 追及する tsuíkyū suru

folly [fɑ:l'i:] *n* (foolishness) ばかな事 bákà na kotó

fond [fɑ:nd] *adj* (memory) 楽しい tanóshiì; (smile, look) 愛情に満ちた aijō ni michita; (hopes, dreams) 愚かな órōka na

to be fond of …が好きである …ga sukí de arù

fondle [fɑ:n'dəl] *vt* 愛ぶする aíbù suru

font [fɑ:nt] *n* (in church) 洗礼盤 señreíban; (TYP) フォント fóñto

food [fu:d] *n* 食べ物 tabémonò

food mixer *n* ミキサー míkīsā

food poisoning [-pɔi'zəniŋ] *n* 食中毒 shokúchùdoku

food processor [-prɑ:s'esər] *n* ミキサー míkīsā ◇食べ物を混ぜたりひいたりおろしたりするための家庭電気製品 tabemono no mazetari hiitari oroshitari suru tame no katei denki seihin

foodstuffs [fu:d'stʌfs] *npl* 食料 shokúryō

fool [fu:l] *n* (idiot) ばか bákà; (CULIN)

フール fūru ◇果物入りムースの一種 kudámono-iri mūsu no ísshù

♦*vt* (deceive) だます damásù

♦*vi* (*also*: **fool around**: be silly) ふざける fuzákerù

foolhardy [fu:l'hɑːrdiː] *adj* (conduct) 無謀な mubō na

foolish [fu:'liʃ] *adj* (stupid) ばかな bákà na; (rash) 無茶な muchá na

foolproof [fu:l'pru:f] *adj* (plan etc) 絶対確実な zettáikakújitsu na

foot [fut] (*pl* **feet**) *n* (of person, animal) 足 ashí; (of bed, cliff) ふもと fumóto; (measure) フィート fìto

♦*vt* (bill) 支払う shiháraù

on foot 徒歩で tóhò de

footage [fut'idʒ] *n* (CINEMA) 場面 bámèn

football [fut'bɔːl] *n* (ball: round) サッカーボール sakkábòru; (: oval) フットボール futtóbòru; (sport: BRIT) サッカー sakká; (: US) フットボール futtóbòru

football player *n* (BRIT: also: **footballer**) サッカー選手 sakká señshu; (US) フットボール選手 futtóbòru señshu

footbrake [fut'breik] *n* 足ブレーキ ashíbùreki

footbridge [fut'bridʒ] *n* 橋 hashí ◇歩行者しか渡れない狭い物を指す hokōsha shika watárenài semáî monó wo sasú

foothills [fut'hilz] *npl* 山ろくの丘陵地帯 safíroku nò kyūryōchìtai

foothold [fut'hould] *n* 足場 ashíba

footing [fut'iŋ] *n* (*fig*: position) 立場 tachíba

to lose one's footing 足を踏み外す ashí wo fumihazusù

footlights [fut'laits] *npl* (THEATER) フットライト futtóraìto

footman [fut'mən] (*pl* **footmen**) *n* (servant) 下男 genán

footnote [fut'nout] *n* 脚注 kyakúchū

footpath [fut'pæθ] *n* 遊歩道 yūhodō

footprint [fut'print] *n* (of person, animal) 足跡 ashíato

footstep [fut'step] *n* (sound) 足音 ashíoto; (footprint) 足跡 ashíato

footwear [fut'weər] *n* (shoes, sandals

etc) 履物 hakímono

KEYWORD
---

for [fɔːr] *prep* **1** (indicating destination, intention) ...行きの ...yuki no, ...に向かって ...ni mùkátte, ...のために〔の〕...notámèni〔no〕

the train for London ロンドン行きの電車 róndonyuki no densha

he left for Rome 彼はローマへ出発しました kárè wa rōmà e shúppatsu shimashíta

he went for the paper 彼は新聞を取りに行きました kárè wa shínbun wo torí ni ikímashíta

is this for me? これは私に? koré wa wàtákushi nî?

there's a letter for you あなた宛の手紙が来ています ànáta ate no tegami ga kîté ìmasù

it's time for lunch 昼食の時間です chúshoku no jikan desù

2 (indicating purpose) ...のために〔の〕...no tamé nì〔no〕

what's it for? それは何のためですか soré wa nàn no tamé dèsu ká

give it to me - what for? それをよこせ–何で? soré wo yòkósè - nàndé?

clothes for children 子供服 kodómofùku

to pray for peace 平和を祈る héiwa wo inorù

3 (on behalf of, representing) ...の代理として ...no daíri toshite

the MP for Hove ホーブ選出の議員 hōbùsénshutsu no gǐn

he works for the government/a local firm 彼は政府〔地元の会社〕に雇われています kárè wa séifu〔jimóto no kaisha〕ni yatówarete ìmasù

I'll ask him for you あなたに代って私が彼に聞きましょう anátà ni kawátte wàtákushi ga karè ni kikímashǒ

G for George G はジョージの G G wà jǒjì no G

4 (because of) ...の理由で ...no riyǔ de, ...のために ...no tamé nì

for this reason このため kònó tame

for fear of being criticized 批判を恐れて hìhán wo ôsórète

the town is famous for its canals 町は運河で有名です machî wà úngà de yūmei desù

5 (with regard to) ...にしては ...ni shité wà

it's cold for July 7月にしては寒い shichígatsu nî shité wà samúî

he's mature for his age 彼はませている kárè wa másète iru

a gift for languages 語学の才能 gógàku no saínô

for everyone who voted yes, 50 voted no 賛成1に対して反対50だった sánsei ìchí nì táî shite hántaihyô gojú dàtta

6 (in exchange for) ...と交換して ...to kôkan shite

I sold it for $5 5ドルでそれを売りました gódòru de soré wo ùrímashîta

to pay $2.50 for a ticket 切符を2ドル50セントで買う kìppú wo nídòru gojússeñto de kaú

7 (in favor of) ...に賛成して ...ni sánsei shite

are you for or against us? あなたは我々に賛成なのか反対なのかはっきり言いなさい anátà wa waréware ni sánsei na nò ka hántai na nò ka hakkírí ìnasaî

I'm all for it 私は無条件で賛成です watákushi wa mùjōkèn de sánsei desù

vote for X X に投票する ékkùsu ni tóhyō suru

8 (referring to distance): *there are roadworks for 5 km* 5キロもの区間が工事中です gókìro mo no kúkàn ga kǒjichū desù

we walked for miles 何マイルも歩きました nánmaîru mo arúkimashîta

9 (referring to time) ...の間 ...no aída

he was away for 2 years 彼は2年間家を離れていました kárè wa ninéñkan iê wò hanárete imashîta

she will be away for a month 彼女は1か月間出掛ける事になっています kánòjo wa ikkágetsukàn dekákeru kotó ni natté imasù

it hasn't rained for 3 weeks 雨は3週間も降っていません áme wa sanshūkan mo futté imaseñ

I have known her for years 何年も前から彼女とは知り合いです nánnen mo máe kara kánojo to wa shirái desù

can you do it for tomorrow? 明日までに出来ますか asú madè ni dekímasù ká

10 (with infinitive clause): *it is not for me to decide* 私が決める事ではありません watakushi gà kiméru kotò de wa arímaseñ

it would be best for you to leave あなたは帰った方がいい anátá wa káetta hō ga íi

there is still time for you to do it あなたはまだまだそれをする時間があります anátá wa mádàmada soré wò suru jikañ ga arímasù

for this to be possible ... これが可能になるのには... koré gà kanō ni narù no ni wa...

11 (in spite of) ...にもかかわらず ...ní mò kakáwarazù

for all his complaints, he is very fond of her 彼は色々と文句を言うが、結局彼女を愛しています kárè wa iróiro tò mónku wo iú gà, kekkyóku kanōjo wo ái shite imásù

for all he said he would write, in the end he didn't 手紙を書く書くと言っていましたけれども、結局書いてくれませんでした tegami wò kákù kákù to itté imashìtà keredomo, kekkyóku kaité kurémasen deshìta

◆*conj* (since, as: rather formal) なぜならば...だから názènaraba ...dá kàra

she was very angry, for he was late again 彼女はかんかんになっていました、というのは彼はまたも遅刻したからです kánòjo wa kañkan ni natté imashìta, to iú no wà kárè wa matá mò chikóku shita kara desù

forage [fɔːr'idʒ] *vi* (search: for food, interesting objects etc) ...をあさる ...wo asárù

foray [fɔːr'ei] *n* (raid) 侵略 shiñryaku

forbad(e) [fɔːrbæd'] *pt of* **forbid**

forbid [fɔːrbid'] (*pt* **forbad(e)**, *pp* **forbidden**) *vt* (sale, marriage, event etc) 禁ずる kiñzurù

to forbid someone to do something ...に...するのを禁ずる ...ni ...surú no wò kiñzurù

forbidden [fərbid'ən] *pp of* **forbid**

forbidding [fərbid'iŋ] *adj* (look, prospect) 怖い kowái

force [fɔːrs] *n* (violence) 暴力 bóryoku; (PHYSICS, *also* strength) 力 chikára

◆*vt* (compel) 強制する kyōsei suru; (push) 強く押す tsúyòku osú; (break open: lock, door) こじ開ける kojíakerù

in force (in large numbers) 大勢で ōzei de; (LAW) 有効で yūkō de

to force oneself to do 無理して...する múrī shite ...suru

forced [fɔːrst] *adj* (labor) 強制的な kyōseiteki na; (smile) 作りの tsukúri no

forced landing (AVIAT) 不時着 fujíchaku

force-feed [fɔːrs'fiːd] *vt* (animal, prisoner) ...に強制給餌をする ...ni kyōseikyù-ji wo suru

forceful [fɔːrs'fəl] *adj* (person) 力強い chikárazuyoî; (attack) 強烈な kyōretsu na; (point) 説得力のある settókuryoku no arù

forceps [fɔːr'səps] *npl* ピンセット piñsettò

forces [fɔːrs'iz] (*BRIT*) *npl*: *the Forces* (MIL) 軍隊 guñtai

forcibly [fɔːr'səbliː] *adv* (remove) 力ずくで chikárazukù de; (express) 力強く chikárazuyokù

ford [fɔːrd] *n* (in river) 浅瀬 asáse ◆ (船を使わないで川を渡れる場所を指す fúnè wo tsukáwanaìde kawá wò watáreru bashò wo sásù

fore [fɔːr] *n*: *to come to the fore* 前面に出て来る zeñmen ni dete kurù

forearm [fɔːr'ɑːrm] *n* 前腕 maéude

foreboding [fɔːrbou'diŋ] *n* (of disaster) 不吉な予感 fukítsu na yokañ

forecast [fɔːr'kæst] *n* (of profits, prices,

weather) 予報 yohó
♦vt (pt, pp **forecast**) (predict) 予報する yohó suru

forecourt [fɔːrˈkɔːrt] n (of garage) 前庭 maéniwa

forefathers [fɔːrˈfɑːðəːrz] npl (ancestors) 先祖 señzo

forefinger [fɔːrˈfiŋgəːr] n 人差指 hitósashiyùbi

forefront [fɔːrˈfrʌnt] n: **in the forefront of** (industry, movement) ...の最前線で ...no saízeñsen de

forego [fɔːrgou'] (pt **forewent** pp **foregone**) vt (give up) やめる yamérù; (go without) ...なしで我慢する ...náshì de gámàn suru

foregone [fɔːrgɔːn'] adj: **it's a foregone conclusion** 結果は決まっている kekká wa kimattè irú

foreground [fɔːrˈgraund] n (of painting) 前景 zeñkei

forehead [fɔːrˈhed] n 額 hitái

foreign [fɔːrˈin] adj (country) 外国の gaíkoku no; (trade) 対外の taígai no; (object, matter) 異質の ishítsu no

foreigner [fɔːrˈənəːr] n 外国人 gaíkokujìn

foreign exchange n 外国為替 gaíkokukawàse; (currency) 外貨 gaíka

Foreign Office (BRIT) n 外務省 gaímushō

Foreign Secretary (BRIT) n 外務大臣 gaímudaìjin

foreleg [fɔːrˈleg] n (of animal) 前足 maéàshi

foreman [fɔːrˈmən] (pl **foremen**) n (in factory, on building site etc) 現場監督 geñbakaňtoku

foremost [fɔːrˈmoust] adj (most important) 最も大事な mottómò dáiji na
♦adv: **first and foremost** 先ず第一に mázù dáiichi ni

forensic [fərenˈsik] adj (medicine, test) 法医学的な hóigàkuteki na

forerunner [fɔːrˈrʌnəːr] n 先駆者 señkushà

foresee [fɔːrsiː'] (pt **foresaw** pp **foreseen**) vt (problem, development) 予想する yosó suru

foreseeable [fɔːrsiː'əbəl] adj (problem, development) 予想出来る yosó dekirù

foreshadow [fɔːrˈʃædou] vt (event) ...の前兆となる ...no zeñchō to narù

foresight [fɔːrˈsait] n 先見の明 señken nò meí

forest [fɔːrˈist] n 森 mórì

forestall [fɔːrstɔːl'] vt (person) 出し抜く dashínuku; (discussion) 防ぐ fuségù

forestry [fɔːrˈistriː] n 林業 riñgyō

foretaste [fɔːrˈteist] n 前兆 zeñchō

foretell [fɔːrtel'] (pt, pp **foretold**) vt (predict) 予言する yogén suru

forever [fərevˈəːr] adv (for good) 永遠に eíen ni; (continually) いつも ítsùmo

forewent [fɔːrwent'] pt of **forego**

foreword [fɔːrˈwəːrd] n (in book) 前書 maégaki

forfeit [fɔːrˈfit] vt (lose: right, friendship etc) 失う ushínaù

forgave [fərgeiv'] pt of **forgive**

forge [fɔːrdʒ] n (smithy) 鍛冶屋 kajíyà
♦vt (signature, money) 偽造する gizó suru; (wrought iron) 鍛えて作る kitáetè tsukúrù

forge ahead vi (country, person) 前進する zeñshin suru

forger [fɔːrˈdʒəːr] n 偽造者 gizóshà

forgery [fɔːrˈdʒəːriː] n (crime) 偽造 gizó; (object) 偽物 nisémono

forget [fərget'] (pt **forgot**, pp **forgotten**) vt (fact, face, skill, appointment) 忘れる wasúrerù; (leave behind: object) 置忘れる okíwasurerù; (put out of mind: quarrel, person) 考えない事にする kañgaenài kotó ni surù
♦vi (fail to remember) 忘れる wasúrerù

forgetful [fərget'fəl] adj (person) 忘れっぽい wasúreppòi

forget-me-not [fərget'miːnɑːt] n ワスレナグサ wasúrenagùsa

forgive [fərgiv'] (pt **forgave**, pp **forgiven**) vt (pardon) 許す yurúsù
to forgive someone for something (excuse) ...の...を許す ...no ...wo yurúsù

forgiveness [fərgiv'nis] n 許し yurúshi

forgo [fɔːrgou'] vt = **forego**

forgot [fəˈrɡɑːt'] *pt of* **forget**

forgotten [fəˈrɡɑːt'ən] *pp of* **forget**

fork [fɔːrk] *n* (for eating) フォーク fôku; (for gardening) ホーク hôku; (in road, river, railway) 分岐点 buńkiteǹ
♦*vi* (road) 分岐する buńki suru

fork-lift truck [fɔːrk'lift-] *n* フォークリフト fôkurifûto

fork out (*inf*) *vt* (pay) 払う haráù

forlorn [fəˈrlɔːrn'] *adj* (person, place) わびしい wabíshiì; (attempt) 絶望的な zetsúbōteki na; (hope) 空しい munáshiì

form [fɔːrm] *n* (type) 種類 shúrùi; (shape) 形 katáchì; (SCOL) 学年 gakúnen; (questionnaire) 用紙 yôshi
♦*vt* (make: shape, queue, object, habit) 作る tsukúrù; (make up: organization, group) 構成する kôsei suru; (idea) まとめる matómerù
in top form 調子が最高で chôshi gà saíkō de

formal [fɔːr'məl] *adj* (offer, statement, occasion) 正式な seíshiki na; (person, behavior) 堅苦しい katágurushiì; (clothes) 正装の seísō no; (garden) 伝統的な dentôteki na ◇極めて幾何学的な配置の庭園について言う kiwámetè kikágakuteki na haíchi nò teien ni tsuìtè iú; (education) 正規の seíki no

formalities [fɔːrmæl'iti:z] *npl* (procedures) 手続き tetsúzùki

formality [fɔːrmæl'iti:] *n* (procedure) 形式 keíshiki

formally [fɔːr'məli:] *adv* (make offer etc) 正式に seíshiki ni; (act) 堅苦しく katágurushikù; (dress): *to dress formally* 正装する seísō suru

format [fɔːr'mæt] *n* (form, style) 形式 keíshiki
♦*vt* (COMPUT: disk) 初期化する shókìka suru, フォーマットする fômatto suru

formation [fɔːrmeí'ʃən] *n* (creation: of organization, business) 創立 sôritsu; (: of theory) 考案 kôan; (pattern) 編隊 heńtai; (of rocks, clouds) 構造 kôzō

formative [fɔːr'mətiv] *adj* (years, influence) 形成的な keíseiteki na

former [fɔːr'məːr] *adj* (one-time) かつて の kátsùte no; (earlier) 前の mâè no
the former ... the latter ... 前者...後者... zeńshà... kôshà...

formerly [fɔːr'məːrli:] *adv* (previously) 前は mâè wa

formidable [fɔːr'midəbəl] *adj* (task, opponent) 手ごわい tegówaì

formula [fɔːr'mjələ] (*pl* **formulae** *or* **formulas**) *n* (MATH, CHEM) 公式 kôshiki; (plan) 方式 hôshiki

formulate [fɔːr'mjəleit] *vt* (plan, strategy) 練る nérù; (opinion) 表現する hyôgen suru

forsake [fɔːrseik'] (*pt* **forsook**, *pp* **forsaken**) *vt* (abandon: person) 見捨てる misúterù; (: belief) 捨てる sutérù

forsook [fɔːrsuk'] *pt of* **forsake**

fort [fɔːrt] *n* (MIL) とりで toríde

forte [fɔːr'tei] *n* (strength) 得意 tokúî

forth [fɔːrθ] *adv* (out) 外へ sôtò e
back and forth 行ったり来たりして ittárì kitárì shité
and so forth など nádò

forthcoming [fɔːrθ'kʌm'iŋ] *adj* (event) 今度の końdo no; (help, evidence) 手に入る té ni hairù; (person) 率直な sotchóku na

forthright [fɔːrθ'rait] *adj* (condemnation, opposition) はっきりした hakkírì to shitá

forthwith [fɔːrθwiθ'] *adv* 直ちに tádàchi ni

fortify [fɔːr'təfai] *vt* (city) ...の防備を固める ...no bôbi wo katámerù; (person) 力付ける chikárazukerù

fortitude [fɔːr'tətuːd] *n* 堅忍 keńnin

fortnight [fɔːrt'nait] *n* (two weeks) 2週間 nishúkan

fortnightly [fɔːrt'naitli:] *adj* (payment, visit, magazine) 2週間置きの nishúkan-oki no
♦*adv* (pay, meet, appear) 2週間置きに nishúkan-oki ni

fortress [fɔːr'tris] *n* 要塞 yôsai

fortuitous [fɔːrtuː'itəs] *adj* (discovery, result) 偶然の gûzen no

fortunate [fɔːr'tʃənit] *adj* (person) 運の いい úǹ no íi; (event) 幸運な kôun na

it is fortunate that ... 幸いに... saíwai ni ...

fortunately [fɔːr'tʃənitli:] *adv* (happily, luckily) 幸いに saíwai ni

fortune [fɔːr'tʃən] *n* (luck) 運 úñ; (wealth) 財産 zaísan

fortune-teller [fɔːr'tʃəntelər] *n* 易者 e-kísha

forty [fɔːr'ti:] *num* 40 (の) yóñjū (no)

forum [fɔːr'əm] *n* フォーラム fôramu

forward [fɔːr'wərd] *adj* (in position) 前方の zeñpō no; (in movement) 前方への zeñpō e no; (in time) 将来のための shôrai nò tame no; (not shy) 出過ぎた desúgitā
♦*n* (SPORT) フォワード fowádo
♦*vt* (letter, parcel, goods) 転送する teñsō suru; (career, plans) 前進させる zeñshin saserú

to move forward (progress) 進歩する shiñpo suru

forward(s) [fɔːr'wərd(z)] *adv* 前へ máe e

fossil [fɑs'əl] *n* 化石 kaséki

foster [fɔs'tər] *vt* (child) 里親として育てる satóoya toshitè sodáterù; (idea, activity) 助成する joséi suru

foster child *n* 里子 satógo

fought [fɔːt] *pt, pp* of **fight**

foul [faul] *adj* (state, taste, smell, weather) 悪い warúi; (language) 汚い kitánaì; (temper) ひどい hidôì
♦*n* (SPORT) 反則 hañsoku, ファウル fáūru
♦*vt* (dirty) 汚す yogósù

foul play *n* (LAW) 殺人 satsújin

found [faund] *pt, pp* of **find**
♦*vt* (establish: business, theater) 設立する setsúritsu suru

foundation [faundei'ʃən] *n* (act) 設立 setsúritsu; (base) 土台 dodái; (organization) 財団 zaídan; (also: **foundation cream**) ファンデーション fañdềshon

foundations [faundei'ʃənz] *npl* (of building) 土台 dodái

founder [faun'dər] *n* (of firm, college) 設立者 setsúritsushà
♦*vi* (ship) 沈没する chiñbotsu suru

foundry [faun'dri:] *n* 鋳造工場 chūzōkō-

jồ

fountain [faun'tin] *n* 噴水 fuñsui

fountain pen *n* 万年筆 mañneñhitsu

four [fɔːr] *num* 4 (の) yóñ (no), 四つ (の) yotsu (no)

on all fours 四つんばいになって yotsúnbai ni nattè

four-poster [fɔːr'pous'tər] *n* (*also:* **four-poster bed**) 天がい付きベット teñgaitsukibetto

foursome [fɔːr'səm] *n* 4人組 yoníngumi

fourteen [fɔːr'tiːn'] *num* 14 (の) jûyon (no)

fourth [fɔːrθ] *num* 第4(の) daíyon (no)

fowl [faul] *n* 家きん kakín

fox [fɑks] *n* キツネ kitsúne
♦*vt* (baffle) 困らす komárasu

foyer [fɔi'ər] *n* (of hotel, theater) ロビー rôbī

fraction [fræk'ʃən] *n* (portion) 一部 ichíbù; (MATH) 分数 buñsū

fracture [fræk'tʃər] *n* (of bone) 骨折 kossétsu
♦*vt* (bone) 折る órù

fragile [frædʒ'əl] *adj* (breakable) 壊れやすい kowáreyasuì

fragment [fræg'mənt] *n* (small piece) 破片 hahén

fragrance [freig'rəns] *n* (scent) 香り kaóri

fragrant [freig'rənt] *adj* 香り高い kaóritakaì

frail [freil] *adj* (person, invalid) か弱い kayówaì; (structure) 壊れやすい kowáreyasuì

frame [freim] *n* (of building, structure) 骨組 honégumi; (of human, animal) 体格 taíkaku; (of door, window) 枠 wakú; (of picture) 額縁 gakúbuchi; (of spectacles: *also:* **frames**) フレーム fúrēmu
♦*vt* (picture) 額縁に入れる gakúbuchi ni irerú

frame of mind *n* 気分 kibúñ

framework [freim'wərk] *n* (structure) 骨組 honégumi

France [fræns] *n* フランス furánsu

franchise [fræn'tʃaiz] *n* (POL) 参政権 sañseikèn; (COMM) フランチャイズ fu-

furánchaīzu

frank [fræŋk] *adj* (discussion, look) 率直 な sotchóku na, フランクな furáṅku na
♦*vt* (letter) ...に料金別納の判を押す ...ni ryókinbetsunó no háṅ wo osú

frankly [fræŋk'li:] *adv* (honestly) 正直に shójikī ni; (candidly) 率直に sotchóku ni

frankness [fræŋk'nis] *n* (honesty) 正直 さ shójikisà; (candidness) 率直さ sotchókukusa

frantic [fræn'tik] *adj* (distraught) 狂乱 した kyóran shita; (hectic) てんてこ舞い の teṅtekomài no

fraternal [frətəːr'nəl] *adj* (greetings, relations) 兄弟の様な kyódai no yó na

fraternity [frətəːr'niti:] *n* (feeling) 友愛 yúai; (group of people) 仲間 nakáma

fraternize [fræt'əːrnaiz] *vi* 付き合う tsukíaù

fraud [frɔːd] *n* (crime) 詐欺 sagí; (person) ぺてん師 peténshi

fraudulent [frɔː'dʒələnt] *adj* (scheme, claim) 不正な fuséi na

fraught [frɔːt] *adj*: *fraught with* (danger, problems) ...をはらんだ ...wo haráṅda

fray [frei] *n* (battle, fight) 戦い tatákai
♦*vi* (cloth, rope) 擦切れる suríkirerù; (rope end) ほつれる hotsúrerù
tempers were frayed 皆短気になって いた miná táṅki ni nátte itá

freak [friːk] *n* (person: in attitude, behavior) 変人 heñjin; (: in appearance) 奇形 kikéi
♦*adj* (event, accident) まぐれの mágùre no

freckle [frek'əl] *n* そばかす sobákasù

free [friː] *adj* (person, press, movement) 自由な jíyū na; (not occupied: time) 暇な hímà na; (: seat) 空いている aíte irù; (costing nothing: meal, pen etc) 無料の muryó no
♦*vt* (prisoner etc) 解放する kaího suru; (jammed object) 動ける様にする ugókeru yó ni suru
free (of charge) 無料で muryó de
for free = *free of charge*

freedom [friː'dəm] *n* (liberty) 自由 jíyū

free-for-all [friː'fəːrɔːl'] *n* 乱闘 raṅtō

free gift *n* 景品 keíhin

freehold [friː'hould] *n* (of property) 自由 保有権 jiyúhoyûken

free kick *n* (SPORT) フリーキック furíkikkù

freelance [friː'læns] *adj* (journalist, photographer, work) フリーランサーの furíraṅsā no

freely [friː'li:] *adv* (without restriction, limits) 自由に jíyū ni; (liberally) 気ままに kimáma ni

Freemason [friː'meisən] *n* フリーメーソ ン furímēson

Freepost [friː'poust] ® *BRIT n* (postal service) 料金受取人払い ryókin uketorininbarài

free-range [friː'reindʒ] *adj* 放し飼いの hanáshigài no ◇特にニワトリやその卵に ついて言う tókù ni niwátori yà sonó tamagó ni tsuíte iú

free trade *n* 自由貿易 jiyúbóeki

freeway [friː'wei] (*US*) *n* 高速道路 kósōkudóro

free will *n* 自由意志 jiyúishì
of one's own free will 自発的に jihátsuteki ni

freeze [friːz] (*pt* **froze**, *pp* **frozen**) *vi* (weather) 氷点下になる hyóteṅka ni nárù; (liquid, pipe) 凍る kórù; (person: with cold) 冷える hiérù; (: stop moving) 立ち すくむ tachísukumù
♦*vt* (water, lake) 凍らせる kóraserù; (food) 冷凍にする reítō ni surù; (prices, salaries) 凍結する tóketsu suru
♦*n* (weather) 氷点下の天気 hyóteṅka no téṅki; (on arms, wages) 凍結 tóketsu

freeze-dried [friːz'draid'] *adj* 凍結乾燥 の tóketsukaṅsō no

freezer [friː'zəːr] *n* フリーザー furízā

freezing [friː'ziŋ] *adj* (wind, weather, water) 凍る様な kóru yó na
3 degrees below freezing 氷点下3度 hyóteṅka sáṅdo

freezing point *n* 氷点 hyóten

freight [freit] *n* (goods) 貨物 kámòtsu; (money charged) 運送料 uṅsóryo

freight train (*US*) *n* (goods train) 貨物

列車 kamótsuresshā

French [frentʃ] *adj* フランス の furánsu no; (LING) フランス語の furánsugo no
♦*n* (LING) フランス語 furánsugo
♦*npl*: **the French** (people) フランス人 furánsujìn

French bean *n* サヤインゲン sayá-iñgen

French fried potatoes *npl* フレンチフライ (ポテト) furénchifurài(pótèto)

French fries [-fraiz] (*US*) *npl* = **French fried potatoes**

Frenchman/woman [fren'tʃmən /wumən] (*pl* **Frenchmen/women**) *n* フランス人男性〔女性〕furánsujin dañsei 〔jòsei〕

French window *n* フランス窓 furánsu madò

frenetic [frənet'ik] *adj* (activity, behavior) 熱狂的な nekkyōteki na

frenzy [fren'zi:] *n* (of violence) 逆上 gyakújō; (of joy, excitement) 狂乱 kyōran

frequency [fri:'kwənsi:] *n* (of event) 頻度 híñdo; (RADIO) 周波数 shūhasū

frequent [*adj* fri:'kwint *vb* frikwent'] *adj* (intervals, visitors) 頻繁な hiñpan na
♦*vt* (pub, restaurant) ...によく行く ...ni yókù ikú

frequently [fri:'kwintli:] *adv* (often) しばしば shíbàshiba

fresco [fres'kou] *n* フレスコ画 furésukoga

fresh [freʃ] *adj* (food, vegetables, bread, air etc) 新鮮な shiñsen na; (memories, footprint) 最近の saíkin no; (instructions) 新たな árata na; (paint) 塗立ての nurítate no; (new: approach, start) 新しい atárashiì; (cheeky: person) 生意気な namáiki na

freshen [freʃ'ən] *vi* (wind) 強くなる tsuyóku narù; (air) 涼しくなる suzúshiku narù

freshen up *vi* (person) 化粧直しをする keshōnaòshi wo suru

fresher [freʃ'əːr] (*BRIT*: *inf*) *n* = **freshman**

freshly [freʃ'li:] *adv* (made, cooked, painted) ...されたばかりで ...saréta bakàri de

freshman [freʃ'mən] (*pl* **freshmen**) *n* (*US*: SCOL) 1年生 ichínensei ◇大学生や高校生について言う daígakùsei ya kōkōsei ni tsuitè iú

freshness [freʃ'nis] *n* 新鮮さ shiñsensà

freshwater [freʃ'wɔːtəːr] *adj* (lake, fish) 淡水の tañsui no

fret [fret] *vi* (worry) 心配する shiñpai suru

friar [frai'əːr] *n* (REL) 修道士 shúdōshì

friction [frik'ʃən] *n* (resistance, rubbing) 摩擦 masátsu; (between people) 不仲 fúnàka

Friday [frai'dei] *n* 金曜日 kiñ-yòbi

fridge [fridʒ] (*BRIT*) *n* 冷蔵庫 reízòko

fried [fraid] *adj* (steak, eggs, fish etc) 焼いた yaítà; (chopped onions etc) いためた itámetà; (in deep fat) 揚げた agétà, フライした furái shita

friend [frend] *n* 友達 tomódachi

friendly [frend'li:] *adj* (person, smile) 愛想のいい aísō no íi; (government) 友好的な yūkōteki na; (place, restaurant) 居心地の良い igókochi no yoì; (game, match) 親善の shiñzen no

friendship [frend'ʃip] *n* 友情 yújō

frieze [fri:z] *n* フリーズ fúrīzu ◇壁の一番高い所に付ける細長い飾り、彫刻などを指す kabé no ichíban takái tokórò ni tsukérù hosónagaì kazárì, chōkoku nadò wo sásù

frigate [frig'it] *n* フリゲート艦 furígètokan

fright [frait] *n* (terror) 恐怖 kyōfu; (scare) 驚き odóroki
to take fright 驚く odórokù

frighten [frait'ən] *vt* 驚かす odórokasù

frightened [frait'ənd] *adj* (afraid) 怖がった kowágattà; (worried, nervous) 不安に駆られた fúan ni karáreta

frightening [frait'niŋ] *adj* (experience, prospect) 恐ろしい osóroshiǐ

frightful [frait'fəl] *adj* (dreadful) 恐ろしい osóroshiǐ

frightfully [frait'fəli:] *adv* 恐ろしく osóroshikù

frigid [fridʒ'id] *adj* (woman) 不感症の fukánshō no

frill [fril] n (of dress, shirt) フリル fúriru

fringe [frindʒ] n (BRIT: of hair) 前髪 maégami; (decoration: on shawl, lampshade etc) 縁飾り fuchíkazàri; (edge: of forest etc) へり herí

fringe benefits npl 付加給付 fukákyū̀fu

frisk [frisk] vt (suspect) ボディーチェックする bodíchekkù suru

frisky [fris'ki:] adj (animal, youngster) はつらつとした hatsúratsu to shitá

fritter [frit'ə:r] n (CULIN) フリッター furíttā

fritter away vt (time, money) 浪費する rōhi suru

frivolous [friv'ələs] adj (conduct, person) 軽率な keísotsu na; (object, activity) 下らない kudáranaì

frizzy [friz'i:] adj (hair) 縮れた chijíretà

fro [frou] see to

frock [fra:k] n (dress) ドレス dórèsu

frog [frɔ:g] n カエル kaérù

frogman [frɔ:g'mæn] (pl **frogmen**) n ダイバー dáìbā

frolic [fra:l'ik] vi (animals, children) 遊び回る asóbimawarù

---

from [frʌm] prep **1** (indicating starting place) ...から ...kárà

where do you come from?, where are you from? (asking place of birth) ご出身はどちらですか go-shússhìn wa dóchìra désù ká

from London to Glasgow ロンドンからグラスゴーへ róndon kara gurásugò e

to escape from something/someone ...から逃げる ...kárà nigérù

2 (indicating origin etc) ...から ...kárà

a letter/telephone call from my sister 妹からの手紙〔電話〕imóto karà no tegámi〔deñwa〕

tell him from me that ... 私からの伝言で彼に...と言って下さい watákushi karà no deñgon dè kárè ni ...to itté kudasaì

a quotation from Dickens ディケンズからの引用 díkènzu kara no iñyō

to drink from the bottle 瓶から飲む bíñ kara nómù

3 (indicating time) ...から ...kárà

from one o'clock to/until/till two 1時から2時まで ichíji karà níji madè

from January (on) 1月から(先) ichígatsu karà (sakí)

4 (indicating distance) ...から ...kárà

the hotel is 1 km from the beach ホテルは浜辺から1キロ離れています hótèru wa hamabè kárà ichíkiro hanarète imásù

we're still a long way from home まだまだ家まで遠い mádàmada iè madè tōi

5 (indicating price, number etc) ...から ...kárà, ...ないし... ...náìshi ...

prices range from $10 to $50 値段は10ドルないし50ドルです nedán wà júdòru náìshi gojúdòru désù

there were from 20 to 30 people there 20ないし30人いました níjù náìshi sañjūnìn imáshìta

the interest rate was increased from 9% to 10% 公定歩合は9パーセントから10パーセントに引き上げられました kōteibùai wa kyúpāsèñto kara juppásèñto ni hikíageraremashìta

6 (indicating difference) ...と ...tò

he can't tell red from green 彼は赤と緑の区別ができません kárè wa ákà to mídòri no kúbètsu ga dekímaseñ

to be different from someone/something ...と違っている ...tò chigátte irù

7 (because of, on the basis of) ...から ...kárà, ...によって ...ni yotté

from what he says 彼の言う事によると kárè no iú kotò ni yorú tò

from what I understand 私が理解したところでは watákushi gà ríkài shita tokóro de wà

to act from conviction 確信に基づいて行動する kakúshin ni motozuìte kṓdō suru

weak from hunger 飢えでぐったりになって ué dè guttári ni náttè

---

front [frʌnt] n (of house, dress) 前面 zeń-

meǹ; (of coach, train, car) 最前部 saízeǹbu; (promenade: *also*: **sea front**) 海岸沿いの遊歩道 kaígaǹzoi no yúhodò; (MIL) 戦線 seǹseñ; (METEOROLOGY) 前線 zeǹseñ; (*fig*: appearances) 外見 gaíkeñ

♦*adj* (*gen*) 前の máè no, 一番前の ichíbanmaè no; (gate) 正面の shómeñ no

in front (of) (...の) 前に (...no) máè ni

front tooth 前歯 máèba

frontage [frʌn'tidʒ] *n* (of building) 正面 shómeñ

frontal [frʌn'təl] *adj* 真っ向からの makkō kara no

front door *n* 正面玄関 shómengeǹkan

frontier [frʌnti:r'] *n* (between countries) 国境 kokkyō

front page *n* (of newspaper) 第一面 dáiichimen

front room (*BRIT*) *n* 居間 imá

front-wheel drive [frʌnt'wi:l-] *n* (AUT) 前輪駆動 zeńrinkùdō

frost [frɔːst] *n* (weather) 霜が降りる事 shimó ga oríru koto; (*also*: **hoarfrost**) 霜 shímò

frostbite [frɔːst'bait] *n* 霜焼け shimóyake

frosted [frɔːs'tid] *adj* (glass) 曇りの kumóri no

frosty [frɔːs'tiː] *adj* (weather, night) 寒い samúi ◇気温が氷点下であるが雪が降っていない状態について言う kíon ga hyōtenka de arù ga yukí ga futte inái jōtai ni tsuíte iú; (welcome, look) 冷たい tsumétaì

froth [frɔːθ] *n* (on liquid) 泡 awá

frown [fraun] *vi* 顔をしかめる káò wo shikámerù

froze [frouz] *pt of* **freeze**

frozen [frou'zən] *pp of* **freeze**

frugal [fru:'gəl] *adj* (person) 倹約的な keń-yakuteki na; (meal) つましい tsumáshiì

fruit [fru:t] *n inv* (AGR, BOT) 果物 kudámono; (*fig*: results) 成果 seíkà

fruiterer [fru:t'ə:rə:r] (*BRIT*) *n* 果物屋 kudámonoyà

fruiterer's (shop) [fru:t'ə:rə:rz-] (*BRIT*) *n* 果物屋 kudámonoyà

fruitful [fru:t'fəl] *adj* (meeting, discussion) 有益な yū́eki na

fruition [fru:iʃ'ən] *n*: *to come to fruition* 実る minórù

fruit juice *n* 果汁 kajū́, フルーツジュース furū́tsujùsu

fruit machine (*BRIT*) *n* スロットマシン suróttomashìñ

fruit salad *n* フルーツサラダ furū́tsusaràda

frustrate [frʌs'treit] *vt* (upset) ...に欲求不満を起させる ...ni yokkyū́fumàn wo okósaserù; (block) ざ折させる zasétsu saserù

frustration [frʌstrei'ʃən] *n* (irritation) 欲求不満 yokkyū́fumàn; (disappointment) がっかり gakkárì

fry [frai] (*pt*, *pp* **fried**) *vt* (CULIN: steak, eggs etc) 焼く yákù; (: chopped onions etc) いためる itámerù; (: in deep fat) 揚げる agérù ¶ *see also* **small fry**

frying pan [frai'iŋ-] *n* フライパン furáipan

ft. *abbr* = **foot**; **feet**

fuddy-duddy [fʌd'iː:dʌdiː] (*pej*) *n* 古臭い人 furúkusaî hitð

fudge [fʌdʒ] *n* (CULIN) ファッジ fájjì

fuel [fju:'əl] *n* 燃料 neńryō

fuel oil *n* 重油 jū́yu

fuel tank *n* 燃料タンク neńryòtaǹku

fugitive [fju:'dʒətiv] *n* (runaway, escapee) 逃亡者 tōbōsha

fulfil [fulfil'] *vt* (function) 果す hatásù; (condition) 満たす mitásù; (request, wish, desire) かなえる kanáerù; (order) 実行する jikkō suru

fulfilment [fulfil'mənt] *n* (satisfaction) 満足 máñzoku; (of promise, desire) 実現 jitsúgen

full [ful] *adj* (container, cup, car, cinema) 一杯の ippái no; (maximum: use, volume) 最大限の saídaìgen no; (complete: details, information) 全ての súbete no; (price) 割引なしの waríbikinashì no; (skirt) ゆったりした yuttárì shitá

♦*adv*: *to know full well that* ...という事を重々承知している ...to iú kotò wo jū́jù shōchi shite irù

I'm full (up) 満腹だ mañpuku da

a full two hours 二時間も nijíkàn mo

at full speed 全速力で zeñsokuryóku de

in full (reproduce, quote, pay) 完全に kañzen ni

full employment n 100パーセントの就業率 hyakú pāseñto no shúgyōrìtsu

full-length [ful'leŋkθ'] adj (film, novel etc) 長編の chōhen no; (coat) 長い nágài; (portrait) 全身の zeñshin no

full moon n 満月 mâñgetsu

full-scale [ful'skeil'] adj (attack, war) 全面的な zeñmenteki na; (model) 実物大の jitsúbutsudai no

full stop n 終止符 shúshifù, ピリオド pírìodo

full-time [ful'taim] adj (work, study) 全時間制の zeñjikáñsei no

♦adv 全時間で zeñjikàn de

fully [ful'i:] adv (completely) 完全に kañzen ni; (at least): *fully as big as* 少なくとも…と同じぐらいの大きさの sukúnàkutomo ...to onaji gurai no ōkisa no

fully-fledged [ful'i:fledʒd'] adj (teacher, barrister) 一人前の ichíninmaè no

fulsome [ful'səm] (pej) adj (praise, compliments) 大げさな ōgesa na

fumble [fʌm'bəl] vi: *to fumble with* (key, catch) …でもたもたする ...de mótàmota suru

fume [fju:m] vi (rage) かんかんに怒る káñkan ni okórù

fumes of fire, fuel, car) ガス gásù

fun [fʌn] n (amusement) 楽しみ tanóshimi

to have fun 楽しむ tanóshimù

for fun 冗談として jōdan toshité

to make fun of (ridicule, mock) ばかにする bákà ni suru

function [fʌŋk'ʃən] n (role) 役割 yakúwari, 機能 kinō; (product) …による物 ...ni yórù monó; (social occasion) 行事 gyóji

♦vi (operate) 作動する sadō suru

functional [fʌŋk'ʃənəl] adj (operational) 作動できる sadō dekirù; (practical) 機能的な kinōteki na

fund [fʌnd] n (of money) 基金 kikíñ; (source, store) 貯蓄 chochíku

fundamental [fʌndəmen'təl] adj (principle, change, mistake) 基本的な kihôntekina na

fundamentalist [fʌndəmen'təlɪst] n 原理主義者 geñrishugìsha

funds [fʌndz] npl (money) 資金 shikíñ

funeral [fju:'nə:rəl] n 葬式 sôshiki

funeral parlor n 葬儀屋 sôgiya

funeral service n 葬式 sôshiki

funfair [fʌn'fe:r] (BRIT) n 移動遊園地 idôyūeñchi

fungi [fʌn'dʒai] npl of **fungus**

fungus [fʌŋ'gəs] (pl **fungi**) n (plant) キノコ kínòko; (mold) かび kabî

funnel [fʌn'əl] n (for pouring) じょうご jôgo; (of ship) 煙突 eñtotsu

funny [fʌn'i:] adj (amusing) こっけいな kokkéi na; (strange) 変な héñ na

fur [fə:r] n (on animal) 毛 ke; (animal skin for clothing etc) 毛皮 kegáwa; (BRIT: in kettle etc) 湯あか yuáka

fur coat n 毛皮コート kegáwakòto

furious [fju:r'i:əs] adj 猛烈な mōretsu na

furlong [fə:r'lɔ:ŋ] n (HORSE-RACING) ハロン hárõn ◇距離の単位で、約201メーター kyórì no táñ-i de, yakú 201 mêta

furlough [fə:r'lou] n (MIL: leave) 休暇 kyûka

furnace [fə:r'nis] n (in foundry) 炉 ro; (in power plant) ボイラー bôirā

furnish [fə:r'niʃ] vt (room, building) …に家具調度を備える ...ni kagúchòdo wo sonáerù; (supply) …に供給する ...ni kyôkyū suru

furnishings [fə:r'niʃiŋz] npl 家具と設備 kágù to sétsùbi

furniture [fə:r'nitʃə:r] n 家具 kágù

piece of furniture 家具一点 kágù itteñ

furrow [fə:r'ou] n (in field) 溝 mizó; (in skin) しわ shiwá

furry [fə:r'i:] adj 毛で覆われた ke de ốwaretà

further [fə:r'ðə:r] adj (additional) その上の sonó ue no, 追加の tsuíka no

♦adv (farther) もっと遠くに móttò tôku ni; (more) それ以上 soré ijõ; (moreover) 更に sárà ni, なお náõ

♦*vt* (career, project) 促進する sokúshin suru

further education (*BRIT*) *n* 成人教育 seíjin kyőiku

furthermore [fəːrˈðɔːrmɔːr] *adv* (moreover) 更に sárà ni, なお nao

furthest [fəːrˈðist] *superl of* **far**

furtive [fəːrˈtiv] *adj* (glance, movement) こっそりとする kossőri to surú

fury [fjuːrˈiː] *n* (anger, rage) 憤慨 fuñgai

fuse [fjuːz] *n* (ELEC: in plug, circuit) ヒューズ hyűzu; (for bomb etc) 導火線 dőkasen

♦*vt* (metal) 融合させる yúgō saserù; (*fig*: ideas, systems) 混合する koñgō suru

♦*vi* (metal: *also fig*) 融合する yúgō suru

to fuse the lights (*BRIT*: ELEC) ヒューズを飛ばす hyűzu wo tobásu

fuse box *n* (ELEC) ヒューズ箱 hyűzubàko

fuselage [fjuːˈsəlɑːʒ] *n* (AVIAT) 胴体 dőtai

fusion [fjuːˈʒən] *n* (of ideas, qualities) 混合 koñgō; (*also*: **nuclear fusion**) 核融合 kakúyūgō

fuss [fʌs] *n* (anxiety, excitement) 大騒ぎ ősawàgi; (complaining, trouble) 不平 fuhéi

to make a fuss 大騒ぎをする ősawàgi wo suru

to make a fuss of someone ...をちやほやする ...wo chíyàhoya suru

fussy [fʌsˈiː] *adj* (person) 小うるさい koúrusaì; (clothes, room etc) 凝った kőttà

futile [fjuːˈtəl] *adj* (attempt, comment, existence) 無駄な mudá na

future [fjuːˈtʃər] *adj* (date, generations) 未来の mírài no; (president, spouse) 将来の shőrai no

♦*n* (time to come) 未来 mírài; (prospects) 将来 shőrai; (LING) 未来形 mirái-kei

in future 将来に shőrai ni

fuze [fjuːz] (*US*) = **fuse**

fuzzy [fʌzˈiː] *adj* (PHOT) ぼやけた boyáketa; (hair) 縮れた chijíretà

G

G [dʒiː] *n* (MUS: note) ト音 to-óñ; (: key) ト調 tóchō

g. *abbr* = **gram(s)**

gabble [gæbˈəl] *vi* ぺちゃくちゃしゃべる péchàkucha shábèru

gable [geiˈbəl] *n* (of building) 切妻 kirízùma

gadget [gædʒˈit] *n* 装置 sőchi

Gaelic [geiˈlik] *adj* ゲール語の gérugo no

♦*n* (LING) ゲール語 gérugo

gaffe [gæf] *n* (in words) 失言 shitsúgen; (in actions) 失態 shittái

gag [gæg] *n* (on mouth) 猿ぐつわ sarúgutsùwa; (joke) ギャグ gyágù

♦*vt* (prisoner) ...に猿ぐつわをはめる ...ni sarúgutsùwa wo hamérù

gaiety [geiˈəti:] *n* お祭り騒ぎ o-mátsuri sawàgi

gaily [geiˈli:] *adv* (talk, dance, laugh) 楽しそうに tanóshisò ni; (colored) 華やかに hanáyàka ni

gain [gein] *n* (increase) 増加 zōka; (improvement) 進歩 shíñpo; (profit) 利益 ríèki

♦*vt* (speed, weight, confidence) 増す masú

♦*vi* (benefit): *to gain from something* ...から利益を得る ...kara ríèki wo érù; (clock, watch) 進む susúmù

to gain on someone ...に迫る ...ni semárù

to gain 3lbs (in weight) （体重が）3 ポンド増える (taíjū ga) sañpoñdo fuérù

gait [geit] *n* 歩調 hochő

gal. *abbr* = **gallon**

gala [geiˈlə] *n* (festival) 祝祭 shukúsai

galaxy [gælˈəksi:] *n* (SPACE) 星雲 seíun

gale [geil] *n* (wind) 強風 kyőfu

gallant [gælˈənt] *adj* (brave) 勇敢な yúkan na; (polite) 紳士的な shiñshiteki na

gallantry [gælˈəntri:] *n* (bravery) 勇気 yúki; (politeness) 礼儀正しさ reígitadashìsa

gall bladder [gɔːl-] *n* 胆のう tañnő

gallery [gǽlˈəːriː] n (also: **art gallery**: public) 美術博物館 bijútsu hakubutsukán; (: private) 画廊 garó; (in hall, church, theater) 二階席 nikáiseki

galley [gǽliː] n (ship's kitchen) 調理室 chórishìtsu

gallon [gǽlən] n (= 8 pints; BRIT = 4.5 l; US = 3.8 l) ガロン gárðn

gallop [gǽləp] n ギャロップ gyáróppu
◆vi (horse) ギャロップで走る gyáróppu de hashírù

gallows [gǽlouz] n 絞首台 kőshudai

gallstone [gɔ́ːlstoun] n (MED) 胆石 tañseki

galore [gəlɔ́ːr] adv どっさり dossárì

galvanize [gǽlvənaiz] vt (audience) ぎょっとさせる győttð saséru; (support) 求める motómerù

gambit [gǽmˈbit] n (fig): (opening) **gambit** 皮切り kawákiri

gamble [gǽmˈbəl] n (risk) かけ kaké
◆vt (money) かける kakérù
◆vi (take a risk) 冒険をする bőken wo surù; (bet) ばくちをする bakúchi wo surù, ギャンブルをする gyáñburu wo suru
to gamble on something (horses, race, success etc) ...にかける ...ni kakérù

gambler [gǽmˈbləːr] n (punter) ばくち打ち bakúchiuchi

gambling [gǽmˈbliŋ] n (betting) ばくち bakúchi, ギャンブル gyáñburu

game [geim] n (activity, sport) 遊び asóbi; (match) 試合 shiái; (part of match: esp TENNIS: also: **board game**) ゲーム gēmu; (strategy, scheme) 策略 sakúryaku; (HUNTING) 猟鳥獣 ryőchōjù; (CULIN) 猟鳥獣の肉 ryőchōjù no nikú
◆adj (willing): **game (for)** (...をする) 気がある (...wo suru) kí ga arù
big game 大型猟獣 ögataryòjū

gamekeeper [geimˈkiːpəːr] n 猟番 ryőban

gammon [gǽmˈən] n (bacon) ベーコン běkon; (ham) スモークハム sumőkuhamù

gamut [gǽmˈət] n (range) 範囲 háñ-i

gang [gæŋ] n (of criminals, hooligans) 一味 ichímì; (of friends, colleagues) 仲間 nakama; (of workmen) 班 háñ

gangrene [gǽŋˈgriːn] n (MED) えそ ésð

gangster [gǽŋˈstəːr] n (criminal) 暴力団員 bőryokudaň-in, ギャング gyáñgu

gang up vi: **to gang up on someone** 寄ってたかって...をやっつける yotté takattè ...wo yattsukeru

gangway [gǽŋˈwei] n (from ship) タラップ taráppù; (BRIT: in cinema, bus, plane etc) 通路 tsúro

gaol [dʒeil] (BRIT) n, vt = **jail**

gap [gæp] n (space) すき間 sukíma, ギャップ gyappu; (: in time) 空白 kúhaku; (difference): **gap (between)** (...の) 断絶 (...no) dañzetsu

gape [geip] vi (person) ぽかんと口を開けて見詰める pokáñ to kuchí wo aketè mitsúmerù; (shirt, hole) 大きく開いている ökiku aíte irù

gaping [geiˈpiŋ] adj (shirt, hole) 大きく開いた ökiku aíta

garage [gərɑːʒ] n (of private house) 車庫 shákð; (for car repairs) 自動車修理工場 jidőshashūrikōjō

garbage [gɑːrˈbidʒ] n (US: rubbish) ごみ gomí; (inf: nonsense) でたらめ detáramè

garbage can (US) n ごみ容器 gomíyöki

garbled [gɑːrˈbəld] adj (account, message) 間違った machígattà

garden [gɑːrˈdən] n (private) 庭 niwá

gardener [gɑːrdˈnəːr] n 庭師 niwáshì

gardening [gɑːrˈdəniŋ] n 園芸 éñgei

gardens [gɑːrˈdənz] npl (public park) 公園 köeñ

gargle [gɑːrˈgəl] vi うがいする ugái suru

garish [geːrˈiʃ] adj けばけばしい kebákebashiì

garland [gɑːrˈlənd] n (also: **garland of flowers**) 花輪 hanáwa

garlic [gɑːrˈlik] n (BOT, CULIN) ニンニク nifiniku

garment [gɑːrˈmənt] n (dress) 衣服 ífuku

garnish [gɑːrˈniʃ] vt (food) 飾る kazáru

garrison [gǽrˈisən] n (MIL) 守備隊 shubítai

garrulous [gǽrˈələs] adj (talkative) 口数の多い kuchíkazu no ői

garter [gɑːrˈtəːr] n (for sock etc) 靴下止

め kutsúshitadome, ガーター gǎtā; (US: suspender) ガーターベルト gǎtāberùto

gas [gæs] n (CHEM) 気体 kítài; (fuel) ガス gásù; (US: gasoline) ガソリン gasórin
♦vt (kill) ガスで殺す gásù de korósù

gas cooker (BRIT) n ガスレンジ gasúreñji

gas cylinder n ガスボンベ gasúboñbe

gas fire (BRIT) n ガスストーブ gasúsutōbu

gash [gæʃ] n (wound) 切り傷 kiríkìzu; (tear) 裂け目 sakéme
♦vt (wound) 傷を負わせる kizú wò owáserù

gasket [gæs'kit] n (AUT) ガスケット gasúkettò

gas mask n ガスマスク gasúmasùku

gas meter n ガスメーター gasúmètā

gasoline [gæsəli:n'] (US) n ガソリン gasórin

gasp [gæsp] n (breath) 息切れ ikígire; (of shock, horror) はっとする事 háttò suru kotó
♦vi (pant) あえぐ aégù

gasp out vt (say) あえぎながら言う aéginagàra iú

gas station (US) n ガソリンスタンド gasórinsutañdo

gassy [gæs'i:] adj (beer etc) 炭酸ガスの入った tañsangasù no haítta

gastric [gæs'trik] adj 胃の f no

gastroenteritis [gæstrouentərai'tis] n 胃腸炎 ichóen

gate [geit] n (of garden, field, grounds) 門 móñ; (at airport) ゲート gèto

gatecrash [geit'kræʃ] (BRIT) vt ...に押し掛ける ...ni oshíkakerù

gateway [geit'wei] n (entrance: also fig) 入口 iríguchi

gather [gæð'əːr] vt (flowers, fruit) 摘む tsúmù; (pick up) 拾う hiróù; (assemble, collect: objects, information) 集める atsúmerù; (understand) 推測する suísoku suru; (SEWING) ...にギャザーを寄せる ...ni gyázà wo yoserù
♦vi (assemble) 集まる atsúmerù
to gather speed スピードを上げる supído wo agerù

gathering [gæð'əːriŋ] n 集まり atsúmarì

gauche [gouʃ] adj (adolescent, youth) ぎごちない gigóchinài

gaudy [gɔːd'iː] adj 派手な hadé na

gauge [geidʒ] n (instrument) 計器 keíki
♦vt (amount, quantity) 計る hakárù; (fig: feelings, character etc) 判断する hañdan suru

gaunt [gɔːnt] adj (haggard) やせこけた yasékoketà; (bare, stark) 荒涼とした kóryō to shita

gauntlet [gɔːnt'lit] n (glove) 長手袋 nagátebukùro; (fig): **to run the gauntlet** 方々からやられる hōbō kara yaráreru
to throw down the gauntlet 挑戦する chósen suru

gauze [gɔːz] n (fabric: also MED) ガーゼ gāze

gave [geiv] pt of **give**

gay [gei] adj (homosexual) 同性愛の dóseīai no, ホモの hómò no; (cheerful) 陽気な yōki na; (color, music, dress etc) 華やかな hanáyàka na

gaze [geiz] n (look, stare) 視線 shisén
♦vi: **to gaze at something** ...をじっと見る ...wo jíttò mírù

gazelle [gəzel'] n ガゼル gázèru

gazetteer [gæziti:r'] n (index) 地名辞典 chiméijitèn

gazumping [gəzʌm'piŋ] (BRIT) n (of house buyer) 詐欺 sági

GB [dʒi:bi:'] abbr = **Great Britain**

GCE [dʒi:si:i:'] (BRIT) n abbr (= General Certificate of Education) 普通教育証書 futsúkyōikushōsho ◊16才の時に受けるOレベルと大学入学前に受けるAレベルの2種類がある júrokusài no tokí nì ukérù O rèbèru to daígaku nyūgaku máè ni ukérù A rèbèru no nishúrui ga arù

GCSE [dʒi:si:esi:'] (BRIT) n abbr (= General Certificate of Secondary Education) ◊1988年からGCEのOレベルはGCSEに置換えられた señkyūhyakuhachijūhachi nèn ni GCE no O rèbèru wa GCSE ni okíkaeraretà

gear [giːr] n (equipment) 道具 dōgu; (TECH) 歯車 hagúrùma; (AUT) ギヤ gí-

yà

♦vt (fig: adapt): **to gear something to**
...に...を適応させる ...ni ...wo tekíō saserù

high (US) or **top** (BRIT) / **low gear** ハ
イ（ロー）ギヤ haí(ró)giyà

in gear ギヤを入れて gíyà wo iréte

gear box n ギヤボックス giyábokkùsu

gear shift (BRIT **gear lever**) n シフト
レバー shífutorebā

geese [giːs] npl of **goose**

gel [dʒel] n (for hair) ジェル jérù;
(CHEM) ゲル gérù

gelatin(e) [dʒel'ətin] n (CULIN) ゼラチ
ン zeráchìn

gelignite [dʒel'ignait] n (explosive) ゼリ
グナイト zerígunaìto

gem [dʒem] n (stone) 宝石 hōseki

Gemini [dʒem'ənai] n (ASTROLOGY) 双
子座 futágoza

gender [dʒen'dəːr] n (sex: also LING) 性
seí

gene [dʒiːn] n (BIO) 遺伝子 idénshi

general [dʒen'əːrəl] n (MIL) 大将 taíshō

♦adj (overall, non-specific, miscellaneous) 一般の ippán no, 一般的な ippánteki
na; (widespread: movement, interest) 全
面的な zenmenteki na

in general 一般に ippán ni

general delivery (US) n (poste restante) 局留 kyokúdome

general election n 総選挙 sōsenkyo

generalization [dʒenəːrələzei'ʃən] n 一
般化 ippánkà

generally [dʒen'əːrəliː] adv (in general)
一般に ippán ni; (usually) 普通は futsū
wa

general practitioner n 一般開業医 ippán kaigyòi

generate [dʒen'əːreit] vt (power, energy)
発生させる hasséi saserù; (jobs, profits)
生み出す umídasù

to generate electricity 発電する hatsúden suru

generation [dʒenəːrei'ʃən] n (period of
time) 世代 sedái; (of people, family) 同じ
世代の人々 onáji sedài no hitobìto; (of
heat, steam, gas etc) 発生 hasséi; (of

electricity) 発電 hatsúden

generator [dʒen'əːreitəːr] n (ELEC) 発電
機 hatsúdeñki

generosity [dʒenəraːs'əti:] n 寛大さ kañdaisa

generous [dʒen'əːrəs] adj (person, measure, remuneration etc) 寛大な kañdai
na

genetics [dʒənet'iks] n (science) 遺伝学
idéngàku

Geneva [dʒəni:'və] n ジュネーブ júnèbu

genial [dʒi:'ni:əl] adj (host, smile) 愛想の
良い aíso no yoì

genitals [dʒen'itəlz] npl (ANAT) 性器
seíki

genius [dʒi:n'jəs] n (ability, skill, person)
天才 teñsai

genocide [dʒen'əsaid] n 民族虐殺 miñzo-
kugyakusàtsu, ジェノサイド jénòsaido

gent [dʒent] n abbr = **gentleman**

genteel [dʒenti:l'] adj (person, family) 家
柄の良い iégara no yoì

gentle [dʒen'təl] adj (person) 優しい yasáshiì; (animal) 大人しい otónashiì;
(movement, shake) 穏やかな odáyàka
na, 静かな shizùka na; (slope, curve) 緩
やかな yurúyàka na

a gentle breeze そよ風 soyókàze

gentleman [dʒen'təlmən] (pl **gentlemen**) n (man) 男の方 otóko no katà;
(referring to social position: also well-
mannered man) 紳士 shiñshì, ジェントル
マン jéñtoruman

gentleness [dʒen'təlnis] n (of person) 優
しさ yasáshisà; (of animal) 大人しさ otó-
nashisà; (of movement, breeze, shake)
穏やかさ odáyàkasa, 静かさ shizúkàsa;
(of slope, curve) 緩やかさ yurúyàkasa

gently [dʒen'tli:] adv (subj: person) 優し
く yasáshikù; (: animal) 大人しく otóna-
shikù; (: breeze etc) 静かに shizúkàni
(: slope, curve) 緩やかに yurúyàka ni

gentry [dʒen'tri:] n 紳士階級 shiñshikaì-
kyū

gents [dʒents] (BRIT) n (men's toilet) 男
性トイレ dañseitoirè

genuine [dʒen'ju:in] adj (real) 本物の hoñ-
monò no; (person) 誠実な seíjitsu na

geographic(al) [dʒiːəgræf'ik(əl)] *adj* 地理の chírī no

geography [dʒiːɑːg'rəfiː] *n* (of town, country etc: *also* SCOL) 地理 chírī

geological [dʒiːələːdʒ'ikəl] *adj* 地質学の chishítsugàku no

geologist [dʒiːɑːl'ədʒist] *n* 地質学者 chishítsugakushà

geology [dʒiːɑːl'ədʒiː] *n* (of area, rock etc) 地質 chíshìtsu; (SCOL) 地質学 chishítsugàku

geometric(al) [dʒiːəmet'rik(əl)] *adj* (problem, design) 幾何学的な kikágakuteki na

geometry [dʒiːɑːm'ətriː] *n* (MATH) 幾何学 kikágaku

geranium [dʒəreiːni'əm] *n* ゼラニウム zeráníumu

geriatric [dʒeːriːæt'rik] *adj* (of old people) 老人の rōjin no

germ [dʒəːrm] *n* ばい菌 baíkin

German [dʒəːr'mən] *adj* (of Germany) ドイツの dóìtsu no; (LING) ドイツ語の dóìtsugo no
♦*n* ドイツ人 dóìtsujin; (LING) ドイツ語 dóìtsugo

German measles *n* (rubella) 風しん fúshin

Germany [dʒəːr'məniː] *n* ドイツ dóìtsu

germination [dʒəːrmeneiˈʃən] *n* (of seed) 発芽 hatsúga

gesticulate [dʒestikˈjəleit] *vi* (with arms, hands) 手振りをする tébùri wo suru

gesture [dʒesˈtʃəːr] *n* (movement) 手振り tébùri, ジェスチャー jésùchā; (symbol, token) ジェスチャー jésùchā

KEYWORD

get [get] (*pt, pp* **got**, (*US*) *pp* **gotten**) *vi* 1 (become, be) ...になる ...ni nárù
to get old (thing) 古くなる fúrùku naru; (person) 年を取る toshí wò toru
to get cold 寒くなる sámùku naru
to get annoyed/bored/tired 怒る〔退屈する, 疲れる〕okórù(taíkutsu surù, tsukárerù)
to get drunk 酔っ払う yopparau

to get dirty 汚れる yogórerù
to get killed 殺される korósarerù
to get married 結婚する kekkón surù
when do I get paid? 金はいつ払ってくれますか kané wà ítsù harátte kuremasù ká
it's getting late 遅くなってきました osóku nattè kimáshìta

2 (go): *to get to/from* ...へ〔から〕行く ...é〔kará〕iku
to get home 家に帰る ié ni kaerù
how did you get here? あなたはどうやってここへ来ましたか anátà wa dó yattè kokó è kimáshìtà ká

3 (begin): *to get to know someone* ...と親しくなる ...tò shitáshikù naru
I'm getting to like him 彼を好きになってきました kárè wo sukí ni nattè kimáshìta
let's get going/started さあ, 行きましょう sâ, ikímashō

♦*modal aux vb*: *you've got to do it* あなたはどうしてもそれをしなければなりません anátà wa dóshite mò soré wò shinákereba narimaseñ
I've got to tell the police 警察に知らせなければなりません keísatsu nì shirásenakereba narimaseñ

♦*vt* 1: *to get something done* (do) ...を済ます ...wò sumásù; (have done) ...をしてもらう ...wò shité moraù
to get the washing/dishes done 洗濯〔皿洗い〕を済ます señtaku〔saráarài〕wò sumásù
to get one's hair cut 散髪してもらう sañpatsu shite moraù
to get the car going/to go 車のエンジンをかける kurúma no eñjin wo kakérù
to get someone to do something ...に...をさせる ...ní ...wò saserù
to get something ready ...を用意する ...wò yóì suru
to get someone ready ...に用意をさせる ...nì yóì wo saserù
to get someone drunk/into trouble ...を酔っ払わせる〔困らせる〕...wò yoppárawaserù〔komáraserù〕

2 (obtain: money) 手に入れる té ni irerù;

(: permission, results) 得る érù; (find: job, flat) 見付ける mitsúkerù; (fetch: person, doctor) 呼んで来る yónde kuru; (: object) 持って来る mótté kurù

to get something for someone ...のために...を持って来る ...no tamé nì ...wò mótté kurù

he got a job in London 彼はロンドンに仕事を見付けました kárè wa róndon ni shigóto wò mitsúkemashìta

get me Mr Jones, please (TEL) ジョーンズさんをお願いしたいんですが jónzu san wo o-négai shitaiñ desù ga

I think you should see the doctor 医者を呼んだ方がいいと思います ishá wò yoñda hồ ga ší to omóimasù

can I get you a drink? 何か飲みませんか nánìka nomímaseñ ka

3 (receive: present, letter) 受ける ukérù; (acquire: reputation, prize) 得る érù, 獲得する kakútoku suru

what did you get for your birthday? お誕生日に何をもらいましたか o-tánjòbi ni nánì wo moráimashìta ká

he got a prize for French 彼はフランス語の成績で賞をもらいました kárè wa furánsugồ no seíseki dè shồ wò moráimashìta

how much did you get for the painting? 絵画はいくらで売れましたか káìga wa íkùra de urémashìta ká

4 (catch) つかむ tsukámù; (hit: target etc) ...に当る ...ni atárù

to get someone by the arm/throat ...の腕〔のど〕をつかむ ...no udé〔nódò〕wò tsukámù

get him! やつを捕まえろ yátsù wo tsukámaerò

the bullet got him in the leg 弾丸は彼の脚に当った dañgan wà kárè no ashí ni atattà

5 (take, move) 連れて〔持って〕いく tsuréte〔mótté〕ikù, 移動する idồ suru

to get something to someone ...に...を持って行く ...ní ...wò mótté ikù

do you think we'll get it through the door? それは戸口から入ると思いますか soré wà tồguchi kara háìru to omó-

imasù ká

I'll get you there somehow 何とかしてあなたを連れて行きます náñ to ka shite anátà wo tsuréte ikimasù

we must get him to (US the) hospital どうしても彼を病院に連れて行かなくちゃ dồshitè mo kárè wo byồìn ni tsuréte ikanakùcha

6 (catch, take: plane, bus etc) 乗る norú

where do I get the train - Birmingham? 電車はどこで乗ればいいんですか -バーミンガムですか deñsha wà dókò de noréba iin desù ká - bámìñgamu desu ká

7 (understand) 理解する ríkai suru; (hear) 聞き取る kikítorù

I've got it 分かった wakáttá

I don't get your meaning あなたが言おうとしている事が分かりません anáta ga iố to shite iru kotố ga wakárimaseñ

I'm sorry, I didn't get your name 済みませんが、お名前を聞き取れませんでした sumímaseñ ga, o-námae wò kikítoremasen deshìta

8 (have, possess): *to have got* 持つ mótsù

how many have you got? いくつ持っていますか íkùtsu mótté imasù ká

---

get about *vi* 動き回る ugókimawarù; (news) 広まる hirómarù

get along *vi* (agree) 仲良くする nákàyoku suru; (depart) 帰る káèru; (manage) = **get by**

get at *vt fus* (attack, criticize) 批判する hihán suru; (reach) ...に手が届く ...ni té gà todókù

get away *vi* (leave) 帰る káèru; (escape) 逃げる nigérù

get away with *vt fus* ...をうまくやりおおせる ...wò úmàku yaríōseru

get back *vi* (return) 帰る káèru

♦*vt* 返す káèsu

get by *vi* (pass) 通る tồrù; (manage) やって行く yatté ikù

get down *vi* 降りる orírù

♦*vt fus* 降りる orírù

♦*vt* 降ろす orósù; (depress: person) がっかりさせる gakkárì saseru

get down to vt fus (work) ...に取り掛る ...ni toríkakarù

get in vi 入る háirù; (train) 乗る norú; (arrive home) 帰って来る kaétte kurù

get into vt fus ...に入る ...ni háirù; (vehicle) ...に乗る ...ni norú; (clothes) 着る kirú

to get into bed ベッドに入る béddò ni háirù

to get into a rage かんかんに怒る kańkan nì okórù

get off vi (from train etc) 降りる orírù; (depart: person, car) 出発する shuppátsu suru; (escape punishment etc) 逃れる nogárerù

♦vt (remove: clothes) 脱ぐ núgù; (: stain) 消す kesú, 落す otósù; (send off) 送る okúrù

♦vt fus (train, bus) 降りる orírù

get on vi (at exam etc) *how are you getting on?* 万事うまく行っていますか báńji úmàku itté imasù ká; (agree): *to get on (with)* (...と) 気が合う (...tò) ki gá aù

♦vt fus ...に乗る ...ni norú

get out vi 出る dérù; (of vehicle) 降りる orírù

♦vt 取り出す torídasù

get out of vt fus ...から出る ...kara dérù; (vehicle) ...から降りる ...kara orírù; (bed) ...から起きる ...kara okírù; (duty etc) 避ける sakérù, 逃れる nogárerù

get over vt fus (illness) ...が直る ...ga naórù

get round vt fus (problem, difficulty) 避ける sakérù; (law, rule) ...に触れないようにする ...ni furénai yò ni suru; (fig: person) 言いくるめる iíkurumerù

get through vi (TEL) 電話が通じる deńwa gà tsújirù

get through to vt fus (TEL) ...に電話が通じる ...ni deńwa gà tsújiru

get together vi (people) 集まる atsúmarù

♦vt 集める atsúmerù

get up vi (rise) 起きる okírù

♦vt fus 起す okósù

get up to vt fus (reach) ...に着く ...ni tsukú; (BRIT: prank etc) 仕出かす shidékasù

geyser [gai'zəːr] n (GEO) 間欠温泉 kańketsu oñsen; (BRIT: water heater) 湯沸かし器 yuwákashikì

Ghana [gɑːnə] n ガーナ gàna

ghastly [gæst'liː] adj (horrible: person, behavior, situation) いやな fyà na, ひどい hídòi; (: building, appearance) 薄気味悪い usúkimiwaruì; (pale: complexion) 青白い aójiroì

gherkin [gəːr'kin] n キュウリのピクルス kyúri no píkùrusu

ghetto [get'ou] n (ethnic area) ゲットー géttò

ghost [goust] n (spirit) 幽霊 yúrei, お化け o-bákè

giant [dʒai'ənt] n (in myths, children's stories) 巨人 kyojín, ジャイアント jáìanto; (fig: large company) 大企業 daíkigyò

♦adj (enormous) 巨大な kyodái na

gibberish [dʒib'əːriʃ] n (nonsense) でたらめ detárame

gibe [dʒaib] n = **jibe**

giblets [dʒib'lits] npl 鳥の内臓 torí nò naízō

Gibraltar [dʒibrɔːl'təːr] n ジブラルタル jíbùrarutaru

giddy [gid'iː] adj (dizzy) めまいがする memái ga suru

gift [gift] n (present) 贈り物 okúrimonò, プレゼント purézènto, ギフト gífùto; (ability) 才能 saínō

gifted [gif'tid] adj (actor, sportsman, child) 才能ある saínō arù

gift token n ギフト券 gifútokèn

gift voucher n = **gift token**

gigantic [dʒaigæn'tik] adj 巨大な kyodái na

giggle [gig'əl] vi くすくす笑う kusúkùsu waráù

gill [dʒil] n (= 0.25 pints; BRIT = 0.15 l; US = 0.12 l) ギル gírù

gills [gilz] npl (of fish) えら erá

gilt [gilt] adj (frame, jewelery) 金めっきした kińmekkì shita

♦n 金めっき kińmekkì

gilt-edged [gilt'edʒd] adj (stocks, secu-

rities) 優良な yūryō na

gimmick [gim'ik] n (sales, electoral) 仕掛け shikáke

gin [dʒin] n ジン jín

ginger [dʒin'dʒəːr] n (spice) ショウガ shōga

ginger ale n ジンジャーエール jíñjàèru

ginger beer n ジンジャービール jíñjàbīru

gingerbread [dʒin'dʒəːrbred] n (cake) ジンジャーブレッドケーキ jíñjàbureddo-kèki; (biscuit) ジンジャーブレッドクッキー jíñjàbureddokukkì

gingerly [dʒin'dʒəːrliː] adv (tentatively) 慎重に shiñchō ni

gipsy [dʒip'siː] n = **gypsy**

giraffe [dʒəræf'] n キリン kirín

girder [gəːr'dəːr] n 鉄骨 tekkótsu

girdle [gəːr'dəl] n (corset) ガードル gắdoru

girl [gəːrl] n (child) 女の子 oñna nò ko, 少女 shōjo; (young unmarried woman) 若い女性 wakái joséi, ガール gầru; (daughter) 娘 musúme

an English girl 若いイングランド人女性 wakái iñgurandojìn joséi

girlfriend [gəːrl'frend] n (of girl) 女友達 oñna tomodàchi; (of boy) ガールフレンド gầrufureñdo

girlish [gəːr'liʃ] adj 少女の様な shōjo nó yō na

giro [dʒai'rou] n (also: **bank giro**) 銀行振替 o 替 giñkōfurikaekawàse; (also: **post office giro**) 郵便振替 o 替 yūbinfurikaekawàse; (BRIT: welfare check) 生活保護の小切手 seíkatsuhogò no kogíttè

girth [gəːrθ] n (circumference) 周囲 shūi; (of horse) 腹帯 haráobi

gist [dʒist] n (of speech, program) 骨子 kósshì

KEYWORD

give [giv] (pt gave, pp given) vt 1 (hand over): *to give someone something, give something to someone* ...に...を与える ...nî ...wò atáerù, ...に...を渡す ...nî ...wò watásu

I gave David the book, I gave the book to David 私は本をデービッドに渡しました watákushi wà hóñ wò débìddo ni watáshimashìta

give him your key あなたのかぎを彼に渡しなさい anátá no kagí wò kárè ni watáshinasaì

he gave her a present 彼は彼女にプレゼントをあげた kárè wa kánòjo ni puré-zeñto wo agéta

give it to him, give him it それを彼に渡しなさい soré wò kárè ni watáshi nasaì

I'll give you £5 for it それを5ポンドで私に売ってくれませんか soré wò go-póñdo de watákushi nì utté kuremaseñ ká

2 (used with noun to replace a verb): *to give a sigh* ため息をつく taméikì wo tsuku

to give a cry/shout 叫ぶ sakébù

to give a push 押す osú

to give a groan うめく umékù

to give a shrug 肩をすくめる kátà wo sukúmerù

to give a speech/a lecture 演説〔講演〕をする eñzetsu〔kōen〕wo surù

to give three cheers 万歳三唱をする bañzaisañshō wo suru

3 (tell, deliver: news, advice, message etc) 伝える tsutáerù, 言う iú, 与える atáerù

did you give him the message/the news? 彼にメッセージ〔ニュース〕を伝えましたか kárè ni mésseji〔nyūsù〕wo tsutáemashìta ká

let me give you some advice ちょっと忠告をあげよう chóttò chūkoku wo age-yō

he gave me his new address over the phone 彼は電話で新しい住所を教えてくれました kárè wa deñwa dè atárashii jūsho wo oshíete kuremashìta

to give the right/wrong answer 正しい〔間違った〕答を言う tadáshii〔machí-gatta〕kotàe wo iú

4 (supply, provide: opportunity, surprise, job etc) 与える atáerù, 提供する teíkyō suru; (bestow: title) 授与する júyò suru;

(: honor, right) 与える atáerù

I gave him the chance to deny it それを否定するチャンスを彼に与えました soré wò hitéi suru chañsu wo kárè ni atáemashìta

the sun gives warmth and light 太陽は熱と光を我々に与えてくれる táiyō wa netsú tò hikári wò waréware nì atáete kurerù

what gives you the right to do that? 何の権利でそんな事をするのか nán no keñri de soñna kotò wo suru nò ka

that's given me an idea あれでいい事を思い付いたんですが aré de ii kotò wo omóitsuitan desù ga

5 (dedicate: time) 当てる atérù; (: one's life) 捧げる saságerù; (: attention) 払う haráù

you'll need to give me more time もっと時間を下さい móttò jikán wo kudasaì

she gave it all her attention 彼女はそれに専念した kánòjo wa soré nì señnen shità

6 (organize): *to give a party/dinner etc* パーティ〔晩さん会〕を開催する pátì〔bañsañkai〕wo kaísai suru

♦*vi* **1** (*also*: **give way**: break, collapse) 崩れる kuzúrerù

his legs gave beneath him 彼は突然立てなくなった kárè wa totsúzen taténaku nattà

the roof/floor gave as I stepped on it 私が踏んだとたん屋根〔床〕が抜け落ちた watákushi ga funda totañ yáně〔yuká〕ga nukéochità

2 (stretch: fabric) 伸びる nobírù

give away *vt* (money) 人にやる hitó nì yarú; (opportunity) 失う ushínaù; (secret, information) 漏らす morásù; (bride) 新郎に渡す shiñrō nì watásu

give back *vt* 返す káesu

give in *vi* (yield) 降参する kósan suru

♦*vt* (essay etc) 提出する teíshutsu suru

give off *vt* (heat) 放つ hanátsù; (smoke) 出す dásù

give out *vt* (distribute: prizes, books,

drinks etc) 配る kubárù; (make known: news etc) 知らせる shiráserù

give up *vi* (surrender) 降参する kósan suru

♦*vt* (renounce: job, habit) やめる yamérù; (boyfriend) ...との交際をやめる ...to no kósai wò yamérù; (abandon: idea, hope) 捨てる sutérù

to give up smoking タバコをやめる tabáko wò yamérù

to give oneself up 自首する jishú suru

give way *vi* (yield) 譲る yuzúrù; (break, collapse: floor, ladder etc) 崩れる kuzúrerù, 壊れる kowárerù; (: rope) 切れる kirérù; (*BRIT*: AUT) 道を譲る michí wò yuzúru

glacier [glei'ʃəːr] *n* 氷河 hyóga

glad [glæd] *adj* (happy, pleased) うれしい uréshiì

gladly [glæd'liː] *adv* (willingly) 喜んで yorókoñde

glamorous [glæm'əːrəs] *adj* 魅惑的な miwákuteki na

glamour [glæm'əːr] *n* 魅惑 miwáku

glance [glæns] *n* (look) ちらっと見る事 chiráttò mírù koto

♦*vi*: *to glance at* ...をちらっと見る ...wo chiráttò mírù

glance off *vt fus* ...に当って跳ね返る ...ni attátè hanékaerù

glancing [glæn'siŋ] *adj* (blow) かすめる kasúmerù

gland [glænd] *n* せん séñ

glare [gleːr] *n* (of anger) にらみ nirámi; (of light) まぶしさ mabúshisà; (of publicity) 脚光 kyakkō

♦*vi* (light) まぶしく光る mabúshikù hikárù

to glare at (glower) ...をにらみ付ける ...wo nirámitsukerù

glaring [gleːr'iŋ] *adj* (mistake) 明白な meíhaku na

glass [glæs] *n* (substance) ガラス garásu; (container) コップ koppú, グラス gúrásu; (contents) コップ一杯 koppú ippài

glasses [glæs'iz] *npl* 眼鏡 mégàne

glasshouse [glæs'haus] *n* 温室 oñshitsu

glassware [glæs'weːr] *n* グラス類 gurá-

surui

glassy [glæs'i:] *adj* (eyes) うつろな utsúro na

glaze [gleiz] *vt* (door, window) ...に ガラスをはめる ...ni garásu wò hamérù; (pottery) ...にうわぐすりを掛ける ...ni uwágusùri wo kakérù

♦*n* (on pottery) うわぐすり uwágusùri

glazed [gleizd] *adj* (eyes) うつろな utsúro na; (pottery, tiles) うわぐすりを掛けた uwágusùri wo kakéta

glazier [glei'ʒəːr] *n* ガラス屋 garásuyà

gleam [gliːm] *vi* (shine: light, eyes, polished surface) 光る hikárù

glean [gliːn] *vt* (information) かき集める kakíatsumerù

glee [gliː] *n* (joy) 喜び yorókobi

glen [glen] *n* 谷間 taníaì

glib [glib] *adj* (person) 口達者な kuchídasshà na; (promise, response) 上辺だけの uwábe dake no

glide [glaid] *vi* (snake, dancer, boat etc) 滑る様に動く subéru yǒ ni ugókù; (AVIAT, birds) 滑空する kakkǜ suru

glider [glai'dəːr] *n* (AVIAT) グライダー guráidà

gliding [glai'diŋ] *n* (AVIAT) 滑空 kakkǜ

glimmer [glim'əːr] *n*: *a glimmer of light* かすかな光 kásùka na hikári

a glimmer of interest かすかな表情 kásùka na hyójò

a glimmer of hope かすかな希望 kásùka na kibǒ

glimpse [glimps] *n* (of person, place, object) ...がちらっと見える事 ...ga chiráttò miérù koto

♦*vt* ...がちらっと見える ...ga chiráttò miérù

glint [glint] *vi* (flash: light, eyes, shiny surface) ぴかっと光る pikáttò hikárù

glisten [glis'ən] *vi* (with sweat, rain etc) ぎらぎらする gíràgira suru

glitter [glit'əːr] *vi* (sparkle: light, eyes, shiny surface) 輝く kagáyakù

gloat [glout] *vi*: *to gloat (over)* (exult) ...にほくそえむ ...ni hokúsoemu

global [glou'bəl] *adj* (worldwide) 世界的な sekáiteki na

globe [gloub] *n* (world) 地球 chikyǜ; (model) 地球儀 chikyǘgì; (shape) 球 kyǜ

gloom [gluːm] *n* (dark) 暗やみ kuráyami; (sadness) 失望 shitsúbò

gloomy [gluː'mi:] *adj* (dark) 薄暗い usúguraì; (sad) 失望した shitsúbò shita

glorious [glɔːr'i:əs] *adj* (sunshine, flowers, weather) 素晴らしい subárashiǐ; (victory, future) 栄光の eíkō no

glory [glɔːr'i:] *n* (prestige) 栄光 eíkō; (splendor) 華々しさ hanábanashisà

gloss [glɔːs] *n* (shine) つや tsuyá; (also: **gloss paint**) つや出しペイント tsuyádashipeìnto

glossary [glɑːs'əːri:] *n* 用語集 yǒgoshǜ

gloss over *vt fus* (error) 言繕う iítsukuroù; (problem) 言いくるめる iíkurumerù

glossy [glɑːs'i:] *adj* (hair) つやつやした tsuyátsùya shitá; (photograph) つや出しの tsuyádashi no; (magazine) アート紙の átoshì no

glove [glʌv] *n* (gen) 手袋 tebúkùro; (in baseball) グローブ gúròbu, グラブ gúràbu

glove compartment *n* (AUT) グローブボックス gurôbubokkùsu

glow [glou] *vi* (embers) 赤く燃える akákù moérù; (stars) 光る hikárù; (face, eyes) 輝く kagáyakù

glower [glau'əːr] *vi*: *to glower at* ...をにらみ付ける ...wo nirámitsukerù

glucose [gluː'kous] *n* ブドウ糖 budótō, グルコース gurúkòsu

glue [gluː] *n* (adhesive) 接着剤 setcháku-zài

♦*vt* 接着する setchákù suru

glum [glʌm] *adj* (miserable) ふさぎ込んだ fuságikoǹda

glut [glʌt] *n* (of oil, goods etc) 生産過剰 seísankajò

glutton [glʌt'ən] *n* 大食らい ǒgurai

a glutton for work 仕事の鬼 shigóto nò oní

gluttony [glʌt'əni:] *n* 暴食 bǒshoku

glycerin(e) [glis'əːrin] *n* グリセリン guríserìn

gnarled [nɑːrld] *adj* (tree, hand) 節くれだった fushíkuredattà

gnat [næt] n ブヨ búyò

gnaw [nɔː] vt (bone) かじる kajírù

gnome [noum] n 地の小鬼 chi no koôni

KEYWORD
---

go [gou] (pt **went**, pp **gone**) vi **1** (travel, move) 行く ikú

she went into the kitchen 彼女は台所に行った kánòjo wa daídokoro ni ittá

shall we go by car or train? 車で行きましょうか, それとも電車で行きましょうか kurúma dè ikímashō ka, soréto-mò deñsha dè ikímashō ka

a car went by 車が通り過ぎた kurúma gà tóri sugitá

to go round the back 裏へ回る urá e mawáru

to go by the shop 店の前を通る misé no maè wo tốrù

he has gone to Aberdeen 彼はアバディーンへ行きました kárè wa abádìn e ikímashìta

2 (depart) 出発する shuppátsu suru, たつ tátsù, 帰る káèru, 行ってしまう itté shimaù

"I must go," she said 「帰ります」と彼女は言った "kaérimasù" to kánòjo wa ittá

our plane went at 6 pm 我々の飛行機は夕方6時に出発しました waréware no hikōki wa yūgata rokujī ni shuppátsu shimashìta

they came at 8 and went at 9 彼らは8時に来て9時に帰った kárèra wa hachíji ni kitè kújī ni kaérimashìta

3 (attend) 通う kayóu

she went to university in Aberdeen 彼女はアバディーンの大学に通った kánòjo wa abádìn no daígaku ni kayótta

she goes to her dancing class on Tuesdays 彼女がダンス教室に通うのは火曜日です kánòjo ga dañsukyōshitsu ni kayóu no wà kayóbì desu

he goes to the local church 彼は地元の教会に通っています kárè wa jimóto no kyōkai ni kayótte imasù

4 (take part in an activity) ...に行く ...ni ikú, ...をする ...surù

to go for a walk 散歩に行く sañpo ni ikù, 散歩する sanpo suru

to go dancing ダンスに行く dáñsu ni iku

5 (work) 作動する sadó suru

the clock stopped going 時計が止りました tokéi gà tomárimashìta

is your watch going? あなたの時計は動いていますか anátà no tokéi wà ugóite imasù ká

the bell went just then 丁度その時ベルが鳴りました chôdo sono tokì bérù ga narímashìta

the tape recorder was still going テープレコーダーはまだ回っていました tē-purekōdà wa mádà mawátte imashìta

6 (become) ...になる ...ni nárù

to go pale 青白くなる aójiroku narù

to go moldy かびる kabíru

7 (be sold): *to go for $10* 10ドルで売れる jūdòru de urérù

8 (fit, suit) 合う áù

to go with ...に合う ...ni áù

that tie doesn't go with that shirt そのネクタイはシャツと合いません sonó nekùtai wa shátsù to aímaseñ

9 (be about to, intend to): *he's going to do it* 彼は今それをやる所です kárè wa ímà soré wò yarú tokorò desu

we're going to leave in an hour 1時間したら出発します ichíjikan shitarà shup-pátsu shimasù

are you going to come? あなたも一緒に来ますか anátà mo isshó nì kimásù ká

10 (time) 経つ tátsù

time went very slowly/quickly 時間が経つのがとても遅く〔早く〕感じられました jikán ga tátsù no ga totémò osóku 〔háyàku〕 kanjiraremashìta

11 (event, activity) 行く ikú

how did it go? うまく行きましたか úmàku ikímashìta ká

12 (be given) 与えられる atáerarerù

the job is to go to someone else そのポストは他の人のところへいきました sonó posùto wa hoká no hito no tokorò e ikímashìta

13 (break etc: glass etc) 割れる warérù;

(: stick, leg, pencil etc) 折れる　oréru;
(: thread, rope, chain etc) 切れる kiréru

the fuse went ヒューズが切れた〔飛んだ〕hyúzu ga kiréta(tónda)

the leg of the chair went いすの脚が折れた isú no ashì ga óreta

14 (be placed) ...にしまう事になっている ...ni shimáu kotò ni nátte irù

where does this cup go? このカップはどこにしまうのですか konó kappù wa dókò ni shimáu no desu ká

the milk goes in the fridge ミルクは冷蔵庫にしまう事になっています mírùku wa reízòko ni shimáu kotò ni nátte imasù

♦*n* (*pl* **goes**) **1** (try): *to have a go (at)* (...を) やってみる (...wo) yatté mirù

2 (turn) 番 bán

whose go is it? だれの番ですか dáre no bán desu ká

3 (move): *to be on the go* 忙しくする isógashiku surù

go about *vi* (*also*: **go around**: rumor) 流れる nagáreru

♦*vt fus*: *how do I go about this?* どういう風にやればいいんですか dó iu fû ni yareba íin desu ká

goad [goud] *vt* 刺激する shigéki suru

go ahead *vi* (make progress) 進歩する shíñpo suru; (get going) 取り掛かる toríkakarù

go-ahead [gou'əhed] *adj* (person, firm) 進取の気に富んだ shíñshu no ki ni tóñda

♦*n* (for project) 許可 kyóka, ゴーサイン gòsaiñ

goal [goul] *n* (SPORT) ゴール gòru; (aim) 目標 mokúhyō

goalkeeper [goul'ki:pə:r] *n* ゴールキーパー gòrukìpā

go along *vi* ついて行く tsuíte ikú

♦*vt fus* ...を行く ...wò ikú

to go along with (agree with: plan, idea, policy) ...に賛成する ...ni sañsei surù

goalpost [goul'poust] *n* ゴールポスト gòrupòsuto

goat [gout] *n* ヤギ yágì

go away *vi* (leave) どこかへ行く dókò ka e ikú

go back *vi* (return) 帰る káeru; (go again) また行く matá ikú

go back on *vt fus* (promise) 破る yabúrù

gobble [gɑːbʼəl] *vt* (*also*: **gobble down**, **gobble up**) むさぼり食う musáborikuù

go-between [gouʼbitwi:n] *n* 仲介者 chúkaishà

go by *vi* (years, time) 経つ tátsù

♦*vt fus* (book, rule) ...に従う ...ni shitágaù

God [gɑːd] *n* (REL) 神 kámì

god [gɑːd] *n* (MYTHOLOGY, *fig*) 神 kámì

godchild [gɑːdʼtʃaild] *n* 名付け子 nazúkegò

goddaughter [gɑːdʼdɔːtəːr] *n* 名付け娘 nazúkemusùme

goddess [gɑːdʼis] *n* (MYTHOLOGY, REL, *fig*) 女神 mégàmi

godfather [gɑːdʼfɑːðəːr] *n* 名付け親 nazúkeoyà, 代父 daífù, 教父 kyófù

godforsaken [gɑːdʼfəːrseiʼkən] *adj* (place, spot) 荒れ果てた aréhatetà

godmother [gɑːdʼmʌðəːr] *n* 名付け親 nazúkeoyà, 代母 daíbò, 教母 kyóbò

go down *vi* (descend) 降りる orírù; (ship) 沈む shizúmu, 沈没する chiñbotsu suru; (sun) 沈む shizúmu

♦*vt fus* (stairs, ladder) ...を降りる ...wo orírù

godsend [gɑːdʼsend] *n* (blessing) 天の恵み teñ nò megúmì

godson [gɑːdʼsʌn] *n* 名付け息子 nazúkemusùko

go for *vt fus* (fetch) 取りに行く tórì ni ikú; (like) 気に入る kí ní irù; (attack) ...に襲い掛る ...ni osóikakarù

goggles [gɑːgʼəlz] *npl* (for skiing, motorcycling) ゴーグル gòguru

go in *vi* (enter) 入る háiru

go in for *vt fus* (competition) ...に参加する ...ni sañka suru; (like) ...が好きである ...ga sukí de arù, ...を気に入る ...wò ki ní irù

going [gouʼiŋ] *n* (conditions) 状況 jókyō

♦*adj: the going rate* 相場 sōba

go into *vt fus* (enter) ...に入る ...ni haíru; (investigate) 調べる shiráberù; (embark on) ...に従事する ...ni jūjī suru

gold [gould] *n* (metal) 金 kíñ

♦*adj* (jewelery, watch, tooth etc) 金の kíñ no

gold reserves 金の正貨準備 kíñ no seíka juñbi

golden [goul'dən] *adj* (made of gold) 金の kíñ no; (gold in color) 金色の kiñ-iro no

goldfish [gould'fiʃ] *n* 金魚 kíñgyo

goldmine [gould'main] *n* 金山 kíñzan; *(fig)* ドル箱 dorúbako

gold-plated [gouldplei'tid] *adj* 金めっきの kiñmekkì no

goldsmith [gould'smiθ] *n* 金細工師 kiñzaikushì

golf [ga:lf] *n* ゴルフ gőrùfu

golf ball *n* (for game) ゴルフボール gorúfubőrù; (on typewriter) 電動タイプライターのボール deñdōtaipuraītā no bőru

golf club *n* (organization, stick) ゴルフクラブ gorúfukuràbu

golf course *n* ゴルフコース gorúfukòsu

golfer [ga:l'fə:r] *n* ゴルファー gőrùfā

gondola [ga:n'dələ] *n* (boat) ゴンドラ goñdora

gone [gɔ:n] *pp of* go

gong [gɔ:ŋ] *n* どら dorá, ゴング góñgu

good [gud] *adj* (pleasant, satisfactory etc) 良い yoî; (high quality) 高級な kố-kyū na; (tasty) おいしい oíshiì; (kind) 親切な shiñsetsu na; (well-behaved: child) 行儀の良い győgi no yoî; (morally correct) 正当な seítō na

♦*n* (virtue, morality) 善 zéñ; (benefit) 利益 ríèki

good! よろしい！ yoróshiî!

to be good at ...が上手である ...ga jőzu dè árù

to be good for (useful) ...に使える ...ni tsukáerù

it's good for you あなたのためにいい anáta no tamè ni íi

would you be good enough to ...? 済みませんが...して下さいませんか sumímaseñ ga ...shite kudásaimaseñ ká

a good deal (of) 沢山（の）takúsan (no)

a good many 沢山の takúsan no

to make good (damage, loss) 弁償する beñshō suru

it's no good complaining 不平を言ってもしようがない fuhéi wo ittě mo shiyő ga nài

for good (forever) 永久に eíkyū ni

good morning! お早うございます o-háyō gozaimasù

good afternoon! 今日は koñnichi wa

good evening! 今晩は koñban wa

good night! お休みなさい o-yásumi nasaî

goodbye [gudbai'] *excl* さようなら sayőnarà

to say goodbye 別れる wakárerù

Good Friday *n* (REL) 聖金曜日 seíkinyőbi

good-looking [gud'luk'iŋ] *adj* (woman) 美人の bijín no; (man) ハンサムな háñsamu na

good-natured [gud'nei'tʃə:rd] *adj* (person, pet) 気立ての良い kidáte no yoî

goodness [gud'nis] *n* (of person) 優しさ yasáshisà

for goodness sake! 後生だから goshő da kara

goodness gracious! あらまあ！ará mấ

goods [gudz] *npl* (COMM) 商品 shőhin

goods train (*BRIT*) *n* 貨物列車 kamótsuresshà

goodwill [gud'wil'] *n* (of person) 善意 zéñ-i

go off *vi* (leave) どこかへ行く dőkò ka é ikù; (food) 悪くなる warúku naru; (bomb) 爆発する bakúhatsu suru; (gun) 暴発する bőhatsu suru; (event): *to go off well* うまくいく úmàku iku

♦*vt fus* (person, place, food etc) 嫌いになる kirái ni narù

go on *vi* (continue) 続く tsuzúku; (happen) 起る okórù

to go on doing something ...をし続ける ...wò shitsúzukerù

goose [gu:s] *n* (*pl* **geese**) ガチョウ gachő

gooseberry [gu:s'be:ri:] *n* (tree, fruit) ス

グリ súgùri

to play gooseberry (*BRIT*) アベックの邪魔をする abékkù no jamá wo surù

gooseflesh [gu:s'fleʃ] *n* 鳥肌 toríhada

goose pimples *npl* = **gooseflesh**

go out *vi* (leave: room, building) 出る dérù; (for entertainment): **are you going out tonight?** 今夜どこかへ出掛けますか kôn-ya dókòka e dekákemasù ká; (couple): **they went out for 3 years** 彼らは3年交際した kárèra wa sañneñ kōsai shita; (fire, light) 消える kiérù

go over *vi* (ship) 転覆する teñpuku suru
◆*vt fus* (check) 調べる shiráberù

gore [gɔːr] *vt* (subj: bull, buffalo) 角で刺す tsunó dè sásù
◆*n* (blood) 血のり chinóri

gorge [gɔːrdʒ] *n* (valley) 峡谷 kyôkoku
◆*vt*: **to gorge oneself (on)** (...を) たらふく食う (...wo) taráfùku kúù

gorgeous [gɔːr'dʒəs] *adj* (necklace, dress etc) 豪華な gốka na; (weather) 素晴らしい subárashiì; (person) 美しい utsúkushiì

gorilla [gəril'ə] *n* ゴリラ gőrìra

gorse [gɔːrs] *n* ハリエニシダ haríenishìda

gory [gɔːr'iː] *adj* (details, situation) 血みどろの chimídoro no

go-slow [gou'slou'] (*BRIT*) *n* 遵法闘争 juñpốtōsō

gospel [gɑːs'pəl] *n* (REL) 福音 fukúìn

gossip [gɑːs'əp] *n* (rumors) うわさ話 uwásabanashi, ゴシップ goshíppù; (chat) 雑談 zatsúdan; (person) おしゃべり o-sháberi, ゴシップ屋 goshíppùya
◆*vi* (chat) 雑談する zatsúdan suru

got [gɑːt] *pt*, *pp of* **get**

go through *vt fus* (town etc) ...を通る ...wò tốrù; (search through: files, papers) ...を一つ一つ調べる ...wò hitótsu hitotsu shiráberù; (examine: list, book, story) 調べる shiráberù

gotten [gɑːt'ən] (*US*) *pp of* **get**

go up *vi* (ascend) 登る nobórù; (price, level) 上がる agárù

gout [gaut] *n* 通風 tsúfū

govern [gʌv'əːrn] *vt* (country) 統治する tốchi suru; (event, conduct) 支配する shi-

hái suru

governess [gʌv'əːrnis] *n* (children's) 女性家庭教師 joséikateikyōshì

government [gʌv'əːrnmənt] *n* (act of governing) 政治 seíji; (governing body) 政府 seífu; (*BRIT*: ministers) 内閣 naíkaku

governor [gʌv'əːrnəːr] *n* (of state) 知事 chíjì; (of colony) 総督 sốtoku; (of bank, school, hospital) 理事 ríjì; (*BRIT*: of prison) 所長 shochố

go without *vt fus* (food, treats) ...無しで済ます ...náshì de sumásù

gown [gaun] *n* (dress: *also* of teacher) ガウン gáùn; (*BRIT*: of judge) 法服 hốfuku

GP [dʒiːpiː'] *n abbr* = **general practitioner**

grab [græb] *vt* (seize) つかむ tsukámù
◆*vi*: **to grab at** ...をつかもうとする ...wo tsukámó to suru

grace [greis] *n* (REL) 恩恵 oñkei; (gracefulness) しとやかさ shitóyakasà
◆*vt* (honor) ...に栄誉を与える ...ni eíyo wo atáerù; (adorn) 飾る kazárù

5 days' grace 5日間の猶予 itsúkakañ no yúyo

graceful [greis'fəl] *adj* (animal, athlete) しなやかな shináyàka na; (style, shape) 優雅な yūga na

gracious [grei'ʃəs] *adj* (person) 親切な shiñsetsu na

grade [greid] *n* (COMM: quality) 品質 hiñshitsu; (in hierarchy) 階級 kaíkyū; (SCOL: mark) 成績 seíseki; (*US*: school class) 学年 gakúnen
◆*vt* (rank, class) 格付けする kakúzuke suru; (exam papers etc) 採点する saíten suru

grade crossing (*US*) *n* 踏切 fumíkiri

grade school (*US*) *n* 小学校 shốgakkồ

gradient [grei'diːənt] *n* (of road, slope) こう配 kốbai

gradual [grædʒ'uːəl] *adj* (change, evolution) 少しずつの sukóshizutsù no

gradually [grædʒ'uːəliː] *adv* 徐々に jójò ni

graduate [*n* grædʒ'uːit *vb* grædʒ'uːeit] *n* (*also*: **university graduate**) 大学の卒

業生 daígaku nò sotsúgyòsei; (*US: also:* **high school graduate**) 高校の卒業生 kókō nò sotsúgyòsei

♦*vi* 卒業する sotsúgyō suru

graduation [grædʒuːeiʃ'ən] *n* (*also:* **graduation ceremony**) 卒業式 sotsúgyòshiki

graffiti [grəfiː'tiː] *npl* 落書 rakúgaki

graft [græft] *n* (AGR) 接木 tsugíki; (MED) 移植 ishóku; (*BRIT: inf:* hard work) 苦労 kúrō; (bribery) 汚職 oshóku

♦*vt* (AGR) 接木する tsugíki suru; (MED) 移植する ishóku suru

grain [grein] *n* (of rice, wheat, sand, salt) 粒 tsúbù; (no pl: cereals) 穀物 kokúmòtsu; (of wood) 木目 mokúme

gram [græm] *n* グラム gúràmu

grammar [græm'əːr] *n* (LING) 文法 buńpō; (book) 文法書 buńpōsho

grammar school (*BRIT*) *n* 公立高等学校 kóritsukōtōgakkō ◇大学進学教育をする公立高校 daígakushingakukyōiku wo suru kóritsukōkō; (*US*) 小学校 shógakkō

grammatical [grəmæt'ikəl] *adj* (LING) 文法の buńpō no

gramme [græm] *n* = **gram**

gramophone [græm'əfoun] *n* 蓄音機 chikúoǹki

grand [grænd] *adj* (splendid, impressive) 壮大な sódai na; (*inf:* wonderful) 素晴らしい subárashiì; (*also* humorous: gesture etc) 大げさな ógesa na

grandchildren [græn'tʃil'drən] *npl* 孫 mágò

granddad [græn'dæd] *n* (*inf*) おじいちゃん ojíichan

granddaughter [græn'dɔːtəːr] *n* 孫娘 magómusùme

grandeur [græn'dʒəːr] *n* (of scenery etc) 壮大さ sódaisa

grandfather [græn'fɑːðəːr] *n* 祖父 sófù

grandiose [græn'diːous] *adj* (scheme, building) 壮大な sódai na; (*pej*) 大げさな ógesa na

grandma [græm'ə] *n* (*inf*) おばあちゃん obáàchan

grandmother [græn'mʌðəːr] *n* 祖母 só-bò

grandpa [græn'pə] *n* (*inf*) = **granddad**

grandparents [græn'peːrənts] *npl* 祖父母 sófùbo

grand piano *n* グランドピアノ gurándopiàno

grandson [græn'sʌn] *n* 孫息子 magómusùko

grandstand [græn'stænd] *n* (SPORT) 観覧席 kańrañseki, スタンド sutáǹdo

granite [græn'it] *n* 御影石 mikágeìshi

granny [græn'iː] *n* (*inf*) おばあちゃん o-báàchan

grant [grænt] *vt* (money) 与える atáerù; (request etc) かなえる kanáerù; (visa) 交付する kófu suru; (admit) 認める mitómerù

♦*n* (SCOL) 助成金 joséìkin; (ADMIN: subsidy) 交付金 kófùkin

to take someone/something for granted ...を軽く見る ...wo karúkù mírù

granulated sugar [græn'jəleitid-] *n* グラニュー糖 gurányùtō

granule [græn'juːl] *n* (of coffee, salt) 粒 tsúbù

grape [greip] *n* ブドウ budó

grapefruit [greip'fruːt] (*pl* **grapefruit** *or* **grapefruits**) *n* グレープフルーツ gurḗpufurùtsu

graph [græf] *n* (diagram) グラフ gúràfu

graphic [græf'ik] *adj* (account, description) 写実的な shajítsuteki na; (art, design) グラフィックの guráfikkù no

graphics [græf'iks] *n* (art, process) グラフィックス guráfikkùsu

♦*npl* (drawings) グラフィックス guráfikkùsu

grapple [græp'əl] *vi*: **to grapple with someone** ...ともみ合う ...to momíaù

to grapple with something (problem etc) ...と取組む ...to toríkumù

grasp [græsp] *vt* (hold, seize) 握る nigírù; (understand) 理解する rikái suru

♦*n* (grip) 握り nigírì; (understanding) 理解 rikái

grasping [græs'piŋ] *adj* (money-grabbing) 欲深い yokúfukaì

grass [græs] n (BOT) 草 kusá; (lawn) 芝生 shibáfu

grasshopper [græs'hɑ:pər] n バッタ battá

grass-roots [græs'ru:ts] adj (level, opinion) 一般人の ippánjìn no

grate [greit] n (for fire) 火格子 higóshi
♦vi (metal, chalk): **to grate (on)** (...にすれて) きしる (...ni surḗte) kishíru
♦vt (CULIN) すりおろす suríorosù

grateful [greit'fəl] adj (thanks) 感謝の kánsha no; (person) 有難く思っている a-rígatakù omótte irù

grater [grei'tər] n (CULIN) 卸し金 oróshigàne

gratifying [græt'əfaiiŋ] adj (pleasing, satisfying) 満足な mánzoku na

grating [grei'tiŋ] n (iron bars) 鉄格子 tetsúgōshi
♦adj (noise) きしる kishírù

gratitude [græt'ətu:d] n 感謝 kánsha

gratuity [grətu:'iti:] n (tip) 心付け kokórozùke, チップ chíppù

grave [greiv] n (tomb) 墓 haká
♦adj (decision, mistake) 重大な jūdai na; (expression, person) 重々しい omóomoshiì

gravel [græv'əl] n 砂利 jarí

gravestone [greiv'stoun] n 墓石 hakáishi

graveyard [greiv'jɑ:rd] n 墓場 hakába, 墓地 bóchi

gravity [græv'iti:] n (PHYSICS) 引力 ínryoku; (seriousness) 重大さ jūdaisa

gravy [grei'vi:] n (juice of meat) 肉汁 nikújū; (sauce) グレービーソース gurḗbīsōsu

gray [grei] adj = **grey**

graze [greiz] vi (animal) 草を食う kusá wo kuú
♦vt (touch lightly) かすめる kasúmerù; (scrape) こする kosúrù
♦n (MED) かすり傷 kasúrikìzu

grease [gri:s] n (lubricant) グリース gurḗsù; (fat) 脂肪 shibō
♦vt ...にグリースを差す ...ni gurḗsù wo sásù

greaseproof paper [gri:s'pru:f-] (BRIT)

n パラフィン紙 paráfiñshi

greasy [gri:'si:] adj (food) 脂っこい abúrakkoì; (tools) 油で汚れた abúra dè yogóretà; (skin, hair) 脂ぎった abúragittà

great [greit] adj (large: area, amount) 大きい ōkii; (intense: heat, pain) 強い tsuyóì; (important, famous: city, man) 有名な yūmei na; (inf: terrific) 素晴らしい subárashiì

Great Britain n 英国 eíkoku, イギリス igírisu

great-grandfather [greit'græn'fɑːðər] n そう祖父 sṓsofù

great-grandmother [greit'græn'mʌðər] n そう祖母 sṓsobò

greatly [greit'li:] adv とても totémo

greatness [greit'nis] n (importance) 偉大さ idáisa

Greece [gri:s] n ギリシア gírìshia

greed [gri:d] n (also: **greediness**) どん欲 dóñ-yoku

greedy [gri:'di:] adj どん欲な dóñ-yoku na

Greek [gri:k] adj ギリシアの gírìshia no; (LING) ギリシア語の giríshiago no
♦n (person) ギリシア人 giríshiajìn; (LING) ギリシア語 giríshiago

green [gri:n] adj (color) 緑 (色) の mídðri(iro) no; (inexperienced) 未熟な mijúku na; (POL) 環境保護の kañkyōhogò no
♦n (color) 緑 (色) mídðri(iro); (stretch of grass) 芝生 shibáfu; (on golf course) グリーン guríñ

green belt n (round town) 緑地帯 ryokúchitài, グリーンベルト gurínberùto

green card n (BRIT: AUT) グリーンカード gurínkàdo ◇海外自動車保険証 kaígai jidōsha hokeñshō; (US: ADMIN) グリーンカード gurínkàdo ◇外国人入国就労許可書 gaíkokujìn nyūkoku shūrō kyokàsho

greenery [gri:'nəːri:] n 緑 mídðri ◇主に人為的に植えた樹木などを指す ómò ni jiñ-iteki ni ueta júmòku nádà wo sásù

greengrocer [gri:n'grousər] (BRIT) n 八百屋 yaóya

greenhouse [gri:n'haus] n 温室 oñshitsu

greenish [gri:'niʃ] adj 緑がかった mídòri-

gakattà

Greenland [gri:n'lənd] *n* グリーンランド gurînrando

greens [gri:nz] *npl* (vegetables) 葉物 hamóno, 菜葉 yōsai

greet [gri:t] *vt* (welcome: person) ...にあいさつする ...ni áĩsatsu suru, 歓迎する kañgei suru; (receive: news) 受けとめる ukétomerù

greeting [gri:'tiŋ] *n* (welcome) あいさつ áĩsatsu, 歓迎 kañgei

greeting(s) card *n* グリーティングカード gurítingukādo

gregarious [grige:r'i:əs] *adj* (person) 社交的な shakōteki na

grenade [grineid'] *n* (also: **hand grenade**) 手りゅう弾 teryűdan, shuryűdan

grew [gru:] *pt of* **grow**

grey [grei] *adj* (color) 灰色 haíiro; (dismal) 暗い kuráī

grey-haired [grei'he:rd] *adj* 白髪頭の shirágaatama no, 白髪の hakúhatsu no

greyhound [grei'haund] *n* グレーハウンド gurêhaundo

grid [grid] *n* (pattern) 碁盤の目 góbàn no me; (ELEC: network) 送電網 sōdenmō

grief [gri:f] *n* (distress, sorrow) 悲しみ kanáshimǐ

grievance [gri:'vəns] *n* (complaint) 苦情 kujō

grieve [gri:v] *vi* (feel sad) 悲しむ kanáshimù

◆*vt* (cause sadness or distress to) 悲しませる kanáshimaserù

to grieve for (dead spouse etc) ...を嘆く ...wo nagékù

grievous [gri:'vəs] *adj*: *grievous bodily harm* (LAW) 重傷 jūshō

grill [gril] *n* (on cooker) グリル gúrīru; (grilled food: *also*: **mixed grill**) グリル料理 gurírüryòri

◆*vt* (BRIT: food) グリルで焼く gúrīru de yakù; (*inf*: question) 尋問する jiñmon suru

grille [gril] *n* (screen: on window, counter etc) 鉄格子 tetsúgồshi; (AUT) ラジエーターグリル rajḗtāgùriru

grim [grim] *adj* (unpleasant: situation) 厳しい kibíshiǐ; (unattractive: place) 陰気な fñki na; (serious, stern) 険しい kewáshiǐ

grimace [grim'əs] *n* (ugly expression) しかめっ面 shikámetsura

◆*vi* しかめっ面をする shikámetsura wo surù

grime [graim] *n* (dirt) あか aká

grin [grin] *n* (smile) にやにや笑い níyàniyawarai

◆*vi* にやにやと笑う níyàniya to waráù

grind [graind] (*pt, pp* **ground**) *vt* (crush) もみつぶす momítsubusù; (coffee, pepper etc: *also* US: meat) 挽く hikú; (make sharp: knife) 研ぐ tógù

◆*n* (work) 骨折れ仕事 honéoreshigòto

grip [grip] *n* (hold) 握り nigíri; (control, grasp) 支配 shihái; (of tire, shoe) グリップ guríppù; (handle) 取っ手 tottě; (holdall) 旅行かばん ryokőkabàn

◆*vt* (object) つかむ tsukámù, 握る nigírù; (audience, attention) 引付ける hikítsukerù

to come to grips with (problem, difficulty) ...と取組む ...to toríkumù

gripping [grip'iŋ] *adj* (story, film) 引付ける hikítsukerù

grisly [griz'li:] *adj* (death, murder) ひどい hidóì

gristle [gris'əl] *n* (on meat) 軟骨 nańkotsu

grit [grit] *n* (sand, stone) 砂利 jarí; (determination, courage) 根性 kofjō

◆*vt* (road) ...に砂利を敷く ...ni jarí wo shíkù

to grit one's teeth 歯を食いしばる há wo kuíshibarù

groan [groun] *n* (of person) うめき声 umékigoè

◆*vi* うめく umékù

grocer [grou'sə:r] *n* 食料品商 shokúryōhiñshō

groceries [grou'sə:ri:z] *npl* (provisions) 食料品 shokúryōhin

grocer's (shop) [grou'sə:rz-] *n* 食料品店 shokúryōhiñten

groggy [gra:g'i:] *adj* ふらふらする fúrafura suru, グロッキーの gurókkǐ no

groin [grɔin] n そけい部 sokéibu

groom [gruːm] n (for horse) 馬丁 batéi;
(also: **bridegroom**) 花婿 hanámukò
♦vt (horse) ...の手入れをする ...no teíre
wò suru; (fig): **to groom someone for**
(job) 仕込む shikómù
well-groomed (person) 身だしなみのい
い midáshìnami no íi

groove [gruːv] n 溝 mizó

grope [group] vi (fumble): **to grope for**
手探りで探す teságuri de sagásù

gross [grous] adj (flagrant: neglect, injustice) 甚だしい hanáhadashiì; (vulgar:
behavior, building) 下品な gehín na;
(COMM: income, weight) 全体の zeńtai
no

grossly [grous'liː] adv (greatly) 甚だしく
hanáhadashikù

grotesque [groutesk'] adj (exaggerated,
ugly) 醜悪な shúaku na, グロテスクな
gurótesùku na

grotto [grɑːt'ou] n (cave) 小さな洞穴 chíisana horáana

grotty [grɑːt'iː] (BRIT inf) adj (dreadful) ひどい hídòi

ground [graund] pt, pp of **grind**
♦n (earth, soil) 土 tsuchí; (land) 地面 jímèn; (SPORT) グランド gurándo; (US:
also: **ground wire**) アース線 ásùsen;
(reason: gen pl) 根拠 koñkyo
♦vt (plane) 飛べない様にする tobénai yò
ni suru; (US: ELEC) ...のアースを取付け
る ...no ásu wò torítsukerù
on the ground 地面に〔で〕jímèn ni
〔de〕
to the ground 地面へ jímèn e
to gain/lose ground 前進〔後退〕する
zeńshin〔kótai〕surù
ground cloth (US) n = **groundsheet**
grounding [graun'diŋ] n (in education)
基礎 kisó
groundless [graund'lis] adj (fears, suspicions) 根拠のない koñkyo no nàì
grounds [graundz] npl (of coffee etc) か
す kásù; (gardens etc) 敷地 shikíchi
groundsheet [graund'ʃiːt] n グラウンド
シート guráundoshìto
ground staff n (AVIAT) 整備員 seíbiìn

◇総称 sóshō
ground swell n (of opinion) 盛り上がり
moríagarì
groundwork [graund'wəːrk] n (preparation) 準備 júñbi
group [gruːp] n (of people) 集団 shúdan,
グループ gurúpu; (of trees etc) 一群れ
hitómùre; (of cars etc) 一団 ichídan;
(also: **pop group**) グループ gurúpu;
(COMM) グループ gurúpu
♦vt (also: **group together**: people,
things etc) 一緒にする isshð ni suru, グル
ープにする gurúpu ni suru
♦vi (also: **group together**) 群がる murágarù, グループになる gurúpu ni nárù
grouse [graus] n inv (bird) ライチョウ
raíchō
♦vi (complain) 不平を言う fuhéi wò iú
grove [grouv] n 木立 kodáchì
grovel [grʌv'əl] vi (fig): **to grovel**
(before) (boss etc) (...に) ぺこぺこす
る (..ni) pékòpeko suru
grow [grou] (pt grew, pp grown) vi
(plant, tree) 生える haérù; (person, animal) 成長する seíchō suru; (increase) 増
える fuérù; (become) なる nárù; (develop): **to grow (out of/from)** (...から)
発生する (...kara) hasséi suru
♦vt (roses, vegetables) 栽培する saíbai
suru; (beard) 生やす hayásù
grower [grou'əːr] n (BOT, AGR) 栽培者
saíbaishà
growing [grou'iŋ] adj (fear, awareness,
number) 増大する zódai suru
growl [graul] vi (dog, person) うなる u-
nárù
grown [groun] pp of **grow**
grown-up [groun'ʌp'] n (adult) 大人 otóna
growth [grouθ] n (development, increase: of economy, industry) 成長 seíchō; (what has grown: of weeds, beard
etc) 生えた物 haéta monò; (growing: of
child, animal etc) 発育 hatsúiku; (MED)
しゅよう shuyó
grow up vi (child) 育つ sodátsù
grub [grʌb] n (larva) 幼虫 yóchū; (inf:
food) 飯 meshí

grubby [grʌb'i:] *adj* (dirty) 汚い kitánaî

grudge [grʌdʒ] *n* (grievance) 恨み urámî
♦*vt*: *to grudge someone something* (be unwilling to give) ...に...を出し惜しみする ...ni ...wo dashíoshimi suru; (envy) ...の...をねたむ ...no ...wo netámù
to bear someone a grudge ...に恨みがある ...ni urámi ga arù

gruelling [gru:'əliŋ] *adj* (trip, journey, encounter) きつい kitsúi

gruesome [gru:'səm] *adj* (tale, scene) むごたらしい mugótarashiî

gruff [grʌf] *adj* (voice, manner) ぶっきらぼうな bukkírabò na

grumble [grʌm'bəl] *vi* (complain) 不平を言う fuhéi wò iú

grumpy [grʌm'pi:] *adj* (bad-tempered) 機嫌が悪い kigéñ ga warúî

grunt [grʌnt] *vi* (pig) ぶーぶー言う bûbū iú; (person) うなる unáru

G-string [dʒi:'striŋ] *n* (garment) バタフライ bátàfurai

guarantee [gærənti:'] *n* (assurance) 保証 hoshố; (COMM: warranty) 保証書 hoshố-shò
♦*vt* 保証する hoshố suru

guard [gɑ:rd] *n* (one person) 警備員 keíbiñ、ガードマン gấdoman; (squad) 護衛隊 goéitai; (BRIT: RAIL) 車掌 shashố; (on machine) 安全カバー añzenkabà; (also: **fireguard**) 安全格子 añzenkôshi
♦*vt* (protect: place, person, secret etc)
to guard (against) (...から) 守る (...kara) mamórù; (prisoner) 見張る mihárù
to be on one's guard 警戒する keíkai suru

guard against *vt fus* (prevent: disease, damage etc) 防ぐ fuségù

guarded [gɑ:r'did] *adj* (statement, reply) 慎重な shíñchō na

guardian [gɑ:r'di:ən] *n* (LAW: of minor) 保護者 hốgòsha; (defender) 監視人 kañshiñin

guard's van (BRIT) *n* (RAIL) 乗務員車 jốmuiñsha

guerrilla [gəril'ə] *n* ゲリラ gérìra

guess [ges] *vt, vi* (estimate: number, dis-

tance etc) 推定する suítei suru; (correct answer) 当ててみる atétè mírù; (US: think) ...だと思う ...da to omóù
♦*n* (attempt at correct answer) 推定 suítei
to take/have a guess 推定する suítei suru, 当ててみる atétè mírù

guesswork [ges'wə:rk] *n* (speculation) 当て推量 atézuiryố

guest [gest] *n* (visitor) 客 kyákù; (in hotel) 泊り客 tomárikyaku

guest-house [gest'haus] *n* 民宿 míñshuku

guest room *n* 客間 kyakúma

guffaw [gʌfɔ:'] *vi* ばか笑い bakáwaraî

guidance [gaid'əns] *n* (advice) 指導 shidố

guide [gaid] *n* (person: museum guide, tour guide, mountain guide) 案内人 annáiñin、ガイド gấido; (book) ガイドブック gaídobukkù; (BRIT: also: **girl guide**) ガールスカウト gấrusukaùto
♦*vt* (round city, museum etc) 案内する annái suru; (lead) 導く michíbikù; (direct) ...に道を教える ...ni michí wò oshíerù

guidebook [gaid'buk] *n* ガイドブック gaídobukkù

guide dog *n* 盲導犬 mốdōkèn

guidelines [gaid'lainz] *npl* (advice) 指針 shishín、ガイドライン gaídoraìn

guild [gild] *n* (association) 組合 kumíaî、協会 kyốkai

guile [gail] *n* (cunning) 悪意 akúî

guillotine [gil'əti:n] *n* (for execution) 断頭台 dañtốdai、ギロチン giróchin; (for paper) 裁断機 saídañki

guilt [gilt] *n* (remorse) 罪の意識 tsumí nò ishíki; (culpability) 有罪 yûzai

guilty [gil'ti:] *adj* (person) 有罪の yûzai no; (expression) 後ろめたそうな ushíro-metasō na; (secret) やましい yamáshiî

guinea [gin'i:] (BRIT) *n* (old money) ギニー gínî

guinea pig *n* (animal) モルモット morúmottò; (fig: person) 実験台 jikkéñdai

guise [gaiz] *n*: *in/under the guise of* ...の装いで ...no yosốoî de

guitar [gɪtɑːr'] n ギター gítǎ

gulf [gʌlf] n (GEO) 湾 wán; (abyss: *also fig*: difference) 隔たり hedátarì

gull [gʌl] n カモメ kamóme

gullet [gʌl'it] n 食道 shokúdō

gullible [gʌl'əbəl] adj (naive, trusting) だまされやすい damásareyàsui

gully [gʌl'iː] n (ravine) 峡谷 kyôkoku

gulp [gʌlp] vi (swallow) 息を飲込む íkì wo nomíkomù
♦vt (*also*: **gulp down**: drink) がぶがぶ飲込む gábùgabu nomíkomù; (: food) 急いで食べる isóìde tabérù

gum [gʌm] n (ANAT) 歯茎 hágùki; (glue) アラビア糊 arábia nòri; (sweet: *also*: **gumdrop**) ガムドロップ gamúdoroppù; (*also*: **chewing-gum**) チューインガム chúingugàmu, ガム gámù
♦vt (stick): **to gum (together)** 張り合わせる harfawaserù

gumboots [gʌm'buːts] (BRIT) npl ゴム靴 gomúgùtsu

gumption [gʌmp'ʃən] n (sense, wit) 度胸 dokyô

gun [gʌn] n (small: revolver, pistol) けん銃 kenjū, ピストル písùtoru, ガン gáñ; (medium-sized: rifle) 銃 jū, ライフル raífùru; (: *also*: **airgun**) 空気銃 kûkijū; (large: cannon) 大砲 taíhō

gunboat [gʌn'bout] n 砲艦 hôkan

gunfire [gʌn'faiəːr] n 銃撃 jûgeki

gunman [gʌn'mən] (pl gunmen) n (criminal) ガンマン gáñman

gunpoint [gʌn'point] n: **at gunpoint** (pointing a gun) ピストルを突付けて písùtoru wo tsukítsuketè; (threatened with a gun) ピストルを突付けられて písùtoru wo tsukísukerarète

gunpowder [gʌn'paudəːr] n 火薬 kayákù

gunshot [gʌn'ʃɑːt] n (act) 発砲 happô; (sound) 銃声 jûsei

gurgle [gəːr'gəl] vi (baby) のどを鳴らす nodó wò narásù; (water) ごぼごぼ流れる góbògobo nagárerù

guru [guː'ruː] n (REL: *also fig*) 教師 kyôshi

gush [gʌʃ] vi (blood, tears, oil) どっと流れ出る dóttò nagárederù; (person) 大げさに言う ôgesa ni iu

gusset [gʌs'it] n (SEWING) まち máchì

gust [gʌst] n (*also*: **gust of wind**) 突風 toppû; (of smoke) 渦巻 uzúmàki

gusto [gʌs'tou] n (enthusiasm) 楽しみ tanóshimì

gut [gʌt] n (ANAT: intestine) 腸 chô

guts [gʌts] npl (ANAT: of person, animal) 内臓 naízō; (*inf*: courage) 勇気 yúki, ガッツ gáttsù

gutter [gʌt'əːr] n (in street) どぶ dobu; (of roof) 雨どい amádòi

guttural [gʌt'əːrəl] adj (accent, sound) のどに絡まった様な nódò ni karámatta yô na

guy [gai] n (*inf*: man) 野郎 yarô, やつ yátsù; (*also*: **guyrope**) 支線 shisén; (figure) ガイフォークスの人形 gaífôkusu no niñgyō

guzzle [gʌz'əl] vt (drink) がぶがぶ飲む gábùgabu nómù; (food) がつがつ食う gátsùgatsu kúù

gym [dʒim] n (building, room: *also*: **gymnasium**) 体育館 taíikukàn; (activity: *also*: **gymnastics**) 体操 taísō

gymnast [dʒim'næst] n 体操選手 taísō-señshu

gymnastics [dʒimnæs'tiks] n 体操 taísō

gym shoes npl 運動靴 uñdōgùtsu, スニーカー súnikà

gym slip (BRIT) n (tunic) スモックスモックku◇そで無しの上っ張りでかつて女子学童の制服として使われた物 sodénashi no uwápparì de katsútè joshí gakudô no seífuku toshite tsukáwaretà monó

gynecologist [gainəkɑːl'ədʒist] (BRIT **gynaecologist**) n 婦人科医 fujíñka-i

gypsy [dʒip'siː] n ジプシー jípùshi

gyrate [dʒai'reit] vi (revolve) 回転する kaíten suru

H

haberdashery [hæb'əːrdæʃəːriː] n (US) 紳士服店 shiñshifukutèn; (BRIT) 小間物店 komámonotèn

habit [hǽb'it] *n* (custom, practice) 習慣 shúkan; (addiction) 中毒 chúdoku; (REL: costume) 修道服 shúdōfūku

habitable [hǽb'itəbəl] *adj* 住める sumérù

habitat [hǽb'itæt] *n* 生息地 seísokuchì

habitual [həbitʃ'uːəl] *adj* (action) 習慣的な shúkanteki na; (drinker, liar) 常習的な jóshūteki na

hack [hæk] *vt* (cut, slice) ぶった切る buttágirù

◆*n* (*pej*: writer) 三文文士 sańmonbunshi

hacker [hæk'əːr] *n* (COMPUT) コンピュータ破り koñpyūtayaburì, ハッカー hákkā

hackneyed [hæk'niːd] *adj* 陳腐な chíñpu na

had [hæd] *pt, pp of* have

haddock [hæd'ək] (*pl* **haddock** *or* **haddocks**) *n* タラ tárà

hadn't [hæd'ənt] = **had not**

haemorrhage [hem'əːridʒ] (*BRIT*) *n* = **hemorrhage**

haemorrhoids [hem'əːrɔidz] (*BRIT*) *npl* = **hemorrhoids**

haggard [hæg'əːrd] *adj* (face, look) やつれた yatsúretà

haggle [hæg'əl] *vi* (bargain) 値切る negírù

Hague [heig] *n*: **The Hague** ハーグ hágù

hail [heil] *n* (frozen rain) ひょう hyồ; (of objects, criticism etc) 降り注ぐ物 furísosogù monó

◆*vt* (call: person) 呼ぶ yobú; (flag down: taxi) 呼止める yobítomerù; (acclaim: person, event etc) ほめる homérù

◆*vi* (weather) ひょうが降る hyồ ga fúrù

hailstone [heil'stoun] *n* ひょうの粒 hyồ no tsubú

hair [heːr] *n* (of animal: *also gen*) 毛 ke; (of person's head) 髪の毛 kamí no kè

to do one's hair 髪をとかす kamí wò tokásu

hairbrush [heːr'brʌʃ] *n* ヘアブラシ heáburashì

haircut [heːr'kʌt] *n* (action) 散髪 sańpatsu; (style) 髪型 kamígata, ヘアスタイル heásutaìru

hairdo [heːr'duː] *n* 髪型 kamígata, ヘアスタイル heásutaìru

hairdresser [heːr'dresəːr] *n* 美容師 biyóshì

hairdresser's [heːr'dresəːrz] *n* (shop) 美容院 biyóìn

hair dryer *n* ヘアドライヤー heádoraìyā

hairgrip [heːr'grip] *n* 髪止め kamídome

hairnet [heːr'net] *n* ヘアネット heánettò

hairpin [heːr'pin] *n* ヘアピン heápiñ

hairpin curve (*BRIT* **hairpin bend**) *n* ヘアピンカーブ heápinkàbu

hair-raising [heːr'reiziŋ] *adj* (experience, tale) ぞっとする様な zóttò suru yồ na

hair remover [-rimuː'vəːr] *n* (cream) 脱毛クリーム datsúmōkurìmù

hair spray *n* ヘアスプレー heásupurè

hairstyle [heːr'stail] *n* 髪型 kamígata, ヘアスタイル heásutaìru

hairy [heːr'iː] *adj* (person, animal) 毛深い kebúkaì; (*inf*: situation) 恐ろしい osóroshìì

hake [heik] (*pl inv or* **hakes**) *n* タラ tárà

half [hæf] (*pl* **halves**) *n* (of amount, object) 半分 hańbuñ; (of beer etc) 半パイント hańpaìnto; (RAIL, bus) 半額 hańgaku

◆*adj* (bottle, fare, pay etc) 半分の hańbuñ no

◆*adv* (empty, closed, open, asleep) 半ば nakábà

two and a half 2と2分の1 ní tò nibún no ichi

two and a half years/kilos/hours 2年〔キロ, 時間〕半 ninén〔kíro, jíkan〕hàn

half a dozen 半ダース hańdàsu

half a pound 半ポンド hańpoñdo

to cut something in half ...を半分に切る ...wo hańbuñ ni kírù

half-baked [hæf'beikt'] *adj* (idea, scheme) ばかげた bakágetà

half-caste [hæf'kæst] *n* 混血児 końketsujì, ハーフ hàfu

half-hearted [hæf'hɑːr'tid] *adj* (attempt) いい加減な iíkagen na

half-hour [hæf'au'ər] n 半時間 hañjikàn

half-mast [hæf'mæst']: *a flag at half-mast* 半旗 háñki

halfpenny [hei'pəni:] (*BRIT*) n 半ペニー hañpenī

half-price [hæf'prais'] *adj* 半額の hañgaku no
◆*adv* 半額で hañgaku de

half term (*BRIT*) n (SCOL) 中間休暇 chúkankyùka

half-time [hæf'taim'] n (SPORT) ハーフタイム háfutaimù

halfway [hæf'wei'] *adv* (between two points in place, time) 中途で chúto de

halibut [hæl'əbət] n *inv* オヒョウ ohyṓ

hall [hɔ:l] n (entrance way) 玄関ホール geñkanhòru; (for concerts, meetings etc) 講堂 kṓdō, ホール hòru

hall of residence (*BRIT*) n 学生寮 gakúseiryō

hallmark [hɔ:l'mɑːrk] n (on metal) 太鼓判 taíkoban; (of writer, artist etc) 特徴 tokúchō

hallo [həlou'] *excl* = **hello**

Hallowe'en [hælʌwi:n'] n ハロウィーン haróuīn

hallucination [həlu:sənei'ʃən] n 幻覚 geñkaku

hallway [hɔ:l'wei] n (entrance hall) 玄関ホール geñkanhòru

halo [hei'lou] n (of saint) 後光 gokṓ

halt [hɔ:lt] n (stop) 止る事 tomáru kotò
◆*vt* (progress, activity, growth etc) 止める tomérù
◆*vi* (stop) 止る tomárù

halve [hæv] *vt* (reduce) 半分に減らす hañbuñ ni herásù; (divide) 半分に切る hañbuñ ni kírù

halves [hævz] *pl of* **half**

ham [hæm] n (meat) ハム hámù

hamburger [hæm'bə:rgə:r] n ハンバーガー hañbāgā

hamlet [hæm'lit] n (village) 小さな村 chíisana murá

hammer [hæm'ə:r] n (tool) 金づち kanázuchì, とんかち toñkáchì
◆*vt* (nail) たたく tatákù
◆*vi* (on door, table etc) たたく tatákù

to hammer an idea into someone ...にある考え方をたたき込む ...ni árù kañgàekata wo tátakikomù

to hammer a message across ある考えを繰返し強調する aru kañgaè wo kuríkaeshì kyóchō suru

hammock [hæm'ək] n (on ship, in garden) ハンモック hañmokkù

hamper [hæm'pə:r] *vt* (person, movement, effort) 邪魔する jamá suru
◆n (basket) ふた付きバスケット futátsukibasukettò

hamster [hæm'stə:r] n ハムスター hámùsutā

hand [hænd] n (ANAT) 手 tế; (of clock) 針 hárì; (handwriting) 筆跡 hissékì; (worker) 使用人 shíyðnin; (of cards) 持札 mochífùda
◆*vt* (pass, give) 渡す watásù

to give/lend someone a hand ...の手伝いをする ...no tetsúdaì wo suru

at hand 手元に temóto nì

in hand (time) 空いていて aíte itè; (job, situation) 当面の tōmen no

on hand (person, services etc) 利用できる ríyō dekirù

to hand (information etc) 手元に temóto nì

on the one hand ..., on the other hand ... 一方では...他方では... ippṓ de wa ..., táhō de wa ...

handbag [hænd'bæg] n ハンドバッグ hañdobaggù

handbook [hænd'buk] n (manual) ハンドブック hañdobukkù

handbrake [hænd'breik] n (AUT) サイドブレーキ saídoburèki

handcuffs [hænd'kʌfs] *npl* (POLICE) 手錠 tejṓ

handful [hænd'ful] n (of soil, stones) 一握り hitónigirì

a handful of people 数人 sűnin

handicap [hæn'di:kæp] n (disability) 障害 shṓgai; (disadvantage) 不利 fúrì; (SPORT) ハンデ háñde
◆*vt* (hamper) 不利にする fúrì ni suru

mentally/physically handicapped 精神的〔身体〕障害のある seíshinteki 〔shiñ-

tai) shōgai no árù

handicraft [hænˈdi:kræft] n (activity) 手芸 shúgei; (object) 手芸品 shugéihiǹ

hand in vt (essay, work) 提出 する teíshutsu suru

handiwork [hænˈdi:wəːrk] n やった事 yattá kotò

handkerchief [hæŋˈkəːrtʃif] n ハンカチ haňkachi

handle [hænˈdəl] n (of door, window, drawer etc) 取っ手 tottè; (of cup, knife, brush etc) 柄 e; (for winding) ハンドル haňdòru

♦vt (touch: object, ornament etc) いじる ijírù; (deal with: problem, responsibility etc) 処理する shórì suru; (treat: people) 扱う atsúkaù

「handle with care」取扱い注意 toríatsukai chùi

to fly off the handle 怒る okórù

handlebar(s) [hænˈdəlbɑːr(z)] n(pl) ハンドル haňdòru

hand luggage n 手荷物 teními̇tsu

handmade [hænˈdˈmeid] adj (clothes, jewellery, pottery etc) 手作りの tezúkùri no

hand out vt (object, information) 配る kubárù; (punishment) 与える atáerù

handout [hænˈdaut] n (money, clothing, food) 施し物 hodókoshimono; (publicity leaflet) パンフレット páňfuretto; (summary: of lecture) 講演の要約 kóeǹ nò yóyaku

hand over vt (thing) 引渡す hikíwatasù; (responsibility) 譲る yuzúrù

handrail [hænˈdreil] n (on stair, ledge) 手すり tesúri

handshake [hændˈʃeik] n 握手 ákùshu

handsome [hænˈsəm] adj (man) 男前の otófomaè no, ハンサムな háǹsamu na; (woman) きりっとした kirftto shita; (building) 立派な rippá na; (fig: profit, return) 相当な sótō na

handwriting [hændˈraitiŋ] n (style) 筆跡 hisséki

handy [hænˈdi:] adj (useful) 便利な béǹri na; (skilful) 手先の器用な tesáki nò kíyō na; (close at hand) 手元にある temóto nì

árù

handyman [hænˈdi:mæn] (pl handymen) n (at home) 手先の器用な人 tesáki nò kíyō na hitò; (in hotel etc) 用務員 yōmuin

hang [hæŋ] (pt, pp hung) vt (painting, coat etc) 掛ける kakérù; (criminal: pt, pp hanged) 絞首刑にする kōshukei ni surù

♦vi (painting, coat, drapery etc) 掛っている kakátte irù; (hair etc) 垂れ下がる tarésagarù

to get the hang of something (inf) ...のこつが分かる ...no kótsù ga wakárù

hang about vi (loiter) ぶらつく burátsukù

hangar [hæŋˈəːr] n (AVIAT) 格納庫 kakúnōko

hang around vi = hang about

hanger [hæŋˈəːr] n (for clothes) 洋服掛け yōfukukàke, ハンガー háǹga

hanger-on [hæŋˈərɑːn] n (parasite) 取巻き torímaki

hang-gliding [hæŋˈglaidiŋ] n (SPORT) ハンググライダー haňguguraídā

hang on vi (wait) 待つ mátsù

hangover [hæŋˈouvəːr] n (after drinking) 二日酔い futsúkayoì

hang up vi (TEL) 電話を切る deňwa wò kírù

♦vt (coat, painting etc) 掛ける kakérù

hang-up [hæŋˈʌp] n (inhibition) ノイローゼ noírōze

hanker [hæŋˈkəːr] vi: to hanker after (desire, long for) 渇望する katsúbō suru

hankie [hæŋˈkiː] n abbr = handkerchief

hanky [hæŋˈkiː] n abbr = handkerchief

haphazard [hæpˈhæzˈəːrd] adj (system, arrangement) いい加減な iŋkagen na

happen [hæpˈən] vi (event etc: occur) 起る okórù; (chance): to happen to do something 偶然に...する gūzen ni ...surù

as it happens 実は jitsú wà

happening [hæpˈəniŋ] n (incident) 出来事 dekígòto

happily [hæpˈiliː] adv (luckily) 幸い saíwai; (cheerfully) 楽しそうに tanóshisò ni

happiness [hæp'i:nis] *n* (contentment) 幸せ shiáwase

happy [hæp'i:] *adj* (pleased) うれしい uréshiì; (cheerful) 楽しい tanóshiì

to be happy (with) (content) (...に) 満足する (...ni) mańzoku suru

to be happy to do (willing) 喜んで...する yorókoǹde ...surù

happy birthday! 誕生日おめでとう! tafijóbi omédetò!

happy-go-lucky [hæp'i:goulʌk'i:] *adj* (person) のんきな nóǹki na

harangue [həræŋ'] *vt* (audience, class) ...に向かって熱弁を振るう ...ni mukáttè netsúben wò furúù

harass [həræs'] *vt* (annoy, pester) ...にいやがらせをする ...ni iyágarase wo surù

harassment [həræs'mənt] *n* (hounding) 嫌がらせ iyágarase

harbor [hɑːr'bər] (*BRIT* **harbour**) *n* (NAUT) 港 mináto

♦*vt* (hope, fear etc) 心に抱く kokórò ni idákù; (criminal, fugitive) かくまう ka-kúmaù

hard [hɑːrd] *adj* (surface, object) 堅い katáì; (question, problem) 難しい muzúkashiì; (work) 骨の折れる honé no orérù; (life) 苦しい kurúshiì; (person) 非情な hijó na; (facts, evidence) 確実な kakújitsu na

♦*adv* (work, think, try) 一生懸命に isshókeǹmei ni

to look hard at ...を見詰める ...wo mitsúmerù

no hard feelings! 悪く思わないから warúkù omówanai karà

to be hard of hearing 耳が遠い mimí ga tòi

to be hard done by 不当な扱いを受けた futó na atsukài wo ukétà

hardback [hɑːrd'bæk] *n* (book) ハードカバー hádokabà

hard cash *n* 現金 geńkin

hard disk *n* (COMPUT) ハードディスク hádodisùku

harden [hɑːr'dən] *vt* (wax, glue, steel) 固める katámerù; (attitude, person) かたくなにする katákùna ni suru

♦*vi* (wax, glue, steel) 固まる katámarù; (attitude, person) かたくなになる katákùna ni nárù

hard-headed [hɑːrd'hed'id] *adj* (businessman) 現実的な geńjitsuteki na

hard labor *n* (punishment) 懲役 chóeki

hardly [hɑːrd'li:] *adv* (scarcely) ほとんど...ない hotóndo ...náì; (no sooner) ...するや否や ...surú ya inà ya

hardly ever ほとんど...しない hotóndo ...shináì

hardship [hɑːrd'ʃip] *n* (difficulty) 困難 kofinaǹ

hard up (*inf*) *adj* (broke) 金がない kané ga naì, 懐が寂しい futókoro ga sabishìì

hardware [hɑːrd'weːr] *n* (ironmongery) 金物 kanámono; (COMPUT) ハードウエア hádoueà; (MIL) 兵器 hêiki

hardware shop *n* 金物屋 kanámonoya

hard-wearing [hɑːrd'weːr'iŋ] *adj* (clothes, shoes) 丈夫な jôbu na

hard-working [hɑːrd'wəːr'kiŋ] *adj* (employee, student) 勤勉な kińben na

hardy [hɑːr'di:] *adj* (plants, animals, people) 丈夫な jôbu na

hare [heːr] *n* ノウサギ noúsàgi

hare-brained [heːr'breind] *adj* (scheme, idea) バカげた bakágetà

harem [heːr'əm] *n* (of wives) ハーレム háremu

harm [hɑːrm] *n* (injury) 害 gáì; (damage) 損害 sońgai, ダメージ daméjī

♦*vt* (person) ...に危害を加える ...ni kígaì wo kuwáerù; (thing) 損傷する sońshō su-ru

out of harm's way 安全な場所に ańzen na bashò ni

harmful [hɑːrm'fəl] *adj* (effect, toxin, influence etc) 有害な yúgai na

harmless [hɑːrm'lis] *adj* (animal, person) 無害な mugái na; (joke, pleasure, activity) たわいのない tawai no nai

harmonica [hɑːrmɑːn'ikə] *n* ハーモニカ hámonika

harmonious [hɑːrmou'ni:əs] *adj* (discussion, relationship) 友好的な yúkōteki na; (layout, pattern) 調和の取れた chôwa no torétà; (sound, tune) 調子の良い chôshi

no yoì

harmonize [hɑːr'mənaiz] vi (MUS) ハー
モニーを付ける hámonī wo tsukérù;
(colors, ideas): *to harmonize (with)*
(...と)調和する (...to) chówa suru

harmony [hɑːr'məni:] n (accord) 調和
chówa; (MUS) ハーモニー hámonī

harness [hɑːr'nis] n (for horse) 馬具 bágù; (for child, dog) 胴輪 dówa, ハーネス
hánesù; (safety harness) 安全ハーネス aǹ-
zenhànesu

♦vt (resources, energy etc) 利用する riyó-
suru; (horse) ...に馬具をつける ...ni bágù
wo tsukérù; (dog) ...にハーネスを付ける
...ni hánesù wo tsukérù

harp [hɑːrp] n (MUS) たて琴 tatégòto, ハ
ープ hápu

♦vi: *to harp on about* (pej) ...の事をく
どくどと話し続ける ...no kotó wò kúdò-
kudo to hanáshitsuzukerù

harpoon [hɑːrpuːn'] n もり mórì

harrowing [hær'ouiŋ] adj (experience,
film) 戦りつの seńritsu no

harsh [hɑːrʃ] adj (sound) 耳障りな mimízawàri na; (light) どぎつい dogítsui;
(judge, criticism) か酷な kakóku na;
(life, winter) 厳しい kibíshiî

harvest [hɑːr'vist] n (harvest time) 収穫
期 shúkakukì; (of barley, fruit etc) 収穫
shúkaku

♦vt (barley, fruit etc) 収穫する shúkaku
suru

has [hæz] vb see **have**

hash [hæʃ] n (CULIN) ハッシュ hásshù;
(fig: mess) めちゃめちゃな有様 mechámecha na arisama

hashish [hæʃ'iːʃ] n ハシシ háshîshi

hasn't [hæz'ənt] = **has not**

hassle [hæs'əl] (inf) n (bother) 面倒 meńdò

haste [heist] n (hurry) 急ぎ isógi

hasten [hei'sən] vt (decision, downfall)
早める hayámerù

♦vi (hurry): *to hasten to do something*
急いで...する isóide ...surù

hastily [heis'tili:] adv (hurriedly) 慌ただ
しく awátadashikù; (rashly) 軽はずみに
karúhazùmi ni

hasty [heis'ti:] adj (hurried) 慌ただしい
awátadashiî; (rash) 軽はずみの karúhazùmi no

hat [hæt] n (headgear) 帽子 bôshi

hatch [hætʃ] n (NAUT: also: **hatchway**)
倉口 sôkō, ハッチ hátchì; (also: **service
hatch**) サービス口 sábisugùchi, ハッチ
hátchì

♦vi (bird) 卵からかえる tamágò kara kaérù; (egg) かえる kaérù, ふ化する fuká
suru

hatchback [hætʃ'bæk] n (AUT) ハッチ
バック hatchíbakkù

hatchet [hætʃ'it] n (axe) おの ónò

hate [heit] vt (wish ill to: person) 憎む
nikúmù; (dislike strongly: person, thing,
situation) 嫌う kiráu

♦n (illwill) 増悪 zôo; (strong dislike) 嫌
悪 kéñ-o

hateful [heit'fəl] adj ひどい hidôî

hatred [hei'trid] n (illwill) 増悪 zôo;
(strong dislike) 嫌悪 kéñ-o

haughty [hɔː'ti:] adj (air, attitude) 尊大
な soñdai na

haul [hɔːl] vt (pull) 引っ張る hippáru

♦n (of stolen goods etc) 獲物 emóno;
(also: **a haul of fish**) 漁獲 gyokáku

haulage [hɔː'lidʒ] n (business, costs) 運送
uńsō

hauler [hɔːl'əːr] (BRIT **haulier**) n 運送屋
uńsōya

haunch [hɔːntʃ] n (ANAT) 腰 koshí; (of
meat) 腰肉 koshíniku

haunt [hɔːnt] vt (subj: ghost) (place) ...に
出る ...ni dérù; (person) ...に付きまとう
...ni tsukímatou; (: problem, memory
etc) 悩ます nayámasù

♦n (of crooks, childhood etc) 行き付けの
場所 ikítsuke nò bashó

haunted house お化け屋敷 obákeyashì-
ki

KEYWORD

have [hæv] (pt, pp **had**) aux vb **1** (gen)
to have arrived/gone/eaten/slept 着
いた〔行った，食べた，眠った〕tsuîta〔it-
tá, tábèta, nemúttà〕
he has been kind/promoted 彼は親切

だった〔昇格した〕kárè wa shínsetsu dáttā〔shōkaku shita〕

has he told you? 彼はあなたにそれを話しましたか kárè wa anátà ni soré wò hanáshimashìta ká

having finished/when he had finished, *he left* 仕事が済むと彼は帰った shigóto ga sumù to kárè wa káètta

2 (in tag questions): ***you've done it, haven't you?*** あなたはその仕事をやったんでしょう anátà wa sonó shigòto wo yattáñ deshṓ

he hasn't done it, has he? 彼は仕事をやらなかったんでしょう kárè wa shigóto wò yaránakattañ deshṓ

3 (in short answers and questions): ***you've made a mistake - no I haven't/so I have*** あなたは間違いをしました-違いますよ〔そうですね〕anátà wa machígaì wo shimáshìta - chigáimasù yó〔sò desu né〕

we haven't paid - yes we have! 私たちはまだ金を払っていません-払いましたよ watákushitàchi wa mádà kanè wo harátte imaseñ - haráimashìta yó

I've been there before, have you? 私は前にあそこへ行った事がありますが、あなたは？watákushi wà máè ni asóko è ittà kotó ga arímasù ga, anátà wá?

◆*modal aux vb* (be obliged): ***to have (got) to do something*** ...をしなければならない ...wò shinákereba naranaì

she has (got) to do it 彼女はどうしてもそれをしなければなりません kánòjo wa dōshitè mo soré wò shinákereba narimaseñ

I have (got) to finish this work 私はこの仕事を済まさなければなりません watákushi wà konó shigòto wo sumásanakereba narimaseñ

you haven't to tell her 彼女に言わなくてもいい〔言ってはならない〕kánòjo ni iwánakute mò íi〔itté wa naranaì〕

I haven't got/I don't have to wear glasses 私は眼鏡を掛けなくてもいい watákushi wà mégàne wo kakénakute mò íi

this has to be a mistake これは何かの

間違いに違いない koré wa nánìka no machígaì ni chigái naì

◆*vt* **1** (possess) 持っている móttè iru, ...がある ...gá arù

he has (got) blue eyes/dark hair 彼は目が青い〔髪が黒い〕kárè wa mé gà aóì〔kamí gà kuróì〕

do you have/have you got a car/phone? あなたは車〔電話〕を持っていますか anátà wa kurúma〔deñwa〕wò móttè imasu ká

I have (got) an idea いい考えがあります íi kañgaè ga arímasù

have you any more money? もっとお金がありませんか móttò o-káne gà arímaseñ ká

2 (take: food) 食べる tabérù; (: drink) 飲む nómù

to have breakfast/lunch/dinner 朝食〔昼食、夕食〕を食べる chōshoku〔chūshoku, yūshoku〕wò tabérù

to have a drink 何かを飲む nánìka wo nómù

to have a cigarette タバコを吸う tabáko wo suù

3 (receive, obtain etc) 受ける ukérù, 手に入れる té ni irerù

may I have your address? ご住所を教えて頂けますか go-júsho wò oshíete itadakemasù ká

you can have it for $5 5ドルでそれを譲ります gódòru de soré wò yuzúrimasù

I must have it by tomorrow どうしても明日までにそれをもらいたいのです dōshite mò ashíta made nì soré wò moráitai no desù

to have a baby 子供を産む kodómo wo umù

4 (maintain, allow) 主張する shuchṓ suru, 許す yurúsù

he will have it that he is right 彼は自分が正しいと主張している kárè wa jibún gà tadáshiì to shuchṓ shite irù

I won't have it/this nonsense! それ〔こんなばかげた事〕は許せません soré〔koñna bakageta kotò〕wà yurúsemaseñ

we can't have that そんな事は許せません soñna kotò wa yurúsemaseñ

5: *to have something done* ...をさせる
...wŏ sasérù, ...をしてもらう ...wŏ shité
mòraù

to have one's hair cut 散髪をしてもら
う sañpatsu wŏ shité moraù

to have a house built 家を建てる ié wŏ
tatérù

to have someone do something ...に
...をさせる ...nî ...wŏ sasérù

*he soon had them all laughing/
working* まもなく彼は皆を笑わせて〔働
かせて〕いた ma mŏ nàku kárè wa miná
wŏ waráwasete〔határakasete〕itá

6 (experience, suffer) 経験する keíken
suru

to have a cold 風邪を引いている kazé
wŏ hîfte irù

to have (the) flu 感冒にかかっている
kañbō nî kakátte irù

*she had her bag stolen/her arm
broken* 彼女はハンドバッグを盗まれた
〔腕を折った〕kánòjo wa hañdobaggù wo
nusúmaretà〔udé wo ottà〕

to have an operation 手術を受ける
shújùtsu wo ukérù

7 (+ noun: take, hold etc) ...する ... suru

to have a swim/walk/bath/rest 泳ぐ
〔散歩する、風呂に入る、ひと休みする〕
oyógù〔sañpo suru, fúrò ni hâîru, hitóya-
sumi suru〕

let's have a look 見てみましょう mîtè
mimashō

to have a meeting/party 会議〔パーテ
ィ〕を開く kâîgi〔pátì〕wo hirákù

let me have a try 私に試させて下さい
watákushi nî tamésasete kudasaí

8 (inf: dupe) だます damásù

he's been had 彼はだまされた kárè wa
damásaretà

haven [hei'vən] *n* (harbor) 港 mináto;
(safe place) 避難所 hináñjo

haven't [hæv'ənt] = have not

have out *vt*: *to have it out with
someone* (settle a problem etc) ...と決着
をつける ...tŏ ketcháku wŏ tsukérù

haversack [hæv'ə:ræk] *n* (of hiker, soldier) リュックサック ryukkúsakkù

havoc [hæv'ək] *n* (chaos) 混乱 koñran

Hawaii [həwai'ji:] *n* ハワイ háwài

hawk [hɔ:k] *n* タカ takâ

hay [hei] *n* 干草 hoshîkusa

hay fever *n* 花粉症 kafúñshō

haystack [hei'stæk] *n* 干草の山 hoshíku-
sa no yama

haywire [hei'waiə:re] (inf) *adj*: *to go
haywire* (machine etc) 故障する koshō
suru; (plans etc) とんざする tóñza suru

hazard [hæz'ə:rd] *n* (danger) 危険 kikén
♦*vt* (risk: guess, bet etc) やってみる yatté mirù

hazardous [hæz'ə:rdəs] *adj* (dangerous)
危険な kikén na

hazard (warning) lights *npl* (AUT)
非常点滅灯 hijôtenmetsutō

haze [heiz] *n* (of heat, smoke, dust) かす
み kasúmi

hazelnut [hei'zəlnʌt] *n* ヘーゼルナッツ
hēzerunattsù

hazy [hei'zi:] *adj* (sky, view) かすんだ ka-
súnda; (idea, memory) ぼんやりとした
boñ-yarî to shita

he [hi:] *pron* 彼は〔が〕 kárè wa〔ga〕

he who ... ...する人は ...surú hitò wa

head [hed] *n* (ANAT, mind) 頭 atáma;
(of table) 上席 jōseki; (of queue) 先頭 señtō; (of company, organization) 最高責任
者 saíkōsekinìñsha; (of school) 校長 kô-
chō

♦*vt* (list, queue) ...の先頭にある〔いる〕
...no señtō ni arù〔irù〕; (group, company) 取仕切る toríshikirù

heads (or tails) 表か〔裏か〕omóte
kà〔urá kà〕

head first (fall) 真っ逆様に massákàsama ni; (rush) 向こう見ずに mukó mîzu ni

head over heels (in love) ぞっこん zok-
kôn

to head a ball ボールをヘディングで飛
ばす bŏru wo hedíngu de tobásu

headache [hed'eik] *n* 頭痛 zutsū

headdress [hed'dres] (BRIT) *n* (of
bride) ヘッドドレス heddôdoresù

head for *vt fus* (place) ...に向かう ...ni
mukáù; (disaster) ...を招く ...wo manékù

heading [hed'iŋ] *n* (of chapter, article)

表題 hyṓdai, タイトル táìtoru

headlamp [hed'læmp] (*BRIT*) *n* = **headlight**

headland [hed'lænd] *n* 岬 misáki

headlight [hed'lait] *n* ヘッドライト heddóraìto

headline [hed'lain] *n* (PRESS, TV) 見出 し midáshi

headlong [hed'lɔːŋ] *adv* (fall) 真っ逆様に massákàsama ni; (rush) 向こう見ずに mukṓ mìzu ni

headmaster [hed'mæs'tər] *n* 校長 kṓchō ◊男性の場合 dańsei nò baái

headmistress [hed'mis'tris] *n* 校長 kṓchō ◊女性の場合 joséi nò baái

head office *n* (of company etc) 本社 hóñsha

head-on [hed'ɑːn'] *adj* (collision, confrontation) 正面の shṓmen no

headphones [hed'founz] *npl* ヘッドホン heddóhòn

headquarters [hed'kwɔːrtəːrz] *npl* (of company, organization) 本部 hóñbu; (MIL) 司令部 shiréìbu

headrest [hed'rest] *n* (AUT) ヘッドレス ト heddórèsuto

headroom [hed'ruːm] *n* (in car) 天井の高 さ teñjō no takàsa; (under bridge) 通行可 能な高さ tsúkōkanð na takàsa

headscarf [hed'skɑːrf] *n* スカーフ sukā́fù

headstrong [hed'strɔːŋ] *adj* (determined) 強情な gṓjō na

head waiter *n* (in restaurant) 給仕頭 kyúǰigashira

headway [hed'wei] *n*: **to make headway** 進歩する shíñpo suru

headwind [hed'wind] *n* 向かい風 mukáikaze

heady [hed'iː] *adj* (experience, time) 陶酔 の tōsui no; (drink, atmosphere) 酔わせ る yowáserù

heal [hiːl] *vt* (injury, patient) 治す naósù
◆*vi* (injury, damage) 治る naórù

health [helθ] *n* (condition: *also* MED) 健 康状態 keñkōjōtai; (good health) 健康 keñkō

health food *n* 健康食品 keñkōshokùhin

Health Service (*BRIT*) *n*: **the Health Service** 公共衛生機構 kṓkyōeiseikikō

healthy [hel'θiː] *adj* (person, appetite etc) 健康な keñkō na; (air, walk) 健康に 良い keñkō ni yoì; (economy) 健全な keñzen na; (profit etc) 大いなる ṓi naru

heap [hiːp] *n* (pile: of clothes, papers, sand etc) 山 yamá
◆*vt* (stones, sand etc): **to heap (up)** 積 み上げる tsumíagerù
to heap something with (plate) ...に ...を山盛りする ...ni ...wo yamámori suru; (sink, table etc) ...に...を山積みする ...ni ...wo yamázumi suru
to heap something on (food) ...を...に山 盛りする ...wo ...ni yamámori suru; (books etc) ...を...に山積みする ...wo ...ni yamázumi suru
heaps of (*inf*: time, money, work etc) 一杯の ippái no

hear [hiːr] (*pt, pp* **heard**) *vt* (sound, voice etc) ...を聞く ...wo kikú, ...が聞える ...ga kikóeru; (news, information) ...を聞く ...wo kikú, ...で聞いて知る ...de kiíte shirú; (LAW: case) 審理する shiñri suru
to hear about (event, person) ...の事を 聞く ...no kotó wo kikú
to hear from someone ...から連絡を受 ける ...kara reñraku wð ukérù

heard [həːrd] *pt, pp* of **hear**

hearing [hiːˈriŋ] *n* (sense) 聴覚 chṓkaku; (of facts, witnesses etc) 聴聞会 chṓmoñkai

hearing aid *n* 補聴器 hochṓkì

hearsay [hiːrˈsei] *n* (rumor) うわさ uwása

hearse [həːrs] *n* 霊きゅう車 reíkyùsha

heart [hɑːrt] *n* (ANAT) 心臓 shiñzō; (*fig*: emotions, character) 心 kokórò; (of problem) 核心 kakúshin; (of city) 中心部 chūshiñbu; (of lettuce) しん shíñ; (shape) ハート形 hátogata
to lose heart (courage) 落胆する rakútan suru
to take heart (courage) 勇気を出す yū́ki wð dásù
at heart (basically) 根は... né wà ...
by heart (learn, know) 暗記で añki de

heart attack n (MED) 心臓発作 shińzō-hossà

heartbeat [haːrtˈbiːt] n 心拍 shiñpaku

heartbreaking [haːrtˈbreikiŋ] adj (news, story) 悲痛な hitsū na

heartbroken [haːrtˈbroukən] adj: **to be heartbroken** 悲嘆に暮れている hitán ni kurete irù

heartburn [haːrtˈbəːrn] n (indigestion) 胸焼け muñyake

heart failure n (MED) 心不全 shiñfùzen

heartfelt [haːrtˈfelt] adj (prayer, wish) 心からの kokórò kara no

hearth [haːrθ] n (fireplace) 炉床 roshó

heartland [haːrtˈlænd] n (of country, region) 中心地 chūshiñchi

heartless [haːrtˈlis] adj (person, attitude) 非情な hijó na

hearts [haːrts] npl (CARDS) ハート hắto

hearty [haːrˈtiː] adj (person) 明朗な meírō na; (laugh) 大きな ōkina; (appetite) お う盛な ōsei na; (welcome) 熱烈な netsúretsu na; (dislike) 絶対的な zettáiteki na; (support) 心からの kokórò kara no

heat [hiːt] n (warmth) 暑さ átsùsa; (temperature) 温度 óñdo; (excitement) 熱気 nekkí; (SPORT: also: **qualifying heat**) 予選 yosén

♦vt (water) 沸かす wákasù; (food) ...に火 を通す ...ni hí wò tōsu; (room, house) 暖 める atátamerù

heated [hiːˈtid] adj (pool) 温水の oñsui no; (room etc) 暖房した dañbō shita; (argument) 激しい hagéshiì

heater [hiːˈtəːr] n ヒーター hītā

heath [hiːθ] (BRIT) n 荒野 aréno

heathen [hiːˈðən] n (REL) 異教徒 ikyótò

heather [heˈðəːr] n エリカ érìka, ヒース hísù

heating [hiːˈtiŋ] n (system, equipment) 暖房 dáñbō

heatstroke [hiːtˈstrouk] n (MED) 熱射病 nesshábyō

heat up vi (water, room) 暖まる atátamarù

♦vt (food, water, room) 暖める atátamerù

heatwave [hiːtˈweiv] n 熱波 néppà

heave [hiːv] vt (pull) 強く引く tsúyòku hikú; (push) 強く押す tsúyòku osú; (lift) ぐ いと持上げる gúì to mochíagerù

♦vi (vomit) 吐く hákù; (feel sick) むかつ く mukátsukù

♦n (of chest) あえぎ aēgi; (of stomach) むかつき mukátsuki

to heave a sigh ため息をつく tameíkì wo tsukú

his chest was heaving 彼はあえいでい た kárè wa aéide ità

heaven [hevˈən] n (REL: also fig) 天国 téñgoku

heavenly [hevˈənliː] adj (REL) 天からの téñ kara no; (fig: day, place) 素晴らしい subárashiì

heavily [hevˈiliː] adv (land, fall) どしんと dóshìn to; (drink, smoke) 大量に taíryō ni; (sleep) ぐっすりと gussúrì to; (sigh) 深く fukákù; (depend, rely) すっかり sukkárì

heavy [hevˈiː] adj (person, load, responsibility) 重い omói; (clothes) 厚い atsúi; (rain, snow) 激しい hagéshiì; (of person: build, frame) がっしりした gasshírī shita; (blow) 強い tsúyòi; (breathing) 荒い aráî; (sleep) 深い fukáî; (schedule, week) 過密な kamítsu na; (work) きつい kitsúi; (weather) 蒸し暑い mushíatsuì; (food, meal) もたれる motárerù

a heavy drinker 飲兵衛 nóñbē

a heavy smoker ヘビースモーカー hebísumōkā

heavy goods vehicle (BRIT) n 大型トラック ōgatatoràkku

heavyweight [hevˈiːweit] n (SPORT) ヘビー級選手 hebíkyūseñshu

Hebrew [hiːˈbruː] adj ヘブライの hebúrài no; (LING) ヘブライ語の hebúraigo no

♦n (LING) ヘブライ語 hebúraigo

Hebrides [hebˈridiːz] npl: **the Hebrides** ヘブリディーズ諸島 hebúridìzushotō

heckle [hekˈəl] vt (speaker, performer) 野次る yajírù

hectic [hekˈtik] adj (event, week) やたら に忙しい yatára ni isogashiì

he'd [hiːd] = **he would; he had**

hedge [hedʒ] n (in garden, on roadside)

生け垣 ikégàki
♦*vi* (stall) あいまいな態度を取る aímai nà táìdo wo tórù
to hedge one's bets (*fig*) 失敗に備える shippái nì sonáerù

hedgehog [hedʒ'hɑːg] *n* ハリネズミ harínezùmi

heed [hiːd] *vt* (*also*: **take heed of**: advice, warning) 聞き入れる kikíirerù

heedless [hiːd'lis] *adj*: **heedless (of)** (...を) 無視して (...wo) múshì shité

heel [hiːl] *n* (of foot, shoe) かかと kakáto
♦*vt*: *to heel shoes* 靴のかかとを修理する kutsú nò kakáto wo shúrì suru

hefty [hef'tiː] *adj* (person) がっしりした gasshírì shita; (parcel etc) 大きくて重い ōkikute omóì; (profit) 相当な sōtō na

heifer [hef'əːr] *n* 若い雌ウシ wakáī méùshi ◇まだ子を生んだ事のない物を指す mádà ko wo uńda kotò no náī monó wo sásù

height [hait] *n* (of tree, building, mountain) 高さ takása; (of person) 身長 shińchō; (of plane) 高度 kōdo; (high ground) 高地 kōchi; (*fig*: of powers) 絶頂期 zetchōkì; (: of season) 真っ最中 massáìchū; (: of luxury, stupidity) 極み kiwámi

heighten [hait'ən] *vt* (fears, uncertainty) 高める takámerù

heir [eːr] *n* (to throne) 継承者 keíshōshà; (to fortune) 相続人 sōzokuniñ

heiress [eːr'is] *n* 大遺産の相続人 daísan no sōzokuniñ ◇女性について言う joséi ni tsuitè iú

heirloom [eːr'luːm] *n* 家宝 kahō

held [held] *pt, pp* of **hold**

helicopter [hel'əkɑːptəːr] *n* (AVIAT) ヘリコプター heríkopùtā

heliport [hel'əpɔːrt] *n* (AVIAT) ヘリポート herípòto

helium [hiː'liːəm] *n* ヘリウム heríùmu

he'll [hiːl] = **he will, he shall**

hell [hel] *n* (life, situation: *also* REL) 地獄 jigóku
hell! (*inf*) 畜生! chikúshò!, くそ! kusó!

hellish [hel'iʃ] (*inf*) *adj* (traffic, weather, life etc) 地獄の様な jigóku no yō na

hello [helou'] *excl* (as greeting) やあ yā, 今日は końnichi wa; (to attract attention) おい óì; (on telephone) もしもし móshìmoshi; (expressing surprise) おや oyá

helm [helm] *n* (NAUT: stick) かじ棒 kajíbō, チラー chírā; (: wheel) だ輪 daríñ

helmet [hel'mit] *n* (*gen*) ヘルメット herúmettò

help [help] *n* (assistance, aid) 助け tasúke, 手伝い tetsúdaì; (charwoman) お手伝いさん o-tétsùdaisan
♦*vt* (person) 助ける tasúkerù, 手伝う tétsudau; (situation) ...に役に立つ ...ni yakú ni tatsù
help! 助けてくれ! tasúketè kuré!
help yourself (to) (...を) 自由に取って下さい (...wo) jiyū ni tottè kudásai
he can't help it 彼はそうせざるを得ない kárè wa sō sezarù wo énài

helper [hel'pəːr] *n* (assistant) 助手 joshú, アシスタント ashísùtanto

helpful [help'fəl] *adj* (person, advice, suggestion etc) 役に立つ yakú ni tatsù

helping [hel'piŋ] *n* (of food) 一盛り hitómòri
a second helping お代り o-káwarì

helpless [help'lis] *adj* (incapable) 何もできない naní mo dekínài; (defenceless) 無防備の mubóbi no

hem [hem] *n* (of skirt, dress) すそ susó
♦*vt* (skirt, dress etc) ...のすそ縫いをする ...no susónui wo suru

hem in *vt* 取囲む toríkakomù

hemisphere [hem'isfiːr] *n* 半球 hańkyū

hemorrhage [hem'əːridʒ] (*BRIT* **haemorrhage**) *n* 出血 shukkétsu

hemorrhoids [hem'əːrɔidz] (*BRIT* **haemorrhoids**) *npl* じ痔 ji

hen [hen] *n* (female chicken) メンドリ meńdori; (female bird) 雌の鳥 mesú no torí

hence [hens] *adv* (therefore) 従って shitágattè
2 years hence 今から2年先 ímà kara nínen saki

henceforth [hens'fɔːrθ] *adv* (from now on) 今後 kóñgo; (from that time on) その

後 sonō go

henchman [hentʃ'mən] (*pej*: *pl* **henchmen**) *n* (of gangster, tyrant) 手下 teshíta, 子分 kóbùn

henpecked [hen'pekt] *adj* (husband) 妻のしりに敷かれた tsúmà no shirí ni shikaretà

hepatitis [hepətai'tis] *n* (MED) 肝炎 kánen

her [həːr] *pron* (direct) 彼女を kánòjo wo; (indirect) 彼女に kánòjo ni
◆*adj* 彼女の kánòjo no ¶ *see also* **me**; **my**

herald [heːr'əld] *n* (forerunner) 兆し kizáshi
◆*vt* (event, action) 予告する yokóku suru

heraldry [heːr'əldriː] *n* (study) 紋章学 moñshōgàku; (coat of arms) 紋章 moñshō ◇総称 sóshō

herb [əːrb] *n* (*gen*) ハーブ hābu; (BOT, MED) 薬草 yakúsō; (CULIN) 香草 kōsō

herd [həːrd] *n* (of cattle, goats, zebra etc) 群れ muré

here [hiːr] *adv* (this place): *she left here yesterday* 彼女は昨日ここを出ました kanójo wa kínō kokó wò demáshità; (beside me): *I have it here* ここに持っています kokó ni mottè imásù; (at this point): *here he stopped reading ...* そ の時彼は読むのをやめて... sonó tokí kárè wa yómù no wo yaméte ...
here! (I'm present) はい！ hái!; (take this) はいどうぞ hái dòzo
here is/are はい、...です hái, ...désù
here she is! 彼女はここにいました！ kanójo wa kokó ni imáshità!

hereafter [hiːræf'təːr] *adv* (in the future) 今後 kóñgo

hereby [hiːrbai'] *adv* (in letter) これをもって koré wo mottè

hereditary [həred'iteːriː] *adj* (disease) 先天的な señtenteki na; (title) 世襲の seshú no

heredity [həred'itiː] *n* (BIO) 遺伝 idén

heresy [heːr'isiː] *n* (opposing belief: *also* REL) 異端 itán

heretic [heːr'itik] *n* 異端者 itáñsha

heritage [heːr'itidʒ] *n* (of country, nation) 遺産 isán

hermetically [həːrmet'ikliː] *adv*: *hermetically sealed* 密閉した mippéi shita

hermit [həːr'mit] *n* 隠とん者 iñtoñsha

hernia [həːr'niːə] *n* (MED) 脱腸 datchō

hero [hiː'rou] (*pl* **heroes**) *n* (in book, film) 主人公 shujíñkō, ヒーロー hírō ◇男性を指す dansei wo sasu; (of battle, struggle) 英雄 eíyū; (idol) アイドル aídoru

heroic [hirou'ik] *adj* (struggle, sacrifice, person) 英雄的な eíyūteki na

heroin [heːr'ouin] *n* ヘロイン heróīn

heroine [heːr'ouin] *n* (in book, film) 女主人公 oñnashujíñkō, ヒロイン hiróīn; (of battle, struggle) 英雄的女性 eíyūtekijosei; (idol) アイドル aídoru

heroism [heːr'ouizəm] *n* (bravery, courage) 勇敢さ yúkansa

heron [heːr'ən] *n* アオサギ aósagi

herring [heːr'iŋ] *n* (fish) ニシン níshin

hers [həːrz] *pron* 彼女の物 kanójo no mono ¶ *see also* **mine**

herself [həːrself'] *pron* 彼女自身 kanójojishìn ¶ *see also* **oneself**

he's [hiːz] = **he is**; **he has**

hesitant [hez'ətənt] *adj* (smile, reaction) ためらいがちな taméraigachi na

hesitate [hez'əteit] *vi* (pause) ためらう taméraù; (be unwilling) 後込みする shirígomì suru

hesitation [hezətei'ʃən] *n* (pause) ためらい tamérai; (unwillingness) 後込み shirígomì

heterosexual [hetə·rəsek'ʃuːəl] *adj* (person, relationship) 異性愛の iséiai no

hew [hjuː] *vt* (stone, wood) 刻む kizámu

hexagonal [heksæg'ənəl] *adj* (shape, object) 六角形の rokkákukèi no

heyday [hei'dei] *n*: *the heyday of ...* ...の全盛時代 ...no zeñseijidài

HGV [eitʃgiːviː'] (*BRIT*) *n* *abbr* = **heavy goods vehicle**

hi [hai] *excl* (as greeting) やあ yá, 今日は koñnichi wa; (to attract attention) おい ói

hiatus [haiei'təs] *n* (gap: in manuscript etc) 脱落個所 datsúrakukashò; (pause)

中断 chūdan
hibernate [hai'bə:rneit] *vi* (animal) 冬眠
する tōmin suru
hiccough [hik'ʌp] *vi* しゃっくりする
shákkùri suru
hiccoughs [hik'ʌps] *npl* しゃっくり
shákkùri
hiccup [hik'ʌp] *vi* = **hiccough**
hiccups [hik'ʌps] *npl* = **hiccoughs**
hid [hid] *pt of* **hide**
hidden [hid'ən] *pp of* **hide**
hide [haid] *n* (skin) 皮 kawá
♦*vb* (*pt* **hid**, *pp* **hidden**)
♦*vt* (person, object, feeling, information)
隠す kakúsù; (obscure: sun, view) 覆い隠
す ōikakusù
♦*vi*: **to hide (from someone)** (...に見
つからない様に) 隠れる (...ni mitsúkara-
nai yṑ ni) kakúrerù
hide-and-seek [haid'ənsi:k'] *n* (game)
隠れん坊 kakúreǹbo
hideaway [haid'əwei] *n* (retreat) 隠れ家
kakúregà
hideous [hid'i:əs] *adj* (painting, face) 醜
い miníkui
hiding [hai'diŋ] *n* (beating) むち打ち muchíuchi
to be in hiding (concealed) 隠れている
kakúrete irù
hierarchy [hai'ə:rɑ:rki:] *n* (system of
ranks) 階級制 kaíkyūseì; (people in
power) 幹部 káǹbu ◇総称 sōshō
hi-fi [hai'fai'] *n* ステレオ sutéreo
♦*adj* (equipment, system) ステレオの sutéreo no
high [hai] *adj* (gen) 高い takáì; (speed) 速
い hayáì; (wind) 強い tsuyóì; (quality) 上
等な jōtō na; (principles) 崇高な sū́kō na
♦*adv* (climb, aim etc) 高く tákàku
it is 20 m high その高さは20メーター
です sonó takàsa wa nijū́ mḕtā desu
high in the air 空高く sórataàkaku
highbrow [hai'brau] *adj* (intellectual) 知
的な chitéki na
highchair [hai'tʃe:r] *n* (for baby) ベビー
チェア bebíchèa
higher education [hai'ə:r-] *n* 高等教育
kōtōkyōìku

high-handed [hai'hæn'did] *adj* (decision, rejection) 横暴な ōbō na
high-heeled [hai'hi:ld] *adj* (shoe) ハイヒ
ールの haíhìru no
high jump *n* (SPORT) 走り高飛び ha-
shíritakàtobi
highlands [hai'ləndz] *npl*: **the Highlands** スコットランド高地地方 sukótto-
raǹdo kōchichihō
highlight [hai'lait] *n* (*fig*: of event) 山場
yamába, ハイライト haíraìto; (of news
etc) 要点 yōten, ハイライト haíraìto; (in
hair) 光る部分 hikárù búbùn, ハイライト
haíraìto
♦*vt* (problem, need) ...に焦点を合せる
...ni shṓten wò awáserù
highly [hai'li:] *adv* (critical, confidential)
非常に hijō ni; (a lot): **to speak highly
of** ...をほめる ...wo homérù
to think highly of ...を高く評価する
...wo tákàku hyōka suru
highly paid 高給取りの kōkyūtòri no
highly strung (*BRIT*) *adj* = **high-
strung**
highness [hai'nis] *n*: **Her (or His)
Highness** 陛下 héìka
high-pitched [hai'pitʃt'] *adj* (voice,
tone, whine) 調子の高い chōshi no tákaì
high-rise block [hai'raiz'-] *n* 摩天楼
matéǹrō
high school *n* (*US*: for 14-18 year-olds)
高等学校 kōtōgakkṑ, ハイスクール haí-
sūkùru; (*BRIT*: for 11-18 year-olds) 総合
中学校 sōgōchūtōgakkṑ
high season (*BRIT*) *n* 最盛期 saiseiki,
シーズン shīzun
high street (*BRIT*) *n* 本通り hoǹdōri
high-strung [hai'strʌŋ'] (*US*) *adj* 神経
質な shiǹkeishitsu na
highway [hai'wei] *n* 幹線道路 kaǹsendō-
ro, ハイウエー haíueē
Highway Code (*BRIT*) *n* 道路交通法
dōrokōtsūhṑ
hijack [hai'dʒæk] *vt* (plane, bus) 乗っ取
る nottórù, ハイジャックする haíjakkù
suru
hijacker [hai'dʒækə:r] *n* 乗っ取り犯 not-
tórihaǹ

hike [haik] *vi* (go walking) ハイキングする haíkingu suru
♦*n* (walk) ハイキング haíkingu

hiker [hai'kə:r] *n* ハイカー haíkā

hilarious [hile:r'i:əs] *adj* (account, adventure) こっけいな kokkéi na

hill [hil] *n* (small) 丘 oká; (fairly high) 山 yamá; (slope) 坂 saká

hillside [hil'said] *n* 丘の斜面 oká no shamèn

hilly [hil'i:] *adj* 丘の多い oká no ōí
a hilly area 丘陵地帯 kyūryōchitái

hilt [hilt] *n* (of sword, knife) 柄 e
to the hilt (*fig*: support) とことんまで tokótoñ made

him [him] *pron* (direct) 彼を kárè wo; (indirect) 彼に kárè ni ¶ *see also* **me**

himself [himself'] *pron* 彼自身 kárèjishin ¶ *see also* **oneself**

hind [haind] *adj* (legs, quarters) 後ろの ushíro no

hinder [hin'də:r] *vt* (progress, movement) 妨げる samátagerù

hindrance [hin'drəns] *n* 邪魔 jamá

hindsight [haind'sait] *n*: *with hindsight* 後になってみると átò ni nátte mirù to

Hindu [hin'du:] *adj* ヒンズーの hiñzú no

hinge [hindʒ] *n* (on door) ちょうつがい chōtsugái
♦*vi* (*fig*): *to hinge on* ...による ...ni yorú

hint [hint] *n* (suggestion) 暗示 añji, ヒント híñto; (advice) 勧め susúme, 提言 teígen; (sign, glimmer) 兆し kizáshi
♦*vt*: *to hint that* (suggest) ...だとほのめかす ...da to honómekasù
♦*vi*: *to hint at* (suggest) ほのめかす honómekasù

hip [hip] *n* (ANAT) 腰 koshí, ヒップ híppù

hippopotamus [hipəpɑ:t'əməs] (*pl* **hippopotamuses** *or* **hippopotami**) *n* カバ kábà

hire [haiə:r] *vt* (*BRIT*: car, equipment, hall) 賃借りする chíñgari suru; (worker) 雇う yatóù
♦*n* (*BRIT*: of car, hall etc) 賃借り chíñgari

for hire (taxi, boat) 賃貸し用の chíñgashiyō no

hire purchase (*BRIT*) *n* 分割払い購入 buñkatsubaraikōnyū

his [hiz] *pron* 彼の物 kárè no monó
♦*adj* 彼の kárè no ¶ *see also* **my; mine**

hiss [his] *vi* (snake, gas, roasting meat) しゅうっと言う shúttò iú; (person, audience) しーっと野次る shíttò yajírù

historian [histɔ:r'i:ən] *n* 歴史学者 rekíshigakushà

historic(al) [histɔ:r'ik(əl)] *adj* (event, person) 歴史上の rekíshijō no, 歴史的な rekíshiteki na; (novel, film) 歴史に基づく rekíshi ni motózukù

history [his'tə:ri:] *n* (of town, country, person: *also* SCOL) 歴史 rekíshi

hit [hit] (*pt*, *pp* **hit**) *vt* (strike: person, thing) 打つ utsú, たたく tatáku; (reach: target) ...に当る ...ni atárù; (collide with: car) ...にぶつかる ...ni butsúkarù; (affect: person, services, event etc) ...に打撃を与える ...ni dagéki wò atáerù
♦*n* (knock) 打撃 dagéki; (success: play, film, song) 大当り ōatàri, ヒット híttò
to hit it off with someone ...と意気投合する ...to íkitōgō suru

hit-and-run driver [hit'ənrʌn'-] *n* ひき逃げ運転者 hikínige unteñsha

hitch [hitʃ] *vt* (fasten) つなぐ tsunágù; (*also*: **hitch up**: trousers, skirt) 引上げる hikíagerù
♦*n* (difficulty) 問題 moñdai
to hitch a lift ヒッチハイクをする hitchíhaìku wo suru

hitch-hike [hitʃ'haik] *vi* ヒッチハイクをする hitchíhaìku wo suru

hitch-hiker [hitʃ'haikə:r] *n* ヒッチハイクをする人 hitchíhaìku wo suru hitò

hi-tech [hai'tek'] *adj* ハイテクの haíteku no
♦*n* ハイテク haíteku

hitherto [hið'ə:rtu:] *adv* (until now) 今まで imá madè

hive [haiv] *n* (of bees) ミツバチの巣箱 mitsúbachi no súbàko

hive off (*inf*) *vt* (company) ...の一部を切放す ...no ichíbu wo kiríhanasù

HMS [eitʃemes'] *abbr* (= *Her/His Majesty's Ship*) 軍艦...号 guńkaǹ ...gṍ ◇英国海軍の軍艦の名前の前に付ける eíkoku-kaigún no guńkaǹ no namáe no máe ni tsukérù

hoard [hɔːrd] *n* (of food etc) 買いだめ kaídame; (of money, treasure) 蓄え takúwae

◆*vt* (food etc) 買いだめする kaídamesuru

hoarding [hɔːr'diŋ] (*BRIT*) *n* (for posters) 掲示板 keíjiban

hoarfrost [hɔːr'frɔːst] *n* (on ground) 霜 shimó

hoarse [hɔːrs] *adj* (voice) しわがれた shiwágaretà

hoax [houks] *n* (trick) いんちき íńchiki, いかさま ikásama

hob [haːb] *n* (of cooker, stove) レンジの上部 reńji no jõbu

hobble [haːb'əl] *vi* (limp) びっこを引く bíkkò wo hikú

hobby [haːb'i:] *n* (pastime) 趣味 shúmì

hobby-horse [haːb'i:hɔːrs] *n* (*fig*: favorite topic) 十八番の話題 oháko nò wadái

hobo [hou'bou] (*US*) *n* (tramp) ルンペン rúńpen

hockey [haːk'i:] *n* (game) ホッケー hókkè

hoe [hou] *n* (tool) くわ kuwá, ホー hṍ

hog [hɔːg] *n* (pig) ブタ butá ◇去勢した雄ブタを指す kyoséi shita osobùta wo sasu

◆*vt* (*fig*: road, telephone etc) 独り占めにする hitórijime nì suru

to go the whole hog とことんまでやる tokótoǹ made yarú

hoist [hɔist] *n* (apparatus) 起重機 kijúkì, クレーン kuréǹ

◆*vt* (heavy object) 引上げる hikíagerù; (flag) 掲げる kakágerù; (sail) 張る harú

hold [hould] (*pt, pp* **held**) *vt* (bag, umbrella, someone's hand etc) 持つ mótsù; (contain: subj: room, box etc) ...が入っている ...ni ...ga háitte iru; (have: power, qualification, opinion) ...を持っている ...wo móttè iru, ...がある ...ga árù; (meeting) 開く hirákù; (detain: prisoner, hostage) 監禁する kańkin suru; (consider): *to hold someone responsible/liable etc* ...の責任と見なす ...no sekínin tò minásù; (keep in certain position): *to hold one's head up* 頭を上げる atáma wò agérù

◆*vi* (withstand pressure) 持ちこたえる mochíkotaeru; (be valid) 当てはまる atéhamaru

◆*n* (grasp) 握り nigíri; (of ship) 船倉 seńsō; (of plane) 貨物室 kamótsushìtsu; (control): *to have a hold over* ...の急所を握っている ...no kyúsho wò nigítte irù

to hold a conversation with ...と話し合う ...to hanáshiaù

hold the line! (*TEL*) 少々お待ち下さい shōshō o-máchi kudasai

hold on! ちょっと待って chótto mátte

to hold one's own (*fig*) 引けを取らない hiké wò toránaí, 負けない makénaí

to catch/get (a) hold of ...に捕まる ...ni tsukámarù

holdall [hould'ɔːl] (*BRIT*) *n* 合切袋 gassáibukùro

hold back *vt* (person, thing) 制止する seíshi suru; (thing, emotion) 押さえる osáerù; (secret, information) 隠す kakúsù

hold down *vt* (person) 押さえつける o-sáetsukerù; (job) ...についている ...ni tsúìte iru

holder [houl'dəːr] *n* (container) 入れ物 irémono, ケース kḕsu, ホールダー hṓrudā; (of ticket, record, title) 保持者 hojísha; (of office) 在職者 zaíshokusha

holding [houl'diŋ] *n* (share) 持株 mochíkabu; (small farm) 小作農地 kosákunōchi

hold off *vt* (enemy) ...に持ちこたえる ...ni mochíkotaerù

hold on *vi* (hang on) 捕まる tsukámarù; (wait) 待つ mátsù

hold on to *vt fus* (for support) ...に捕まる ...ni tsukámarù; (keep) 預かる azúkarù

hold out *vt* (hand) 差伸べる sashínoberù; (hope, prospect) 持たせる motáserù

◆*vi* (resist) 抵抗する teíkō suru

hold up *vt* (raise) 上げる agérù; (sup-

port) 支える sasáerù; (delay) 遅らせる o-kúraserù; (rob: person, bank) 武器を突付けて...から金を奪う búki wo tsukftsuketè ...kara kané wò ubáù

hold-up [hould'ʌp] *n* (robbery) 強盗 gótō; (delay) 遅れ okúre; (BRIT: in traffic) 渋滞 jútai

hole [houl] *n* 穴 aná
♦*vt* (ship, building etc) ...に穴を開ける ...ni aná wò akéru

holiday [hɑ:l'idei] *n* (BRIT: vacation) 休暇 kyúka; (day off) 休暇の日 kyúka no hi; (public holiday) 祝日 shukújitsu
on holiday 休暇中 kyúkachū

holiday camp (BRIT) *n* (also: **holiday centre**) 休暇村 kyúkamùra

holiday-maker [hɑ:l'ideimeikə:r] (BRIT) *n* 行楽客 kórakukyàku

holiday resort *n* 行楽地 kórakuchì, リゾート rizótò

holiness [hou'li:nis] *n* (of shrine, person) 神聖さ shiñseisa

Holland [hɑ:l'ənd] *n* オランダ oráñda

hollow [hɑl'ou] *adj* (container) 空っぽの karáppo no; (log, tree) うろのある uró no arù; (cheeks, eyes) くぼんだ kubóñda; (laugh) わざとらしい wazátorashiì; (claim) 根拠のない kofikyo no naì; (sound) うつろな utsúro na
♦*n* (in ground) くぼみ kubómi
♦*vt: to hollow out* (excavate) がらんどうにする garándō ni surù

holly [hɑl'i:] *n* (tree, leaves) ヒイラギ híiragi

holocaust [hɑl'əkɔ:st] *n* 大虐殺 daígyakùsatsu

hologram [hou'ləgræm] *n* ホログラム horógurāmu

holster [houl'stə:r] *n* (for pistol) ホルスター horúsutā

holy [hou'li:] *adj* (picture, place, person) 神聖な shiñsei na
holy water 聖水 seísui

homage [hɑ:m'idʒ] *n* (honor, respect) 敬意 kéìi
to pay homage to (hero, idol) ...に敬意を表す ...ni kéìi wo aráwasù

home [houm] *n* (house) 家 ié, 住い sumáì;

(area, country) 故郷 kokyó; (institution) 収容施設 shúyōshisètsu
♦*cpd* (domestic) 家庭の katéi no; (ECON, POL) 国内の kokúnài no; (SPORT: team, game) 地元の jimóto no
♦*adv* (go, come, travel etc) 家に ié ni
at home (in house) 家に〔で〕 ié ni (de); (in country) 本国に〔で〕 hóñgoku ni (de); (in situation) ...に通じて ...ni tsújite
make yourself at home どうぞお楽に dózo o-ráku ni
to drive something home (nail etc) ...を打込む ...wo uchíkomù; (fig: point etc) ...を強調する ...wo kyóchō suru

home address *n* 自宅の住所 jitáku no júsho

home computer *n* パーソナルコンピュータ pásonarukonpyúta, パソコン pasókon

homeland [houm'lænd] *n* 母国 bókòku

homeless [houm'lis] *adj* (family, refugee) 家のない ié no naì

homely [houm'li:] *adj* (simple, plain) 素朴な sobóku na; (US: not attractive: person) 不器量な bukíryò na

home-made [houm'meid'] *adj* (bread, bomb) 手製の teséi no, 自家製の jikásei no

Home Office (BRIT) *n* 内務省 naímushō

homeopathy [houmi:ɑ:p'əθi:] (BRIT **homoeopathy**) *n* (MED) ホメオパシー homéopashī

home rule *n* (POL) 自治権 jichíkèn

Home Secretary (BRIT) *n* 内務大臣 naímudaìjin

homesick [houm'sik] *adj* ホームシックの hómushikkù no

hometown [houmtaun'] *n* 故郷 kokyó

homeward [houm'wə:rd] *adj* (journey) 家に帰る ié ni kaerù

homework [houm'wə:rk] *n* (SCOL) 宿題 shukúdai

homicide [hɑ:m'isaid] (US) *n* 殺人 satsújin

homoeopathy [houmi:ɑ:p'əθi:] (BRIT) *n* = **homeopathy**

homogeneous [houmədʒi:'ni:əs] *adj*

(group, class) 均質の kinshitsu no

homosexual [houməsek'ʃuːəl] *adj* (person, relationship: *gen*) 同性愛の dōseiai no; (man) ホモの hómo no; (woman) レズの rézu no
♦*n* (man) 同性愛者 dōseiaishà, ホモ hómò; (woman) 同姓愛者 dōseiaishà, レズ rézù

honest [ɑːn'ist] *adj* (truthful, trustworthy) 正直な shōjiki na; (sincere) 率直な sotchoku na

honestly [ɑːn'istliː] *adv* (truthfully) 正直に shōjiki ni; (sincerely, frankly) 率直に sotchoku ni

honesty [ɑːn'istiː] *n* (truthfulness) 正直 shōjiki; (sincerity, frankness) 率直さ sotchōkusa

honey [hʌn'iː] *n* (food) はちみつ hachímitsu

honeycomb [hʌn'iːkoum] *n* (of bees) ミツバチの巣 mitsúbachi no su

honeymoon [hʌn'iːmuːn] *n* (holiday, trip) 新婚旅行 shinkonryokō, ハネムーン hanémùn

honeysuckle [hʌn'iːsʌkəl] *n* (BOT) スイカズラ suíkazùra

honk [hɑːŋk] *vi* (AUT: horn) 鳴らす narásu

honorary [ɑːn'əːreːriː] *adj* (unpaid: job, secretary) 無給の mukyū no; (title, degree) 名誉の meíyo no

honor [ɑːn'əːr] (*BRIT* **honour**) *vt* (hero, author) ほめたたえる homětataeru; (commitment, promise) 守る mamóru
♦*n* (pride, self-respect) 名誉 meíyo; (tribute, distinction) 光栄 kōei

honorable [ɑːn'əːrəbəl] *adj* (person, action, defeat) 名誉ある meíyo aru

honors degree [ɑːn'əːrz-] *n* (SCOL) 専門学士号 senmongakushigō

hood [hud] *n* (of coat, cooker etc) フードfùdo; (*US*: AUT: engine cover) ボンネット bonnettò; (*BRIT*: AUT: folding roof) 折畳み式トップ orítatamishiki toppù

hoodlum [huːd'ləm] *n* (thug) ごろつき gorótsuki, 暴力団員 bōryokudan-ìn

hoodwink [hud'wiŋk] *vt* (con, fool) だます damásu

hoof [huf] (*pl* **hooves**) *n* ひずめ hizúme

hook [huk] *n* (for coats, curtains etc) かぎ kagí, フック fúkkù; (on dress) ホックhókkù; (*also*: **fishing hook**) 釣針 tsuríbàri
♦*vt* (fasten) 留める toméru; (fish) 釣る tsurú

hooligan [huː'ligən] *n* ちんぴら chínpira

hoop [huːp] *n* (ring) 輪 wá

hooray [həreiʹ] *excl* = **hurrah, hurray**

hoot [huːt] *vi* (AUT: horn) クラクションを鳴らす kurákùshon wo narásù; (siren) 鳴る narú; (owl) ほーほーと鳴く hōhō to nakú

hooter [huː'təːr] *n* (*BRIT*: AUT) クラクション kurákùshon, ホーン hôn; (NAUT, factory) 警報機 keíhōkì

hoover [huː'vəːr] ®(*BRIT*) *n* (vacuum cleaner) (真空) 掃除機 (shiñkū)sōjikì
♦*vt* (carpet) ...に掃除機を掛ける ...ni sōjikì wo kakérù

hooves [huvz] *npl* of **hoof**

hop [hɑːp] *vi* (on one foot) 片足で跳ぶ katáashi de tobù; (bird) ぴょんぴょん跳ぶ pyónpyon tobú

hope [houp] *vt*: **to hope that/to do** ...だと〔する事を〕望む ...da to 〔surú kotò wo〕nozómù
♦*vi* 希望する kibō suru
♦*n* (desire) 望み nozómi; (expectation) 期待 kitái; (aspiration) 希望 kibō
I hope so/not そうだ〔でない〕といいが sō dà 〔de náì〕to íi ga

hopeful [houp'fəl] *adj* (person) 楽観的な rakkánteki na; (situation) 見込みのある mikómi no arù

hopefully [houp'fəliː] *adv* (expectantly) 期待して kitái shite; (one hopes) うまくいけば úmàku ikébà

hopeless [houp'lis] *adj* (grief, situation, future) 絶望的な zetsúbōteki na; (person: useless) 無能な munôna

hops [hɑːps] *npl* (BOT) ホップ hóppù

horde [hɔːrd] *n* (of critics, people) 大群 taígun

horizon [həraiʹzən] *n* (skyline) 水平線 suíheìsen

horizontal [hɔːrizɑːn'təl] *adj* 水平の suí-

hei no

hormone [hɔːrˈmoun] *n* (BIO) ホルモン hórùmon

horn [hɔːrn] *n* (of animal) 角 tsunó; (material) 角質 kakúshitsu; (MUS: *also*: **French horn**) ホルン hórùn; (AUT) クラクション kurákùshon, ホーン hồn

hornet [hɔːrˈnit] *n* (insect) スズメバチ suzúmebàchi

horny [hɔːrˈniː] (*inf*) *adj* (aroused) セックスをしたがっている sékkùsu wo shitágatte irú

horoscope [hɔːrˈəskoup] *n* (ASTROLOGY) 星占い hoshíurànai

horrendous [hɔːrenˈdəs] *adj* (crime) 恐ろしい osóroshiì; (error) ショッキングな shókkìngu na

horrible [hɔːrˈəbəl] *adj* (unpleasant: color, food, mess) ひどい hidóì; (terrifying: scream, dream) 恐ろしい osóroshiì

horrid [hɔːrˈid] *adj* (person, place, thing) いやな iyá na

horrify [hɔːrˈəfai] *vt* (appall) ぞっとさせる zóttò sasérù

horror [hɔːrˈəːr] *n* (alarm) 恐怖 kyófù; (abhorrence) 憎悪 zồo; (of battle, warfare) むごたらしさ mugótarashisà

horror film *n* ホラー映画 horáeìga

hors d'oeuvre [ɔːr dəːrv'] *n* (CULIN: *gen*) 前菜 zeńsai; (: Western food) オードブル ồdobùru

horse [hɔːrs] *n* 馬 umá

horseback [hɔːrsˈbæk]: **on horseback** *adj* 乗馬の jồba no

◆*adv* 馬に乗って umá ni nottè

horse chestnut *n* (tree) トチノキ tochí no kì; (nut) とちの実 tochí no mì

horseman/woman [hɔːrsˈmən/wumən] (*pl* **horsemen/women**) *n* (rider) 馬の乗り手 umá nò norìte

horsepower [hɔːrsˈpauəːr] *n* (of engine, car etc) 馬力 baríki

horse-racing [hɔːrsˈreisiŋ] *n* (SPORT) 競馬 keíba

horseradish [hɔːrsˈrædiʃ] *n* (BOT, CULIN) ワサビダイコン wasábidaìkon, セイヨウワサビ seíyōwasàbi

horseshoe [hɔːrsˈʃuː] *n* てい鉄 teítetsu

horticulture [hɔːrˈtəkʌltʃəːr] *n* 園芸 eńgei

hose [houz] *n* ホース hồsu

hosiery [houˈʒəːriː] *n* (in shop) 靴下類 kutsúshitaruì

hospice [hɑːsˈpis] *n* (for the dying) ホスピス hósùpisu

hospitable [hɑːspitˈəbəl] *adj* (person) 持て成しの良い moténashi no yoì; (behavior) 手厚い teátsuì

hospital [hɑːsˈpitəl] *n* 病院 byốin

hospitality [hɑːspətælˈitiː] *n* (of host, welcome) 親切な持て成し shińsetsu nà moténashi

host [houst] *n* (at party, dinner etc) 主人 shújìn, ホスト hósùto; (TV, RADIO) 司会者 shikáìsha; (REL) 御聖体 go-séitai; (large number): **a host of** 多数の tasú no

hostage [hɑːsˈtidʒ] *n* (prisoner) 人質 hitójichi

hostel [hɑːsˈtəl] *n* (for homeless etc) 収容所 shúyòjo; (*also*: **youth hostel**) ユースホステル yūsuhosùteru

hostess [housˈtis] *n* (at party, dinner etc) 女主人 ońnashujìn, ホステス hósùtesu; (*BRIT*: air hostess) スチュワーデス suchúwàdesu; (TV, RADIO) (女性) 司会者 (joséi)shikáìsha

hostile [hɑːsˈtəl] *adj* (person, attitude: aggressive) 敵対する tekítai suru, 敵意のある tékì no árù; (: unwelcoming): **hostile to** ...に対して排他的な ...ni táìshite haítateki na; (conditions, environment) か酷な kakóku na

hostilities [hɑːstilˈətiːz] *npl* (fighting) 戦闘 seńtó

hostility [hɑːstilˈətiː] *n* (antagonism) 敵対 tekítai, 敵意 tékì-i; (lack of welcome) 排他的態度 haítatekitaìdo; (of conditions, environment) か酷さ kakókusa

hot [hɑːt] *adj* (moderately hot) 暖かい atátakaì; (very hot) 熱い atsúi; (weather, room etc) 暑い atsúi; (spicy: food) 辛い karáì; (fierce: temper, contest, argument etc) 激しい hagéshiì

it is hot (weather) 暑い atsúì; (object) 熱い atsúì

I am hot (person) 私は暑い watákushi wà atsúî

he is hot 彼は暑がっている kárè wa atsúgatte irú

hotbed [hɑːt'bed] *n* (*fig*) 温床 oñshō

hot dog *n* (snack) ホットドッグ hottó-doggù

hotel [houtel'] *n* ホテル hótèru

hotelier [ɔːteljei'] *n* (owner) ホテルの経営者 hótèru no keíeîsha; (manager) ホテルの支配人 hótèru no shiháînin

hotheaded [hɑːt'hedid] *adj* (impetuous) 気の早い kí no hayáî

hothouse [hɑːt'haus] *n* (BOT) 温室 oñshitsu

hot line *n* (POL) ホットライン hottóraìn

hotly [hɑːt'liː] *adv* (speak, contest, deny) 激しく hagéshikù

hotplate [hɑːt'pleit] *n* (on cooker) ホットプレート hottópurèto

hot-water bottle [hɑːtwɔːt'əːr-] *n* 湯たんぽ yutáñpo

hound [haund] *vt* (harass, persecute) 迫害する hakúgai suru
♦*n* (dog) 猟犬 ryóken, ハウンド haúndo

hour [au'əːr] *n* (sixty minutes) 1時間 ichí jikàn; (time) 時間 jíkàn

hourly [au əːr'liː] *adj* (service, rate) 1時間当りの ichí jikan atàri no

house [*n* haus *vb* hauz] *n* (home) 家 ié, うち uchí; (household) 家族 kázòku; (company) 会社 kaísha; (POL) 議院 gíin; (THEATER) 客席 kyakúseki; (dynasty) ...家 ...kê
♦*vt* (person) ...に住宅を与える ...ni júutaku wò atáerù; (collection) 収容する shúyō suru

on the house (*fig*) サービスで sàbisu de

house arrest *n* (POL, MIL) 軟禁 nañkin

houseboat [haus'bout] *n* 屋形船 yakáta-bunè, ハウスボート haúsubòto ◊住宅用の船を指す júutakuyō no funè wo sásù

housebound [haus'baund] *adj* (invalid) 家から出られない ié kara derárenaî

housebreaking [haus'breikiŋ] *n* 家宅侵入 kátakushiñnyū

housecoat [haus'kout] *n* 部屋着 heyági

household [haus'hould] *n* (inhabitants)

家族 kazóku; (home) 家 ié

housekeeper [haus'kiːpəːr] *n* (servant) 家政婦 kaséifu

housekeeping [haus'kiːpiŋ] *n* (work) 家事 kájì; (money) 家計費 kakéìhi

house-warming party [haus'wɔːrmiŋ-] *n* 新居祝いのパーティ shiñkyo-iwaî no pâti

housewife [haus'waif] (*pl* **housewives**) *n* 主婦 shúfu

housework [haus'wəːrk] *n* (chores) 家事 kájì

housing [hau'ziŋ] *n* (houses) 住宅 júutaku; (provision) 住宅供給 júutakukyōkyū

housing development *n* 住宅団地 júuta-kudañchi

housing estate (*BRIT*) *n* 住宅団地 júuta-kudañchi

hovel [hʌv'əl] *n* (shack) あばら屋 abára-ya

hover [hʌv'əːr] *vi* (bird, insect) 空中に止る kúuchū ni tomarú

hovercraft [hʌv'əːrkræft] *n* (vehicle) ホバークラフト hobákurafùto

KEYWORD

how [hau] *adv* **1** (in what way) どうdò, どの様に donó yō ni, どうやって dó yattè

how did you do it? どうやってそれができたんですか dó yattè soré gà dekítan desù ká

I know how you did it あなたがどの様にしてそれができたか私には分かっています anáta ga donó yō ni shite soré gà dekíta kà watákushi ni wà wakátte imasù

to know how to do something ...の仕方を知っている ...no shikáta wò shitté irù

how is school? 学校はどうですか gakkō wa dó desu ká

how was the film? 映画はどうでしたか eíga wa dó deshita ká

how are you? お元気ですか o-géñki desu ká

2 (to what degree) どのくらい donó kurai

how much milk? どのくらいのミルク

donó kurai nò mírúku
how many people? 何人の人々 nánnin no hitôbito
how much does it cost? 値段はいくらですか nedán wà íkùra desu ká
how long have you been here? いつらからここにいますか ítsù kara kokó nì imásù ká
how old are you? お幾つですか o-íkùtsu desu ká
how tall is he? 彼の身長はどれくらいですか kárè no shifíchō wà doré gùrai desu ká
how lovely/awful! なんて美しい〔ひどい〕nánte utsúkushiì〔hidóì〕

---

howl [haul] *vi* (animal) 遠ぼえする tôboe suru; (baby, person) 大声で泣く ôgoè de nakú; (wind) うなる unárú

H.P. [eitʃpi:'] *abbr* = **hire purchase**

h.p. *abbr* = **horsepower**

HQ [eitʃkju:'] *abbr* = **headquarters**

hub [hʌb] *n* (of wheel) ハブ hábù; (*fig*: centre) 中心 chûshin

hubbub [hʌb'ʌb] *n* (din, commotion) どよめき doyómeki

hubcap [hʌb'kæp] *n* (AUT) ホイールキャップ hoírukyappù

huddle [hʌd'əl] *vi*: *to huddle together* (for heat, comfort) 体を寄せ合う karáda wò yoséaù

hue [hju:] *n* (color) 色 iró; (shade of color) 色合い iróaì

hue and cry *n* (outcry) 騒ぎ sáwàgi

huff [hʌf] *n*: *in a huff* (offended) 怒っておくって okôtte

hug [hʌg] *vt* (person, thing) 抱締める dakíshimerù

huge [hju:dʒ] *adj* (enormous) ばく大な bakúdai na

hulk [hʌlk] *n* (ship) 廃船 haísen; (person) 図体ばかり大きい人 zûtai bakari ôkiì hitô, うどの大木 udo no taiboku; (building etc) ばかでかい物 bakádekai monò

hull [hʌl] *n* (of ship) 船体 sefítai, ハル hárù

hullo [həlou'] *excl* = **hello**

hum [hʌm] *vt* (tune, song) ハミングで歌う hamingu de utau
♦*vi* (person) ハミングする hámìngu suru; (machine) ぶーんと鳴る bûn to narú; (insect) ぶんぶんいう bûnbun iu

human [hju:'mən] *adj* (existence, body) 人の hitô no, 人間の nifígen no; (weakness, emotion) 人間的な nifígenteki na
♦*n* (person) 人 hitô, 人間 nifígen

humane [hju:mein'] *adj* (treatment, slaughter) 苦痛を与えない kutsû wò atáenai

humanitarian [hju:mænite:r'i:ən] *adj* (aid, principles) 人道的な jifídōteki na

humanity [hju:mæn'iti:] *n* (mankind) 人類 jifírui, 人間 nifígen; (human nature) 人間性 nifígensei; (humaneness, kindness) 思いやり omóiyari

humble [hʌm'bəl] *adj* (modest) 謙虚な kêñkyo na; (lowly: background) 身分の低い míbùn no hikûì
♦*vt* (humiliate, crush) ...の高慢な鼻を折る ...no kôman na haná wò órù

humbug [hʌm'bʌg] *n* (of statement, writing) でたらめ detárame; (*BRIT*: sweet) はっかあめ hakká-ame

humdrum [hʌm'drʌm] *adj* (dull, boring) 退屈な tafkutsu na

humid [hju:'mid] *adj* (atmosphere, climate) 湿度の高い shitsúdò no takáì

humidity [hju:mid'əti:] *n* 湿度 shitsúdò

humiliate [hju:mil'i:eit] *vt* (rival, person) ...の高慢な鼻を折る ...no kôman na haná wò órù

humiliation [hju:mili:ei'ʃən] *n* (embarrassment) 恥 hajî; (situation, experience) 恥辱 chijôku

humility [hju:mil'əti:] *n* (modesty) 謙そん kefíson

humor [hju:'mə:r] (*BRIT* **humour**) *n* (comedy, mood) ユーモア yûmoa
♦*vt* (child, person) ...の機嫌を取る ...no kigén wo tôrù

humorous [hju:'mə:rəs] *adj* (remark, book) おどけた odôketa; (person) ユーモアのある yûmoa no árù

hump [hʌmp] *n* (in ground) 小山 koyáma; (of camel: *also* deformity) こぶ kobú

humpbacked [hʌmp'bækt] *adj*: *hump-*

backed bridge 反り橋 soríhàshi

hunch [hʌntʃ] *n* (premonition) 直感 chokkán

hunchback [hʌntʃˈbæk] *n* せむしの人 semúshi nò hitó ◇べつ称 besshố

hunched [hʌntʃt] *adj* (bent, stooped: shoulders) 曲げた magéta; (: person) 肩を落した kátà wo otóshità

hundred [hʌnˈdrid] *num* 百（の）hyakú (no); (before *n*): *a/one hundred books* 100冊の本 hyakúsatsu nò hón: *a/one hundred people* 100人の人 hyakúnin nò hitó: *a/one hundred dollars* 100ドル hyakú doru

hundreds of 何百もの nañbyaku mo no

hundredweight [hʌnˈdridweit] *n* (*US = 45.3 kg, 100 lb; BRIT = 50.8 kg, 112 lb*)

hung [hʌŋ] *pt, pp of* **hang**

Hungarian [hʌŋɡəˈri:ən] *adj* ハンガリーの hañgarí no; (LING) ハンガリー語の hañgaríŋo no
♦*n* (person) ハンガリー人 hañgaríjìn; (LING) ハンガリー語 hañgaríŋo

Hungary [hʌŋˈɡəːri:] *n* ハンガリー hañgarí

hunger [hʌŋˈɡəːr] *n* (lack of food) 空腹 kúfuku; (starvation) 飢餓 kígà
♦*vi*: *to hunger for* (desire) ...に飢える ...ni uérù

hunger strike *n* ハンガーストライキ hañgāsutoraíki, ハンスト hañsuto

hungry [hʌŋˈɡri:] *adj* (person, animal) 空腹な kúfuku na; (keen, avid): *hungry for* ...に飢えた ...ni uétà

to be hungry おなかがすいた onáka ga suità

hunk [hʌŋk] *n* (of bread etc) 塊 katámari

hunt [hʌnt] *vt* (for food: subj: animal) 捜し求める sagáshimotomerù, あさる asárù; (SPORT) 狩る kárù, ...の狩りをする ...no kárì wo suru; (criminal, fugitive) 捜す sagásu, 捜索する sósaku suru
♦*vi* (search): *to hunt (for)* (...を) 捜す (...wo) sagásu; (SPORT) (...の) 狩りをする (...no) kárì wo suru
♦*n* (for food: *also* SPORT) 狩り kárì; (search) 捜す事 sagásu kotò; (for crimi-

nal) 捜索 sósaku

hunter [hʌnˈtəːr] *n* (sportsman) ハンター hañtā

hunting [hʌnˈtiŋ] *n* (for food: *also* SPORT) 狩り kárì

hurdle [həːrˈdəl] *n* (difficulty) 障害 shốgai; (SPORT) ハードル hấdoru

hurl [həːrl] *vt* (object) 投げる nagérù; (insult, abuse) 浴びせ掛ける abísekakerù

hurrah [həˈrɑː] *n* (as cheer) 歓声 kañsei

hurray [həreí] *n* = **hurrah**

hurricane [həːrˈəkein] *n* (storm) ハリケーン haríkèn

hurried [həːrˈiːd] *adj* (hasty, rushed) 大急ぎの ốisògi no

hurriedly [həːrˈiːdliː] *adv* 大急ぎで ốisògi de

hurry [həːrˈiː] *n* (haste, rush) 急ぎ isógi
♦*vi* (*also*: **hurry up**: hasten, rush) 急ぐ isógù
♦*vt* (*also*: **hurry up**: person) 急がせる isógaserù; (: work) 急いでする isóide suru

to be in a hurry 急いでいる isóide irù

hurt [həːrt] (*pt, pp* **hurt**) *vt* (cause pain to) 痛める itámerù; (injure, *fig*) 傷付ける kizútsukerù
♦*vi* (be painful) 痛む itámù

it hurts! 痛い！itái!

hurtful [həːrtˈfəl] *adj* (remark) 傷付ける様な kizútsukeru yố na

hurtle [həːrˈtəl] *vi*: *to hurtle past* (train, car) 猛スピードで通り過ぎる mốsupìdo de tốrisugirù

to hurtle down (fall) 落ちる ochírù

husband [hʌzˈbənd] *n* 夫 ottó

hush [hʌʃ] *n* (silence) 沈黙 chiñmoku; (stillness) 静けさ shizúkesà
♦*vt* (silence) 黙らせる damáraserù

hush! 静かに shízùka ni

hush up *vt* (scandal etc) もみ消す momíkesù

husk [hʌsk] *n* (of wheat, rice) 殻 kará; (of maize) 皮 kawá

husky [hʌsˈkiː] *adj* (voice) しわがれた shiwágaretà, ハスキーな hásùkī na
♦*n* (dog) ハスキー hásùkī

hustle [hʌsˈəl] *vt* (hurry) 急がせる isóga-

serù

♦*n: hustle and bustle* 雑踏 zattô

hut [hʌt] *n* (house) 小屋 koyá; (shed) 物置 monô-oki

hutch [hʌtʃ] *n* (*also*: **rabbit hutch**) ウサギ小屋 uságigoya

hyacinth [hai'əsinθ] *n* ヒヤシンス hiyáshiñsu

hybrid [hai'brid] *n* (plant, animal) 交雑種 kôzatsushù, ハイブリッド haíbɯriddò; (mixture) 混成物 koñseibùtsu

hydrant [hai'drənt] *n* (*also*: **fire hydrant**) 消火栓 shôkasen

hydraulic [haidrɔ:'lik] *adj* (pressure, system) 油圧の yuátsu no

hydroelectric [haidrouilek'trik] *adj* (energy, complex) 水力発電の suíryokuhatsùden no

hydrofoil [hai'drəfoil] *n* (boat) 水中翼船 suíchùyokùsen

hydrogen [hai'drədʒən] *n* (CHEM) 水素 suîso

hyena [haii:'nə] *n* ハイエナ haíena

hygiene [hai'dʒi:n] *n* (cleanliness) 衛生 eísei

hygienic [haidʒi:en'ik] *adj* 衛生的な eíseiteki na

hymn [him] *n* 賛美歌 sañbika

hype [haip] (*inf*) *n* 売込み口上 urîkomi-kôjô

hypermarket [hai'pə:rmɑ:rkit] (*BRIT*) *n* 大型スーパー ôgatasūpā

hyphen [hai'fən] *n* (dash) ハイフン hâifun

hypnosis [hipnou'sis] *n* 催眠 saímin

hypnotic [hipnɑ:t'ik] *adj* (trance) 催眠術の saímiñjutsu no; (rhythms) 催眠的な saímiñteki na

hypnotism [hip'nətizəm] *n* 催眠術 saímiñjutsu

hypnotist [hip'nətist] *n* (person) 催眠術師 saíminjutsushî

hypnotize [hip'nətaiz] *vt* (MED etc) ...に催眠術を掛ける ...ni saímiñjutsu wo kakérù; (*fig*: mesmerise) 魅惑する miwáku suru

hypochondriac [haipəkɑ:n'dri:æk] *n* 心気症患者 shiñkishōkañja

hypocrisy [hipɑ:k'rəsi:] *n* (falseness, in-sincerity) 偽善 gizén

hypocrite [hip'əkrit] *n* (phoney) 偽善者 gizéñsha

hypocritical [hipəkrit'ikəl] *adj* (person) 偽善の gizén no; (behavior) 偽善者的な gizéñshateki na

hypothermia [haipəθə:r'mi:ə] *n* (MED) 低体温症 teftaioñshō

hypothesis [haipɑ:θ'əsis] (*pl* **hypotheses**) *n* (theory) 仮説 kasétsu

hypothetic(al) [haipəθet'ik(əl)] *adj* (question, situation) 仮定の katéi no

hysteria [histi'ri:ə] *n* (panic: *also* MED) ヒステリー hisúterī

hysterical [histe:r'ikəl] *adj* (person, rage) ヒステリックな hisúterikkù na; (situation: funny) 笑いが止らない様な warái gà tomáranai yô na

hysterical laughter ばか笑い bakáwarài

hysterics [histe:r'iks] *npl* (anger, panic) ヒステリー hisúterī; (laughter) 大笑い ô-warài

I

I [ai] *pron* 私は〔が〕watákushi wa〔ga〕

ice [ais] *n* (frozen water) 氷 kôri; (*also*: **ice cream**) アイスクリーム aísukurîmu

♦*vt* (cake) ...にアイシングを掛ける ...ni âîshingu wo kakérù

♦*vi* (*also*: **ice over**, **ice up**: road, window etc) 氷に覆われる kôri nì ôwarerù

iceberg [ais'bə:rg] *n* 氷山 hyôzan

icebox [ais'bɑ:ks] *n* (*US*: fridge) 冷蔵庫 reízōko; (*BRIT*: compartment) 冷凍室 reítôshitsu; (insulated box) クーラー kūrā

ice cream *n* アイスクリーム aísukurîmu

ice cube *n* 角氷 kakúgôri

iced [aist] *adj* (cake) アイシングを掛けた âîshingu wo kâkèta; (beer) 冷した hiyáshìta

iced tea アイスティー aísutî

ice hockey *n* (SPORT) アイスホッケー aísuhokkê

Iceland [ais'lənd] *n* アイスランド aísurañ-

do

ice lolly [-lɑːˈliː] (BRIT) n アイスキャンディー aísukyandī

ice rink n スケートリンク suketorinku

ice-skating [aisˈskeitiŋ] n アイススケート afsusukēto

icicle [aiˈsikəl] n (on gutter, ledge etc) つらら tsurára

icing [aiˈsiŋ] n (CULIN) 砂糖衣 satőgorðmo, アイシング aíshingu

icing sugar (BRIT) n 粉砂糖 konázatð

icon [aiˈkɑːn] n (REL) 聖像画 seízðga, イコン íkon

icy [aiˈsiː] adj (air, water, temperature) 冷たい tsumétai; (road) 氷に覆われた kőri ni őwareta

I'd [aid] = **I would; I had**

idea [aidiːˈə] n (scheme, notion) 考え kañgae; (opinion) 意見 íkèn; (objective) つもり tsumőri

ideal [aidiːˈəl] n (principle) 理想 riső; (epitome) 模範 mohán
♦adj (perfect) 理想的な risőteki na

idealist [aidiːˈəlist] n 理想主義者 risőshugishà

identical [aidenˈtikəl] adj 同一の dőitsu no

identification [aidentəfəkeiˈʃən] n (process) 識別 shikíbetsu; (of person, dead body) 身元の確認 mimőto nð kakúnin
(means of) identification 身分証明書 mibúnshōmeĩsho

identify [aidenˈtəfai] vt (recognize) 見分ける miwákerù; (distinguish) 識別する shikíbetsu suru; (associate): ***to identify someone/something (with)*** ...と (...と) 関連付ける ...wo (...to) kañrenzukerù

Identikit [aidenˈtakit] ® n: ***Identikit (picture)*** モンタージュ写真 moñtājushashìn

identity [aidenˈtiti] n (of person, suspect etc) 身元 mimőto, 正体 shőtai; (of group, culture, nation etc) 特性 tokúsei

identity card n 身分証明書 mibúnshōmeĩsho

ideology [aidiːɑːlˈədʒiː] n (beliefs) 思想

shiső, イデオロギー ídeorðgī

idiom [idˈiːəm] n (style) 作風 sakúfū; (phrase) 熟語 jukúgo, イディオム ídiomu

idiomatic [idiːəmætˈik] adj 熟語的な jukúgoteki na

idiosyncrasy [idiːəsiŋˈkrəsiː] n (foible) 特異性 tokúisei

idiot [idˈiːət] n (fool) ばか bákà

idiotic [idiːɑːtˈik] adj (stupid) ばかな bákà na

idle [aiˈdəl] adj (inactive) 暇な himá na; (lazy) 怠惰な taída na; (unemployed) 失業中の shitsúgyōchū no; (machinery) 動いていない ugőite inái; (factory) 休業中の kyűgyōchū no; (question, conversation) 無意味な muími na; (pleasure) むなしい munáshiĩ
♦vi (machine, engine) 空回りする káramawàri suru, アイドリングする aídoriñgu suru

idle away vt: ***to idle away the time*** のらくらする nőràkura suru

idol [aiˈdəl] n (hero) アイドル aídoru; (REL) 偶像 gűzō

idolize [aiˈdəlaiz] vt ...に心酔する ...ni shifñsui suru

idyllic [aidilˈik] adj のどかな nődðka na

i.e. [aiiˈ] abbr (= id est: that is) 即ち sunáwàchi

KEYWORD

---

if [if] conj **1** (conditional use: given that, providing that etc) (もし)...すれば〔するならば〕(móshì) ...surébà〔surú naràba〕
I'll go if you come with me あなたが一緒に来れば、私は行ってもいいです anátà ga isshő ni kurèba watákushi wà itté mò íi desu
I'd be pleased if you could do it あなたがそれをやって下されば私は助かりますが anátà ga soré wð yatté kudasarèba watákushi wà tasúkarimasù ga
if anyone comes in だれかが入って来れば dárèka ga háìtte kurèba
if necessary 必要であれば hitsúyō de arèba
if I were you 私があなただったら watákushi gà anátà dáttàra

2 (whenever) ...の時...no tókì
*if we are in Scotland, we always go
to see her* スコットランドにいる時私た
ちは必ず彼女に会いに行きます sukótto-
rañdo ni irú tokì watákushitàchi wa
kanárazù kánòjo ni áì ni ikímasù

3 (although): *(even) if* たとえ...でも tatôè ...dé mò
*I am determined to finish it, (even)
if it takes all week* たとえ今週いっぱ
いかかっても私はこの仕事を片付けたい
tatôè koñshū ippài kakátte mò watákushi wà konó shigoto wò katázuketaì
I like it, (even) if you don't あなた
がいやでも、私はこれが好きです anátà
ga iyá de mò, watákushi wà koré gà
sukí desù

4 (whether) ...かどうか ...ka dò ka
I don't know if he is here 彼がここに
いるかどうか私には分かりません kárè
ga kokó nì irú ka dòka watákushi ni wà
wakárimaseñ
ask him if he can come 来られるかど
うか彼に聞いて下さい koráreru ka dò
ka kárè ni kííte kudasaì

5: *if so/not* そうであれば〔なければ〕só
de arèba〔nakerèba〕
if only ...であったらなあ ...dè áttara ná
if only I could 私にそれができたらな
あ watákushi nì soré gà dékìtara ná
¶ *see also* **as**

igloo [ig'lu:] *n* イグルー ígùrū

ignite [ignait'] *vt* (set fire to) ...に火をつ
ける ...ni hí wò tsukérù
♦*vi* 燃出す moédasù

ignition [igniʃ'ən] *n* (AUT: process) 点火
teñka; (: mechanism) 点火装置 teñkasô-
chi
to switch on/off the ignition エンジ
ンスイッチを入れる〔切る〕eñjinsuìtchi
wo irérù〔kírù〕

ignition key *n* (AUT) カーキー kâkî

ignorance [ig'nə:rəns] *n* (lack of knowledge) 無知 múchì

ignorant [ig'nə:rənt] *adj* (uninformed,
unaware) 無学な múgàku na, 無知な mú-
chì na

to be ignorant of (subject, events) ...を
知らない ...wo shiránaî

ignore [ignɔːr'] *vt* (person, advice, event,
fact) 無視する mushí suru

I'll [ail] = **I will**; **I shall**

ill [il] *adj* (sick) 病気の byóki no; (harmful: effects) 悪い warúî
♦*n* (evil) 悪 ákù; (trouble) 凶兆 kyóchō
♦*adv*: *to speak ill of someone* ...の悪口
を言う ...no warúgùchi wo iú
to think ill (of someone) (...を) 悪
く思う (...wo) warúkù omóù
to be taken ill 病気になる byóki ni
narù, 倒れる taórerù

ill-advised [il'ædvaizd'] *adj* (decision) 軽
率な keísotsu na; (person) 無分別な mu-
fúñbetsu na

ill-at-ease [il'əti:z'] *adj* (awkward, uncomfortable) 落着かない ochítsukanaî

illegal [ili:'gəl] *adj* (not legal: activity,
organization, immigrant etc) 不法の fu-
hô no

illegible [iledʒ'əbəl] *adj* (writing) 読めな
い yoménaî

illegitimate [ilidʒit'əmit] *adj*: *an illegitimate child* 私生児 shiséiji

ill-fated [il'fei'tid] *adj* (doomed) 不運な
fúùn na

ill feeling *n* (animosity, bitterness) 恨み
urámi

illicit [ilis'it] *adj* (unlawful: sale, association, substance) 不法の fuhô no

illiterate [ilit'ə:rit] *adj* (person) 文盲の
moñmô no; (letter) 無学な múgàku na

ill-mannered [il'mæn'ə:rd] *adj* (rude:
child etc) 行儀の悪い gyôgi no warùi

illness [il'nis] *n* 病気 byóki

illogical [ilɑːdʒ'ikəl] *adj* (fear, reaction,
argument) 不合理な fugôri na

ill-treat [il'tri:t] *vt* (child, pet, prisoner)
虐待する gyakútai suru

illuminate [ilu:'məneit] *vt* (light up:
room, street) 明るくする akárukù suru;
(decorate with lights: building, monument etc) ライトアップする raítoappù
suru; (shine light on) 照らす terásù

illumination [ilu:mənei'ʃən] *n* (lighting)
照明 shômei

illuminations [ilu:mənei'ʃənz] *npl* (decorative lights) 電飾 deñshoku, イルミネーション irúmiñeshon

illusion [ilu:'ʒən] *n* (false idea, belief) 錯覚 sakkáku; (trick) いんちき iñchiki, トリック toríkkù

illusory [ilu:'sə:ri:] *adj* (hopes, prospects) 錯覚の sakkáku no

illustrate [il'əstreit] *vt* (point) 例を挙げて説明する rei wò agéte setsúmei suru; (book) ...に挿絵を入れる ...ni sashíe wo iréru; (talk) ...にスライド（など）を使う ...ni suráido (nádò) wo tsukáu

illustration [iləstrei'ʃən] *n* (act of illustrating) 図解 zukái; (example) 例 reí; (in book) 挿絵 sashíe

illustrious [ilʌs'tri:əs] *adj* (career) 輝かしい kagáyakashiì; (predecessor) 著名な choméi na

ill will *n* (hostility) 恨み urámi

I'm [aim] = **I am**

image [im'idʒ] *n* (picture) 像 zṓ; (public face) イメージ ímēji; (reflection) 姿 sugáta

imagery [im'idʒri:] *n* (in writing, painting etc) 比ゆ híyu

imaginary [imædʒ'əne:ri:] *adj* (being, danger) 想像上の sṓzōjō no

imagination [imædʒənei'ʃən] *n* (part of the mind) 想像 sṓzō; (inventiveness) 想像力 sṓzōryoku

imaginative [imædʒ'ənətiv] *adj* (person) 想像力に富んだ sṓzōryoku ni toñdà; (solution) 奇抜な kibátsu na

imagine [imædʒ'in] *vt* (visualise) 想像する sṓzō suru; (dream) ...だと錯覚する ...da to sakkáku suru; (suppose) ...だと思う ...da to omóu

imbalance [imbæl'əns] *n* (inequality) 不均等 fukíhìtō, アンバランス añbaránsu

imbecile [im'bəsil] *n* (idiot) ばか bákà

imbue [imbju:'] *vt*: **to imbue someone/something with** ...に ...を吹き込む ...ni ...wo fukíkomù

imitate [im'əteit] *vt* (copy) まねる manérù; (mimic) ...の物まねをする ...no monómane wò suru

imitation [imətei'ʃən] *n* (act of copying) まね mané; (act of mimicking) 物まね monómane; (copy) 偽物 nisémono

immaculate [imæk'jəlit] *adj* (room) 汚れ一つない yogóre hitotsù náì; (appearance) 清潔な seíketsu na; (piece of work) 完璧な kañpeki na; (REL) 原罪のない geñzai nò náì

immaterial [imæti:'ri:əl] *adj* (unimportant) どうでもいい dṓ dè mo íi

immature [imətur'] *adj* (fruit, cheese) 熟していない jukú shite inái; (organism) 未成熟の miséijuku no; (person) 未熟な mijúku na

immediate [imi:'di:it] *adj* (reaction, answer) 即時の sokúji no; (pressing: need) 緊迫した kíñpaku shita; (nearest: neighborhood, family) 最も近い mottómò chikáì

immediately [imi:'di:itli:] *adv* (at once) 直ぐに súgù ni, 直ちに tádàchi ni; (directly) 真っ直ぐに massúgù ni

immediately next to ...の直ぐ隣に ...no súgù tonárì ni

immense [imens'] *adj* (huge: size) 巨大な kyodái na; (: progress, importance) 大変な taíheñ na

immerse [imə:rs'] *vt* (submerge) 浸す hitásù

to be immersed in (*fig*: work, study etc) ...に熱中している ...ni netchū shite irú

to be immersed in thought 考え込んでいる kañgaekoñde irú

immersion heater [imə:r'ʒən-] (*BRIT*) *n* 投込式湯沸かし器 tṓnyūshiki yuwakashikí

immigrant [im'əgrənt] *n* 移民 imíñ

immigration [iməgrei'ʃən] *n* (process) 移住 ijū; (control: at airport etc) 入国管理局 nyūkoku kañrikyoku

imminent [im'ənənt] *adj* (arrival, departure) 差迫った sashísematta

immobile [imou'bəl] *adj* (motionless) 動かない ugókanaì

immobilize [imou'bəlaiz] *vt* (person, machine) 動けなくする ugókenakù suru

immoral [imɔːr'əl] *adj* (person, behavior, idea etc) 不道徳な fudōtoku na

immorality [iməræl'iti:] *n* 不道徳 fudō-toku

immortal [imɔ:r'təl] *adj* (living for ever: god) 永遠に生きる eíen ní ikírù; (unforgettable: poetry, fame) 不滅の fumétsu no

immortalize [imɔ:r'təlaiz] *vt* (hero, event) ...に不朽の名声を与える ...ni fukyū no meísei wo atáerù

immune [imju:n'] *adj*: **immune (to)** (disease) (...に) 免疫がある (...ni) meñ-eki ga arù; (flattery) (...が) ...に通じない (...ga) ...ni tsūjinài; (criticism, attack) ...に (...の) しようがない ...ni (...no) shíyō ga nai

immunity [imju:'niti:] *n* (to disease etc) 免疫 meñ-eki; (from prosecution, taxation etc) 免除 méñjo

diplomatic immunity 外交特権 gaíkoutokkèn

immunize [im'jənaiz] *vt* (MED: *gen*) ...に免疫性を与える ...ni meñ-ekisei wò atáerù; (with injection) ...に予防注射をする ...ni yobōchūsha wo suru

imp [imp] *n* (small devil) 小鬼 ko-óni; (child) いたずらっ子 itázurakkò

impact [im'pækt] *n* (of bullet, crash) 衝撃 shōgeki, インパクト íñpakuto; (of law, measure) 影響 eíkyō

impair [impe:r'] *vt* (vision, judgement) 損なう sokónaù

impale [impeil'] *vt* くし刺しにする kushízashi ni suru

impart [impɑ:rt'] *vt* (make known: information) 与える atáerù; (bestow: flavor) 添える soérù

impartial [impɑ:r'ʃəl] *adj* (judge, observer) 公平な kōhei na

impassable [impæs'əbəl] *adj* (river) 渡れない watárenaî; (road, route etc) 通行不可能な tsūkōfukanō na

impasse [im'pæs] *n* (in war, negotiations) 行き詰り ikízumari

impassive [impæs'iv] *adj* (face, expression) 無表情な muhyōjō na

impatience [impei'ʃəns] *n* (annoyance due to waiting) じれったさ jiréttasà; (irritation) 短気 táñki; (eagerness) 意欲 f-

yòku

impatient [impei'ʃənt] *adj* (annoyed by waiting) じれったい jiréttaî; (irritable) 短気な táñki na; (eager, in a hurry): **impatient to ...** ...従っている ...shitágatte irù

to get/grow impatient もどかしがる modōkashigarù

impeccable [impek'əbəl] *adj* (perfect: manners, dress) 申分のない mōshibùn no naî

impede [impi:d'] *vt* (progress, development etc) 妨げる samátagerù

impediment [impe'dəmənt] *n* (to growth, movement) 障害 shōgai; (*also*: **speech impediment**) 言語障害 geñgoshō-gai

impending [impen'diŋ] *adj* (arrival, catastrophe) 差迫る sashísemarù

impenetrable [impen'itrəbəl] *adj* (wall, jungle) 通れない tōrenaî; (*fig*: law, text) 難解な nañkai na

imperative [imper'ətiv] *adj* (need) 緊急の kiñkyū no; (tone) 命令的な meíreiteki na

♦*n* (LING) 命令形 meíreikei

imperceptible [impərsep'təbəl] *adj* (change, movement) 気付かれない kizúkarenaî

imperfect [impər'fikt] *adj* (goods, system etc) 不完全な fukánzen na

♦*n* (LING: *also*: **imperfect tense**) 過去進行形 kakóshinkōkei

imperfection [impərfek'ʃən] *n* (failing, blemish) 欠点 kettéñ

imperial [impi:r'i:əl] *adj* (history, power) 帝国の teíkoku no; (*BRIT*: measure) ヤードポンド法の yádopondohō no

imperialism [impi:r'i:əlizəm] *n* 帝国主義 teíkokushùgi

impersonal [impər'sənəl] *adj* (place, organization) 人間味のない niñgeñmi no naî

impersonate [impər'səneit] *vt* (another person, police officer etc) ...の名をかたる ...no ná wò katárù, ...に成り済ます ...ni narísumasù; (THEATER) ...にふんする ...ni fuñ surù

impertinent [impər'tənənt] *adj* (pupil, question) 生意気な namáiki na

impervious [impər'vi:əs] *adj* (*fig*): **impervious to** (criticism etc) ...に影響されない ...ni eíkyō sarenái

impetuous [impetʃ'u:əs] *adj* (impulsive) 無鉄砲な mutéppō na

impetus [im'pitəs] *n* (momentum: of flight, runner) 惰性 daséi; (*fig*: driving force) 原動力 gefídōryoku

impinge [impindʒ']: **to impinge on** *vt fus* (person) ...の行動を制限する ...no kṓdō wò seígen suru; (rights) 侵害する shiñgai suru

implacable [implæk'əbəl] *adj* (hatred, anger etc) なだめがたい nadámegàtai; (opposition) 執念深い shúnenbukai

implement
[*n* im'pləmənt *vb* im'pləment] *n* (tool: for farming, gardening, cooking etc) 道具 dṓgu
♦*vt* (plan, regulation) 実行する jikkṓ suru

implicate [im'plikeit] *vt* (in crime, error) ...のかかわり合いを立証する ...no kakáwariaì wo risshṓ suru

implication [implikei'ʃən] *n* (inference) 含み fukúmi; (involvement) 係り合い kakáwariai

implicit [implis'it] *adj* (inferred: threat, meaning etc) 暗黙の afímoku no; (unquestioning: belief, trust) 盲目的な mṓmokuteki na

implore [implɔ:r'] *vt* (beg) ...に嘆願する ...ni tafígan suru

imply [implai'] *vt* (hint) ...の意味を含む ...no ímì wo fukúmù; (mean) ...を意味する ...wo ímì suru

impolite [impəlait'] *adj* (rude, offensive) 失礼な shitsúrei na

import [*vb* impɔ:rt' *n* im'pɔ:rt] *vt* (goods etc) 輸入する yunyū suru
♦*n* (COMM: article) 輸入品 yunyū́hin; (: importation) 輸入 yunyū́

importance [impɔ:r'təns] *n* (significance) 重大さ jūdaisa; (of person) 有力 yū́ryoku

important [impɔ:r'tənt] *adj* (significant: decision, difference etc) 重要な jū́yō na, 重大な jū́dai na; (influential: person) 偉い erái

it's not important 大した事じゃない taíshita kotò ja naí

importer [impɔ:r'tər] *n* (COMM) 輸入業者 yunyū́gyōsha

impose [impouz'] *vt* (sanctions, restrictions, discipline etc) 負わせる owáserù
♦*vi*: *to impose on someone* ...に付込む ...ni tsukékomù, ...に迷惑を掛ける ...ni mêlwaku wo kakérù

imposing [impou'ziŋ] *adj* (building, person, manner) 貫ろくある kañroku arù

imposition [impəzi'ʃən] *n* (of tax etc) 賦課 fuká

to be an imposition on (person) ...に付込む ...ni tsukékomù, ...に迷惑を掛ける ...ni mêlwaku wo kakérù

impossible [impɑ:s'əbəl] *adj* (task, demand etc) 不可能な fukánō na; (situation) 厄介な yakkáî na; (person) どうようもない dṓ shiyṓ mo nai

impostor [impɑ:s'tər] *n* 偽者 nisémono

impotence [im'pətəns] *n* (lack of power) 無力 múryòku; (MED) 性交不能 seíkōfùnō, インポテンツ iñpoteñtsu

impotent [im'pətənt] *adj* (powerless) 無力な múryòku na; (MED) 性交不能の seíkōfùnō no

impound [impaund'] *vt* (belongings, passports) 没収する bosshū suru

impoverished [impɑ:v'əriʃt] *adj* (country, person etc) 貧しくなった mazúshiku nattà

impracticable [impræk'tikəbəl] *adj* (idea, solution) 実行不可能な jikkṓfukanṓ na

impractical [impræk'tikəl] *adj* (plan) 実用的でない jitsúyōteki de naî; (person) 不器用な bukíyō na

imprecise [imprisais'] *adj* (inexact) 不正確な fuséikaku na

impregnable [impreg'nəbəl] *adj* (castle, fortress) 難攻不落の nañkōfùraku no

impregnate [impreg'neit] *vt* (saturate) ...に染込ませる ...ni shimíkomaserù

impresario [imprəsɑ:'ri:ou] *n* (THEA-

TER) 興業師 kógyōshì

impress [impres'] vt (person) ...に印象を
与える ...ni ińshō wò atáerù; (mark) ...に
押付ける ...ni oshítsukerù

to impress something on someone ...に
...を強く言い聞かす ...ni ...wo tsuyókù
iíkikasù

impression [impreʃ'ən] n (of place, situation, person) 印象 ińshō; (of stamp,
seal) 判 hán, 刻印 kokúiǹ; (idea) 思い込
み omóikomi; (effect) 効果 kóka; (mark)
跡 átò; (imitation) まね monómane

to be under the impression that ...だ
と思い込んでいる ...da to omóikoǹde irú

impressionable [impreʃ'ənəbəl] adj
(child, person) 感じやすい kańjiyasui

impressionist [impreʃ'ənist] n (entertainer) 物真似芸人 monómanegeínin;
(ART): *Impressionist* 印象派画家 ińshō-
hagaka

impressive [impres'iv] adj (reputation,
collection) 印象的な ińshōteki na

imprint [im'print] n (outline: of hand
etc) 跡 ato; (PUBLISHING) 奥付 okúzu-
ke

imprison [impriz'ən] vt (criminal) 拘置
する kóchi suru, 刑務所に入れる keímu-
shò ni irérù

imprisonment [impriz'ənmənt] n 拘置
kóchi

improbable [imprɑːb'əbəl] adj (unlikely:
outcome) ありそうもない arísō mò nái;
(: explanation, story) 本当らしくない hoń-
tōrashikù nái

impromptu [imprɑːmp'tuː] adj (celebration, party) 即席の sokúseki no

improper [imprɑːp'əːr] adj (unsuitable:
conduct, procedure) 不適切な futékisetsu na; (dishonest: activities) 不正な fuséi na

improve [impruːv'] vt (make better:
character, housing, result) 改善する kaízen suru

♦vi (get better: weather, pupil, patient,
health etc) 良くなる yókù naru

improvement [impruːv'mənt] n (mak-
ing better) 改善する事 kaízen suru kotó; (getting better)
良くなる事 yókù naru kotó; *improve-*

ment (in) (making better) (...を) 改善
する事 (...wo) kaízen surù kotó; (getting
better) (...が) 良くなる事 (...ga) yókù
naru kotó

improvise [im'prəvaiz] vt (meal, bed
etc) 有り合せの物で作る aríawase no
mono dè tsukúrù

♦vi (THEATER, MUS) 即興的にしゃべ
る〔演奏する〕sokkyóteki nǐ shabérù
〔eńsō suru〕, アドリブする adóribu suru

imprudent [impruːd'ənt] adj (unwise) 賢
明でない keńmei de naí

impudent [im'pjədənt] adj (child, comment, remark) 生意気な namáiki na

impulse [im'pʌls] n (urge: gen) 衝動 shó-
dō; (: to do wrong) 出来心 dekígokòro;
(ELEC) 衝撃 shógeki, インパルス íñparu-
su

to act on impulse 衝動的に行動する
shódōteki ni kōdō suru

impulsive [impʌl'siv] adj (purchase, gesture, person) 衝動的な shódōteki na

impunity [impjuː'niti:] n: *with impu-*
nity 罰せられずに bassérarezù ni

impure [impjuːr'] adj (adulterated) 不純
な fujún na; (sinful) みだらな mídàra na

impurity [impjuːr'iti:] n (foreign substance) 不純物 fujúnbutsu

KEYWORD

in [in] prep 1 (indicating place, position)
...に〔で〕... nǐ〔dè〕

in the house/garden 家〔庭〕に〔で〕ié
〔niwá〕nǐ〔dè〕

in the box/fridge/drawer 箱〔冷蔵庫,
引き出し〕に〔で〕hakó〔reízōko, hikída-
shi〕nǐ〔dè〕

I have it in my hand 手に持っていま
す té nǐ móttè imasu

to spend a day in town/the country
町〔田舎〕で1日を過ごす machí〔ináka〕dè
ichínichi wò sugósù

in school 学校に〔で〕gakkó nǐ〔dè〕

in here/there ここ〔あそこ〕に〔で〕ko-
kó〔asóko〕nǐ〔dè〕

2 (with place names: of town, region,
country) ...に〔で〕... nǐ〔dè〕

in London ロンドンに〔で〕róǹdon ni

〔de〕

in England/Japan/Canada/the United States 英国〔日本, カナダ, アメリカ〕に〔で〕 eíkoku(nippóñ, kánàda, amérìka) nî(de)

in Burgundy バーガンディーに〔で〕 bágañdì ni(de)

3 (indicating time: during) ...に ...nî

in spring/summer 春〔夏〕に hárù(natsú)ni

in 1998 1998年 に señkyùhyakukyújùhachi néñ ni

in May 5月に gógàtsu ni

I'll see you in July 7月に会いましょう shichígàtsu ni aímashǒ

in the afternoon 午後に gógò ni

at 4 o'clock in the afternoon 午後4時に gógò yójì ni

4 (indicating time: in the space of) ...で ...dè

I did it in 3 hours/days 3時間〔3日〕でやりました sañjikàn(mikkà)de yarímashìta

I'll see you in 2 weeks/in 2 weeks' time 2週間したらまた会いましょう nishùkàn shitara matá aimashǒ

5 (indicating manner etc) ...で ...dè

in a loud/soft voice 大きな〔小さな〕声で ŏkìna(chíisana)kǒè de

in pencil/ink 鉛筆〔インク〕で eñpitsu (íñku)dè

in English/French 英語〔フランス語〕で eígo(furánsugo)dè

the boy in the blue shirt 青いシャツの少年 aóì shátsù no shǒnen

6 (indicating circumstances): *in the sun* 直射日光に当って chokúshanikkǒ ni atáttè, 日なたに hinátà ni

in the rain 雨の中 ámè no nákà

in the shade 日陰で hikáge de

a change in policy 政策の変更 seísaku nò heñkǒ

a rise in prices 物価の上昇 búkkà no jǒshǒ

7 (indicating mood, state): *in tears* 泣いて naíte

in anger 怒って okóttè

in despair 失望して shitsúbō shitè

in good condition 無事に bují nî

to live in luxury ぜいたくに暮す zeítaku ni kurásu

8 (with ratios, numbers): *1 in 10 households has a second car, 1 household in 10 has a second car* 10世帯中1世帯は車を2台持っている jussétaichù issétai wà kurúma wò nídài mótte irù

6 months in the year 1年の内6か月 ichínen no uchì rokkágètsu

they lined up in twos 彼らは2人ずつ並んだ kárèra wa futárizùtsu naráñda

9 (referring to people, works): *the disease is common in children* この病気は子供によく見られる konó byōki wa kodómo nì yòkù mirárerù

in (the works of) Dickens ディケンズの作品の中に díkenzu no sakúhin no nakà ni

she has it in her to succeed 彼女には成功する素質がある kánòjo ni wa seíkō suru soshítsu ga árù

they have a good leader in him 彼らにとって彼は素晴らしいリーダーです kárèra ni tóttè kárè wa subárashìi rídà desu

10 (indicating profession etc): *to be in teaching* 教員である kyǒìn de árù

to be in publishing 出版関係の仕事をしている shuppánkañkei no shigóto wò shitè irù

to be in the army 軍人である guñjìn de árù

11 (after superlative): *the best pupil in the class* クラスで最優秀の生徒 kúràsu de saíyùshū no seíto

the biggest/smallest in Europe ヨーロッパ中で最も大きな〔小さな〕物 yǒroppajù de mottómò ŏkìna(chíisana)monò

12 (with present participle): *in saying this* こう言って kǒ ittè

in doing things the way she did, she alienated everyone 彼女のやり方は皆の反感を買った kánòjo no yaríkata wà miná nò hañkan wo kattá

♦*adv: to be in* (person: at home) 在宅である zaítaku de árù; (: at work) 出社して

いる shusshá shite irú; (train, plane) 到着
している tōchaku shite irú; (ship) 入港し
ている nyūkō shite irú; (in fashion) 流行
している ryūkō shite irú

he'll be in later today 2-3時間したら
出社すると思います nisánjikàn shitárà
shusshá suru tò omóimasù

miniskirts are in again this year 今
年ミニスカートが再び流行しています
kotóshi mínísukàto ga futátabi ryūkō
shite imasù

to ask someone in ...を家に上がらせる
...wò ié nì agáraserù

to run/limp etc in 走って〔びっこを引
いて〕入って来る hashíttè〔bíkkò wo hií-
tè〕háittè kuru

♦*n: the ins and outs* (of proposal,
situation etc) 詳細 shōsai

*he explained all the ins and outs of
the deal to me* 彼は私に取引の詳細を
説明してくれました kárè wa watákushi
nì toríhiki no shōsai wo setsúmei shite
kuremashìta

in. *abbr* = **inch**

inability [inəbil'əti:] *n* (incapacity): *inability (to do)* (...する事が) できない
事 (...surú kotò ga) dekínai kotó

inaccessible [inækses'əbəl] *adj* (place)
入りにくい hafrinikùi, 近付きにくい chi-
kázukinikùi; (*fig*: text, music) 難解な nañkai na

inaccurate [inæk'jə:rit] *adj* (account,
answer, person) 不正確な fuséikaku na

inactivity [inæktiv'iti:] *n* (idleness) 活動
しない事 katsúdōshìnai kotó

inadequate [inæd'əkwit] *adj* (income,
amount, reply) 不十分な fujūbùn na;
(person) 無能な munō na

inadvertently [inədvə:r'təntli:] *adv* (unintentionally) うっかり ukkárì

inadvisable [inədvai'zəbəl] *adj* 得策でな
い tokúsaku de naì

inane [inein'] *adj* (smile, remark) 愚かな
óròka na

inanimate [inæn'əmit] *adj* 生命のない
seímei no naì

inappropriate [inəprou'pri:it] *adj* (un-

suitable) 不適切な futékisetsu na; (improper: word, expression) 非難すべき hinánsubeki

inarticulate [ina:rtik'jəlit] *adj* (person)
口下手な kuchíbeta na; (speech) 分かり
にくい wakárinikuì

inasmuch as [inəzmʌtʃ'-] *adv* (in that)
...という点で ...to iú teñ de; (insofar as)
できる限り dekíru kagìri

inaudible [inɔ:'dəbəl] *adj* (voice, aside)
聞取れない kikítorenaì

inaugural [inɔ:'gjə:rəl] *adj* (speech) 就任
の shūnin no; (meeting) 発会の hakkái
no

inaugurate [inɔ:'gjə:reit] *vt* (president,
official) ...の就任式を行う ...no shūniñshiki wo okonau; (system, measure) 始
める hajímeru; (organization) 発足させ
る hossóku saserù

inauguration [inɔ:gjə:rei'ʃən] *n* (of president, official) 就任式 shūniñshiki; (of
system, measure) 開始 kaíshi; (of organization) 発足 hossóku

in-between [in'bitwi:n'] *adj* (intermediate) 中間的な chūkanteki na

inborn [in'bɔ:rn] *adj* (quality) 生れ付きの
umáretsuki no

inbred [in'bred] *adj* (quality) 生まれつき
の umaretsuki no; (family) 近親交配の
kiñshinkōhai no

Inc. *abbr* = **incorporated**

incalculable [inkæl'kjələbəl] *adj* (effect,
loss) 途方もない tohō mo naì

incapable [inkei'pəbəl] *adj* (helpless) 無
能な munō na; (unable to): *to be incapable of something/doing something* ...が〔する事が〕できない ...ga〔surú
kotò ga〕dekínaì

incapacitate [inkəpæs'əteit] *vt* 不具に
する fúgù ni suru

incapacity [inkəpæs'iti:] *n* (weakness)
弱さ yówàsa; (inability) 不能 funō

incarcerate [inka:r'sə:rit] *vt* 拘置する
kōchi suru, 刑務所に入れる keímushò ni
irérù

incarnation [inka:rnei'ʃən] *n* (of beauty)
化身 késhìn; (of evil) 権化 góñge; (REL)
神が人間の姿を取る事 kámì ga niñgen

no sugatá wo tórù kotó

incendiary [insen'di:e:ri:] *adj* (device) 放
火の hőka no
an incendiary bomb 焼い弾 shőidàn

incense [*n* in'sens *vb* insens'] *n* (perfume: *also* REL) 香 kő
♦*vt* (anger) 怒らせる okóraserù

incentive [insen'tiv] *n* (inducement) 動機
dőkì, 刺激 shigékì

incessant [inses'ənt] *adj* (bickering, criticism) 引っ切り無しの hikkíri nashí no

incessantly [inses'əntli:] *adv* 引っ切り無
しに hikkíri nashí ni

incest [in'sest] *n* 近親相かん kinshinső-
kan

inch [intʃ] *n* (measurement) インチ ínchi
to be within an inch of doing 危うく
...するところである ayáuku ...surú tokôro de árù
he didn't give an inch (*fig*: back
down, yield) 一寸も譲ろうとしなかった
issún mo yuzúrő to shinákatta

inch forward *vi* 一寸刻みに進む issú-
ñkizami ni susúmù

incidence [in'sidəns] *n* (of crime, disease) 発生率 hasséiritsu

incident [in'sidənt] *n* (event) 事件 jíken

incidental [insiden'təl] *adj* (additional,
supplementary) 付随的な fuzúiteki na
incidental to ...に対して二次的な ...ni
táishite nijíteki na

incidentally [insiden'təli:] *adv* (by the
way) ところで tokóro dè

incinerator [insin'ə:reitə:r] *n* (for
waste, refuse) 焼却炉 shőkyakurð

incipient [insip'i:ənt] *adj* (baldness, madness) 初期の shőkì no

incision [insiʒ'ən] *n* (cut: *also* MED) 切開
sékkài

incisive [insai'siv] *adj* (comment, criticism) 痛烈な tsúretsu na

incite [insait'] *vt* (rioters, violence) 扇動
する señdő suru; (hatred) あおりたてる
aóritatèru

inclination [inklənei'ʃən] *n* (tendency)
傾向 keíkő; (disposition, desire) 望み nozómi

incline [in'klain] *n* (slope) 坂 saká

♦*vt* (bend: head) 下げる sagérù
♦*vi* (surface) 傾斜する keísha suru
to be inclined to (tend) ...する傾向があ
る ...suru keíkő ga árù

include [inklu:d'] *vt* (incorporate: in
plan, team etc) 入れる irérù; (: in price)
含む fukúmù

including [inklu:d'iŋ] *prep* ...を含めて
...wo fukúmète

inclusion [inklu:'ʒən] *n* (incorporation:
in plan etc) 入れる事 irérù kotó; (: in
price) 含む事 fukúmù kotó

inclusive [inklu:'siv] *adj* (price, terms)
含んでいる fukúnde irù
inclusive of ...を含めて ...wo fukúmète

incognito [inka:gni:'tou] *adv* (travel) 御
忍びで o-shínobi de

incoherent [inkouhi:'rənt] *adj* (argument, speech, person) 分かりにくい wakárinikuì

income [in'kʌm] *n* 収入 shúnyū

income tax *n* 所得税 shotőkuzèi

incoming [in'kʌmiŋ] *adj* (flight, passenger) 到着の tőchaku no; (call, mail) 着信
の chakúshin no; (government, official)
新任の shínìnin no; (wave) 寄せて来る yo-
séte kurù
the incoming tide 上げ潮 agéshio

incomparable [inka:m'pə:rəbəl] *adj*
(genius, efficiency etc) 類のない rúì no
náì

incompatible [inkəmpæt'əbəl] *adj* (life-
styles, systems, aims) 相容れない áìré-
nai

incompetence [inka:m'pitəns] *n* 無能
munő

incompetent [inka:m'pitənt] *adj* (person) 無能な munő na; (job) 下手な hetá
na

incomplete [inkəmpli:t'] *adj* (unfinished:
book, painting etc) 未完成の mikánsei
no; (partial: success, achievement) 部分
的な bubúnteki na

incomprehensible [inka:mprihen'səbəl]
adj (conduct) 不可解な fukákai na; (language) 分からない wakáranaì

inconceivable [inkənsi:'vəbəl] *adj* (unthinkable) 考えられない kañgaerarenaì

incongruous [inkɑːŋ'gruːəs] *adj*
(strange: situation, figure) 変った kawátta; (inappropriate: remark, act) 不適
当な futékitō na

inconsiderate [inkənsíd'ərit] *adj* (person, action) 心ない kokóronaì

inconsistency [inkənsís'tənsiː] *n* (of
behavior, person etc) 一貫しない事 ikkán
shinai koto; (in work) むら mura; (in
statement, action) 矛盾 mujún

inconsistent [inkənsís'tənt] *adj* (behavior, person) 変りやすい kawáriyasuì;
(work) むらの多い murá no ōi; (statement, action) 矛盾した mujún shita
inconsistent with (beliefs, values) ...と
矛盾する ...to mujún suru

inconspicuous [inkənspík'juːəs] *adj*
(person, color, building etc) 目立たない
medátanaì

incontinent [inkɑːn'tənənt] *adj* (MED)
失禁の shikkín no

inconvenience [inkənviːn'jəns] *n* (problem) 問題 mondai; (trouble) 迷惑 meíwaku
♦*vt* ...に迷惑を掛ける ...ni meíwaku wò
kakérù

inconvenient [inkənviːn'jənt] *adj* (time,
place, house) 不便な fubén na; (visitor,
incident etc) 厄介な yakkái na

incorporate [inkɔːr'pəːrit] *vt* (make
part of) 取入れる toríirerù; (contain) 含
む fukúmù

incorporated company [inkɔːr'-
pəːreitid-] (*US*) *n* (*abbr* **Inc.**) 会社 kaísha

incorrect [inkərekt'] *adj* (information,
answer, attitude etc) 間違った machígattà

incorrigible [inkɔːr'idʒəbəl] *adj* (liar,
crook) 救い様のない sukúiyō no naì

incorruptible [inkərʌp'təbəl] *adj* (not
open to bribes) 買収のできない baíshū
no dekinaì

increase [*n* in'kriːs *vb* inkriːs'] *n* (rise):
increase (in/of) (...の) 増加 (...no) zō-
ka
♦*vi* (: price, level, productivity etc) 増す
masú
♦*vt* (make greater: price, knowledge

etc) 増す masú

increasing [inkriːs'iŋ] *adj* (number, use)
増加する zōka suru

increasingly [inkriːs'iŋliː] *adv* (more
intensely, more often) ますます masú-
mású

incredible [inkred'əbəl] *adj* (unbelievable) 信じられない shinjirarenaì; (enormous) ばく大な bakúdai na

incredulous [inkredʒ'ələs] *adj* (tone,
expression) 半信半疑の hanshihhangi no

increment [in'krəmənt] *n* (in salary) 定
期昇給 teíkishōkyū

incriminate [inkrim'əneit] *vt* (LAW)
...の罪を立証する ...no tsúmi wo risshō
suru

incubation [inkjəbei'ʃən] *n* (of eggs) ふ
卵 furán; (of illness) 潜伏期間 seńpukuki-
kàn

incubator [in'kjəbeitəːr] *n* (for babies)
保育器 hoíkukì

incumbent [inkʌm'bənt] *n* (official:
POL, REL) 現役 gén-eki
♦*adj*: *it is incumbent on him to ...*
...するのが彼の義務である ...surú no gà
kárè no gímù de árù

incur [inkəːr'] *vt* (expenses) ...が掛る ...ga
kakárù; (loss) 受ける ukérù; (debt) こし
らえる koshíraerù; (disapproval, anger)
被る kômurù

incurable [inkjuːr'əbəl] *adj* (disease) 不
治の fújì no

incursion [inkəːr'ʒən] *n* (MIL: invasion)
侵入 shińnyū

indebted [indet'id] *adj*: *to be indebted
to someone* (grateful) ...に感謝している
...ni kánsha shité irù

indecent [indiː'sənt] *adj* (film, book) み
だらな mídàra na

indecent assault (*BRIT*) *n* 強制わいせ
つ罪 kyōsei waisetsuzài

indecent exposure *n* 公然わいせつ罪
kōzen waisetsuzài

indecisive [indisai'siv] *adj* (person) 決断
力のない ketsúdanryoku no naì

indeed [indiːd'] *adv* (certainly) 確かに tá-
shīka ni, 本当に hońtō ni; (in fact) 実は
jitsú wà; (furthermore) なお nâò

yes indeed! 確かにそうだ! táshìka ni ső dá!

indefinite [indef'ǝnit] *adj* (answer, view) 不明確な fuméikaku na; (period, number) 不定の futéi no

indefinitely [indef'ǝnitli:] *adv* (continue, wait) いつまでも ítsù made mo

indelible [indel'ǝbǝl] *adj* (mark, stain, ink) 消せない kesénaì
indelible pen 油性フェルトペン yuséi ferútopen

indemnity [indem'niti:] *n* (insurance) 賠償保険 baíshōhoкèn; (compensation) 賠償 baíshō

independence [indipen'dǝns] *n* (of country, person etc) 独立 dokúritsu; (of thinking etc) 自主性 jishúsei

independent [indipen'dǝnt] *adj* (country, business etc) 独立した dokúritsu shita; (person, thought) 自主的な jishúteki na; (school) 私立の shírìtsu no; (broadcasting company) 民間の míñkan no; (inquiry) 独自の dokúji no

indestructible [indistrʌk'tǝbǝl] *adj* 破壊できない hakái dekinaì

indeterminate [indita:r'mǝnit] *adj* (number, nature) 不明の fuméi no

index [in'deks] (*pl* **indexes**) *n* (in book) 索引 sakúin, インデックス iñdekkùsu; (in library etc) 蔵書目録 zōshomokùroku; (*pl*: **indices**: ratio) 率 rítsù, 指数 shísù; (: sign) 印 shírushi

index card *n* インデックスカード iñdekkusukàdo

indexed [in'dekst] (*BRIT* **index-linked**) *adj* (income, payment) スライド制のsuráidosei no

index finger *n* 人差指 hitósashiyùbi

India [in'di:ǝ] *n* インド íñdo

Indian [in'di:ǝn] *adj* インドの íñdo no
Red Indian アメリカインディアン amérika iñdian

Indian Ocean *n: the Indian Ocean* インド洋 iñdoyő

indicate [in'dikeit] *vt* (show) 示す shimésù; (point to) 指す sásù; (mention) 示唆する shisá suru

indication [indikei'ʃǝn] *n* (sign) しるし

shirúshi

indicative [indik'ǝtiv] *adj*: *indicative of* ...のしるしである ...no shirúshi de aru
♦*n* (LING) 直接法 chokúsetsuhō

indicator [in'dikeitǝːr] *n* (marker, signal) しるし shirúshi; (AUT) 方向指示器 hốkōshijìki, ウインカー uíñkā

indices [in'disi:z] *npl of* **index**

indictment [indait'mǝnt] *n* (denunciation) 避難 hínan; (charge) 起訴 kisó

indifference [indif'ǝrǝns] *n* (lack of interest) 無関心 mukáñshin

indifferent [indif'ǝrǝnt] *adj* (uninterested: attitude) 無関心な mukáñshin na; (mediocre: quality) 平凡な heíbon na

indigenous [indidʒ'ǝnǝs] *adj* (wildlife) 固有の koyű no
the indigenous population 原住民 geñjūmin

indigestion [indidʒes'tʃǝn] *n* 消化不良 shōkafuryὸ

indignant [indig'nǝnt] *adj*: *to be indignant at something/with someone* (angry) ...に怒っている ...ni okótte irù

indignation [indignei'ʃǝn] *n* (outrage, resentment) 立腹 rippúku

indignity [indig'niti:] *n* (humiliation) 侮辱 bujóku

indigo [in'dǝgou] *n* (color) あい áì

indirect [indirekt'] *adj* (way, route) 遠回しの tőmawashì no; (answer, effect) 間接的な kañsetsuteki na

indirectly [indirekt'li:] *adv* (responsible) 間接的に kañsetsuteki ni

indiscreet [indiskri:t'] *adj* (person, behavior, comment) 軽率な keísotsu na

indiscriminate [indiskrim'ǝnit] *adj* (bombing) 無差別の musábetsu no; (taste) はっきりしない hakkírì shináì

indispensable [indispen'sǝbǝl] *adj* (tool, worker) 掛替えのない kakégae no naì

indisposed [indispouzd'] *adj* (unwell) 体調の悪い taíchō no warúì

indisputable [indispju:'tǝbǝl] *adj* (undeniable) 否めない inámenaì

indistinct [indistiŋkt'] *adj* (image, memory) ぼんやりした boñ-yarî shita; (noise) かすかな kásùka na

individual [indəvídʒu:əl] n (person: different from all others) 個人 kójìn; (: with adj) 人 hitô, 人物 jinbutsu

♦adj (personal) 個人個人の kójìnkòjin no; (single) それぞれの sorézòre no; (particular: characteristic) 独特な dokútoku na

individualist [indəvídʒu:əlist] n 個人主義者 kojínshugìsha

individually [indəvídʒu:əli:] adv (singly: persons) 一人一人で hitórihitorî de; (: things) 一つ一つで hitótsuhitotsù de

indivisible [indəvízəbəl] adj (matter, power) 分割できない buṅkatsu dekinâi

indoctrinate [indɑːktrəneit] vt ...に ...を教え込む ...ni ...wo oshíekomù, 洗脳する señnō suru

indoctrination [indɑːktrənéiʃən] n 教え込む事 oshíekomù kotó, 洗脳 señnō

indolent [índələnt] adj (lazy) 怠惰な táìda na

Indonesia [indəníːʒə] n インドネシア iñdoneshìa

indoor [índɔːr] adj 屋内の okúnai no

indoors [indɔːrz'] adv (inside) 屋内で o-kúnai de

induce [indus'] vt (bring about) 引起こす hikíokosù; (persuade) 説得する settóku suru; (MED: birth) 誘発する yúhatsu suru

inducement [indus'mənt] n (incentive) 動機 dôki, 刺激 shigéki; (pej: bribe) 賄ろ wâîro

indulge [indʌldʒ'] vt (desire, whim) 満たす mitásù; (person, child) 気ままにさせる kimáma ni saserù

♦vi: **to indulge in** (vice, hobby) ...にふける ...ni fukérù

indulgence [indʌl'dʒəns] n (pleasure) 楽しみ tanóshimi; (leniency) 寛大さ kañdaisa

indulgent [indʌl'dʒənt] adj (parent, smile) 甘やかす amáyakasù

industrial [indʌs'tri:əl] adj 産業の saṅgyō no, 工業の kôgyō no

industrial action (BRIT) n 争議行為 sôgikôi

industrial estate (BRIT) n = **industrial park**

industrialist [indʌs'tri:əlist] n 実業家 jitsúgyōka

industrialize [indʌs'tri:əlaiz] vt (country, society) 工業化する kôgyōka suru

industrial park (US) n 工業団地 kôgyōdañchi

industrious [indʌs'tri:əs] adj (student, worker) 勤勉な kíñben na

industry [in'dəstri:] n (manufacturing) 産業 saṅgyō, 工業 kôgyō; (oil industry, textile industry etc) ...業界 ...gyōkai; (diligence) 勤勉さ kíñbensa

inebriated [ini:b'ri:eitid] adj (drunk) 酔っ払った yoppáratta

inedible [ined'əbəl] adj (disgusting) 食べられない tabérarenài; (poisonous) 食用に適さない shokúyō nì tekísanaì

ineffective [inifek'tiv] adj (policy, government) 効果のない kôka no naì

ineffectual [inifek'tʃu:əl] adj = **ineffective**

inefficiency [inifiʃ'ənsi:] n 非能率 hinôritsu

inefficient [inifiʃ'ənt] adj (person, machine, system) 能率の悪い nôritsu no waruì

inept [inept'] adj (politician, management) 無能な munô na

inequality [inikwɑːl'iti:] n (of system) 不平等 fubyôdō; (of amount, share) 不等 futô

inert [inəːrt'] adj (immobile) 動かない u-gókanaì; (gas) 不活性の fukássei no

inertia [inəːr'ʃə] n (apathy) 物臭 monôgusa; (PHYSICS) 惰性 daséi

inescapable [inəskei'pəbəl] adj (conclusion, impression) 避けられない sakérarenaì

inevitable [inev'itəbəl] adj (outcome, result) 避けられない sakérarenaì, 必然的な hitsúzenteki na

inevitably [inev'itəbli:] adv 必然的に hitsúzenteki ni

inexcusable [inikskju:'zəbəl] adj (behavior, error) 許されない yurúsarenaì

inexhaustible [inigzɔːs'təbəl] adj (wealth, resources) 無尽蔵の mujíñzō no

inexorable [inek'sə:rəbəl] *adj* (progress, decline) 止め様のない toméyō no naî

inexpensive [inikspen'siv] *adj* (cheap) 安い yasúî

inexperience [inikspi:r'i:əns] *n* (of person) 不慣れ fúnàre

inexperienced [inikspi:r'i:ənst] *adj* (swimmer, worker) 不慣れの fúnàre no

inexplicable [ineks'plikəbəl] *adj* (decision, mistake) 不可解な fukákài na

inextricably [ineks'trikəbli:] *adv* (entangled, linked) 分けられない程 wakérarenài hodo

infallible [infæl'əbəl] *adj* (person, guide) 間違いのない machígaî no naî

infamous [in'fəməs] *adj* (crime, murderer) 悪名高い akúmeidakaî

infamy [in'fəmi:] *n* (notoriety) 悪評 akúhyō

infancy [in'fənsi:] *n* (of person) 幼年時代 yōnenjidài

infant [in'fənt] *n* (baby) 赤ちゃん ákàchan; (young child) 幼児 yōjì

infantile [in'fəntail] *adj* (disease) 幼児の yuꓸ no; (foolish) 幼稚な yōchî na

infantry [in'fəntri:] *n* (MIL) 歩兵隊 hohéitai

infant school (*BRIT*) *n* 幼稚園 yōchien

infatuated [infætʃ'u:eitid] *adj*: **to be infatuated with** ...にのぼせている ...ni nobósete irù

infatuation [infætʃu:ei'ʃən] *n* (passion) ...にのぼせる事 ...ni nobóseru koto

infect [infekt'] *vt* (person, animal) ...に感染させる ...ni kańsen saserù; (food) 汚染する osén suru

infection [infek'ʃən] *n* (MED: disease) 感染 kańsen; (contagion) 伝染 defìsen

infectious [infek'ʃəs] *adj* (person, animal) 伝染病にかかった defìsenbyō ni kakáttà; (disease) 伝染性の defìsensei no; (*fig*: enthusiasm, laughter) 移りやすい utsúriyasuî

infer [infə:r'] *vt* (deduce) 推定する suítei suru; (imply) ...の意味を含む ...no ímì wo fukúmù

inference [in'fə:rəns] *n* (deduction) 推定 suítei; (implication) 含み fukúmi

inferior [infi:'ri:ər] *adj* (in rank) 下級の kakyū no; (in quality, quantity) 劣った otóttà
♦*n* (subordinate) 下の者 shitá no mònò; (junior) 年下の者 toshíshita no monò

inferiority [infi:ri:ɔ:r'iti:] *n* (in rank) 下級である事 kakyū de arù kotò; (in quality) 品質の悪さ hiñshitsu nò wárùsa

inferiority complex *n* (PSYCH) 劣等感 rettókan

infernal [infə:r'nəl] *adj* (racket, temper) ひどい hidóî

inferno [infə:r'nou] *n* (blaze) 大火事 ōkajì

infertile [infə:r'təl] *adj* (soil) 不毛の fumō no; (person, animal) 不妊の funín no

infertility [infə:rtil'əti:] *n* (of soil) 不毛 fumō; (of person, animal) 不妊症 funíñshō

infested [infes'tid] *adj*: **infested with** (vermin, pests) ...がうじゃうじゃいる ...ga újàuja irú

infidelity [infidel'iti:] *n* (unfaithfulness) 浮気 uwáki

in-fighting [in'faitiŋ] *n* 内紛 naífun, 内ゲバ uchígeba

infiltrate [infil'treit] *vt* ...に潜入する ...ni seńnyū suru

infinite [in'fənit] *adj* (very great: variety, patience) ばく大な bakúdai na; (without limits: universe) 無限の mugén no

infinitive [infin'ətiv] *n* (LING) 不定詞 futéishi

infinity [infin'əti:] *n* (infinite number) 無限大 mugéndai; (infinite point) 無限 mugén

infirm [infə:rm'] *adj* (weak) 虚弱な kyojáku na; (ill) 病弱な byójaku na

infirmary [infə:r'mə:ri:] *n* (hospital) 病院 byóin

infirmity [infə:r'miti:] *n* (weakness) 虚弱さ kyojákusa; (being ill) 病弱さ byójakusa; (specific illness) 病気 byóki

inflamed [infleimd'] *adj* (tongue, appendix) 炎症を起した eńshō wò okóshità

inflammable [inflæm'əbəl] *adj* (fabric, chemical) 可燃性の kanénsei no, 燃えや

すい moéyasuì

inflammation [infləmei'(ʃən] n (of throat, appendix etc) 炎症 eñshō

inflatable [inflei'təbəl] adj (life jacket, dinghy, doll) 膨らます事のできる fukúramasu kotò no dekírù

inflate [infleit'] vt (tire, balloon) 膨らます fukúramasù; (price) つり上げる tsuríagerù

inflation [inflei'ʃən] n (ECON) インフレ iñfure

inflationary [inflei'ʃəne:ri:] adj (spiral) インフレの iñfure no; (demand) インフレを引起こす iñfure wò hikíokosù

inflexible [inflek'səbəl] adj (rule, timetable) 融通が利かない yúzū ga kikànai; (person) 譲らない yuzúranaì

inflict [inflikt'] vt: **to inflict something on someone** (damage, suffering) ...に...を加える ...ni ...wo kuwáerù

influence [in'flu:əns] n (power) 実力 jitsúryoku; (effect) 影響 eíkyō
◆vt (person, situation, choice etc) 左右する sáyū suru
under the influence of alcohol 酒に酔って saké ni yottè

influential [influ:en't'ʃəl] adj (politician, critic) 有力な yúryoku na

influenza [influ:en'zə] n (MED) 流感 ryúkan

influx [in'flʌks] n (of refugees, funds) 流入 ryúnyū

inform [infɔ:rm'] vt: **to inform someone of something** (tell) ...に...を知らせる ...ni ...wo shiráserù
◆vi: **to inform on someone** (to police, authorities) ...を密告する ...wo mikkóku suru

informal [infɔ:r'məl] adj (manner, discussion, party) 寛いだ kutsúroida; (clothes) 普段の fúdàn no; (unofficial: visit, meeting) 非公式の hikóshiki no

informality [infɔ:rmæl'iti:] n (of manner, party etc) 寛いだ雰囲気 kutsúroida fuñ-iki

informant [infɔ:r'mənt] n (source) 情報提供者 jōhōteikyōsha, インフォーマント iñfōmañto

information [infə:rmei'(ʃən] n 情報 jōhō
a piece of information 1つの情報 hitótsu no jōhō

information office n 案内所 añnaijo

informative [infɔ:r'mətiv] adj (report, comment) 有益な yúeki na

informer [infɔ:r'mər] n (also: **police informer**) 密告者 mikkókusha, スパイ supáì

infra-red [in'frəred] adj (rays, light) 赤外線の sekígaisen no

infrastructure [in'frəstrʌk't'ʃər] n (of system etc) 下部構造 kabúkōzō, インフラストラクチャー iñfurasutorakùchā

infrequent [infri:'kwint] adj (visits) 間遠な madò na; (buses) 本数の少ない hoñsū nò sukúnaì

infringe [infrindʒ'] vt (law) 破る yabúrù
◆vi: **to infringe on** (rights) ...を侵す ...wo okásù

infringement [infrindʒ'mənt] n (of law) 違反 ihán; (of rights) 侵害 shiñgai

infuriating [infju:r'i:eitiŋ] adj (habit, noise) いらいらさせる íràira saséru

ingenious [indʒi:n'jəs] adj (idea, solution) 巧妙な kōmyō na

ingenuity [indʒənu:'iti:] n (cleverness, skill) 才能 saínō

ingenuous [indʒen'ju:əs] adj (innocent, trusting) 無邪気な mújàki na

ingot [iŋ'gət] n (of gold, platinum) 延べ棒 nobébō, インゴット iñgótto

ingrained [ingreind'] adj (habit, belief) 根深い nebúkaì

ingratiate [ingrei'ʃi:eit] vt: **to ingratiate oneself with** ...に取入る ...ni toríiru

ingratitude [ingræt'ətu:d] n (of beneficiary, heir) 恩知らず oñshirāzu

ingredient [ingri:'di:ənt] n (of cake) 材料 zaíryò; (of situation) 要素 yōso

inhabit [inhæb'it] vt (town, country) ...に住む ...ni súmù

inhabitant [inhæb'ətənt] n (of town, street, house, country) 住民 júmin

inhale [inheil'] vt (breathe in: smoke, gas etc) 吸込む suíkomù
◆vi (breathe in) 息を吸う íkì wo suu; (when smoking) 煙を吸込む kemúri wo

suíkomù

inherent [inhə:r'ent] *adj*: *inherent in* ...に固有の ...ni koyū no

inherit [inher'it] *vt* (property, money) 相続する sōzoku suru; (characteristic) 遺伝で受継ぐ idén de ukétsugù

inheritance [inher'itəns] *n* (property, money etc) 相続財産 sōzoku zaisàn; (characteristics etc) 遺伝 idén

inhibit [inhib'it] *vt* (growth: also PSYCH) 抑制 yokúsei

inhibited [inhib'itid] *adj* (PSYCH) 抑制の多い yokúsei no ōì

inhibition [inibiʃ'ən] *n* 抑制 yokúsei

inhospitable [inha:spit'əbəl] *adj* (person) もてなしの悪い moténashi nò warui; (place, climate) 住みにくい sumínikuì

inhuman [inhju:'mən] *adj* (behavior) 残忍な zańnin na; (appearance) 非人間的な hińningenteki na

inimitable [inim'itəbəl] *adj* (tone, style) まねのできない mané no dekinai

iniquity [inik'witi:] *n* (wickedness) 悪 ákù; (injustice) 不正 fuséi

initial [iniʃ'əl] *adj* (stage, reaction) 最初の saísho no
♦*n* (letter) 頭文字 kashíramojì
♦*vt* (document) ...に頭文字で署名する ...ni kashíramojì de shoméi surù

initials [iniʃ'əlz] *npl* (of name) 頭文字 kashíramojì; (as signature) 頭文字の署名 kashíramojì no shoméi

initially [iniʃ'əli:] *adv* (at first) 最初は saísho wa; (first) まず最初に mázù saísho ni

initiate [iniʃ'i:it] *vt* (begin: talks, process) 始める hajímerù; (new member) 入会させる nyúkai saserù
to initiate someone into a secret ...に秘密を教える ...ni himítsu wò oshíerù
to initiate proceedings against someone (LAW) ...を起訴する ...wo kisó suru

initiation [iniʃi:ei'ʃən] *n* (beginning) 開始 kaíshi; (into organization etc) 入会式 nyúkaìshiki; (into secret etc) 伝授 dénju

initiative [iniʃ'i:ətiv] *n* (move) 企画 kikáku; (enterprise) 進取の気 shíńshu no kí
to take the initiative 先手を打つ seńte

inject [indʒekt'] *vt* (drugs, poison) 注射する chúsha suru; (patient): *to inject someone with something* ...に...を注射する ...ni ...wo chúsha suru; (funds) つぎ込む tsugíkomù

injection [indʒek'ʃən] *n* (of drugs, medicine) 注射 chúsha; (of funds) つぎ込む事 tsugíkomù kotó

injunction [indʒʌŋk'ʃən] *n* (LAW) 差止め命令 sashítomemeìrei

injure [in'dʒə:r] *vt* (hurt: person, leg etc) 傷付ける kizútsukerù; (: feelings, reputation) 害する gaí surù

injured [in'dʒə:rd] *adj* (person, arm) 傷付いた kizútsuità; (feelings) 害された gaí saretà; (tone) 感情を害された kańjō wò gaí saretà

injury [in'dʒə:ri:] *n* (wound) 傷 kizú, けが kegá

injury time *n* (SPORT) 延長時間 eńchōjikàn ◇傷の手当てなどに使った分の延長時間 kizú no teàte nádò ni tsukátta buň no eńchōjikàn

injustice [indʒʌs'tis] *n* (unfairness) 不公平 fukóhei

ink [iŋk] *n* (in pen, printing) インク íñku

inkling [iŋk'liŋ] *n* (idea, clue) 薄々と気付く事 usúsu tò kizúku kotó

inlaid [in'leid] *adj* (with gems, wood etc) ...をちりばめた ...wo chiríbametà

inland [in'lænd] *adj* (port, sea, waterway) 内陸の naíriku no
♦*adv* (travel) 内陸へ naíriku e

Inland Revenue (*BRIT*) *n* 国税庁 kokúzeichō

in-laws [in'lɔ:z] *npl* 義理の親せき girí nò shińseki, 姻せき iňseki

inlet [in'let] *n* (GEO) 入江 iríe

inmate [in'meit] *n* (in prison) 受刑者 jukéìsha; (in asylum) 入院患者 nyúinkaňja

inn [in] *n* 旅館 ryokán

innate [ineit'] *adj* (skill, quality, characteristic) 生来の seírai no

inner [in'ə:r] *adj* (office, courtyard) 内側の uchígawa no; (calm, feelings) 内心の naíshin no

inner city *n* インナーシティー íñnāshì-

ti◇スラム化した都心部を指す súramu-ka shita toshínbu wo sásù

inner tube n (of tire) チューブ chúbu

inning [in'iŋ] n (BASEBALL) イニング íninŋu

innings [in'iŋz] n (CRICKET) イニング íninŋu

innocence [in'əsəns] n (LAW) 無罪 múzāi; (naivety: of child, person) 純真さ juñshinsa

innocent [in'əsənt] adj (not guilty: of crime etc) 無罪の múzāi no, 潔白な keppáku na; (naive: child, person) 純真な juñshin na; (not involved: victim) 罪のない tsúmì no náì; (remark, question) 無邪気な mújàki na

innocuous [ina:k'ju:əs] adj (harmless) 無害の múgài no

innovation [inəvei'ʃən] n (change) 刷新 sasshín

innuendo [inju:en'dou] (pl innuendoes) n (insinuation) 当てこすり atékosuri

innumerable [inu:'mə:rəbəl] adj (countless) 無数の musū no

inoculation [ina:kjəlei'ʃən] n (MED) 接種 sesshú

inopportune [ina:pə:rtu:n'] adj (event, moment) 都合の悪い tsugō no warúi

inordinately [inɔ:r'dənitli:] adv (proud, long, large etc) 極度に kyokúdò ni

in-patient [in'peiʃənt] n (in hospital) 入院患者 nyúinkañja

input [in'put] n (information) 情報 jóhò; (resources etc) つぎ込む事 tsugíkomù kotó; (COMPUT) 入力 nyúryoku, インプット íñputtò

inquest [in'kwest] n (on someone's death) 検死諮問 keñshishimòn

inquire [inkwaiə:r'] vi (ask) 尋ねる tazúnerù, 聞く kíkù
◆vt (ask) ...に尋ねる ...ni tazúnerù, ...に聞く ...ni kíkù
to inquire about (person, fact) ...について問い合せる ...ni tsúîte toíawase surù

inquire into vt fus (death, circumstances) 調べる shiráberù

inquiry [inkwaiə:r'i:] n (question) 質問 shitsúmon; (investigation) 調査 chósa

inquiry office (BRIT) n 案内所 añnaijò

inquisitive [inkwiz'ətiv] adj (curious) せん索好きな señsakuzuki na

inroads [in'roudz] npl: **to make inroads into** (savings, supplies) ...を消費する ...wo shóhi suru

ins abbr = **inches**

insane [insein'] adj (foolish, crazy) 気違い染みた kichígaijimità; (MED) 狂気の kyóki no

insanity [insæn'iti:] n (foolishness) 狂気のさた kyóki nò satá; (MED) 狂気 kyóki

insatiable [insei'ʃəbəl] adj (greed, appetite) 飽く事のない akú kotò no nái

inscription [inskrip'ʃən] n (on gravestone, memorial etc) 碑文 hibún; (in book) 献呈の言葉 keñtei no kotòba

inscrutable [inskru:'təbəl] adj (comment, expression) 不可解な fukákài na

insect [in'sekt] n 虫 mushi, 昆虫 koñchū

insecticide [insek'tisaid] n 殺虫剤 satchúzài

insecure [insikju:r'] adj (structure, lock, door: weak) 弱い yówài; (: unsafe) 安全でない añzen de naì; (person) 自信のない jishín no naì

insecurity [insikju:r'iti:] n (of structure, lock etc: weakness) 弱さ yówàsa; (: lack of safety) 安全でない事 añzen de naì kotó; (of person) 自信欠如 jishínketsujò

insemination [inseminei'ʃən] n: **artificial insemination** (AGR, MED) 人工授精 jiñkōjùsei

insensible [insen'səbəl] adj (unconscious) 意識を失った íshìki wo ushínattà

insensitive [insen'sətiv] adj (uncaring, indifferent) 思いやりのない omóiyarì no náì

inseparable [insep'ə:rəbəl] adj (ideas, elements) 分離できない buñri dekinài; (friends) いつも一緒の ítsùmo isshó no

insert [insə:rt'] vt (between two things) ...の間に入れる ...no aídà ni irérù; (into something) 差込む sashíkomù, 挿入する sónyū suru

insertion [insə:r'ʃən] n (of needle, comment, peg etc) 差込む事 sashíkomù kotó, 挿入 sónyū

in-service [in'sə:r'vis] *adj* (training, course) 現職の geñshoku no

inshore [in'ʃɔːr] *adj* (fishing, waters) 近海の kiñkai no
♦*adv* (be) 岸の近くに kishí no chikakù ni; (move) 岸の近くへ kishí no chikakù e

inside [in'said'] *n* (interior) 中 nákà, 内側 uchígawa
♦*adj* (interior) 中 [内側] nákà [uchigawa] no
♦*adv* (go) 中 [内側] へ nákà [uchígawa] e; (be) 中 [内側] に nákà [uchígawa] ni
♦*prep* (of location) …の中へ [に] …no nákà e[ni]; (of time): *inside 10 minutes* 10分以内に juppún inài ni

inside forward *n* (SPORT) インサイドフォワード iñsaidofowàdo

inside information *n* 内部情報 naíbujòhō

inside lane *n* (AUT) 内側車線 uchígawashaseñ

inside out *adv* (be, turn) 裏返しで urágaèshi de; (know) すっかり sukkárì

insides [in'saidz] *npl* (*inf*: stomach) おなか onáka

insidious [insid'i:əs] *adj* (effect, power) 潜行的な señkōteki na

insight [in'sait] *n* (into situation, problem) 洞察 dōsatsu

insignia [insig'ni:ə] *npl* 記章 kishō

insignificant [insignif'ikənt] *adj* (extent, importance) ささいな sasái na

insincere [insinsi:r'] *adj* (smile, welcome) 偽りの itsúwarì no

insinuate [insin'ju:eit] *vt* (imply) 当てこする atékosurù

insipid [insip'id] *adj* (person, activity, color) 面白くない omóshirokunài; (food, drink) 風味のない fùmi no nái

insist [insist'] *vi* (maintain) 主張する shuchō suru, 言い張る iíharù
to insist on (demand) …を要求する …wo yōkyū suru
to insist that (demand) …する様要求する …surú yō yōkyū suru; (claim) …だと言い張る …da to iíharù

insistence [insis'təns] *n* (determination) 強要 kyōyō

insistent [insis'tənt] *adj* (determined: person) しつこい shitsúkoì; (continual: noise, action) 絶間ない taémanaì

insole [in'soul] *n* (of shoe) 敷皮 shikíkawa

insolence [in'sələns] *n* (rudeness) 横柄さ ōheisa

insolent [in'sələnt] *adj* (attitude, remark) 横柄な ōhei na

insoluble [insɑ:l'jəbəl] *adj* (problem) 解決のできない kaíketsu nò dekínaì

insolvent [insɑ:l'vənt] *adj* (bankrupt) 破産した hasán shita

insomnia [insɑ:m'ni:ə] *n* 不眠症 fumíñshō

inspect [inspekt'] *vt* (examine: *gen*) 調べる shiráberù; (premises) 捜査する sōsa suru; (equipment) 点検する teñken suru; (troops) 査閲する saétsu suru; (*BRIT*: ticket) 改札する kaísatsu suru

inspection [inspek'ʃən] *n* (examination: *gen*) 検査 keñsa; (of premises) 捜査 sōsa; (of equipment) 点検 teñken; (of troops) 査閲 saétsu; (*BRIT*: of ticket) 改札 kaísatsu

inspector [inspek'tə:r] *n* (ADMIN) 検査官 keñsakàn; (*BRIT*: on buses, trains) 車掌 shashō; (: POLICE) 警部 keibu

inspiration [inspərei'ʃən] *n* (encouragement) 発憤 happún; (influence, source) 発憤させる物 happún saserù mono; (idea) 霊感 reíkan, インスピレーション iñsupirēshon

inspire [inspaiə:r'] *vt* (workers, troops) 奮い立たせる furúitataserù; (confidence, hope etc) 持たせる motáserù

instability [instəbil'əti:] *n* (of place, person, situation) 不安定 fuáñtei

install [instɔ:l'] *vt* (machine) 取付ける torítsukerù; (official) 就任させる shūnin saserù

installation [instəlei'ʃən] *n* (of machine, equipment) 取付け torítsuke, 設置 sétchì; (plant: INDUSTRY) 工場施設 kójōshisètsu, プラント puráñto; (: MIL) 基地 kichí

installment [instɔ:l'mənt] (*BRIT* **instalment**) *n* (of payment, story, TV

serial etc) 1回分 ikkáíbun
in installments (pay, receive) 分割払い
で buńkatsubarài de
instance [in'stəns] *n* (example) 例 réi
for instance 例えば tatóèba
in the first instance まず最初に mázù
saísho ni
instant [in'stənt] *n* (moment) 瞬間 shuń-
kan
♦*adj* (reaction, success) 瞬間的な shuńkanteki na; (coffee, food) 即席の sokúseki no, インスタントの fńsutanto no
instantaneous [instəntei'ni:əs] *adj*
(immediate) 即時の sokúji no
instantly [in'stəntli:] *adv* (immediately)
即時に sokúji ni
instead [insted'] *adv* (in place of) (そ
の) 代りに (sonó) kawári ni
instead of ...の代りに ...no kawári ni
instep [in'step] *n* (of foot) 足の甲 ashí no
kō; (of shoe) 靴の甲 kutsú no kō
instigate [in'stəgeit] *vt* (rebellion etc) 起
させる okósaserù; (talks etc) 始めさせる
hajímesaserù
instil(l) [instil'] *vt*: *to instil something
into* (confidence, fear etc) ...を...に吹込
む ...wo ...ni fukíkomù
instinct [in'stiŋkt] *n* 本能 hońnō
instinctive [instiŋk'tiv] *adj* (reaction,
feeling) 本能的な hońnōteki na
institute [in'stitu:t] *n* (for research,
teaching) 施設 shisétsu; (professional
body: of architects, planners etc) 協会
kyōkai
♦*vt* (system, rule, course of action) 設ける
mṓkerù; (proceedings, inquiry) 始める
hajímerù
institution [institu:'ʃən] *n* (of system
etc) 開設 kaísetsu; (custom, tradition) 伝
統 deńtō; (organization: financial, religious, educational) 協会 kyōkai; (hospital, mental home) 施設 shisétsu
instruct [instrʌkt] *vt*: *to instruct
someone in something* (teach) ...に...を
教える ...ni ...wo oshíerù
to instruct someone to do something
(order) ...する様に...に命令する ...surú yō
...ni meírei suru

instruction [instrʌk'ʃən] *n* (teaching) 教
育 kyōiku
instructions [instrʌk'ʃənz] *npl* (orders)
命令 meírei
instructions (for use) 取扱い説明 toríatsukai setsúmei
instructive [instrʌk'tiv] *adj* (lesson,
response) 有益な yūeki na
instructor [instrʌk'tər] *n* (teacher) 先
生 seńsei; (for skiing, driving etc) 指導者
shidōshā
instrument [in'strəmənt] *n* (tool) 道具
dōgu; (measuring device etc) 計器 keíki;
(MUS) 楽器 gakkí
instrumental [instrəmen'təl] *adj* (MUS)
器楽の kígaku no
to be instrumental in ...に大きな役割
を果す ...ni ōkina yakúwari wo hatasù
instrument panel *n* 計器盤 keíkiban
insubordination [insəbɔ:rdənei'ʃən] *n*
(disobedience) 不服従 fufúkujū
insufferable [insʌf'ə:rəbəl] *adj* (arrogance, laziness) 耐えがたい taégataì;
(person) 我慢のならない gámàn no naránaì
insufficient [insəfiʃ'ənt] *adj* (funds,
data, research) 不十分な fujūbùn na
insular [in'sələ:r] *adj* (outlook, person)
狭量な kyōryō na
insulate [in'səleit] *vt* (protect: person,
group) 孤立させる korítsu saserù;
(against cold: house, body) 断熱する dań-
netsu suru; (against sound) 防音にする
bōon ni suru; (against electricity) 絶縁す
る zetsúen suru
insulating tape [in'səleitiŋ-] *n* (ELEC)
絶縁テープ zetsúentèpu
insulation [insəlei'ʃən] *n* (of person,
group) 孤立させる事 korítsu saserù ko-
tó; (against cold) 断熱材 dańnetsuzài;
(against sound) 防音材 bōonzài; (against
electricity) 絶縁材 zetsúenzài
insulin [in'səlin] *n* (MED) インシュリン iń-
shurin
insult [*n* in'sʌlt *vb* insʌlt'] *n* (offence) 侮
辱 bujóku
♦*vt* (offend) 侮辱する bujóku suru
insulting [insʌl'tiŋ] *adj* (attitude, lan-

guage) 侮辱的な bujōkuteki na

insuperable [insu:'pə:rəbəl] *adj* (obstacle, problem) 乗越えられない noríkoerarenaì

insurance [inʃə:r'əns] *n* (on property, car, life etc) 保険 hokén

fire/life insurance 火災〔生命〕保険 kasái〔seímei〕hokèn

insurance agent *n* 保険代理店 hokéndairitèn

insurance policy *n* 保険証書 hokénshòsho

insure [inʃu:r'] *vt* (life, property): *to insure (against)* ...に (...の) 保険を掛ける ...ni (...no) hokén wò kakérù

to insure (oneself) against (disappointment, disaster) ...に備える ...ni sonáerù

insurrection [insərek'ʃən] *n* (uprising) 反乱 hañran

intact [intækt'] *adj* (whole) 元のままの mótò no mamá no; (unharmed) 無傷の múkìzu no

intake [in'teik] *n* (gen) 取込み toríkomi; (of food etc) 摂取 sésshù; (of air) 吸入 kyúnyū; (BRIT: SCOL): *an intake of 200 a year* 毎年の新入生は200人 maítoshi nò shifinyūsei wa nihyakúnìn

intangible [intæn'dʒəbəl] *adj* (quality, idea, benefit) ばく然とした bakúzen to shita

integral [in'təgrəl] *adj* (feature, element) 不可欠な fukákètsu na

integrate [in'təgreit] *vt* (newcomer) 溶け込ませる tokékomaserù; (ideas, systems) 取入れる toríirerù

◆*vi* (groups, individuals) 溶け込む tokékomù

integrity [integ'riti:] *n* (morality: of person) 誠実さ seíjitsusa

intellect [in'təlekt] *n* (intelligence) 知性 chiséi; (cleverness) 知能 chinō

intellectual [intəlek'tʃuːəl] *adj* (activity, interest, pursuit) 知的な chitéki na

◆*n* (intelligent person) 知識人 chishíkijìn, インテリ ifiteri

intelligence [intel'idʒəns] *n* (cleverness, thinking power) 知能 chinō; (MIL etc) 情報 jōhō

intelligence service *n* 情報部 jōhōbu

intelligent [intel'idʒənt] *adj* (person) 知能の高い chinō no takaì; (decision) 利口な rikō na; (machine) インテリジェントの ifiterijento no

intelligentsia [intelidʒen'tsi:ə] *n* 知識階級 chishíkikaìkyū, インテリ階級 ifiterikaìkyū

intelligible [intel'idʒəbəl] *adj* (clear, comprehensible) 分かりやすい wakáriyasuì

intend [intend'] *vt* (gift etc): *to intend something for* ...を...に上げようと思っている ...wo ...ni agéyò to omótte irù

to intend to do something (mean) ...する決心でいる ...suru kesshíñ de irú; (plan) ...するつもりである ...suru tsumóri de arù

intended [inten'did] *adj* (effect, insult) 意図した ítò shita; (journey) 計画した keíkaku shita; (victim) ねらった nerátta

intense [intens'] *adj* (heat, effort, anger, joy) 猛烈な mōretsu na; (person) 情熱的な jōnetsuteki na

intensely [intens'li:] *adv* (extremely) 激しく hagéshikù

intensify [inten'səfai] *vt* (efforts, pressure) 増す másù

intensity [inten'siti:] *n* (of heat, anger, effort) 激しさ hagéshisa

intensive [inten'siv] *adj* (concentrated) 集中的な shūchūteki na

intensive care unit *n* (MED) 集中治療室 shūchūchiryōshitsu, ICU aishíyū

intent [intent'] *n* (intention) 意図 ítò; (LAW) 犯意 hán-i

◆*adj* (absorbed): *intent (on)* (...しようとして) 余念がない (...shíyò to shite) yonén ga naì; (attentive) 夢中な muchū na

to all intents and purposes 事実上 jijítsujō

to be intent on doing something (determined) ...しようとして余念がない ...shíyò to shite yonén ga naì

intention [inten'tʃən] *n* (purpose) 目的 mokúteki; (plan) 意図 ítò

intentional [inten't∫ənəl] adj (deliberate) 意図的な ítòteki na

intentionally [inten't∫ənəli:] adv (deliberately) 意図的に ítòteki ni, わざと wázà to

intently [intent'li:] adv (listen, watch) 熱心に nesshín ni

inter [intə:r'] vt (bury) 埋葬する maísō suru

interact [intə:rækt'] vi: **to interact (with)** (people, things, ideas) (...と) 相互に反応し合う (...to) sṓgo ni hañnō shiaù

interaction [intə:ræk't∫ən] n 相互反応 sṓgohañnō

intercede [intə:rsi:d'] vi: **to intercede (with)** (...に) 取りなしをする (...ni) torínashi wo surú

intercept [in'tə:rsept] vt (person, car) 途中で捕まえる tochū de tsukamaerù; (message) 傍受する bṓju suru

interchange [in'tə:rt∫eindʒ] n (exchange) 交換 kṓkan; (on motorway) インターチェンジ iñtāchieñji

interchangeable [intə:rt∫ein'dʒəbəl] adj (terms, ideas, things) 置換えられる okíkaerarerù

intercom [in'tə:rkɑ:m] n (in office etc) インターホーン iñtāhōn

intercourse [in'tə:rkɔ:rs] n (also: **sexual intercourse**) 性交 seíkō

interest [in'trist] n (in subject, idea, person etc) 興味 kyṓmi; (pastime, hobby) 趣味 shúmì; (advantage, profit) 利益 ríèki; (COMM: in company) 株 kábù; (: sum of money) 利息 risóku

♦vt (subject: work, subject, idea etc) ...の興味をそそる ...no kyṓmi wo sosórù
...no kyṓmi wo sosórù

to be interested in ...に興味がある ...ni kyṓmi ga árù

interesting [in'tristiŋ] adj (idea, place, person) 面白い omóshiroì

interest rate n 利率 rirítsu

interface [in'tə:rfeis] n (COMPUT) インターフェース iñtāfēsu

interfere [intə:rfi:r'] vi: **to interfere in** (quarrel, other people's business) ...に干渉する ...ni kañshō suru

to interfere with (object) ...をいじる

...wo ijírù; (plans, career, duty, decision) ...を邪魔する ...wo jamá suru

interference [intə:rfi:r'əns] n (in someone's affairs etc) 干渉 kañshō; (RADIO, TV) 混信 koñshin

interim [in'tə:rim] adj (agreement, government) 暫定的な zañteiteki na

♦n: **in the interim** (meanwhile) その間 sonó aidà

interior [inti:'ri:ə:r] n (of building, car, box etc) 内部 naíbu; (of country) 内陸 naíriku

♦adj (door, window, room etc) 内部の naíbu no; (minister, department) 内務の naímu no

interior designer n インテリアデザイナー iñteriadezaínā

interjection [intə:rdʒek't∫ən] n (interruption) 野次 yájì; (LING) 感嘆詞 kañtañshi

interlock [in'tə:rlɑ:k] vi かみ合う kamíaù

interloper [intə:rlou'pə:r] n (in town, meeting etc) ちん入者 chíñnyùsha

interlude [in'tə:rlu:d] n (break) 休憩 kyṻkei; (THEATER) 休憩時間 kyṻkeijikàn

intermarry [intə:rmær'i:] vi 交婚する kṓkon suru

intermediary [intə:rmi:'di:e:ri:] n 仲介者 chūkaísha

intermediate [intə:rmi:'di:it] adj (stage, student) 中間の chūkan no

interminable [intə:r'mənəbəl] adj (process, delay) 果てし無い hatéshinaì

intermission [intə:rmi∫'ən] n (pause) 休止 kyū́shi; (THEATER, CINEMA) 休憩時間 kyṻkeijikàn

intermittent [intə:rmit'ənt] adj (noise, publication etc) 断続的な dañzokuteki na

intern [in'tə:rn] vt (imprison) 拘置する kṓchi suru

♦n (US: houseman) 研修医 keñshūi

internal [intə:r'nəl] adj (layout, structure, memo etc) 内部の naíbu no; (pipes etc) 埋め込みの umékomi no; (bleeding, injury) 体内の taínai no; (security, politics) 国内の kokúnai no

internally [intə:r'nəli:] *adv* 「*not to be taken internally*」内服外用薬 naffuku-gaiyōyaku

Internal Revenue Service (*US*) *n* 国税庁 kokúzeichō

international [intə:rnæʃ'ənəl] *adj* (trade, agreement etc) 国際的な kokúsaiteki na, 国際... kokúsai...
♦ *n* (*BRIT*: SPORT: match) 国際試合 kokúsaijiái

interplay [in'tə:rplei] *n*: *interplay (of/between)* (...の) 相互反応 (...no) sōgohannō

interpret [intə:r'prit] *vt* (explain, understand) 解釈する káishaku suru; (translate) 通訳する tsūyaku suru
♦ *vi* (translate) 通訳する tsūyaku suru

interpretation [intə:rpritei'ʃən] *n* (explanation) 解釈 káishaku; (translation) 通訳 tsūyaku

interpreter [intə:r'pritə:r] *n* (translator) 通訳 (者) tsūyaku(sha)

interrelated [intə:rilei'tid] *adj* (causes, factors etc) 相互関係のある sōgokankèi no aru

interrogate [inte:r'əgeit] *vt* (question: witness, prisoner, suspect) 尋問する jińmon suru

interrogation [inte:rəgei'ʃən] *n* (of witness, prisoner etc) 尋問 jińmon

interrogative [intərɑːg'ətiv] *adj* (LING) 疑問の gímon no

interrupt [intərʌpt'] *vt* (speaker) ...の話に割込む ...no hanáshi nì waríkomù; (activity) 邪魔する jamá suru
♦ *vi* (during someone's conversation etc) 話に割込む hanáshi ni waríkomù; (during activity) 邪魔する jamá suru

interruption [intərʌp'ʃən] *n* (act) 邪魔する事 jamá suru kotò; (instance) 邪魔jamá

intersect [intə:rsekt'] *vi* (roads) 交差する kōsa suru

intersection [intə:rsek'ʃən] *n* (of roads) 交差点 kōsatèn

intersperse [intə:rspə:rs'] *vt*: *to intersperse with* ...を所々に入れる ...wo tokórodokòro ni irérù

intertwine [intə:rtwain'] *vi* 絡み合う karámiaù

interval [in'tə:rvəl] *n* (break, pause) 間隔 kańkaku; (*BRIT*: SCOL: *also* THEATER, SPORT) 休憩時間 kyūkeijikàn
at intervals (periodically) 時々 tokídoki

intervene [intə:rvi:n'] *vi* (person: in situation: interfere) 介入する kaínyu suru; (: : to help) 仲裁に入る chūsai ni hairù; (: in speech) 割込む waríkomù; (event) 間に起る aída ni okorù; (time) 経つ tátsù

intervention [intə:rven'tʃən] *n* (of person: interference) 介入 kaínyu; (help) 仲裁 chūsai

interview [in'tə:rvju:] *n* (for job etc) 面接 meńsetsu; (RADIO, TV etc) インタビュー íńtabyū
♦ *vt* (for job etc) ...と面接する ...to meńsetsu suru; (RADIO, TV etc) ...にインタビューする ...ni ińtabyū suru

interviewer [in'tə:rvju:ə:r] *n* (of candidate, job applicant) 面接者 meńsetsushà; (RADIO, TV etc) インタビューア ińtabyūa

intestine [intes'tin] *n* 腸 chō

intimacy [in'təməsi:] *n* (closeness) 親しみ shitáshimi

intimate [*adj* in'təmit *vb* in'təmeit] *adj* (friendship, relationship) 親しい shitáshiì; (detail) 知られざる shirárezarù; (restaurant, dinner, atmosphere) こじんまりした kojínmarì shita; (knowledge) 詳しい kuwáshiì
♦ *vt* (announce) ほのめかす honōmekasù

intimidate [intim'ideit] *vt* (frighten) 脅す odósu

intimidation [intimidei'ʃən] *n* 脅し odóshi

KEYWORD

into [in'tu:] *prep* 1 (indicating motion or direction) ...の中に〔へ〕...no nákà ni(e)
come into the house/garden 家〔庭〕に入って来て下さい ié(niwá)nì háitte kité kudasaì
go into town 町に出掛ける machí ni dekakerù

he got into the car 彼は車に乗った kárè wa kurúma ni nottá

throw it into the fire 火の中へ捨てて下さい hí no nakà e sutéte kudasaí

research into cancer がんの研究 gáñ no kefíkyū

he worked late into the night 彼は夜遅くまで働いた kárè wa yórù osóku madè határaìta

the car bumped into the wall 車は塀にぶつかった kurúma wà heí nì butsúkattà

she poured tea into the cup 彼女は紅茶をカップについだ kánòjo wa kócha wò káppù ni tsuída

2 (indicating change of condition, result): *she burst into tears* 彼女は急に泣き出した kánòjo wa kyū̀ nì nakídashìta

he was shocked into silence 彼はショックで物も言えなかった kárè wa shókkù de monó mò íenakatta

it broke into pieces ばらばらに割れたbarábara nì warétà

she translated into French 彼女はフランス語に訳した kánòjo wa furánsugo nì yakúshità

they got into trouble 彼らは問題を起した kárèra wa mofídai wò okóshità

---

intolerable [intɑːl'ə:rəbəl] *adj* (extent, quality) 我慢できない gámàn dekínaì

intolerance [intɑːl'ə:rəns] *n* (bigotry, prejudice) 偏狭さ hefíkyōsa

intolerant [intɑːl'ə:rənt] *adj*: *intolerant (of)* (...に対して) 偏狭な (...ni táìshite) hefíkyō na

intonation [intounei'ʃən] *n* (of voice, speech) 抑揚 yokúyō, イントネーション ifítonēshon

intoxicated [intɑːk'sikeitid] *adj* (drunk) 酔っ払った yoppárattà

intoxication [intɑːksikei'ʃən] *n* 泥酔 deísui

intractable [intræk'təbəl] *adj* (child, problem) 手に負えない té ni oenài

intransigent [intræn'sidʒənt] *adj* (attitude) 頑固な gafíko na

intransitive [intræn'sətiv] *adj* (LING): *intransitive verb* 自動詞 jidóshì

intravenous [intrəvi:'nəs] *adj* (injection, drip) 静脈内の jómyakunaì no

in-tray [in'trei] *n* (in office) 着信のトレー chakúshin nò torḗ

intrepid [intrep'id] *adj* (adventurer, explorer) 勇敢な yūkan na

intricate [in'trəkit] *adj* (pattern, design) 複雑な fukúzatsu na

intrigue [intri:g'] *n* (plotting) 策略 sakúryàku
♦*vt* (fascinate) ...の好奇心をそそる ...no kókishin wò sosórù

intriguing [intri:'giŋ] *adj* (fascinating) 面白い omóshiroì

intrinsic [intrin'sik] *adj* (quality, nature) 本質的な hofíshitsuteki na

introduce [intrədus'] *vt* (new idea, measure etc) 導入する dốnyū suru; (speaker, TV show etc) 紹介する shókai suru
to introduce someone (to someone) (...に) ...を紹介する (...ni) ...wo shókai suru
to introduce someone to (pastime, technique) ...に...を初めて経験させる ...ni ...wo hajímète keíken saserù

introduction [intrədʌk'ʃən] *n* (of new idea, measure etc) 導入 dốnyū; (of person) 紹介 shókai; (to new experience) 初めて経験させる事 hajímète keíken saserù kotó; (to book) 前書 maégaki

introductory [intrədʌk'tə:ri:] *adj* (lesson) 導入の dốnyū no; (offer) 初回の shokái no

introspective [intrəspek'tiv] *adj* (person, mood) 内省的な naíseiteki na

introvert [in'trəvə:rt] *n* 内向性の人 naíkōsei no hitò
♦*adj (also: introverted*: behavior, child etc) 内向性の naíkōsei no

intrude [intru:d'] *vi* (person) 邪魔する jamá suru
to intrude on (conversation, grief, party etc) ...のところを邪魔する ...no tokóro wò jamá suru

intruder [intru:'də:r] *n* (into home, camp) 侵入者 shifínyūshà

intrusion [intru:'ʒən] n (of person, outside influences) 邪魔 jamá

intuition [intu:í'ʃən] n (feeling, hunch) 直感 chokkán

intuitive [intu:'ətiv] adj (instinctive) 直感的な chokkánteki na

inundate [in'ʌndeit] vt: **to inundate with** (calls, letters etc) …が殺到する …ga sattó suru

invade [inveid'] vt (MIL) …を侵略する …wo shińryaku suru

invalid [n in'vəlid adj invæ'lid] n (MED: disabled person) 身障者 shińshōsha; (: sick and weak person) 病弱な人 byójaku na hitò

◆adj (not valid) 無効の mukó no

invaluable [invæl'ju:əbəl] adj (person, thing) 貴重な kichō na

invariable [inve:r'i:əbəl] adj 変らない kawáranaì, 不変の fuhén no

invariably [inve:r'i:əbli:] adv 必ず kanárazù

invasion [invei'ʒən] n (MIL) 侵略 shińryaku

invent [invent'] vt (machine, game, phrase etc) 発明する hatsúmei suru; (fabricate: lie, excuse) でっち上げる detchíagerù

invention [inven'tʃən] n (machine, system) 発明品 hatsúmeihin; (untrue story) 作り話 tsukúribanàshi; (act of inventing: machine, system) 発明 hatsúmei

inventor [inven'tə:r] n (of machines, systems) 発明家 hatsúmeika

inventory [in'vəntɔ:ri:] n (of house, ship etc) 物品目録 buppínmokùroku

inverse [inve:rs'] adj (relationship) 逆の gyakú no

invert [inve:rt'] vt (turn upside down) 逆さにする sakása ni surù

invertebrate [inve:r'təbrit] n 無せきつい動物 musékitsuidōbutsu

inverted commas [inve:r'tid-] (BRIT) npl 引用符 ińyōfù

invest [invest'] vt (money) 投資する tóshi suru; (fig: time, energy) つぎ込む tsugíkomù

◆vi: **invest in** (COMM) …に投資する

…ni tóshi suru; (fig: something useful) 購入する kónyū suru

investigate [inves'təgeit] vt (accident, crime, person) 取調べる toríshiraberù, 捜査する sósa suru

investigation [inves'təgeiʃən] n 取調べ toríshirabe, 捜査 sósa

investigator [inves'təgeitə:r] n (of events, situations, people) 捜査官 sósakàn

investiture [inves'titʃə:r] n (of chancellor) 就任式 shúniñshiki; (of prince) たい冠式 taíkañshiki

investment [invest'mənt] n (activity) 投資 tóshi; (amount of money) 投資額 tóshigàku

investor [inves'tə:r] n (COMM) 投資者 tóshishà

inveterate [invet'ə:rit] adj (liar, cheat etc) 常習的な jóshūteki na

invidious [invid'i:əs] adj (task, job: unpleasant) 憎まれ役の nikúmareyàku no; (comparison, decision: unfair) 不公平な fukóhei na

invigilator [invidʒ'əleitə:r] (BRIT) n (in exam) 試験監督 shikéñkañtoku

invigorating [invig'ə:reitiŋ] adj (air, breeze etc) さわやかな sawáyàka na; (experience etc) 元気が出る様な geńki ga deru yō na

invincible [invin'səbəl] adj (army, team: unbeatable) 無敵の mútèki no

invisible [inviz'əbəl] adj 目に見えない mé ni mienài

invitation [invitei'ʃən] n (to party, meal, meeting etc) 招待 shótai; (written card, paper) 招待状 shótaijō

invite [in'vait] vt (to party, meal, meeting etc) 招く manékù, 招待する shótai suru; (encourage: discussion, criticism) 求める motómerù

to invite someone to do …に…するよう求める …ni …surú yō motómerù

inviting [invai'tiŋ] adj (attractive, desirable) 魅力的な miryókuteki na

invoice [in'vɔis] n (COMM) 請求書 seíkyūsho

◆vt …に請求書を送る …ni seíkyūsho wo

okúrù

invoke [invouk'] *vt* (law, principle) ...に訴える ...ni uttáerù

involuntary [inva:l'ənte:ri:] *adj* (action, reflex etc) 反射的な hañshateki na

involve [inva:lv'] *vt* (person, thing: include, use) 伴う tomónaù, 必要とする hitsúyō to surù; (: concern, affect) ...に関係する ...ni kañkei suru

to involve someone (in something) (...に) ...を巻き込む (...ni) ...wo makíkomù

involved [inva:lvd'] *adj* (complicated) 複雑な fukúzatsu na

to be involved in (take part: in activity etc) ...にかかわる ...ni kakáwarù; (be engrossed) ...に夢中になっている ...ni muchū ni nattè irú

involvement [inva:lv'mənt] *n* (participation) 参加 sañka; (concern, enthusiasm) 感情的かかわり合い kañjōteki nà kakáwariaì

inward [in'wə:rd] *adj* (thought, feeling) 内心の naíshin no; (movement) 中の方への nákà no hố e no

inward(s) [in'wə:rd(z)] *adv* (move, face) 中の方へ nákà no hố e

I/O [ai'ou'] *abbr* (*COMPUT*: = *input/ output*) 入出力 nyūshutsuryóku

iodine [ai'ədain] *n* (chemical element) ヨウ素 yōso, ヨード yōdo; (disinfectant) ヨードチンキ yódochiñki

ion [ai'ən] *n* イオン íòn

iota [aiou'tə] *n: not one/an iota* 少しも ...ない sukóshī mo ...náì

IOU [aiouju:'] *n abbr* (= *I owe you*) 借用証 shakúyōshō

IQ [aikju:'] *n abbr* (= *intelligence quotient*) 知能指数 chínōshisū, IQ aikyū

IRA [aia:rei'] *n abbr* (= *Irish Republican Army*) アイルランド共和国軍 aírurando kyōwakakugùn

Iran [iræn'] *n* イラン íràn

Iranian [irei'ni:ən] *adj* イランの íràn no
◆*n* イラン人 iráñjin

Iraq [ira:k'] *n* イラク íràku

Iraqi [ira:k'i:] *adj* イラクの íràku no
◆*n* イラク人 iráküjin

irascible [iræs'əbəl] *adj* 怒りっぽい okó-

rippoì

irate [aireit'] *adj* 怒っている okótte irù

Ireland [aiə:r'lənd] *n* アイルランド aírurando

iris [ai'ris] (*pl* **irises**) *n* (ANAT) こう彩 kốsai; (BOT) アヤメ ayáme, アイリス áìrisu

Irish [ai'riʃ] *adj* アイルランドの aírurando no
◆*npl: the Irish* アイルランド人 aíruran-dojìn ◇総称 sōshō

Irishman/woman [ai'riʃmən/wumən] (*pl* **Irishmen/women**) *n* アイルランド人男性〔女性〕 aírurandojìn dañsei〔joséi〕

Irish Sea *n: the Irish Sea* アイリッシュ海 aírisshukaì

irksome [ə:rk'səm] *adj* いらいらさせるí-ràira saséru

iron [ai'ə:rn] *n* (metal) 鉄 tetsú; (for clothes) アイロン aíron
◆*cpd* (bar, railings) 鉄の tetsú no; (will, discipline etc) 鉄の様な tetsú no yố na
◆*vt* (clothes) ...にアイロンを掛ける ...ni aíron wò kakérù

Iron Curtain *n: the Iron Curtain* 鉄のカーテン tetsú no kấten

ironic(al) [aira:n'ik(əl)] *adj* (remark, gesture, situation) 皮肉な hínìku na

ironing [ai'ə:rniŋ] *n* (activity) アイロン掛け aíronkake; (clothes) アイロンを掛けるべき衣類 aíron wò kakérubeki irúi

ironing board *n* アイロン台 aírondai

ironmonger [ai'ə:rnmʌŋgə:r] (*BRIT*) *n* 金物屋 kanámonoya ◇人を指す hitó wò sásù

ironmonger's (shop) [ai'ə:rnmʌŋgə:rz-] *n* 金物屋 kanámonoya ◇店を指す misé wò sásù

iron out *vt* (*fig*: problems) 打開する dakái suru

irony [ai'rəni:] *n* 皮肉 hínìku

irrational [iræʃ'ənəl] *adj* (feelings, behavior) 不合理な fugốri na

irreconcilable [irek'ənsailəbəl] *adj* (ideas, views) 両立しない ryőritsu shinaì; (disagreement) 調和不可能な chốwafukanố na

irrefutable [irifju:'təbəl] *adj* (fact) 否め

られない inámerarenaì; (argument) 反ば
くできない hañbaku dekinài

irregular [ireg'jələr] *adj* (surface) 凸 凹
の dekóboko no; (pattern, action, event
etc) 不規則な fukísoku na; (not acceptable: behavior) 良くない yókùnai; (verb,
noun, adjective) 不規則変化の fukísoku-
heñka no

irregularity [iregjəlær'iti:] *n* (of surface) 凸凹 dekóboko; (of pattern, action
etc) 不規則 fukísoku; (instance of behavior) 良くない行為 yókunai kôi

irrelevant [irel'əvənt] *adj* (fact, information) 関係のない kañkei no naì

irreparable [irep'ərəbəl] *adj* (harm,
damage etc) 取返しの付かない toríkae-
shi no tsukanài

irreplaceable [iriplei'səbəl] *adj* 掛替え
のない kakégae no naì

irrepressible [iripres'əbəl] *adj* 陽気な
yôki na

irresistible [irizis'təbəl] *adj* (force) 抵抗
できない teíkô dekinài; (urge, desire) 抑
えきれない osáekirenaì; (person, thing)
とても魅惑的な totémô miwákuteki na

irresolute [irez'əlu:t] *adj* 決断力のない
ketsúdanryòku no naî

irrespective [irispek'tiv]: *irrespective
of prep* ...と関係なく ...to kañkei nakù

irresponsible [irispɑːn'səbəl] *adj* (person, action) 無責任な musékinin na

irreverent [irev'ə:rənt] *adj* 不敬な fukéi
na

irrevocable [irev'əkəbəl] *adj* (action,
decision) 変更できない heñkô dekinài

irrigate [ir'igeit] *vt* (AGR) かんがいする
kañgai suru

irrigation [irigei'ʃən] *n* (AGR) かんがい
kañgai

irritable [ir'itəbəl] *adj* 怒りっぽい okô-
rippoì

irritate [ir'əteit] *vt* (annoy) いらいらさ
せる íraìra saséru; (MED) 刺激する shigéki suru

irritating [ir'əteitiŋ] *adj* (person, sound
etc) いらいらさせる íraira saséru

irritation [iritei'ʃən] *n* (feeling of annoyance) いら立ち irádachi; (MED) 刺激 shi-

géki; (annoying thing) いら立ちの元 irádachi no motò

IRS [aiɑːres'] (*US*) *n abbr* = **Internal
Revenue Service**

is [iz] *vb see* **be**

Islam [iz'lɑːm] *n* イスラム教 isúramukyò

Islamic [izlɑːm'ic] *adj* イスラム教の isúramukyò no

island [ai'lənd] *n* (GEO) 島 shimá

islander [ai'ləndə:r] *n* 島の住民 shimá no
júmin

isle [ail] *n* (GEO) 島 shimá

isn't [iz'ənt] = **is not**

isolate [ai'səleit] *vt* (physically, socially:
set apart) 孤立させる korítsu saserù;
(substance) 分離する buñri suru; (sick
person, animal) 隔離する kakúri suru

isolated [ai'səleitid] *adj* (place) へんぴな
heñpi na; (person) 孤立した korítsu shita; (incident) 単独の tañdoku no

isolation [aisəlei'ʃən] *n* 孤立 korítsu

isotope [ai'sətoup] *n* (PHYSICS) 同位体
dôitai, アイソトープ aísotôpu

Israel [iz'reiəl] *n* イスラエル isúraèru

Israeli [izrei'li:] *adj* イスラエルの isúraèru no
♦*n* イスラエル人 isúraerujìn

issue [iʃ'u:] *n* (problem, subject, most
important part) 問題 moñdai; (of newspaper, magazine etc) 号 gô; (of book) 版
hâñ; (of stamp) 発行部数 hakkôbûsu
♦*vt* (statement) 発表する happyô suru;
(rations, equipment, documents) 配給す
る kañkyû suru
at issue 問題は〔の〕 moñdai wa〔no〕
to take issue with someone (over)
(...について) ...と争う (...ni tsúìte) ...to
arásoù

isthmus [is'məs] *n* (GEO) 半島 hañtô

<u>KEYWORD</u>

it [it] *pron* **1** (specific: subject) それは
〔が〕 soré wà〔gà〕; (: direct object) それ
を soré wò; (: indirect object) それに soré
nì ◊通常日本語では表現しない tsújô ni-
hongo de wa hyôgen shínài
where's my book? - it's on the table
私の本はどこですか-テーブルにあります

watákushi no hoñ wa dókò desu ká - tēbùru ni arímasù

I can't find it 見当りません miátarimaseñ

give it to me それを私に渡して下さい soré wò watákushi nì watáshite kudasaì

about/from/in/of/to it それについて〔から、の中に、の、の方へ〕soré ni tsuíte(kárà, no nákà ni, nó, no hố è)

I spoke to him about it その件について私は彼に話しました sonó keñ ni tsúìte watákushi wà kárè ni hanáshimashìta

what did you learn from it? その事からあなたは何を学びましたか sonó kotò kara anátà wa nánì wo manábimashìta ká

what role did you play in it? その件に関してあなたはどんな役割をしましたか sonó keñ ni káñ shite anátà wa doñna yakùwari wo shimáshìta ká

I'm proud of it それを誇りに思っています soré wò hokóri nì omótte imasù

did you go to it? (party, concert etc) 行きましたか ikímashìta ká

2 (impersonal): *it's raining* 雨が降っている ámè ga futté irù

it's cold today 今日は寒い kyố wà samúì

it's Friday tomorrow 明日は金曜日です asú wà kiñ-yòbi desu

it's 6 o'clock/the 10th of August 6時(8月10日)です rokújì(hachígàtsu tốkà)desu

how far is it? - it's 10 miles/2 hours on the train そこまでどのぐらいありますか-10マイル〔列車で2時間です〕sokó madè donó gurai arimasù ká - jūmaìru arímasù(resshá dè nijíkàn desu)

who is it? - it's me どなたですか-私です dóñàta desu ká - watákushi desù

Italian [itæl'jən] *adj* イタリアの itária no; (LING) イタリア語の itáriago no
♦*n* (person) イタリア人 itáriajìn; (LING) イタリア語 itáriago

italics [itæl'iks] *npl* (TYP) 斜体文字 shatáimòji, イタリック体 itárikkutai

Italy [it'əli:] *n* イタリア itária

itch [itʃ] *n* (irritation) かゆみ kayúmi
♦*vi* (person) かゆがる kayúgarù; (part of body) かゆい kayúî

to itch to do something ...をしたくてむずむずしている ...wo shitákutè múzùmuzu shité irù

itchy [itʃ'i:] *adj* (person) かゆがっている kayúgatte irù; (skin etc) かゆい kayúî

it'd [it'əd] = **it would**; **it had**

item [ai'təm] *n* (one thing: of list, collection) 品目 hiñmoku; (on agenda) 項目 kốmoku; (*also*: **news item**) 記事 kíjì

itemize [ai'təmaiz] *vt* (list) 明細に書く meísai ni kakù, リストアップする risútoappù suru

itinerant [aitin'ə:rənt] *adj* (laborer, salesman, priest etc) 巡回する juñkai suru

itinerary [aitin'əre:ri:] *n* 旅程 ryotéi

it'll [it'əl] = **it will**; **it shall**

its [its] *adj* それ〔あれ〕の soré(arè)no

it's [its] = **it is**; **it has**

itself [itself'] *pron* それ〔あれ〕自身 soré(arè)jishiñ

ITV [ait:vi:'] *n abbr* (BRIT: = *Independent Television*) 民間テレビ放送 míñkan terebi hōsò

IUD [aiju:di:'] *n abbr* (= *intra-uterine device*) 子宮内避妊具 shikyúnaihininìgu, IUD aiyūdī

I've [aiv] = **I have**

ivory [ai'və:ri:] *n* (substance) 象げ zốge; (color) アイボリー áibòrī

ivory tower *n* (*fig*) 象げの塔 zốge no tồ

ivy [ai'vi:] *n* (BOT) キヅタ kízùta, アイビー áibī

J

jab [dʒæb] *vt* (poke: with elbow, stick) 突く tsukú
♦*n* (*inf*: injection) 注射 chúsha

to jab something into something ...を...に突っ込む ...wo...ni tsukkốmù

jabber [dʒæb'ə:r] *vi* (*also*: **jabber away**) ぺちゃくぺちゃしゃべる péchàkucha

shabérù

jack [dʒæk] n (AUT) ジャッキ jákkì; (CARDS) ジャック jákkù

jackal [dʒæk'əl] n ジャッカル jákkàru

jackdaw [dʒæk'dɔ:] n コクマルガラス kokúmarugaràsu

jacket [dʒæk'it] n (garment) ジャケット jákètto; (of book) ジャケット jákètto, カバー kábà

potatoes in their jackets 皮ごと料理 したジャガイモ kawágòto ryōri shita jagáimo

jack-knife [dʒæk'naif] vi (trailer truck) ジャックナイフ現象を起す jakkúnaifu genshō wo okósù ◇鋭角に折り曲って動けなくなる eíkaku ni orímagatte ugokenàku nárù

jack plug n (ELEC: for headphones etc) プラグ purágù

jackpot [dʒæk'pɑ:t] n 大賞金 daíshōkin
to hit the jackpot 大賞金を当てる daíshōkin wo atérù, 大当りする ōatári suru

jack up vt (AUT) ジャッキで持上げる jákkì de mochíagerù

jade [dʒeid] n (stone) ひすい hisúi

jaded [dʒei'did] adj (tired) 疲れ切った tsukárekittà; (fed-up) うんざりした uñzaríshita

jagged [dʒæg'id] adj (outline, edge) ぎざぎざの gízàgiza no

jail [dʒeil] n 刑務所 keímusho
◆vt 刑務所に入れる keímusho ni irérù

jam [dʒæm] n (food) ジャム jámù; (also: *traffic jam*) 交通渋滞 kōtsūjūtai; (inf: difficulty): *to be in a jam* 困っている komátte irù
◆vt (passage etc) ふさぐ fuságù; (mechanism, drawer etc) 動けなくする ugókenàku suru; (RADIO) 妨害する bōgai suru
◆vi (mechanism, drawer etc) 動けなくなる ugókenàku nárù
to jam something into something (cram, stuff) ...に...を押込む ...ni...wo oshíkomù

Jamaica [dʒəmei'kə] n ジャマイカ jámaìka

jangle [dʒæŋ'gəl] vi (keys, bracelets etc) じゃらじゃら鳴る járàjara narú

janitor [dʒæn'itə:r] n (caretaker: of building) 管理人 kañrinin

January [dʒæn'ju:we:ri:] n 1月 ichígatsu

Japan [dʒəpæn'] n 日本 nihóñ〔nippóñ〕

Japanese [dʒæpəni:z'] adj 日本の nihóñ〔nippóñ〕no; (LING) 日本語の nihóngo no
◆n inv (person) 日本人 nihóñ〔nippóñ〕jin; (LING) 日本語 nihóngo

jar [dʒɑ:r] n (container: glass with wide mouth) 瓶 bíñ; (: stone, earthenware) つぼ tsubó, かめ kamé
◆vi (sound) 耳ざわりである mimízawàri de aru, きしる kishírù; (colors) 釣合わない tsuríawanài

jargon [dʒɑ:r'gən] n 専門用語 señmonyōgo, 隠語 iñgo

jasmine [dʒæz'min] n ジャスミン jásùmin

jaundice [dʒɔ:n'dis] n (MED) 黄だん ōdan

jaundiced [dʒɔ:n'dist] adj *to view with a jaundiced eye* 白い目で見る shiróì me de mírù

jaunt [dʒɔ:nt] n (trip, excursion) 遠足 eñsoku

jaunty [dʒɔ:n'ti:] adj (attitude, tone) 陽気な yōki na; (step) 軽やかな karóyàka na

javelin [dʒæv'lin] n (SPORT) やり投げ yarínage

jaw [dʒɔ:] n (ANAT) あご agó

jay [dʒei] n カケス kakésu

jaywalker [dʒei'wɔ:kə:r] n ◇交通規則を無視して道路を横断する人 kótsukisòku wo mushí shite dōro wo ōdan surù hitó

jazz [dʒæz] n (MUS) ジャズ jázù

jazz up vt (liven up: party) 活気付ける kakkízukerù; (: taste) ぴりっとさせる pirítto saséru; (: image) 派手にする hadé ni surù

jazzy [dʒæz'i:] adj (shirt, pattern) 派手な hadé na

jealous [dʒel'əs] adj (suspicious: husband etc) 嫉妬深い shittóbukài; (envious: person) うらやましい uráyamashiì, うらやましがっている uráyamashigàtte irú; (look etc) うらやましそうな uráyamashisōna

jealousy [dʒel'əsi:] n (resentment) ねた

み netámi; (envy) うらやむ事 uráyamù
kotó

jeans [dʒiːnz] *npl* (trousers) ジーパン jípañ

jeep [dʒiːp] *n* (AUT, MIL) ジープ jípù

jeer [dʒiːr] *vi* (mock, scoff): *to jeer (at)*
野次る yajírù

jelly [dʒel'iː] *n* (CULIN) ゼリー zérī

jellyfish [dʒel'iːfiʃ] *n* クラゲ kuráge

jeopardize [dʒep'əːrdaiz] *vt* 危険にさら
す kikén ni sarásù

jeopardy [dʒep'əːrdiː] *n*: *to be in jeopardy* 危険にさらされる kikén ni sarása-
rerù

jerk [dʒəːrk] *n* (jolt, wrench) ◇ 急な動き
kyū na ugóki; (*inf*: idiot) 間抜け manúke
◆*vt* (pull) ぐいと引っ張る guí to hippárù
◆*vi* (vehicle, person, muscle) 急に動く
kyū ni ugókù

jerkin [dʒəːr'kin] *n* チョッキ chokkí

jersey [dʒəːr'ziː] *n* (pullover) セーター sè-
tā; (fabric) ジャージー jājī

jest [dʒest] *n* 冗談 jódañ

Jesus [dʒiː'səs] *n* イエス iésù

jet [dʒet] *n* (of gas, liquid) 噴射 fuñsha, ジ
ェット jéttò; (AVIAT) ジェット機 jétto-
kì

jet-black [dʒet'blæk'] *adj* 真っ黒な mak-
kúrð na

jet engine *n* ジェットエンジン jétto eñjin

jet lag *n* 時差ぼけ jisábòke

jettison [dʒet'əsən] *vt* (fuel, cargo) 捨て
る sutéru

jetty [dʒet'iː] *n* 波止場 hatóba

Jew [dʒuː] *n* ユダヤ人 yudáyajìn

jewel [dʒuː'əl] *n* (*also fig*) 宝石 hóseki; (in
watch) 石 ishí

jeweler [dʒuː'ələːr] (*BRIT* **jeweller**) *n*
(dealer in jewelery) 宝石商 hósekishò;
(dealer in watches) 時計屋 tokéiya

jeweler's (shop) [dʒuː'ələːrz-] *n*
(jewelery shop) 宝石店 hósekitèn; (watch
shop) 時計店 tokéitèn

jewelry [dʒuː'əlriː] (*BRIT* **jewellery**) *n*
装身具 sōshìngu

Jewess [dʒuː'is] *n* ユダヤ人女性 yudáyajin
jðsei

Jewish [dʒuː'iʃ] *adj* ユダヤ人の yudáyajiñ
no

jibe [dʒaib] *n* 野次 yájì

jiffy [dʒif'iː] (*inf*) *n*: *in a jiffy* 直ぐ súgù

jig [dʒig] *n* (dance) ジグ jígù ◇ 動きの早い
活発なダンス ugóki nò hayáî kappátsu
na dáñsu

jigsaw [dʒig'sɔː] *n* (*also*: **jigsaw puzzle**)
ジグソーパズル jígùsō-pazùru

jilt [dʒilt] *vt* (lover etc) 振る furú

jingle [dʒiŋ'gəl] *n* (for advert) コマーシ
ャルソング komásharu soñgu
◆*vi* (bells, bracelets) ちりんちりんと鳴る
chírìnchirin to narú

jinx [dʒiŋks] *n* ジンクス jíñkusu

jitters [dʒit'əːrz] (*inf*) *npl*: *to get the
jitters* びびる bibíru

job [dʒɑːb] *n* (chore, task) 仕事 shigóto;
(post, employment) 職 shokú

it's not my job (duty, function) それは
私の仕事ではない soré wà watákushi nò
shigóto de wa naî

it's a good job that ... (*BRIT*) ...して
良かったね ...shite yókàtta né

just the job! (*BRIT*: *inf*) おあつらえ向
きだ o-átsurae muki da, 丁度いい chódo
iî

job centre (*BRIT*) *n* 公共職業安定所
kốkyōshokugyò anteishò

jobless [dʒɑːb'lis] *adj* (ECON) 失業の shitsúgyō no

jockey [dʒɑːk'iː] *n* (SPORT) 騎手 kíshu
◆*vi*: *to jockey for position* (rivals,
competitors) 画策する kakúsaku suru

jocular [dʒɑːk'jələːr] *adj* (p e r s o n,
remark) ひょうきんな hyốkiñ na

jog [dʒɑːg] *vt* (bump) 小突く kozúkù
◆*vi* (run) ジョギングする jógìngu suru

to jog someone's memory ...に...を思い
起させる ...ni...wo omóí okosaserù

jog along *vi* (person, vehicle) のんびり
と進む noñbirî to susúmù

jogging [dʒɑːg'iŋ] *n* ジョギング jógìngu

join [dʒɔin] *vt* (queue) ...に加わる ...ni kuwáwarù; (party) ...に参加する ...ni sañka
suru; (club etc) ...に入会する ...ni nyůkai
suru; (put together: things, places) つな
ぐ tsunágu; (meet: group of people) 一緒

になる isshō ni narù

♦vi (roads, rivers) 合流する gṓryū suru

♦n つなぎ目 tsunágimè

joiner [dʒɔi'nə:r] (BRIT) n 建具屋 tatéguya

joinery [dʒɔi'nə:ri:] n 建具職 tatégushokku

join in vi 参加する sañka suru

♦vt fus (work, discussion etc) ...に参加する ...ni sañka surù

joint [dʒɔint] n (TECH: in woodwork, pipe) 継ぎ目 tsugíme; (ANAT) 関節 kañsetsu; (of meat) ブロック肉 búrðkku niku; (inf: nightclub, pub, cheap restaurant etc) 店 misé; (: of cannabis) マリファナタバコ marífana tabakò

♦adj (common) 共通の kyṓtsu no; (combined) 共同の kyṓdō no

joint account n (at bank etc) 共同預金口座 kyṓdō yokin kòza

join up vi (meet) 一緒になる isshō ni narù; (MIL) 入隊する nyū́tai suru

joist [dʒɔist] n はり harí

joke [dʒouk] n (gag) 冗談 jṓdañ; (also: practical joke) いたずら itázura

♦vi 冗談を言う jṓdañ wo iú

to play a joke on ...をからかう ...wo karákaù

joker [dʒou'kə:r] n (inf) 冗談を言う人 jṓdañ wo iu hitð; (pej: person) 野郎 yárð; (cards) ジョーカー jṓkằ

jolly [dʒɑ'li:] adj (merry) 陽気な yṓki na; (enjoyable) 楽しい tanóshiì

♦adv (BRIT: inf) とても totémo

jolt [dʒoult] n (physical) 衝撃 shṓgeki; (emotional) ショック shôkkù

♦vt (physically) ...に衝撃を与える ...ni shṓgeki wð atáerù; (emotionally) ショックを与える shôkkù wo atáerù

Jordan [dʒɔ:r'dʌn] n ヨルダン yórùdan

jostle [dʒɑːs'əl] vt: to be jostled by the crowd 人込みにもまれる hitógomi ni momárerù

jot [dʒɑːt] n: not one jot 少しも...ない sukóshì mo ...naì

jot down vt (telephone number etc) 書留める kakítomerù

jotter [dʒɑːt'ə:r] (BRIT) n (notebook,

pad) ノート (ブック) nṓto(búkkù), メモ帳 memôchō

journal [dʒə:r'nəl] n (magazine, periodical) 雑誌 zasshí; (diary) 日記 nikkí

journalese [dʒə:rnəli:z'] n (pej) 大衆新聞調 taíshūshinbunchō

journalism [dʒə:r'nəlizəm] n ジャーナリズム jánarizùmu

journalist [dʒə:r'nəlist] n ジャーナリスト jánarisùto

journey [dʒə:r'ni:] n (trip, route) 旅行 ryokṓ; (distance covered) 道のり michínori

jovial [dʒou'vi:əl] adj (person, air) 陽気な yṓki na

joy [dʒɔi] n (happiness, pleasure) 喜び yorôkobi

joyful [dʒɔi'fəl] adj (news, event) うれしい uréshiì; (look) うれしそうな uréshisṑ na

joyride [dʒɔi'raid] n (AUT: US) 無謀運転のドライブ mubṓuñten no doráibù; (: BRIT) 盗難車でのドライブ tõnanshà de no doráibù

joystick [dʒɔi'stik] n (AVIAT) 操縦かん sṓjūkan; (COMPUT) 操縦レバー sṓjū rebằ, ジョイスティック joísùtikku

JP [dʒeipi:'] n abbr = Justice of the Peace

Jr abbr = junior

jubilant [dʒu:'bələnt] adj 大喜びの ṓyorokobi no

jubilee [dʒu:'bəli:] n (anniversary) ...周年記念日 ...shū́nen kinenbi

judge [dʒʌdʒ] n (LAW) 裁判官 saíbankan; (in competition) 審査員 shiñsa-in; (fig: expert) 通 tsū́

♦vt (LAW) 裁く sabákù; (competition) 審査する shiñsa suru; (person, book etc) 評価する hyṓka suru; (consider, estimate) 推定する suítei suru

judg(e)ment [dʒʌdʒ'mənt] n (LAW) 判決 hañketsu; (REL) 審判 shiñpan; (view, opinion) 意見 ikén; (discernment) 判断力 hañdañryoku

judicial [dʒu:diʃ'əl] adj (LAW) 司法の shihṓ no

judiciary [dʒu:diʃ'i:eri:] n 司法部 shihṓ

bù

judicious [dʒuːdíʃˈəs] *adj* (action, decision) 分別のある fuñbetsu no árù

judo [dʒuːˈdou] *n* 柔道 júdò

jug [dʒʌg] *n* 水差し mizúsashi

juggernaut [dʒʌgˈəːrnɔːt] (*BRIT*) *n* (huge truck) 大型トラック ōgata torakkù

juggle [dʒʌgˈəl] *vi* 品玉をする shinádama wo surù ◊幾つもの玉などを投上げて受止める曲芸 íkutsu mo no tamá nadò wo nagéagetè ukétomerù kyokúgei

juggler [dʒʌgˈləːr] *n* 品玉をする曲芸師 shinádama wo suru kyokúgeishì

Jugoslav [juːˈgouslɑːv] *etc* = **Yugoslav** *etc*

juice [dʒuːs] *n* (of fruit, plant, meat) 汁 shírù; (beverage) ジュース jùsu

juicy [dʒuːˈsiː] *adj* (food) 汁の多い shírù no ōi; (*inf*: story, details) エッチな étchì na

jukebox [dʒuːkˈbɑːks] *n* ジュークボックス júkùbokkusu

July [dʒuˈlai] *n* 7月 shichí gatsu

jumble [dʒʌmˈbəl] *n* (muddle) ごたまぜ gotámaze
◊*vt* (*also*: **jumble up**) ごたまぜにする gotámaze ni suru

jumble sale (*BRIT*) *n* 慈善バザー jizén bazà

jumbo (**jet**) [dʒʌmˈbou] *n* ジャンボジェット機 jánbo jettókì

jump [dʒʌmp] *vi* (into air) 飛び上る tobíagarù; (with fear, surprise) ぎくっとする gíkùtto suru; (increase: price etc) 急上昇する kyújōshō suru; (: population etc) 急増する kyúzō suru
◊*vt* (fence) 飛び越える tobíkoeru
◊*n* (into air etc) 飛び上る事 tobíagarù kotó; (increase: in price etc) 急上昇 kyújōshō; (: in population etc) 急増 kyúzō
to jump the queue (*BRIT*) 列に割込む rétsù ni waríkomù

jumper [dʒʌmˈpəːr] *n* (*BRIT*: pullover) セーター sētà; (*US*: dress) ジャンパースカート jañpāsukàto

jumper cables *npl* (*US*) ブースターケーブル bŭsutākèburu ◊外のバッテリーから電気を得るために用いるコード hoká nò báttèrī kara dénki wo érù tamé nì mochíìru kôdo

jump leads (*BRIT*) [-liːdz] *npl* = **jumper cables**

jumpy [dʒʌmˈpiː] *adj* (nervous) びくびくしている bíkùbiku shité írù

Jun. *abbr* = **junior**

junction [dʒʌŋkˈʃən] *n* (*BRIT*: of roads) 交差点 kōsatèn; (*RAIL*) 連絡駅 reñrakuèki

juncture [dʒʌŋkˈtʃəːr] *n*: *at this juncture* この時 konó tokí

June [dʒuːn] *n* 6月 rokúgatsu

jungle [dʒʌŋˈgəl] *n* ジャングル jáñguru; (*fig*) 弱肉強食の世界 jakúniku kyōshoku nò sékai

junior [dʒuːnˈjəːr] *adj* (younger) 年下の toshíshita no; (subordinate) 下位の kái no; (*SPORT*) ジュニアの jùnia no
◊*n* (office junior) 後輩 kôhai; (young person) 若者 wakámono
he's my junior by 2 years 彼は私より2才年下である kárè wa watákushi yorì nísaì toshíshita desu

junior school (*BRIT*) *n* 小学校 shōgakkò

junk [dʒʌŋk] *n* (rubbish, cheap goods) がらくた garákuta; (ship) ジャンク jáñku

junk food *n* ジャンクフード jáñku fúdo ◊ポテトチップス，ファーストフードなど高カロリーだが低栄養のスナック食品 potétochippùsu, fāsuto fùdo nádò kōkarorī da ga teíeiyō no sunákku shokùhin

junkie [dʒʌŋˈkiː] (*inf*) *n* ペイ中 peichū

junk shop *n* 古物商 kobútsushò

Junr. *abbr* = **junior**

jurisdiction [dʒuːrisdikˈʃən] *n* (*LAW*) 司法権 shihōkèn; (*ADMIN*) 支配権 shiháikèn

juror [dʒuːˈrəːr] *n* (person on jury) 陪審員 baíshiñ-in

jury [dʒuːˈriː] *n* (group of jurors) 陪審員 baíshiñ-in

just [dʒʌst] *adj* (fair: decision) 公正な kōsei na; (: punishment) 適切な tekísetsu na

♦adv (exactly) 丁度 chôdo; (only) ただ tádà; (barely) ようやく yôyaku

he's just done it ついさっきそれをやったばかりだ tsuí sakkí sore wo yatta bákàri da

he's just left ついさっき出た〔帰った〕ばかりだ tsuí sakkí détà 〔kaéttà〕 bákàri da

just right 丁度いい chôdo ǐ

just two o'clock 丁度2時 chôdo nǐji

she's just as clever as you 彼女はあなたに負けないぐらい頭がいい kánòjo wa anátà ni makénai gurài atáma ga ǐ

just as well that ... ...して良かった ...shǐtè yokátta

just as he was leaving 丁度出掛けるところに chôdo dekákerù tokórò ni

just before 丁度前に chôdo máè ni

just enough 辛うじて間に合って kárðjite ma nǐ attè

just here ぴったりここに pittárì kokó ni

he just missed わずかの差で外れた wázùka no sá dè hazúreta

just listen ちょっと聞いて chottó kiite

justice [dʒʌsˈtis] n (LAW: system) 司法 shihô; (rightness: of cause, complaint) 正当さ seítòsa; (fairness) 公正さ kôseisa; (US: judge) 裁判官 saíbankan

to do justice to (fig: task) ...をやりこなす ...wo yaríkonasù; (: meal) ...を平らげる ...wo taíragerù; (: person) ...を正当に扱う ...wo seítò ni atsúkaù

Justice of the Peace n 治安判事 chián hanji

justifiable [dʒʌsˈtifaiəbəl] adj (claim, statement etc) もっともな móttòmo na

justification [dʒʌstəfəkeiˈʃən] n (reason) 正当とする理由 seítò to suru riyú

justify [dʒʌsˈtəfai] vt (action, decision) 正当である事を証明する seítò de arù kotô wo shômei suru; (text) 行の長さをそろえる gyô no nágàsa wo soróerù

justly [dʒʌsˈtli] adv (with reason) 正当に seítò ni; (deservedly) 当然 tôzen

jut [dʒʌt] vi (also: **jut out**: protrude) 突出る tsukíderù

juvenile [dʒuːˈvənəl] adj (court) 未成年の

miséinen no; (books) 少年少女向きの shônen shôjo mukí no; (humor, mentality) 子供っぽい kodômoppoì

♦n (LAW, ADMIN) 未成年者 miséinensha

juxtapose [dʒʌkstəpouzˈ] vt (things, ideas) 並べておく narábete okù

K

K [kei] abbr (= *one thousand*) 1000 séñ = **kilobyte**

kaleidoscope [kəlaiˈdəskoup] n 万華鏡 mañgekyô

Kampuchea [kæmpuːtʃiːˈə] n カンプチア káñpuchia

kangaroo [kæŋgəruːˈ] n カンガルー kañgarû

karate [kərɑːˈtiː] n 空手 karáte

kebab [kəbɑːbˈ] n くし刺の焼肉 kushísashi nò yakíniku, シシカバブ shishikababu

keel [kiːl] n 竜骨 ryûkotsu

on an even keel (fig) 安定して afitei shite

keen [kiːn] adj (eager) やりたがっている yarítagattè írù; (intense: interest, desire) 熱心な nesshíñ na; (acute: eye, intelligence) 鋭い surúdoì; (fierce: competition) 激しい hagéshiì; (sharp: edge) 鋭い surúdoì

to be keen to do/on doing something (eager, anxious) ...をやりたがっている ...wo yarítagattè írù

to be keen on something/someone ...に熱を上げている ...ni netsú wò agéte irù

keep [kiːp] (pt, pp **kept**) vt (retain: receipt etc) 保管する hokán suru; (: money etc) 自分の物にする jíbùn no monô ni surù; (: job etc) なくさない様にする nakúsanai yô ni suru, 守る mamórù; (preserve, store) 貯蔵する chozô suru; (maintain: house, garden etc) 管理する káñri suru; (detain) 引留める hikítomerù; (run: shop etc) 経営する keíei suru; (chickens, bees etc) 飼育する shiíku

suru; (accounts, diary etc) ...を付ける ...wo tsukérù; (support: family etc) 養う yashínàù; (fulfill: promise) 守る mamórù; (prevent): **to keep someone from doing something** ...が...をできない様に阻止する ...ga ...wo dekínài yō ni soshí surù

♦vi (remain: in a certain state) ...でいる〔ある〕...de irú 〔árù〕; (: in a certain place) ずっと...にいる zuttó ...ni irú; (last: food) 保存がきく hozón ga kikù

♦n (cost of food etc) 生活費 seíkatsuhì; (of castle) 本丸 hofímaru

to keep doing something ...をし続ける ...wo shitsúzukerù

to keep someone happy ...の期限をとる ...no kígèn wo torú

to keep a place tidy ある場所をきちんとさせておく árù bashó wo kichín to saséte okù

to keep something to oneself ...について黙っている ...ni tsúìte damátte irù

to keep something (back) from someone ...の事を...に隠す ...no kotó wo ...ni kakúsù

to keep time (clock) 時間を正確に計る jíkàn wo seíkaku ni hakárù

for keeps (inf) 永久に eíkyū ni

keeper [ki:'pər] n (in zoo, park) 飼育係 shi-íkugakàri, キーパー kípā

keep-fit [ki:p'fit'] n (BRIT) 健康体操 keñkōtaìsō

keeping [ki:'piŋ] n (care) 保管 hokán

in keeping with ...に合って ...ni áttè, ...に従って ...ni shitagatte

keep on vi (continue): **to keep on doing** ...し続ける ...shitsúzukerù

to keep on (about something) (...を話題に) うるさくしゃべる (...wo wadái ni) urúsakù shabérù

keep out vt (intruder etc) 締出す shimédasù

「**keep out**」立入禁止 tachíiri kinshi

keepsake [ki:p'seik] n 形見 katámi

keep up vt (maintain: payments etc) 続ける tsuzúkerù; (: standards etc) 保持する hojí suru

♦vi: **to keep up (with)** (match: pace)

(...と) 速度を合せる (...to) sókùdo wo a-wáserù; (: level) (...に) 遅れない様にする (...ni) okúrenai yō ni suru

keg [keg] n たる tarú

kennel [ken'əl] n イヌ小屋 inúgoya

kennels [ken'əlz] npl (establishment) イヌ屋 inúyà

Kenya [ken'jə] n ケニア kénìa

Kenyan [ken'jən] adj ケニアの kénìa no
♦n ケニア人 kenîajìn

kept [kept] pt, pp of **keep**

kerb [kə:rb] (BRIT) n = **curb**

kernel [kə:r'nəl] n (BOT: of nut) 実 mi; (fig: of idea) 核 kákù

kerosene [ker'əsi:n] n 灯油 tôyu

ketchup [ketʃ'əp] n ケチャップ kecháppù

kettle [ket'əl] n やかん yakán

kettle drum n ティンパニ tíñpani

key [ki:] n (for lock etc) かぎ kagí; (MUS: scale) 調 chố; (of piano, computer, typewriter) キー kí
♦adj (issue etc) 重要な jûyō na
♦vt (also: **key in**: into computer etc) 打込む uchíkomù, 入力する nyúryoku suru

keyboard [ki:'bɔːrd] n (of computer, typewriter) キーボード kíbòdo; (of piano) けん盤 keñban, キーボード kíbòdo

keyed up [ki:d-] adj (person) 興奮している kôfun shite irù

keyhole [ki:'houl] n 鍵穴 kagíana

keynote [ki:'nout] n (MUS) 主音 shúòn; (of speech) 基調 kichô

key ring n キーホルダー kíhorùdā

kg abbr = **kilogram**

khaki [kæk'i:] n (color) カーキ色 káki i-ro; (also: **khaki cloth**) カーキ色服地 káki iro fukùji

kibbutz [kibuts'] n キブツ kíbùtsu ◇イスラエルの農業共同体 ísùraeru no nôgyō kyōdotai

kick [kik] vt (person, table, ball) ける kérù; (inf: habit, addiction) やめる yamérù
♦vi ける kérù
♦n (from person, animal) けり kéri; (to ball) キック kíkkù; (thrill): **he does it for kicks** 彼はそんな事をやるのはスリ

ルのためだ kárè wa soñna kotó wo yárù no wa surfrù no tamé dà

kick off vi (FOOTBALL, SOCCER) 試合を開始する shiái wò kaíshi suru

kick-off [kik'ɔːf] n (FOOTBALL, SOCCER) 試合開始 shiái kaishi, キックオフ kíkkùofu

kid [kid] n (inf: child) がき gakí, じゃり jarí; (animal) 子ヤギ koyágì; (also: **kid leather**) キッド革 kíddògawa
♦vi (inf) 冗談を言う jódàn wo iú

kidnap [kid'næp] vt 誘拐する yúkai suru

kidnapper [kid'næpəːr] n 誘拐犯人 yúkai hañnin

kidnapping [kid'næpiŋ] n 誘拐事件 yúkai jikèn

kidney [kid'niː] n (ANAT) じん臓 jiñzò; (CULIN) キドニー kídònì

kill [kil] vt (person, animal) 殺す korósù; (plant) 枯らす karásù; (murder) 殺す korosu, 殺害する satsúgai suru
♦n 殺し koróshi
to kill time 時間をつぶす jíkàn wo tsubúsù

killer [kil'əːr] n 殺し屋 koróshiya

killing [kil'iŋ] n (action) 殺す事 korósu kotò; (instance) 殺人事件 satsújin jikèn
to make a killing (inf) 大もうけする ṓmòke suru

killjoy [kil'dʒɔi] n 白けさせる人 shiráke-saserù hitó

kiln [kiln] n 窯 kamá

kilo [kiː'lou] n キロ kírò

kilobyte [kil'əbait] n (COMPUT) キロバイト kiróbaìto

kilogram(me) [kil'əgræm] n キログラム kiróguràmu

kilometer [kil'əmiːtəːr] (BRIT **kilometre**) n キロメーター kirómètā

kilowatt [kil'əwɑːt] n キロワット kiró-wattò

kilt [kilt] n キルト kirúto

kimono [kimou'nou] n 着物 kimóno, 和服 wafúku

kin [kin] n see kith; next-of-kin

kind [kaind] adj 親切な shíñsetsu na
♦n (type, sort) 種類 shúrùi; (species) 種 shú

to pay in kind 現物で支払う geñbutsu de shiháraù

a kind of ...の一種 ...no ísshù

to be two of a kind 似たり寄ったりする nitárì yottárì suru, 似た者同志である nitá mono dōshi de árù

kindergarten [kin'dəːrgɑːrtən] n 幼稚園 yōchìen

kind-hearted [kaind'hɑːr'tid] adj 心の優しい kokóro no yasáshiì

kindle [kin'dəl] vt (light: fire) たく takú, つける tsukeru; (arouse: emotion) 起す okósù, そそる sosórù

kindly [kaind'liː] adj 親切な shíñsetsu na
♦adv (smile) 優しく yasáshiku; (behave) 親切に shíñsetsu ni
will you kindly ... ...して下さいませんか ...shítè kudásaìmasen ká

kindness [kaind'nis] n (personal quality) 親切 shíñsetsu; (helpful act) 親切な行為 shíñsetsu na kṓì

kindred [kin'drid] adj: **kindred spirit** 自分と気の合った人 jíbùn to kí no attà hitó

kinetic [kinet'ik] adj 動的な dṓteki na

king [kiŋ] n (monarch) 国王 kokúṓ; (CARDS, CHESS) キング kíñgu

kingdom [kiŋ'dəm] n 王国 ṓkoku

kingfisher [kiŋ'fiʃəːr] n カワセミ kawá-semi

king-size [kiŋ'saiz] adj 特大の tokúdai no

kinky [kiŋ'kiː] (pej) adj (person, behavior) へんてこな heñteko na, 妙な myṓ na; (sexually) 変態気味の heñtaigimi no

kiosk [kiːɑːsk'] n (shop) キオスク kiósùku; (BRIT: TEL) 電話ボックス deñwa bokkùsu

kipper [kip'əːr] n 薫製ニシン kuñsei ni-shìn

kiss [kis] n キス kísù
♦vt ...にキスする ...ni kísù suru
to kiss (each other) キスする kísù suru

kiss of life n 口移しの人工呼吸 kuchíu-tsushi no jiñkōkokyù

kit [kit] n (clothes: sports kit etc) 運動服一式 uñdōfùku isshíki; (equipment, set of tools: also MIL) 道具一式 dṓgu isshí-

ki; (for assembly) キット kíttò

kitchen [kitʃ'ən] n 台所 daídokoro, キッチン kítchìn

kitchen sink n 台所の流し daídokoro no nagáshi

kite [kait] n (toy) たこ takó

kith [kiθ] n: **kith and kin** 親せき知人 shiñsekichijin

kitten [kit'ən] n 子ネコ konékð

kitty [kit'i:] n (pool of money) お金の蓄え o-káne no takúwae; (CARDS) 総掛金 sōkakekìn

kleptomaniac [kleptəmei'ni:æk] n 盗癖のある人 tōheki no árù hitð

km abbr = **kilometer**

knack [næk] n: **to have the knack of doing something** ...をするのが上手である ...wo suru nð ga jōzu de arù

knapsack [næp'sæk] n ナップサック nappúsakkù

knead [ni:d] vt (dough, clay) 練る nérù

knee [ni:] n ひざ hizá

kneecap [ni:'kæp] n ひざ頭 hizágashìra, ひざ小僧 hizákozð

kneel [ni:l] (pt, pp **knelt**) vi (also: **kneel down**) ひざまずく hizámazukù

knelt [nelt] pt, pp of **kneel**

knew [nu:] pt of **know**

knickers [nik'ə:rz] (BRIT) npl パンティー pânti

knife [naif] (pl **knives**) n ナイフ nâīfu
♦vt ナイフで刺す naífu de sásù

knight [nait] n (HISTORY) 騎士 kishí; (BRIT) ナイト naíto; (CHESS) ナイト naíto

knighthood [nait'hud] (BRIT) n (title): **to get a knighthood** ナイト爵位を与えられる naíto shakùi wo atáerarerù

knit [nit] vt (garment) 編む ámù
♦vi (with wool) 編物をする amímòno wo suru; (broken bones) 治る naórù
to knit one's brows まゆをひそめる máyù wo hisómerù

knitting [nit'iŋ] n 編物 amímòno

knitting machine n 編機 amíkì

knitting needle n 編棒 amíbð

knitwear [nit'we:r] n ニット・ウェアー nittð ueâ

knives [naivz] npl of **knife**

knob [nɑ:b] n (handle: of door) 取っ手 tottê, つまみ tsumámi; (: of stick) 握り nigíri; (on radio, TV etc) つまみ tsumámi

knock [nɑ:k] vt (strike) たたく tatákù; (inf: criticize) 批判する hihán suru
♦vi (at door etc): **to knock at/on** ...にノックする ...ni nókku surù
♦n (blow, bump) 打撃 dagéki; (on door) ノック nókkù

knock down vt (subj: person) 殴り倒す nagúritaosù; (: car) ひき倒す hikítaosù

knocker [nɑ:k'ə:r] n (on door) ノッカー nokkâ

knock-kneed [nɑ:k'ni:d] adj X脚の ekúsukyaku na

knock off vi (inf: finish) やめる yamérù, 終りにする owári ni surù
♦vt (from price) 値引する nebíki suru; (inf: steal) くすねる kusúnerù

knock out vt (subj: drug etc) 気絶させる kizétsu saserù, 眠らせる nemúraserù; (BOXING etc, also fig) ノックアウトする nokkúaùto surù; (defeat: in game, competition) ...に勝つ ...ni kátsù, 敗退させる haítai saséru

knockout [nɑ:k'aut] n (BOXING) ノックアウト nokkúaùto
♦cpd (competition etc) 決定的な kettéiteki na

knock over vt (person, object) 倒す taósù

knot [nɑ:t] n (in rope) 結び目 musúbime; (in wood) 節目 fushíme; (NAUT) ノット nóttð
♦vt 結ぶ musúbù

knotty [nɑ:t'i:] adj (fig: problem) 厄介な yakkái na

know [nou] (pt **knew**, pp **known**) vt (facts, dates etc) 知っている shitté irù; (language) できる dekírù; (be acquainted with: person, place, subject) 知っている shitté irù; (recognize: by sight) 見て分かる mítè wakárù; (: by sound) 聞いて分かる kiite wakaru
to know how to swim 泳げる oyógerù
to know about/of something/some-

one ...の事を知っている ...no kotó wð shitté irù

know-all [nou'ɔːl] *n* 知ったか振りの人 shittákaburi no hitó

know-how [nou'hau] *n* 技術知識 gijútsu-chishìki, ノウハウ nóuhaù

knowing [nou'iŋ] *adj* (look: of complicity) 意味ありげな imíarige na

knowingly [nou'iŋli:] *adv* (purposely) 故意に kôí ni; (smile, look) 意味ありげに ímìarige ni

knowledge [nɑːl'idʒ] *n* (understanding, awareness) 認識 nínshiki; (learning, things learnt) 知識 chíshìki

knowledgeable [nɑːl'idʒəbəl] *adj* 知識の ある chíshìki no árù

known [noun] *pp* of **know**

knuckle [nʌk'əl] *n* 指関節 yubí kaǹsetsu ◊特に指の付根の関節を指す tókù ni yubí no tsukéne no kaǹsetsu wð sásù

KO [kei'ou'] *n abbr* = **knockout**

Koran [kɔːrɑːn'] *n* コーラン kóran

Korea [kɔːri:'ə] *n* 韓国 káǹkoku, 朝鮮 chôseǹ

Korean [kɔːri:'ən] *adj* 韓国の káǹkoku no, 朝鮮の chôseǹ no; (LING) 韓国語の kaǹkokugo no, 朝鮮語の chôsengo no
◆*n* (person) 韓国人 kaǹkokujìn, 朝鮮人 chôsenjìn; (LING) 韓国語 kaǹkokugo, 朝鮮語 chôsengo

kosher [kou'ʒəːr] *adj* 適法の tekíhô no ◊ ユダヤ教の戒律に合った食物などについ て言う yudáyakyô no kaíritsu ni attá shokúmòtsu nádò ni tsuíte iú

L

L (*BRIT*) *abbr* = **learner driver**

l. *abbr* = **liter**

lab [læb] *n abbr* = **laboratory**

label [lei'bəl] *n* (on suitcase, merchandise etc) ラベル rábèru
◆*vt* (thing) ...にラベルを付ける ...ni rábèru wo tsukérù

labor [lei'bəːr] (*BRIT* **labour**) *n* (hard work) 労働 rôdô; (work force) 労働者 rô-dôshà ◊総称 sôshô; (work done by work

force) 労働 rôdô; (MED): **to be in labor** 陣痛が始まっている jińtsū ga hajímatte irù
◆*vi*: **to labor (at something)** (...に) 苦心する (...ni) kushíñ surù
◆*vt*: **to labor a point** ある事を余計に強 調する árù kotó wð yokéi nì kyôchô suru

laboratory [læb'rətɔːri:] *n* (scientific: building, institution) 研究所 keñkyūjo; (: room) 実験室 jikkéñshitsu; (school) 理 科教室 rikákyôshitsu

labored [lei'bəːrd] *adj* (breathing: one's own) 苦しい kurúshìi; (: someone else's) 苦しそうな kurúshisô na

laborer [lei'bəːrəːr] *n* (industrial) 労働者 rôdôshà

farm laborer 農場労務者 nôjôrōmushà

laborious [ləbɔːr'i:əs] *adj* 骨の折れる ho-né no orérù

labour [lei'bəːr] *etc n* = **labor** *etc*

Labour, the Labour Party (*BRIT*) 労 働党 rôdôtô

labyrinth [læb'ərinθ] *n* 迷路 mêíro

lace [leis] *n* (fabric) レース rêsu; (of shoe etc) ひも himó
◆*vt* (shoe etc: *also:* **lace up**) ...のひもを結 ぶ ...no himó wo musúbù

lack [læk] *n* (absence) 欠如 kétsùjo
◆*vt* (money, confidence) ...が 無い ...ga náì; (intelligence etc) 欠いている kaíte irù

through/for lack of ...が無いために ...ga náì tamé ni

to be lacking ...がない ...ga náì

to be lacking in (intelligence, generosity etc) ...を欠いている ...wo kaíte iru

lackadaisical [lækədei'zikəl] *adj* (lacking interest, enthusiasm) 気乗りしない kinóri shinaí

laconic [ləkɑːn'ik] *adj* 言葉数の少ない kotóbakazù no sukúnaì

lacquer [læk'əːr] *n* (paint) ラッカー rák-kà; (*also:* **hair lacquer**) ヘアスプレー he-ásupurě

lad [læd] *n* (boy) 少年 shôneñ; (young man) 若者 wakámonð

ladder [læd'əːr] *n* (metal, wood, rope) は

しご子 hashígo; (*BRIT*: in tights) 伝線 defíseñ

laden [lei'dən] *adj*: **laden (with)** (ship, truck etc) (...を) たっぷり積んだ (...wo) tappúrî tsufída; (person) (...を) 沢山抱 えている (...wo) takúsaň kakáete iru
laden with fruit (tree) 実をたわわに付 けている mi wo tawáwa ni tsukéte irú

ladle [lei'dəl] *n* 玉じゃくし tamájakûshi

lady [lei'di:] *n* (woman) 女性 joséi; (: dignified, graceful etc) 淑女 shukújò, レディ ー rédì; (in address): **ladies and gentlemen ...** 紳士淑女の皆様 shiñshishukujò no minásama
young lady 若い女性 wakáî joseì
the ladies' (room) 女性用トイレ joséiyōtoìre

ladybird [lei'di:bə:rd] *n* テントウムシ teñtōmushi

ladybug [lei'debʌg] (*US*) *n* = **ladybird**

ladylike [lei'di:laik] *adj* (behavior) レデ ィーらしい rédìrashii

ladyship [lei'di:ʃip] *n*: **your ladyship** 奥 様 ókùsama

lag [læg] *n* (period of time) 遅れ okúre
♦*vi* (*also*: **lag behind**: person, thing) ...に 遅れる ...ni okúrerù; (: trade, investment etc) ...の勢いが衰える ...no ikíoî ga otóroerù
♦*vt* (pipes etc) ...に断熱材を巻く ...ni dań-netsuzaì wo makú

lager [lɑː'gə:r] *n* ラガービール ragábìru

lagoon [ləgu:n'] *n* 潟 katá, ラグーン rágùn

laid [leid] *pt, pp of* **lay**[3]

laid back (*inf*) *adj* のんびりした noñbirî shitá

laid up *adj*: **to be laid up (with)** (...で) 寝込んでいる (...de) nekónde irú

lain [lein] *pp of* **lie**

lair [le:r] *n* (ZOOL) 巣穴 suána

lake [leik] *n* 湖 mizú-umì

lamb [læm] *n* (animal) 子ヒツジ kohítsujì; (meat) ラム rámù

lamb chop *n* ラムチャップ ramúchappù, ラムチョップ ramúchoppù

lambswool [læmz'wul] *n* ラムウール ramúûru

lame [leim] *adj* (person, animal) びっこの bíkkò no; (excuse, argument, answer) 下 手な hetá na

lament [ləment'] *n* 嘆き nagéki
♦*vt* 嘆く nagékù

laminated [læm'əneitid] *adj* (metal, wood, glass) 合板の gôhan no; (covering, surface) プラスチック張りの purásuchikkubari no

lamp [læmp] *n* (electric, gas, oil) 明り a-kári, ランプ ráñpu

lamppost [læmp'poust] *n* 街灯 gaîtō

lampshade [læmp'ʃeid] *n* ランプの傘 ráñpu no kasá, シェード shèdo

lance [læns] *n* やり yarí
♦*vt* (MED) 切開する sekkái suru

land [lænd] *n* (area of open ground) 土地 tochí; (property, estate) 土地 tochí, 所有 地 shoyúchî; (as opposed to sea) 陸 rikú; (country, nation) 国 kuní
♦*vi* (from ship) 上陸する jôriku suru; (AVIAT) 着陸する chakúriku suru; (*fig*: fall) 落ちる ochírù
♦*vt* (passengers, goods) 降ろす orósù
to land someone with something (*inf*) ...に...を押付ける ...ni ...wo oshítsukerù

landing [læn'diŋ] *n* (of house) 踊り場 o-dóriba; (AVIAT) 着陸 chakúriku

landing gear *n* (AVIAT) 着陸装置 cha-kúrikusôchi

landing strip *n* 滑走路 kassôro

landlady [lænd'leidi:] *n* (of rented house, flat, room) 女大家 ofinaðya; (of pub) 女 主人 ofinashujìn, おかみ okámi

landlocked [lænd'lɑ:kt] *adj* 陸地に囲ま れた rikúchi ni kakómareta

landlord [lænd'lɔ:rd] *n* (of rented house, flat, room) 大家 ôya; (of pub) 主人 shujìn

landmark [lænd'mɑ:rk] *n* (building, hill etc) 目標 mokúhyō; (*fig*) 歴史的な事件 rekíshiteki na jíken

landowner [lænd'ounə:r] *n* 地主 jinúshi

landscape [lænd'skeip] *n* (view over land, buildings etc) 景色 késhìki; (ART) 風景画 fúkeiga

landscape gardener *n* 造園家 zôenka

landslide [lænd'slaid] *n* (GEO) 地滑り ji-

súběri; (*fig*: electoral) 圧勝 asshō

land up *vi*: **to land up in/at** 結局...に行くはめになる kekkyókù ...ni ikú hame ni narù

lane [lein] *n* (in country) 小道 komíchi; (AUT: of carriageway) 車線 shasén; (of race course, swimming pool) コース kōsu

language [læŋ'gwidʒ] *n* (national tongue) 国語 kokúgo; (ability to communicate verbally) 言語 géngo; (specialized terminology) 用語 yōgo; (style: of written piece, speech etc) 言葉遣 kotóbazukài; (SCOL) 語学 gógaku

bad language 下品な言葉 gehín na kotóba

he is studying languages 彼は外国語を勉強している kare wa gaikokugo wo benkyō shite iru

language laboratory *n* ランゲージラボラトリー rañgéjiraboratòrī, エルエル éruèru

languid [læŋ'gwid] *adj* (person, movement) 元気のない géñki no náî

languish [læŋ'gwiʃ] *vi* 惨めに生きる míjìme ni ikírù

lank [læŋk] *adj* (hair) 長くて手入れしない nagákutè teíre shinai

lanky [læŋ'ki:] *adj* ひょろっとした hyorottó shita

lantern [læn'tə:rn] *n* カンテラ kañtera

lap [læp] *n* (of person) ひざの上 hizá nò ué; (in race) 1周 ísshû, ラップ ráppù
♦*vt* (*also*: **lap up**: drink) ぴちゃぴちゃ飲む pichápìcha nômu
♦*vi* (water) ひたひたと打寄せる hitáhìta to uchíyoserù

lapel [ləpel'] *n* 折えり oríeri, ラペル rápèru

Lapland [læp'lənd] *n* ラップランド ráppùrando

lapse [læps] *n* (bad behavior) 過失 kashítsu; (of memory) 喪失 sōshitsu; (of time) 経過 keíka
♦*vi* (law) 無効になる mukó ni narù; (contract, membership, passport) 切れる kirérù

a lapse of concentration 不注意 fu-

chūi

to lapse into bad habits (of behavior) 堕落する daráku suru

lap up *vt* (*fig*: flattery etc) 真に受ける ma ni ukérù

larceny [lɑ:r'səni:] *n* (LAW) 窃盗罪 settōzai

larch [lɑ:rtʃ] *n* (tree) カラマツ karámàtsu

lard [lɑ:rd] *n* ラード rådo

larder [lɑ:r'də:r] *n* 食料貯蔵室 shokúryōchozōshitsu

large [lɑ:rdʒ] *adj* (big: house, person, amount) 大きい ōkii

at large (as a whole) 一般に ippán ni; (at liberty) 捕まらないで tsukámaranaîde ¶ *see also* **by**

largely [lɑ:rdʒ'li:] *adv* (mostly) 大体 daítai; (mainly: introducing reason) 主に ómò ni

large-scale [lɑ:rdʒ'skeil] *adj* (action, event) 大規模の daíkibò no; (map, diagram) 大縮尺の daíshukùshaku no

largesse [lɑ:rdʒes'] *n* (generosity) 気前さ kimáeyosà; (money etc) 贈り物 okúrimonò

lark [lɑ:rk] *n* (bird) ヒバリ hibári; (joke) 冗談 jōdañ

lark about *vi* ふざけ回る fuzákemawaru

larva [lɑ:r'və] (*pl* **larvae**) *n* 幼虫 yōchū

larvae [lɑ:r'vi:] *npl of* **larva**

laryngitis [lærəndʒai'tis] *n* こうとう炎 kōtōen

larynx [lær'iŋks] *n* (ANAT) こうとう kōtō

lascivious [ləsiv'i:əs] *adj* (person, conduct) みだらな midára na

laser [lei'zə:r] *n* レーザー rēzā

laser printer *n* レーザープリンター rēzāpuriñtā

lash [læʃ] *n* (eyelash) まつげ mátsùge; (blow of whip) むち打ち muchíuchi
♦*vt* (whip) むち打つ muchíutsù; (subj: rain) 激しくたたく hagéshikù tatákù; (: wind) 激しく揺さぶる hagéshikù yusáburù; (tie): **to lash to/together** ...を...に〔...と一緒に〕縛る ...wo ...ni〔...to isshó ni〕

shibárù

lash out vi: *to lash out (at someone)* (hit) (...に) 打ち掛る (...ni) uchíkakarù
to lash out against someone (criticize) ...を激しく非難する ...wo hagéshikù hínàn suru

lass [læs] n (girl) 少女 shòjo; (young woman) 若い女性 wakáì josēi

lasso [læs'ou] n 投縄 nagénawa

last [læst] adj (latest: period of time, event, thing) 前の máè no; (final: bus, hope etc) 最後の saígo no; (end: of series, row) 一番後の ichíban atò no; (remaining: traces, scraps etc) 残りの nokórì no
♦adv (most recently) 最近 saíkin; (finally) 最後に saígo ni
♦vi (continue) 続く tsuzúkù; (: in good condition) もつ mótsù; (money, commodity) ...に足りる ...ni taríru
last week 先週 senshū
last night 昨晩 sakúbàn, 昨夜 sakúyà
at last (finally) とうとう tōtō
last but one 最後から2番目 saígo kara nibánme

last-ditch [læst'ditʃ'] adj (attempt) 絶体絶命の zettáizetsumei no

lasting [læs'tiŋ] adj (friendship, solution) 永続的な eízokuteki na

lastly [læst'li:] adv 最後に saígo ni

last-minute [læst'min'it] adj (decision, appeal etc) 土壇場の dotánba no

latch [lætʃ] n (on door, gate) 掛け金 kakégàne, ラッチ rátchi

late [leit] adj (far on in time, process, work etc) 遅い osóì; (not on time) 遅れた okúreta; (former) 前の máè no, 前... zén...
♦adv (far on in time, process, work etc) 遅く osóku; (behind time, schedule) 遅れて okúrete
of late (recently) 最近 saíkin
in late May 5月の終り頃 gógàtsu no owári gorò
the late Mr X (deceased) 故Xさん ko ékusu san

latecomer [leit'kʌmər] n 遅れて来る人 okúrete kurù hitò

lately [leit'li:] adv 最近 saíkin

latent [lei'tənt] adj (energy, skill, ability) 表に出ない omóte nì dénài

later [lei'tər] adj (time, date, meeting etc) もっと後の móttò átò no; (version etc) もっと新しい móttò atárashiì
♦adv 後で átò de
later on 後で átò de

lateral [læt'ə:rəl] adj (position) 横の yokó no; (direction) 横への yokó e no

latest [lei'tist] adj (train, flight etc) 最後の saígo no; (novel, film, news etc) 最新の saíshin no
at the latest 遅くとも osókùtomo

lathe [leið] n (for wood, metal) 旋盤 señban

lather [læð'ər] n 石けんの泡 sekkén nò awá
♦vt ...に石けんの泡を塗る ...ni sekkén nò awá wò nurú

Latin [læt'in] n (LING) ラテン語 raténgo
♦adj ラテン語の raténgo no

Latin America n ラテンアメリカ raténamèrika

Latin American adj ラテンアメリカの ratén-amèrika no
♦n ラテンアメリカ人 ratén-amerikajìn

latitude [læt'ətu:d] n (GEO) 緯度 ídò; (fig: freedom) 余裕 yoyū

latrine [lətri:n'] n 便所 benjo

latter [læt'ə:r] adj (of two) 後者の kôsha no; (recent) 最近の saíkin no; (later) 後の方の átò no hō no
♦n: *the latter* (of two people, things, groups) 後者 kôsha

latterly [læt'ə:rli:] adv 最近 saíkin

lattice [læt'is] n (pattern, structure) 格子 kôshi

laudable [lɔ:'dəbəl] adj (conduct, motives etc) 感心な kanshin na

laugh [læf] n 笑い warái
♦vi 笑う waráù
(to do something) for a laugh 冗談として (...をする) jōdañ toshité (...wo suru)

laugh at vt fus ...をばかにする ...wo bakâ ni surù

laughable [læf'əbəl] adj (attempt, quality etc) ばかげた bakágeta

laughing stock [læf'iŋ-] n: *to be the laughing stock of* ...の笑い者になる ...no waráimono ni narú

laugh off vt (criticism, problem) 無視する mushí suru

laughter [læf'tər] n 笑い声 waráigoe

launch [lɔːntʃ] n (of rocket, missile) 発射 hasshá; (of satellite) 打上げ uchíage; (COMM) 新発売 shiñhatsubai; (motorboat) ランチ ráñchi

♦vt (ship) 進水させる shiñsui saséru; (rocket, missile) 発射する hasshá suru; (satellite) 打上げる uchíagerù; (fig: start) 開始する kaíshi suru; (COMM) 発売する hatsúbai suru

launch into vt fus (speech, activity) 始める hajímerù

launch(ing) pad [lɔːn'tʃ(iŋ)-] n (for missile, rocket) 発射台 hasshádai

launder [lɔːn'dər] vt (clothes) 洗濯する señtaku suru

launderette [lɔːndəret'] (BRIT) n コインランドリー koínrañdorī

Laundromat [lɔːn'drəmæt] ® US) n コインランドリー koínrañdorī

laundry [lɔːn'driː] n (dirty, clean) 洗濯物 señtakumono; (business) 洗濯屋 señtakuya◊ドライクリーニングはしない doráikuriñingu wa shinái; (room) 洗濯場 señtakuba

laureate [lɔː'riːit] adj see poet laureate

laurel [lɔː'rəl] n (tree) ゲッケイジュ gekkéiju

lava [læv'ə] n 溶岩 yōgan

lavatory [læv'ətɔːriː] n お手洗い otéarai

lavender [læv'əndər] n (BOT) ラベンダー rabéñda

lavish [læv'iʃ] adj (amount) たっぷりの tappúri no, 多量の taryō no; (person): *lavish with* ...を気前良く与える ...wo kimáeyokù atáerù

♦vt: *to lavish something on someone* ...に...を気前よく与える ...ni ...wo kimáeyokù atáerù

law [lɔː] n (system of rules: of society, government) 法 hō; (a rule) 法律 hōritsu; (of nature, science) 法則 hōsoku; (lawyers) 弁護士の職 beñgoshi no shokú;

(police) 警察 keísatsu; (SCOL) 法学 hōgaku

law-abiding [lɔː'əbaidiŋ] adj 法律を遵守する hōritsu wò júñshu suru

law and order n 治安 chíañ

law court n 法廷 hōtei

lawful [lɔː'fəl] adj 合法の gōhō no

lawless [lɔː'lis] adj (action) 不法の fuhō no

lawn [lɔːn] n 芝生 shibáfu

lawnmower [lɔːn'mouər] n 芝刈機 shibákarikì

lawn tennis n ローンテニス rōntenisu

law school (US) n (SCOL) 法学部 hōgakùbu

lawsuit [lɔː'suːt] n 訴訟 soshō

lawyer [lɔː'jər] n (gen) 弁護士 beñgoshi; (solicitor) 事務弁護士 jimúbeñgoshi; (barrister) 法廷弁護士 hōteibeñgoshi

lax [læks] adj (behavior, standards) いい加減な iíkagen na

laxative [læk'sətiv] n 下剤 gezái

lay¹ [lei] pt of lie

lay² [lei] adj (REL) 俗人の zokújin no; (not expert) 素人の shíroto no

lay³ [lei] (pt, pp laid) vt (place) 置く okú; (table) ...に食器を並べる ...ni shokkí wo náraberù; (carpet etc) 敷く shikú; (cable, pipes etc) 埋設する maísetsu suru; (ZOOL: egg) 産む umú

layabout [lei'əbaut] (BRIT: inf) n のらくら者 norákuramono

lay aside vt (put down) わきに置く wakí ni okú; (money) 貯蓄する chochíku suru; (belief, prejudice) 捨てる sutérù

lay by vt = lay aside

lay-by [lei'bai] (BRIT) n 待避所 taíhijo

lay down vt (object) 置く okú; (rules, laws etc) 設ける mōkerù

to lay down the law (pej) 威張り散らす ibárichirasu

to lay down one's life (in war etc) 命を捨てる inóchi wo sutérù

layer [lei'ər] n 層 sō

layman [lei'mən] (pl **laymen**) n (nonexpert) 素人 shíroto

lay off vt (workers) 一時解雇にする i-chíjikaìko ni suru, レイオフにする reío-

fù ni suru

lay on vt (meal, entertainment etc) 提供する teíkyō suru

lay out vt (spread out: things) 並べて置く narábete okù

layout [lei'aut] n (arrangement: of garden, building) 配置 haíchi; (: of piece of writing etc) レイアウト reíaùto

laze [leiz] vi (also: **laze about**) ぶらぶらする búràbura suru

laziness [lei'zi:nis] n 怠惰 taída

lazy [lei'zi:] adj (person) 怠惰な taída na; (movement, action) のろい norói

lb abbr = **pound** (weight)

lead[1] [li:d] n (front position: SPORT, fig) 先頭 seńtō; (piece of information) 手掛りtegákàri; (in play, film) 主演 shuén; (for dog) 引き綱 hikízùna, ひも himó; (ELEC) リード線 rídosen

♦vb (pt, pp **led**)

♦vt (walk etc in front) 先導する seńdō suru; (guide): **to lead someone somewhere** ...を...に案内する ...wo ...ni afínaî suru; (group of people, organization) ...のリーダーになる ...no rídā ni nárù; (start, guide: activity) ...の指揮を取る ...no shikí wo torù

♦vi (road, river, pipe, wire etc) ...に通じる ...ni tsújiru; (SPORT) 先頭に立つ seńtō ni tatsù

in the lead (SPORT, fig) 先頭に立って seńtō ni tatte

to lead the way (also fig) 先導する seńdō suru

lead[2] [led] n (metal) 鉛 namári; (in pencil) しん shíñ

lead away vt 連れ去る tsurésarù

lead back vt 連れ戻す tsurémodosù

leaden [led'ən] adj (sky, sea) 鉛色の namáiiro no

leader [li:'də:r] n (of group, organization) 指導者 shidóshà, リーダー rídā; (SPORT) 先頭を走る選手 seńtō wo hashírù seńshu

leadership [li:'də:rʃip] n (group, individual) 指導権 shidókèn; (position, quality) リーダーシップ rídāshìppu

lead-free [ledfri:'] adj (petrol) 無鉛の

muén no

leading [li:'diŋ] adj (most important: person, thing) 主要な shuyố na; (role) 主演の shuén no; (first, front) 先頭の seńtō no

leading lady n (THEATER) 主演女優 shuénjoyù

leading light n (person) 主要人物 shuyốjinbùtsu

leading man (pl **leading men**) n (THEATER) 主演男優 shuéndañ-yū

lead on vt (tease) からかう karákaù

lead singer n (in pop group) リードシンガー rídoshìngà, リードボーカリスト rídobōkarīsuto

lead to vt fus ...の原因になる ...no geń-in ni narù

lead up to vt fus (events) ...の原因になる ...no geń-in ni narù; (in conversation) 話題を...に向ける wadái wo ...ni mukérù

leaf [li:f] (pl **leaves**) n (of tree, plant) 葉 ha

♦vi: **to leaf through** (book, magazine) ...にさっと目を通す ...ni sátto me wo tốsù

to turn over a new leaf 心を入れ換える kokórò wo irékaerù

leaflet [li:f'lit] n ビラ bírà, 散らし chiráshi

league [li:g] n (group of people, clubs, countries) 連盟 reńmei, リーグ rígu

to be in league with someone ...と手を組んでいる ...to te wo kuńdè irú

leak [li:k] n (of liquid, gas) 漏れ moré; (hole: in roof, pipe etc) 穴 aná; (piece of information) 漏えい rôei

♦vi (shoes, ship, pipe, roof) ...から...が漏れる ...kara ...ga moreru; (liquid, gas) 漏れる moréru

♦vt (information) 漏らす morásù

the news leaked out そのニュースが漏れた sonó nyùsu ga moréta

lean [li:n] adj (person) やせた yaséta; (meat) 赤身の akámi no

♦vb (pt, pp **leaned** or **leant**)

♦vt: **to lean something on something** ...を...にもたせかける ...wo ...ni motásekakerù

♦*vi* (slope) 傾く katámukù

to lean against ...にもたれる ...ni motárerù

to lean on ...に寄り掛る ...ni yoríkakerù

lean back *vi* 後ろへもたれる ushíro e motárerù

lean forward *vi* 前にかがむ máè ni kagámù

leaning [li:'niŋ] *n*: *leaning (towards)* (tendency, bent) (...する) 傾向 (...surú) keíkō

lean out *vi* ...から体を乗出す ...kara karáda wò norídasù

lean over *vi* ...の上にかがむ ...no ué nì kagámù

leant [lent] *pt, pp of* **lean**

leap [li:p] *n* (jump) 跳躍 chóyaku; (in price, number etc) 急上昇 kyújōshō

♦*vi* (*pt, pp* **leaped** *or* **leapt**) (jump: high) 跳ね上がる hanéagarù; (: far) 跳躍する chóyaku suru; (price, number etc) 急上昇する kyújōshō suru

leapfrog [li:p'frɔːg] *n* 馬跳びの umátobi

leapt [lept] *pt, pp of* **leap**

leap year *n* うるう年 urúūdoshi

learn [lə:rn] (*pt, pp* **learned** *or* **learnt**) *vt* (facts, skill) 学ぶ manábù; (study, repeat: poem, play etc) 覚える obóerù, 暗記する añki suru

♦*vi* 習う naráù

to learn about something (hear, read) ...を知る ...wo shírù

to learn to do something ...の仕方を覚える ...no shikáta wò obóerù

learned [lə:r'nid] *adj* (person) 学識のある gakúshiki no arù; (book, paper) 学術の gakújutsu no

learner [lə:r'nə:r] (*BRIT*) *n* (*also:* **learner driver**) 仮免許運転者 karímenkyo unténsha

learning [lə:r'niŋ] *n* (knowledge) 学識 gakúshiki

learnt [lə:rnt] *pt, pp of* **learn**

lease [li:s] *n* (legal agreement, contract: to borrow something) 賃借契約 chíñshakukeíyaku, リース ríisu; (: to lend something) 賃貸契約 chíñtaikeíyaku, リース ríisu

♦*vt* (borrow) 賃借する chíñshaku suru; (lend) 賃貸する chíñtai suru

leash [li:ʃ] *n* (for dog) ひも himó

least [li:st] *adj*: *the least* (+noun: smallest) 最も小さい móttòmo chíīsaì; (: smallest amount of) 最も少ない mottòmo sukúnaì

♦*adv* (+verb) 最も...しない móttòmo ...shináì; (+adjective): *the least* 最も...でない móttòmo ...de náì

the least possible effort 最小限の努力 saíshōgen no dóryòku

at least 少なくとも sukúnakùtomo

you could at least have written 少なくとも手紙をくれたら良かったのに sukúnakùtomo tegámi wò kurétara yokattà no ní

not in the least ちっとも...でない chíttò mo ...de náì

leather [leð'ə:r] *n* なめし革 naméshigàwa, 革 kawá

leave [li:v] (*pt, pp* **left**) *vt* (place: go away from) 行ってしまう itté shimaù, 帰る kaérù; (place, institution: permanently) 去る sárù, 辞める yamérù; (leave behind: person) 置去りにする okízari ni surù, 見捨てる misúterù; (: thing: accidentally) 置忘れる okíwasurerù; (: deliberately) 置いて行く oíte ikù; (husband, wife) ...と別れる ...to wakárerù; (allow to remain: food, space, time etc) 残す nokósù

♦*vi* (go away) 去る sárù, 行ってしまう itté shimaù; (: permanently) 辞める yamérù; (bus, train) 出発する shuppátsu suru, 出る dérù

♦*n* 休暇 kyúka

to leave something to someone (money, property etc) ...に...を残して死ぬ ...ni ...wo nokóshite shinù; (responsibility etc) ...に...を任せる ...ni ...wo makáserù

to be left 残る nokórù

there's some milk left over ミルクは少し残っている mírùku wa sukóshì nokótte irù

on leave 休暇中で kyúkachū de

leave behind *vt* (person, object) 置いて

行く oíte ikú; (object: accidentally) 置忘れる okíwasurerù

leave of absence n 休暇 kyúka, 暇 himá

leave out vt 抜かす nukásù

leaves [li:vz] npl of **leaf**

Lebanon [leb'ənən] n レバノン rebánòn

lecherous [letʃ'ə:rəs] (pej) adj 助平な sukébè na

lecture [lek'tʃə:r] n (talk) 講演 kóen; (SCOL) 講義 kógi
♦vi (talk) 講演する kóen suru; (SCOL) 講義する kógi sùru
♦vt (scold): **to lecture someone on/about something** ...の事で...をしかる ...no kotó de ...wo shikárù
to give a lecture on ...について講演する ...ni tsúite kóen suru

lecturer [lek'tʃə:rə:r] (BRIT) n (at university) 講師 kòshi

led [led] pt, pp of **lead**[1]

ledge [ledʒ] n (of mountain) 岩棚 iwádana; (of window) 桟 sáň; (on wall) 棚 tanā

ledger [ledʒ'ə:r] n (COMM) 台帳 dáichō

lee [li:] n 風下 kazáshimo

leech [li:tʃ] n ヒル hírù

leek [li:k] n リーキ ríki, リーク ríku

leer [li:r] vi: **to leer at someone** ..をいん乱な目で見る ...wo íñran na me de mirù

leeway [li:'wei] n (fig): **to have some leeway** 余裕がある yoyú ga arù

left [left] pt, pp of **leave**
♦adj (direction, position) 左の hidári no
♦n (direction, side, position) 左 hidári
♦adv (turn, look etc) 左に〔へ〕 hidári ni 〔e〕
on the left 左に〔で〕 hidári ni〔de〕
to the left 左に〔へ〕 hidári ni〔e〕
the Left (POL) 左翼 sáyòku

left-handed [left'hæn'did] adj 左利きの hidárikikì no, ぎっちょの gítchò no

left-hand side [left'hænd'-] n 左側 hidárigawa

left-luggage (office) [leftlʌg'idʒ-] (BRIT) n 手荷物預かり所 teńimotsu azukaríshò

leftovers [left'ouvə:rz] npl (of meal) 残り物 nokórimono

left-wing [left'wiŋ] adj (POL) 左翼の sáyòku no

leg [leg] n (gen) 脚 ashí; (CULIN: of lamb, pork, chicken) もも mómò; (part: of journey etc) 区切り kugíri

legacy [leg'əsi:] n (of will: also fig) 遺産 isán

legal [li:'gəl] adj (of law) 法律の hóritsu no; (action, situation) 法的な hóteki na

legal holiday (US) n 法定休日 hóteikyújitsu

legality [li:gæl'iti:] n 合法性 góhōsei

legalize [li:'gəlaiz] vt 合法化する góhōka suru

legally [li:'gəli:] adv (by law) 法的に hóteki ni

legal tender n (currency) 法定通貨 hóteitsūka, 法貨 hóka

legend [ledʒ'ənd] n (story) 伝説 deńsetsu; (fig: person) 伝説的人物 deńsetsutekijinbutsu

legendary [ledʒ'əndeːriː] adj (of legend) 伝説の deńsetsu no; (very famous) 伝説的な deńsetsuteki na

legible [ledʒ'əbəl] adj 読める yomérù

legion [li:'dʒən] n (MIL) 軍隊 guńtai

legislation [ledʒislei'ʃən] n 法律 hóritsu

legislative [ledʒ'isleitiv] adj 立法の rippó no

legislature [ledʒ'isleitʃə:r] n (POL) 議会 gíkai

legitimate [lidʒit'əmit] adj (reasonable) 正当な seítō na; (legal) 合法な góhō na

leg-room [leg'ru:m] n (in car, plane etc) 脚を伸ばせる空間 ashí wo nobáserù kúkan

leisure [li:'ʒə:r] n (period of time) 余暇 yoká, レジャー rejá
at leisure ゆっくり yukkúri

leisure centre (BRIT) n レジャーセンター rejáseňtā ◊スポーツ施設, 図書室, 会議室, 喫茶店などを含んだ文化施設 supótsushisetsù, toshóshìtsu, kaígishìtsu, kissáteñ nadò wo fukúňda buňkashisetsù

leisurely [li:'ʒə:rli:] adj (pace, walk) ゆっくりした yukkúrì shitá

lemon [lem'ən] n (fruit) レモン rémòn

lemonade [leməneid'] *n* (*BRIT*: fizzy drink) ラムネ rámùne; (with lemon juice) レモネード remônêdo

lemon tea *n* レモンティー remôntī

lend [lend] (*pt, pp* **lent**) *vt*: **to lend something to someone** (money, thing) ...に...を貸す ...ni...wo kásù

lending library [len'diŋ-] *n* 貸出し図書館 kashídashitoshokàn

length [leŋkθ] *n* (measurement) 長さ nagása; (distance): **the length of** ...の端から端まで ...no hashí kara hashi madè; (of swimming pool) プールの長さ pūru no nagása; (piece: of wood, string, cloth etc) 1本 ippón; (amount of time) 時間 jikán

at length (at last) とうとう tôtô; (for a long time) 長い間 nagaî aída

lengthen [leŋk'θən] *vt* 長くする nágàku suru

♦*vi* 長くなる nágàku naru

lengthways [leŋkθ'weiz] *adv* (slice, fold, lay) 縦に tátè ni

lengthy [leŋk'θi:] *adj* (meeting, explanation, text) 長い nagaî

lenient [li:'ni:ənt] *adj* (person, attitude) 寛大な kañdai na

lens [lenz] *n* (of spectacles, camera) レンズ rêñzu; (telescope) 望遠鏡 bôeñkyō

Lent [lent] *n* 四旬節 shijúñsetsu

lent [lent] *pt, pp of* **lend**

lentil [len'təl] *n* ヒラマメ hirámame

Leo [li:'ou] *n* (ASTROLOGY) しし座 shishíza

leopard [lep'ə:rd] *n* (ZOOL) ヒョウ hyô

leotard [li:'ətɑ:rd] *n* レオタード reôtàdo

leprosy [lep'rəsi:] *n* らい病 raîbyō, ハンセン病 hañsenbyō

lesbian [lez'bi:ən] *n* 女性同性愛者 joséidōseiaishà, レスビアン resúbiàn

less [les] *adj* (in size, degree) ...より小さい ...yórì chiîsai; (in amount, quality) ...より少ない ...yórì sukúnaì

♦*pron* ...より少ないもの ...yórì sukúnaì monó

♦*adv* ...より少なく ...yórì sukúnakù

♦*prep*: **less tax/10% discount** ...から税金〔1割り〕を引いて ...kara zeîkin〔ichíwàri〕wo hiîte

less than half 半分以下 hañbùn íka

less than ever 更に少なく sárà ni sukúnàku

less and less ますます少なく masúmàsu sukúnàku

the less he talks the better ... 彼はできるだけしゃべらない方がいい kárè wa dekíru dake shabéranai hō ga íi

lessen [les'ən] *vi* 少なくなる sukúnaku narù

♦*vt* 少なくする sukúnaku suru

lesser [les'ə:r] *adj* (smaller: in degree, importance, amount) 小さい〔少ない〕方の chiîsai〔sukúnài〕hō no

to a lesser extent それ程ではないが ...sorê hodò de wa naî ga ...no

lesson [les'ən] *n* (class: history etc) 授業 jugyō; (: ballet etc) けいこ kêîko, レッスン rêssùn; (example, warning) 見せしめ miséshime

to teach someone a lesson (*fig*) ...に思い知らせてやる ...ni omôishirasete yarù

lest [lest] *conj* ...しない様に ...shinái yô ni

let [let] (*pt, pp* **let**) *vt* (allow) 許す yurúsù; (*BRIT*: lease) 賃貸する chiñtai suru

to let someone do something ...に...するのを許す ...ni...surú no wò yurúsù

to let someone know something ...に...を知らせる ...ni...wo shiráserù

let's go 行きましょう ikímashô

let him come (permit) 彼が来るのを邪魔しないで下さい kárè ga kúrù no wo jamá shinàide kudásaî

「***to let***」貸し家 kashíya

let down *vt* (tire etc) ...の空気を抜く ...no kũki wo nuku; (person) がっかりさせる gakkárî saséru

let go *vi* (stop holding: thing, person) 手を放す te wo hanásù

♦*vt* (release: person, animal) 放す hanásu

lethal [li:'θəl] *adj* (chemical, dose etc) 致命的な chiméiteki na

a lethal weapon 凶器 kyôki

lethargic [ləθɑ:r'dʒik] *adj* 無気力の mukíryòku no

let in *vt* (water, air) ...が漏れる ...ga mo-

rérù; (person) 入らせる haíraserù

let off *vt* (culprit) 許す yurúsù; (firework, bomb) 爆発させる bakúhatsu saseru; (gun) 撃つ útsù

let on *vi* 漏らす morásù

let out *vt* (person, dog) 外に出す sótò ni dásù; (breath) 吐く hákù; (water, air) 抜く núkù; (sound) 出す dásù

letter [let'ə:r] *n* (correspondence) 手紙 tegámi; (of alphabet) 文字 mójì

letter bomb *n* 手紙爆弾 tegámibakùdan

letterbox [let'ə:rbɑːks] (*BRIT*) *n* (for receiving mail) 郵便受け yūbìn-uke; (for sending mail) 郵便ポスト yūbinposùto, ポスト pósùto

lettering [let'ə:riŋ] *n* 文字 mójì

lettuce [let'is] *n* レタス rétàsu

let up *vi* (cease) やむ yámù; (diminish) 緩む yurúmù

let-up [let'ʌp] *n* (of violence, noise etc) 減少 geńshō

leukemia [luːkiːˈmiːə] (*BRIT* **leukaemia**) *n* 白血病 hakkétsubyō

level [lev'əl] *adj* (flat) 平らな taíra na
♦*adv*: **to draw level with** (person, vehicle) ...に追い付く ...ni oítsukù
♦*n* (point on scale, height etc) 高さ tákàsa, レベル rébèru; (of lake, river) 水位 súìi
♦*vt* (land: make flat) 平らにする taíra ni suru; (building, forest etc: destroy) 破壊する hakái suru

to be level with ...と同じぐらいである ...to onáji guraì de árù

"A" levels (*BRIT*) 学科の上級試験 gakká no jōkyū shikèn ◇大学入学資格を得るための試験 daígakunyūgaku shikakù wo érù tamé nò shikéñ

"O" levels (*BRIT*) 学科の普通級試験 gakká no futsūkyū shikèn ◇中等教育を5年受けた後に受ける試験 chūtōkyōìku wò gonéñ ukéta nochi ni ukérù shikéñ

on the level (*fig*: honest) 正直で shōjiki de

level crossing (*BRIT*) *n* 踏切 fumíkiri

level-headed [lev'əlhed'id] *adj* (calm) 分別のある fúñbetsu no árù

level off *vi* (prices etc) 横ばい状態にな

る yokóbaijōtai ni nárù

level out *vi* = **level off**

lever [lev'ə:r] *n* (to operate machine) レバー rébā; (bar) バール bárù; (*fig*) 人を動かす手段 hitó wò ugókasù shúdàn, てこ tékò

leverage [lev'ə:rid3] *n* (using bar, lever) てこの作用 tékò no sáyò; (*fig*: influence) 影響力 eíkyōryòku

levity [lev'iti:] *n* (frivolity) 不真面目さ fumájimesa

levy [lev'i:] *n* (tax, charge) 税金 zeíkin
♦*vt* 課する ka súrù

lewd [luːd] *adj* (look, remark etc) わいせつな waísetsu na

liabilities [laiəbil'əti:z] *npl* (COMM) 債務 saímu

liability [laiəbil'əti:] *n* (person, thing) 負担 fután; (LAW: responsibility) 責任 sekínin

liable [lai'əbəl] *adj* (subject): **liable to** ...の罰則が適用される ...no bassóku ga tekíyō sarerù; (responsible): **liable for** ...の責任を負うべきである ...no sekínin wò oúbeki de arù; (likely): **liable to do** ...しがちである ...shigáchi ni arù

liaise [liːeiz'] *vi*: **to liaise (with)** (...と) 連携する (...to) reñkei suru

liaison [liːei'zɑːn] *n* (cooperation, coordination) 連携 reñkei; (sexual relationship) 密通 mittsū

liar [lai'ə:r] *n* うそつき usótsùki

libel [lai'bəl] *n* 名誉棄損 meíyokisòn
♦*vt* 中傷する chúshō suru

liberal [lib'ə:rəl] *adj* (tolerant) 開放的なkaíhōteki na; (large: offer, amount etc) 寛大な kañdai na

liberate [lib'ə:reit] *vt* 解放する kaíhō suru

liberation [libərei'ʃən] *n* 解放 kaíhō

liberty [lib'ə:rti:] *n* (*gen*) 自由 jiyú; (criminal): **to be at liberty** 捕まらないでいる tsukámaranàide írù, 逃走中である tōsōchū de arù

to be at liberty to do 自由に...できる jiyú ni ...dekírù

to take the liberty of doing something 勝手に...する katté ni ...surú

Libra [li:'brə] *n* (ASTROLOGY) 天びん座 teñbinza

librarian [laibre:r'i:ən] *n* (worker) 図書館員 toshókañ-in; (qualified) 司書 shíshò

library [lai'bre:ri:] *n* (institution, SCOL: building) 図書館 toshókàn; (: room) 図書室 toshóshìtsu; (private collection) 蔵書 zōsho

libretto [libret'ou] *n* (OPERA) 脚本 kyakúhon

Libya [lib'i:ə] *n* リビア ríbìa

Libyan [lib'i:ən] *adj* リビアの ríbìa no
♦*n* リビア人 ribíajìn

lice [lais] *npl of* **louse**

licence [lai'səns] (*US also*: **license**) *n* (official document) 免許 méñkyo; (AUT) 運転免許証 uñtenmenkyoshō

license [lai'səns] *n* (*US*) = **licence**
♦*vt* (person, organization, activity) 認可する nñíka suru

licensed [lai'sənst] *adj* (driver, pilot etc) 免許を持った méñkyo wo mottá; (for alcohol) 酒類販売許可を持った sakéruihanbaikyòka wo mottá

license plate (*US*) *n* ナンバープレート nañbāpurèto

licentious [laisen't∫əs] *adj* いん乱な iñran na

lichen [lai'kən] *n* 地衣 chíi

lick [lik] *vt* (stamp, fingers etc) なめる namérù; (*inf*: defeat) ...に楽勝する ...ni rakúshò suru
to lick one's lips (*also fig*) 舌なめずりする shitánamèzuri suru

licorice [lik'ə:ris] (*US*) *n* カンゾウあめ kañzōame

lid [lid] *n* (of box, case, pan) ふた futá; (eyelid) まぶた mábùta

lie [lai] (*pt* **lay**, *pp* **lain**) *vi* (person) 横になる yokó ni narù; (be situated: place, object: *also fig*) ...にある ...ni árù; (be placed: in race, league etc) 第...位である dáì ...i de arù; (tell lies: *pt*, *pp* **lied**) うそをつく usó wo tsúkù
♦*n* (untrue statement) うそ usó
to lie low (*fig*) 人目を避ける hitóme wo sakéru

lie about/around *vi* (things) 散らばっ

ている chirábatte iru; (people) ごろりと寝ている goróri to neté iru

lie-down [lai'daun] (*BRIT*) *n*: *to have a lie-down* 昼寝する hirúne suru

lie-in [lai'in] (*BRIT*) *n*: *to have a lie-in* 寝坊する nebō suru

lieu [lu:]: *in lieu of* prep ...の代りに ...no kawári ni

lieutenant [lu:ten'ənt] *n* (MIL) (*also*: **first lieutenant**) 中尉 chūi; (*also*: **second lieutenant**) 小尉 shōi

life [laif] (*pl* **lives**) *n* (quality of being alive) 生命 seímeì; (live things) 生物 seíbùtsu; (state of being alive) 命 ínòchi; (lifespan) 一生 isshō; (events, experience, activities) 生活 seíkatsu
to come to life (*fig*: person, party etc) 活気付く kakkízukù

life assurance (*BRIT*) *n* = **life insurance**

lifebelt [laif'belt] *n* 救命具 kyūmeìgu

lifeboat [laif'bout] *n* (rescue launch) 巡視艇 juñshitèi; (on ship) 救命ボート kyūmeibòto

lifeguard [laif'gɑ:rd] *n* (at beach, swimming pool) 看視員 kañshiìn

life imprisonment *n* 無期懲役 mukíchòeki

life insurance *n* 生命保険 seímeihokèn

life jacket *n* 救命胴衣 kyūmeidòi

lifeless [laif'lis] *adj* (dead: person, animal) 死んだ shínda; (*fig*: person) 元気のない géñki no naí; (: party etc) 活気のない kakkí no naì

lifelike [laif'laik] *adj* (model, dummy, robot etc) 生きている様な íkìte irú yòna; (realistic: painting, performance) 写実的な shajítsuteki na

lifeline [laif'lain] *n* (means of surviving) 命綱 ínóchizùna

lifelong [laif'lɔ:ŋ] *adj* (friend, ambition etc) 一生の isshō no

life preserver (*US*) *n* = **lifebelt**; **life jacket**

life sentence *n* 無期懲役 mukíchòeki

life-size(d) [laif'saiz(d)] *adj* (painting, model etc) 実物大の jitsúbutsudaì no

life-span [laif'spæn] *n* (of person, ani-

mal, plant: *also fig*) 寿命 jumyṓ
life style n 生き方 ikíkata, ライフスタイル raffusutaîru
life support system n (MED) 生命維持装置 seímeiijisóchi
lifetime [laif'taim] n (of person) 生涯 shṓgai; (of thing) 寿命 jumyṓ
lift [lift] vt (raise: thing, part of body) 上げる agéru; (end: ban, rule) 撤廃する teppái suru
♦vi (fog) 晴れる harérù
♦n (BRIT: machine) エレベーター erébētā
to give someone a lift (AUT) ...を車に乗せて上げる ...wo kurúma ni nosête agerù
lift-off [lift'ɔːf] n (of rocket) 離昇 rishṓ
ligament [lig'əmənt] n じん帯 jíntai
light [lait] n (brightness: from sun, moon, lamp, fire) 光 hikári; (ELEC) 電気 defíki; (AUT) ライト ráito; (for cigarette etc): *have you got a light?* 火をお持ちですか hí wò o-móchî desu ká
♦vt (pt, pp **lit**) (fire) たく takú; (candle, cigarette) ...に火を付ける ...ni hí wo tsukérù; (room): *to be lit by* ...で照明されている ...de shṓmei sarête irù
♦adj (pale) 淡い awáì; (not heavy: object) 軽い karúì; (: rain) 細かい komákaì; (: traffic) 少ない sukúnaì; (not strenuous: work) 軽い karúì; (bright: building, room) 明るい akárui; (graceful, gentle: movement, action) 軽やかな karóyaka na; (not serious: book, play, film, music) 肩の凝らない katá no kóranaì
to come to light 明るみに出る akárumi ni derù
in the light of (discussions, new evidence etc) ...を考慮して ...wo kṓryo shite
light bulb n 電球 defíkyū
lighten [lai'tən] vt (make less heavy) 軽くする karúku surù
lighter [lai'təːr] n (also: **cigarette lighter**) ライター ráitā
light-headed [lait'hed'id] adj (dizzy) 頭がふらふらする atáma ga fúrafura suru; (excited) 浮わついた uwátsuita
light-hearted [lait'hɑːr'tid] adj (person) 陽気な yṓki na; (question, remark etc) 気楽な kiráku na
lighthouse [lait'haus] n 燈台 tṓdai
lighting [lai'tiŋ] n (system) 照明 shṓmei
lightly [lait'liː] adv 軽く karúku; (thoughtlessly) 軽率に keísotsu ni; (slightly) 少し sukóshì
to get off lightly 軽い罰だけで逃れる karúi bátsù dáke de nogárerù
lightness [lait'nis] n (in weight) 軽さ karúsa
lightning [lait'niŋ] n (in sky) 稲妻 inázùma
lightning conductor (BRIT) n = **lightning rod**
lightning rod (US) n 避雷針 hiráìshin
light pen n ライトペン raítopeñ
lights [laits] npl (AUT: traffic lights) (交通)信号 (kṓtsū)shiñgō
light up vi (face) 輝く kagáyakù
♦vt (illuminate) 明るくする akáruku suru
lightweight [lait'weit] adj (suit) 薄いusúi
♦n (BOXING) ライト級のボクサー raítokyū no bókùsa
light year n (PHYSICS) 光年 kṓnen
like [laik] vt (find pleasing, attractive, acceptable: person, thing) ...が好きである ...ga sukí de arù
♦prep (similar to) ...の様な ...no yṓ na; (in comparisons) ...の様に ...no yṓ ni; (such as) 例えば...などの様な〔に〕tatóeba ...nádò no yṓ na〔ni〕
♦adj 似た nitá
♦n: *and the like* など nádò
his likes and dislikes 彼の好きな物と嫌いな物 kárè no sukí na monò to kirái na monò
I would like, I'd like ...が欲しいのですが ...ga hoshíi no desu ga
would you like a coffee? コーヒーはいかがですか kṓhì wa ikága desu ká
to be/look like someone/something ...に似ている ...ni nité irù
what does it look/taste/sound like? どんな格好〔味、音〕ですか dóñna kákkō〔ají, otó〕dèsu ká

that's just like him 彼らしいね karé rashìi né

do it like this やり方はこうです yari-kata wa kó desu

it is nothing like … …とは全く違います …to wa mattáku chigaìmasu

likeable [lai'kəbəl] *adj* (person) 人好きのする hitózuki no suru

likelihood [laik'li:hud] *n* 可能性 kanósei

likely [laik'li:] *adj* (probable) ありそうな arísō na

to be likely to do …しそうである …shi-só de arù

not likely! 何があっても…しない nánì ga atté mo …shínài, とんでもない toñde-monài

likeness [laik'nis] *n* (similarity) 似ている事 nité irù kotó

that's a good likeness (photo, portrait) 実物そっくりだ jitsúbùtsu sokkúrì da

likewise [laik'waiz] *adv* (similarly) 同じく onájiku

to do likewise 同じ様にする onáji yó ni suru

liking [lai'kiŋ] *n*: *to have a liking for* (person, thing) …が好きである …ga sukí de arù

to be to someone's liking …の気に入っている …no kí ni itte irù

lilac [lai'lək] *n* (BOT: tree, flower) ライラック raírakkù, リラ rírà

lily [lil'i:] *n* (plant, flower) ユリ yurí

lily of the valley *n* スズラン suzúrañ

limb [lim] *n* (ANAT) 手足 téàshi, 肢 shí

limber up [lim'bə:r-] *vi* (SPORT) 準備運動をする juñbiuñdō wo suru, ウォーミングアップする uóminguappù suru

limbo [lim'bou] *n*: *to be in limbo* (*fig*) 忘れ去られている wasúresararete irù

lime [laim] *n* (fruit) ライム raímu; (*also*: **lime tree**) ライムの木 raímu no ki; (*also*: **lime juice**) ライムジュース raímujùsu; (for soil) 石灰 sekkái; (rock) 石灰岩 sek-káìgan

limelight [laim'lait] *n*: *to be in the limelight* 注目を浴びている chúmoku wò abíte irù

limerick [lim'ə:rik] *n* 五行わい歌 gogyówaìka

limestone [laim'stoun] *n* 石灰岩 sekkáìgan

limit [lim'it] *n* (greatest amount, extent, degree) 限界 geñkai; (restriction: of time, money etc) 制限 seígen; (of area) 境界 kyókai

♦*vt* (production, expense etc) 制限する seígen suru

limitation [limitei'ʃən] *n* (control, restriction) 制限 seígen; (of person, thing) 限界 geñkai

limited [lim'itid] *adj* (small: choice, resources etc) 限られた kagírarèta

to be limited to …に限られる …ni kagírarerù

limited (liability) company (*BRIT*) *n* 有限会社 yúgengaìsha

limousine [lim'əzi:n] *n* リムジン rímùjin

limp [limp] *n*: *to have a limp* びっこを引く bíkkò wo hikú

♦*vi* (person, animal) びっこを引く bíkkò wo hikú

♦*adj* (person) ぐにゃぐにゃの gúnyàgu-nya no

limpet [lim'pit] *n* カサガイ kaságai

line [lain] *n* (long thin mark) 線 séñ; (wrinkle: on face) しわ shiwá; (row: of people, things) 列 rétsù; (of writing, song) 行 gyó; (rope) 綱 tsuná, ロープ rópu; (*also*: **fishing line**) 釣糸 tsurííto; (*also*: **power line**) 送電線 sódeñsen; (*also*: **telephone line**) 電話線 deñwasen; (TEL) 回線 kaísen; (railway track) 線路 séñro; (bus, coach, train route) …線 …séñ; (*fig*: attitude, policy) 方針 hóshìn; (: business, work) 分野 búñ-ya; (COMM: of product(s)) シリーズ shírìzu

♦*vt* (road, room) …に並ぶ …ni narábù; (subj: person: container) …の内側に…を張る …no uchigawa ni …wo hárù; (: clothing) …に裏地を付ける …ni uráji wo tsu-kérù

to line something with …に…の裏を付ける …ni …no urá wo tsukérù

to line the streets 道路の両側に並ぶ dóro no ryógawa ni narábù

in line (in a row) 1列に ichíretsu ni

in line with (according to) ...に従って ...ni shitágatte

linear [lin'i:ə:r] *adj* (process, sequence) 一直線の itchōkusen no; (shape, form) 線形の senkei no

lined [laind] *adj* (face) しわのある shiwá no arū; (paper) 線を引いた sén wo hiíta

linen [lin'ən] *n* (cloth) リンネル ríñneru, リネン rínèn; (tablecloths, sheets etc) リネン rínèn

liner [lai'nə:r] *n* (ship) 豪華客船 gōkakyakùsen; (for bin) ごみ袋 gomíbukuro

linesman [lainz'mən] (*pl* **linesmen**) *n* (SPORT) 線審 séñshin, ラインズマン raíñzuman

line up *vi* 列を作る rétsu wo tsukúrù

♦*vt* (people) 1列に並ばせる ichíretsu ni narábaserù; (prepare: event, celebration) 手配する tehái suru

line-up [lain'ʌp] *n* (US: queue) 行列 gyṓretsu; (SPORT) ラインアップ raíñ-appù

linger [liŋ'gə:r] *vi* (smell, tradition etc) 残る nokórù; (person) ぐずぐずする gúzùguzu suru

lingerie [lɑ:n'dʒə:rei] *n* 女性下着類 joséishitagirùi, ランジェリー ráñjerī

lingo [liŋ'gou] (*pl* **lingoes**: *inf*) *n* (language) 言葉 kotóba

linguist [liŋ'gwist] *n* (person who speaks several languages) 数カ国語を話せる人 sūkakokùgo wo hanáserù hitó

linguistic [liŋgwis'tik] *adj* (studies, developments, ideas etc) 語学の gógàku no

linguistics [liŋgwis'tiks] *n* 語学 gógàku

lining [lai'niŋ] *n* (cloth) 裏地 uráji; (ANAT) 粘膜 néñmaku

link [liŋk] *n* (relationship) 関係 kañkei; (of a chain) 輪 wá

♦*vt* (join) つなぐ tsunágu; (associate): *to link with/to* ...と関連付ける ...to kañren-zukerù

links [liŋks] *npl* (GOLF) ゴルフ場 gorúfujō

link up *vt* (machines, systems) つなぐ tsunágu

♦*vi* 合流する gṓryū suru

lino [lai'nou] *n* = **linoleum**

linoleum [linou'li:əm] *n* リノリウム rínòriumu

lion [lai'ən] *n* (ZOOL) ライオン ráìon

lioness [lai'ənis] *n* 雌ライオン mesúràion

lip [lip] *n* (ANAT) 唇 kuchíbiru

lip-read [lip'ri:d] *vi* 読唇する dokúshin suru

lip salve *n* 唇の荒れ止め kuchíbiru no arédome

lip service *n*: *to pay lip service to something* (*pej*) 上辺だけ...に賛成する u-wábe dake ...ni sañsei suru

lipstick [lip'stik] *n* 口紅 kuchíbeni

liqueur [likə:r'] *n* リキュール ríkyùru

liquid [lik'wid] *adj* 液体の ekítai no

♦*n* 液 ékì, 液体 ekítai

liquidate [lik'wideit] *vt* (opponents, rivals) 消す késù, 殺す korósù; (company) つぶす tsubúsù

liquidize [lik'widaiz] *vt* (CULIN) ミキサーに掛ける míkìsā ni kakérù

liquidizer [lik'widaizə:r] (*BRIT*) *n* ミキサー míkìsā

liquor [lik'ə:r] *n* 酒 saké

liquorice [lik'ə:ris] (*BRIT*) *n* = **licorice**

liquor store (*US*) *n* 酒屋 sákàya

Lisbon [liz'bən] *n* リスボン rísùbon

lisp [lisp] *n* 舌足らずの発音 shitátaràzu no hatsúòn

♦*vi* 舌足らずに発音する shitátaràzu ni hatsúòn suru

list [list] *n* (catalog: of things) 目録 mokúroku, リスト rísùto; (: of people) 名簿 meíbo, リスト rísùto

♦*vt* (mention) 並べてあげる narábete agérù; (put on list) ...のリストを作る ...no rísùto wo tsukúrù

listed building [lis'tid-] (*BRIT*) *n* 指定建造物 shitéikenzòbutsu

listen [lis'ən] *vi* 聞く kikú

to listen to someone/something ...を〔...の言う事を〕聞く ...wo〔...no iú kotò wo〕kikú

listener [lis'ənə:r] *n* (person listening to speaker) 聞いている人 kiíte irù hitó; (RADIO) 聴取者 chṓshushà

listless [list'lis] *adj* 物憂い monóuì

lit [lit] *pt, pp of* **light**

liter [liːˈtəːr] (*US*) *n* (unit of volume) リットル ríttoru

literacy [litˈəːrəsiː] *n* 識字 shikíji

literal [litˈəːrəl] *adj* (exact: sense, meaning) 厳密な geñmitsu na; (word for word: translation) 逐語的な chikúgoteki na

literally [litˈəːrəliː] *adv* (in fact) 本当に hoñtō ni; (really) 文字通りに mojídōri ni

literary [litˈəːreːriː] *adj* 文学の buñgaku no

literate [litˈəːrit] *adj* (able to read etc) 読み書きできる yomíkaki dekirù; (educated) 教養のある kyōyō no arù

literature [litˈəːrətʃəːr] *n* (novels, plays, poetry) 文学 buñgaku; (printed information: scholarly) 文献 buñken; (: brochures etc) 印刷物 iñsatsubùtsu, カタログ katárogu

lithe [laið] *adj* (person, animal) しなやかな shináyaka na

litigation [litəgeiˈʃən] *n* 訴訟 soshō

litre [liːˈtəːr] (*BRIT*) *n* = **liter**

litter [litˈəːr] *n* (rubbish) 散らばっているごみ chirábatte irù gomi; (young animals) 一腹 hitóhara

litter bin (*BRIT*) *n* ごみ入れ gomíire

littered [litˈəːrd] *adj*: **littered with** (scattered) ...を散らかされた ...wo chirákasareta

little [litˈəl] *adj* (small: thing, person) 小さい chíisài; (young: child) 幼い osánài; (short: distance) 近い chikáì; (time, event) 短い mijíkaì

♦*adv* 少ししか...ない sukóshì shika ...nái

a little (amount) 少し(の) sukóshì (no)

a little bit 少し sukóshì

little brother/sister 弟[妹] otóto[imóto]

little by little 少しずつ sukóshizùtsu

little finger *n* 小指 koyúbi

live [*vb* liv *adj* laiv] *vi* (reside: in house, town, country) 住む súmù; (lead one's life) 暮す kurásù; (be alive) 生きている ikíte irù

♦*adj* (animal, plant) 生きている ikíte irù; (TV, RADIO) 生の namá no, ライブの ráibu no; (performance) 実演の jitsúen

no; (ELEC) 電流が通じている deñryū ga tsújite irù, 生きている ikíte irù; (bullet, bomb, missile) 使用可能状態の shiyōkanōjōtai no, 実の jitsú no

to live with someone (cohabit) ...と同せいする ...to dōsei suru

live down *vt* (defeat, error, failure): *I'll never live it down* 一生の恥だ isshō no hájì da

livelihood [laivˈliːhud] *n* (income source) 生計 seíkei

lively [laivˈliː] *adj* (person) 活発な kappátsu na; (interesting: place etc) 活気に満ちた kakkí ni michità; (: event) にぎやかな nigíyaka na; (: book) 面白い omóshiroì; (enthusiastic: interest, admiration etc) 熱心な nesshín na

liven up [laivˈən-] *vt* (person) ...に元気を付ける ...ni géñki wo tsukérù; (discussion, evening etc) 面白くする omóshirokù suru

♦*vi* (person) 元気になる géñki ni nárù; (discussion, evening etc) 面白くなる omóshirokù nárù

live on *vt fus* (food) ...を食べて暮す ...wo tábète kurásu

liver [livˈəːr] *n* (ANAT) 肝臓 kañzō; (CULIN) レバー rébà

livery [livˈəːriː] *n* (of servant) お仕着せ o-shíkise

lives [laivz] *npl of* **life**

livestock [laivˈstɑːk] *n* (AGR) 家畜 kachíku

live together *vi* (cohabit) 同せいする dōsei suru

live up to *vt fus* (fulfil) 守る mamórù

livid [livˈid] *adj* (color: of bruise) 青黒い aóguroì; (: of angry face) どす黒い dosúguroì; (: of sky) 鉛色の namáiro no; (furious: person) 激怒した gékìdo shitá

living [livˈiŋ] *adj* (alive: person, animal) 生きている íkìte iru

♦*n*: *to earn/make a living* 生計を立てる seíkei wo tatérù

living conditions *npl* 暮しの状況 kuráshi no jōkyō

living room *n* 居間 imá

living standards *npl* 生活水準 seíka-

tsusuijùn

living wage n 生活賃金 seíkatsuchiǹgin

lizard [liz'ərd] n トカゲ tokáge

load [loud] n (thing carried: of person) 荷物 nímòtsu; (: of animal) 荷 ní; (: of vehicle) 積荷 tsumíni; (weight) 負担 fután

♦vt (also: **load up**: vehicle, ship etc): **to load (with)** (...を) ...に積む (...wo) ...ni tsúmù; (COMPUT: program) メモリーに読込む mémòrī ni yomíkomù, ロードする rôdo suru; (gun) ...に弾丸を込める ...ni dañgan wo komérù; (camera) ...にフィルムを入れる ...ni fírùmu wo iréru; (tape recorder) ...にテープを入れる ...ni têpu wo iréru

a load of rubbish (inf) でたらめ detárame

loads of/a load of (fig) 沢山の takúsaǹ no

loaded [lou'did] adj (vehicle): **to be loaded with** ...を積んでいる ...wo tsuñde iru; (question) 誘導的な yúdòteki na; (inf: rich) 金持の kanémochi no

loaf [louf] (pl **loaves**) n 一かたまりのパン hitókàtamari no pan

loan [loun] n (sum of money) 貸付金 kashítsukekin, ローン ròn

♦vt (money, thing) 貸す kasú

on loan (borrowed) 借りている karíte irú

loath [louθ] adj: **to be loath to do something** ...をしたくない ...wo shitáku naí

loathe [louð] vt (person, activity) ...が大嫌いである ...ga daíkirai de árù

loaves [louvz] npl of **loaf**

lobby [lɑ:b'i:] n (of building) ロビー robí; (POL: pressure group) 圧力団体 atsúryokudaǹtai

♦vt (POL) ...に圧力を掛ける ...ni atsúryoku wò kakérù

lobe [loub] n (also: **earlobe**) 耳たぶ mimítabù

lobster [lɑ:b'stər] n ロブスター róbùsutā

local [lou'kəl] adj (council, paper, police station) 地元の jimóto no

♦n (BRIT: pub) 地元のパブ jimóto no

pábù

local anesthetic n (MED) 局部麻酔 kyokúbumasùi

local authority n 地方自治体 chihójichitài

local call n (TEL) 市内通話 shináitsùwa

local government n 地方自治体 chihójichitài

locality [loukæl'iti:] n 場所 basho

locally [lou'kəli:] adv 地元で jimóto de

locals [lou'kəlz] npl: **the locals** (local inhabitants) 地元の住民 jimóto no júmiǹ

locate [lou'keit] vt (find: person, thing) 見付ける mitsúkeru; (situate): **to be located in** ...にある〔いる〕 ...ni árù〔irú〕

location [loukei'ʃən] n (particular place) 場所 basho

on location (CINEMA) ロケで roké de

loch [lɑ:k] n 湖 mizúumì

lock [lɑ:k] n (of door, drawer, suitcase) 錠 jô; (on canal) こう門 kômon; (also: **lock of hair**) 髪の一房 kamí no hitófùsa

♦vt (door, drawer, suitcase: with key) ...のかぎを掛ける ...no kagí wo kakérù

♦vi (door etc) かぎが掛る kagí ga kakárù; (wheels) 回らなくなる mawáranaku narù

locker [lɑ:k'ər] n (in school, railway station etc) ロッカー rókkà

locket [lɑ:k'it] n ロケット rokéttò

lock in vt 閉じ込める tojíkomerù

lock out vt (person) 閉出す shimédasu

locksmith [lɑ:k'smiθ] n 錠前師 jômaeshì

lock up vt (criminal) 刑務所に入れる keímushò ni iréru; (mental patient) 施設に預ける shisétsu ni azúkerù; (house) ...のかぎを掛ける ...no kagí wo kakérù

♦vi ...のかぎが掛ける ...no kagí wo kakérù

lockup [lɑ:k'ʌp] n (jail) 刑務所 keímushò

locomotive [loukəmou'tiv] n 機関車 kikáñsha

locum tenens [lou'kəm ti:'nenz] (BRIT **locum**) n (MED) 代診 dashín

locust [lou'kəst] n イナゴ inágo

lodge [lɑ:dʒ] n (small house) 守衛室 shuéishìtsu; (hunting lodge) 山小屋 yamágoya

◆*vi* (person): *to lodge (with)* (...の家に) 下宿する (...no ĭe ni) geshúku suru; (bullet, bone etc) ...に支える ...ni tsukáerù

◆*vt* (complaint, protest etc) 提出する teíshutsu suru

lodger [lɑ:dʒˈəːr] *n* 下宿人 geshúkunin

lodgings [lɑ:dʒˈiŋz] *npl* 下宿 geshúku

loft [lɔːft] *n* (attic) 屋根裏部屋 yanéurabèya

lofty [lɔːfˈtiː] *adj* (noble: ideal, aim) 高尚な kốshō na; (self-important: manner) 横柄な ôhei na

log [lɔːg] *n* (piece of wood) 丸太 marúta; (written account) 日誌 nisshí

◆*vt* (event, fact) 記録する kiróku suru

logarithm [lɔːgˈəriðəm] *n* (MATH) 対数 taísū

logbook [lɔːgˈbuk] *n* (NAUT) 航海日誌 kōkainisshì; (AVIAT) 航空日誌 kôkūnisshi; (*BRIT*: of car) 登録帳 tôrokuchō

loggerheads [lɔːgˈəːrhedz] *npl*: *to be at loggerheads* 対立している taíritsu shite iru

logic [lɑːdʒˈik] *n* (method of reasoning) 論理学 roñrigàku; (process of reasoning) 論理 rôñri

logical [lɑːdʒˈikəl] *adj* (argument, analysis) 論理的な roñriteki na; (conclusion, result) 当然な tốzen na; (course of action) 合理的な gốriteki na

logistics [loudʒis'tiks] *n* (planning and organization) 仕事の計画と実行 shigóto nò keíkaku tò jikkố

logo [lou'gou] *n* (of firm, organization) シンボルマーク shíñborumàku, ロゴ rôgò

loin [lɔin] *n* (of meat) 腰肉 koshíniku

loiter [lɔi'təːr] *vi* (linger) ぶらつく burátsuku

loll [lɑːl] *vi* (person: *also*: **loll about**) ごろ寝する goróne suru

lollipop [lɑːl'iːpɑːp] *n* 棒あめ bôame

lollipop lady (*BRIT*) *n* 緑のおばさん midóri no obasàn ◊学童道路横断監視員 gakúdō dōroôdan kañshiin

lollipop man (*BRIT*: *pl* **lollipop men**) *n* ◊緑のおばさんの仕事をする男性 midó-

ri no obasàn no shigóto wò suru dansei

London [lʌn'dən] *n* ロンドン rôñdon

Londoner [lʌn'dənəːr] *n* ロンドンっ子 rôñdonkko

lone [loun] *adj* (person) たったひとりの tattá hitóri no; (thing) たったひとつの tattá hitótsu no

loneliness [loun'liːnis] *n* 孤独 kodóku

lonely [loun'liː] *adj* (person) 寂しい sabíshiĭ; (situation) 孤独な kodóku na; (place) 人気のない hitóke no naĭ

long [lɔːŋ] *adj* 長い nagáĭ

◆*adv* 長く nagáku

◆*vi*: *to long for something* ...を恋しがる ...wo koíshigarù

so/as long as ...さえすれば ...sáè suréba

don't be long! 早く帰って来て下さいね háyàku kaétte kite kudàsai nê

how long is the street? この道の端から端までどのぐらいありますか konő michî no hashí kara hashí madè donő guraî arímasù ká

how long is the lesson? レッスンの時間はどのぐらいですか rèssùn no jíkàn wa donő guraĭ desu ká

6 meters long 長さは6メーター nágàsa wa rokú mētā

6 months long 期間は6か月 kíkàn wa rokkágetsu

all night long ひと晩中 hitóbanjū

he no longer comes 彼はもう来ない kárè wa mồ kónaĭ

long before ずっと前に zuttố máè ni

before long (+future, +past) まもなく mamónàku

at long last やっと yattố

long-distance [lɔːŋ'dis'təns] *adj* (travel, phone call) 長距離の chốkyori no

longevity [lɑːndʒev'itiː] *n* 長生き nagáiki

long-haired [lɔːŋ'he'rd] *adj* (person) 長髪の chốhatsu no

longhand [lɔːŋ'hænd] *n* 普通の書き方 futsũ no kakíkata

longing [lɔːŋ'iŋ] *n* あこがれ akógare

longitude [lɑːn'dʒətuːd] *n* 経度 keído

long jump *n* 走り幅跳び hashírihabàtobi

long-life [lɔːŋˈlaif] *adj* (batteries etc) 寿命の長い jumyō no nagaî; (milk) ロングライフの roñguraîfu no

long-lost [lɔːŋˈlɔːst] *adj* (relative, friend) 長年会わなかった nagánen awánakattà

long-playing record [lɔːŋˈpleiˈiŋ-] *n* L Pレコード erúpīrekòdo

long-range [lɔːŋˈreindʒ] *adj* (plan, forecast) 長期の chōki no; (missile, plane etc) 長距離の chōkyori no

long-sighted [lɔːŋˈsaitid] *adj* (MED) 遠視の eñshi no

long-standing [lɔːŋˈstændiŋ] *adj* 長年にわたる nagánen ni watárù

long-suffering [lɔːŋˈsʌfˈəːriŋ] *adj* (person) 忍耐強い niñtaizuyoi

long-term [lɔːŋˈtəːrmˈ] *adj* (project, solution etc) 長期の chōki no

long wave *n* (RADIO) 長波 chōha

long-winded [lɔːŋˈwinˈdid] *adj* (speech, text) 長たらしい nagátarashiì

loo [luː] (*BRIT: inf*) *n* トイレ tôîre

look [luk] *vi* (see) 見る mírù; (seem, appear) ...に見える ...ni miérù; (building etc): **to look south/(out) onto the sea** 南〔海〕に面している minámi〔úmì〕ni mén shite irú

 ♦*n* (*gen*): **to have a look** 見る mírù; (glance: expressing disapproval etc) 目付き mêtsùki; (appearance, expression) 様子 yôsu

 look (here)! (expressing annoyance etc) おい ôi

 look! (expressing surprise: male language) 見てくれ mítè kurê; (: female language) 見て mítè

look after *vt fus* (care for) ...の面倒を見る ...no mefñdō wo mírù; (deal with) 取扱う toríatsukaù

look at *vt fus* (see) ...を見る ...wo mírù; (read quickly) ...にさっと目を通す ...ni sattó me wo tôsù; (study: problem, subject etc) 調べる shiráberù

look back *vi* (remember) 振返ってみる furíkaette mirù

look down on *vt fus* (*fig*) 軽べつする keíbetsu suru

look for *vt fus* (person, thing) 捜す sa-

gásu

look forward to *vt fus* ...を楽しみにする ...wo tanóshimi ni suru; (in letters): **we look forward to hearing from you** ご返事をお待ちしております go-héñji wo o-máchi shitè orímasù

look into *vt* (investigate) ...を調べる ...wo shiráberù

look on *vi* (watch) 傍観する bôkan suru

look out *vi* (beware): **to look out (for)** (...に) 注意する (...ni) chūì suru

lookout [lukˈaut] *n* (tower etc) 看視所 kañshijò; (person) 見張り人 mihárinìn

 to be on the lookout for something ...を警戒する ...wo keíkai suru

look out for *vt fus* (seek) 捜す sagásu

look round *vi* 見回す mimáwasù

looks [luks] *npl* (good looks) 容ぼう yō-bō

look through *vt fus* (examine) ...を調べる ...wo shiráberù

look to *vt fus* (rely on) ...を頼りにする ...wo tayóri ni surù

look up *vi* (with eyes) 見上げる miágerù; (situation) ...の見通しがよくなる ...no mitōshi ga yokù naru

 ♦*vt* (piece of information) 調べる shiráberù

look up to *vt fus* (hero, idol) ...を尊敬する ...wo soñkei suru

loom [luːm] *vi* (*also*: **loom up**: object, shape) ぼんやりと姿を現す boñ-yarî to sugáta wò aráwasù; (: event: approach) 迫っている semátte irù

 ♦*n* (for weaving) 機織機 hatáorikì

loony [luːˈniː] (*inf*) *adj* 狂っている kurútte irù

 ♦*n* 気違い kichígaì

loop [luːp] *n* (in string, ribbon etc) 輪 wá

 ♦*vt*: **to loop something round something** ...に...を巻付ける ...ni ...wo makítsukerù

loophole [luːpˈhoul] *n* (*fig*) 抜け穴 nukéana

loose [luːs] *adj* (not firmly fixed) 緩い yurûì; (not close fitting: clothes etc) ゆったりした yuttárî shita; (not tied back: long hair) 縛ってない shibátte naî; (promiscu-

ous: life, morals) ふしだらな fushídàra na

♦*n*: *to be on the loose* (prisoner, maniac) 逃亡中である tôbōchū de arù

loose change *n* 小銭 kozéni

loose chippings [-'tʃip'iŋz] *npl* (on road) 砂利 jarí

loose end *n*: *to be at loose ends* (*US*) *or a loose end* (*BRIT*) 暇を持て余している himá wo motéamashite irù

loosely [luːs'liː] *adv* 緩く yúrùku

loosen [luː'sən] *vt* 緩める yurúmerù

loot [luːt] *n* (*inf*) 分捕り品 buńdorihìn

♦*vt* (steal from: shops, homes) 略奪する ryakúdatsu suru

lop off [lɑːp-] *vt* (branches etc) 切り落す kirīotosù

lopsided [lɑːp'saiˈdid] *adj* (crooked) 偏った katáyottà

lord [lɔːrd] *n* (*BRIT*: peer) 貴族 kízòku

Lord Smith スミス卿 sumísukyō

the Lord (REL) 主 shú

my lord (to bishop, noble, judge) 閣下 kákkà

good Lord! えっ êt

the (House of) Lords (*BRIT*) 上院 jôin

lordship [lɔːrd'ʃip] *n*: *your Lordship* 閣下 kákkà

lore [lɔːr] *n* (of particular culture) 伝承 deńshō

lorry [lɔːr'iː] (*BRIT*) *n* トラック torákkù

lorry driver (*BRIT*) *n* トラック運転手 torákkù unteńshu

lose [luːz] (*pt, pp* **lost**) *vt* (object) 紛失する fuńshitsu suru, なくす nakúsù; (job) 失う ushínaù; (weight) 減らす herásù; (friend, relative through death) 失う ushínaù, なくす nakusu; (waste: time) 無駄にする mudá ni surù; (: opportunity) 逃す nogásù; (money) 損する sóń suru

♦*vi* (competition, argument) ...に負ける ...ni makérù

to lose (time) (clock) 遅れる okúrerù

loser [luː'zəːr] *n* (in game, contest) 敗者 háisha; (*inf*: failure: person, thing) 出来損ない dekísokonai

loss [lɔːs] *n* (act of losing something) 紛失 fuńshitsu; (occasion of losing something) 喪失 sôshitsu; (death) 死亡 shibô; (COMM): *to make a loss* 損する sóń suru

heavy losses (MIL) 大きな損害 ôkina sońgai

to be at a loss 途方に暮れる tohô ni kuréru

lost [lɔːst] *pt, pp of* **lose**

♦*adj* (person, animal: in unknown place) 道に迷った michí ni mayôtta; (: missing) 行方不明の yukûe fuméi no; (object) なくした nakúshita

lost and found (*US*) *n* 遺失物 ishítsubùtsu

lost property (*BRIT*) *n* = **lost and found**

lot [lɑːt] *n* (set, group: of things) ひと組 hitôkùmi; (at auctions) ロット rôttò

the lot (everything) 全部 zéñbu

a lot (large number, amount) 沢山 takusan

a lot of 沢山の takusan no

lots of (things, people) 沢山の takúsañ no

I read a lot 私は沢山の本を読みます watákushi wa takúsań no hoń wò yomímasù

to draw lots (for something) (...のために) くじを引く (...no tamé nì) kújì wo hîkù

lotion [lou'ʃən] *n* (for skin, hair) ローション rôshon

lottery [lɑːt'əːriː] *n* (game) 宝くじ takárakùji

loud [laud] *adj* (noise, voice, laugh) 大きい ôkii; (support, condemnation) 強い tsuyôi; (clothes) 派手な hadé na

♦*adv* (speak etc) 大きな声で ôkina kôe de

out loud (read, laugh, pray etc) 声を出して kôe wo dâshite

loudhailer [laud'heilə:r] (*BRIT*) *n* = **bullhorn**

loudly [laud'liː] *adv* 大きな声で ôkina kôe de

loudspeaker [laud'spiːkəːr] *n* 拡声器 kakúseïki, スピーカー súpìkā

lounge [laundʒ] *n* (*BRIT*: in house) 居間

imá; (in hotel, at airport, station) ロビー róbì; (BRIT: also: lounge bar) ラウンジバー raúnjibà

♦vi ぐったりもたれる guttárì motárerù

lounge about vi ぶらぶらする búrabura suru

lounge around vi = **lounge about**

lounge suit (BRIT) n 背広 sebíro, スーツ sútsu

louse [laus] (pl **lice**) n (insect) シラミ shirámi

lousy [lau'zi:] adj (inf: bad quality: show, meal etc) 最低の saítei no; (: ill) 気持が悪い kimóchi gà waruî

lout [laut] n ちんぴら chínpira

lovable [lʌv'əbəl] adj 愛らしい aírashiî

love [lʌv] n (gen) 愛 áî, 愛情 aíjō; (romantic) 恋 愛 reñ-ai; (sexual) 性 愛 seíai; (strong liking: for music, football, animals etc) 愛着 aíchaku, 好み konómi

♦vt (gen) 愛する aí surù; (thing, activity etc) ...が大好きである ...ga daísuki de arù

love (from) Anne (on letter) 愛を込めて, アン (より) áî wo kométe, áñ (yórì)

to love to do ...するのが大好きである ...surú nò ga daísuki de arù

to be in love with ...にほれている ...ni horéte irù, ...が好きである ...ga sukí de arù

to fall in love with ...と恋に落ちる ...to kóî ni ochírù, ...が好きになる ...ga sukí ni narù

to make love (have sex) 性交する seíkō suru, セックスする sékkùsu suru

15 love (TENNIS) 15対0 jūgo taî zérò, フィフティーンラブ fífftìn rabu

I love chocolate 私はチョコレートが大好きです watákushi wà chokórēto ga daísuki desù

love affair n 情事 jōji

love letter n ラブレター rábùretā

love life n 性生活 seíseikàtsu

lovely [lʌv'li:] adj (beautiful) 美しい utsúkushiî; (delightful) 楽しい tanóshiî

lover [lʌv'ə:r] n (sexual partner) 愛人 aíjin; (person in love) 恋人 koíbito

a lover of art/music 美術〔音楽〕の愛好者 bíjutsu〔óñgaku〕no aíkōsha

loving [lʌv'iŋ] adj (person) 愛情深い aíjōbukaî; (actions) 愛情のこもった aíjō no komótta

low [lou] adj (gen) 低 い hikui; (income, price etc) 安い yasúî; (quality) 粗悪な soáku na; (sound: deep) 深い fukáî; (: quiet) 低い hikúî

♦adv (sing) 低音で teíon de; (fly) 低く hikúkù

♦n (METEOROLOGY) 低気圧 teíkiatsu

to be low on (supplies etc) ...が少なくなっている ...ga sukúnàku natté irù

to feel low (depressed) 元気がない géñki ga náî

low-alcohol [lou'æl'kəhɔːl] adj (wine, beer) 度の低い do no hikúî

low-cut [lou'kʌt] adj (dress) 襟ぐりの深い eríguri no fukáî, ローカットの rókattò no

lower [lou'ə:r] adj (bottom, less important) 下の shitá no

♦vt (object, price etc) 下 げる sagérù; (voice) 低くする hikúkù suru; (eyes) 下に向ける shitá ni mukérù

low-fat [lou'fæt] adj 低脂肪の teíshibō no, ローファットの rófattò no

lowlands [lou'ləndz] npl (GEO) 低 地 teíchi

lowly [lou'li:] adj (position, origin) 卑しい iyáshiî

loyal [lɔi'əl] adj (friend, support etc) 忠実な chūjitsu na

loyalty [lɔi'əlti:] n 忠誠 chūsei

lozenge [lɑːz'indʒ] n (MED) ドロップ dóròppu

LP [el'piː'] n abbr = **long-playing record**

L-plates [el'pleits] (BRIT) npl 仮免許運転中の表示プレート karímenkyo untenchū no hyójipurēto

Ltd abbr (COMM) = **limited (liability) company**

lubricate [luː'brikeit] vt (part of machine, chain etc) ...に油を差す ...ni abúra wo sásù

lucid [luː'sid] adj (writing, speech) 分かりやすい wakáriyasuî; (able to think clear-

ly) 正気な shṓki na

luck [lʌk] n (also: **good luck**) 運 úñ
  bad luck 悪運 akúuñ
  good luck! 成功を祈るよ seíkō wò inórù yò
  bad/hard/tough luck! 残念だね zañneñ da né

luckily [lʌk'ili:] adv 幸いに saíwai ni

lucky [lʌk'i:] adj (person: fortunate) 運の良い úñ no yóì; (: at cards etc) ...に強い ...ní tsuyóì; (situation, event) まぐれの magúrè no; (object) 好運をもたらす kṓuñ wo motárasù

lucrative [lu:'krətiv] adj もうかる mṓkarù

ludicrous [lu:'dəkrəs] adj (feeling, situation, price etc) ばかばかしい bakábakashii

lug [lʌg] (inf) vt (heavy object, suitcase etc) 引きずる hikízuru

luggage [lʌg'idʒ] n 手荷物 tenímòtsu

luggage rack n (on car) ルーフラック rūfurakku; (in train) 網棚 amidana

lukewarm [lu:k'wɔːrm'] adj (liquid) ぬるい nurúì; (person, reaction etc) 気乗りしない kinóri shinai

lull [lʌl] n (break: in conversation, fighting etc) 途切れる事 togírerù kotó
  ♦vt: **to lull someone to sleep** ゆすって ...を寝付かせる yusútte ...wo netsúkaserù
  to be lulled into a false sense of security 油断する yudán suru

lullaby [lʌl'əbai] n 子守歌 komóriùta

lumbago [lʌmbei'gou] n (MED) 腰痛 yṓtsū

lumber [lʌm'bəːr] n (wood) 材木 zaímoku; (BRIT: junk) 粗大ごみ sodáigomi

lumberjack [lʌm'bəːrdʒæk] n きこり kikóri

lumber with vt: **to be lumbered with something** ...を押付けられる ...wo oshítsukerarerù

luminous [lu:'minəs] adj (fabric, color, dial, instrument etc) 蛍光の keíkō no

lump [lʌmp] n (of clay, butter etc) 塊 katámari; (on body) しこり shikóri; (on head) こぶ kobú; (also: **sugar lump**) 角砂

糖 kakúzatō
  ♦vt: **to lump together** 一緒くたに扱う isshōkuta ni atsúkaù
  a lump sum 一時払い金額 ichíjibaraikiñgaku

lumpy [lʌm'pi:] adj (sauce) 塊だらけの katámaridaràke no; (bed) ごつごつの gotsúgotsuno

lunar [lu:'nəːr] adj (landscape, module, landing etc) 月の tsukí no

lunatic [lu:'nətik] adj (behavior) 気違い染みた kichígaijimità

lunch [lʌntʃ] n 昼食 chūshoku

luncheon [lʌn'tʃən] n (formal meal) 昼食会 chūshokukài

luncheon meat n ランチョンミート rañchonmìto

luncheon voucher (BRIT) n 昼食券 chūshokukèn

lunch time n 昼食時 chūshokudoki

lung [lʌŋ] n (ANAT) 肺 haí

lunge [lʌndʒ] vi (also: **lunge forward**) 突進する tosshín suru
  to lunge at ...を目掛けて突っ掛る ...wo megákete tsukkákarù

lurch [ləːrtʃ] vi (person) よろめく yorómekù; (vehicle) 揺れる yurérù
  ♦n (movement: of person) よろめき yorómeki; (: of vehicle) 揺れる事 yurérù kotó
  to leave someone in the lurch 見捨てる misúterù

lure [lu:r] n (attraction) 魅惑 miwáku
  ♦vt (entice, tempt) 魅惑する miwáku suru

lurid [lu:'rid] adj (violent, sexually graphic: story etc) どぎつい dogítsuì; (pej: brightly colored: dress etc) けばけばしい kebákebashiì

lurk [ləːrk] vi (animal, person) 待ち伏せする machíbuse surù

luscious [lʌʃ'əs] adj (attractive: person, thing) 魅力的な miryókuteki na; (food) おいしそうな oíshisō na

lush [lʌʃ] adj (fields, gardens) 生茂った oíshigettà

lust [lʌst] (pej) n (sexual desire) 性欲 seíyoku; (desire for money, power etc) 欲望

yokúbō

lust after vt fus (desire: strongly) ...の欲に駆られる ...no yokú ni karárerù; (: sexually) ...とセックスをしたがる ...to sekkúsù wo shitágarù

luster [lʌs'tər] (BRIT **lustre**) n (shining: of metal, polished wood etc) つや tsuyá

lust for vt fus = **lust after**

lusty [lʌs'ti:] adj (healthy, energetic) 元気一杯の geñkíippaì no

Luxembourg [lʌk'səmbə:rg] n ルクセンブルク rukúseñburuku

luxuriant [lʌgʒu:r'i:ənt] adj (plants, trees) 生茂った oíshigettà; (gardens) 植込みの生茂った uékomi no oíshigettà; (hair) 豊富な hőfu na

luxurious [lʌgʒu:r'i:əs] adj (hotel, surroundings etc) 豪華な gőka na

luxury [lʌk'ʃə:ri:] n (great comfort) ぜいたく zeítaku; (expensive extra) ぜいたく品 zeítakuhìn; (infrequent pleasure) 得難い楽しみ egátaì tanóshimì

◆cpd (hotel, car etc) 豪華... gőka...

lying [lai'iŋ] n うそをつく事 usó wo tsúkù kotó

◆adj うそつきの usótsuki no

lynch [lintʃ] vt (prisoner, suspect) 勝手に絞り首にする katté ni shibárikùbi ni suru

lyrical [lir'ikəl] adj (poem) 叙情の jojő no; (fig: praise, comment) 叙情的な jojőteki na

lyrics [lir'iks] npl (of song) 歌詞 káshì

M

m. abbr = **meter**; **mile**; **million**

M.A. [emei'] abbr = **Master** of **Arts**

mac [mæk] (BRIT) n = **mackintosh**

macabre [məkɑ:'brə] adj 背筋の凍る様な sesúji no kőru yő na

macaroni [mækərou'ni:] n マカロニ makároni

machine [məʃi:n'] n (piece of equipment) 機械 kikáì; (fig: party machine, war machine etc) 組織 sőshìki

◆vt (TECH) 機械で作る kikáì de tsukú-

rù; (dress etc) ミシンで作る míshìn de tsukúrù

machine gun n 機関銃 kikánjū

machine language n (COMPUT) 機械語 kikáigo

machinery [məʃi:'nə:ri:] n (equipment) 機械類 kikáiruì; (fig: of government) 組織 sőshìki

macho [mɑ:tʃou] adj (man, attitude) 男っぽい otőkoppoi

mackerel [mæk'ə:rəl] n inv サバ sabá

mackintosh [mæk'intɑʃ] (BRIT) n レーンコート rénkòto

mad [mæd] adj (insane) 気の狂った ki no kurúttà; (foolish) ばかげた bakágetà; (angry) 怒っている okőtte irù; (keen: to be mad about (person, football etc) ...に夢中になっている ...ni muchű ni nátte iru

madam [mæd'əm] n (form of address) 奥様 őkùsama

madden [mæd'ən] vt 怒らせる okőraserù

made [meid] pt, pp of **make**

Madeira [mədei'rə] n (GEO) マデイラ madéira; (wine) マデイラ madéira

made-to-measure [meid'təmeʒ'ə:r] (BRIT) adj = **made-to-order**

made-to-order [meid'tu:ɔ:r'dɔ:r] (US) adj オーダーメードの ődàmèdo no

madly [mæd'li:] adv (frantically) 死物狂いで shinímonogurùi de
madly in love ぞっこんほれ込んで zokkón horékoňde

madman [mæd'mæn] (pl **madmen**) n 気違い kichígai

madness [mæd'nis] n (insanity) 狂気 kyőki; (foolishness) 気違い沙汰 kichígaizata

Madrid [mədrid'] n マドリード madőrìdo

Mafia [mɑ:f'i:ə] n マフィア máfìa

magazine [mægəzi:n'] n (PRESS) 雑誌 zasshí; (RADIO, TV) 放送ジャーナル hősō jānarù

maggot [mæg'ət] n ウジムシ ujímùshi

magic [mædʒ'ik] n (supernatural power) 魔法 mahő; (conjuring) 手品 téjìna, マジック májìkku

♦*adj* (powers, ritual) 魔法の mahō no

magical [mædʒ'ikəl] *adj* (powers, ritual) 魔法の mahō no; (experience, evening) 夢の様な yumé no yṓ na

magician [mədʒiʃ'ən] *n* (wizard) 魔法使い mahṓtsukaí; (conjurer) マジシャン májìshan

magistrate [mædʒ'istreit] *n* 軽犯罪判事 keíhanzai hañji

magnanimous [mægnæn'əməs] *adj* (person, gesture) 寛大な kañdai na

magnate [mæg'neit] *n* 大立者 ṓdatemóno, ...王 ...ṓ

magnesium [mægni:'zi:əm] *n* マグネシウム magúneshiùmu

magnet [mæg'nit] *n* 磁石 jíshaku

magnetic [mægnet'ik] *adj* (PHYSICS) 磁石の jíshaku no; (personality) 魅力的な miryókuteki na

magnetic tape *n* 磁気テープ jikí tèpu

magnetism [mæg'nitizəm] *n* 磁気 jíkì

magnificent [mægnif'əsənt] *adj* 素晴らしい subárashiî

magnify [mæg'nəfai] *vt* (enlarge: object) 拡大する kakúdai suru; (increase: sound) 大きくする ṓkiku suru

magnifying glass [mæg'nəfaiíŋ-] *n* 拡大鏡 kakúdaikyō

magnitude [mæg'nətu:d] *n* (size) 大きさ ṓkisa; (importance) 重要性 júyōsei

magnolia [mægnoul'jə] *n* マグノリア magúnorìa ◇モクレン, コブシ, タイサンボクを含む植物の類 mókùren, kóbùshi, taísanboku wo fukúmù shokúbùtsu no ruí

magpie [mæg'pai] *n* カササギ kasásagi

mahogany [məhɑ:g'əni:] *n* マホガニー mahógànī

maid [meid] *n* (servant) メイド meídò

old maid (*pej*: spinster) ハイミス haímìsu

maiden [meid'ən] *n* (literary: girl) 少女 shṓjo

♦*adj* (aunt etc) 未婚の mikón no; (speech, voyage) 処女... shṓjo ...

maiden name *n* 旧姓 kyúsei ◇既婚女性について使う kikónjòsei ni tsuîte tsukáù

mail [meil] *n* (postal service) 郵便 yūbin;

(letters etc) 郵便物 yúbiñbutsu

♦*vt* (post) 投かんする tṓkan suru

mailbox [meil'bɑ:ks] (*US*) *n* ポスト pósùto

mailing list [mei'liŋ-] *n* 郵送先名簿 yúsōsaki meíbo

mail-order [meil'ɔ:rdə:r] *n* (system) 通信販売 tsūshinhañbai

maim [meim] *vt* 重傷を負わせる júshō wo owáserù ◇その結果不具になる場合について言う sonó kekkà fúgù ni nárù baái ni tsuîte iú

main [mein] *adj* 主な ṓmò na, 主要な shuyṓ na, メーンの mēn no

♦*n* (pipe) 本管 hofìkan

in the main (in general) 概して gaî shite

mainframe [mein'freim] *n* (COMPUT) メインフレーム meínfurèmu

mainland [mein'lənd] *n* 本土 hóndo

mainly [mein'li:] *adv* 主に ṓmò ni

main road *n* 幹線道路 kañsendṓro

mains [meinz] *npl*: *the mains* (gas, water) 本管 hofìkan; (ELEC) 本線 hofìsen

mainstay [mein'stei] *n* (*fig*: prop) 大黒柱 daíkokubàshira

mainstream [mein'stri:m] *n* (*fig*) 主流 shuryū

maintain [meintein'] *vt* (preserve: contact, friendship, system) 続ける tsuzúkeru, 保持する hojí suru; (keep up: momentum, output) 維持する ijí suru; (provide for: dependant) 養う yashínaù; (look after: building) 管理する kañri suru; (affirm: belief, opinion) 主張する shuchō suru

maintenance [mein'tənəns] *n* (of contact, friendship, system) 保持 hojí; (of momentum, output) 維持 ijí; (provision for dependent) 扶養 fuyṓ; (looking after building) 管理 kañri; (affirmation: of belief, opinion) 主張する事 shuchō suru koto; (*BRIT*: LAW: alimony) 離婚手当 rikónteate

maize [meiz] *n* トウモロコシ toúmoròkoshi

majestic [mədʒes'tik] *adj* (splendid: scenery etc) 壮大な sodái na; (dignified)

堂々とした dōdō to shitá

majesty [mædʒ'isti:] n (title): *Your Majesty* 陛下 héĭka; (sovereignty) 王位 ŏi; (splendor) 威厳 igén

major [mei'dʒəːr] n (MIL) 少佐 shṓsa
♦*adj* (important, significant: event, factor) 重要な jŭyṓ na; (MUS: key) 長調の chṓchō no

Majorca [məjɔːr'kə] n マジョルカ majórùka

majority [mədʒɔːr'iti:] n (larger group: of people, things) 過半数 kahánsū; (margin: of votes) 得票差 tokúhyōsa

make [meik] (*pt, pp* **made**) *vt* (produce, form: object, clothes, cake) 作る tsukúrù; (: noise) 立てる tatérù; (: speech, mistake) する surú; (: remark) 言う iú; (manufacture: goods) 作る tsukúrù, 製造する seízō suru; (cause to be): *to make someone sad* ...を悲しくさせる ...wo kanáshikù saséru; (force): *to make someone do something* ...に...をさせる ...ni ...wo saseru; (earn: money) もうける mṓkerù; (equal): *2 and 2 make 4* 2足す2は4 2 tásù 2 wà 4
♦*n* (brand): *it's a Japanese make* 日本製です nihónsei desu

to make the bed ベッドを整える béddò wo totónoerù

to make a fool of someone ...をばかにする ...wo bákà ni suru

to make a profit 利益を得る ríèki wo érù

to make a loss 損をする sóñ wo suru

to make it (arrive on time) 間に合う ma ní aù; (achieve something) 成功する sefkō suru

what time do you make it? 今何時ですか imá náñji desu ká

to make do with ...で間に合せる ...de ma ní awaserù

make-believe [meik'bili:v] n (pretense) 見せ掛け mìsékake

make for *vt fus* (place) ...に向かう ...ni mukáù

make out *vt* (decipher) 解読する kaídoku suru; (understand) 分かる wakárù; (see) 見る mírù; (write: cheque) 書く kákù

maker [mei'kəːr] n (of program, film etc) 制作者 sefsakushà; (manufacturer) 製造者 seízōshà, メーカー mḗkā

makeshift [meik'ʃift] adj (temporary) 間に合せの ma ní awase no

make up *vt* (constitute) 構成する kṓsei suru; (invent) でっち上げる detchíagerù; (prepare: bed) 用意する yóĭ suru; (: parcel) 包む tsutsúmù
♦*vi* (after quarrel) 仲直りする nakánaori suru; (with cosmetics) 化粧する keshṓ suru

make-up [meik'ʌp] n (cosmetics) メーキャップ mḗkyappù

make up for *vt fus* (loss, disappointment) ...の埋め合せをする ...no uméawase wò suru

make-up remover n 化粧落し keshṓ otòshi

making [mei'kiŋ] n (*fig*): *a doctor etc in the making* 医者の卵 ishá no tamágo

to have the makings of ...の素質がある ...no soshítsu ga arù

malaise [mæleiz'] n 倦怠 keñtai

malaria [məleːr'i:ə] n マラリア marária

Malaya [məlei'jə] n マラヤ máràya

Malaysia [məlei'ʒə] n マレーシア marḗshīa

male [meil] n (BIOL: not female) 雄 osú
♦*adj* (animal) 雄の osú no; (human) 男の otóko no, 男性の dañsei no; (attitude etc) 男性的な dañseiteki na

malevolent [məlev'ələnt] adj (evil, harmful: person, intention) 悪魔の様な ákùma no yṓ na

malfunction [mælfʌŋk'ʃən] n (of computer, machine) 故障 koshṓ

malice [mæl'is] n (ill will) 悪意 ákùi; (rancor) 恨み urámi

malicious [məliʃ'əs] adj (spiteful: person, gossip) 悪意に満ちた ákùi ni michíta

malign [məlain'] *vt* (slander) 中傷する chúshō suru

malignant [məlig'nənt] adj (MED: tumor, growth) 悪性の akúsei no

mall [mɔːl] n (*also*: **shopping mall**) ショ

ッピング・モール shoppíngu mòru

mallet [mæl'it] *n* 木づち kízùchi

malnutrition [mælnu:triʃ'ən] *n* 栄養失調 eíyōshìtchō

malpractice [mælpræk'tis] *n* (MED) 医療過誤 iryókagò; (LAW) 不正行為 fuséikòi

malt [mɔːlt] *n* (grain) もやし moyáshi, モルト mórùto; (*also:* **malt whisky**) モルトウイスキー morúto uisùkī

Malta [mɔːl'tə] *n* マルタ márùta

Maltese [mɔːltiːzʻ] *adj* マルタの márùta no
♦*n inv* マルタ人 marútajìn

maltreat [mæltri:t'] *vt* (treat badly, violently: child, animal) 虐待する gyakútai suru

mammal [mæm'əl] *n* ほ乳類 honyúrùi

mammoth [mæm'əθ] *n* (animal) マンモス máñmosu
♦*adj* (colossal, enormous: task) ばく大な bakúdai na

man [mæn] (*pl* **men**) *n* (adult male) 男 otóko, 男性 dañsei; (mankind) 人類 jíñrui
♦*vt* (NAUT: ship) 乗組ませる noríkumaserù; (MIL: gun, post) 配置につく haíchi ni tsúkù; (operate: machine) 操作する sósa suru

an old man 老人 rójìñ
man and wife 夫婦 fùfu

manage [mæn'idʒ] *vi* (succeed) うまくなんとかする úmàku nàñtoka suru; (get by financially) なんとかして暮す nàñtoka shite kurásù
♦*vt* (be in charge of: business, shop, organization) 管理する káñri suru; (control: ship) 操縦する sójū suru; (: person) うまくあしらう úmàku ashíraù

manageable [mæn'idʒəbəl] *adj* (task, number) 扱いやすい atsúkaiyasuì

management [mæn'idʒmənt] *n* (of business etc: control, organization) 管理 káñri; (: persons) 管理職 kañrishòku

manager [mæn'idʒəːr] *n* (of business etc) 支配人 shihaínin; (of pop star) マネージャー manéjà; (SPORT) 監督 kañtoku

manageress [mæn'idʒəːris] *n* (of business etc) 女性支配人 joséishihaìnin; (of pop star) 女性マネージャー joséi manèjà; (SPORT) 女性監督 joséi kañtoku

managerial [mænidʒiːri:əl] *adj* (role, skills) 管理職の kañrishòku no

managing director [mæn'idʒiŋ-] *n* 専務取締役 séñmutoríshimariyàku

mandarin [mæn'dəːrin] *n* (*also:* **mandarin orange**) みかん mîkàn; (high-ranking bureaucrat) 高級官僚 kókyù kañryō

mandate [mæn'deit] *n* (authority) 権限 keñgen; (task) 任務 nîñmu

mandatory [mæn'dətɔːri:] *adj* (obligatory) 義務的な gimúteki na

mane [mein] *n* (of horse, lion) たてがみ tatégami

maneuver [mənu:'vəːr] (*US*) *vt* (move: car, bulky, object) 巧みに動かす tákùmi ni ugókasù; (manipulate: person, situation) 操る ayátsuru
♦*vi* (move: car, plane) 巧みに動く tákùmi ni ugókù; (MIL) 軍事演習を行う guñjieñshū wo okonau
♦*n* 巧みな動き tákùmi na ugóki

manfully [mæn'fəli:] *adv* (valiantly) 勇ましく isámashikù

mangle [mæŋ'gəl] *vt* (crush, twist) めちゃくちゃにする mechákucha ni suru

mango [mæŋ'gou] (*pl* **mangoes**) *n* マンゴー máñgō

mangy [mein'dʒiː] *adj* (animal) 汚らしい kitánarashiì

manhandle [mæn'hændəl] *vt* (mistreat) 手荒に扱う teára ni atsúkaù

manhole [mæn'houl] *n* マンホール mañhòru

manhood [mæn'hud] *n* (age) 成人時代 seíjin jidài; (state) 成人である事 seíjin de arù kotó ◇男性のみについて言う dañsei nomì ni tsútte iú

man-hour [mæn'auəːr] *n* (time) 人時 nîñji

manhunt [mæn'hʌnt] *n* (POLICE) 人間狩り niñgeñgari

mania [mei'niːə] *n* (craze) ...狂 ...kyò; (illness) そう病 sóbyō

maniac [mei'niːæk] *n* (lunatic) 狂人 kyójin; (*fig*) 無謀な人 mubó na hitò

manic [mæn'ik] *adj* (behavior, activity) 猛烈な mōretsu na

manic-depressive [mæn'ikdipres'iv] *n* そううつ病患者 sōutsubyō kaǹja

manicure [mæn'əkju:r] *n* マニキュア maníkyùa

manicure set *n* マニキュア・セット maníkyua settò

manifest [mæn'əfest] *vt* (show, display) 表す aráwasù
♦*adj* (evident, obvious) 明白な meíhaku na

manifestation [mænəfestei'ʃən] *n* 現れ aráware

manifesto [mænəfes'tou] *n* 声明書 seímeisho

manipulate [mənip'jəleit] *vt* (people) 操る ayátsurù; (system, situation) 操作する sōsa suru

mankind [mæn'kaind'] *n* (human beings) 人類 jíǹrui

manly [mæn'li:] *adj* (masculine) 男らしい otókorashiĩ

man-made [mæn'meid] *adj* (environment, satellite etc) 人工の jiǹkō no; (fiber, lake etc) 人造の jiǹzō no

manner [mæn'ə:r] *n* (way) やり方 yaríkata; (behavior) 態度 taído; (type, sort): **all manner of things** あらゆる物 aráyuru monò

mannerism [mæn'ə:rizəm] *n* 癖 kusé

manners [mæn'ə:rz] *npl* (conduct) 行儀 gyōgi, マナー mánā
bad manners 行儀の悪い事 gyōgi no warúĩ kotò

manoeuvre [mənu:'və:r] (*BRIT*) = maneuver

manor [mæn'ə:r] *n* (*also:* **manor house**) 屋敷 yashíki

manpower [mæn'pauə:r] *n* (workers) 人手 hitóde

mansion [mæn'tʃən] *n* 豪邸 gōtei

manslaughter [mæn'slɔ:tə:r] *n* (LAW) 殺意なき殺人 satsúinaki satsùjin

mantelpiece [mæn'təlpi:s] *n* マントルピース maǹtorupīsu

manual [mæn'ju:əl] *adj* (work, worker) 肉体の nikútai no; (controls) 手動の shu-

dō no
♦*n* (book) マニュアル mányùaru

manufacture [mænjəfæk'tʃə:r] *vt* (make, produce: goods) 製造する seízō suru
♦*n* (making) 製造 seízō

manufacturer [mænjəfæk'tʃə:rə:r] *n* 製造業者 seízōgyòsha, メーカー mḗkā

manure [mənu:r'] *n* 肥やし koyáshi

manuscript [mæn'jəskript] *n* (of book, report) 原稿 geǹkō; (old document) 写本 shahón

many [men'i:] *adj* (a lot of: people, things, ideas) 沢山の takúsaǹ no
♦*pron* (several) 多数 tasú
a great many 非常に沢山の hijō ni takúsaǹ no
many a time 何回も naǹkai mo

map [mæp] *n* (of town, country) 地図 chízù

maple [mei'pəl] *n* (tree) カエデ kaéde; (wood) カエデ材 kaédezài

map out *vt* (plan, task) 計画する keíkaku suru

mar [mɑ:r] *vt* (spoil: appearance) 損なう sokónaù; (: day, event) ぶち壊す buchí kowasù

marathon [mær'əθɑ:n] *n* (race) マラソン marásoǹ

marauder [mərɔ:d'ə:r] *n* (robber, killer)◊殺人、略奪などを繰返しながら荒し回る無法者 satsújin, ryakúdatsu nado wo kuríkaeshinagara arashimawarù muhōmòno

marble [mɑ:r'bəl] *n* (stone) 大理石 daíriseki; (toy) ビー玉 bídama

March [mɑ:rtʃ] *n* 3月 saǹgatsu

march [mɑ:rtʃ] *vi* (MIL: soldiers) 行進する kōshin suru; (*fig*: protesters) デモ行進をする demó kōshin wo suru; (walk briskly) 足音も高く歩く ashíoto mo takakù arúkù
♦*n* (MIL) 行進 kōshin; (demonstration) デモ行進 demó kōshin

mare [me:r] *n* 牝ウマ mesú uma

margarine [mɑ:r'dʒə:rin] *n* マーガリン mǎgarin

margin [mɑ:r'dʒin] *n* (difference: of

votes) 差 sa; (extra amount) 余裕 yoyū; (COMM: profit) 利ざや rizáya, マージン májin; (space: on page) 余白 yoháku; (edge: of area, group) 外れ hazúre

marginal [mɑːrˈdʒinəl] adj (unimportant) 二次的な nijíteki na

marginal (seat) n (POL) 不安定な議席 fuántei na giséki ◇わずかな票の差で得たので，次の選挙で失う可能性のある議席 wázùka na hyố nò sá de età node, tsugí nò seńkyo de ushínaù kanốsei no arù giséki

marigold [mærˈəgould] n マリーゴールド marígōrudo

marijuana [mærəwɑːˈnə] n マリファナ marífāna

marina [məriˈnə] n (harbor) マリーナ marínà

marinate [mærˈəneit] vt (CULIN) マリネにする márìne ni suru

marine [məriˈnː] adj (life, plant, biology) 海の umí no; (engineer, engineering) 船舶の seńpaku no
◆n (US: sailor) 海兵隊員 kaíheitaìin; (BRIT: soldier) 海兵隊員 kaíheitaìin

marital [mærˈitəl] adj (problem, relations) 夫婦の fűfu no
marital status ◇未婚，既婚，離婚を尋ねる時に使う言葉 mikón, kikón, ríkòn wo tazúnerù tokí ni tsukaù kotóba

maritime [mærˈitaim] adj 海事の káìji no

marjoram [mɑːrˈdʒəːrəm] n マヨラナ mayónàra, マージョラム mājóramu

mark [mɑːrk] n (symbol: cross, tick etc) 印 shirúshi; (stain) 染み shimí; (of shoes, fingers, tires: in snow, mud etc) 跡 átò; (sign: of friendship, respect etc) 印 shirúshi; (SCOL) 成績 seíseki; (level, point): **the halfway mark** 中間点の目印 chūkanteñ no mejírùshi; (currency) マルク márùku
◆vt (make a mark on: with pen etc) 印を書く shirúshi wo kákù; (: with shoes, tires etc) 跡を残す átò wo nokósù; (damage: furniture etc) 傷を付ける kizú wo tsukérù; (stain: clothes, carpet etc) 染みを付ける shimí wo tsukérù; (indicate:

place, time, price) 示す shimésù; (commemorate: event) 記念する kinén suru; (BRIT: SCOL) 成績をつける seíseki wò tsukérù

to mark time (MIL, fig) 足踏みする a-shíbumi suru

marked [mɑːrkt] adj (obvious) 著しい i-chíjirushiī

marker [mɑːrˈkəːr] n (sign) 目印 mejírùshi; (bookmark) しおり shiốri
marker pen サインペン saínpen

market [mɑːrˈkit] n (for fish, cattle, vegetables etc) 市場 íchìba; (in proper names) 市場 íchìba, 市場 shijố; (COMM: business and trading activity) 市場 shijố; (: demand) 需要 juyố
◆vt (COMM: sell) 市場に出す shijố ni dásù

market garden (BRIT) n 野菜農園 ya-sáinồen ◇主に市場向けの野菜や果物を栽培する小規模農場 ốmò ni shijốmuke nò yasái ya kudámono wò saíbai surù shố-kibo nồjò

marketing [mɑːrˈkitiŋ] n (COMM) 販売 hañbai

marketplace [mɑːrˈkitpleis] n (area, site: also COMM) 市場 íchìba

market research n 市場調査 shijốchồsa

marksman [mɑːrksˈmən] (pl **marksmen**) n 射撃の名手 shagéki no meíshù

marmalade [mɑːrˈməleid] n マーマレード mámarèdo

maroon [məruːˈn] vt: **to be marooned** (shipwrecked) 遭難で置去りになる sốnan dè okízari ni narù; (fig: abandoned) 置去りにされる okízari ni sarèru
◆adj (color) クリ色 kuríiro

marquee [mɑːrkiːˈ] n (tent) テント tến-to ◇運動会，野外パーティなどで使う物を指す uñdốkai, yagái pàti nádò de tsukáù monố wo sásù

marquess [mɑːrˈkwis] n 侯爵 kốshaku

marquis [mɑːrˈkwis] n = **marquess**

marriage [mærˈidʒ] n (relationship, institution) 結婚 kekkón; (wedding) 結婚式 kekkóñshiki

marriage bureau n 結婚相談所 kekkón-

sōdanjo

marriage certificate n 結婚証明書 kekkónshōmeishò

married [mær'i:d] adj (man, woman) 既婚の kikón no; (life, love) 結婚の kekkón no

marrow [mær'ou] n (vegetable) セイヨ ウカボチャ seíyōkabòcha; (also: **bone marrow**) 骨髄 kotsúzui

marry [mær'i:] vt (man, woman) ...と結婚する ...to kekkón surù; (subj: father, priest etc) ...の結婚式を行う ...no kekkónshiki wo okónaù

♦vi (also: **get married**) 結婚する kekkón suru

Mars [ma:rz] n (planet) 火星 kaséi

marsh [ma:rʃ] n (bog) 沼沢地 shótakùchi; (also: **salt marsh**) 塩性沼沢地 eńsei shótakuchi

marshal [ma:r'ʃəl] n (MIL: also: **field marshal**) 陸軍元帥 rikúgun geńsui; (official: at sports meeting etc) 役員 yakúin; (US: of police, fire department) 長官 chōkan

♦vt (organize: thoughts) 整理する seíri suru; (: support) 集める atsúmerù; (: soldiers) 整列させる seíretsu saserù

marshy [ma:r'ʃi:] adj 沼沢の多い shótakunò oi

martial [ma:r'ʃəl] adj (military) 軍の gún no

martial arts npl 武術 bújùtsu

martial law n 戒厳令 kaígeñrei

martyr [ma:r'tə:r] n (for beliefs) 殉教者 juńkyōsha

martyrdom [ma:r'tə:rdəm] n 殉教 juńkyō

marvel [ma:r'vəl] n (wonder) 驚異 kyói

♦vi: **to marvel (at)** 驚嘆する kyótan suru

marvelous [ma:r'vələs] (BRIT **marvellous**) adj 素晴らしい subárashiì

Marxism [ma:rk'sizəm] n マルクス主義 marúkusushùgi

Marxist [ma:r'ksist] adj マルクス主義の marúkusushùgi no

♦n マルクス主義者 marúkusushùgisha

marzipan [ma:r'zəpæn] n マジパン mají-

pan

mascara [mæskæ:r'ə] n マスカラ masúkara

mascot [mæs'kɔ:t] n マスコット masúkòtto

masculine [mæs'kjəlin] adj (male: characteristics, pride) 男性の dańsei no; (: atmosphere) 男性的な dańseiteki na; (woman) 男の様な otóko no yō na; (LING: noun, pronoun etc) 男性の dańsei no

mash [mæʃ] vt つぶす tsubúsu

mashed potatoes [mæʃt-] npl マッシュポテト masshú potèto

mask [mæsk] n (disguise) 覆面 fukúmen; (shield: gas mask, face mask) マスク másuku

♦vt (cover: face) 覆い隠す óikakùsu; (hide: feelings) 隠す kakúsù

masochist [mæs'əkist] n マゾヒスト mazóhisùto

mason [mei'sən] n (also: **stone mason**) 石屋 ishíya; (also: **freemason**) フリーメーソン furímèson

masonic [məsɑn'ik] adj (lodge, dinner) フリーメーソンの furímèson no

masonry [mei'sənri:] n (stonework) 石造部 sekízòbu ◊建物の石やれんがなどで造られた部分 tatémono no ishí yà reñga nadò de tsukúrarèta búbun

masquerade [mæskəreid'] vi: **to masquerade as** ...を装う ...wo yosóoù

mass [mæs] n (large number: of papers, people etc) 多数 tasú; (large amount: of detail, hair etc) 大量 taíryò; (amount: of air, liquid, land) 集団 shúdan; (PHYSICS) 物量 butsúryò; (REL) ミサ聖祭 misá seisài

♦cpd (communication, unemployment etc) 大量の taíryo no

♦vi (troops, protesters) 集合する shúgō suru

massacre [mæs'əkə:r] n 大虐殺 daígyakùsatsu

massage [məsɑːʒ'] n マッサージ massáji

♦vt (rub) マッサージする massáji suru

masses [mæs'iz] npl: **the masses** (ordinary people) 大衆 taíshū

masses of (*inf*: food, money, people) 一杯の ippái no

masseur [mæsə:r'] *n* マッサージ師 massájishì

masseuse [məsu:s'] *n* マッサージ嬢 massájijò

massive [mæs'iv] *adj* (large and heavy: furniture, door, person) どっしりした dosshírì shita; (huge: support, changes, increase) 膨大な bódai na

mass media [-mi:'di:ə] *npl* マスメディア masúmèdia

mass production (*BRIT* **mass-production**) *n* 大量生産 taíryōseisan, マスプロ masúpuro

mast [mæst] *n* (NAUT) マスト másùto; (RADIO etc) 放送アンテナ hósō àntena

master [mæs'tə:r] *n* (of servant, slave) 主人 shujíñ; (in secondary school) 先生 señseì; (title for boys): ***Master X*** X君 ékusu kùn

♦*vt* (control: situation) 掌握する shóaku suru; (: one's feelings etc) 抑える osáerù; (learn: skills, language) 修得する shútoku suru, マスターする masútā suru

to be master of the situation (*fig*) 事態を掌握している jíttai wo shóaku shite irù

master key *n* マスターキー masútā kī

masterly [mæs'tə:rli:] *adj* あっぱれな appárè na

mastermind [mæs'tə:rmaind] *n* (of crime etc) 首謀者 shubóshà, 黒幕 kurómaku

♦*vt* 計画を練って実行させる keíkaku wò nettè jikkó saserù

Master of Arts/Science *n* (person) 文学〔理学〕修士 buñgaku 〔rigaku〕 shūshi; (qualification) 文学〔理学〕修士号 buñgaku 〔rigaku〕 shūshigō

masterpiece [mæs'tə:rpi:s] *n* 傑作 kessáku

mastery [mæs'tə:ri:] *n* (of skill, language) 修得 shútoku

masturbate [mæs'tə:rbeit] *vi* マスターベーション〔オナニー〕をする masútābèshon〔onánì〕wo suru

masturbation [mæstə:rbei'ʃən] *n* マスタ

ーベーション masútābèshon, オナニー onánì

mat [mæt] *n* (on floor) マット máttò; (at door: *also*: **doormat**) ドアマット doámattò; (on table: *also*: **table mat**) テーブルマット téburumattò

♦*adj* = **matt**

match [mætʃ] *n* (game: of football, tennis etc) 試合 shiái, マッチ mátchì; (for lighting fire, cigarette) マッチ mátchì; (equal) 力が同等な人 chikára ga dōtō na hitð

♦*vt* (go well with: subj: colors, clothes) ...に合う ...ni áù; (equal) ...と同等である ...to dōtō de arù; (correspond to) ...に合う ...ni áù; (pair: *also*: **match up**) ...と合せる ...to awáserù, ...と組ませる ...to kumáserù

♦*vi* (colors, materials) 合う áù

to be a good match (colors etc) よく合う yokú áù; (couple) 似合いの...である niáì no ...de arù

matchbox [mætʃ'bɑ:ks] *n* マッチ箱 matchíbàko

matching [mætʃ'iŋ] *adj* (clothes etc) そろいの soról no

mate [meit] *n* (workmate) 仲間 nakáma; (*inf*: friend) 友達 tomódachi; (animal) 相手 aíte; (in merchant navy: first, second) ...等航海士 ...tó kōkaishì

♦*vi* (animals) 交尾する kóbi suru

material [məti:'ri:əl] *n* (substance) 物質 busshítsu; (cloth) 生地 kijí; (information, data) 情報 jóhð

♦*adj* (possessions, existence) 物質的な busshítsuteki na

materialistic [məti:ri:əlis'tik] *adj* 唯物主義的な yuíbutsushugiteki na

materialize [məti:r'i:əlaiz] *vi* (happen) 起る okórù; (appear) 現れる aráwarerù

materials [məti:'ri:əlz] *npl* (equipment) 材料 zaíryō

maternal [mətə:r'nəl] *adj* (feelings, role) 母性の boséi no

maternity [mətə:r'niti:] *n* 母性 boséi

maternity dress *n* マタニティドレス matánitidorèsu

maternity hospital *n* 産院 sañ-in

math [mæθ] (*BRIT* **maths**) *n* 数学 sūgaku

mathematical [mæθəmæt'ikəl] *adj* (formula) 数学の sūgaku no; (mind) 数学的な sūgakuteki na

mathematician [mæθəmətiʃ'ən] *n* 数学者 sūgakushà

mathematics [mæθəmæt'iks] *n* 数学 sūgaku

maths [mæθs] (*BRIT*) *n* = **math**

matinée [mætənei'] *n* マチネー machínē

mating call [mei'tiŋ-] *n* (of animals) 求愛の声 kyúai no kóè

matrices [meit'risi:z] *npl of* **matrix**

matriculation [mətrikjəlei'ʃən] *n* (enrollment) 大学入学 daígakunyūgaku

matrimonial [mætrəmou'ni:əl] *adj* 結婚の kekkón no

matrimony [mæt'rəmouni:] *n* (marriage) 結婚 kekkón

matrix [mei'triks] (*pl* **matrices**) *n* (context, environment) 環境 kañkyō

matron [mei'trən] *n* (in hospital) 婦長 fuchō; (in school) 養護員 yǒgoiñ

mat(t) [mæt] *adj* つや消しの tsuyákeshi no

matted [mæt'id] *adj* もつれた motsúretà

matter [mæt'əːr] *n* (event) 事件 jikéñ; (situation) 事情 jijō; (problem) 問題 moñdai; (PHYSICS) 物質 busshítsu; (substance, material) 素材 sozái; (written material: reading matter etc) 印刷物 iñsatsubùtsu, 本 hóñ; (MED: pus) うみ umí
♦*vi* (be important: family, job etc) 大切である taísetsu de arù

it doesn't matter 構わない kamáwanài

what's the matter? どうしましたか dō shimashita ká

no matter what (whatever happens) 何があっても nánì ga atté mo

as a matter of course (automatically) 当然ながら tōzen nagara

as a matter of fact 実は jitsú wa

matter-of-fact [mæt'əːrʌvfækt'] *adj* 無味乾燥な mumíkañsō na

matters [mæt'əːrz] *npl* (affairs) 物事 monógòto; (situation) 状況 jōkyō

mattress [mæt'ris] *n* マットレス mattórèsu

mature [mətuːr'] *adj* (person) 成熟した seíjuku shita; (cheese, wine etc) 熟成した jukúsei shita
♦*vi* (develop: child, style) 成長する seíchō suru; (grow up: person) 成熟する seíjuku suru; (ripen, age: cheese, wine etc) 熟成する jukúsei suru

maturity [mətuːr'iti:] *n* (adulthood) 成熟 seíjuku; (wisdom) 分別 fúñbetsu

maul [mɔːl] *vt* ...に大けがをさせる ...ni ōkega wo saséru

mausoleum [mɔːsəliː'əm] *n* 納骨堂 nōkotsudō

mauve [mouv] *adj* フジ色の fujíiro no

maverick [mæv'əːrik] *n* 一匹オオカミ ippíki ōkami

maxim [mæk'sim] *n* 格言 kakúgeñ

maximum [mæk'səməm] (*pl* **maxima**) *adj* (efficiency, speed, dose) 最大の saídai no
♦*n* 最大限 saídaigèn

May [mei] *n* 5月 gógàtsu

may [mei] (*conditional*: **might**) *vi* (indicating possibility): *he may come* 彼は来るかも知れない kárè wa kurú ka mo shirenài; (be allowed to): *may I smoke?* タバコをすってもいいですか tabáko wo sutté mò íi desu ká; (wishes): *may God bless you!* 神の祝福をあなたに! kamí nò shukúfuku wò anáta ni
you may as well go 行ってもいいかも知れない itté mò íi ka mo shirenai; (dismissive) 行った方がいいかも知れない itta hō ga íi ka mo shirénài

maybe [mei'biː] *adv* 事によると kotó ni yorù to

May Day *n* メーデー mèdē

mayhem [mei'hem] *n* 混乱 koñran

mayonnaise [meiəneiz'] *n* マヨネーズ mayónèzu

mayor [mei'əːr] *n* (of city, town) 市〔町, 村〕長 shi〔chō, son〕chō

mayoress [mei'əːris] *n* (partner) 市〔町, 村〕長夫人 shi〔chō, son〕chō fujiñ

maze [meiz] *n* (labyrinth, puzzle) 迷路 mèiro

M.D. [emdi:ʰ] *abbr* = **Doctor of Medicine**

KEYWORD

---

me [mi:] *pron* **1** (direct) 私 を watákushi wo
can you hear me? 私の声が聞えますか watákushi no koè ga kikóemasù ká
he heard me 彼は私の声を聞いた kárè wa watákushi no koè wo kiítà
he heard ME! (not anyone else) 彼が聞いたのは私の声だった kárè ga kiítà no wa watákushi no koè dáttà
it's me 私です watákushi desù
2 (indirect) 私に watákushi nì
he gave me the money, he gave the money to me 彼は私に金を渡した kárè wa watákushi nì kané wo watáshità
give them to me それらを私に下さい sorérà wo watákushi nì kudásaì
3 (after prep): *the letter's for me* 手紙は私宛てです tegámi wà watákushi ate dèsu
with me 私と一緒に watákushi tò isshó nì
without me 私抜きで watákushi nukì de

---

meadow [med'ou] *n* 草原 kusáhara
meager [mi:'gəːr] (*BRIT* **meagre**) *adj* 乏しい tobóshiì
meal [mi:l] *n* (occasion, food) 食事 shokúji; (flour) 粉 koná
mealtime [mi:l'taim] *n* 食事時 shokújidòki
mean [mi:n] *adj* (with money) けちな kechí na; (unkind: person, trick) 意地悪な ijíwarù na; (shabby: street, lodgings) 見すぼらしい misúborashiì; (average: height, weight) 中位の chúgurai no
♦*vt* (*pt, pp* **meant**) (signify) 意味する imî suru; (refer to): *I thought you meant her* あなたは彼女の事を言っていると私は思った anátà wa kanójò no kotó wò itté irù to watákushi wà omóttà; (intend): *to mean to do something* ...をするつもりでいる ...wo suru tsumórì de irú

♦*n* (average) 平均 heíkin
do you mean it? 本当ですか hofitō desù ká
what do you mean? それはどういう事ですか sorè wa dò iú kotò desu ká
to be meant for someone/something ...に当てた物である ...ni atéta monò de árù
meander [mi:æn'dəːr] *vi* (river) 曲がりくねって流れる magárikunettè nagárerù
meaning [mi:'niŋ] *n* (of word, gesture, book) 意味 imî; (purpose, value) 意義 ígi
meaningful [mi:'niŋfəl] *adj* (result) 意味のある imî no árù; (explanation) 納得できる nattóku dekirù; (glance, remark) 意味ありげな imíarige na; (relationship, occasion) 意味深い imíbùkai
meaningless [mi:'niŋlis] *adj* 無意味な muími na
meanness [mi:n'nis] *n* (with money) けちけちさ kechí; (unkindness) 意地悪 ijíwàru; (shabbiness) 見すぼらしさ misúborashisà
means [mi:nz] *npl* (way) 方法 hóhō; (money) 財産 zaísan
by means of ...を使って ...wo tsukátte
by all means! ぜひどうぞ zéhì dózò
meant [ment] *pt, pp* of **mean**
meantime [mi:n'taim] *adv* (also: **in the meantime**) その間に sonó aìda ni
meanwhile [mi:n'wail] *adv* (meantime) その間に sonó aìda ni
measles [mi:'zəlz] *n* はしか hashíka
measly [mi:z'li:] (*inf*) *adj* ちっぽけな chippókè na
measure [meʒ'əːr] *vt* (size, weight, distance) 計る hakárù
♦*vi* (room, person) ...だけの寸法がある ...dakè nò sufipō ga árù
♦*n* (amount: of protection etc) ある程度 árù teídò; (: of whisky etc) 定量 teíryō; (ruler, *also*: **tape measure**) 巻尺 makíjaku, メジャー mejáː; (action) 処置 shochí
measured [meʒ'əːrd] *adj* 慎重な shíñchō na
measurements [meʒ'əːrmənts] *npl* (size) 寸法 sufipō
meat [mi:t] *n* 肉 nikú

cold meat コールドミート kṓrudomìto

meatball [mi:t'bɔ:l] *n* ミートボール mītobŏru

meat pie *n* ミートパイ mītopài

Mecca [mek'ə] *n* (city) メッカ mékkà; (*fig*) あこがれの地 akógare nð chí

mechanic [məkæn'ik] *n* 自動車整備士 jidṓsha seĩbishi

mechanical [məkæn'ikəl] *adj* 機械仕掛の kikáijikakè no

mechanics [məkæn'iks] *n* (PHYSICS) 力学 rikígaku

♦*npl* (of reading, government etc) 機構 kikṓ

mechanism [mek'ənizəm] *n* (device) 装置 sṓchi; (procedure) 方法 hṓhō; (automatic reaction) 反応 haĩnō

mechanization [mekənizei'ʃən] *n* 機械化 kikáika

medal [med'əl] *n* (award) メダル médàru

medallion [mədæl'jən] *n* メダリオン medáriòn

medalist [med'list] (*BRIT* **medallist**) *n* (SPORT) メダリスト medárisùto

meddle [med'əl] *vi*: **to meddle in** ...にちょっかいを出す ...ni chokkáì wo dásù

to meddle with something ...をいじる ...wo ijírù

media [mi:'di:ə] *npl* マスメディア masúmedìa

mediaeval [mi:di:i:'vəl] *adj* = **medieval**

median [mi:'di:ən] (*US*) *n* (*also*: **median strip**) 中央分離帯 chũō buñritai

mediate [mi:'di:it] *vi* (arbitrate) 仲裁する chũsai suru

mediator [mi:'di:eitəːr] *n* 仲裁者 chũsaishà

Medicaid [med'əkeid] (*US*) *n* メディケイド medíkeìdo ◇低所得者への医療扶助 teíshotðkushà e no iryṓfujo

medical [med'ikəl] *adj* (treatment, care) 医学的な igákuteki na

♦*n* (*BRIT*: examination) 健康診断 keñkōshìñdan

Medicare [med'əkeːr] (*US*) *n* メディケア medíkèa ◇高齢者への医療扶助 kṓreishà e no iryṓfujo

medicated [med'ikeitid] *adj* 薬用の yakúyō no

medication [medikei'ʃən] *n* (drugs etc) 薬 kusúri

medicinal [mədis'ənəl] *adj* 薬効のある yakkṓ no arù

medicine [med'isin] *n* (science) 医学 ígàku; (drug) 薬 kusúri

medieval [mi:di:i:'vəl] *adj* 中世の chũsei no

mediocre [mi:'di:oukəːr] *adj* (play, artist) 粗末な sṓmatsu na

mediocrity [mi:di:ɑ:k'riti:] *n* (poor quality) 粗末さ sómatsusà

meditate [med'əteit] *vi* (think carefully) 熟考する jukkṓ suru; (REL) めい想する meĩsō suru

meditation [meditei'ʃən] *n* (thinking) 熟考 jukkṓ; (REL) めい想 meĩsō

Mediterranean [meditərei'ni:ən] *adj* 地中海の chichũkai no

the Mediterranean (Sea) 地中海 chichũkai

medium [mi:'di:əm] *adj* (average: size, color) 中位の chũgurai no

♦*n* (*pl* media: means) 手段 shúdàn; (*pl* mediums: people) 霊媒 reĩbai

medium wave *n* 中波 chũha

medley [med'li:] *n* (mixture) ごったまぜ gottámaze; (MUS) メドレー médðrē

meek [mi:k] *adj* 穏和な ofíwa na

meet [mi:t] (*pt, pp* **met**) *vt* (friend: accidentally) ...に出会う ...ni deáù; (: by arrangement) ...に会う ...ni áù; (stranger: for the first time) ...と知合いになる ...to shíriai ni naru; (go and fetch: at station, airport) 出迎える demúkaerù; (opponent) ...と試合をする ...to shiái wo surù; (obligations) 果す hatásù; (problem, need) 解決する kaíketsu suru

♦*vi* (friends: accidentally) 出会う deáù; (: by arrangement) 会う áù; (strangers: for the first time) 知合いになる shíriai ni narù; (for talks, discussion) 会合する kaígō suru; (join: lines, roads) 合流する gṓryū suru

meeting [mi:'tiŋ] *n* (assembly: of club, committee etc) 会合 kaígō; (: of people) 集会 shúkai; (encounter: with friend) 出

会い deál; (COMM) 会議 káigi; (POL) 集会 shúkai

meet with *vt fus* (encounter: difficulty) 合う aú
to meet with success 成功する seíkō suru

megabyte [meg'əbait] *n* (COMPUT) メガバイト megábaìto

megaphone [meg'əfoun] *n* メガホン megáhòn

melancholy [mel'ənkɑ:li:] *n* (sadness) 憂うつ yúutsu, メランコリー meráñkorī
♦*adj* (sad) 憂鬱な yúutsu na

mellow [mel'ou] *adj* (sound, light, color) 柔らかい yawárakaì; (wine) 芳じゅんな hōjun na
♦*vi* (person) 角が取れる kádò ga torérù

melodrama [mel'ədræmə] *n* メロドラマ meródòrama

melody [mel'ədi:] *n* 旋律 señritsu, メロディー méròdī

melon [mel'ən] *n* メロン méròn

melt [melt] *vi* (metal, snow) 溶ける tokérù
♦*vt* (metal, snow, butter) 溶かす tokásù

melt down *vt* (metal) 溶かす tokásù

meltdown [melt'daun] *n* (in nuclear reactor) メルトダウン merútodàun

melting pot [melt'iŋ-] *n* (*fig*: mixture) るつぼ rútsùbo

member [mem'bə:r] *n* (of group, family) 一員 ichí-in; (of club) 会員 kaíin, メンバー méñbā; (ANAT) 体の一部 karáda no íchìbu
Member of Parliament (*BRIT*) 国会議員 kokkái giìn
Member of the European Parliament (*BRIT*) 欧州議会議員 ōshūgikai giìn

membership [mem'bə:rʃip] *n* (members) 会員一同 kaíin ichídò; (state) 会員である事 kaíin de arù kotó

membership card *n* 会員証 kaíiñshō

membrane [mem'brein] *n* 膜 makú

memento [məmen'tou] *n* 記念品 kinéñhin

memo [mem'ou] *n* 覚書 obóegaki, メモ mémò

memoirs [mem'wɑ:rz] *npl* 回顧録 kaíko-

roku

memorable [mem'ə:rəbəl] *adj* 記念すべき kinéñsubeki

memorandum [meməræn'dəm] (*pl* **memoranda**) *n* (official note) 覚書 obóegaki; (order to employees etc) 社内通達 shanái tsūtatsu

memorial [məmɔ:'ri:əl] *n* (statue, monument) 記念碑 kinéñhi
♦*adj* (service) 追悼の tsuítō no; (prize) 記念の kinén no

memorize [mem'ə:raiz] *vt* (learn) 暗記する añki suru

memory [mem'ə:ri:] *n* (ability to remember) 記憶 kióku; (things one remembers) 思い出 omóide; (instance) 思い出 omóide; (of dead person: memory) 思い出 omóide
in memory of ... ...を記念して ...wo kinén shitè; (COMPUT) 記憶装置 kiókusòchi, メモリー mémòrī

men [men] *pl of* **man**

menace [men'is] *n* (threat) 脅威 kyói; (nuisance) 困り者 komárimono
♦*vt* (threaten) 脅かす odókasu; (endanger) 危険にさらす kikén ni saràsu

menacing [men'isiŋ] *adj* (person, gesture) 脅迫的な kyóhakuteki na

mend [mend] *vt* (repair) 修理する shúri suru; (darn: socks etc) 繕う tsukúroù, 修繕する shúzen suru
♦*n*: *to be on the mend* 回復に向かっている kaífuku nî mukátte irù
to mend one's ways 心を入替える kokórò wo irékaerù

mending [mend'iŋ] *n* (repairing) 修繕 shúzen; (clothes) 繕い物 tsukúroimòno

menial [mi:'ni:əl] *adj* (lowly: often *pej*) 卑しい iyáshiì

meningitis [menindʒai'tis] *n* 脳膜炎 nómakuèn

menopause [men'əpɔ:z] *n* 更年期 kóneñki

menstruation [menstruːei'ʃən] *n* 月経 gekkéi, 生理 seíri, メンス méñsu

mental [men'təl] *adj* (ability, effort) 精神的な seíshinteki na; (illness, health) 精神の seíshin no
mental arithmetic/calculation 暗算 añzan

mentality [mentæl'iti:] *n* (attitude) 考え方 kañgaekàta

menthol [men'θɔːl] *n* メントール mefitōru

mention [men'tʃən] *n* (reference) 言及 gefikyū
♦*vt* (speak of) ...に言及する ...ni gefikyū suru
don't mention it! どういたしまして dō itáshimashitè

mentor [men'tər] *n* 良き指導者 yokí shidōsha

menu [men'juː] *n* (set menu) 献立 kofidate; (printed) 献立表 kofidatehyō, メニュー ményū; (COMPUT) メニュー ményū

MEP [emiːpiː'] (*BRIT*) *n abbr* = **Member of the European Parliament**

mercenary [məˈr'sənriː] *adj* 金銭ずくの kifisenzuku no
♦*n* (soldier) よう兵 yōhei

merchandise [məˈr'tʃəndais] *n* 商品 shōhin

merchant [məˈr'tʃənt] *n* (trader) 貿易商 bōekishō

merchant bank (*BRIT*) *n* マーチャントバンク máchantobañku

merchant marine (*BRIT* **merchant navy**) *n* 商船 shōsen ◇一国の全商船を集合的に指す ikkōku no zefishōsen wò shūgōteki ni sasù

merciful [məˈr'sifəl] *adj* (kind, forgiving) 情け深い nasákebukaì; (fortunate): *merciful release* 苦しみからの解放 kurúshimì kara no kaíhō ◇重病人などの死亡について言う jūbyōnin nado no shibō ni tsuitè iú

merciless [məˈr'silis] *adj* (person, regime) 冷酷な reíkoku na

mercury [məˈr'kjəriː] *n* 水銀 suígin

mercy [məˈr'siː] *n* (clemency: *also* REL) 情け nasáke, 慈悲 jihí
at the mercy of ...のなすがままになって ...no násù ga mamá ni nattè

mere [miːr] *adj* (emphasizing insignificance: child, trifle, amount) ほんの hoñno; (emphasizing significance): *his mere presence irritates her* 彼がそこにいるだけで彼女は頭に来る kárè ga sokó ni

irú dakè de kánòjo wa atáma ni kurù

merely [miːr'liː] *adv* ただ ...だけ tádà ...dakè

merge [məːrdʒ] *vt* (combine: companies, institutions etc) 合併させる gappéi saserù
♦*vi* (COMM) 合併する gappéi suru; (colors, sounds, shapes) 次第に溶け合う shidái ni tokéaù; (roads) 合流する gōryū suru

merger [məːr'dʒər] *n* (COMM) 合併 gappéi

meringue [məræŋ'] *n* メレンゲ meréñge

merit [me:r'it] *n* (worth, value) 価値 kachí; (advantage) 長所 chōsho, 利点 ritén
♦*vt* ...に値する ...ni atái suru

mermaid [məˈr'meid] *n* 人魚 níñgyo

merry [me:r'iː] *adj* (happy: laugh, person) 陽気な yōki na; (cheerful: music) 活気ある kakkí arù
Merry Christmas! メリークリスマス merí kurisùmasu

merry-go-round [me:r'iːgouraund] *n* 回転木馬 kaífeñmokuba

mesh [meʃ] *n* (net) メッシュ mésshù

mesmerize [mez'məraiz] *vt* 魅惑する miwáku suru

mess [mes] *n* (muddle: in room) 散らかしっ放し chirákashippanashi, めちゃくちゃ mechákucha; (: of situation) 混乱 koñran; (dirt) 汚れ yogóre; (MIL) 食堂 shokúdō

mess about/around (*inf*) *vi* (fool around) ぶらぶらする búrabura suru

mess about/around with *vt fus* (play around with) いじる ijírù

message [mes'idʒ] *n* (piece of information) 伝言 deñgon, メッセージ méssèji; (meaning: of play, book etc) 教訓 kyōkun

messenger [mes'indʒənr] *n* 使者 shíshà, メッセンジャー messéñjā

Messrs. [mes'əːrz] *abbr* (on letters) ◇Mr. の複数形 Mr. no fukúsūkeì

mess up *vt* (spoil) 台無しにする daínashi ni suru; (dirty) 汚す yogósù

messy [mes'iː] *adj* (dirty) 汚れた yogóreta; (untidy) 散らかした chirákashita

met [met] *pt, pp of* **meet**

metabolism [mətǽb'əlizəm] *n* 新陳代謝
shińchintaĩsha

metal [met'əl] *n* 金属 kińzoku

metallic [mitǽl'ik] *adj* (made of metal)
金属の kińzoku no; (sound, color) 金属的
な kińzokuteki na

metallurgy [met'ələːrdʒi:] *n* や 金 学 ya-
kińgaku

metamorphosis [metəmɔːr'fəsis] (*pl*
metamorphoses) *n* 変態 heńtai

metaphor [met'əfɔːr] *n* 隠 ゆ iń-yu, メタ
ファー metáfā

mete [mi:t] *vt*: **to mete out** (punishment,
justice) 与える atáerù, 加える kuwáerù

meteor [mi:'ti:our] *n* 流れ星 nagárebòshi

meteorite [mi:'ti:ərait] *n* いん石 ińseki

meteorology [mi:ti:ərəl'ədʒi:] *n* 気象学
kishŏgaku

meter [mi:'təːr] *n* (instrument: gas
meter, electricity meter) ...計 ...kéi, メー
ター métā; (*also*: **parking meter**) パーキ
ングメーター pākingumétā; (*US*: unit) メ
ートル métoru

method [meθ'əd] *n* (way) 方法 hŏhō

methodical [məθɑːd'ikəl] *adj* (careful,
thorough) 慎重な shińchō na

Methodist [meθ'ədist] *n* メソジスト教徒
mesŏjisuto kyŏto

methodology [meθədɑːl'ədʒi:] *n* 方 法 論
hŏhōrōn

meths [meθs] (*BRIT*) *n* = **methylated
spirit**

methylated spirit [meθ'əleitid-] (*BRIT*)
n 変性アルコール heńsei arukŏru

meticulous [mətik'jələs] *adj* 厳密な geńmitsu na

metre [mi:'təːr] (*BRIT*) *n* (unit) = **meter**

metric [met'rik] *adj* メートル法の méto-
ruhŏ no

metropolis [mitrɑːp'əlis] *n* 大都会 daítokai

metropolitan [metrəpɑːl'itən] *adj* 大 都
会の daítokai no

Metropolitan Police (*BRIT*) *n*: **the
Metropolitan Police** ロンドン市警察
rońdon shikeísatsu

mettle [met'əl] *n* (spirit, courage): **to be
on one's mettle** 張切っている haríkitte

irù

mew [mju:] *vi* (cat) にゃあと鳴く nyấ tò
nakú

mews [mju:z] *n* (*BRIT*): **mews flat** アパ
ート apáto ◇昔の馬屋をアパートに改造
した物を指す mukáshi nò umáya wò
apáto ni kaízō shita monò wo sásù

Mexican [mek'səkən] *adj* メキシコの
mekíshiko no
◆人 メキシコ人 mekíshikojìn

Mexico [mek'səkou] *n* メ キ シ コ mekíshiko

Mexico City *n* メキシコ市 mekíshiko-
shi

miaow [miau'] *vi* (cat) にゃあと鳴く nyấ
tò nakú

mice [mais] *pl of* **mouse**

micro- [mai'krou] *prefix* 微小... bishŏ...

microbe [mai'kroub] *n* 細菌 saíkin

microchip [mai'krətʃip] *n* マイクロチッ
プ maíkurochippù

micro(computer) [maikrou(kəmpju:'-
təːr)] *n* マイクロコンピュータ maíkuro-
kompyùta, パソコン pasókon

microcosm [mai'krəkɑːzəm] *n* 小 字 宙
shŏuchū, ミクロコスモス mikúrokosu-
mòsu

microfilm [mai'krəfilm] *n* マイクロフィ
ルム maíkurofirùmu

microphone [mai'krəfoun] *n* マイクロホ
ン maíkurohòn

microprocessor [maikrouprɑːs'esəːr] *n*
マイクロプロセッサー maíkuropurosès-
sā

microscope [mai'krəskoup] *n* 顕微鏡 keń-
bikyŏ

microscopic [mai'krəskɑːp'ik] *adj* 微 小
の bishŏ no

microwave [mai'krouweiv] *n* (*also*:
microwave oven) 電子レンジ deńshi reñ-
ji

mid [mid] *adj*: **in mid May** 5月半ばに
gogátsu nakàba ni
in mid afternoon 昼下がりに hirúsaga-
ri ni
in mid air 空中に kúchū ni

midday [mid'dei] *n* 正午 shŏgo

middle [mid'əl] *n* (center) 真ん中 mańna-

ka, 中央 chūō; (half-way point) 中間 chū-kan; (waist) ウエスト uésuto

♦adj (of place, position) 真ん中の mañnaka no; (average: quantity, size) 中位の chūgurai no

in the middle of the night 真夜中に mayónaka ni

middle-aged [mid'əleidʒd'] *adj* 中年の chūnen no

Middle Ages *npl: the Middle Ages* 中世 chūsei

middle-class [mid'əlklæs] *adj* 中流の chūryū no

middle class(es) [mid'əlklæs(iz)] *n(pl): the middle class(es)* 中流階級 chūryū-kaíkyū

Middle East *n: the Middle East* 中東 chūtō

middleman [mid'əlmæn] (*pl* **middlemen**) *n* 仲買人 nakágainin

middle name *n* ミドルネーム midórunè-mu

middle-of-the-road [mid'əlɔvðəroud'] *adj* (politician, music) 中道の chūdō no

middleweight [mid'əlweit] *n* (BOX-ING) ミドル級の midórukyū no

middling [mid'liŋ] *adj* 中位の chūgurai no

midge [midʒ] *n* ブヨ búyo ◊ ブヨの様な小さい虫の総称 búyo no yō na chíīsaī mushí no sōshō

midget [midʒ'it] *n* 小人 kobíto

Midlands [mid'ləndz] (*BRIT*) *npl: the Midlands* イングランド中部地方 íngurañdo chūbu chihō

midnight [mid'nait] *n* 真夜中 mayónaka

midriff [mid'rif] *n* おなか onáka ◊ ウエストから胸までの部分を指す uésuto kara muné madè no búbùn wo sásù

midst [midst] *n: in the midst of* (crowd, group) ...の中に〔で〕 ...no nákà ni〔de〕; (situation, event) ...のさなかに ...no sanákà ni; (action) ...をしている所 ...wo shité irù tokóro

midsummer [mid'sʌm'əːr] *n* 真夏 manátsu

midway [mid'wei] *adj: midway (between/through)* ...の途中で ...no to-

chū de

♦*adv: midway (between/through)* ...の途中に〔で〕 ...no tochū ni〔de〕

midweek [mid'wiːk] *adv* 週半ば shū nakabà

midwife [mid'waif] (*pl* **midwives**) *n* 助産婦 josáñpu

midwinter [mid'win'təːr] *n: in midwinter* 真冬に mafúyu ni

might[1] [mait] *see* **may**

might[2] [mait] *n* (power) 力 chikára

mighty [mai'tiː] *adj* 強力な kyóryoku na

migraine [mai'grein] *n* 偏頭痛 heñzutsū

migrant [mai'grənt] *adj: migrant bird* 渡り鳥 watáridòri

migrant worker 渡り季節労働者 watári kisetsurōdōshà

migrate [mai'greit] *vi* (bird etc) 移動する idō suru; (person) 移住する ijū suru

migration [maigrei'ʃən] *n* (bird etc) 移動 idō; (person) 移住 ijū

mike [maik] *n abbr* = **microphone**

Milan [milæn'] *n* ミラノ miráno

mild [maild] *adj* (gentle: character) 大人しい otónashiī; (climate) 穏やかな odáyàka na; (slight: infection, illness) 軽い karúi; (: interest) 少しの sukóshī no; (taste) 甘口の amákuchi no

mildew [mil'duː] *n* かび kabí

mildly [maild'liː] *adv* (gently) 優しく yasáshikù; (somewhat) 少し sukóshī

to put it mildly 控え目に言って hikáe-me ni ittè

mile [mail] *n* (unit) マイル maírù

mileage [mai'lidʒ] *n* (number of miles) マイル数 maírùsū

mileometer [mailɑːm'itəːr] (*BRIT*) *n* = **odometer**

milestone [mail'stoun] *n* (marker) 一里塚 ichírizùka; (*fig*: important point) 画期的な出来事 kakkíteki na dekígoto

milieu [miːlju:'] *n* 環境 kañkyō

militant [mil'ətənt] *adj* 戦闘的な señtō-teki na

military [mil'iteːriː] *adj* 軍隊の gúntai no

militate [mil'əteit] *vi: to militate against* (prevent) 邪魔する jamá suru

militia [miliʃ'ə] *n* 民兵 miñpei

milk [milk] *n* (of any mammal) 乳 chichí; (of cow) 牛乳 gyúnyū, ミルク mírùku
◆*vt* (cow, goat) ...の乳を搾る ...no chichí wò shibórù; (*fig*: situation, person) 食い物にする kuímonò ni suru

milk chocolate *n* ミルクチョコレート mirúkuchokorēto

milkman [milk'mæn] (*pl* **milkmen**) *n* 牛乳配達人 gyúnyūhaitatsunìn

milkshake [milk'ʃeik] *n* ミルクセーキ mirúkusēki

milky [mil'ki:] *adj* (color) 乳白色の nyúhakùshoku no; (drink) ミルク入りの mirúku iri no

Milky Way *n* 銀河 gíñga

mill [mil] *n* (windmill etc: for grain) 製粉機 seífunki; (*also*: **coffee mill**) コーヒーひき kóhīhikì; (factory: steel mill, saw mill) 製...工場 seí...kójō
◆*vt* (grind: grain, flour) ひく híkù
◆*vi* (*also*: **mill about**: people, crowd) 右往左往する uósaò suru

woolen mill 織物工場 orímonokòjō

miller [mil'ə:r] *n* 製粉業者 seífungyòsha

milligram(me) [mil'əgræm] *n* ミリグラム miríguràmu

millimeter [mil'əmi:tə:r] (*BRIT* **millimetre**) *n* ミリメートル mirímētoru

millinery [mil'əne:ri:] *n* 婦人帽子店 fujínbōshiten

million [mil'jən] *n* 100万 hyakúmaǹ

a million times 何回も nañkai mo

millionaire [miljəne:r'] *n* 大富豪 daífugò

milometer [mai'loumi:tə:r] *n* = **mileometer**

mime [maim] *n* (action) パントマイム pañtomaìmu; (actor) パントマイム役者 pañtomaimu yakùsha
◆*vt* (act) 身振り手振りでまねる mibúritebùri de manérù
◆*vi* (act out) パントマイムを演ずる pañtomaìmu wo eñzurù

mimic [mim'ik] *n* 物まね師 monómaneshì
◆*vt* (imitate) ...のまねをする ...no mané wo surù

min. *abbr* **minute(s); minimum**

minaret [minəret'] *n* ミナレット miná-

rètto ◇モスクのせん塔 mósùku no señtō

mince [mins] *vt* (meat) ひく híkù
◆*vi* (in walking) 気取って歩く kidòtte arukù
◆*n* (*BRIT*: CULIN) ひき肉 hikíniku

mincemeat [mins'mi:t] *n* (fruit) ミンスミート míñsumìto ◇ドライフルーツなどの細切り doráifurūtsu nádò no komágiri; (*US*: meat) ひき肉 hikíniku

mincemeat pie (*US*) *n* (sweet) ミンスミートパイ míñsumìtopaì

mince pie (*BRIT*) *n* (sweet) = **mincemeat pie**

mincer [min'sə:r] *n* 肉ひき器 nikúhikikì

mind [maind] *n* (thoughts) 考え kañgaè; (intellect) 頭脳 zunő; (opinion): *to my mind* 私の意見では watákushi no ikén de wa; (sanity): *to be out of one's mind* 気が狂っている ki ga kurútte irù
◆*vt* (attend to, look after: shop, children, pets etc) ...の番をする ...no báǹ wo suru; (: children, pets etc) ...の面倒を見る ...no meñdō wò mírù; (be careful of) ...に注意する ...ni chúi suru; (object to): *I don't mind the noise* その音を気にしません sonó otó wo kí ni shimáseǹ

it is on my mind 気に掛っている kí ni kakátte irù

to keep/bear something in mind ...を気にする ...wo kí ni suru

to make up one's mind 決心する kesshín suru

I don't mind 構いませんよ kamáimaseǹ yó

mind you, ... でもこれだけ言っておく ... de mo koré dakè itté okù ...

never mind! (it makes no odds) 気にしないで下さい kí ni shináìde kudásaì; (don't worry) ほうっておきなさい hôtte oki nasaì, 心配しないで下さい shiñpai shinaidè kudásaì

「*mind the step*」階段に注意 kaídan ni chúi

minder [maind'ə:r] *n* (childminder) ベビーシッター bebíshittà; (*BRIT inf*: bodyguard) ボディーガード bodígàdo

mindful [maind'fəl] *adj*: *mindful of* ...を気に掛ける ...wo kí ni kakérù

mindless [maɪnd'lɪs] *adj* (violence) 愚かな óròka na, 愚劣な gurétsu na; (boring: job) 退屈な taíkutsu na

KEYWORD

mine¹ [maɪn] *pron* 私 の 物 watákushi no monó

that book is mine その本は私のです sonó hoñ wa watákushi no děsu

these cases are mine それらのケースは私のです sorérà no kḗsù wa watákushi no děsu

this is mine これは私の物です koré wà watákushi no monó desu

yours is red, mine is green あなたのは赤いが、私のは緑色です anátà no wa akái ga, watákushi no wà midóri irò desu

a friend of mine 私のある友達 watákushi nò árù tomódàchi

mine² [maɪn] *n* (gen) 鉱 山 kózan; (also: land mine) 地雷 jirái; (bomb in water) 機雷 kírái

♦*vt* (coal) 採掘する saíkutsu suru; (beach) 地雷を敷設する jirái wo fusétsu suru; (harbor) 機雷を敷設する kírái wo fusétsu suru

coal mine 炭坑 tañkō

gold mine 金坑 kiñkō

minefield [maɪn'fiːld] *n* (area: land) 地雷原 jiráigeñ; (: water) 機雷敷設水域 kírái-fusetsu suíiki; (*fig*: situation) 危険をはらんだ事態 kikéñ wò haráñda jítai

miner [maɪn'əːr] *n* 鉱山労働者 kózanrōdōshà

mineral [mɪn'əːrəl] *adj* (deposit, resources) 鉱物の kóbutsu no

♦*n* (in earth) 鉱物 kóbutsu no; (in food) ミネラル mínérarù

minerals [mɪn'əːrəlz] (*BRIT*) *npl* (soft drinks) 炭酸飲料水 tañsan-inryòsui

mineral water *n* ミネラルウォーター mínéraru uòtā

mingle [mɪŋ'gəl] *vi*: *to mingle with* ...と交わる ...to majíwaru ◇特にパーティなどで多くの人に声を掛けて回るなどの意味で使う tókù ni páti nádò de ókù no

miniature [mɪn'iːətʃəːr] *adj* (small, tiny) ミニチュアの miníchùa no

♦ミニチュア miníchùa

minibus [mɪn'iːbʌs] *n* マイクロバス maíkurobàsu

minim [mɪn'əm] *n* (MUS) 二分音符 níbun oñpu

minimal [mɪn'əməl] *adj* 最小限(度)の saíshōgen(do) no

minimize [mɪn'əmaiz] *vt* (reduce: risks, disease) 最小限(度)に抑える saíshōgen (do) ni osáerù; (play down: role) 見くびる mikúbirù; (: weakness) 問題にしない moñdai ni shináì, 避けて通る sakéte tōru

minimum [mɪn'əməm] (*pl* **minima**) *n* 最小限(度) saíshōgen(do)

♦*adj* 最小限(度)の saíshōgeñ(do) no

mining [maɪ'niŋ] *n* 鉱業 kógyō

miniskirt [mɪn'iːskəːrt] *n* ミニスカート minísukàto

minister [mɪn'istəːr] *n* (POL) 大臣 daíjin; (REL) 牧師 bókùshi

♦*vi*: *to minister to* (people, needs) ...に仕える ...ni tsukáerù

ministerial [ministiːr'iːəl] (*BRIT*) *adj* (POL) 大臣の daíjin no

ministry [mɪn'istriː] *n* (POL) ...省 ...shò; (REL) 聖職 seíshoku

mink [mɪŋk] *n* (fur) ミンクの毛皮 míñku no kegáwa; (animal) ミンク míñku

mink coat *n* ミンクのコート míñku no kōto

minnow [mɪn'ou] *n* 小魚 kozákàna

minor [maɪ'nəːr] *adj* (unimportant: repairs) ちょっとした chottó shità; (: injuries) 軽い karúi; (: poet) 二流の niryū no; (MUS) 短調の tanchō no

♦*n* (LAW) 未成年 misếneñ

minority [minɔːr'itiː] *n* (less than half: of group, society) 少数派 shōsūha

mint [mint] *n* (plant) ハッカ hakká; (sweet) ハッカあめ hakká amé

♦*vt* (coins) 鋳造する chúzō suru

the (US) Mint (US), the (Royal) Mint (BRIT) 造幣局 zōheíkyoku

in mint condition 新品同様で shíñpin-

dòyō de

minus [mai'nəs] n (also: **minus sign**) マイナス記号 maínasu kigò

♦prep: *12 minus 6 equals 6* 12引く6は6 jûni hikù rokú wà rokú; (temperature): *minus 24* 零下24度 reíka nijûyoñ do

minuscule [min'əskju:l] adj 微々たる bíbìtaru

minute [min'it] n (unit) 分 fún; (fig: short time) ちょっと chottó

♦adj (search, detail) 細かい komákaì
at the last minute 土壇場に dotánba ni

minutes [min'its] npl (of meeting) 会議録 kaígìròku

miracle [mir'əkəl] n (REL, fig) 奇跡 kiséki

miraculous [miræk'jələs] adj 奇跡的な kisékiteki na

mirage [mira:ʒ'] n しん気楼 shiñkirò

mirror [mir'ə:r] n (in bedroom, bathroom) 鏡 kagámi, ミラー mírà; (in car) バックミラー bakkúmirà

mirth [mə:rθ] n (laughter) 笑い warái

misadventure [misədven'tʃə:r] n 災難 saínañ

misapprehension [misæprihen'tʃən] n 誤解 gokái

misappropriate [misəprou'pri:eit] vt (funds, money) 横領する ōryō suru

misbehave [misbiheiv'] vi 行儀悪くする gyōgiwarukù suru

miscalculate [miskæl'kjəleit] vt 見込み違いする mikómichigaì suru

miscarriage [miskær'idʒ] n (MED) 流産 ryūzan; (failure): *miscarriage of justice* 誤審 goshíñ

miscellaneous [misəlei'ni:əs] adj (collection, group: of tools, people) 雑多な zattá na; (subjects, items) 種々の shujú no

mischance [mistʃæns'] n (misfortune) 不運 fúùn

mischief [mis'tʃif] n (naughtiness: of child) いたずら itázura; (playfulness, fun) いたずら itázura; (maliciousness) 悪さ wárùsa

mischievous [mis'tʃəvəs] adj (naughty, playful) いたずらな itázura na

misconception [miskənsep'ʃən] n 誤解 gokái

misconduct [miska:n'dʌkt] n (behavior) 非行 hikō

professional misconduct 背任 haínin, 職権乱用 shokken rañyō

misdemeanor [misdimi:'nə:r] (*BRIT* **misdemeanour**) n 軽犯罪 keíhañzai

miser [mai'zə:r] n けちん坊 kéchìnbō, 守銭奴 shuséñdo

miserable [miz'ə:rəbəl] adj (unhappy: person, expression) 惨めな míjìme na, 不幸な fukō na; (wretched: conditions) 哀れな fukō na; (unpleasant: weather, person) いやな iyá na; (contemptible: offer, donation) ちっぽけな chippókè na; (: failure) 情けない nasákenaì

miserly [mai'zə:rli:] adj けちな kechí na

misery [miz'ə:ri:] n (unhappiness) 惨めさ mijímesà, 不幸せ fushiawase; (wretchedness) 哀れな状態 āware na jōtai

misfire [misfair'] vi (plan etc) 失敗する shippái suru

misfit [mis'fit] n (person) 適応不能者 tekíōfunòsha

misfortune [misfɔ:r'tʃən] n (bad luck) 不運 fúùn

misgiving [misgiv'iŋ] n (apprehension) 心もとなさ kokóromotonasà, 疑念 ginéñ
to have misgivings about something ...を疑問に思う ...wo gimón nì omóù

misguided [misgai'did] adj (opinion, view) 心得違いの kokóroechigaì no

mishandle [mishæn'dəl] vt (mismanage: problem, situation) ...の処置を誤る ...no shóchì wo ayámarù

mishap [mis'hæp] n 事故 jíkò

misinform [misinfɔ:rm'] vt ...にうそを伝える ...ni úsò wo tsutáerù

misinterpret [misintə:r'prit] vt 誤解する gokái suru

misjudge [misdʒʌdʒ'] vt ...の判断を誤る ...no hañdañ wo ayámarù

mislay [mislei'] (*pt, pp* **mislaid**) vt (lose) なくす nakúsù, 置忘れる okíwasurerù

mislead [misli:d'] (*pt, pp* **misled**) vt うそを信じ込ませる úsò wo shíñjikomaserù

misleading [misli:'diŋ] adj (information)

誤解させる gokái saserù

mismanage [mismæn'idʒ] *vt* (manage badly: business, institution) 下手な管理をする hétà na kánri wo suru; (: problem, situation) …の処置を誤る …no shóchì wo ayámarù

misnomer [misnou'mər] *n* (term) 誤った名称 ayámattà meíshō

misogynist [misɑːdʒ'ənist] *n* 女嫌い onnágirai

misplace [mispleis'] *vt* (lose) なくす nakúsù, 置忘れる okíwasurerù

misprint [mis'print] *n* 誤植 goshóku

Miss [mis] *n* …さん …sán ◇ 未婚の女性に対する敬称 míkòn no joséi ni taí surù keíshō

miss [mis] *vt* (train, bus etc) …に乗遅れる …ni noríokurerù; (fail to hit: target) …に当て損なう …ni atésokonaù; (fail to see): *you can't miss it* 見落しっこない miótoshikkonài; (regret the absence of) …が恋しい …ga koíshiì, …が懐かしい …ga natsúkashiì; (chance, opportunity) 逃す nigásù, の がす nogásù; (class, meeting) …に欠席する …ni kesséki suru
◆*vi* (fail to hit) 当り損なう atárisokonaù, それる sorérù
◆*n* (failure to hit) 当て損ない atésokonài, ミス mísù

misshapen [misʃei'pən] *adj* 不格好なbukákkō na

missile [mis'əl] *n* (weapon: MIL) ミサイル misáiru; (: object thrown) 飛道具 tobídōgu

missing [mis'iŋ] *adj* (lost: person, pupil) 行方不明の yukúefumèi no; (: object) なくなっている nakúnatte irù; (removed: tooth) 抜かれた nukáretà; (: wheel) 外された hazúsaretà; (MIL) 行方不明の yukúefumèi no
to be missing 行方不明である yukúefumèi de aru

mission [miʃ'ən] *n* (task) 任務 nímmu; (official representatives) 代表団 daíhyōdan; (MIL) 出撃 shutsúgeki ◇特に爆撃機について言う tókù ni bakúgekikì ni tsuite iú; (REL: activity) 伝道 dendō; (: building) 伝道所 dendōjō

missionary [miʃ'əne:ri:] *n* 伝道師 dendóshi

miss out (*BRIT*) *vt* (leave out) 落す otósù

misspent [misspent'] *adj*: *his misspent youth* 浪費した彼の青春 rōhi shità kárè no seíshun

mist [mist] *n* (light) も や móyà; (heavy) 濃霧 nómu
◆*vi* (*also*: **mist over**, **mist up**) (eyes) 涙ぐむ namídagumu; (windows) 曇る kumórù

mistake [misteik'] *n* (error) 間違い machígaì
◆*vt* (*pt* **mistook**, *pp* **mistaken**) (be wrong about) 間違える machígaerù
by mistake 間違って machígattè
to make a mistake 間違いをする machígaì wo suru
to mistake A for B AをBと間違える A wo B to machígaerù

mistaken [mistei'kən] (*pp of* **mistake**) *adj* (idea, belief etc) 間違った machígattà
to be mistaken 間違っている machígattè irú

mister [mis'tə:r] (*inf*) *n* ◇男性への呼び掛け dañsei e no yobíkake ¶ *see* **Mr.**

mistletoe [mis'əltou] *n* ヤドリギ yadórigì

mistook [mistuk'] *pt of* **mistake**

mistress [mis'tris] *n* (lover) 愛人 aíjin; (of house, servant) 女主人 ofína shùjin; (in primary, secondary schools) 先生 señsei
to be mistress of the situation (*fig*) 事態を掌握している jítài wo shóaku shite irú

mistrust [mistrʌst'] *vt* 信用しない shiñyō shinài

misty [mis'ti:] *adj* (day etc) もやった moyáttà; (glasses, windows) 曇った kumóttà

misunderstand [misʌndəːrstænd'] (*irreg*) *vt* (fail to understand: person, book) 誤解する gokái suru
◆*vi* (fail to understand) 誤解する gokái suru

misunderstanding [misʌndəːrstæn'diŋ]

n (failure to understand) 誤 解 gokái; (disagreement) 口げんか kuchígeñka

misuse [misju:s'] *n* (of power) 乱 用 rañ-yō; (of funds) 悪用 akúyō
◆*vt* (power) 乱 用 す る rañ-yō suru; (funds) 悪用する akúyō suru

mitigate [mit'əgeit] *vt* 和らげる yawára-gerù

mitt(en) [mit'(ən)] *n* ミ ト ン mítòn

mix [miks] *vt* (combine: liquids, ingredients, colors) 混ぜる mazérù; (cake, cement) こねる konérù; (drink, sauce) 作る tsukúrù
◆*vi* (people): *to mix (with)* ...と交わる ...to majíwarù ◇特にパーティなどで多くの人に声を掛けて回るなどの意味で使う tōkú ni pātì nádò de ōku no hitó nì kóè wo kakétè máwarù nádò no ímì de tsukáù
◆*n* (combination) 混合物 koñgóbutsu; (powder) ミックス míkkùsu

mixed [mikst] *adj* (salad) コンビネーションの koñbinéshon no; (grill) 盛り合せのmoríawase no; (feelings, reactions) 複雑な fukúzatsu na; (school, education etc) 共学の kyōgaku no
a mixed marriage (religion) 異なった宗教の信徒間の結婚 kotónatta shūkyō no shinto kan no kekkon; (race) 異なった人種間の結婚 kotónatta jiñshu kan no kekkon

mixed-up [mikst'ʌp] *adj* (confused) 混乱している koñran shite irù

mixer [mik'sə:r] *n* (for food) ミキサーmíkìsā; (person): *to be a good mixer* 付合い上手である tsukíaijôzu de aru

mixture [miks'tʃə:r] *n* (combination) 混合物 koñgóbutsu; (MED: for cough etc) 飲薬 nomígusùri

mix up *vt* (confuse: people, things) 混同する koñdō suru

mix-up [miks'ʌp] *n* (confusion) 混乱 koñran

mm *abbr* = **millimeter**

moan [moun] *n* (cry) うめき uméki
◆*vi* (*inf*: complain): *to moan (about)* (...について) 愚痴を言う (...ni tsuítě) guchí wo iù

moat [mout] *n* 堀 horí

mob [mɑːb] *n* (crowd) 群衆 guñshū
◆*vt* (person) ...の回りにわっと押し寄せる ...no mawárì ni wáttò oshíyoserù

mobile [mou'bəl] *adj* (able to move) 移動式の idóshiki no
◆*n* (decoration) モビール móbìru

mobile home *n* モビールハウス mobíru-haùsu

mobility [moubil'əti:] *n* 移動性 idósei

mobilize [mou'bəlaiz] *vt* (friends, work force) 動員する dōin suru; (MIL: country, army) 戦時態勢を取らせる señji taísei wo toráserù

moccasin [mɑːk'əsin] *n* モカシン mokáshìn

mock [mɑːk] *vt* (ridicule) ばかにする bákà ni suru; (laugh at) あざ笑う azáwaraù
◆*adj* (fake) 見せ掛けの misékake no; (exam, battle) 模擬の mógì no

mockery [mɑːk'ə:ri:] *n* (derision) あざけり azákeri
to make a mockery of ...をばかにする ...wo bákà ni suru

mock-up [mɑːk'ʌp] *n* (model) 模型 mo-kéi

mod [mɑːd kɑːnz] *adj see* **convenience**

mode [moud] *n* (form: of life) 様式 yóshi-ki; (: of transportation) 手段 shùdan

model [mɑːd'əl] *n* (representation: of boat, building etc) 模型 mokéi; (fashion model, artist's model) モデル módèru; (example) 手本 téhòn
◆*adj* (excellent) 模範的な mohánteki na
◆*vt* (clothes) ...のモデルをする ...no mó-dèru wo suru; (with clay etc) ...の模型を作る ...no mokéi wo tsukúrù; (copy): *to model oneself on* ...の模範に習う ...no móhàn ni naráù
◆*vi* (for designer, photographer etc) モデルをする móděru wo suru

model railway *n* 模型鉄道 mokéi tetsu-dō

modem [mou'dem] *n* (COMPUT) モデム módèmu

moderate [*adj* mɑːd'ə:rit *vb* mɑːd'ə:reit] *adj* (views, opinion) 穏健な oñken na; (amount) 中位の chūgurai no; (change)

ある程度の arú teído no

♦vi (storm, wind etc) 弱まる yawámarù

♦vt (tone, demands) 和らげる yawáragerù

moderation [mɑːdəreiʃən] n 中庸 chǔyō

modern [mɑːd'ərn] adj 現代的な geńdaiteki na, 近代的な kińdaiteki na, モダンな modáñ na

modernize [mɑːd'ərnaiz] vt 現代的にする geńdaiteki ni suru

modest [mɑːd'ist] adj (small: house, budget) 質素な shíssò na; (unassuming: person) 謙虚な keńkyo na

modesty [mɑːd'isti:] n 慎み tsutsúshimi

modicum [mɑːd'əkəm] n: **a modicum of** ちょっとだけの... chóttò dake no ...

modification [mɑːdəfəkeiʃən] n (alteration: of law) 改正 kaísei; (: of building) 改修 kaíshū; (: of car, engine etc) 改造 kaízō

modify [mɑːd'əfai] vt (law) 改正する kaísei suru; (building, car, engine) 改造する kaízō suru

module [mɑːdʒ'uːl] n (unit, component, SPACE) モジュール mojúrù

mogul [mou'gəl] n (fig) 大立者 ōdatemòno

mohair [mou'heːr] n モヘア móheà

moist [moist] adj (slightly wet: earth, eyes, lips) 湿った shiméttà

moisten [mois'ən] vt (lips, sponge) 湿らす shimérasù

moisture [mois'tʃəːr] n 湿り気 shimérike

moisturizer [mois'tʃəːraizəːr] n (cream) モイスチュアクリーム moísuchua kurīmu; (lotion) モイスチュアローション moísuchua rōshon

molar [mou'ləːr] n きゅう歯 kyúshi

mold [mould] (BRIT **mould**) n (cast: for jelly, metal) 型 katá; (mildew) かび kabí

♦vt (shape: plastic, clay etc) ...で...の形を作る ...de ...no katáchi wò tsukúrù; (fig: influence: public opinion, character) 作り上げる tsukúriagerù

moldy [moul'di:] (BRIT **mouldy**) adj (bread, cheese) かびた kabítà; (smell) か び臭い kabíkusaì

mole [moul] n (spot) ほくろ hokúro; (ani-

mal) モグラ mogúra; (fig: spy) 秘密工作員 himítsukōsakuìn

molecule [mɑːl'əkjuːl] n 分子 búñshi

molest [məlest'] vt (assault sexually) ...にいたずらをする ...ni itázura wo surù; (harass) いじめる ijímerù

mollycoddle [mɑːl'iːkɑːdəl] vt (pamper) 甘やかす amáyakasù

molt [moult] (BRIT **moult**) vi (animal, bird) 換毛する kańmō suru

molten [moul'tən] adj (metal, rock) 溶解の yōkai no

mom [mɑːm] (US: inf) n かあちゃん kàchan, ママ mámà

moment [mou'mənt] n (period of time): **for a moment** ちょっと chóttò; (point in time): **at that moment** 丁度その時 chódò sonó tokì

at the moment 今の所 imá no tokòro

momentary [mou'mənte:ri:] adj (brief: pause, glimpse) 瞬間的な shuńkanteki na

momentous [moumen'təs] adj (occasion, decision) 重大な jūdai na

momentum [moumen'təm] n (PHYSICS) 運動量 uńdōryò; (fig: of events, movement, change) 勢い ikíòi, 惰性 daséi

to gather momentum (lit, fig) 勢いが付く ikíòi ga tsúkù

mommy [mɑːm'iː] (US) n ママ mámà ◇幼児用語 yōjiyògo

Monaco [mɑːn'əkou] n モナコ mónàko

monarch [mɑːn'əːrk] n 君主 kúnshu

monarchy [mɑːn'əːrkiː] n (system) 王制 ōsei; (royal family) 王室 ōshitsu, 王族 ōzoku

monastery [mɑːn'əste:riː] n 修道院 shúdōìn

Monday [mʌn'dei] n 月曜日 getsúyòbi

monetary [mɑːn'iteːriː] adj (system, policy, control) 金融の kiń-yū no

money [mʌn'iː] n (coins and notes) 金 kané; (currency) 通貨 tsūka

to make money (earn) 金をもうける kané wo mōkerù

money order n 郵便為替 yúbinkawàse

money-spinner [mʌn'iːspinəːr] (BRIT:

inf) *n* (person, idea, business) ドル箱 do-rúbako

mongol [mɑː'ŋgəl] *adj* モンゴルの móñgoru no
♦*n* (MED) ダウン症候群患者 daúnshōkōgun kañja

mongrel [mʌŋ'grəl] *n* (dog) 雑種 zasshú

monitor [mɑːn'itəːr] *n* (machine) モニター装置 monítāsōchi; (screen: *also*: **television monitor**) ブラウン管 buráuñkan; (of computer) モニター móñītā
♦*vt* (broadcasts) 傍受する bóju suru; (heartbeat, pulse) モニターする móñītā suru; (progress) 監視する kañshi suru

monk [mʌŋk] *n* 修道師 shúdoshi

monkey [mʌŋ'kiː] *n* (animal) サル sarú

monkey nut (*BRIT*) *n* ピーナッツ pínattsu

monkey wrench *n* モンキーレンチ móñkīreñchi

mono [mɑːn'ou] *adj* (recording) モノラルの móñoraru no

monochrome [mɑːn'əkroum] *adj* (film, photograph) 白黒の shírōkuro no, モノクロの monókùro no

monogram [mɑːn'əgræm] *n* モノグラム monógùramu

monologue [mɑːn'əlɔːg] *n* 会話の独占 kaíwa no dokúsen; (THEATER) 独白 dokúhaku, モノローグ monórògu

monopolize [mənɑːp'əlaiz] *vt* 独占する dokúsen suru

monopoly [mənɑːp'əli] *n* (domination) 独占 dokúsen; (COMM) 専売 señbai, モノポリー monópòrī

monosyllable [mɑːn'əsiləbəl] *n* 単音節語 tañ-onsetsugò

monotone [mɑːn'ətoun] *n*: **to speak in a monotone** 単調な声で話す tañchō na kóè de hanású

monotonous [mənɑːt'ənəs] *adj* (life, job etc) 退屈な taíkutsu na; (voice, tune) 単調な tañchō na

monotony [mənɑːt'əniː] *n* 退屈 taíkutsu

monsoon [mɑːnsuːn'] *n* モンスーン móñsūn

monster [mɑːn'stəːr] *n* (animal, plant: misshapen) 奇形 kikéi; (: enormous) 怪物

kaíbùtsu, お化け obákè; (imaginary creature) 怪物 kaíbùtsu; (person: cruel, evil) 怪物 kaíbùtsu

monstrosity [mɑːnstrɑːs'əti:] *n* (hideous object, building) 見るに堪えない代物 mírù ni taénài shirómòno

monstrous [mɑːn'strəs] *adj* (huge) 巨大な kyodái na; (ugly) 見るに堪えない mírù ni taénài; (atrocious) 極悪な gokúaku na

month [mʌnθ] *n* 月 tsukí

monthly [mʌnθ'liː] *adj* (ticket etc) 一カ月の ikkágetsu no; (magazine) 月刊の gekkán no; (payment etc) 毎月の maítsuki no; (meeting) 月例の getsúrei no
♦*adv* 毎月 maítsuki

monument [mɑːn'jəmənt] *n* (memorial) 記念碑 kinéñhi; (historical building) 史的記念物 shitékikinenbutsu

monumental [mɑːnjəmen'təl] *adj* (large and important: building, statue) 歴史的な rekíshiteki na; (important: book, piece of work) 画期的な kakkíteki na; (terrific: storm, row) すごい sugóì, すさまじい susámajiì

moo [muː] *vi* (cow) もーと鳴く mó tò nakú

mood [muːd] *n* (humor: of person) 機嫌 kigén; (: of crowd, group) 雰囲気 fuñ-ikì, ムード mùdo
to be in a good/bad mood (temper) 機嫌がいい（悪い）kigén gà íi（warúi）

moody [muː'diː] *adj* (variable) むら気な muráki na; (sullen) 不機嫌な fukígèn na

moon [muːn] *n* 月 tsukí

moonlight [muːn'lait] *n* 月光 gekkō

moonlighting [muːn'laitiŋ] *n* (work) アルバイト arúbaito ◇本職の外にする仕事で, 特に規定, 規則違反の仕事を指す hoñshòku no hoká nì suru shigóto dè, tókù ni kitéi, kisóku ihàn no shigóto wò sásù

moonlit [muːn'lit] *adj*: **a moonlit night** 月夜 tsukíyò

moor [muːr] *n* (heath) 荒れ野 aréno
♦*vt* (ship) つなぐ tsunágù
♦*vi* 停泊する teíhaku suru

moorland [muːr'lænd] *n* 荒れ野 aréno

moose [mu:s] *n inv* アメリカヘラジカ a-mérikaherajīka

mop [mɑ:p] *n* (for floor) モップ moppú; (for dishes) スポンジたわし supónjitawàshi ◇短い柄の付いた皿洗い用を指す mijíkai̯ e no tsùita saráarai yṑ wo sásù
♦*vt* (floor) モップでふく moppú de fukú; (eyes, face) ふく fukú, ぬぐう nugúù
a mop of hair もじゃもじゃ頭 mojámoja atáma

mope [moup] *vi* ふさぎ込む fuságikomù

moped [mou'ped] *n* モペット mopéttò ◇ペダルで動かす事も出来る小型オートバイ pédarù de ugókasù kotó mo dekirù kogáta ṓtobài

mop up *vt* (liquid) ふく fukú

moral [mɔ:r'əl] *adj* 倫理的な rińriteki na
♦*n* (of story etc) 教訓 kyṓkun
moral support (encouragement) 精神的支え seíshinteki sasáe

morale [məræl'] *n* (of army, staff) 士気 shikí

morality [məræl'iti:] *n* (good behavior) 品行 hińkō; (system of morals: *also* correctness, acceptability) 倫理 rińri

morals [mɔ:r'əlz] *npl* (principles, values) 倫理 rińri

morass [məræs'] *n* (*lit*, *fig*) 泥沼 dorónuma

morbid [mɔ:r'bid] *adj* (imagination, ideas) 陰気な fńki na

KEYWORD

more [mɔ:r] *adj* **1** (greater in number etc) より多くの yorí ōku no
more people/work/letters than we expected 私たちが予定していたより多くの人々〔仕事，手紙〕watákushitàchi ga yotéi shite ita yorí ōku no hitóbito (shigòto, tegámi)
I have more books/money than you 私はあなたより沢山の本〔金〕を持っています watákushi wà anátà yori takúsan nò hoń〔kané〕wo mótte imasù
this store has more wine than beer この店はビールよりワインが沢山あります konó mise wà bírù yori waín ga takúsan arimasù

2 (additional) もっと móttò
do you want (some) more tea? もっと紅茶をいかがですか móttò kṓcha wò ikága desù ká
is there any more wine? ワインはまだありますか wáĩn wa mádà arímasù ká
I have no/I don't have any more money お金はもうありません o-káne wa mṓ arímaseň
it'll take a few more weeks あと数週間掛けります átò sūshṹkàn kakárimasù
♦*pron* **1** (greater amount) もっと沢山 móttò takúsan
more than 10 10以上 jū́ijō ◇この成句の英語には「10」が含まれないが，日本語の場合「10」も含まれる konó seíku no éigo ni wà "jū́" gà fukúmarenaì ga, nihóngo no baái "jū́" mò fukúmarerù. (Note: The English phrase indicates a quantity of 11 and above, but the Japanese indicates 10 and above.)
it cost more than we expected 予想以上に金が掛りました yosṓ ijō ni kané gà kakárimashìta

2 (further or additional amount) もっと沢山 móttò takúsaň
is there any more? まだありますか mádà arímasù ká
there's no more もうありません mṓ arímaseň
a little more もう少し mṓ sukoshî
many/much more ...よりずっと沢山 ...yorí zuttò takúsaň
♦*adv* ...よりもっと... ...yorí mottò...
more dangerous/difficult etc (than) ...より危ない〔難しい〕...yorí abúnai〔muzūkashiî〕
more easily/economically/quickly (than) ...よりたやすく〔経済的に，早く〕...yorí tayasukù〔keizaiteki ni, hayáku〕
more and more ますます masúmasu
more and more excited/friendly/expensive ますます興奮して〔親しくなって，高くなって〕masúmasu kṓfun shitè〔shitáshiku nattè, tákàku natte〕
he grew to like her more and more 彼はますます彼女が好きになった kárè wa masúmasu kánòjo ga sukí ni nattà

more or less 大体 daítai, 大よそ ṓyoso

the job's more or less finished 仕事は大体できています shigóto wà daítai dékìte imasu

it should cost £ 500, more or less 大よそ500ポンド掛りそうです ṓyoso gohyákupoǹdo kakárisṑ desu

more than ever ますます masúmàsu, より一層 yorí issṓ

more beautiful than ever ますます美しい masúmàsu utsúkushiì

more quickly than ever ますます早く masúmàsu háyàku

he loved her more than ever 彼はより一層彼女を愛する様になった kárè wa yorí issṓ kánòjo wo aí suru yṓ ni nátta

moreover [mɔːrouˈvəːr] *adv* なお náò

morgue [mɔːrg] *n* 死体保管所 shitáihokaǹjo, モルグ morúgù

moribund [mɔːrˈəbʌnd] *adj* (organization, industry) 斜陽の shayṓ no

Mormon [mɔːrˈmən] *n* モルモン教徒 morúmon kyṓto

morning [mɔːrˈniŋ] *n* (period after daybreak) 朝 asá; (from midnight to noon) 午前 gózeǹ

in the morning 朝に asá ni, 午前中に gozénchū ni

7 o'clock in the morning 午前7時 gózeǹ shichíji

morning paper 朝刊 chṓkan

morning sun 朝日 ásàhi

morning walk 朝の散歩 ásà no saǹpo

morning sickness n つわり tsuwári

Morocco [məˈrɑːkou] *n* モロッコ morókkò

moron [mɔːrˈɑːn] *(inf) n* ばか bákà

morose [məˈrous] *adj* (miserable) 陰気な íǹki na

morphine [mɔːrˈfiːn] *n* モルヒネ morúhìne

Morse [mɔːrs] *n* (*also*: **Morse code**) モールス信号 mṓrusu shiǹgō

morsel [mɔːrˈsəl] *n* (of food) 一口 hitókùchi

mortal [mɔːrˈtəl] *adj* (man) いつか死ぬ ítsùka shinú; (wound) 致命的な chiméiteki na; (danger) 命にかかわる ínòchi ni kakáwarù

♦*n* (human being) 人間 niǹgen

mortal combat 死闘 shitṓ

mortal enemy 宿敵 shukúteki

mortal remains 遺骨 ikótsu

mortal sin 大罪 taízai

mortality [mɔːrˈtælˈitiː] *n* いつか死ぬ事 ítsùka shinú kotò; (number of deaths) 死亡率 shibṓrìtsu

mortar [mɔːrˈtəːr] *n* (cannon) 迫撃砲 hakúgekihṓ; (CONSTR) モルタル mórùtaru; (bowl) 乳鉢 nyūbachi

mortgage [mɔːrˈgidʒ] *n* 住宅ローン jūtakurōn

♦*vt* (house, property) 抵当に入れて金を借りる teítō ni irète kané wo karírù

mortify [mɔːrˈtəfai] *vt*: *to be mortified* 恥を感じる hají wo kaǹjirù

mortuary [mɔːrˈtʃuːeːriː] *n* 霊安室 reíaǹshitsu

mosaic [mouzeiˈik] *n* モザイク mozáìku

Moscow [mɑːsˈkau] *n* モスクワ mosúkuwa

Moslem [mɑːzˈləm] *adj*, *n* = **Muslim**

mosque [mɑːsk] *n* イスラム教寺院 isúramukyō jìin, モスク mósùku

mosquito [məskiːˈtou] (*pl* **mosquitoes**) *n* 蚊 ká

moss [mɔːs] *n* (plant) コケ koké

most [moust] *adj* 1 (almost all: people, things etc) ほとんどの hotóǹdo no

most people ほとんどの人 hotóǹdo no hitó

most men/dogs behave like that ほとんどの男性(イヌ)はそういう振舞をする hotóǹdo no daǹsei(inú)wà sṓ iù furúmai wo surù

most houses here are privately owned ここのほとんどの家は個人所有の物です kokó nò hotóǹdo no ié wà kojínshoyū nò monó desù

2 (largest, greatest: interest, money etc) 最も沢山の mottómò takúsan no

who has (the) most money? 最も多くの金を持っているのは誰でしょう mottó-

mò ōku no kane wo motte iru no wa dare deshò

he derived the most pleasure from her visit 最も彼を喜ばせたのは彼女の訪問だった mottómð kárè wo yorókobaseta no wà kánòjo no hòmon dattà

♦*pron* (greatest quantity, number) ほとんど hotóñdo

most of it/them それ〔それら〕のほとんど soré〔sorérà〕no hotóñdo

most of the money/her friends 金〔彼女の友達〕のほとんど kané〔kánòjo no tomódàchi〕nò hotóñdo

most of the time ほとんどの場合 hotóñdo no baái

do the most you can できるだけの事をして下さい dekíru dakè no kotó wò shité kudasaì

I saw the most 私が一番沢山見ました watákushi gà ichíban takùsan mimáshìta

to make the most of something ...を最大限に利用する ...wò saídaìgen ni riyð surù

at the (very) most 最大に見積っても saídai nì mitsúmotte mð

♦*adv* (+ verb: spend, eat, work etc) 最も多く mottómð ōkù; (+ adjective: *the most intelligent/expensive* etc 最も利口〔高価〕な mottómð rikó〔kóka〕nà; (+ adverb: carefully, easily etc) 最も注意深く〔たやすく〕mottómð chúibukakù〔tayásukù〕; (very: polite, interesting etc) とても totémo

a most interesting book とても面白い本 totémo omoshiroì hóñ

mostly [moust'li:] *adv* (chiefly) 主に ómò ni; (usually) 普段は fúdàn wa, 普通は futsú wa

MOT [emouti:'] *n abbr* = **Ministry of Transport**: *the MOT (test)* (*BRIT*) 車検 shakéñ

motel [moutel'] *n* モーテル mòteru

moth [mɔ:θ] *n* (insect) ガ gá; (clothes moth) イガ igá

mothball [mɔ:θ'bɔ:l] *n* 防虫剤 bóchūzài

mother [mʌð'ə:r] *n* 母 háhà, 母親 haháo-

ya, お母さん o-káasan

♦*adj*: *mother country* 母国 bókðku

♦*vt* (act as mother to) 母親として育てる haháoya toshitè sodáterù; (pamper, protect) 甘やかす amáyakasù

mother company 親会社 oyágaìsha

motherhood [mʌð'ə:rhud] *n* 母親である事 haháoya de arù kotó

mother-in-law [mʌð'ə:rinlɔ:] (*pl* **mothers-in-law**) *n* しゅうと shùto

motherly [mʌð'ə:rli:] *adj* 母の様な háhà no yð na

mother-of-pearl [mʌð'ə:rəvpə:rl'] *n* 真珠母 shiñjùbo

mother-to-be [mʌð'ə:rtəbi:'] (*pl* **mothers-to-be**) *n* 妊婦 níñpu

mother tongue *n* 母国語 bokókugð

motif [mouti:f'] *n* (design) 模様 moyð

motion [mou'ʃən] *n* (movement) 動き ugóki; (gesture) 合図 aízù; (at meeting) 動議 dðgi

♦*vt*: *to motion (to) someone to do something* ...する様に...に合図をする ...surú yð ni ...ni aízù wo suru

motionless [mou'ʃənlis] *adj* 動かない ugókanaì

motion picture *n* (film) 映画 eìga

motivated [mou'təveitid] *adj* (enthusiastic) 張切っている haríkitte irù; (impelled): *motivated by* (envy, desire) ...の動機で ...no dðki de

motivation [moutəvei'ʃən] *n* (drive) 動機 dðki

motive [mou'tiv] *n* (aim, purpose) 目標 mokúhyō

motley [mɑ:t'li:] *adj* 雑多で奇妙な zattá dè kimyó na

motor [mou'tə:r] *n* (of machine) 原動機 geñdòki, モーター mðta; (of vehicle) エンジン éñjin; (*BRIT*: inf: vehicle) 車 kurúma

♦*cpd* (industry, trade) 自動車の jídòsha no

motorbike [mou'tə:rbaik] *n* オートバイ ðtòbai

motorboat [mou'tə:rbout] *n* モーターボート mðtābòto

motorcar [mou'tə:rkɑ:r] (*BRIT*) *n* 自動

車 jídōsha

motorcycle [mou'tə:rsai'kəl] *n* オートバイ ōtóbai

motorcycle racing *n* オートバイレーシング ōtóbairḗshiǹgu

motorcyclist [mou'tə:rsaiklist] *n* オートバイのライダー ōtóbai no raídā

motoring [mou'tə:riŋ] (*BRIT*) *n* 自動車運転 jídōsha uǹten

motorist [mou'tə:rist] *n* 運転者 uǹteǹsha

motor racing (*BRIT*) *n* カーレース kā́rēsu

motor vehicle *n* 自動車 jídōsha

motorway [mou'tə:rwei] (*BRIT*) *n* ハイウェー haíuē

mottled [mɑt'əld] *adj* ぶちの buchí no

motto [mɑt'ou] (*pl* **mottoes**) *n* 標語 hyó-go, モットー mottṓ

mould [mould] (*BRIT*) *n, vt* = **mold**

mouldy [moul'di:] (*BRIT*) *adj* = **moldy**

moult [moult] (*BRIT*) *vi* = **molt**

mound [maund] *n* (heap: of blankets, leaves, earth etc) 一山 hitóyama

mount [maunt] *n* (mountain in proper names): *Mount Carmel* カルメル山 karúmeruzàn

♦*vt* (horse) ...に乗る ...ni norú; (exhibition, display) 開催する kaísai suru; (fix: jewel) 台座にはめる daíza ni hamérù; (: picture) 掛ける kakérù; (staircase) 昇る nobórù

♦*vi* (increase: inflation) 上昇する jōshō suru; (: tension) つのる tsunoru; (: problems) 増える fuérù

mountain [maun'tən] *n* (GEO) 山 yamá

♦*cpd* (road, stream) 山の yamá no

mountaineer [mauntəni:r'] *n* 登山家 tozáñka

mountaineering [mauntəni:'riŋ] *n* 登山 tōzán

mountainous [maun'tənəs] *adj* (country, area) 山の多い yamá no ōi

mountain rescue team *n* 山岳救助隊 saǹgaku kyū̀jotai

mountainside [maun'tənsaid] *n* 山腹 saǹpuku

mount up *vi* (bills, costs, savings) たま

る tamárù

mourn [mɔ:rn] *vt* (death) 悲しむ kanáshimù

♦*vi*: *to mourn for* (someone) ...の死を悲しむ ...no shí wo kanáshimù

mourner [mɔ:r'nə:r] *n* 会葬者 kaísōsha

mournful [mɔ:rn'fəl] *adj* (sad) 悲しそうな kanáshisō na

mourning [mɔ:r'niŋ] *n* 喪 mo

in mourning 喪中で mochū̀ de

mouse [maus] (*pl* **mice**) *n* (animal) ハツカネズミ hatsúkanezùmi; (COMPUT) マウス máusu

mousetrap [maus'træp] *n* ネズミ取り nezúmitòri

mousse [mu:s] *n* (CULIN) ムース mū̀su; (*also:* **hair mousse**) ヘアムース heámūsu

moustache [məstæʃ'] (*BRIT*) *n* = **mustache**

mousy [mau'si:] *adj* (hair) 薄汚い茶色の usugitanai cha-íro no

mouth [mauθ] (*pl* **mouths**) *n* (ANAT) 口 kuchí; (of cave, hole) 入口 iríguchi; (of river) 河口 kakṑ

mouthful [mauθ'ful] *n* (amount) 口一杯 kuchí ippai

mouth organ *n* ハーモニカ hā́monika

mouthpiece [mauθ'pi:s] *n* (of musical instrument) 吹口 fukíguchi; (spokesman) スポークスマン supṓkusumàn

mouthwash [mauθ'wɔʃ] *n* マウスウォッシュ máusu uósshù ◇口臭防止洗口液 kṓshūbōshi senkòeki

mouth-watering [mauθ'wɔ:tə:riŋ] *adj* おいしそうな oíshisō na

movable [mu:'vəbəl] *adj* 可動な kadṓ na

move [mu:v] *n* (movement) 動き ugóki; (in game: change of position) 手 tê; (: turn to play) 番 báñ; (change: of house) 引っ越し hikkṓshi; (: of job) 転職 teñshoku

♦*vt* (change position of: furniture, car, curtains etc) 動かす ugókasù; (chessmen etc: in game) 動かす ugókasù; (emotionally) 感動させる kañdō saserù; (POL: resolution etc) 提議する teígi suru

♦*vi* (person, animal) 動く ugókù; (traffic) 流れる nagárerù; (*also:* **move house**)

引っ越す hikkósù; (develop: situation, events) 進展する shiñten suru
to get a move on 急ぐ isógù
to move someone to do something ...に ...をする気を起こさせる ...ni ...wo suru ki wò okósaserù

moveable [muːˈvəbəl] *adj* = movable

move about/around *vi* (change position) そわそわする sówàsowa suru; (travel) 頻繁に旅行する hiñpan ni ryokó suru; (change: residence) 頻繁に引っ越す hiñpan ni hikkósù; (: job) 頻繁に転職する hiñpan ni teñshoku suru

move along *vi* 立ち去る tachísarù
move along! 立ち止まるな tachídomarù ná

move away *vi* (leave: town, area) よそへ引っ越す yosó e hikkósù

move back *vi* (return) 元の所へ引っ越す mótò no tokóro e hikkósù

move forward *vi* (advance) 前進する zeñshin suru

move in *vi* (to a house) 入居する nyúkyo suru; (police, soldiers) 攻撃を加える kó̄geki wò kuwáerù

movement [muːvˈmənt] *n* (action: of person, animal) 動き ugóki, 動作 dósa; (: of traffic) 流れ nagáre; (gesture) 合図 aízu; (transportation: of goods etc) 運輸 úñ-yu; (shift: in attitude, policy) 変化 heñka; (group of people: esp REL, POL) 運動 uñdó; (MUS) 楽章 gakúshō

move on *vi* 立ち去る tachísarù
move on! 立ち止まるな tachídomarù ná

move out *vi* (of house) 引っ越す hikkósù

move over *vi* (to make room) 横へどいて場所を空ける yokó è dóite bashó wò akérù

move up *vi* (employee, deputy) 昇進する shóshin suru; (pupil) 進級する shiñkyū suru

movie [muːˈviː] *n* 映画 eíga
to go to the movies 映画を見に行く eíga wo mí ni ikù

movie camera *n* 映画カメラ eíga kaméra

moving [muːˈviŋ] *adj* (emotional) 感動的

に kañdōteki ni; (that moves) 動く ugóku

mow [mou] (*pt* **mowed**, *pp* **mowed** *or* **mown**) *vt* (grass, corn) 刈る karú

mow down *vt* (kill) なぎ払う様に殺す nagíharaù yó̄ nì korósu

mower [mouˈəːr] *n* (*also*: **lawnmower**) 芝刈機 shibákarikì

MP [empiːʹ] (*BRIT*) *n abbr* = **Member of Parliament**

m.p.h. [empieitʃʹ] *abbr* (= *miles per hour*) 時速...マイル jísoku ...maîru

Mr, Mr. [misˈtəːr] *n*: *Mr. Smith* スミスさん sumisu sán ◇男性の敬称 dañsei no kefshō

Mrs, Mrs. [misˈiz] *n*: *Mrs Smith* スミスさん sumisu sán ◇既婚女性の敬称 kíkòñjoséi no keíshō

Ms, Ms. [miz] *n*: *Ms. Smith* スミスさん sumisu sán ◇既婚・未婚を問わず女性の敬称 kíkòn, míkòn wo towázù joséi no keíshō

M.Sc. [emessiːʹ] *abbr* = **Master of Science**

KEYWORD

much [mʌtʃ] *adj* (time, money, effort) 沢山の takúsañ no, 多くの ṓkù no
we haven't got much time/money あまり多くの時間〔金〕はありません amári ṓku no jikáñ〔kané〕wà arímaseñ
much effort was expended on the project その企画に多くの努力を費やした sonó kikáku ni ṓkù no dóryòku wo tsuíyashìta
how much money/time do you need? お金〔時間〕はどのぐらい必要ですか o-káne〔jikán〕wà dóǹo gurai hitsúyō desù ká
he's done so much work for the charity その慈善事業のために彼は様々な仕事をしてくれました sonó jizéñjigyō no tamé nì kárè wa samázàma na shigóto wò shitè kuremashìta
it's too much あんまりだ añmarì da
it's not much 大した事じゃない táìshita kotó jà nai
to have too much money/free time 金

〔暇〕が有り余る kane(himá)gà aríamarù
as much as ...と同じぐらい ...to onáji
gurài

*I have as much money/intelligence
as you* 私はあなたと同じぐらいの金〔知
識〕を持っています watákushi wà anáta
to onáji gurài no kane(chíshĭki)wò
móttè imasu

◆*pron* 沢山の物 takúsan no monò
there isn't much to do あまりする事は
ありません amári suru kotò wa arímaseň
*much has been gained from our
discussions* 我々の話し合いは多くの成
果を産みました warewarè no hanáshiai
wà ōku no seíka wò umímashìta
how much does it cost? - too much
値段はいくらですか-べらぼうさ nedán
wà íkura desu ká - berábō sà
how much is it? いくらですか íkùra
desu ká

◆*adv* 1 (greatly, a great deal) とても totémo

thank you very much 大変有難うござ
います taíhen arígatò gózaimasù
much bigger (than) (...より) はるか
に大きい (...yori) haruka ni ōkii
*we are very much looking forward
to your visit* あなたが来られるのを首
を長くして待っております anáta ga ko-
rárerù no wo kubí wò nágaku shite
matté orimasù

*he is very much the gentleman/poli-
tician* 彼はれっきとした紳士〔政治家〕で
す kárè wa rekkí tò shita shíňshi(seíjika)desu

however much he tries 彼はどんなに努
力しても kárè wa dóňna ni doryóku
shite mò

as much as ...と同じぐらい沢山 ...tò o-
náji gurài takúsaň

I read as much as ever 私はいつもと
同じぐらい沢山の本を読んでいます wa-
tákushi wà ítsumo to onáji gurài takúsaň no hóň wo yóňde imásù

I read as much as possible/as I can
私はできるだけ沢山の本を読む事にして
います watákushi wà dekíru dakè takúsaň no hóň wo yómù koto ni shité imasù

*he is as much a part of the commu-
nity as you* 彼はあなたと同様ここの社
会の一員です kárè wa anáta to dōyō
kokô no shakài no ichíň desù

2 (by far) ずっと zúttò
I'm much better now 私はずっと元気
になっています watákushi wà zúttò gé-
ňki ni natté imasù
much reduced in price ずっと安くなっ
て zuttó yasúku natte
*it's much the biggest publishing
company in Europe* あれはヨーロ
ッパ最大の出版社です arë wa dañzen
yōroppasaidài no shuppáňsha desu

3 (almost) ほとんど hotóňdo
*the view is much as it was 10 years
ago* 景色は10年前とほとんど変っていま
せん késhĭki wa jūnen maè to hotóňdo
kawátte imaseň
the 2 books are much the same その
2冊の本はどちらも同じ様な物です sonô
nisàtsu no hóň wa dóchìra mo onáji yō
na monô desù

*how are you feeling? - much the
same* ご気分はいかがですか-大して変り
ません go-kíbùn wa ikága dèsu ká -
táïshite kawárimaseň

muck [mʌk] *n* (dirt) 泥 doró; (excrement)
くそ kusó
muck about/around *vi* (*inf*: fool a-
bout) ぶらぶらする búràbura suru
muck up *vt* (*inf*: ruin) 台無しにする daínashi ni suru
mucus [mjuːˈkəs] *n* 粘液 néň-eki
mud [mʌd] *n* 泥 doró
muddle [mʌdˈəl] *n* (mess, mix-up) めちゃ
くちゃ mechákucha, 混乱 koňran
◆*vt* (*also*: **muddle up**): (confuse: person,
things) 混乱させる koňran saserù;
(: story, names) ごちゃごちゃにする go-
chágocha ni suru
muddle through *vi* (get by) どうにかし
て切抜ける dō ni ka shite kirínukerù
muddy [mʌdˈiː] *adj* (floor, field) どろどろ
の doródoro no
mudguard [mʌdˈgɑːrd] *n* フェンダー féň-
dā

muesli [mju:z'li:] *n* ムースリ mūsuri ◇朝食用のナッツ，ドライフルーツ，穀物の混合 chōshoku yō no náttsu, doráifurū-tsu, kokúmotsu no kóngō

muffin [mʌf'in] *n* (*US*) マドレーヌ madórēnu; (*BRIT*) マフィン máfin

muffle [mʌf'əl] *vt* (sound) 弱める yowámerù; (against cold) ...に防寒具を付ける ...ni bōkangu wo tsukérù

muffled [mʌf'əld] *adj* (sound) 弱い yowáì

muffler [mʌf'lər] (*US*) *n* (*AUT*) マフラー máfurā

mug [mʌg] *n* (cup) マグ mágù; (for beer) ジョッキ jókkì; (*inf*: face) 面 tsurá; (: *BRIT*: fool) ばか bákà

◆*vt* (assault) 襲う osóù ◇特に強盗行為について言う tókù ni gōtōkòi ni tsúîte iú

mugging [mʌg'iŋ] *n* 強盗事件 gōtōjikèn

muggy [mʌg'i:] *adj* (weather, day) 蒸暑い mushíatsuì

mule [mju:l] *n* ラバ rábà

mull [mʌl] *vt*: **to mull over** ...について考え込む ...ni tsúîte kangaekomù

multi... [mʌl'ti:] *prefix* 複数の ... fukúsū no ...

multicolored [mʌl'tikʌlə:rd] (*BRIT* **multicoloured**) *adj* 多色の tashóku no

multilateral [mʌltilæt'ə:rəl] *adj* (disarmament, talks) 多国間の takókukan no

multi-level [mʌlti:lev'əl] (*US*) *adj* = **multistory**

multinational [mʌltənæʃ'ənəl] *adj* (company, business) 多国籍の takókuseki no

multiple [mʌl'təpəl] *adj* (collision) 玉突きの tamátsuki no; (interests) 複数の fukúsū no

◆*n* (MATH) 倍数 baísū

multiple sclerosis [-sklirou'sis] *n* 多発性硬化症 tahátsusei kōkashō

multiplication [mʌltəpləkei'ʃən] *n* (MATH) 掛算 kakézàn; (increase) 増加 zōka

multiply [mʌl'təplai] *vt* (MATH): *4 multiplied by 2 is 8* 4掛ける2は8 yón kakérù nî wa hachí

◆*vi* (increase) 増える fuérù

multistory [mʌlti:stɔ:r'i:] (*BRIT* **multistorey**) *adj* (building etc) 高層の kōsō no

multitude [mʌl'tətu:d] *n* (crowd) 群衆 gunshū; (large number): *a multitude of* (reasons, ideas) 沢山の takúsaǹ no

mum [mʌm] (*BRIT*: *inf*) *n* = **mom**

◆*adj*: **to keep mum** 黙っている damátte irù

mumble [mʌm'bəl] *vt* (speak indistinctly) もぐもぐ言う mógùmogu iú

◆*vi* ぶつぶつ言う bútsùbutsu iú

mummy [mʌm'i:] *n* (embalmed) ミイラ míira; (*BRIT*: mother) = **mommy**

mumps [mʌmps] *n* おたふく風邪 otáfukukàze

munch [mʌntʃ] *vt* (chew) かむ kámù

◆*vi* かむ kámù

mundane [mʌndein'] *adj* (task, life) 平凡な heíbon na

municipal [mju:nis'əpəl] *adj* 市の shí no

munitions [mju:niʃ'ənz] *npl* 兵器弾薬 heíkidañ-yaku

mural [mju:r'əl] *n* 壁画 hekíga

murder [mə:r'də:r] *n* (killing) 殺人 satsújin

◆*vt* (kill) 殺す korósù

murderer [mə:r'də:rə:r] *n* 人殺し hitógoroshi

murderous [mə:r'də:rəs] *adj* (person) 殺人も辞さない satsújin mo jisanài; (attack) 殺しを目的とする koróshi wò mokúteki to surù

murky [mə:r'ki:] *adj* (street, night) 暗い kurái; (water) 濁った nigótta

murmur [mə:r'mə:r] *n*: *a murmur of voices* かすかな人声 kásùkana hitógòe; (of wind, waves) さざめき sazámeki

◆*vt* (speak quietly) 声をひそめて言う kóè wo hisómetè iú

◆*vi* 声をひそめて話す kóè wo hisómetè hanásù

muscle [mʌs'əl] *n* (ANAT) 筋肉 kíñniku; (*fig*: strength) 力 chikára

muscle in *vi* 割込む warīkomù

muscular [mʌs'kjələ:r] *adj* (pain) 筋肉の kíñniku no; (build) たくましい takúmashiì; (person) 強そうな tsuyósō na

muse [mjuːz] *vi* (think) 考え込む kańgaekomù

♦*n* (MYTHOLOGY) ミューズ myûzu ◊ 人間の知的活動をつかさどるという女神 niñgen no chitékikatsudő wo tsukásadorù to iú mégàmi

museum [mjuːziːˈəm] *n* 博物館 hakúbùtsukan

mushroom [mʌˈʃruːm] *n* (fungus: edible, poisonous) キノコ kínòko

♦*vi* (fig: town, organization) 急速に成長する kyûsoku ni seíchō suru

music [mjuːˈzik] *n* (sound, art) 音楽 óñgaku; (written music, score) 楽譜 gakúfu

musical [mjuːˈzikəl] *adj* (career, skills, person) 音楽の óñgaku no; (sound, tune) 音楽的な oñgákuteki na

♦*n* (show, film) ミュージカル myûjikaru

musical instrument *n* 楽器 gakkí

music hall *n* (place) ボードビル劇場 bôdobiru gekijő

musician [mjuːziˈʃən] *n* ミュージシャン myûjishàn

musk [mʌsk] *n* じゃ香 jakô

Muslim [mʌzˈlim] *adj* イスラム教の isúramukyô no

♦*n* イスラム教徒 isúramukyôto

muslin [mʌzˈlin] *n* モスリン mósùrin

mussel [mʌsˈəl] *n* ムールガイ mûrugai

must [mʌst] *aux vb* (necessity, obligation): *I must do it* 私はそれをしなければならない watákushi wa soré wo shinákereba naranài; (probability): *he must be there by now* もう彼はあそこに着いているでしょう mô kárè wa asőko ni tsúite írù deshő; (suggestion, invitation): *you must come and see me soon* そのうち是非遊びに来て下さい sonő uchi zéhì asőbi ni kite kudasaí; (indicating something unwelcome): *why must he behave so badly?* どうしてまたあの子はそんなに行儀悪くするのだろう dôshite mata áñő ko wa sofína ni győgiwarukù suru no darő

♦*n* (necessity): *it's a must* 必需品だ hitsújuhin da

mustache [məstæʃˈ] (*US*) *n* 鼻ひげ hanáhige

mustard [mʌsˈtəːrd] *n* (Japanese) 辛子 karáshi, 和辛子 wagáràshi; (Western) 辛子 karáshi, 洋辛子 yőgaràshi, マスタード masútado

muster [mʌsˈtəːr] *vt* (support) 求める motómerù; (energy, strength) 奮い起す furúiokosù; (MIL) 召集する shőshū suru

mustn't [mʌsˈənt] = **must not**

musty [mʌsˈti] *adj* かび臭い kabíkusaì

mutation [mjuːteiˈʃən] *n* (alteration) 変化 heñka

mute [mjuːt] *adj* (silent) 無言の mugón no

muted [mjuːˈtid] *adj* (color) 地味な jimí na; (reaction) ひそめた hisómeta

mutilate [mjuːˈtəleit] *vt* (person, thing) 傷付ける kizútsukerù ◊ 特に体の部分を切断する場合に使う tőkù ni karáda no búbùn wo setsúdan suru baái ni tsukáù

mutiny [mjuːˈtəniː] *n* (rebellion: of soldiers, sailors) 反乱 hañran

♦*vi* 反乱を起す hañran wő okősù

mutter [mʌtˈəːr] *vt* (speak quietly) つぶやく tsubúyakù

♦*vi* ぶつぶつ不平を言う bútsùbutsu fuhéi wő iú

mutton [mʌtˈən] *n* (meat) マトン mátòn

mutual [mjuːˈtʃuːəl] *adj* (shared: benefit, interest) 共通の kyőtsū no; (reciprocal: feeling, attraction) 相互の sốgo no

mutually [mjuːˈtʃuːəliː] *adv* 相互に sốgo ni

muzzle [mʌzˈəl] *n* (mouth: of dog) ふん fûñ, 鼻づら hanázura; (: of gun) 銃口 jûkō; (guard: for dog) 口輪 kuchíwa

♦*vt* (dog) ...に口輪をはめる ...ni kuchíwa wo hamérù

KEYWORD

my [mai] *adj* 私の watákushi nò

this is my house/car/brother これは私の家〔車, 兄〕です koré wà watákushi nò ié〔kurúma, áñì〕desù

I've washed my hair/cut my finger 私は髪を洗いました〔指を切りました〕 watákushi wà kamí wờ aráimashìta 〔yubí wờ kirímashìta〕

is this my pen or yours? これは私の

ペンですか，それともあなたのですか korě wà watákushi nò péñ desu ká, sorétomò anátà no desu ká

Myanmar [mai'ænmɑ:r] *n* ミャンマー myáñmā

myopic [maiɑːp'ik] *adj* 近眼の kiñgan no

myriad [mir'i:əd] *n* (of people, things) 無数 musú

myself [maiself'] *pron* 私自身 watákushi-jishìn ¶ *see also* **oneself**

mysterious [misti:r'i:əs] *adj* (strange) なぞの nazó no

mystery [mis'tə:ri:] *n* (puzzle) なぞ nazó
shrouded in mystery (place) なぞに包まれた nazó nì tsutsúmareta

mystic [mis'tik] *n* (person) 神秘主義者 shiñpishùgisha

mystic(al) [mis'tik(əl)] *adj* 神秘的な shiñpiteki na

mystify [mis'təfai] *vt* (perplex) ...の理解を越える ...no rikái wò koérù

mystique [misti:k'] *n* 神秘 shiñpí

myth [miθ] *n* (legend, story) 神話 shiñwa; (fallacy) 俗信 zokúshin

mythology [miθɑ:l'ədʒi:] *n* 神話集 shiñwàshū

N

n/a *abbr* (= *not applicable*) ◇申請用紙などで空欄にしておく場合に書く shiñsei yōshi nádò de kúran ni shite oku baài ni kákù

nag [næg] *vt* (scold) がみがみ言う gámìgami iú

nagging [næg'iŋ] *adj* (doubt) 晴れない harénaî; (pain) しつこい shitsúkoì

nail [neil] *n* (on fingers, toes) つめ tsumé; (metal) くぎ kugí
♦*vt: to nail something to something* ...を...にくぎで留める ...wo ...ni kugí dè toméru
to nail someone down to doing something 強制的に...に...をさせる kyōseiteki ni ...ni ...wò sasérù

nailbrush [neil'brʌʃ] *n* つめブラシ tsu-

méburàshi

nailfile [neil'fail] *n* つめやすり tsuméya-sùri

nail polish *n* マニキュア maníkyùa

nail polish remover *n* 除光液 jokōeki, マニキュア落し maníkyua otóshi

nail scissors *npl* つめ切りばさみ tsumé-kiribasàmi

nail varnish (*BRIT*) *n* = **nail polish**

naive [naii:v'] *adj* (person, ideas) 無邪気な mújàki na, ナイーブな naíbù na

naked [nei'kid] *adj* 裸の hadáka no

name [neim] *n* (of person, animal, place) 名前 namáe; (surname) 名字 myōjì, 姓 séì; (reputation) 評判 hyōban
♦*vt* (child) ...に名前を付ける ...ni namáe wò tsukérù; (identify: accomplice, criminal) 名指す nazásù; (specify: price, date etc) 指定する shitéi suru
what's your name? お名前は何とおっしゃいますか o-námae wà náñto ósshái-masù ká
by name 名指しで nazáshi dè
in the name of (*fig*) ...の名において ...no ná ni oìte
to give one's name and address (to police etc) 名前と住所を知らせる namáe tò jūshó wo shiráserù

nameless [neim'lis] *adj* (unknown) 無名の muméi no; (anonymous: witness, contributor) 匿名の tokúmei no

namely [neim'li:] *adv* 即ち sunáwàchi

namesake [neim'seik] *n* 同姓同名の人 dōseidōmei no hitó

nanny [næn'i:] *n* 養育係 yōikugakàri

nap [næp] *n* (sleep) 昼寝 hirúne
to be caught napping (*fig*) 不意を突かれる fuí wò tsukárerù

napalm [nei'pɑ:m] *n* ナパーム napámù

nape [neip] *n*: *nape of the neck* えり首 eríkùbi

napkin [næp'kin] *n* (*also*: **table napkin**) ナプキン nápùkin

nappy [næp'i:] (*BRIT*) *n* おむつ o-mútsù

nappy rash (*BRIT*) *n* おむつかぶれ o-mútsukabùre

narcissus [nɑ:rsis'əs] (*pl* **narcissi**) *n* (BOT) スイセン suísen

narcotic [nɑːrkɑːtˈik] *adj* 麻酔性の masúisei no
♦*n* 麻薬 mayáku

narrative [nærˈətiv] *n* 物語 monógatàri

narrator [nærˈeitəːr] *n* (in book) 語り手 katárite; (in film etc) ナレーター narḗtā

narrow [nærˈou] *adj* (space, road etc) 狭い semáì; (*fig*: majority, advantage) ぎりぎりの girígiri no; (: ideas, attitude) 狭量な kyóryō na
♦*vi* (road) 狭くなる sémàku naru; (gap, difference: diminish) 小さくなる chíisaku naru

to have a narrow escape 間一髪で逃れる káǹ-ippátsu dè nogárerù

to narrow something down to (choice, possibility) ...を...に絞る ...wo ...ni shíbórù

narrowly [nærˈouli:] *adv* (miss) 辛うじて karṓjìte, 間一髪で káǹ-ippátsu dè

narrow-minded [nærˈoumainˈdid] *adj* 狭量な kyóryō na

nasal [neiˈzəl] *adj* (of the nose) 鼻の haná no; (voice, sound) 鼻にかかった haná ni kakattà

nasty [næsˈtiː] *adj* (unpleasant: remark, person) いやな iyá nà; (malicious) 腹黒い haráguroì; (rude) 無礼な búrèi na; (revolting: taste, smell) むかつI かせる mukátsukaserù; (wound, disease etc) ひどい hidóì

nation [neiˈʃən] *n* (country) 国 kuní, 国家 kókkà; (people) 国民 kokúmin

national [næʃˈənəl] *adj* 国の kuní no
♦*n: a foreign national* 外国人 gaíkokujìn

national dress *n* 民族衣装 mìnzokuishṓ

National Health Service (*BRIT*) *n* 国民医療制度 kokúmin iryōseìdo

National Insurance (*BRIT*) *n* 国民保険 kokúminhokèn

nationalism [næʃˈənəlizəm] *n* 国家主義 kokkáshugì, 民族主義 mínzokushugì

nationalist [næʃˈənəlist] *adj* 国家主義の kokkáshugì no, 民族主義 mínzokushugì no
♦*n* 国家主義者 kokkáshugishà, 民族主義者 mìnzokushugishà

nationality [næʃənælˈətiː] *n* 国籍 kokúseki

nationalization [næʃənələzeiˈʃən] *n* 国有化 kokúyūka, 国営化 kokúeika

nationalize [næʃˈnəlaiz] *vt* 国営にする kokúei ni surù

nationally [næʃˈnəliː] *adv* (nationwide) 全国的に zeńkokuteki ni; (as a nation) 国として kuní toshite

nationwide [neiˈʃənwaidˈ] *adj* (problem, campaign) 全国的な zeńkokuteki na
♦*adv* (campaign, search) 全国的に zeńkokuteki ni

native [neiˈtiv] *n* (local inhabitant) 地元の人 jimóto no hitò; (of tribe etc) 原住民 geńjūmin
♦*adj* (indigenous) 地元の jimóto no, 地元生れの jimóto umàre no; (of one's birth) 生れの umáre no; (innate) 生れつきの umáretsuki no

a native of Russia ロシア生れの人 roshía umare no hitò

a native speaker of French フランス語を母国語とする人 furánsugo wò bokókugo to surù hitò

native language *n* 母国語 bokókugo

Nativity [nətivˈətiː] *n: the Nativity* キリストの降誕 kirísuto nò kótan

NATO [neiˈtou] *n abbr* (= *North Atlantic Treaty Organization*) 北大西洋条約機構 kitátaiseiyō jōyaku kikō

natural [nætʃˈəːrəl] *adj* (*gen*) 自然の shizén no; (innate) 生れつきの umáretsuki no

natural gas *n* 天然ガス teńnengasù

naturalist [nætʃˈəːrəlist] *n* 博物学者 hakúbutsugakushà

naturalize [nætʃˈəːrəlaiz] *vt: to become naturalized* (person, plant) 帰化する kiká suru

naturally [nætʃˈəːrəliː] *adv* (*gen*) 自然に shizén ni; (of course) もちろん mochíròn, 当然 tṓzen

nature [neiˈtʃəːr] *n* (*also:* **Nature**) 自然 shizén, 大自然 daíshizen; (character) 性質 seíshitsu; (type, sort) 種類 shúrùi
by nature 生れつき umáretsuki

naught [nɔːt] *n* 零 reí, ゼロ zérò

naughty [nɔː'tiː] *adj* (child) 行 儀 の 悪 い gyōgi no waruí

nausea [nɔː'ziːə] *n* 吐気 hakíke

nauseate [nɔː'zieit] *vt* むかつかせる mukátsukaserù, 吐気を起させる hakíke wò okósaserù; (*fig*) いやな感じを与える iyá na kanjì wo atáerù

nautical [nɔː'tikəl] *adj* (uniform) 船員 の señ-in no; (people) 海洋の kaíyō no
a nautical mile 海里 kaíri

naval [nei'vəl] *adj* (uniform, academy) 海 軍の kaígun no
a naval battle 海戦 kaísen
naval forces 海軍力 kaígunryòku

naval officer *n* 海軍将校 kaígunshōkō

nave [neiv] *n* 外陣 gaíjìn

navel [nei'vəl] *n* へそ hesó

navigate [næv'əgeit] *vi* (NAUT, AVIAT) 航行する kōkō suru; (AUT) 道 案内する michíannai suru

navigation [nævəgei'ʃən] *n* (action) 航行 kōkō; (science) 航海術 kōkaijùtsu

navigator [næv'əgeitər] *n* (NAUT) 航 海長 kōkaíchō; (AVIAT) 航空士 kōkū-shi; (AUT) 道案内をする人 michíannai wo suru hitð

navvy [næv'iː] *n* (BRIT) 労働者 rōdōsha

navy [nei'viː] *n* 海軍 kaígun

navy(-blue) *adj* 濃紺の nókon no

Nazi [nɑːt'siː] *n* ナチ náchì

NB [enbi'] *abbr* (= *nota bene*) 注 chū ◇脚 注などに使う略語 kyakúchū nadð ni tsukáù ryakúgo

near [niːr] *adj* (place, time, relation) 近い chikáì
♦*adv* 近く chikákù
♦*prep* (*also*: **near to**: space, time) ...の近 くに ...no chikákù ni
♦*vt* (place, event) ...に近づく ...ni chikázukù

nearby [niːr'bai] *adj* 近くの chikákù no
♦*adv* 近くに chikákù ni

nearly [niːr'liː] *adv* (not totally) ほとんど hotóñdo; (on the point of) 危うく ayáukù
I nearly fell 危うく転ぶところだった ayáukù koróbu tokoro dattá

near miss *n* (narrow escape) ニアミス niámisù; (of planes) 異常接近 ijōsekkìn,

ニアミス niámisù; (of cars etc): *that was a near miss!* 危ないところだった abúnai tokoro dattá

nearside [niːr'said] *n* (AUT: in Britain, Japan) 左側 hidárigawa; (: in US, Europe etc) 右側 migígawa

near-sighted [niːr'saitid] *adj* 近眼の kiñgan no, 近視の kiñshi no

neat [niːt] *adj* (place, person) きちんとし た kichíñ to shita; (skillful: work, plan) 上手な jōzu na; (spirits) ストレートの su-tōrēto no

neatly [niːt'liː] *adv* (tidily) きちんと ki-chíñ to; (skillfully) 上手に jōzu nì

necessarily [nesəsɛ:r'iliː] *adv* (inevi-tably) 必然的に hitsúzenteki ni
not necessarily 必ずしも...でない kanárazushìmo ...de náì

necessary [nes'iseri:] *adj* (required: skill, quality, measure) 必要な hitsúyō na; (inevitable: result, effect) 必然の hi-tsúzen no
it is necessary to/that ...する必要があ る ...suru hitsúyō ga arù

necessitate [nəses'əteit] *vt* 必要とする hitsúyō to surù

necessities [nəses'iti:z] *npl* (essentials) 必需品 hitsújuhin

necessity [nəses'iti:] *n* (thing needed) 必 需品 hitsújuhin; (compelling circum-stances) 必然 hitsúzen

neck [nek] *n* (of person, animal, gar-ment, bottle) 首 kubí
♦*vi* (*inf*) ペッティングする pettíñgu su-ru
neck and neck 接戦して sessén shite

necklace [nek'lis] *n* ネックレス nékkùre-su

neckline [nek'lain] *n* ネックライン nek-kúraìn

necktie [nek'tai] (US) *n* ネクタイ nékù-tai

née [nei] *adj*: *née Scott* 旧姓スコット kyúsei sukóttò

need [niːd] *n* (lack) 欠乏 ketsúbō; (neces-sity) 必要 hitsúyō; (thing needed) 必需品 hitsújuhin
♦*vt* (require) ...を必要とする ...wo hitsú-

yō to surù

I need to do it 私はそれをしなければ
ならない watákushi wà sorè wò shinákereba naranaì, 私はそれをする必要があ
る watákushi wà sorè wò suru hitsuyō
ga arù

you don't need to go 行かなくてもい
い ikánakute mo iì

needle [ni:'dəl] *n* (*gen*) 針 hárì; (for knitting) 編棒 amíbō

♦*vt* (*fig: inf*) からかう karákaù

needless [ni:d'lis] *adj* (criticism, risk) 不
必要な fuhítsuyō na

needless to say 言うまでもなく iú made mo nakù

needlework [ni:d'əlwə:rk] *n* (item(s) of
needlework) 縫い物 nuímonò; (activity)
針仕事 haríshigòto

needn't [ni:d'ənt] = **need not**

needy [ni:'di:] *adj* 貧しい mazúshiì

negation [nigei'ʃən] *n* 否定 hitéi

negative [neg'ətiv] *adj* (answer) 否定の
hitéi no; (attitude) 否定的な hitéiteki na;
(reaction) 消極的な shōkyokuteki na;
(ELEC) 陰極の iñkyoku no, マイナスの
maínasu no

♦*n* (LING) 否定形 hitéikei; (PHOT) 陰画
iñga, ネガ négà

neglect [niglekt'] *vt* (child) 放任する hōnin suru, ほったらかす hottárakasù;
(one's duty) 怠る okótarù

♦*n* (of child) 放任 hōnin; (of area, house,
garden) ほったらかす事 hottárakasu ko-
tò; (of duty) 怠る事 okótaru kotò

negligee [neg'ləʒei] *n* (dressing gown) ネ
グリジェ negúrijè

negligence [neg'lidʒəns] *n* (carelessness)
不注意 fuchūi

negligible [neg'lidʒəbəl] *adj* (cost, difference) わずかな wázùka na

negotiable [nigou'ʃəbəl] *adj* (check) 譲渡
できる jōto dekirù

negotiate [nigou'ʃi:eit] *vi*: *to negotiate
(with)* (...と) 交渉する (...to) kōshō su-
ru

♦*vt* (treaty, transaction) 協議して決める
kyōgi shite kimerù; (obstacle) 乗越える
noríkoerù; (bend in road) 注意して通る

negotiation [nigouʃi:ei'ʃən] *n* 交渉 kōshō

negotiator [nigou'ʃi:eitə:r] *n* 交渉する人
kōshō suru hitò

Negress [ni:g'ris] *n* 黒人女性 kokújinjo-
sèi

Negro [ni:g'rou] *adj* 黒人の kokújin no
♦*n* 黒人 kokújin

neigh [nei] *vi* いななく inánakù

neighbor [nei'bə:r] (*BRIT* **neighbour**) *n*
(next door) 隣の人 tonári no hitò; (in
vicinity) 近所の人 kíñjo no hitò

neighborhood [nei'bə:rhud] *n* (place) 近
所 kíñjo, 界隈 kaíwai; (people) 近所の
人々 kíñjo no hitóbito

neighboring [nei'bə:riŋ] *adj* (town,
state) 隣の tonári no

neighborly [nei'bə:rli:] *adj* (person, attitude) 親切な shíñsetsu na

neighbour [nei'bə:r] *etc* (*BRIT*) *n* =
neighbor *etc*

neither [ni:'ðə:r] *adj* どちらの...も...でな
い dóchìra no ...mo ...de naì

neither story is true どちらの話も本当
ではない dóchìra no hanáshi mò hoñtō
de wa naì

♦*conj*: *I didn't move and neither did
John* 私も動かなかったしジョンも動か
なかった watákushi mò ugókanakattà
shi, jóñ mo ugókanakattà

♦*pron* どちらも...でない dóchìra mo ...de
naì

neither is true どちらも本当でない dóchìra mo hoñtō de naì

♦*adv*: *neither good nor bad* よくも悪
くもない yókù mo warúkù mo naì

neon [ni:'ɑːn] *n* ネオン néòn; (*also*: **neon
sign**) ネオンサイン neónsaìn

neon light *n* ネオン灯 neóntō

nephew [nef'ju:] *n* おい oi

nerve [nə:rv] *n* (ANAT) 神経 shíñkei;
(courage) 勇気 yūki; (impudence) 厚かま
しさ atsúkamashisà, 図々しさ zúzùshisà

to have a fit of nerves 神経質になる
shiñkeishitsu ni narù

nerve-racking [nə:rv'rækiŋ] *adj* いらい
らさせる íraira saserù

nervous [nər'vəs] *adj* (ANAT) 神経の shínkei no; (anxious) 神経質な shínkei-shitsu na; (timid: person) 気の小さいki no chíisai; (: animal) おく病な okúbyō na

nervous breakdown *n* 神経衰弱 shínkeisuijáku

nest [nest] *n* 巣 sú
◆*vi* 巣を作る sú wò tsukúrù

nest egg *n* (fig) へそくり hesókuri

nestle [nes'əl] *vi*: *to nestle in a valley/the mountains* (village etc) 谷間〔山あい〕に横たわる taníma〔yamá-ai〕nì yokótawarù

net [net] *n* (gen) 網 amí; (fabric) レース résù; (TENNIS, VOLLEYBALL etc) ネット néttò; (fig) わな wánà
◆*adj* (COMM) 正味の shómi no
◆*vt* (fish, game) 網で取る amí dè tórù; (profit) 得る érù

netball [net'bɔːl] *n* ネットボール nettóbōru ◇英国で行われるバスケットボールに似た球技 eíkoku de okonawarerù basúkettobōru ni nítà kyúgì

net curtains *npl* レースのカーテン résù no kátèn

Netherlands [neð'ə:rləndz] *npl*: *the Netherlands* オランダ oránda

nett [net] (*BRIT*) *adj* = **net**

netting [net'iŋ] *n* 網 amí

nettle [net'əl] *n* イラクサ irákusa

network [net'wə:rk] *n* (of roads, veins, shops) ネットワーク nettówàku; (TV, RADIO) 放送網 hósōmō, ネットワーク nettówàku

neurotic [nurɑː'tik] *adj* 神経過敏な shínkeikabìn na, ノイローゼの noírōze no
◆*n* ノイローゼの人 noírōze no hitó

neuter [nuː'tə:r] *adj* (LING) 中性の chúsei no
◆*vt* (cat etc) 去勢する kyoséi suru

neutral [nuː'trəl] *adj* (person) 中立の chúritsu no; (color etc) 中間色の chúkanshoku no; (ELEC) 中性の chúsei no
◆*n* (AUT) ニュートラル nyútòraru

neutrality [nuːtræl'iti:] *n* 中立 chúritsu

neutralize [nuː'trəlaiz] *vt* (acid, poison etc) 中和する chúwa suru; (campaign, goodwill) 台無しにする daínashi ni surù

never [nev'ə:r] *adv* どんな時でも ...ない dóñna toki de mo ...náî
I never went 行かなかった ikánakatta
never in my life ...したことがない ...shitá kotò ga náî ¶ *see also* **mind**

never-ending [nev'ə:ren'diŋ] *adj* 終りのない owári no naî, 果てしない hatéshinaî

nevertheless [nevə:rðəles'] *adv* それにもかかわらず soré ni mò kakáwarazù, それでもやはり soré de mò yahárî

new [nu:] *adj* (brand new) 新しい atárashiî; (recent) 最近の saíkin no; (different) 今までになかった imá madè ni nákàtta; (inexperienced) 新入りの shiñ-iri no

newborn [nuː'bɔːrn] *adj* 生れたばかりの umáreta bakàri no

newcomer [nuː'kʌmə:r] *n* 新顔 shiñgao, 新入り shiñ-iri

new-fangled [nuː'fæŋ'gəld] (*pej*) *adj* 超モダンな chómodàn na

new-found [nuː'faund] *adj* (enthusiasm, confidence) 新たに沸いた árata ni waîta; (friend) 新しくできた atárashikù dékîta

newly [nuː'liː] *adv* 新しく atárashikù

newly-weds [nuː'liːwedz] *npl* 新婚者 shiñkoñsha

new moon *n* 新月 shíñgetsu

news [nuːz] *n* ニュース nyúsu
a piece of news ニュース項目 nyúsukōmoku, ニュース nyúsu
the news (RADIO, TV) ニュース nyúsu

news agency *n* 通信社 tsúshiñsha

newsagent [nuːz'eidʒənt] (*BRIT*) *n* = **newsdealer**

newscaster [nuːz'kæstə:r] *n* ニュースキャスター nyúsukyasùtā

newsdealer [nuːz'diːlə:r] (*US*) *n* (shop) 新聞販売店 shiñbunhanbaitèn; (person) 新聞販売業者 shiñbunhanbaigyòsha

newsflash [nuːz'flæʃ] *n* ニュース速報 nyúsusokuhò

newsletter [nuːz'letə:r] *n* ニュースレター nyúsuretà

newspaper [nuːz'peipə:r] *n* 新聞 shiñbun

newsprint [nuːz'print] *n* 新聞印刷用紙 shiñbun insatsuyòshi

newsreader [nuːz'riːdə:r] *n* = **newscaster**

newsreel [nuːzˈriːl] n ニュース映画 nyūsueīga

newsstand [nuːzˈstænd] n (in station etc) 新聞スタンド shiñbun sutañdo

newt [nuːt] n イモリ imórī

New Year n 新年 shíñnen

New Year's Day n 元旦 gañtan, 元日 gañjitsu

New Year's Eve n 大みそ日 ōmisòka

New York [-jɔːrk] n ニューヨーク nyúyòku

New Zealand [-ziːlənd] n ニュージーランド nyújīrando

New Zealander [-ziːləndər] n ニュージーランド人 nyújīrandojìn

next [nekst] adj (in space) 隣の tonári no; (in time) 次の tsugí no

♦adv (place) 隣に tonári ni; (time) 次に tsugí ni, 今度 kóñdo

the next day 次の日 tsugí no hì, 翌日 yokújitsu

next time 次回に jíkai ni, 今度 kóñdo

next year 来年 raínen

next to ...の隣に ...no tonári ni

to cost next to nothing ただ同然である tádà dōzen de arù

to do next to nothing ほとんど何もしない hotóñdo naní mo shinài

next please! (at doctor's etc) 次の方 tsugí no katà

next door adv 隣の家に tonári nò ié nì

♦adj (neighbor, flat) 隣の tonári no

next-of-kin [nekstˈəvkin] n 最も近い親せき mottómo chikaì shiñseki

NHS [eneitʃes] n abbr = National Health Service

nib [nib] n ペン先 peñsakì

nibble [nibˈəl] vt 少しずつかじる sukóshizutsù kajírù, ちびちび食べる chíbìchibi tabérù

Nicaragua [nikərɑːgˈwə] n ニカラグア nikáragua

nice [nais] adj (likeable) 感じのよい kañji no yoī; (kind) 親切な shiñsetsu na; (pleasant) 天気のよい téñki no yoī; (attractive) 魅力的な miryōkuteki na

nicely [naisˈliː] adv (pleasantly) 気持よく kimóchi yokù; (kindly) 親切に shíñsetsu ni; (attractively) 魅力的に miryōkuteki ni

niceties [naiˈsətiːz] npl 細かい点 komákaì teñ

nick [nik] n (wound) 切傷 kiríkìzu; (cut, indentation) 刃の跡 há no atò

♦vt (BRIT inf: steal) かっ払う kappáraù

in the nick of time 際どい時に kiwádoì tókì ni, 危ういところで ayáui tokoro dè

nickel [nikˈəl] n (metal) ニッケル nikkéru; (US) 5セント玉 5 señto dama

nickname [nikˈneim] n あだ名 adána, 愛称 aíshō, ニックネーム nikkúnēmu

♦vt ...に...のあだ名をつける ...ni ...no adána wò tsukérù

nicotine [nikˈətiːn] n ニコチン nikóchin

niece [niːs] n めい meí

Nigeria [naidʒiˈriːə] n ナイジェリア naíjeria

Nigerian [naidʒiˈriːən] adj ナイジェリアの naíjeria no

♦n ナイジェリア人 naíjeriajìn

nigger [nigˈəːr] (inf) n (highly offensive) 黒ん坊 kuróñbō

niggling [nigˈliŋ] adj (trifling) つまらない tsumáranaì; (annoying) いらいらさせる íràira sasérù

night [nait] n (period of darkness) 夜 yórù; (evening) 夕方 yūgata

the night before last おとといの夜 otótoì no yórù

at night 夜（に）yórù (ni)

by night 夜に yórù ni

nightcap [naitˈkæp] n (drink) 寝酒 nezáke, ナイトキャップ naítokyappù

nightclub [naitˈklʌb] n ナイトクラブ naítokurabu

nightdress [naitˈdres] n 寝巻 nemáki ◇女性用のを指す joséiyō no wò sásù

nightfall [naitˈfɔːl] n 夕暮 yūgure

nightgown [naitˈgaun] n = nightdress

nightie [naiˈtiː] n = nightdress

nightingale [naitˈəngeil] n ヨナキウグイス yonákiuguìsu, サヨナキドリ sayónakidòri, ナイチンゲール naíchingèru

nightlife [naitˈlaif] n 夜の生活 yórù no seíkatsu

nightly [nait'li:] *adj* 毎晩の máiban no
♦*adv* 毎晩 máiban

nightmare [nait'me:r] *n* 悪夢 ákùmu

night porter *n* 夜間のフロント係 yákàn no furóntogakàri

night school *n* 夜間学校 yakángakkò

night shift *n* 夜間勤務 yakánkìnmu

night-time [nait'taim] *n* 夜 yórù

night watchman *n* 夜警 yakéi

nil [nil] *n* ゼロ zérò; (*BRIT: SPORT*) 零点 reíteñ, ゼロ zérò

Nile [nail] *n*: *the Nile* ナイル川 naírugà-wa

nimble [nim'bəl] *adj* (agile) 素早い subáyaì, 軽快な keíkai na; (skillful) 器用な kíyò na

nine [nain] *num* 9 (の) kyū́ (no), 九つ (の) kokónòtsu (no)

nineteen [nain'ti:n'] *num* 19 (の) júku (no)

ninety [nain'ti:] *num* 90 (の) kyū́jū (no)

ninth [nainθ] *adj* 第9 (の) daíku (no)

nip [nip] *vt* (pinch) つねる tsunérù; (bite) かむ kámù

nipple [nip'əl] *n* (ANAT) 乳首 chikúbì

nitrogen [nai'trədʒən] *n* 窒素 chíssò

KEYWORD

no [nou] (*pl* **noes**) *adv* (opposite of "yes") いいえ íife

are you coming? - no (I'm not) 一緒に来ませんか-いいえ (行きません) isshó ni kimaseñ ká - íife (ikímaseñ)

would you like some? - no thank you いりませんか-いいえ，結構です irímaseñ ká - íife, kékkò desu

♦*adj* (not any) 何も...ない naní mò ...náì

I have no money/time/books 私には金(時間，本)がありません watákushi ni wà kané(jikán, hóñ)ga arimaseñ

no other man would have done it 他の人ならだれもしてくれなかったでしょう hoká no hitò nara daré mò sorê wò shité kurenakatta deshò

「*no entry*」立入禁止 tachíirikìnshi

「*no smoking*」禁煙 kiñ-en

♦*n* 反対意見 hañtai ikèn, 反対票 hañtai-

there were 20 noes and one "don't know" 反対意見20に対し，「分からない」は1つだった hañtai ikèn níjù ni tai shi, "wakáranaì" wa hitótsu dattà

nobility [noubil'əti:] *n* (dignity) 気高さ kedákasà; (social class) 貴族 kízòku

noble [nou'bəl] *adj* (person, character: worthy) 気高い kedákaì; (title, family: of high social class) 貴族の kízòku no

nobody [nou'bɑːdi:] *pron* だれも...ない daré mò ...náì

nocturnal [nɑːktəːr'nəl] *adj* (tour, visit) 夜の yórù no, 夜間の yákàn no; (animal) 夜行性の yakõsei no

nod [nɑːd] *vi* (gesture) 頭で合図する atáma dè aízu suru; (*also: nod in agreement*) うなずく unázukù; (doze) うとうとする útòuto suru

♦*vt*: *to nod one's head* うなずく unázukù

♦*n* うなずき unazuki

nod off *vi* 居眠りする inémuri suru

noise [nɔiz] *n* (sound) 音 otó; (din) 騒音 sóon

noisy [nɔi'zi:] *adj* (audience, child, machine) うるさい urúsaì

nomad [nou'mæd] *n* 遊牧民 yúbokumìn

nominal [nɑːm'ənəl] *adj* (leader) 名目上の meímokujõ no; (rent, price) わずかな wázùka na

nominate [nɑːm'əneit] *vt* (propose) 推薦する suísen suru; (appoint) 任命する niñmei suru

nomination [nɑːmənei'ʃən] *n* (proposal) 推薦 suísen; (appointment) 任命 niñmei

nominee [nɑːməni:'] *n* (proposed person) 推薦された人 suísen sareta hitò; (appointed person) 任命された人 niñmei sareta hitò

non... [nɑːn] *prefix* 非... hí..., 無... mú..., 不... fú...

non-alcoholic [nɑːnælkəhɔːl'ik] *adj* アルコールを含まない arúkōru wò fukúmanaì

non-aligned [nɑːnəlaind'] *adj* 非同盟の hidõmei no

nonchalant [nɑ:nʃəlɑ:nt'] *adj* 平然とした heízen to shita

noncommittal [nɑ:nkəmit'əl] *adj* (person, answer) どっちつかずの dotchí tsukazù no

nondescript [nɑ:n'diskript] *adj* (person, clothes, color) 特徴のない tokúchō no naî

none [nʌn] *pron* (person) だれも ...ない daré mò ...náî; (thing) どれも...ない dôrè mo ...náî

none of you あなたたちの1人も...ない anátatàchi no hitóri mò ...náî

I've none left 何も残っていません naní mò nokótte imaseñ

he's none the worse for it それでも彼は大丈夫です soré de mò kare wa daíjōbu desu

nonentity [nɑ:nen'titi:] *n* 取るに足らない人 tôrù ni taránai hitò

nonetheless [nʌn'ðəles'] *adv* それにもかかわらず soré ni mò kakáwarazù, それでもやはり soré de mò yahárî

non-existent [nɑ:nigzis'tənt] *adj* 存在しない soñzai shinaî

non-fiction [nɑ:nfik'ʃən] *n* ノンフィクション noñfikùshon

nonplussed [nɑ:nplʌst'] *adj* 困惑した koñwaku shita, 困った komáttà

nonsense [nɑ:n'sens] *n* でたらめ detárame, ナンセンス náñsensu

nonsense! そんな事はない sofina koto wà naî, ナンセンス náñsensu

non-smoker [nɑ:nsmou'kə:r] *n* タバコを吸わない人 tabáko wò suwánai hitò, 非喫煙者 híkitsueñsha

non-stick [nɑ:nstik'] *adj* (pan, surface) こげつかない kogétsukanaî

non-stop [nɑ:n'stɑ:p'] *adj* (conversation) 止らない tomáranaî; (flight, train) 直行の chokkô no, ノンストップの noñsutoppù no

♦*adv* 止らずに tomárazu ni

noodles [nu:'dəlz] *npl* ヌードル nûdòru

nook [nuk] *n: every nook and cranny* 隅々 sumízùmi

noon [nu:n] *n* 正午 shôgò

no one (*BRIT* **no-one**) *pron* = **nobody**

noose [nu:s] *n* (loop) 引結び hikímusùbi

hangman's noose 絞首刑用の縄 kôshukeiyô no nawà

nor [nɔ:r] *conj* = **neither**

♦*adv see* **neither**

norm [nɔ:rm] *n* (convention) 慣習 kañshū; (rule, requirement) ノルマ nôrùma

normal [nɔ:r'məl] *adj* (usual, ordinary: life, behavior, result) 普通の futsū no; (child: not abnormal) 異常のない ijô no naî, ノーマルな nômàru na

normally [nɔ:r'məli:] *adv* 普通は futsū wa, 普通に futsū ni

north [nɔ:rθ] *n* 北 kitá

♦*adj* 北の kitá no

♦*adv* 北へ kitá e

North America *n* 北米 hokúbei

north-east [nɔ:rθi:st'] *n* 北東 hokútō

northerly [nɔ:r'ðə:rli:] *adj* (point) 北方の hoppô no; (direction) 北方への hoppô e nò

a northerly wind 北からの風 kitá kara nò kazé

northern [nɔ:r'ðə:rn] *adj* 北の kitá no

the northern hemisphere 北半球 kitáhañkyū

Northern Ireland *n* 北アイルランド kitá airurañdo

North Pole *n* 北極 hokkyôku

North Sea *n* 北海 hokkái

northward(s) [nɔ:rθ'wə:rd(z)] *adv* 北へ kitá e

north-west [nɔ:rθwest'] *n* 北西 hokúsei

Norway [nɔ:r'wei] *n* ノルウェー norúuè

Norwegian [nɔ:rwi:'dʒən] *adj* ノルウェーの norúuè no; (LING) ノルウェー語の norúuègo no

♦*n* (person) ノルウェー人 norúuèjìn; (LING) ノルウェー語 norúuègo

nose [nouz] *n* (ANAT, ZOOL) 鼻 haná; (sense of smell) きゅう覚 kyûkaku

♦*vi: nose about* せん索する señsaku suru

nosebleed [nouz'bli:d] *n* 鼻血 hanáji

nose-dive [nouz'daiv] *n* (of plane) 急降下 kyûkôka

nosey [nou'zi:] (*inf*) *adj* = **nosy**

nostalgia [nəstæl'dʒə] *n* 郷愁 kyôshū, ノ

スタルジア nosútarùjia

nostalgic [nəstæl'dʒik] *adj* (person, book, film) 懐かしい natsúkashiǐ

nostril [nɑːs'trəl] *n* (of person, animal) 鼻のあな haná no anà, 鼻孔 bikó

nosy [nou'zi:] (*inf*) *adj* せん索好きな seńsakuzùki na

KEYWORD
---

not [nɑːt] *adv* ...でない ...de naǐ

he is not/isn't here 彼はいません kárè wa imáseǹ

you must not/you mustn't do that それをしてはいけません soré wò shité wà ikémaseǹ

it's too late, isn't it? 遅過ぎますよね osósugimasù yo né, 遅過ぎるでしょう osósugirù deshō

he asked me not to do it それをしないで下さいと彼に頼まれました soré wò shináide kudasaǐ to kárè ni tanómaremashǐta

not that I don't like him/he isn't interesting 彼を嫌い〔面白くない〕というのではないが kárè wo kirái(omóshirokùnai)tò iú no de wa naǐ gá

not yet まだ mádà

not now 今は駄目 ímà wa damé ¶ *see also* **only**

---

notably [nou'təbli:] *adv* (particularly) 特に tókù ni; (markedly) 著しく ichíjirushikù

notary [nou'tə:ri:] *n* 公証人 kôshōnin

notch [nɑːtʃ] *n* (in wood, blade, saw) 刻み目 kizámime, ノッチ notchí

note [nout] *n* (record) 覚書 obóegaki, ノート nôto, メモ mémð; (letter) 短い手紙 mijíkaǐ tegámi; (banknote) 紙幣 shíheǐ, 札 satsú; (MUS) 音符 ońpu; (tone) 音 otó
♦*vt* (observe) ...に気が付く ...ni ki gá tsukù; (write down) 書留める kakítomerù

notebook [nout'buk] *n* 帳面 chômen, ノート nôto

noted [nou'tid] *adj* (famous) 有名な yúmei na

notepad [nout'pæd] *n* メモ用紙 memóyòshi ◊糊などでつづった物を指す norí

notepaper [nout'peipə:r] *n* 便せん biǹsen

nothing [nʌθ'iŋ] *n* (not anything) 何も...ない naní mò ...naǐ; (zero) ゼロ zérð

he does nothing 彼は何もしない kárè wa naní mò shináǐ

nothing new/much/special 目新しい〔大した,特別な〕ことはない meátarashiǐ〔tàǐshita, tokúbetsu nà〕kotó wa naǐ

for nothing (free) 無料で muryó de, ただで tádà ḍe; (in vain) 無駄に mudá ni

notice [nou'tis] *n* (announcement) 通知 tsúchi; (warning) 通告 tsúkoku; (dismissal) 解雇通知 kaíkotsùchi; (resignation) 辞表 jihyô; (period of time) 予告 yokóku
♦*vt* (observe) ...に気が付く ...ni ki gá tsukù

to bring something to someone's notice (attention) ...を...に知らせる ...wo ...ni shiráserù

to take notice of ...に気が付く ...ni ki gá tsukù

at short notice 急に kyú ni

until further notice 追って通知があるまで otté tsúchi ga aru madè

to hand in one's notice 辞表を出す jihyô wò dásù

noticeable [nou'tisəbəl] *adj* (mark, effect) はっきりした hakkírì shita

noticeboard [nou'tisbɔːrd] (*BRIT*) *n* 掲示板 keíjiban

notify [nou'təfai] *vt*: *to notify someone (of something)* (...を)...に知らせる (...wo)...ni shiráserù

notion [nou'ʃən] *n* (idea) 考え kańgaè, 概念 gáǐnen; (opinion) 意見 íkèn

notorious [noutɔːr'iːəs] *adj* (criminal, liar, place) 悪名高い akúmeitakaǐ

notwithstanding [nɑːtwiθstæn'diŋ] *adv* ...にもかかわらず ...ní mò kakáwarazù
♦*prep* ...にもかかわらず ...ní mò kakáwarazù

nougat [nuː'gət] *n* ヌガー núgà ◊クルミなどの入ったキャラメル風のお菓子 kurúmi nadò no haǐtta kyarámerufù no okáshì

nought [nɔ:t] n = **naught**

noun [naun] n 名詞 meíshi

nourish [nəːr'iʃ] vt (feed) 養う yashínaù; (fig: foster) 心中にはぐくむ shíñchū ni hagúkumù

nourishing [nəːr'iʃiŋ] adj (food) 栄養のある eíyō no arù

nourishment [nəːr'iʃmənt] n (food) 栄養 eíyō

novel [nɑ:v'əl] n 小説 shōsetsu
♦adj (new, fresh: idea, approach) 目新しい meátarashiì, 新鮮な shiñsen na

novelist [nɑːv'əlist] n 小説家 shōsetsuka

novelty [nɑːv'əlti:] n (newness) 新鮮さ shiñsensa; (object) 変ったもの kawátta monð

November [nouvem'bəːr] n 11月 júichigatsu

novice [nɑːv'is] n (beginner) 初心者 shoshíñsha; (REL) 修練者 shúreñsha

now [nau] adv 今 ímà
♦conj: now (that) ...であるから ...de árù kara
right now (immediately) 今すぐ ímà súgù; (at the moment) 今の所 imá no tokoro
by now 今ごろはもう imágoro wà mõ
just now 今の所 imá no tokoro
now and then, now and again 時々 tokídoki
from now on 今後 kőñgo

nowadays [nau'ədeiz] adv このごろ(は) konőgoro (wa)

nowhere [nou'weːr] adv (be, go) どこにも...ない dőkò ni mo ...náì

nozzle [nɑːz'əl] n (of hose, fire extinguisher etc) ノズル nőzùru; (of vacuum cleaner) 吸口 suíkuchi

nuance [nuː'ɑːnts] n ニュアンス nyúañsu

nubile [nuː'bail] adj (woman) セクシーな sékùshī na

nuclear [nuː'kli:əːr] adj (fission, weapons) 核... kákù...
the nuclear industry 原子力産業界 geñshiryoku sangyőkai
nuclear physics 原始物理学 geñshibutsurigàku, 核物理学 kakúbutsurigàku
nuclear power 原子力 geñshiryòku

nucleus [nuː'kli:əs] (pl **nuclei**) n (of atom, cell) 核 kákù; (of group) 中心 chúshin

nude [nuːd] adj 裸の hadáka no
♦n ヌード nûdo
in the nude (naked) 裸で hadáka de

nudge [nʌdʒ] vt (person) 小突く kozúkù

nudist [nuː'dist] n 裸体主義者 ratáishugishà, ヌーディスト nûdisùto

nudity [nuː'diti:] n 裸 hadáka

nuisance [nuː'səns] n (state of affairs) 厄介な事情 yákkaì na jijő; (thing) 厄介な物 yákkaì na monő; (person: irritating) 迷惑な人 meíwaku na hitð
what a nuisance! 困ったもんだ komátta moñ da

null [nʌl] adj: **null and void** (contract, agreement) 無効な mukő na

numb [nʌm] adj: **numb (with)** (with cold etc) ...でしびれた ...de shibíretà; (fig: with fear etc) ...で気が動転した ...de ki ga dőten shitā

number [nʌm'bəːr] n (MATH) 数字 sūji; (quantity) 数 kázù; (of house, bank account etc) 番号 bañgő
♦vt (pages etc) ...に番号を付ける ...ni bañgő wo tsukérù; (amount to) 総数は...である sősū wa ...de árù
to be numbered among ...の1人である ...no hitőrì de árù
a number of (several) 数...の sū... no
they were ten in number (people) 彼らは10人だった kárèra wa júnìn datta; (things) 10個あった júkkð atta

number plate (BRIT) n (AUT) ナンバープレート nañbāpurēto

numeral [nuː'məːrəl] n 数詞 sūshi

numerate [nuː'məreit] adj 数学ができる súgaku gà dekírù

numerical [nuːmeː'ikəl] adj (value) 数字で表した sūji dè aráwashità; (order) 数字の sūji no

numerous [nuː'məːrəs] adj (many, countless) 多くの őkù no, 多数の tasū no

nun [nʌn] n (Christian) 修道女 shúdðjo; (Buddhist) 尼 ámà

nurse [nəːrs] n (in hospital) 看護婦 kañgofù; (also: **nursemaid**) 保母 hóbð

♦*vt* (patient) 看護する kángo suru; (baby) ...に乳を飲ませる ...ni chichí wŏ nomáserù

nursery [nəːrˈsəːriː] *n* (institution) 保育園 hoíkuèn; (room) 育児室 ikújishìtsu; (for plants: commercial establishment) 種苗園 shubyóèn

nursery rhyme *n* 童謡 dóyō

nursery school *n* 保育園 hoíkuèn

nursery slope (*BRIT*) *n* (SKI) 初心者用ゲレンデ shoshínshayŏ gerènde

nursing [nəːrsˈiŋ] *n* (profession) 看護職 kaňgoshòku; (care) 看病 kaňbyŏ

nursing home *n* (*gen*) 療養所 ryŏyòjo; (for old people) 老人ホーム rŏjinhòmu

nursing mother *n* 授乳している母親 junyû shite irù haháoya

nurture [nəːrˈtʃəːr] *vt* (child, plant) 育てる sodáterù

nut [nʌt] *n* (TECH) ナット náttò; (BOT) 木ノ実 kínòmi(kónòmi), ナッツ náttsù

nutcracker [nʌtˈkrækəːr] *npl* クルミ割り kurúmiwarì

nutmeg [nʌtˈmeg] *n* ニクズク nikúzùku, ナツメグ natsúmeggù ◇香辛料の一種 kŏshìnryŏ no fsshù

nutrient [nuːˈtriːənt] *n* 養分 yóbùn

nutrition [nuːtriʃˈən] *n* (diet, nourishment) 栄養 efyŏ; (proteins, vitamins etc) 養分 yóbùn

nutritious [nuːtriʃˈəs] *adj* (food) 栄養価の高い efyŏka no takáì

nuts [nʌts] (*inf*) *adj* 頭がおかしい atáma gà okáshiì

nutshell [nʌtˈʃel] *n* クルミの殻 kurúmi no karà

in a nutshell (*fig*) 簡単に言えば kańtan nì iébà

nylon [naiˈlɑːn] *n* ナイロン náìron

♦*adj* ナイロンの náìron no

O

oak [ouk] *n* オーク ŏkù

♦*adj* (table) オークの ŏkù no

O.A.P. [oueipiːˈ] (*BRIT*) *n abbr* = **old-age pensioner**

oar [ɔːr] *n* かい kaî, オール ŏrú

oasis [oueiˈsis] (*pl* **oases**) *n* (in desert) オアシス oáshìsu

oath [ouθ] *n* (promise) 誓い chikái; (swear word) 悪態 akútaì

under or *on* (*BRIT*) *oath* 宣誓して seňsei shite

oatmeal [outˈmiːl] *n* オートミール ŏtómìru

oats [outs] *n* カラスムギ karásumugì

obedience [oubiːˈdiːəns] *n* 服従 fukújū

obedient [oubiːˈdiːənt] *adj* (child, dog etc) 素直な sunáo na, よく言う事を聞く yokú iú koto wo kikú

obesity [oubiːˈsitiː] *n* 肥満 himán

obey [oubeiˈ] *vt* (instructions, person) ...に従う ...ni shitágau; (regulations) 守る mamóru

obituary [oubitʃˈuːeːriː] *n* 死亡記事 shibŏkijì

object [*n* ɑːbˈdʒikt *vt* əbdʒektˈ] *n* (thing) 物 monó; (aim, purpose) 目的 mokúteki; (of affection, desires) 対象 taishō; (LING) 目的語 mokútekigo

♦*vi*: *to object to* ...に反対する ...ni haňtai suru

to object that ...だと言って反対する ...da to ittě haňtai suru

expense is no object 費用にはこだわらない hiyŏ ni wa kodáwaranaî

I object! 反対です haňtai dèsu

objection [əbdʒekˈʃən] *n* 異議 igì

I have no objection to ... ...に異議はありません ...ni gì iwa arímasèn

objectionable [əbdʒekˈʃənəbəl] *adj* (person, language, conduct) いやな iyá na

objective [əbdʒekˈtiv] *adj* (impartial: person, information) 客観的な kyákùkanteki na

♦*n* (aim, purpose) 目的 mokúteki

obligation [ɑːbləgeiˈʃən] *n* (duty, commitment) 義務 gimù

without obligation (COMM) 買う義務なしで kaú gimù nashi de

obligatory [əblígˈətɔːriː] *adj* 強制的な kyŏseiteki na

oblige [əblaidʒˈ] *vt* (force): *to oblige someone to do something* 強制的に

...に..をさせる kyōseiteki ni ...ni ...wo
saserù; (do a favor for) ...の頼みを聞く
...no tanómi wo kikú
to be obliged to someone for something (grateful) ...の事で...に感謝してい
る ...no kotó de ...ni kañsha shité irù

obliging [əblai'dʒiŋ] *adj* (helpful) 親切な
shínsetsu na

oblique [əbli:k'] *adj* (line) 斜めの nanáme
no; (comment, reference) 間接的な kañsetsuteki na

obliterate [əblit'əːreit] *vt* 跡形もなくす
る atókata mo nakúsuru

oblivion [əbliv'i:ən] *n* (unawareness) 無
意識 muíshìki; (being forgotten) 忘却 bō-
kyaku

oblivious [əbliv'i:əs] *adj*: *oblivious of/
to* ...を意識していない ...wo ishíki shité
inai

oblong [ɑːb'lɔːŋ] *adj* 長方形の chōhōkei
no
◆*n* 長方形 chōhōkei

obnoxious [əbnɑːk'ʃəs] *adj* (unpleasant:
behavior, person) 不愉快な fuyúkài na;
(: smell) いやな iyá na

oboe [ou'bou] *n* オーボエ ōboe

obscene [əbsi:n'] *adj* (gesture, remark,
behavior) わいせつな waísetsu na

obscenity [əbsen'iti:] *n* (of book, behavior etc) わいせつ waísetsu; (offensive
word) 卑語 hígo

obscure [əbskju:r'] *adj* (little known:
place, author etc) 無名の muméi no; (difficult to understand) 難解な nañkai na
◆*vt* (obstruct: view, sun etc) 覆い隠す
ōíkakusù; (conceal: truth, meaning etc)
隠す kakúsù

obsequious [əbsi:'kwi:əs] *adj* ぺこぺこす
る pekòpeko suru

observance [əbzəːr'vəns] *n* (of law) 遵守
juñshu; (of custom) 守る事 mamórù koto

observant [əbzəːr'vənt] *adj* (person) 観
察力の優れた kañsatsuryòku no sugure-
ta; (remark) 鋭い surúdoì

observation [ɑːbzəːrvei'ʃən] *n* (remark)
意見 ikèn; (act of observing) 観察 kañsatsu; (MED) 監視 kañshi

observatory [əbzəːr'vətɔːri:] *n* 観測所

kañsokujo

observe [əbzəːrv'] *vt* (watch) 観察する
kañsatsu suru; (comment) 意見を述べる
ikèn wo nobérù; (abide by: rule) 守る
mamórù, 遵守する juñshu suru

observer [əbzəːr'vəːr] *n* 観察者 kañsa-
tsushà

obsess [əbses'] *vt* ...に取付く ...ni torítsu-
ku

obsession [əbseʃ'ən] *n* 強迫観念 kyōha-
kukannen

obsessive [əbses'iv] *adj* (person, tendency, behavior) 妄想に取付かれた様な
mōsō ni torítsukareta yō na

obsolescence [ɑːbsəles'əns] *n* 旧式化
kyūshikika

obsolete [ɑːbsəli:t'] *adj* (out of use: word
etc) 廃れた sutáreta; (: machine etc) 旧式
の kyūshiki no

obstacle [ɑːb'stəkəl] *n* (obstruction) 障害
物 shōgaibutsù; (*fig*: problem, difficulty)
障害 shōgai

obstacle race *n* 障害物競走 shōgaibu-
tsukyōsō

obstetrics [əbstet'riks] *n* 産科 sañka

obstinate [ɑːb'stənit] *adj* (determined:
person, resistance) 頑固な gañko na

obstruct [əbstrʌkt'] *vt* (block) ふさぐ fuságu; (*fig*: hinder) 妨害する bōgai suru

obstruction [əbstrʌk'ʃən] *n* (action) 妨
害 bōgai; (object) 障害物 shōgaibutsu

obtain [əbtein'] *vt* (get) 手に入れる te nì
iréru, 獲得する kakútoku suru; (achieve)
達成する tasséi suru

obtainable [əbtein'əbəl] *adj* (object) 入
手できる nyūshu dekírù

obvious [ɑːb'vi:əs] *adj* (clear) 明かな akíràka na; (self-evident) 分かり切った wa-
kárikitta

obviously [ɑːb'vi:əsli:] *adv* 明らかに akíràka ni
obviously not 明らかに...でない akíraka ni ...de nai

occasion [əkei'ʒən] *n* (point in time) 時
tokí, 時点 jitén; (event, celebration etc)
行事 gyōji, イベント ibénto; (opportunity) 機会 kikái, チャンス chañsu

occasional [əkei'ʒənəl] *adj* (infrequent)

時々の tokídokì no

occasionally [əkei'ʒənəli:] *adv* 時々 to-kídokì

occult [əkʌlt'] *n*: *the occult* 超自然 chô-shizen, オカルト okárùto

occupant [ɑːk'jəpənt] *n* (long-term: of house etc) 居住者 kyojūshà; (of office etc) テナント tenánto; (temporary: of car, room etc) 中にいる人 nakà ni irù hitô

occupation [ɑːkjəpei'ʃən] *n* (job) 職業 shokúgyò; (pastime) 趣味 shumì; (of building, country etc) 占領 señryō

occupational hazard [ɑːkjəpei'ʃənəl-] *n* 職業上の危険 shokúgyōjō no kikén

occupier [ɑːk'jəpaiəːr] *n* 居住者 kyojū-shà

occupy [ɑːk'jəpai] *vt* (inhabit: house) ...に住む ...ni sumù; (take: seat, place etc) ...に居る ...ni irú; (take over: building, country etc) 占領する señryō suru; (take up: time) ...が掛る ...ga kakárù; (: attention) 奪う ubáù; (: space) 取る torù

   to occupy oneself in doing (to be busy with) ...に専念する ...ni sénnen suru

occur [əkəːr'] *vi* (event: take place) 起る okórù; (phenomenon: exist) 存在する soñzai suru

   to occur to someone ...の頭に浮ぶ ...no atáma ni ukábu

occurrence [əkəːr'əns] *n* (event) 出来事 dekígoto; (existence) 存在 soñzai

ocean [ou'ʃən] *n* 海 umì

   Indian Ocean インド洋 iñdoyō ¶ *see also* **Atlantic; Pacific**

ocean-going [ou'ʃəngouiŋ] *adj* 外洋の gaíyō no

ocher [ou'kəːr] (*BRIT*: **ochre**) *adj* (color) 黄土色の ōdòiro no, オークルの ōkùru no

o'clock [əklɑːk'] *adv*: *it is 5 o'clock* 5時です gojì desu

OCR [ousiɑːr'] *n abbr* (COMPUT: = *optical character recognition*) 光学読取り kōgakuyomitorì (: = *optical character reader*) 光学読取り装置 kōgakuyomisō-chì

octagonal [ɑːktæg'ənəl] *adj* 八角形の hákkakukèi no

octave [ɑːk'tiv] *n* (MUS) オクターブ o-kútābù

October [ɑːktou'bəːr] *n* 10月 jūgatsu

octopus [ɑːk'təpəs] *n* タコ takò

odd [ɑːd] *adj* (strange: person, behavior, expression) 変な heñ na, 妙な myō na; (uneven: number) 奇数の kísū no; (not paired: sock, glove, shoe etc) 片方の kátahò no

   60-odd 60幾つ rokújū ikutsu

   at odd times 時々 tokídokì

   to be the odd one out 例外である reígai de aru

oddity [ɑːd'iti:] *n* (person) 変り者 kawa-rimono; (thing) 変った物 kawatta mono

odd-job man [ɑːdʒɑːb'-] *n* 便利屋 beñriya

odd jobs *npl* 雑用 zatsúyō

oddly [ɑːd'li:] *adv* (strangely: behave, dress) 変な風に heñ na fū ni ¶ *see also* **enough**

oddments [ɑːd'mənts] *npl* (COMM) 残り物 nokórimono

odds [ɑːdz] *npl* (in betting) かけ率 kaké-rìtsu, オッズ ozzū

   it makes no odds 構いません kamáî-masen

   at odds 仲たがいして nakátagàishite

odds and ends *npl* 半端物 hañpamono

ode [oud] *n* しょう歌 shōkà, オード ōdō

odious [ou'di:əs] *adj* 不快な fukái na

odometer [oudɑːm'itəːr] *n* 走行距離計 sōkōkyorikeì

odor [ou'dəːr] (*BRIT* **odour**) *n* (smell) におい níòi; (: unpleasant) 悪臭 akúshū

KEYWORD

of [ʌv] *prep* 1 (gen) ...の ...nò

   the history of France フランスの歴史 furánsu nò rekíshi

   a friend of ours 私たちのある友達 wa-tákushitàchi no árù tomódachi

   a boy of 10 10才の少年 jússai no shṍnen

   that was kind of you ご親切にどうも go-shíñsetsu ni dṑmo

   a man of great ability 才能抜群の人 saínō batsugùn no hitô

the city of New York ニューヨーク市 nyúyōkushì

south of Glasgow グラスゴーの南 gurásugồ no mínámi

2 (expressing quantity, amount, dates etc): *a kilo of flour* 小麦粉1キロ komúgiko ichíkiro

how much of this do you need? これはどのぐらい要りますか koré wà donó gurai irimasù ká

there were 3 of them (people) 3人いました sańnin imáshìta; (objects) 3個ありました sáñko arímashìta

3 of us went 私たちの内から3人行きました watákushitàchi no uchí karà sáńnin ikímashìta

the number of road accidents is increasing 交通事故の数が増えています kồtsūjikồ no kázù ga fúete imásù

a cup of tea お茶1杯 o-chá ippài

a vase of flowers 花瓶に生けた花 kabín nì íkèta haná

the 5th of July 7月5日 shichígatsu itsúkà

the winter of 1987 1987年の冬 señkyūhyakuhachíjūnánàneñ no fuyú

3 (from, out of): *a bracelet of solid gold* 純金の腕輪 juñkín nò udéwa

a statue of marble 大理石の彫像 daírisèki no chồzồ

made of wood 木製の mokúsei no

KEYWORD

off [ɔːf] *adv* 1 (referring to distance, time) 離れて hanárète

it's a long way off あれは遠い aré wà tồi

the game is 3 days off 試合は3日先です shiái wà mikká saki desù

2 (departure) 出掛けて dekáketè

to go off to Paris/Italy パリ〔イタリア〕へ出掛ける párì〔itária〕de dekárerù

I must be off そろそろ出掛けます sorósoro dekákemasù

3 (removal) 外して hazúshitè

to take off one's hat/coat/clothes 帽子〔コート, 服〕を脱ぐ bốshi〔kồto, fukú〕wo núgù

the button came off ボタンが取れた botán gà tốrèta

10% off (COMM) 10パーセント引き juppásentobiki

4 (not at work: on holiday) 休暇中で kyúkachū dè; (: due to sickness) 欠勤して kekkín shitè

I'm off on Fridays 私の休みは金曜日です watákushi nò yasúmi wa kiñ-yồbi desu

he was off on Friday (on holiday) 金曜日には彼は休みでした kiñ-yồbi ni wa kárè wa yasúmi deshìta; (sick etc) 金曜日には彼は欠勤しました kiñ-yồbi ni wa kárè wa kékkin shimashìta

to have a day off (from work) 1日の休みを取る ichínichi nò yasúmi wồ tồrù

to be off sick 病欠する byồketsu suru

♦*adj* 1 (not turned on: machine, engine, water, gas etc) 止めてある tomête arù; (: tap) 締めてある shimête arù; (: light) 消してある keshíte arù

2 (cancelled: meeting, match, agreement) 取消された toríkesàreta

3 (BRIT: not fresh: milk, cheese, meat etc) 悪くなった wárùku natta

4: *on the off chance* (just in case) ...の場合に備えて ...no baái ni sonaete

to have an off day (not as good as usual) 厄日である yakúbì de árù

♦*prep* 1 (indicating motion, removal etc) ...から ...kárà

to fall off a cliff 崖から落ちる gakè karà ochírù

the button came off my coat コートのボタンが取れた kồtồ no botán gà tốrèta

to take a picture off the wall 壁に掛けてある絵を降ろす kabè nì kákète aru é wồ orósù

2 (distant from) ...から離れて ...kárà hanárète

it's just off the M1 国道M1を降りて直ぐの所にあります kokúdō emúwañ wo ồrìte súgù no tokórồ ni arímasù

it's 5 km off the main road 幹線道路から5キロの所にあります kañsendồro

kara gókìro no tokórò ni arímasù

an island off the coast 沖合の島 okí-ai nò shimá

to be off meat (no longer eat it) 肉をやめている nikú wð yaméte irù; (no longer like it) 肉が嫌いになっている nikú gà kirái nì natté irù

offal [ɔː'fəl] *n* (CULIN) もつ motsù

off-color [ɔː'kʌl'əːr] (*BRIT* **off-colour**) *adj* (ill) 病気の byôki no

offend [əfend'] *vt* (upset: person) 怒らせる okóraserù

offender [əfen'dəːr] *n* (criminal) 犯罪者 hañzaísha, 犯人 hañnin, ...犯 ...hañ

offense [əfens'] (*BRIT* **offence**) *n* (crime) 犯罪 hañzaí

to take offense at ...に怒る ...ni okórù

offensive [əfen'siv] *adj* (remark, gesture, behavior) 侮辱的な bujôkuteki na; (smell etc) いやな iyá na; (weapon) 攻撃用の kôgekiyō no

♦*n* (MIL) 攻撃 kôgeki

offer [ɔː'fəːr] *n* (proposal: to help etc) 申出 môshide; (: to buy) 申込み môshikomi

♦*vt* (advice, help, information) ...すると申出る ...surú to môshideru; (opportunity, service, product) 提供する teíkyo suru

on offer (*BRIT*: COMM) 値下げ品で neságehin de

offering [ɔː'fəːriŋ] *n* (of a company: product) 売物 urímono; (REL) 供物 sonáemono

off-hand [ɔː'hænd'] *adj* (behavior etc) いい加減な ikágen na

♦*adv* 即座に sokúza ni

office [ɔː'fis] *n* (place) 事務所 jimúshò, オフィス ofisu; (room) 事務室 jimúshìtsu; (position) 職 shoku

doctor's office (*US*) 医院 ìn

to take office 職に就く shokú ni tsuku

office automation *n* オフィスオートメーション ofisu ōtōmêshon

office building (*BRIT* **office block**) *n* オフィスビル offsubiru

office hours *npl* (COMM) 業務時間 gyômujikan; (*US*: MED) 診察時間 shiñsatsujikan

officer [ɔː'fisəːr] *n* (MIL etc) 将校 shôkò; (*also*: **police officer**) 警官 keíkan; (of organization) 役員 yakúin

office worker *n* 事務員 jimúin

official [əfiʃ'əl] *adj* (authorized) 公認の kônin no; (visit, invitation, letter etc) 公式の kôshiki no

♦*n* (in government) 役人 yakúnin; (in trade union etc) 役員 yakúin

official residence 官邸 kañtei

officialdom [əfiʃ'əldəm] (*pej*) *n* 官僚の世界 kañryō no sekái

officiate [əfiʃ'iːeit] *vi* 司会する shikái suru

officious [əfiʃ'əs] *adj* (person, behavior) 差出がましい sashídegamashii

offing [ɔː'fiŋ] *n*: *in the offing* (*fig*: imminent) 差迫って sashísemattè

off-licence [ɔː'laisəns] *BRIT n* (shop selling alcohol) 酒屋 sakáya

off-line [ɔː'lain'] *adj* (COMPUT) オフラインの ofúrain no

♦*adv* オフラインで ofúrain de

off-peak [ɔː'piːk'] *adj* (heating) オフピークの ofúpīku no; (train, ticket) 混んでいない時の koñde inai tokí no

off-putting [ɔː'put'iŋ] (*BRIT*) *adj* (person, remark etc) 気を悪くさせる kì wo warúku saseru

off-season [ɔː'siːzən] *adj* (holiday, ticket) オフシーズンの ofúshīzun no

♦*adv* (travel, book etc) オフシーズンに ofúshīzun ni

offset [ɔː'fset'] (*pt, pp* **offset**) *vt* (counteract) 補う ogínaù

offshoot [ɔː'fʃuːt] *n* (*fig*) 副産物 fukúsañbutsu

offshore [ɔː'fʃɔːr'] *adj* (breeze) 陸からの rikú kara no; (oilrig, fishing) 沖合の okí-ai no

offside [ɔː'fsaid'] *adj* (SPORT) オフサイドの ofúsaido no; (AUT: with right-hand drive) 右の migí no; (: with left-hand drive) 左の hidári no

offspring [ɔː'fspriŋ] *n inv* 子孫 shisón

offstage [ɔː'fsteidʒ'] *adv* 舞台裏に〔で〕 butáiura ni〔de〕

off-the-rack [ɔːfˈðəræk'] (*BRIT* **off-the-peg**) *adj* (clothing) 出来合いの dekíai no, 既製の kiséi no

off-white [ɔːfˈwait] *adj* (grayish white) 灰色がかった白の haíirogakatta shirð no; (yellowish white) 黄色がかった白の kiírogakatta shirð no

often [ɔːfˈən] *adv* (frequently) よく yokù, しょっちゅう shotchū, 度々 tabítabi
how often do you go? どのぐらい行きますか donð gurai ikímasu ká

ogle [ouˈgəl] *vt* 色目で見る irðmè de mirù

oh [ou] *excl* あっ át

oil [ɔil] *n* (*gen*) 油 abúra, オイル oíru; (CULIN) サラダ油 sarádayu; (petroleum) 石油 sekíyu; (crude) 原油 geñyu; (for heating) 石油 sekíyu, 灯油 tðyu
◆*vt* (lubricate: engine, gun, machine) ...に油を差す ...ni abúra wo sasù

oilcan [ɔil'kæn] *n* 油差し abúrasashi

oilfield [ɔil'fiːld] *n* 油田 yudén

oil filter *n* (AUT) オイルフィルター oírufirutå

oil painting *n* 油絵 abúrae

oil refinery [-riːfainˈəːriː] *n* 精油所 seíyujo

oil rig *n* 石油掘削装置 sekíyu kússakusōchi

oilskins [ɔil'skinz] *npl* 防水服 bðsuifuku

oil tanker *n* (ship) オイルタンカー oírutankā; (truck) タンクローリー tañkurðrī

oil well *n* 油井 yuséi

oily [ɔi'liː] *adj* (rag) 油染みた abúrajimità; (substance) 油の様な abúra no yð na; (food) 脂っこい abúrakkoi

ointment [ɔint'mənt] *n* 軟こう nañkō

O.K., okay [oukei'] (*inf*) *excl* (agreement: alright) よろしい yoróshii, オーケー ōkè; (: don't fuss) 分かったよ wakáttà yo
◆*adj* (average: film, book, meal etc) まあまあの māmā no
◆*vt* (approve) 承認する shðnin suru

old [ould] *adj* (aged: person) 年寄の toshíyori no; (: thing) 古い furúì; (former: school, home etc) 元の motð no, 前の maè no

how old are you? お幾つですか o-íkutsu desu ká
he's 10 years old 彼は10才です karè wa jussái desu

older brother (one's own) 兄 ani; (of person spoken to) お兄さん o-níisan; (of third party) 兄さん níisan

old age *n* 老齢 rðrei

old-age pensioner [ould'eidʒ-] (*BRIT*) *n* 年金で生活している老人 neñkin dè seíkatsu surù rðjìn, 年金暮しの人 neñkingurashi no hitð

old-fashioned [ould'fæʃ'ənd] *adj* (style, design) 時代遅れの jidáiokùre no, 古くさい furúkusai; (person, values) 保守的な hoshùteki na

olive [ɑːl'iv] *n* (fruit) オリーブ oríbù; (*also*: **olive tree**) オリーブの木 oríbù no ki
◆*adj* (*also*: **olive-green**) オリーブ色の o-ríbùiro no

olive oil *n* オリーブ油 oríbùyu

Olympic [oulim'pik] *adj* 五輪の gorín no, オリンピックの orínpikkù no

Olympic Games *npl*: *the Olympic Games* 五輪 gorín, オリンピック orínpikkù
the Olympics 五輪 gorín, オリンピック orínpikkù

omelet(te) [ɑːm'lit] *n* オムレツ omúretsu

omen [ou'mən] *n* (sign) 兆し kizáshi, 前触れ maébure

ominous [ɑːm'ənəs] *adj* (worrying) 不気味な bukìmi na

omission [oumiʃ'ən] *n* 省略 shðryaku

omit [oumit'] *vt* (deliberately) 省略する shðryaku suru; (by mistake) うっかりして抜かす ukkárì shite nukásu

---

KEYWORD

---

on [ɑːn] *prep* **1** (indicating position) ...(の上)に(で) ...(no uè) ni(de)
on the wall 壁に kabé ni
it's on the table テーブル(の上)にあります tèburu (no uè) nì arímasù
on the left 左に hidári nì
the house is on the main road 家は幹線道路に面しています iè wà kañsendòro

ni mén shite imásu

2 (indicating means, method, condition etc) ...で ...dè

on foot (go, be) 歩いて arúite

on the train/plane (go) 電車〔飛行機〕で dénsha〔hikṓki〕de; (be) 電車〔飛行機〕に乗って dénsha〔hikṓki〕ni notté

on the telephone/radio/television 電話〔ラジオ，テレビ〕で dénwa〔rájio, térèbi〕de

she's on the telephone 彼女は電話しています〔電話中です〕kánòjo wa dénwa ni détè imasu〔deṅwachū desù〕

I heard it on the radio/saw him on television 私はラジオで聞きました〔テレビで彼を見ました〕watákushi wà rájio o kikímashìta〔térèbi de kárè wo mimáshita〕

to be on drugs 麻薬をやっている mayáku wò yatté irú

to be on holiday 休暇中である kyūka-chū de arù

to be away on business 商用で出掛けている shṓyō dè dekákete irù

3 (referring to time) ...に ...ni

on Friday 金曜日に kiń-yòbi ni

on Fridays 金曜日に kiń-yòbi ni, 毎週金曜日に maíshū kiń-yòbi ni, 金曜日毎に kiń-yòbi gótò ni

on June 20th 6月20日に rokúgatsu hatsúka ni

on Friday, June 20th 6月20日金曜日に rokúgatsu hatsúka ni kiń-yòbi ni

a week on Friday 来週の金曜日に raíshū nò kiń-yòbi ni

on arrival he went straight to his hotel 到着すると彼は真っ直ぐにホテルへ行きました tṓchaku suru tò kárè wa massúgù ni hótèru e ikímashìta

on seeing this これを見ると koré wò mírù to

4 (about, concerning) ...について ...ni tsuíte, ...に関して ...ni káń shite

information on train services 列車に関する情報 resshá nì kań surù jṓhō

a book on physics 物理の本 bútsùri no hóñ

♦*adv* **1** (referring to dress) 身につけて mi ní tsukète

to have one's coat on コートを着ている kṓto wo kité irù

what's she got on? 彼女は何を着ていますか kánòjo wa náni wo kité imasù ká

she put her boots/gloves/hat on 彼女はブーツを履いた〔手袋をはめた，帽子をかぶった〕kánòjo wa būtsu wo haíta〔tebúkuro wò haméta, bṓshi wo kabútta〕

2 (referring to covering): *screw the lid on tightly* ふたをしっかり締めて下さい futá wò shikkárì shímète kudásaì

3 (further, continuously) 続けて tsuzúkete

to walk/drive/go on 歩き〔車で走り，行き〕続ける arúkì〔kuruma dè hashíri, ikí〕tsuzukéru

to read on 読み続ける yomítsuzukèru

♦*adj* **1** (functioning, in operation: machine) 動いている ugóite irù; (: radio, TV, light) ついている tsuíte iru; (: faucet) 水が出ている mizú gà deté irù; (: brakes) かかっている kakátte irù; (: meeting) 続いている tsuzúite irù

is the meeting still on? (in progress) まだ会議中ですか mádà kaígichū desù ká; (not cancelled) 会議は予定通りにやるんですか káìgi wa yotéi dòri ni yarún desù ká

there's a good film on at the cinema 映画館で今いい映画をやっています eígakàn de ímà iì eíga wò yatté imasù

2: *that's not on!* (*inf*: of behavior) それはいけません soré wà ikémaseñ

once [wʌns] *adv* (on one occasion) 一度 ichído, 一回 ikkái; (formerly) 前は maè wa, かつて katsúte

♦*conj* (immediately afterwards) ...した後 ...shitá ato, ...してから ...shité kara

once he had left/it was done 彼が出て〔事が済んで〕から kare ga detè〔kotó ga suṅde〕kara

at once (immediately) 直ちに tadáchi ni, 直ぐに sugù ni; (simultaneously) 同時に dṓji ni

once a week 週一回 shū ikkái

once more もう一度 mố ichído

once and for all 断然 dañzen

once upon a time 昔々 mukáshi mukashi

oncoming [ɑːnˈkʌmiŋ] *adj* (approaching: traffic etc) 向ってくる mukátte kurú

KEYWORD

one [wʌn] *num* 一（の）ichí (no), 1つ（の）hitótsu (no)

one hundred and fifty 150 hyakúgojū

I asked for two coffees, not one 注文したのは1つじゃなくて2つのコーヒーです chūmon shita no wà hitótsu jànakutè futátsu nò kốhī desu

one day there was a sudden knock at the door ある日突然だれかがドアをノックした árù hi totsúzen dárèka ga dóà wo nókkù shita

one by one 1つずつ hitótsu zùtsu

◆*adj* **1** (sole) ただ一つの tádà hitótsu no, 唯一の yúītsu no

it's the one book which interests me 私が興味を感じる唯一の本です watákushi gà kyốmi wo kañjiru yúītsu no hốn desu

that is my one worry 私が心配しているのはそれだけです watákushi gà shiñpai shite iru nò wa soré dake dèsu

the one man who ... ...する唯一の人 ...suru yúītsu no hitó

2 (same) 同じ onájì

they came in the one car 彼らは皆同じ車で来ました kárèra wa mínà onáji kurùma de kimáshìta

they all belong to the one family 彼らは皆身内です kárèra wa mínà miúchi desù

◆*pron* **1** 物 monó

this one これ koré

that one それ soré, あれ aré

I've already got one/a red one 私は既に1つ（赤いのを）持っています watákushi wà súdè ni hitótsù (akái nò wo) mốttè imasu

2: *one another* お互いに o-tágai nì

do you two ever see one another? お二人は付合っていますか o-fútàri wa tsu-

kíattè imasu ká

the boys didn't dare look at one another 少年たちはあえて顔を合せる事ができなかった shốnentàchi wa áète kaố wò awáseru kotò ga dekínakattà

3 (impersonal): *one never knows* どうなるか分かりませんね dố naru ka wakárimaseñ nế

to cut one's finger 指を切る yubí wò kírù

one needs to eat 人は食べる必要がある hitő wa tabérù hitsúyō ga arù

one-day excursion [wʌnˈdei-] (*US*) *n* (day return) 日帰り往復券 higáeri ốfukuken

one-man [wʌnˈmæn] *adj* (business) 1人だけの hitóri dake no, ワンマンの wañman no

one-man band *n* ワンマンバンド wañmanbando

one-off [wʌnˈɔːf] (*BRIT*: *inf*) *n* 一つだけの物 hitótsù dake no mono

KEYWORD

oneself [wʌnselfˈ] *pron* (reflexive) 自分自身を jibúnjishìn wo; (after prep) 自分自身に jibúnjishìn ni; (alone: often after prep) 自分一人で jibún hitóri de; (emphatic) 自分で jibún dè

to hurt oneself けがする kegá surù

to keep something for oneself 自分のために...を取って置く jibún no tamè ni ...wò tóttè oku

to talk to oneself 独り言を言う hitórigotò wo iú

one-sided [wʌnˈsaidid] *adj* (argument) 一方的な ippốteki na

one-to-one [wʌnˈtəwʌnˈ] *adj* (relationship) 一対一の ittáiichi no

one-upmanship [wʌnʌpˈmənʃip] *n* 自分の方が一枚上だと見せ付ける事 jibún no hố ga ichímai uế da to misétsukerù koto

one-way [wʌnˈwei] *adj* (street, traffic) 一方通行の ippốsūkō no

ongoing [ɑnˈgouiŋ] *adj* (project, situation etc) 進行中の shiñkōchū no

onion [ʌn'jən] *n* タマネギ tamánegì

on-line [ɑːn'lain] *adj* (COMPUT) オンラインの ofirain no
♦*adv* (COMPUT) オンラインで ofirain de

onlooker [ɑːn'lukəːr] *n* 見物人 kefibutsunìn

only [oun'li:] *adv* ...だけ ...dake
♦*adj* (sole, single) ただ一つ〔一人〕の tada hitótsù[hitórì] no
♦*conj* (but) しかし shikáshì
an only child 一人っ子 hitórikkð
not only ... but also ... ...ばかりでなく...も ...bakári de naku ...mo

onset [ɑːn'set] *n* (beginning: of war, winter, illness) 始まり hajímari, 始め hajíme

onshore [ɑːn'ʃɔːr] *adj* (wind) 海からの umì kara no

onslaught [ɑːn'slɔːt] *n* 攻撃 kōgeki

onto [ɑːn'tu:] *prep* = **on to**

onus [ou'nəs] *n* 責任 sekínin

onward(s) [ɑːn'wəːrd(z)] *adv* (forward: move, progress) 先へ sakí e
from that time onward(s) それ以後 soré igo

onyx [ɑːn'iks] *n* オニキス onîkisu

ooze [u:z] *vi* (mud, water, slime) にじみでる nijímideru

opal [ou'pəl] *n* オパール opárù

opaque [oupeik'] *adj* (substance) 不透明な futómèi na

OPEC [ou'pek] *n abbr* (= *Organization of Petroleum-Exporting Countries*) 石油輸出国機構 sekíyu yushutsukoku kikð

open [ou'pən] *adj* (not shut: window, door, mouth etc) 開いた aíta; (: shop, museum etc) 営業中の eígyōchū no, 開いている aíte iru; (unobstructed: road) 開通している kaítsū shite iru; (: view) 開けた hirákéta; (not enclosed: land) 囲いのない kakói no nai; (*fig*: frank: person, manner, face) 率直な sótchoku na; (unrestricted: meeting, debate, championship) 公開の kōkai no
♦*vt* 開ける akéru, 開く hiráku
♦*vi* (flower, eyes, door, shop) 開く akú, 開く hiráku; (book, debate etc: commence) 始まる hajímaru

in the open (air) 野外に yagài ni
an open car オープンカー ōpùnkā

opening [ou'pəniŋ] *adj* (commencing: speech, remarks etc) 開会の kaíkai no, 冒頭の bōtō no
♦*n* (gap, hole) 穴 aná; (start: of play, book etc) 始め hajíme, 冒頭 bōtō; (opportunity) 機会 kikái, チャンス chañsu

openly [ou'pənli:] *adv* (speak, act) 公然と kōzen to; (cry) 人目をはばからず hitóme wo habákarazu

open-minded [ou'pənmain'did] *adj* 偏見のない henkén no nai

open-necked [ou'pənnekt'] *adj* (shirt) 開きんの kaíkin no

open on to *vt fus* (subj: room, door) ...に面している ...ni mén shite iru

open-plan [ou'pənplæn'] *adj* 間仕切のない majíkiri no nai

open up *vt* (building, room: unlock) 開ける akéru; (blocked road) ...の障害物を取除く ...no shōgaibutsu wo torínozokù
♦*vi* (COMM: shop, business) 開く akú

opera [ɑːp'rə] *n* 歌劇 kagèki, オペラ opèra

opera singer *n* オペラ歌手 opèrakashu

operate [ɑːp'əːreit] *vt* (machine) 操作する sōsa suru; (vehicle) 運転する ufiten suru
♦*vi* (machine) 動く ugòkù; (vehicle) 走る hashiru, 動く ugòkù; (company, organization) 営業する eígyō suru
to operate on someone (for) (MED) ...に (...の) 手術をする ...ni (...no) shujùtsu wo suru

operatic [ɑːpəræt'ik] *adj* 歌劇の kagèki no, オペラの opèra no

operating [ɑːp'əːreitiŋ] *adj*: *operating table* 手術台 shujùtsudai
operating theater 手術室 shujùtsushitsu

operation [ɑːpərei'ʃən] *n* (of machine etc) 操作 sōsa; (of vehicle) 運転 ufiten; (MIL, COMM etc) 作戦 sakúsen; (MED) 手術 shujùtsu
to be in operation (law, regulation) 実施されている jisshí sarete iru
to have an operation (MED) 手術を受

ける shujùtsu wo ukérù

operational [ɑːpərei'ʃənəl] *adj* (working: machine, vehicle etc) 使用可能な shíyō-kanō na

operative [ɑːp'ərətiv] *adj* (law, measure, system) 実施されている jisshí sarete iru

operator [ɑːp'əːreitəːr] *n* (TEL) 交 換 手 kókanshu, オ ペ レ ー タ ー opérētā; (of machine) 技師 gishì

ophthalmic [ɑːfθæl'mik] *adj* 眼科の gàñka no

opinion [əpin'jən] *n* (point of view, belief) 意見 ikén
  in my opinion 私の意見では watákushi no ikèn de wa

opinionated [əpin'jəneitid] (*pej*) *adj* 独善的な dokúzenteki na

opinion poll *n* 世論調査 yorónchōsa

opium [ou'piːəm] *n* あへん ahèn

opponent [əpou'nənt] *n* (person not in favor) 反 対 者 hañtaisha; (MIL) 敵 tekí; (SPORT) 相手 aìte

opportunism [ɑːpəːrtuː'nizəm] (*pej*) *n* 日 和見主義 hiyórimishugí

opportunist [ɑːpəːrtuː'nist] (*pej*) *n* 日 和 見主義者 hiyórimishugishà

opportunity [ɑːpəːrtjuː'niti:] *n* 機 会 ki-kái, チャンス chañsu
  to take the opportunity of doing 折 角の機会を利用して...する sekkáku no kikái wo riyó shite ...suru

oppose [əpouz'] *vt* (object to: wish, opinion, plan) ...に反対する ...ni hañtai suru
  to be opposed to something ...に反対である ...ni hañtai de aru
  as opposed to ...ではなくて ...de wa nakutè

opposing [əpouz'iŋ] *adj* (side, ideas) 反対の hañtai no; (team) 相手の aìte no

opposite [ɑːp'əzit] *adj* (house) 向かい側の mukáigawa no; (end, direction, side) 反対の hañtai no; (point of view, effect) 逆の gyakú no
  ♦*adv* (live, stand, work, sit) 向い側に〔で〕mukáigawa ni(de)
  ♦*prep* (in front of) ...の向い側に〔で〕...no mukáigawa ni(de)

  ♦*n*: *the opposite* (say, think, do etc) 反対 hañtai
  the opposite sex 異性 iséi

opposition [ɑːpəziʃ'ən] *n* (resistance) 反 対 hañtai; (those against) 反対勢力 hañtaiseiryokù; (POL) 野党 yatō

oppress [əpres'] *vt* 抑圧する yokúatsu suru

oppression [əpreʃ'ən] *n* 抑圧 yokúatsu

oppressive [əpres'iv] *adj* (political regime) 抑 圧 的 な yokúatsuteki na; (weather, heat) 蒸し暑い mushíatsuì

opt [ɑːpt] *vi*: *to opt for* ...を 選 ぶ ...wo erábù
  to opt to do ...する事にする ...surú koto ni suru

optical [ɑːp'tikəl] *adj* (instrument, device etc) 光学の kógaku no

optical illusion *n* 目の錯覚 mé no sak-káku

optician [ɑːptiʃ'ən] *n* 眼鏡屋 méganeya

optimism [ɑːp'təmizəm] *n* 楽観 rakkán, 楽天主義 rakútenshugì

optimist [ɑːp'təmist] *n* 楽天家 rakúten-ka

optimistic [ɑːptəmis'tik] *adj* 楽観的な rakkánteki na

optimum [ɑːp'təməm] *adj* (conditions, number, size) 最良の saíryō no, 最善の saízen no

option [ɑːp'ʃən] *n* (choice) 選択 señtaku, オプション opúshon

optional [ɑːp'ʃənəl] *adj* (not obligatory) 自由選択の jiyűsentakuno

opt out *vi*: *to opt out of* ...から手を引く ...kara te wò hiku

opulent [ɑːp'jələnt] *adj* (very wealthy: person, society etc) 大金持の ồganemochi no

or [ɔːr] *conj* (linking alternatives: up or down, in or out etc) それとも sorétomò, または matá wa; (otherwise) でないと de naî to, さもないと sa mò nai to; (with negative): *he hasn't seen or heard anything* 彼は何一つ見ても聞いてもいない karè wa nanì hitótsu mitè mo kiíte mo inai
  or else (otherwise) でないと de naî to

oracle [ɔːrˈəkəl] n 予言者 yogénsha

oral [ɔːrˈəl] adj (spoken: test, report) 口頭の kótô no; (MED: vaccine, medicine) 経口の keíkô no
♦n (spoken examination) 口頭試問 kótôshimon

orange [ɔːrˈindʒ] n (fruit) オレンジ orénji
♦adj (color) だいだい色の daídaiiro no, オレンジ色の orénjiiro no

orator [ɔːrˈətəːr] n 雄弁家 yúbenka

orbit [ɔːrˈbit] n (SPACE) 軌道 kidô
♦vt (circle: earth, moon etc) ...の周囲を軌道を回って回る ...no shúî wo kidô wo egaite mawaru

orchard [ɔːrˈtʃəːrd] n 果樹園 kajúen

orchestra [ɔːrˈkistrə] n (MUS) 楽団 gakúdan, オーケストラ ókesùtora; (US: THEATER: seating) 舞台前の特等席 butáimae no tokútôseki

orchestrate [ɔːrˈkistreit] vt (stage-manage) 指揮する shikí suru

orchid [ɔːrˈkid] n ラン rań

ordain [ɔːrˈdein] vt (REL) 聖職に任命する seíshoku ni nińmei suru

ordeal [ɔːrdiːl] n 試練 shíren

order [ɔːrˈdəːr] n (command) 命令 meírei; (COMM: from shop, company etc: also in restaurant) 注文 chúmon; (sequence) 順序 juñjo; (good order) 秩序 chitsújò; (law and order) 治安 chìàn
♦vt (command) 命ずる mèízuru; (COMM: from shop, company etc: also in restaurant) 注文する chúmon suru; (also: put in order) 整理する seíri suru

in order (gen) 整理されて seíri sarete; (of document) 規定通りで kitéidôri de

in (working) order 整備されて seíbi sarete

in order to do/that ...するために ...surú tame ni

on order (COMM) 発注してあって hatchú shite atte

out of order (not in correct order) 順番が乱れて juñban ga midáretè; (not working) 故障して koshô shite

to order someone to do something ...に...する様に命令する ...ni ...suru yō ni meírei suru

order form n 注文用紙 chúmon yōshi

orderly [ɔːrˈdəːrliː] n (MIL) 当番兵 tôbànhei; (MED) 雑役夫 zatsúekifu
♦adj (well-organized: room) 整とんされた seíton sareta; (: person, system etc) 規則正しい kisókutadashii

ordinary [ɔːrˈdəneːriː] adj (everyday, usual) 普通の futsû no; (pej: mediocre) 平凡な heíbon na

out of the ordinary (exceptional) 変った kawátta

Ordnance Survey [ɔːrˈdnəns-] (BRIT) n 英国政府陸地測量局 eíkokuseifu rikúchi sokuryôkyoku

ore [ɔːr] n 鉱石 kóseki

organ [ɔːrˈgən] n (ANAT: kidney, liver etc) 臓器 zóki; (MUS) オルガン orúgan

organic [ɔːrˈgænˈik] adj (food, farming etc) 有機の yúkî no

organism [ɔːrˈgənizəm] n 有機体 yúkîtai, 生物 seíbutsu

organist [ɔːrˈgənist] n オルガン奏者 orúgansôsha, オルガニスト orúganisuto

organization [ɔːrgənəzeiˈʃən] n (business, club, society) 組織 soshíki, 機構 kikô, オーガニゼーション ôganizêshon

organize [ɔːrˈgənaiz] vt (arrange: activity, event) 企画する kikáku suru

organizer [ɔːrˈgənaizəːr] n (of conference, party etc) 主催者 shusáisha

orgasm [ɔːrˈgæzəm] n オルガズム orúgazumù

orgy [ɔːrˈdʒiː] n 乱交パーティ rañkôpâti

Orient [ɔːrˈiːent] n: *the Orient* 東洋 tóyō

oriental [ɔːriːenˈtəl] adj 東洋の tôyō no

orientate [ɔːrˈiːenteit] vt: *to orientate oneself* (in place) 自分の居場所を確認する jibún no ibásho wo kakúnin suru; (in situation) 環境になれる kańkyô ni narérù

origin [ɔːrˈidʒin] n (beginning, source) 起源 kigén; (of person) 生れ umare

original [əridʒˈənəl] adj (first: idea, occupation) 最初の saísho no; (genuine: work of art, document etc) 本物の hoňmono no; (fig: imaginative: thinker, writer, artist) 独創的な dokúsôteki na

◆*n* (genuine work of art, document) 本物 honmono

originality [ərɪdʒənæl'ɪti:] *n* (imagination: of artist, writer etc) 独創性 dokúsōsei

originally [ərɪdʒ'ənəli:] *adv* (at first) 最初は saísho wa, 当初 tōsho

originate [ərɪdʒ'əneit] *vi*: **to originate from** (person, idea, custom etc) ...から始まる ...karā hajímaru

to originate in ...で始まる ...dè hajímaru

Orkneys [ɔːrk'ni:z] *npl*: **the Orkneys** (*also*: **the Orkney Islands**) オークニー諸島 ōkúnīshotō

ornament [ɔːr'nəmənt] *n* (gen) 飾りkazári, 装飾 sōshoku; (to be worn) 装身具 sōshíngu

ornamental [ɔːrnəmen'təl] *adj* (decorative: garden, pond) 装飾的な sōshokuteki na

ornate [ɔːrneit'] *adj* (highly decorative: design, style) 凝った kottà

ornithology [ɔːrnəθɑːl'ədʒi:] *n* 鳥類学 chōruigaku

orphan [ɔːr'fən] *n* 孤児 kojì

orphanage [ɔːr'fənidʒ] *n* 孤児院 kojìin

orthodox [ɔːr'θədɑːks] *adj* (REL: *also fig*) 正統派の seítōha no

orthodoxy [ɔːr'θədɑːksi:] *n* (traditional beliefs) 正統思想 seítōshisō

orthopedic [ɔːrθəpi:'dik] (*BRIT* **orthopaedic**) *adj* 整形外科の seíkeigeka no

oscillate [ɑːs'əleit] *vi* (ELEC) 発振する hasshín suru; (PHYSICS) 振動する shindō suru; (*fig*: mood, person, ideas) 頻繁に変る hinpan ni kawáru

ostensibly [ɑːsten'səbli:] *adv* 表面上 hyōmenjō

ostentatious [ɑːstentei'ʃəs] *adj* (showy: building, car etc) 派手な hadé na; (: person) 万事に派手な banji ni hadé na

osteopath [ɑːs'ti:əpæθ] *n* 整骨療法医 seíkotsuryōhōi

ostracize [ɑːs'trəsaiz] *vt* のけ者にする nokémono ni suru

ostrich [ɔːs'tritʃ] *n* ダチョウ dachō

other [ʌð'əːr] *adj* (that which has not been mentioned: person, thing) 外の hoká no; (second of 2 things) もう一つの mō hitotsu no

◆*pron*: **the other (one)** 外の物 hoká no mono

◆*adv*: **other than** ...を除いて ...wo nozóite

others (other people) 他人 tanín

the other day (recently) 先日 senjitsu, この間 konó aida

otherwise [ʌð'əːrwaiz] *adv* (in a different way) 違ったやり方で chígatta yarikata dè; (apart from that) それを除けば soré wo nozókeba

◆*conj* (if not) そうでないと sō dè nai to

otter [ɑːt'əːr] *n* カワウソ kawáuso

ouch [autʃ] *excl* 痛い itáì

ought [ɔːt] (*pt* ought) *aux vb*: **she ought to do it** 彼女はそれをやるべきです kanòjo wa soré wo yarubeki desu

this ought to have been corrected これは直すべきだった koré wa naósubeki datta

he ought to win (probability) 彼は勝つはずです karè wa katsù hazu desu

ounce [auns] *n* (unit of weight) オンス onsu

our [au'əːr] *adj* 私たちの watákushitachi no ¶ *see also* **my**

ours [au'əːrz] *pron* 私たちの物 watákushitachi no mono ¶ *see also* **mine**

ourselves [auəːrselvz'] *pron* 私たち自身 watákushitachi jishìn ¶ *see also* **oneself**

oust [aust] *vt* (forcibly remove: government, MP etc) 追放する tsuíhō suru

---
KEYWORD
---

out [aut] *adv* **1** (not in) 外に〔で, へ〕sótò ni〔de, e〕

they're out in the garden 彼らは庭にいます kárèra wa niwà ni imasù

(to stand) out in the rain/snow 雨〔雪〕の降る中に立っている ámè〔yukí〕no fúrù nákà ni tátte irù

it's cold out here/out in the desert 外〔砂漠〕は寒い sótò〔sabáku〕wa samúì

out here/there ここ〔あそこ〕だ-外の方に kokó〔asóko〕dà - sótò no hō nì

to go/come etc out 出て行く〔来る〕dé-tè iku〔kuru〕

(to speak) out loud 大きな声で言う ókina koè de iú

2 (not at home, absent) 不在で fuzái de, 留守で rúsù de

Mr Green is out at the moment グリーンさんはただ今留守ですが gurín san wa tadáìma rúsù desu ga

to have a day/night out 1日〔1晩〕外出して遊ぶ ichínichì〔hitóbàn〕gaíshutsu shitè asóbù

3 (indicating distance): *the boat was 10 km out* 船は10キロ沖にあった fúnè wa jukkíró okí ni attà

3 days out from Plymouth プリマスを出港して3日の所 purímàsu wo shukkō shitè mikká no tokorò

4 (SPORT) アウトで áùto de

the ball is/has gone out ボールはアウトだ〔出た〕bōru wa áùto da〔détà〕

out! (TENNIS etc) アウト áùto

♦*adj* **1**: *to be out* (person: unconscious) 気絶〔失神〕している kizétsu〔shisshín〕shite irù; (: SPORT) アウトである áùto de árù; (out of fashion: style) 流行遅れである ryūkōokùre de árù, 廃れている sutárete irù; (: singer) 人気がなくなった nińki gà nakúnattà

2 (have appeared: flowers): *to be out* 咲いている saíte irù; (: news) 報道されているhōdō sarete irù; (: secret) ばれている báretà, 発覚した hakkáku shità

3 (extinguished: fire, light, gas) 消えた kiétà

before the week was out (finished) その週が終らない内に sonó shū ga owáranai uchi nì

4: *to be out to do something* (intend) …しようとしている …shiyō to shité irù

to be out in one's calculations (wrong) 計算が間違っている keísan gà machígatte irù

out-and-out [aut'əndaut'] *adj* (liar, thief etc) 全くの mattáku no, 根っからの nekkára no

outback [aut'bæk] *n* (in Australia) 奥地 okúchi

outboard [aut'bɔːrd] *adj*: *outboard motor* アウトボードエンジン aùtobōdo-enjin

outbreak [aut'breik] *n* (of war, disease, violence etc) ぽっ発 boppátsu

outburst [aut'bəːrst] *n* (sudden expression of anger etc) 爆発 bakúhatsu

outcast [aut'kæst] *n* のけ者 nokémono

outcome [aut'kʌm] *n* (result) 結果 kekká

outcrop [aut'krɑːp] *n* (of rock) 露頭 rotō

outcry [aut'krai] *n* 反発 hañpatsu

outdated [autdei'tid] *adj* (old-fashioned) 時代遅れの jidáiokùre no

outdo [autduː'] (*pt* **outdid** *pp* **outdone**) *vt* しのぐ shinógu

outdoor [aut'dɔːr] *adj* (open-air: activities, games etc) 野外の yagài no, 屋外の okúgài no; (clothes) 野外用の yagáiyō no

outdoors [autdɔːrz'] *adv* (play, stay, sleep: in the open air) 野外に〔で〕yagài ni〔de〕

outer [aut'əːr] *adj* (exterior: door, wrapping, wall etc) 外側の sotógawa no

outer space *n* 宇宙空間 uchūkūkan

outfit [aut'fit] *n* (set of clothes) 衣装 ishō

outgoing [aut'gouiŋ] *adj* (extrovert) 外向性の gaíkōsei no; (retiring: president, mayor etc) 退陣する taíjin suru

outgoings [aut'gouiŋz] (*BRIT*) *npl* 出費 shuppí

outgrow [autgrou'] (*pt* **outgrew** *pp* **outgrown**) *vt* (one's clothes) 大きくなって…が着られなくなる ōkiku natte …ga kirárenaku naru

outhouse [aut'haus] *n* 納屋 nayà; (*US*) 屋外便所 okùgaibenjo

outing [aut'iŋ] *n* (excursion: family outing, school outing) 遠足 eńsoku

outlandish [autlæn'diʃ] *adj* (strange: looks, behavior, clothes) 奇妙な kimyò na

outlaw [aut'lɔː] *n* 無法者 muhōmono

♦*vt* (person, activity, organization) 禁止する kiñshi suru

outlay [aut'lei] *n* (expenditure) 出費

shuppí

outlet [aut'let] n (hole, pipe) 排水口 haísuíkō; (US: ELEC) コンセント koñseñto; (COMM: also: **retail outlet**) 販売店 hañbaíten

outline [aut'lain] n (shape: of object, person etc) 輪郭 riñkaku, アウトライン aútoraiñ; (brief explanation: of plan) あらまし arámashi, アウトライン aútoraiñ; (rough sketch) 略図 ryakúzu
♦vt (fig: theory, plan etc) ...のあらましを説明する ...no arámashi wo setsúmei suru

outlive [autliv'] vt (survive: person) ...より長生きする ...yorí naga-ikí suru; (: war, era) 生き延びる ikínobiru

outlook [aut'luk] n (view, attitude) 見方 mikáta; (fig: prospects) 見通し mitóshi; (: for weather) 予報 yohő

outlying [aut'laiiŋ] adj (away from main cities: town etc) 中心部を離れた chūshinbu wo hanáreta

outmoded [autmou'did] adj (old-fashioned: custom, theory) 時代遅れの jidáiokūre no

outnumber [autnʌm'bə:r] vt ...より多い ...yorí ōí

KEYWORD

out of prep 1 (outside, beyond) ...の外へ〔に, で〕 ..no sótò e[ni, de]
to go out of the house 家から外へ出る ié kara sótò e dérù
to look out of the window 窓から外を見る mádò kara sótò wo mírù
to be out of danger (safe) 危険がなくなった kikén gà nakúnattà
2 (cause, motive) ...に駆られて ...ni karáretè
out of curiosity/fear/greed 好奇心〔恐怖, どん欲〕に駆られて kókishìn〔kyōfu, dóñ-yoku〕ni karáretè
3 (origin) ...から ...kara
to drink something out of a cup カップから...を飲む káppù kara ...wo nomù
to copy something out of a book 本から...を写す hóñ kara ...wð utsúsù
4 (from among) ...の中から ...no nákà

kara, ...の内 ...no uchí
1 out of every 3 smokers 喫煙者3人に1人 kitsúeñsha sañnin nì hitórì
out of 100 cars sold, only one had any faults 売れた100台の車の内、1台だけに欠陥があった uréta hyakúdài no kurúma no uchi, íchídai dake ni kekkán ga atta
5 (without) ...が切れて ...ga kírète, ...がなくなって ...ga nakúnattè
to be out of milk/sugar/gas (US)/petrol (BRIT) etc ミルク〔砂糖, ガソリン〕が切れている mírùku〔satő, gasórin〕ga kírète iru

out-of-date [autəvdeit'] adj (passport) 期限の切れた kigèn no kiréta; (clothes etc) 時代遅れの jidáiokūre no

out-of-the-way [autəvðəwei'] adj (place) へんぴな heñpi na

outpatient [aut'peiʃənt] n (MED) 外来患者 gaíraikanja

outpost [aut'poust] n (MIL, COMM) 前しょう zeñshō; (COMM) 前進基地 zeñshinkichi

output [aut'put] n (production: of factory, mine etc) 生産高 seísañdaka; (: of writer) 作品数 sakúhinsū; (COMPUT) 出力 shutsúryoku, アウトプット aútoputto

outrage [aut'reidʒ] n (action: scandalous) 不法行為 fuhōkōī; (: violent) 暴力行為 bőryokukōī; (anger) 激怒 gekído
♦vt (shock, anger) 激怒させる gekído saseru

outrageous [autrei'dʒəs] adj 非難すべき hinánsubeki

outright [adv autrait' adj aut'rait] adv (absolutely: win) 圧倒的に attőteki ni; (at once: kill) 即座に sokúza ni; (openly: ask, deny, refuse) はっきりと hakkíri to
♦adj (absolute: winner, victory) 圧倒的な attőteki na; (open: refusal, denial, hostility) 明白な meíhaku na

outset [aut'set] n (start) 始め hajíme

outside [aut'said'] n (exterior: of container, building) 外側 sotðgawa
♦adj (exterior) 外側の sotðgawa no
♦adv (away from the inside: to be, go,

wait) 外に〔で〕sotó ni(de)
♦*prep* (not inside) ...の外に〔で〕...no sotó ni(de); (not included in) ...の 外 に ...no hoká ni; (beyond) ...を越えて ...wo koéte
at the outside (fig) せいぜい seízei

outside lane *n* (AUT) 追越し車線 oíkoshishaseñ

outside line *n* (TEL) 外線 gaíseñ

outsider [autsai'də:r] *n* (stranger) 部外者 bugáisha

outside-left/-right [aut'saidleft'/rait'] *n* (SOCCER) レフト〔ライト〕ウイング refúto〔raíto〕uíñgu

outsize [aut'saiz] *adj* (clothes) キング サ イズの kíñgusaìzu no

outskirts [aut'skə:rts] *npl* (of city, town) 外れ hazúre

outspoken [aut'spou'kən] *adj* (statement, opponent, reply) 遠慮のない eñryo no nai

outstanding [autstæn'diŋ] *adj* (exceptional) 並外れた namíhazureta, 優れた sugúretà; (remaining: debt, work etc) 残っている nókotte iru

outstay [autstei'] *vt*: *to outstay one's welcome* 長居して嫌われる nagái shite kiráwareru

outstretched [autstretʃt'] *adj* (hand) 伸ばした nobáshìta; (arms) 広げた hirógetà

outstrip [autstrip'] *vt* (competitors, demand) 追抜く oínuku

out-tray [aut'trei] *n* 送信のトレー sóshin no torè

outward [aut'wə:rd] *adj* (sign, appearances) 外部の gaíbu no; (journey) 行きの ikí no

outwardly [aut'wə:rdli:] *adv* 外部的に gaíbuteki ni

outweigh [autwei'] *vt* ...より重要である ...yórì júyō de aru

outwit [autwit'] *vt* ...の裏をかく ...no urá wo kaku

oval [ou'vəl] *adj* (table, mirror, face) だ円形の daéñkei no
♦*n* だ円形 daéñkei

ovary [ou'və:ri:] *n* 卵巣 rañsō

ovation [ouvei'ʃən] *n* 大喝さい daíkassai

oven [ʌv'ən] *n* (CULIN) 天火 teñpi, オーブン ōbùn; (TECH) 炉 ro

ovenproof [ʌv'ənpru:f] *adj* (dish etc) オーブン用の ōbùn yō no

KEYWORD

over [ou'və:r] *adv* **1** (across: walk, jump, fly etc) ...を越えて ...wò koétè
to cross over to the other side of the road 道路を横断する dòro wo ōdan suru
over here/there ここ〔あ そ こ〕に〔で〕kokó〔asóko〕nì(dè)
to ask someone over (to one's house) ...を家に招く ...wò ié nì manékù
2 (indicating movement from upright: fall, knock, turn, bend etc) 下へ shitá è, 地面へ jímèn e
3 (excessively: clever, rich, fat etc) 余り amári, 過度に kádò ni
she's not over intelligent, is she? 彼女はあまり頭が良くないね kánòjo wa amári atáma gà yókùnai né
4 (remaining: money, food etc) 余って amáttè, 残って nokóttè
there are 3 over 3個が残っている sáñko ga nokótte irù
is there any cake (left) over? ケーキが残っていませんか kèki ga nokótte imaseñ ká
5: *all over* (everywhere) 至る所に〔で〕itárù tokoró ni(de), どこもかしこも dókò mo káshikò mo
over and over (again) (repeatedly) 何度〔何回, 何返〕も nâñdo〔náñkai, náñben〕mo
♦*adj* (finished): *to be over* (game, life, relationship etc) 終りである owári de arù
♦*prep* **1** (on top of) ...の上に〔で〕...no ué nì(de); (above) ...の上方に〔で〕...no jôhō nì(de)
to spread a sheet over something ...の上にシーツを掛ける ...no ué nì shìtsu wo kakérù
there's a canopy over the bed ベッドの上に天がいがある béddò no ué nì teñgai ga arù
2 (on the other side of) ...の向こう側に

〔で〕...no mukốgawa nī〔dè〕
the pub over the road 道路の向こう側
にあるパブ dốrồ no mukốgawa ni arù
pábù
he jumped over the wall 彼は塀を飛
越えた kárè wa heí wồ tobíkoèta
3 (more than) ...以上 ijồ
over 200 people came 200人以上の人
が来ました nihyákunìn íjồ no hitồ gã
kimáshìtā
over and above ...の外に ...no hốkằ ni,
...に加えて ...ni kuwáetè
*this order is over and above what
we have already ordered* この注文は
これまでの注文への追加です konố chừ-
mon wa korế madề no chừmon e no
tsuíka desù
4 (during) ...の間 ...no aída
over the last few years 過去数年の間
kákồ sûnèn no aída
over the winter 冬の間 fuyú nồ aída
let's discuss it over dinner 夕食をし
ながら話し合いましょう yûshoku wồ
shinágàra hanáshiaimashồ

overall [*adj, n* ou'vər:ɔːl *adv* ouvər:ɔːl]
adj (length, cost etc) 全体の zeńtai no;
(general: study, survey) 全面的な zeńmen-
teki na
♦*adv* (view, survey etc) 全面的に zeńmen-
teki ni; (measure, paint) 全体に zeńtai ni
♦*n* (*BRIT*: woman's, child's, painter's)
上っ張り uwáppari

overalls [ou'vər:ɔːlz] *npl* オーバーオール
ōbāồrū

overawe [ouvər:ɔː'] *vt* 威圧する iátsu suru

overbalance [ouvər:bæl'əns] *vi* バラン
スを失う baránsu wo ushínau

overbearing [ouvər:ber'iŋ] *adj* (person,
behavior, manner) 横暴な ốbồ na

overboard [ou'vər:bɔːrd] *adv* (NAUT):
to fall overboard 船から水に落ちる fu-
nề kara mizú ni ochírù

overbook [ou'vər:buk] *vt* 予約を取り過
ぎる yoyáku wo torísugìru

overcast [ou'vər:kæst] *adj* (day, sky) 曇
った kumóttà

overcharge [ouvər:rtʃɑːrdʒ] *vt* ...に不当
な金額を請求する ...ni futố na kińgaku
wo seíkyū suru

overcoat [ou'vər:kout] *n* オーバーコー
ト ōbằkoto, オーバー ōbằ

overcome [ouvər:rkʌm'] (*pt* **overcame** *pp*
overcome) *vt* (defeat: opponent, enemy)
...に勝つ ...ni katsù; (*fig*: difficulty, problem) 克服する kokúfuku suru

overcrowded [ouvər:rkrau'did] *adj*
(room, prison) 超満員の chốman-in no;
(city) 過密な kamítsu na

overdo [ouvər:rdu'] (*pt* **overdid** *pp* **over-
done**) *vt* (exaggerate: concern, interest)
誇張する kochố suru; (overcook) 焼き過
ぎる yakísugiru
to overdo it (work etc) やり過ぎる yarí-
sugirù

overdose [ou'vər:rdous] *n* (MED: dangerous dose) 危険量 kikénryồ; (: fatal dose)
致死量 chíshìryō

overdraft [ou'vər:rdræft] *n* 当座借越 tố-
zakarikoshi

overdrawn [ouvər:rdrɔːn'] *adj* (account)
借越した karíkoshi shita

overdue [ouvər:rduː'] *adj* (late: person,
bus, train) 遅れている okúrete iru;
(change, reform etc) 待望の taíbồ no

overestimate [ouvər:res'təmeit] *vt* (cost,
importance, time) 高く見積りすぎる ta-
kắku mitsúmorisugirù; (person's ability,
skill etc) 買いかぶる kaíkaburu

overexcited [ouvər:riksai'tid] *adj* 過度に
興奮した kadồ ni kốfun shita

overflow [*vb* ouvər:rflou' *n* ou'vər:rflou]
vi (river) はん濫する hańran suru; (sink,
vase etc) あふれる afúreru
♦*n* (*also*: **overflow pipe**) 放出パイプ hố-
shutsupaipu

overgrown [ouvər:rgroun'] *adj* (garden)
草がぼうぼうと生えた kusa ga bốbō ni
haềta

overhaul [*vb* ouvər:rhɔːl' *n* ou'vər:rhɔːl]
vt (engine, equipment etc) 分解検査する
buńkaikensa suru, オーバーホールする
ōbằhōru suru
♦*n* オーバーホール ōbằhōru

overhead [*adv* ouvər:rhed' *adj*, *n*

ou'və:rhed] *adv* (above) 頭上に〔で〕zujố ni〔de〕; (in the sky) 上空に〔で〕jōkū ni〔de〕
♦*adj* (lighting) 上からの ué kara no; (cables, railway) 高架の kōkà no
♦*n* (*US*) = **overheads**

overheads [ou'və:rhedz] *npl* (expenses) 経費 keíhi

overhear [ouvə:rhiə:r'] (*pt, pp* **overheard**) *vt* 耳にする mimí ni suru

overheat [ouvə:rhi:t'] *vi* (engine) 過熱する kanétsu suru, オーバーヒートする ōbāhīto suru

overjoyed [ouvə:rdʒɔid'] *adj* 大喜びした ốyðrokobi shita

overkill [ou'və:rkil] *n* やり過ぎ yarísugi

overland [ou'və:rlænd] *adj* (journey) 陸路の rikùro no
♦*adv* (travel) 陸路で rikùro de

overlap [ouvə:rlæp'] *vi* (edges) 部分的に重なる bubúnteki ni kasánaru, オーバーラップする ōbārappu suru; (*fig*: ideas, activities etc) 部分的に重複する bubúnteki ni chốfuku suru, オーバーラップする ōbārappu suru

overleaf [ou'və:rli:f] *adv* ページの裏に pếji no urá ni

overload [ou'və:rloud] *vt* (vehicle) ...に積み過ぎる ...ni tsumísugiru; (ELEC) ...に負荷を掛け過ぎる ...ni fuká wo kakésugiru; (*fig*: with work, problems etc) ...に負担を掛け過ぎる ...ni fután wo kakésugiru

overlook [ou'və:rluk] *vt* (have view over) 見下ろす miốrosu; (miss: by mistake) 見落す miótosu; (excuse, forgive) 見逃がす minógasu

overnight [*adv* ouvə:rnait' *adj* ou'və:rnait] *adv* (during the whole night) 一晩中 hitóbanjū; (*fig*: suddenly) いつの間にか itsù no ma ni ka
♦*adj* (bag, clothes) 1泊用の ippákuyð no
to stay overnight 一泊する ippáku suru

overpass [ou'və:rpæs] *n* 陸橋 ríkkyō

overpower [ouvə:rpau'ə:r] *vt* (person) 腕力で抑え込む wañryoku de osáekomù; (subj: emotion, anger etc) 圧倒する attố suru

overpowering [ouvə:rpau'ə:riŋ] *adj* (heat, stench) 圧倒する様な attố suru yō na

overrate [ouvə:rreit'] *vt* (person, film, book) 高く評価し過ぎる takáku hyồka shisúguru

override [ouvə:raid'] (*pt* **overrode** *pp* **overridden**) *vt* (order) 無効にする mukố ni suru; (objection) 無視する mushí suru

overriding [ouvə:raid'iŋ] *adj* (importance) 最大の saídai no; (factor, consideration) 優先的な yūsénteki na

overrule [ouvə:rru:l'] *vt* (decision, claim, person) 無効にする mukố ni suru; (person) ...の提案を退ける ...no teían wo shirízokerù

overrun [ou'və:rʌn] (*pt* **overran** *pp* **overrun**) *vt* (country) 侵略する shifryaku suru; (time limit) 越える koéru

overseas [*adv* ouvə:rsi:z' *adj* ou'və:rsi:z] *adv* (live, travel, work: abroad) 海外に〔で〕kaígai ni〔de〕
♦*adj* (market, trade) 海外の kaígai no; (student, visitor) 外国人の gaíkokujìn no

overshadow [ouvə:rʃæd'ou] *vt* (throw shadow over: place, building etc) ...の上にそびえる ...no ué ni sobíerù; (*fig*) ...の影を薄くさせる ...no kagè wo usúku saseru

overshoot [ouvə:rʃu:t'] (*pt, pp* **overshot**) *vt* (subj: plane, train, car etc) ...に止らずに行き過ぎる ...ni tomárazu ni ikísugirù

oversight [ou'və:rsait] *n* 手落ち teóchi

oversleep [ouvə:rsli:p'] (*pt, pp* **overslept**) *vi* 寝過ごす nesúgðsu, 寝坊する nebố suru

overstate [ouvə:rsteit'] *vt* (exaggerate: case, problem, importance) 誇張する kochố suru

overstep [ouvə:rstep'] *vt*: *to overstep the mark* (go too far) 行き過ぎをやる ikísugi wo yaru

overt [ouvə:rt'] *adj* あからさまな akárasama na

overtake [ouvə:rteik'] (*pt* **overtook** *pp* **overtaken**) *vt* (AUT) 追越す oíkðsu

overthrow [ouvə:rθrou'] *vt* (govern-

ment, leader) 倒す taósù

overtime [ou'və:rtaim] *n* 残業 zañgyō

overtone [ou'və:rtoun] *n* (*fig*) 含み fukúmī

overture [ou'və:rtʃə:r] *n* (MUS) 序曲 jokyóku; (*fig*) 申出 móshide

overturn [ouvə:rtə:rn'] *vt* (car, chair) 引っ繰り返す hikkúrikaèsu; (*fig*: decision, plan, ruling) 翻す hirúgaèsu; (: government, system) 倒す taósù

♦*vi* (car, train, boat etc) 転覆する teńpuku suru

overweight [ouvə:rweit'] *adj* (person) 太り過ぎの futórìsugi no

overwhelm [ouvə:rwelm'] *vt* 圧倒する attó suru

overwhelming [ouvə:rwel'miŋ] *adj* (victory, heat, feeling) 圧倒的な attóteki na

overwork [ouvə:rwə:rk'] *n* 働き過ぎ határakisugī, 過労 karó

overwrought [ou'vərɔ:t'] *adj* 神経が高ぶった shiñkei ga tákabuttā

owe [ou] *vt*: *to owe someone something, to owe something to someone* (money) ...に...を借りている ...ni ...wo karíte iru, ...に...を払う義務がある ...ni ...wo haráù gimù ga aru; (*fig*: gratitude, respect, loyalty) ...に...しなければならない ...ni ...shinákereba naranaì; (: life, talent, good looks etc) ...は...のおかげである ...wa ...no o-kagé de aru

owing to [ou'iŋ tu:] *prep* (because of) ...のために ...no tamé nì

owl [aul] *n* フクロウ fukúrō, ミミズク mimízuku

own [oun] *vt* (possess: house, land, car etc) 所有する shoyū́ suru, 保有する hoyū́ suru

♦*adj* (house, work, style etc) 自分の jibún no, 自分自身の jubúnjishìn no

a room of my own 自分の部屋 jibún no heyá

to get one's own back (take revenge) 復しゅうする fukushū́ suru

on one's own (alone) 自分で jibun de, 自分の力で jibún no chikára de

owner [ou'nə:r] *n* (*gen*) 所有者 shoyū́sha, 持主 móchìnushi, オーナー ōnā; (of shop)

主人 shujîn, 経営者 kéieìsha; (of pet) 飼主 kaínushi

ownership [ou'nə:rʃip] *n* (possession) 所有 shoyū́

own up *vi* (admit: guilt, error) ...を認める ...wo mitómeru

ox [ɑ:ks] (*pl* **oxen**) *n* ウシ ushî ◊通常去勢した牡ウシを指す tsujō kyoséi shita oùshi wo sasu

oxtail [ɑ:ks'teil] *n*: *oxtail soup* オックステールスープ okkùsutērusūpu

oxygen [ɑ:k'sidʒən] *n* 酸素 sañso

oxygen mask/tent *n* 酸素マスク〔テント〕 sañsomasuku〔tento〕

oyster [ois'tə:r] *n* カキ kaki

oz. *abbr* = **ounce(s)**

ozone [ou'zoun] *n* オゾン ozòn

ozone layer *n* オゾン層 ozònsō

P

p [pi:] *abbr* = **penny; pence**

P.A. [pi:ei'] *n abbr* = **personal assistant; public address system**

p.a. *abbr* = **per annum**

pa [pɑ:] (*inf*) *n* 父ちゃん tōchan, パパ pápà

pace [peis] *n* (step) 1歩 îppò; (distance) 歩幅 hohába; (speed) 早さ háyàsa, 速度 sókùdo, ペース pḕsu

♦*vi*: *to pace up and down* (walk around angrily or impatiently) うろうろする úròuro suru

to keep pace with (person) ...と足並をそろえる ...to ashínami wò soróerù

pacemaker [peis'meikə:r] *n* (MED) ペースメーカー pḕsumèkā; (SPORT: *also*: **pacesetter**) ペースメーカー pḕsumèkā

Pacific [pəsîf'ik] *n*: *the Pacific (Ocean)* 太平洋 taíheìyō

pacifist [pæs'əfist] *n* 平和主義者 heíwashugìshà

pacify [pæs'əfai] *vt* (soothe: person) なだめる nadámerù; (: fears) 鎮める shizúmerù

pack [pæk] *n* (packet) 包み tsutsúmi; (*US*: of **cigarettes**) 1箱 hitóhàko; (group:

of hounds) 群れ muré; (: of people) グループ gúrūpu; (back pack) リュックサック ryukkúsakkù; (of cards) 1組 hitókùmi

◆*vt* (fill: box, container, suitcase etc) ...に詰込む ...ni tsumékomù; (cram: people, objects): *to pack into* ...を...に詰込む ...wo ...ni tsumékomù

to pack (one's bags) 荷造りをする nízūkùri wo suru

to pack someone off ...を追出す ...wo oídasù

pack it in! (*inf*: stop it!) やめなさい! yaménasai!

package [pæk'idʒ] *n* (parcel) 小包 kozútsumi; (*also*: **package deal**) 一括取引 ikkátsutorihìki

package holiday *n* = **package tour**

package tour *n* パッケージツアー pakkéjitsuà, パックツアー pakkútsuà

packed lunch [pækt-] *n* 弁当 beńtō

packet [pæk'it] *n* (box) 1箱 hitóhàko; (bag) 1袋 hitófùkuro

packing [pæk'iŋ] *n* (act) 詰込む事 tsumékomù kotó; (external: paper, plastic etc) 包装 hōsō

packing case *n* 木箱 kíbàko

pact [pækt] *n* 協定 kyótei

pad [pæd] *n* (block of paper) 一つづり hitótsùzuri; (to prevent friction, damage) こん包材 końpōzài; (in shoulders of dress, jacket etc) パッド páddò; (*inf*: home) 住い súmài

◆*vt* (SEWING: cushion, soft toy etc) ...に詰物をする ...ni tsumémòno wo suru

padding [pæd'iŋ] *n* (material) 詰物 tsumémòno

paddle [pæd'əl] *n* (oar) かい kái, パドル pádòru; (*US*: for table tennis) ラケット rakéttò

◆*vt* (boat, canoe etc) こぐ kógù

◆*vi* (with feet) 水の中を歩く mízù no nakà wo arúkù

paddle steamer *n* (on river) 外輪船 gaírinsen

paddling pool [pæd'liŋ-] (*BRIT*) *n* (children's) 子供用プール kodómoyò pūru

paddock [pæd'ək] *n* (for horse: small field) 放牧場 hōbokujō; (: at race course)

パドック pádòkku

paddy field [pæd'i:-] *n* 水田 suíden, 田んぼ tańbo

padlock [pæd'lɑːk] *n* (on door, bicycle etc) 錠 (前) jō(mae)

paediatrics [piːdiːæt'riks] (*BRIT*) *n* = **pediatrics**

pagan [pei'gən] *adj* (gods, festival, worship) 異教の ikyō no ◇キリスト教, ユダヤ教, イスラム教以外の宗教をさげすんで言う語 kirísutokyō, yudáyakyō, isúramukyō igài no shúkyō wo sagésuñde iú go

◆*n* (worshipper of pagan gods) 異教徒 ikyōto

page [peidʒ] *n* (of book, magazine, newspaper) ページ pēji; (*also*: **page boy**) 花嫁付添いの少年 hanáyòmetsukisoi no shōnen

◆*vt* (in hotel etc) ボーイ bōi

pageant [pædʒ'ənt] *n* (historical procession, show) ページェント pèjento

pageantry [pædʒ'əntri:] *n* 見世物 misémono

paid [peid] *pt, pp of* **pay**

◆*adj* (work) 有料の yūryō no; (staff, official) 有給の yūkyū no; (gunman, killer) 雇われた yatówaretà

a paid holiday 有給休暇 yūkyūkyùka

to put paid to (*BRIT*: end, destroy) ...を台無しにする ...wo daínashi ni surù

pail [peil] *n* (for milk, water etc) バケツ bakétsu

pain [pein] *n* (unpleasant physical sensation) 痛み itámi, 苦痛 kutsū; (*fig*: unhappiness) 苦しみ kurúshimi, 心痛 shińtsū

to be in pain (person, animal) 苦痛を感じている kutsū wò kañjite irù, 苦しんでいる kurúshinde irù

to take pains to do something (make an effort) 苦心して...する kushín shite ...surù

pained [peind] *adj* (expression) 怒った okóttà

painful [pein'fəl] *adj* (back, wound, fracture etc) 痛い itái, 痛む itámù; (upsetting, unpleasant: sight etc) 痛々しい itáitashii; (memory) 不快な fukái na; (deci-

sion) 苦しい kurúshiȋ; (laborious: task, progress etc) 骨の折れる honé no orerù

painfully [pein'fəli:] *adv* (*fig*: very) 痛い程 itáihodo

painkiller [pein'kilər] *n* (aspirin, paracetamol etc) 鎮痛剤 chíntsūzai

painless [pein'lis] *adj* (operation, childbirth) 無痛の mutsū no

painstaking [peinz'teikiŋ] *adj* (work) 骨折れの honéore no; (person) 勤勉な kíñben na

paint [peint] *n* (decorator's: for walls, doors etc) 塗料 toryó, ペンキ peńki, ペイント peńto; (artist's: oil paint, watercolor paint etc) 絵の具 e nó gu
♦*vt* (wall, door, house etc) ...にペンキを塗る ...ni peńki wo nurù; (picture, portrait) 描く kákù
to paint the door blue ドアに水色のペンキを塗る dóa ni mizúiro nò peńki wò nurú

paintbrush [peint'brʌʃ] *n* (decorator's) 刷毛 haké, ブラシ búrashi; (artist's) 絵筆 éfude

painter [pein'tər] *n* (artist) 画家 gaká; (decorator) ペンキ屋 peńkiya

painting [pein'tiŋ] *n* (activity: decorating) ペンキ塗り peńkinùri; (: art) 絵描き ekáki; (picture) 絵画 kaíga
an oil painting 油絵 abúraè

paintwork [peint'wərk] *n* (painted parts) 塗装の部分 tosó no bubùn

pair [per] *n* (of shoes, gloves etc) 対 tsuí
a pair of scissors はさみ hasámi
a pair of trousers ズボン zubóñ

pajamas [pədʒɑːm'əz] (*US*) *npl* パジャマ pájàma

Pakistan [pæk'istæn] *n* パキスタン pakísùtan

Pakistani [pæk'əstæn'iː] *adj* パキスタンの pakísùtan no
♦*n* パキスタン人 pakísutanjìn

pal [pæl] (*inf*) *n* (friend) 友達 tomódachi

palace [pæl'is] *n* (residence: of monarch) 宮殿 kyúdeñ; (: of president etc) 官邸 kañtei; (: of Japanese emperor) 皇居 kókyo, 御所 góshò

palatable [pæl'ətəbəl] *adj* (food, drink)

おいしい oíshiȋ

palate [pæl'it] *n* 口がい kógai

palatial [pəlei'ʃəl] *adj* (surroundings, residence) 豪華な góka na

palaver [pəlæv'əːr] *n* (*US*) 話し合い hanáshiai; (*BRIT*: *inf*: fuss) 大騒ぎ ósawàgi

pale [peil] *adj* (whitish: color) 白っぽい shíróppoì; (: face) 青白い aójiroì, 青ざめた aózametà; (: light) 薄暗い usúgurai
♦*n*: *beyond the pale* (unacceptable) 容認できない yónin dekinài

Palestine [pæl'istain] *n* パレスチナ parésùchina

Palestinian [pælistin'iːən] *adj* パレスチナの parésùchina no
♦*n* パレスチナ人 parésuchinajìn

palette [pæl'it] *n* (ART: paint mixing board) パレット paréttò

palings [pei'liŋz] *npl* (fence) さく sakú

pall [pɔːl] *n*: *a pall of smoke* 一面の煙 ichímen no kemuri
♦*vi* ...が詰まらなくなる ...ga tsumáranakù naru, ...に飽きる ...ni akírù

pallet [pæl'it] *n* (for goods) パレット paréttò

pallid [pæl'id] *adj* (person, complexion) 青白い aójiroì

pallor [pæl'əːr] *n* そう白 sóhaku

palm [pɑːm] *n* (*also*: **palm tree**) ヤシ yáshì; (of hand) 手のひら tenóhira
♦*vt*: *to palm something off on someone* (*inf*) ...に ...をつかませる ...ni ...wo tsukámaserù

Palm Sunday *n* 枝の主日 edá nò shujítsu

palpable [pæl'pəbəl] *adj* (obvious: lie, difference etc) 明白な meíhaku na

palpitations [pælpitei'ʃənz] *npl* (MED) 動き dóki

paltry [pɔːl'tri:] *adj* (amount: tiny, insignificant) ささいな sásài na

pamper [pæm'pəːr] *vt* (cosset: person, animal) 甘やかす amáyakasù

pamphlet [pæm'flit] *n* (political, literary etc) 小冊子 shósasshì, パンフレット páñfuretto

pan [pæn] *n* (CULIN: *also*: **saucepan**) 片

手なべ katátenabè; (: also: **frying pan**)
フライパン furáipan

panacea [pænəsi:'ə] n 万能薬 baṅnōyàku

panache [pənæʃ'] n 気取り kidóri

Panama [pæn'əmɑː] n パナマ pánama

Panama Canal n: *the Panama Canal* パナマ運河 panáma uṅga

pancake [pæn'keik] n パンケーキ paṅkēki, ホットケーキ hottókēki

pancreas [pæn'kri:əs] n すい臓 suízō

panda [pæn'də] n (ZOOL) ジャイアントパンダ jaíantopaṅda

panda car (BRIT) n (police car) パトカー patókā

pandemonium [pændəmou'ni:əm] n (noisy confusion) 大混乱 daíkoṅran

pander [pæn'də:r] vi: *to pander to* (person, whim, desire etc) ...に迎合する ...ni geígō suru

pane [pein] n (of glass) 窓ガラス madógaràsu

panel [pæn'əl] n (oblong piece: of wood, metal, glass etc) 羽目板 hameíta, パネル pánèru; (group of judges, experts etc) ...の一団 ...no ichídàn, パネル pánèru

paneling [pæn'əliŋ] (BRIT **panelling**) n 羽目板 hameíta ◇総称 sṓshō

pang [pæŋ] n: *a pang of regret* 悔恨の情 kaíkon no jō
hunger pangs (physical pain) 激しい空腹感 hagéshiì kúfukukan

panic [pæn'ik] n (uncontrollable terror, anxiety) パニック pánìkku
◆vi (person) うろたえる urótaerù; (crowd) パニック状態になる paníkkujōtai ni nárù

panicky [pæn'iki:] adj (person) うろたえる urótaerù

panic-stricken [pæn'ikstrikən] adj (person, face) パニックに陥った pánìkku ni ochíttà

panorama [pænəræm'ə] n (view) 全景 zeñkei, パノラマ panórama

pansy [pæn'zi:] n (BOT) サンシキスミレ sañshikisumìre, パンジー páñjī; (inf: pej) 弱虫 yowámùshi

pant [pænt] vi (gasp: person, animal) あえぐ aégù

panther [pæn'θə:r] n ヒョウ hyṓ

panties [pæn'ti:z] npl パンティー páñtī

pantomime [pæn'təmaim] (BRIT) n クリスマスミュージカル kurísumasu myūjikaru

pantry [pæn'tri:] n 食料室 shokúryōshìtsu, パントリー páñtorī

pants [pænts] n (BRIT: underwear: woman's) パンティー páñtī; (: man's) パンツ páñtsu; (US: trousers) ズボン zubóñ

panty hose n パンティーストッキング páñtīsutokkìṅgu

papal [pei'pəl] adj ローマ法王の rṓmahṑō no

paper [pei'pə:r] n (gen) 紙 kamí; (also: **newspaper**) 新聞 shiñbun; (exam) 試験 shikéñ; (academic essay) 論文 roñbun, ペーパー pḗpā; (also: **wallpaper**) 壁紙 kabégami
◆adj (made from paper: hat, plane etc) 紙の kamí no
◆vt (room: with wallpaper) ...に壁紙を張る ...ni kabégami wò hárù

paperback [pei'pə:rbæk] n ペーパーバック pḗpābakku

paper bag n 紙袋 kamíbukùro

paper clip n クリップ kuríppù

paper hankie n ティッシュ tísshù

papers [pei'pə:rz] npl (documents) 書類 shórùi; (also: **identity papers**) 身分証明書 mibúnshōmeishò

paperweight [pei'pə:rweit] n 文鎮 buñchin

paperwork [pei'pə:rwə:rk] n (in office: dealing with letters, reports etc) 机上の事務 kijṓ no jìmu, ペーパーワーク pḗpāwāku

papier-mâché [pei'pə:rməʃei'] n 張り子 haríko

paprika [pɑːpriː'kə] n パプリカ papúrìka

par [pɑːr] n (equality of value) 同等 dṓtō; (GOLF) 基準打数 kijúndasù, パー pā
to be on a par with (be equal with) ...と同等である ...to dṓtō de arù

parable [pær'əbəl] n たとえ話 tatóebanàshi

parachute [pær'əʃuːt] n 落下傘 rakkásàn, パラシュート paráshūto

parade [pəreid'] *n* (public procession) パ
レード parḗdò
◆*vt* (show off: wealth, knowledge etc) 見
せびらかす misḗbirakasù
◆*vi* (MIL) 行進する kṓshin suru

paradise [pær'ədais] *n* (REL: heaven,
nirvana etc: *also fig*) 天国 tḗñgoku, 極楽
gokúraku

paradox [pær'ədɑːks] *n* (thing, statement) 逆説 gyakúsetsu

paradoxically [pærədɑːk'sikli:] *adv* 逆
説的に言えば gyakúsetsuteki nì iébà

paraffin [pær'əfin] (*BRIT*) *n* (*also*: **paraffin oil**) 灯油 tṓyu

paragon [pær'əgɑːn] *n* (of honesty, virtue etc) 模範 moháñ, かがみ kagámi

paragraph [pær'əgræf] *n* 段落 dañrakù,
パラグラフ parágùrafu

Paraguay [pær'əgwei] *n* パラグアイ pa-
rágùai

parallel [pær'əlel] *adj* (lines, walls,
streets etc) 平行の heḯkō no; (*fig*: similar) 似た nitá
◆*n* (line) 平行線 heḯkòsen; (surface) 平行
面 heḯkòmen; (GEO) 緯度線 idòsen; (*fig*:
similarity) 似た所 nitá tokoro

paralysis [pəræl'isis] *n* (MED) 麻ひ máhì

paralyze [pær'əlaiz] *vt* (MED) 麻ひさせ
る máhì saséru; (*fig*: organization, production etc) 麻ひ状態にする mahíjòtai ni
suru

parameters [pəræm'itəːrz] *npl* (*fig*) 限
定要素 geñteiyṓso

paramilitary [pærəmil'ite:ri:] *adj* (organization, operations) 準軍事的な juñguñ-
jiteki na

paramount [pær'əmaunt] *adj*: **of paramount importance** 極めて重要な kiwá-
mète jūyō na

paranoia [pærənɔi'ə] *n* 被害妄想 higáimòsò

paranoid [pær'ənɔid] *adj* (person, feeling) 被害妄想の higáimòsò no

parapet [pær'əpit] *n* 欄干 rañkan

paraphernalia [pærəfəːrneil'jə] *n* (gear)
道具 dṓgu

paraphrase [pær'əfreiz] *vt* (poem, arti-

cle etc) やさしく言替える yasáshikù iī-
kaerù

paraplegic [pærəpli:'dʒik] *n* 下半身麻ひ
患者 kahánshinmahi kañja

parasite [pær'əsait] *n* (insect: *also fig*:
person) 寄生虫 kiséichū; (plant) 寄生植物
kiséishokùbutsu

parasol [pær'əsɔ:l] *n* 日傘 higasa, パラソ
ル párāsoru

paratrooper [pær'ətru:pə:r] *n* (MIL) 落
下傘兵 rakkásanhei

parcel [pɑr'səl] *n* (package) 小包 kozútsùmi
◆*vt* (object, purchases: *also*: **parcel up**)
小包にする kozútsùmi ni suru

parch [pɑːrtʃ] *vt* (land) 干上がらす hiága-
rasu; (crops) からからに枯らす karákara
ni karasù

parched [pɑːrtʃt] *adj* (person) のどがから
からの nódò ga karákara no

parchment [pɑːrtʃ'mənt] *n* (animal skin)
羊皮紙 yṓhishì; (thick paper) 硫酸紙 ryū-
sanshì

pardon [pɑːr'dən] *n* (LAW) 赦免 shamén
◆*vt* (forgive: person, sin, error etc) 許す
yurúsù

pardon me!, I beg your pardon! (I'm
sorry) 済みません sumímaseñ, 失礼しま
した shitsúrèi shimashita, ご免なさい
gomén nasaì

(I beg your) pardon?, pardon me?
(what did you say?) もう一度言って下さ
い mṓ ichido ittè kudásaì

parent [pe:r'ənt] *n* (mother or father) 親
oyá; (mother) 母親 haháoya; (father) 父
親 chichíoya

parental [pəren'təl] *adj* (love, control,
guidance etc) 親の oyá no

parenthesis [pəren'θəsis] (*pl* **parentheses**) *n* 括弧 kákkò

parents [pe:r'ənts] *npl* (mother and
father) 両親 ryōshin

Paris [pær'is] *n* パリ párì

parish [pær'iʃ] *n* (REL) 教区 kyókù;
(*BRIT*: civil) 行政教区 győseikyōku

Parisian [pəriʒ'ən] *adj* パリの párì no
◆*n* パリっ子 paríkkò

parity [pær'iti:] *n* (equality: of pay, con-

ditions etc) 平等 byōdō

park [pɑːrk] n (public) 公園 kṓen
♦vt (AUT) 駐車させる chū́sha saséru
♦vi (AUT) 駐車する chū́sha suru

parka [pɑːr'kə] n パーカ pắkà, アノラック anórakkù

parking [pɑːr'kiŋ] n 駐車 chū́sha
「no parking」駐車禁止 chū́shakinshi

parking lot (US) n 駐車場 chū́shajō

parking meter n パーキングメーター pākingumḗtā

parking ticket n (fine) 駐車違反切符 chū́shaihan kippù

parlance [pɑːr'ləns] n 用語 yṓgo

parliament [pɑːr'ləmənt] (BRIT) n (institution) 議会 gíkài

parliamentary [pɑːrləmen'tɑːri:] adj (business, behavior etc) 議会の gíkài no

parlor [pɑːr'ləːr] (BRIT parlour) n (in house) 居間 imá, 応接間 ṓsetsuma

parochial [pərou'ki:əl] (pej) adj (person, attitude) 偏狭な henkyō na

parody [pær'ədi:] n (THEATER, LITERATURE, MUS) パロディー páròdī

parole [pəroul'] n: on parole (LAW) 仮釈放で karíshakuhō de

paroxysm [pær'əksizəm] n (of rage, jealousy, laughter) 爆発 bakúhatsu

parquet [pɑːrkei'] n: parquet floor(ing) 寄せ木張りの床 yoségibari nò yuká

parrot [pær'ət] n オウム ṓmu

parry [pær'i:] vt (blow) かわす kawásu

parsimonious [pɑːrsəmou'ni:əs] adj けちな kechí na

parsley [pɑːrz'li:] n パセリ pásèri

parsnip [pɑːrs'nip] n 白にんじん shironinjin, パースニップ pắsunippù

parson [pɑːr'sən] n (REL) 牧師 bókùshi

part [pɑːrt] n (section, division) 部分 búbùn; (of machine, vehicle) 部品 buhín; (THEATER, CINEMA etc: role) 役 yakú; (PRESS, RADIO, TV: of serial) 第...部 dái...bù; (US: in hair) 分け目 wakéme
♦adv = **partly**
♦vt (separate: people, objects, hair) 分ける wakérù

♦vi (people: leave each other) 別れる wákarerù; (crowd) 道を開ける michí wo akerù

to take part in (participate in) ...に参加する ...ni sańka suru

to take something in good part ...を怒らない ...wo okóranaì

to take someone's part (support) ...の肩を持つ ...no kátà wo mótsù

for my part 私としては watákushi toshite wà

for the most part (usually, generally) ほとんどは hotóndo wa

part exchange n: **in part exchange** (BRIT: COMM) 下取りで shitádòri de

partial [pɑːr'ʃəl] adj (not complete: victory, support, solution) 部分的な bubúnteki na
to be partial to (like: person, food, drink etc) ...が大好きである ...ga daísuki de arù

participant [pɑːrtis'əpənt] n (in competition, debate, campaign etc) 参加者 sańkashà

participate [pɑːrtis'əpeit] vi: **to participate in** (competition, debate, campaign etc) ...に参加する ...ni sańka suru

participation [pɑːrtisəpei'ʃən] n (in competition, debate, campaign etc) 参加 sańka

participle [pɑːr'tisipəl] n (LING) 分詞 búnshi

particle [pɑːr'tikəl] n (tiny piece: gen) 粒子 ryū́shi; (: of dust) 一片 ippén; (of metal) 砕片 saíhen; (of food) 粒 tsúbù

particular [pərtik'jələːr] adj (distinct from others: person, time, place etc) 特定の tokútei no; (special) 特別な tokúbetsu na; (fussy, demanding) やかましい yakámashiì
in particular 特に tókù ni

particularly [pərtik'jələːrli:] adv 特に tókù ni

particulars [pərtik'jələːrz] npl (facts) 詳細 shōsai; (personal details) 経歴 keíreki

parting [pɑːr'tiŋ] n (action) 分ける事 wakérù kotó; (farewell) 別れ wakáre;

(BRIT: hair) 分け目 wakéme

♦adj (words, gift etc) 別れの wakáre no

partisan [pɑːr'tizən] adj (politics, views) 党派心の tóhashiñ no

♦n (supporter) 支援者 shiéñsha; (fighter) パルチザン parúchizañ

partition [pɑːtiʃ'ən] n (wall, screen) 間仕切 majíkìri; (POL: of country) 分割buñkatsu

partly [pɑːrt'liː] adv (to some extent) 幾分か ikúbun ka

partner [pɑːrt'nər] n (wife, husband) 配偶者 háigūsha; (girlfriend, boyfriend) 交際の相手 kósai nò aíte; (COMM) 共同経営者 kyódōkeièisha; (SPORT) パートナー pátònā; (at dance) 相手 aíte

partnership [pɑːrt'nərʃip] n (COMM) 共同経営事業 kyódōkeieijigyò; (POL etc) 協力 kyóryoku

partridge [pɑːr'tridʒ] n ウズラ uzúra

part-time [pɑːrt'taim] adj (work, staff) 非常勤の hijókin no, パートタイムの pátotaìmu no

♦adv (work, study) パートタイムで pátotaìmu de

part with vt fus (money, possessions) ...を手放す ...wo tebánasù

party [pɑːr'tiː] n (POL) 政党 seítō; (celebration, social event) パーティ pátì; (group of people) 一行 ikkó, パーティ pátì; (LAW) 当事者 tójishà; (individual) 人 hitó

♦cpd (POL) 党の tó no

party dress n パーティドレス pátidòresu

party line n (TEL) 共同線 kyódōsen

pass [pæs] vt (spend: time) 過ごす sugósù; (hand over: salt, glass, newspaper etc) 渡す watásù; (go past: place) 通り過ぎる tórisugirù; (overtake: car, person etc) 追越す oíkosù; (exam) ...に合格する ...ni gókaku suru; (approve: law, proposal) 可決する kakétsu suru

♦vi (go past) 通る tóru; (in exam) 合格する gókaku suru, パスする pásù suru

♦n (permit) 許可証 kyokáshò; (membership card) 会員証 kaíinshò; (in mountains) 峠 tóge; (SPORT) パス pásù;

(SCOL: also: **pass mark**): **to get a pass in** ...で及第する ...de kyúdai suru, ...でパスする ...de pásù suru

to pass something through something ...を...に通す ...wo ...ni tósu

to make a pass at someone (inf) ...にモーションを掛ける ...ni móshon wo kakérù

passable [pæs'əbəl] adj (road) 通行できる tsúkō dekirù; (acceptable: work) まずまずの mázùmazu no

passage [pæs'idʒ] n (also: **passageway**: indoors) 廊下 róka; (: outdoors) 通路 tsúro; (in book) 一節 issétsu; (ANAT): **the nasal passages** 鼻こう bikó; (act of passing) 通過 tsúka; (journey: on boat) 船旅 funátabi

pass away vi (die) 死ぬ shinú

passbook [pæs'buk] n 銀行通帳 giñkōtsúchō

pass by vi (go past) ...のそばを通る ...no sóba wo tòru

♦vt (ignore) 無視する múshì suru

passenger [pæs'indʒər] n (in car, boat, plane etc) 乗客 jókyaku

passer-by [pæsər'bai'] n 通行人 tsúkōnin

pass for vt fus ...で通る ...de tóru

passing [pæs'iŋ] adj (fleeting: moment, glimpse, thought etc) 束の間の tsuká no ma no

in passing (incidentally) ついでに tsuíde ni

passing place n (AUT) 待避所 taíhijò

passion [pæʃ'ən] n (love: for person) 情欲 jóyoku; (fig: for cars, football, politics etc) 熱狂 nekkyó, マニア mánìa

passionate [pæʃ'ənit] adj (affair, embrace, person etc) 情熱的な jónetsuteki na

passive [pæs'iv] adj (person, resistance) 消極的な shókyokuteki na; (LING) 受動態の judótai no, 受け身の ukémi no

pass on vt (news, object) 伝える tsutáerù; (illness) 移す utsúsù

pass out vi (faint) 気絶する kizétsu suru

Passover [pæs'ouvər] n 過越し祭 sugíkòshisai

passport [pæs'pɔːrt] n (official docu-

ment) 旅券 ryoken, パスポート pasúpòto

passport control n 出入国管理所 shutsúnyūkoku kañrijo

pass up vt (opportunity) 逃す nogásù

password [pæs'wə:rd] n (secret word, phrase) 合言葉 aíkotòba, パスワード pasúwàdo

past [pæst] prep (drive, walk, run: in front of) ...を通り過ぎて ...wo tōrisugìte; (: beyond: also in time: later than) ...を過ぎて ...wo sugíte

♦adj (previous: government, monarch etc) 過去の kákò no; (: week, month etc) この前の konó maè no, 先... señ...

♦n (period and events prior to the present: also of person) 過去 kákò

he's past forty (older than) 彼は40才を過ぎている kárè wa yoñjussaì wo sugíte irù

ten/quarter past eight 8時10分〔15分〕過ぎ hachíji juppùn(júgofun)sugí

for the past few/3 days この数日〔3日〕の間 konó sūjitsu(mikkà) no aída

pasta [pɑ:s'tə] n パスタ pásùta

paste [peist] n (wet mixture) 練り物 nerímòno; (glue) のり norí; (CULIN: fish, meat, tomato etc paste) ペースト pèsuto

♦vt (stick: paper, label, poster etc) 張る harú

pastel [pæstel'] adj (color) パステルの pásùteru no

pasteurized [pæs'tʃə:raizd] adj (milk, cream) 低温殺菌された teíonsakkìn sareta

pastille [pæsti:l'] n (sweet) ドロップ dóròppu

pastime [pæs'taim] n (hobby) 趣味 shúmì

pastoral [pæs'tə:rəl] adj (REL: duties, activities) 牧師としての bókùshi toshite

pastry [peis'tri:] n (dough) 生地 kíjì; (cake) 洋菓子 yōgashi, ケーキ kèki

pasture [pæs'tʃə:r] n (grassland) 牧場 bokújō

pasty [n pæs'ti: adj peis'ti:] n (meat and vegetable pie) ミートパイ mítopaì

♦adj (complexion, face) 青ざめた aóza-

metà

pat [pæt] vt (with hand: dog, someone's back etc) 軽くたたく karúkù tatákù

patch [pætʃ] n (piece of material) 継ぎ tsugí; (also: **eye patch**) 眼帯 gañtai; (area: damp, bald, black etc) 一部 ichíbu; (repair: on tire etc) 継ぎはぎ tsugíhagi

♦vt (clothes) ...に継ぎを当てる ...ni tsugí wo aterú

to go through a bad patch 不運の時期に合う fúùn no jíkì ni áù

patch up vt (mend temporarily) 応急的に直す ōkyūteki ni naosù; (quarrel) ...をやめて仲直りする ...wo yamétè nakánaorì surù

patchwork [pætʃ'wə:rk] n (SEWING) パッチワーク patchíwàku

patchy [pætʃ'i:] adj (uneven: color) むらの多い murá no ōì; (incomplete: information, knowledge etc) 不完全な fukánzen na

pâté [pɑ:tei'] n パテ pátè ◇肉、魚などを香辛料とすり合せて蒸焼きにして冷ました物 nikú, sakana nadò wo kōshiñryō to suráwasetè mushíyaki ni shitè samáshita monò

patent [pæt'ənt] n (COMM) 特許 tókkyo

♦vt (COMM) ...の特許を取る ...no tókkyo wo tórù

♦adj (obvious) 明白な meíhaku na

patent leather n: *patent leather shoes* エナメル靴 enámerugùtsu

paternal [pətə:r'nəl] adj (love, duty) 父親の chichíoya no; (grandmother etc) 父方の chichígata no

paternity [pətə:r'niti:] n 父親である事 chichíoya de arù kotó

path [pæθ] n (trail, track) 小道 kómìchi; (concrete path, gravel path etc) 道 michí; (of planet, missile) 軌道 kidō

pathetic [pəθet'ik] adj (pitiful: sight, cries) 哀れな áwàre na; (very bad) 哀れな程悪い áwàre na hódò warui

pathological [pæθələdʒ'ikəl] adj (liar, hatred) 病的な byōteki na; (of pathology: work) 病理の byōri no

pathology [pəθɑ:l'ədʒi:] n (medical field) 病理学 byōrigàku

pathos [peiˈθɑːs] n 悲哀 hiái

pathway [pæθˈwei] n (path) 歩道 hodố

patience [peiˈʃəns] n (personal quality) 忍耐 níñtai; (BRIT: CARDS) 一人トランプ hitóritorañpu

patient [peiˈʃənt] n (MED) 患者 kañja
♦adj (person) 忍耐強い niñtaizuyoì

patio [pætˈiːou] n テラス tếrasu

patriot [peiˈtriːət] n 愛国者 aíkokushà

patriotic [peitriːɑːˈtik] adj (person) 愛国心の強い aíkokushìn no tsuyóì; (song, speech etc) 愛国の aíkoku no

patriotism [peiˈtriːətizəm] n 愛国心 aíkokushìñ

patrol [pətroulˈ] n (MIL, POLICE) 巡回 juñkai, パトロール patốrōru
♦vt (MIL, POLICE: city, streets etc) 巡回する juñkai suru, パトロールする patốrōru suru

patrol car n (POLICE) パトカー patốkā

patrolman [pətroulˈmən] (pl patrolmen: US) n (POLICE) 巡査 juńsa

patron [peiˈtrən] n (customer, client) 客 kyakú; (benefactor: of charity) 後援者 kốeñsha
patron of the arts 芸術のパトロン geíjùtsu no pátòron

patronage [peiˈtrənidʒ] n (of artist, charity etc) 後援 kốen

patronize [peiˈtrənaiz] vt (pej: look down on) 尊大にあしらう soñdai nì ashíraù; (artist, writer, musician) 後援する kốen suru; (shop, club, firm) ひいきにする hiíki ni surù

patron saint n (REL) 守護聖人 shugóseijìn

patter [pætˈəːr] n (sound: of feet) ぱたぱたという音 pátàpata to iú oto; (of rain) パラパラという音 páràpara to iú otò; (sales talk) 売込み口上 uríkomikòjō
♦vi (footsteps) ぱたぱたと歩く pátàpata to arúkù; (rain) ぱらぱらと降る páràpara to fúrù

pattern [pætˈəːrn] n (design) 模様 moyố; (SEWING) 型紙 katágami, パターン patáñ

paunch [pɔːntʃ] n 太鼓腹 taíkobara

pauper [pɔːˈpəːr] n 貧乏人 biñbônin

pause [pɔːz] n (temporary halt) 休止 kyúshi, ポーズ pốzu
♦vi (stop temporarily) 休止する kyúshi suru; (: while speaking) 間を置く má wò okú

pave [peiv] vt (street, yard etc) 舗装する hosố suru
to pave the way for (fig) ...を可能にする ...wo kanố ni suru

pavement [peivˈmənt] n (US) 路面 romén; (BRIT) 歩道 hodố

pavilion [pəvilˈjən] n (BRIT: SPORT) 選手更衣所 señshukõijõ

paving [peiˈviŋ] n (material) 舗装材 hosốzai

paving stone n 敷石 shikíishi

paw [pɔː] n (of animal) 足 ashí

pawn [pɔːn] n (CHESS) ポーン pôn; (fig) 操り人形 ayátsuriniñgyō
♦vt 質に入れる shichí ni irerù

pawnbroker [pɔːnˈbroukəːr] n 質屋 shichíyà

pawnshop [pɔːnˈʃɑːp] n 質屋 shichíyà

pay [pei] n (wage, salary etc) 給料 kyúryō
♦vb (pt, pp paid)
♦vt (sum of money, debt, bill, wage) 払う haráù
♦vi (be profitable) 利益になる ríèki ni nárù
to pay attention (to) (...に) 注意する (...ni) chûi suru
to pay someone a visit ...を訪問する ...wo hốmon suru
to pay one's respects to someone ...にあいさつをする ...ni aísatsu wo suru

payable [peiˈəbəl] adj (sum of money) 支払うべき shiháraubeki
payable to bearer (check) 持参人払いの jisánninbaraì no

pay back vt (money) 返す kaếsù; (person) ...に仕返しをする ...ni shikáeshi wò suru

payday [peiˈdei] n 給料日 kyúryōbi

payee [peiiːˈ] n (of check, postal order) 受取人 ukétorinìn

pay envelope (US) n 給料袋 kyúryōbukùro

pay for vt fus (purchases) ...の代金を払う ...no daíkin wò haráù; (fig) 償う tsugúnaù

pay in vt (money, check etc) 預け入れる azúkeirerù, 入金する nyúkin suru

payment [pei'mənt] n (act) 支払い shiháraì; (amount of money) 支払い金額 shiháraikiṅgaku

a monthly payment 月賦 géppù

pay off vt (debt) 返済する heñsai suru; (person: with bribe etc) 買収する baíshū suru

♦vi (scheme, decision) 成功する seíkō suru

pay packet (BRIT) n = **pay envelope**

pay phone n 公衆電話 kṓshūdeñwa

payroll [pei'roul] n 従業員名簿 jūgyōinmeíbo

pay slip n 給料明細書 kyúryōmeisaishò

pay up vt 払う haráù

PC [pi:si:'] n abbr = **personal computer**; (BRIT: police constable) 巡査 júñsa

p.c. abbr = **per cent**

pea [pi:] n エンドウマメ eñdṓmame

peace [pi:s] n (not war) 平和 heíwa; (calm: of place, surroundings) 静けさ shizúkesà; (: personal) 心の平和 kokórò no heíwa

peaceful [pi:s'fəl] adj (calm: place, time) 静寂な seíjaku na; (: person) 穏和な oñwa na

peach [pi:tʃ] n モモ momó

peacock [pi:'kɑ:k] n クジャク kujáku

peak [pi:k] n (of mountain: top) 頂上 chṓjō; (of cap) つば tsúbà; (fig: physical, intellectual etc) 頂点 chṓten, ピーク pḭku

peak hours npl ピーク時 pḭkuji

peak period n ピーク時 pḭkuji

peal [pi:l] n (of bells) 響き hibḭki

peal of laughter 大きな笑い声 ṑkina waráigoè

peanut [pi:'nʌt] n 落花生 rakkáseì, ピーナッツ pḭnattsù

peanut butter n ピーナッツバター pḭnattsubatā

pear [pe:r] n セイヨウナシ seíyōnashḭ

pearl [pə:rl] n 真珠 shiñju, パール pằru

peasant [pez'ənt] n 百姓 hyakúshò, 農夫 nṓfu

peat [pi:t] n 泥炭 deítan

pebble [peb'əl] n 小石 koíshi

peck [pek] vt (also: **peck at**: subj: bird) つつく tsutsúkù

♦n (of bird) つつく事 tsutsúkù kotó; (kiss) 軽いキス karúi kísù

pecking order [pek'iŋ-] n (fig: hierarchy) 序列 jorétsu

peckish [pek'iʃ] (BRIT: inf) adj (hungry): *to be peckish* おなかがすいた onáka ga suità

peculiar [pikju:l'jə:r] adj (strange: person, taste, shape etc) 変った kawátta; (belonging exclusively): *peculiar to* 独特な dokútoku na

peculiarity [pikju:li:ær'iti:] n (strange habit, characteristic) 癖 kusé; (distinctive feature: of person, place etc) 特徴 tokúchō

pedal [ped'əl] n (on bicycle, car, machine) ペダル pédaru

♦vi (on bicycle) こぐ kógù

pedantic [pədæn'tik] adj げん学的な geñgakuteki na

peddler [ped'lə:r] n (also: **drug peddler**) 麻薬の売人 mayáku nò baínìñ

pedestal [ped'istəl] n 台座 daíza

pedestrian [pədes'tri:ən] n 歩行者 hokṓshà

♦adj 歩行者の hokṓshà no

pedestrian crossing (BRIT) n 横断歩道 ṓdanhodṓ

pediatrics [pi:di:æt'riks] (BRIT paediatrics) n (hospital department) 小児科 shṓnika; (subject) 小児科学 shṓnikagàku

pedigree [ped'əgri:] n (of animal) 血統 kettṓ; (fig: background) 経歴 keíreki

♦cpd (animal) 純血の juñketsu no

pee [pi:] (inf) vi おしっこする o-shíkkò suru

peek [pi:k] vi のぞく nozóku

peel [pi:l] n (of orange, apple, potato) 皮 kawá

♦vt (vegetables, fruit) ...の皮をむく ...no kawá wo mukù

♦vi (paint, wallpaper) はげる hagérù; (skin) むける mukérù

peep [pi:p] *n* (look) のぞき見 nozókimi; (sound) 鳴き声 nakígoè
♦*vi* (look) のぞく nozóku

peephole [pi:p'houl] *n* のぞき穴 nozókiàna

peep out *vi* (be visible) のぞく nozóku

peer [pi:r] *vi*: **to peer at** ...をじっと見る ...wo jíttò mírú
♦*n* (noble) 貴族 kízòku; (equal) 同等の人 dótō nò hitó; (contemporary) 同輩 dóhai

peerage [pi:'ridʒ] *n* (rank) 貴族の地位 kízòku no chíi

peeved [pi:vd] *adj* (annoyed) 怒った okóttà

peevish [pi:'viʃ] *adj* (bad-tempered) 機嫌の悪い kigén nò warúî

peg [peg] *n* (hook, knob: for coat etc) フック fúkkù; (BRIT: also: **clothes peg**) 洗濯ばさみ sefitakubasámi

pejorative [pidʒɔ:r'ətiv] *adj* (word, expression) 軽べつ的な keíbetsuteki na

Peking [pi:kiŋ'] *n* 北京 pékìn

Pekin(g)ese [pi:kəni:z'] *n* (dog) ペキニーズ pekínîzu

pelican [pel'ikən] *n* (ZOOL) ペリカン períkàn

pelican crossing (BRIT) *n* (AUT) 押しボタン式信号 oshíbotanshiki shìńgō

pellet [pel'it] *n* (of paper, mud etc) 丸めた球 marúmeta tamà; (also: **shotgun pellet**) 散弾銃の弾 safidañjū no tamá

pelt [pelt] *vt*: **to pelt someone with something** ...に...を浴びせ掛ける ...ni ...wo abísekakerù
♦*vi* (rain) 激しく降る hagéshikù fúrù; (*inf*: run) 駆ける kakérù
♦*n* (animal skin) 毛皮 kegáwa

pelvis [pel'vis] *n* 骨盤 kotsúban

pen [pen] *n* (for writing: fountain pen, ballpoint pen) ペン péǹ; (: felt-tip pen etc) サインペン saíǹpen; (enclosure: for sheep, pigs etc) 囲い kakói

penal [pi:'nəl] *adj* (colony, institution) 刑罰の keíbatsu no; (system, code, reform) 刑法の keíhō no

penalize [pi:'nəlaiz] *vt* (punish) 罰する bassúrù; (: SPORT) ...にペナルティーを科する ...ni penárutî wo kasúrù

penalty [pen'əlti:] *n* (punishment) 罰 bátsù; (fine) 罰金 bakkíň; (SPORT) ペナルティー penárutî

penalty (kick) *n* (RUGBY, SOCCER) ペナルティーキック penárutî kíkkù

penance [pen'əns] *n* 償い tsugúnai

pence [pens] *pl of* **penny**

pencil [pen'səl] *n* (for writing, drawing) 鉛筆 eñpitsu

pencil case *n* 筆入れ fudéîre

pencil sharpener *n* 鉛筆削り eñpitsu-kezùri, シャープナー shâpunà

pendant [pen'dənt] *n* ペンダント péňdanto

pending [pen'diŋ] *prep* ...を待つ間 ...wo mátsù aída
♦*adj* (business) 未決の mikétsu no; (lawsuit) 審理中の shifirichū no; (exam) 差迫った sashísemattà

pendulum [pen'dʒələm] *n* (of clock) 振子 furíko

penetrate [pen'itreit] *vt* (subj: person: enemy territory) ...に侵入する ...ni shiñnyū suru; (forest etc) ...に入り込む ...ni haírikomù; (: water etc) 染込む shimíkomù; (: light) 通る tôru

penetrating [pen'itreitiŋ] *adj* (sound, glance, mind, observation) 鋭い surúdoî

penetration [penitrei'ʃən] *n* (action) 入り込む事 haírikomù kotó

penfriend [pen'frend] (BRIT) *n* = **pen pal**

penguin [pen'gwin] *n* ペンギン péňgin

penicillin [penisil'in] *n* ペニシリン penî-shirin

peninsula [pənin'sələ] *n* 半島 hańtō

penis [pi:'nis] *n* 陰茎 ińkei, ペニス pénîs

penitent [pen'itənt] *adj* (person: very sorry) 後悔している kōkai shite irú

penitentiary [peniten'tʃə:ri:] (US) *n* 刑務所 keímushò

penknife [pen'naif] *n* ペンナイフ peñnaî-fu

pen name *n* ペンネーム peñnêmu

penniless [pen'i:lis] *adj* (person) 一文無しの ichímoňnashi no

penny [pen'i:] (*pl* **pennies** *or BRIT* **pence**) *n* (US) ペニー pénî, セント séňto;

(*BRIT*: after 1971: = one hundredth of a pound) ペニ péni

pen pal *n* ペンパル pénparu, ペンフレンド pénfuréndo

pension [pen'tʃən] *n* (state benefit) 年金 nénkin; (company pension etc) 恩給 ońkyū

pensioner [pen'tʃənər] (*BRIT*) *n* (old-age pensioner) 年金で生活する老人 nénkin dè sefkatsu surū rōjìn, 年金暮らしの人 nénkingurāshi no hitó

pension fund *n* 年金基金 nénkinkikìn

pensive [pen'siv] *adj* (person, expression etc) 考え込んだ kańgaekonda

pentagon [pen'təgɑːn] *n*: **the Pentagon** (*US*: POL) 国防総省 kokúbōsōshò, ペンタゴン péntàgon

Pentecost [pen'təkɔːst] *n* 聖霊降臨祭 seíreikōrìnsai

penthouse [pent'haus] *n* (flat) 屋上階 okújōkai

pent-up [pent'ʌp'] *adj* (feelings) たまった tamátta

penultimate [pinʌl'təmit] *adj* 最後から2番目の saígo kara nibánme no

people [piː'pəl] *npl* (persons) 人々 hitóbìto; (inhabitants) 住民 júmin; (citizens) 市民 shímin; (POL): **the people** 国民 kokúmin

♦*n* (nation) 国民 kokúmin; (race) 民族 mínzoku

several people came 数人来ました sūnin kimashìta

people say that ... ...だと言われている ...da to iwáreté irù, ...だそうだ ...da sō dà

pep [pep] (*inf*) *n* (energy, vigor) 元気 génki

pepper [pep'əːr] *n* (spice) こしょう koshō; (hot pepper) トウガラシ tōgarashi; (sweet pepper) ピーマン pīman

♦*vt* (*fig*): **to pepper with** ...を振掛ける ...wo furíkakerù

peppermint [pep'əːrmint] *n* (sweet) ハッカあめ hakkáamè

peptalk [pep'tɔːk] (*inf*) *n* (encouraging talk) 激励演説 gekíreienzetsù

pep up *vt* (enliven) 活気付ける kakkízukerù

per [pəːr] *prep* (of amounts, prices etc: for each) ...につき ...ni tsukí

per day/person 1日〔1人〕につき... ichínichi〔hitórì〕ni tsukí...

per annum 1年につき... ichínèn ni tsukí...

per capita [-kæp'itə] *adj* (income) 一人当りの hitóri atarì no

♦*adv* 一人当り hitóri atarì

perceive [pərsiːv'] *vt* (sound) 聞く kíkù; (light) 見る mírù; (difference) 認識する nińshiki suru; (notice) ...に気が付く ...ni ki gá tsukù; (realize, understand) 分かる wakárù

per cent *n* パーセント pásento

percentage [pərsen'tidʒ] *n* (amount) 割合 waríai, 率 rítsù

perception [pərsep'ʃən] *n* (insight) 洞察力 dōsatsuryòku; (opinion, understanding) 理解 rikái; (faculty) 知覚 chikáku

perceptive [pərsep'tiv] *adj* (person) 洞察力のある dōsatsuryòku no árù, 鋭敏な eíbin na; (analysis, assessment) 鋭い surúdoì

perch [pəːrtʃ] *n* (for bird) 止り木 tomárigì; (fish) パーチ pāchi ◇スズキに似た淡水魚 suzúki ni nitá tańsuigyò

♦*vi*: **to perch (on)** (bird) (...に) 止る (...ni) tomárù; (person) (...に) 腰掛ける (...ni) koshíkakerù

percolator [pəːr'kəleitər] *n* (also: **coffee percolator**) パーコレーター pákorètā

percussion [pərkʌʃ'ən] *n* 打楽器 dagákki ◇総称 sōshō

peremptory [pəremp'təːriː] (*pej*) *adj* (person) 横柄な ōhei na; (order, instruction) 断固たる dańkotarù

perennial [pəren'iːəl] *adj* (flower, plant) 多年生の tanénsei no; (*fig*: problem, feature etc) ありがちな arígachi na

perfect [*adj, n* pəːr'fikt *vb* pəːrfekt'] *adj* (without fault: person, weather, behavior etc) 完璧な kańpeki na; (utter: nonsense, stranger etc) 全くの mattáku no

♦*n* (also: **perfect tense**) 完了形 kańryōkei

♦*vt* (technique) 仕上げる shiágerù

perfection [pərˈfekˈʃən] *n* (faultlessness) 完璧さ kañpekisa

perfectionist [pərˈfekˈʃənist] *n* 完璧主義者 kañpekishugishà

perfectly [pərˈfiktli:] *adv* (emphatic) 全く mattákù; (faultlessly: perform, do etc) 完璧に kañpeki ni; (completely: understand etc) 完全に kañzen ni

perforate [pərˈfəˌreit] *vt* ...に穴を開ける ...ni aná wò akérù

perforations [pərˈfəreiˈʃənz] *npl* (series of small holes) ミシン目 mishíńme

perform [pərˈfɔːrm] *vt* (carry out: task, operation, ceremony etc) 行う okónaù, する surú; (piece of music) 演奏する eñsō suru; (play etc) 上演する jōen suru

♦*vi* (well, badly) する surú, やる yarú

performance [pərˈfɔːrˈməns] *n* (of actor) 演技 eñgi; (of dancer) 踊り odóri; (of musician) 演奏 eñsō; (of singer) 歌い方 utáikata; (of play, show) 上演 jōen; (of car, engine) 性能 seínō; (of athlete, company, economy) 成績 seíseki

performer [pərˈfɔːrˈmər] *n* (actor, dancer, singer etc) 芸能人 geínōjìn

perfume [pərˈfjuːm] *n* (cologne, toilet water, essence) 香水 kōsui; (pleasant smell: of flowers etc) 香り kaórì

perfunctory [pərˈfʌŋkˈtəriː] *adj* (kiss, remark etc) いい加減な iíkagen na

perhaps [pərˈhæps] *adv* (maybe) たぶん ...だろう tábùn ...daró

peril [perˈəl] *n* (great danger) 危険 kikén

perimeter [pərimˈitər] *n* 周辺 shūhen

period [piːrˈiːəd] *n* (length of time) 期間 kikáñ; (SCOL) 時限 jigén; (full stop) 終止符 shūshifù, ピリオド píriòdo; (MED) 月経 gekkéi, メンス méñsu, 生理 seíri

♦*adj* (costume, furniture) 時代の jidái no

periodic(al) [piːriːɑːdˈik(əl)] *adj* (event, occurrence) 周期的な shūkiteki na, 定期的な teíkiteki na

periodical [piːriːɑːdˈikəl] *n* (magazine) 雑誌 zasshí

periodically [piːriːɑːdˈikliː] *adv* 定期的に teíkiteki ni

peripheral [pərifˈəːrəl] *adj* 二次的な nijí-

teki na; (on the edge: *also* COMPUT) 周辺の shūhen no

♦*n* (COMPUT) 周辺機器 shūhenkikì

periphery [pərifˈəːriː] *n* (edge) 周辺 shūhen

periscope [peːrˈiskoup] *n* 潜望鏡 señbōkyō

perish [peːrˈiʃ] *vi* (die) 死ぬ shinú; (die out) 滅びる horóbirù; (rubber, leather etc) 腐る kusárù

perishable [peːrˈiʃəbəl] *adj* (food) いたみやすい itámiyasuì

perjury [pəːrˈdʒəˌriː] *n* (LAW) 偽証 gishō

perk [pəːrk] (*inf*) *n* (extra) 役得 yakútoku

perk up *vi* (cheer up) 元気を出す géñki wo dásù

perky [pəːrˈkiː] *adj* (cheerful) 朗らかな hogáraka na

perm [pəːrm] *n* (for hair) パーマ pāma

permanent [pəːrˈmənənt] *adj* 永久的な eíkyūteki na

permeate [pəːrˈmiːeit] *vi* (pass through) 浸透する shiñtō suru; (*fig*: spread) 広がる hirógarù

♦*vt* (subj: liquid) ...に染込む ...ni shimíkomù; (: idea) ...に広まる ...ni hirómarù

permissible [pəːrˈmisˈəbəl] *adj* (action, behavior) 許される yurúsarerù

permission [pəːrˈmiʃˈən] *n* (consent, authorization) 許可 kyókà

permissive [pəːrˈmisˈiv] *adj* (person, behavior, society) 甘い amái

permit [*n* pəːrˈmit *vb* pəːrˈmit] *n* (official authorization) 許可証 kyokáshō

♦*vt* (allow) 許可する kyókà suru; (make possible) 可能にする kanō ni surù

permutation [pəːrmjəteiˈʃən] *n* 置換え o-kíkae

pernicious [pəːrniʃˈəs] *adj* (very harmful: attitude, influence etc) 有害な yūgai na; (MED) 悪性の akúsei na

perpendicular [pəːrpəndikˈjələːr] *adj* (line, surface) 垂直の suíchoku no; (cliff, slope) 険しい kewáshiì

perpetrate [pəːrˈpitreit] *vt* (commit: crime) 犯す okásù

perpetual [pəːrˈpetʃˈuːəl] *adj* (constant:

motion, darkness) 永久の eíkyū no; (: noise, questions) 年がら年中の neñgaraneñjū no

perpetuate [pə:rpetʃ'uːeit] vt (situation, custom, belief etc) 永続させる eízoku saserù

perplex [pə:rpleks'] vt (person) まごつかせる magótsukaserù

persecute [pə:r'səkjuːt] vt (harass, oppress: minorities etc) 迫害する hakúgai suru

persecution [pə:rsəkjuː'ʃən] n (of minorities etc) 迫害 hakúgai

perseverance [pə:rsəviːr'əns] n 根気 koñki

persevere [pə:rsəviːr'] vi 辛抱強く続ける shiñbōzuyokù tsuzúkerù

Persian [pə:r'ʒən] adj ペルシアの pérùshia no
◆n ペルシア人 perúshiajìn
the (Persian) Gulf ペルシア湾 perúshiawàn

persist [pə:rsist'] vi: *to persist (in doing something)* (...をし) 続ける (...wo shi)tsuzúkerù

persistence [pə:rsis'təns] n (determination) 根気強さ koñkizuyòsa

persistent [pə:rsis'tənt] adj (noise, smell, cough etc) いつまでも続く ítsùmademo tsuzúkù; (person: determined) 根気強い koñkizuyoì

person [pə:r'sən] n 人 hitó
in person (appear, sing, recite etc) 本人が hoñnin ga

personal [pə:r'sənəl] adj (belongings, phone etc) 個人の kojín no; (opinion, life, habits etc) 個人的な kojínteki na; (in person: visit) 本人自身の hoñninjishiñ no

personal assistant n 秘書 hishó

personal call n (TEL) 私用の電話 shiyó no deñwa

personal column n 私信欄 shishíñrañ

personal computer n パーソナルコンピュータ pāsonarukoñpyūta, パソコン pasókòn

personality [pə:rsənæl'itiː] n (character) 人格 jiñkaku; (famous person) 有名人 yūmeíjìn

personally [pə:r'sənəliː] adv (for my etc part) 個人的には kojínteki ni wà; (in person) 本人が hoñnin ga
to take something personally ...を個人攻撃と受止める ...wo kojínkōgeki to ukétomerù

personal organizer n 予定帳 yotéichò

personify [pə:rsɑːn'əfai] vt (evil) ...の権化である ...no góñge de árù; (good) ...の化身である ...no késhìn de árù

personnel [pə:rsənel'] n 職員 shokúin ◇総称 sóshō

perspective [pə:rspek'tiv] n (ARCHIT, ART) 遠近法 eñkinhō; (way of thinking) 見方 mikáta
to get something into perspective (fig) 事情を考えて...を見る jijó wò kañgaetè ...wo mírù

Perspex [pə:rs'peks] ® n アクリル ákùriru

perspiration [pə:rspərei'ʃən] n 汗 ásè

persuade [pə:rsweid'] vt: *to persuade someone to do something* ...する様に...を説き伏せる ...surú yò ni ...wo tokífuserù

persuasion [pə:rswei'ʒən] n (act) 説得 settóku; (creed) 信条 shiñjō

persuasive [pə:rswei'siv] adj (person, argument) 説得力のある settókuryòku no árù

pertaining [pə:rtein'iŋ]: *pertaining to* prep (relating to) ...に関する ...ni kañ suru

pertinent [pə:r'tənənt] adj (answer, remark) 適切な tekísetsu na

perturb [pə:rtəːrb'] vt (person) 不安にする fuán ni surù

Peru [pəruː'] n ペルー pérù

peruse [pəruːz'] vt (newspaper, documents etc) ...に目を通す ...ni mé wo tòsù

Peruvian [pəruː'viːən] adj ペルーの pérù no
◆n ペルー人 perújìn

pervade [pə:rveid'] vt (subj: smell, feeling) ...に充満する ...ni júman suru

perverse [pə:rvəːrs'] adj (contrary: behavior) 天のじゃくの amá no jàku no

perversion [pə:rvəːr'ʒən] n (sexual) 変態

hentai; (of truth) 曲解 kyokkái; (of justice) 悪用 akúyō

pervert [n pəːr'vəːrt vb pəːrvəːrt'] n (sexual pervert) 変態 hentai

♦vt (person, mind) 堕落させる daráku saseru; (truth, someone's words) 曲解する kyokkái suru

pessimism [pes'əmizəm] n 悲観主義 hikánshùgi, ペシミズム peshímizùmu

pessimist [pes'əmist] n 悲観主義者 hikánshugisha, ペシミスト peshímisùto

pessimistic [pesəmis'tik] adj (person) 悲観的な hikánteki na, ペシミスティックな peshímisutikkū na

pest [pest] n (insect) 害虫 gaíchū; (fig: nuisance) うるさいやつ urúsai yatsù

pester [pes'təːr] vt (bother) 悩ませる nayámaserù

pesticide [pes'tisaid] n 殺虫剤 satchūzài

pet [pet] n (domestic animal) 愛がん動物 aígandòbùtsu, ペット péttò

♦cpd (theory, hate etc) 十八番の oháko no

♦vt (stroke: person, animal) 愛ぶする aíbu suru

♦vi (inf: sexually) ペッティングする pettíngu suru

teacher's pet (favorite) 先生のお気に入り seńsei nò o-kí ni irí

petal [pet'əl] n 花びら hanábirà

peter [piː'təːr]: **peter out** vi (road, stream etc) だんだんなくなる dańdan nakúnarù; (conversation, meeting) いつすぼまりに終る shirísubomari ni owárù

petite [pətiːt'] adj (referring to woman: small) 小柄な kogára na

petition [pətiʃ'ən] n (signed document) 陳情書 chińjōshò; (LAW) 請願 seígan

petrified [pet'rəfaid] adj (fig: terrified) 恐怖に駆られた kyòfu ni karáreta

petrol [pet'rəl] (BRIT) n (fuel) ガソリン gasórin

two/four-star petrol レギュラー〔ハイオク〕ガソリン regyúrà(haíoku)gasórin

petrol can n ガソリン缶 gasórinkan

petroleum [pətrou'liːəm] n 石油 sekíyu

petrol pump (BRIT) n (in garage) ガソリンポンプ gasórinponpu

petrol station (BRIT) n ガソリンスタンド gasórinsutando

petrol tank (BRIT) n ガソリンタンク gasórintanku

petticoat [pet'iːkout] n (underskirt) ペチコート péchikōto

petty [pet'iː] adj (small, unimportant) さいさいな sásài na; (small-minded) 狭量な kyóryō na

petty cash n (in office) 小口現金 kogúchigenkin

petty officer n (in navy) 下士官 kashíkan

petulant [petʃ'ələnt] adj せっかちな sekkáchi na

pew [pjuː] n (in church) 長いす nagáisu

pewter [pjuː'təːr] n しろめ shíròme

phallic [fæl'ik] adj (object, symbol) 陰茎状の ińkeijō no

phantom [fæn'təm] n (ghost) お化け obáke

pharmaceutical [fɑːrməsuː'tikəl] adj 製薬の seíyaku no

pharmacist [fɑːr'məsist] n 薬剤師 yakúzaishì

pharmacy [fɑːr'məsiː] n 薬局 yakkyóku

phase [feiz] n (stage) 段階 dańkai

♦vt: **to phase something in/out** ...を段階的に取入れる〔なくす〕 ...wo dańkaiteki nì toríirerù〔nakúsù〕

Ph.D. [piː'eitʃ'diː'] abbr = **Doctor of Philosophy**

pheasant [fez'ənt] n キジ kijí

phenomena [finɑːm'ənə] npl of **phenomenon**

phenomenal [finɑːm'ənəl] adj 驚異的な kyóiteki na

phenomenon [finɑːm'ənɑːn] (pl **phenomena**) n 現象 geńshō

philanthropist [filæn'θrəpist] n 慈善家 jizénka

Philippines [fil'ipiːnz] npl: **the Philippines** フィリピン fírìpin

philosopher [filɑːs'əfəːr] n (scholar) 哲学者 tetsúgakushà

philosophical [filəsɑːf'ikəl] adj (ideas, conversation etc) 哲学的な tetsúgakuteki na; (fig: calm, resigned) 冷静な reísei

na

philosophy [filɑːsˈəfiː] *n* (SCOL) 哲学 tetsúgaku; (set of ideas: of philosopher) ...の哲学 ...no tetsúgaku; (theory: of any person) 考え方 kañgaekatà, 思想 shisō

phlegm [flem] *n* (substance) たん tañ

phlegmatic [flegmætˈik] *adj* (person) の ろまな noróma na

phobia [fouˈbiːə] *n* (irrational fear: of insects, flying, water etc) 恐怖症 kyōfushō

phone [foun] *n* (system) 電話 deñwa; (apparatus) 電話器 deñwakì
♦*vt* ...に電話を掛ける ...ni deñwa wò kakérù
to be on the phone (*BRIT*: possess a phone) 電話を持っている deñwa wò motté irù; (be calling) 電話中である deñwachū de arù

phone back *vt* ...に電話を掛け直す ...ni deñwa wò kakénaosù
♦*vi* 電話を掛け直す deñwa wò kakénaosù

phone book *n* (directory) 電話帳 deñwachō

phone booth *n* 電話ボックス deñwabokkùsu

phone box (*BRIT*) *n* 電話ボックス deñwabokkùsu

phone call *n* 電話 deñwa

phone-in [founˈin] (*BRIT*) *n* (RADIO, TV) 視聴者が電話で参加する番組 shichōsha ga deñwa dè sañka suru bañgumi

phonetics [fənetˈiks] *n* 音声学 oñseigàku

phone up *vt* ...に電話を掛ける ...ni deñwa wò kakérù
♦*vi* 電話を掛ける deñwa wò kakérù

phoney [founˈiː] *adj* (false: address) うその úsò no; (: accent) 偽の nisé no; (person) 信用できない shiñ-yō dekinài

phonograph [founˈəgræf] (*US*) *n* 蓄音機 chikúonkì

phosphorus [fɑːsˈfərəs] *n* りん ríñ

photo [fouˈtou] *n* (photograph) 写真 shashíñ

photocopier [fouˈtəkɑːpiːər] *n* (machine)

写真複写機 shashíñfukushakì, コピー機 kopíkì

photocopy [fouˈtəkɑːpiː] *n* コピー kópì
♦*vt* (picture, document etc) ...のコピーを 取る ...no kópì wo tórù

photogenic [foutədʒenˈik] *adj* (person) 写真写りの良い shashíñ-utsurì no yóì

photograph [fouˈtəgræf] *n* 写真 shashíñ
♦*vt* (person, object, place etc) 撮影する satsúei suru

photographer [fətɑːgˈrəfəːr] *n* カメラマ ン kaméramàn

photographic [foutəgræfˈik] *adj* (equipment etc) 写真の shashíñ no

photography [fətɑːgˈrəfiː] *n* (art, subject) 写真撮影 shashíñsatsùei

phrase [freiz] *n* (group of words, expression) 言方 iíkàta; (LING) 句 kú
♦*vt* (express) 表現する hyốgen suru

phrase book *n* (foreign language aid) 表現集 hyốgenshū

physical [fizˈikəl] *adj* (of the body: needs, punishment, exercise etc) 肉体的 な nikútaiteki na; (geography, properties) 物理的な butsúriteki na; (world, universe, object) 自然の shizén no; (sciences) 物理学の butsúrigàku no

physical education *n* 体育 taíiku

physically [fizˈikliː] *adv* (fit, attractive) 肉体的に nikútaiteki ni

physician [fiziʃˈən] *n* (doctor) 医者 ishá

physicist [fizˈəsist] *n* 物理学者 butsúrigakushà

physics [fizˈiks] *n* 物理学 butsúrigàku

physiology [fiziɑːlˈədʒiː] *n* (science) 生 理学 seírigàku; (functioning: of animal, plant) 生理 seíri

physiotherapy [fiziːouθeˈrəpiː] *n* (MED) 物理療法 butsúriryồhồ

physique [fiziˈkʼ] *n* (build: of person) 体格 taíkaku

pianist [piːˈænist] *n* (MUS) ピアニスト piánisùto

piano [piːænˈou] *n* (MUS) ピアノ piáno

piccolo [pikˈəlou] *n* (MUS) ピッコロ pikkóro

pick [pik] *n* (tool: *also*: **pick-axe**) つるは し tsurúhashi

♦*vt* (select) 選ぶ erábù; (gather: fruit, flowers) 摘む tsúmù; (remove, take) 取る tórù; (lock) こじ開ける kojíakerù

take your pick (choose) 選ぶ erábù

the pick of (best) ...からえり抜かれた物 ...kara erínukaretà mónò

to pick one's nose/teeth 鼻〔歯〕をほじる haná(há)wò hojírù

to pick a quarrel (with someone) (...に) けんかを売る (...ni) kefika wò urú

pick at *vt fus* (food) ちびちび食べる chíbìchibi tabérù

picket [pik'it] *n* (in strike) ピケ piké

♦*vt* (factory, workplace etc) ...にピケを張る ...ni piké wò hárù

pickle [pik'əl] *n* (*also*: **pickles**: as condiment) ピクルス píkurusu; (*fig*: mess) 苦境 kukyó

♦*vt* (CULIN: in vinegar) 酢漬けにする suzúke ni surù; (: in salt water) 塩漬けにする shiózuke ni surù

pick on *vt fus* (person: criticize) 非難する hinán suru; (: treat badly) いじめる ijímerù

pick out *vt* (distinguish) 識別する shikfbetsu suru; (choose from a group) 選び出す erábidasù, ピックアップする pikkúappù suru

pickpocket [pik'pɑːkit] *n* すり súrì

pick up *vi* (improve: health, economy, trade) 良くなる yókù naru

♦*vt* (object: from floor) 拾う hiróu; (POLICE: arrest) 逮捕する taího suru; (collect: person, parcel etc) 引取る hikítorù; (AUT: passenger) 乗せる nosérù; (person: for sexual encounter) 引っ掛ける hikkákerù; (learn: language, skill etc) 覚える obóerù; (RADIO) 受信する jushín suru

to pick up speed 加速する kasóku suru

to pick oneself up (after falling etc) 起き上る okíagarù

pickup [pik'ʌp] *n* (small truck) ピックアップ pikkúappù

picnic [pik'nik] *n* (outdoor meal) ピクニック pikunikku

picture [pik'tʃər] *n* (painting, drawing, print) 絵 é; (photograph) 写真 shashín;

(TV) 画像 gazó; (film) 映画 éìga; (*fig*: description) 描写 byósha; (: situation) 事態 jítài

♦*vt* (imagine) 想像する sózó suru

picture book *n* 絵本 ehóñ

pictures [pik'tʃərz] (*BRIT*) *npl*: *the pictures* (cinema) 映画 éìga

picturesque [piktʃəresk'] *adj* (place, building) 風情のある fúzèi no árù

pie [pai] *n* (CULIN: vegetable, meat, fruit) パイ pái

piece [piːs] *n* (bit or part of larger thing) かけら kakéra; (portion: of cake, chocolate, bread etc) 一切れ hitókìre; (length: of string, ribbon) 一本 íppòn; (item): *a piece of clothing/furniture/advice* 1つ hitótsu

♦*vt*: *to piece together* (information) 総合する sógo suru; (parts of a whole) 継ぎ合せる tsugíawaserù

to take to pieces (dismantle) 分解する buñkai suru

piecemeal [piːs'miːl] *adv* (irregularly) 少しずつ sukóshizutsù

piecework [piːs'wəːrk] *n* 出来高払いの仕事 dekídakabaràì no shigóto

pie chart *n* 円形グラフ eñkeiguràfu

pier [piːr] *n* 桟橋 sañbashi

pierce [piːrs] *vt* (puncture: surface, material, skin etc) 貫通する kañtsū suru

piercing [piːrs'iŋ] *adj* (*fig*: cry) 甲高い kañdakaì; (: eyes, stare) 鋭い surúdoì; (wind) 刺す様な sásù yō na

piety [pai'əti:] *n* (REL) 信心 shiñjiñ

pig [pig] *n* (ZOOL) ブタ butá; (*pej*: unkind person) 畜生 chikúshó; (: greedy person) 欲張り目 yokúbarimè

pigeon [pidʒ'ən] *n* (bird) ハト hátò

pigeonhole [pidʒ'ənhoul] *n* (for letters, messages) 小仕切り kojíkìri

piggy bank [pig'iː-] *n* (money box) 貯金箱 chokíñbako

pigheaded [pig'hedid] (*pej*) *adj* (stubborn) 頑固な gañko na

piglet [pig'lit] *n* 子ブタ kobúta

pigment [pig'mənt] *n* 色素 shikíso

pigskin [pig'skin] *n* ブタのなめし革 butá no naméshigàwa

pigsty [pig'stai] n (on farm) ブタ小屋 butágoya

pigtail [pig'teil] n (plait) お下げ o-ságe

pike [paik] n (fish) カワカマス kawákamàsu, パイク páiku

pilchard [pil'tʃərd] n (fish) イワシ iwáshi

pile [pail] n (heap, stack) 山 yamá; (of carpet, cloth) 毛足 keáshi, パイル páiru

♦vt (also: **pile up**: objects) 積上げる tsumíagerù

♦vi (also: **pile up**: objects) 積重なる tsumíkasanarù; (problems, work) たまる tamárù

pile into vt fus (car) ...に乗込む ...ni noríkomù

piles [pailz] npl (MED) じ痔 ji

pile-up [pail'ʌp] n (AUT) 衝突事故 shótotsujikò

pilfering [pil'fəriŋ] n (petty thieving) くすねる事 kusúnerù kotó

pilgrim [pil'grim] n (REL) 巡礼者 juńreishà

pilgrimage [pil'grəmidʒ] n (REL) 巡礼 juńreì

pill [pil] n (MED: tablet) 錠剤 jôzai

the pill (contraceptive pill) 経口避妊薬 keíkōhinin̄-yaku, ピル pírù

pillage [pil'idʒ] vt (loot: house, town etc) 略奪する ryakúdatsu suru

pillar [pil'ər] n (ARCHIT) 柱 hashíra

pillar box (BRIT) n (MAIL) ポスト pósùto

pillion [pil'jən] n: **to ride pillion** (on motorcycle) 後ろに相乗りする ushíro nì aínori surù

pillory [pil'ə:ri:] vt (criticize strongly) 非難する hínan suru

pillow [pil'ou] n (cushion: for head) まくら makúra

pillowcase [pil'oukeis] n (cover: for pillow) 枕カバー makúrakabà, ピロケース pirókèsu

pilot [pai'lət] n (AVIAT) 操縦士 sôjùshi, パイロット páìrotto

♦cpd (scheme, study etc) 試験的な shikénteki na

♦vt (aircraft) 操縦する sôjū suru

pilot light n (on cooker, boiler, fire) 口火 kuchíbi

pimp [pimp] n ポン引き poñbiki, ひも himó

pimple [pim'pəl] n にきび níkìbi

pin [pin] n (metal: for attaching, fastening) ピン píñ

♦vt (fasten with pin) ピンで止める píñ de tomérù

pins and needles (in arms, legs etc) しびれが切れる事 shibíre gà kirérù kotó

to pin someone down (fig) ...に約束させる ...ni yakúsoku saserù, ...にくぎを刺す ...ni kugí wò sásù

to pin something on someone (fig) ...に...のぬれぎぬを着せる ...ni ...no nuréginù wo kisérù

pinafore [pin'əfɔ:r] n (also: **pinafore dress**) エプロンドレス epúrondorèsu

pinball [pin'bɔ:l] n (game) スマートボール sumátobòru; (machine) スマートボール機 sumátobòruki

pincers [pin'sə:rz] npl (TECH) やっとこ yattóko, ペンチ péñchi; (of crab, lobster etc) はさみ hasámi

pinch [pintʃ] n (small amount: of salt etc) 一つまみ hitótsùmami

♦vt (person: with finger and thumb) つねる tsunérù; (inf: steal) くすねる kusúnerù

at a pinch 緊急の場合 kiñkyū nò baái

pincushion [pin'kuʃən] n (SEWING) 針刺し harísashì

pine [pain] n (also: **pine tree**) マツ mátsù; (wood) マツ材 matsúzài

♦vi: **to pine for** (person, place) 思い焦がれる omóikogarerù

pineapple [pain'æpəl] n (fruit) パイナップル paínappùru

pine away vi (gradually die) 衰弱して死ぬ suíjaku shite shinù

ping [piŋ] n (noise) ぴゅーんという音 pyūn to iú otò

ping-pong [piŋ'pɔ:ŋ] ® n (sport) 卓球 takkyū, ピンポン píñpon

pink [piŋk] adj ピンク色の piñkuiro no

♦n (color) ピンク色 piñkuiro; (BOT) ナデシコ nadéshìko

pinnacle [pin'əkəl] *n* (of building, mountain) 天辺 teppéñ; (*fig*) 頂点 chôteñ

pinpoint [pin'pɔint] *vt* (discover) 発見する hakkéñ suru; (explain) 説明する setsúmei suru; (position of something) 正確に示す seíkaku nì shimésù

pint [paint] *n* (US: = 473 cc; BRIT: = 568 cc) パイント paíñto

a pint of beer, (BRIT: inf) a pint ビール1パイント bíru ichípaìñto

pin-up [pin'ʌp] *n* (picture) ピンナップ写真〔絵〕 piñnappushashiñ(e)

pioneer [paiəni:r'] *n* (initiator: of scheme, science, method) 先駆者 señkushà, パイオニア paíonìa; (early settler) 開拓者 kaítakushà

pious [pai'əs] *adj* (person) 信心深い shíñjiñbukai

pip [pip] *n* (seed of fruit) 種 tané; (BRIT: time signal on radio) 時報 jihô

pipe [paip] *n* (gen, also for smoking) パイプ paípu; (also: **water pipe**) 水道管 suídōkan; (also: **gas pipe**) ガス管 gasúkan

◆*vt* (water, gas, oil) パイプで運ぶ paípu de hakóbù

pipes [paipz] *npl* (also: **bagpipes**) バグパイプ bagúpaìpu

pipe cleaner *n* パイプクリーナー paípukurìnà

pipe down (*inf*) *vi* (be quiet) 黙る damárù

pipe dream *n* (hope, plan) 夢想 musô

pipeline [paip'lain] *n* (for oil, gas) パイプライン paípuraìn

piper [pai'pə:r] *n* (bagpipe player) バグパイプ奏者 bagúpaìpu sòsha

piping [pai'piŋ] *adv*: **piping hot** (water, food, coffee) うんと熱い úñto atsúì

piquant [pi:'kənt] *adj* (food: spicy) ぴりっとした piríttò shitá; (*fig*: interesting, exciting) 興味深い kyômibùkai

pique [pi:k] *n* 立腹 rippúku

pirate [pai'rit] *n* (sailor) 海賊 kaízoku

◆*vt* (book, video tape, cassette etc) ...の海賊版を作る ...no kaízokubañ wo tsukúrù

pirate radio (BRIT) *n* 海賊放送 kaízokuhòsō

pirouette [piru:et'] *n* つま先旋回 tsumásakiseñkai

Pisces [pai'si:z] *n* (ASTROLOGY) 魚座 uózà

piss [pis] (*inf!*) *vi* (urinate) おしっこする oshíkkò suru

pissed [pist] (*inf!*) *adj* (US) 怒った okóttà; (BRIT: drunk) 酔っ払った yoppárattà

pistol [pis'təl] *n* けん銃 keñjū, ピストル pisútoru

piston [pis'tən] *n* ピストン písùton

pit [pit] *n* (hole in ground) 穴 aná; (in surface of something) くぼみ kubómi; (also: **coal pit**) 炭坑 tañkō; (quarry) 採石場 saísekijō

◆*vt*: *to pit one's wits against someone* ...と知恵比べをする ...to chiékuràbe wo suru

pitch [pitʃ] *n* (BRIT: SPORT: ground) グラウンド guráundo; (MUS) 調子 chôshi, ピッチ pitchi; (*fig*: level, degree) 度合 doai; (tar) ピッチ pítchì

◆*vt* (throw) 投げる nagérù

◆*vi* (fall forwards) つんのめる tsuñnomerù

to pitch a tent (erect) テントを張る téñto wo hárù

pitch-black [pitʃ'blæk'] *adj* (night, place) 真っ暗な makkúra na

pitched battle [pitʃt-] *n* (violent fight) 激戦 gekísen

pitchfork [pitʃ'fɔ:rk] *n* ホーク hôku

piteous [pit'i:əs] *adj* (sight, sound etc) 悲惨な hisán na

pitfall [pit'fɔ:l] *n* (difficulty, danger) 落し穴 otóshiàna, 危険 kikén

pith [piθ] *n* (of orange, lemon etc) わた watá

pithy [piθ'i:] *adj* (comment, saying etc) 中身の濃い nakámì no kôi

pitiful [pit'ifəl] *adj* (touching: appearance, sight) 哀れな awáre na

pitiless [pit'ilis] *adj* (person) 冷酷な reíkoku na

pits [pits] *npl* (AUT) ピット pitto

pittance [pit'əns] *n* (very small income) スズメの涙 suzúme no namída

pity [pit'i:] n (compassion) 哀れみ awáre-mì

♦vt 哀れむ awáremù

what a pity! (expressing disappointment) 残念だ zafinen da

pivot [piv'ət] n (TECH) 旋回軸 señkaijì-ku, ピボット píbòtto; (fig) 中心 chúshin

pizza [pi:t'sə] n ピッツァ píttsà, ピザ pí-zà

placard [plæk'ɑ:rd] n (sign: in public place) 看板 kañban; (: in march etc) プラカード purákàdo

placate [plei'keit] vt (person, anger) なだめる nadámerù

place [pleis] n (in general: point, building, area) 所 tokóro, 場所 bashó; (position: of object) 位置 íchì; (seat) 席 sékì; (job, post etc) 職 shokú, ポスト pósùto; (home): *at/to his place* 彼の家で(へ) kárè no ié de(e); (role: in society, system etc) 役割 yakúwarì

♦vt (put: object) 置く okú; (identify: person) 思い出す omóidasù

to take place (happen) 起る okórù

out of place (not suitable) 場違いの bachígai no

in the first place (first of all) まず第一 に mázù daíchi nì

to change places with someone ...と交代する ...to kótai suru

to be placed (in race, exam) 入賞する nyúshō suru

place of birth n 出生地 shusséichì

placenta [pləsen'tə] n 胎盤 taíban

placid [plæs'id] adj (person) 穏和な ofíwa na

plagiarism [plei'dʒə:rizəm] n ひょう窃 hyósetsu, 盗作 tósaku

plague [pleig] n (MED) 伝染病 deñsen-byò; (fig: of locusts etc) 異常発生 ijóhas-sèi

♦vt (fig: subj: problems, difficulties) 悩ます nayámasù

plaice [pleis] n inv (fish) カレイ kárèi

plaid [plæd] n (cloth) チェックの生地 chékkù no kíjì

plain [plein] adj (unpatterned) 無地の mújì no; (simple: dress, food) 質素な shís-sò na; (clear, easily understood) 明白な meíhaku na; (not beautiful) 不器量な bu-kíryò na

♦adv (wrong, stupid etc) 全く mattáku

♦n (area of land) 平原 heígen

plain chocolate n ブラックチョコレート burákku chokorèto

plain-clothes [plein'klouz] adj (police officer) 私服の shifúku no

plainly [plein'li:] adv (obviously) 明白に meíhaku ni; (hear, see, smell: easily) はっきりと hakkírì to; (state: clearly) ざっくばらんに zákkùbaran ni

plaintiff [plein'tif] n (LAW) 原告 geñko-ku

plaintive [plein'tiv] adj (cry, voice) 哀れっぽい awáreppoì

plait [plæt] n (of hair) お下げ o-ságe; (of rope, leather) 編みひも状の物 amíhimo-jō no monó

plan [plæn] n (scheme, project) 計画 keí-kaku, プラン púràn; (drawing) 図面 zú-mèn; (schedule) 予定表 yotéihyō

♦vt (work out in advance: crime, holiday, future etc) 計画する keíkaku suru

♦vi (think ahead) 計画する keíkaku suru

to plan to do ...しようと計画する ...shi-yó tò keíkaku suru

plane [plein] n (AVIAT) 飛行機 híkòki; (MATH) 面 mén; (fig: level) 段階 dañkai-i; (tool) かんな kanna; (also: **plane tree**) スズカケノキ suzúkake no ki, プラタナス purátanàsu

planet [plæn'it] n 惑星 wakúsei

plank [plæŋk] n (of wood) 板 ítà

planner [plæn'ə:r] n (gen) 計画をする人 keíkaku wo suru hitò; (also: **town planner**) 都市計画担当者 toshíkeikaku tantò-shà; (of TV program, project) 計画者 keíkakushà •

planning [plæn'iŋ] n (of future, project, event etc) 計画 keíkaku; (also: **town planning**) 都市計画 toshíkeìkaku

family planning 家族計画 kazókukeí-kaku

planning permission n 建築許可 keñ-chikukyòka

plant [plænt] n (BOT) 植物 shokúbùtsu;

(machinery) 設備 sétsùbi; (factory) プラント puránto

♦vt (seed, plant, sapling) 植える uérù; (field, garden) ...に植える ...ni uérù; (secretly: microphone, bomb, incriminating evidence etc) 仕掛ける shikákerù

plantation [plæntei'ʃən] n (of tea, rubber, sugar etc) 農園 nốen; (area planted out with trees) 植林地 shokúrìnchi

plaque [plæk] n (commemorative plaque: on building etc) 銘板 meíban; (on teeth) 歯こう shíkō

plasma [plæz'mə] n 血清 kesséi

plaster [plæs'tə:r] n (for walls) しっくい shikkúì; (also: **plaster of Paris**) 石こう sekkố; (BRIT: also: **sticking plaster**) ばんそうこう bańsōkō

♦vt (wall, ceiling) ...にしっくいを塗る ...ni shikkúì wo nurú; (cover: **to plaster with** ...に...をべったり張る ...ni ...wo bettárì hárù

plastered [plæs'tə:rd] (inf) adj 酔っ払った yopparáttà

plasterer [plæs'tərə:r] n (of walls, ceilings) 左官屋 sakáñ-ya

plastic [plæs'tik] n 合成樹脂 gốseijushî, プラスチック purásuchikkù

♦adj (made of plastic: bucket, chair, cup etc) プラスチック製の purásuchikkusei no

plastic bag n ポリ袋 poríbùkuro

Plasticine [plæs'tisi:n]® n 合成粘土 gốseineñdo

plastic surgery n 整形手術 seíkeishujùtsu

plate [pleit] n (dish) 皿 sará; (plateful: of food, biscuits etc) 一皿 hitósàra; (in book: picture, photograph) 1ページ大の挿絵 ichípèjidai nò sashíè, プレート púrèto; (dental plate) 入れ歯 iréba

gold/silver plate 貴金属の食器類 kikínzoku no shokkírùi

plateau [plætou'] (pl **plateaus** or **plateaux**) n (GEO) 高原 kốgen

plate glass n (for window, door) 板ガラス itágaràsu

platform [plæt'fɔ:rm] n (at meeting, for band) 演壇 eńdan; (raised structure: for landing, loading on etc) 台 dáì; (RAIL) ホーム hốmu; (BRIT: of bus) 踏段 fumídan, ステップ sutéppù; (POL) 綱領 kốryō

platinum [plæt'ənəm] n 白金 hakkín, プラチナ puráchina

platitude [plæt'ətu:d] n 決り文句 kimárimoñku

platonic [plətɑ:'nik] adj 純粋に精神的な juñsui nî seíshinteki na, プラトニックな purátonikkù na

platoon [plətu:n'] n 小隊 shốtai

platter [plæt'ə:r] n 盛皿 morízara

plausible [plɔ:'zəbəl] adj (theory, excuse, statement) もっともらしい mottómorashiì; (person) 口先のうまい kuchísaki nò umaì

play [plei] n (THEATER, RADIO, TV) 劇 gékì

♦vt (subj: children: game) ...して遊ぶ ...shite asóbù; (football, tennis, chess) やる yarú; (compete against) ...と試合をする ...to shiái wò suru; (part, role: in play, film etc) 演ずる eñzurù, ...にふんする ...ni funsuru; (instrument, tune) 演奏する eñsō suru; (listen to: tape, record) 聞く kíkù

♦vi (children: on beach, swings etc) 遊ぶ asóbù; (MUS: orchestra, band) 演奏する eñsō suru; (: record, tape, radio) かかる kakárù

to play safe 大事を取る daíji wò tôrù

playboy [plei'bɔi] n プレーボーイ purébòi

play down vt 軽く扱う karúku atsukaù

player [plei'ə:r] n (SPORT) 選手 sénshu, プレーヤー puréyà; (MUS) 奏者 sốsha; (THEATER) 役者 yakúsha

playful [plei'fəl] adj (person, animal) 遊び好きの asóbizuki no

playground [plei'graund] n (in park) 遊び場 asóbiba; (in school) 校庭 kốtei, 運動場 uñdōjō

playgroup [plei'gru:p] (BRIT) n 保育園 hoíkuèn

playing card [plei'iŋ-] n トランプ toráñpu

playing field n グラウンド guráundo

playmate [plei'meit] n 遊び友達 asóbitomodachi

mŏdachi

play-off [plei'ɔːf] n (SPORT) 優勝決定戦 yúshōketteïsen, プレーオフ puréofù

playpen [plei'pen] n ベビーサークル bebísākuru

plaything [plei'θiŋ] n おもちゃ omóchà

playtime [plei'taim] n (SCOL) 休み時間 yasúmijikàn

play up vi (cause trouble: machine) 調子が悪くなる chŏshi gà wárùku naru; (: children) 行儀を悪くする gyŏgi wò wárùku suru

playwright [plei'rait] n 劇作家 gekísakka

plc [piːelsiː'] abbr (= public limited company) 有限株式会社 yúgen kabushikigaishà

plea [pliː] n (request) 懇願 koñgan; (LAW) 申立て mŏshitate

plead [pliːd] vt (LAW) 申立てる mŏshitaterù; (give as excuse: ignorance, ill health etc) ...だと言い訳する ...dá tò iíwake surù

♦vi (LAW) 申立てる mŏshitaterù; (beg): **to plead with someone** ...に懇願する ...ni koñgan suru

pleasant [plez'ənt] adj (agreeable, nice: weather, chat, smile etc) 気持の良い kimóchi no yoì; (agreeable: person) 愛想の良い aíso no yoì

pleasantries [plez'əntriːz] npl: **to exchange pleasantries** あいさつを交わす aísatsu wo kawásù

please [pliːz] excl (polite request) どうぞ dŏzo, どうか dŏka; (polite acceptance): **yes, please** ええ, 有難う eé, arígàtō; (to attract someone's attention) 済みません sumímaseñ

♦vt (give pleasure or satisfaction to) 喜ばす yorókobasù

♦vi (give pleasure, satisfaction) 人を喜ばす hitó wò yorókobasù; (think fit): **do as you please** お好きな様にして下さい o-súki na yŏ ni shité kudasaì

please yourself! (inf) ご勝手に go-kátte nì

pleased [pliːzd] adj (happy, satisfied): **pleased (with)** (...で) 満足している

(...de) mañzoku shite irú

pleased to meet you 初めまして hajímemashìte

pleasing [pliː'ziŋ] adj (remark etc) 愉快な yúkài na, うれしい uréshiì; (picture) 楽しい tanóshiì; (person) 愛敬のある aíkyō no arù

pleasure [pleʒ'əːr] n (happiness, satisfaction) 快楽 kaíraku; (activity of enjoying oneself, enjoyable experience) 楽しみ tanóshimì

it's a pleasure どういたしまして dŏ itáshimashìte

pleasure boat n 遊覧船 yúransen

pleat [pliːt] n ひだ hídà, プリーツ purítsù

pledge [pledʒ] n (promise) 約束 yakúsoku

♦vt (promise: money, support, help) 約束する yakúsoku suru

plentiful [plen'tifəl] adj (food, supply, amount) 豊富な hŏfù na

plenty [plen'tiː] n: **plenty of** (much, many) 沢山の takúsan no; (sufficient) 十分な jŭbun na

pleurisy [pluːr'isiː] n ろく膜炎 rokúmakueñ

pliable [plai'əbəl] adj (material) しなやかな shináyàka na; (fig: person) 素直な súnào na

pliant [plai'ənt] adj = **pliable**

pliers [plai'əːrz] npl ペンチ péñchi

plight [plait] n (of person, country) 苦境 kukyŏ

plimsolls [plim'səlz] (BRIT) npl 運動靴 uñdŏgutsu, スニーカー suníkà

plinth [plinθ] n 台座 daíza

plod [plɑːd] vi (walk) とぼとぼ歩く tóbòtobo arúkù; (fig) 何とかやる nán to ka yarú

plonk [plɑːŋk] (inf) n (BRIT: wine) 安ワイン yasúwaìn

♦vt: **to plonk something down** たたきつける様に...を置く tatákitsukeru yŏ ni ...wo ókù

plot [plɑːt] n (secret plan) 陰謀 iñbō; (of story, play, film) 筋 súji, プロット puróttò; (of land) 区画 kukáku

♦vt (sb's downfall etc) たくらむ takúra-

mù; (AVIAT, NAUT: position on chart) 地図に書き込む chízù ni kakíkomù; (MATH: point on graph) グラフにする gúráfu ni suru

♦vi (conspire) 陰謀を企てる iñbō wò kuwádarusù

plotter [plɑːˈtəːr] n (instrument) 製図道具 seízudōgu

plough [plau] (US also: **plow**) n (AGR) すき sukí

♦vt (earth) 耕す tagáyasù

to plough money into (company, project etc) ...に金をつぎ込む ...ni kané wò tsugíkomù

ploughman's lunch [plauˈmənz-] (BRIT) n 軽食 keíshoku ◇パブのランチで、パン、チーズ、ピクルスからなる pábù no ráñchi de, páñ, chízu, píkùrusu kara nárù

plough through vt fus (crowd) ...をかき分けて歩く ...wo kakíwakete arukù

plow [plau] (US) = **plough**

ploy [plɔi] n 策略 sakúryaku

pluck [plʌk] vt (fruit, flower, leaf) 摘む tsúmù; (musical instrument) つま弾く tsumábikù; (bird) ...の羽をむしる ...no hane wò mushírù; (remove hairs from: eyebrow) ...の毛を抜く ...no ké wò nukú

♦n (courage) 勇気 yúki

to pluck up courage 勇気を出す yúki wo dásù

plug [plʌg] n (ELEC) 差込み sashíkomi, プラグ púràgu; (stopper: in sink, bath) 栓 séñ; (AUT: also: **spark(ing) plug**) スパークプラグ supákupuràgu

♦vt (hole) ふさぐ fuságù; (inf: advertise) 宣伝する señden suru

plug in vt (ELEC) ...のプラグを差込む ...no púràgu wo sashíkomù

plum [plʌm] n (fruit) プラム púràmu

♦cpd (inf): **plum job** 甘い汁を吸える職 amái shirù wo suérù shoku

plumage [pluːˈmidʒ] n 羽 hane ◇鳥の体を覆う羽の総称 torí nò karáda wo ōù hane no sōshō

plumb [plʌm] vt: **to plumb the depths** (fig) (of unpleasant emotion) 辛酸をなめ尽す shiñsan wò namétsukusù; (of un-

pleasant expression) ...を極端に表現する ...wo kyokútan nì hyōgen suru

plumber [plʌmˈəːr] n 配管工 haíkankō

plumbing [plʌmˈiŋ] n (piping) 水道設備 suídōsetsubì; (trade, work) 配管業 haíkangyō

plume [pluːm] n (of bird) 羽 hane; (on helmet, horse s head) 前立 maédate

plummet [plʌmˈit] vi: **to plummet (down)** (bird, aircraft) 真っ直ぐに落下する massúgù ni rakká surù; (price, amount, rate) 暴落する bóraku suru

plump [plʌmp] adj (person) ぽっちゃりした potchári shita

♦vi: **to plump for** (inf: choose) 選ぶ erábù

plump up vt (cushion, pillow) 膨らませる fukúramaserù

plunder [plʌnˈdəːr] n (activity) 略奪 ryakúdatsu; (stolen things) 分捕り品 buñdorihiñ

♦vt (steal from: city, tomb) 略奪する ryakúdatsu suru

plunge [plʌndʒ] n (dive: of bird, person) 飛込み tobíkomi; (fig: of prices, rates etc) 暴落 bóraku

♦vt (hand, knife) 突っ込む tsukkómù

♦vi (fall: person, thing) 落ちる ochírù; (dive: bird, person) 飛込む tobíkomù; (fig: prices, rates etc) 暴落する bóraku suru

to take the plunge 冒険する bóken suru

plunger [plʌnˈdʒəːr] n (for sink) プランジャー puráñja ◇長い棒の付いたゴムカップ nagáî bó no tsuità gomúkappù

plunging [plʌnˈdʒiŋ] adj (neckline) 切込みの深い kiríkomi no fukaí

pluperfect [pluːpəːrˈfikt] n 過去完了形 kakókanryōkei

plural [pluːrˈəl] adj 複数の fukúsū no

♦n 複数形 fukúsūkei

plus [plʌs] n (also: **plus sign**) 加符号 kafúgō, プラス púràsu

♦prep (MATH) ...に ...を加算して ...ni ...wo kasán shite, ...に ...を足して ...ni ...wo tashíte; (in addition to) ...に加えて ...ni kuwáete

2 plus 2 is 4 2足す2は4 ní tasù ní wà yőñ

ten/twenty plus (more than) 10〔20〕以上 jú(nijú)ijő

plush [plʌʃ] *adj* (car, hotel etc) 豪華な gő-ka na

plutonium [plu:tou'ni:əm] *n* プルトニウム purútonìumu

ply [plai] *vt* (a trade) 営む itónamù
◆*vi* (ship) 往復する őfuku suru
◆*n* (of wool, rope) 太さ futósa

to ply someone with drink ...に強引に酒を勧める ...ni gőin nì saké wò susúmerù

plywood [plai'wud] *n* ベニヤ板 benîyaità

P.M. [pi:'em'] *abbr* = **Prime Minister**

p.m. [pi:'em'] *adv abbr* (= *post meridiem*) 午後 gőgo

pneumatic [nu:mæt'ik] *adj* (air-filled) 空気で膨らませた kűki dè fukúramasetà; (powered by air) 空気... kűki...

pneumatic drill *n* 空気ドリル kűkidorì-ru

pneumonia [nu:moun'jə] *n* 肺炎 haîen

poach [poutʃ] *vt* (steal: fish) 密漁する mitsúryō suru; (: animals, birds) 密猟する mitsúryō suru; (cook: egg) 落し卵にする otóshitamagò ni suru, ポーチエッグにする pőchitoeggù ni suru; (: fish) 煮る nirú
◆*vi* (steal: fish) 密漁する mitsúryō suru; (: animals, birds) 密猟する mitsúryō suru

poached [poutʃt] *adj*: *poached egg* 落し卵 otóshitamagò, ポーチエッグ pőchitoeggù

poacher [pou'tʃəːr] *n* (of fish) 密漁者 mitsúryōshà; (of animals, birds) 密猟者 mitsúryōshà

P.O. Box [pi:'ou-] *n abbr* = **Post Office Box**

pocket [pɑ:k'it] *n* (on jacket, trousers, suitcase, car door etc) ポケット pokéttò; (*fig*: small area) 孤立地帯 korítsuchitài
◆*vt* (put in one's pocket) ポケットに入れる pokéttò ni irérù; (steal) くすねる kusúnerù

to be out of pocket (*BRIT*) 損をする sőñ suru

pocketbook [pɑ:k'itbuk] (*US*) *n* (wallet) 財布 saífu; (handbag) ハンドバッグ hañdobaggù

pocket calculator *n* 電卓 deñtaku

pocket knife *n* ポケットナイフ pokéttonaìfu

pocket money *n* 小遣い kózùkai

pod [pɑ:d] *n* さや sáyà

podgy [pɑ:dʒ'i:] *adj* 小太りの kobútòri no

podiatrist [pədai'ətrist] (*US*) *n* 足治療医 ashíchiryòi

poem [pou'əm] *n* 詩 shi

poet [pou'it] *n* 詩人 shijín

poetic [pouet'ik] *adj* (relating to poetry) 詩の shi no; (like poetry) 詩的な shitéki na

poet laureate *n* 桂冠詩人 keikanshijin

poetry [pou'itri:] *n* (LITERATURE) 詩歌 shíika

poignant [pɔin'jənt] *adj* (emotion, look, grief etc) 痛ましい itámashìi

point [pɔint] *n* (*gen*) 点 teñ, ポイント poíñto; (sharp end: of needle, knife etc) せん端 señtan; (purpose) 目的 mokúteki; (significant part) 要点 yőten; (detail, aspect, quality) 特徴 tokúchō; (particular place or position) 地点 chitéñ; (moment) 時点 jítèn; (stage in development) 段階 dañkai; (score: in competition, game, sport) 得点 tokúten, 点数 teñsū; (*BRIT*: ELEC: socket) コンセント kőñsento; (*also*: **decimal point**) 小数点 shősùten; (in numbers): *2 point 3 (2.3)* 2点3 ní teñ sañ
◆*vt* (show, mark) 指す sásù; (gun etc) 向ける mukérù

to point something at someone ...に...を向ける ...ni ...wo mukérù
◆*vi*: *to point at* (with finger, stick etc) ...を指す ...wo sásù

to be on the point of doing something ...をする所である ..wo suru tokoró de árù

to make a point of doing 努めて...する tsutőmete ...surù

to get/miss the point 相手が言わんとする事が分かる〔分からない〕 afte gà iwáñ to suru kotő ga wakárù〔wakáranaì〕

to come to the point 要点を言う yőten

wǒ iú

there's no point (in doing) (...するのは) 無意味だ (...surú no wà) muímì dà

point-blank [pɔint'blæŋk'] adv (say, ask) ずばり zubárì; (refuse) あっさり assárì; (also: **at point-blank range**) 至近距離で shikínkyorì de

pointed [pɔin'tid] adj (stick, pencil, chin, nose etc) とがった togátta; (fig: remark) 辛らつな shinratsu na

pointedly [pɔin'tidli:] adv (reply etc) 意味深長に ímìshinchō ni

pointer [pɔin'tə:r] n (on chart, machine) 針 hárì; (fig: piece of information or advice) ヒント hínto

pointless [pɔint'lis] adj (useless, senseless) 無意味な muími na

point of view n (opinion) 観点 kánten

point out vt (in debate etc) ...を指摘する ...wo shitéki suru

points [pɔints] npl (AUT) ポイント pofnto; (RAIL) 転てつ機 teñtetsukì, ポイント pofnto

point to vt fus (fig) ...を指摘する ...wo shitéki suru

poise [pɔiz] n (composure) 落ち着き ochítsuki

poison [pɔi'zən] n (harmful substance) 毒 dokú

♦vt (person, animal: kill with poison) 毒殺する dokúsatsu suru; (: give poison to) ...に毒を飲ませる ...ni dokú wò nomáserù

poisonous [pɔi'zənəs] adj 有毒な yúdoku na, 毒... dokú...

poke [pouk] vt (jab with finger, stick etc) つつく tsutsúkù; (put): **to poke something in(to)** ...の中へ...を突っ込む ...no nákà e ...wo tsukkómù

poke about vi (search) 物色する busshókù suru

poker [pou'kə:r] n (metal bar) 火かき棒 hikákibò; (CARDS) ポーカー pòkā

poky [pou'ki:] adj (room, house) 狭苦しい semákurushiì

Poland [pou'lənd] n ポーランド pòrando

polar [pou'lə:r] adj (GEO, ELEC) 極地の kyókùchi no

polar bear n 北極グマ hokkyókugùma

polarize [pou'lə:raiz] vt 分裂させる buñretsu saserù

Pole [poul] n ポーランド人 pòrandojìn

pole [poul] n (post, stick) 棒 bò, さお sáò; (GEO, ELEC) 極 kyókù

flag pole 旗ざお hatázao

telegraph/telephone pole 電柱 deñchū

pole bean (US) n (runner bean) インゲン ińgen

pole vault n 棒高飛び bòtakàtobi

police [pəli:s'] n (organization) 警察 keísatsu; (members) 警官 keíkan

♦vt (street, area, town) ...の治安を維持する ...no chián wò fjí suru

police car n パトカー patókà

policeman [pəli:s'mən] (pl **policemen**) n 警官 keíkan

police state n (POL) 警察国家 keísatsukokkà

police station n 警察署 keísatsusho

policewoman [pəli:s'wumən] (pl **policewomen**) n 婦人警官 fujínkeìkan, 婦警 fukéi

policy [pɑ:l'isi:] n (POL, ECON: set of ideas, plans) 政策 seísaku; (also: **insurance policy**) 保険証券 hokéñshōken

polio [pou'li:ou] n 小児麻ひ shóⁿimahì, ポリオ pórìo

Polish [pou'liʃ] adj ポーランドの pòrando no; (LING) ポーランド語の pòrandogo no

♦n (LING) ポーランド語 pòrandogo

polish [pɑ:l'iʃ] n (also: **shoe polish**) 靴墨 kutsúzùmi; (for furniture, floors etc) 光沢剤 kótakuzài; (shine: on shoes, floors, furniture etc) 光沢 kótaku; (fig: refinement) 洗練 señren

♦vt (put polish on, make shiny) 磨く migáku

polished [pɑ:l'iʃt] adj (fig: person, style) 洗練された señren sareta

polish off vt (work) 仕上げる shiágerù; (food) 平らげる taíragerù

polite [pəlait'] adj (person: well-mannered) 礼儀正しい reígitadashiì; (socially superior: company, society) 上流の jóryū no

politeness [pəlait'nis] n 礼儀正しさ reígitadashisa

political [pəlit'ikəl] adj (relating to politics) 政治の seíji no; (person) 政治に関心ある seíji ní kańshin arù

politically [pəlit'ikli:] adv 政治的に seíjiteki ni

politician [pɑ:litiʃ'ən] n 政治家 seíjika

politics [pɑ:l'itiks] n (activity) 政治 seíji; (subject) 政治学 seíjigàku
♦npl (beliefs, opinions) 政治的思想 seíjitekishisồ

poll [poul] n (also: opinion poll) 世論調査 yoróñchòsa; (political election) 選挙 séñkyo
♦vt (in opinion poll) ...の意見を聞く ...no íkèn wo kikú; (number of votes) 獲得する kakútoku suru

pollen [pɑ:l'ən] n 花粉 kafún

polling day [pou'liŋ-] (BRIT) n 投票日 tóhyòbi

polling station (BRIT) n 投票所 tóhyòjo

pollute [pəlu:t'] vt (air, water, land) 汚染する osén suru

pollution [pəlu:'ʃən] n (process) 汚染 osén; (substances) 汚染物質 osénbusshìtsu

polo [pou'lou] n (sport) ポロ pórò

polo-necked [pou'lounekt] adj (sweater) とっくりえりの tokkúrierì no

poltergeist [poul'tə:rgaist] n けん騒霊 keńsòrei, ポルターガイスト porútàgaisuto

polyester [pɑ:li:es'tə:r] n ポリエステル poríesùteru

polyethylene [pɑ:li:eθ'əli:n] (US) n ポリエチレン poríechìren

polystyrene [pɑ:li:stai'ri:n] n ポリスチレン porísuchìren

polytechnic [pɑ:li:tek'nik] n 科学技術専門学校 kagákugijùtsu senmongakkồ ◊ 英国では大学レベルの高等教育機関 efkoku de wà daígakurebèru no kồtōkyòiku kikàn

polythene [pɑ:l'əθi:n] (BRIT) n = **polyethylene**

pomegranate [pɑ:m'əgrænit] n ザクロ zákùro

pomp [pɑ:mp] n 華やかさ hanáyàkasa

pompom [pɑ:m'pɑ:m] n ポンポン póñpon

pompon [pɑ:m'pɑ:n] n = **pompom**

pompous [pɑ:m'pəs] (pej) adj (person, piece of writing) もったい振った mottáibuttà

pond [pɑ:nd] n (natural, artificial) 池 iké

ponder [pɑ:n'də:r] vt 熟考する jukkồ suru

ponderous [pɑ:n'də:rəs] adj (large and heavy) 大きくて重い ồkikute omóì; (speech, writing) 重苦しい omókurushiì

pong [pɔ:ŋ] (BRIT: inf) n 悪臭 akúshū

pontificate [pɑ:ntif'ikeit] vi (fig): **to pontificate (about)** (...について) もったい振って話す ...ni tsúìte) mottáibuttè hanásù

pontoon [pɑ:ntu:n'] n (platform) ポンツーン poñtsùn; (for seaplane etc) フロート fúròto

pony [pou'ni:] n ポニー pónì

ponytail [pou'ni:teil] n (person's hairstyle) ポニーテール ponítèru

pony trekking [-trek'iŋ] (BRIT) n 乗馬旅行 jồbaryokò

poodle [pu:'dəl] n プードル pùdoru

pool [pu:l] n (also: pool of water) 水たまり mizútamari; (pond) 池 iké; (also: swimming pool) プール pùru; (fig: of light, liquid) たまり tamári; (SPORT) 玉突 tamátsuki, ビリヤード biríyàdo
♦vt (money, knowledge, resources) 出し合う dashíaù, プールする pùru suru
typing pool タイピストのプール taípisùto no pùru

pools [pu:lz] npl (football pools) トトカルチョ totókaruchò

poor [pur] adj (not rich: person, place, country) 貧しい mazúshiì, 貧乏な bíñbō na; (bad) 粗末な sómàtsu na
♦npl: **the poor** 貧乏人 biñbònin ◊総称 sồshō
poor in (resources etc) ...が不足している ...ga fusóku shite irù

poorly [pur'li:] adj (ill) 病気の byồki no
♦adv (badly: designed) 粗末に sómàtsu ni; (paid, furnished) 不十分に fujûbùn ni

pop [pɑ:p] n (MUS) ポップス póppùsu;

(fizzy drink) 炭酸飲料 tañsan-iñryō, ソーダ水 sṓdasùi; (*inf*: father) 父 chìchaん tṓchan, パパ pápà; (sound) ぽんという音 pôñ to iú otò

♦*vt* (put quickly) 突っ込む tsukkómù

♦*vi* (balloon) 破裂する harétsu suru; (cork) 飛出す tobídasù

popcorn [paːpˈkɔːrn] *n* ポップコーン poppúkòñ

pope [poup] *n* 法王 hṓ ṓ

pop in *vi* 立寄る tachíyorù

poplar [paːpˈlər] *n* ポプラ pópùra

poplin [paːpˈlin] *n* ポプリン pópùriñ

pop out *vi* 飛出る tobíderù

popper [paːpˈər] (*BRIT*) *n* (for fastening) スナップ sunáppù

poppy [paːpˈiː] *n* ケシ keshí

Popsicle [paːpˈsikəl] (℞ *US*) *n* (ice lolly) アイスキャンディー aísukyàñdī

pop star *n* ポップスター poppúsutà

populace [paːpˈjələs] *n* 大衆 taíshū

popular [paːpˈjələr] *adj* (well-liked: person, place, thing) 人気のある niñki no arù; (of ordinary people: idea, belief) 一般の ippán no, 流行の ryū́kō no; (non-academic) 一般向けの ippánmuke no; (POL) 国民の kokúmin no

popularity [paːpjəlærˈitiː] *n* (of person, thing, activity) 人気 niñki

popularize [paːpˈjələraiz] *vt* (sport, music, fashion) 普及させる fukyū́ saserù; (science, ideas) 分かりやすくする wakáriyasukù suru

population [paːpjəleiˈʃən] *n* (inhabitants: of country, area) 住民 jū́min; (number of inhabitants) 人口 jiñkō

populous [paːpˈjələs] *adj* (country, city, area) 人口の多い jiñkō no ṓi

pop up *vi* 現れる aráwarerù

porcelain [pɔːrˈsəlin] *n* 磁器 jíkì

porch [pɔːrtʃ] *n* (ARCHIT: entrance) 玄関 genkan; (*US*) ベランダ beránda

porcupine [pɔːrˈkjəpain] *n* ヤマアラシ yamáaràshi

pore [pɔːr] *n* (ANAT) 毛穴 keánà, 気孔 kikṓ; (GEO) 小穴 koánà

♦*vi*: **to pore over** (book, article etc) 熟読する jukúdoku suru

pork [pɔːrk] *n* 豚肉 butániku

pornographic [pɔːrnəgrǽfˈik] *adj* (film, book, magazine) わいせつな waísetsu na, ポルノの poruno no

pornography [pɔːrnɑːˈgrəfiː] *n* (films, books, magazines) ポルノ pórùno

porous [pɔːrˈəs] *adj* (soil, rock, clay etc) 小穴の多い koánà nò ṓi

porpoise [pɔːrˈpəs] *n* イルカ irúka

porridge [pɔːrˈidʒ] *n* オートミール ṓtomīru

port [pɔːrt] *n* (harbor) 港 minátò; (NAUT: left side) 左げん sagéñ; (wine) ポートワイン pótowaìn

port of call 寄港地 kikṓchì

portable [pɔːrˈtəbəl] *adj* (television, typewriter, telephone etc) 携帯用の keítai yṓ no, ポータブルの pótaburu no

porter [pɔːrˈtər] *n* (for luggage) 赤帽 akákabō, ポーター pótà; (doorkeeper) 門番 moñban

portfolio [pɔːrtfouˈliːou] *n* (case) かばん kabáñ; (POL) 大臣の職 dáìjin no shokú; (FINANCE) ポートフォリオ pótoforìo; (of artist) 代表作品集 daíhyōsakuhìnshū

porthole [pɔːrtˈhoul] *n* げん窓 geñsō

portion [pɔːrˈʃən] *n* (part) 部分 búbùn; (helping of food) 一人前 ichíninmaè

portly [pɔːrtˈliː] *adj* (man) 太った futóttà

portrait [pɔːrˈtrit] *n* (picture) 肖像 shṓzō, ポートレート pótorèto

portray [pɔːrˈtrei] *vt* (subj: artist) 描く egákù; (: actor) 演じる eñjirù

portrayal [pɔːrˈtreiˈəl] *n* (artist's: *also* representation in book, film etc) 描写 byṓsha; (actor's) 演技 eñgi

Portugal [pɔːrˈtʃəgəl] *n* ポルトガル porútogàru

Portuguese [pɔːrtʃəgiːzˈ] *adj* ポルトガルの porútogàru no; (LING) ポルトガル語の porútogarugò no

♦*n inv* ポルトガル人 porútogarujìn; (LING) ポルトガル語 porútogarugò

pose [pouz] *n* (posture) ポーズ pṓzu

♦*vi* (pretend): **to pose as** ...を装う ...wo yosóoù, ...の名をかたる ...no ná wo katárù

♦*vt* (question) 持出す mochídasù; (prob-

lem, danger) ...である ...de árù

to pose for (painting etc) ...のためにポーズを取る ...no tamé nì pōzu wo tórù

posh [pɑːʃ] (*inf*) *adj* (smart: hotel, restaurant etc) 高級な kókyū na; (upper class: person, behavior) 上流階級の jōryūkaikyū no

position [pəziʃ'ən] *n* (place: of house, thing, person) 位置 íchì; (of person's body) 姿勢 shiséi; (social status) 地位 chíi; (job) 職 shokù; (in race, competition) 第...位 dái ...i; (attitude) 態度 táido; (situation) 立場 tachíba
♦*vt* (person, thing) 置く okú

positive [pɑːz'ətiv] *adj* (certain) 確かな táshìka na; (hopeful, confident) 確信している kakúshin shite irù; (definite: decision, action, policy) 積極的な sekkyókuteki na

posse [pɑːs'iː] (*US*) *n* 捜索隊 sōsakutai

possess [pəzes'] *vt* (have, own: car, watch, radio etc) 所有する shoyū suru, 保有する hoyū suru; (quality, ability) ...がある ...ga árù, ...を持っている ...wo móttè irù; (subj: feeling, belief) 支配する shíhai suru

possession [pəzeʃ'ən] *n* (state of possessing) 所有 shoyū
to take possession of 占領する senryō suru

possessions [pəzeʃ'ənz] *npl* (belongings) 持物 mochímòno

possessive [pəzes'iv] *adj* (of another person) ...の愛情を独占したがる ...no aijō wò dokúsen shitagarù; (of things) 他人に使わせたがらない tanín nì tsukáwasetagaranài; (LING) 所有を表す shoyū wò aráwasù

possibility [pɑːsəbil'əti:] *n* 可能性 kanōsei; (possible event) 可能な事 kanō na kotð

possible [pɑːs'əbəl] *adj* (which can be done) 可能な kanō na; (event, reaction) 有り得る aríurù; (candidate, successor) 成り得る naríurù
it's possible (may be true) そうかも知れない sō ka mò shirénài
as fast as possible できるだけ早く de-

kíru dakè hayákù

possibly [pɑːs'əbliː] *adv* (perhaps) あるいは arúiwa; (expressing surprise, shock, puzzlement) ...が考えられない ...ga kañgaerarenài; (emphasizing someone's efforts) できる限り dekíru kagirì
I cannot possibly come どう合っても私は行かれません dōattè mo watákushi wà ikáremaseñ

post [poust] *n* (*BRIT*: service, system) 郵便 yūbin; (: letters) 郵便（物） yūbin (bùtsu); (delivery) 配達 haítatsu ◊1回分の配達郵便を指す ikkáìbun no haítatsuyūbin wo sásù; (pole) 柱 hashíra; (job, situation) 職 shokù; (MIL) 持場 mochíba
♦*vt* (*BRIT*: send by post) 郵送する yūsō suru; (: put in mailbox) 投かんする tōkan suru; (: appoint): *to post someone to* ...を...へ配置する ...wo ...e haíchi suru

postage [pous'tidʒ] *n* (charge) 郵便料金 yūbin ryōkin

postage stamp *n* （郵便）切手 (yūbin) kitté

postal [pous'təl] *adj* (charges, service, strike) 郵便の yūbin no

postal order *n* 郵便為替 yūbin kawàse

postbox [poust'bɑːks] (*BRIT*) *n* （郵便）ポスト (yūbin)pósùto

postcard [poust'kɑːrd] *n* （郵便）葉書 (yūbin) hagáki

postcode [poust'koud] (*BRIT*) *n* 郵便番号 yūbin bañgō

postdate [poust'deit] *vt* (check) ...に先の日付を付ける ...ni sakí nò hizúke wò tsukérù

poster [pous'tər] *n* ポスター pósùtā

poste restante [poust res'tɑːnt] (*BRIT*) *n* 局留 kyokúdome

posterity [pɑːster'itiː] *n* 後世 kōsei

postgraduate [poustgrædʒ'uːit] *n* 大学院生 daígakuiñsei

posthumous [pɑːs'tʃəməs] *adj* (award, publication) 死後の shígò no

postman [poust'mən] (*pl* **postmen**) *n* 郵便屋 yūbin-ya

postmark [poust'mɑːrk] *n* 消印 keshíin

post-mortem [poustmɔːr'təm] *n* 司法解剖 shihōkaibō, 検死解剖 keñshikaibō

post office n (building) 郵便局 yūbiṅkyoku; (organization): *the Post Office* 郵政省 yūseíshō

Post Office Box n 私書箱 shishóbàko

postpone [poustpoun'] vt 延期する eṅki suru

postscript [poust'skript] n 追伸 tsuíshin

posture [pɑːs'tʃəːr] n (position of body) 姿勢 shiséi; (fig) 態度 táído

postwar [poust'wɔːr'] adj (building, period, politics) 戦後の séngo no

posy [pou'ziː] n 花束 hanátàba ◇小さい花束を指す chíísaī hanátàba wo sásù

pot [pɑːt] n (for cooking) な べ nábè; (also: **teapot**) ティーポット típottò; (also: **coffeepot**) コーヒーポット kōhīpottò; (tea/coffee in pot) ティー[コーヒー]ポット一杯 tí[kóhī]pottò íppaì; (bowl, container: for paint etc) つぼ tsubó; (flowerpot) 植木鉢 uékibàchi; (inf: marijuana) マリファナ marífàna

◆vt (plant) 鉢に植える hachí ni uérù

to go to pot (inf: work, performance) 駄目になる damé ni narù

potato [pətei'tou] (pl **potatoes**) n ジャガイモ jagáimo

potato peeler [-piː'ləːr] n 皮むき器 kawámukikì

potent [pout'ənt] adj (powerful: weapon, argument, drink) 強力な kyóryokù na; (man) 性的能力のある seítekinōryoku no árù

potential [pəten'tʃəl] adj (candidate) 成り得る narfurù; (sales, success) 可能な kanō na; (danger etc) 潜在する seṅzai suru

◆n (talents, abilities) 潜在能力 seṅzainōryoku; (promise, possibilities) 将来性 shōraisei

potentially [pəten'tʃəliː] adv 潜在的に seṅzaiteki ni

pothole [pɑːt'houl] n (in road) 穴ぼこ anábòko; (BRIT: underground) 洞くつ dókutsu

potholing [pɑːt'houliŋ] (BRIT) n: *to go potholing* 洞くつを探検する dókutsu wò taṅken suru

potion [pou'ʃən] n (of medicine, poison etc) 水薬 mizúgusùri

potluck [pɑːt'lʌk] n: *to take potluck* 有り合せの物で間に合せる aríawase no monò de ma ní awaserù

potted [pɑːt'id] adj (food) つぼ詰めの tsubózume no; (plant) 鉢植えの hachíue no; (abbreviated: account, biography etc) 要約した yóyaku shita

potter [pɑːt'əːr] n (pottery maker) 陶芸家 tōgeika

◆vi: *to potter around/about in the garden* (BRIT) ぶらぶらと庭いじりをする búràbura to niwáíjiri wo suru

pottery [pɑːt'əːriː] n (pots, dishes etc) 陶器 tōki; (factory, workshop) 陶器製造所 tōkiseizōjo

potty [pɑːt'iː] adj (inf: mad) 狂った kurúttà

◆n (for child) おまる o-máru

pouch [pautʃ] n (for tobacco, coins etc) 小袋 kobúkuro; (ZOOL) 袋 fukúro

poultry [poul'triː] n (live chickens, ducks etc) 家きん kakín; (meat from chickens etc) 鳥肉 toríniku

pounce [pauns] vi: *to pounce on* (animal, person) …に襲い掛る …ni osóikakarù; (fig: mistake, idea etc) 攻撃する kōgeki suru

pound [paund] n (unit of weight) ポンド póṅdo; (BRIT: unit of money) ポンド póṅdo

◆vt (beat: table, wall etc) 強くたたく tsúyòku tatákù; (crush: grain, spice etc) 砕く kudákù

◆vi (heart) どきどきする dókìdoki suru

pound sterling n ポンド póṅdo

pour [pɔːr] vt (tea, wine, cereal etc) つぐ tsugú

◆vi (water, blood, sweat etc) 流れ出る nagárederù

to pour someone a drink …に酒をついでやる …ni saké wò tsuíde yarù

pour away/off vt 流して捨てる nagáshite suterù

pour in vi (people) ぞろぞろと入って来る zórozoro to haítte kurù; (information) 続々と入る zókùzoku to háíru

pouring [pɔːr'iŋ] adj: *pouring rain* 土砂

降りの雨 dosháburi no amê

pour out vi (people) ぞろぞろと出て来る zórôzoro to detê kurû

♦vt (tea, wine etc) つぐ tsugú; (fig: thoughts, feelings, etc) せきを切った様に吐き出す séki wo kittá yô ni hakídasù

pout [paut] vi 膨れっ面をする fukúrettsura wô suru

poverty [pɑːvˈəːrtiː] n 貧乏 bíñbō

poverty-stricken [pɑːvˈəːrtiːstrikən] adj (people, town, country) 非常に貧しい hijō nì mazúshiî

powder [pauˈdəːr] n (tiny particles of solid substance) 粉 koná; (face powder) おしろい oshíroi, パウダー páùdā

♦vt: to powder one's face 顔におしろいをつける kaó nì oshíroi wò tsukérù

powder compact n コンパクト kóñpakuto

powdered milk [pauˈdəːrd-] n 粉ミルク konámirùku

powder puff n パフ páfù

powder room n 化粧室 keshóshìtsu

power [pauˈəːr] n (control: over people, activities) 権力 kéñryoku; (ability, opportunity) 能力 nōryoku; (legal right) 権利 kéñri; (of explosion, engine) 威力 íryòku; (electricity) 電力 déñryoku

to be in power (POL etc) 権力を握っている kéñryoku wo nigítte irû

power cut (BRIT) n 停電 teíden

powered [pauˈəːrd] adj: powered by ...で動く ...de ugókù

power failure n 停電 teíden

powerful [pauˈəːrfəl] adj (person, organization) 有力な yúryoku na; (body) 力強い chikárazuyoî; (blow, kick etc) 強力な kyóryoku na; (engine) 馬力の強い barîki no tsuyoî; (speech, piece of writing) 力強い chikárazuyoî

powerless [pauˈəːrlis] adj (without control or influence) 無力な múryòku na

powerless to do ...する力がない ...súrù chikára ga naî

power point (BRIT) n コンセント kóñsento

power station n 発電所 hatsúdensho

p.p. [piːpiː] abbr (= per procurationem):

p.p. J. Smith J.Smithの代理として jē sumísù no daíri tòshité; (= pages) ページ pēji

PR [piːɑːr] abbr = **public relations**

practicable [prækˈtikəbəl] adj (scheme, task, idea) 実用的な jitsúyōteki na

practical [prækˈtikəl] adj (not theoretical: difficulties, experience etc) 実際の jissái no; (person: sensible) 現実的な geñjitsuteki na; (: good with hands) 器用な kíyô na; (ideas, methods) 現実的な geñjitsuteki na; (clothes, things: sensible) 実用的な jitsúyōteki na

practicality [præktikælˈitiː] n (no pl) 現実主義 geñjitsushùgi; (of situation etc) 現実 geñjitsu

practical joke n 悪ふざけ warúfuzàke

practically [prækˈtikliː] adv (almost) ほとんど hotôñdo

practice [prækˈtis] n (habit) 習慣 shúkan; (of profession) 業務 gyómu; (REL) おきてを守る事 okíte wo mamóru kotò; (exercise, training) 練習 reñshū; (MED, LAW: business) 開業 kaígyō

♦vt (train at: musical instrument, sport etc) 練習する reñshū suru; (carry out: custom, craft etc) 行う okónaù; (religion) ...のおきてを守る ...no okite wo mamoru; (profession) ...に従事する ...ni jûji suru

♦vi (train) 練習する reñshū suru; (lawyer, doctor etc) ...の業務をする ...no gyómu wo suru

in practice (in reality) 実際には jissái ni wà

out of practice 腕が鈍って udé gà nibúttè

practicing [prækˈtisiŋ] (BRIT **practising**) adj (Christian etc) おきてを守っている okíte wò mamótte irù; (doctor, lawyer) 業務をしている gyómu wo shité irù

practise [prækˈtis] vt, vi (BRIT) = **practice**

practitioner [præktiʃˈənəːr] n (MED): **medical practitioner** 医者 ishá

pragmatic [prægmætˈik] adj (person, reason etc) 現実的な geñjitsuteki na

prairie [preˈriː] n 草原 sôgen

praise [preiz] *n* (expression of approval, admiration) 賞賛 shṓsan

♦*vt* (express approval, admiration: of person, thing, action etc) ほめる homérù

praiseworthy [preiz'wəːrði:] *adj* (person, act etc) ほめるべき homérùbeki

pram [præm] (*BRIT*) *n* 乳母車 ubágurùma

prance [præns] *vi* (person) 威張って歩く ibátte arúku; (horse) 躍る様に歩く odóru yṓ ni arúkù

prank [præŋk] *n* いたずら itázura

prawn [prɔːn] *n* エビ ebí

pray [prei] *vi* (REL) 祈る inórù; (*fig*) 祈る inórù, 願う negáù

prayer [preːr] *n* (REL: activity, words) 祈り inóri

preach [priːtʃ] *vi* (REL) 説教する sékkyō suru; (*pej*: moralize) お説教する o-sékkyō suru

♦*vt* (peace, doctrine etc) 説く tókù

to preach a sermon 説教する sékkyō suru

preacher [priːtʃəːr] *n* (REL) 説教者 sekkyṓsha

preamble [priːæmbəl] *n* (to spoken words) 前置き maéoki; (to written words) 前書 maégaki

precarious [prikeːrʼiːəs] *adj* (dangerous: position, situation) 不安定な fuántei na; (*fig*) 危険な kikén na

precaution [prikɔːʼʃən] *n* 用心 yṓjin

precede [prisiːdʼ] *vt* (event, period of time) ...の前に起る ...no máè ni okórù; (person) ...の前を歩く ...no máè wo arúkù; (sentence, paragraph, chapter) ...の前にある ...no máè ni árù

precedence [presʼidəns] *n* (priority) 優先 yūsen

precedent [presʼidənt] *n* (action, official decision) 判例 hańrei; (something that has happened before) 先例 seńrei

preceding [prisiːʼdiŋ] *adj* (chapter, programme, day) 前の máè no

precept [priːʼsept] *n* おきて okíte

precinct [priːʼsiŋkt] *n* (*US*: part of city) 管区 káňku

pedestrian precinct (*BRIT*) 歩行者天

国 hokṓshateńgoku

shopping precinct (*BRIT*) ショッピングセンター shóppìngu séñtā ◇車が閉出される kurúma gà shimédasarerù

precincts [priːʼsiŋkts] *npl* (of a large building) 構内 kṓnai

precious [preʃʼəs] *adj* (commodity: valuable, useful) 貴重な kichṓ na; (object, material) 高価な kṓka na

precious stone n 宝石 hōseki

precipice [presʼəpis] *n* 断崖 dańgai

precipitate [prisipʼiteit] *vt* (hasten) 早める hayámerù

precise [prisais'] *adj* (exact: time, nature etc) 正確な seíkaku na; (detailed: instructions, plans etc) 細かい komákaì

precisely [prisaisʼliː] *adv* (accurately) 正確に seíkaku ni; (exactly) その通り sonó tōri

precision [prisiʒʼən] *n* 正確さ seíkakusa

preclude [prikluːdʼ] *vt* (action, event) 不可能にする fukánō ni suru

precocious [prikouʼʃəs] *adj* (child, talent) 早熟な sōjuku na

preconceived [priːkənsiːvdʼ] *adj*:
preconceived idea 先入観 seńnyūkan

precondition [priːkəndiʃʼən] *n* 前提条件 zeńteijōken

precursor [prikəːrʼsəːr] *n* (person) 先駆者 seńkushà; (thing) 前触れ maébure

predator [predʼətəːr] *n* 捕食者 hoshókushà

predecessor [predʼisesəːr] *n* (person) 前任者 zeńniñsha

predestination [priːdestineiʼʃən] *n* 予定 yotéisètsu

predicament [pridikʼəmənt] *n* 苦境 kukyṓ

predict [pridikt] *vt* 予言する yogén suru

predictable [pridiktʼəbəl] *adj* (event, behavior etc) 予知できる yóchì dekírù

prediction [pridikʼʃən] *n* 予言 yogén

predominantly [pridaːmʼənəntliː] *adv* 圧倒的に attṓteki ni

predominate [pridaːmʼəneit] *vi* (person, thing) ...が圧倒的に多い ...ga attṓteki nì ōì; (feature, quality) 目立つ medátsù

pre-eminent [priːemʼənənt] *adj* (person,

thing) 優れた sugúretà

pre-empt [pri:'empt] vt (decision, action, statement) 先取りする sakídori suru

preen [pri:n] vt: *to preen itself* (bird) 羽繕いをする hazúkùroi wo suru

to preen oneself 得意がる tokúîgaru

prefab [pri:'fæb] n プレハブ住宅 puréhabujûtaku

prefabricated [pri:'fæb'rikeitid] adj (buildings) プレハブの puréhabu no

preface [pref'is] n (in book) 前書 maégaki

prefect [pri:'fekt] (BRIT) n (in school) 監督生 kañtokuseì

prefer [prifər'] vt (like better: person, thing, activity) ...の方を好む ...no hố wò konômù

to prefer doing/to do ...する方が好きである ...suru hố gà sukí de arù

preferable [pref'ə:rəbəl] adj ...が望ましい ...ga nozômashiî

preferably [prifə:r'əbli:] adv できれば dekírèba

preference [pref'ə:rəns] n (liking) 好み konômi

to give preference to ...を優先的に扱う ...wo yūsenteki nì atsúkaù

preferential [prefəren'tʃəl] adj: *preferential treatment* 優先的な取扱い yūsenteki nà torîatsukai

prefix [pri:'fiks] n 接頭辞 settôjì

pregnancy [preg'nənsi:] n (of woman, female animal) 妊娠 ninshin

pregnant [preg'nənt] adj (woman, female animal) 妊娠している nifhshin shite irù

prehistoric [pri:histɔ:r'ik] adj (person, dwelling, monster etc) 有史以前の yûshiizèn no

prejudice [predʒ'ədis] n (unreasonable dislike) 偏見 heñken; (bias in favor) ひいき hîiki

prejudiced [predʒ'ədist] adj (person: prejudiced against) ...に対して偏見のある ...ni tâîshite heñken no arù; (: prejudiced in favor) ...をひいきにした ...wo hîiki ni shitá

preliminary [prilim'əne:ri:] adj (action, discussion) 予備的な yobíteki na

prelude [prei'lu:d] n (preliminary event) 前兆 zeñchō; (MUS) 序曲 jókyòku

premarital [pri:mær'itəl] adj 婚前の koñzen no

premature [pri:mətʃu:r'] adj (earlier than expected: baby) 早産の sôzan no; (death, arrival) 早過ぎた hayásugita; (too early: action, event etc) 時期尚早の jíkìshōsō no

premature aging 早老 sôrō

premeditated [primed'əteitid] adj 計画的な keíkakuteki na

premier [primji:r'] adj (best) 最良の saíryō no

♦n (POL) 総理大臣 sôridaìjin, 首相 shushô

première [primji:r'] n (of film) 初公開 hatsúkòkai; (of play) 初演 shoén

premise [prem'is] n 前提 zeñtei

premises [prem'isiz] npl (of business, institution) 構内 kônai

on the premises 構内で kônai de

premium [pri:'mi:əm] n (COMM: extra sum of money) 割増金 warîmashikin, プレミアム purémîamu; (: sum paid for insurance) 掛金 kakékin

to be at a premium (expensive) 高価である kôka de arù; (hard to get) 手に入りにくい té nì haírinikùi

premium bond (BRIT) n 割増金付き債券 warîmashikintsukisaîken ◇抽選による賞金が付く chûsen ni yorù shôkin ga tsukù

premonition [preməniʃ'ən] n 予感 yokán

preoccupation [pri:ɑ:kjəpei'ʃən] n (obsession) 専念する事 señnen surù kotô; (worry) 気掛かりな事 kigákàri na kotô

preoccupied [pri:ɑ:k'jəpaid] adj (person) 上の空になった uwánosorà ni nátta

prep [prep] n (SCOL: study) 勉強 beñkyō

prepaid [pri:peid'] adj (paid in advance) 支払い済みの shiháraizumi no

preparation [prepərei'ʃən] n (activity) 準備 júnbi; (food) 料理 ryôri; (medicine) 薬品 yakúhin; (cosmetic) 化粧品 keshôhin

preparations [prepərei'ʃənz] npl (arrangements) 準備 júnbi

preparatory [pripǽr'ətɔːriː] *adj* (report) 予備の yóbì no; (training) 準備の júnbì no

preparatory school *n* (*US*) 予備校 yo-bíkồ; (*BRIT*) 私立小学校 shiritsu shố-gakkồ

prepare [pripeːr'] *vt* (make ready: plan, speech, room etc) 準備する júnbi suru; (CULIN) 調理する chốri suru

♦*vi*: **to prepare for** (event, action) ...の準備をする ...no júnbì wo suru

prepared to (willing) ...する用意がある ...surú yồi ga árù

prepared for (ready) ...の用意ができている ...no yồi ga dékìte irú

preponderance [pripɑːn'dərəns] *n* (of people, things) 大多数 daítasū

preposition [prepəziʃ'ən] *n* 前置詞 zeńchishi

preposterous [pripɑːs'tərəs] *adj* (suggestion, idea, situation) 途方もない tohố-monaí

prep school *n* = **preparatory school**

prerequisite [prirek'wizit] *n* 必要条件 hitsúyồjồken

prerogative [prərɑːg'ətiv] *n* (of person, group) 特権 tokkén

Presbyterian [prezbitiːr'iːən] *adj* 長老派の chốrồha no

♦*n* 長老派の信者 chốrồha no shiñja

preschool [priːˈskuːl'] *adj* (age, child, education) 就学前の shúgakumaè no

prescribe [priskraib'] *vt* (MED: medicine) 処方する shohố suru; (treatment) 命ずる meízurù

prescription [priskrip'ʃən] *n* (MED: slip of paper) 処方せん shohốsen; (: medicine) 処方薬 shohốyầku

presence [prez'əns] *n* (state of being somewhere) ...に居る事 ...ni irú kotò; (*fig*: strong personal quality) 風さい fúsai; (spirit, invisible influence) 霊 reí

in someone's presence ...の居る前で ...no irú maè de

presence of mind *n* 機転 kitén

present [*adj, n* prez'ənt *vb* prizent'] *adj* (current: person, thing) 現在の geñzai no; (in attendance) 出席している shussé-

ki shite irú

♦*n* (actuality): **the present** 現在 geñzai; (gift) 贈り物 okúrimono, プレゼント pu-rézènto

♦*vt* (give: prize, award etc) 贈る okúrù; (cause, provide: difficulty, threat etc) ...になる ...ni nárù; (information) 与える atáerù; (describe: person, thing) 描写する byốsha suru; (RADIO, TV) 提供する teíkyồ suru; (formally introduce: person) 紹介する shốkai suru

to give someone a present ...にプレゼントを上げる ...ni puréztènto wo agérù

at present 今の所 imá no tokoro

presentable [prizen'təbəl] *adj* (person) 人前に出られる hitómae nì derárerù

presentation [prezəntei'ʃən] *n* (of plan, proposal, report etc) 提出 teíshutsu; (appearance) 体裁 teísai; (formal ceremony) 贈呈式 zốteishìki

present-day [prez'əntdei] *adj* 現代の geñdai no

presenter [prizen'tər] *n* (RADIO, TV) 司会者 shikáìsha

presently [prez'əntliː] *adv* (soon) 間もなく mamónàku; (now) 現在 geñzai

preservation [prezəːrvei'ʃən] *n* (act of preserving) 保存 hozón; (state of being preserved) 保存状態 hozóñjồtai

preservative [prizəːr'vətiv] *n* (for food, wood, metal etc) 保存剤 hozóñzài

preserve [prizəːrv'] *vt* (maintain: situation, condition) 維持する ijí suru; (: building, manuscript) 保存する hozón suru; (food) 保存する hozón suru

♦*n* (*often pl*: jam, marmalade) ジャム jámù

preside [prizaid'] *vi*: **to preside (over)** (meeting, event etc) (...の) 議長をする (...no) gichồ wồ suru

presidency [prez'idənsiː] *n* (POL: post) 大統領職 daítồryồshokù; (: time in office) 大統領の任期 daítồryồ no niñki

president [prez'idənt] *n* (POL) 大統領 daítồryồ; (of organization) ...長 ...chồ

presidential [preziden'tʃəl] *adj* 大統領の daítồryồ no

press [pres] *n*: **the Press** (newspapers)

報道機関 hōdōkikàn; (journalists) 報道陣 hōdōjin; (printing press) 印刷機 iñsatsukī; (of switch, button, bell) 押す事 osú kotð

♦vt (hold one thing against another) 押付ける oshítsukerù; (button, switch, bell etc) 押す osú; (iron: clothes) ...にアイロンを掛ける ...ni aíron wò kakérù; (put pressure on: person) せき立てる sekítaterù; (insist): *to press something on someone* ...に...を押付ける ...ni ...wo o-shítsukerù

♦vi (squeeze) 押える osáerù; (pressurize): *to press for* (improvement, change etc) ...のために働く ...no tamé nì határakù; (forcibly) 強要する kyōyō suru
we are pressed for time/money 時間〔金〕が足りない jíkàn〔kanè〕ga tarínai

press agency n 通信社 tsūshíñsha

press conference n 記者会見 kishákaìken

pressing [pres'iŋ] adj (engagement, decision etc) 緊急の kíñkyū no

press on vi (despite problems etc) ひるまずに続ける hirúmazù ni tsuzúkerù

press stud (BRIT) n スナップ sunáppù

press-up [pres'ʌp] (BRIT) n 腕立て伏せ udétefusè

pressure [preʃ'ə:r] n (physical force: also fig) 圧力 atsúryòku; (also: **air pressure**) 気圧 kiátsu; (also: **water pressure**) 水圧 suíatsu; (also: **oil pressure**) 油圧 yuátsu; (stress) 圧迫 appáku, プレッシャー purésshā
to put pressure on someone (to do) (...する様に) ...に圧力を掛ける (...surú yō ni) ...ni atsúryòku wo kakérù

pressure cooker n 圧力ガマ atsúryokugàma

pressure gauge n 圧力計 atsúryokukei

pressure group n (POL) 圧力団体 atsúryokudañtai, プレッシャーグループ purésshāgurùpu

pressurized [preʃ'əraizd] adj (cabin, container, spacesuit) 気圧を一定に保った kiátsu wò ittéi ni tamottà

prestige [presti:ʒ'] n 名声 meísei

prestigious [prestidʒ'əs] adj 著名な cho-

méi na

presumably [prizu:'məbli:] adv たぶん tábùn, おそらく osóràku

presume [prizu:m'] vt: *to presume (that)* (suppose) (...だと) 推定する (...dá tò) suítei suru

presumption [prizʌmp'ʃən] n (supposition) 推定 suítei

presumptuous [prizʌmp'tʃuəs] adj せん越な señ-etsu na

presuppose [pri:səpouz'] vt ...を前提とする ...wo zeñtei tò suru

pretence [pritens'] (US also: **pretense**) n (false appearance) 見せ掛け misékake
under false pretences うそを言って úsò wo itté

pretend [pritend'] vt (feign) ...の振りをする ...no furí wò suru
♦vi (feign) 見せ掛ける misékakerù
to pretend to do ...する振りをする ...suru furí wò suru

pretense [pritens'] (US) n = **pretence**

pretentious [priten'tʃəs] adj (claiming importance, significance: person, play, film etc) うぬぼれた unúboreta

pretext [pri:'tekst] n 口実 kōjitsu

pretty [prit'i:] adj (person, thing) きれいな kírèi na
♦adv (quite) かなり kánàri

prevail [priveil'] vi (be current: custom, belief) はやる hayárù; (gain acceptance, influence: proposal, principle) 勝つ kátsù

prevailing [privei'liŋ] adj (wind) 卓越風 takúetsufù; (dominant: fashion, attitude etc) 一般の ippán no

prevalent [prev'ələnt] adj (common) 一般的な ippánteki na

prevent [privent'] vt: *to prevent someone from doing something* ...が...をするのを妨げる ...ga ...wo suru no wò samátagerù
to prevent something from happening ...が起るのを防ぐ ...ga okórù no wò fuségù

preventative [priven'tətiv] adj = **preventive**

prevention [priven'tʃən] n 予防 yobō

preventive [priven'tiv] *adj* (measures, medicine) 予防の yobō no

preview [pri:'vju:] *n* (of film) 試写会 shishákài; (of exhibition etc) 招待展示内覧 shōtaitenjināran

previous [pri:'vi:əs] *adj* (earlier: event, thing, period of time) 前の máè no

previously [pri:'vi:əsli:] *adv* 前に máè ni

pre-war [pri:'wɔ:r] *adj* 戦前の señzen no

prey [prei] *n* 獲物 emóno

♦*vi: to prey on* (animal: feed on) ...を捕食する ...wo hoshóku suru

it was preying on his mind 彼はそれを気にしていた kárè wa soré wò ki ní shite itá

price [prais] *n* (amount of money) 値段 nedán; (*fig*) 代償 daíshō

♦*vt* (goods) ...に値段を付ける ...ni nedán wò tsukérù

priceless [prais'lis] *adj* 非常に貴重な hijō nì kichō na

price list *n* 値段表 nedánhyō

prick [prik] *n* (short, sharp pain) ちくっとする痛み chikúttō suru itámi

♦*vt* (make hole in) 鋭い物で刺す surúdoì monó dè sásù; (cause pain) ちくっと刺す chikúttō sásù

to prick up one's ears (listen eagerly) 耳を澄まして聞く mimí wò sumáshite kikú

prickle [prik'əl] *n* (of plant) とげ togé; (sensation) ちくちくする痛み chíkùchiku suru itámi

prickly [prik'li:] *adj* (plant) とげだらけの togédaràke no; (fabric) ちくちくする chíkùchiku suru

prickly heat *n* 汗も asémo

pride [praid] *n* (satisfaction) 誇り hokóri; (dignity, self-respect) 自尊心 jisóñshin, プライド puráido; (*pej*: feeling of superiority) 高慢 kōman

♦*vt: to pride oneself on* ...を誇りとする ...wo hokóri tò suru

priest [pri:st] *n* (Christian: Catholic, Anglican etc) 司祭 shisáì; (non-Christian) 僧侶 sōryo

priestess [pri:s'tis] *n* (non-Christian) みこ míkò

priesthood [pri:st'hud] *n* (position) 司祭職 shisáishokù

prig [prig] *n* 気取り屋 kidóriyà

prim [prim] (*pej*) *adj* (formal, correct) 堅苦しい katákurushiì; (easily shocked) 上品ぶった jōhìñbutta

primarily [praime:r'ili:] *adv* (above all) 主に ōmò ni

primary [prai'me:ri:] *adj* (first in importance) 主要な shuyō na

♦*n* (*US*: election) 予備選挙 yobíseñkyo

primary school *n* 小学校 shōgakkō

primate [prai'meit] *n* (ZOOL) 霊長類 reíchōrui

prime [praim] *adj* (most important) 最も重要な mottómò jūyō na; (best quality) 最上の saíjō no

♦*n* (of person's life) 盛り sakári

♦*vt* (wood) ...に下塗りをする ...ni shitánuri wò suru; (*fig*: person) ...に教え込む ...ni oshíekomù

prime example (typical) 典型的な例 teñkeiteki nà reí

Prime Minister *n* 総理大臣 sōridaìjin, 首相 shushō

primeval [praimi:'vəl] *adj* (existing since long ago): *primeval forest* 原生林 geñseìrin; (feelings, tribe) 原始的な geñshiteki na

primitive [prim'ətiv] *adj* 原始的な geñshiteki na

primrose [prim'rouz] *n* ツキミソウ tsukímisō

primus (stove) [prai'məs-] (*BRIT*) *n* 石油こんろ sekíyukoñro

prince [prins] *n* (son of king etc) 王子 ōji; (son of Japanese emperor) 親王 shiññō

princess [prin'sis] *n* (daughter of king etc) 王女 ōjo; (daughter of Japanese emperor) 内親王 naíshinnō

principal [prin'səpəl] *adj* (most important: reason, character, aim etc) 主要な shuyō na

♦*n* (of school) 校長 kōchō; (of college) 学長 gakúchō

principle [prin'səpəl] *n* (moral belief) 信念 shiññen; (general rule) 原則 geñsoku; (scientific law) 法則 hōsoku

in principle (theoretically) 原則として gensoku tòshité

on principle (morally) 主義として shugí tòshité

print [print] *n* (letters and numbers on page) 印刷文字 insatsumojì; (ART) 版画 hanga; (PHOT) 陽画 yǒga, プリント purìnto; (footprint) 足跡 ashíatò; (fingerprint) 指紋 shimón

◆*vt* (produce: book, newspaper, leaflet) 印刷する insatsu suru; (publish: story, article etc) 記載する kisái suru; (cloth) ...になっ染する ...ni nassén suru; (write in capitals) 活字体で書く katsújitai dè kákù

out of print 絶版で zeppán de

printed matter [print'tid-] *n* 印刷物 insatsubùtsu

printer [prin'tə:r] *n* (person, firm) 印刷屋 insatsuyà; (machine) 印刷機 insatsukì

printing [prin'tiŋ] *n* (act, art) 印刷 insatsu

printout [print'aut] *n* (COMPUT) プリントアウト purìntoaùto

prior [prai'ə:r] *adj* (previous: knowledge, warning, consent etc) 事前の jízen no; (more important: claim, duty) より重要な yorí jùyó na

prior to ...の前に ...no máè ni

priority [praiɔ:r'iti:] *n* (most urgent task) 優先課題 yūsenkadài; (most important thing, task) 最重要課題 saíjūyōkadài

to have priority (over) (...に) 優先する (...ni) yūsen suru

prise [praiz] *vt*: *to prise open* こじ開ける kojíakerù

prism [priz'əm] *n* プリズム purízùmu

prison [priz'ən] *n* (building) 刑務所 keímusho

◆*cpd* 刑務所の keímusho no

prisoner [priz'ənə:r] *n* (in prison) 囚人 shújin; (captured person) 捕虜 hóryò

prisoner of war *n* 戦争捕虜 sensōhoryò

pristine [pris'ti:n] *adj* (condition: new) 真新しい maátarashiì; (: like new) 新品同様の shínpindòyó no

privacy [prai'vəsi:] *n* プライバシー puráibashī

private [prai'vit] *adj* (not public: property, club etc) 私有の shiyū no, プライベートの puráibèto no; (not state-owned: industry, service) 民間の minkan no; (discussion, sitting etc) 非公開の hikókai no; (personal: activities, belongings) 個人の kójìn no; (: thoughts, plans) 心の中の kokóro no naka no; (quiet: place) 奥まった okúmattà; (: person) 内気な uchíki na; (confidential) 内密の naímitsu no; (intimate) 部外者立入禁止の bugáishà tachíirikinshi no

◆*n* (MIL) 兵卒 heísotsu

「*private*」(on envelope) 親展 shínten; (on door) 部外者立入禁止 bugáishà tachíirikinshi

in private 内密に naímitsu ni

private enterprise *n* (not state owned) 民間企業 minkan kigyò; (owned by individual) 個人企業 kójin kigyò

private eye *n* 私立探偵 shirítsutantei

private property *n* 私有地 shiyūchì

private school *n* (fee-paying) 私立学校 shirítsugakkò

privatize [prai'vətaiz] *vt* (government-owned company etc) 民間に払い下げる minkan nì harái sagerù

privet [priv'it] *n* イボタノキ ibótanoki

privilege [priv'əlidʒ] *n* (advantage) 特権 tokkén; (opportunity) 光栄な機会 kóei na kikaì

privileged [priv'əlidʒd] *adj* (having advantages) 特権のある tokkén no arù; (having special opportunity) 光栄な機会を得た kóei na kikaì wo età

privy [priv'i:] *adj*: *to be privy to* 内々に関知している naínai nì kánchi shité irù

prize [praiz] *n* (reward) 賞 shó

◆*adj* (first class) 典型的な tenkeiteki na

◆*vt* 重宝する chóhō suru

prize-giving [praiz'giviŋ] *n* 表彰式 hyóshōshìki

prizewinner [praiz'winə:r] *n* 受賞者 jushóshà

pro [prou] *n* (SPORT) 職業選手 shokúgyōseńshu, プロ púrò

♦**prep** (in favor of) ...に賛成して ...ni sañsei shite

the pros and cons 賛否両論 sáñpiryōron

probability [prɑːbəbil'əti:] *n* (likelihood): *probability of/that* ...の〔...が起る〕公算 ...no 〔...ga okórù〕kōsan

in all probability たいてい taítei

probable [prɑːb'əbəl] *adj* (likely to happen) 起りそうな okórisò na; (likely to be true) ありそうな arísò na

probably [prɑːb'əbli:] *adv* たぶん tábùn, おそらく osóràku

probation [prəbei'ʃən] *n*: *on probation* (LAW) 保護観察で hogókañsatsu de; (employee) 見習いで mináraì de

probe [proub] *n* (MED) ゾンデ zóñde; (SPACE) 探査衛星 tañsaeisèi; (enquiry) 調査 chōsa

♦**vt** (investigate) 調査する chōsa suru; (poke) つついて探る tsutsúîte sagúrù

problem [prɑːb'ləm] *n* 問題 mofidai

problematic(al) [prɑːbləmæt'ik(əl)] *adj* 問題になる mofidai ni narù

procedure [prəsi:'dʒər] *n* (way of doing something) やり方 yaríkata; (ADMIN, LAW) 手続き tetsúzuki

proceed [prəsi:d'] *vi* (do afterwards): *to proceed to do something* ...をし始める ...wo shihájimerù; (continue): *to proceed (with)* (...を) 続ける (...wo) tsuzúkerù; (activity, event, process: carry on) 続ける tsuzúkerù; (person: go) 行く ikú

proceedings [prəsi:'diŋz] *npl* (organized events) 行事 gyōji; (LAW) 訴訟手続き soshōtetsuzùki

proceeds [prou'si:dz] *npl* 収益 shúeki

process [prɑːs'es] *n* (series of actions: *also* BIOL, CHEM) 過程 katéi, プロセス purósèsu

♦**vt** (raw materials, food) 加工する kakō suru; (information) 処理する shórì suru

processing [prɑːs'esiŋ] *n* (PHOT) 現像 geñzō

procession [prəseʃ'ən] *n* 行列 gyóretsu

proclaim [prəkleim'] *vt* (announce) 宣言する señgen suru

proclamation [prɑːkləmei'ʃən] *n* 宣言 señgen

procrastinate [prəkræs'təneit] *vi* 先に延ばす sakí nì nobásù

procreation [proukri:ei'ʃən] *n* 生殖 seíshoku

procure [prəkju:r'] *vt* 調達する chótatsu suru

prod [prɑːd] *vt* (push: with finger, stick, knife etc) つつく tsutsúkù

♦**n** (with finger, stick, knife etc) 一突き hitótsuki

prodigal [prɑːd'əgəl] *adj*: *prodigal son/daughter* 放とう息子〔娘〕hótōmusùko 〔musúme〕

prodigious [prədidʒ'əs] *adj* 巨大な kyódai na

prodigy [prɑːd'ədʒi:] *n* 天才 teñsai

produce [*n* prou'du:s *vb* prədu:s'] *n* (AGR) 農産物 nōsanbùtsu

♦**vt** (cause: effect, result etc) 起す okósù; (make, create: object) 作る tsukúrù; (BIOL: fruit, seeds) つける tsukérù, ...は...がなる ...ní wà ...ga narù; (: young) 産む umú; (CHEM) 作り出す tsukúridasù; (fig: evidence, argument) 示す shimésù; (: bring or take out) 取出す torídasù; (play, film, program) 製作する seísaku suru

producer [prədu:'sər] *n* (of film, play, program, record) 製作者 seísakushà, プロデューサー puródyūsà; (country: of food, material) 生産国 seísankòku; (company: of food, material) 生産会社 seísangaìsha

product [prɑːd'əkt] *n* (thing) 産物 safibutsu; (result) 結果 kekká

production [prədʌk'ʃən] *n* (process of manufacturing, growing) 生産 seísan; (amount of goods manufactured, grown) 生産高 seísañdaka; (THEATER) 上演 jóen

electricity production 発電 hatsúden

production line *n* 工程ライン kóteiraìn, ライン raìn

productive [prədʌk'tiv] *adj* (person, thing: *also fig*) 生産的な seísanteki na

productivity [prɑːdəktiv'əti:] *n* 生産能

力 seísannōryoku

profane [prəfein'] *adj* (secular, lay) 世俗的な sezókuteki na; (language etc) 下品な gehín na

profess [prəfes'] *vt* (claim) 主張する shuchō suru; (express: feeling, opinion) 明言する meígen suru

profession [prəfeʃ'ən] *n* (job requiring special training) 知的職業 chitékishokugyō; (people) 同業者仲間 dōgyōshanakama

professional [prəfeʃ'ənəl] *adj* (skill, organization, advice) 専門職の seímonshoku no; (not amateur: photographer, musician etc) プロの púrò no; (highly trained) 専門家の seímonka no; (of a high standard) 本職らしい honshokurashiì

♦*n* (doctor, lawyer, teacher etc) 知的職業者 chitékishokugyōshà; (SPORT) プロ púrò; (skilled person) 玄人 kúròto

professor [prəfes'ə:r] *n* (US) 教師 kyōshi, 先生 señsei; (BRIT) 教授 kyōju

proficiency [prəfiʃ'ənsi:] *n* 熟練 jukúren

proficient [prəfiʃ'ənt] *adj* 熟練した jukúren shita

profile [prou'fail] *n* (of person's face) 横顔 yokógaò; (fig: article) 経歴 keíreki

profit [pra:f'it] *n* (COMM) 利益 ríeki

♦*vi*: **to profit by/from** (fig) …がために なる …ga tamé nì nárù

profitability [pra:fitəbil'əti:] *n* (ECON) 収益性 shúekisei

profitable [pra:f'itəbəl] *adj* (ECON) 利益になる ríeki ni nárù

profound [prəfaund'] *adj* (great: shock, effect) 強い tsuyóì; (intellectual: idea, work) 深遠な shiń-en na

profusely [prəfju:s'li:] *adv* (bleed) 多量に taryō ni; (thank) 重ね重ね kasáneqasàne

profusion [prəfju:'ʒən] *n* 大量 taíryō

prognoses [pra:gnou'si:z] *npl of* **prognosis**

prognosis [pra:gnou'səs] (*pl* **prognoses**) *n* (forecast) 予想 yosō; (of illness) 予後 yógò

program [prou'græm] (BRIT **programme**) *n* (of actions, events) 計画 keí-kaku; (RADIO, TV) 番組 bañgumi; (leaflet) プログラム puróguràmu; (COMPUT) プログラム puróguràmu

♦*vt* (machine, system) …にプログラムを入れる …ni puróguràmu wo irérù

programing [prou'græmiŋ] (BRIT **programming**) *n* (COMPUT) プログラム作成 puróguramu sakuseì, プログラミング puróguramiñgu

programmer [prou'græmə:r] *n* (COMPUT) プログラマー purógurámā

progress [*n* pra:g'res *vb* prəgres'] *n* (process of getting nearer to objective) 前進 zeńshin; (changes, advances in society) 進歩 shíñpo; (development) 発展 hattén

♦*vi* (become more advanced, skilled) 進歩する shíñpo suru; (become higher in rank) 昇進する shōshin suru; (continue) 続く tsuzúkù

in progress (meeting, battle, match) 進行中で shiñkōchū de

progression [prəgreʃ'ən] *n* (gradual development) 進展 shiñten; (series) 連続 reñzoku

progressive [prəgres'iv] *adj* (person) 進歩的な shiñpoteki na; (change) 段階的な dañkaiteki na

prohibit [prouhib'it] *vt* (forbid, make illegal) 禁じる kiñjirù

prohibition [prouəbiʃ'ən] *n* (law, rule) 禁則 kiñsoku; (forbidding: of strikes, alcohol etc) 禁止 kiñshi; (US): **Prohibition** 禁酒法時代 kiñshuhōjidài

prohibitive [prouhib'ətiv] *adj* (price etc) 法外な hōgai na, 手が出ない様な té gà dénài yō na

project [*n* pra:dʒ'ekt *vb* prədʒekt'] *n* (large-scale plan, scheme) 計画 keíkaku; (SCOL) 研究テーマ keñkyūtēma

♦*vt* (plan) 計画する keíkaku suru; (estimate: figure, amount) 見積る mitsúmorù; (light) 投射する tōsha suru; (film, picture) 映写する eísha suru

♦*vi* (stick out) 突出る tsukíderù

projectile [prədʒek'təl] *n* 弾丸 dañgan

projection [prədʒek'ʃən] *n* (estimate) 見積り mitsúmori; (overhang) 突起 tokkí;

(CINEMA) 映写 eísha

projector [prədʒek'tə:r] n 映写機 eíshakī

proletarian [prouliteːr'iːən] adj 無産階級の musánkaìkyū no, プロレタリアの purôretarìa no

proletariat [prouliteːr'iːət] n 無産階級 musánkaìkyū, プロレタリア purôretarìa

proliferate [proulif'əːreit] vi 急増する kyūzō suru

prolific [proulif'ik] adj (artist, composer, writer) 多作の tasáku no

prologue [prou'lɔːg] n (of play) 序幕 jomáku, プロローグ purôrôgu; (of book) 序言 jogén

prolong [prəlɔːŋ'] vt (life, meeting, holiday) 引延ばす hikínobasù, 延長する eńchō suru

prom [prɑːm] n abbr = promenade; (US: ball) 学生舞踏会 gakúseibutôkai

promenade [prɑːməneid'] n (by sea) 海岸の遊歩道 kaígan nò yūhôdō

promenade concert (BRIT) n 立見席のある音楽会 tachímisèki no árù oñgakukài

prominence [prɑːm'ənəns] n (importance) 重要性 jūyōsei

prominent [prɑːm'ənənt] adj (important) 重要な jūyō na; (very noticeable) 目立つ medátsù

promiscuous [prəmis'kjuːəs] adj (person) 相手構わずにセックスをする aíte kamawazù ni sékkùsu wo suru

promise [prɑːm'is] n (vow) 約束 yakúsoku; (talent) 才能 saínō; (hope) 見込み mikômi

♦vi (vow) 約束する yakúsoku suru

♦vt: to promise someone something, promise something to someone ...に...を約束する ...ni ...wo yakúsoku suru

to promise (someone) to do something/that (...に) ...すると約束する (...ni) ...surú tò yakúsoku suru

promising [prɑːm'isiŋ] adj (person, thing) 有望な yūbō na

promote [prəmout'] vt (employee) 昇進させる shôshin saserù; (product, pop star) 宣伝する señden suru; (ideas) 促進する sokúshin suru

promoter [prəmou'təːr] n (of event) 興業主 kôgyōshù, プロモーター purômôtā; (of cause, idea) 推進者 suíshiñsha

promotion [prəmou'ʃən] n (at work) 昇進 shôshin; (of product, event, idea) 宣伝 señden

prompt [prɑːmpt] adj (rapid: reaction, response etc) 迅速な jiñsoku na

♦adv (exactly) 丁度 chôdo

♦n (COMPUT) プロンプト purôñputo

♦vt (cause) ...の原因となる ...no geń-in tò nárù; (when talking) ...に水を向ける ...ni mizú wò mukérù

to prompt someone to do something ...が...をするきっ掛けとなる ...ga ...wo suru kikkáke to narù

promptly [prɑːmpt'liː] adv (immediately) 直ちに tádàchi ni; (exactly) 丁度 chôdo

prone [proun] adj (lying face down) うつ伏せの utsúbuse no

prone to (inclined to) ...しがちな ...shigáchi na

prong [prɔːŋ] n (of fork) 歯 há

pronoun [prou'naun] n 代名詞 daímeìshi

pronounce [prənauns'] vt (word) 発音する hatsúon suru; (declare) 宣言する señgen suru; (give verdict, opinion) 言渡す iíwatasù

pronounced [prənaunst'] adj (marked) 著しい ichíjirushiì

pronunciation [prənʌnsiːeiʃən] n 発音 hatsúon

proof [pruːf] n (evidence) 証拠 shôko; (TYP) 校正刷り kôseizuri, ゲラ gerá

♦adj: proof against ...に耐えられる ...ni taérarerù

prop [prɑːp] n (stick, support: also fig) 支え sasáe

♦vt (also: prop up) 支える sasáerù; (lean): to prop something against ...を...に立掛ける ...wo ...ni tatékakerù

propaganda [prɑːpəgæn'də] n 宣伝 señden, プロパガンダ purôpagañda

propagate [prɑːp'əgeit] vt (idea, information) 普及させる fukyú saserù

propel [prəpel'] vt (vehicle, boat,

machine) 推進する suíshin suru; (*fig*: person) 駆立てる karítaterù

propeller [prəpél'əːr] *n* プロペラ puropérà

propensity [prəpen'siti:] *n* 傾向 keíkō

proper [prɑː'pəːr] *adj* (real, authentic) ちゃんとした chấnto shita; (correct) 正しい tadáshiì; (suitable) 適当な tekítō na; (socially acceptable) 社会の通念にかなった shákài no tsúnen ni kanáttà; (referring to place): *the village proper* 村そのもの murá sono monò

properly [prɑː'pəːrli:] *adv* (adequately: eat, study) 充分に júbun ni; (decently: behave) 正しく tadáshìku

proper noun *n* 固有名詞 koyúmeìshi

property [prɑː'pəːrti:] *n* (possessions) 財産 zaísan; (building and its land) 物件 bukkén; (land owned) 所有地 shoyúchì; (quality: of substance, material etc) 特性 tokúsei

property owner *n* 地主 jinúshi

prophecy [prɑːf'isi:] *n* 予言 yogén

prophesy [prɑːf'isai] *vt* (predict) 予言する yogén suru

prophet [prɑːf'it] *n* (REL) 予言者 yogénsha

prophetic [prəfet'ik] *adj* (statement, words) 予言的な yogénteki na

proportion [prəpɔːr'ʃən] *n* (part: of group, amount) 割合 waríai; (number: of people, things) 数 kázù; (ratio) 率 rítsu

proportional [prəpɔːr'ʃənəl] *adj*: *proportional (to)* (...に) 比例する (...ni) hiréi suru

proportional representation *n* 比例代表制 hiréidaihyōsei

proportionate [prəpɔːr'ʃənit] *adj*: *proportionate (to)* (...に) 比例する (...ni) hiréi suru

proposal [prəpou'zəl] *n* (plan) 提案 teían

a proposal (of marriage) 結婚の申込み kekkón nò móshikomi, プロポーズ puropốzu

propose [prəpouz'] *vt* (plan, idea) 提案する teían suru; (motion) 提出する teíshutsu suru; (toast) ...の音頭を取る ... no óndo wo tórù

♦*vi* (offer marriage) 結婚を申込む kekkón wò móshikomù, プロポーズする puropốzu suru

to propose to do ...するつもりでいる ...suru tsumóri de irù

proposition [prɑːpəziʃ'ən] *n* (statement) 主張 shuchō; (offer) 提案 teían

proprietor [prəprai'ətəːr] *n* (of hotel, shop, newspaper etc) 持主 mochínushi, オーナー ốnā

propriety [prəprai'əti:] *n* (seemliness) 礼儀正しさ reígitadashìsa

pro rata [-rɑː'tə] *adv* 比例して hiréi shite

prosaic [prouzei'ik] *adj* (person, piece of writing) 散文的な safibunteki na

prose [prouz] *n* (not poetry) 散文 safibun

prosecute [prɑːs'əkjuːt] *vt* (LAW) 訴追する sotsúi suru

prosecution [prɑːsəkju:'ʃən] *n* (action) 訴追 sotsúi; (accusing side) 検察側 keńsatsugàwa

prosecutor [prɑːs'əkju:təːr] *n* (*also*: **public prosecutor**) 検察官 keńsatsukàn

prospect [prɑːs'pekt] *n* (possibility) 可能性 kańōsei; (outlook) 見込み mikómi

♦*vi*: *to prospect (for)* (gold) etc (...を) 探鉱する (...wo) tańkō suru

prospecting [prɑːs'pektiŋ] *n* (for gold, oil etc) 探鉱 tańkō

prospective [prəspek'tiv] *adj* (son-in-law, customer, candidate etc) ...になろうとしている ...ni narố tò shité irù

prospects [prɑːs'pekts] *npl* (for work etc) 見込み mikómi

prospectus [prəspek'təs] *n* (of college, school, company) 要綱 yốkō

prosper [prɑːs'pəːr] *vi* (person, business, city etc) 繁栄する hań-ei suru

prosperity [prɑːsper'iti:] *n* 繁栄 hań-ei

prosperous [prɑːs'pəːrəs] *adj* (person, city etc) 裕福な yúfuku na; (business etc) 繁盛している hańjō shite irù

prostitute [prɑːs'titu:t] *n* (female) 売春婦 baíshuñfu; (male) 男娼 dańshō

prostrate [prɑːs'treit] *adj* (face down) うつ伏せの utsúbuse no

protagonist [proutæg'ənist] *n* (sup-

porter) 支援者 shiéñsha; (leading participant: in event, movement) リーダー格の人 rídākaku nò hitð; (THEATER) 主役 shuyáku; (in story etc) 主人公 shujíñkõ

protect [prətekt'] vt (person, thing) 守る mamórù, 保護する hógð suru

protection [prətek'ʃən] n 保護 hógð

protective [prətek'tiv] adj (clothing, layer, etc) 防護の bõgo no; (gesture) 防衛の bõei no; (person) 保護的な hogóteki na

protégé [prou'təʒei] n 偉い人のひいきを受ける人 erâî hitð nò híki wò ukérù hitð

protein [prou'ti:n] n たんぱく質 tañpakushìtsu

protest [n prou'test vb prətest'] n (strong expression of disapproval, opposition) 抗議 kõgi
♦vi: **to protest about/against/at** ...に抗議する ...ni kõgi suru
♦vt (insist): **to protest (that)** (...だと) 主張する (...dá tò) shuchõ suru

Protestant [prɑt'istənt] adj 新教の shíñkyō no, プロテスタントの purótesùtanto no
♦n 新教徒 shiñkyðto, プロテスタント教徒 purótesùtanto kyðto

protester [prətes'tə:r] n 抗議者 kõgishà

protocol [prou'təkɔ:l] n 外交儀礼 gaíkōgirèi

prototype [prou'tətaip] n 原型 geñkei

protracted [proutræk'tid] adj (absence, meeting etc) 長引いた nagábiità

protrude [proutru:d'] vi (rock, ledge, teeth etc) 突出る tsukíderù

proud [praud] adj (pleased): **proud of** ...を誇りとする ...wo hokóri tò suru; (dignified) プライドのある puráido no arù; (arrogant) 尊大な soñdai na

prove [pru:v] vt (verify) 立証する risshõ suru
♦vi: **to prove (to be) correct** etc 結局...が正しいと判明する kekkyóku ...ga tadáshiî to hañmei suru
to prove oneself 自分の才能を立証する jibún nò saínõ wò risshõ suru

proverb [prɑ:v'ə:rb] n ことわざ kotówaza

proverbial [prəvə:r'bi:əl] adj ことわざの kotówaza no

provide [prəvaid'] vt (give) 与える atáerù; (make available) 供給する kyõkyū suru
to provide someone with something ...に...を供給する ...ni ...wo kyõkyō suru

provided (that) [prəvai'did-] conj ...という条件で ...tō iû jõken de

provide for vt fus (person) ...の面倒を見る ...no meñdō wò mírù
♦vt (future event) ...に備える ...ni sonáerù

Providence [prɑ:v'idəns] n 摂理 sétsùri

providing [prəvai'diŋ] conj: **providing (that)** ...という条件で ...tō iû jõken de

province [prɑ:v'ins] n (of country) 県 kéñ; (fig) 管轄 kañkatsu

provincial [prəvin'tʃəl] adj (town, newspaper etc) 地方の chihõ no; (pej) 田舎じみた inákajimità

provision [prəviʒ'ən] n (supplying) 供給 kyõkyū; (of contract, agreement) 規定 kitéi

provisional [prəviʒ'ənəl] adj (government, agreement, arrangement etc) 暫定的な zañteiteki na

provisions [prəviʒ'ənz] npl (food) 食料 shokúryō

proviso [prəvai'zou] n 規定 kitéi

provocation [prɑ:vəkei'ʃən] n 挑発 chõhatsu

provocative [prəvɑ:k'ətiv] adj (remark, article, gesture) 挑発的な chõhatsuteki na; (sexually stimulating) 扇情的な señjōteki na

provoke [prəvouk'] vt (annoy: person) 怒らせる okóraserù; (cause: fight, argument etc) 引起こす hikíokosù

prow [prau] n へさき hesáki, 船首 séñshu

prowess [prau'is] n (outstanding ability) 手腕 shúwàn

prowl [praul] vi (also: **prowl about**, **prowl around**) うろつく urótsukù
♦n: **on the prowl** あさり歩いて asária-ruitè

prowler [prau'lə:r] n うろつく人 urótsuku hitð

proximity [prɔːksimˈiti:] *n* 近さ chikása

proxy [prɑːkˈsi:] *n*: *by proxy* 代理を通じて daíri wò tsûjite

prude [pruːd] *n* 上品ぶる人 jôhiñburu hitô

prudence [pruːˈdəns] *n* (care, sense) 慎重さ shiñchôsa

prudent [pruːˈdənt] *adj* (careful, sensible) 慎重な shiñchô na

prune [pruːn] *n* 干しプラム hoshîpurāmu
♦*vt* (bush, plant, tree) せん定する señtei suru

pry [prai] *vi*: *to pry (into)* (...を) せん索する (...wo) señsaku suru

PS [piːˈes] *abbr* = **postscript**

psalm [sɑːm] *n* 詩編 shihén

pseudo- [suːˈdou] *prefix* 偽... nisé...

pseudonym [suːˈdənim] *n* 筆名 hitsúmei, ペンネーム peñnêmu

psyche [saiˈkiː] *n* 精神 seíshin

psychiatric [saikiætˈrik] *adj* (hospital, problem, treatment) 精神科の seíshinka no

psychiatrist [sikaiˈətrist] *n* 精神科医 seíshinka-ì

psychiatry [sikaiˈətriː] *n* 精神医学 seíshin-igàku

psychic [saiˈkik] *adj* (person: *also*: **psychical**) 霊媒の reíbai no; (of the mind) 精神の seíshin no

psychoanalysis [saikouənælˈisis] *n* 精神分析 seíshinbuñseki

psychoanalyst [saikouænˈəlist] *n* 精神分析医 seíshinbunseki-ì

psychoanalyze [saikouæn'əlaiz] *vt* ...の精神分析をする ...no seíshinbuñseki wo suru

psychological [saikələːdʒˈikəl] *adj* (related to the mind: difference, problem etc) 精神的な seíshinteki na; (related to psychology: test, treatment etc) 心理的な shiñriteki na

psychologist [saikɑːlˈədʒist] *n* 心理学者 shiñrigakùsha

psychology [saikɑːlˈədʒiː] *n* (study) 心理学 shiñrigàku; (mind) 心理 shiñri

psychopath [saiˈkəpæθ] *n* 精神病質者 seíshinbyōshitsushà

psychosomatic [saikousoumætˈik] *adj* 精神身体の seíshinshiñtai no

psychotic [saikɑːtˈik] *adj* 精神病の seíshinbyō no

PTO [piːˈtiːˈou] *abbr* (= *please turn over*) 裏面に続く rímen ni tsuzukù

pub [pʌb] *n* *abbr* (= *public house*) 酒場 sakába, パブ pábù

puberty [pjuːˈbəːrtiː] *n* 思春期 shishúñki

pubic [pjuːˈbik] *adj*: *pubic hair* 陰毛 iñmō

public [pʌbˈlik] *adj* (of people: support, opinion, interest) 国民の kokúmin no; (for people: building, service) 公共の kôkyō no; (for people to see: statement, action etc) 公の ôyake no
♦*n*: *the public* (all people of country, community) 公衆 kôshū; (particular set of people) ...層 ...sô; (fans, supporters) 支持者 shijíshà

in public 公に ôyake ni, 人前で hitómaè de

to make public 公表する kôyō suru

public address system *n* 場内放送 (装置) jônaihôsô(sôchi)

publican [pʌbˈlikən] *n* パブの亭主 pábù no teíshu

publication [pʌblikeiˈʃən] *n* (act) 出版 shuppán; (book, magazine) 出版物 shuppáñbutsu

public company *n* 株式会社 kabúshiki-gaìsha

public convenience (*BRIT*) *n* 公衆便所 kôshūbeñjo

public holiday *n* 休日 kyûjitsu

public house (*BRIT*) *n* 酒場 sakába, パブ pábù

publicity [pʌblisˈətiː] *n* (information) 宣伝 señden; (attention) 広く知られる事 híròku shiráreru kotò

publicize [pʌbˈləsaiz] *vt* (fact, event) 報道する hôdō suru

publicly [pʌbˈlikliː] *adv* 公に ôyake ni, 人前で hitómaè de

public opinion *n* 世論 yóròn

public relations *n* 広報活動 kôhōkatsu-dô, ピーアール píàru

public school *n* (*US*) 公立学校 kôritsu-

gakkő; (*BRIT*) 私立学校 shiritsugakkő

public-spirited [pʌb'likspir'itid] *adj* 公共心のある kőkyōshin nò árù

public transport *n* 公共輸送機関 kőyō-yusōkikaǹ

publish [pʌb'liʃ] *vt* (book, magazine) 出版する shuppán suru, 発行する hakkő suru; (letter etc: in newspaper) 記載する kisái suru; (subj: person: article, story) 発表する happyő suru

publisher [pʌb'liʃəːr] *n* (person) 発行者 hakkőshà; (company) 出版社 shuppán-sha

publishing [pʌb'liʃiŋ] *n* (profession) 出版業 shuppangyō

puce [pjuːs] *adj* 暗かっ色の aǹkasshoku no

pucker [pʌk'əːr] *vt* (part of face) ...をしかめる ...wo shikámerù; (fabric etc) ...にしわを寄せる ...ni shiwà wò yosérù

pudding [pud'iŋ] *n* (cooked sweet food) プディング púdìngu; (*BRIT*: dessert) デザート dezàto

black pudding ブラッドソーセージ buráddosōsēji

puddle [pʌd'əl] *n* (*also*: **a puddle of water**) 水溜まり mizutamari; (of blood etc) 溜まり tamari

puff [pʌf] *n* (of cigarette, pipe) 一服 ippúku; (gasp) あえぎ aégi; (of air, smoke) 一吹き hitófuki

♦*vt*: *to puff one's pipe* パイプをふかす páìpu wo fukásù

♦*vi* (breathe loudly) あえぐ aégù

puffed [pʌft] (*inf*) *adj* (out of breath) 息を切らせた ikì wo kirásetà

puff out *vt* (fill with air: one's chest, cheeks) 膨らます fukúramasù

puff pastry *n* パイ皮 paíkawa

puffy [pʌf'i] *adj* (eye) はれぼったい harébottaì; (face) むくんだ mukúnda

pull [pul] *n* (tug): *to give something a pull* ...を引っ張る ...wo hippárù

♦*vt* (*gen*) 引く hikú; (tug: rope, hair etc) 引っ張る hippárù

♦*vi* (tug) 引く hikú, 引っ張る hippárù

to pull to pieces 引裂く hikísakù

to pull one's punches 手加減する teká-

gen suru

to pull one's weight 仲間同様に働く nakámadòyō ni határakù

to pull oneself together 落着きを取り戻す ochítsuki wò torímodosù

to pull someone's leg (*fig*) ...をからかう ...wo karákaù

pull apart *vt* (break) ばらばらにする barábara nì suru

pull down *vt* (building) 取壊す toríko-wasù

pulley [pul'i:] *n* 滑車 kasshá

pull in *vi* (AUT: at the curb) ...に停車する ...ni teísha suru; (RAIL) 到着する tő-chaku suru

pull off *vt* (take off: clothes etc) 脱ぐ núgù; (*fig*: difficult thing) ...に成功する ...ni seíkō suru

pull out *vi* (AUT: from curb) 発進する hasshín suru; (RAIL) 出発する shuppátsu suru

♦*vt* (extract) 取出す torídasù

pull over *vi* (AUT) 道路わきに寄せて停車する dőrowaki ni yosetè teísha suru

pullover [pul'ouvəːr] *n* セーター sḗta

pull through *vi* (MED) 治る naórù

pull up *vi* (AUT, RAIL: stop) 停車する teísha suru

♦*vt* (raise: object, clothing) 引上げる hikíagerù; (uproot) 引抜く hikínukù

pulp [pʌlp] *n* (of fruit) 果肉 kaníku

pulpit [pul'pit] *n* 説教壇 sekkyődaǹ

pulsate [pʌl'seit] *vi* 脈動する myakúdō suru

pulse [pʌls] *n* (ANAT) 脈拍 myakúhaku; (rhythm) 鼓動 kodő; (BOT) 豆類 mamé-rùi

pulverize [pʌl'vəːraiz] *vt* (crush to a powder) 砕く kudákù; (*fig*: destroy) 破壊する hakái suru

puma [puː'mə] *n* ピューマ pyűma

pummel [pʌm'əl] *vt* 続け様にげんこつで打つ tsuzúkezama ni geńkotsu de utsú

pump [pʌmp] *n* (for water, air, petrol) ポンプ pőǹpu; (shoe) パンプス pánpusu

♦*vt* (force: in certain direction: liquid, gas) ポンプで送る pőǹpu de okúrù; (obtain supply of: oil, water, gas) ポンプ

で汲む pónpu de kúmù

pumpkin [pʌmp'kin] *n* カボチャ kabócha

pump up *vt* (inflate) ポンプで膨らます pónpu de fukúramasù

pun [pʌn] *n* しゃれ sharé

punch [pʌntʃ] *n* (blow) げんこつで打つ事 geñkotsu dè útsù kotó, パンチ páñchi; (tool: for making holes) パンチ páñchi; (drink) ポンチ póñchi

♦*vt* (hit): **to punch someone/something** げんこつで...を打つ geñkotsu de ...wo útsù

punchline [pʌntʃ'lain] *n* 落ち ochí

punch-up [pʌntʃ'ʌp] (*BRIT*: *inf*) *n* けんか keñka

punctual [pʌŋk'tʃuːəl] *adj* 時間を厳守する jíkàn wo geñshu suru

punctuation [pʌŋktʃuːei'ʃən] *n* 句読法 kutóhō

puncture [pʌŋk'tʃər] *n* パンク páñku

♦*vt* ...に穴を開ける ...ni aná wò akérù

pundit [pʌn'dit] *n* 物知り monóshiri

pungent [pʌn'dʒənt] *adj* (smell, taste) 刺激的な shigékiteki na

punish [pʌn'iʃ] *vt* (person, crime) 罰する bassúrù

punishment [pʌn'iʃmənt] *n* (act) 罰する事 bassúrù kotó; (way of punishing) 罰 bátsù

punk [pʌŋk] *n* (*also*: **punk rock**) パンクロック pañkurokkù; (*also*: **punk rocker**) パンクロッカー pañkurokkà; (*US*: *inf*: hoodlum) ちんぴら chiñpira

punt [pʌnt] *n* (boat) ボート bòto ◇底が平らでさおで川底を突いて進める物を指す sokó ga taira dè sáò de kawázoko wo tsuitè susúmeru mono wò sásù

punter [pʌn'tər] *n* (*BRIT*: gambler) ばくち打ち bakúchiùchi; (*inf*: client, customer) 客 kyakú

puny [pjuː'niː] *adj* (person, effort) ちっぽけな chippókè na

pup [pʌp] *n* (young dog) 子イヌ koínu

pupil [pjuː'pəl] *n* (SCOL) 生徒 seíto; (of eye) どう孔 dōkó

puppet [pʌp'it] *n* (doll) 操り人形 ayátsuriniñgyō; (*fig*: person) かいらい kaírai

puppy [pʌp'iː] *n* 子イヌ koínu

purchase [pər'tʃis] *n* (act of buying) 購入 kónyū; (item bought) 買い物 kaímono

♦*vt* (buy: house, book, car etc) 買う káù

purchaser [pər'tʃisər] *n* 買い手 kaíte

pure [pjuːr] *adj* (not mixed with anything: silk, gold etc) 純粋な juñsui na; (clean, healthy: water, air etc) 清潔な seíketsu na; (*fig*: woman, girl) 純潔な juñketsu na; (complete, total: chance, bliss) 全くの mattáku no

purée [pjuːrei'] *n* (of tomatoes, potatoes, apples etc) ピューレ pyūre

purely [pjuːr'liː] *adv* 単に tán ni

purgatory [pər'gətɔːriː] *n* (REL) れん獄 reñgoku; (*fig*) 地獄 jigóku

purge [pərdʒ] *n* (POL) 粛正 shukúsei, パージ pāji

♦*vt* (organization) 粛正する shukúsei suru, パージする pāji suru

purify [pjuːr'əfai] *vt* (air, water etc) 浄化する jōka suru

purist [pjuːr'ist] *n* 純正主義者 juñseishugishà

puritan [pjuːr'itən] *n* 禁欲主義者 kiñyoku shugishà

purity [pjuːr'itiː] *n* (of silk, gold etc) 純粋さ juñsuisa; (of water, air etc) 清潔 seíketsu; (*fig*: of woman, girl) 純潔 juñketsu

purple [pər'pəl] *adj* 紫色の murásakiiro no

purport [pər'pɔːrt] *vi*: **to purport to be/do** ...である(...する)と主張する ...de árù(...ga dekírù)to shuchō suru

purpose [pər'pəs] *n* (reason) 目的 mokúteki; (objective: of person) 目標 mokúhyō

on purpose 意図的に itóteki ni, わざと wáza to

purposeful [pər'pəsfəl] *adj* (person, look, gesture) 果敢な kakán na

purr [pər] *vi* (cat) ごろごろとのどを鳴らす górògoro to nódò wo narásù

purse [pərs] *n* (for money) 財布 saífu; (*US*: handbag) ハンドバッグ hañdobaggù

♦*vt* (lips) すぼめる subómerù

purser [pəːrˈsəːr] n (NAUT) 事務長 jimúchō, パーサー pāsā

pursue [pəːrsuː'] vt (follow: person, thing) 追う óu, 追跡する tsuíseki suru; (fig: activity, interest) 行う okonau; (: plan) 実行する jikkṓ suru; (: aim, result) 追い求める oímotomerù

pursuer [pəːrsuː'əːr] n 追跡者 tsuísekishà

pursuit [pəːrsuː'] n (chase: of person, thing) 追跡 tsuíseki; (fig: of happiness, pleasure etc) 追求 tsuíkyū; (pastime) 趣味 shúmì

pus [pʌs] n うみ umí

push [puʃ] n 押す事 osú kotð
◆vt (press, shove) 押す osú; (promote) 宣伝する seńden suru
◆vi (press, shove) 押す osú; (fig: demand urgently): **to push for** 要求する yṓkyū suru

push aside vt 押しのける oshínokerù

pushchair [puʃ'tʃeːr] (BRIT) n いす型ベビーカー isúgata bebìkā

pusher [puʃ'əːr] n (drug pusher) 売人 baínin

push off (inf) vi: **push off!** 消えうせろ kiéuserð

push on vi (continue) 続ける tsuzúkerù

pushover [puʃ'ouvəːr] (inf) n: **it's a pushover** 朝飯前だ asámeshimaè da

push through vi (crowd etc) ...を押し分けて進む ...wo oshíwakete susumù
◆vt (measure, scheme etc) 押し通す oshítōsu

push up vt total, prices 押し上げる oshíagerù

push-up [puʃ'ʌp] (US) n (press-up) 腕立て伏せ udétatefùse

pushy [puʃ'iː] (pej) adj 押しの強い oshí no tsuyoì

puss [pus] (inf) n ネコちゃん nékòchan

pussy(cat) [pus'i:(kæt)] (inf) n ネコちゃん nékòchan

put [put] (pt, pp **put**) vt (place: thing) 置く okú; (: person: in institution etc) 入れる irérù; (express: idea, remark etc) 表現する hyṓgen suru; (present: case, view) 説明する setsúmei suru; (ask: question) する súrù; (place: person: in state, situation) 追込む oíkomù, 置く okú; (estimate) 推定する suítei suru; (write, type: word, sentence etc) 書く kákù

put about/around vt (rumor) 広める hirómerù

put across vt (ideas etc) 分からせる wakáraserù

put away vt (store) 仕舞っておく shimátte okù

put back vt (replace) 戻す modósù; (postpone) 延期する eńki suru; (delay) 遅らせる okúraserù

put by vt (money, supplies etc) 蓄えておく takúwaete okù

put down vt (on floor, table) 下ろす orósù; (in writing) 書く kákù; (riot, rebellion) 鎮圧する chiń-atsu suru; (kill: animal) 安楽死させる ańrakushi saserù; (attribute): **to put something down to** ...を...のせいにする ...wo ...no seí ni surù

put forward vt (ideas, proposal) 提案する teían suru

put in vt (application, complaint) 提出する teíshutsu suru; (time, effort) つぎ込む tsugíkomù

put off vt (delay) 延期する eńki suru; (discourage) いやにさせる iyá ni saserù

put on vt (shirt, blouse, dress etc) 着る kírù; (hat etc) かぶる kabúrù; (shoes, pants, skirt etc) はく hakú; (gloves etc) はめる hamérù; (make-up, ointment etc) つける tsukérù; (light etc) つける tsukérù; (play etc) 上演する jōen suru; (brake) かける kakérù; (record, tape, video) かける kakérù; (kettle, dinner etc) 火にかける hí nì kakérù; (assume: look, behavior etc) 装う yosóoù; (gain): **to put on weight** 太る futórù

put out vt (fire, candle, cigarette, light) 消す kesú; (take out: rubbish, cat etc) 出す dásù; (one's hand) 伸ばす nobásù; (inf: person): **to be put out** 怒っている okótte irù

putrid [pjuː'trid] adj 腐った kusáttà

putt [pʌt] n (GOLF) パット pátto

put through vt (TEL: person, call) つなぐ tsunágù; (plan, agreement) 成功させる seíkō saserù

putting green [pʌt'iŋ-] *n* (GOLF: smooth area around hole) グリーン gurín; (: for practice) パット練習場 páttðreñshūjō

putty [pʌt'i:] *n* パテ pátè

put up *vt* (build) 建てる tatérù; (raise: umbrella) 広げる hirógerù; (: tent) 張る hárù; (: hood) かぶる kabúrù; (poster, sign etc) 張る harú; (increase: price, cost) 上げる agérù; (accommodate) 泊める tomérù

put-up [put'ʌp]: *put-up job* (*BRIT*) *n* 八百長 yaóchō

put up with *vt fus* 我慢する gámàn suru

puzzle [pʌz'əl] *n* (question, game) なぞなぞ nazónazo; (toy) パズル pázùru; (mystery) なぞ nazó
♦*vt* 当惑させる tówaku saserù
♦*vi*: *to puzzle over something* ...を思案する ...wo shían suru

puzzling [pʌz'liŋ] *adj* (thing, action) 訳の分からない wákè no wakáranaì

pyjamas [pədʒɑːm'əz] (*BRIT*) *npl* = **pajamas**

pylon [pai'lɑːn] *n* (for electric cables) 鉄塔 tettő

pyramid [pir'əmid] *n* (ARCHIT) ピラミッド pirámiddð; (shape, object, pile) ピラミッド状の物 pirámiddojõ no monõ

Pyrenees [pir'əni:z] *npl*: *the Pyrenees* ピレネー山脈 pírēnē sáñmyaku

python [pai'θɑːn] *n* ニシキヘビ nishíkihebì

Q

quack [kwæk] *n* (of duck) がーがー gāgā; (*pej*: doctor) やぶ医者 yabúisha

quad [kwɑːd] *abbr* = **quadrangle; quadruplet**

quadrangle [kwɑːd'ræŋgəl] *n* (courtyard) 中庭 nakániwa

quadruple [kwɑːdru:'pəl] *vt* (increase fourfold) 4倍にする yoñbai ni suru
♦*vi* 4倍になる yoñbai ni naru

quadruplets [kwɑːdrʌ'plits] *npl* 四つ子

yotsúgo

quagmire [kwæg'maiə:r] *n* (bog) 湿地 shitchí; (muddy place) ぬかるみ nukárumi

quail [kweil] *n* (bird) ウズラ uzúra
♦*vi*: *to quail at/before* (anger, prospect) ...の前でおじけづく ...no maè de ojíkezùku

quaint [kweint] *adj* (house, village) 古風で面白い kofū de omóshiroì; (ideas, customs) 奇妙な kimyõ na

quake [kweik] *vi* (with fear) 震える furúeru
♦*n abbr* = **earthquake**

Quaker [kwei'kə:r] *n* クエーカー教徒 kuēkākyōto

qualification [kwɑːləfəkei'ʃən] *n* (often pl: training, degree, diploma) 資格 shikáku; (skill, quality) 能力 nōryðku; (reservation, modification) 限定 geñtei, 条件 jōken

qualified [kwɑːl'əfaid] *adj* (trained) 資格のある shikáku no aru; (fit, competent): *qualified to* ...する能力がある ...suru nōryðku ga aru; (limited) 条件付きの jōkentsuki no

qualify [kwɑːl'əfai] *vt* (make competent) ...に資格を与える ...ni shikáku wo ataerù; (modify) 限定する geñtei suru
♦*vi* (pass examination(s)): *to qualify (as)* ...の資格を取る ...no shikáku wo torù; (be eligible): *to qualify (for)* (...の) 資格がある (...no) shikáku ga aru; (in competition): *to qualify (for)* (...に進む) 資格を得る (...ni susúmu) shikáku wo eru

quality [kwɑːl'iti:] *n* (standard: of work, product) 品質 hiñshitsu; (characteristic: of person) 性質 seíshitsu; (: of wood, stone etc) 特徴 tokúchō

qualm [kwɑːm] *n* (doubt) 疑問 gimón
qualms of conscience 良心のかざ ryóshin nò kasháku

quandary [kwɑːn'dri:] *n*: *to be in a quandary* 途方に暮れる tohő ni kuréru

quantity [kwɑːn'titi:] *n* (amount: of uncountable thing) 量 ryő; (: of countable things) 数 kazù

quantity surveyor n 積算士 sekīsanshi ◇工事などの費用を見積りで計算する人 kṓji nadð no hĩyṓ wo mitsúmori dè keísan suru hitð

quarantine [kwɔːr'əntiːn] n (isolation) 隔離 kakúri

quarrel [kwɔːr'əl] n (argument) けんか keńka
♦vi: **to quarrel (with)** (...と) けんかする (...to) keńka suru

quarrelsome [kwɔːr'əlsəm] adj けんかっ早い keńkappayaǐ

quarry [kwɔːr'iː] n (for stone) 石切り場 ishíkiriba, 採石場 saísekijṓ; (animal) 獲物 emóno

quart [kwɔːrt] n クォート kwṓto

quarter [kwɔːr'tər] n (fourth part) 4分の1 yoǹbun no ichi; (US: coin) 25セント玉 nijúgosentodamà; (of year) 四半期 shihánki; (district) 地区 chikú
♦vt (divide by four) 4等分する yoǹtōbun suru; (MIL: lodge) 宿泊させる shukúhaku saseru
a quarter of an hour 15分 jūgófun

quarter final n 準々決勝 juňjunkesshṓ

quarterly [kwɔːr'tərliː] adj (meeting, payment) 年4回の neǹ-yoǹkai no
♦adv (meet, pay) 年4回に neǹ-yoǹkai ni

quarters [kwɔːr'tərz] npl (barracks) 兵舎 heísha; (living quarters) 宿舎 shúkusha

quartet(te) [kwɔːrtet'] n (group: of instrumentalists) 四重奏団 shijūsṓdan, カルテット karútetto; (: of singers) 四重唱団 shijúshōdan, カルテット karútetto; (piece of music) 四重奏曲 shijúsōkyokù

quartz [kwɔːrts] n 水晶 suíshō

quash [kwɑːʃ] vt (verdict, judgement) 破棄する hakí suru

quasi- [kwei'zai] prefix 疑似... gijí...

quaver [kwei'vər] n (BRIT: MUS) 八分音符 hachífbun oñpu
♦vi (voice) 震える furúeru

quay [kiː] n (also: **quayside**) 岸壁 gañpeki

queasy [kwiː'ziː] adj (nauseous) 吐気がする hakíkè ga suru

queen [kwiːn] n (monarch) 女王 joṓ; (king's wife) 王妃 ṓhǐ; (ZOOL: also:

queen bee 女王バチ joōbachi; (CARDS, CHESS) クイーン kuíñ

queen mother n 皇太后 kṓtaigṓ

queer [kwiːr] adj (odd) 変な heñ na
♦n (inf: homosexual) ホモ homó

quell [kwel] vt (opposition) 鎮める shizúmeru; (unease, fears) なだめる nadámeru, 静める shizúmeru

quench [kwentʃ] vt: **to quench one's thirst** のどの乾きをいやす nodð no kawákǐ wo iyásù

querulous [kwer'ələs] adj (person, voice) 愚痴っぽい guchíppoǐ

query [kwiər'iː] n (question) 質問 shitsúmon
♦vt (question) ...に聞く ...ni kikú, ...に質問する ...ni shitsúmon suru

quest [kwest] n 探求 tañkyū

question [kwes'tʃən] n (query) 質問 shitsúmon; (doubt) 疑問 gimón; (issue) 問題 moñdai; (in test: problem) 問 toǐ
♦vt (ask) ...に聞く ...ni kikú, ...に質問する ...ni shitsúmon suru; (interrogate) 尋問する jiñmon suru; (doubt) ...に疑問を投げ掛ける ...ni gimón wo nagékakeru
beyond question 疑いもなく utágai mo naku
out of the question 全く不可能で mattáku fúkanð de

questionable [kwes'tʃənəbəl] adj (doubtful) 疑わしい utágawashii

question mark n 疑問符 gimóñfu

questionnaire [kwestʃəner'] n 調査票 chṓsahyō, アンケート añkḗto

queue [kjuː] n (BRIT) 列 retsù
♦vi (also: **queue up**) 列を作る retsù wo tsukúru

quibble [kwib'əl] vi 詰まらない議論をする tsumáranaǐ giròn wo suru

quiche [kiːʃ] n キッシュ kisshù ◇パイの一種 paǐ no isshù

quick [kwik] adj (fast: person, movement, action etc) 早い hayáǐ; (agile) 素早い subáyaǐ; (: mind) 理解の早い rikáǐ no hayáǐ; (brief: look, visit) 短い mijíkaì, ちょっとした chottó shita
♦n: **cut to the quick** (fig) ...の感情を害する ...no kañjō wo gaí sùru

be quick! 急いで isóíde

quicken [kwik'ən] *vt* (pace, step) 早める hayámeru

♦*vi* (pace, step) 早くなる hayáku naru

quickly [kwik'li:] *adv* 早く hayáku

quicksand [kwik'sænd] *n* 流土砂 ryúdo-sha, クイックサンド kuíkkùsando

quick-witted [kwik'wit'id] *adj* (alert) 機敏な kibín na

quid [kwid] (*BRIT*: *inf*) *n inv* ポンド po-ńdo

quiet [kwai'it] *adj* (not loud or noisy) 静かな shizúka na; (silent) 何も言わない nanî mo iwânai; (peaceful: place) 平和な heiwa na; (calm: person) もの静かな mo-nóshizuka na; (without fuss etc: ceremony) 簡単な kańtan na

♦*n* (peacefulness) 静けさ shizúkesa; (silence) 静かにする事 shizúka ni suru koto

♦*vi* (*US*: *also*: **quiet down**) (grow calm) 落着く ochitsuku; (grow silent) 静かになる shizúka ni naru

♦*vt* (person, animal) 落着かせる ochítsukaserù

quieten [kwai'itən] (*BRIT*) = **quiet** *vi*, *vt*

quietly [kwai'itli:] *adv* (speak, play) 静かに shizúka ni; (silently) 黙って damáttè

quietness [kwai'itnis] *n* (peacefulness) 静けさ shizúkesa; (silence) 静かにする事 shizúka ni suru koto

quilt [kwilt] *n* (covering) ベッドカバー beddòkabā; (*also*: **continental quilt**) 掛布団 kakebuton, キルト kirúto

quin [kwin] *n abbr* = **quintuplet**

quinine [kwai'nain] *n* キニーネ kinínè

quintet(te) [kwintet'] *n* (group) 五重奏団 gojúsōdan, クインテット kuíntetto; (piece of music) 五重奏曲 gojúsōkyoku

quintuplets [kwintʌ'plits] *npl* 五つ子 i-tsútsugo

quip [kwip] *n* 警句 keíku

quirk [kwə:rk] *n* (unusual characteristic) 癖 kusé; (accident: of fate, nature) 気まぐれ kimágure

quit [kwit] (*pt*, *pp* **quit** *or* **quitted**) *vt* (smoking, grumbling) やめる yaméru; (job) 辞める yaméru; (premises) ...から出ていく ...kara detè iku

♦*vi* (give up) やめる yaméru; (resign) 辞める yaméru

quite [kwait] *adv* (rather) かなり kanàri; (entirely) 全く mattàku, 完全に kańzen ni; (following a negative: almost): *that's not quite big enough* それはちょっと小さい soré wa chottó chiisai

I saw quite a few of them 私はそれらをかなり沢山見ました watákushi wa soréra wo kanári takúsan mimashita

quite (so)! 全くその通り mattáku sonó tōri

quits [kwits] *adj*: *quits (with)* (...と) おあいこである (...to) o-áiko de aru

let's call it quits (call it even) おあいこにしましょう o-aíko ni shimáshō; (stop working etc) やめましょう yamé-mashō

quiver [kwiv'ə:r] *vi* (tremble) 震える fu-rúerù

quiz [kwiz] *n* (game) クイズ kuízu; (*US*: short test) 小テスト shótesùto

♦*vt* (question) 尋問する jiñmon suru

quizzical [kwiz'ikəl] *adj* (look, smile) なぞめいた nazómeìta

quorum [kwɔ:r'əm] *n* (of members) 定足数 teísokusū

quota [kwou'tə] *n* 割当数〔量〕 waríatesū〔ryō〕

quotation [kwoutei'ʃən] *n* (from book, play etc) 引用文 iñ-yōbuñ; (estimate) 見積り mitsúmori

quotation marks *npl* 引用符 iñyōfù

quote [kwout] *n* (from book, play etc) 引用文 iñyōbuñ; (estimate) 見積り mitsú-mori

♦*vt* (sentence, proverb etc) 引用する iñ-yō suru; (figure, example) 引合いに出す hikíai ni dasù; (price) 見積る mitsúmorù

♦*vi*: *to quote from* (book, play etc) ...から引用する ...kara iñ-yō suru

quotes [kwouts] *npl* (quotation marks) 引用符 iñ-yōfù

quotient [kwou'ʃənt] *n* (factor) 指数 shi-sū

R

rabbi [ræb'ai] n ラビ rábì ◇ユダヤ教の聖職者 yudáyakyō nò seíshokushà

rabbit [ræb'it] n ウサギ usági

rabbit hutch n ウサギ小屋 uságigoyà

rabble [ræb'əl] (pej) n 群衆 guńshū

rabies [rei'bi:z] n 恐犬病 kyókeñbyō

RAC [ɑːreisiz'] (BRIT) n abbr (= Royal Automobile Club) 英国自動車連盟 eíkoku jidōsha reñmei

raccoon [ræku:n'] n アライグマ aráigùma

race [reis] n (species) 人種 jińshu; (competition: for speed) 競走 kyōsō, レース résù; (: for power, control) 競争 kyósō; (public gambling event: also: **horse race**) 競馬 keíba; (: also: **bicycle race**) 競輪 keírin; (: also: **motorboat race**) 競艇 kyótei
♦vt (horse) 競馬に出場させる keíba nì shutsújō saserù; (compete against: person) ...と競走する ...to kyósō suru
♦vi (compete: for speed) 競走する kyósō suru; (: for power, control) 競争する kyósō suru; (hurry) 急いで行く isóide ikù; (pulse) どきどきする dókìdoki suru; (engine) 空回りする karámawarì suru

race car (US) n レーシングカー réshingukà

race car driver (US) n レーサー résà

racecourse [reis'kɔ:rs] n 競馬場 keíbajō

racehorse [reis'hɔ:rs] n 競走馬 kyósōba

racetrack [reis'træk] n (for people) トラック torákkù; (for cars) サーキット sákitto

racial [rei'ʃəl] adj 人種の jińshu no, 人種... jińshu...

racing [rei'siŋ] n (horses) 競馬 keíba; (bicycles) 競輪 keírin; (motorboats) 競艇 kyótei; (cars) 自動車レース jidósharèsu; (motorcycles) オートレース ótorèsu

racing car (BRIT) n = **race car**

racing driver (BRIT) n = **race car driver**

racism [rei'sizəm] n 人種差別 jińshusabètsu

racist [rei'sist] adj (statement, policy) 人種差別的な jińshusabetsuteki na
♦n 人種差別主義者 jińshusabetsushugishà

rack [ræk] n (also: **luggage rack**) 網棚 amídana; (shelf) 棚 taná; (also: **roof rack**) ルーフラック rúfurakkù; (dish rack) 水切りかご mizúkirikago
♦vt: **racked by** (pain, anxiety) ...でもだえ苦しんで ...de modáekurushiñde
to rack one's brains 知恵を絞る chié wò shibórù

racket [ræk'it] n (for tennis, squash etc) ラケット rakéttò; (noise) 騒音 sóon; (swindle) 詐欺 ságì

racoon [ræku:n'] n = **raccoon**

racquet [ræk'it] n (for tennis, squash etc) ラケット rakéttò

racy [rei'si:] adj きびきびした kíbìkibi shita

radar [rei'dɑ:r] n レーダー rédā

radial [rei'di:əl] adj (also: **radial-ply**) ラジアルの rájìaru no

radiance [rei'di:əns] n (glow) 光 hikári

radiant [rei'di:ənt] adj (happy, joyful) 輝く kagáyakù

radiate [rei'di:eit] vt (heat) 放射する hōsha suru; (emotion) ...で輝く ...de kagáyakù
♦vi (lines) 放射状に広がる hōshajō nì hirógarù

radiation [reidi:ei'ʃən] n (radioactive) 放射能 hōshanō; (from sun etc) 放射 hōsha

radiator [rei'di:eitər] n ラジエーター rajíètā

radical [ræd'ikəl] adj (change etc) 抜本的な bappónteki na; (person) 過激な kagéki na; (organization) 過激派の kagékiha no, 過激派... kagékiha...

radii [rei'di:ai] npl of **radius**

radio [rei'di:ou] n (broadcasting) ラジオ放送 rajíohòsō; (device: for receiving broadcasts) ラジオ rájìo; (: for transmitting and receiving signals) 無線通信機 muséntsūshiñki
♦vt (person) ...と無線で通信する ...to musén dè tsúshin suru
on the radio ラジオで rájìo de

radioactive [reidi:ouæk'tiv] *adj* 放射性 の hōshasei no

radiography [reidi:ɑːg'rəfi:] *n* レントゲン撮影 reńtogensatsuèi

radiology [reidi:ɑːl'ədʒi:] *n* 放射線医学 hōshasen-igàku

radio station *n* ラジオ放送局 rajío hō-sōkyòku

radiotherapy [reidi:ouθe:r'əpi:] *n* 放射線療法 hōshasenryòhō

radish [ræd'iʃ] *n* はつかだいこん hatsú-kadaìkon

radius [rei'di:əs] (*pl* **radii**) *n* (of circle) 半径 haǹkei; (from point) 半径内の範囲 haǹkeinai nò háǹ-i

RAF [ɑːrei:ef'] *n abbr* = **Royal Air Force**

raffle [ræf'əl] *n* 宝くじ takárakùji ◇当と金ではなく賞品をもらえる物を指す a-tárù to kané de wa nakù shóhin wò moráerù monó wò sásù

raft [ræft] *n* (craft) いかだ ikáda; (*also*: **life raft**) 救命いかだ kyúmei ikàda

rafter [ræf'tə:r] *n* はり harí

rag [ræg] *n* (piece of cloth) ぞうきん zó-kin; (torn cloth) ぼろ bòrð; (*pej*: newspaper) 三流紙 sańryūshi; (*BRIT*: UNIVERSITY: for charity) 慈善募金運動 ji-zénbokin-uńdð

rag-and-bone man [rægənboun'-] (*BRIT*) *n* = **ragman**

rag doll *n* 縫いぐるみ人形 nuíguruminiǹ-gyð

rage [reidʒ] *n* (fury) 憤怒 fúǹdo ◆*vi* (person) 怒り狂う ikárikuruù; (storm) 荒れ狂う arékuruù; (debate) 荒れる arérù

it's all the rage (very fashionable) 大流行している daíryūkō shite irù

ragged [ræg'id] *adj* (edge) ぎざぎざの gi-zágiza no; (clothes) ぼろぼろの boróboro no; (appearance) 不ぞろいの fuzórði no

ragman [ræg'mæn] (*pl* **ragmen**) *n* くず屋 kuzúyà

rags [rægz] *npl* (torn clothes) ぼろぼろの衣服 boróboro no ifúku

raid [reid] *n* (MIL) 襲撃 shúgeki; (criminal) 不法侵入 fuhóshiǹnyū; (by police) 手

入れ teíre ◆*vt* (MIL) 襲撃する shúgeki suru; (criminally) ...に不法侵入する ...ni fuhóshiǹnyū suru; (subj: police) 手入れする teíre suru

rail [reil] *n* 手すり tesúri

by rail (by train) 列車で resshá de

railing(s) [rei'liŋ(z)] *n(pl)* (fence) さく sakú

railroad [reil'roud] (*US*) *n* (track) 線路 seńro; (company) 鉄道 tetsúdō

railroader [reil'roudə:r] (*US*) *n* 鉄道員 tetsúdōìn

railroad line (*US*) *n* 鉄道線 tetsúdōsen

railroad station (*US*) *n* 駅 ekí

rails [reilz] *npl* (for train) レール rèru

railway [reil'wei] (*BRIT*) *n* = **railroad** *etc*

railwayman [reil'weimən] (*BRIT*: *pl* **railwaymen**) *n* = **railroader**

rain [rein] *n* 雨 ámè ◆*vi* 雨が降る ámè ga fúrù

in the rain 雨の中で ámè no nákà de

it's raining 雨が降っている ámè ga fut-tè irù

rainbow [rein'bou] *n* にじ nijí

raincoat [rein'kout] *n* レーンコート rèń-kōto

raindrop [rein'drɑːp] *n* 雨の一滴 ámè no ittéki

rainfall [rein'fɔːl] *n* 降雨量 kóuryð

rainy [rei'ni:] *adj* 雨模様の amémoyð no

raise [reiz] *n* (payrise) 賃上げ chíń-age ◆*vt* (lift) 持上げる mochíagerù; (increase: salary) 上げる agérù; (: production) 増やす fuyásù; (improve: morale) 高める takámerù; (: standards) 引上げる hikíagerù; (produce: doubts, question) 引起こす hikíokosù; (rear: cattle) 飼育する shiíku suru; (: family) 育てる sodáterù; (cultivate: crop) 栽培する saíbai suru; (get together: army, funds, loan) 集める atsúmerù

to raise one's voice 声を大きくする kóè wo ókiku suru

raisin [rei'zin] *n* 干しぶどう hoshíbudð, レーズン rèzun

rake [reik] *n* (tool) レーキ rèki ◆*vt* (garden) レーキで...の土をならす rè-

ki de ...no tsuchí wǒ narásu; (leaves) かき集める kakísatsumerù; (with machine gun) 掃射する sōsha suru

rally [ræl'i:] *n* (POL etc) 集会 shūkai; (AUT) ラリー rarī; (TENNIS etc) ラリー rarī

♦*vt* (support) 集める atsúmerù

♦*vi* (sick person, Stock Exchange) 持直す mochínaosù

rally round *vt fus* (fig: give support to) ...の支援に駆け付ける ...no shién ni kakétsukerù

RAM [ræm] *n abbr* = **(random access memory)** ラム rámù

ram [ræm] *n* (ZOOL) 雄ヒツジ osúhitsùji

♦*vt* (crash into) ...に激突する ...ni gekítotsu suru; (push: bolt, fist etc) 押込む oshíkomù

ramble [ræm'bəl] *n* (walk) ハイキング haíkingu

♦*vi* (walk) ハイキングする haíkingu suru; (talk: *also*: **ramble on**) だらだらしゃべる dáradara shabérù

rambler [ræm'blə:r] *n* (walker) ハイカー haíkà; (BOT) ツルバラ tsurúbara

rambling [ræm'bliŋ] *adj* (speech) 取留めのない torítome no naì; (house) だだっ広い dadáppiroì; (BOT) つる性の tsurúsei no

ramp [ræmp] *n* 傾斜路 keísharo

on/off ramp (*US*: AUT) 入口(出口)ランプ iríguchi(degúchi)raǹpu

rampage [ræm'peidʒ] *n*: **to be on the rampage** 暴れ回っている abáremawatte irù

♦*vi*: **they went rampaging through the town** 彼らは町中暴れ回った kárèra wa machíjū abaremawattà

rampant [ræm'pənt] *adj* (crime) はびこる habíkorù; (disease) まん延する mañ-en suru

rampart [ræm'pɑːrt] *n* (fortification) 城壁 jōheki

ramshackle [ræm'ʃækəl] *adj* (house, car, table) がたがたの gatágata no

ran [ræn] *pt of* **run**

ranch [ræntʃ] *n* 牧場 bokújō

rancher [ræn'tʃə:r] *n* 牧場主 bokújōshu

rancid [ræn'sid] *adj* (butter, bacon etc) 悪くなった wárùku natta

rancor [ræŋ'kə:r] (*BRIT* **rancour**) *n* 恨み urámi

random [ræn'dəm] *adj* (arrangement, selection) 手当り次第の teátarishidài no; (COMPUT, MATH) 無作為の musákùi no

♦*n*: **at random** 手当り次第に teátarishidài ni

random access *n* (COMPUT) ランダムアクセス rañdamuakùsesu

randy [ræn'di:] (*inf*) *adj* セックスをしたがっている sékkùsu wo shitágatte irù

rang [ræŋ] *pt of* **ring**

range [reindʒ] *n* (*also*: **mountain range**) 山脈 sañmyaku; (of missile) 射程距離 shatéikyorì; (of voice) 声域 seíiki; (series: of proposals, offers, products) 一連の... ichíren no ...; (MIL: *also*: **shooting range**) 射撃場 shagékijō; (*also*: **kitchen range**) レンジ réñji

♦*vt* (place) 歩き回る arúkimawarù; (arrange) 並べる naráberù

♦*vi*: **to range over** (extend) ...にわたる ...ni watárù

to range from ... to ... ...から...までにわたる ...kárà ...mádè ni watárù

ranger [rein'dʒə:r] *n* 森林警備隊員 shiñrinkeibitaiin, レンジャー réñjā

rank [ræŋk] *n* (a row) 列 rétsù; (MIL) 階級 kaíkyū; (status) 地位 chíi; (*BRIT*: *also*: **taxi rank**) タクシー乗場 takúshinorîba

♦*vi*: **to rank among** ...のうちに数えられる ...no uchí ni kazóerarerù

♦*adj* (stinking) 臭い kusáì

the rank and file (fig: ordinary members) 一般の人 ippán no hitó, 一般人 ippánjin

rankle [ræŋ'kəl] *vi* (insult) わだかまる wadákamarù

ransack [ræn'sæk] *vt* (search) 物色する busshóku suru; (plunder) 略奪する ryakúdatsu suru

ransom [ræn'səm] *n* (money) 身代金 minóshirokiñ

to hold to ransom (fig: nation, company, individual) ...に圧力を掛ける ...ni

atsúryóku wo kakérù

rant [rænt] *vi* (rave) わめく wamékù

rap [ræp] *vt* (on door, table) たたく tatáku

rape [reip] *n* (of woman) 強かん gókan; (BOT) アブラナ abúranà
♦*vt* (woman) 強かんする gókan suru

rape(seed) oil [reip'(si:d)-] *n* ナタネ油 natáneabùra

rapid [ræp'id] *adj* (growth, development, change) 急速な kyúsoku na

rapidity [rəpid'iti:] *n* (speed) 速さ háyàsa

rapidly [ræp'idli:] *adv* (grow, develop, change) 急速に kyúsoku ni

rapids [ræp'idz] *npl* (GEO) 早瀬 hayáse

rapist [rei'pist] *n* 強かん者 gókansha

rapport [ræpɔːr'] *n* 親和関係 shińwakaǹkei

rapture [ræp'tʃəːr] *n* (delight) 歓喜 káñki

rapturous [ræp'tʃəːrəs] *adj* (applause) 熱狂的な nekkyóteki na

rare [re:r] *adj* (uncommon) まれな maré na; (unusual) 珍しい mezúrashiì; (CULIN) レアの réa no

rarely [rea:r'li:] *adv* (seldom) めったに …ない méttà ni …naì

raring [re:r'iŋ] *adj*: **raring to go** (*inf*: keen) 意気込んでいる ikígonde irù

rarity [re:r'iti:] *n* (exception) 希有な物 kéù na monó; (scarcity) 希少性 kishósei

rascal [ræs'kəl] *n* (rogue) ごろつき górótsuki; (mischievous child) いたずらっ子 itázurakkò

rash [ræʃ] *adj* (person) 向こう見ずの mukómìzu no; (promise, act) 軽率な keísotsu na
♦*n* (MED) 発しん hasshín; (spate: of events, robberies) 多発 tahátsu

rasher [ræʃ'əːr] *n* (of bacon) 一切れ hitókìre

raspberry [ræz'be:ri:] *n* キイチゴ kiíchìgo

rasping [ræs'piŋ] *adj*: **a rasping noise** きしむ音 kishímù otó

rat [ræt] *n* ネズミ nezúmi

rate [reit] *n* (speed) 速度 sókùdo; (of change, inflation) 進行度 shińkòdo;

(ratio: *also* of interest) 率 rítsù; (price: at hotel etc) 料金 ryókin
♦*vt* (value, estimate) 評価する hyóka suru

to rate someone/something as …を …と評価する …wo …to hyóka suru

rateable value [rei'təbəl-] (*BRIT*) *n* 課税評価額 kazéi hyókagàku

ratepayer [reit'peiəːr] (*BRIT*) *n* 納税者 nózeìsha◇固定資産税の納税者について言う kotéishisaǹzei no nózeìsha ni tsuíte iú

rates [reits] *npl* (*BRIT*: property tax) 固定資産税 kotéishisaǹzei; (fees) 料金 ryókin

rather [ræð'əːr] *adv* (quite, somewhat) かなり kánàri; (to some extent) 少し sukóshì; (more accurately): **or rather** 正確に言えば seíkaku nì iébà

it's rather expensive (quite) かなり値段が高い kánàri nedán gà takáì; (too) 値段が高過ぎる nedán gà takásugirù

there's rather a lot かなり沢山ある kánàri takúsan arù

I would rather go どちらかというと行きたいと思う dóchìra ka to iú tò ikítaì to omóù

ratify [ræt'əfai] *vt* (agreement, treaty) 批准する hijún suru

rating [rei'tiŋ] *n* (assessment) 評価 hyóka; (score) 評点 hyóten; (NAUT: *BRIT*: sailor) 海軍兵卒 kaígunheìsotsu

ratings [rei'tiŋz] *npl* (RADIO, TV) 視聴率 shichóritsu

ratio [rei'ʃou] *n* 率 rítsù

in the ratio of 100 to 1 100に1つという割合で hyakú ni hitotsù to iu waríai de

ration [ræʃ'ən] *n* (allowance: of food, petrol etc) 配給分 haíkyùbun
♦*vt* (food, petrol etc) 配給する haíkyù suru

rational [ræʃ'ənəl] *adj* (solution, reasoning) 合理的な góriteki na; (person) 訳の分かる wáke no wakárù

rationale [ræʃənæl'] *n* 根拠 kóñkyo

rationalize [ræʃ'ənəlaiz] *vt* (justify) 正当化する seítōka suru

rationally [ræʃˈənəliː] *adv* (sensibly) 合理的に gṓriteki ni

rationing [ræʃˈəniŋ] *n* (of food, petrol etc) 配給 haíkyū

rations [reiˈʃənz] *npl* (MIL) 兵糧 hyṓrō

rat race *n* 競争の世界 kyṓsō no sékài

rattle [ræt'əl] *n* (of door, window) がたがたという音 gátàgata to iú oto; (of train, car, engine etc) ごう音 gṓon; (of coins) じゃらじゃらという音 járàjara to iú oto; (of chain) がらがらという音 gáràgara to iú oto; (object: for baby) がらがら garágarà

♦*vi* (small objects) がらがら鳴る gáràgara narú; (car, bus): **to rattle along** がたがた走る gatagata hashírù

♦*vt* (unnerve) どぎまぎさせる dógìmagi sasérù

rattlesnake [ræt'əlsneik] *n* ガラガラヘビ garágarahebì

raucous [rɔːˈkəs] *adj* しゃがれ声の shagáregoè no

ravage [ræv'idʒ] *vt* (damage) 荒す arásù

ravages [ræv'idʒiz] *npl* (of time, weather) 荒廃 kṓhai

rave [reiv] *vi* (in anger) わめく wamékù; (with enthusiasm) ...をべたほめする ...wo betábòme suru; (MED) うわごとを言う uwágoto wo iú

raven [rei'vən] *n* ワタリガラス watárigaràsu

ravenous [ræv'ənəs] *adj* 猛烈におなががすいた mōretsu ní onáka ga suìta

ravine [rəvin'] *n* 渓谷 keíkoku

raving [rei'viŋ] *adj*: **raving lunatic** ど気違い dokíchigài

ravishing [ræv'iʃiŋ] *adj* (beautiful) 悩殺する nṓsatsu suru

raw [rɔː] *adj* (uncooked) 生の námà no; (not processed: cotton, sugar etc) 原料のままの gefiryṓ no mamá no; (sore) 赤むけした akámuke shità; (inexperienced) 青二才の aónisài no; (weather, day) 肌寒い hadázamuì

raw deal (*inf*) *n* ひどい仕打 hidóì shiúchi

raw material *n* (coal, oil, gas etc) 原料 gefiryṓ

ray [rei] *n* (*also*: **ray of light**) 光線 kṓsen; (*also*: **ray of heat**) 熱線 nessen

the rays of the sun 太陽の光線 táiyō no kṓsen

a ray of hope 希望のひらめき kibṓ nò hirámeki

rayon [rei'ɑːn] *n* レーヨン rèyon

raze [reiz] *vt* 根こそぎ破壊する nekósògi hakái suru

razor [rei'zəːr] *n* (open razor) かみそり kamísorì; (safety razor) 安全かみそり afizenkamisòri; (electric razor) 電気かみそり defikikamisòri

razor blade *n* かみそりの刃 kamísorì no há

Rd *n abbr* = **road**

re [rei] *prep* (with regard to) ...に関して ...ni káñ shite

reach [riːtʃ] *n* (range: of arm) 手が届く範囲 té gà todókù hán-i; (scope: of imagination) 範囲 hán-i; (stretch: of river etc) 区域 kúìki

♦*vt* (arrive at: place) ...に到着する ...ni tṓchaku suru; (: conclusion, agreement, decision, end) ...に達する ...ni tassúrù; (be able to touch) ...に手が届く ...ni té gà todókù; (by telephone) ...に連絡する ...ni refiraku suru

♦*vi* (stretch out one's arm) 手を伸ばす té wò nobásù

within reach 手の届く所に té nò todókù tokórò ni

out of reach 手の届かない所に té nò todókanaì tokórò ni

within reach of the shops/station 商店街〔駅〕の近くに shóteñgai〔ékì〕no chikákù ni

「**keep out of the reach of children**」子供の手が届かない所に保管して下さい kodómo nò té gà todókanaì tokórò ni hokán shitè kudásaí

reach out *vt* (hand) 伸ばす nobásù

♦*vi* 手を伸ばす té wò nobásù

to reach out for something ...を取ろうとして手を伸ばす ...wo toró tò shite té wò nobásù

react [riːækt'] *vi* (CHEM): **to react (with)** (...と) 反応する (...to) hafinō su-

ru; (MED): *to react (to)* (...に対して)
副作用が起る (...ni táishite) fukúsayō ga
okóru; (respond): *to react (to)* (...に)
反応する (...ni) hańnō suru; (rebel): *to
react (against)* (...に) 反発する (...ni)
hańpatsu suru

reaction [ri:æk'ʃən] *n* (response): *reaction (to)* (...に対する) 反応 (...ni taísu-
rù) hańnō; (rebellion): *reaction
(against)* (...に対する) 反発 (...ni taí-
surù) hańpatsu; (belief in conservatism)
反動 hańdō; (CHEM) 反応 hańnō; (MED)
副作用 fukúsayō

reactionary [ri:æk'ʃəneːri:] *adj* (forces,
attitude) 反動的な hańdōteki na

reactions [ri:æk'ʃənz] *npl* (reflexes) 反
応 hańnō

reactor [ri:æk'tə:r] *n* (*also*: **nuclear
reactor**) 原子炉 geńshirò

read [ri:d] (*pt*, *pp* **read**) *vi* (person, child)
...を読む ...wo yómù; (piece of writing,
letter etc) ...と書いてある ...to káîte árù
♦*vt* (book, newspaper, music etc) 読む
yómù; (mood, thoughts) 読取る yomíto-
rù; (meter, thermometer etc) 読む yómù;
(study: at university) 学ぶ manábù

readable [ri:'dəbəl] *adj* (writing) 読める
yomérù; (book, author etc) 読ませる yo-
máserù

reader [ri:'də:r] *n* (of book, newspaper
etc) 読者 dókùsha; (book) リーダー rídà;
(*BRIT*: at university) 助教授 jokyójù
an avid reader 読書家 dokúshòka

readership [ri:'də:rʃip] *n* (of newspaper
etc) 読者 dókùsha ◇総称 sōsho

readily [red'əli:] *adv* (willingly) 快く ko-
kóroyokù; (easily) たやすく tayásukù;
(quickly) 直ぐに súgu ni

readiness [red'i:nis] *n* (preparedness) 用
意ができている事 yōi ga dekíte iru koto;
(willingness) ...する意志 ...suru ishi
in readiness (prepared) 用意ができて
yōi ga dekite

reading [ri:d'iŋ] *n* (of books, newspapers
etc) 読書 dokusho; (in church, as entertainment) 朗読 rōdoku; (on meter, thermometer etc) 記録 kiroku

readjust [ri:ədʒʌst'] *vt* (alter: position,

knob, mirror etc) 調節する chōsetsu suru
♦*vi* (adapt): *to readjust (to)* (...に) な
れる (...ni) nareru

read out *vt* 朗読する rōdoku suru

ready [red'i:] *adj* (prepared) 用意ができ
ている yōi ga dekíte iru; (willing) ...する
意志がある ...surú ishì ga árù; (available)
用意されている yōi sárete irù
♦*n*: *at the ready* (MIL) 銃を構えて jū
wo kamáetè
to get ready
♦*vi* 支度する shitáku suru
♦*vt* 準備する júnbi suru

ready-made [red'i:meid'] *adj* 既製の kiséi no

ready money *n* 現金 geńkiǹ

ready reckoner [-rek'ənə:r] *n* 計算表
keísaǹhyō

ready-to-wear [red'i:təweːr'] *adj* 既製
の kiséi no

reaffirm [ri:əfə:rm'] *vt* 再び言明する futátabi geńmei suru

real [ri:l] *adj* (actual, true: reason, interest, result etc) 本当の hońtō no; (not artificial: leather, gold etc) 本物の hońmono
no; (not imaginary: life, feeling) 実際の
jissái no; (for emphasis): *a real idiot/
miracle* 正真正銘のばか〔奇跡〕shōshin-
shōmei no bákà〔kiséki〕
in real terms 事実は jíjìtsu wa

real estate *n* 不動産 fudósan

realism [ri:'əlizəm] *n* (practicality) 現実
主義 geńjitsushugì; (ART) リアリズム ri-
árizùmu

realist [ri:'əlist] *n* 現実的な人 geńjitsuteki nà hitó

realistic [ri:əlis'tik] *adj* (practical) 現実
的な geńjitsuteki na; (true to life) 写実的
な shajítsuteki na

reality [ri:æl'iti:] *n* (actuality, truth) 事
実 jíjìtsu
in reality 事実は jíjìtsu wa

realization [ri:ələzei'ʃən] *n* (understanding: of situation) 実感 jikkán; (fulfilment: of dreams, hopes) 実現 jitsúgen;
(of asset) 現金化 geńkiǹka

realize [ri:'əlaiz] *vt* (understand) 実感す

る jikkán suru; (fulfil: a dream, hope, project etc) 実現する jitsúgen suru; (COMM: asset) 現金に替える geñkin ni kaéru

really [ri:'əli:] *adv* (for emphasis) 実に jitsú ni, とても totémo; (actually): *what really happened* 実際に起った事は jissái ni okótta kotó wa

really? (indicating interest) そうですか sô desu ka; (expressing surprise) 本当ですか hoñtó desu kà

really! (indicating annoyance) うんも う！úñ mő!

realm [relm] *n* (of monarch) 王国 ő koku; (*fig*: area of activity or study) 分野 búñ ya

realtor [ri:'əltər] (*US*) *n* 不動産業者 fudősangyősha

reap [ri:p] *vt* (crop) ...の刈入れをする ...no karíre wò suru; (*fig*: benefits, rewards) 収穫する shúkaku suru

reappear [ri:əpi:r'] *vi* 再び現れる futátabi arawarerù

rear [ri:r] *adj* (back) 後ろの ushíro no
♦*n* (back) 後ろ ushíro
♦*vt* (cattle) 飼育する shíku suru; (family) 育てる sodáterù
♦*vi* (*also*: **rear up**: animal) 後足で立ち上る atóashi de tachíagarù

rearguard [ri:r'gɑ:rd] *n* (MIL) 後衛 kőei

rearmament [ri:ɑ:rm'əmənt] *n* 再軍備 saíguñbi

rearrange [ri:əreindʒ'] *vt* 並べ直す narábenaosù

rear-view mirror [ri:r'vju:'-] *n* (AUT) バックミラー bakkúmirà

reason [ri:'zən] *n* (cause) 理由 riyú; (ability to think) 理性 riséi
♦*vi*: *to reason with someone* ...の説得に当る ...no settóku nì atárù

it stands to reason that ...という事は当然である ...to iú kotó wa tőzen de arù

reasonable [ri:'zənəbəl] *adj* (sensible) 訳の分かる wákè no wakárù; (fair: number, amount) 程々の hodóhodo no; (: quality) まあまあの mâmà no; (: price) 妥当な datő na

reasonably [ri:'zənəbli:] *adv* (sensibly)

常識的に jőshikiteki ni; (fairly) 程々に hodóhodo ni

reasoned [ri:'zənd] *adj* (argument) 筋の通った sújì no tőttà

reasoning [ri:'zəniŋ] *n* (process) 推理 súri

reassurance [ri:əʃu:r'əns] *n* 安ど áñdo

reassure [ri:əʃu:r'] *vt* (comfort) 安心させる añshin saserù

to reassure someone of ...に...だと安心させる ...ni ...dá tò añshin saserù

reassuring [ri:əʃu:r'iŋ] *adj* (smile, manner) 安心させる añshin saserù

rebate [ri:'beit] *n* (on tax etc) リベート ribéto

rebel [*n* reb'əl *vb* ribel'] *n* (against political system) 反逆者 hañgyakushà; (against society, parents etc) 反抗分子 hañkóbuñshi
♦*vi* (against political system) 反乱を起す hañran wò okósù; (against society, parents etc) 反抗する hañkő suru

rebellion [ribel'jən] *n* (against political system) 反乱 hañran; (against society, parents etc) 反抗 hañkő

rebellious [ribel'jəs] *adj* (subject) 反逆者の hañgyakushà no; (child, behavior) 反抗的な hañkóteki na

rebirth [ri:bə:rθ'] *n* 復活 fukkátsu

rebound [*vb* ri:baund' *n* ri:'baund] *vi* (ball) 跳ね返る hanékaerù
♦*n*: *on the rebound* (ball) 跳ね返った所を hanékaettà tokórð wo; (*fig*: person) ...した反動で ...shítà hañdő de

rebuff [ribʌf'] *n* 拒絶 kyozétsu

rebuild [ri:bild'] (*pt*, *pp* **rebuilt**) *vt* (town, building etc) 建直す taténaosù; (economy, confidence) 立直す taténaosù

rebuke [ribju:k'] *vt* しかる shikárù

rebut [ribʌt'] *vt* しりぞける shirízokerù

recalcitrant [rikæl'sitrənt] *adj* (child, behavior) 反抗的な hañkóteki na

recall [ri:kɔ:l'] *vt* (remember) 思い出す omőidasù; (parliament, ambassador etc) 呼戻す yobímodosù
♦*n* (ability to remember) 記憶 kíoku; (of ambassador etc) 召還 shőkan

recant [rikænt'] *vi* 自説を取消す jisétsu

wǒ toríkesù

recap [riːˈkæp] *vt* (summarize) 要約する yōyaku suru
♦*vi* ...を要約する ...wo yōyaku suru

recapitulate [riːkəpitʃˈuːleit] *vt, vi* = **recap**

recapture [riːkæpˈtʃəːr] *vt* (town, territory etc) 奪環する dakkán suru; (atmosphere, mood etc) 取戻す torímodosù

rec'd *abbr* = **received**

recede [risiːˈdʲ] *vi* (tide) ひく hikú; (lights etc) 遠のく tōnokù; (memory) 薄らぐ usúragù; (hair) はげる hagérù

receding [risiːˈdiŋ] *adj* (hair) はげつつある hagétsutsu arù; (chin) 無いに等しい naí ni hitóshiì

receipt [risiːtˈ] *n* (document) 領収書 ryōshūsho; (from cash register) レシート reshītò; (act of receiving) 受取る事 ukétorù kotó

receipts [risiːtsˈ] *npl* (COMM) 収入 shúnyū

receive [risiːvˈ] *vt* (get: money, letter etc) 受け取る ukétorù; (criticism, acclaim) 受ける ukérù; (visitor, guest) 迎える mukáerù
to receive an injury けがする kegá surù

receiver [risiːˈvəːr] *n* (TEL) 受話器 juwákì; (RADIO, TV) 受信機 jushínkì; (of stolen goods) 故買屋 kobáiya; (COMM) 管財人 kañzainìn

recent [riːˈsənt] *adj* (event, times) 近ごろの chikágòro no

recently [riːˈsəntliː] *adv* 近ごろ chikágòro

receptacle [risepˈtəkəl] *n* 容器 yṓkì

reception [risepˈʃən] *n* (in hotel, office, hospital etc) 受付 ukétsuke; (party) レセプション resépùshon; (welcome) 歓迎 kañgei; (RADIO, TV) 受信 jushín

reception desk *n* 受付 ukétsuke, フロント furóñto

receptionist [risepˈʃənist] *n* 受付係 ukétsukegakàri

receptive [risepˈtiv] *adj* (person, attitude) 前向きの maémuki no

recess [riːˈses] *n* (in room) 壁のくぼみ

kabé nò kubómi; (secret place) 奥深い所 okúfukaì tokórò; (POL etc: holiday) 休憩時間 kyūkeijikàn

recession [riseˈʃən] *n* 景気後退 keíkikōtai

recharge [riːtʃɑːrdʒˈ] *vt* (battery) 充電する jǔden suru

recipe [resˈəpi] *n* (CULIN) 調理法 chṓrihō; (fig: for success) 秘けつ hikétsu; (: for disaster) やり方 yaríkata

recipient [risipˈiːənt] *n* (of letter, payment etc) 受取人 ukétorinìn

reciprocal [risipˈrəkəl] *adj* (arrangement, agreement) 相互の sṓgò no

recital [risaitˈəl] *n* (concert) リサイタル risáìtaru

recite [risaitˈ] *vt* (poem) 暗唱する añshō suru

reckless [rekˈlis] *adj* (driving, driver) 無謀な mubṓ na; (spending) 無茶な múchà na

recklessly [rekˈlisliː] *adv* (drive) 無謀に mubṓ ni; (spend) むやみに múyàmi ni

reckon [rekˈən] *vt* (calculate) 計算する keísan suru; (think): *I reckon that ...* ...だと思う ...dá tò omóu

reckoning [rekˈəniŋ] *n* (calculation) 計算 keísan

reckon on *vt fus* (expect) 当てにする até nì suru

reclaim [rikleimˈ] *vt* (demand back) ...の返還を要求する ...no heñkan wò yṓkyū suru; (land: by filling in) 埋め立てる umétaterù; (: by draining) 干拓する kañtaku suru; (waste materials) 再生する saísei suru

reclamation [rekləmeiˈʃən] *n* (of land: by filling in) 埋め立て umétate; (: by draining) 干拓 kañtaku

recline [riklainˈ] *vi* (sit or lie back) もたれる motárerù

reclining [riklainˈiŋ] *adj*: *reclining seat* リクライニングシート rikúrainingushìto

recluse [rekˈluːs] *n* 隠とん者 iñtoñsha

recognition [rekəgniˈʃən] *n* (of person, place) 認識 niñshiki; (of problem, fact) 意識 íshìki; (of achievement) 認める事

mitómeru kotó

transformed beyond recognition 見分けが付かない程変化した miwáke ga tsukanái hodo hénka shita

recognizable [rekəgnai'zəbəl] *adj*: *recognizable (by)* (...で) 見分けが付く (...de) miwáke ga tsukú

recognize [rek'əgnaiz] *vt* (person, place, attitude, illness) ...だと分かる ...dá tò wakárù; (problem, need) 意識する íshìki suru; (qualification, achievement) 認める mitómerù; (government) 承認する shónin suru

to recognize by/as ...で〔として〕分かる ...de 〔toshítè〕wakárù

recoil [rikɔil'] *vi* (person): *to recoil from doing something* ...するのをいやがる ...surú no wò iyágarù

◆*n* (of gun) 反動 handó

recollect [rekəlekt'] *vt* (remember) 思い出す omóidasù

recollection [rekəlek'ʃən] *n* (memory) 思い出 omóide; (remembering) 思い出す事 omóidasu kotó

recommend [rekəmend'] *vt* (book, shop, person) 推薦する suísen suru; (course of action) 勧める susúmerù

recommendation [rekəmendei'ʃən] *n* (of book, shop, person) 推薦 suísen; (of course of action) 勧告 kańkoku

recompense [rek'əmpens] *n* (reward) 報酬 hóshū

reconcile [rek'ənsail] *vt* (two people) 仲直りさせる nakánaðri sasérù; (two facts, beliefs) 調和させる chówa saserù

to reconcile oneself to something (unpleasant situation, misery etc) ...だとあきらめる ...dá tò akframerù

reconciliation [rekənsili:ei'ʃən] *n* (of people etc) 和解 wakái; (of facts etc) 調和 chówa

recondition [ri:kəndi'ʃən] *vt* (machine) 修理する shūri suru

reconnaissance [rikɑːn'isəns] *n* (MIL) 偵察 teísatsu

reconnoiter [ri:kənɔi'tə:r] (*BRIT* **reconnoitre**) *vt* (MIL: enemy territory) 偵察する teísatsu suru

reconsider [ri:kənsid'əːr] *vt* (decision, opinion etc) 考え直す kańgaenaosù

reconstruct [ri:kənstrʌkt'] *vt* (building) 建直す taténaosù; (policy, system) 練り直す nerínaosù; (event, crime) 再現する saígen suru

reconstruction [ri:kənstrʌk'ʃən] *n* (of building, country) 再建 saíken; (of crime) 再現 saígen

record [*n* rek'əːrd *vb* rekɔːrd'] *n* (*gen*) 記録 kiróku; (MUS: disk) レコード rekódð; (history: of person, company) 履歴 riréki; (*also*: **criminal record**) 前科 zénka

◆*vt* (write down) 記録する kiróku suru; (temperature, speed etc) 表示する hyóji suru; (MUS: song etc) 録音する rokúon suru

in record time 記録的な速さで kirókuteki hayása de

off the record adj (remark) オフレコの ofúreko no

◆*adv* (speak) オフレコで ofúreko de

record card *n* (in file) ファイルカード faírukàdo

recorded delivery [rikɔːr'did-] (*BRIT*) *n* (MAIL) 簡易書留 kań-i kakítome

recorder [rikɔːr'dəːr] *n* (MUS: instrument) リコーダー rikódā

record holder *n* (SPORT) 記録保持者 kiróku hojishà

recording [rikɔːr'diŋ] *n* 録音 rokúon

record player *n* レコードプレーヤー rekódopurèyā

recount [rikaunt'] *vt* (story, event etc) 述べる nobérù

re-count [*n* ri:'kaunt *vb* ri:kaunt'] *n* (POL: of votes) 数え直し kazóenaoshi

◆*vt* (votes etc) 数え直す kazóenaosù

recoup [riku:p'] *vt*: *to recoup one's losses* 損失を取戻す sofishitsu wò torímodosù

recourse [ri:'kɔːrs] *n*: *to have recourse to* ...を用いる ...wo mochíirù

recover [rikʌv'əːr] *vt* (get back: stolen goods, lost items, financial loss) 取戻す torímodosù

◆*vi*: *to recover (from)* (illness) (...が)

治る (...ga) naóru; (operation, shock, experience) (...から) 立直る (...kará) tachínaorù

recovery [rikʌv'ə:ri:] n (from illness, operation: in economy etc) 回復 kaífuku; (of stolen, lost items) 取戻し torímodoshi

re-create [ri:kri:eit'] vt 再現する saígen suru

recreation [rekri:ei'ʃən] n (play, leisure activities) 娯楽 goráku

recreational [rekri:ei'ʃənəl] adj 娯楽の goráku no

recrimination [rikrimənei'ʃən] n 責合い seméai

recruit [rikru:t'] n (MIL) 新兵 shiñpei; (in company, organization) 新入社〔会〕員 shiñnyūsha〔kai〕ìn
♦vt 募集する boshū suru

recruitment [rikru:t'mənt] n 募集 boshū

rectangle [rek'tæŋgəl] n 長方形 chốhōkei

rectangular [rektæŋ'gjələ:r] adj (shape, object etc) 長方形の chốhōkei no

rectify [rek'təfai] vt (correct) 正す tadásù

rector [rek'tə:r] n (REL) 主任司祭 shuniñshisài

rectory [rek'tə:ri:] n (house) 司祭館 shisáikan

recuperate [riku:'pə:reit] vi (recover: from illness etc) 回復する kaífuku suru

recur [rikə:r'] vi (error, event) 繰返される kuríkaesarerù; (illness, pain) 再発する saíhatsu suru

recurrence [rikə:r'əns] n (of error, event) 繰返し kuríkaeshi; (of illness, pain) 再発 saíhatsu

recurrent [rikə:r'ənt] adj 頻繁に起る hiñpan ni okórù

red [red] n (color) 赤 ákà; (pej: POL) 過激派 kagékiha
♦adj 赤い akái
to be in the red (bank account, business) 赤字になっている akáji ni natté irù
red carpet treatment n 盛大な歓迎式 seídai nà kañgeishìki

Red Cross n 赤十字 sekíjūji

redcurrant [red'kʌr'ənt] n アカフサスグリ akáfusasugùri

redden [red'ən] vt (turn red) 赤くする a-kákù suru
♦vi (blush) 赤面する sekímen suru

reddish [red'iʃ] adj 赤っぽい akáppòi

redeem [ridi:m'] vt (fig: situation, reputation) 救う sukúù; (something in pawn, loan) 請出す ukédasù; (REL: rescue) 救う sukúù

redeeming [ridi:'miŋ] adj: **redeeming feature** 欠点を補う取柄 kettén wò ogínaù toríe

redeploy [ri:diplɔi'] vt (resources) 配置し直す haíchi shinaosù

red-haired [red'he:rd] adj 赤毛の akáge no

red-handed [red'hæn'did] adj: **to be caught red-handed** 現行犯で捕まる geñkôhan de tsukámarù

redhead [red'hed] n 赤毛の人 akáge no hitò

red herring n (fig) 本論から注意をそらす物 hoñron karà chū̃i wo sorásù monó

red-hot [red'hɑ:t'] adj (metal) 真っ赤に焼けた makká nì yakétà

redirect [ri:dərekt'] vt (mail) 転送する teñsō suru

red light n: **to go through a red light** (AUT) 信号無視をする shiñgōmùshi wo suru

red-light district [red'lait-] n 赤線地区 akásenchikù

redo [ri:du:'] (pt redid pp redone) vt やり直す yarínaosù

redolent [red'ələnt] adj: **redolent of** (smell: also fig) ...臭い ...kusáì

redouble [ri:dʌb'əl] vt: **to redouble one's efforts** 一層努力する issō doryòku suru

redress [ridres'] n (compensation) 賠償 baíshō
♦vt (error, wrong) 償う tsugúnaù

Red Sea n: **the Red Sea** 紅海 kốkai

redskin [red'skin] n (pej) インディアン fñdian

red tape n (fig) 形式的手続き keíshikite-

ki tetsuzŭki

reduce [ridu:s'] *vt* (decrease: spending, numbers etc) 減らす herásù

to reduce someone to (begging, stealing) ...を余儀なくさせる ...wo yogínaku saserù

to reduce someone to tears 泣かせる nakáserù

to reduce someone to silence 黙らせる damáraserù

「*reduce speed now*」(AUT) 徐行 jokŏ

at a reduced price (goods) 割引で warîbiki de

reduction [ridʌk'ʃən] *n* (in price) 値下げ neságe; (in numbers etc) 減少 geńshō

redundancy [ridʌn'dənsi:] *n* (dismissal) 解雇 káīko; (unemployment) 失業 shitsúgyō

redundant [ridʌn'dənt] *adj* (worker) 失業中の shitsúgyōchū no; (detail, object) 余計な yokéi na

to be made redundant 解雇される káīko sarérù

reed [ri:d] *n* (BOT) アシ ashí; (MUS: of clarinet etc) リード rĩdo

reef [ri:f] *n* (at sea) 暗礁 ańshō

reek [ri:k] *vi: to reek (of)* (...の) におい がぷんぷんする (...no) nióí ga púñpun suru

reel [ri:l] *n* (of thread, string) 巻 makí; (of film, tape: *also* on fishing-rod) リール rīru; (dance) リール rīru

♦*vi* (sway) よろめく yorómekù

reel in *vt* (fish, line) 手繰り寄せる tagúriyoserù

ref [ref] (*inf*) *n abbr* = **referee**

refectory [rifek'tə:ri:] *n* 食堂 shokúdō

refer [rifə:r'] *vt* (person, patient): *to refer someone to* ...を...に回す ...wo ...ni mawásù; (matter, problem): *to refer something to* ...を...に委託する ...wo ...ni itáku suru

♦*vi: to refer to* (allude to) ...に言及する ...ni geńkyū suru; (consult) ...を参照する ...wo sańshō suru

referee [refəri:'] *n* (SPORT) 審判員 shińpań-in, レフェリー réfèrī; (*BRIT:* for job application) 身元保証人 mimótohoshōnìn

♦*vt* (football match etc) ...のレフェリーをやる ...no réfèrī wo yárù

reference [ref'ə:rəns] *n* (mention) 言及 geńkyū; (in book, paper) 引用文献 iń-yō buńken; (for job application: letter) 推薦状 suíseńjō

with reference to (COMM: in letter) ...に関しては ...ni kańshite wa

reference book *n* 参考書 sańkōsho

reference number *n* 整理番号 seíribańgō

referenda [refəren'də] *npl of* **referendum**

referendum [refəren'dəm] (*pl* **referenda**) *n* 住民投票 jŭmintóhyō

refill [*vb* ri:fil' *n* ri:'fil] *vt* (glass etc) ...にもう一杯つぐ ...ni mŏ ippaí tsugú; (pen etc) ...に...を詰替える ...ni ...wo tsumékaerù

♦*n* (of drink etc) お代り o-káwari; (for pen etc) スペアー supéā

refine [rifain'] *vt* (sugar, oil) 精製する seísei suru; (theory, idea) 洗練する señren suru

refined [rifaind'] *adj* (person, taste) 洗練された señren saretà

refinement [rifain'mənt] *n* (of person) 優雅さ yŭgasa; (of system) 精度 seído

reflect [riflekt'] *vt* (light, image) 反射する hańsha suru; (situation, attitude) 反映する hań-ei suru

♦*vi* (think) じっくり考える jikkúrì kańgaerù

it reflects badly/well on him それは彼の悪い〔いい〕所を物語っている soré wā kárè no warúí 〔íí〕 tokórò wo monógatatte irù

reflection [riflek'ʃən] *n* (of light, heat) 反射 hańsha; (image) 影 kágè; (of situation, attitude) 反映する物 hań-ei suru monò; (criticism) 非難 hínàn; (thought) 熟考 jukkŏ

on reflection よく考えると yókù kańgaerù to

reflector [riflek'tə:r] *n* 反射器 hańshakì

reflex [ri:'fleks] *adj* (action, gesture) 反射的な hańshateki na

♦*n* (PHYSIOLOGY, PSYCH) 反射 hań-

sha

reflexive [riflek'siv] *adj* (LING) 再帰の saíki no

reform [rifɔːrm'] *n* (of sinner, character) 改心 kaíshin; (of law, system) 改革 kaíkaku
◆*vt* (sinner) 改心させる kaíshin saserù; (law, system) 改革する kaíkaku suru

Reformation [refərmei'ʃən] *n : the Reformation* 宗教改革 shúkyōkaìkaku

reformatory [rifɔːr'mətɔːri:] (*US*) *n* 感化院 kańkaìn

refrain [rifrein'] *vi : to refrain from doing* ...をしない様にする ...wo shinái yô ni suru
◆*n* (of song) 繰返し kuríkaeshi, リフレイン rifúreìn

refresh [rifreʃ'] *vt* (subj: sleep, drink) 元気付ける geńkizukerù
to refresh someone's memory ...に思い出させる ...ni omóidasaserù

refresher course [rifreʃ'əːr-] (*BRIT*) *n* 研修会 keńshūkài

refreshing [rifreʃ'iŋ] *adj* (drink) 冷たくておいしい tsumétakùte oíshiî; (sleep) 気分をさわやかにする kíbùn wo sawáyàka ni suru

refreshments [rifreʃ'mənts] *npl* (food and drink) 軽食 keíshoku

refrigeration [rifridʒərei'ʃən] *n* (of food) 冷蔵 reízō

refrigerator [rifridʒ'əːreitəːr] *n* 冷蔵庫 reízōko

refuel [ri:fju:'əl] *vi* 燃料を補給する neńryò wo hokyû suru

refuge [refju:dʒ] *n* (shelter) 避難場所 hináñbasho
to take refuge in ...に避難する ...ni hínàn suru

refugee [refjudʒi:'] *n* 難民 nańmin

refund [*n* ri:'fʌnd *vb* rifʌnd'] *n* 払い戻し haráimodoshi
◆*vt* (money) 払い戻す haráimodosù

refurbish [ri:fəːr'biʃ] *vt* (shop, theater) 改装する kaísō suru

refusal [rifju:'zəl] *n* 断り kotówari, 拒否 kyóhì
first refusal (option) オプション権 o-

púshoñken

refuse¹ [rifju:z'] *vt* (request, offer, gift) 断る kotówarù; (invitation) 辞退する jítài suru; (permission, consent) 拒む kobámù
◆*vi* (say no) 断る kotówarù; (horse) 飛越を拒否する hiétsu wò kyóhì suru
to refuse to do something ...するのを拒む ...surú no wò kobámù

refuse² [ref'ju:s] *n* (rubbish) ごみ gomí

refuse collection *n* ごみ収集 gomíshūshū

refute [rifju:t'] *vt* (argument) 論破する roñpa suru

regain [rigein'] *vt* (power, position) 取戻す torímodosù

regal [ri:'gəl] *adj* 堂々とした dôdo to shitá

regalia [rigei'li:ə] *n* (costume) 正装 seísō

regard [rigɑːrd'] *n* (gaze) 視線 shisén; (attention, concern) 関心 kańshin; (esteem) 尊敬 soñkei
◆*vt* (consider) 見なす minásù
to give one's regards to ...から...によろしく伝える ...kará ...nì yoróshiku tsutáerù
with kindest regards 敬具 keígu
regarding, as regards, with regard to (with reference to, concerning) ...に関して ...ni kańshitè

regardless [rigɑːrd'lis] *adv* (carry on, continue) 構わずに kamáwazù ni
regardless of (danger, consequences) ...を顧みず ...wo kaérimizù

regatta [rigɑ:t'ə] *n* ヨット〔ボート〕競技会 yottó 〔bôto〕kyōgikài

regenerate [ri:dʒen'əːreit] *vt* (inner cities, arts) よみがえらせる yomígaeraserù

regent [ri:'dʒənt] *n* 摂政 sesshô

regime [reiʒi:m'] *n* (system of government) 政治体制 seíjitaìsei

regiment [redʒ'əmənt] *n* (MIL) 連隊 reńtai

regimental [redʒəmen'təl] *adj* 連隊の reńtai no

region [ri:'dʒən] *n* (area: of land) 地区 chíkù; (: of body) ...部 ...bù; (administra-

tive division of country) 行政区 gyṓsei-ku

in the region of (*fig*: approximately) 約 yákù

regional [ri:'dʒənəl] *adj* (organization, wine, geography) 地元の jimóto no; (provincial) 地方の chihṓ no

register [redʒ'istəːr] *n* (list: of births, marriages, deaths, voters) 登録簿 tṓroku-bo; (SCOL: of attendance) 出席簿 shussékibo; (MUS: of voice) 声域 seíiki; (: of instrument) 音域 oń-iki

◆*vt* (birth, death, marriage) 届出る todó-kederù; (car) 登録する tṓroku suru; (MAIL: letter) 書留にする kakítome nì suru; (subj: meter, gauge) 示す shimésù

◆*vi* (at hotel) チェックインする chekkúìn suru; (for work) 名前を登録する namáè wo tóroku suru; (as student) 入学手続きをする nyúgakutetsuzuki wò suru; (make impression) ぴんと来る píñ tò kúrù

registered [redʒ'istəːrd] *adj* (MAIL: letter, parcel) 書留の kakítome no

registered trademark *n* 登録商標 tórokushōhyō

registrar [redʒ'istrɑːr] *n* (official) 戸籍係 kosékigakàri; (in college, university) 教務係 kyṓmugakàri; (*BRIT*: in hospital) 医務吏員 imúrìin

registration [redʒistrei'ʃən] *n* (gen) 登録 tṓroku; (of birth, death) 届出 todókede; (AUT: *also*: **registration number**) ナンバー náñbā

registry [redʒ'istri:] *n* 登記所 tṓkisho

registry office (*BRIT*) *n* 戸籍登記所 kosékitòkisho

to get married in a registry office 戸籍登記所で結婚する kosékitōkisho dè kekkóñ suru

regret [rigret'] *n* (sorrow) 悔み kuyámi

◆*vt* (decision, action) 後悔する kṓkai suru; (loss, death) 悔む kuyámù; (inability to do something) 残念に思う zañnen nì omóù; (inconvenience) 済まないと思う sumánài to omóù

regretfully [rigret'fəli:] *adv* (sadly) 残念ながら zañnen nagàra

regrettable [rigret'əbəl] *adj* (unfortunate: mistake, incident) あいにくの aíniku no

regular [reg'jələːr] *adj* (even: breathing, pulse etc) 規則的な kisókuteki na; (evenly-spaced: intervals, meetings etc) 定期的な teíkiteki na; (symmetrical: features, shape etc) 対称的な taíshōteki na; (frequent: raids, exercise etc) 頻繁な hiñpan na; (usual: time, doctor, customer etc) 通常の tsújō no; (soldier) 正規の sefki no; (LING) 規則変化の kisókuheñka no

◆*n* (client etc) 常連 jṓren

regularity [regjəlær'iti:] *n* (frequency) 高頻度 kṓhìndo

regularly [reg'jələːrli:] *adv* (at evenly-spaced intervals) 規則的に kisókuteki ni; (symmetrically: shaped etc) 対称的に taíshōteki ni; (often) 頻繁に hiñpan ni

regulate [reg'jəleit] *vt* (conduct, expenditure) 規制する kiséi suru; (traffic, speed) 調整する chṓsei suru; (machine, oven) 調節する chṓsetsu suru

regulation [regjəlei'ʃən] *n* (of conduct, expenditure) 規制 kiséi; (of traffic, speed) 調整 chṓsei; (of machine, oven) 調節 chṓsetsu; (rule) 規則 kisóku

rehabilitation [ri:həbilətei'ʃən] *n* (of criminal, addict) 社会復帰 shakáifukkì, リハビリテーション rihábiritḕshon

rehearsal [rihəːr'səl] *n* リハーサル rihā́saru

rehearse [rihəːrs'] *vt* (play, dance, speech etc) ...のリハーサルをする ...no rihā́saru wo suru

reign [rein] *n* (of monarch) 治世 chiséi; (*fig*: of terror etc) 支配 shíhài

◆*vi* (monarch) 君臨する kuñrin suru; (*fig*: violence, fear etc) はびこる habíkorù; (: peace, order etc) 行渡る ikíwatarù

reimburse [ri:imbəːrs'] *vt* (pay back) ...に弁償する ...ni beñshō suru

rein [rein] *n* (for horse) 手綱 tazúna

reincarnation [ri:inkɑːrnei'ʃən] *n* (belief) 輪ね ríñne

reindeer [rein'diːr] *n inv* トナカイ tonákài

reinforce [ri:inforrs'] *vt* (strengthen: object) 補強する hokyṓ suru; (: situation) 強化する kyṓka suru; (support: idea, statement) 裏付ける urázukerù

reinforced concrete [ri:inforrst'-] *n* 鉄筋コンクリート tekkín konkurīto

reinforcement [ri:inforrs'mənt] *n* (strengthening) 補強 hokyṓ

reinforcements [ri:inforrs'mənts] *npl* (MIL) 援軍 eñgun

reinstate [ri:insteit'] *vt* (worker) 復職させる fukúshoku saserù; (tax, law, text) 元通りにする motṓdōri ni surù

reiterate [ri:it'əreit] *vt* (repeat) 繰返すkuríkaesù

reject [*n* ri:'dʒekt *vb* ridʒekt'] *n* (COMM) 傷物 kizúmono

♦*vt* (plan, proposal etc) 退ける shirízokerù; (offer of help) 断る kotówarù; (belief, political system) 拒絶する kyozétsu suru; (candidate) 不採用にする fusáiyō ni suru; (coin) 受付けない ukétsukenài; (goods, fruit etc) 傷物として処分する kizúmono toshitè shóbùn suru

rejection [ridʒek'ʃən] *n* (of plan, proposal, offer of help etc) 拒否 kyóhì; (of belief etc) 拒絶 kyozétsu; (of candidate) 不採用 fusáiyō

rejoice [ridʒɔis'] *vi*: **to rejoice at/over** ...を喜ぶ ...wo yorókobù

rejuvenate [ridʒu:'vəneit] *vt* (person) 若返らせる wakágaeraserù

relapse [rilæps'] *n* (MED) 再発 saíhatsu

relate [rileit'] *vt* (tell) 話す hanásù; (connect) 結び付ける musúbitsukerù

♦*vi*: **to relate to** (person, subject, thing) ...に関係がある ...ni kañkei ga arù

related [rilei'tid] *adj* (person) 血縁がある ketsúen ga arù; (animal, language) 近縁の kiñ-en no

related to ...に関係がある ...ni kañkei ga arù

relating [rilei'tiŋ]: **relating to** *prep* ...に関する ...ni kañ suru

relation [rilei'ʃən] *n* (member of family) 親せき shiñseki; (connection) 関係 kañkei

relations [rilei'ʃənz] *npl* (dealings) 関係

relationship [rilei'ʃəñʃip] *n* (between two people, countries, things) 関係 kañkei; (*also*: **family relationship**) 親族関係 shiñzokukañkei

relative [rel'ətiv] *n* (member of family) 親類 shíñrui, 親せき shiñseki

♦*adj* (comparative) 相対的な sṓtaiteki na; (connected): **relative to** ...に関する ...ni kañ suru

relatively [rel'ətivli:] *adv* (comparatively) 比較的 hikákuteki

relax [rilæks'] *vi* (person: unwind) くつろぐ kutsúrogù; (muscle) 緩む yurúmù

♦*vt* (one's grip) 緩める yurúmerù; (mind, person) くつろがせる kutsúrogaserù; (rule, control etc) 緩める yurúmerù

relaxation [ri:læksei'ʃən] *n* (rest) 休みyasúmi; (of muscle, grip) 緩み yurúmi; (of rule, control etc) 緩和 kañwa; (recreation) 娯楽 goráku

relaxed [rilækst'] *adj* (person) 落着いたochítsuità; (discussion, atmosphere) くつろいだ kutsúroìda

relaxing [rilæks'iŋ] *adj* (holiday, afternoon) くつろいだ kutsúroìda

relay [ri:'lei] *n* (race) リレー rírē

♦*vt* (message, question) 伝える tsutáerù; (programme, signal) 中継する chúkei suru

release [rili:s'] *n* (from prison) 釈放 shakúhō; (from obligation) 免除 méñjo; (of gas, water etc) 放出 hōshutsu; (of film) 封切 fúkiri; (of book, record) 発売 hatsúbai

♦*vt* (prisoner: from prison) 釈放する shakúhō suru; (: from captivity) 解放する kaíhō suru; (gas etc) 放出する hōshutsu suru; (free: from wreckage etc) 救出する kyúshutsu suru; (TECH: catch, spring etc) 外す hazúsù; (book, record) 発売する hatsúbai suru; (film) 公開する kṓkai suru; (report, news) 公表する kṓhyō suru

relegate [rel'əgeit] *vt* (downgrade) 格下げする kakúsage suru; (*BRIT*: SPORT): **to be relegated** 格下げされる kakúsage sarerù

relent [rilent'] *vi* (give in) ...の態度が軟化

する ...no taído ga nafika suru

relentless [rilent'lis] *adj* (unceasing) 絶間ない taémanaì; (determined) 執念深い shúnenbukai

relevance [rel'əvəns] *n* (of remarks, information) 意義 ígì; (of question etc) 関連 kańren

relevant [rel'əvənt] *adj* (fact, information, question) 意義ある ígì árù
  relevant to (situation, problem etc) ...に関連のある ...ni kańren no arù

reliability [rilaiəbil'əti:] *n* (of person, machine) 信頼性 shińraisei; (of information) 信ぴょう性 shińpyōsei

reliable [rilai'əbəl] *adj* (person, firm) 信頼できる shińrai dekirù; (method, machine) 信頼性のある shińraisei no arù; (news, information) 信用できる shiń-yō dekirù

reliably [rilai'əbli:] *adv*: **to be reliably informed that ...** 確かな情報筋による と... táshìka na jōhōsùji ni yorú tò ...

reliance [rilai'əns] *n*: **reliance (on)** (...への) 依存 (...è nò) izón

relic [rel'ik] *n* (REL) 聖遺物 seíbutsu; (of the past) 遺物 ibútsu

relief [rili:f'] *n* (from pain, anxiety etc) 緩和 kańwa; (help, supplies) 救援物資 kyúenbusshì; (ART) 浮彫 ukíbori, レリーフ reríifu; (GEO) 際立つ事 kiwádatsu kotò

relieve [rili:v'] *vt* (pain, fear, worry) 緩和する kańwa suru; (patient) 安心させる afshin saserù; (bring help to: victims, refugees etc) ...に救援物資を届ける ...ni kyúenbusshì wo todókerù; (take over from: colleague, guard) ...と交替する ...to kótai suru
  to relieve someone of something (load) ...の ...を持って上げる ...no ...wo móttè agérù; (duties, post) ...を解任する ...wo kańnin suru
  to relieve oneself 小便する shóben suru

religion [rilidʒ'ən] *n* 宗教 shúkyō

religious [rilidʒ'əs] *adj* (activities, faith) 宗教の shúkyō no; (person) 信心深い shińjinbukai

relinquish [riliŋ'kwiʃ] *vt* (authority) ...から手を引く ...kara té wò hikú; (plan, habit) やめる yamérù

relish [rel'iʃ] *n* (CULIN) レリッシュ rerísshù; (enjoyment) 楽しみ tanóshimi
  ◆*vt* (enjoy: food, competition) 楽しむ tanóshimù
  to relish the thought/idea/prospect of something/doing something ...を〔...するのを〕心待ちに待つ ...wo 〔... surú nò wo〕 kokóromachi nì mátsù

relocate [ri:lou'keit] *vt* 移動させる idó saserù
  ◆*vi* 移動する idó suru

reluctance [rilʌk'təns] *n* (unwillingness) 気が進まない事 kí gà susúmanai kotò

reluctant [rilʌk'tənt] *adj* (unwilling) 気が進まない kí gà susúmanai

reluctantly [rilʌk'təntli:] *adv* (unwillingly) いやいやながら iyáiyanagàra

rely on [rilai'-] *vt fus* (be dependent on) ...に頼る ...ni tayórù; (trust) ...を信用する ...wo shiń-yō suru

remain [rimein'] *vi* (survive, be left) 残る nokórù; (continue to be) 相変らず...である aíkawarazù ...de árù; (stay) とどまる todómaru

remainder [rimein'də:r] *n* (rest) 残り nokóri

remaining [rimei'niŋ] *adj* 残りの nokóri no

remains [rimeinz'] *npl* (of meal) 食べ残り tabénokori; (of building) 廃虚 haíkyo; (corpse) 遺体 itái

remand [rimænd'] *n*: **on remand** 拘置中で kóchichū de
  ◆*vt*: **to be remanded in custody** 拘置される kóchi sarerù

remand home (*BRIT*) *n* 少年院 shónen-ìn

remark [rimɑrk'] *n* (comment) 発言 hatsúgen
  ◆*vt* (comment) 言う iú

remarkable [rimɑ:r'kəbəl] *adj* (outstanding) 著しい ichíjirushìì

remarry [ri:mær'i:] *vi* 再婚する saíkon suru

remedial [rimi:'di:əl] *adj* (tuition, clas-

ses) 補修の hoshū no; (exercise) 矯正の kyōsei no

remedy [rem'idi:] n (cure) 治療法 chiryō-hō

♦vt (correct) 直す naósù

remember [rimem'bə:r] vt (call back to mind) 思い出す omóidasù; (bear in mind) 忘れない様にする wasúrenai yố ni suru; (send greetings): **remember me to him** 彼によろしくお伝え下さい kárè ni yoróshikù o-tsútaè kudasái

remembrance [rimem'brəns] n (memory: of dead person) 思い出 omóide; (souvenir: of place, event) 記念品 kinénhin

remind [rimaind'] vt: **to remind someone to do something** ...するのを忘れない様に...に注意する ...surú no wò wasúrenai yố ni ...ni chúì suru

to remind someone of something ...に ...を思い出させる ...ni ...wo omóidasaséru

she reminds me of her mother 彼女を見ると彼女の母親を思い出す kánòjo wo mírù to kánòjo no haháoya wò omóidasù

reminder [rimaind'ə:r] n (souvenir) 記念品 kinénhin; (letter) 覚書 obóegaki

reminisce [remənis'] vi (about the past) 追憶する tsuíoku suru

reminiscent [remənis'ənt] adj: **to be reminiscent of something** ...を思い出させる ...wo omóidasaserù

remiss [rimis'] adj (careless) 不注意な fuchúì na

it was remiss of him 彼は不注意だった kárè wa fuchúì dáttà

remission [rimiʃ'ən] n (of debt) 免除 mêñjo; (of prison sentence) 減刑 geñkei; (of illness) 緩解 kañkai; (REL: of sins) 許し yurúshi

remit [rimit'] vt (send: money) 送金する sókin suru

remittance [rimit'əns] n (payment) 送金 sókin

remnant [rem'nənt] n (small part remaining) 残り nokóri; (of cloth) 切れ端 kiréhashi

remnants [rem'nənts] npl (COMM) 端切れ hagíre

remorse [rimɔːrs'] n (guilt) 後悔 kôkai

remorseful [rimɔːrs'fəl] adj (guilty) 後悔 している kôkai shite irù

remorseless [rimɔːrs'lis] adj (fig: noise, pain) 絶間ない taémanaì

remote [rimout'] adj (distant: place, time) 遠い tôì; (person) よそよそしい yosóyososhiì; (slight: possibility, chance) かすかな kásùka na

remote control n 遠隔操作 eñkakusôsa, リモートコントロール rimótokontorōru

remotely [rimout'li:] adv (distantly) 遠くに tôku ni; (slightly) かすかに kásùka ni

remould [ri:'mould] (BRIT) n (tire) 再生タイヤ saíseitaiya

removable [rimu:'vəbəl] adj (detachable) 取外しのできる toríhazushi nò dekírù

removal [rimu:'vəl] n (taking away) 取除く事 torínozoku kotò; (of stain) 消し取る事 keshítoru kotò; (BRIT: from house) 引っ越し hikkóshi; (from office: dismissal) 免職 meñshoku; (MED) 切除 sétsùjo

removal van (BRIT) n 引っ越しトラック hikkóshi torakkù

remove [rimu:v'] vt (gen) 取除く torínozokù; (clothing) 脱ぐ núgù; (bandage etc) 外す hazúsù; (stain) 消し取る keshítorù; (employee) 解雇する kaíko suru; (MED: lung, kidney, appendix etc) 切除する sétsùjo suru

removers [rimu:'və:rz] (BRIT) npl (company) 引っ越し屋 hikkóshiyà

remuneration [rimju:nərei'ʃən] n (payment) 報酬 hôshù

Renaissance [ren'isɑːns] n: **the Renaissance** ルネッサンス runéssànsu

render [ren'də:r] vt (give: thanks, service) する surú; (make) させる sasérù

rendering [ren'də:riŋ] n (MUS: instrumental) 演奏 eñsō; (: song) 歌い方 utáikatà

rendez-vous [rɑːn'deivuː] n (meeting) 待ち合せ machíawase; (place) 待ち合せの

場所 machíawase nò báshò

renegade [ren'əgeid] n (裏切者) urágirimono

renew [rinu:'] vt (resume) 再び始める futátabi hajimerù; (loan, contract etc) 更新する kôshin suru; (negotiations) 再開する saíkai suru; (acquaintance, relationship) よみがえらせる yomígaeraserù

renewal [rinu:'əl] n (resumption) 再開 saíkai; (of license, contract etc) 更新 kôshin

renounce [rinauns'] vt (belief, course of action) 捨てる sutérù; (claim, right, peerage) 放棄する hôki suru

renovate [ren'əveit] vt (building, machine) 改造する kaízō suru

renovation [renəvei'ʃən] n 改造 kaízō

renown [rinaun'] n (fame) 名声 meísei

renowned [rinaund'] adj (famous) 有名な yúmei na

rent [rent] n (for house) 家賃 yáchìn
♦vt (take for rent: house) 賃借する chínshaku suru; (: television, car) レンタルで借りる rêñtaru de karírù; (also: **rent out**: house) 賃貸する chíñtai suru; (: television, car) 貸出す kashídasù

rental [ren'təl] n (for television, car) レンタル rêñtaru

renunciation [rinʌnsi:ei'ʃən] n 放棄 hôki

reorganize [ri:ɔ:r'gənaiz] vt 再編成する saíheñsei suru

rep [rep] n abbr (COMM) = **representative**; (THEATER) = **repertory**

repair [riper'] n (of clothes, shoes) 修繕 shúzen; (of car, road, building etc) 修理 shúri
♦vt (clothes, shoes) 修繕する shúzen suru; (car, engine, road, building) 修理する shúri suru

in good/bad repair 整備が行届いている〔いない〕seíbi gà ikítodoite irù 〔ínài〕

repair kit n 修理キット shúrikittò

repatriate [ri:pei'tri:eit] vt (refugee, soldier) 送還する sôkan suru

repay [ripei'] (pt, pp **repaid**) vt (money, debt, loan) 返済する heñsai suru; (person) ...に借金を返済する ...ni shakkíñ wo

heñsaì suru; (sb's efforts) ...に答える ...ni kotáerù; (favor) ...の恩返しをする ...no oñgaeshi wò suru

repayment [ripei'mənt] n (amount of money) 返済金 heñsaikiñ; (of debt, loan etc) 返済 heñsai

repeal [ripi:l'] n (of law) 廃止する haíshi suru
♦vt (law) 廃止 haíshi

repeat [ripi:t'] n (RADIO, TV) 再放送 saíhōsō
♦vt (say/do again) 繰返す kuríkaesù; (RADIO, TV) 再放送する saíhōsō surù
♦vi 繰返る kuríkaesù

repeatedly [ripi:t'idli:] adv (again and again) 再三 saísan

repel [ripel'] vt (drive away: enemy, attack) 撃退する gekítai suru; (disgust: subj: appearance, smell) ...に不快な感じを与える ...ni fukaî na kañji wò atáerù

repellent [ripel'ənt] adj いやな iyá nà
♦n: *insect repellent* 虫よけ mushíyoke

repent [ripent'] vi: *to repent (of)* (sin, mistake) (...を) 後悔する (...wo) kôkai suru

repentance [ripen'təns] n 後悔 kôkai

repercussions [ri:pə:rkʌʃ'ənz] npl 反響 hañkyō

repertoire [rep'ə:rtwɑ:r] n レパートリー repátòrī

repertory [rep'ə:rtɔ:ri:] n (also: **repertory theater**) レパートリー演劇 repátorīeñgeki

repetition [repitiʃ'ən] n (repeat) 繰返し kuríkaeshi

repetitive [ripet'ətiv] adj (movement, work) 単純反復の tañjunhañpuku no; (speech) くどい kudôî; (noise) 反復される hañpuku sarerù

replace [ripleis'] vt (put back) 元に戻す mótò ni modósù; (take the place of) ...に代る ...ni kawárù

replacement [ripleis'mənt] n (substitution) 置き換え okíkae; (substitute) 代りの物 kawári no monò

replay [ri:plei'] n (of match) 再試合 saíshiai; (of tape, film) 再生 saísei

replenish [riplen'iʃ] vt (glass) ...にもう一

杯つぐ ...ni mŏ ippài tsugú; (stock etc) 補
充する hojū suru

replete [ripli:t'] *adj* (well-fed) 満腹の mañpuku no

replica [rep'ləkə] *n* (copy) 複製 fukúsei,
レプリカ repúrĭka

reply [riplai'] *n* (answer) 答え kotáè
♦*vi* (to question, letter) 答える kotáèrù

reply coupon *n* 返信券 heñshiñken ◇切
手と交換できる券 kitté tò kŏkan dekirù
kêñ

report [ripɔ:rt'] *n* (account) 報告書 hŏko-
kushò; (PRESS, TV etc) 報道 hŏdō;
(BRIT: also: **school report**) レポート
repŏtò; (of gun) 銃声 jūsei
♦*vt* (give an account of: event, meeting)
報告する hŏkoku suru; (PRESS, TV etc)
報道する hŏdō suru; (theft, accident,
death) 届け出る todŏkederù
♦*vi* (make a report) 報告する hŏkoku
suru; (present oneself): **to report (to
someone)** (...ni) 出頭する (...ni) shuttŏ
suru; (be responsible to): **to report to
someone** ...が直属の上司である ...ga cho-
kúzoku nò jŏshi de arù

report card (US, SCOTTISH) *n* 通知表
tsūchihyŏ

reportedly [ripɔ:r'tidli:] *adv* うわさによ
ると uwása ni yoru tò

reporter [ripɔ:r'tər] *n* (PRESS, TV etc)
記者 kishá

repose [ripouz'] *n*: **in repose** (face,
mouth) 平常で heĵō de

reprehensible [reprihen'səbəl] *adj* (behavior) 不届きな futŏdŏki na

represent [reprizent'] *vt* (person, nation)
代表する daĬhyŏ suru; (view, belief) ...の
典型的な例である ...no teñkeiteki nà rêi
de árù; (symbolize: idea, emotion) ...のシ
ンボルである ...no shîñboru de árù; (constitute) ...である ...de árù; (describe): **to
represent something as** ...を...として描
写する ...wo ...toshite byŏsha suru;
(COMM) ...のセールスマンである ...no
sérusumàn de árù

representation [reprizentei'ʃən] *n*
(state of being represented) 代表を立て
ている事 daĬhyŏ wò tátète irú kotò; (pic-

ture) 絵 é; (statue) 彫像 chŏzō; (petition)
陳情 chiñĵō

representations [reprizentei'ʃənz] *npl*
(protest) 抗議 kŏgi

representative [reprizen'tətiv] *n* (of
person, nation) 代表者 daĬhyŏsha; (of
view, belief) 典型 teñkei; (COMM) セー
ルスマン sérusumàn; (US: POL) 下院議
員 kaíngiìn
♦*adj* (group, survey, cross-section) 代表
的な daĬhyŏteki na

repress [ripres'] *vt* (people, revolt) 抑圧
する yokúatsu suru; (feeling, impulse) 抑
制する yokúsei suru

repression [ripreʃ'ən] *n* (of people, country) 抑圧 yokúatsu; (of feelings) 抑制 yokúsei

repressive [ripres'iv] *adj* (society, measures) 抑圧的な yokúatsuteki na

reprieve [ripri:v'] *n* (LAW) 執行延期
shikkŏeñki ◇特に死刑について言う tókù
ni shikêi ni tsuitè iú; (fig: delay) 延期
eñki

reprimand [rep'rəmænd] *n* (official
rebuke) 懲戒 chŏkai
♦*vt* 懲戒する chŏkai suru

reprint [*n* ri:'print *vb* ri:print'] *n* 復刻版
fukkŏkuban
♦*vt* 復刻する fukkŏku suru

reprisal [riprai'zəl] *n* 報復 hŏfuku

reprisals [riprai'zəlz] *npl* (acts of
revenge) 報復行為 hŏfukukŏi

reproach [riproutʃ'] *n* (rebuke) 非難 hínàn
♦*vt*: **to reproach someone for something** ...の...を非難する ...no ...wo hínàn
suru

reproachful [riproutʃ'fəl] *adj* (look,
remark) 非難めいた hinánmeìta

reproduce [ri:prədus'] *vt* (copy: document etc) 複製する fukúsei suru; (sound)
再生する saísei suru
♦*vi* (mankind, animal, plant) 繁殖する
hañshoku suru

reproduction [ri:prədʌk'ʃən] *n* (copy: of
document, report etc) 複写 fukúsha; (of
sound) 再生 saísei; (of painting, furniture) 複製品 fukúseihin; (of mankind,

animal etc) 繁殖 hańshoku

reproductive [ri:prədʌk'tiv] *adj* (system, process) 繁殖の hańshoku no

reproof [ripru:f'] *n* しっ責 shisséki

reprove [ripru:v'] *vt: to reprove someone for something* ...の事で...をしっ責する ...no kotó dè ...wo shisséki suru

reptile [rep'tail] *n* は虫類 hachûrùi

republic [ripʌb'lik] *n* 共和国 kyówakòku

republican [ripʌb'likən] *adj* (system, government etc) 共和国の kyówakòku no; *(US: POL)*: *Republican* 共和党の kyówatō no

repudiate [ripju:'di:eit] *vt* (accusation, violence) 否定する hitéi suru

repugnant [ripʌg'nənt] *adj* 不愉快な fuyúkài na

repulse [ripʌls'] *vt* (enemy, attack) 撃退する gekítai suru

repulsive [ripʌl'siv] *adj* (sight, idea) 不愉快な fuyúkài na

reputable [rep'jətəbəl] *adj* 評判の良い hyōban no yoî

reputation [repjətei'ʃən] *n* 評判 hyōban

reputed [ripju:'tid] *adj* (supposed) ...とされる ...to sarérù

reputedly [ripju:'tidli:] *adv* (supposedly) 人の言うには hitó nò iú ni wà

request [rikwest'] *n* (polite demand) 願い negái; (formal demand) 要望 yōbō; (RADIO, TV) リクエスト ríkùesùto

♦*vt: to request something of/from someone* (politely) ...に...をお願いする ...ni ...wo o-négai suru; (formally) ...に...を要望する ...ni ...wo yōbō suru; (RADIO, TV) リクエストする ríkùesùto suru

request stop *(BRIT)* *n* 随時停留所 zuíjiteiryùjo ◊乗降客がいる時だけバスが留まる停留所 jōkōkyaku ga irú toki dakè básù ga tomárù teíryùjo

requiem [rek'wi:əm] *n* (REL) 死者のためのミサ shíshà no tamé nò mísà; (MUS) 鎮魂曲 chíñkoñkyoku, レクイエム rekúîemu

require [rikwaiə:r'] *vt* (need) ...が必要である ...ga hitsúyō de arù; (order): *to*

require someone to do something ...に...する事を要求する ...ni ...surú kotò wo yōkyū suru

requirement [rikwaiə:r'mənt] *n* (need) 必要条件 hitsúyōjōken; (want) 要求 yōkyū

requisite [rek'wizit] *n* (requirement) 必要条件 hitsúyōjōken

♦*adj* (required) 必要な hitsúyō na

requisition [rekwizi'ʃən] *n*: *requisition (for)* (demand) (...の) 請求 (...no) seíkyū

♦*vt* (MIL) 徴発する chōhatsu suru

resale [ri:'seil] *n* 転売 teńbai

rescind [risind'] *vt* (law) 廃止する haíshi suru; (contract, order etc) 破棄する hákì suru

rescue [res'kju:] *n* (help) 救援 kyúen; (from drowning, accident) 人命救助 jińmeikyùjo

♦*vt: to rescue (from)* (person, animal) (...から) 救う (...kara) sukûù; (company) 救済する kyúsai suru

rescue party *n* 救援隊 kyúentai, レスキュー隊 resúkyūtai

rescuer [res'kju:ə:r] *n* 救助者 kyújoshà

research [risə:rtʃ'] *n* 研究 keńkyū

♦*vt* (story, subject) 研究する keńkyū suru; (person) ...について情報を集める ...ni tsuíte jōhō wò atsúmerù

researcher [risə:r'tʃə:r] *n* 研究者 keńkyūsha

resemblance [rizem'bləns] *n* (likeness) 似ている事 nité iru kotò

resemble [rizem'bəl] *vt* ...に似ている ...ni nité irù

resent [rizent'] *vt* ...に対して腹を立てる ...ni táishite hará wò tatérù

resentful [rizent'fəl] *adj* 怒っている o-kótte irù

resentment [rizent'mənt] *n* 恨み urámi

reservation [rezə:rvei'ʃən] *n* (booking) 予約 yoyáku; (doubt) 疑い utágai; (for tribe) 居留地 kyoryúchì

reserve [rizə:rv'] *n* (store) 備蓄 bichíku, 蓄え takúwae; (SPORT) 補欠 hokétsu; (game reserve) 保護区 hogókù; (restraint) 遠慮 eńryo

♦*vt* (keep) 取って置く tóttè oku; (seats, table etc) 予約する yoyáku suru

in reserve 蓄えてあって takúwaete attè

reserved [rizəːrvd'] *adj* (restrained) 遠慮深い eńryobukai

reserves [rizəːrvz'] *npl* (MIL) 予備軍 yobígùn

reservoir [rez'əːrvwɑːr] *n* (of water) 貯水池 chosúichi

reshuffle [riːʃʌf'əl] *n*: *Cabinet reshuffle* (POL) 内閣改造 naíkakukaizò

reside [rizaid'] *vi* (person: live) 住む súmù

residence [rez'idəns] *n* (formal: home) 住い sumáì; (length of stay) 滞在 taízai

residence permit (*BRIT*) *n* 在留許可 zaíryukyokà

resident [rez'idənt] *n* (of country, town) 住民 júmin; (in hotel) 泊り客 tomárikyakù

♦*adj* (population) 現住の geńjū no; (doctor) レジデントの réjidento no

residential [reziden'tʃəl] *adj* (area) 住宅の jútaku no; (course) 住込みの sumíkomi no; (college) 全寮制の zeńryōsei no

residue [rez'iduː] *n* (remaining part) 残留物 zańryūbutsu

resign [rizain'] *vt* (one's post) 辞任する jinín suru

♦*vi* (from post) 辞任する jinín suru

to resign oneself to (situation, fact) あきらめて...を認める akírametè ...wo mitómerù

resignation [rezignei'ʃən] *n* (post) 辞任 jinín; (state of mind) あきらめ akírame

resigned [rizaind'] *adj* (to situation etc) あきらめている akíramete irù

resilience [rizil'jəns] *n* (of material) 弾力 dańryoku; (of person) 回復力 kaífukuryòku

resilient [rizil'jənt] *adj* (material) 弾力のある dańryoku no arù; (person) 立直りの速い tachínaori nò hayáì

resin [rez'in] *n* 樹脂 júshi

resist [rizist'] *vt* 抵抗する teíkō suru

resistance [rizis'təns] *n* (*gen*) 抵抗 teíkō; (to illness, infection) 抵抗力 teíkōryoku

resolute [rez'əluːt] *adj* (person) 意志の強い íshì no tsuyóì; (refusal) 断固とした dáñko to shitá

resolution [rezəluː'ʃən] *n* (decision) 決心 kesshín; (determination) 決意 kétsùi; (of problem, difficulty) 解決 kaíketsu

resolve [rizɑːlv'] *n* (determination) 決意 kétsùi

♦*vt* (problem, difficulty) 解決する kaíketsu suru

♦*vi: to resolve to do* ...しようと決心する ...shiyó tò kesshín suru

resolved [rizɑːlvd'] *adj* (determined) 決心している kesshín shité irù

resonant [rez'ənənt] *adj* 朗朗たる rórò taru

resort [rizɔːrt'] *n* (town) リゾート rizótò; (recourse) 利用 riyó

♦*vi: to resort to* ...を利用する ...wo riyó suru

in the last resort 結局 kekkyókù

resound [rizaund'] *vi: to resound (with)* (...の音が...中に) 鳴り響く (...no otó ga ...jū ni) naríhibikù

resounding [rizaun'diŋ] *adj* (noise) 響き渡る hibíkiwatarù; (*fig*: success) 完全な kańzen na

resource [riː'sɔːrs] *n* (raw material) 資源 shígen

resourceful [risɔːrs'fəl] *adj* (quick-witted) やり手の yaríte no

resources [riː'sɔːrsiz] *npl* (coal, iron, oil etc) 天然資源 teńnenshìgen; (money) 財産 zaísan

respect [rispekt'] *n* (consideration, esteem) 尊敬 sońkei

♦*vt* 尊敬する sońkei suru

with respect to ...に関して ...ni káñ shite

in this respect この点では konó ten de wà

respectability [rispektəbil'əti:] *n* 名声 meísei

respectable [rispek'təbəl] *adj* (morally correct) 道理にかなった dóri nì kanáttà; (large: amount) かなりの kánàri no; (passable) まあまあの mámà no

respectful [rispekt'fəl] *adj* (person, behavior) 礼儀正しい reígitadashiì

respective [rispek'tiv] *adj* (separate) そ
れぞれの sorézòre no

respectively [rispek'tivli:] *adv* それぞれ
sorézòre

respects [rispekts'] *npl* (greetings) あい
さつ áisatsu

respiration [respərei'ʃən] *n see* **artificial respiration**

respite [res'pit] *n* (rest) 休息 kyúsoku

resplendent [risplen'dənt] *adj* 華やかな
hanáyàka na

respond [rispɑ:nd'] *vi* (answer) 答える
kotáerù; (react: to pressure, criticism)
反応する hańnō suru

response [rispɑ:ns'] *n* (answer) 答え kotáè; (reaction) 反応 hańnō

responsibility [rispɑ:nsəbil'əti:] *n* (liability) 責任 sekínin; (duty) 義務 gímù

responsible [rispɑ:n'səbəl] *adj* (liable):
responsible (for) (...の) 責任がある
(...no) sekínin gà árù; (character, person)
責任感のある sekíniñkan no aru; (job) 責
任の重い sekínin nò omóì

responsive [rispɑ:n'siv] *adj* (child, gesture) 敏感な bíñkan na; (to demand,
treatment) よく応じる yókù ōjírù

rest [rest] *n* (relaxation) 休み yasúmi;
(pause) 休止 kyúshi; (remainder) 残り nokóri; (object: to support something) 台
dái; (MUS) 休止符 kyúshifu

♦*vi* (relax) 休む yasúmù; (stop) 休止する
kyúshi suru; *to rest on* (idea) ...に基づく
...ni motózukù; (weight, object) ...に置か
れている ...ni okárete irù

♦*vt* (head, eyes, muscles) 休ませる yasú-
maserù; (lean): *to rest something on/
against* ...を...に置く〔寄り掛ける〕...wo
...ni okú (yorīkakerù)

the rest of them (people) 残りの人たち
nokóri nò hitótàchi; (objects) 残りの物
nokóri no monò

it rests with him to ... ...するのは彼の
責任だ ...surú no wà kárè no sekínin dà

restaurant [res'tə:rənt] *n* レストラン rḗ-
sùtoran

restaurant car (*BRIT*) *n* 食堂車 shokúdōsha

restful [rest'fəl] *adj* 心を落着かせる ko-

rest home *n* 養老院 yōrōìn

restitution [restitu:'ʃən] *n*: *to make
restitution to someone for something*
(compensate) ...に対して...の弁償をする
...ni táìshite ...no beńshō wo surù

restive [res'tiv] *adj* (person, crew) 反抗
的な hańkōteki na; (horse) 言う事を聞か
ない iú kotò wo kikánài

restless [rest'lis] *adj* (person, audience)
落着かない ochítsukanaì

restoration [restərei'ʃən] *n* (of building
etc) 修復 shúfuku; (of law and order,
faith, health) 回復 kaífuku; (of something stolen) 返還 heñkan; (to power,
former state) 復旧 fukkyū

restore [ristɔ:r'] *vt* (building) 修復する
shúfuku suru; (law and order, faith,
health) 回復する kaífuku suru; (something stolen) 返す káesu; (to power, former state) 元に戻す mótò ni modósù

restrain [ristrein'] *vt* (feeling, growth,
inflation) 抑制する yokúsei suru; (per-
son): *to restrain (from doing)* (...し
ない様に) 抑える (...shinái yō ni) osáerù

restrained [ristreind'] *adj* (style, person)
控え目な hikáeme na

restraint [ristreint'] *n* (restriction) 抑制
yokúsei; (moderation) 程々 hodóhodo;
(of style) 控え目な調子 hikáeme nà chōshi

restrict [ristrikt'] *vt* (limit: growth,
numbers etc) 制限する seígen suru;
(: vision) 邪魔する jámà suru; (confine:
people, animals) ...の動きを制限する
...no ugóki wò seígen suru; (: activities,
membership) 制限する seígen suru

restriction [ristrik'ʃən] *n* (gen) 制限 seígen; (of vision) 妨げ samátagè; (limitation): *restriction (on)* (...の) 制限
(...no) seígen

restrictive [ristrik'tiv] *adj* (environment) 束縛的な sokúbakuteki na; (clothing) きつい kitsúì

restrictive practices *npl* (INDUS-
TRY) 制限的慣行 seígentekikañkō

rest room (*US*) *n* お手洗 o-téarài

restructure [ri:strʌk'tʃər] *vt* (business,

economy) 再編成する saíheńsei suru

result [rizʌlt'] *n* (of event, action) 結果 kekká; (of match) スコア sukóà; (of exam, competition) 成績 seíseki

♦*vi*: **to result in** ...に終る ...ni owárù

as a result of ...の結果... no kekká

resume [ri:zu:m'] *vt* (work, journey) 続ける tsuzúkerù

♦*vi* (start again) また始まる matá hàjimaru

résumé [rez'u:mei] *n* (summary) 要約 yóyaku; (*US*: curriculum vitae) 履歴書 rirékishò

resumption [rizʌmp'ʃən] *n* (of work, activity) 再開 saíkai

resurgence [risə:r'dʒəns] *n* 復活 fukkátsu

resurrection [rezərek'ʃən] *n* (of hopes, fears) よみがえらせる事 yomígaeraserù kotŏ; (REL): **the Resurrection** キリストの復活 kirísuto no fukkátsu

resuscitate [risʌs'əteit] *vt* (MED) そ生させる soséi saserù

resuscitation [risʌsətei'ʃən] *n* そ生 soséi

retail [ri:'teil] *adj* (trade, department, shop, goods) 小売の koúri no

♦*adv* 小売で koúri de

retailer [ri:'teilə:r] *n* (trader) 小売業者 koúrigyòsha

retail price *n* 小売価格 koúrikakàku

retain [ritein'] *vt* (keep) 保つ tamótsù

retainer [ritei'nə:r] *n* (fee) 依頼料 iráiryò

retaliate [ritæl'i:eit] *vi*: **to retaliate (against)** (attack, ill-treatment) (...に対して) 報復する (...ni taíshite) hófuku suru

retaliation [ritæli:ei'ʃən] *n* 報復 hófuku

retarded [ritɑ:r'did] *adj* (child) 知恵遅れの chiékohre no; (development, growth) 遅れた okúretà

retch [retʃ] *vi* むかつく mukátsukù

retentive [riten'tiv] *adj* (memory) 優れた sugúretà

reticent [ret'isənt] *adj* 無口な múkuchi na

retina [ret'ənə] *n* (ANAT) 網膜 mómaku

retire [ritaiə:r'] *vi* (give up work: *gen*) 引

退する iñtai suru; (: at a certain age) 定年退職する teínentaìshoku suru; (withdraw) 引下がる hikísagarù; (go to bed) 寝る nérù

retired [ritaiə:rd'] *adj* (person: *gen*) 引退した iñtai shita; (: at certain age) 定年退職した teínentaìshoku shita

retirement [ritaiə:r'mənt] *n* (giving up work: *gen*) 隠退 iñtai; (: at certain age) 定年退職 teínentaìshoku

retiring [ritaiə:r'iŋ] *adj* (leaving) 退職する taíshoku suru; (shy) 内気な uchíki na

retort [ritɔ:rt'] *vi* しっぺ返しをする shippégaèshi wo suru

retrace [ri:treis'] *vt*: **to retrace one's steps** 来た道を戻る kitá michì wo modórù

retract [ritrækt'] *vt* (statement, offer) 撤回する tekkái suru; (claws, aerial etc) 引っ込める hikkómerù

retrain [ri:trein'] *vt* 再訓練する saíkuñren suru

retraining [ri:trei'niŋ] *n* 再訓練 saíkuñren

retread [ri:'tred] *n* (tire) 再生タイヤ saíseitaìya

retreat [ritri:t'] *n* (place) 隠れ家 kakúregà; (withdrawal) 避難 hínàn; (MIL) 退却 taíkyaku

♦*vi* (from danger, enemy) 避難する hínàn suru; (MIL) 退却する taíkyaku suru

retribution [retrəbju:'ʃən] *n* 天罰 teñbatsu

retrieval [ritri:'vəl] *n* (of object) 回収 kaíshū; (of situation) 繕う事 tsukúrou kotŏ; (of honor) ばん回 bañkai; (of error) 償い tsugúnaì; (loss) 取返し toríkaeshi

retrieve [ritri:v'] *vt* (object) 回収する kaíshū suru; (situation) 繕う tsukúroù; (honor) ばん回する bañkai suru; (error) 償う tsugúnaù; (loss) 取返す toríkaesù

retriever [ritri:'və:r] *n* (dog) リトリーバ犬 ritórībakèn

retrograde [ret'rəgreid] *adj* 後戻りの atómodòri no

retrospect [ret'rəspekt] *n*: **in retrospect** 振返ってみると furíkaette miru tŏ

retrospective [retrəspek'tiv] *adj* (exhi-

bition) 回顧的な kaíkoteki na; (feeling, opinion) 過去にさかのぼる kákò ni sakánoborù; (law, tax) 及ぼする sokyú suru

return [ritə:rn'] *n* (going or coming back) 帰り kaéri; (of something stolen, borrowed etc) 返還 heñkan; (FINANCE: from land, shares, investment) 利回り rimáwari

♦*cpd* (journey) 帰りの kaéri no; (BRIT: ticket) 往復の ốfuku no; (match) 雪辱の setsújoku no

♦*vi* (person etc: come or go back) 帰る kaérù; (feelings, symptoms etc) 戻る modórù; (regain): **to return to** (consciousness) ...を回復する ...wo kaífuku suru; (power) ...に返り咲く ...ni kaérizakù

♦*vt* (favor, love etc) 返す kaésù; (something borrowed, stolen etc) 返却する heñkyaku suru; (LAW: verdict) ...と答申する ...to tōshin suru; (POL: candidate) 選出する señshutsu suru; (ball) 返す kaésù

in return (for) (...の) お返しに (...no) o-káèshi ni

by return of post 折返し郵便で oríkaeshiyūbin de

many happy returns (of the day)! お誕生日おめでとう o-táñjòbi omédetò

returns [ritə:rnz'] *npl* (COMM) 利益 rſeki

reunion [ri:ju:n'jən] *n* (of family) 集い tsudói; (of school, class etc) 同窓会 dōsōkai; (of two people) 再会 saíkai

reunite [ri:ju:nait'] *vt* (bring or come together again) 元のさやに収めさせる mótò no sáyà ni osámesaserù; (reconcile) 和解させる wakái saserù

rev [rev] *n abbr* (AUT: = *revolution*) 回転 kaíten

♦*vt* (also: **rev up**: engine) ふかす fukásù

revamp [ri:væmp'] *vt* (organization, company, system) 改革する kaíkaku suru

reveal [rivi:l'] *vt* (make known) 明らかにする akírakà ni suru; (make visible) 現す aráwasù

revealing [rivi:'liŋ] *adj* (action, statement) 手の内を見せる tế nò uchí wò misérù; (dress) 肌をあらわにする hádà

wo arawá ni suru

reveille [rev'əli:] *n* (MIL) 起床らっぱ kishō rappā

revel [rev'əl] *vi*: **to revel in something/ in doing something** (enjoy) ...を〔...する のを〕楽しむ ...wo〔...surú no wò〕tanóshimù

revelation [revəlei'ʃən] *n* (fact, experience) 意外な新知識 igái nà shifchishīki

revelry [rev'əlri:] *n* どんちゃん騒ぎ doñchan sawàgi

revenge [rivend3'] *n* (for injury, insult) 復しゅう fukúshū

to take revenge on (enemy) ...に復しゅうする ...ni fukúshū suru

revenue [rev'ənu:] *n* (income: of individual, company, government) 収入 shūnyū

reverberate [rivə:r'bə:reit] *vi* (sound, thunder etc: *also fig*) 響く hibſkù

reverberation [rivə:rbərei'ʃən] *n* (of sound, etc: *also fig*) 響き hibſki

revere [rivi:r'] *vt* 敬愛する keſai suru

reverence [rev'ə:rəns] *n* 敬愛 keſai

Reverend [rev'ə:rənd] *adj* (in titles) ...師 ...shī ◇聖職者の名前に付ける敬称 seſshokushà no namáè ni tsukérù keſshō

reversal [rivə:r'səl] *n* (of order) 反転 hañten; (of direction) 逆戻り gyakúmodòri; (of decision, policy) 逆転 gyakúten; (of roles) 入れ代り irékawari

reverse [rivə:rs'] *n* (opposite) 反対 hañtai; (back) 裏 urá; (AUT: *also*: **reverse gear**) バック bákkù; (setback, defeat) 失敗 shippái

♦*adj* (opposite: order, direction, process) 反対の hañtai no, 逆の gyakú no; (: side) 裏の urá no

♦*vt* (order, position, direction) 逆にする gyakú ni surù; (process, policy, decision) 引っ繰り返す hikkúrikaèsu; (roles) 入れ替える irékaerù; (car) バックさせる bákkù saserù

♦*vi* (BRIT: AUT) バックする bákkù suru

reverse-charge call [rivə:rs'tʃɑ:rdʒ-] (BRIT) *n* 受信人払い電話 jushſnninbarai deñwa

reversing lights [rivə:r'siŋ-] (BRIT)

npl (AUT) バックライト bakkúraìto

revert [rivə:rt'] *vi*: *to revert to* (former state) ...に 戻る ...ni modórù; (LAW: money, property) ...に帰属する ...ni kizóku surù

review [rivju:'] *n* (magazine) 評論雑誌 hyóronzasshì; (MIL) 閲兵 eppéi; (of book, film etc) 批評 hihyō̂; (examination: of situation, policy etc) 再検討 saíkentō

♦*vt* (MIL) 閲兵する eppéi suru; (book, film etc) ...の批評を書く ...no hihyō̂ wò kákù; (situation, policy etc) 再検討する saíkentō suru

reviewer [rivju:'ə:r] *n* (of book, film etc) 批評者 hihyṓshà

revile [rivail'] *vt* (insult) 侮辱する bujóku suru

revise [rivaiz'] *vt* (manuscript) 修正する shúsei suru; (opinion, price, procedure) 変える kaérù

♦*vi* (*BRIT*: study) 試験勉強する shikénbeñkyō suru

revision [riviʒ'ən] *n* (amendment) 修正 shúsei; (for exam) 試験勉強 shikénbeñkyō

revitalize [ri:vai'təlaiz] *vt* ...に新しい活力を与える ...ni atárashìi katsúryòku wo atáerù

revival [rivai'vəl] *n* (recovery) 回復 kaífuku; (of interest, faith) 復活 fukkátsu; (THEATER) リバイバル ribáibaru

revive [rivaiv'] *vt* (person) ...の意識を回復させる ...no íshìki wo kaífuku saserù; (economy, industry) 復興させる fukkō̂ saserù; (custom, hope, courage) 復活させる fukkátsu saserù; (play) 再上演する saíjōen suru

♦*vi* (person: from faint) 意識を取り戻す í-shìki wo torímodosù; (: from ill-health) 元気になる géñki ni nárù; (activity, economy etc) 回復する kaífuku suru; (faith, interest etc) 復活する fukkátsu suru

revoke [rivouk'] *vt* 取消す toríkesù

revolt [rivoult'] *n* (rebellion) 反逆 hañgyaku

♦*vi* (rebel) 反逆する hañgyaku suru

♦*vt* (disgust) むかつかせる mukátsukaserù

revolting [rivoul'tiŋ] *adj* (disgusting) むかつかせる mukátsukaserù

revolution [revəlu:'ʃən] *n* (POL) 革命 kakúmei; (rotation: of wheel, earth etc: *also* AUT) 回転 kaíten

revolutionary [revəlu:'ʃəne:ri:] *adj* (method, idea) 革命的な kakúmeiteki na; (leader, army) 革命の kakúmei no

♦*n* (POL: person) 革命家 kakúmeika

revolutionize [revəlu:'ʃənaiz] *vt* (industry, society etc) ...に大変革をもたらす ...ni daíhenkaku wò motárasù

revolve [rivɑ:lv'] *vi* (turn: earth, wheel etc) 回転する kaíten suru; (life, discussion): *to revolve (a)round* ...を中心に展開する ...wo chúshin nì teñkai suru

revolver [rivɑ:l'və:r] *n* けん銃 keñjū, リボルバー ribórùbā ◇回転式の物を指す kaítenshiki no monṑ wò sásù

revolving [rivɑ:l'viŋ] *adj* (chair etc) 回転式の kaítenshiki no

revolving door *n* 回転ドア kaíten doà

revue [rivju:'] *n* (THEATER) レビュー rébyū

revulsion [rivʌl'ʃən] *n* (disgust) 嫌悪 kéñ-o

reward [riwɔ:rd'] *n* (for service, merit, work) 褒美 hóbi; (money for capture of criminal, information etc) 賞金 shókin

♦*vt*: *to reward (for)* (effort) (...のために) 褒美を与える (... no tamé nì) hóbi wò atáerù

rewarding [riwɔ:rd'iŋ] *adj* (*fig*: worthwhile) やりがいのある yarígai no arù

rewind [ri:waind'] (*pt, pp* **rewound**) *vt* (tape, cassette) 巻戻す makímodosù

rewire [ri:waiə:r'] *vt* (house) ...の電気配線をし直す ...no deñki haìsen wo shínaosù

rewrite [ri:rait'] (*pt* **rewrote**, *pp* **rewritten**) *vt* 書き直す kakínaosù

rhapsody [ræp'sədi:] *n* (MUS) 狂詩曲 kyóshikyòku, ラプソディー rápùsodī

rhetorical [ritɔ:r'ikəl] *adj* (question, speech) 修辞的な shújiteki na

rheumatic [ru:mæt'ik] *adj* リューマチの ryúmachi no

rheumatism [ruːˈmətizəm] n リューマチ ryûmachi

Rhine [rain] n: *the Rhine* ライン川 raíñgawa

rhinoceros [rainɑːsˈəːrəs] n サイ sáì

rhododendron [roudədenˈdrən] n シャクナゲ shakúnage

Rhone [roun] n: *the Rhone* ローヌ川 rônùgawa

rhubarb [ˈruːbɑːrb] n ルバーブ rubâbù

rhyme [raim] n (of two words) 韻 iñ; (verse) 詩 shi; (technique) 韻を踏む事 iñ wò fumú kotò

rhythm [ˈriðəm] n リズム rízùmu

rhythmic(al) [ˈriðˈmik(əl)] adj リズミカルな rizúmikàru na

rib [rib] n (ANAT) ろっ骨 rokkótsu
♦vt (tease) からかう karákaù

ribbon [ˈribən] n リボン ríbòn
in ribbons (torn) ずたずたになって zutázuta ni nattè

rice [rais] n (grain) 米 komé; (cooked) 御飯 góhàn

rice pudding n ライスプディング raísu pudìñgu ◇御飯にミルク、卵、砂糖などを加えたデザート góhàn ni mírùku, tamágo, satô nadò wo kuwáeta dezâtò

rich [ritʃ] adj (person, country) 金持の kanémochi no; (clothes, jewels) 高価な kôka na; (soil) 肥えた koétà, 肥よくな hiyóku na; (food, diet) 濃厚な nôkô na; (color, voice, life) 豊かな yútàka na; (abundant): *rich in* (minerals, resources etc) ...に富んだ ...ni tóñda
♦npl: *the rich* 金持 kanémochi ◇総称 sôshô

riches [ˈritʃiz] npl (wealth) 富 tómì

richly [ˈritʃliː] adv (dressed, decorated) 豪華に gôka ni; (rewarded, deserved, earned) 十分に júbuñ ni

rickets [ˈrikits] n くる病 kurúbyô

rickety [ˈrikətiː] adj (shaky) がたがたの gatágata no

rickshaw [ˈrikʃɔː] n 人力車 jiñrikishà

ricochet [rikəʃeiˈ] vi (bullet, stone) 跳ね飛ぶ hanétobù

rid [rid] (pt, pp rid) vt: *to rid someone of something* ...の...を取除く ...no ...wo

torínozokù
to get rid of (something no longer required) 捨てる sutérù; (something unpleasant or annoying) ...を取除く ...wo torínozokù

ridden [ˈridən] pp of ride

riddle [ˈridəl] n (conundrum) なぞなぞ nazónazo; (mystery) なぞ nazó
♦vt: *to be riddled with* ...だらけである ...dáràke de árù

ride [raid] n (in car, on bicycle, horse) 乗る事 norú kotò; (distance covered) 道のり michínori
♦vb (pt rode, pp ridden)
♦vi (as sport) 乗馬をする jôba wo suru; (go somewhere: on horse, bicycle, bus) 乗って行く nottê ikú
♦vt (a horse, bicycle, motorcycle) ...に乗る ...ni nórù; (distance) 行く ikú
to take someone for a ride (fig: deceive) ぺてんに掛ける petén nì kakérù
to ride a bicycle 自転車に乗る jitéñsha ni norú
to ride at anchor (NAUT) 停泊する teíhaku suru

rider [ˈraidəːr] n (on horse) 乗り手 noríte; (on bicycle, motorcycle) 乗る人 norú hitò, ライダー ráìdā

ridge [ridʒ] n (of hill) 尾根 ônè; (of roof) 天辺 teppéñ; (wrinkle) うね uné

ridicule [ˈridəkjuːl] n あざけり azákerì
♦vt あざける azákerù

ridiculous [ridikˈjələs] adj (foolish) ばかげた bakágetà

riding [ˈraidiŋ] n (sport, activity) 乗馬 jôba

riding school n 乗馬学校 jôbagakkô

rife [raif] adj: *to be rife* (bribery, corruption, superstition) はびこる habíkorù
to be rife with (rumors, fears) ...がはびこっている ...ga habíkotte irù

riffraff [ˈrifræf] n (rabble) ろくでなしの連中 rokúdenashi nò reñchú

rifle [ˈraifəl] n (gun) ライフル ráìfuru
♦vt (steal from: wallet, pocket etc) ...の中身を盗む ...no nakámi wò nusúmù

rifle range n (for sport) 射撃場 shagékijô; (at fair) 射的 shatéki

rifle through vt fus (papers) ...をかき回して捜す ...wo kakímawashite sagásù

rift [rift] n (split: in ground) 亀裂 kíretsu; (: in clouds) 切れ間 kiréma; (fig: disagreement) 仲たがい nakátagaì

rig [rig] n (also: **oil rig**) 油井掘削装置 yuséi kussaku sôchi

♦vt (election, game etc) 不正操作する fuséisòsa suru

rigging [rig'iŋ] n (NAUT) 索具 sakúgù

right [rait] adj (correct: answer, solution, size etc) 正しい tadáshiì; (suitable: person, clothes, time) 適当な tekítō na; (: decision etc) 適切な tekísetsu na; (morally good) 正当な seítō na; (fair, just) 公正な kôsei na; (not left) 右の migí no

♦n (what is morally right) 正義 seígi; (entitlement) 権利 keńri; (not left) 右 migí

♦adv (correctly: answer etc) 正しく tadáshìku; (properly, fairly: treat etc) 公正に kôsei ni; (not on the left) 右に migí ni; (directly, exactly): **right now** 今すぐ ímà súgù

♦vt (put right way up: ship, car etc) 起す okósù; (correct: fault, situation, wrong) 正す tadásù

♦excl では dê wà

to be right (person) ...の言う事が合っている ...no iú kotò ga atté irù; (answer) 正解である seíkai de arù; (clock, reading etc) 合っている atté irù

by rights 当然 tôzen

on the right 右に migí ni

to be in the right ...の方が正しい ...no hô gà tadáshiì

right away すぐに súgù ni

right in the middle 丁度真ん中に chôdo mańnaka ni

right angle n (MATH) 直角 chokkáku

righteous [rait'tʃəs] adj (person) 有徳な yútoku na; (anger) 当然な tôzen na

rightful [rait'fəl] adj (heir, owner) 合法の gôhō no; (place, share) 正当な seítō na

right-handed [rait'hæendid] adj (person) 右利きの migíkiki no

right-hand man [rait'hæend'-] n 右腕 migíude

right-hand side n 右側 migígawa

rightly [rait'li:] adv (with reason) 当然 tôzen

right of way n (on path etc) 通行権 tsúkōken; (AUT) 先行権 seńkōken

right-wing [rait'wiŋ] adj (POL) 右翼の úyðku no

rigid [ridʒ'id] adj (structure, back etc) 曲らない magáranaì; (attitude, views etc) 厳格な geńkaku na; (principle, control etc) 厳しい kibíshiì

rigmarole [rig'məroul] n (procedure) 手続 tetsúzùki

rigor [rig'ɔːr] (BRIT **rigour**) n (strictness) 厳格さ geńkakusa; (severity): **rigors of life/winter** 生活[冬]の厳しさ seíkatsu(fuyú)nò kibíshisa

rigorous [rig'ɔːrəs] adj (control, test) 厳密な geńmitsu na; (training) 厳しい kibíshiì

rig out (BRIT) vt: **to rig out as** ...の仮装をする ...no kasô wò suru

to rig out in ...を着る ...wo kírù

rig up vt 作り上げる tsukúriagerù

rile [rail] vt (annoy) ...を怒らせる ...wo okóraserù

rim [rim] n (of glass, dish) 縁 fuchí; (of spectacles) フレーム furêmù; (of wheel) リム rímù

rind [raind] n (of bacon, fruit, cheese) 皮 kawá

ring [riŋ] n (of metal, light, smoke) 輪 wá; (for finger) 指輪 yubíwà; (of spies, drug-dealers etc) 組織 sôshìki; (for boxing, of circus) リング ríngu; (bullring) 闘牛場 tôgyūjō; (sound of bell) ベルの音 bérù no otó

♦vb (pt **rang**, pp **rung**)

♦vi (person: by telephone) 電話を掛ける deńwa wo kakérù; (telephone, bell, doorbell) 鳴る narú; (also: **ring out**: voice, words) 鳴り響く naríhibikù

♦vt (BRIT: TEL) ...に電話を掛ける ...ni deńwa wð kakérù; (bell etc) 鳴らす narásù

a ring of people 車座になった人々 kurúmaza ni nattá hitóbìto

a ring of stones 環状に並んだ石 kańjō

ni naraňda ishí

to give someone a ring (BRIT: TEL)
...に電話を掛ける ...ni deňwa wò kakérù

my ears are ringing 耳鳴りがする mimínari ga surù

ring back (BRIT) vt (TEL) ...に電話を
掛け直す ...ni deňwa wò kakénaosù

◆vi (TEL) 電話を掛け直す deňwa wò kakénaosù

ringing [riŋ'iŋ] n (of telephone, bell) 鳴
る音 narú otò; (in ears) 耳鳴り mimínari

ringing tone n (TEL) ダイヤルトーン
daíyarutòn

ringleader [riŋ'li:də:r] n (of gang) 主犯
shuhán

ringlets [riŋ'lits] npl (of hair) 巻き毛 makíge

ring off (BRIT) vi (TEL) 電話を切る
deňwa wò kírù

ring road (BRIT) n 環状線 kaňjōsen

ring up (BRIT) vt (TEL) ...に電話を掛け
る ...ni deňwa wò kakérù

rink [riŋk] n (also: **ice rink**) スケートリ
ンク sukétorìnku

rinse [rins] n (of dishes, hands) すすぎ
susúgi; (of hair) リンスする事 ríñsu suru
kotò; (dye: for hair) リンス ríñsu

◆vt (dishes, hands etc) すすぐ susúgù;
(hair etc) リンスする ríñsu suru; (also:
rinse out: clothes) すすぐ susúgù;
(: mouth) ゆすぐ yusúgù

riot [rai'ət] n (disturbance) 騒動 sódō

◆vi (crowd, protestors etc) 暴動を起す
bódō wò okósù

a riot of colors 色取り取り irótoridòri

to run riot (children, football fans etc)
大騒ぎをする ōsawàgi wo suru

riotous [rai'ətəs] adj (mob, assembly
etc) 暴動的な bódōteki na; (behavior, living) 遊とうざんまい yútōzaňmai; (party)
どんちゃん騒ぎの doñchan sawàgi no

rip [rip] n (tear) 破れ目 yabúremè

◆vt (paper, cloth) 破る yabúrù

◆vi (paper, cloth) 破れる yabúrerù

ripcord [rip'kɔ:rd] n (on parachute) 引き
網 hikízùna

ripe [raip] adj (fruit, grain, cheese) 熟し
た jukú shità

ripen [rai'pən] vt (subj: sun) 熟させる jukú saserù

◆vi (fruit, crop) 熟する jukú suru

ripple [rip'əl] n (wave) さざ波 sazánami;
(of laughter, applause) ざわめき zawá-
meki

◆vi (water) さざ波が立つ sazánami gà
tátsù

rise [raiz] n (slope) 上り坂 nobórizaka;
(hill) 丘 oká; (increase: in wages: BRIT)
賃上げ chiň-age; (: in prices, temperature) 上昇 jóshō; (fig: to power etc) 出世
shussé

◆vi (pt rose, pp risen) (prices, numbers)
上がる agárù; (waters) 水かさが増す mi-
zúkasa gà masú; (sun, moon) 昇る nobórù; (person: from bed etc) 起きる okírù;
(sound, voice) 大きくなる ōkiku nárù;
(also: **rise up**: tower, building) そびえる
sobíerù; (: rebel) 立ち上がる tachíagarù;
(in rank) 昇進する shōshin suru

to give rise to ...を起す ...wo okósù

to rise to the occasion 腕前を見せる
udémaè wo misérù

risen [riz'ən] pp of **rise**

rising [rai'ziŋ] adj (increasing: number,
prices) 上がる agárù; (tide) 満ちる michírù; (sun, moon) 昇る nobórù

risk [risk] n (danger) 危険 kikén;
(INSURANCE) リスク rísùku

◆vt (endanger) 危険にさらす kikén nì sarásù; (chance) ...の危険を冒す ...no kinén
wò okásù

to take/run the risk of doing ...する
危険を冒す ...súrù kikén wò okásù

at risk 危険にさらされて kikén nì sara-
sárete

at one's own risk 自分の責任で jibún
nò sekínin de

risky [ris'ki:] adj (dangerous) 危険な kikén na

risqué [riskei'] adj (joke) わいせつがかっ
た waísetsugakattà

rissole [ris'ɑ:l] n (of meat, fish etc) メン
チカツ meňchikatsù

rite [rait] n 儀式 gíshìki

last rites (REL) 終油の秘蹟 shúyu nò
hiséki

ritual [ritʃˈuːəl] adj (law, dance) 儀式的な gishíkiteki na
♦n 儀式 gíshìki
rival [raiˈvəl] n ライバル ráìbaru
♦adj ライバルの ráìbaru no
♦vt (match) ...に匹敵する ...ni hittéki suru
rivalry [raiˈvəlriː] n (competition) 競争 kyósō
river [rivˈəːr] n 川 kawá
♦cpd (port, traffic) 川の kawá no
up/down river 川上〔下〕へ kawákami [shimo] e
riverbank [rivˈəːrbæŋk] n 川岸 kawágishi
riverbed [rivˈəːrbed] n 河原 kawára
rivet [rivˈit] n (bolt) リベット ribéttò
♦vt (fig): to rivet one's eyes/attention on ...に注目する ...ni chúmoku suru
Riviera [riviːeːrˈə] n: the (French) Riviera リビエラ ribîèra
the Italian Riviera イタリアのリビエラ itária nò ribîèra
road [roud] n (gen) 道 michî, 道路 dóro
♦cpd (accident, sense) 道路の kótsū no
major/minor road 優先〔非優先〕道路 yúsen (hiyúsen)dòro
roadblock [roudˈblɑːk] n 検問所 keñmonjo
roadhog [roudˈhɔːg] n マナーの悪いドライバー mánā no warúî doráìbā
road map n 道路地図 dórochìzu
road safety n 交通安全 kótsūañzen
roadside [roudˈsaid] n 道路端 dórowaki
roadsign [roudˈsain] n 道路標識 dórohyòshiki
road user n ドライバー doráìbā
roadway [roudˈwei] n 車道 shadó
roadworks [roudˈwəːrks] npl 道路工事 dórokòji
roadworthy [roudˈwəːrðiː] adj (car) 整備状態のいい seíbijòtai no íi
roam [roum] vi (wander) さまよう samáyoù
roar [rɔːr] n (of animal) ほえ声 hoégoè; (of crowd) どよめき doyómeki; (of vehicle, storm) とどろき todóroki
♦vi (animal) ほえる hoérù; (person) どな

る donárù; (crowd) どよめく doyómekù; (engine, wind etc) とどろく todórokù
a roar of laughter 大笑い ówarài
to roar with laughter 大笑いする ówarài suru
to do a roaring trade ...の商売が繁盛する ...no shóbai gà hañjó suru
roast [roust] n (of meat) ロースト rósuto
♦vt (meat, potatoes) オーブンで焼く óbun de yakú; (coffee) いる frú
roast beef n ローストビーフ rósutobìfu
rob [rɑːb] vt (person, house, bank) ...から盗む ...kara nusúmù
to rob someone of something ...から...を盗む ...kará ...wo nusúmù; (fig: deprive) 奪う ubáù
robber [rɑːbˈəːr] n 泥棒 doróbō
robbery [rɑːbˈəːriː] n (theft) 盗み nusúmi
robe [roub] n (for ceremony etc) ローブ róbu; (also: bath robe) バスローブ basúróbu; (US) 肩掛け hizákake
robin [rɑːbˈin] n コマドリ komádòri
robot [rouˈbət] n ロボット robóttò
robust [roubʌstˈ] adj (person) たくましい takúmashiì; (economy) 健全な keñzen na; (appetite) おう盛な ósei na
rock [rɑːk] n (substance) 岩石 gañseki; (boulder) 岩 iwá; (US: small stone, pebble) 小石 koíshi; (BRIT: sweet) 氷砂糖 kórizatò
♦vt (swing gently: cradle) 優しく揺する yasáshiku yusurù; (: child) あやす ayásù; (shake: subj: explosion, waves etc) 激しく揺すぶる hagéshiku yusuburù
♦vi (object) 揺れる yurérù; (person) 震える furúerù
on the rocks (drink) オンザロックで oñzarokkù de; (marriage etc) 危ぶまれて ayábumaretè
rock and roll n ロックンロール rokkúnròru
rock-bottom [rɑːkˈbɑːtˈəm] adj (fig: lowest point) 最低の saítei no
rockery [rɑːkˈəːriː] n (in garden) 庭石 niwá-ishi ◇総称 sóshō
rocket [rɑːkˈit] n (space rocket) ロケット rokéttò; (missile) ロケット弾 rokéttodañ; (firework) ロケット花火 rokétto ha-

nàbi
rocking chair [rɑːkʼiŋ-] *n* 揺りいす yu-
ríisu
rocking horse *n* 揺り木馬 yurímokùba
rocky [rɑːkʼiː] *adj* (covered with rocks)
岩だらけの iwádaràke no; (unsteady:
table) 不安定な fuántei na; (unstable:
business, marriage) 危ぶまれている ayá-
bumarete irù
rod [rɑːd] *n* (pole) さお saó; (*also:* **fishing
rod**) 釣ざお tsurízao
rode [roud] *pt of* **ride**
rodent [rouʼdənt] *n* げっ歯類 gesshírùi
rodeo [rouʼdiːou] *n* ロデオ ródèo
roe [rou] *n* (species: *also:* **roe deer**) ノロ
ジカ norójìka; (of fish) 卵 tamágò
    hard roe 腹子 haráko
    soft roe 白子 shirákò
rogue [roug] *n* 野郎 yarő
role [roul] *n* 役 yakú
roll [roul] *n* (of paper, cloth etc) 巻き
makí; (of banknotes) 札束 satsútabà;
(*also:* **bread roll**) ロールパン rőrupàn;
(register, list) 名簿 meíbo; (sound: of
drums etc) とどろき todőroki
    ♦*vt* (ball, stone etc) 転がす korógasù;
(*also:* **roll up**: string) 巻く makú;
(: sleeves) まくる makúrù; (cigarette) 巻
く makú; (eyes) 白黒させる shírōkuro
sasérù; (*also:* **roll out**: pastry) 延ばす nobásù; (flatten: lawn, road, surface) なら
す narásù
    ♦*vi* (ball, stone etc) 転がる korógarù;
(drum) 鳴り響く naríhibikù; (vehicle:
also: **roll along**) 走る hashírù; (ship) 揺れ
る yurérù
roll about/around *vi* 転がる korógarù
roll by *vi* (time) 過ぎる sugírù
roll call *n* 点呼 tếnko
roller [rouʼləːr] *n* (*gen*) ローラー rőrā;
(for hair) カーラー kắrā
roller coaster [-kousʼtəːr] *n* ジェットコ
ースター jettőkōsutā
roller skates *npl* ローラースケート rő-
rāsukèto
roll in *vi* (mail, cash) 大量に入る taíryō
nì haírù
rolling [rouʼliŋ] *adj* (landscape) うねりの

多い unéri no ői
rolling pin *n* めん棒 mếnbō
rolling stock *n* (RAIL) 車両 sharyő◇総
称 sőshō
roll over *vi* 寝返りを打つ negáeri wò
útsù
roll up *vi* (*inf*: arrive) やって来る yatté
kurù
    ♦*vt* (carpet, newspaper, umbrella etc) 巻
く makú
ROM [rɑːm] *n abbr* (*COMPUT:* = *read
only memory*) ロム rómù
Roman [rouʼmən] *adj* ローマの rőma no
Roman Catholic *adj* ローマカトリック
の rőmakatorikkù no
    ♦*n* ローマカトリック信者 rőmakatorik-
ku shiñja
romance [roumæns'] *n* (love affair) 恋愛
reñ-ai; (charm) ロマンス rőmànsu;
(novel) 恋愛小説 reñ-ai shősetsu
Romania [roumei'niːə] *n* = **Rumania**
Roman numeral *n* ローマ数字 rőmasù-
ji
romantic [roumæn'tik] *adj* ロマンチッ
クな románchikkù na
Rome [roum] *n* ローマ rőma
romp [rɑːmp] *n* 騒々しい遊び sőzōshiì a-
sőbi
    ♦*vi* (*also:* **romp about**: children, dogs
etc) はしゃぎ回る hashágimawarù
rompers [rɑːm'pəːrz] *npl* ロンパース roñ-
pāsu
roof [ruːf] (*pl* **roofs**) *n* 屋根 yánè, ルーフ
rűfu
    ♦*vt* (house, building etc) 屋根を付ける
yánè wo tsukérù
    the roof of one's mouth 口がい kőgai
roofing [ruːʼfiŋ] *n* 屋根ふき材 yanéfuki-
zài
roof rack *n* (AUT) ルーフラック rűfu-
rakkù
rook [ruk] *n* (bird) ミヤマガラス miyá-
magaràsu; (CHESS) ルック rúkkù
room [ruːm] *n* (in house, hotel etc) 部屋
heyá; (space) 空間 kűkan, 場所 bashő;
(scope: for improvement, change etc) 余
地 yőchì
    「*rooms for rent*」, 「*rooms to let*」 貸間

あり kashíma arì

single/double room シングル〔ダブル〕部屋 shínguru〔dabúru〕beyà

rooming house [ruːˈmiŋ-] (US) n 下宿屋 geshúkuya

roommate [ruːmˈmeit] n ルームメート rúmumèto ◇寄宿舎などで同室に泊まる人 kishúkushà nádò de dōshitsu nì tomárù hitò

rooms [ruːmz] npl (lodging) 下宿 geshúku

room service n (in hotel) ルームサービス rūmusābisu

roomy [ruːˈmiː] adj (building, car) 広々とした hiróbiro to shità; (garment) ゆったりした yuttári shità

roost [ruːst] vi (birds) ねぐらにつく negúra ni tsukù

rooster [ruːsˈtəːr] n オンドリ oñdòri

root [ruːt] n (BOT) 根 nế; (MATH) 根 kốñ; (of problem, belief) 根源 koñgen
  ♦vi (plant) 根を下ろす nế wò orósù; (belief) 定着する teíchaku suru
  the root of a hair 毛根 mốkon
  the root of a tooth 歯根 shikón

root about vi (fig: search) かき回す kakímawasù

root for vt fus (support) ...を応援する ...wo ốeñ surù

root out vt (find) 捜し出す sagáshidasù

roots [ruːts] npl (family origins) ルーツ rūtsu

rope [roup] n (thick string) ロープ rôpu; (NAUT) 綱 tsunâ; (for climbing) ザイル zāīru
  ♦vt (tie) 縛る shibárù; (climbers: also: **rope together**) ザイルでつなぐ zāīru de tsunágù; (an area: also: **rope off**) 綱で仕切る nawá dè shikírù
  to know the ropes (fig: know how to do something) こつが分かっている kotsú gà wakátte irù

rope in vt (fig: person) 誘い込む sasóikomù

rope ladder n 縄ばしご nawábashigo

rosary [rouˈzəːriː] n ロザリオ rozárìo

rose [rouz] pt of **rise**
  ♦n (single flower) バラ bará; (shrub) バ

ラの木 bará nò kí; (on watering can) はす口 hasúkuchi

rosé [rouzei'] n ロゼワイン rozéwàin

rosebud [rouz'bʌd] n バラのつぼみ bará nò tsubómi

rosebush [rouz'buʃ] n バラの木 bará no ki

rosemary [rouz'me:ri:] n ローズマリー rôzumarì

rosette [rouzet'] n ロゼット rozéttò

roster [ras'təːr] n: **duty roster** 勤務当番表 kíñmutōbañhyō

rostrum [ras'trəm] n 演壇 eñdan

rosy [rou'ziː] adj (color) バラ色の bará-iro no; (face, cheeks) 血色のいい kesshóku no iì; (situation) 明るい akáruì
  a rosy future 明るい見通し akáruì mitóshi

rot [rɑːt] n (decay) 腐敗 fuhái; (fig: pej: rubbish) でたらめ detárame
  ♦vt (cause to decay: teeth, wood, fruit etc) 腐らす kusárasù
  ♦vi (decay: teeth, wood, fruit etc) 腐る kusárù

rota [rou'tə] (BRIT) n 勤務当番表 kíñmutōbañhyō

rotary [rou'tə:ri:] adj (movement) 回転式の kaíteñshiki no

rotate [rou'teit] vt (revolve) 回転させる kaíteñ saserù; (change round: jobs) 交替でやる kôtai de yarù
  ♦vi (revolve) 回転する kaíteñ suru

rotating [rou'teitiŋ] adj (movement) 回転する kaíteñ suru

rotation [routei'ʃən] n (revolving) 回転 kaíteñ; (changing round: jobs) 交替 kôtai; (of crops) 輪作 ríñsaku

rote [rout] n: **by rote** 暗記で añki de

rotor [rou'təːr] n (also: **rotor blade**) 回転翼 kaíteñyoku, ローター rôtā

rotten [rɑːt'ən] adj (decayed: fruit, meat, wood, eggs etc) 腐った kusáttà; (fig: person, situation) いやな iyá nà; (inf: bad) ひどい hidóì
  a rotten tooth 虫歯 mushíba
  to feel rotten (ill) 気分が悪い kíbùn ga warúì

rotund [routʌnd'] adj (person) 丸々と太

った marúmaru to futótta

rouble [ru:'bəl] (*BRIT*) *n* = **ruble**

rouge [ru:ʒ] *n* ほお紅 hôbeni

rough [rʌf] *adj* (skin, surface, cloth) 粗い
araî; (terrain, road) 凸凹の dekóboko no;
(voice) しゃがれた shagáretà; (person,
manner: violent) 荒っぽい aráppoì;
(: brusque) ぶっきらぼうな bukkírabò na;
(treatment) 荒い araî; (weather, sea) 荒
れた aréta; (town, area) 治安の悪い chiân-
nò warúì; (plan, sketch) 大まかな ômaka
na; (guess) 大よその ôyoso no

♦*n* (GOLF): **in the rough** ラフに ráfù ni

to rough it 原始的な生活をする geñshiteki nà seíkatsu wð suru

to sleep rough (*BRIT*) 野宿する nójùku
suru

roughage [rʌf'idʒ] *n* 繊維 séñ-i

rough-and-ready [rʌf'ənred'i:] *adj* 原
始的な geñshiteki na

roughcast [rʌf'kæst] *n* (for wall) 小石を
混ぜたしっくい koíshi wð mazéta shik-
kûì

rough copy *n* 下書き shitágaki

rough draft *n* 草案 soán

roughly [rʌf'li:] *adv* (handle) 荒っぽく a-
ráppokù; (make) 大まかに ômaka ni;
(speak) ぶっきらぼうに bukkírabò ni;
(approximately) 大よそ ôyoso

roughness [rʌf'nis] *n* (of surface) 荒さ
arása; (of manner) がさつさ gasátsusa

roulette [ru:let'] *n* ルーレット rûretto

Roumania [ru:mei'ni:ə] *n* = **Rumania**

round [raund] *adj* 丸い marûì; (figures,
sum) 概数の gaísū no

♦*n* (*BRIT*: of toast) 一切 hitókire; (of
policeman, milkman, doctor) 巡回 juñkai; (game of cards) 一勝負 hitóshòbu; (:
in competition) ...回戦 ...kaîsen; (of
ammunition) 一発 ippátsu; (BOXING) ラ
ウンド ráundo; (*also*: **round of golf**) ラウ
ンド ráundo; (of talks) 一連 ichíren

♦*vt* (corner) 回る mawáru

♦*prep* (surrounding): **round his neck/
the table** 首[家]の回りに kubî(iế)nð
mawári ni; (in a circular movement): **to
move round the room** 部屋の中を一回
りする heyá no nakà wo hitómawarî

suru: **to sail round the world** 世界一
周の航海をする sékàiisshū nð kôkai wð
suru; (in various directions): **to move
round a room/house** 部屋[家]の中を動
き回る heyá (iế)no nakà wo ugôkima-
warù; (approximately): **round about
300** 大よそ300 ôyoso sañbyaku

♦*adv*: **all round** 回りに mawári ni

a round of golf ゴルフのワンラウンド
gôrùfu no wañraùndo

the long way round 遠回り tômawari

all the year round 一年中 ichínenjū

it's just round the corner (*fig*) 直ぐそ
こまで来ている súgù sokó madè kitê irú

round the clock 24時間 nijû-yo jîkan

to go round to someone's (house) ...の
うちへ行く ...no uchî è ikú

to go round the back 裏に回る urá nî
mawáru

to go round a house ある家を訪ねる
árù iế wð tazúnerù

enough to go round みんなに足りる程
mínna nì tarírù hodó

a round of applause 拍手 hákùshu

a round of drinks/sandwiches みん
なに一通りの飲み物[サンドウイッチ]を
おごる事 mínna nì hitótòri nð nomímòno
(sañdouicchì)wo ogórù kotó

roundabout [raund'əbaut] (*BRIT*) *n*
(AUT) ロータリー rôtarî; (at fair) メリー
ゴーラウンド merîgòraundo

♦*adj* (route) 遠回りの tômawàri no;
(means) 遠回しの tômawàshi no

rounders [raun'dəːrz] *npl* (game) ラウン
ダーズ raúndazu ◇野球に似た英国のゲー
ム yakyû ni nità eîkoku no gêmu

roundly [raund'li:] *adv* (*fig*: criticize) 厳
しく kibíshikù

round off *vt* (speech etc) 終える oéru

round-shouldered [raund'ʃouldəːrd] *adj*
ねこ背の nekôze no

round trip *n* 往復旅行 ôfukuryokò

round up *vt* (cattle, people) 駆集める
karísatsumerù; (price, figure) 概数にする
gaísū ni suru

roundup [raund'ʌp] *n* (of news, information) まとめ matôme; (of animals) 駆集
め karísatsume; (of criminals) 一斉逮捕

isséitaīho

rouse [rauz] vt (wake up) 起す okósù; (stir up) 引起す hikíokosù

rousing [rau'ziŋ] adj (cheer, welcome) 熱狂的な nekkyōteki na

rout [raut] n (MIL) 敗走 haísō
♦vt (defeat) 敗走させる haísō saserù

route [ru:t] n (way) ルート rūto; (of bus, train) 路線 rosén; (of shipping) 航路 kōro; (of procession) 通り道 tōrimìchi

route map (BRIT) n (for journey) 道路地図 dōrochizù

routine [ru:ti:n'] adj (work) 日常の nichíjō no; (procedure) お決りの o-kímari no
♦n (habits) 習慣 shūkan; (drudgery) 反復作業 hañpukusagyō; (THEATER) お決りの演技 o-kímari nò eñgi

rove [rouv] vt (area, streets) はいかいする haíkai suru

row[1] [rou] n (line of people, things) 列 rétsu; (KNITTING) 段 dáñ; (in boat) こぐ事 kogú kotò
♦vi (in boat) こぐ kogú
♦vt (boat) こぐ kogú
in a row (fig) 一列に ichíretsu ni

row[2] [rau] n (racket) 騒ぎ sáwagi; (noisy quarrel) 口論 kōron; (dispute) 論争 rofísō; (BRIT inf: scolding): **to give someone a row** ...に大目玉を食らわす ...ni ōmedàma wo kuráwasù
♦vi (argue) 口論する kōron suru

rowboat [rou'bout] (US) n ボート bōto

rowdy [rau'di:] adj (person: noisy) 乱暴な rañbō na; (occasion) 騒々しい sōzōshìī

rowing [rou'iŋ] n (sport) ボートレース bōtorēsu

rowing boat (BRIT) n = **rowboat**

royal [rɔi'əl] adj 国王〔女王〕の kokúō〔jō-ō〕 no

Royal Air Force (BRIT) n 英国空軍 eíkokukūgun

royalty [rɔi'əlti:] n (royal persons) 王族 ōzoku; (payment to author) 印税 iñzei

rpm [ɑːrpiːem'] abbr (= revolutions per minute) 毎分回転数 maífunkaiteñsū

RSVP [ɑːresviːpiː'] abbr (= répondez s'il vous plaît) 御返事を請う go-héñji wò kóū

Rt Hon. (BRIT) abbr (= Right Hon-

ourable) 閣下 kákkà

rub [rʌb] vt こする kosúrù
♦n: **to give something a rub** こする kosúrù
to rub one's hands (together) もみ手をする momíde wò suru
to rub someone the wrong way (US) or **to rub someone up the wrong way (BRIT)** 怒らせる okóraserù

rubber [rʌb'əːr] n (substance) ゴム gómù; (BRIT: eraser) 消しゴム keshígomu

rubber band n 輪ゴム wagómu

rubber plant n ゴムの木 gómù no ki

rubbery [rʌb'əːri:] adj (material, substance) ゴムの様な gómù no yō na; (meat, food) 固い katáì

rubbish [rʌb'iʃ] n (waste material) ごみ gomí; (junk) 廃品 haíhin; (fig: pej: nonsense) ナンセンス náñsensu

rubbish bin (BRIT) n ごみ箱 gomíbako

rubbish dump n ごみ捨て場 gomísute-ba

rubble [rʌb'əl] n (debris) がれき garéki; (CONSTR) バラス bárasu

ruble [ru:'bəl] (BRIT **rouble**) n (currency) ルーブル rūburu

rub off vi (paint) こすり取る kosúritorù

rub off on vt fus ...に移る ...ni utsúrù

rub out vt (erase) 消す kesú

ruby [ru:'bi:] n ルビー rúbì

rucksack [rʌk'sæk] n リュックサック ryukkúsakkù

rudder [rʌd'əːr] n (of ship) かじ kajī; (of plane) 方向かじ hōkōda

ruddy [rʌd'i:] adj (face, complexion) 血色の良い kesshóku no yoì; (BRIT: inf: damned) くそったれの kusóttarè no

rude [ru:d] adj (impolite: person, manners, word) 無礼な buréi na; (shocking: word, behavior) 下品な gehín na

rudeness [ru:d'nis] n (impoliteness) 無礼 buréi

rudimentary [ru:dəmən'tə:ri:] adj (equipment, knowledge) 原始的な geñshiteki na

rudiments [ru:'dəmənts] npl (basics) 基本 kihón

rueful [ru:'fəl] adj 悲しい kanáshìī

ruffian [rʌf'i:ən] n ごろつき gorótsuki

ruffle [rʌf'əl] vt (hair) 乱す midásù; (clothes) しわくちゃにする shiwákucha ni surù; (fig: person) 怒らせる okóraserù

rug [rʌg] n (on floor) じゅうたん jútan; (BRIT: blanket) ひざ掛け hizákake

rugby [rʌg'bi:] n (also: **rugby football**) ラグビー rágùbī

rugged [rʌg'id] adj (landscape) 岩だらけ の iwádaràke no; (features) ごつい go-tsúì; (character) 無愛想な buáisō na

rugger [rʌg'ə:r] (BRIT: inf) n ラグビー rágùbī

ruin [ru:'in] n (destruction: of building) 破壊 hakái; (: of hopes, plans) ざ折 zasé-tsu; (downfall) 失墜 shittsúi; (bank-ruptcy) 破産 hasán; (remains: of build-ing) 廃虚 haíkyo

♦vt (destroy: building) 破壊する hakái suru; (: hopes, plans, health) 壊す kowá-sù; (: future) 台無しにする daínashi ni surù; (: person) 失墜させる shittsúi sase-rù; (: financially) 破産に追込む hasán ni oikomù

ruinous [ru:'inəs] adj (expense, interest) 破滅的な hamétsuteki na

ruins [ru:'inz] npl (of building, castle etc) 廃虚 haíkyo

rule [ru:l] n (norm, regulation) 規則 kisó-ku; (government) 君臨 kuńrin; (ruler) 物差し monósashi

♦vt (country, person) 支配する shíhài su-ru

♦vi (leader, monarch etc) 君臨する kuń-rin suru; (LAW) 裁定する saítei suru

as a rule 普通は futsú wà

ruled [ru:ld] adj (paper) けい紙 keíshi

rule out vt (idea, possibility etc) 除外する jogái suru

ruler [ru:'lə:r] n (sovereign) 元首 géńshu; (for measuring) 物差し monósashi

ruling [ru:'liŋ] adj 支配する shíhài suru

♦n (LAW) 決定 kettéi

ruling party 与党 yótò

ruling class 支配階級 shiháikaìkyū

rum [rʌm] n ラム酒 ramúshu

Rumania [ru:mei'ni:ə] n ルーマニア rú-mania

Rumanian [ru:mei'ni:ən] adj ルーマニア の rúmania no; (LING) ルーマニア語の rúmaniagò no

♦n (person) ルーマニア人 rúmaniajìn; (LING) ルーマニア語 rúmaniagò

rumble [rʌm'bəl] n ごう音 góon, とどろ き todóroki

♦vi (make rumbling noise: heavy truck) ごう音を響かせて走る góon wò hibíkasè-te hashírù; (: stomach) 鳴る narú; (: pipes) ゴボゴボいう góbògobo íù; (: thunder) とどろく todórokù

rummage [rʌm'idʒ] vi (search) 引っかき 回して捜す hikkákimawashitè sagásù

rumor [ru:'mə:r] (BRIT **rumour**) n うわ さ uwása

♦vt: *it is rumored that ...* ...だとうわ さされている ...dá tò uwása sarete irù

rump [rʌmp] n (of animal) しり shirí; (of group, political party) 残党 zańtō

rump steak n ランプステーキ rańpusu-tēki

rumpus [rʌm'pəs] n 騒ぎ sawági

run [rʌn] n (fast pace) 駆け足 kakéàshi; (for exercise) ジョギング jogíngu; (in car) ドライブ dóràibu; (distance trav-eled) 行程 kótei; (journey) 区間 kukáń; (series) 継続 keízoku; (SKI) ゲレンデ ge-rénde; (CRICKET, BASEBALL) 得点 tokúten; (THEATER) 上演期間 jōenkikàn; (in tights, stockings) ほころび ho-kórobi

♦vb (pt **ran**, pp **run**)

♦vt (race, distance) 走る hashírù; (oper-ate: business, hotel) 経営する keíei suru; (: competition, course) 行う okónaù; (: house) ...の切盛りをする ...no kirímori wò suru; (COMPUT) 走らせる hashíra-serù; (pass: hand) 通す tōsù; (water) 出す dásù; (bath) ...に水をはる ...ni mizú wò hárù; (PRESS: feature) 載せる nosérù

♦vi (move quickly) 走る hashírù; (flee) 逃げる nigérù; (work: machine) 作動する sadō suru; (bus, train: operate) 動く ugó-kù; (: travel) 走る hashírù; (continue: play) 上演される jōen sarerù; (: contract) 継続する keízoku suru; (flow: river, liq-uid) 流れる nagárerù; (colors) 落ちる o-

chírù; (washing) 色落ちする iróochi suru; (in election) 立候補する rikkóho suru; (nose) 鼻水が出る hanámizu ga derù

there was a run on ... (meat, tickets) 人々は...を買いに殺到した hitóbìto wa ...wo kaí nì sattó shità

in the long run 行く行く（は）yukú-yuku (wà)

on the run 逃亡中で tóbōchū de

I'll run you to the station 駅まで車で送ろう ékì made kurúma dè okúrò

to run a risk 危険を冒す kikén wò okásù

run about/around *vi* (children) はしゃぎ回る hashágimawarù

run across *vt fus* (find) 偶然に見付ける gűzen nì mitsúkerù

run away *vi* (from home, situation) 逃げる nigérù

runaway [rʌn'əwei] *adj* (horse, truck) 暴走の bósō no; (person) 逃走中の tósōchū no

run down *vt* (production, factory) ...の規模を縮小する ...no kíbō wo shukúshō suru; (AUT: person) ひく hikú; (criticize) けなす kenásù

to be run down (person: tired) へとへとになっている hetóheto nì natté irù

rung [rʌŋ] *pp* of **ring**

♦*n* (of ladder) 一段 ichídàn

run in (*BRIT*) *vt* (car) ...のならし運転をする ...no naráshiuǹten wo suru

run into *vt fus* (meet: person, trouble) ...に出会う ...ni deàu; (collide with) ...にぶつかる ...ni butsúkarù

runner [rʌn'əːr] *n* (in race: person) 競走の選手 kyósō nì seńshu, ランナー ráǹnā; (: horse) 競走馬 kyósōba; (on sledge) 滑り木 subérigi, ランナー ráǹnā; (for drawer etc) レール rḕru

runner bean (*BRIT*) *n* サヤインゲン sayáiǹgen

runner-up [rʌnəːrʌp'] *n* 第2位入賞者 daí ni-i nyūshōsha

running [rʌn'iŋ] *n* (sport) ジョギング jogíngu; (of business, organization) 経営 keíei

♦*adj* (water) 水道の suídō no

to be in/out of the running for something ...の候補者である〔でなくなっている〕...no kóhoshà de árù〔de nakúnatte irù〕

6 days running 連続6日間 reńzoku muikakàn

running commentary *n* 生中継 namáchūkei

running costs *npl* (of car, machine etc) 維持費 ijíhi

runny [rʌn'i:] *adj* (honey, egg) 緩い yurúì; (nose) 垂れる tarérù; (eyes) 目やにの出る meyáni nò dérù

run off *vt* (water) ...から流れ落ちる ...kara nagáreochirù; (copies) 印刷する ińsatsu suru

♦*vi* (person, animal) 逃げる nigérù

run-of-the-mill [rʌnəvðəmil'] *adj* (ordinary) ごく普通の gókù futsű no

run out *vi* (person) 走って出る hashítte derù; (liquid) 流れ出る nagárederù; (lease, passport) 切れる kirérù; (money) なくなる nakúnarù

run out of *vt fus* (money, time, ideas) ...がなくなる ...ga nakúnarù

run over *vt* (AUT) ひく hikú

♦*vt fus* (revise) おさらいする o-sárai suru

runt [rʌnt] *n* (animal) 未熟児 mijúkujì; (*pej*: person) どちび dochíbi

run through *vt fus* (instructions) ...に目を通す ...ni mé wo tósù; (rehearse, practice: play) 一通り練習する hitótōri reńshū suru

run up *vt* (debt) ...がかさむ ...ga kasámù

to run up against (difficulties) ...にぶつかる ...ni butsúkarù

run-up [rʌn'ʌp] *n* (*BRIT*): *run-up to* (election etc) ...への準備期間 ...é nò juńbikikàn

runway [rʌn'wei] *n* (AVIAT) 滑走路 kassórò

rupee [ru:'pi:] *n* (currency) ルピー rúpī

rupture [rʌp'tʃəːr] *n* (MED) ヘルニア herúnia

rural [ru:r'əl] *adj* (area) 田舎の ináka no; (economy) 地方の chíhō no

ruse [ru:z] *n* 策略 sakúryaku

rush [rʌʃ] n (hurry) 大急ぎ ṓisogi; (COMM: sudden demand) 急激な需要 kyū́geki nà juyṓ; (of water, current) 奔流 hoñryū; (of feeling, emotion) 高まり takámari; (BOT) イグサ igúsa
♦vt (hurry) 急がせる isógaserù
♦vi (person) 急ぐ isógù; (air, water) 速く流れる háyaku nagárerù

rush hour n ラッシュアワー rasshúawầ

rusk [rʌsk] n (biscuit) ラスク rásùku

Russia [rʌ́ʃə] n ロシア róshìa

Russian [rʌ́ʃən] adj ロシアの róshìa no; (LING) ロシア語の roshíagò no
♦n (person) ロシア人 roshíajìn; (LING) ロシア語 roshíagò

rust [rʌst] n さび sabí
♦vi (iron, machine etc) さびる sabírù

rustic [rʌ́stik] adj (style, furniture) 田舎風の inákafū no

rustle [rʌ́səl] vi (leaves) かさかさいう kásàkasa iú
♦vt (paper) かさかさ動かす kásàkasa ugókasù; (US: cattle) 盗む nusúmù

rustproof [rʌ́st'pruːf] adj (car, machine) さびない sabínaì

rusty [rʌ́sti] adj (car) さびた sabíta; (fig: skill) ...の勘が鈍くなった ...no kañ gà níbùku natta

rut [rʌt] n (groove) わだち wadáchi; (ZOOL: season) 発情期 hatsújòki
to be in a rut 型にはまっている katá nì hamátte irù

ruthless [rʌ́θlis] adj (person) 血も涙もない chí mò namída mò náì; (action) 残酷な zañkoku na

rye [rai] n (cereal) ライ麦 raímugì

rye bread n ライパン raípañ

S

Sabbath [sæb'əθ] n (Jewish) 土曜日 doyṓbì; (Christian) 日曜日 nichíyòbi

sabbatical [səbæt'ikəl] n (also: **sabbatical year**) 一年休暇 ichíneñ kyū́ka ◇7年置きに大学教授などに与えられる1年の長期有給休暇 nanáneñ okí nì daígakukyòju nádò ni atáerarerù ichíneñ no chṓkyu-

kyū́kyùka

sabotage [sæb'ətɑːʒ] n 破壊工作 hakáikòsaku
♦vt (machine, building) 破壊する hakái suru; (plan, meeting) 妨害する bṓgai suru

saccharin(e) [sæk'əːrin] n サッカリン sakkárìn

sachet [sæʃei'] n (of shampoo, sugar, etc) 小袋 kobúkùro ◇一回分ずつのシャンプー、砂糖などを入れた小さな包 ikkáìbun zutsu no sháñpū, satṓ nádò wo iréta chíìsana tsutsúmi

sack [sæk] n (bag: for flour, coal, grain, etc) 袋 fukúro
♦vt (dismiss) 首にする kubí ni surù; (plunder) 略奪する ryakúdatsu suru
to get the sack 首になる kubí ni narù

sacking [sæk'iŋ] n (dismissal) 解雇 káìko; (material) ズック zúkkù

sacrament [sæk'rəmənt] n (ceremony: Protestant) 聖礼典 seíreiteñ; (: Catholic) 秘跡 hiséki

sacred [sei'krid] adj (of religion: music, history, writings) 宗教の shū́kyō no; (holy: animal, building, memory) 神聖な shiñsei na

sacrifice [sæk'rəfais] n (offering of someone/something) 犠牲 giséi; (thing/person offered) いけにえ ikénie
♦vt (animal) 殺す korósu; (fig: human lives, health, career) 犠牲にする giséi ni surù

sacrilege [sæk'rəlidʒ] n 冒とく bṓtoku

sacrosanct [sæk'rousæŋkt] adj (also fig) 神聖な shiñsei na

sad [sæd] adj (unhappy: person, day, story, news) 悲しい kanáshii; (: look) 悲しそうな kanáshisō na; (deplorable: state of affairs) 嘆かわしい nagékawashiì

saddle [sæd'əl] n (for horse) くら kurá; (of bicycle) サドル sadoru
♦vt (horse) ...にくらを付ける ...ni kurá wò tsukérù
to be saddled with (inf) ...の重荷を負わされる ...no omóni wò owásarerù

saddlebag [sæd'əlbæg] n (on bicycle) サ

ドルバッグ sadórubaggù
sadism [sei'dizəm] *n* サディズム sadízù-
mu
sadistic [sədis'tik] *adj* サディスティック
な sadísutikkù na
sadly [sæd'li:] *adv* (unhappily) 悲しそう
に kanáshisò ni; (unfortunately) 残念な
がら zañneñnagara; (seriously: mistaken, neglected) ひどく hídòku
sadly lacking (in) 残念ながら (...が)
ない zañneñnagara (...ga) náì
sadness [sæd'nis] *n* 悲しみ kanáshimi
sae [eseii'] *abbr* (= *stamped addressed
envelope*) 返信用封筒 heñshin-yō fútò ◇
宛先を書き，切手を張った物を指す até-
saki wò kákì, kitté wò hattá mono wò
sásù
safari [səfɑː'ri:] *n* サファリ sáfàri
safe [seif] *adj* (out of danger) 安全な場所
にいる〔ある〕añzen na bashò ni irú
〔árù〕; (not dangerous, sure: place) 安全
な añzen na; (unharmed: return, journey)
無事な bují na; (without risk: bet, subject, appointment) 安全な añzen na, 安心
できる añshin dekirù; (: seat in parliament) 落選する恐れのない rakúsen suru
osore nò náì
♦*n* (for valuables, money) 金庫 kíñko
safe from (attack) ...される心配のない
場所にいる〔ある〕...saréru shiñpai no
náì bâshò ni irú 〔árù〕
safe and sound (return, sleep, etc) 無事
で bují de
(just) to be on the safe side 念のため
に neñ no tame nì
safe-conduct [seif'kɑːn'dʌkt] *n* (right
to pass) 通行許可 tsūkōkyokà
safe-deposit [seif'dipæːzit] *n* (vault) 貸
金庫室 kashíkìñkoshitsu; (*also*: **safe
deposit box**) 貸金庫 kashíkìñko
safeguard [seif'gɑːrd] *n* 保護手段 hogó-
shudàn
♦*vt* 保護する hógò suru
safekeeping [seifki:'piŋ] *n* 保管 hokán
safely [seif'li:] *adv* (without risk:
assume, say) 安心して añshin shite;
(without mishap: drive) 安全に añzen ni;
(arrive) 無事に bují ni

safety [seif'ti:] *n* 安全 añzen
safety belt *n* 安全ベルト añzenberùto,
シートベルト shítoberùto
safety pin *n* 安全ピン añzeñpin
safety valve *n* 安全弁 añzeñben
saffron [sæf'rən] *n* (powder) サフラン
sáfùran
sag [sæg] *vi* (breasts, hem) 垂れ下がる
tarésagarù; (roof) 凹む kubómu
saga [sæg'ə] *n* (long story, *also fig*) 長編
物語 chōheñmonogatàri
sage [seidʒ] *n* (herb) セージ sèji; (wise
man) 賢人 keñjiñ
Sagittarius [sædʒite:r'i:əs] *n* (sign of
Zodiac) 射手座 itéza
Sahara [səher:'ə] *n*: *the Sahara (Desert)* サハラ砂漠 sahára sabàku
said [sed] *pt, pp of* **say**
sail [seil] *n* (on boat) 帆 hó; (trip): *to go
for a sail* ヨットに乗る yóttò ni noru
♦*vt* (boat) 操縦する sōjū suru
♦*vi* (travel: ship) 航海する kókai suru;
(SPORT) ヨットに乗る yóttò ni norú;
(begin voyage: ship) 出航する shukkó
suru; (: passenger) 船で出発する fúnè de
shuppátsu suru
they sailed into Copenhagen 彼らはコ
ペンハーゲンに入港した kárèra wa ko-
pénhàgen ni nyúkò shità
sailboat [seil'bout] (*US*) *n* ヨット yóttò
sailing [sei'liŋ] *n* (SPORT) ヨット遊び
yottóasòbi
to go sailing ヨットに乗る yóttò ni norú, ヨット遊びをする yottóasòbi wo suru
sailing boat *n* ヨット yóttò
sailing ship *n* 帆船 hañsen
sailor [sei'lər] *n* (seaman) 船乗り funánòri
sail through *vt fus* (*fig*: exams, interview etc) ...に楽々と合格する ...ni rakú-
rakù to gókaku suru
saint [seint] *n* (*also fig*) 聖人 sêjin
saintly [seint'li:] *adj* (person, life,
expression) 聖人の様な sêjin no yó nà
sake [seik] *n*: *for the sake of some-
one/something* ...のために ...no tamé nì
salad [sæl'əd] *n* サラダ sáràda
salad bowl *n* サラダボール sarádabòru

salad cream (*BRIT*) n マヨネーズ mayónēzu

salad dressing n サラダドレッシング saràdadoresshìngu

salami [səlɑː'miː] n サラミ sárãmi

salary [sæl'əriː] n 給料 kyúryô

sale [seil] n (act of selling: commercial goods etc) 販売 hañbai; (: house, land etc) 売却 baíkyaku; (at reduced prices) 安売り yasúuri, セール sḕru; (auction) 競売 kyóbai

「for sale」 売物 urímono

on sale 発売中 hatsúbaichū

on sale or return (goods) 委託販売で itákuhañbai de

saleroom [seil'ruːm] *BRIT* n = **salesroom**

sales [seilz] npl (total amount sold) 売上 uríage

sales clerk (*BRIT* **sales assistant**) n 店員 teñ-in

salesman [seilz'mən] (pl **salesmen**) n (in shop) 男子店員 dañshiteñ-in; (representative) セールスマン sḕrusumàn

salesroom [seilz'ruːm] (*US*) n 競売場 kyóbaijò

saleswoman [seilz'wumən] (pl **saleswomen**) n 女子店員 joshíteñ-in

salient [sei'liːənt] adj (features, points) 重要な júyô na

saliva [səlaiv'ə] n だ液 daéki

sallow [sæl'ou] adj (complexion) 血色の悪い kesshóku nò warúi

salmon [sæm'ən] n inv サケ sákè

salon [səlɑːn'] n (hairdressing salon, beauty salon) 美容院 biyóin

saloon [səluːn'] n (*US*: bar) 酒場 sakába; (*BRIT*: AUT) セダン sédàn; (ship's lounge) 広間 hírðma

salt [sɔːlt] n 塩 shiő

♦vt (preserve: fish, beef, etc) 塩漬にする shiózukè ni suru; (put salt on) ...に塩を掛ける ...ni shiő wð kakérù

salt cellar n 塩入れ shiő-ire

saltwater [sɔːlt'wɔːtər] adj (fish, plant) 海水の kaísui no

salty [sɔːl'tiː] adj しょっぱい shoppái

salutary [sæl'jətɛːriː] adj (lesson, reminder) ためになる tamé ni narù

salute [səluːt'] n (MIL) 敬礼 keírei; (with guns) 礼砲 reíhō; (gen: greeting) あいさつ áìsatsu

♦vt (MIL) ...に敬礼する ...ni keírei suru; (fig) ...に敬意を現す ...ni kếì wo aráwasù

salvage [sæl'vidʒ] n (action: gen) 救助作業 kyúĵo sagyð; (: of shipwreck) 海難救助作業 kaínan kyúĵo sagyð; (things saved) サルベージ sarúbēji, 救助された物 kyúĵo sareta monð

♦vt 救助する kyúĵo suru; (fig: situation etc) 収拾する shúshū suru

salvation [sælvei'ʃən] n (REL) 霊魂の救い reíkon no sukúi; (economic etc) 救済 kyúsai

Salvation Army n 救世軍 kyúseigùn

salvo [sæl'vou] n (in battle) 一斉射撃 isséishagèki; (ceremonial) 一斉祝砲 isséishukùhō

same [seim] adj 同じ onáji

♦pron: **the same** 同じ物 onáji monð

the same book as ...と同じ本 ...to onáji hoñ

at the same time (at the same moment) 同時に dðjì ni; (yet) とはいえ tố wà ie

all/just the same それにしても soré ni shite mð

to do the same (as someone) (...と) 同じ事をする (...to) onáji koto wð suru

the same to you! お前もだ omáe mo dã ◇侮辱を返す時に言う bujóku wð kaésu toki nì iű

sample [sæm'pəl] n (MED: blood/urine sample) 検体 keñtai, サンプル sáñpuru; (of work, merchandise) 見本 mihóñ, サンプル sáñpuru

♦vt (food) 試食する shishóku suru; (drink) 試飲する shiíñ suru

sanatoria [sænətɔːr'iːə] npl of **sanatorium**

sanatorium [sænətɔːr'iːəm] (pl **sanatoria**) n = **sanitarium**

sanctify [sæŋk'təfai] vt 神聖にする shiñsei ni surù

sanctimonious [sæŋktəmou'niːəs] adj

(person, remarks) 宗教心を装う shúkyō-shiǹ wo yosóoù

sanction [sæŋk'ʃən] n (approval) お墨付き osúmitsùki, 認可 nínka

♦vt (give approval to) 認可する nínka suru

sanctions [sæŋk'ʃənz] npl (severe measures) 制裁処置 seísaishochì

sanctity [sæŋk'titi:] n 神聖さ shínseisa

sanctuary [sæŋk'tʃuːeːri:] n (also: **bird sanctuary**) 鳥類保護区 chōruihogokù, サンクチュアリ saǹkuchùari; (place of refuge) 避難所 hináǹjo; (REL: in church) 内陣 naíjin

sand [sænd] n (material, fine grains) 砂 sunà; (beach: also: **sands**) 砂浜 sunáhama

♦vt (piece of furniture: also: **sand down**) 紙やすりで磨く kamíyasùri de migáku

sandal [sæn'dəl] n (shoe) サンダル saǹdaru

sandbox [sænd'bɑːks] US n (for children) 砂場 sunába

sandcastle [sænd'kæsəl] n 砂の城 suná no shirò

sand dune n 砂丘 sakyǔ

sandpaper [sænd'peipəːr] n 紙やすり kamíyasùri, サンドペーパー saǹdopèpā

sandpit [sænd'pit] (BRIT) n = **sandbox**

sandstone [sænd'stoun] n 砂岩 ságàn

sandwich [sænd'witʃ] n サンドイッチ saǹdoitchì

♦vt: **sandwiched between** ...の間に挟まれて ...no aída nì hasámarète

cheese/ham sandwich チーズ〔ハム〕サンドイッチ chízù〔hámù〕saǹdoitchì

sandwich course (BRIT) n サンドイッチコース saǹdoitchikōsu ◇勉強と現場実習を交互に行う課程 beǹkyō tò geǹbajisshū wo kōgo nì okónaù katéi

sandy [sæn'di:] adj (beach) 砂の sunà no; (color) 砂色の suná-iro no

sane [sein] adj (person) 正気の shōki no; (sensible: action, system) 合理的な gōriteki na

sang [sæŋ] pt of **sing**

sanitarium [sæniteːr'iːəm] (US) n 療養所 ryōyōjo, サナトリウム sanátoriùmu

sanitary [sæn'iteːri:] adj (system, arrangements, inspector) 衛生の eísei no; (clean) 衛生的な eíseiteki na

sanitary napkin (BRIT **sanitary towel**) n 生理用ナプキン seíriyō napùkin

sanitation [sænitei'ʃən] n (in house) 衛生設備 eíseisetsùbi; (in town) 下水道設備 gesúidōsetsùbi

sanitation department (US) n 清掃局 seísōkyòku

sanity [sæn'iti:] n (quality of being sane: of person) 正気 shōki; (common sense: of suggestion etc) 合理性 gōrisei

sank [sæŋk] pt of **sink**

Santa Claus [sæn'tə klɔ:z] n サンタクロース saǹtakurōsu

sap [sæp] n (of plants) 樹液 juéki

♦vt (strength, confidence) 失わせていく ushínawasete ikù

sapling [sæp'liŋ] n 苗木 naégi

sapphire [sæf'aiəːr] n サファイア safáia

sarcasm [sɑːr'kæzəm] n 皮肉 hiníku

sarcastic [sɑːrkæs'tik] adj (person) いやみ好きな iyámizùki na; (remark, smile) 皮肉な hiníku na

sardine [sɑːrdiːn'] n イワシ iwáshi

Sardinia [sɑːrdin'iːə] n サルディニア島 sarúdiniatō

sardonic [sɑːrdɑːn'ik] adj (smile) あざける様な azákeru yō na

sari [sɑː'ri:] n サリー sárī

sash [sæʃ] n (Western) サッシュ sásshù; (Japanese) 帯 óbì

sat [sæt] pt, pp of **sit**

Satan [sei'tən] n 大魔王 daímaō, サタン sátàn

satchel [sætʃ'əl] n (child's) かばん kabáñ

satellite [sæt'əlait] n (body in space) 衛星 eísei; (communications satellite) 通信衛星 tsūshin-eisèi

satellite dish n パラボラアンテナ parábora aǹtena

satin [sæt'ən] n サテン sátèn

♦adj サテンの sátèn no

satire [sæt'aiəːr] n (form of humor) 風刺 fúshi; (novel) 風刺小説 fúshishōsètsu; (play) 風刺劇 fúshigekì

satirical [sətir'ikəl] adj (remarks, draw-

ings etc) 風刺の fúshi no

satisfaction [sætisfæk'ʃən] *n* (pleasure) 満足 mánzoku; (refund, apology etc) 謝罪 shazai

satisfactory [sætisfæk'tə:ri:] *adj* (patient's condition) 良い yóì; (results, progress) 満足できる mánzoku dekiru

satisfy [sæt'isfai] *vt* (please) 満足させる mánzoku saserù; (meet: needs, demand) ...に応じる ...ni ōjirù; (convince) 納得させる nattóku saserù

satisfying [sæt'isfaiiŋ] *adj* (meal, job, feeling) 満足な mánzoku na

saturate [sætʃ'ə:reit] *vt*: *to saturate (with)* (*also fig*) (...で)一杯にする (...de) ippái ni surù

saturation [sætʃərei'ʃən] *n* (*also fig*) 飽和状態 hōwajōtai

Saturday [sæt'ə:rdei] *n* 土曜日 doyóbi

sauce [sɔːs] *n* (sweet, savory) ソース sōsù

saucepan [sɔːs'pæn] *n* ソースパン sōsupàn

saucer [sɔː'sə:r] *n* 受皿 ukézàra, ソーサー sōsā

saucy [sɔːs'iː] *adj* (cheeky) ずうずうしい zūzūshiī

Saudi [sau'diː]: *Saudi Arabia n* サウジアラビア saújiaràbia

Saudi (Arabian) *adj* サウジアラビアの saújiaràbia no

sauna [sɔː'nə] *n* サウナ sáùna

saunter [sɔːn'tə:r] *vi* のんびりと歩く noñbirī to árùku

sausage [sɔː'sidʒ] *n* ソーセージ sōséji

sausage roll *n* ソーセージパン sōséjipàñ

sauté [sɔːtei'] *adj*: *sauté potatoes* フライポテト furáipotèto

savage [sæv'idʒ] *adj* (cruel, fierce: dog) どうもうな dōmō na; (: attack) 残忍な zañnin na; (primitive: tribe) 未開な mikái na
♦*n* 野蛮人 yabáñjiñ

savagery [sæv'idʒri:] *n* 残忍さ zanninsa

save [seiv] *vt* (rescue: someone, someone's life, marriage) 救う sukúù; (economize on: money, time) 節約する setsúyaku suru; (put by: receipts etc) 取って置く tóttè oku; (: money) 蓄える takúwaeru;

(COMPUT) 格納する kakúnō suru, セーブする sébu suru; (avoid: work, trouble) 省く habúkù; (keep: seat) 確保する kákùho suru; (SPORT: shot, ball) セーブする sébu suru
♦*vi* (*also*: **save up**) 貯金する chokín suru
♦*n* (SPORT) セーブ sébu
♦*prep* (except) (...を)除いて (...wo) nozóite

saving [sei'viŋ] *n* (on price etc) 節約 setsúyaku
♦*adj*: *the saving grace of something* ...の唯一の長所 ...no yúìtsu no chōsho

savings [sei'viŋz] *npl* (money) 貯金 chokín

savings account *n* 普通預金口座 futsūyokinkōza

savings bank *n* 普通銀行 futsūgiñkō

savior [seiv'jə:r] (*BRIT* **saviour**) *n* (gen) 救い主 sukúìnùshi; (REL) 救世主 kyúseìshu

savor [sei'və:r] (*BRIT* **savour**) *vt* (food, drink, experience) 味わう ajíwaù

savory [sei'və:ri:] (*BRIT* **savoury**) *adj* (dish: not sweet: spicy) ぴりっとした pírìttò shita; (: salt-flavored) 塩味の shióaji no

saw [sɔː] *n* (tool) のこぎり nokógirì
♦*vt* (*pt* **sawed**, *pp* **sawed** *or* **sawn**) のこぎりで切る nokógirì de kírù
♦*pt* of **see**

sawdust [sɔː'dʌst] *n* のこくず nokókuzù

sawed-off [sɔːd'ɔːf] *n* (*US*): *sawed-off shotgun* 短身散弾銃 tañshin sandañjū ◊ のこぎりで銃身を短く切った散弾銃 nokógirì de júshin wò mijíkaku kittà sandañjū

sawmill [sɔː'mil] *n* 製材所 seízaisho

sawn-off [sɔːn'ɔːf] *adj* (*BRIT*) = **sawed-off**

saxophone [sæk'səfoun] *n* サキソホーン sakísohòn

say [sei] *n*: *to have one's say* 意見を言う íkèn wo iú
♦*vt* (*pt*, *pp* **said**) 言う iú
to have a/some say in something ...についてある程度の発言権がある ...ni tsúìte áru teidò no hatsúgeñken ga árù

to say yes/no 承知する〔しない〕shóchi suru〔shinaї〕

could you say that again? もう一度言ってくれませんか mố ichidồ itté kuremaseň ka

that is to say つまり tsúmari

that goes without saying それは言うまでもない soré wà iú made mo naї

saying [sei'iŋ] *n* (proverb) ことわざ kotówaza; (words of wisdom) 格言 kakúgen; (often repeated phrase) 愛用の言葉 aíyō no kotoba

scab [skæb] *n* (on wound) かさぶた kasábuta; (*pej*: strike-breaker) スト破り sutó-yabùri

scaffold [skæf'əld] *n* (for execution) 死刑台 shikéidai; (for building etc) = **scaffolding**

scaffolding [skæf'əldiŋ] *n* 足場 ashíba

scald [skɔːld] *n* やけど yakédo ◊熱湯や蒸気などによるやけどを指す nettố yà jồkì nado ni yôrù yakédo wò sásù

◆*vt* (burn: skin) やけどさせる yakédo saserù

scale [skeil] *n* (*gen*: set of numbers) 目盛 memóri; (of salaries, fees etc) 表 hyố; (of fish) うろこ uróko; (MUS) 音階 oňkai; (of map, model) 縮小率 shukúshōrìtsu; (size, extent) 規模 kíbo

◆*vt* (mountain, tree) 登る nobórù

on a large scale 大規模で daíkibo de

scale of charges 料金表 ryókinhyồ

scale down *vt* 縮小する shukúshō suru

scales [skeilz] *npl* (for weighing) 量り hakári

scallop [skɑːl'əp] *n* (ZOOL) ホタテガイ hotátegài; (SEWING) スカラップ sukárappù

scalp [skælp] *n* 頭の皮膚 atáma no hifù, 頭皮 tôhi

◆*vt* ...の頭皮をはぐ ...no tốhì wo hágù

scalpel [skæl'pəl] *n* メス mésù

scamper [skæm'pəːr] *vi*: *to scamper away/off* (child, animal) ぱたぱた走って行く pátapata hashítte ikù

scampi [skæm'piː] *npl* エビフライ ebífurài

scan [skæn] *vt* (examine: horizon) 見渡す miwátasu; (glance at quickly: newspaper) ...にさっと目を通す ...ni sáttồ mé wồ tốsù; (TV, RADAR) 走査する sốsa suru

◆*n* (MED) スキャン sukyán

scandal [skæn'dəl] *n* (shocking event) 醜聞 shûbun, スキャンダル sukyáňdaru; (defamatory: reports, rumors) 陰口 kagéguchi; (gossip) うわさ uwása; (*fig*: disgrace) 恥ずべき事 hazúbeki kotố

scandalize [skæn'dəlaiz] *vt* 慣慨させる fuňgai saserù

scandalous [skæn'dələs] *adj* (disgraceful, shocking: behavior etc) 破廉恥な harénchi na

Scandinavian [skændənei'viːən] *adj* スカンディナビアの sukándinabìa no

scant [skænt] *adj* (attention) 不十分な fujûbun na

scanty [skæn'tiː] *adj* (meal) ささやかな sasáyàka na; (underwear) 極めて小さい kiwámète chísaì

scapegoat [skeip'gout] *n* 身代り migáwari

scar [skɑːr] *n* (on skin: *also fig*) 傷跡 kizúato

◆*vt* (*also fig*) 傷跡を残す kizúato wò nokósù

scarce [skeːrs] *adj* (rare, not plentiful) 少ない sukúnaї

to make oneself scarce (*inf*) 消えうせる kiéuserù

scarcely [skeːrs'liː] *adv* (hardly) ほとんど...ない hotóňdo ...naї; (with numbers: barely) わずかに wázùka ni

scarcity [skeːr'sitiː] *n* (shortage) 不足 fusóku

scare [skeːr] *n* (fright) 恐怖 kyốfu; (public fear) 恐慌 kyốkō

◆*vt* (frighten) 怖がらす kowágarasù

bomb scare 爆弾騒ぎ bakúdan sawàgi

to scare someone stiff ...に怖い思いをさせる ...ni kowái omoì wo sasérù

scarecrow [skeːr'krou] *n* かかし kakáshi

scared [skeːrd] *adj*: *to be scared* 怖がる kowágarù

scare off/away *vt* おどかして追払う o-

dókashite oiharaù

scarf [skɑːrf] (*pl* **scarfs** *or* **scarves**) *n* (long) マフラー máfūrā; (square) スカーフ sukáfù

scarlet [skɑːr'lit] *adj* (color) ひ色 hiíro

scarlet fever *n* しょう紅熱 shōkōnetsu

scarves [skɑːrvz] *npl of* **scarf**

scary [sker'iː] (*inf*) *adj* 怖い kowáî

scathing [skei'ðiŋ] *adj* (comments, attack) 辛らつな shíratsu na

scatter [skæt'əːr] *vt* (spread: seeds, papers) まき散らす makíchirasù; (put to flight: flock of birds, crowd of people) 追散らす oíchirasù

♦*vi* (crowd) 散る chirú

scatterbrained [skæt'əːrbreind] (*inf*) *adj* (forgetful) おつむの弱い o-tsúmù no yowáî

scavenger [skæv'indʒəːr] *n* (person) くず拾い kuzúhiròi

scenario [sinɛːr'iːou] *n* (THEATER, CINEMA) 脚本 kyakúhon, シナリオ shinário; (*fig*) 筋書 sujígaki

scene [siːn] *n* (THEATER, *fig*) 場 ba, シーン shíìn; (of crime, accident) 現場 geńba; (sight, view) 景色 késhìki; (fuss) 騒ぎ sáwàgi

scenery [siː'nəːriː] *n* (THEATER) 大道具 ōdògu; (landscape) 景色 késhìki

scenic [siː'nik] *adj* (picturesque) 景色の美しい késhìki no utsúkushiî

scent [sent] *n* (pleasant smell) 香り kaóri; (track) 通った後のにおい tôtta átò no nióì; (*fig*) 手がかり tegákàri; (liquid perfume) 香水 kốsui

scepter [sep'təːr] (*BRIT* **sceptre**) *n* しゃく shaku

sceptic [skep'tik] (*BRIT*) *n* = **skeptic** *etc*

schedule [skedʒ'uːl] *n* (of trains, buses) 時間割 jikánwari; (list of events and times) 時刻表 jikōkuhyō; (list of prices, details etc) 表 hyố

♦*vt* (timetable, visit) 予定する yotéi suru

on schedule (trains, buses) 定刻通りに teíkokudòri ni; (project etc) 予定通りに yotéidòri ni

to be ahead of schedule 予定時間より

早い yotéijikàn yórì hayáî

to be behind schedule 予定時間に遅れる yotéijikàn ni okúrerù

scheduled flight [skedʒ'uːld-] *n* 定期便 teíkibin

schematic [skiːmæt'ik] *adj* (diagram etc) 模式的な moshíkiteki na

scheme [skiːm] *n* (personal plan, idea) もくろみ mokúromi; (dishonest plan, plot) 陰謀 iñbō; (formal plan: pension plan etc) 計画 keíkaku, 案 áñ; (arrangement) 配置 haíchi

♦*vi* (intrigue) たくらむ takúramù

scheming [skiː'miŋ] *adj* 腹黒い haráguroî

♦*n* たくらむ事 takúramù kotó

schism [skiz'əm] *n* 分裂 buńretsu

schizophrenic [skitsəfren'ik] *adj* 精神分裂症の seíshinbunretsushō no

scholar [skɑːl'əːr] *n* (pupil) 学習者 gakúshūsha; (learned person) 学者 gakúsha

scholarly [skɑːl'əːrliː] *adj* (text, approach) 学問的な gakúmonteki na; (person) 博学的な hakúgakuteki na

scholarship [skɑːl'əːrʃip] *n* (academic knowledge) 学問 gakúmon; (grant) 奨学金 shốgakukìn

school [skuːl] *n* (place where children learn: *gen*) 学校 gakkố; (*also:* **elementary school**) 小学校 shốgakkố; (*also:* **secondary school**: lower) 中学校 chúgakkố; (: higher) 高(等学)校 kố(tốgak)kō; (*US:* university) 大学 daígaku

♦*cpd* 学校の gakkố no

school age *n* 学齢 gakúrei

schoolbook [skuːl'buk] *n* 教科書 kyốkashò

schoolboy [skuːl'bɔi] *n* 男子生徒 dańshiseìto

schoolchildren [skuːl'tʃildrən] *npl* 生徒 seíto

schooldays [skuːl'deiz] *npl* 学校時代 gakkốjidài

schoolgirl [skuːl'gəːrl] *n* 女子生徒 joshíseìto

schooling [skuːl'liŋ] *n* (education at school) 学校教育 gakkốkyồiku

schoolmaster [skuːl'mæstəːr] *n* 教員

kyṓshi, 教員 kyṓin, 先生 seńsei ◇男子教員 dańshikyṓin

schoolmistress [sku:l'mistris] *n* 教師 kyṓshi, 教員 kyṓin, 先生 seńsei ◇女子教員 joshíkyṓin

schoolteacher [sku:l'ti:tʃər] *n* 教師 kyṓshi, 教員 kyṓin, 先生 seńsei ◇男女を問わず使う dáñjo wo tṓwàzu tsukáù

schooner [sku:'nə:r] *n* (ship) 帆船 hańsen

sciatica [saiæt'ikə] *n* 座骨神経痛 zakṓtsushinkeítsū

science [sai'əns] *n* (study of natural things) 科学 kágàku; (branch of such knowledge) ...学 ...gàku

science fiction *n* 空想科学物語 kūsōkagakumonogatàri, SF esuefu

scientific [saiəntif'ik] *adj* (research, instruments) 科学の kágàku no

scientist [sai'əntist] *n* 科学者 kagákushà

scintillating [sin'təleitiŋ] *adj* (*fig*: conversation, wit, smile) 輝く様な kagáyakù yō na

scissors [siz'ə:rz] *npl* (*also*: **a pair of scissors**) はさみ hasámi

scoff [ska:f] *vt* (*BRIT*: *inf*: eat) がつがつ食う gátsùgatsu kúù
♦*vi*: **to scoff (at)** (mock) ...をあざける ...wo azákerù

scold [skould] *vt* しかる shikárù

scone [skoun] *n* スコーン sukṓn ◇小さなホットケーキの一種 chíisa na hottṓkèki no ísshū

scoop [sku:p] *n* (measuring scoop: for flour etc) スコップ sukóppù; (for ice cream) サーバー sầbầ; (*PRESS*) スクープ sukṓpù

scoop out *vt* すくい出す sukúidasù

scoop up *vt* すくい上げる sukúiagerù

scooter [sku:'tə:r] *n* (*also*: **motor scooter**) スクーター sukū̀tầ; (toy) スクーター sukū̀tầ ◇片足を乗せて走る遊び道具 katáashi wo nosetè hashírù asóbidṑgu

scope [skoup] *n* (opportunity) 機会 kikái; (range: of plan, undertaking) 範囲 háñ-i; (: of person) 能力 nōryoku

scorch [sko:rtʃ] *vt* (clothes) 焦がす kogásù; (earth, grass) 枯らす karásù

score [sko:r] *n* (total number of points etc) 得点 tokúteñ, スコア sukṓà; (*MUS*) 楽譜 gakúfu; (twenty) 20 níjū̀
♦*vt* (goal, point, mark) 取る tórù; (achieve: success) 収める osámerù
♦*vi* (in game) 得点する tokúteñ suru; (*FOOTBALL* etc) トライする toráí suru; (keep score) 得点を記録する tokúteñ wo kirókù suru

scores of (very many) 多数の tasū́ no
on that score その点に関して sonó teñ ni kańshitè
to score 6 out of 10 10回中6回成功する jukkáichū rokkáí seíkō suru

scoreboard [sko:r'bo:rd] *n* スコアボード sukóabòdo

score out *vt* 線を引いて消す séñ wo hiítè kesù

scorn [sko:rn] *n* 軽べつ keíbetsu
♦*vt* 軽べつする keíbetsu suru

scornful [sko:rn'fəl] *adj* (laugh, disregard) 軽べつ的な keíbetsuteki na

Scorpio [sko:r'pi:ou] *n* (sign of Zodiac) さそり座 sasórizầ

scorpion [sko:r'pi:ən] *n* サソリ sasori

Scot [ska:t] *n* スコットランド人 sukóttorandojìn

Scotch [ska:tʃ] *n* (whisky) スコッチ sukótchī

scotch [ska:tʃ] *vt* (end: rumor) 消し止める keshítomerù; (plan, idea) 没にする bótsū ni suru

scot-free [ska:t'fri:'] *adv*: **to get off scot-free** (unpunished) 何の罰も受けない náñ no bátsù mo ukénaí

Scotland [ska:t'lənd] *n* スコットランド sukóttorando

Scots [ska:ts] *adj* (accent, people) スコットランドの sukóttorando no

Scotsman [ska:ts'mən] (*pl* **Scotsmen**) *n* スコットランドの男性 sukóttorando no dansei

Scotswoman [ska:ts'wumən] (*pl* **Scotswomen**) *n* スコットランドの女性 sukóttorando no joséi

Scottish [ska:t'iʃ] *adj* (history, clans, people) スコットランドの sukóttorando no

scoundrel [skaun'drəl] *n* 悪党 akútō

scour [skaur] *vt* (search: countryside etc) くまなく捜し回る kumánàku sagáshimawarù

scourge [skə:rdʒ] *n* (cause of trouble: *also fig*) 悩みの種 nayámi no tanè

scout [skaut] *n* (MIL) 斥候 sekkō; (*also*: **boy scout**) ボーイスカウト bōisukaùto
girl scout (*US*) ガールスカウト gárusukaùto

scout around *vi* 捜し回る sagáshimawarù

scowl [skaul] *vi* 顔をしかめる káò wo shikámerù
to scowl at someone しかめっつらをして ...をにらむ shikámettsura wò shité ...wo nirámù

scrabble [skræb'əl] *vi* (claw): *to scrabble (at)* (...を)引っかく (...wo) hikkákù; (*also*: **scrabble around**: search) 手探りで探す teságuri de sagásù
n: *Scrabble* ® スクラップブーる sukúrabbùru ◇単語作りゲーム tañgozukurigēmu

scraggy [skræg'i:] *adj* (animal, body, neck etc) やせこけた yasékoketà

scram [skræm] (*inf*) *vi* (get away fast) うせる userù

scramble [skræm'bəl] *n* (difficult climb) よじ上り yojínobori; (struggle, rush) 奪い合い ubáiai
vi: *to scramble out/through* 慌てて出る〔通る〕 awátete derù [tōru]
to scramble for ...の奪い合いをする ...no ubáiai wo surù

scrambled eggs [skræm'bəld-] *npl* いり卵 iritamago, スクランブルエッグ sukúranburu eggù

scrap [skræp] *n* (bit: of paper, material etc) 切れ端 kiréhashi; (: of information) 少し sukóshi; (*fig*: of truth) 欠けら kakéra; (fight) けんか keñka; (*also*: **scrap iron**) くず鉄 kuzútetsu
vt (discard: machines etc) くず鉄にする kuzútetsu ni surù; (*fig*: plans etc) 捨てる sutérù
vi (fight) けんかする keñka suru

scrapbook [skræp'buk] *n* スクラップブック sukúrappubukkù

scrap dealer *n* くず鉄屋 kuzútetsuyà

scrape [skreip] *n* (*fig*: difficult situation) 窮地 kyūchì
vt (scrape off: potato skin etc) むく mukú; (scrape against: hand, car) こする kosúrù
vi: *to scrape through* (exam etc) ...をどうにか切抜ける ...wo dō ni ka kirínukerù

scrape together *vt* (money) かき集める kakíatsumerù

scrap heap *n* (*fig*): *on the scrap heap* 捨てられて sutérarete

scrap merchant *n* (*BRIT*) = **scrap dealer**

scrap paper *n* 古い紙 furúì kamí, 古紙 kóshì, ほご紙 hógò

scrappy [skræp'i:] *adj* (piece of work) 雑な zatsú na

scraps [skræps] *npl* (leftovers: food, material etc) くず kúzù

scratch [skrætʃ] *n* (cut: on body, furniture: *also* from claw) かき傷 kakízu
cpd: *scratch team* 寄集めチーム yoséatsumechìmu
vt (rub: one's nose etc) かく kákù; (damage: paint, car) 傷付ける kizútsukerù; (with claw, nail) ひっかく hikkákù
vi (rub one's body) ...をかく ...wo kákù
to start from scratch 何もない所から始める naní mo naì tokóro karà hajímerù
to be up to scratch いい線をいっている íi séñ wo itté irù

scrawl [skrɔ:l] *n* なぐり書き nagúrigaki
vi なぐり書きする nagúrigaki suru

scrawny [skrɔ:'ni:] *adj* (person, neck) やせこけた yasékoketà

scream [skri:m] *n* 悲鳴 himéi
vi 悲鳴を上げる himéi wo agerù

scree [skri:] *n* 岩くず iwákuzu ◇崩れ落ちてたい積した岩くずを指す kuzúreochìte taíseki shitá iwákuzu wo sasù

screech [skri:tʃ] *vi* (person) 金切り声を出す kanákirigoè wo dásù; (bird) きーきー声で鳴く kíkígoè de nákù; (tires, brakes) きーきーと鳴る kíkī to narù

screen [skri:n] *n* (CINEMA) スクリーン

sukúrìn; (TV, COMPUT) ブラウン管 buráunkan; (movable barrier) ついたて tsuítate; (fig: cover) 幕 makú

♦vt (protect, conceal) 覆い隠す ōikakusù; (from the wind etc) ...の...よけになる ...no...yoké ni narù; (film) 映写する eísha suru; (television program) 放映する hōei suru; (candidates etc) 審査する shíñsa suru

screening [skri:'niŋ] n (MED) 健康診断 keñkōshiñdan

screenplay [skri:n'plei] n 映画脚本 eígakyakùhon

screw [skru:] n (for fixing something) ねじ néjì

♦vt (fasten) ねじで留める neji de tomérù

screwdriver [skru:'draivə:r] n ねじ回し nejímawashì

screw up vt (paper etc) くしゃくしゃにする kushákùsha ni suru

to screw up one's eyes 目を細める mé wò hosómerù

scribble [skrib'əl] n 走り書き hashírigakì

♦vt (write carelessly: note etc) 走り書きする hashírigaki suru

♦vi (make meaningless marks) 落書きする rakúgakì suru

script [skript] n (CINEMA etc) 脚本 kyakúhon, スクリプト sukúripùto; (system of writing) 文字 mójì

scripture(s) [skrip'tʃə:r(z)] n(pl) (holy writing(s) of a religion) 聖典 seíten

scroll [skroul] n (official paper) 巻物 makímono

scrounge [skraundʒ] vt (inf): *to scrounge something off/from someone* ...に...をねだる ...ni...wo nedárù

♦n: *on the scrounge* たかって takáttè

scrub [skrʌb] n (land) 低木地帯 teíbokuchitài

♦vt (rub hard: floor, hands, pan, washing) ごしごし洗う goshígoshi aráù; (inf: reject: idea) 取り止める toríyamerù

scruff [skrʌf] n: *by the scruff of the neck* 首筋をつかんで kubísuji wò tsukáñde

scruffy [skrʌf'i:] adj (person, object,

appearance) 薄汚い usúgitanaì

scrum(mage) [skrʌm('idʒ)] n (RUGBY) スクラム sukúramu

scruple [skru:'pəl] n (gen pl) 良心のとがめ ryōshìn no togáme

scrupulous [skru:'pjələs] adj (painstaking: care, attention) 細心の saíshin no; (fair-minded: honesty) 公正な kōsei na

scrutinize [skru:'tənaiz] vt (examine closely) 詳しく調べる kuwáshikù shiráberù

scrutiny [skru:'təni:] n (close examination) 吟味 gíñmi

to keep someone under scrutiny ...を監視する ...wo kañshi suru

scuff [skʌf] vt (shoes, floor) すり減らす suríherasù

scuffle [skʌf'əl] n (fight) 乱闘 rañtō

sculptor [skʌlp'tə:r] n 彫刻家 chōkokuka

sculpture [skʌlp'tʃə:r] n 彫刻 chōkoku

scum [skʌm] n (on liquid) 汚い泡 kitánaì awà; (pej: people) 人間のくず niñgen nò kúzù

scupper [skʌp'ə:r] (BRIT: inf) vt (plan, idea) 邪魔して失敗させる jamá shitè shippái saserù

scurrilous [skə:r'ələs] adj 口汚い kuchígitanaì

scurry [skə:r'i:] vi ちょこちょこ走る chókòchoko hashírù

scurry off vi ちょこちょこ走って行く chókòchoko hashítte ikù

scuttle [skʌt'əl] n (also: **coal scuttle**) 石炭入れ sekítan-ire

♦vt (ship) 沈没させる chíñbotsu saserù

♦vi (scamper): *to scuttle away/off* ちょこちょこ走っていく chókòchoko hashítte ikù

scythe [saið] n 大がま ōgamà ◊柄も刃も長いかま é mò há mò nagáì kámà

sea [si:] n 海 úmì; (fig: very many) 多数 tasū; (: very much) 多量 taryō

♦cpd (breeze, bird etc) 海の úmì no

by sea (travel) 海路で kaíro de

on the sea (boat) 海上で kaíjō de; (town) 海辺の umíbe no

out to/at sea 沖に okí ni
to be all at sea (fig) 頭が混乱している atáma gà końran shite irù
a sea of faces (fig) 顔の海 kaó nò úmì
seaboard [si:'bo:rd] n 海岸 kaígan
seafood [si:'fu:d] n 魚介類 gyokáirùi, シーフード shífùdo ◇料理に使う魚介類を指す ryóri ni tsukáù gyokáirùi wo sásù
seafront [si:'frʌnt] n 海岸 kaígan ◇海辺の町などの海沿いの部分を指す umíbe nò machí nadò no umízoi no bubùn wo sásù
sea-going [si:'gouiŋ] adj (ship) 遠洋航海用の eń-yōkōkaiyō no
seagull [si:'gʌl] n カモメ kamóme
seal [si:l] n (animal) アザラシ azárashi ◇セイウチを除いて全てのひれ足類を含む sefuchì wo nozóìte súbète no hiréashirùi wo fúkumù; (official stamp) 印章 ińshō; (closure) 封印 fúin
◆vt (close: envelope) ...の封をする ...no fū wò suru; (: opening) 封じる fújirù
sea level n 海抜 kaíbatsu
sea lion n トド tódò
seal off vt (place) 封鎖する fúsa suru
seam [si:m] n (line of stitches) 縫目 nuíme; (where edges meet) 継目 tsugíme, 合せ目 awáseme; (of coal etc) 薄層 hakúsō
seaman [si:'mən] (pl **seamen**) n 船乗り funánòri
seamy [si:'mi:] adj: **the seamy side of** ...の汚い裏面 ...no kitánaì rímèn, ...の恥部 ...no chíbù
seance [sei'ɑ:ns] n 降霊会 kōreíkai
seaplane [si:'plein] n 水上飛行機 suíjōhikōki
seaport [si:'po:rt] n 港町 minátomachi
search [sə:rtʃ] n (hunt: for person, thing) 捜索 sōsaku; (COMPUT) 探索 tańsaku, 検索 keńsaku; (inspection: of someone's home) 家宅捜査 katákusōsa
◆vt (look in: place) ...の中を捜す ...no nakà wo sagásù; (examine: memory) 捜す sagásù; (person) ...の身体検査をする ...no shíntaikeñsa wo suru
◆vi: **to search for** ...を捜す ...wo sagásù
in search of ...を求めて ...wo motómetè
searching [sə:r'tʃiŋ] adj (question, look) 鋭い surúdoì

searchlight [sə:rtʃ'lait] n サーチライト sáchiraìto
search party n 捜索隊 sōsakutai
search through vt fus ...の中をくまなく捜す ...no nakà wo kumánàku sagásù
search warrant n 捜査令状 sōsareijō
seashore [si:'ʃo:r] n 海岸 kaígan
seasick [si:'sik] adj 船酔いになった funáyòi ni náttà
seaside [si:'said] n 海辺 umíbe
seaside resort n 海辺の行楽地 umíbe nò kòrakuchì
season [si:'zən] n (of year) 季節 kisétsu; (time of year for something: football season etc) シーズン shízun; (series: of films etc) シリーズ shírīzu
◆vt (food) ...に味を付ける ...ni ají wò tsukérù
in season (fruit, vegetables) しゅんで shúǹ de
out of season (fruit, vegetables) 季節外れで kisétsuhàzure de
seasonal [si:'zənəl] adj (work) 季節的な kisétsuteki na
seasoned [si:'zənd] adj (fig: traveler) 経験豊かな keíken yutàka na
seasoning [si:'zəniŋ] n 調味料 chōmiryò, 薬味 yakúmi
season ticket n (RAIL) 定期券 teíkikèn; (THEATER) シーズン入場券 shízun nyūjōken
seat [si:t] n (chair) いす isú; (in vehicle, theater: space) 席 sékì; (PARLIAMENT) 議席 giséki; (buttocks: also of trousers) しり shirí
◆vt (place: guests etc) 座らせる suwáraserù; (subj: table, theater: have room for) ...人分の席がある ...nínbun no sékì ga árù
to be seated 座る suwárù
seat belt n シートベルト shítoberùto
sea water n 海水 kaísui
seaweed [si:'wi:d] n 海草 kaísō
seaworthy [si:'wə:rði:] adj (ship) 航海に耐えられる kōkai nì taérarerù
sec. abbr = **second(s)**
secluded [siklu:'did] adj (place) 人里離れた hitózato hanaretà; (life) 隠とんの iń-

ton no

seclusion [siklu:'ʒən] *n* 隔離 kákùri

second [sek'ənd] *adj* (after first) 第二 (の) dái ní (no)

♦*adv* (come, be placed: in race etc) 二番 に níbàn ni; (when listing) 第二に dái ní ni

♦*n* (unit of time) 秒 byō; (AUT: *also*: **second gear**) セカンド sekándo; (COMM: imperfect) 二流品 niryūhìn; (*BRIT*: SCOL: degree) 2級優等卒業学位 níkyū yūtō sotsugyō gakùi ¶ *see also* **first**

♦*vt* (motion) ...に支持を表明する ...ni shí-jì wo hyōmei suru; (*BRIT*: worker) 派遣 する hakén suru

secondary [sek'əndeːriː] *adj* (less important) 二次的な nijíteki na

secondary school *n* 中等高等学校 chū-tōkōtōgakkō

second-class [sek'əndklæs'] *adj* (hotel, novel, work) 二流の niryū no; (tickets, transport) 2等の nitō no

♦*adv* (travel) 2等で nitō de

secondhand [sek'əndhænd'] *adj* (clothing, car) 中古の chūko no

second hand *n* (on clock) 秒針 byōshìn

secondly [sek'əndliː] *adv* 2番目に nibán-me ni

secondment [sek'əndmənt] (*BRIT*) *n* 派 遣 hakén

second-rate [sek'əndreit'] *adj* (film etc) 二流の niryū no

second thoughts *npl* ためらい tamérai

on second thought (US) or thoughts (BRIT) 気が変って ki gá kawattè

secrecy [si:'krisi:] *n*: *to swear someone to secrecy* ...に秘密を誓わせる ...ni himí-tsu wò chikáwaserù

secret [si:'krit] *adj* (plan, passage, agent) 秘密の himítsu no; (admirer, drinker) ひ そかな hisókà na

♦*n* 秘密 himítsu

in secret 内密に naímitsu ni

secretarial [sekriteːrˈiːəl] *adj* (work, course, staff, studies) 秘書の hishō no

secretariat [sekriteːrˈiːət] *n* 事 務 局 ji-mūkyòku

secretary [sek'riteːriː] *n* (COMM) 秘 書 hishō; (of club) 書記 shokí

Secretary of State (for) (BRIT: POL) (...) 大臣 (...)dáìjin

secretion [sikri:'ʃən] *n* (substance) 分 泌 物 buńpitsubùtsu

secretive [si:'kritiv] *adj* 秘密主義の hi-mítsushùgi no

secretly [si:'kritli:] *adv* (tell, marry) 内密 に naímitsu ni

sect [sekt] *n* 宗派 shūha

sectarian [sekteːrˈiːən] *adj* (riots etc) 宗 派間の shūhakàn no

section [sek'ʃən] *n* (part) 部分 búbùn; (department) ...部 ...bù; (of document) 章 shō; (of opinion) 一 部 ichíbù; (cross-section) 断面図 dańmenzù

sector [sek'təːr] *n* (part) 部 門 búmòn; (MIL) 戦闘地区 seńtōchikù

secular [sek'jələːr] *adj* (music, society etc) 世俗の sezóku no; (priest) 教区の kyōku no

secure [sikju:r'] *adj* (safe: person) 安全な 場所にいる ańzen na bashò ni irú; (: money) 安全な場所にある ańzen na bashò ni árù; (: building) 防犯対策完備の bōhantaisakukaňbi no; (firmly fixed, strong: rope, shelf) 固定された kotéi sa-retà

♦*vt* (fix: rope, shelf etc) 固定する kotéi suru; (get: job, contract etc) 確保する kákùho suru

security [sikju:r'iti:] *n* (protection) 警 備 kéìbi; (for one's future) 保証 hoshō; (FINANCE) 担保 táñpo

sedan [sidæn'] (*US*) *n* (AUT) セダン sé-dàn

sedate [sideit'] *adj* (person, pace) 落着い た ochítsuità

♦*vt* (MED: with injection) ...に鎮静剤を 注射する ...ni chińseizài wo chūshà suru; (: with pills etc) ...に鎮静剤を飲ませる ...ni chińseizài wo nomáserù

sedation [sidei'ʃən] *n* (MED): *under sedation* 薬で鎮静されて kusúrò dè chiń-sei saretè

sedative [sed'ətiv] *n* 鎮静剤 chińseizài

sedentary [sed'ənteːri:] *adj* (occupation,

work) 座ってする suwátte surù

sediment [sed'əmənt] *n* (in bottle) おり orí; (in lake etc) 底のたい積物 sokó nò taísekibùtsu

seduce [sidu:s'] *vt* (entice: *gen*) 魅了する miryő suru; (: sexually) 誘惑する yūwaku suru, たらし込む taráshikomù

seduction [sidʌk'ʃən] *n* (attraction) 魅惑 miwàku; (act of seducing) 誘惑 yūwaku

seductive [sidʌk'tiv] *adj* (look, voice, *also fig* offer) 誘惑的な yūwakuteki na

see [si:] (*pt* **saw**, *pp* **seen**) *vt* (*gen*) 見る mírù; (accompany): **to see someone to the door** ...を戸口まで送る ...wo tóguchi máde okúrù; (understand) 分かる wakárù

♦*vi* (*gen*) 見える miérù; (find out) 調べる shiráberù

♦*n* (REL) 教区 kyőkù

to see that someone does something ...が...する様に気を付ける ...ga...surú yő ni kí wo tsukérù

see you soon! またね matá nè

see about *vt fus* ...の問題を調べて片付ける ...no mońdai wò shirábete katazùkeru

seed [si:d] *n* (of plant, fruit) 種 tánè; (sperm) 精液 seíeki; (*fig*: *gen pl*) 種 tánè; (TENNIS) シード shído

to go to seed (plant) 種ができる tánè ga dekírù; (*fig*) 衰える otóroerù

seedling [si:d'liŋ] *n* 苗 náè

seedy [si:'di:] *adj* (shabby: person, place) 見すぼらしい misúborashiî

seeing [si:'iŋ] *conj*: **seeing (that)** ...だから ...dákara

seek [si:k] (*pt, pp* **sought**) *vt* (truth, shelter, advice, post) 求める motómerù

seem [si:m] *vi* ...に見える ...ni miérù

there seems to be ... ...がある様です ...ga árù yő desù

seemingly [si:'miŋli:] *adv* ...らしく ...rashíkù

seen [si:n] *pp of* **see**

see off *vt* ...を見送る ...wo miőkurù

seep [si:p] *vi* (liquid, gas) 染み透る shimítồru

seesaw [si:'sɔ:] *n* シーソー shísồ

seethe [si:ð] *vi* (place: with people/things) 騒然としている sőzen shite irù

to seethe with anger 怒りで煮え繰り返る ikári dè niékurikaerù

see through *vt* 最後までやり通す sáigo made yaritốsu

♦*vt fus* 見抜く minúkù

see-through [si:'θru:] *adj* (blouse etc) すけすけルックの sukésukerukkù no

see to *vt fus* ...の世話をする ...no sewá wò suru

segment [seg'mənt] *n* (part: *gen*) 一部 ichíbu; (of orange) ふさ fusá

segregate [seg'rəgeit] *vt* 分ける wakérù

seismic [saiz'mik] *adj* (activity) 地震の jishín no

seize [si:z] *vt* (grasp) つかむ tsukámù; (take possession of: power, control, territory) 奪う ubáù; (: hostage) 捕まえる tsukámaerù; (opportunity) 捕える toráerù

seize up *vi* (TECH: engine) 焼け付く yakétsukù

seize (up)on *vt fus* ...に飛付く ...ni tobítsukù

seizure [si:'ʒə:r] *n* (MED) 発作 hossá; (LAW) 没収 bosshű; (: of power) 強奪 gődatsu

seldom [sel'dəm] *adv* めったに...ない méttà ni...náî

select [silekt'] *adj* (school, group, area) 一流の ichíryū no

♦*vt* (choose) 選ぶ erábù

selection [silek'ʃən] *n* (being chosen) 選ばれる事 erábareru kotð; (COMM: range available) 選択 seńtaku

selective [silek'tiv] *adj* (careful in choosing) 選択的な seńtakuteki na; (not general: strike etc) 限られた範囲の kagírareta háń-i no

self [self] (*pl* **selves**) *n*: **the self** 自我 jígà

♦*prefix* 自分で(の)... jibún de (no) ...

self-assured [self'əʃu:rd'] *adj* 自信のある jishín no arù

self-catering [self'kei'tə:riŋ] *adj* (BRIT: holiday, apartment) 自炊の jisúi no

self-centered [self'sen'tə:rd] (BRIT **self-centred**) *adj* 自己中心の jikóchūshin-

no

self-colored [self'kʌl'ə:rd] (*BRIT* **self-coloured**) *adj* (of one color) 単色の tañshoku no

self-confidence [self'kɑ:n'fidəns] *n* 自信 jishín

self-conscious [self'kɑ:n'tʃəs] *adj* (nervous) 照れる teréru

self-contained [self'kənteind'] (*BRIT*) *adj* (flat) 設備完備の setsúbikañbi no

self-control [self'kəntroul'] *n* 自制 jiséi

self-defense [self'difens'] (*BRIT* **self-defence**) *n* 自己防衛 jikóbōei
  in self-defense 自己防衛で jikóbōei de

self-discipline [self'dis'əplin] *n* 気力 kíryōku

self-employed [self'imploid'] *adj* 自営業の jiéigyō no

self-evident [self'ev'idənt] *adj* 自明の jiméi no

self-governing [self'gʌv'ə:rniŋ] *adj* 独立の dokúritsu no

self-indulgent [self'indʌl'dʒənt] *adj* 勝手気ままな kattékimama na

self-interest [self'in'trist] *n* 自己利益 jikórièki

selfish [sel'fiʃ] *adj* 身勝手な migátte na

selfishness [sel'fiʃnis] *n* 利己主義 rikóshùgi

selfless [self'lis] *adj* 献身的な keñshinteki na

self-made [self'meid'] *adj*: *self-made man* 自力でたたき上げた人 jiríki dè tatákiageta hitò

self-pity [self'pit'i:] *n* 自己れんびん jikóreñbin

self-portrait [self'po:r'trit] *n* 自画像 jigázō

self-possessed [self'pəzest'] *adj* 落着いた ochítsuita

self-preservation [self'prezə:rvei'ʃən] *n* 本能的自衛 hoñnōtekijièi

self-respect [self'rispekt'] *n* 自尊心 jisóñshin

self-righteous [self'rai'tʃəs] *adj* 独善的な dokúzenteki na

self-sacrifice [self'sæk'rəfais] *n* 献身 keñshin

self-satisfied [self'sæt'isfaid] *adj* 自己満足の jikómañzoku no

self-service [self'sə:r'vis] *adj* (shop, restaurant, service station) セルフサービスの serúfusābisu no

self-sufficient [self'səfiʃ'ənt] *adj* (farm, country) 自給自足の jikyúujisòku no; (person) 独立独歩の dokúritsudoppò no

self-taught [self'tɔ:t'] *adj* 独学の dokúgaku no

sell [sel] (*pt, pp* **sold**) *vt* (*gen*) 売る urú; (*fig*: idea) 売込む uríkomù
  ♦*vi* (goods) 売れる uréru
  to sell at/for $10 値段は10ドルである nedán wà 10 dórù de árù

sell-by date [sel'bai-] (*BRIT*) *n* 賞味期限 shōmikigèn

seller [sel'ə:r] *n* 売手 uríte

selling price [sel'iŋ-] *n* 値段 nedán

sell off *vt* 売払う uríharaù

sell out *vi* (use up stock): *to sell out (of something)* (...が) 売切れる (...ga) uríkirerù
  the tickets are sold out 切符は売切れだ kippú wà uríkire da

sellotape [sel'əteip]® (*BRIT*) *n* セロテープ serótēpu

selves [selvz] *pl of* **self**

semaphore [sem'əfɔ:r] *n* 手旗 tebáta

semblance [sem'bləns] *n* 外観 gaíkan

semen [si:'mən] *n* 精液 seíeki

semester [simes'tə:r] (*US*) *n* 学期 gakkí

semi... [sem'i:] *prefix* 半分の... hañbùn no

semicircle [sem'i:sə:rkəl] *n* 半円形 hañeñkei

semicolon [sem'i:koulən] *n* セミコロン semíkoròn

semiconductor [semi:kəndʌk'tə:r] *n* 半導体 hañdōtai

semidetached (house) [semi:ditætʃt'] (*BRIT*) *n* 二戸建て住宅 nikódate jūtaku

semifinal [semi:fai'nəl] *n* 準決勝 juñkesshō

seminar [sem'ənɑ:r] *n* セミナー sémìnā

seminary [sem'əne:ri:] *n* (REL) 神学校 shiñgakkō

semiskilled [semi:skild'] *adj* (work,

worker) 半熟練の hañjukúren no

senate [sen'it] *n* 上院 jōin

senator [sen'ətər] *n* 上院議員 jōingiìn

send [send] (*pt, pp* **sent**) *vt* (dispatch) 送る okúrù; (transmit: signal) 送信する sōshin suru

send away *vt* (letter, goods) 送る okúrù; (unwelcome visitor) 追払う oíharaù

send away for *vt fus* 郵便で注文する yūbin dè chūmon suru

send back *vt* 送り返す okúrikaesù

sender [send'ər] *n* 差出人 sashídashinìn

send for *vt fus* (thing) 取寄せる torīyoseru; (person) 呼寄せる yobíyoserù

send off *vt* (goods) 送る okúrù; (*BRIT*: SPORT: player) 退場させる taíjō saserù

send-off [send'ɔːf] *n*: *a good send-off* 素晴らしい送別 subárashiì sōbetsu

send out *vt* (invitation) 送る okúrù; (signal) 発信する hasshín suru

send up *vt* (price, blood pressure) 上昇させる jōshō saserù; (astronaut) 打上げる uchíagerù; (*BRIT*: parody) 風刺する fūshi suru

senile [si:'nail] *adj* 老いぼれた oíboretà, ぼけた bōketa; (*MED*) 老人性の rōjinsei no

senior [si:n'jə:r] *adj* (older) 年上の toshíue no; (on staff: position, officer) 幹部の kánbu no; (of higher rank: partner) 上級の jōkyū no

senior citizen *n* 老人 rōjin, 高齢者 kōreishā

seniority [si:njɔːr'iti:] *n* (in service) 年功 nefíkō

sensation [sensei'(ə]n *n* (feeling) 感覚 kañkaku; (great success) 大成功 daíseikō

sensational [sensei'(ə]nəl] *adj* (wonderful) 素晴らしい subárashiì; (causing much interest: headlines) 扇情的な señjōteki na; (: result) センセーショナルな señsēshōnaru na

sense [sens] *n* (physical) 感覚 kañkaku; (feeling: of guilt, shame etc) 感じ kañji; (good sense) 常識 jōshiki; (meaning: of word, phrase etc) 意味 ímì

♦*vt* (become aware of) 感じる kañjirù

it makes sense (can be understood) 意味が分かる ímì ga wakáru; (is sensible) 賢明だ keñmei dà

sense of humor ユーモアを解する心 yūmoa wo kaí surù kokóro, ユーモアのセンス yūmoa no sénsu

senseless [sens'lis] *adj* (pointless: murder) 無意味な muími na; (unconscious) 気絶した kizétsu shità

sensible [sen'səbəl] *adj* (person) 利口な rikō na; (reasonable: price, advice) 合理的な gōriteki na; (: decision, suggestion) 賢明な keñmei na

sensitive [sen'sətiv] *adj* (understanding) 理解のある rīkai no árù; (nerve, skin) 敏感な bíñkan no; (instrument) 高感度の kōkando no; (fig: touchy: person) 怒りっぽい okōrippoì; (: issue) 際どい kiwádoī

sensitivity [sensətiv'əti:] *n* (understanding) 理解 rīkai; (responsiveness: to touch etc) 敏感さ bíñkansa; (: of instrument) 感度 kándo; (touchiness: of person) 怒りっぽさ okórripposà; (delicate nature: of issue etc) 際どさ kiwádosà

sensual [sen'ju:əl] *adj* (of the senses: rhythm etc) 官能的な kañnōteki na; (relating to sexual pleasures) 肉感的な nikkánteki na

sensuous [sen'ju:əs] *adj* (lips, material etc) 官能的な kañnōteki na

sent [sent] *pt, pp of* **send**

sentence [sen'təns] *n* (LING) 文 búñ; (LAW) 宣告 señkoku

♦*vt*: *to sentence someone to death/to 5 years in prison* ...に死刑〔懲役5年〕の判決を言渡す ...ni shikéi〔chōeki gonèn〕nò hañketsu wò iíwatasù

sentiment [sen'təmənt] *n* (tender feelings) 感情 kañjō; (opinion, *also* pl) 意見 íkèn

sentimental [sentəmen'təl] *adj* (song) 感傷的な kañshōteki na, センチメンタルな señchimeñtaru na; (person) 情にもろい jō nī moróì

sentry [sen'tri:] *n* 番兵 bañpei

separate [*adj* sep'rit *vb* sep'əreit] *adj* (distinct: piles, occasions, ways, rooms) 別々の betsúbetsu no

◆*vt* (split up: people, things) 分ける wakérù; (make a distinction between: twins) 見分ける miwákerù; (: ideas etc) 区別する kubétsu suru

◆*vi* (split up, move apart) 分かれる wakárerù

separately [sep'ritli:] *adv* 別々に betsúbetsu ni

separates [sep'rits] *npl* (clothes) セパレーツ sepárētsu

separation [sepərei'ʃən] *n* (being apart) 分離 bunri; (time spent apart) 別れ別れになっている期間 wakárewakáre ni natté irù kikáñ; (LAW) 別居 bekkyò

September [septem'bəːr] *n* 9月 kúgàtsu

septic [sep'tik] *adj* (wound, finger etc) 感染した kañsen shita

septic tank *n* 浄化槽 jòkasò

sequel [si:'kwəl] *n* (follow-up) 後日談 gojítsudàn; (of film, story) 続編 zokúhen

sequence [si:'kwins] *n* (ordered chain) 連続 reñzoku; (*also*: **dance sequence, film sequence**) 一場面 ichíbameñ, シークエンス shíkueñsu

sequin [si:'kwin] *n* シークイン shíkuìn, スパンコール supáñkòru

serene [səri:n'] *adj* (smile, expression etc) 穏やかな odáyàka na

serenity [səren'iti:] *n* 穏やかさ odáyàkasa

sergeant [sɑːr'dʒənt] *n* (MIL etc) 軍曹 gúñsò; (POLICE) 巡査部長 juñsàbùchò

serial [si:r'i:əl] *n* 連続物 reñzokumono

serialize [si:r'i:əlaiz] *vt* (in newspaper, magazine) 連載する reñsai suru; (on radio, TV) 連続物として放送する reñzokumono toshitè hòsò suru

serial number *n* 製造番号 seízòbañgò

series [si:r'i:z] *n inv* (group) 一連 ichíren; (of books, TV programs) シリーズ shirízù

serious [si:r'i:əs] *adj* (person, manner) 真剣な shiñken na; (important: matter) 大事な daíjì na; (grave: illness, condition) 重い omóì

seriously [si:'ri:əsli:] *adv* (talk, take) 真剣に shiñken ni; (hurt) ひどく hídòku

seriousness [si:'ri:əsnis] *n* (of person,

manner) 真剣さ shiñkensa; (importance) 重大さ jùdaisa; (gravity) 重さ omósa

sermon [səːr'mən] *n* (*also fig*) 説教 sekkyò

serrated [se:rei'tid] *adj* (edge, knife) のこぎり状の nokógirijò no

serum [si:r'əm] *n* 血清 kesséi

servant [səːr'vənt] *n* (gen) 召使い meshítsukài; (*fig*) 人に仕える物 hitó nì tsukáerù monò

serve [səːrv] *vt* (gen: company, country) 仕える tsukáerù; (in shop: goods) 売る urú; (: customer) ...の用を うかがう ...no yò wò ukágaù; (subj: train) ...の足になる ...no ashí nì naru; (apprenticeship) 務める tsutómerù

◆*vi* (at table) 給仕する kyùji suru; (TENNIS) サーブする sàbu suru; (be useful): *to serve as/for* ...として役に立つ ...toshité yakú ni tatsù

◆*n* (TENNIS) サーブ sàbu

to serve to do ...をするのに役に立つ ...wo suru nò ni yakú ni tatsù

it serves him right 自業自得だ jigòjitòku da

to serve a prison term 服役する fukúeki suru

serve out/up *vt* (food) 出す dásù

service [səːr'vis] *n* (gen: help) 役に立つ事 yakú ni tatsù koto; (in hotel) サービス sàbisu; (REL) 式 shikí; (AUT) 整備 seíbi; (TENNIS) サーブ sàbu; (plates, dishes etc) 一そろい hitósoroì; (*also*: **train service**) 鉄道の便 tetsúdò nò béñ; (*also*: **plane service**) 空の便 sòrà no béñ

◆*vt* (car, washing machine) 整備する seíbi suru

military/national service 兵役 heíeki

to be of service to someone ...に役に立つ ...ni yakú ni tatsù

serviceable [sə:r'visəbəl] *adj* 役に立つ yakú ni tatsù

service area *n* (on motorway) サービスエリア sàbisu erìa

service charge (*BRIT*) *n* サービス料 sàbisuryò

serviceman [sə:r'vismæn] (*pl* **servicemen**) *n* (MIL) 軍人 guñjin

Services [səːrˈvisiz] *npl*: *the Services* (army, navy etc) 軍隊 gúntai

service station *n* ガソリンスタンド gasórinsutaňdo; (*BRIT*: on motorway) サービスエリア sábisu erīa

serviette [səːrviːetˈ] (*BRIT*) *n* 紙ナプキン kamínapùkin

servile [səːrˈvail] *adj* (person, obedience) おもねる様な omóneru yố na

session [sefˈən] *n* (period of activity: recording/drinking session) ...するために集まる事 ...surú tame nì atsúmaru kotð

to be in session (court) 開廷中である kaíteichū de arù; (Parliament etc) 開会中である kaíkaichū de arù

set [set] *n* (collection of things) 一そろい hitósoroì, 一式 isshíki, セット séttð; (radio set) ラジオ rájìo; (TV set) テレビ térèbi; (TENNIS) セット séttð; (group of people) 連中 reńchū; (MATH) セット séttð; (CINEMA, THEATER) 舞台装置 butáisòchi, セット séttð; (HAIRDRESSING) セット séttð

♦*adj* (fixed: rules, routine) 決りの kimári no; (ready) 用意ができた yối ga dekítà

♦*vb* (*pt, pp* **set**)

♦*vt* (place) 置く ókù; (fix, establish: time, price, rules etc) 決める kimérù; (: record) 作る tsukúrù; (adjust: alarm, watch) セットする séttð suru; (impose: task) 命ずる meízurù; (: exam) 作る tsukúrù

♦*vi* (sun) 沈む shizúmù; (jam, jelly, concrete) 固まる katámarù; (broken bone) 治る naôru

to set the table 食卓の用意をする shokútaku nò yối wo suru

to be set on doing something どうしても...をすると決めている dồshite mo ... wo suru tð kiméte irù

to set to music ...に曲を付ける ...ni kyokú wo tsukérù

to set on fire ...に火を付ける ...ni hí wð tsukérù

to set free 放してやる hanáshite yarù, 自由にする jiyú ni surù

to set something going ...を始めさせる

...wo hajímesaserù

to set sail 出航する shukkố suru

set about *vt fus* (task) 始める hajímerù

set aside *vt* (money etc) 取って置く tốttè oku; (time) 空けておく akétè okù

set back *vt* (cost): *to set someone back $5* 5ドル払わなければならない go dốrù haráwànakereba naránaî; (in time): *to set someone back (by)* ...を (...) 遅らせる ...wo (...) okúraserù

setback [setˈbæk] *n* (hitch) 苦難 kúnàn

set menu *n* 定食メニュー teíshokumenyū

set off *vi* 出発する shuppátsu suru

♦*vt* (bomb) 爆発させる bakúhatsu saserù; (alarm) 鳴らす narásù; (chain of events) ...の引金となる ...no hikígane to narù; (show up well: jewels) 引立たせる hikítataserù

set out *vi* (depart) 出発する shuppátsu suru

♦*vt* (arrange: goods etc) 並べて置く narábete okù; (state: arguments) 述べる nobérù

to set out to do something ...をするつもりである ...wo suru tsumori de arù

settee [setiːˈ] *n* ソファー sófà

setting [setˈiŋ] *n* (background) 背景 haíkei; (position: of controls) セット séttð; (of jewel) はめ込み台 hamékomidài

the setting of the sun 日没 nichíbotsu

settle [setˈəl] *vt* (argument, matter) ...に決着を付ける ...ni ketcháku wð tsukérù; (accounts) 清算する seísan suru; (MED: calm: person) 落着かせる ochítsukaserù

♦*vi* (*also*: **settle down**) 一カ所に落着く ikkáshò ni ochítsukù; (bird) 降りる orírù; (dust etc) つく tsukú; (calm down: children) 静まる shizúmarù

to settle for something ...で我慢する ...de gámàn suru

to settle on something ...に決める ...ni kimérù

settle in *vi* 新しい所に落着く atárashiî tokôro ni ochítsukù

settle up *vi*: *to settle up with someone* ...に借金を返す ...ni shakkíñ wo káèsu

settlement [set'əlmənt] n (payment) 清算 seísan; (agreement) 和解 wakái; (village etc) 集落 shúraku

settler [set'lə:r] n 入植者 nyúshokushà

set up vt (organization) 設立する setsúritsu suru

setup [set'ʌp] n (organization) 機構 kikó; (situation) 様子 yósu, 状況 jókyō

seven [sev'ən] num 七(の) nánà (no), 七つ(の) nanátsù (no)

seventeen [sev'ənti:n'] num 十七(の) júnanà (no)

seventh [sev'ənθ] num 第七(の) dái nanà (no)

seventy [sev'ənti:] num 七十(の) nanájū (no)

sever [sev'ə:r] vt (artery, pipe) 切断する setsúdan suru; (relations) 切る kírù, 断つ tátsù

several [sev'ə:rəl] adj (things) 幾つかの íkùtsu ka no; (people) 幾人かの íkùnin ka no
♦pron 幾つか íkùtsu ka
several of us 私たちの中から幾人か watákushitàchi no nákà kara íkùnin ka

severance [sev'ə:rəns] n (of relations) 断交 dankō

severance pay n 退職金 taíshokukìn

severe [sivi:r'] adj (serious: pain) 激しい hagéshiì; (: damage) 大きな ókì na; (: shortage) 深刻な shiñkoku na; (hard: winter, climate) 厳しい kibíshiì; (stern) 厳格な geñkaku na; (plain: dress) 簡素な káñso na

severity [sive:r'iti:] n (seriousness: of pain) 激しさ hagéshisà; (: of damage) 大きさ ókisa; (: of shortage) 深刻さ shiñkoku-sa; (bitterness: of winter, climate) 厳しさ kibíshisa; (sternness) 厳格さ geñkaku-sa; (plainness: of dress) 簡素さ kañso-sa

sew [sou] (pt sewed, pp sewn) vt 縫う núù

sewage [su:'idʒ] n (waste) 汚水 osúi

sewer [su:'ə:r] n 下水道 gesúidō

sewing [sou'iŋ] n (activity) 裁縫 saíhō; (items being sewn) 縫物 nuímono

sewing machine n ミシン míshìn

sewn [soun] pp of sew

sew up vt (item of clothing) 縫い合せる nuíawaserù

sex [seks] n (gender) 性別 seíbetsu; (lovemaking) セックス sékkùsu
to have sex with someone ...とセックスをする ...to sékkùsu wo suru

sexist [seks'ist] adj 性差別の seísabètsu no

sextet [sekstet'] n (group) セクステット sekúsutettò

sexual [sek'ʃu:əl] adj (of the sexes: reproduction) 有性の yúsei no; (: equality) 男女の dáñjo no; (of sex: attraction) 性的な seíteki na; (: relationship) 肉体の nikútai no

sexy [sek'si:] adj (pictures, underwear etc) セクシーな sékùshī na

shabby [ʃæb'i:] adj (person, clothes) 見すぼらしい misúborashiī; (trick, treatment) 卑劣な hirétsu na

shack [ʃæk] n バラック barákkù

shackles [ʃæk'əlz] npl (on foot) 足かせ ashíkasè; (on hands) 手かせ tékàse; (fig) 束縛 sokúbaku

shade [ʃeid] n (shelter) 日陰 hikáge; (also: lampshade) ランプのかさ ráñpu no kásà; (of colour) 色合 iróaì; (small quantity): **a shade too large** ちょっと大き過ぎる chottó ōkisugirù
♦vt (shelter) ...の日よけになる ...no hiyóke ni narù; (eyes) ...に手をかざす ...ni té wò kazásù
in the shade 日陰に hikáge ni
a shade more もうちょっと mó chottó

shadow [ʃæd'ou] n 影 kágè
♦vt (follow) 尾行する bikó suru

shadow cabinet (BRIT) n (POL) 影の内閣 kágè no náìkaku

shadowy [ʃæd'oui:] adj (in shadow) 影の多い kágè no ōi; (dim: figure, shape) 影の様な kágè no yó nà

shady [ʃei'di:] adj (place) 日陰のある hikáge no arù; (trees) 日よけになる hiyóke ni narù; (fig: dishonest: person, deal) いかがわしい ikágawashiī

shaft [ʃæft] n (of arrow) 矢柄 yagára; (of spear) 柄 e; (AUT, TECH) 回転軸 kaíteñjiku, シャフト sháfùto; (of mine) 縦坑 ta-

tēkō; (of elevator) 通路 tsūrò
a shaft of light 一条の光 ichíjō no
hikarì

shaggy [ʃæg'i:] *adj* (appearance, beard,
dog) ぼさぼさの bosábosa no

shake [ʃeik] (*pt* **shook**, *pp* **shaken**) *vt*
(*gen*) 揺さぶる yusúburù; (bottle) 振る fú-
rù; (cocktail) シェイクする sheíkù suru;
(building) 揺るがす yurúgasù; (weaken:
beliefs, resolve) ぐらつかせる gurátsu-
kaserù; (upset, surprise) ...にショックを
与える ...ni shókkù wo atáerù
♦*vi* (tremble) 震える furúerù
to shake one's head (in refusal, dismay) 頭を振る atáma wò fúrù
to shake hands with someone ...と握
手をする ...to ákùshu wo suru

shaken [ʃei'kən] *pp of* shake

shake off *vt* (lit) 振り落す furíotosù;
(*fig*: pursuer) まく makú

shake up *vt* (lit: ingredients) よく振る
yókù furu; (*fig*: organization) 一新する
isshín suru

shaky [ʃei'ki:] *adj* (hand, voice) 震える furúerù; (table, building) ぐらぐらする gú-
ràgura suru

shall [ʃæl] *aux vb*: *I shall go* 行きます
ikímasù
shall I open the door? ドアを開けま
しょうか dóà wo akémashò ka
I'll get some, shall I? 少し取ってきま
しょうか sukóshì totté kimashò ka

shallow [ʃæl'ou] *adj* (water, box, breathing) 浅い asáì; (*fig*: ideas etc) 浅薄な seńpaku na

sham [ʃæm] *n* いんちき íñchiki
♦*vt* ...の振りをする ...no furí wò suru

shambles [ʃæm'bəlz] *n* 大混乱 daíkoñran

shame [ʃeim] *n* (embarrassment) 恥 hají;
(disgrace) 不面目 fuméñboku
♦*vt* 辱める hazúkashimerù
it is a shame that ... ...であるのは残
念だ ...de árù no wa zañneñ da
it is a shame to do ... ...するのはもっ
たいない ...súrú no wà mottáinaì
what a shame! 残念だ zañneñ da

shamefaced [ʃeim'feist] *adj* 恥ずかしそ
うな hazúkashisō na

shameful [ʃeim'fəl] *adj* (disgraceful) 恥
ずべき hazúbeki

shameless [ʃeim'lis] *adj* (liar, deception)
恥知らずの hajíshirazù no

shampoo [ʃæmpuː'] *n* シャンプー sháñpū
♦*vt* シャンプーする sháñpū suru
shampoo and set シャンプーとセット
sháñpū to séttò

shamrock [ʃæm'rɑːk] *n* ツメクサ tsumé-
kusa, クローバー kurôbà

shandy [ʃæn'diː] *n* シャンディー sháñdī ◇
ビールをレモネードで割った飲物 bírù
wo remóñèdo de wattá nomimonò

shan't [ʃænt] = shall not

shanty town [ʃæn'tiː-] *n* バラック集落
barákkushùraku

shape [ʃeip] *n* (form, outline) 形 katáchi
♦*vt* (fashion, form) 形作る katáchizuku-
rù; (someone's ideas, life) 方向付ける hô-
kōzukerù
to take shape (painting) 段々格好がつ
く dañdañ kakkô ga tsukù; (plan) 具体化
してくる gutáika shite kurù

-shaped [ʃeipt] *suffix*: *heart-shaped* ハ
ート形の hátògata no

shapeless [ʃeip'lis] *adj* 不格好な bukákk-
ō na

shapely [ʃeip'liː] *adj* (woman, legs) 美し
い utsúkushiì

shape up *vi* (events) 具体化してくる gutáika shite kurù; (person) 期待通りに進
歩する kitáidòri ni shiñpo suru

share [ʃeːr] *n* (part received) 分け前 wa-
kémaè; (part contributed) 持分 mochíbùn,
負担分 futáñbun; (COMM) 株 kabú
♦*vt* (books, toys, room) 共用する kyōyō
suru; (cost) 分担する buñtan suru; (one's
lunch) 分けてやる wakéte yarù; (have in
common: features, qualities etc) ...の点
で似ている ...no téñ de nité irù

shareholder [ʃeːr'houldəːr] *n* 株主 kabú-
nùshi

share out *vi* 分配する buñpai suru

shark [ʃɑːrk] *n* サメ samé

sharp [ʃɑːrp] *adj* (razor, knife) よく切れ
る yókù kirérù; (point, teeth) 鋭い surúdoì; (nose, chin) とがった togátta; (outline) くっきりした kukkíri shitá; (pain)

鋭い surúdoì; (cold) 身を切る様な mí wò kírù yō na; (taste) 舌を刺す様な shitá wò sásù yō na; (MUS) ピッチが高過ぎる pítchì ga takásugirù; (contrast) 強い tsuyóì; (increase) 急な kyū na; (voice) 甲高い kandakaì; (person: quick-witted) 抜け目のない nukéme no naì; (dishonest: practice etc) 不正な fuséi na

♦n (MUS) えい音記号 eíonkigò, シャープ shápù

♦adv (precisely): **at 2 o'clock sharp** 2時きっかりに níjì kikkárì ni

sharpen [ʃɑːrˈpən] vt (stick etc) とがらせる togáraserù; (pencil) 削る kezúrù; (fig: appetite) そそる sosórù

sharpener [ʃɑːrˈpənəːr] n (also: **pencil sharpener**) 鉛筆削り eńpitsukezúrì

sharp-eyed [ʃɑːrpˈaid] adj 目の鋭い mé nò surudoì

sharply [ʃɑːrpˈliː] adv (turn, stop) 急にkyū ni; (stand out) くっきりと kukkírì to; (contrast) 強く tsuyókù; (criticize, retort) 辛らつに shińratsu ni

shatter [ʃætˈəːr] vt (break) 割る warú, 木っ端みじんにする kóppàmijin ni surù; (fig: ruin) 台無しにする daínashi ni surù; (: upset) がっくりさせる gakkúrì sasérù

♦vi (break) 割れる warérù

shave [ʃeiv] vt (person, face, legs etc) そる sórù

♦vi ひげをそる higé wò sórù

♦n: **to have a shave** (at barber's) ひげをそってもらう higé wò sóttè moráù; (oneself) ひげをそる higé wò sórù

shaver [ʃeiˈvəːr] n (also: **electric shaver**) 電気かみそり deńkikamìsori

shaving [ʃeiˈviŋ] n (action) ひげをそる事 higé wò sórù kotó

shaving brush n シェービングブラシ shébinguburàshi

shaving cream, shaving foam n シェービングクリーム shébingukurìimu

shavings [ʃeiˈviŋz] npl (of wood etc) かんなくず kańnakuzù

shawl [ʃɔːl] n 肩掛 katákàke, ショール shórù

she [ʃiː] pron 彼女は〔が〕kánòjo wa 〔ga〕

sheaf [ʃiːf] (npl **sheaves**) n (of corn, papers)

束 tábà

shear [ʃiːˈəːr] (pt **sheared**, pp **shorn**) vt (sheep) ...の毛を刈る ...noké wò karú

shear off vi 折れる orérù

shears [ʃiːˈəːrz] npl (for hedge) はさみ hasámi

sheath [ʃiːθ] n (of knife) さや sáyà; (contraceptive) コンドーム końdòmu, スキン sukíñ

sheaves [ʃiːvz] npl of **sheaf**

she-cat [ʃiːˈkæt] n 雌ネコ mesúneko

shed [ʃed] n 小屋 koyá

♦vt (leaves, fur, hair etc) 落す otósù; (skin) 脱皮する dappí suru; (tears) 流す nagásù

to shed blood 人を殺す hitó wò korósù

to shed a load (subj: truck etc) 荷崩れを起す nikúzure wo okósù

she'd [ʃiːd] = **she had; she would**

sheen [ʃiːn] n つや tsuyá

sheep [ʃiːp] n inv ヒツジ hitsúji

sheepdog [ʃiːpˈdɔːg] n 牧用犬 bokúyōken

sheepish [ʃiːˈpiʃ] adj 恥ずかしそうな hazúkashisò na

sheepskin [ʃiːpˈskin] n ヒツジの毛皮 hitsúji nò kegáwa, シープスキン shípusukiñ

sheer [ʃiːr] adj (utter) 全くの mattáku no; (steep) 垂直の suíchoku no; (almost transparent) ごく薄手の gokù usúde no

♦adv (straight up: rise) 垂直に suíchoku ni

sheet [ʃiːt] n (on bed) シーツ shítsù; (of paper, glass, metal) 一枚 ichímaì

a sheet of ice アイスバーン aísubàn

sheik(h) [ʃiːk] n 首長 shuchó

shelf [ʃelf] (pl **shelves**) n 棚 taná

shell [ʃel] n (on beach) 貝殻 kaígara; (of egg, nut etc) 殻 kará; (explosive) 弾丸 dańgan; (of building) 外壁 sotókabe

♦vt (peas) むく múkù; (MIL: fire on) 砲撃する hógeki suru

she'll [ʃiːl] = **she will; she shall**

shellfish [ʃelˈfiʃ] n inv (crab) カニ kaní; (prawn, shrimp etc) エビ ebí; (lobster) ロブスター robúsùtà; (scallop, clam etc) 貝 kái ◊料理用語として殻のある海の生物を指す ryóriyogo toshite kará no arù úmi

no séîbutsu wo sásù

shelter [ʃel'tər] n (building) シェルター shérútā; (protection: for hiding) 隠れ場所 kakúrebashð; (: from rain) 雨宿りの場所 amáyàdori no bashó

♦vt (protect) 守る mamórù; (give lodging to: homeless, refugees) ...に避難の場所を提供する ...ni hínàn no bashó wð teíkyð surù; (: wanted man) かくまう kakúmaù

♦vi (from rain etc) 雨宿りをする amáyàdori wo surù; (from danger) 避難する hínàn surù; (hide) 隠れる kakúrerù

sheltered [ʃel'tərd] adj (life) 世間の荒波から守られた sékèn no aránami karà mamóraretà; (spot) 雨風を避けられる ámèkaze wo sakérarerù

sheltered housing 老人・身障者用住宅 rójìñ, shíñshōshayō jūtaku

shelve [ʃelv] vt (fig: plan) 棚上げにする taná-age ni surù

shelves [ʃelvz] npl of **shelf**

shepherd [ʃep'ərd] n ヒツジ飼い hitsújikài

♦vt (guide) 案内する añnai surù

shepherd's pie (BRIT) n シェパードパイ shepádopaì ◇ひき肉にマッシュポテトを乗せて焼いた料理 hikíniku nî masshúpotèto wo noséte yaità ryórì

sheriff [ʃer'if] (US) n 保安官 hoáñkan

sherry [ʃer'i:] n シェリー酒 sheríshù

she's [ʃi:z] = **she is**; **she has**

Shetland [ʃet'lənd] n (also: **the Shetlands, the Shetland Isles**) シェットランド諸島 shettórando shotð

shield [ʃi:ld] n (MIL) 盾 tátè; (SPORT: trophy) 盾型トロフィー tatégata toròfī; (protection) ...よけ ...yóke

♦vt: **to shield (from)** ...の(...)よけになる ...no (...) yóke ni narù

shift [ʃift] n (change) 変更 heñkō; (work-period) 交替 kótai; (group of workers) 交替組 kótaigùmi

♦vt (move) ...の位置を変える ...no íchì wo kaérù; (remove: stain) 抜く nukú

♦vi (move: wind, person) 変る kawárù

shiftless [ʃift'lis] adj (person) ろくでなしの rokúdenashi no

shift work n 交替でする作業 kótai de suru sagyò

shifty [ʃif'ti:] adj (person, eyes) うさん臭い usáñkusaì

shilling [ʃil'iŋ] (BRIT) n シリング shírìngu ◇かつての英国の硬貨でポンドの1/20 kátsùte no eíkoku no kóka de póñdo no nijúbùn no ichí

shilly-shally [ʃil'i:ʃæli:] vi ぐずぐずする gúzùguzu suru

shimmer [ʃim'ər] vi ちらちら光る chíràchira hikárù

shin [ʃin] n 向こうずね mukózune

shine [ʃain] n つや tsuyá

♦vb (pt, pp **shone**)

♦vi (sun) 照る térù; (torch, light, eyes) 光る hikárù; (fig) 優れる sugúrerù

♦vt (glasses) ふく fukú; (shoes) 磨く migákù

to shine a torch on something ...を懐中電燈で照す ...wo kaíchūdèntō de terásù

shingle [ʃiŋ'gəl] n (on beach) 砂利 jarí

shingles [ʃiŋ'gəlz] n (MED) 帯状ヘルペス taíjōherupèsu

shiny [ʃai'ni:] adj (coin) ぴかぴかの pikápika no; (shoes, hair, lipstick) つやつやの tsuyátsuya no

ship [ʃip] n 船 fúnè

♦vt (transport by ship) 船で運ぶ fúnè de hakóbù; (send: goods) 輸送する yusó surù

shipbuilding [ʃip'bildiŋ] n 造船 zósen

shipment [ʃip'mənt] n (goods) 輸送貨物 yusókamòtsu

shipper [ʃip'ər] n 送り主 okúrinùshi

shipping [ʃip'iŋ] n (transport of cargo) 運送 uñsó; (ships collectively) 船舶 séñpaku

shipshape [ʃip'ʃeip] adj きちんとした kichíñ to shita

shipwreck [ʃip'rek] n (event) 難破 nañpa; (ship) 難破船 nañpasen

♦vt: **to be shipwrecked** 難破する nañpa suru

shipyard [ʃip'jɑːrd] n 造船所 zósenjo

shire [ʃaiə:r] (BRIT) n 郡 gúñ

shirk [ʃə:rk] vt (work, obligations) 怠る

okótarù

shirt [ʃəːrt] n (man's) ワイシャツ waíshatsu; (woman's) シャツブラウス shatsúburaùsu

in (one's) shirt sleeves 上着を脱いで uwági wò núìde

shit [ʃit] (*inf!*) excl くそっ kusót

shiver [ʃívˈəːr] n (act of shivering) 身震い mibúruì

♦vi 震える furúerù

shoal [ʃoul] n (of fish) 群れ muré; (*fig: also*: **shoals**) 大勢 özeí

shock [ʃɑːk] n (start, impact) 衝撃 shốgeki; (ELEC) 感電 kañden; (emotional) 打撃 dagéki, ショック shókkù; (MED) ショック shókkù

♦vt (upset, offend) ...にショックを与える ...ni shókkù wo atáerù

shock absorber n 緩衝器 kańshōkì

shocking [ʃɑːkiŋ] adj (awful: standards, accident) ひどい hidóì; (outrageous: play, book) 衝撃的な shốgekiteki na

shod [ʃɑːd] pt, pp of **shoe**

shoddy [ʃɑːdiː] adj (goods, workmanship) 粗雑な sozátsu na

shoe [ʃuː] n (for person) 靴 kutsú; (for horse) てい鉄 teítetsu

♦vt (pt, pp **shod**) (horse) ...にてい鉄を付ける ...ni teítetsu wò tsukérù

shoebrush [ʃuːˈbrʌʃ] n 靴ブラシ kutsúburàshi

shoelace [ʃuːˈleis] n 靴ひも kutsúhìmo

shoe polish n 靴磨き kutsúmigàki

shoeshop [ʃuːˈʃɑːp] n 靴屋 kutsúyà

shoestring [ʃuːˈstriŋ] n (*fig*): *on a shoestring* わずかの金で wázùka no kané de

shone [ʃoun] pt, pp of **shine**

shoo [ʃuː] excl しっ shítt ◊動物を追っ払う時に言う言葉 dóbutsu wò oíharaù toki ni iú kotoba

shook [ʃuk] pt of **shake**

shoot [ʃuːt] n (on branch, seedling) 若枝 wakáeda

♦vb (pt, pp **shot**)

♦vt (gun) 撃つ utsù; (arrow) 射る írù; (kill: bird, robber etc) 撃ち殺す uchíkorosù; (wound) そ撃する sogéki suru; (execute) 銃殺する júsatsu suru; (film) 撮

影する satsúei suru

♦vi (with gun/bow): *to shoot (at)* (...を目掛けて) 撃つ〔射る〕 (...wo megákete) útsù 〔írù〕; (SOCCER) シュートする shúto suru

shoot down vt (plane) 撃ち落とす uchíotosù

shoot in/out vi (rush) 飛込む〔飛出す〕 tobíkomù 〔tobídasù〕

shooting [ʃuːtiŋ] n (shots) 発砲事件 happójikèn; (HUNTING) 狩猟 shuryố

shooting star n 流れ星 nagárebòshi

shoot up vi (*fig*) 急上昇する kyújōshō suru

shop [ʃɑːp] n (selling goods) 店 misé; (*also*: **workshop**) 作業場 sagyốbà

♦vi (*also*: **go shopping**) 買物する kaímono suru

shop assistant (BRIT) n 店員 teñ-in

shop floor (BRIT) n 労働側 rốdōgawa

shopkeeper [ʃɑːpˈkiːpəːr] n 店主 teñshu

shoplifting [ʃɑːpˈliftiŋ] n 万引 mañbiki

shopper [ʃɑːpˈəːr] n (person) 買物客 kaímonokyàku

shopping [ʃɑːpˈiŋ] n (goods) 買物 kaímono

shopping bag n ショッピングバッグ shoppíngubaggù

shopping center (BRIT **shopping centre**) n ショッピングセンター shoppíngusentā

shop-soiled [ʃɑːpˈsɔild] adj (goods) 棚ざらしの tanázarashi no

shop steward (BRIT) n (INDUSTRY) 職場代表 shokúbadaihyố

shop window n ショーウインドー shốuindò

shore [ʃɔːr] n 岸 kishí

♦vt: *to shore up* 補強する hokyố suru

on shore 陸に rikú ni

shorn [ʃɔːrn] pp of **shear**

short [ʃɔːrt] adj (not long) 短い mijíkaì; (person: not tall) 背の低い sé nò hikúì; (curt) ぶっきらぼうな bukkírabō na; (insufficient) 不足している fusóku shite irù

to be short of something ...が不足している ...ga fusóku shite irù

in short 要するに yố surù ni

short of doing ... ...をしなければ ...wo shinákereba

it is short for それは...の短縮形です soré wà ... no tańshukukei desu

to cut short (speech, visit) 予定より短くする yotéi yorì mijíkakù suru

everything short of ... ...を除いて何でも ...wo nozóîte náñ de mo

to fall short of ...に達しない ...ni tasshínaî

to run short of ...が足りなくなる ...ga tarínakunarù

to stop short (while walking etc) 急に立ち止まる kyū ni tachidomarù; (while doing something) 急にやめる kyū ni yamerù

to stop short of ...まではしない ...máde wa shináî

shortage [ʃɔːˈtɪdʒ] *n*: *a shortage of* ...不足 ...busóku

shortbread [ʃɔːtˈbred] *n* ショートブレッド shótobureddò ◇小麦粉、バター、砂糖で作った菓子 komúgiko, bátà, satő dè tsukútta kashì

short-change [ʃɔːtˈtʃeindʒ] *vt* ...に釣銭を少なく渡す ...ni tsurísen wò sukúnakù watásù

short-circuit [ʃɔːtˈsəːˈkɪt] *n* (ELEC) ショート shóto

shortcoming [ʃɔːtˈkʌmɪŋ] *n* 欠点 kettén

short(crust) pastry [ʃɔːt(ˈkrʌst)-] *(BRIT) n* パイ生地 páikijì

shortcut [ʃɔːtˈkʌt] *n* 近道 chikámichi

shorten [ʃɔːrˈtən] *vt* (clothes, visit) 短くする mijíkakù suru

shortfall [ʃɔːtˈfɔːl] *n* 不足 fusóku

shorthand [ʃɔːtˈhænd] *n* 速記 sokkí

shorthand typist *(BRIT) n* 速記もできるタイピスト sokkí mo dekirù taípisùto

shortlist [ʃɔːtˈlɪst] *(BRIT) n* (for job) 予備審査の合格者リスト yobíshiñsa no gőkakusha risùto

short-lived [ʃɔːtˈlɪvd] *adj* つかの間の tsuká no ma no

shortly [ʃɔːtˈliː] *adv* 間もなく ma mó nàku

shorts [ʃɔːts] *npl*: *(a pair of) shorts* (short trousers) 半ズボン hañzubon; (men's underwear) パンツ páñtsu

short-sighted [ʃɔːtˈsaiˈtid] *(BRIT) adj* 近眼の kiñgan no; *(fig)* 先見の明のない señken no meî no nai

short-staffed [ʃɔːtˈstæft] *adj*: *to be short-staffed* 人手不足である hitódebusoku de aru

short story *n* 短編小説 tañpenshősetsu

short-tempered [ʃɔːtˈtempərd] *adj* 短気な táñki na

short-term [ʃɔːtˈtəːˈrm] *adj* (effect, borrowing) 短期の táñki no

shortwave [ʃɔːtˈweiv] *n* (RADIO) 短波 táñpa

shot [ʃɑːt] *pt, pp of* **shoot**
♦*n* (of gun) 発砲 happő; (try, *also* SOCCER etc) シュート shūto; (injection) 注射 chūsha; (PHOT) ショット shőttò

a good/poor shot (person) 射撃のうまい〔下手な〕人 shagéki no umaî〔hetà na〕hitő

like a shot (without any delay) 鉄砲玉の様に teppődama no yő ni

shotgun [ʃɑːtˈgʌn] *n* 散弾銃 sañdañjū

should [ʃud] *aux vb*: *I should go now* もうおいとましなくては mő o-ítoma shinakute wà

he should be there now 彼は今あそこにいるはずです káre wa ímà asóko nì irú hazù desu

I should go if I were you 私だったら，行きますよ watákushi dattàra, ikímasù yő

I should like to ... ...をしたいと思いますが ...wo shitái tò omóimasù ga

shoulder [ʃoulˈdəːr] *n* (ANAT) 肩 kátà
♦*vt (fig:* responsibility, blame) 負う őù

shoulder bag *n* ショルダーバッグ shorúdābaggù

shoulder blade *n* 肩甲骨 keñkőkotsu

shoulder strap *n* ショルダーストラップ shorúdāsutorappù

shouldn't [ʃudˈənt] = **should not**

shout [ʃaut] *n* 叫び声 sakébigoè
♦*vt* 大声で言う őgoè de iú
♦*vi (also:* shout out) 叫ぶ sakébù

shout down *vt* (speaker) どなって黙らせる donátte damáraserù

shouting [ʃautɪŋ] n 叫び声 sakébigoè

shove [ʃʌv] vt 押す osú; (inf: put): **to shove something in** ...を...に押込む ...wo...ni oshíkomù

shovel [ʃʌvəl] n (gen) スコップ sukóppù, シャベル shábèru; (mechanical) パワーシャベル pawáshabèru

♦vt (snow) かく kákù; (coal, earth) すくう sukúù

shove off vi: **shove off!** (inf) うせろ usérò

show [ʃou] n (demonstration: of emotion) 表現 hyōgen; (semblance) 見せ掛け misékake; (exhibition: flower show etc) 展示会 teñjikài, ショー shō; (THEATER, TV) ショー shō

♦vb (pt showed, pp shown)

♦vt (indicate) 示す shimésù, 見せる misérù; (exhibit) 展示する teñji suru; (courage etc) 示す shimésù; (illustrate, depict) 描写する byōsha suru; (film: in movie theater) 上映する jōei suru; (program, film: on television) 放送する hōsō suru

♦vi (be evident) 見える miérù; (appear) 現れる aráwarerù

for show 格好だけの kakkō dake no

on show (exhibits etc) 展示中 teñjichù

show business n 芸能界 geínōkài

showdown [ʃou'daun] n 対決 taíketsu

shower [ʃau'əːr] n (of rain) にわか雨 niwákaamè; (of stones etc) ...の雨 ...no ámè; (for bathing in) シャワー sháwà

♦vi 降ってくる futté kurù

♦vt: **to shower someone with** ...の上に...を降らす ...no ué nì...wo furásù

to have a shower シャワーを浴びる sháwà wo abírù

showerproof [ʃau'əːrpruːf] adj 防水の bōsui no ◇にわか雨程度なら耐えられるが強い雨にはぬれてしまうコートなどについて言う niwákaamè téido nara taérarerù ga tsuyói amè ni wa nuréteshimau kōto nado ni tsúite iú

show in vt (person) 中へ案内する nákà e añnaì suru

showing [ʃou'ɪŋ] n (of film) 上映 jōei

show jumping [-dʒʌmp'iŋ] n (of horses) 障害飛越 shōgaihiètsu

shown [ʃoun] pp of **show**

show off vi (pej) 気取る kidóru

♦vt (display) 見せびらかす misébirakasù

show-off [ʃou'ɔːf] (inf) n (person) 自慢屋 jimán-yà

show out vt (person) 出口へ案内する dégùchi e añnaì suru

showpiece [ʃou'piːs] n (of exhibition etc) 立派な見本 rippá nà mihón

showroom [ʃou'ruːm] n ショールーム shōrùmu

show up vi (stand out) 目立つ medátsù; (inf: turn up) 現れる aráwarerù

♦vt (uncover: imperfections etc) 暴露する bákùro suru

shrank [ʃræŋk] pt of **shrink**

shrapnel [ʃræp'nəl] n 弾丸の破片 dañgan nò hahén

shred [ʃred] n (gen pl) 切れ端 kiréhashi

♦vt (gen) ずたずたにする zutázuta ni surù; (CULIN) 刻む kizámù

shredder [ʃred'əːr] n (vegetable shredder) 削り器 kezúrikì; (document shredder) シュレッダー shuréddà

shrewd [ʃruːd] adj (businessman) 抜け目のない nukéme no naì; (assessment) 賢明な keñmei na

shriek [ʃriːk] n 金切り声 kanákirigoè

♦vi 金切り声を出す kanákirigoè wo dásù

shrill [ʃril] adj (cry, voice) 甲高い kañdakaì

shrimp [ʃrimp] n (shellfish) えび ebí

shrine [ʃrain] n (place of worship) 礼拝堂 reíhaidò; (for relics) 聖遺物容器 seíbutsuyōkì; (fig: building) 殿堂 deñdò; (: place) 聖地 seichi

shrink [ʃriŋk] (pt shrank, pp shrunk) vi (cloth) 縮む chijímù; (be reduced: profits, audiences) 減る herú; (move: also: **shrink away**) 縮こまって逃げる chijíkomattè nigérù

♦vt (cloth) 縮める chijímerù

♦n (inf: pej: psychiatrist) 精神科医 seíshinka-ì

to shrink from (doing) something ...を(するのを)いやがる ...wo (surú no wò) iyágarù

shrinkage [ʃriŋk'idʒ] *n* 縮まる分 chijímarù bún

shrinkwrap [ʃriŋk'ræp] *vt* ラップで包む ráppù de tsutsúmù

shrivel [ʃriv'əl] (*also*: **shrivel up**) *vt* しおれさせる shióresaserù
♦*vi* しおれる shiórerù

shroud [ʃraud] *n* 覆い ôi
♦*vt*: **shrouded in mystery** なぞに包まれて nazó nì tsutsúmaretè

Shrove Tuesday [ʃrouv-] *n* 謝肉祭の火曜日 shaníkusài no kayóbi

shrub [ʃrʌb] *n* 低木 teíboku

shrubbery [ʃrʌb'əːri:] *n* 植込み uékomi

shrug [ʃrʌg] *n* 肩をすくめる事 kátà wo sukúmerù kotó
♦*vt, vi*: **to shrug (one's shoulders)** 肩をすくめる kátà wo sukúmerù

shrug off *vt* (criticism) 受流す ukénagasù; (illness) 無視する múshì suru

shrunk [ʃrʌŋk] *pp of* **shrink**

shudder [ʃʌd'əːr] *n* 身震い mibúrùi
♦*vi* (person: with fear, revulsion) 身震いする mibúrùi suru

shuffle [ʃʌf'əl] *vt* (cards) 混ぜる mazérù
♦*vi* (walk) 足を引きずって歩く ashí wò hikízutte arukù
to shuffle (one's feet) (while standing, sitting) 足をもぞもぞ動かす ashí wò mózòmozo ugókasù

shun [ʃʌn] *vt* (publicity, neighbors etc) 避ける sakérù

shunt [ʃʌnt] *vt* (train) 分岐線に入れる buńkisen ni irerù; (object) 動かす ugókasù

shut [ʃʌt] (*pt, pp* **shut**) *vt* (door) 閉める shimérù; (shop) しまう shimáù; (mouth, eyes) 閉じる tojírù
♦*vi* (door, eyes, shop) 閉る shimárù

shut down *vt* (for a time) 休業させる kyúgyo saserù; (forever) 閉鎖する heísa suru
♦*vi* (for a time) 休業する kyúgyo surù; (forever) 閉鎖になる heísa ni narù

shut off *vt* (supply etc) 遮断する shadán suru

shutter [ʃʌt'əːr] *n* (on window: *also* PHOT) シャッター sháttà

shuttle [ʃʌt'əl] *n* (plane etc) シャトル

shátòru; (*also*: **space shuttle**) スペースシャトル supésushatòru; (*also*: **shuttle service**) 折り返し運転 oríkaeshi uñten

shuttlecock [ʃʌt'əlkɑːk] *n* シャットルコック shattórukokkù

shut up *vi* (*inf*: keep quiet) 黙る damárù
♦*vt* (close) しまう shimau; (silence) 黙らせる damáraserù

shy [ʃai] *adj* (timid: animal) 臆病な okúbyò na; (reserved) 内気な uchíka na

shyness [ʃai'nis] *n* (timidity: of animal) 臆病 okúbyò; (reservedness) 内気 uchíki

Siamese [saiəmi:z'] *adj*: **Siamese cat** シャムネコ shamúneko

Siberia [saibí:'riːə] *n* シベリア shibéria

sibling [sib'liŋ] *n* 兄弟 kyódai ◇男兄弟にも兄弟（姉妹）にも使う otókokyòdai ni mo oñnakyòdai (shímai) ni mo tsukáù

Sicily [sis'iliː] *n* シチリア shichíria

sick [sik] *adj* (ill) 病気の byóki no; (nauseated) むかついた mukátsuita; (humor) 病的な byóteki na; (vomiting):
to be sick 吐く hákù
to feel sick むかつく mukátsukù
to be sick of (*fig*) ...にうんざりしている ...ni uñzari shite irù

sick bay *n* (on ship) 医務室 imúshìtsu

sicken [sik'ən] *vt* むかつかせる mukátsukaserù

sickening [sik'əniŋ] *adj* (*fig*) 不快な fukái na

sickle [sik'əl] *n* かま kámà

sick leave *n* 病気休暇 byókikyùka

sickly [sik'liː] *adj* (child, plant) 病気がちな byókigachi na; (causing nausea: smell) むかつかせる mukátsukaserù

sickness [sik'nis] *n* (illness) 病気 byóki; (vomiting) おう吐 ôto

sick pay *n* 病気手当 byókiteàte

side [said] *n* (of object) 横 yokó; (of body) 脇腹 wakíbara; (of lake) 岸 kishí; (aspect) 側面 sokúmen; (team) 側 gawá
♦*adj* (door, entrance) 横の yokó no
♦*vi*: **to side with someone** ...の肩を持つ ...no kátà wo mótsù
the side of the road 路肩 rokáta
the side of a hill 山腹 sañpuku
by the side of ...の横に ...no yokó ni

side by side 横に並んで yokó ni naráñ-de

from side to side 左右に sáyū ni

from all sides 四方八方から shihôhap-pô kara

to take sides (with) (...に)味方する (...ni) mikáta suru

sideboard [said'bɔːrd] *n* 食器戸棚 shok-kítodàna, サイドボード saídobòdo

sideboards [said'bɔːrdz] (*BRIT*) *npl* = **sideburns**

sideburns [said'bəːrnz] *npl* もみあげ mo-míage

side drum *n* (MUS) 小太鼓 kodáīko

side effect *n* (MED, *fig*) 副作用 fukúsa-yō

sidelight [said'lait] *n* (AUT) 車幅灯 sha-fúkutō

sideline [said'lain] *n* (SPORT) サイドライン saídoraìn; (*fig*: supplementary job) 副業 fukúgyō

sidelong [said'lɔːŋ] *adj*: *to give some-one/something a sidelong glance* ...を横目で見る ...wo yokóme de mirú

sidesaddle [said'sædəl] *adv*: *to ride sidesaddle* 馬に横乗りする umá ni yo-kónori surù

side show *n* (stall at fair, circus) 見世物屋台 misémonoyatài

sidestep [said'step] *vt* (*fig*) 避けて通る sakétetoru

side street *n* わき道 wakímìchi

sidetrack [said'træk] *vt* (*fig*) ...の話を脱線させる ...no hanáshi wò dassén saserù

sidewalk [said'wɔːk] (*US*) *n* 歩道 hodố

sideways [said'weiz] *adv* (go in) 横向きに yokómuki ni; (lean) 横へ xɔ̀ e

siding [sai'diŋ] *n* (RAIL) 側線 sokúsen

sidle [sai'dəl] *vi*: *to sidle up (to)* (...に) こっそり近寄る (...ni) kossórì chikáyorù

siege [siːdʒ] *n* (gen, MIL) 包囲 hối

siesta [siːes'tə] *n* 昼寝 hirúne .

sieve [siv] *n* ふるい furúi

♦*vt* ふるう furúu

sift [sift] *vt* (*fig*: *also*: **sift through**: information) ふるい分ける furúiwakerù; (sieve) ふるう furúu

sigh [sai] *n* ため息 taméikì

♦*vi* ため息をつく taméikì wo tsukú

sight [sait] *n* (faculty) 視覚 shikáku; (spectacle) 光景 kốkei; (on gun) 照準器 shôjunki

♦*vt* 見掛ける mikákerù

in sight 見える所に miérù tokóro ni

on sight (shoot) 見付け次第 mitsúkeshi-dài

out of sight 見えない所に miénaì tokó-rò ni

sightseeing [sait'siːiŋ] *n* 名所見物 meí-shokeñbutsu

to go sightseeing 名所見物に行く meí-shokeñbutsu ni ikú

sign [sain] *n* (with hand) 合図 aízu; (indication: of present condition) しるし shi-rúshi; (: of future condition) 兆し kizá-shi; (notice) 看板 kañban; (written) 張紙 harígami

♦*vt* (document) ...に署名〔サイン〕する ...ni shoméi 〔sáīn〕 suru; (player) 雇う yatóù

to sign something over to someone ...を...に譲渡する ...wo...ni jốto suru

signal [sig'nəl] *n* (gen) 信号 shiñgō; (equipment on highway, railway) 信号機 shiñgòki

♦*vi* (make signs: *also* AUT) 合図をする aízu wo suru

♦*vt* (person) ...に合図をする ...ni aízu wo suru; (message) ...する様に合図をする ...suru yō ni aizu wo suru

signalman [sig'nəlmən] (*pl* **signalmen**) *n* (RAIL) 信号手 shiñgòshu

signature [sig'nətʃəːr] *n* 署名 shoméi, サイン sáîn

signature tune *n* テーマ音楽 têmaoñ-gaku

signet ring [sig'nit-] *n* 印章指輪 iñshō-yubiwà

significance [signif'əkəns] *n* (impor-tance) 重要性 jūyōsei

significant [signif'ikənt] *adj* (full of meaning: look, smile) 意味深い imíbukà-i; (important: amount, discovery) 重要な jūyō na

signify [sig'nəfai] *vt* 意味する ímì suru

sign language *n* 手話 shúwà

sign on *vi* (MIL) 入隊する nyútai surù; (*BRIT*: as unemployed) 失業手当を請求する shitsúgyoteàte wo seíkyu suru; (for course) 受講手続をする jukótetsuzùki wo suru

◆*vt* (MIL: recruits) 入隊させる nyútai saserù; (employee) 雇う yatóù

signpost [sain'poust] *n* 案内標識 annaihyóshiki

sign up *vi* (MIL) 入隊する nyútai suru; (for course) 受講手続をする jukótetsuzùki wo suru

silence [sai'ləns] *n* (of person) 沈黙 chímmoku; (of place) 静けさ shizúkesà

◆*vt* (person, opposition) 黙らせる damáraserù

silencer [sai'lənsə:r] *n* (on gun) 消音器 shóoñki, サイレンサー saíreñsà; (*BRIT*: AUT) 消音器 shóoñki, マフラー máfùrā

silent [sai'lənt] *adj* (person) 黙っている damátte irù; (place) しんとした shiñtó shitá; (machine) 音のない otó no naì; (film) 無声の muséi no

to remain silent 黙っている damátte irù

silent prayer 黙とう mokútoð

silent partner *n* (COMM) 出資者 shusshísha ◇資本金の一部を出すが, 業務に直接関与しない社員について言う shihóñkin no ichíbù wo dásù ga, gyómù ni chokúsetsu kañyo shináì shá-ìn ni tsuite iú

silhouette [silu:et'] *n* シルエット shírùetto

silicon chip [sil'ikən-] *n* シリコンチップ shírikonchippù

silk [silk] *n* 絹 kínù

◆*adj* (scarf, shirt) 絹の kínù no

silky [sil'ki:] *adj* (material, skin) 絹の様な kínù no yó nà

silly [sil'i:] *adj* (person, idea) ばかな bákà na

silo [sai'lou] *n* (on farm, for missile) サイロ sáìro

silt [silt] *n* (in harbor, river etc) 沈泥 chíñdei

silver [sil'və:r] *n* (metal) 銀 gíñ; (coins) 硬貨 kốkà; (items made of silver) 銀製品 gíñseìhin

◆*adj* (color) 銀色の gíñ-iro no; (made of silver) 銀の gíñ no

silver paper (*BRIT*) *n* 銀紙 gíñgami

silver-plated [sil'və:rplei'tid] *adj* 銀めっきの gíñmekkì no

silversmith [sil'və:rsmiθ] *n* 銀細工師 gíñzaikushì

silvery [sil'və:ri:] *adj* (like silver) 銀の様な gíñ no yó nà

similar [sim'ələ:r] *adj*: **similar (to)** (...に)似た (...ni) nitá

similarity [siməlær'iti:] *n* 似ている事 nité irù kotó

similarly [sim'ələ:rli:] *adv* 同じ様に onáji yố ni

simile [sim'əli:] *n* 例え tatóè

simmer [sim'ə:r] *vi* (CULIN) ぐつぐつ煮える gútsùgutsu niérù

simpering [sim'pə:riŋ] *adj* (person) ばかみたいな作り笑いをする bákàmitai na tsukúriwaraì wo suru

a simpering smile ばかみたいな作り笑い bákàmitai na tsukúriwaraì

simple [sim'pəl] *adj* (easy) 簡単な kañtan na; (plain: dress, life) 素朴な sobóku na, シンプルな shíñpuru na; (foolish) ばかな bákà na; (COMM: interest) 単純な tañjun na

simplicity [simplis'əti:] *n* (ease) 簡単さ kañtansa; (plainness) 素朴さ sobókusa; (foolishness) 白痴 hakuchi

simplify [sim'pləfai] *vt* 簡単にする kañtan ni surù

simply [sim'pli:] *adv* (in a simple way: live) 素朴に sobóku ni; (talk) 平易に heíi ni; (just, merely) 単に tán ni

simulate [sim'jəleit] *vt* (enthusiasm, innocence) 装う yosóoù

simulated [sim'jəleitid] *adj* (hair, fur) 偽の nisé no, 人工の jiñkó no; (nuclear explosion) 模擬の mógì no

simultaneous [saimətlei'ni:əs] *adj* (translation, broadcast) 同時の dójì no

simultaneously [saimətlei'ni:əsli:] *adv* 同時に dójì ni

sin [sin] *n* 罪 tsúmì

◆*vi* 罪を犯す tsúmì wo okásù

since [sins] *adv* それ以来 soré irài
♦*prep* ...以来 ...îrài
♦*conj* (time) ...して以来 ...shité irài; (because) ...ので ...nódè
since then, ever since それ以来 soré irài

sincere [sinsi:r'] *adj* 誠実な seíjitsu na

sincerely [sinsi:r'li:] *adv*: *yours sincerely* (in letters) 敬具 keígu

sincerity [sinser'iti:] *n* 誠実さ seíjitsusa

sinew [sin'ju:] *n* (of person, animal) けんkéñ, 筋 sújì

sinful [sin'fəl] *adj* (thought, person) 罪深い tsumíbukaì

sing [siŋ] (*pt* **sang**, *pp* **sung**) *vt* 歌う utáù
♦*vi* (gen) 歌う utáù; (bird) 鳴く nakú

Singapore [siŋ'gəpɔ:r] *n* シンガポール shíñgapōru

singe [sindʒ] *vt* 焦がす kogásù

singer [siŋ'ə:r] *n* 歌手 káshù

singing [siŋ'iŋ] *n* (noise: of people) 歌声 utágoè; (: of birds) 鳴声 nakígoè; (art) 声楽 seígaku

single [siŋ'gəl] *adj* (individual) 一つ一つの hitótsuhitotsù no; (unmarried) 独身の dokúshin no; (not double) 一つだけの hitótsu dake nò
♦*n* (*BRIT*: *also*: **single ticket**) 片道乗車券 katámichijōshakèn; (record) シングル盤 shíñguruban

single-breasted [siŋ'gəlbres'tid] *adj* (jacket, suit) シングルの shíñguru no

single file *n*: *in single file* 一列縦隊で ichíretsujūtai de

single-handed [siŋ'gəlhæn'did] *adv* (sail, build something) 一人で hitórì de

single-minded [siŋ'gəlmain'did] *adj* 一つだけの目的を追う hitótsu dake nò mokúteki wò oú

single out *vt* (choose) 選び出す erábidasù; (distinguish) 区別する kúbètsu suru

single room *n* シングル部屋 shíñgurubeya

singles [siŋ'gəlz] *n* (TENNIS) シングルス shíñgurusu

singly [siŋ'gli:] *adv* (alone, one by one: people) 一人ずつ hitórì zutsu; (: things) 一つずつ hitótsu zutsu

singular [siŋ'gjələ:r] *adj* (odd: occurrence) 変ったkawátta; (outstanding: beauty) 著しい ichíjirushiì; (LING) 単数の tañsū no
♦*n* (LING) 単数 tañsū

sinister [sin'istə:r] *adj* 怪しげな ayáshigè na

sink [siŋk] *n* 流し nagáshi
♦*vb* (*pt* **sank**, *pp* **sunk**)
♦*vt* (ship) 沈没させる chiñbotsu saserù; (well, foundations) 掘る hórù
♦*vi* (ship) 沈没する chiñbotsu suru; (heart, spirits) しょげる shogérù, がっかりする gakkárì suru; (ground) 沈下する chiñka suru; (*also*: **sink back**, **sink down**: into chair) 身を沈める mí wò shizúmerù; (: to one's knees etc) しゃがみ込む shágamikomù; (: head etc) うなだれる unádarerù
to sink something into (teeth, claws etc) ...に...を食込ませる ...ni...wo kuíkomaserù

sink in *vi* (*fig*: words) 理解される ríkài sarérù, 身にしみる mí nì shimírù

sinner [sin'ə:r] *n* 罪人 tsumíbîto

sinus [sai'nəs] *n* (ANAT) 副鼻こう fukúbikò

sip [sip] *n* 一口 hitókùchi
♦*vt* ちびりちびり飲む chibírìchibiri nómù

siphon [sai'fən] *n* サイホン sáîhon

siphon off *vt* (liquid) サイホンで汲み出す sáîhon de kumídasù; (money etc) ほかへ回す hoká è mawásù

sir [sə:r] *n* ◇男性に対する丁寧な呼び掛け。日本語では表現しない dañsei ni taí surù teínei na yobíkake. nihóñgo de wa hyógen shinaì
Sir John Smith ジョン・スミス卿 jóñ sumísukyò
yes sir はい hâî

siren [sai'rən] *n* サイレン sâîren

sirloin [sə:r'lɔin] *n* (*also*: **sirloin steak**) サーロインステーキ sároinsutèki

sissy [sis'i:] *n* (*inf*) 弱虫 yowámùshi

sister [sis'tə:r] *n* (relation: *gen*) 女きょうだい ofinakyôdai, 姉妹 shímai; (*also*: **older sister**) 姉 anê, 姉さん nêêsan; (*also*:

younger sister) 妹 imóto; (nun) 修道女 shūdōjo; (BRIT: nurse) 婦長 fuchō

sister-in-law [sis'tə:rinlɔ:] (pl **sisters-in-law**) n (older) 義理の姉 girí nò ané; (younger) 義理の妹 girí nò imóto

sit [sit] (pt, pp **sat**) vi (sit down) 座る suwárù, 腰掛ける koshíkakerù; (be sitting) 座っている suwátte irù, 腰掛けている koshíkakerù; (assembly) 会期中である kaíkichū de arù; (for painter) モデルになる módèru ni nárù
♦vt (exam) 受ける ukérù

sitcom [sit'kɑ:m] n abbr (= situation comedy) 連続放送コメディー refízoku hōsōkomèdī

sit down vi 座る suwárù, 腰掛ける koshíkakerù

site [sait] n (place) 場所 bashó; (also: **building site**) 用地 yōchì
♦vt (factory, cruise missiles) 置く ókù

sit-in [sit'in] n (demonstration) 座り込み suwárikomi

sit in on vt fus (meeting) 傍聴する bōchō suru

sitting [sit'iŋ] n (of assembly etc) 開会 kaíkai; (in canteen) 食事の時間 shokúji nò jikán
we have two sittings for lunch 昼食は2交代で出されます chúshoku wà nikōtai de dasáremasù

sitting room n 居間 ímà

situated [sitʃ'u:eitid] adj ...にある ...ni árù

situation [sitʃu:ei'ʃən] n (state) 状況 jōkyō; (job) 職 shokú; (location) 立地条件 ritchíjōken
「**situations vacant**」 (BRIT) 求人欄 kyūjin ◇新聞などの求人欄のタイトル shínbun nadò no kyūjinran no taítoru

sit up vi (after lying) 上体を起す jōtai wò okósù; (straight) きちんと座る kichíñto suwárù; (not go to bed) 起きている ókìte irú

six [siks] num 六 (の) rokú (no), 六つ (の) múttsù (no)

sixteen [siks'ti:n'] num 十六 (の) júroku (no)

sixth [siksθ] num 第六(の) daí roku (no)

sixty [siks'ti:] num 六十 (の) rokújū (no)

size [saiz] n (gen) 大きさ ōkisa; (extent: of project etc) 規模 kíbò; (of clothing, shoes) サイズ saízu; (glue) サイズ saízu ◇紙のにじみ止め kamí nò nijímidome

sizeable [sai'zəbəl] adj (crowd, income etc) かなり大きい kánàri ōkiì

size up vt (person, situation) 判断する hańdan suru

sizzle [siz'əl] vi (sausages etc) じゅうじゅうと音を立てる jújū to otó wò tatérù

skate [skeit] n (ice skate) スケート sukéto; (roller skate) ローラースケート rōrā-sukèto; (fish) エイ éì
♦vi スケートをする sukéto wo suru

skateboard [skeit'bɔ:rd] n スケートボード sukétobōdo

skater [skei'tə:r] n スケートをする人 sukéto wo suru hito, スケーター sukétā

skating [skei'tiŋ] n (SPORT) スケート sukéto

skating rink n スケートリンク sukéto-riñku

skeleton [skel'itən] n (bones) がい骨 gaíkotsu; (TECH: framework) 骨組 honégumi; (outline) 骨子 kósshì

skeleton staff n 最小限度の人員 saíshōgendo no jiñ-in

skeptic [skep'tik] (US) n 疑い深い人 utágaibukaì hitó

skeptical [skep'tikəl] (US) adj 疑っている utagátte irù, 信用しない shiñ-yō shinaì

skepticism [skep'tisizəm] (US) n 疑問 gímon

sketch [sketʃ] n (drawing) スケッチ sukétchì; (outline) 骨子 kósshì; (THEATER, TV) 寸劇 suñgeki, スキット sukítto
♦vt スケッチする sukétchì suru; (also: **sketch out**: ideas) ...のあらましを言う ...no arámashi wò iú

sketchbook [sketʃ'buk] n スケッチブック sukétchibukkù

sketchy [sketʃ'i:] adj (coverage, notes etc) 大雑把な ōzappà na

skewer [skju:'ə:r] n くし kushí

ski [ski:] *n* スキー sukí

♦*vi* スキーをする sukí wo surú

ski boot *n* スキー靴 sukígùtsu

skid [skid] *n* (AUT) スリップ suríppù

♦*vi* (*gen*, AUT) スリップする suríppù suru

skier [ski:'ə:r] *n* スキーヤー sukíyầ

skiing [ski:'iŋ] *n* スキー sukí

ski jump *n* スキージャンプ sukíjaǹpu

skilful [skil'fəl] (*BRIT*) *adj* = **skillful**

ski lift *n* スキーリフト sukírifùto

skill [skil] *n* (ability, dexterity) 熟練 jukúren; (work requiring training: computer skill etc) 技術 gíjùtsu

skilled [skild] *adj* (able) 上手な jốzu na; (worker) 熟練の jukúren no

skillful [skil'fəl] (*BRIT*: **skilful**) *adj* 上手な jốzu na

skim [skim] *vt* (milk) ...の上澄みをすくい取る ...no uwázumi wð sukúitorù; (glide over) ...すれすれに飛ぶ ...surésure nì tobú

♦*vi*: **to skim through** (book) ...をざっと読む ...wo záttò yómù

skimmed milk [skimd-] *n* 脱脂乳 dasshínyù

skimp [skimp] *vt* (*also*: **skimp on**: work) いいかげんにする iíkagen nì suru; (: cloth etc) けちる kechírù

skimpy [skim'pi:] *adj* (meager: meal) 少な過ぎる sukúnasugirù; (too small: skirt) 短過ぎる mijíkasugirù

skin [skin] *n* (*gen*: of person, animal) 皮膚 hífù; (: of fruit) 皮 kawá; (complexion) 顔の肌 kaó nò hádà

♦*vt* (fruit etc) ...の皮をむく ...no kawá wð múkù; (animal) ...の皮を剥ぐ ...no kawá wð hágù

skin-deep [skin'di:p'] *adj* (superficial) 表面だけの hyốmeǹ daké no

skin-diving [skin'daiviŋ] *n* スキンダイビング sukíndaìbingu

skinny [skin'i:] *adj* (person) やせた yasétà

skintight [skin'tait] *adj* (jeans etc) 体にぴったりの karáda nì pittárì no

skip [skip] *n* (movement) スキップ sukíppù; (*BRIT*: container) ごみ箱 gomíbàko

♦*vi* (jump) スキップする sukíppù suru; (with rope) 縄跳びする nawátobì suru

♦*vt* (pass over: boring parts) とばす tobásù; (miss: lunch) 抜く nukú; (: lecture) すっぽかす suppókasù

ski pants *npl* スキーズボン sukízubòn

ski pole *n* スキーストック sukísutokkù

skipper [skip'ə:r] *n* (NAUT) 船長 seńchō; (SPORT) 主将 shushố, キャプテン kyáputen

skipping rope [skip'iŋ-] (*BRIT*) *n* 縄跳の縄 nawátobì nò nawá

skirmish [skə:r'miʃ] *n* (*also* MIL) こぜりあい kozérìai

skirt [skə:rt] *n* スカート sukátò

♦*vt* (*fig*: go round) 避けて通る sákète tốrù

skirting board [skə:r'tiŋ-] (*BRIT*) *n* 幅木 habáki

ski slope *n* ゲレンデ geréňde

ski suit *n* スキー服 sukífùku

skit [skit] *n* スキット sukíttò

skittle [skit'əl] *n* スキットルのピン sukíttòru no píň

skittles [skit'əlz] *n* (game) スキットル sukíttòru ◊9本のピンを木のボールで倒すボーリングに似た遊び kyúhòn no píň wo kí no bồru de taosu bồringu ni nita asobì

skive [skaiv] (*BRIT*: *inf*) *vi* サボる sabórù

skulk [skʌlk] *vi* うろつく urótsukù

skull [skʌl] *n* (ANAT) 頭がい骨 zugáìkotsu

skunk [skʌŋk] *n* (animal) スカンク sukáňku

sky [skai] *n* 空 sórà

skylight [skai'lait] *n* 天窓 teñmado

skyscraper [skai'skreipə:r] *n* 摩天楼 matéňrō

slab [slæb] *n* (stone) 石板 sekíban; (of cake, cheese) 厚い一切れ atsúi hitokìre

slack [slæk] *adj* (loose: rope, trousers etc) たるんでいる tarúnde irù; (slow: period) 忙しくない isógashikunaì; (careless: security, discipline) いい加減な iíkagen na

slacken [slæk'ən] (*also*: **slacken off**) *vi*

(demand) 減る herú; (speed) 落ちる ochírù

♦vt (trousers) 緩める yurúmeru; (speed) 緩める yurúmerù, 落す otósù

slacks [slæks] npl ズボン zubóñ, スラックス surákkùsu

slag heap [slæg-] n ぼた山 botáyama

slag off (BRIT: inf) vt (criticize) ...の悪口を言う ...no warúgùchi wo iú

slain [slein] pp of slay

slalom [slɑːˈləm] n 回転競技 kaítenkyōgi, スラローム surárōmu

slam [slæm] vt (door) ばたんと閉める batáñ to shimérù; (throw) 投付ける nagétsukerù; (criticize) 非難する hínan suru

♦vi (door) ばたんと閉まる batáñ to shimárù

slander [slænˈdəːr] n 中傷 chúshō

slang [slæŋ] n (informal language) 俗語 zokúgo, スラング suráñgu; (jargon: prison slang etc) 符丁 fuchō

slant [slænt] n (sloping: position) 傾斜 keísha; (fig: approach) 見方 mikáta

slanted [slænˈtid] adj (roof) 傾斜のある keísha no aru; (eyes) つり上った tsuríagattà

slanting [slænˈtiŋ] adj = slanted

slap [slæp] n (hit) 平手打ち hiráteuchi, びんた bíñta

♦vt (child, face) ぴしゃりと打つ pishári to útsù

♦adv (directly) まともに matómo nì

to slap something on something (paint etc) ...を...にいい加減に塗り付ける ...wo ...ni iíkagen nì nurítsukerù

slapdash [slæpˈdæʃ] adj (person, work) いい加減な iíkagen na

slapstick [slæpˈstik] n (comedy) どたばた喜劇 dotábata kigèki

slap-up [slæpˈʌp] adj: a slap-up meal (BRIT) 御馳走 gochísō

slash [slæʃ] vt (cut: upholstery, wrists etc) 切る kírù ◇特に長くて深い切傷を付けるという意味で使う tōkù ni nágàkute fukáì kiríkìzu wo tsukérù to iú imì de tsukáù; (fig: prices) 下げる sagérù

slat [slæt] n (of wood, plastic) 板 ítà ◇百葉箱に使われる様な薄くて細い板を指す

hyakúyōbàko ni tsukáwareru yṑ na usúkùte hosóì ítà wo sásù

slate [sleit] n (material) 粘板岩 neñbañgan; (piece: for roof) スレート surétò

♦vt (fig: criticize) けなす kenásù

slaughter [slɔːˈtəːr] n (of animals) と殺 tosátsu; (of people) 虐殺 gyakúsatsu

♦vt (animals) と殺する tosátsu suru; (people) 虐殺する gyakúsatsu suru

slaughterhouse [slɔːˈtəːrhaus] n と殺場 tosátsujō

Slav [slɑːv] adj スラブ民族の surábumiñzoku no

slave [sleiv] n 奴隷 doréi

♦vi (also: slave away) あくせく働く ákùseku határakù

slavery [sleiˈvəːri] n (system) 奴隷制度 doréiseìdo; (condition) 奴隷の身分 doréi no mìbun

slavish [sleiˈviʃ] adj (obedience) 卑屈な hikútsu na; (copy) 盲目的な mṓmokuteki na

slay [slei] (pt slew, pp slain) vt 殺す korósù

sleazy [sliˈziː] adj (place) 薄汚い usúgitanaì

sledge [sledʒ] n そり sórì

sledgehammer [sledʒˈhæməːr] n 大づち ózùchi

sleek [sliːk] adj (shiny, smooth: hair, fur etc) つやつやの tsuyátsuyà no; (car, boat etc) 優雅な yū́ga na

sleep [sliːp] n 睡眠 suímin

♦vi (pt, pp slept) (gen) 眠る nemúrù, 寝る nerú; (spend night) 泊る tomárù

to go to sleep (person) 眠る nemúrù, 寝る neru

sleep around vi 色々な人とセックスをする iróiro na hito tò sékkùsu wo suru

sleeper [sliːˈpəːr] (BRIT) n (RAIL: on track) まくら木 makúragi; (: train) 寝台列車 shiñdairesshà

sleep in vi (oversleep) 寝坊する nebṓ suru

sleeping bag [sliːˈpiŋ-] n 寝袋 nebúkùro

sleeping car n (RAIL) 寝台車 shiñdaishà

sleeping partner (BRIT) n (COMM)

= **silent partner**
sleeping pill *n* 睡眠薬 suímiñ-yaku
sleepless [sli:p'lis] *adj*: ***a sleepless night*** 眠れない夜 nemúrenai yorù
sleepwalker [sli:p'wɔ:kə:r] *n* 夢遊病者 muyū́byōshà
sleepy [sli:'pi:] *adj* (person) 眠い nemúi; (*fig*: village etc) ひっそりとした hissórì to shita
sleet [sli:t] *n* みぞれ mizóre
sleeve [sli:v] *n* (of jacket etc) そで sodé; (of record) ジャケット jákètto
sleeveless [sli:v'lis] *adj* (garment) そでなしの sodénashi no, スリーブレスの surī́burèsu no
sleigh [slei] *n* そり sórì
sleight [slait] *n*: ***sleight of hand*** 奇術 kī́jùtsu
slender [slen'də:r] *adj* (slim: figure) ほっそりした hossórì shita, スリムな súrìmu na; (small: means, majority) わずかな wā́zùka na
slept [slept] *pt, pp of* **sleep**
slew [slu:] *vi* (*BRIT*) = **slue**
♦*pt of* **slay**
slice [slais] *n* (of meat, bread, lemon) スライス suráìsu; (utensil: fish slice) フライ返し furáigaèshi; (: cake slice) ケーキサーバー kḗkisābā
♦*vt* (bread, meat etc) スライスする surá-ìsu suru
slick [slik] *adj* (skillful: performance) 鮮やかな azáyàka na; (clever: salesman, answer) 抜け目のない nukéme no naì
♦*n* (*also*: **oil slick**) 油膜 yumáku
slid [slid] *pt, pp of* **slide**
slide [slaid] *n* (downward movement) 下落 geráku; (in playground) 滑り台 subéri-dāi; (PHOT) スライド suráìdo; (*BRIT*: *also*: **hair slide**) 髪留 kamídòme, ヘアクリップ heákurìppu
♦*vb* (*pt, pp* **slid**)
♦*vt* 滑らせる subéraserù
♦*vi* (slip) 滑る subérù; (glide) 滑る様に動く subéru yṑ ni ugókù
slide rule *n* 計算尺 keísanjaku
sliding [slai'diŋ] *adj*: ***sliding door*** 引戸 hikídò
sliding scale *n* スライド制 suráidosei
slight [slait] *adj* (slim: figure) やせ型の yaségata no; (frail) か弱い kayṓwaì; (small: increase, difference) わずかな wā́zùka na; (error, accent, pain etc) ちょっとした chṓttò shita; (trivial) ささいな sásài na
♦*n* (insult) 侮辱 bujṓku
not in the slightest 少しも…ない sukṓshì mo ...nâì
slightly [slait'li:] *adv* (a bit, rather) 少し sukṓshì
slim [slim] *adj* (person, figure) ほっそりした hossórì shita; (chance) わずかな wá-zùka na
♦*vi* (lose weight) やせる yasérù
slime [slaim] *n* ぬるぬるした物 núrùnuru shita monṓ
slimming [slim'iŋ] *n* (losing weight) そう身 sṓshin
slimy [slai'mi:] *adj* (pond) ぬるぬるした物に覆われた núrùnuru shita monṓ nì ṓwaretà
sling [sliŋ] *n* (MED) 三角きん sañkakùkin; (for baby) 子守り帯 komṓriobì; (weapon) 石投げ器 ishínagekì
♦*vt* (*pt, pp* **slung**) (throw) 投げる nagérù
slip [slip] *n* (while walking) 踏外し fumí-hazushi; (of vehicle) スリップ suríppù; (mistake) 過ち ayámachì; (underskirt) スリップ suríppù; (*also*: **slip of paper**) 一枚の紙 ichímài no kamí ◊通常メモ用紙, 伝票などの様な小さい紙を指す tsū́jō me-moyṑshi, deñpyō nadò no yṓ nà chiísaì kamí wò sásù
♦*vt* (slide) こっそり…を…にやる kossórì ...wo ...ni yarú
♦*vi* (slide) 滑る subérù; (lose balance) 踏外す fumíhazusù; (decline) 悪くなる wá-rùku nárù; (move smoothly): ***to slip into/out of*** (room etc) そっと入る〔出て行く〕sóttò háìru 〔détè iku〕
to give someone the slip …をまく ...wo mákù
a slip of the tongue うっかり言ってしまう事 ukkárì itté shimaù kotó
to slip something on/off さっと…を着る〔脱ぐ〕sáttò ...wo kírù 〔nugu〕

slip away vi (go) そっと立ち去る sótto tachísaru

slip in vt (put) こっそり入れる kossórì irérù

♦vi (errors) いつの間にか入ってしまう itsú no ma ni ka haítte shimaù

slip out vi (go out) そっと出て行く sótto détè ikú

slipped disc [slipt-] n つい間板ヘルニア tsuíkañbanherunìa

slipper [slip'ə:r] n (carpet slipper) スリッパ suríppà

slippery [slip'ə:ri:] adj (road) 滑りやすい subériyasuì; (fish etc) つかみにくい tsukáminikuì

slip road (BRIT) n (on motorway: access road) 入路 nyúro; (: exit road) 出口 deguchi

slipshod [slip'ʃɑ:d] adj いい加減な iíkagen na

slip up vi (make mistake) 間違いをする machígai wò suru

slip-up [slip'ʌp] n (error) 間違い machígaì

slipway [slip'wei] n 造船台 zósendaì

slit [slit] n (cut) スリット suríttò; (opening) すき間 sukíma

♦vt (pt, pp slit) 切り開く kiríhiraku

slither [sliθ'ə:r] vi (person) 足を取られながら歩く ashí wò torárenagara arukú; (snake etc) はう háù

sliver [sliv'ə:r] n (of glass, wood) 破片 hahén; (of cheese etc) 一切れ hitókìre

slob [slɑ:b] (inf) n (man) だらしない野郎 daráshinai yarò; (woman) だらしないあま daráshinaì ámà

slog [slɑ:g] (BRIT) vi (work hard) あくせく働く ákùseku határakù

♦n: it was a hard slog 苦労した kuró shità

slogan [slou'gən] n スローガン surógàn

slop [slɑ:p] vi (also: slop over) こぼれる kobórerù

♦vt こぼす kobósù

slope [sloup] n (gentle hill) 坂道 sakámìchi; (side of mountain) 山腹 sañpuku; (ski slope) ゲレンデ geréñde; (slant) 傾斜 keísha

♦vi: to slope down 下り坂になる kudárizaka ni narù

slope up vi 上り坂になる nobórizaka ni narù

sloping [slou'piŋ] adj (ground, roof) 傾斜になっている keísha ni natte irù; (handwriting) 斜めの nanáme no

sloppy [slɑ:p'i:] adj (work, appearance) だらしない daráshinaì

slot [slɑ:t] n (in machine) 投入口 tónyùguchi, スロット suróttò

♦vt: to slot something into ... (のスロットなど) に...を入れる ... (no suróttò nado) ni ...wo irérù

sloth [slɔ:θ] n (laziness) 怠惰 táìda

slot machine n (BRIT: vending machine) 自動販売機 jidóhanbaikì; (for gambling) スロットマシーン suróttomashìn

slouch [slautʃ] vi (person) だらしない姿勢で...する daráshinaì shiséi dè ... suru

slovenly [slʌv'ənli:] adj (dirty: habits, conditions) 汚い kitánaì; (careless: piece of work) だらしない daráshinaì

slow [slou] adj (music, journey) ゆっくりした yukkúrì shita; (service) 遅い osóì, のろい noróì; (person: not clever) 物覚えの悪い monóobòe no warúì; (watch, clock): to be slow 遅れている okúrete irù

♦adv ゆっくりと yukkúrì to, 遅く osókù

♦vt (also: slow down, slow up): ...のスピードを落す ...no supídò wo otósù; (: business etc) 低迷させる teímei saserù

♦vi (also: slow down, slow up: vehicle) スピードを落す supídò wo otósù; (: business etc) 下火になる shitábi nì narù

「slow」(road sign) 徐行 jokó

slowly [slou'li:] adv ゆっくりと yukkúrì to, 遅く osókù

slow motion n: in slow motion スローモーションで surómòshon de

sludge [slʌdʒ] n (mud) へどろ hedóro

slue [slu:] (US veer) vi スリップする suríppù suru

slug [slʌg] n (creature) なめくじ namékujì; (bullet) 弾丸 dañgan, 鉄砲玉 teppó-

dama

sluggish [slʌg'iʃ] *adj* (stream, engine, person) 緩慢な kaṅman na; (COMM: trading) 不活発な fukáppatsu na

sluice [sluːs] *n* (*also*: **sluicegate**) 水門 suímon; (channel) 水路 suíro

slum [slʌm] *n* (house) 汚い家 kitánaì ié; (area) 貧民街 hiṅmiṅgai, スラム súramu

slump [slʌmp] *n* (economic) 不景気 fukéiki; (COMM) スランプ suráṅpu
♦*vi* (fall: person) 崩れ落ちる kuzúreochirù; (: prices) 暴落する bóraku suru

slung [slʌŋ] *pt*, *pp* of **sling**

slur [sləːr] *n* (*fig*): **slur (on)** (...の)悪口 (...no) warúkuchi
♦*vt* (words) 口ごもって言う kuchígomottè iú

slush [slʌʃ] *n* (melted snow) 溶けかかった雪 tokékakattà yukí

slush fund *n* 裏金用資金 uráganeyōshikiṅ

slut [slʌt] (*inf!*) *n* ばいた baítà

sly [slai] *adj* (smile, expression, remark) 意味ありげな imíarige na; (person: clever, wily) ずるい zurúi

smack [smæk] *n* (slap) 平手打ち hiráteuchi; (on face) びんた bíṅta
♦*vt* (hit: *gen*) 平手で打つ hiráte dè útsù; (: child) ぶつ bútsù; (: on face) ...にびんたを食らわす ...ni bíṅta wo kurawásù
♦*vi*: **to smack of** (smell of) ...くさい ...kusáì; (remind one of) ...を思わせる ...wo omówaserù

small [smɔːl] *adj* (person, object) 小さい chíisaì; (child: young) 幼い osánaì; (quantity, amount) 少しの sukóshì no

small ads (*BRIT*) *npl* 分類広告 buṅruikōkoku

small change *n* 小銭 kozéni

small fry *npl* (unimportant people) 下っ端 shitáppa

smallholder [smɔːl'houldəːr] (*BRIT*) *n* 小自作農 shójisakunō

small hours *npl*: **in the small hours** 深夜に shíṅya ni

smallpox [smɔːl'pɑːks] *n* 天然痘 teṅnentō

small talk *n* 世間話 sekéṅbanàshi

smart [smɑːrt] *adj* (neat, tidy) きちんとした kichíṅ to shitá; (fashionable: clothes etc) しゃれた sharéta, いきな ikí na, スマートな sumáto na; (: house, restaurant) しゃれた shareta, 高級な kókyū na; (clever) 頭がいい atáma ga iì; (quick) 早い hayáì

smarten up [smɑːr'tən-] *vi* 身なりを直す mínari wo naósù
♦*vt* きれいにする kírèi ni suru

smash [smæʃ] *n* (collision: *also*: **smash-up**) 衝突 shótotsu; (smash hit) 大ヒット daíhittò
♦*vt* (break) めちゃめちゃに壊す mechámecha ni kowásù; (car etc) 衝突してめちゃめちゃにする shótotsu shitè mechámecha ni surù; (SPORT: record) 破る yabúrù
♦*vi* (break) めちゃめちゃに壊れる mechámecha nì kowárerù; (against wall etc) 激突する gekítotsu suru

smashing [smæʃ'iŋ] (*inf*) *adj* 素晴らしい subárashiì

smattering [smæt'əːriŋ] *n*: **a smattering of** ...をほんの少し ...wo hoṅno sukoshī

smear [smiːʔəːr] *n* (trace) 染み shimí; (MED) スミア sumíà
♦*vt* (spread) 塗る nurú; (make dirty) 汚す yogósù

smear campaign *n* 中傷作戦 chúshōsakuseṅ

smell [smel] *n* (odor) におい nióì; (sense) 臭覚 kyūkaku
♦*vb* (*pt*, *pp* **smelt** *or* **smelled**)
♦*vt* (become aware of odor) ...のにおいがする ...no nioi ga suru; (sniff) かぐ kagú
♦*vi* (*pej*) におう nióù, 臭い kusáì; (food etc) ...においがする ...nióì ga suru
to smell of ...のにおいがする ...no nióì ga suru

smelly [smel'iː] *adj* (cheese, socks) 臭い kusáì

smile [smail] *n* ほほえみ hohóemi
♦*vi* ほほえむ hohóemù

smirk [smə:rk] n にやにや笑い niyániya warài

smithy [smiθ'i:] n 鍛冶屋の仕事場 kajíyà no shigótobà

smock [smɑ:k] n (gen) 上っ張り uwápparì; (children's) スモック sumókkù; (US: overall) 作業着 sagyṓgì

smog [smɑ:g] n スモッグ sumóggù

smoke [smouk] n 煙 kemúri
♦vi (person) タバコを吸う tabáko wò súù; (chimney) 煙を出す kemúri wò dásù
♦vt (cigarettes) 吸う súù

smoked [smoukt] adj (bacon etc) 薫製の kuńsei no; (glass) いぶした ibúshita

smoker [smou'kə:r] n (person) タバコを吸う人 tabáko wò súù hito, 喫煙者 kitsúeñsha; (RAIL) 喫煙車 kitsúeñsha

smokescreen [smouk'skri:n] n (also fig) 煙幕 éñmaku

smoking [smou'kiŋ] n (act) 喫煙 kitsúen 「no smoking」(sign) 禁煙 kiń-en

smoky [smou'ki:] adj (atmosphere, room) 煙い kemúi; (taste) 薫製の (様な) kuńsei no (yṓ na)

smolder [smoul'də:r] (US) vi (fire: also fig: anger, hatred) くすぶる kusúburù

smooth [smu:ð] adj (gen) 滑らかな naméràka na; (sauce) つぶつぶのない tsubútsubu no nái; (flat: sea) 穏やかな odáyàka na; (flavor, whisky) まろやかな maróyàka na; (movement) 滑らかな naméràka na; (pej: person) 口先のうまい kuchísaki no umáì
♦vt (also: smooth out): skirt, piece of paper etc) ...のしわを伸ばす ...no shiwá wò nobásù; (: creases) 伸ばす nobásù; (: difficulties) 取除く torínozokù

smother [smʌð'ə:r] vt (fire) ...に...をかぶせて消す ...ni ...wo kabúsete kesù; (suffocate: person) 窒息させる chissóku saserù; (repress: emotions) 抑える osáerù

smoulder [smoul'də:r] (BRIT) vi = smolder

smudge [smʌdʒ] n 汚れ yogóre
♦vt 汚す yogósù

smug [smʌg] adj 独り善がりの hitóriyogarì no

smuggle [smʌg'əl] vt (diamonds etc) 密輸する mitsúyu suru; (refugees) 密入国させる mitsúnyūkoku saserù

smuggler [smʌg'lə:r] n 密輸者 mitsúyushà

smuggling [smʌg'liŋ] n (traffic) 密輸 mitsúyu

smutty [smʌt'i:] adj (fig: joke, book) わいせつな waísetsu na

snack [snæk] n (light meal) 軽食 keíshoku; (food) スナック sunákkù

snack bar n スナックバー sunákkubà, スナック sunákkù

snag [snæg] n 障害 shṓgai

snail [sneil] n カタツムリ katátsumùri ◊ 一般に水生の巻貝をも指す ippán nì suísei nò makígai wo mo sásù

snake [sneik] n (gen) ヘビ hébì

snap [snæp] n (sound) ぱちっという音 pachíttò iú otò; (photograph) 写真 shashín
♦adj (decision etc) 衝動的な shṓdōteki na
♦vt (break) 折る órù; (fingers) 鳴らす narásù
♦vi (break) 折れる orérù; (fig: person: speak sharply) 辛らつな事を言う shiníratsu na kotó wo iú
to snap shut (trap, jaws etc) がちゃっと閉まる gacháttò shimárù

snap at vt fus (subj: dog) かみつこうとする kamítsukò to suru

snap off vt (break) 折れる orérù ◊ 折れて取れる場合に使う órète torérù baái nì tsukáù

snappy [snæp'i:] (inf) adj (answer, slogan) 威勢のいい iséi no ií
make it snappy (hurry up) 早くしなさい háyàku shinásaì

snapshot [snæp'ɑːt] n 写真 shashín

snap up vt (bargains) すぐ買う súgù káù

snare [sne:r] n わな wánà

snarl [snɑ:rl] vi (animal) うなる unárù; (person) どなる donárù

snatch [snætʃ] n (small piece: of conversation, song etc) 断片 dañpeñ
♦vt (snatch away: handbag, child etc) ったくる hittákurù; (fig: opportunity) 利用する riyṓ suru; (: look, some sleep etc)

急いでやる isóide yarù

sneak [sniːk] (*pt, pp* **sneaked** *also US* **snuck**) *vi*: **to sneak in/out** こっそり入る〔出る〕 kossórì háīru〔deru〕

♦*n* (*inf*) 告げ口するひと tsugéguchi suru hitò

to sneak up on someone ...に忍び寄る ...ni shinóbiyorù

sneakers [sniː'kəːrz] *npl* 運動靴 uńdōgutsu, スニーカー sunîkā

sneer [sniːr] *vi* (laugh nastily) 冷笑する reíshō suru; (mock): **to sneer at** ...をあざわらう ...wo azáwaraù

sneeze [sniːz] *n* くしゃみ kushámì

♦*vi* くしゃみをする kushámì wo suru

sniff [snif] *n* (sound) 鼻をくんくん鳴らす音 haná wò kúńkun narásù otó; (smell: by dog, person) くんくんかぐ事 kúńkun kagú kotò

♦*vi* (person: when crying etc) 鼻をくんくん鳴らす haná wò kúńkun narásù

♦*vt* (*gen*) かぐ kagú; (glue, drugs) 鼻で吸う haná dè súù

snigger [snig'əːr] *vi* くすくす笑う kúsùkusu waráu

snip [snip] *n* (cut) はさみで切る事 hasámì dè kírù koto; (*BRIT*: *inf*: bargain) 掘出し見 horídashimonð

♦*vt* (cut) はさみで切る hasámì dè kírù

sniper [snai'pəːr] *n* そ撃兵 sogékihèi

snippet [snip'it] *n* (of information, news) 断片 dańpen

snivelling [sniv'əliŋ] *adj* (whimpering) めそめそ泣く mésòmeso nakú

snob [snɑːb] *n* 俗物 zokúbutsu

snobbery [snɑːb'əːri] *n* 俗物根性 zokúbutsukoñjō

snobbish [snɑːb'iʃ] *adj* 俗物的な zokúbutsuteki na

snooker [snuk'əːr] *n* ビリヤード bíryàdo

snoop [snuːp] *vi*: **to snoop about** こっそりのぞき回る kossórì nozókimawarù

snooty [snuː'tiː] *adj* (person, letter, reply) 横柄な ốhèi na

snooze [snuːz] *n* 昼寝 hirúne

♦*vi* 昼寝する hirúne suru

snore [snɔːr] *n* いびき ibíki

♦*vi* いびきをかく ibíki wò kákù

snorkel [snɔːr'kəl] *n* (for swimming) シュノーケル shunôkèru

snort [snɔːrt] *n* 鼻を鳴らす事 haná wò narásù koto

♦*vi* (animal, person) 鼻を鳴らす haná wò narásù

snout [snaut] *n* ふん fúñ

snow [snou] *n* 雪 yukí

♦*vi* 雪が降る yukí gà fúrù

snowball [snou'bɔːl] *n* 雪のつぶて yukí nò tsubúte

♦*vi* (*fig*: problem, campaign) どんどん大きくなる dôńdon ốkìku nárù

snowbound [snou'baund] *adj* (people) 雪に閉じ込められた yukí ni tojíkomerarèta; (vehicles) 雪で立ち往生した yukí dè tachíōjō shita

snowdrift [snou'drift] *n* 雪の吹きだまり yukí nò fukídamarì

snowdrop [snou'drɑːp] *n* 雪の花 yukínohanà

snowfall [snou'fɔːl] *n* (amount) 降雪量 kõsetsuryō; (a fall of snow) 降雪 kõsetsu

snowflake [snou'fleik] *n* 雪のひとひら yukí nò hitóhìra

snowman [snou'mæn] (*pl* **snowmen**) *n* 雪だるま yukídaruma

snowplow [snou'plau] (*BRIT* **snowplough**) *n* 除雪車 josétsushà

snowshoe [snou'ʃuː] *n* かんじき kańjiki

snowstorm [snou'stɔːrm] *n* 吹雪 fúbùki

snub [snʌb] *vt* (person) 鼻であしらう haná dè ashíraù

♦*n* 侮辱 bujóku

snub-nosed [snʌb'nouzd] *adj* 鼻先の反った hanásaki nò sottá

snuck [snʌk] (*US*) *pt, pp of* **sneak**

snuff [snʌf] *n* かぎタバコ kagítabàko

snug [snʌg] *adj* (sheltered: person, place) こじんまりした kojínmarì shita; (person) 心地好い kokóchiyoì; (well-fitting) ぴったりした pittárì shita

snuggle [snʌg'əl] *vi*: **to snuggle up to someone** ...に体を擦り付ける ...ni karáda wò surítsukerù

KEYWORD

so [sou] *adv* **1** (thus, likewise) そう só, その通り sonó tòri

so saying he walked away そう言って彼は歩き去った só ittè kárè wa arúki-sattà

while she was so doing, he ... 彼女がそれをやっている間彼は... kánòjo ga soré wò yatté iru aìda kárè wa...

if so だとすれば dá tò suréba

do you enjoy soccer? if so, come to the game フットボールが好きですか、だったら試合を見に来て下さい futtóbòru ga sukí desù ka, dáttàra shiái wò mì nì kite kudasaì

I didn't do it - you did so! やったのは私じゃない -iyá, お前 did so! yatté no wà watákushi ja naì -iyá, omáe dà

so do I, so am I etc 私もそうです watákushi mò só desù

I like swimming - so do I 私は水泳が好きです -私もそうです watákushi wà suíei gà sukí desù -watákushi mò só desù

I'm still at school - so am I 私はまだ学生です -私もそうです watákushi wà mádà gakúsei desù -watákushi mò só desù

I've got work to do - so has Paul 私には仕事がありますから -ポールもそうですよ watákushi ni wà shigóto gà arímasu karà -pōru mo só desù yó

it's 5'clock - so it is! 5時です -あっ、そうですね góji desu -át, só desù né

I hope so そう希望します só kibō shimasù

I think so そうだと思います só da tò omóimasù

so far これまで koré màde

how do you like the book so far? これまでその本はどうでしたか koré màde sonó hoñ wa dó deshìta ka

so far I haven't had any problems ここまでは問題はありません kokó màde wa mońdai wà arímaseñ

2 (in comparisons etc: to such a degree) そんなに sofína nì

so quickly (that) (...がある程) 素早く (...ga árù hodo) subáyàku, とても素早く (...した ので...) totémo subáyàku (...shitá no dè ...)

so big (that) (...がある程) 大きな (...ga árù hodo) ōkina, とても大きい (ので...) totémo ōkii (nó dè ...)

she's not so clever as her brother 彼女は兄さん程利口ではない kánòjo wa niīsañ hodo ríkò de wa naí

we were so worried 私たちはとても心配していましたよ watákushitàchi wa totémo shiñpai shite imashìta yó

I wish you weren't so clumsy あなたの不器用さはどうにかなりませんかね anátà no bukíyòsa wa dō nì kà narímasen kà né

I'm so glad to see you あなたを見てほっとしました anátà wo mítè hóttò shimáshìta

3: *so much* *adv* そんなに沢山で sofína nì takúsañ de

♦*adj* そんなに沢山の sofína nì takúsañ de

I've got so much work 私は仕事が山程あります watákushi wà shigóto gà yamá hodò arímasù

I love you so much あなたを心から愛しています anátà wo kokórò kara áì shite imasu

so many そんなに沢山 (の) sofína nì takúsañ (no)

there are so many things to do する事が山程あります surú kotò ga yamá hodò arímasù

there are so many people to meet 私が会うべき人たちは余りにも大勢です watákushi gà aúbeki hitótàchi wa amári ni mò ōzei desù **4** (phrases): *10 or so* 10個ぐらい júkkò gurai

so long! (*inf*: goodbye) じゃね já nè, またね matá nè

♦*conj* **1** (expressing purpose): *so as to do* ...する様〔ため〕に ...surú yò〔tamè〕ni

we hurried so as not to be late 遅れない様に急いで行きました okúrenai yò ni isóìde ikímashìta

so (that) ...する様〔ため〕に ...surú yò

〔tamè〕ni

I brought it so (that) you could see it あなたに見せるために持ってきました anátā ni misérù tame ni mottě kimashìta

2 (expressing result) ...であるから... ...de árù kara ..., ...ので... ...nô dè ...

he didn't arrive so I left 彼が来なかったので私は帰りました kárè ga kónakatta nó de watákushi wā kaérimashìta

so I was right after all 結局私の言った通りでした kekkyókù watákushi nò ittá tôri deshita

so you see, I could have gone ですからね、行こうと思えば行けたんです désù kara né, ikô tô omóebà ikétan desù

---

soak [souk] *vt* (drench) ずぶぬれにする zubúnure nǐ suru; (steep in water) 水に漬ける mizú nǐ tsukéru

♦*vi* (dirty washing, dishes) 漬かる tsukárù

soak in *vi* (be absorbed) 染み込む shimíkomù

soak up *vt* (absorb) 吸収する kyúshū surù

soap [soup] *n* 石けん sekkén

soapflakes [soup'fleiks] *npl* フレーク石けん furékusekkén ◊洗濯用の固形石けんをフレークにした物を指す sentakuyô no kokéisekkén wo furékù ni shitá monò wo sásù

soap opera *n* メロドラマ meródorāma ◊テレビやラジオの連続物を指す térèbi ya rájìo no renzokumonò wo sásù

soap powder *n* 粉石けん konásekkén

soapy [sou'pi:] *adj* (hands etc) 石けんのついた sekkén no tsuità

soapy water 石けん水 sekkénsui

soar [sɔ:r] *vi* (on wings) 舞上がる maíagarù; (rocket) 空中に上がる kúchū nǐ agárù; (price, production, temperature) 急上昇する kyúshōshō suru; (building etc) そびえたつ sobíetatsù

sob [sɑ:b] *n* しゃくり泣き shakúrinaki

♦*vi* 泣きじゃくる nakíjakurù

sober [sou'bə:r] *adj* (serious) まじめな majíme na; (dull: color, style) 地味な ji-

mí na; (not drunk) しらふの shíràfu no

sober up *vt* ...の酔いを覚ます ...no yoí wò samásù

♦*vi* 酔いが覚める yoí gà samérù

so-called [sou'kɔ:ld'] *adj* (friend, expert) いわゆる iwáyurù ◊多くの場合不信や軽べつなどを表す ōkù no baái fushín yà keíbetsu nadò wo aráwasù

soccer [sɑ:k'ə:r] *n* サッカー sákkā

sociable [sou'ʃəbəl] *adj* 愛想の良い aísō no yoì

social [sou'ʃəl] *adj* (gen: history, structure, background) 社会の shákài no; (leisure: event, life) 社交的な shakóteki na; (sociable: animal) 社会性のある shakáisei no arù

♦*n* (party) 懇親会 konshínkai

social club *n* 社交クラブ shakókurabù

socialism [sou'ʃəlizəm] *n* 社会主義 shakáishugī

socialist [sou'ʃəlist] *adj* 社会主義の shakáishugī no

♦*n* 社会主義者 shakáishugishà

socialize [sou'ʃəlaiz] *vi*: *to socialize (with)* (...と) 交際する (...to) kôsai suru

socially [sou'ʃəli:] *adv* (visit) 社交的に shakóteki ni; (acceptable) 社会的に shakáiteki ni

social security (*BRIT*) *n* 社会保障 shakáihoshō

social work *n* ソーシャルワーク sósharuwãku

social worker *n* ソーシャルワーカー sósharuwākā

society [sasai'əti:] *n* (people, their lifestyle) 社会 shákài; (club) 会 kāi; (*also:* **high society**) 上流社会 jōryūshakái

sociologist [sousi:ɑ:l'ədʒist] *n* 社会学者 shakáigakushà

sociology [sousi:ɑ:l'ədʒi:] *n* 社会学 shakáigāku

sock [sɑ:k] *n* 靴下 kutsúshita

socket [sɑ:k'it] *n* (gen: cavity) 受け口 ukégùchi; (ANAT: of eye) 眼か gánka; (ELEC: for light bulb) ソケット sokéttò; (*BRIT*: ELEC: wall socket) コンセント kônsento

sod [sɑːd] *n* (of earth) 草の生えた土 kusá nò hâeta tsuchí; (*BRIT: inf!*) くそ kusó

soda [sou'də] *n* (CHEM) ナトリウム化合物 natóriumu kagōbutsu ◇一般にか性ソーダ, 重曹などを指す ippán nì kaséisōda, jūsó nadò wo sásù; (*also:* **soda water**) ソーダ水 sōdàsui; (*US: also:* **soda pop**) 清涼飲料 seíryōinryō

sodden [sɑːd'ən] *adj* びしょぬれの bishónure no

sodium [sou'diːəm] *n* ナトリウム natóriumu

sofa [sou'fə] *n* ソファー sófà

soft [sɔːft] *adj* (not hard) 柔らかい yawárakaî; (gentle, not loud: voice, music) 静かな shízùka na; (not bright: light, color) 柔らかな yawárakà na; (kind: heart, approach) 優しい yasáshii

soft drink *n* 清涼飲料水 seíryōinryōsui

soften [sɔːf'ən] *vt* (*gen:* make soft) 柔らかくする yawárakàku suru; (effect, blow, expression) 和らげる yawáragerù
◆*vi* (*gen:* become soft) 柔らかくなる yawárakaku narù; (voice, expression) 優しくなる yasáshiku narù

softly [sɔːft'liː] *adv* (gently) 優しく yasáshiku; (quietly) 静かに shízùka ni

softness [sɔːft'nis] *n* (gen) 柔らかさ yawárakasa; (gentleness) 優しさ yasáshisa

soft spot *n: to have a soft spot for someone* ...が大好きである ...ga dáîsuki de árù

software [sɔːft'weːr] *n* (COMPUT) ソフトウエア sofútoueà

soggy [sɑːg'iː] *adj* (ground, sandwiches etc) ぐちゃぐちゃの guchágucha no

soil [sɔil] *n* (earth) 土壌 dójō; (territory) 土地 tochí
◆*vt* 汚す yogósù

solace [sɑːl'is] *n* 慰め nagúsame

solar [sou'lər] *adj* (eclipse, power etc) 太陽の táîyo no

sold [sould] *pt, pp of* **sell**

solder [sɑːd'əːr] *vt* はんだ付けにする hañdazuke nì suru
◆*n* はんだ hañda

soldier [soul'dʒəːr] *n* (in army) 兵隊 heftai; (not a civilian) 軍人 guñjin

sold out *adj* (COMM: goods, tickets, concert etc) 売切れで uríkire de

sole [soul] *n* (of foot) 足の裏 ashí nò urá; (of shoe) 靴の底 kutsú nò sokó; (fish: pl inv) シタビラメ shitábiràme
◆*adj* (unique) 唯一の yúîtsu no

solely [soul'liː] *adv* ...だけ ...dáke

solemn [sɑːl'əm] *adj* (person) 謹厳な kiñgen na; (music) 荘重な sōchō na; (promise) 真剣な shiñken na

sole trader *n* (COMM) 自営業者 jiéigyōsha

solicit [səlis'it] *vt* (request) 求める motómerù
◆*vi* (prostitute) 客引きする kyakúbiki suru

solicitor [səlis'itəːr] (*BRIT*) *n* (for wills etc, in court) 弁護士 beñgoshì

solid [sɑːl'id] *adj* (not hollow) 中空でない chūkū de naî; (not liquid) 固形の kokéi no; (reliable: person, foundations etc) しっかりした shikkárî shita; (entire) まる... marú...; (pure: gold etc) 純粋の juñsui no
◆*n* (solid object) 固体 kotái

solidarity [sɑːlidær'itiː] *n* 団結 dañketsu

solidify [səlid'əfai] *vi* (fat etc) 固まる katámarù

solids [sɑːl'idz] *npl* (food) 固形食 kokéishōku

solitaire [sɑːl'iteːr] *n* (gem) 一つはめの宝石 hitótsuhame nò hōseki; (game) 一人遊び hitóriasobì

solitary [sɑːl'iteːriː] *adj* (person, animal, life) 単独の tañdoku no; (alone: walk) 一人だけでする hitórî dake de suru; (isolated) 人気のない hitóke no naî; (single: person) 一人だけの hitórî dake no; (: animal, object) 一つだけの hitótsu dake no

solitary confinement *n* 独房監禁 dokúbō kañkin

solitude [sɑːl'ətuːd] *n* 人里を離れている事 hitózato wò hanárete iru kotò

solo [sou'lou] *n* (piece of music, performance) 独奏 dokúsō
◆*adv* (fly) 単独で tañdoku de

soloist [sou'louist] *n* 独奏者 dokúsōshà

soluble [sɑːl'jəbəl] *adj* (aspirin etc) 溶ける tokérù

solution [səluː'ʃən] n (of puzzle, problem, mystery: answer) 解決 kaíketsu; (liquid) 溶液 yṓeki

solve [saːlv] vt (puzzle, problem, mystery) 解決する kaíketsu suru

solvent [saːl'vənt] adj (COMM) 支払い能力のある shiháraiñōryoku no aru
♦n (CHEM) 溶剤 yṓzai

somber [saːm'bəːr] (BRIT **sombre**) adj (dark: color, place) 暗い kuráì; (serious: person, view) 陰気な íñki na

KEYWORD

some [sʌm] adj 1 (a certain amount or number of) 幾らかの íkuraka no, 幾つかの íkùtsuka no, 少しの sukóshī no

some tea/water/biscuits お茶〔水, ビスケット〕o-chá〔mizú, bisúkettò〕◇この用法では日本語で表現しない場合が多い konó yṓhō de wa nihóngo dè hyṓgen shinaì baái ga ōì

some children came 何人かの子供が来た nánninka no kodómo ga kítà

there's some milk in the fridge 冷蔵庫にミルクがあります reízōko ni mírùku ga arímasu

he asked me some questions 彼は色々な事を聞きました kárè wa iróiro na kotò wo kikímashìta

there were some people outside 数人の人が外に立っていた sūnìn no hitó gà sótò ni tatté ità

I've got some money, but not much 金はあるにはありますが, 少しだけです kané wà árù ni wa arímasù gá, sukóshi dake désu

2 (certain: in contrasts) ある árù

some people say that ... ...と言っている人がいます ...tò itté irù hitó ga imasù

some people hate fish, while others love it 魚の嫌いな人もいれば大好きな人もいます sakána nò kiráì na hitó mo irébà daísuki na hitó mo imásù

some films were excellent, but most were mediocre 中には優れた映画もあったが, 大半は平凡な物だった nákà ni wa sugúreta eìga mo attá gà, taíhan wa heíbon na monò dáttà

3 (unspecified) 何かの nánika no, だれかの dárèka no

some woman was asking for you だれか女の人があなたを訪ねていましたよ dárèka oñna nó hitò ga anátà wo tazúnete imashìta yó

he was asking for some book (or other) 彼は何かの本を捜していました kárè wa nánika no hòñ wo sagáshite imashìta

some day いつか ítsùka, そのうち sonó uchì

we'll meet again some day そのうちまた会うチャンスがあるでしょう sonó uchì matá áù cháñsu ga árù deshō

shall we meet some day next week? 来週のいつかに会いましょうか raíshū nò ítsùka ni aímashō ká
♦pron 1 (a certain number) 幾つか íkùtsuka

I've got some (books etc) 私は幾つか持っています watákushi wà íkùtsuka móttè imasu

some (of them) have been sold 数個は売れてしまいました sū̀kò wa uréte shimaimashìta

some went for a taxi and some walked 何人かはタクシーを拾いに行ったが, 残りの人は歩いた náñninka wa tákùshī wo hiróì ni itta gà, nokóri nò hitó wà arúìta

2 (a certain amount) 幾分か ikúbun kà

I've got some (money, milk) 私は幾分か持っています watákushi wà ikúbun kà móttè imasu

some was left 少し残っていた sukóshi nokótte ità

could I have some of that cheese? そのチーズを少しもらっていいかしら sonó chìzu wo sukóshi morátte ii kashìra

I've read some of the book その本の一部を読みました sonó hoñ no ichíbù wo yomímashìta
♦adv: *some 10 people* 10人ぐらい jū́nin gurai

somebody [sʌm'baːdiː] pron = someone

somehow [sʌm'hau] adv (in some way)

何とかして náñ to ka shite; (for some reason) どういう訳か dō iu wákè ka

---

KEYWORD

someone [sʌm'wʌn] *pron* だれか dáreka, 人 hitó

there's someone coming 人が来ます hitó gà kimásù

I saw someone in the garden だれか庭にいました dáreka niwá nì imáshìta

---

someplace [sʌm'pleis] (*US*) *adv* = **somewhere**

somersault [sʌm'əːrsɔːlt] *n* とんぼ返り toñbogaèri

♦*vi* (person, vehicle) とんぼ返りする toñbogaèri suru

KEYWORD

something [sʌm'θiŋ] *pron* 何か nánìka

something nice 何かいい物 nánìka íi mono

something to do 何かする事 nánìka suru kotð

there's something wrong 何かおかしい nánìka okáshiì

would you like something to eat/drink? 何か食べませんか(飲みませんか) nánìka tabémaseñ(nomímaseñ)ká

---

sometime [sʌm'taim] *adv* (in future) いつか ítsuka; (in past): *sometime last month* 先月のいつか señgetsu no ítsuka

sometimes [sʌm'taimz] *adv* 時々 tokídoki

somewhat [sʌm'wʌt] *adv* 少し sukóshì

KEYWORD

somewhere [sʌm'weːr] *adv* (be) どこかに(で) dókòka ni(de); (go) どこかへ dókòka e

I must have lost it somewhere どこかに落した様です dókòka ni otóshita yō desu

it's somewhere or other in Scotland スコットランドのどこかにあります sukóttorañdo no dókòka ni arímasù

somewhere else (be) どこか外の所に

(で) dókòka hoká no tokorò ni(de); (go) どこか外の所へ dókòka hoká no tokorò e

son [sʌn] *n* 息子 musúko

sonar [sou'nɑːr] *n* ソナー sónà

song [sɔːŋ] *n* (MUS) 歌 utá; (of bird) さえずり saézurì

sonic [sɑːn'ik] *adj*: *sonic boom* ソニックブーム soníkkubūmu

son-in-law [sʌn'inlɔː] (*pl* **sons-in-law**) *n* 義理の息子 no musuko

sonnet [sɑːn'it] *n* ソネット sonéttò

sonny [sʌn'iː] (*inf*) *n* 坊や bōya

soon [suːn] *adv* (in a short time) もうすぐ mō sugù; (a short time after) 間もなく mamónàku; (early) 早く hayákù

soon afterwards それから間もなく soré karà mamónàku ¶ *see also* **as**

sooner [suː'nəːr] *adv* (time) もっと早く móttò hayáku; (preference): *I would sooner do that* 私はむしろあれをやりたい watákushi wà múshìro aré wò yarítaì

sooner or later 遅かれ早かれ osókare hayákàre

soot [sut] *n* すす súsù

soothe [suːð] *vt* (calm: person, animal) 落着かせる ochítsukaserù; (reduce: pain) 和らげる yawáragerù

sophisticated [səfis'tikeitid] *adj* (woman, lifestyle, audience) 世慣れた yonárèta; (machinery) 精巧な seíkō na; (arguments) 洗練された señren saréta

sophomore [sɑːf'əmɔːr] (*US*) *n* 2年生 ninéñsei

soporific [sɑːpərif'ik] *adj* (speech) 眠気を催させる nemúke wò moyóosaserù; (drug) 睡眠の suímin no

sopping [sɑːp'iŋ] *adj*: *sopping (wet)* (hair, clothes etc) びしょぬれの bishónure no

soppy [sɑːp'iː] (*pej*) *adj* (sentimental) センチな señchi na

soprano [səpræn'ou] *n* (singer) ソプラノ sopúrano

sorcerer [sɔːr'sərəːr] *n* 魔法使い mahō-tsukài

sordid [sɔːr'did] *adj* (dirty: bed-sit etc) 汚らしい kitánarashiì; (wretched: story etc) 浅ましい asámashiì, えげつない egétsunaì

sore [sɔːr] *adj* (painful) 痛い itáì
♦*n* (shallow) ただれ tadáre; (deep) かいよう kaíyō

sorely [sɔːr'liː] *adv*: **I am sorely tempted to** よほど...しようと思っている yohódo ...shiyō to omótte irù

sorrow [sɑːr'ou] *n* (regret) 悲しみ kanáshimi

sorrowful [sɑːr'oufəl] *adj* (day, smile etc) 悲しい kanáshiì

sorrows [sɑːr'ouz] *npl* (causes of grief) 不幸 fúkō

sorry [sɑːr'iː] *adj* (regretful) 残念な zańneñ na; (condition, excuse) 情けない nasákenaì

sorry! (apology) 済みません sumímaseñ

sorry? (pardon) はい？ haí? ◇相手の言葉を聞取れなかった時に言う aíte no kotóba wo kikítorenakatta tokí ni iú

to feel sorry for someone ...に同情する ...ni dōjō suru

sort [sɔːrt] *n* (type) 種類 shúrùi
♦*vt* (*also*: **sort out**: papers, mail, belongings) より分ける yoríwakerù; (: problems) 解決する kaíketsu suru

sorting office [sɔːr'tiŋ-] *n* 郵便物振分け場 yūbinbutsufuriwakejō

SOS [esoues'] *n* エスオーエス esú ō esù

so-so [sou'sou'] *adv* (average) まあまあ maámaà

soufflé [suːflei'] *n* スフレ súfure

sought [sɔːt] *pt*, *pp of* **seek**

soul [soul] *n* (spirit etc) 魂 támàshii; (person) 人 hitó

soul-destroying [soul'distrɔiiŋ] *adj* (work) ぼけさせる様な bokésaseru yō na

soulful [soul'fəl] *adj* (eyes, music) 表情豊かな hyōjō yutàka na

sound [saund] *adj* (healthy) 健康な keñkō na; (safe, not damaged) 無傷の múkizu no; (secure: investment) 安全な añzen na; (reliable, thorough) 信頼できる shińrai dekirù; (sensible: advice) 堅実な keñjitsu na

♦*adv*: **sound asleep** ぐっすり眠って gussúrì nemútte
♦*n* (noise) 音 otó; (volume on TV etc) 音声 óñsei; (GEO) 海峡 kaíkyo
♦*vt* (alarm, horn) 鳴らす narásù
♦*vi* (alarm, horn) 鳴る narú; (*fig*: seem) ...の様である ...no yō de árù

to sound like ...の様に聞える ...no yō ni kikóerù

sound barrier *n* 音速障害 oñsokushṑgai

sound effects *npl* 音響効果 oñkyōkōka

soundly [saund'liː] *adv* (sleep) ぐっすり gussúrì; (beat) 手ひどく tehídokù

sound out *vt* (person, opinion) 打診する dashín suru

soundproof [saund'pruːf] *adj* (room etc) 防音の bōon no

soundtrack [saund'træk] *n* (of film) サウンドトラック saúndotorakkù

soup [suːp] *n* スープ sū̀pu

in the soup (*fig*) 困って komátte

soup plate *n* スープ皿 sū̀puzarà

soupspoon [suːp'spuːn] *n* スープスプーン sū̀pusupùn

sour [sau'ər] *adj* (bitter) 酸っぱい suppáì; (milk) 酸っぱくなった suppákù náttà; (*fig*: bad-tempered) 機嫌の悪い kigén no waruì

it's sour grapes (*fig*) 負け惜しみだ makéoshimi da

source [sɔːrs] *n* (*also fig*) 源 minámoto

south [sauθ] *n* 南 minámi
♦*adj* 南の minámi no
♦*adv* (movement) 南へ minámi e; (position) 南に minámi ni

South Africa *n* 南アフリカ minámi afùrika

South African *adj* 南アフリカの minámi afùrika no
♦*n* 南アフリカ人 minámi afurikajìn

South America *n* 南米 nañbei

South American *adj* 南米の nañbei nò
♦*n* 南米人 nañbeijìn

south-east [sauθiːst'] *n* 南東 nañtō

southerly [sʌð'əːrliː] *adj* (to/towards the south: aspect) 南への minámi e nò; (from the south: wind) 南からの minámi kara

nò

southern [sʌð'ə:rn] adj (in or from the south of region) 南の minámi no; (to/towards the south) 南向きの minámimuki no

the southern hemisphere 南半球 mínámihañkyū

South Pole n 南極 nañkyoku

southward(s) [sauθ'wə:rd(z)] adv 南へ mínámi e

south-west [sauθwest'] n 南西 nañsei

souvenir [su:vəni:r'] n (memento) 記念品 kíněñhin

sovereign [sɑ:v'rin] n (ruler) 君主 kúñshu

sovereignty [sɑ:v'rənti:] n 主権 shukéñ

soviet [sou'vi:it] adj ソビエトの sobíetò no

the Soviet Union ソ連 sóreñ

sow[1] [sau] n (pig) 牝豚 mesúbùta

sow[2] [sou] (pt **sowed**, pp **sown**) vt (gen: seeds) まく mákù; (fig: spread: suspicion etc) 広める hirómerù

soy [sɔi] (BRIT **soya**) n: **soy bean** 大豆 dáìzu

soy sauce しょう油 shôyu

spa [spɑ:] n (also: **spa town**) 鉱泉町 kôseñmachi; (US: also: **health spa**) ヘルスセンター herúsuseñtà

space [speis] n (gap) すき間 sukíma, ギャップ gyáppù; (place) 空所 kúsho, 余白 yoháku; (room) 空間 kúkan; (beyond Earth) 宇宙空間 uchúkukan, スペース supésu; (interval, period) 間 ma

♦cpd 宇宙... úchū...

♦vt (also: **space out**: text, visits, payments) 間隔を置く kañkaku wò okú

spacecraft [speis'kræft] n 宇宙船 uchúsen

spaceman [speis'mæn] (pl **spacemen**) n 宇宙飛行士 uchúhikòshi

spaceship [speis'ʃip] n = **spacecraft**

spacewoman [speis'wumən] (pl **spacewomen**) n 女性宇宙飛行士 joséi uchúhikòshi

spacing [spei'siŋ] n (between words) スペース supésu

spacious [spei'ʃəs] adj (car, room etc) 広

い hiróî

spade [speid] n (tool) スコップ sukóppù; (child's) おもちゃのスコップ omóchà no sukóppù

spades [speidz] npl (CARDS: suit) スペード supédo

spaghetti [spəget'i:] n スパゲッティ supágettì

Spain [spein] n スペイン supéîn

span [spæn] n (of bird, plane) 翼長 yokúchō; (of arch) スパン supáñ; (in time) 期間 kíkáñ

♦vt (river) ...にまたがる ...ni matágarù; (fig: time) ...に渡る ...ni watárù

Spaniard [spæn'jə:rd] n スペイン人 supéinjìn

spaniel [spæn'jəl] n スパニエル supánièru

Spanish [spæn'iʃ] adj スペインの supéîn no; (LING) スペイン語の supéingo no

♦n (LING) スペイン語 supéingo

♦npl: **the Spanish** スペイン人 supéinjìn ◇総称 sôshō

spank [spæŋk] vt (someone, someone's bottom) ...のしりをたたく ...no shirí wò tatákù

spanner [spæn'ə:r] (BRIT) n スパナ supánà

spar [spɑ:r] n (pole) マスト másùto

♦vi (BOXING) スパーリングする supáriñgu suru

spare [spe:r] adj (free) 空きの akí no; (surplus) 余った amáttà

♦n = **spare part**

♦vt (do without: trouble etc) ...なしで済ます ...náshì de sumásù; (make available) 与える atáerù; (refrain from hurting: person, city etc) 助けてやる tasúkete yarù

to spare (surplus: time, money) 余った amáttà

spare part n 交換用部品 kôkan-yōbuhìn

spare time n 余暇 yókà

spare wheel n (AUT) スペアタイア supéataià

sparing [spe:r'iŋ] adj: **to be sparing with** ...を倹約する ...wo keñ-yaku suru

sparingly [spe:r'iŋli:] adv (use) 控え目に

hikáeme ni

spark [spɑːrk] n 火 花 híbàna, スパーク supákù; (fig: of wit etc) ひらめき hirámekì

spark(ing) plug [spɑːrk'(iŋ)-] n スパークプラグ supákupuràgu

sparkle [spɑːr'kəl] n きらめき kirámekì
♦vi (shine: diamonds, water) きらめく kirámekù

sparkling [spɑːr'kliŋ] adj (wine) 泡立つ awádatsù; (conversation, performance) きらめく様な kirámeku yṑ na

sparrow [spær'ou] n スズメ suzúme

sparse [spɑːrs] adj (rainfall, hair, population) 少ない sukúnaì

spartan [spɑːr'tən] adj (fig) 簡素な kánso na

spasm [spæz'əm] n (MED) けいれん keíren

spasmodic [spæzmɑːd'ik] adj (fig: not continuous, irregular) 不規則な fukísoku na

spastic [spæs'tik] n 脳性麻ひ患者 nṓseimahikaǹja

spat [spæt] pt, pp spit

spate [speit] n (fig): **a spate of** (letters, protests etc) 沢山の takúsañ no

spatter [spæt'əːr] vt (liquid, surface) ...を...にはねかす ...wo ...ni hanékasù

spatula [spætʃ'ələ] n (CULIN, MED) へら hérà

spawn [spɔːn] vi (fish etc) 産卵する sañran suru
♦n (frog spawn etc) 卵 tamágò

speak [spiːk] (pt **spoke**, pp **spoken**) vt (language) 話す hanásù; (truth) 言う iú
♦vi (use voice) 話す hanásù; (make a speech) 演説する eñzetsu suru

to speak to someone ...に話し掛ける ...ni hanáshikakerù

to speak to someone of/about something ...に...のことを話す ...ni ...no kotó wò hanásù

speak up! もっと大きな声で話しなさい móttò ṓkìna kóè de hanáshi nasaì

speaker [spiː'kəːr] n (in public) 演説者 eñzetsushà; (also: **loudspeaker**) スピーカー supíkà; (POL): **the Speaker** (US,

BRIT) 下院議長 ka-íngichṓ

spear [spiːr] n (weapon) やり yarí
♦vt 刺す sásù

spearhead [spiːr'hed] vt (attack etc) ...の先頭に立つ ...no señtō nì tátsù

spec [spek] (inf) n: **on spec** 山をかけて yamá wo kakète

special [speʃ'əl] adj 特別な tokúbetsu na
special delivery 速達 sokútatsu
special school (BRIT) 特殊学校 tokúshugakkṑ
special adviser 特別顧問 tokúbetsukomòn
special permission 特別許可 tokúbetsukyokà

specialist [speʃ'əlist] n (gen) 専門家 señmonka; (MED) 専門医 señmoñ-i

speciality [speʃiːæl'əti:] n = **specialty**

specialize [speʃ'əlaiz] vi: **to specialize (in)** (...を) 専門的にやる (...wo) señmonteki ni yarù

specially [speʃ'əli:] adv (especially) 特にtṓkù ni; (on purpose) 特別に tokúbetsu ni

specialty [speʃ'əlti:] n (dish) 名物 meíbutsu; (study) 専門 señmon

species [spiː'ʃiːz] n inv 種 shú

specific [spisif'ik] adj (fixed) 特定の tokútei no; (exact) 正確な seíkaku na

specifically [spisif'ikli:] adv (especially) 特に tṓkù ni; (exactly) 明確に meíkaku ni

specification [spesəfəkei'ʃən] n (TECH) 仕様 shiyṓ; (requirement) 条件 jṓkeǹ

specifications [spesəfəkei'ʃənz] npl (TECH) 仕様 shiyṓ

specify [spes'əfai] vt (time, place, color etc) 指定する shitéi suru

specimen [spes'əmən] n (single example) 見本 mihón; (sample for testing, also MED) 標本 hyṓhon

speck [spek] n (of dirt, dust etc) 粒 tsúbù

speckled [spek'əld] adj (hen, eggs) 点々模様の teñteñmoyṓ no

specs [speks] (inf) npl 眼鏡 mégàne

spectacle [spek'təkəl] n (scene) 光景 kṓkei; (grand event) スペクタクル supékùtakuru

spectacles [spek'təkəlz] *npl* 眼鏡 mégàne

spectacular [spektæk'jələr] *adj* (dramatic) 劇的な gekíteki na; (success) 目覚しい mezámashiî

spectator [spek'teitər] *n* 観客 kańkyaku

specter [spek'tər] (*US*) *n* (ghost) 幽霊 yūrei

spectra [spek'trə] *npl of* **spectrum**

spectre [spek'tər] (*BRIT*) = **specter**

spectrum [spek'trəm] (*pl* **spectra**) *n* (color/radio wave spectrum) スペクトル supékutoru

speculate [spek'jəleit] *vi* (FINANCE) 投機をする tōki wo suru; (try to guess): *to speculate about* ...についてあれこれと憶測する ...ni tsúîte arékòre to okúsoku suru

speculation [spekjəlei'ʃən] *n* (FINANCE) 投機 tōki; (guesswork) 憶測 okúsoku

speech [spi:tʃ] *n* (faculty) 話す能力 hanásu nōryoku; (spoken language) 話し言葉 hanáshikotòba; (formal talk) 演説 eńzetsu, スピーチ supíchi; (THEATER) せりふ serífù

speechless [spi:tʃ'lis] *adj* (be, remain etc) 声も出ない kôe mo denáî

speed [spi:d] *n* (rate, fast travel) 速度 sókùdo, スピード supídò; (haste) 急ぎ isógi; (promptness) 素早さ subáyasà

at full/top speed 全速力で zeńsokuryòku de

speed boat *n* モーターボート mótàbòto

speedily [spi:'dili:] *adv* 素早く subáyakù

speeding [spi:'diŋ] *n* (AUT) スピード違反 supído-ihàn

speed limit *n* 速度制限 sokúdoseìgen

speedometer [spi:dɑ:m'itər] *n* 速度計 sokúdokèi

speed up *vi* (*also fig*) 速度を増す sókùdo wo masú

♦*vt* (*also fig*) ...の速度を増す ...no sókùdo wo masú, 速める hayámerù

speedway [spi:d'wei] *n* (sport) オートレース ótorèsu

speedy [spi:'di:] *adj* (fast: car) スピードの出る supídò no dérù; (prompt: reply,

recovery, settlement) 速い hayáî

spell [spel] *n* (*also*: **magic spell**) 魔法 mahō; (period of time) 期間 kikáñ

♦*vt* (*pt*, *pp* **spelled** *or* (*Brit*) **spelt**) (*also*: **spell out**) ...のつづりを言う ...no tsuzúri wò iú; (*fig*: advantages, difficulties) ...の兆しである ...no kizáshi de arù

to cast a spell on someone ...に魔法を掛ける ...ni mahō wò kakérù

he can't spell 彼はスペルが苦手だ kárè wa supérù ga nigáte dà

spellbound [spel'baund] *adj* (audience etc) 魅せられた miséraretà

spelling [spel'iŋ] *n* つづり tsuzúri, スペリング supéringu

spend [spend] (*pt*, *pp* **spent**) *vt* (money) 使う tsukáù; (time, life) 過す sugósù

spendthrift [spend'θrift] *n* 浪費家 rōhika

spent [spent] *pt*, *pp of* **spend**

sperm [spə:rm] *n* 精子 sêîshi

spew [spju:] *vt* 吐き出す hakídasù

sphere [sfi:r] *n* (round object) 球 kyū; (area) 範囲 hán-i

spherical [sfe:r'ikəl] *adj* (round) 丸い marúî

sphinx [sfiŋks] *n* スフィンクス sufíñkusu

spice [spais] *n* 香辛料 kōshiñryō, スパイス supáîsu

♦*vt* (food) ...にスパイスを入れる ...ni supáîsu wo irérù

spick-and-span [spik'ənspæn'] *adj* きちんときれいな kichíñ to kírèi na

spicy [spai'si:] *adj* (food) スパイスの利いた supáîsu no kiítà

spider [spai'də:r] *n* クモ kúmò

spike [spaik] *n* (point) くい kuí; (BOT) 穂 hó

spill [spil] (*pt*, *pp* **spilt** *or* **spilled**) *vt* (liquid) こぼす kobósù

♦*vi* (liquid) こぼれる kobórerù

spill over *vi* (liquid: *also fig*) あふれる afúrerù

spin [spin] *n* (trip in car) ドライブ doráîbu; (AVIAT) きりもみ kirímomi; (on ball) スピン supíñ

♦*vb* (*pt*, *pp* **spun**)

♦*vt* (wool etc) 紡ぐ tsumúgù; (ball, coin) 回転させる kaíten saserù

♦*vi* (make thread) 紡ぐ tsumúgù; (person, head) 目が回る mé gà mawárù

spinach [spin'itʃ] *n* (plant, food) ホウレンソウ hôreñsō

spinal [spai'nəl] *adj* (injury etc) 背骨の sebóne no

spinal cord *n* せき髄 sekízùi

spindly [spind'li:] *adj* (legs, trees etc) か細い kabósoì

spin-dryer [spindrai'ə:r] (*BRIT*) *n* 脱水機 dassúikì

spine [spain] *n* (ANAT) 背骨 sebóne; (thorn: of plant, hedgehog etc) とげ togé

spineless [spain'lis] *adj* (*fig*) 意気地なしの ikújinàshi no

spinning [spin'iŋ] *n* (art) 紡績 bóseki

spinning top *n* こま kómà

spinning wheel *n* 紡ぎ車 tsumúgigurùma

spin-off [spin'ɔ:f] *n* (*fig*: by-product) 副産物 fukúsaňbutsu

spin out *vt* (talk, job, money, holiday) 引延ばす hikínobasù

spinster [spin'stə:r] *n* オールドミス ốrudomisù

spiral [spai'rəl] *n* ら旋形 raséñkei

♦*vi* (*fig*: prices etc) うなぎ登りに上る unáginobòri ni nobórù

spiral staircase *n* ら旋階段 raséñkaidàn

spire [spai'ə:r] *n* せん塔 señtō

spirit [spir'it] *n* (soul) 魂 támàshii; (ghost) 幽霊 yūrei; (energy) 元気 géñki; (courage) 勇気 yũki; (frame of mind) 気分 kíbùn; (sense) 精神 seíshin

  in good spirits 気分上々で kíbùn jốjō de

spirited [spir'itid] *adj* (performance, retort, defense) 精力的な seíryokuteki na

spirit level *n* 水準器 suíjuňki

spirits [spir'its] *npl* (drink) 蒸留酒 jốryūshu

spiritual [spir'itʃu:əl] *adj* (of the spirit: home, welfare, needs) 精神的な seíshinteki na; (religious: affairs) 霊的な reíteki

na

♦*n* (*also*: **Negro spiritual**) 黒人霊歌 kokújinreìka

spit [spit] *n* (for roasting) 焼きぐし yakígushi; (saliva) つばき tsubáki

♦*vi* (*pt, pp* **spat**) (throw out saliva) つばを吐く tsubá wo hákù; (sound: fire, cooking) じゅうじゅういう jũjũ iu; (rain) ぱらつく parátsukù

spite [spait] *n* 恨み urámi

♦*vt* (person) ...に意地悪をする ...ni ijíwarù wo suru

  in spite of ...にもかかわらず ...ní mò kakáwarazù

spiteful [spait'fəl] *adj* (child, words etc) 意地悪な ijíwarù na

spittle [spit'əl] *n* つばき tsubáki

splash [splæʃ] *n* (sound) ざぶんという音 zabúñ to iú otò; (of color) 派手なはん点 hadé nà hañten

♦*vt* はね掛ける hanékakerù

♦*vi* (*also*: **splash about**) ぴちゃぴちゃ水をはねる pichápìcha mízù wò hanérù

spleen [spli:n] *n* (ANAT) ひ臓 hizố

splendid [splen'did] *adj* (excellent: idea, recovery) 素晴らしい subárashiĩ; (impressive: architecture, affair) 立派な rippá nà

splendor [splen'də:r] (*BRIT* **splendour**) *n* (impressiveness) 輝き kagáyakì

splendors [splen'də:rz] *npl* (features) 特色 tokúshoku

splint [splint] *n* 副木 fukúboku

splinter [splin'tə:r] *n* (of wood, glass) 破片 hahéñ; (in finger) とげ togé

♦*vi* (bone, wood, glass etc) 砕ける kudákerù

split [split] *n* (crack) 割れ目 waréme; (tear) 裂け目 sakéme; (*fig*: division) 分裂 buñretsu; (: difference) 差異 sá-ì

♦*vb* (*pt, pp* **split**)

♦*vt* (divide) 割る wárù, 裂く sákù; (party) 分裂させる buñretsu saserù; (share equally: work) 手分けしてやる tewáke shite yarù; (: profits) 山分けする yamáwake suru

♦*vi* (divide) 割れる warérù

split up *vi* (couple) 別れる wakárerù;

(group, meeting) 解散する kaísan suru

splutter [splʌt'əːr] vi (engine etc) ぱちぱ
ち音を立てる páchipachi otó wò tatérù;
(person) どもる domórù

spoil [spoil] (pt, pp **spoilt** or **spoiled**) vt
(damage, mar) 台無しにする daínashi ni
surù; (child) 甘やかす amáyakasù

spoils [spoilz] npl (loot: also fig) 分捕り
品 buńdorihìn

spoilsport [spoil'spɔːrt] n 座を白けさせ
る人 zá wò shirákesaserù hitó

spoke [spouk] pt of **speak**

◆n (of wheel) スポーク supókù

spoken [spou'kən] pp of **speak**

spokesman [spouks'mən] (pl **spokes-
men**) n スポークスマン supókusumàn

spokeswoman [spouks'wumən] (pl
spokeswomen) n 女性報道官 joséi hōdō-
kan, 女性スポークスマン joséi supókusumàn

sponge [spʌndʒ] n (for washing with) ス
ポンジ supóñji; (also: **sponge cake**) スポ
ンジケーキ supóñjikèki

◆vt (wash) スポンジで洗う supóñji de a-
ráù

◆vi: **to sponge off/on someone** ...にた
かる ...ni takárù

sponge bag (BRIT) n 洗面バッグ seń-
menbaggù ◇洗面道具を入れて携帯する
バッグ seńmendōgu wo iréte keitai surù
bággù

sponsor [spɑn'səːr] n (of player, event,
club, program) スポンサー supóñsà; (of
charitable event etc) 協賛者 kyósañsha;
(for application) 保証人 hoshónin; (for
bill in parliament etc) 提出者 teíshutsu-
shà

◆vt (player, event, club, program etc)
...のスポンサーになる ...no supóñsà ni
nárù; (charitable event etc) ...の協賛者に
なる ...no kyósañsha ni nárù; (applicant)
...の保証人になる ...no hoshónin ni nárù;
(proposal, bill etc) 提出する teíshutsu
suru

sponsorship [spɑn'səːrʃip] n (financial
support) 金銭的な援助 kińsentekieñjo

spontaneous [spɑːntei'niːəs] adj (un-
planned: gesture) 自発的な jihátsuteki
na

spooky [spuː'kiː] (inf) adj (place, atmosphere) お化けが出そうな o-bàke gà de-
só nà

spool [spuːl] n (for thread) 糸巻 itómàki;
(for film, tape etc) リール rīru

spoon [spuːn] n さじ sají, スプーン supùn

spoon-feed [spuːn'fiːd] vt (baby, patient)
スプーンで食べさせる supūn de tabésa-
serù; (fig: students etc) ...に一方的に教え
込む ...ni ippóteki nì oshíekomù

spoonful [spuːn'ful] n スプーン一杯分
supūn ippáibun

sporadic [spɔːræd'ik] adj (glimpses,
attacks etc) 散発的な sańpatsuteki na

sport [spɔːrt] n (game) スポーツ supótsu;
(person) 気さくな人 kisáku nà hitó

◆vt (wear) これみよがしに身に付ける
korémiyogàshi ni mi ni tsukérù

sporting [spɔːr'tiŋ] adj (event etc) スポ
ーツの supótsù no; (generous) 気前がい
い kimáe ga íi

to give someone a sporting chance
...にちゃんとしたチャンスを与える ...ni
chańtò shita cháñsu wo atáerù

sport jacket (US) n スポーツジャケッ
ト supótsujakettò

sports car [spɔːrts-] n スポーツカー su-
pótsukà

sports jacket (BRIT) n = **sport
jacket**

sportsman [spɔːrts'mən] (pl **sportsmen**)
n スポーツマン supótsumàn

sportsmanship [spɔːrts'mənʃip] n スポ
ーツマンシップ supótsumanshippù

sportswear [spɔːrts'weəːr] n スポーツウ
エア supótsuuèa

sportswoman [spɔːrts'wumən] (pl
sportswomen) n スポーツウーマン supó-
tsuūman

sporty [spɔːr'tiː] adj (good at sports) ス
ポーツ好きの supótsuzuki no

spot [spɑːt] n (mark) 染み shimí; (on pattern, skin etc) はん点 hañten; (place) 場
所 bashó; (RADIO, TV) コーナー kōnä;
(small amount): **a spot of** 少しの sukóshì no

◆vt (notice: person, mistake etc) ...に気

が付く ...ni kí gà tsúkù

on the spot (in that place) 現場に geńba ni; (immediately) その場で sonó ba de, 即座に sókùza ni; (in difficulty) 困って komáttè

spot check n 抜取り検査 nukítorikeǹsa

spotless [spɑ:t'lis] adj (shirt, kitchen etc) 清潔な seíketsu na

spotlight [spɑ:t'lait] n スポットライト supóttoraìto

spotted [spɑ:t'id] adj (pattern) はん点模様の hańtenmoyô no

spotty [spɑ:t'i:] adj (face, youth: with freckles) そばかすだらけの sobákasudaràke no; (: with pimples) にきびだらけの nikíbidaràke no

spouse [spaus] n (male/female) 配偶者 haígùsha

spout [spaut] n (of jug) つぎ口 tsugígùchi; (of pipe) 出口 dégùchi
♦vi (flames, water etc) 噴出す fukídasù

sprain [sprein] n ねんざ neńza
♦vt: **to sprain one's ankle/wrist** 足首〔手首〕をねんざする ashíkùbi(tékùbi)wo neńza suru

sprang [spræŋ] pt of **spring**

sprawl [sprɔ:l] vi (person: lie) 寝そべる nesóberù; (: sit) だらしない格好で座る daráshinai kakkô de suwárù; (place) 無秩序に広がる muchítsujo ni hirógarù

spray [sprei] n (small drops) 水煙 mizúkemùri; (sea spray) しぶき shíbùki; (container: hair spray etc) スプレー supúrè; (garden spray) 噴霧器 fuńmukì; (of flowers) 小枝 koéda
♦vt (sprinkle) 噴霧器で...に...を掛ける fuńmukî de ...ni ...wo kakérù; (crops) 消毒する shôdoku suru

spread [spred] n (range, distribution) 広がり hirógarì; (CULIN: for bread) スプレッド supúreddò; (inf: food) ごちそう gochísò
♦vb (pt, pp **spread**)
♦vt (lay out) 並べる naráberù; (butter) 塗る núrù; (wings, arms, sails) 広げる hirógerù; (workload, wealth) 分配する buńpai suru; (scatter) まく mákù
♦vi (disease, news) 広がる hirógarù;

(also: **spread out**: stain) 広がる hirógarù

spread-eagled [spred'i:gəld] adj 大の字に寝た daí no jî ni netá

spread out vi (move apart) 散らばる chirábarù

spreadsheet [spred'ʃi:t] n (COMPUT) スプレッドシート supúreddoshìto

spree [spri:] n: **to go on a spree** ...にふける ...ni fukérù

sprightly [sprait'li:] adj (old person) かくしゃくとした kakúshaku to shità

spring [spriŋ] n (leap) 跳躍 chôyaku; (coiled metal) ばね bánè; (season) 春 hárù; (of water) 泉 izúmi
♦vi (pt **sprang**, pp **sprung**) (leap) 跳ぶ tobú

in spring (season) 春に hárù ni

springboard [spriŋ'bɔ:rd] n スプリングボード supúringubòdo

spring-cleaning [spriŋ'kli:'niŋ] n 大掃除 ôsôji ◇春とは関係なく言う hárù to wa kańkeinakù iú

springtime [spriŋ'taim] n 春 hárù

spring up vi (thing: appear) 現れる aráwarerù

sprinkle [spriŋ'kəl] vt (scatter: liquid) まく mákù; (: salt, sugar) 振り掛ける furíkakerù

to sprinkle water on, sprinkle with water ...に水をまく ...ni mizú wò mákù

sprinkler [spriŋ'klər] n (for lawn, to put out fire) スプリンクラー supúrinkurà

sprint [sprint] n (race) 短距離競走 tańkyorikyôsō, スプリント supúriǹto
♦vi (gen: run fast) 速く走る háyàku hashírù; (SPORT) スプリントする supúriǹto suru

sprinter [sprin'tər] n スプリンター supúriǹtà

sprout [spraut] vi (plant, vegetable) 発芽する hatsúga suru

sprouts [sprauts] npl (also: **Brussels sprouts**) 芽キャベツ mekyábètsu

spruce [spru:s] n inv (BOT) トウヒ tôhì
♦adj (neat, smart) スマートな sumâtò na

sprung [sprʌŋ] pp of **spring**

spry [sprai] adj (old person) かくしゃく

とした kakúshaku to shitá

spun [spʌn] *pt, pp* of **spin**

spur [spəːr] *n* 拍車 hakúsha; (*fig*) 刺激 shigéki
♦*vt* (*also*: **spur on**) 激励する gekírei suru
on the spur of the moment とっさに tossá ni

spurious [spjuːrˈiːəs] *adj* (false: attraction) 見せ掛けの misékake no; (: argument) 間違った machígattá

spurn [spəːrn] *vt* (reject) はねつける hanétsukerù

spurt [spəːrt] *n* (of blood etc) 噴出 fuńshutsu; (of energy) 奮発 fuńpatsu
♦*vi* (blood, flame) 噴出す fukídasù

spy [spai] *n* スパイ supái
♦*vi*: **to spy on** こっそり見張る kossórì mihárù
♦*vt* (see) 見付ける mitsúkerù

spying [spaiˈiŋ] *n* スパイ行為 supáikòi

sq. *abbr* = **square**

squabble [skwɑːbˈəl] *vi* 口げんかする kuchígeñka suru

squad [skwɑːd] *n* (MIL, POLICE) 班 háñ; (SPORT) チーム chímu

squadron [skwɑːdˈrən] *n* (MIL) 大隊 daítai

squalid [skwɑːlˈid] *adj* (dirty, unpleasant: conditions) 汚らしい kitánarashiî; (sordid: story etc) えげつない egétsunaî

squall [skwɔːl] *n* (stormy wind) スコール sukórù

squalor [skwɑːlˈəːr] *n* 汚い環境 kitánai kañkyō

squander [skwɑːnˈdəːr] *vt* (money) 浪費する rôhi suru; (chances) 逃す nogásù

square [skweːr] *n* (shape) 正方形 seíhôkei; (in town) 広場 híròba; (*inf*: person) 堅物 katábutsu
♦*adj* (in shape) 正方形の seíhôkei no; (*inf*: ideas, tastes) 古臭い furúkusaî
♦*vt* (arrange) ...を...に一致させる ...wo ...ni itchí saserù; (MATH) 2乗する nijô suru; (reconcile) ...を...と調和させる ...wo ...to chôwa saserù

all square 貸し借りなし kashíkàri náshì

a square meal 十分な食事 júbùn na

shokúji

2 meters square 2メーター平方 ni métā heíhō

2 square meters 2平方メーター ni heíhō métā

squarely [skweːrˈliː] *adv* (directly: fall, land etc) まともに matómo nî; (fully: confront) きっぱりと kippárî to

squash [skwɑːʃ] *n* (US: marrow etc) カボチャ kabócha; (BRIT: drink): *lemon/orange squash* レモン[オレンジ]スカッシュ remón[oréñji]sukasshù; (SPORT) スカッシュ sukásshu
♦*vt* つぶす tsubúsu

squat [skwɑːt] *adj* ずんぐりした zuńgurì shita
♦*vi* (*also*: **squat down**) しゃがむ shagámù

squatter [skwɑːtˈəːr] *n* 不法居住者 fuhókyojùsha

squawk [skwɔːk] *vi* (bird) ぎゃーぎゃー鳴く gyâgyā nakú

squeak [skwiːk] *vi* (door etc) きしむ kishímù; (mouse) ちゅーちゅー鳴く chúchū nakú

squeal [skwiːl] *vi* (children) きゃーきゃー言う kyâkyā iú; (brakes etc) キーキー言う kîkī iú

squeamish [skwiːˈmiʃ] *adj* やたら...に弱い yatára ...ni yowáî

squeeze [skwiːz] *n* (*gen*: of hand) 握り締める事 nigírishimerù kotó; (ECON) 金融引締め kiń-yúhikishime
♦*vt* (*gen*) 絞る shibórù; (hand, arm) 握り締める nigírishimerù

squeeze out *vt* (juice etc) 絞り出す shibóridasù

squelch [skweltʃ] *vi* ぐちゃぐちゃ音を立てる gúchàgucha otó wò tatérù

squid [skwid] *n* イカ iká

squiggle [skwigˈəl] *n* のたくった線 notákuttà séñ

squint [skwint] *vi* (have a squint) 斜視である sháshì de árù
♦*n* (MED) 斜視 sháshì

squire [skwaiˈəːr] *n* (BRIT) 大地主 ōjínùshi

squirm [skwəːrm] *vi* 身もだえする mi-

módàe suru

squirrel [skwər'əl] *n* リス rísù

squirt [skwə:rt] *vi* 噴出す fukídasù
♦*vt* 噴掛ける fukíkakerù

Sr *abbr* = **senior**

St *abbr* = **saint; street**

stab [stæb] *n* (with knife etc) ひと刺し hitósashì; (*inf*: try): **to have a stab at (doing) something** ...をやってみる ...wo yatté mirù
♦*vt* (person, body) 刺す sásù
a stab of pain 刺す様な痛み sásù yō na itámi

stability [stəbil'əti:] *n* 安定 añtei

stabilize [stei'bəlaiz] *vt* (prices) 安定させる añtei saserù
♦*vi* (prices, one's weight) 安定する añtei suru

stable [stei'bəl] *adj* (prices, patient's condition) 安定した añtei shita; (marriage) 揺るぎない yurúgi naì
♦*n* (for horse) 馬小屋 umágoya

staccato [stəka:'tou] *adv* スタッカート sutákkàto

stack [stæk] *n* (pile) ...の山 ...no yamá
♦*vt* (pile) 積む tsumú

stadium [stei'di:əm] *n* 競技場 kyōgijō, スタジアム sutájìamu

staff [stæf] *n* (work force) 職員 shokúiǹ; (*BRIT*: SCOL) 教職員 kyōshokuìn
♦*vt* ...の職員として働く ...no shokúiǹ toshite határàku

stag [stæg] *n* 雄ジカ ójìka

stage [steidʒ] *n* (in theater etc) 舞台 butái; (platform) 台 dái; (profession): **the stage** 俳優業 haíyùgyō; (point, period) 段階 dañkai
♦*vt* (play) 上演する jóen suru; (demonstration) 行う okónaù
in stages 少しずつ sukóshi zutsù

stagecoach [steidʒ'koutʃ] *n* 駅馬車 ekíbashà

stage manager *n* 舞台監督 butáikaňtoku

stagger [stæg'ə:r] *vi* よろめく yorómekù
♦*vt* (amaze) 仰天させる gyóten saserù; (hours, holidays) ずらす zurásù

staggering [stæg'ə:riŋ] *adj* (amazing) 仰天させる gyóten saserù

stagnant [stæg'nənt] *adj* (water) よどんだ yodóñda; (economy etc) 停滞した teítai shita

stagnate [stæg'neit] *vi* (economy, business, person) 停滞する teítai suru; (person) だれる darérù

stag party *n* スタッグパーティ sutággupàti

staid [steid] *adj* (person, attitudes) 古めかしい furúmekashiì

stain [stein] *n* (mark) 染み shimí; (coloring) 着色剤 chakúshokuzài, ステイン sutéiñ
♦*vt* (mark) 汚す yogósù; (wood) ...にステインを塗る ...ni sutéiñ wo núrù

stained glass window [steind-] *n* ステンドグラスの窓 suténdogurasu no mádò

stainless steel [stein'lis-] *n* ステンレス sutéñresu

stain remover [-rimu:'və:r] *n* 染み抜き shimínuki

stair [ste:r] *n* (step) 段 dáñ, ステップ sutéppù

staircase [ste:r'keis] *n* 階段 kaídan

stairs [ste:rz] *npl* (flight of steps) 階段 kaídan

stairway [ste:r'wei] *n* = **staircase**

stake [steik] *n* (post) くい kúì; (COMM: interest) 利害関係 rigáikaňkei; (BETTING: *gen pl*) 賞金 shōkin
♦*vt* (money, life, reputation) かける kakérù
to stake a claim to ...に対する所有権を主張する ...ni taí surù shoyúken wò shuchō suru
to be at stake 危ぶまれる ayábumarerù

stalactite [stəlæk'tait] *n* しょう乳石 shōnyūseki

stalagmite [stəlæg'mait] *n* 石じゅん石 sekíjun

stale [steil] *adj* (bread) 固くなった katákù nattá; (food, air) 古くなった fúrùku natta; (air) よどんだ yodóñda; (smell) か び臭い kabíkusaì; (beer) 気の抜けた kí nò nukétà

stalemate [steil'meit] n (CHESS) ステールメート sutérumĕto; (fig) 行き詰り ikízumari

stalk [stɔ:k] n (of flower, fruit) 茎 kukí
♦vt (person, animal) ...に忍び寄る ...ni shinóbiyorù

stalk off vi 威張って行く ibátte ikú

stall [stɔ:l] n (in market) 屋台 yátai; (in stable) 馬房 babő
♦vt (AUT: engine, car) エンストを起す ensuto wò okósù; (fig: delay: person) 引止める hikítomerù; (: decision etc) 引延ばす hikínobasù
♦vi (AUT: engine, car) エンストを起す ensuto wò okósù; (fig: person) 時間稼ぎをする jikánkasegì wò suru

stallion [stæl'jən] n 種ウマ tanéuma

stalls [stɔ:lz] (BRIT) npl (in cinema, theater) 特別席 tokúbetsusèki

stalwart [stɔ:l'wə:rt] adj (worker, supporter, party member) 不動の fudő no

stamina [stæm'inə] n スタミナ sutámina

stammer [stæm'ə:r] n どもり dómòri
♦vi どもる domórù

stamp [stæmp] n (postage stamp) 切手 kitté; (rubber stamp) スタンプ sutánpu; (mark, also fig) 特徴 tokúchō
♦vi (also: **stamp one's foot**) 足を踏み鳴らす ashí wò fumínarasù
♦vt (letter) ...に切手を張る ...ni kitté wò harú; (mark) 特徴付ける tokúchōzukerù; (with rubber stamp) ...にスタンプを押す ...ni sutánpu wo osú

stamp album n 切手帳 kittéchō

stamp collecting [-kəlek'tiŋ] n 切手収集 kittéshūshū

stampede [stæmpi:d'] n (of animal herd) 暴走 bősō; (fig: of people) 殺到 sattő

stance [stæns] n (way of standing) 立っている姿勢 tatté irù shisèi; (fig) 姿勢 shiséi

stand [stænd] n (position) 構え kámàe; (for taxis) 乗場 noríba; (hall, music stand) 台 dái; (SPORT) スタンド sutándo; (stall) 屋台 yátai
♦vb (pt, pp **stood**)
♦vi (be: person, unemployment etc) ...になっている ...ni natté irù; (be on foot) 立

つ tátsù; (rise) 立ち上る tachíagarù; (remain: decision, offer) 有効である yűkō de arù; (in election etc) 立候補する rikkőhò suru
♦vt (place: object) 立てる tatérù; (tolerate, withstand: person, thing) ...に耐える ...ni taérù; (treat, invite to) おごる ogőrù

to make a stand (fig) 立場を執る tachíba wò tórù

to stand for parliament (BRIT) 議員選挙に出馬する gíinsenkyo ni shutsúba suru

standard [stæn'də:rd] n (level) 水準 suíjun; (norm, criterion) 基準 kijún; (flag) 旗 hatá
♦adj (normal: size etc) 標準的な hyőjunteki na; (text) 権威のある kén'i no arù

standardize [stæn'də:rdaiz] vt 規格化する kikákuka suru

standard lamp (BRIT) n フロアスタンド furőasutàndo

standard of living n 生活水準 seíkatsusuijùn

standards [stæn'də:rdz] npl (morals) 道徳基準 dőtoku kijún

stand by vi (be ready) 待機する táiki suru
♦vt fus (opinion, decision) 守る mamórù; (person) ...の力になる ...no chikára ni narú

stand-by [stænd'bai] n (reserve) 非常用の物 hijőyō no monő

to be on stand-by 待機している táiki shité irù

stand-by ticket n (AVIAT) キャンセル待ちの切符 kyánserumachi nò kippú

stand down vi (withdraw) 引下がる hikísagarù

stand for vt fus (signify) 意味する ímì suru; (represent) 代表する daíhyō suru; (tolerate) 容認する yőnin suru

stand-in [stænd'in] n 代役 daíkō

stand in for vt fus (replace) ...の代役を務める ...no daíyaku wò tsutómerù

standing [stæn'diŋ] adj (on feet: ovation) 立ち上ってする tachíagatte surù; (permanent: invitation) 持続の jizóku no, 継続の keízoku no

♦*n* (status) 地位 chíi

of many years' standing 数年前から続いている sǘnen maè kara tsuzúite irù

standing joke *n* お決りの冗談 o-kímari nò jódàñ

standing order (*BRIT*) *n* (at bank) 自動振替 jidófurīkae ◊支払額が定額である場合に使う shiháraīgaku ga teígaku de arù bàaì ni tsukáù

standing room *n* 立見席 tachímiseki

stand-offish [stændɔːˈfiʃ] *adj* 無愛想な buáìsō na

stand out *vi* (be prominent) 目立つ medátsù

standpoint [stændˈpɔint] *n* 観点 kañteñ

standstill [stændˈstil] *n*: *at a standstill* (*also fig*) 滞って todókòtte

to come to a standstill 止ってしまう tomátte shimaù

stand up *vi* (rise) 立ち上る tachíagarù

stand up for *vt fus* (defend) 守る mamórù

stand up to *vt fus* (withstand: *also fig*) ...に立向かう ...ni tachímukaù

stank [stæŋk] *pt of* **stink**

staple [steiˈpəl] *n* (for papers) ホチキスの針 hóchìkisu no hárì

♦*adj* (food etc) 主要の shuyŏ no

♦*vt* (fasten) ホチキスで留める hóchìkisu de tomérù

stapler [steiˈplɚr] *n* ホチキス hóchìkisu

star [stɑːr] *n* (in sky) 星 hoshí; (celebrity) スター sutá

♦*vi*: *to star in* ...で主演する ...de shuén suru

♦*vt* (THEATER, CINEMA) 主役とする shuyáku to surù

starboard [stɑːrˈbɚrd] *n* 右げん úgeñ

starch [stɑːrtʃ] *n* (for shirts etc) のり noría; (CULIN) でんぷん deñpun

stardom [stɑːrˈdəm] *n* スターの身分 sutá no mibùn

stare [steːr] *n* じろじろ見る事 jíròjiro mírù koto

♦*vi*: *to stare at* じろじろ見る jíròjiro mírù

starfish [stɑːrˈfiʃ] *n* ヒトデ hitode

stark [stɑːrk] *adj* (bleak) 殺風景な sappúkèi na

♦*adv*: *stark naked* 素っ裸の suppádàka no

starling [stɑːrˈliŋ] *n* ムクドリ mukúdòri

starry [stɑːrˈiː] *adj* (night, sky) 星がよく見える hoshí gà yókù miérù

starry-eyed [stɑːrˈiːaid] *adj* (innocent) 天真らん漫な teñshinranman na

stars [stɑːrz] *npl*: *the stars* (horoscope) 星占い hoshíuranaì

start [stɑːrt] *n* (beginning) 初め hajíme; (departure) 出発 shuppátsu; (sudden movement) ぎくっとする事 gikúttð suru kotð; (advantage) リード rídò

♦*vt* (begin) 始める hajímerù; (cause) 引起こす hikíokosù; (found: business etc) 創立する sóritsu suru; (engine) かける kakérù

♦*vi* (begin) 始まる hajímarù; (with fright) ぎくっとする gikúttð suru; (train etc) 出発する shuppátsu suru

to start doing/to do something ...を し始める ...wo shihájimerù

starter [stɑːrˈtɚr] *n* (AUT) スターター sutátà; (SPORT: official) スターター sutátà; (*BRIT*: CULIN) 最初の料理 saísho no ryóri

starting point [stɑːrˈtiŋ-] *n* 出発点 shuppátsuteñ

startle [stɑːrˈtəl] *vt* 驚かす odórokasù

startling [stɑːrtˈliŋ] *adj* (news etc) 驚く様な odóroku yð na

start off *vi* (begin) 始める hajímerù; (begin moving) 出発する shuppátsu suru

start up *vi* (business etc) 開業する kaígyō suru; (engine) かかる kakárù; (car) 走り出す hashíridasù

♦*vt* (business etc) 創立する sóritsu suru; (engine) かける kakérù; (car) 走らせる hashíraserù

starvation [stɑːrveiˈʃən] *n* 飢餓 kígà

starve [stɑːrv] *vi* (*inf*: be very hungry) おなかがぺこぺこである onáka gà pekópeko dè árù; (*also*: **starve to death**) 餓死する gáshì suru

♦*vt* (person, animal: not give food to) 飢えさせる uésaserù; (: to death) 餓死させる gáshì saserù

state [steit] n (condition) 状態 jõtai; (government) 国 kuní

♦vt (say, declare) 明言する meígen suru
 to be in a state 取乱している torímidashite irù

stately [steit'li:] adj (home, walk etc) 優雅な yũga na

statement [steit'mənt] n (declaration) 陳述 chiñjutsu

States [steits] npl: *the States* 米国 beíkoku

statesman [steits'mən] (pl **statesmen**) n リーダー格の政治家 rídākaku nò seíjika

static [stæt'ik] n (RADIO, TV) 雑音 zatsúon

♦adj (not moving) 静的な seíteki na

static electricity n 静電気 seídeñki

station [stei'ʃən] n (RAIL) 駅 ékî; (police station etc) 署 shó; (RADIO) 放送局 hõsõkyoku

♦vt (position: guards etc) 配置する haíchi suru

stationary [stei'ʃəne:ri:] adj (vehicle) 動いていない ugõite inaî

stationer [stei'ʃənə:r] n 文房具屋 buñbõguya

stationer's (shop) [stei'ʃənə:rz-] n 文房具店 buñbõguteñ

stationery [stei'ʃəne:ri:] n 文房具 buñbõgu

stationmaster [stei'ʃənmæstə:r] n (RAIL) 駅長 ekíchõ

station wagon (US) n ワゴン車 wagõñsha

statistic [stətis'tik] n 統計値 tõkeichî

statistical [stətis'tikəl] adj (evidence, techniques) 統計学的な tõkeigakuteki na

statistics [stətis'tiks] n (science) 統計学 tõkeígaku

statue [stætʃ'u:] n 像 zõ

stature [stætʃ'ə:r] n 身長 shiñchõ

status [stei'təs] n (position) 身分 míbun; (official classification) 資格 shikáku; (importance) 地位 chíi
 the status quo 現状 geñjõ

status symbol n ステータスシンボル sutétasushiñboru

statute [stætʃ'u:t] n 法律 hõritsu

statutory [stætʃ'u:tɔ:ri:] adj (powers, rights etc) 法定の hõtei no

staunch [stɔ:ntʃ] adj (ally) 忠実な chũjitsu na

stave off [steiv-] vt (attack, threat) 防ぐ fuségù

stay [stei] n (period of time) 滞在期間 taízaikikàn

♦vi (remain) 居残る inőkorù; (with someone, as guest) 泊る tomárù; (in place: spend some time) とどまる todőmarù
 to stay put とどまる todőmarù
 to stay the night 泊る tomárù

stay behind vi 居残る inőkorù

stay in vi (at home) 家にいる ié nî irù

staying power [stei'iŋ-] n 根気 koñki

stay on vi 残る nokőrù

stay out vi (of house) 家に戻らない ié nî modőranaî

stay up vi (at night) 起きている őkîte irù

stead [sted] n: *in someone's stead* ...の代りに ...no kawári ni
 to stand someone in good stead ...の役に立つ ...no yakú ni tatsù

steadfast [sted'fæst] adj 不動の fudő no

steadily [sted'ili:] adv (firmly) 着実に chakújitsu ni; (constantly) ずっと zuttő; (fixedly) じっと jittő; (walk) しっかりと shikkárî to

steady [sted'i:] adj (constant: job, boyfriend, speed) 決った kimátta, 変らない kawáranaî; (regular: rise in prices) 着実な chakújitsu na; (person, character) 堅実な keñjitsu na; (firm: hand etc) 震えない furűenaî; (calm: look, voice) 落着いた ochítsùita

♦vt (stabilize) 安定させる añtei saserù; (nerves) 静める shizúmerù

steak [steik] n (also: **beefsteak**) ビーフステーキ bífusutēkì; (beef, fish, pork etc) ステーキ sutēkì

steal [sti:l] (pt **stole**, pp **stolen**) vt 盗む nusúmù

♦vi (thieve) 盗む nusúmù; (move secretly) こっそりと行く kossőrî to ikú

stealth [stelθ] *n*: *by stealth* こっそりと kossórî to

stealthy [stel'θi:] *adj* (movements, actions) ひそかな hisókà na

steam [sti:m] *n* (mist) 水蒸気 suíjòki; (on window) 曇り kumóri
♦*vt* (CULIN) 蒸す músù
♦*vi* (give off steam) 水蒸気を立てる suíjòki wo tatérù

steam engine *n* 蒸気機関 jòkikikàn

steamer [sti:'mə:r] *n* 汽船 kisén

steamroller [sti:m'roulə:r] *n* ロードローラー rôdorôrā

steamship [sti:m'ʃip] *n* = **steamer**

steamy [sti:'mi:] *adj* (room) 湯気でもうもうとした yúge de mômô no; (window) 湯気で曇った yúge de kumóttà; (heat, atmosphere) 蒸暑い mushíatsuì

steel [sti:l] *n* 鋼鉄 kôtetsu
♦*adj* 鋼鉄の kôtetsu no

steelworks [sti:l'wə:rks] *n* 製鋼所 seíkôjo

steep [sti:p] *adj* (stair, slope) 険しい kewáshiì; (increase) 大幅な ôhaba na; (price) 高い takáì
♦*vt* (fig: soak) 浸す hitásù

steeple [sti:'pəl] *n* せん塔 señtō

steeplechase [sti:'pəltʃeis] *n* 障害レース shôgairèsu

steer [sti:r] *vt* (vehicle) 運転する uñten suru; (person) 導く michíbikù
♦*vi* (maneuver) 車を操る kurúma wò ayátsurù

steering [sti:r'iŋ] *n* (AUT) ステアリング sutéariñgu

steering wheel *n* ハンドル hañdoru

stem [stem] *n* (of plant) 茎 kukí; (of glass) 足 ashí
♦*vt* (stop: blood, flow, advance) 止める tomérù

stem from *vt fus* (subj: condition, problem) ...に由来する ...ni yurái suru

stench [stentʃ] *n* 悪臭 akúshū

stencil [sten'səl] *n* (lettering) ステンシルで書いた文字 suténshiru de káita mójì; (pattern used) ステンシル suténshiru
♦*vt* (letters, designs etc) ステンシルで書く suténshiru de kákù

stenographer [stənɑ:g'rəfə:r] (*US*) *n* 速記者 sokkíshà

step [step] *n* (footstep, *also fig*) 一歩 íppò; (sound) 足音 ashíoto; (of stairs) 段 dáñ, ステップ sutéppù
♦*vi*: *to step forward* 前に出る máè ni dérù *to step back* 後ろに下がる ushíro ni sagárù
in/out of step (with) (...と) 歩調が合って〔ずれて〕 (...to) hochô ga attè 〔zurète〕

stepbrother [step'brʌðə:r] *n* 異父〔異母〕兄弟 ífù〔íbò〕kyôdaì

stepdaughter [step'dɔ:tə:r] *n* まま娘 mamámusùme

step down *vi* (*fig*: resign) 辞任する jinín suru

stepfather [step'fɑ:ðə:r] *n* まま父 mamáchichi

stepladder [step'lædə:r] *n* 脚立 kyatátsu

stepmother [step'mʌðə:r] *n* まま母 mamáhaha

step on *vt fus* (something: walk on) 踏む fumú

stepping stone [step'iŋ-] *n* 飛石 tobíishi

steps [steps] (*BRIT*) *npl* = **stepladder**

stepsister [step'sistə:r] *n* 異父〔異母〕姉妹 ífù〔íbò〕shímaì

stepson [step'sʌn] *n* まま息子 mamámusùko

step up *vt* (increase: efforts, pace etc) 増す masú

stereo [ster'i:ou] *n* (system) ステレオ sutéreo; (record player) レコードプレーヤー rekôdopurêyā
♦*adj* (*also*: **stereophonic**) ステレオの sutéreo no

stereotype [ster'i:ətaip] *n* 固定概念 kotéigaìnen

sterile [ster'əl] *adj* (free from germs: bandage etc) 殺菌した sakkín shita; (barren: woman, female animal) 不妊の funín no; (: man, male animal) 子供を作れない kodómo wò tsukúrenaì; (land) 不毛の fumô no

sterilize [ster'əlaiz] *vt* (thing, place) 殺菌する sakkín suru; (woman) ...に避妊手術をする ...ni hinínshujùtsu wo suru

sterling [stəːrˈliŋ] *adj* (silver) 純銀の juń-gin no
◆*n* (ECON) 英国通貨 eíkokutsūka
one pound sterling 英貨1ポンド eíka ichí poňdo

stern [stəːrn] *adj* (father, warning etc) 厳しい kibíshiì
◆*n* (of boat) 船尾 séňbi

stethoscope [steθˈəskoup] *n* 聴診器 chō-shíňki

stew [stuː] *n* シチュー shichū
◆*vt* (meat, vegetables) 煮込む nikómù; (fruit) 煮る nirú

steward [stuːˈəːrd] *n* (on ship, plane, train) スチュワード suchúwàdo

stewardess [stuːˈəːrdis] *n* (especially on plane) スチュワーデス suchúwàdesu

stick [stik] *n* (*gen*: of wood) 棒 bṑ; (as weapon) こん棒 koñbō; (walking stick) つえ tsúè
◆*vb* (*pt, pp* **stuck**)
◆*vt* (with glue etc) 張る harú; (*inf*: put) 置く okú; (: tolerate) ...の最後まで我慢する ...no saígo made gámàn suru; (thrust):
to stick something into ...の中へ...を突っ込む ...no nákà e ...wo tsukkómù
◆*vi* (become attached) くっつく kuttsú-kù; (be immovable) 引っ掛る hikkákarù; (in mind etc) 焼付く yakítsukù
a stick of dynamite ダイナマイト1本 dainamaito ippon

sticker [stikˈəːr] *n* ステッカー sutékkà

sticking plaster [stikˈiŋ-] *n* ばんそうこう bañsōkō

stickler [stikˈləːr] *n*: *to be a stickler for* ...に関してやかましい ...ni káň shite yakámashiì

stick out *vi* (ears etc) 突出る tsukíderù

stick up *vi* (hair etc) 立つ tátsù

stick-up [stikˈʌp] (*inf*) *n* ピストル強盗 písutoru gótō

stick up for *vt fus* (person) ...の肩をもつ ...no kátà wo mótsù; (principle) 守る mamórù

sticky [stikˈiː] *adj* (messy: hands etc) べたべたしている bétàbeta shité irù; (label) 粘着の neñchaku no; (*fig*: situation) 厄介な yákkài na

stiff [stif] *adj* (hard, firm: brush) 堅い katáì; (hard: paste, egg-white) 固まった katámattà; (moving with difficulty: arms, legs, back) こわばった kowábattà; (: door, zip etc) 堅い katáì; (formal: manner, smile) 堅苦しい katágurushiì; (difficult, severe: competition, sentence) 厳しい kibíshiì; (strong: drink, breeze) 強い tsuyóì; (high: price) 高い takáì
◆*adv* (bored, worried, scared) ひどく hídòku

stiffen [stifˈən] *vi* (body, muscles, joints) こわばる kowábarù

stiff neck *n* 首が回らない事 kubí gà mawáranaì kotó

stifle [staiˈfəl] *vt* (cry, yawn) 抑える osáerù; (opposition) 抑圧する yokúatsu suru

stifling [staifˈliŋ] *adj* (heat) 息苦しい ikí-gurushiì

stigma [stigˈmə] *n* (*fig*: of divorce, failure, defeat etc) 汚名 ómèi

stile [stail] *n* 踏段 fumídan ◇牧場のさくの両側に設けられ、人間が越えられるが家畜が出られない様にした物 bokújō nò sakú nò ryṓgawa ní mōkerarè, niñgen gà koérarerù ga kachíku ga derárenai yṑ ni shitá monò

stiletto [stiletˈou] (*BRIT*) *n* (*also*: **stiletto heel**) ハイヒール haíhiru

still [stil] *adj* (person, water, air) 動かない ugókanaì; (place) 静寂な seíjaku na
◆*adv* (up to this time, yet) まだ mádà; (even) 更に sárà ni; (nonetheless) それにしても soré ni shite mò

stillborn [stilˈbɔːrn] *adj* 死産の shízàn no

still life *n* 静物画 seíbutsugà

stilt [stilt] *n* (pile) 脚柱 kyakúchū; (for walking on) 竹馬 takéuma

stilted [stilˈtid] *adj* (behavior, conversation) 堅苦しい katákurushiì

stimulant [stimˈjələnt] *n* 覚せい剤 kakú-seizài

stimulate [stimˈjəleit] *vt* (person, demand) 刺激する shigéki suru

stimulating [stimˈjəleitiŋ] *adj* (conversation, person, experience) 刺激的な shi-gékiteki na

stimuli [stim'jəlai] *npl of* **stimulus**

stimulus [stim'jələs] (*pl* **stimuli**) *n* (encouragement, *also* MED) 刺激 shigéki

sting [stiŋ] *n* (wound) 虫刺され mushísasarè; (pain) 刺す様な痛み sásù yō na itámi; (organ) 針 hárì

♦*vb* (*pt*, *pp* **stung**)

♦*vt* (insect, plant etc) 刺す sásù; (*fig*) 傷付ける kizútsukerù

♦*vi* (insect, plant etc) 刺す sásù; (eyes, ointment etc) しみる shimírù

stingy [stin'dʒi:] *adj* けちな kéchì na

stink [stiŋk] *n* (smell) 悪臭 akúshū

♦*vi* (*pt* **stank**, *pp* **stunk**) (smell) におう niôù

stinking [stiŋ'kiŋ] (*inf*) *adj* (*fig*) くそったれの kusóttàre no

stint [stint] *n* 仕事の期間 shigóto no kikań

♦*vi*: **to stint on** (work, ingredients etc) ...をけちる ..wo kechírù

stipulate [stip'jəleit] *vt* ...の条件を付ける ...no jōken wo tsukérù

stir [stəːr] *n* (*fig*: agitation) 騒ぎ sáwàgi

♦*vt* (tea etc) かき混ぜる kakímazerù; (*fig*: emotions) 刺激する shigéki suru

♦*vi* (move slightly) ちょっと動く chóttò ugókù

stirrup [stəːr'əp] *n* あぶみ abúmi

stir up *vt* (trouble) 引起こす hikíokosù

stitch [stitʃ] *n* (SEWING, MED) 一針 hitóhàri; (KNITTING) ステッチ sutétchì; (pain) わき腹のけいれん wakíbara nò keíren

♦*vt* (sew: *gen*, MED) 縫う núù

stoat [stout] *n* てん téñ

stock [stɑːk] *n* (supply) 資源 shígèn; (COMM) 在庫品 zaíkohìn; (AGR) 家畜 kachíku; (CULIN) 煮出し汁 nidáshijìru, ストック sutókkù; (descent) 血統 kettő; (FINANCE: government stock etc) 株式 kabúshìki

♦*adj* (*fig*: reply, excuse etc) お決りの o-kímàri no

♦*vt* (have in stock) 常備する jóbì suru

stocks and shares 債券 saíken

in/out of stock 在庫がある〔ない〕zaíko gà árù (nai)

to take stock of (*fig*) 検討する keńtō suru

stockbroker [stɑːk'broukəːr] *n* 株式仲買人 kabúshikinakagainìn

stock cube (*BRIT*) *n* 固形スープの素 kokéi sûpu no moto

stock exchange *n* 株式取引所 kabúshikitorihikijò

stocking [stɑːk'iŋ] *n* ストッキング sutôkkiñgu

stockist [stɑːk'ist] (*BRIT*) *n* 特約店 tokúyakutèn

stock market *n* 株式市場 kabúshikishijò

stock phrase *n* 決り文句 kimárimoňku

stockpile [stɑːk'pail] *n* 備蓄 bichíku

♦*vt* 貯蔵する chozó suru

stocktaking [stɑːk'teikiŋ] (*BRIT*) *n* (COMM) 棚卸し tanáoroshi

stock up with *vt* ...を仕入れる ...wo shiírérù

stocky [stɑːk'i:] *adj* (strong, short) がっしりした gasshîrî shita; (short, stout) ずんぐりした zuñgurî shita

stodgy [stɑːdʒ'i:] *adj* (food) こってりした kottérî shita

stoical [stou'ikəl] *adj* 平然とした heízen tò shita

stoke [stouk] *vt* (fire, furnace, boiler) ...に燃料をくべる ...ni neñryô wo kubérù

stole [stoul] *pt of* **steal**

♦*n* ストール sutóru

stolen [stou'lən] *pp of* **steal**

stolid [stɑːl'id] *adj* (person, behavior) 表情の乏しい hyójō no tobóshiì

stomach [stʌm'ək] *n* (ANAT) 胃 i; (belly) おなか onáka

♦*vt* (*fig*) 耐える taérù

stomachache [stʌm'əkeik] *n* 腹痛 fukútsù

stone [stoun] *n* (rock) 石 ishí; (pebble) 小石 koíshi; (gem) 宝石 hőseki; (in fruit) 種 tánè; (MED) 結石 kessékì; (*BRIT*: weight) ストーン sutóñ ◇体重の単位, 約 6.3 kg taíjū no tañ-i, yákù 6.3 kg

♦*adj* (pottery) ストーンウエアの sutôñ-ueâ no

◆vt (person) ...に石を投げ付ける ...ni ishi wo nagetsukeru; (fruit) ...の種を取る ...no táne wo tórù

stone-cold [stoun'kould'] adj 冷え切った hiékittà

stone-deaf [stoun'def'] adj かなつんぼの kanátsuñbo no

stonework [stoun'wə:rk] n (stones) 石造りの物 ishízukùri no mono

stony [stou'ni:] adj (ground) 石だらけの ishídaràke no; (fig: glance, silence etc) 冷淡な reítan na

stood [stud] pt, pp of **stand**

stool [stu:l] n スツール sutsúrù

stoop [stu:p] vi (also: **stoop down**: bend) 腰をかがめる koshí wò kagámerù; (also: **have a stoop**) 腰が曲っている koshí gà magátte irù

stop [sta:p] n (halt) 停止 teíshi; (short stay) 立寄り tachíyori; (in punctuation: also: **full stop**) ピリオド píriòdo; (bus stop etc) 停留所 teíryujo

◆vt (break off) 止める tomérù; (block: pay, check) ...の支払を停止させる ...no shihárai wò teíshi saserù; (prevent: also: **put a stop to**) やめさせる yamésaserù

◆vi (halt: person) 立ち止る tachídomarù; (: watch, clock) 止る tomárù; (end: rain, noise etc) やむ yamú

to stop doing something ...するのをやめる ...surú no wò yamérù

stop dead vi 急に止る kyū́ nì tomárù

stopgap [sta:p'gæp] n (person/thing) 間に合せの人〔物〕ma ní awase nò hitó 〔monó〕

stop off vi 立寄る tachíyorù

stopover [sta:p'ouvə:r] n (gen) 立寄って泊る事 tachíyotte tomáru kotò; (AVIAT) 給油着陸 kyúyuchakùriku

stoppage [sta:p'idʒ] n (strike) ストライキ sutóraìki; (blockage) 停止 teíshi

stopper [sta:p'ə:r] n 栓 séñ

stop press n 最新ニュース saíshinnyùsu

stop up vt (hole) ふさぐ fuságù

stopwatch [sta:p'wa:tʃ] n ストップウオッチ sutóppuuotchì

storage [stɔ:r'idʒ] n 保管 hokán

storage heater n 蓄熱ヒーター chikú-netsuhītā ◇深夜など電気需要の少ない時に熱を作って蓄え、昼間それを放射するヒーター shíñ-ya nádò deñkijuyò no sukúnai tokì ni netsú wo tsukuttè takúwaè, hirúma soré wò hōsha suru hítā

store [stɔ:r] n (stock) 蓄え takúwaè; (depot) 倉庫 sōko; (BRIT: large shop) デパート depātò; (US) 店 misé; (reserve) 備蓄 bichíku

◆vt (provisions, information etc) 蓄える takúwaerù

in store 未来に待構えて mírài ni machíkamaetè

storeroom [stɔ:r'ru:m] n 倉庫 sōko

stores [stɔ:rz] npl (provisions) 物資 bússhi

store up vt (nuts, sugar, memories) 蓄える takúwaerù

storey [stɔ:r'i:] (BRIT: **floor**) n = **story**

stork [stɔ:rk] n コウノトリ kōnotòri

storm [stɔ:rm] n (bad weather) 嵐 áràshi; (fig: of criticism, applause etc) 爆発 bakúhatsu

◆vi (fig: speak angrily) どなる donárù

◆vt (attack: place) 攻撃する kōgeki suru

stormy [stɔ:r'mi:] adj (weather) 荒れ模様の arémoyò no; (fig: debate, relations) 激しい hagéshiì

story [stɔ:r'i:] n (gen: also: **history**) 物語 monógatàri; (lie) うそ úsò; (US) 階 kái

storybook [stɔ:r'i:buk] n 童話の本 dōwa no hoñ

stout [staut] adj (strong: branch etc) 丈夫な jōbu na; (fat) 太った futóttà; (resolute: friend, supporter) 不動の fudō no

◆n (beer) スタウト sutáùto

stove [stouv] n (for cooking) レンジ réñji; (for heating) ストーブ sutōbù

stow [stou] vt (also: **stow away**) しまう shimáù

stowaway [stou'əwei] n 密航者 mikkōshà

straddle [stræd'əl] vt (chair, fence etc: also fig) ...にまたがる ...ni matágarù

straggle [stræg'əl] vi (houses etc) 散在する sañzai suru; (people etc) 落ごする rakúgo suru

straggly [stræg'li:] adj (hair) ぼさぼさし

た bósàbosa shita

straight [streit] *adj* (line, road, back, hair) 真っ直ぐの massúgù no; (honest: answer) 正直な shójiki na; (simple: choice, fight) 簡潔な kańketsu na

♦*adv* (directly) 真っ直ぐに massúgù ni; (drink) ストレートで sutórèto de

to put/get something straight (make clear) 明らかにする akíràka ni suru

straight away, straight off (at once) 直ちに tádàchi ni

straighten [streiten] *vt* (skirt, bed etc) 整える totónoerù

straighten out *vt* (fig: problem, situation) 解決する kańketsu suru

straight-faced [streit'feist] *adj* まじめな顔をした majíme nà kaó wo shità

straightforward [streitfɔːr'wərd] *adj* (simple) 簡単な kańtan na; (honest) 正直な shójiki na

strain [strein] *n* (pressure) 負担 fután; (TECH) ひずみ hizúmi; (MED: tension) 緊張 kińchō; (breed) 血統 kettó

♦*vt* (back etc) 痛める itámerù; (stretch: resources) ...に負担をかける ...ni fután wò kakérù; (CULIN: food) こす kosú

back strain (MED) ぎっくり腰 gikkúri-gòshi

strained [streind] *adj* (back, muscle) 痛めた itámetà; (relations) 緊張した kińpaku shità

a strained laugh 作り笑い tsukúriwarài

strainer [strei'nər] *n* (CULIN) こし器 koshíkì

strains [streinz] *npl* (MUS) 旋律 señritsu

strait [streit] *n* (GEO) 海峡 kaíkyō

strait-jacket [streit'dʒækit] *n* 拘束衣 kósokuì

strait-laced [streit'leist] *adj* しかつめらしい shikátsumerashiì

straits [streits] *npl*: *to be in dire straits* (fig) 困り果てている komárihatete irù

strand [strænd] *n* (of thread, hair, rope) 一本 íppòn

stranded [stræn'did] *adj* (holiday-makers) 足留めされた ashídome sarétà

strange [streindʒ] *adj* (not known) 未知の míchì no; (odd) 変な hén na

strangely [streindʒ'liː] *adv* (act, laugh) 変った風に kawátta fù ni ¶ *see also* enough

stranger [strein'dʒər] *n* (unknown person) 知らない人 shiránai hitò; (from another area) よそ者 yosómono

strangle [stræŋ'gəl] *vt* (victim) 絞殺する shimékorosù; (fig: economy) 圧迫する appáku suru

stranglehold [stræŋ'gəlhould] *n* (fig) 抑圧 yokúatsu

strap [stræp] *n* 肩ひも katáhimo, ストラップ sutórappù

strapping [stræp'iŋ] *adj* たくましい takúmashiì

strata [stræt'ə] *npl of* stratum

stratagem [stræt'ədʒəm] *n* 策略 sakúryàku

strategic [strəti:'dʒik] *adj* (positions, withdrawal, weapons etc) 戦略的な señryakuteki na

strategy [stræt'idʒiː] *n* (plan, *also* MIL) 作戦 sakúsen

stratum [strei'təm] (*pl* **strata**) *n* (*gen*) 層 só; (in earth's surface) 地層 chisó; (in society) 階層 kaísō

straw [strɔː] *n* (dried stalks) わら wárà; (drinking straw) ストロー sutórō

that's the last straw! もう我慢できない mō gámàn dekínaì

strawberry [strɔː'beːriː] *n* イチゴ ichígo

stray [strei] *adj* (animal) のら... norá...; (bullet) 流れ... nagáre...; (scattered) 点在する teńzai suru

♦*vi* (children, animals) はぐれる hagúrerù; (thoughts) 横道にそれる yokómichi nì sorérù

streak [striːk] *n* (stripe: *gen*) 筋 sújì

♦*vt* ...に筋を付ける ...ni sújì wo tsukérù

♦*vi*: *to streak past* 猛スピードで通り過ぎる mōsupído de tórisugirù

stream [striːm] *n* (small river) 小川 ogáwa; (of people, vehicles, smoke) 流れ nagáre; (of questions, insults etc) 連続 reńzoku

◆*vt* (SCOL: students) 能力別に分ける nōryokubétsu ni wakérù

◆*vi* (water, oil, blood) 流れる nagárerù
to stream in/out (people) 流れ込む〔出る〕nagárekomù(derù)

streamer [stri:'mə:r] *n* 紙テープ kamítēpu

streamlined [stri:m'laind] *adj* 流線形の ryūsénkei no

street [stri:t] *n* 道 michí

streetcar [stri:t'kɑ:r] (*US*) *n* 路面電車 roméndeñsha

street lamp *n* 街灯 gaítō

street plan *n* 市街地図 shigáichizù

streetwise [stri:t'waiz] (*inf*) *adj* 裏町の悪知恵を持っている urámachi no warújie wò motté irù

strength [streŋkθ] *n* (physical) 体力 táìryoku; (of girder, knot etc) 強さ tsúyòsa; (*fig*: power, number) 勢力 seíryoku

strengthen [streŋk'θən] *vt* (building, machine) 補強する hokyō suru; (*fig*: group, argument, relationship) 強くする tsúyòku suru

strenuous [stren'ju:əs] *adj* (energetic: exercise) 激しい hagéshiì; (determined: efforts) 精力的な seíryokuteki na

stress [stres] *n* (force, pressure, *also* TECH) 圧力 atsúryòku; (mental strain) ストレス sutórèsu; (emphasis) 強調 kyōchō

◆*vt* (point, importance etc) 強調する kyōchō suru; (syllable) ...にアクセントを置く ...ni ákùsento wo okú

stretch [stretʃ] *n* (area: of sand, water etc) 一帯 ittái

◆*vi* (person, animal) 背伸びする sénòbi suru; (extend): *to stretch to/as far as* ...まで続く ...mádè tsuzúkù

◆*vt* (pull) 伸ばす nobásù; (subj: job, task: make demands of) ...に努力を要求する ...ni dóryòku wo yōkyū suru

stretcher [stretʃ'ə:r] *n* 担架 táñka

stretch out *vi* 体を伸ばす karáda wò nobásù

◆*vt* (arm etc) 伸ばす nobásù; (spread) 広げる hirógerù

strewn [stru:n] *adj*: *strewn with* ...が散らばっている ...ga chirábatte irù

stricken [strik'ən] *adj* (person) 打ちひしがれた uchíhishigaretà; (city, industry etc) 災いに見舞われた wazáwai nì mimáwaretà
stricken with (arthritis, disease) ...にかかっている ...ni kakátte irù

strict [strikt] *adj* (severe, firm: person, rule) 厳しい kibíshiì; (precise: meaning) 厳密な geñmitsu na

strictly [strikt'li:] *adv* (severely) 厳しく kibíshikù; (exactly) 厳密に geñmitsu ni

stridden [strid'ən] *pp of* **stride**

stride [straid] *n* (step) 大またの一歩 ṓmàta no íppò

◆*vi* (*pt* **strode**, *pp* **stridden**) 大またに歩く ṓmàta ni arúkù

strident [straid'ənt] *adj* (voice, sound) 甲高い kañdakaì

strife [straif] *n* 反目 hañmoku

strike [straik] *n* (of workers) ストライキ sutóraìki; (of oil etc) 発見 hakkén; (MIL: attack) 攻撃 kṓgeki

◆*vb* (*pt, pp* **struck**)

◆*vt* (hit: person, thing) 打つ útsù; (*fig*: subj: idea, thought) ...の心に浮ぶ ...no kókòro ni ukábù; (oil etc) 発見する hakkén suru; (bargain, deal) 決める kimérù

◆*vi* (go on strike) ストライキに入る sutóraìki ni háìru; (attack: soldiers) 攻撃する kṓgeki suru; (: illness) 襲う osóù; (: disaster) 見舞う mimáù; (clock) 鳴る narú

on strike (workers) ストライキ中で sutóraikichū de
to strike a match マッチを付ける mátchì wo tsukérù

strike down *vt* (kill) 殺す korósù; (harm) 襲う osóù

striker [strai'kə:r] *n* (person on strike) ストライキ参加者 sutóraikisankashà; (SPORT) 攻撃選手 kṓgekiseñshu

strike up *vt* (MUS) 演奏し始める eñsō shihajimerù; (conversation) 始める hajímerù; (friendship) 結ぶ musúbù

striking [strai'kiŋ] *adj* (noticeable) 目立つ medátsù; (attractive) 魅力的な miryókuteki na

string [striŋ] *n* (thin rope) ひ も himó; (row: of beads etc) 数珠つなぎの物 juzútsunági no monó; (: of disasters etc) 一連 ichíren; (MUS) 弦 gén

♦*vt* (*pt, pp* **strung**): **to string together** つなぐ tsunágù

a string of islands 列島 rettó

to pull strings (*fig*) コネを利用する kónè wo riyó suru

to string out 一列に並べる ichíretsu nì naráberù

string bean *n* さや豆 sayámame

string(ed) instrument [striŋ(d)-] *n* (MUS) 弦楽器 geñgakkì

stringent [strin'dʒənt] *adj* (rules, measures) 厳しい kibíshiì

strings [striŋz] *npl*: **the strings** (MUS: section of orchestra) 弦楽器 geñgakkì

strip [strip] *n* (*gen*) 細長い切れ hosónagaì kiré; (of land, water) 細長い一帯 hosónagaì ittái

♦*vt* (undress) 裸にする hadáka ni surù; (paint) はがす hagásù; (*also*: **strip down**: machine) 分解する buñkai suru

♦*vi* (undress) 裸になる hadáka ni narù

strip cartoon *n* 四こま漫画 yoñkoma mañga

stripe [straip] *n* (*gen*) しま shima; (MIL, POLICE) そで章 sodéshō

striped [straipt] *adj* しま模様の shimámoyó no

strip lighting *n* 蛍光灯 keíkōtō

stripper [strip'ə:r] *n* ストリッパー sutórippà

striptease [strip'ti:z] *n* ストリップショー sutórippushō

strive [straiv] (*pt* **strove**, *pp* **striven**) *vi*: **to strive for something**/**to do something** ...しようと努力する ...shiyó tò dóryoku suru

striven [striv'ən] *pp of* **strive**

strode [stroud] *pt of* **stride**

stroke [strouk] *n* (blow) 一撃 ichígeki; (SWIMMING) ストローク sutóròku; (MED) 脳卒中 nō nósotchū; (of paintbrush) 筆の運び fudé nò hakóbi

♦*vt* (caress) なでる nadérù

at a stroke 一気に íkkì ni

stroll [stroul] *n* 散歩 sañpo

♦*vi* 散歩する sañpo suru

stroller [strou'lə:r] (*US*) *n* (pushchair) いす型ベビーカー isúgata bebíkā

strong [strɔːŋ] *adj* (person, arms, grasp) 強い tsuyóì; (stick) 丈夫な jóbu na; (wind) 強い tsuyóì; (imagination) 想像力のある sózōryoku no árù; (personality) 気性の激しい kishó nò hagéshiì; (influence) 強い tsuyóì; (nerves) 頑丈な gañjō na; (smell) 強烈な kyóretsu na; (coffee) 濃い kóì; (taste) 際立った kiwádattà

they are 50 strong 50人いる gojúnìn irú

stronghold [strɔːŋ'hould] *n* とりで toríde; (*fig*) 根城 néjiro

strongly [strɔːŋ'liː] *adv* (solidly: construct) 頑丈に gañjō ni; (with force: push, defend) 激しく hagéshikù; (deeply: feel, believe) 強く tsuyóku

strongroom [strɔːŋ'ruːm] *n* 金庫室 kiñkoshìtsu

strove [strouv] *pt of* **strive**

struck [strʌk] *pt, pp of* **strike**

structural [strʌk'tʃəːrəl] *adj* (damage, defect) 構造的な kózoteki na

structure [strʌk'tʃəːr] *n* (organization) 組織 sóshìki; (building) 構造物 kózōbùtsu

struggle [strʌg'əl] *n* 闘争 tósō

♦*vi* (try hard) 努力する dóryoku suru; (fight) 戦う tatákaù

strum [strʌm] *vt* (guitar) つま弾く tsumábikù

strung [strʌŋ] *pt, pp of* **string**

strut [strʌt] *n* (wood, metal) 支柱 shichū

♦*vi* 威張って歩く ibátte arukù

stub [stʌb] *n* (of check, ticket etc) 控え hikáè; (of cigarette) 吸殻 suígara

♦*vt*: **to stub one's toe** つま先をぶつける tsumásaki wò butsúkerù

stubble [stʌb'əl] *n* (AGR) 切株 kiríkàbu; (on chin) 不精ひげ bushōhìge

stubborn [stʌb'əːrn] *adj* (child, determination) 頑固な gáñko na

stub out *vt* (cigarette) もみ消す momíkesù

stuck [stʌk] *pt, pp of* **stick**

♦*adj* (jammed) 引っ掛っている hikkákatte iru

stuck-up [stʌk'ʌp'] (*inf*) *adj* 天ぐになっている teñgu nǐ natté iru

stud [stʌd] *n* (on clothing etc) 飾りボタン kazáribotàn; (earring) 丸玉 marúdamà (on sole of boot) スパイク supáìku; (*also*: **stud farm**) 馬の繁殖牧場 umá nò hañshokubokujò; (*also*: **stud horse**) 種馬 tanéùma

♦*vt* (*fig*): **studded with** ...をちりばめた ...wo chiríbametà

student [stu:'dənt] *n* (at university) 学生 gakúsei; (at lower schools) 生徒 seíto

♦*adj* (nurse, life, union) 学生の gakúsei no

student driver (*US*) *n* 仮免許運転者 karímenkyo unteñsha

studies [stʌd'i:z] *npl* (subjects studied) 勉強の科目 beñkyō nò kamóku

studio [stu:'diːou] *n* (TV etc) スタジオ sutájìo; (sculptor's etc) アトリエ atórìe

studio apartment (*BRIT* **studio flat**) *n* ワンルームマンション wañrūmu máñshon

studious [stu:'diːəs] *adj* (person) 勉強家の beñkyòka no; (careful: attention) 注意深い chúibukaì

studiously [stu:'diːəsliː] *adv* (carefully) 注意深く chúibukakù

study [stʌd'iː] *n* (activity) 勉強 beñkyō; (room) 書斎 shosái

♦*vt* (learn about: subjects) 勉強する beñkyō suru; (examine: face, evidence) 調べる shiráberù

♦*vi* 勉強する beñkyō suru

stuff [stʌf] *n* (thing(s)) 物 monò, 事 kotò; (substance) 素質 soshítsu

♦*vt* (soft toy: *also* CULIN) ...に詰める ...ni tsumérù; (dead animals) はく製にする hakúsei ni surù; (*inf*: push: object) 差し込む sashíkomù

stuffing [stʌf'iŋ] *n* (gen, CULIN) 詰物 tsumémòno

stuffy [stʌf'iː] *adj* (room) 空気の悪い kúki nǒ warúì; (person, ideas) 古臭い furúkusaì

stumble [stʌm'bəl] *vi* つまづく tsumázukù

to **stumble across/on** (*fig*) ...に出くわす ...ni dekúwasù

stumbling block [stʌm'bliŋ-] *n* 障害 shǒgai

stump [stʌmp] *n* (of tree) 切株 kiríkabu; (of limb) 断端 dañtan

♦*vt*: **to be stumped** まごつく magótsukù

stun [stʌn] *vt* (subj: news) あ然とさせる azen to saserù; (: blow on head) 気絶させる kizetsu saserù

stung [stʌŋ] *pt, pp of* **sting**

stunk [stʌŋk] *pp of* **stink**

stunning [stʌn'iŋ] *adj* (*fig*: news, event) 仰天させる gyǒten saserù; (: girl, dress) 美しい utsúkushiì

stunt [stʌnt] *n* (in film) スタント sutáñto; (*also*: **publicity stunt**) 宣伝用のトリック señden-yò no toríkkù

stunted [stʌn'tid] *adj* (trees, growth etc) 成長を阻害された seíchō wò sogái saretà

stuntman [stʌnt'mən] (*pl* **stuntmen**) *n* スタントマン sutáñtoman

stupefy [stu:'pəfai] *vt* ぼう然とさせる bǒzen to saserù

stupendous [stu:pen'dəs] *adj* 途方もない tohǒmonaì

stupid [stu:'pid] *adj* (person, question etc) ばかな bákà na

stupidity [stu:pid'iti:] *n* 愚かさ orókasà

stupor [stu:'pəːr] *n* 前後不覚 zeñgofukáku

sturdy [stəːr'diː] *adj* (person, thing) がっちりした gatchírî shita

stutter [stʌt'əːr] *n* どもり dómòri

♦*vi* どもる domórù

sty [stai] *n* (*also*: **pigsty**) 豚小屋 butágoya

stye [stai] *n* (MED) ものもらい monómoraì

style [stail] *n* (way, attitude) やり方 yaríkata; (elegance) 優雅さ yǔgàsa; (design) スタイル sutáìru

stylish [stai'liʃ] *adj* 優雅な yǔgà na

stylus [stai'ləs] *n* (of record player) 針 harí

suave [swɑ:v] *adj* 物腰の丁寧な monógòshi no teínei na

subconscious [sʌbkɑ:n't'ʃəs] *adj* (desire etc) 潜在意識の señzaiishìki no

subcontract [sʌbkəntrækt'] *vt* 下請に出す shitáuke nì dásù

subdivide [sʌbdivaid'] *vt* 小分けする kowáke suru

subdue [səbdu:'] *vt* (rebels etc) 征服する seífuku suru; (passions) 抑制する yokúsei suru

subdued [səbdu:d'] *adj* (light) 柔らかな yawárakà na; (person) 落込んだ ochíkoñda

subject [*n* sʌb'dʒikt *vb* səbjekt'] *n* (matter) 話題 wadái; (SCOL) 学科 gakká; (of kingdom) 臣民 shiñmiñ; (GRAMMAR) 主語 shúgo

♦*vt: to subject someone to something* ...を...にさらす ...wo ...ni sarásù

to be subject to (law) ...に服従しなければならない ...ni fukújū shinakerèba naránaĩ; (heart attacks) ...が起りやすい ...ga okóriyasuĩ

to be subject to tax 課税される kazéi sarerù

subjective [səbdʒek'tiv] *adj* 主観的な shukánteki na

subject matter *n* (content) 内容 naíyō

subjugate [sʌb'dʒəgeit] *vt* (people) 征服する seífuku suru

subjunctive [səbdʒʌŋk'tiv] *n* 仮定法 katéihō

sublet [sʌb'let] *vt* また貸しする matágashi suru

sublime [səblaim'] *adj* 素晴らしい subárashiĩ

submachine gun [sʌbməʃi:n'-] *n* 軽機関銃 keíkikañjū

submarine [sʌb'məri:n] *n* 潜水艦 señsuikan

submerge [səbmə:rdʒ'] *vt* 水中に沈める suíchū nì shizúmerù

♦*vi* (submarine, sea creature) 潜る mogúrù

submission [səbmiʃ'ən] *n* (state) 服従 fukújū; (claim) 申請書 shiñseishò; (of plan) 提出 teíshutsu

submissive [səbmis'iv] *adj* 従順な jújun na

submit [səbmit'] *vt* (proposal, application etc) 提出する teíshutsu suru

♦*vi: to submit to something* ...に従う ...ni shitágaù

subnormal [sʌbnɔ:r'məl] *adj* (below average: temperatures) 通常以下の tsújòikà no

subordinate [səbɔ:r'dənit] *adj* 二次的な nijíteki na

♦*n* 部下 búka

subpoena [səpi:'nə] *n* (LAW) 召喚状 shōkañjō

subscribe [səbskraib'] *vi: to subscribe to* (opinion) ...に同意する ...ni dōí suru; (fund) ...に寄付する ...ni kifú suru; (magazine etc) ...を購読する ...wo kōdoku suru

subscriber [səbskraib'ə:r] *n* (to periodical, telephone) 購読者 kōdokushà; (to telephone) 加入者 kanyūshà

subscription [səbskrip'ʃən] *n* (to magazine etc) 購読契約 kōdokukeiyàku

subsequent [sʌb'səkwənt] *adj* (following) その後の sonó atò no; (resulting) その結果として起る sonó kekkà toshite okórù

subsequently [sʌb'səkwəntli:] *adv* その後 sonó atò

subside [səbsaid'] *vi* (feeling) 収る osámarù; (flood) ひく hikú; (wind) やむ yamú

subsidence [səbsaid'əns] *n* (in road etc) 陥没 kañbotsu

subsidiary [səbsid'i:e:ri:] *adj* (question, details) 二次的な nijíteki na

♦*n (also:* **subsidiary company**) 子会社 kogáĩsha

subsidize [sʌb'sidaiz] *vt* (education, industry etc) ...に補助金を与える ...ni hojókìn wo atáerù

subsidy [sʌb'sidi:] *n* 補助金 hojókìn

subsistence [səbsis'təns] *n* (ability to live) 最低限度の生活水準 saíteigeñdo no seíkatsusuijùn

subsistence allowance (*BRIT*) *n* (advance payment) 支度金 shitákukìn;

(for expenses etc) 特別手当 tokúbetsu teáte

substance [sʌb'stəns] n (product, material) 物質 busshítsu

substantial [səbstæn'tʃəl] adj (solid) 頑丈な gañjō na; (fig: reward, meal) 多い ōí

substantially [səbstæn'tʃəli:] adv (by a large amount) 大いに ōí ni; (in essence) 本質的に hoñshitsuteki ni

substantiate [səbstæn'tʃi:eit] vt 裏付けする urázukerù

substitute [sʌb'stitu:t] n (person) 代人 daínin; (thing) 代用品 daíyōhìn
♦vt: **to substitute A for B** Bの代りにAを置く B nò kawári nì A wò okú

substitution [sʌbstitu:'ʃən] n (act of substituting) 置換え okíkae; (SOCCER) 選手交代 señshukōtai

subterfuge [sʌb'tə:rfju:dʒ] n 策略 sakúryàku

subterranean [sʌbtərei'ni:ən] adj 地下の chiká no

subtitle [sʌb'taitəl] n 字幕スーパー jimákusūpà

subtle [sʌt'əl] adj (slight: change) 微妙な bimyō na; (indirect: person) 腹芸のうまい harágeì no umáì

subtlety [sʌt'əlti:] n (small detail) 微妙な所 bimyō nà tokórò; (art of being subtle) 腹芸 harágeì

subtotal [sʌbtou'təl] n 小計 shōkei

subtract [səbtræk't'] vt ...から ...を引く ...kárà ...wò hikú

subtraction [səbtræk'ʃən] n 引算 hikízan

suburb [sʌb'ə:rb] n 都市周辺の自治体 toshíshūhen no jichítai

suburban [səbə:r'bən] adj (train, lifestyle etc) 郊外の kōgài no

suburbia [səbə:r'bi:ə] n 郊外 kōgài

suburbs [sʌb'ə:rbz] npl: **the suburbs** (area) 郊外 kōgài

subversive [səbvə:r'siv] adj (activities, literature) 破壊的な hakáiteki na

subway [sʌb'wei] n (US: underground railway) 地下鉄 chikátetsu; (BRIT: underpass) 地下道 chikádō

succeed [səksi:d'] vi (plan etc) 成功する

seíkō suru; (person: in career etc) 出生する shusshō suru
♦vt (in job) ...の後任になる ...no kōnin ni narù; (in order) ...の後に続く ...no átò ni tsuzúkù

to succeed in doing ...する事に成功する ...surú kotò ni seíkō suru

succeeding [səksi:'diŋ] adj (following) その後の sonó atò no

success [səkses'] n (achievement) 成功 seíkō; (hit, also person) 大ヒット daíhittò

successful [səkses'fəl] adj (venture) 成功した seíkō shita; (writer) 出生した shusshō shita

to be successful 成功する seíkō suru
to be successful in doing ...する事に成功する ...surú kotò ni seíkō suru

successfully [səkses'fəli:] adv (complete, do) うまく úmàku

succession [səkseʃ'ən] n (series) 連続 reñzoku; (to throne etc) 継承 keíshō

in succession 立続けに tatétsuzuke ni

successive [səkses'iv] adj 連続の reñzoku no

successor [səkses'ə:r] n 後任 kōnin

succinct [səksiŋkt'] adj 簡潔な kañketsu na

succulent [sʌk'jələnt] adj 汁が多くておいしい shírù ga ōkùte oíshiì

succumb [səkʌm'] vi (to temptation) 負ける makérù; (to illness: become very ill) ...で倒れる ...de taórerù; (: die) ...で死ぬ ...de shinú

such [sʌtʃ] adj (emphasizing similarity) この（その、あの）様な konó (sonó, anó) yō na; (of that kind): **such a book** そんな本 soñna hoñ; (so much): **such courage** そんな勇気 soñna yūki
♦adv こんな（そんな、あんな）に konna (soñna, añna) nì

such books そんな本 soñna hoñ

such a long trip あんなに長い旅行 añna nì nagái ryokō

such a lot of そんなに沢山の soñna nì takúsan no

such as (like) ...の様な ...no yō na

as such その物 sonó monò

such-and-such [sʌtʃ'ənsʌtʃ] adj しかじ かの shikájìka no

suck [sʌk] vt (gen: ice-lolly etc) なめる namérù; (bottle, breast) 吸う súù

sucker [sʌk'əːr] n (ZOOL) 吸盤 kyúban; (inf: easily cheated person) かも kámò

suction [sʌk'ʃən] n 吸引 kyúin

Sudan [suːdæn'] n スーダン sũdan

sudden [sʌd'ən] adj (unexpected, rapid: increase, shower, change) 突然の totsúzen no

all of a sudden (unexpectedly) 突然 totsúzen

suddenly [sʌd'ənliː] adv (unexpectedly) 突然 totsúzen

suds [sʌdz] npl 石けんの泡 sekkén no a- wà

sue [suː] vt ...を相手取って訴訟を起す ...wo aítedottè soshố wò okósù

suede [sweid] n スエード suếdo

suet [suː'it] n 脂肪 shibố◇料理に使うウ シやヒツジの堅い脂肪を指す ryốri ni tsukáù ushí yà hitsúji nò katáì shibố wò sásù

Suez [suː'ez] n: **the Suez Canal** スエズ 運河 suézu uñga

suffer [sʌf'əːr] vt (undergo: hardship etc) 経験する keíken suru; (bear: pain, rudeness) 我慢する gámàn suru

◆vi (be harmed: person, results etc) 苦しむ kurúshimù; (results etc) 悪くなる wárùku nárù

to suffer from (illness etc) ...の病気にかかっている ...no byốkì ni kakátte irù

sufferer [sʌf'əːrəːr] n (MED) 患者 kañja

suffering [sʌf'əːriŋ] n (hardship) 苦しみ kurúshimi

suffice [səfais'] vi 足りる tarírù

sufficient [səfiʃ'ənt] adj 十分な júbùn na

sufficiently [səfiʃ'əntliː] adv 十分に jú- bùn ni

suffix [sʌf'iks] n 接尾辞 setsúbijì

suffocate [sʌf'əkeit] vi 窒息する chissố- ku suru

suffocation [sʌfəkei'ʃən] n 窒息 chissố- ku

suffrage [sʌf'ridʒ] n (right to vote) 参政 権 sañseikèn

suffused [səfjuːzd'] adj: **suffused with** (light, color, tears) ...で満たされた ...de mitásaretà

sugar [ʃug'əːr] n 砂糖 satố

◆vt (tea etc) ...に砂糖を入れる ...ni satố wò irérù

sugar beet n サトウダイコン satốdaìkon

sugar cane n サトウキビ satốkìbi

suggest [səgdʒest'] vt (propose) 提案する teían suru; (indicate) 示唆する shísà suru

suggestion [səgdʒes'tʃən] n (proposal) 提案 teían; (indication) 示唆 shísà

suggestive [səgdʒes'tiv] (pej) adj (re- marks, looks) 卑わいな hiwái na

suicide [suː'isaid] n (death, also fig) 自殺 jisátsu; (person) 自殺者 jisátsushà ¶ see also **commit**

suit [suːt] n (man's) 背広 sebíro; (woman's) スーツ sũtsu; (LAW) 訴訟 soshố; (CARDS) 組札 kumífùda

◆vt (gen: be convenient, appropriate) ...に都合がいい ...ni tsugố ga íì; (color, clothes) ...に似合う ...ni niáù; (adapt): **to suit something to** ...を...に合せる ...wo ...ni awáserù

well suited (well matched: couple) お似 合いの o-níaì no

suitable [suː'təbəl] adj (convenient: time, moment) 都合のいい tsugố no íì; (appro- priate: person, clothes etc) 適当な tekítō na

suitably [suː'təbliː] adv (dressed) 適当に tekítō ni; (impressed) 期待通りに kitái- dòri ni

suitcase [suːt'keis] n スーツケース sũtsu- kèsu

suite [swiːt] n (of rooms) スイートルーム suítorùmu; (MUS) 組曲 kumíkyòku; (furniture): **bedroom / dining room suite** 寝室〔食堂〕用家具の一そろい shiñ- shitsu(shokúdō)yố kágù no hitósòroi

suitor [suː'təːr] n 求婚者 kyúkoñsha

sulfur [sʌl'fəːr] (US) n 硫黄 iố

sulk [sʌlk] vi すねる sunérù

sulky [sʌl'kiː] adj (child, silence) すねた sunétà

sullen [sʌl'ən] adj (person, silence) すね た sunétà

sulphur [sʌl'fə:r] *n* = **sulfur**

sultan [sʌl'tən] *n* サルタン sárùtan ◊ イスラム教国の君主 isúramukyōkoku no kúnshu

sultana [sʌltæn'ə] *n* (fruit) 白いレーズン shirōĩ rḗsùn

sultry [sʌl'tri:] *adj* (weather) 蒸暑い mushíatsuĩ

sum [sʌm] *n* (calculation) 計算 keísan; (amount) 金額 kíngaku; (total) 合計 gốkei

summarize [sʌm'ə:raiz] *vt* 要約する yốyaku suru

summary [sʌm'ə:ri:] *n* 要約 yốyaku

summer [sʌm'ə:r] *n* 夏 natsú
♦*adj* (dress, school) 夏の natsú no
in summer 夏に natsú ni

summer holidays *npl* 夏休み natsúyasùmi

summerhouse [sʌm'ə:rhaus] *n* (in garden) 東屋 azúmayà

summertime [sʌm'ə:rtaim] *n* (season) 夏 natsú

summer time *n* (by clock) サマータイム samátaĩmu

summer vacation (*US*) *n* 夏休み natsúyasùmi

summit [sʌm'it] *n* (of mountain) 頂上 chōjō; (*also:* **summit conference/meeting**) 首脳会議 shunốkaĩgi, サミット samíttò

summon [sʌm'ən] *vt* (person, police, help) 呼ぶ yobú; (to a meeting) 召集する shōshū suru; (LAW: witness) 召喚する shōkan suru

summons [sʌm'ənz] *n* (LAW) 召喚書 shōkanshò; (*fig*) 呼出し yobídashi
♦*vt* (JUR) 召喚する shōkan suru

summon up *vt* (strength, energy, courage) 奮い起す furúiokosù

sump [sʌmp] (*BRIT*) *n* (AUT) オイルパン oírupañ

sumptuous [sʌmp'tʃuːəs] *adj* 豪華な gốkà na

sum up *vt* (describe) 要約する yốyaku suru
♦*vi* (summarize) 要約する yốyaku suru

sun [sʌn] *n* (star) 太陽 taíyō; (sunshine) 日光 níkkò

sunbathe [sʌn'beið] *vi* 日光浴する nikkốyòku suru

sunburn [sʌn'bə:rn] *n* (painful) 日焼け hiyáke

sunburnt [sʌn'bə:rnt] *adj* (tanned) 日に焼けた hi ní yaketà; (painfully) ひどく日焼けした hídòku hiyáke shita

Sunday [sʌn'dei] *n* 日曜日 nichíyòbi

Sunday school *n* 日曜学校 nichíyōgakkò

sundial [sʌn'dail] *n* 日時計 hidốkèi

sundown [sʌn'daun] *n* 日没 nichíbotsu

sundries [sʌn'dri:z] *npl* (miscellaneous items) その他 sonó tà

sundry [sʌn'dri:] *adj* (various) 色々な iróiro na
all and sundry だれもかも dárè mo kámò

sunflower [sʌn'flauə:r] *n* ヒマワリ himáwàri

sung [sʌŋ] *pp of* **sing**

sunglasses [sʌn'glæsiz] *npl* サングラス sañguràsu

sunk [sʌŋk] *pp of* **sink**

sunlight [sʌn'lait] *n* 日光 níkkò

sunlit [sʌn'lit] *adj* 日に照らされた hi ní terasaretà

sunny [sʌn'i:] *adj* (weather, day) 晴れた háreta; (place) 日当りの良い hiátari no yoĩ

sunrise [sʌn'raiz] *n* 日の出 hi nó de

sun roof *n* (AUT) サンルーフ sañrūfu

sunset [sʌn'set] *n* 日没 nichíbotsu

sunshade [sʌn'ʃeid] *n* (over table) パラソル párasoru

sunshine [sʌn'ʃain] *n* 日光 níkkò

sunstroke [sʌn'strouk] *n* 日射病 nisshábyō

suntan [sʌn'tæn] *n* 日焼け hiyáke

suntan lotion *n* 日焼け止めローション hiyákedome ròshon

suntan oil *n* サンタンオイル sañtan oirù

super [su:'pə:r] (*inf*) *adj* 最高の saíkō no

superannuation [su:pə:rænju:ei'ʃən] *n* 年金の掛金 nefikin nò kakékìn

superb [su:pə:rb'] *adj* 素晴らしい subárashiĩ

supercilious [su:pə:rsil'i:əs] *adj* (disdainful, haughty) 横柄な ôhei na

superficial [su:pə:rfiʃ'əl] *adj* (wound) 浅い asái; (knowledge) 表面的な hyômenteki na; (shallow: person) 浅はかな asáhàka na

superfluous [su:pə:r'flu:əs] *adj* 余計な yokéi na

superhuman [su:pə:rhju:'mən] *adj* 超人的な chôjinteki na

superimpose [su:pə:rimpouz'] *vt* 重ね合せる kasáneawaserù

superintendent [su:pə:rinten'dənt] *n* (of place, activity) ...長 ...chô; (POLICE) 警視 keíshi

superior [səpi:r'i:ə:r] *adj* (better) (より) すぐれた (yorí) sugúretà; (more senior) 上位の jôi no; (smug) 偉ぶった erábuttà
♦*n* 上司 jôshì

superiority [səpi:ri:ɔ:r'iti:] *n* 優位性 yúîsei

superlative [səpə:r'lətiv] *n* (LING) 最上級 saíjôkyū

superman [su:'pə:rmæn] (*pl* **supermen**) *n* 超人 chôjin

supermarket [su:'pə:rmɑ:rkit] *n* スーパー sûpā

supernatural [su:pə:rnætʃ'ə:rəl] *adj* (creature, force etc) 超自然の chôshizen no
♦*n*: **the supernatural** 超自然の現象 chôshizen no geñshō

superpower [su:'pə:rpau'ə:r] *n* (POL) 超大国 chôtaikòku

supersede [su:pə:rsi:d'] *vt* ...に取って代る ...ni tôtte kawárù

supersonic [su:pə:rsɑ:n'ik] *adj* (flight, aircraft) 超音速の chôonsoku no

superstar [su:'pə:rstɑ:r] *n* (CINEMA, SPORT etc) スーパースター sûpāsutà

superstition [su:pə:rstiʃ'ən] *n* 迷信 meíshin

superstitious [su:pə:rstiʃ'əs] *adj* (person) 迷信深い meíshinbùkai; (practices) 迷信的な meíshinteki na

supertanker [su:'pə:rtæŋkə:r] *n* スーパータンカー sûpātaǹka

supervise [su:'pə:rvaiz] *vt* (person, activity) 監督する kaǹtoku suru

supervision [su:pə:rviʒ'ən] *n* 監督 kaǹtoku

supervisor [su:'pə:rvaizə:r] *n* (of workers, students) 監督 kaǹtoku

supine [su:'pain] *adj* 仰向きの aómuki no

supper [sʌp'ə:r] *n* (early evening) 夕食 yúshoku; (late evening) 夜食 yashóku

supplant [səplænt'] *vt* (person, thing) ...に取って代る ...ni tôtte kawárù

supple [sʌp'əl] *adj* (person, body, leather etc) しなやかな shináyàka na

supplement [*n* sʌp'ləmənt *vb* sʌp'ləment] *n* (additional amount, e.g. vitamin supplement) 補給品 hokyûhin; (of book) 補遺 hôî; (of newspaper, magazine) 付録 furóku
♦*vt* 補足する hosóku suru

supplementary [sʌpləmen'tə:ri:] *adj* (question) 補足的な hosókuteki na

supplementary benefit (*BRIT*) *n* 生活保護 seíkatsuhogð

supplier [səplai'ə:r] *n* (COMM: person, firm) 供給業者 kyôkyúgyòsha

supplies [səplaiz'] *npl* (food) 食料 shokúryò; (MIL) 軍需品 guñjuhìn

supply [səplai'] *vt* (provide) 供給する kyôkyū suru; (equip): **to supply (with)** (...を) 支給する (...wo) shikyû suru
♦*n* (stock) 在庫品 zaíkohìn; (supplying) 供給 kyôkyū

supply teacher (*BRIT*) *n* 代行教師 daíkôkyòshi

support [səpɔ:rt'] *n* (moral, financial etc) 支援 shién; (TECH) 支柱 shichû
♦*vt* (morally: football team etc) 支援する shién suru; (financially: family etc) 養う yashínaù; (TECH: hold up) 支える saśaerù; (sustain: theory etc) 裏付ける urázukerù

supporter [səpɔ:r'tə:r] *n* (POL etc) 支援者 shieǹshà; (SPORT) ファン fáǹ

suppose [səpouz'] *vt* (think likely) ...だと思う ...dá tò omóù; (imagine) 想像する sôzô suru; (duty): **to be supposed to do something** ...する事になっている ...surú kotò ni natté irù

supposedly [səpou'zidli:] *adv* ...だとされ

て ...dá tò sarétè

supposing [səpou'ziŋ] *conj* もし ... mô-shǐ...

suppress [səpres'] *vt* (revolt) 鎮圧する chiñ-atsu suru; (information) 隠す kakúsù; (feelings, yawn) 抑える osáerù

suppression [səpreʃ'ən] *n* (of revolt) 鎮圧 chiñ-atsu; (of information) 隠ぺい iñ-pei; (of feelings etc) 抑制 yokúsei

supremacy [səprem'əsi:] *n* 優越 yúetsu

supreme [səpri:m'] *adj* (in titles: court etc) 最高の saíkō no; (effort, achievement) 最上の saíjō no

surcharge [sər'tʃɑːrdʒ] *n* (extra cost) 追加料金 tsuíkaryōkin

sure [ʃuːr] *adj* (definite, convinced) 確信している kakúshin shite irù; (aim, remedy) 確実な kakújitsu na; (friend) 頼りになる táyòri ni nárù

to make sure of something ...を確かめる ...wo tashíkamerù

to make sure that ...だと確かめる ...dá tò tashíkamerù

sure! (of course) いいとも ǐi to mo

sure enough 案の定 áñ no jō

sure-footed [ʃuːr'fut'id] *adj* 足のしっかりした ashí nò shikkárì shita

surely [ʃuːr'li:] *adv* (certainly: *US: also*: **sure**) 確かに táshìka ni

surety [ʃuːr'əti:] *n* (money) 担保 táñpo

surf [sərf] *n* 打寄せる波 uchíyoseru namì

surface [sər'fis] *n* (of object) 表面 hyómen; (of lake, pond) 水面 suímen
♦*vt* (road) 舗装する hosó suru
♦*vi* (fish, person in water: *also fig*) 浮上する fujō suru

surface mail *n* 普通郵便 futsúyùbin

surfboard [sərf'bɔːrd] *n* サーフボード sáfubōdo

surfeit [sər'fit] *n*: *a surfeit of* ...の過剰 ...no kajō

surfing [sər'fiŋ] *n* サーフィン sáfìn

surge [sərdʒ] *n* (increase: *also fig*) 高まり takámarì
♦*vi* (water) 波打つ namíutsù; (people, vehicles) 突進する tosshín suru; (emotion) 高まる takámarù

surgeon [sər'dʒən] *n* 外科医 gekáì

surgery [sər'dʒəri:] *n* (treatment) 手術 shújùtsu; (*BRIT*: room) 診察室 shiñsatsushìtsu; (: *also*: **surgery hours**) 診療時間 shiñryō jikan

surgical [sər'dʒikəl] *adj* (instrument, mask etc) 外科用の gekáyō no; (treatment) 外科の gekáno

surgical spirit (*BRIT*) *n* 消毒用アルコール shōdokuyō arúkòru

surly [sər'li:] *adj* 無愛想な buáìsō na

surmount [sər'maunt'] *vt* (*fig*: problem, difficulty) 乗越える noríkoerù

surname [sər'neim] *n* 名字 myóji

surpass [sər'pæs'] *vt* (person, thing) しのぐ shinógù

surplus [sər'pləs] *n* (extra, *also* COMM, ECON) 余剰分 yojóbun
♦*adj* (stock, grain etc) 余剰の yojó no

surprise [sər'praiz'] *n* (unexpected) 思い掛け無い物 omóigakenaì monó; (astonishment) 驚き odóroki
♦*vt* (astonish) 驚かす odórokasù; (catch unawares: army, thief) ...の不意を突く ...no fuí wò tsukú

surprising [sər'praiziŋ] *adj* 驚くべき odórokubèki

surprisingly [sər'praiziŋli:] *adv* (easy, helpful) 驚く程 odóroku hodò

surrealist [səri:'əlist] *adj* (paintings etc) 超現実主義の chōgenjitsushùgi no

surrender [səren'dər] *n* 降伏 kófuku
♦*vi* (army, hijackers etc) 降伏する kófuku suru

surreptitious [sərəptiʃ'əs] *adj* ひそかな hisókà na

surrogate [sər'əgit] *n* 代理の daíri no

surrogate mother *n* 代理母 daírihahà

surround [səraund'] *vt* (subj: walls, hedge etc) 囲む kakómù; (MIL, POLICE etc) 包囲する hóì suru

surrounding [səraun'diŋ] *adj* (countryside) 周囲の shǔi no

surroundings [səraun'diŋz] *npl* 周辺 shǔhen

surveillance [sərvei'ləns] *n* 監視 kañshi

survey [*n* sər'vei *vb* sərvei'] *n* (examination: of land, house) 測量 sokúryō;

(investigation: of habits etc) 調査 chṓsa
♦*vt* (land, house etc) 測量する sokúryō
suru;(look at: scene, work etc) 見渡す
miwátasù

surveyor [sə:rvei'ə:r] *n* (of land, house)
測量技師 sokúryōgishi

survival [sə:rvai'vəl] *n* (continuation of
life) 生存 seízon;(relic) 遺物 ibútsu

survive [sə:rvaiv'] *vi* (person, thing) 助か
る tasúkarù;(custom etc) 残る nokórù
♦*vt* (outlive: person) ...より長生きする
...yóri nagáikì suru

survivor [sə:rvai'və:r] *n* (of illness, accident) 生存者 seízonsha

susceptible [səsep'təbəl] *adj*: *susceptible (to)* (affected by: heat, injury)
(...に) 弱い (...ni) yowáî;(influenced by:
flattery, pressure) (...に) 影響されやす
い (...ni) eíkyō sareyasuî

suspect [*adj, n* sʌs'pekt *vb* səspekt']
adj 怪しい ayáshiî
♦*n* 容疑者 yōgishà
♦*vt* (person) ...が怪しいと思う ...ga ayáshiî to omóù;(think) ...ではないかと思う
...dé wà naî ka to omóù

suspend [səspend'] *vt* (hang) つるす tsu-
rúsù;(delay, stop) 中止する chūshi suru;
(from employment ni) 停職処分にする teí-
shokushobùn ni suru

suspended sentence [səspen'did-] *n*
(LAW) 執行猶予付きの判決 shikkṓyūyo-
tsuki no hañketsu

suspender belt [səspen'də:r-] *n* ガータ
ーベルト gátāberùto

suspenders [səspen'də:rz] *npl* (US) ズボ
ンつり zubóntsuri;(BRIT) ガーターベル
トのストッキング留め gátāberùto no su-
tókkingudòme

suspense [səspens'] *n* (uncertainty) 気掛
り kigakárî;(in film etc) サスペンス sá-
sùpensu

to keep someone in suspense はらはら
させる háràhara sasérù

suspension [səspen'tʃən] *n* (from job,
team) 停職 teíshoku;(AUT) サスペンシ
ョン sasúpeñshon;(of driver's license,
payment) 停止 teíshi

suspension bridge *n* つり橋 tsuríbàshi

suspicion [səspiʃ'ən] *n* (distrust) 疑い u-
tágai;((bad) feeling) 漠然とした感じ bakúzen to shità kañji

suspicious [səspiʃ'əs] *adj* (suspecting:
look) 疑い深い utágaibukaî;(causing
suspicion: circumstances) 怪しげな ayáshigè na

sustain [səstein'] *vt* (continue: interest
etc) 維持する íjî suru;(subj: food, drink)
...に力を付ける ...ni chikára wò tsukérù;
(suffer: injury) 受ける ukérù

sustained [səsteind'] *adj* (effort, attack)
絶間ない taémanaî

sustenance [sʌs'tənəns] *n* 食物 shokúmòtsu

swab [swɑ:b] *n* (MED) 綿球 meñkyū

swagger [swæg'ə:r] *vi* 威張って歩く i-
bátte arukù

swallow [swɑ:l'ou] *n* (bird) ツバメ tsubá-
me
♦*vt* (food, pills etc) 飲込む nomíkomù;
(*fig*: story) 信じ込む shiñjikomù;
(: insult) ...に黙って耐える ...ni damátte
taérù;(one's pride, one's words) 抑える
osáerù

swallow up *vt* (savings etc) 飲込む nomíkomù

swam [swæm] *pt of* **swim**

swamp [swɑ:mp] *n* 沼地 numáchi
♦*vt* (with water etc) 水没させる suíbotsu
saserù;(*fig*: person) 圧倒する attṓ suru

swan [swɑ:n] *n* ハクチョウ hakúchō

swap [swɑ:p] *n* 交換 kṓkan
♦*vt*: *to swap (for)* (exchange (for))
(...) と交換する (...to) kṓkan suru;
(replace (with)) (...と) 取替える (...to)
toríkaerù

swarm [swɔ:rm] *n* (of bees) 群れ muré;
(of people) 群衆 guñshū
♦*vi* (bees) 群れで巣別れする muré dè su-
wákarè suru;(people) 群がる murágarù;
(place): *to be swarming with* ...に...が
うじゃうじゃいる ...ni ...ga újàuja irú

swarthy [swɔ:r'ði:] *adj* 浅黒い aságuroî

swastika [swɑ:s'tikə] *n* かぎ十字 kagíjū-
ji

swat [swɑ:t] *vt* (insect) たたく tatákù

sway [swei] *vi* (person, tree) 揺れる yuré-

rù

♦*vt* (influence) 揺さぶる yusáburù

swear [swe'ə:r] (*pt* **swore**, *pp* **sworn**) *vi* (curse) 悪態をつく akútai wò tsukú

♦*vt* (promise) 誓う chikáù

swearword [swe:r'wə:rd] *n* 悪態 akútai

sweat [swet] *n* 汗 ásè

♦*vi* 汗をかく ásè wo kákù

sweater [swet'ə:r] *n* セーター sétà

sweatshirt [swet'ʃə:rt] *n* トレーナー torénà

sweaty [swet'i:] *adj* (clothes, hands) 汗ばんだ asébànda

Swede [swi:d] *n* スウェーデン人 suédenjìn

swede [swi:d] (*BRIT*) *n* スウェーデンカブ suédeǹkabu

Sweden [swi:d'ən] *n* スウェーデン suéden

Swedish [swi:'diʃ] *adj* スウェーデンの suéden no; (LING) スウェーデン語の suédeǹgo no

♦*n* (LING) スウェーデン語 suédeǹgo

sweep [swi:p] *n* (act of sweeping) 掃く事 hákù kotó; (*also*: **chimney sweep**) 煙突掃除夫 eǹtotsusōjifù

♦*vb* (*pt*, *pp* **swept**)

♦*vt* (brush) 掃く hákù; (with arm) 払う haráù; (subj: current) 流す nagásù

♦*vi* (hand, arm) 振る furú; (wind) 吹きまくる fukímakurù

sweep away *vt* 取除く torínozokù

sweeping [swi:'piŋ] *adj* (gesture) 大振りな óburi na; (generalized: statement) 十把一からげの jíppàhitókàrage no

sweep past *vi* (at great speed) 猛スピードで通り過ぎる mōsupído de tōrisugirù; (majestically) 堂々と通り過ぎる dódō tò tōrisugiru

sweep up *vi* 掃き取る hakítorù

sweet [swi:t] *n* (candy) あめ amé; (*BRIT*: pudding) デザート dezátò

♦*adj* (not savory: taste) 甘い amái; (*fig*: air, water, smell, sound) 快い kokóroyoì; (: kind) 親切な shíñsetsu na; (attractive: baby, kitten) かわいい kawáiì

sweetcorn [swi:t'kɔ:rn] *n* トウモロコシ tómorðkoshi

sweeten [swi:t'ən] *vt* (add sugar to) 甘くする amáku surù; (soften: temper) なだめる nadámerù

sweetheart [swi:t'hɑ:rt] *n* (boyfriend/girlfriend) 恋人 koíbito

sweetness [swi:t'nis] *n* (amount of sugar) 甘さ amása; (*fig*: of air, water, smell, sound) 快さ kokóroyosà; (kindness) 親切 shíñsetsu; (attractiveness: of baby, kitten) かわいさ kawáisà

sweetpea [swi:t'pi:] *n* スイートピー suítopì

swell [swel] *n* (of sea) うねり unéri

♦*adj* (US: *inf*: excellent) 素晴らしい subárashiì

♦*vi* (*pt* **swelled**, *pp* **swollen** *or* **swelled**) (increase: numbers) 増える fuérù; (get stronger: sound, feeling) 増す masú; (*also*: **swell up**: face, ankle etc) はれる harérù

swelling [swel'iŋ] *n* (MED) はれ haré

sweltering [swel'tə:riŋ] *adj* (heat, weather, day) うだる様な udáru yō na

swept [swept] *pt*, *pp of* **sweep**

swerve [swə:rv] *vi* (person, animal, vehicle) それる sorérù

swift [swift] *n* (bird) アマツバメ amátsubàme

♦*adj* (happening quickly: recovery) じん速な jiñsoku na; (moving quickly: stream, glance) 早い hayáî

swiftly [swift'li:] *adv* (move, react, reply) 早く háyàku

swig [swig] (*inf*) *n* (drink) がぶ飲み gabúnomi

swill [swil] *vt* (*also*: **swill out**, **swill down**) がぶがぶ飲む gábùgabu nómù

swim [swim] *n*: *to go for a swim* 泳ぎに行く oyógi nì ikú

♦*vb* (*pt* **swam**, *pp* **swum**)

♦*vi* (person, animal) 泳ぐ oyógù; (head, room) 回る mawárù

♦*vt* (the Channel, a length) 泳いで渡る oyóìde watárù

swimmer [swim'ə:r] *n* 泳ぐ人 oyógù hitó

swimming [swim'iŋ] *n* 水泳 suíei

swimming cap *n* 水泳用の帽子 suíeiyð no bóshi

swimming costume (*BRIT*) *n* 水着 mizúgi

swimming pool *n* 水泳プール suíeipūru

swimming trunks *npl* 水泳パンツ suíeipaǹtsu

swimsuit [swim'su:t] *n* 水着 mizúgi

swindle [swin'dəl] *n* 詐欺 ságì
♦*vt* ぺてんにかける petén nì kakérù

swine [swain] (*inf!*) *n* 畜生め chikúshōme

swing [swiŋ] *n* (in playground) ぶらんこ búranko; (movement) 揺れ yuré; (change: in opinions etc) 変動 heńdō; (MUS: *also* rhythm) スイング suíǹgu
♦*vb* (*pt, pp* **swung**)
♦*vt* (arms, legs) 振る furú; (*also:* **swing round**: vehicle etc) 回す mawásù
♦*vi* (pendulum) 揺れる yurérù; (on a swing) ぶらんこに乗る búranko ni norú; (*also:* **swing round**: person, animal) 振向く furímukù; (: vehicle) 向きを変える múkì wo kaérù

to be in full swing (party etc) たけなわである takénawa de arù

swing bridge *n* 旋回橋 seńkaikyō

swingeing [swin'dʒiŋ] (*BRIT*) *adj* (blow, attack) 激しい hagéshiî; (cuts) 法外な hốgai na

swinging door [swiŋ'iŋ-] (*BRIT* **swing door**) *n* 自在ドア jizáidòa

swipe [swaip] *vt* (hit) たたく tatákù; (*inf:* steal) かっ払う kappáraù

swirl [swə:rl] *vi* (water, smoke, leaves) 渦巻く uzúmakù

swish [swiʃ] *vt* (tail etc) 音を立てて振る otó wò tátète furú
♦*vi* (clothes) 衣ずれの音を立てる kinúzure nò otó wò tatérù

Swiss [swis] *adj* スイスの suísu no
♦*n inv* スイス人 suísujìn

switch [switʃ] *n* (for light, radio etc) スイッチ suítchì; (change) 取替え toríkae
♦*vt* (change) 取替える toríkaerù

switchboard [switʃ'bɔːrd] *n* (TEL) 交換台 kốkandai

switch off *vt* (light, radio) 消す kesú; (engine, machine) 止める tomérù

switch on *vt* (light, radio, machine) つ

ける tsukérù; (engine) かける kakérù

Switzerland [swit'sə:rlənd] *n* スイス suísu

swivel [swiv'əl] *vi* (*also:* **swivel round**) 回る mawárù

swollen [swou'lən] *pp of* **swell**

swoon [swu:n] *vi* 気絶する kizétsu suru

swoop [swu:p] *n* (by police etc) 手入れ te-íre
♦*vi* (*also:* **swoop down**: bird, plane) 舞降りる maíorirù

swop [swa:p] = **swap**

sword [sɔːrd] *n* 刀 katána

swordfish [sɔːrd'fiʃ] *n* メカジキ mekájìki

swore [swɔːr] *pt of* **swear**

sworn [swɔːrn] *pp of* **swear**
♦*adj* (statement, evidence) 宣誓付きの seńseitsuki no; (enemy) 年来の néñrai no

swot [swa:t] *vi* がり勉する garíben suru

swum [swʌm] *pp of* **swim**

swung [swʌŋ] *pt, pp of* **swing**

sycamore [sik'əmɔːr] *n* カエデ kaéde

syllable [sil'əbəl] *n* 音節 oǹsetsu

syllabus [sil'əbəs] *n* 講義概要 kốgigaìyō

symbol [sim'bəl] *n* (sign, *also* MATH) 記号 kigố; (representation) 象徴 shốchō

symbolic(al) [simbɑːl'ik(əl)] *adj* 象徴的な shốchōteki na

symbolism [sim'bəlizəm] *n* 象徴的な意味 shốchōteki imì

symbolize [sim'bəlaiz] *vt* 象徴する shốchō suru

symmetrical [simet'rikəl] *adj* 対称的な taíshōteki na

symmetry [sim'itri:] *n* 対称 taíshō

sympathetic [simpəθet'ik] *adj* (showing understanding) 同情的な dốjōteki na; (likeable: character) 人好きのする hitózuki no surù; (showing support): *sympathetic to(wards)* ...に好意的である ...ni kốiteki de arù

sympathies [sim'pəθi:z] *npl* (support, tendencies) 支援 shíen

sympathize [sim'pəθaiz] *vi*: *to sympathize with* (person) ...に同情する ...ni dốjō suru; (feelings, cause) ...に共感する ...ni kyốkan suru

sympathizer [sim'pəθaizə:r] *n* (POL) 支援者 shiénsha

sympathy [sim'pəθi:] *n* (pity) 同情 dōjō

with our deepest sympathy 心からお悔みを申上げます kokórò kara o-kúyami wò mōshiagemasù

in sympathy (workers: come out) 同情して dōjō shite

symphony [sim'fəni:] *n* 交響曲 kōkyōkyoku

symposia [simpou'zi:ə] *npl of* **symposium**

symposium [simpou'zi:əm] (*pl* **symposiums** *or* **symposia**) *n* シンポジウム shiñpojiùmu

symptom [simp'təm] *n* (indicator: MED) 症状 shōjō; (: *gen*) しるし shirúshi

synagogue [sin'əgɑ:g] *n* ユダヤ教会堂 yudáyakyōkaidō

synchronize [siŋ'krənaiz] *vt* (watches, sound) 合せる awáserù

syncopated [siŋ'kəpeitid] *adj* (rhythm, beat) シンコペートした shiñkopḕto shita

syndicate [sin'dəkit] *n* (of people, businesses, newspapers) シンジケート shiñjikḕto

syndrome [sin'droum] *n* (*also* MED) 症侯群 shōkōgun

synonym [sin'ənim] *n* 同意語 dōigò

synopses [sinɑ:p'si:z] *npl of* **synopsis**

synopsis [sinɑ:p'sis] (*pl* **synopses**) *n* 概要 gaíyō

syntax [sin'tæks] *n* (LING) 統語法 tōgohō, シンタックス shiñtakkùsu

syntheses [sin'θəsi:z] *npl of* **synthesis**

synthesis [sin'θəsis] (*pl* **syntheses**) *n* (of ideas, styles) 総合する sōgō suru

synthetic [sinθet'ik] *adj* (man-made: materials) 合成の gōsei no

syphilis [sif'əlis] *n* 梅毒 baídoku

syphon [sai'fən] = **siphon**

Syria [si:r'i:ə] *n* シリア shírìa

Syrian [si:r'i:ən] *adj* シリアの shírìa no
♦*n* シリア人 shiríàjin

syringe [sərindʒ'] *n* 注射器 chūshakī

syrup [sir'əp] *n* シロップ shiróppù

system [sis'təm] *n* (organization) 組織 sōshíki; (POL): ***the system*** 体制 taísei;

(method) やり方 yaríkata; (the body) 身体 shíntai

the digestive system (MED) 消化器系 shōkakikèi

the nervous system (MED) 神経系 shiñkeikèi

systematic [sistəmæt'ik] *adj* (methodical) 組織的な soshíkiteki na

system disk *n* (COMPUT) システムディスク shisútemu disùku

systems analyst [sis'təmz-] *n* システムアナリスト shisútemu anarisùto

T

ta [tɑ:] (*BRIT*: *inf*) *excl* (thanks) どうも dōmo

tab [tæb] *n* (on file etc) 耳 mimí; (on drinks can etc) プルタブ purútàbu, プルトップ purútoppù; (label: name tab) 名札 nafúda

to keep tabs on (*fig*) 監視する kañshi suru

tabby [tæb'i:] *n* (*also*: **tabby cat**) とら毛のネコ toráge nò nékò

table [tei'bəl] *n* (piece of furniture) テーブル tḕburu; (MATH, CHEM etc) 表 hyō
♦*vt* (*BRIT*: motion etc) 上程する jōtei suru; (*US*: put off: proposal etc) 棚上げにする tana-age ni surù

to lay/set the table 食卓に皿を並べる shokútaku nì sará wò naráberù

tablecloth [tei'bəlklɔ:θ] *n* テーブルクロス tḕburukurosù

table d'hôte [tæb'əl dout'] *adj* (menu, meal) 定食の teíshoku no

table lamp *n* 電気スタンド deñki sutañdo

tablemat [tei'bəlmæt] *n* (for plate) テーブルマット tḕburumattò; (for hot dish) なべ敷 nabéshìki

table of contents *n* 目次 mokúji

tablespoon [tei'bəlspu:n] *n* (type of spoon) テーブルスプーン tḕburusupùn; (*also*: **tablespoonful**: as measurement) 大さじ一杯 ốsaji ippài

tablet [tæb'lit] *n* (MED) 錠剤 jōzai

a stone tablet 石板 sekíban

table tennis n 卓球 takkyú

table wine n テーブルワイン téburuwaìn

tabloid [tæb'lɔid] n (newspaper) タブロイド新聞 tabúroido shiñbun

taboo [təbuː'] n (religious, social) タブー tabū

♦adj (subject, place, name etc) タブーの tabū no

tabulate [tæb'jəleit] vt (data, figures) 表にする hyó ni surù

tacit [tæs'it] adj (agreement, approval etc) 暗黙の añmoku no

taciturn [tæs'itə:rn] adj (person) 無口な múkùchi na

tack [tæk] n (nail) びょう byó; (fig) やり方 yaríkata

♦vt (nail) びょうで留める byó de toméru; (stitch) 仮縫する karínui suru

♦vi (NAUT) 間切る magírù

tackle [tæk'əl] n (gear: fishing tackle etc) 道具 dógù; (for lifting) ろくろ rókùro, 滑車 kásshà; (FOOTBALL, RUGBY) タックル tákkùru

♦vt (deal with: difficulty) ...と取組む ...to toríkumù; (challenge: person) ...に掛合う ...ni kakéaù; (grapple with: person, animal) ...と取組む ...to toríkumù; (FOOTBALL, RUGBY) タックルする tákkùru suru

tacky [tæk'iː] adj (sticky) べたべたする bétàbeta suru; (pej: of poor quality) 安っぽい yasúppoì

tact [tækt] n 如才なさ josáinasà

tactful [tækt'fəl] adj 如才ない josáinaì

tactical [tæk'tikəl] adj (move, withdrawal, voting) 戦術的な señjutsuteki na

tactics [tæk'tiks] n 用兵学 yóheigàku

♦npl 駆引き kakéhìki

tactless [tækt'lis] adj 気転の利かない kitén no kikanaì

tadpole [tæd'poul] n オタマジャクシ otámajakùshi

taffy [tæf'iː] (US) n (toffee) タフィー táfì◇あめの一種 amé nò ísshù

tag [tæg] n (label) 札 fudá

tag along vi ついて行く tsuíte ikú

tail [teil] n (of animal) しっぽ shíppò; (of

plane) 尾部 bíbù; (of shirt, coat) すそ susó

♦vt (follow: person, vehicle) 尾行する bikó suru

tail away/off vi (in size, quality etc) 次第に減る shídai ni herù

tailback [teil'bæk] (BRIT) n (AUT) 交通渋滞 kótsujūtai

tail end n 末端 mattán

tailgate [teil'geit] n (AUT: of hatchback) 後尾ドア kóbidòa

tailor [tei'lə:r] n 仕立屋 shitáteya

tailoring [tei'lə:riŋ] n (cut) 仕立て方 shitátekata; (craft) 仕立職 shitáteshòku

tailor-made [tei'lə:rmeid] adj (suit) あつらえの atsúraè no; (fig: part in play, person for job) おあつらえ向きの o-átsuraemuki no

tails [teilz] npl (formal suit) えん尾服 eñbifùku

tailwind [teil'wind] n 追風 oíkàze

tainted [teint'id] adj (food, water, air) 汚染された osén saretà; (fig: profits, reputation etc) 汚れた yogóretà

Taiwan [tai'wɑ:n'] n 台湾 taíwaǹ

take [teik] (pt **took**, pp **taken**) vt (photo, notes, holiday etc) とる tórù; (shower, walk, decision etc) する surú; (grab: someone's arm etc) 取る tórù; (gain: prize) 得る érù; (require: effort, courage, time) ...が必要である ...ga hitsúyō de arù; (tolerate: pain etc) 耐える taérù; (hold: passengers etc) 収容する shúyō suru; (accompany, bring, carry: person) 連れて行く tsuréte ikù; (: thing) 持って行く motté ikù; (exam, test) 受ける ukérù

to take something from (drawer etc) ...を...から取出す ...wo ...kárà torídasù; (steal from: person) ...を...から盗む ...wo ...kárà nusúmù

I take it that ... ...だと思っていいですね ...dá tò omótte iǐ desu né

take after vt fus (resemble) ...に似ている ...ni nité irù

take apart vt 分解する buñkai suru

take away vt (remove) 下げる sagérù; (carry off) 持って行く motté ikù; (MATH) 引く hikú

takeaway [tei'kəwei] (*BRIT*) *n* = **take-out**

take back *vt* (return) 返す kaésù; (one's words) 取消す toríkesù

take down *vt* (dismantle: building) 解体 する kaítai suru; (write down: letter etc) 書き取る kakítorù

take in *vt* (deceive) だ ま す damásù; (understand) 理 解 す る rikái suru; (include) 含 む fukúmù; (lodger) 泊 め る tomérù

take off *vi* (AVIAT) 離陸する riríku suru; (go away) 行ってしまう itté shimaù
♦*vt* (remove) 外す hazúsù

takeoff [teik'ɔːf] *n* (AVIAT) 離陸 riríku

take on *vt* (work) 引き受ける hikíukerù; (employee) 雇う yatóù; (opponent) ...と戦う ...to tatákaù

take out *vt* (invite) 外食 に連れて行く gaíshoku nì tsuréte ikù; (remove) 取出す torídasù

takeout [teik'aut] (*US*) *n* (shop, restaurant) 持帰り料理店 mochíkaeriryōritèn; (food) 持帰り料理 mochíkaeriryōri

take over *vt* (business, country) 乗っ取る nottórù
♦*vi*: **to take over from someone** ...と交替する ...to kōtai suru

takeover [teik'ouvər] *n* (COMM) 乗っ取り nottóri

take to *vt fus* (person, thing, activity) 気に入る ki nì irù, 好きになる sukí ni narù; (engage in: hobby etc) やり出す yarídasù

take up *vt* (a dress) 短くする mijíkakù suru; (occupy: post, time, space) ...につく ...ni tsukú; (: time) ...がかかる ...ga kakárù; (engage in: hobby etc) やり出す yarídasù
to take someone up on something (offer, suggestion) ...に応じる ...ni ōjirù

takings [tei'kiŋz] *npl* 売上 uríage

talc [tælk] *n* (*also*: **talcum powder**) タルカムパウダー tarúkamupaùdā

tale [teil] *n* (story, account) 物語 monógatàri
to tell tales (*fig*: to teacher, parents etc) 告げ口する tsugéguchi suru

talent [tæl'ənt] *n* 才能 saínō

talented [tæl'əntid] *adj* 才能 あ る saínō arù

talk [tɔːk] *n* (a prepared speech) 演説 eńzetsu; (conversation) 話 hanáshi; (gossip) うわさ uwása
♦*vi* (speak) 話 す hanásù; (give information) しゃべる shabérù
to talk about ...について話す ...ni tsuíte hanásù
to talk someone into doing something ...する様に...を説得する ...surú yō ni ...wo settóku suru
to talk someone out of doing something ...しない様に...を説得する ...shinái yō ni ...wo settóku suru
to talk shop 仕事の話をする shigóto nò hanáshi wo surù

talkative [tɔː'kətiv] *adj* おしゃべりな o-sháberi na

talk over *vt* (problem etc) 話し合う hanáshiaù

talks [tɔːks] *npl* (POL etc) 会談 kaídan

talk show *n* おしゃべり番組 o-sháberi bańgumi

tall [tɔːl] *adj* (person) 背が高い sé gà takáì; (object) 高い takáì
to be 6 feet tall (person) 身長が6フィートである shińchō gà 6 fītò de árù

tall story *n* ほら話 horábanàshi

tally [tæl'i:] *n* (of marks, amounts of money etc) 記録 kiróku
♦*vi*: **to tally (with)** (subj: figures, stories etc) (...と) 合う (...to) áù

talon [tæl'ən] *n* かぎづめ kagízume

tambourine [tæm'bəri:n] *n* タンバリン táñbarin

tame [teim] *adj* (animal, bird) なれた nárèta; (*fig*: story, style) 平凡な heíbon na

tamper [tæm'pəːr] *vi*: **to tamper with something** ...をいじる ...wo ijírù

tampon [tæm'pɑːn] *n* タンポン táñpon

tan [tæn] *n* (*also*: **suntan**) 日焼け hiyáke
♦*vi* (person, skin) 日に焼ける hi nì yakérù
♦*adj* (color) 黄かっ色の ōkasshòku no

tandem [tæn'dəm] *n*: **in tandem** (together) 2人で futári dè

tang [tæŋ] n (smell) 鼻をつくにおい haná wò tsukú niói; (taste) ぴりっとした味 piríttò shita ají

tangent [tæn'dʒənt] n (MATH) 接線 sessén

to go off at a tangent (fig) わき道へそ れる wakímìchi e sorérù

tangerine [tændʒəri:n'] n ミカン mîkan

tangible [tæn'dʒəbəl] adj (proof, bene- fits) 具体的な gutáiteki na

tangle [tæŋ'gəl] n もつれ motsúre

to get in(to) a tangle (also fig) もつれ る motsúreru

tank [tæŋk] n (also: **water tank**) 貯水タ ンク chosúitaǹku; (for fish) 水槽 suísō; (MIL) 戦車 séǹsha

tanker [tæŋk'əːr] n (ship) タンカー táǹ- kā; (truck) タンクローリー taǹkurōrī

tanned [tænd] adj (skin) 日に焼けた hi ní yaketà

tantalizing [tæn'təlaizɪŋ] adj (smell, possibility) 興味をそそる kyômi wò so- sórù

tantamount [tæn'təmaunt] adj: *tanta- mount to* ...も同然である ...mo dôzen de arù

tantrum [tæn'trəm] n かんしゃく kań- shaku

tap [tæp] n (on sink etc) 蛇口 jagúchi; (also: **gas tap**) ガスの元栓 gásù no motó- sen; (gentle blow) 軽くたたく事 karúku tatakú kotó

♦vt (hit gently) 軽くたたく karúku tata- kù; (resources) 利用する riyô suru; (tele- phone) 盗聴する tôchō suru

on tap (fig: resources) いつでも利用でき る ítsùdemo riyô dekirù

tap-dancing [tæp'dænsɪŋ] n タップダン ス tappúdaǹsu

tape [teip] n (also: **magnetic tape**) 磁気 テープ jikítèpu; (cassette) カセットテー プ kaséttotèpu; (sticky tape) 粘着テープ neńchakutèpu; (for tying) ひも hímò

♦vt (record: sound) 録音する rokúon su- ru; (: image) 録画する rokúga suru; (stick with tape) テープで張る tèpu de harú

tape deck n テープデッキ tèpudekkì

tape measure n メジャー méjā

taper [tei'pəːr] n (candle) 細いろうそく hosóî rôsokù

♦vi (narrow) 細くなる hósòku nárù

tape recorder n テープレコーダー té- purekôdā

tapestry [tæp'istri:] n (object) タペスト リー tapésutòrī; (art) ししゅう shishû

tar [taːr] n コールタール kôrutāru

tarantula [təræn'tʃələ] n タランチュラ taráñchura

target [taːr'git] n (thing aimed at, also fig) 的 matố

tariff [tær'if] n (tax on goods) 関税 kań- zei; (BRIT: in hotels, restaurants) 料金 表 ryôkiñhyō

tarmac [taːr'mæk] n (BRIT: on road) ア スファルト asúfarùto; (AVIAT) エプロ ン épùron

tarnish [taːr'niʃ] vt (metal) さびさせる sabísaserù; (fig: reputation etc) 汚す yo- gósù

tarpaulin [taːrpɔː'lin] n シート shīto

tarragon [tær'əgən] n タラゴン táràgon ◇香辛料の一種 kôshiñryō no ísshu

tart [taːrt] n (CULIN) タルト tárùto ◇菓 子の一種 káshì no ísshù; (BRIT: inf: prostitute) ばいた baíta

♦adj (flavor) 酸っぱい suppáî

tartan [taːr'tən] n タータンチェック tá- tanchekkù

♦adj (rug, scarf etc) タータンチェックの tátanchekkù no

tartar [taːr'təːr] n (on teeth) 歯石 shiséki

tartar(e) sauce [taːr'təːr-] n タルタルソ ース tarútarusòsu

tart up (BRIT) vt (inf: object) 派手にす る hadé ni suru

to tart oneself up おめかしをする o-mékashi wò suru

task [tæsk] n 仕事 shigóto

to take to task ...の責任を問う ...no sekínin wò tôù

task force n (MIL, POLICE) 機動部隊 kidôbùtai

Tasmania [tæzmei'ni:ə] n タスマニア ta- súmanìa

tassel [tæs'əl] n 房 fusá

taste [teist] n (also: **sense of taste**) 味覚 mikáku; (flavor; also: **aftertaste**) 味 ajî; (sample) 一口 hitôkùchi; (fig: glimpse, idea) 味わい ajîwaî
♦vt (get flavor of) 味わう ajîwaû; (test) 試食する shishôku suru
♦vi: **to taste of/like** (fish etc) ...の味がする ...no ajî ga surû
you can taste the garlic (in it) (含まれている) ニンニクの味がする (fukúmarete irû) niñniku nò ajî ga surû
in good/bad taste 趣味がいい(悪い) shúmì ga fi(warúî)

tasteful [teist'fəl] adj (furnishings) 趣味の良い shúmì no yôî

tasteless [teist'lis] adj (food) 味がない ajî ga naî; (remark, joke, furnishings) 趣味の悪い shúmì no warúî

tasty [teis'ti:] adj (food) おいしい oíshiî

tatters [tæt'ə:rz] npl: **in tatters** (clothes, papers etc) ずたずたになって zutázuta ni nattê

tattoo [tætu:'] n (on skin) 入れ墨 irézumi; (spectacle) パレード parédò
♦vt (name, design) ...の入れ墨をする ...no irézumi wò suru

tatty [tæt'i:] (BRIT: inf) adj (inf) 薄汚い usúgitanaî

taught [tɔ:t] pt, pp of **teach**

taunt [tɔ:nt] n あざけり azákerì
♦vt あざける azákerù

Taurus [tɔ:r'əs] n 牡牛座 oúshizà

taut [tɔ:t] adj ぴんと張った piñ tò hattá

tavern [tæv'ə:rn] n (old) 酒場 sakába

tax [tæks] n 税金 zeîkin
♦vt (earnings, goods etc) ...に税金をかける ...ni zeîkin wò kakérù; (fig: test: memory) 最大限に使う saídaìgen ni tsukáù; (patience) 試練にかける shîren ni kakérù

taxable [tæk'səbəl] adj (income) 課税される kazéi sarerù

taxation [tæksei'ʃən] n (system) 課税 kazéi; (money paid) 税金 zeîkin

tax avoidance [-əvɔid'əns] n 節税 setsúzei

tax disc (BRIT) n (AUT) 納税ステッカー nôzeisutekkà

tax evasion n 脱税 datsúzei

tax-free [tæks'fri:'] adj (goods, services) 免税の meñzei no

taxi [tæk'si:] n タクシー tákùshī
♦vi (AVIAT: plane) 滑走する kassô suru

taxi driver n タクシーの運転手 tákùshī no uñteñshu

taxi rank (BRIT) n = **taxi stand**

taxi stand n タクシー乗場 takúshīnorìba

tax payer [-pei'ə:r] n 納税者 nôzeishà

tax relief n 減税 geñzei

tax return n 確定申告書 kakúteishinkokushò

TB [ti:bi:'] n abbr = **tuberculosis**

tea [ti:] n (drink: Japanese) お茶 o-chá; (: English) 紅茶 kôchà; (BRIT: meal) おやつ o-yátsù

high tea (BRIT) 夕食 yúshoku ◇夕方早目に食べる食事 yúgata hayáme nì tabérù shokúji

tea bag n ティーバッグ tîbaggù

tea break (BRIT) n 休憩 kyúkei

teach [ti:tʃ] (pt, pp **taught**) vt (gen) 教える oshíerù; (be a teacher of) ...(の)教師をする ...(no)kyôshi wò suru
♦vi (be a teacher: in school etc) 教師をする kyôshi wò suru

teacher [ti:'tʃə:r] n 教師 kyôshi, 先生 señsei

teaching [ti:'tʃiŋ] n (work of teacher) 教職 kyôshoku

tea cosy n お茶帽子 o-chábòshi

tea cup n (Western) ティーカップ tîkappù; (Japanese) 湯飲み茶碗 yunômijawàn, 湯飲み yunômi

teak [ti:k] n チーク chîku

tea leaves npl 茶殻 chagára

team [ti:m] n (of people: gen, SPORT) チーム chîmu; (of animals) 一組 hitôkumi

teamwork [ti:m'wə:rk] n チームワーク chîmuwàku

teapot [ti:'pɑ:t] n きゅうす kyûsu

tear¹ [te:r] n (hole) 裂け目 sakéme
♦vb (pt tore, pp torn)
♦vt (rip) 破る yabúrù
♦vi (become torn) 破れる yabúrerù

tear² [ti:r] n (in eye) 涙 námìda
in tears 泣いている naîte irû

tear along vi (rush) 猛スピードで走って行く mōsupído de hashítte ikù

tearful [tiːˈfəl] adj (family, face) 涙ぐんだ namídaguǹda

tear gas n 催涙ガス saíruigasù

tearoom [tiːˈruːm] n 喫茶店 kissáteǹ

tear up vt (sheet of paper etc) ずたずたに破る zutázuta nì yabúrù

tease [tiːz] vt からかう karákaù

tea set n 茶器セット chakísettò

teaspoon [tiːˈspuːn] n (type of spoon) ティースプーン tísupùn; (also: teaspoonful: as measurement) 小さじ一杯 kosáji ippaì

teat [tiːt] n (ANAT) 乳首 chikúbì; (also: bottle teat) ほ乳瓶の乳首 honyúbìn no chikúbì

teatime [tiːˈtaim] n おやつの時間 o-yátsù no jikàn

tea towel (BRIT) n ふきん fukíñ

technical [tekˈnikəl] adj (terms, advances) 技術の gíjutsu no

technical college (BRIT) n 高等専門学校 kōtōsenmongakkō

technicality [teknikælˈitiː] n (point of law) 法律の専門的細目 hōritsu nò señmonteki saimòku; (detail) 細かい事 komákaì kotó

technically [tekˈnikliː] adv (strictly speaking) 正確に言えば seíkaku nì iébà; (regarding technique) 技術的に gíjutsuteki ni

technician [teknˈiʃən] n 技術者 gijútsushà

technique [teknˈiːk] n 技術 gíjutsu

technological [teknələˈdʒikəl] adj 技術的な gijútsuteki na

technology [teknɑˈlədʒiː] n 科学技術 kagákugijùtsu

teddy (bear) [tedˈiː-] n クマのぬいぐるみ kumá nò nuígurùmi

tedious [tiːˈdiəs] adj (work, discussions etc) 退屈な taíkutsu na

tee [tiː] n (GOLF) ティー tí

teem [tiːm] vi: to teem with (visitors, tourists etc) ...がぞろぞろ来ている ...ga zórozoro kité irù
it is teeming (with rain) 雨が激しく

降っている áme ga hagéshikù futté irù

teenage [tiːnˈeidʒ] adj (children, fashions etc) ティーンエージャーの tíñ-ējà no

teenager [tiːnˈeidʒəːr] n ティーンエージャー tíñ-ējà

teens [tiːnz] npl: to be in one's teens 年齢は10代である neñrei wà júdài de árù

tee-shirt [tiːˈʃəːrt] n = T-shirt

teeter [tiːˈtəːr] vi (also fig) ぐらつく gurátsukù

teeth [tiːθ] npl of tooth

teethe [tiːð] vi (baby) 歯が生える há gà haérù

teething ring [tiːˈðiŋ-] n おしゃぶり o-shábùri ◊リング状の物を指す riñgujō no monó wò sásù

teething troubles npl (fig) 初期の困難 shókì no kónnan

teetotal [tiːtoutˈəl] adj (person) 酒を飲まない sec 酒を飲まない saké wò nománaì

telecommunications [teləkəmjuːnikeiˈʃənz] n 電気通信 deñkitsūshin

telegram [telˈəgræm] n 電報 deñpō

telegraph [telˈəgræf] n (system) 電信 deñshin

telegraph pole n 電柱 deñchū

telepathic [teləpæθˈik] adj テレパシーの terépàshī no

telepathy [telˈepˈəθiː] n テレパシー terépàshī

telephone [telˈəfoun] n 電話 deñwa
♦vt (person) ...に電話をかける ...ni deñwa wò kakérù; (message) 電話で伝える deñwa dè tsutáerù
on the telephone (talking) 電話中で deñwachū de; (possessing phone) 電話を持っている deñwa wò mótte irù

telephone booth n 電話ボックス deñwabokkùsu

telephone box (BRIT) n = telephone booth

telephone call n 電話 deñwa

telephone directory n 電話帳 deñwachō

telephone number n 電話番号 deñwabañgō

telephonist [teləˈfounist] (BRIT) n 電話交換手 deñwakōkañshu

telescope [tel'əskoup] n 望遠鏡 bɔ́enkyō

telescopic [teliskɑ:p'ik] adj (lens) 望遠の bɔ́en no; (collapsible: tripod, aerial) 入れ子式の irékoshìki no

television [tel'əviʒən] n (all senses) テレビ tếrèbi

on television テレビで tếrèbi de

television set n テレビ受像機 terébijuzōki

telex [tel'eks] n テレックス terékkùsu
♦vt (company) ...にテレックスを送る ...ni terékkùsu wo okúrù; (message) テレックスで送る terékkùsu de okúrù

tell [tel] (pt, pp told) vt (say) ...に言う ...ni iú; (relate: story) 述べる nobérù; (distinguish): *to tell something from* ...から ...を区別する ...karà ...wò kúbètsu suru
♦vi (talk): *to tell (of)* ...について話す ...ni tsúìte hanásù; (have an effect) 効果的である kɔ́kateki de arù

to tell someone to do something ...に ...する様に言う ...ni ...surú yɔ̀ ni iú

teller [tel'ə:r] n (in bank) 出納係 suítōgakàri

telling [tel'iŋ] adj (remark, detail) 意味深い imíbukài

tell off vt: *to tell someone off* しかる shikaru

telltale [tel'teil] adj (sign) 証拠の shɔ́ko no

telly [tel'i:] (BRIT: inf) n abbr = **television**

temerity [təme:r'iti:] n ずうずうしさ zū́zūshìsà

temp [temp] n abbr (= *temporary*) 臨時職員 rínjishokuìn

temper [tem'pə:r] n (nature) 性質 seíshitsu; (mood) 機嫌 kigén; (fit of anger) かんしゃく kańshaku
♦vt (moderate) 和らげる yawáragerù

to be in a temper 怒っている okótte irù

to lose one's temper 怒る okórù

temperament [tem'pə:rəmənt] n (nature) 性質 seíshitsu

temperamental [tempə:rəmen'təl] adj (person, fig: car) 気まぐれな kimágùre na

temperate [tem'pə:rit] adj (climate, country) 温暖な oñdan na

temperate zone n 温帯 oñtai

temperature [tem'pə:rətʃə:r] n (of person, place) 温度 óñdo

to have/run a temperature 熱がある netsú ga arù

tempest [tem'pist] n 嵐 áràshi

tempi [tem'pi:] npl of **tempo**

temple [tem'pəl] n (building) 神殿 shiñden; (ANAT) こめかみ komékami

tempo [tem'pou] (pl **tempos** or **tempi**) n (MUS) テンポ téñpo; (fig: of life etc) ペース pếsu

temporarily [tempəre:r'ili:] adv 一時的に ichíjiteki ni

temporary [tem'pə:re:ri:] adj (passing) 一時的な ichíjiteki na; (worker, job) 臨時の rínji no

tempt [tempt] vt 誘惑する yū́waku suru

to tempt someone into doing something ...する様に...を誘惑する ...surú yɔ̀ ni ...wo yū́waku suru

temptation [temptei'ʃən] n 誘惑 yū́waku

tempting [temp'tiŋ] adj (offer) 魅惑的な miwákuteki na; (food) おいしそうな ofshisǒ na

ten [ten] num 十 (の) jū́ (no)

tenacity [tənæs'iti:] n (of person, animal) 根気強さ kofkizúyosa

tenancy [ten'ənsi:] n (possession of room, land etc) 賃借 chíñshaku; (period of possession) 賃借期間 chíñshakukikàn

tenant [ten'ənt] n (rent-payer) 店子 tanáko, テナント tenáñto

tend [tend] vt (crops, sick person) ...の世話をする ...no sewá wò suru
♦vi: *to tend to do something* ...しがちである ...shigáchi de arù

tendency [ten'dənsi:] n (of person, thing) 傾向 keíkō

tender [ten'də:r] adj (person, heart, care) 優しい yasáshiì; (sore) 触ると痛い sawáru tò itáì; (meat) 柔らかい yawárakaì; (age) 幼い osánaì
♦n (COMM: offer) 見積り mitsúmori; (money): *legal tender* 通貨 tsúka

◆*vt* (offer, resignation) 提出する teíshutsu suru
to tender an apology 陳謝する chínsha suru

tenderness [ten'də:rnis] *n* (affection) 優しさ yasáshisà; (of meat) 柔らかさ yawárakasà

tendon [ten'dən] *n* けん kéñ

tenement [ten'əmənt] *n* 安アパート yasúapāto

tenet [ten'it] *n* 信条 shiñjō

tennis [ten'is] *n* テニス téñisu

tennis ball *n* テニスボール teńisubōru

tennis court *n* テニスコート teńisukōto

tennis player *n* テニス選手 teńisuseñshu

tennis racket *n* テニスラケット teńisurakettò

tennis shoes *npl* テニスシューズ teńisushūzu

tenor [ten'ə:r] *n* (MUS) テノール tenőrù

tenpin bowling [ten'pin-] *n* ボウリング bőriñgu

tense [tens] *adj* (person, smile, muscle) 緊張した kiñchō shita; (period) 緊迫した kiñpaku shita
◆*n* (LING) 時制 jiséi

tension [ten'ʃən] *n* (nervousness) 緊張 kiñchō; (between ropes etc) 張力 chőryoku

tent [tent] *n* テント téñto

tentacle [ten'təkəl] *n* (of octopus etc) あし ashí

tentative [ten'tətiv] *adj* (person, step, smile) 自信のない jishíñ no naì; (conclusion, plans) 差し当っての sashíatattè no

tenterhooks [ten'tə:rhuks] *npl*: *on tenterhooks* はらはらして háràhara shite

tenth [tenθ] *num* 第十（の） dáìjū (no)

tent peg *n* テントのくい téñto no kuí

tent pole *n* テントの支柱 téñto no shichū

tenuous [ten'ju:əs] *adj* (hold, links, connection etc) 弱い yowáì

tenure [ten'jə:r] *n* (of land, buildings etc) 保有権 hoyúken; (of office) 在職期間 zaíshokukikàn

tepid [tep'id] *adj* (tea, pool etc) ぬるい nurúì

term [tə:rm] *n* (word, expression) 用語 yőgo; (period in power etc) 期間 kikáñ; (SCOL) 学期 gakkí
◆*vt* (call) ...と言う ...to iú
in the short/long term 短〔長〕期間で tañ(chő)kikàn de

terminal [tə:r'mənəl] *adj* (disease, cancer, patient) 末期の mákkì no
◆*n* (ELEC) 端子 táñshi; (COMPUT) 端末機 tańmatsukì; (*also*: *air terminal*) ターミナルビル tấminarubirù; (BRIT: *also*: *coach terminal*) バスターミナル basútāminaru

terminate [tə:r'məneit] *vt* (discussion, contract, pregnancy) 終らせる owáraserù; (contract) 破棄する hákì suru; (pregnancy) 中絶する chūzetsu suru

termini [tə:r'məni:] *npl of* **terminus**

terminology [tə:rmənɑ:l'ədʒi:] *n* 用語 yőgo ◇総称 sőshō

terminus [tə:r'mənəs] (*pl* -**mini**) *n* (for buses, trains) ターミナル tấminaru

terms [tə:rmz] *npl* (conditions: *also* COMM) 条件 jőken
to be on good terms with someone ...と仲がいい ...to nákà ga íi
to come to terms with (problem) ...と折合いがつく ...to oríaì ga tsukú

terrace [te:r'əs] *n* (BRIT: row of houses) 長屋 nagáyà; (patio) テラス téràsu; (AGR) 段々畑 dañdanbatàke

terraced [te:r'əst] *adj* (house) 長屋の nagáyà no; (garden) ひな壇式の hinádañshiki no

terraces [te:r'əsiz] (BRIT) *npl* (SPORT): *the terraces* 立見席 tachímisèki

terracotta [te:rəkɑ:t'ə] *n* テラコッタ terácottà

terrain [tərein'] *n* 地面 jímèn

terrible [te:r'əbəl] *adj* ひどい hidőì

terribly [te:r'əbli:] *adv* (very) とても totémo; (very badly) ひどく hídòku

terrier [te:r'i:ə:r] *n* テリア térìa

terrific [tərif'ik] *adj* (very great: thunderstorm, speed) 大変な taíheñ na; (wonderful: time, party) 素晴らしい su-

bárashiî

terrify [teːrˈəfai] *vt* おびえさせる obíesaserù

territorial [teːritɔːrˈiːəl] *adj* (waters, boundaries, dispute) 領土の ryõdò no

territory [teːrˈitɔːriː] *n* (gen) 領土 ryõdò; (fig) 縄張 nawábarì

terror [teːrˈəːr] *n* (great fear) 恐怖 kyõfu

terrorism [teːrˈəːrizəm] *n* テロ térò

terrorist [teːrˈəːrist] *n* テロリスト terórisùto

terrorize [teːrˈəːraiz] *vt* おびえさせる obíesaserù

terse [təːrs] *adj* (style) 簡潔な kañketsu na; (reply) そっけない sokkénaî ◇言葉数が少なく無愛想な返事などについて言う kotóbakazù ga sukúnakù buáìsō na heñji nadð ni tsúìte iú

Terylene [teːrˈəliːn] ® *n* テリレン térìren ◇人工繊維の一種 jiñkōseñ-i no ísshù

test [test] *n* (trial, check: *also* MED, CHEM) テスト tésùto; (of courage etc) 試練 shíren; (SCOL) テスト tésùto; (*also*: **driving test**) 運転免許の試験 uñtenmeñkyo no shikéñ
◆*vt* (gen) テストする tésùto suru

testament [tesˈtəmənt] *n* 証拠 shõko
the Old/New Testament 旧(新)約聖書 kyū(shiñ)yaku seishò

testicle [tesˈtikəl] *n* こう丸 kõgan

testify [tesˈtəfai] *vi* (LAW) 証言する shõgen suru
to testify to something ...が...だと証言する ...ga ...dá tò shõgen suru

testimony [tesˈtəmouniː] *n* (LAW: statement) 証言 shõgen; (clear proof) 証拠 shõko

test match *n* (CRICKET, RUGBY) 国際戦 kokúsaisen, 国際試合 kokúsaijiài

test pilot *n* テストパイロット tesútopairottò

test tube *n* 試験管 shikéñkan

tetanus [tetˈənəs] *n* 破傷風 hashõfū

tether [teðˈəːr] *vt* (animal) つなぐ tsunágù
◆*n*: **at the end of one's tether** 行き詰って ikízumattè

text [tekst] *n* 文書 búñsho

textbook [tekstˈbuk] *n* 教科書 kyõkasho

textiles [teksˈtailz] *npl* (fabrics) 織物 orímðno; (textile industry) 織物業界 orímonogyõkai

texture [teksˈtʃəːr] *n* (of cloth, skin, soil, silk) 手触り tezáwari

Thailand [taiˈlənd] *n* タイ tâi

Thames [temz] *n*: **the Thames** テムズ川 témùzugawa

than [ðæn] *conj* (in comparisons) ...より(も) ...yórì(mo)
you have more than 10 あなたは10個以上持っています anátà wa júkkò íjò mõttè imasu
I have more than you/Paul 私はあなた(ポール)より沢山持っています watákushi wà anátà(pórù)yori takúsañ mõttè imasu
I have more pens than pencils 私は鉛筆よりペンを沢山持っています watákushi wà efípitsu yorì péñ wo takúsañ mõttè imasu
she is older than you think 彼女はあなたが思っているより年ですよ káñjo wa anátà ga omóttè irù yórì toshí desù yó
more than once 数回 sū́kài

thank [θæŋk] *vt* (person) ...に感謝する ...ni káñsha suru
thank you (very much) (大変)有難うございました (taíhen) arígatò gozáimashità
thank God! ああ良かった ā̀ yókàtta

thankful [θæŋkˈfəl] *adj*: **thankful (for)** (...を) 有難く思っている (...wo) arígatakù omótte irù

thankless [θæŋkˈlis] *adj* (task) 割の悪い warí no waruì

thanks [θæŋks] *npl* 感謝 káñsha
◆*excl* (also: **many thanks**, thanks a lot) 有難う arígatò

Thanksgiving (Day) [θæŋksgivˈiŋ-] *n* 感謝祭 kañshasaì

thanks to *prep* ...のおかげで ...no o-kágè dè

KEYWORD

that [ðæt] (*demonstrative adj, pron: pl* **those**) *adj* (demonstrative) その sonó, あの anó

that man/woman/book その〔あの〕男性〔女性, 本〕 sonó〔anó〕dañsei〔jòsei, hoñ〕

leave those books on the table その本をテーブルの上に置いていって下さい sonó hoñ wo tḕburu no ué nì oíte ittè kudásaì

that one それ soré, あれ aré

that one over there あそこにある物 asóko nì árù monó

I want this one, not that one 欲しいのはこれです, あれは要りません hoshíi no wà koré desù, aré wà irímaseñ

◆*pron* 1 (demonstrative) それ soré, あれ aré

who's/what's that? あれはだれですか〔何ですか〕aré wà dárè desu ká〔náñ desu ká〕

is that you? あなたですか anátà desu ká

I prefer this to that あれよりこちらの方が好きです aré yorì kochíra no hồ ga sukí desù

will you eat all that? あれを全部食べるつもりですか aré wò zéñbu tabérù tsumóri desù ká

that's my house 私の家はあれです watákushi nò ié wà aré desù

that's what he said 彼はそう言いましたよ kárè wa số iimáshìta yó

what happened after that? それからどうなりましたか soré karà dố narimashìta ká

2 (relative): *the book (that) I read* 私の読んだ本 watákushi nò yóñda hóñ

the books that are in the library 図書館にある本 toshókàn ni árù hóñ

the man (that) I saw 私の見た男 watákushi nò mítà otóko

all (that) I have 私が持っているだけ watákushi gà móttè irú dàke

the box (that) I put it in それを入れた箱 soré wò iréta hakò

the people (that) I spoke to 私が声を掛けた人々 watákushi gà kṓè wo kákète hitóbìto

3 (relative: of time): *the day (that) he came* 彼が来た日 kárè ga kitá hì

the evening/winter (that) he came to see us 彼が私たちの家に来た夜〔冬〕kárè ga watákushitàchi no ié ni kitá yorù〔fuyù〕

◆*conj* ...だと ...dá tò

he thought that I was ill 私が病気だと彼は思っていました watákushi gà byõkì dá tò kárè wa omótte imashìta

she suggested that I phone you あなたに電話する様にと彼女は私に勧めました anátà ni deñwa suru yṓ ni to kánòjo wa watákushi nǐ susúmemashìta

◆*adv* (demonstrative) それ程 soré hodò, あれ程 aré hodò, そんなに soñna nǐ, あんなに añna nǐ

I can't work that much あんなに働けません añna nǐ határakemaseñ

I didn't realize it was that bad 事態があれ程悪くなっているとは思っていませんでした jítai ga aré hodò wárùku natté irù to wa omótte imasen deshìta

that high あんなに高い añna nǐ takáì

the wall's about that high and that thick 塀はこれぐらい高くてこれぐらい厚い heí wà koré gurài tákàkute koré gurài atsúi

---

thatched [θætʃt] *adj* (roof, cottage) わらぶきの warábuki no

thaw [θɔː] *n* 雪解けの陽気 yukídokè no yṓkì

◆*vi* (ice) 溶ける tokérù; (food) 解凍される kaítō sarerù

◆*vt* (food: *also*: **thaw out**) 解凍する kaítō suru

KEYWORD

the [ðə] *def art* 1 (*gen*) その sonó ◇ 通常日本語では表現しない tsūjō nihóngo de wà hyṓgen shinaì

the history of France フランスの歴史

furánsu nò rekíshi

the books/children are in the library 本(子供たち)は図書館にあります〔います〕hôñ(kodômotàchi)wa toshôkàn ni arímasù(imásù)

she put it on the table/gave it to the postman 彼女はテーブルに置きました〔郵便屋さんにあげました〕kánòjo wa têburu ni okímashìta〔yûbin-yasan nì agémashìta〕

he took it from the drawer 彼は引出しから取り出しました kárè wa hikídashi karà torídashimashìta

I haven't the time/money 私にはそれだけの時間〔金〕がありません watákushi ni wà soré dakè no jíkàn(kanê)gà arímaseñ

to play the piano/violin ピアノ〔バイオリン〕をひく piáno(baíorin)wo hikú

the age of the computer コンピュータの時代 koñpyùta no jídài

I'm going to the butcher's/the cinema 肉屋に〔映画を見に〕行って来ます nikúyà ni 〔eíga wò mí nì〕ittè kimasù

2 (+ adjective to form noun)

the rich and the poor 金持と貧乏人 kanémochì to biñbonin

the wounded were taken to the hospital 負傷者は病院に運ばれた fushôshà wa byôìn ni hakóbaretà

to attempt the impossible 不可能な事をやろうとする fukánô na kotò wo yarô to surù

3 (in titles): *Elizabeth the First* エリザベス1世 erízabèsu íssèi

Peter the Great ピョートル大帝 pyôtòru taítei

4 (in comparisons): *the more he works the more he earns* 彼は働けば働く程もうかる kárè wa határakèba határaku hodò môkarù

the more I look at it the less I like it 見れば見る程いやになります míreba míru hodò iyá ni narimasù

---

theater [θiːɑːˈtəːr] (*BRIT* **theatre**) *n* (building with stage) 劇場 gekíjô; (art form) 演劇 eñgeki; (*also*: **lecture thea-**

ter) 講義室 kôgishìtsu; (MED: *also*: **operating theater**) 手術室 shujútsushìtsu

theater-goer [θiːˈətəːrgouəːr] *n* 芝居好き shibáizùki

theatrical [θiːætˈrikəl] *adj* (event, production) 演劇の eñgeki no; (gestures) 芝居染みた shibáijimìta

theft [θeft] *n* 窃盗 settô

their [ðeːr] *adj* 彼らの kárèra no ¶ *see also* **my**

theirs [ðeːrz] *pron* 彼らの物 kárèra no monô ¶ *see also* **mine**

them [ðem] *pron* (direct) 彼らを kárèra wo; (indirect) 彼らに kárèra ni; (stressed, after prep) 彼ら kárèra ¶ *see also* **me**

theme [θiːm] *n* (main subject) 主題 shudái, テーマ têma; (MUS) テーマ têma

theme park *n* テーマ遊園地 têmayuèñchi

theme song *n* 主題歌 shidáìka

themselves [ðəmselvzˈ] *pl pron* (reflexive) 彼ら自身を karèra jishìn wo; (after prep) 彼ら自身 karèra jishìn ¶ *see also* **oneself**

then [ðen] *adv* (at that time) その時(に) sonô tokì (ni); (next, later, and also) それから soré karà

◆*conj* (therefore) だから dá kàra

◆*adj*: *the then president* 当時の大統領 tôjì no daítôryô

by then (past) その時 sonô tokì; (future) その時になったら sonô tokì ni nattárà

from then on その時から sonô tokì kara

theology [θiːɑːlˈədʒiː] *n* 神学 shiñgaku

theorem [θiːrˈəm] *n* 定理 teíri

theoretical [θiːəretˈikəl] *adj* (biology, possibility) 理論的な rirônteki na

theorize [θiːˈəːraiz] *vi* 学説を立てる gakúsetsu wò tatérù

theory [θiəːrˈiː] *n* (all senses) 理論 ríròn

in theory 理論的には rirônteki ni wà

therapeutic(al) [θeːrəpjuːˈtik(əl)] *adj* 治療の chiryô no

therapist [θeːrˈəpist] *n* セラピスト serápisùto

therapy [θeːrʹəpiː] *n* 治療 chiryō

KEYWORD

there [ðeːr] *adv* 1: *there is*, *there are* ...がある〔いる〕 ...ga árù〔irú〕
there are 3 of them (things) 3つあります míttsu arímasù; (people) 3人います sañniñ imásù
there is no one here だれもいません dáre mo imáseñ
there is no bread left パンがなくなりました páñ ga nakúnarimashìta
there has been an accident 事故がありました jíko ga arímashìta
there will be a meeting tomorrow 明日会議があります asú káigi ga arímasù
2 (referring to place) そこに〔で、へ〕 sokó nī〔dè, e〕, あそこに〔で、へ〕asokó nī〔dè, e〕
where is the book? - it's there 本はどこにありますか-あそこにあります hóñ wa dókò ni arímasù ká - asóko nì arímasù
put it down there そこに置いて下さい sokó nī óite kudasaì
he went there on Friday 彼は金曜日に行きました kárè wa kiñ-yóbi ni ikímashìta
I want that book there そこの本が欲しい sokó nò hóñ ga hoshíi
there he is! いました imáshìta
3: *there, there* (especially to child) よしよし yóshì yóshì
there, there, it's not your fault/don't cry よしよし、お前のせいじゃないから〔泣かないで〕yóshì yóshì, omáe nò seí ja naì kara〔nakánaìde〕

thereabouts [ðeːrʹəbauts] *adv* (place) そこら辺 sokórahèñ; (amount) それぐらい soré gurai

thereafter [ðeːræfʹtəːr] *adv* それ以来 soré irài

thereby [ðeːrʹbaiʹ] *adv* それによって soré ni yottè

therefore [ðeːrʹfɔːr] *adv* だから dá kàra

there's [ðeːrz] = there is; there has

thermal [θəːrʹməl] *adj* (underwear) 防寒

用の bōkan-yō no; (paper) 感熱の kañnetsu no; (printer) 熱式の netsúshìki no

thermal spring *n* 温泉 oñsen

thermometer [θəːrmɑːmʹitəːr] *n* (for room/body temperature) 温度計 oñdokèi

Thermos [θəːrʹməs] ® *n* (also: **Thermos flask**) 魔法瓶 mahóbìn

thermostat [θəːrʹməstæt] *n* サーモスタット sámosutattò

thesaurus [θisɔːrʹəs] *n* シソーラス shisórāsu

these [ðiːz] *pl adj* これらの korérà no
♦*pl pron* これらは〔を〕 korérà wa〔wo〕

theses [θiːʹsiːz] *npl of* thesis

thesis [θiːʹsis] (*pl* **theses**) *n* (for doctorate etc) 論文 rôñbun

they [ðei] *pl pron* 彼らは〔が〕 kárèra wa〔ga〕
they say that ... (it is said that) ...と言われている ...to iwárete irù

they'd [ðeid] = they had; they would

they'll [ðeil] = they shall, they will

they're [ðeːr] = they are

they've [ðeiv] = they have

thick [θik] *adj* (in shape: slice, jersey etc) 厚い atsúi; (line) 太い futói; (in consistency: sauce, mud, fog etc) 濃い kôi; (: forest) 深い fukái; (stupid) 鈍い nibúi
♦*n*: *in the thick of the battle* 戦いのさなかに tatákai nò sánàka ni
it's 20 cm thick 厚さは20センチだ atsúsa wà nijússeñchi da

thicken [θikʹən] *vi* (fog etc) 濃くなる kôkù naru; (plot) 込入ってくる komíitte kurù
♦*vt* (sauce etc) 濃くする kôkù suru

thickness [θikʹnis] *n* 厚み atsúmi

thickset [θikʹset'] *adj* (person, body) がっちりした gatchíri shita

thickskinned [θikʹskind'] *adj* (*fig*: person) 無神経な mushíñkei na

thief [θiːf] (*pl* **thieves**) *n* 泥棒 doróbō

thieves [θiːvz] *npl of* thief

thigh [θai] *n* 太もも futómomo

thimble [θimʹbəl] *n* 指抜き yubínuki

thin [θin] *adj* (*gen*) 薄い usúi; (line) 細い hosói; (person, animal) やせた yasétà;

(crowd) まばらな mabára na

♦*vt: to thin (down)* (sauce, paint) 薄める usúmerù

thing [θiŋ] *n* (gen) 物事 monógòto; (physical object) 物 monó; (matter) 事 kotó:

to have a thing about someone/ something (mania) ...が大嫌いである ...ga dáikirai de árù; (fascination) ...が大好きである ...ga dáisuki de árù

poor thing かわいそうに kawáisò ni

the best thing would be to ... ...する のが一番いいだろう ...surú no gà ichíban ií darò

how are things? どうですか dò desu ká

things [θiŋz] *npl* (belongings) 持物 mochímòno

think [θiŋk] (*pt, pp* **thought**) *vi* (reflect) 考える kañgaerù; (believe) 思う omóù

♦*vt* (imagine) ...だと思う ...dá tò omóù

what did you think of them? 彼らの事をどう思いましたか kárèra no kotó wo dò omóimashìtà ka

to think about something/someone ...について考える ...ni tsúìte kañgaerù

I'll think about it 考えておくね kañgaete okù né

to think of doing something ...しよう と思う ...shiyó tò omóù

I think so/not そうだ〔違う〕と思う sò dà〔chigáù〕to omóù

to think well of someone ...に対して 好感を持つ ...ni táìshite kòkan wò mótsù

think over *vt* (offer, suggestion) よく考 える yókù kañgaerù

think tank *n* シンクタンク shiñkutañku

think up *vt* (plan, scheme, excuse) 考え 出す kañgaedasù

thinly [θin'li:] *adv* (cut, spread) 薄く usúkù

third [θə:rd] *num* 第三（の）dáì san (no)

♦*n* (fraction) 3分の1 sañbun no ichi; (AUT: *also:* **third gear**) サードギヤ sádogìyà; (BRIT: SCOL: degree) 3級優等 卒業学位 sañkyū yūtō sotsugyō gakùi

¶ *see also* **first**

thirdly [θə:rd'li:] *adv* 第三に dáì san ni

third party insurance (BRIT) *n* 損害 倍償保険 soñgaibaishōhokèn

third-rate [θə:rd'reit'] *adj* 三流の sañryū no

Third World *n: the Third World* 第 三世界 dáì san sékài

thirst [θə:rst] *n* 渇き kawáki

thirsty [θə:rs'ti:] *adj* (person, animal) の どが渇いた nódò ga kawáità; (work) の どが渇く nódò ga kawákù

to be thirsty (person, animal) のどが渇 いている nódò ga kawáite irù

thirteen [θə:r'ti:n'] *num* 十三（の）jū-san (no)

thirty [θə:r'ti:] *num* 三十（の）sáñjū (no)

KEYWORD

---

this [ðis] (*pl* **these**) *adj* (demonstrative) この konó

this man/woman/book この男性〔女性、本〕konó dansei〔josei, hon〕

these people/children/records この人 たち〔子供たち、レコード〕konó hitotà-chi〔kodomotàchi, rekòdo〕

this one これ koré

it's not that picture but this one that I like 私が好きなのはあの絵ではなくて、この絵です watákushi gà sukí na no wà anó e de wa nakùte, konó e desù

♦*pron* (demonstrative) これ koré

what is this? これは何ですか koré wà náñ desu ká

who is this? この方はどなたですか ko-nó katà wa dónàta desu ká

I prefer this to that 私はあれよりこの 方が好きです watákushi wà aré yorì konó hò ga sukí desù

this is where I live 私の住いはここで す watákushi no sumài wa kokó desù

this is what he said 彼はこう言いました kárè wa kò iimashìta

this is Mr Brown (in introductions/ photo) こちらはブラウンさんです kochí-ra wà buráunsan desu; (on telephone) こ ちらはブラウンですが kochíra wà burá-

ùn desu ga

♦*adv* (demonstrative): *this high/long*
高さ[長さ]はこれぐらいで tákàsa[nágà-sa]wa koré gurài de

it was about this big 大きさはこれぐ
らいでした ókìsa wa korégurài deshita

the car is this long 車の長さはこれぐ
らいです kurúma no nagàsa wa koré
gurài desu

*we can't stop now we've gone this
far* ここまで来たらやめられません ko-
kó madè kitára yaméraremaseǹ

thistle [θisˈəl] *n* アザミ azámi

thong [θɔːŋ] *n* バンド bándo

thorn [θɔːrn] *n* とげ togé

thorny [θɔːrˈniː] *adj* (plant, tree) とげの
多い togé no ói; (problem) 厄介な yákkài
na

thorough [θəːrˈou] *adj* (search, wash) 徹
底的な tettéiteki na; (knowledge,
research) 深い fukái; (person: methodical) きちょうめんな kichómen na

thoroughbred [θəːrˈoubred] *adj* (horse)
サラブレッド sarábureddð

thoroughfare [θəːrˈoufeːr] *n* 目抜き通
り menúkidòri

「*no thoroughfare*」通行禁止 tsúkōkìn-
shi

thoroughly [θəːrˈouliː] *adv* (examine,
study, wash, search) 徹底的に tettéiteki
ni; (very) とても totémo

those [ðouz] *pl adj* それらの sorérà no,
あれらの arérà no

♦*pl pron* それらを sorérà wo, あれらを
arérà wo

though [ðou] *conj* ...にもかかわらず ...ní
mò kákawarazù

♦*adv* しかし shikáshì

thought [θɔːt] *pt, pp of* **think**

♦*n* (idea, reflection) 考え kańgaè; (opinion) 意見 íkèn

thoughtful [θɔːtˈfəl] *adj* (person: deep in
thought) 考え込んでいる kańgaekonde
irù; (: serious) 真剣な shińken na; (considerate: person) 思いやりのある omóiyari no arù

thoughtless [θɔːtˈlis] *adj* (inconsiderate:

behavior, words, person) 心ない kokóronaì

thousand [θauˈzənd] *num* 千（の）sén
(no)

two thousand 二千（の）nisén (no)

thousands of 何千もの... nańzeǹ mo
no ...

thousandth [θauˈzəndθ] *num* 第千
（の）dáì sen (no)

thrash [θræʃ] *vt* (beat) たたく tatákù;
(defeat) ...に快勝する ...ni kaíshō suru

thrash about/around *vi* のたうつ no-
táutsù

thrash out *vt* (problem) 討議する tógi
suru

thread [θred] *n* (yarn) 糸 ítð; (of screw)
ねじ山 nejíyama

♦*vt* (needle) ...に糸を通す ...ni ítð wo tósù

threadbare [θredˈbeːr] *adj* (clothes, carpet) 擦切れた suríkiretà

threat [θret] *n* (*also fig*) 脅し odóshi;
(*fig*) 危険 kikén

threaten [θretˈən] *vi* (storm, danger) 迫
る semárù

♦*vt: to threaten someone with/to do*
...で[...すると言って)...を脅す ...de [...su-
rú tò ittè)...wð odósù

three [θriː] *num* 三（の）sań (no)

three-dimensional [θriːˈdimenˈtʃənəl]
adj 立体の rittái no

three-piece suit [θriːˈpiːs-] *n* 三つぞろ
い mitsúzorði

three-piece suite *n* 応接三点セット ó-
setsu santensettð

three-ply [θriːˈplai] *adj* (wool) 三重織り
の sańjūori no

thresh [θreʃ] *vt* (AGR) 脱穀する dakkó-
ku suru

threshold [θreʃˈould] *n* 敷居 shikíi

threw [θruː] *pt of* **throw**

thrift [θrift] *n* 節約 setsúyaku

thrifty [θrifˈtiː] *adj* 節約家の setsúyaku-
kà no

thrill [θril] *n* (excitement) スリル súrìru;
(shudder) ぞっとする事 zottð suru kotð

♦*vt* (person, audience) わくわくさせる
wákùwaku sasérù

to be thrilled (with gift etc) 大喜びである ỏyorðkobi de árù

thriller [θrílʹəːr] n (novel, play, film) スリラー surírā

thrilling [θrílʹiŋ] adj (ride, performance, news etc) わくわくさせる wákùwaku sasérù

thrive [θraiv] (pt **throve**, pp **thrived** or **thriven**) vi (grow: plant) 生茂る oíshigerù; (: person, animal) よく育つ yókù sodátsù; (: business) 盛んになる sakán ni narù; (do well): ***to thrive on something*** ...で栄える ...de sakáerù

thriven [θráivən] pp of **thrive**

thriving [θráivʹiŋ] adj (business, community) 繁盛している háñjō shité irù

throat [θrout] n のど nódò

to have a sore throat のどが痛い nódò ga itáī

throb [θrɑːb] n (of heart) 鼓動 kodố; (of wound) うずき uzúki; (of engine) 振動 shiñdố

♦vi (heart) どきどきする dókìdoki suru; (head, arm: with pain) ずきずきする zúkìzuki suru; (machine: vibrate) 振動する shiñdố suru

throes [θrouz] npl: ***in the throes of*** (war, moving house etc) ...と取組んでいるさなかに ...to toríkunde irù sánàka ni

thrombosis [θrɑːmbouʹsis] n 血栓症 kesséñshō

throne [θroun] n 王座 ốza

throng [θrɔːŋ] n 群衆 guñshū

♦vt (streets etc) ...に殺到する ...ni sattố suru

throttle [θrɑːtʹəl] n (AUT) スロットル suróttòru

♦vt (strangle) ...ののどを絞める ...no nódò wo shimérù

through [θruː] prep (space) ...を通って ...wo tốttè; (time) ...の間中 ...no aída jū; (by means of) ...を使って ...wo tsukáttè; (owing to) ...が原因で ...ga geñ-in dè

♦adj (ticket, train) 直通の chokútsū no

♦adv 通して tốshite

to put someone through to someone (TEL) ...を...につなぐ ...wo ...ni tsunágù

to be through (TEL) つながれる tsuná-

garerù; (relationship: finished) 終る owáru

「***no through road***」(BRIT) 行き止り ikídomarì

throughout [θruːautʹ] prep (place) ...の至る所に itáru tokoro ni; (time) ...の間中 ...no aída jū

♦adv 至る所に itáru tokoro ni

throve [θrouv] pt of **thrive**

throw [θrou] n (gen) 投げる事 nagéru kotò

♦vt (pt **threw**, pp **thrown**) (object) 投げる nagérù; (rider) 振り落す furíotosù; (fig: person: confuse) 迷わせる mayówasérù

to throw a party パーティをやる pátì wo yárù

throw away vt (rubbish) 捨てる sutérù; (money) 浪費する rốhi suru

throwaway [θrouʹəwei] adj (toothbrush) 使い捨ての tsukáisùte no; (line, remark) 捨てぜりふ染みた sutézerifujimìta

throw-in [θrouʹin] n (SPORT) スローイン suróñ

throw off vt (get rid of: burden, habit) かなぐり捨てる kanágurisuterù; (cold) ...が治る ...ga naórù

throw out vt (rubbish, idea) 捨てる sutérù; (person) ほうり出す hốridasù

throw up vi (vomit) 吐く hákù

thru [θruː] (US) = **through**

thrush [θrʌʃ] n (bird) つぐみ tsugúmi

thrust [θrʌst] n (TECH) 推進力 suíshiñryoku

♦vt (pt, pp **thrust**) (person, object) 強く押す tsuýòku osú

thud [θʌd] n ばたんという音 batáñ to iú otð

thug [θʌg] n (pej) ちんぴら chíñpira; (criminal) 犯罪者 hañzaìsha

thumb [θʌm] n (ANAT) 親指 oyáyubi

♦vt: ***to thumb a lift*** ヒッチハイクする hitchíhaìku suru

thumbtack [θʌmʹtæk] (US) n 画びょう gabyố

thumb through vt fus (book) 拾い読みする hiróiyomi suru

thump [θʌmp] *n* (blow) 一撃 ichígeki; (sound) どしんという音 doshín to iú otò
♦*vt* (person, object) たたく tatákù
♦*vi* (heart etc) どきどきする dókìdoki suru

thunder [θʌn'dər] *n* 雷 kamínari
♦*vi* 雷が鳴る kamínari ga narú; (*fig*: train etc): **to thunder past** ごう音を立てて通り過ぎる góon wò tátète tōrisugirù

thunderbolt [θʌn'də:rboult] *n* 落雷 rakúrai

thunderclap [θʌn'də:rklæp] *n* 雷鳴 raímei

thunderstorm [θʌn'də:rstɔ:rm] *n* 雷雨 ráìu

thundery [θʌn'də:ri:] *adj* (weather) 雷が鳴る kamínarì ga narù

Thursday [θə:rz'dei] *n* 木曜日 mokúyòbi

thus [ðʌs] *adv* (in this way) こうして kố shìte; (consequently) 従って shitágattè

thwart [θwɔ:rt] *vt* (person, plans) 邪魔する jamá suru

thyme [taim] *n* タイム táìmu

thyroid [θai'rɔid] *n* (*also*: **thyroid gland**) 甲状腺 kójōsen

tiara [ti:æ'rə] *n* ティアラ tíàra

Tibet [tibet'] *n* チベット chibéttò

tic [tik] *n* チック chíkkù

tick [tik] *n* (sound: of clock) かちかち káchìkachi; (mark) 印 shirúshi; (ZOOL) だに daní; (*BRIT*: *inf*): **in a tick** もうすぐ mố sugù
♦*vi* (clock, watch) かちかちいう káchìkachi iú
♦*vt* (item on list) ...に印を付ける ...ni shirúshi wò tsukérù

ticket [tik'it] *n* (for public transport, theater etc) 切符 kippú; (in shop: on goods) 値札 nefúda; (for raffle, library etc) チケット chikéttò; (*also*: **parking ticket**) 駐車違反のチケット chūsha-ihàn no chikéttò

ticket collector *n* 改札係 kaísatsugakàri

ticket office *n* (RAIL, theater etc) 切符売場 kippú urìba

tickle [tik'əl] *vt* (person, dog) くすぐる

kusúguru
♦*vi* (feather etc) くすぐったい kusúguttai

ticklish [tik'liʃ] *adj* (person) くすぐったがる kusúguttagàru; (problem) 厄介な yákkài na

tick off *vt* (item on list) ...に印を付ける ...ni shirúshi wò tsukérù; (person) しかる shikárù

tick over *vi* (engine) アイドリングする aídoriñgu suru; (*fig*: business) 低迷する teímei suru

tidal [taid'əl] *adj* (force) 潮の shió no; (estuary) 干満のある kañman no arù

tidal wave *n* 津波 tsunámi

tidbit [tid'bit] (*US*) *n* (food) うまいもの一口 umái monò hitókùchi; (news) 好奇心をあおり立てるうわさ話 kókishìn wo aóritaterù uwásabanàshi

tiddlywinks [tid'li:wiŋks] *n* おはじき oháȷ̃iki

tide [taid] *n* (in sea) 潮 shió; (*fig*: of events, fashion, opinion) 動向 dókō
high/low tide 満(干)潮 mañ(kañ)chō

tide over *vt* (help out) ...の一時的な助けになる ...no ichíjiteki nà tasúke ni narù

tidy [tai'di:] *adj* (room, dress, desk, work) きちんとした kichíñ to shita; (person) きれい好きな kiréìzuki na
♦*vt* (*also*: **tidy up**: room, house etc) 片付ける katázukeru

tie [tai] *n* (string etc) ひも himó; (*BRIT*: *also*: **necktie**) ネクタイ nékùtai; (*fig*: link) 縁 éñ; (SPORT: even score) 同点 dóten
♦*vt* (fasten: parcel) 縛る shibárù; (: shoelaces, ribbon) 結ぶ musúbù
♦*vi* (SPORT etc) 同点になる dóten nì narù
to tie in a bow ちょう結びにする chốmusùbi ni suru
to tie a knot in something ...に結び目を作る ...ni musúbime wò tsukúrù

tie down *vt* (*fig*: person: restrict) 束縛する sokúbaku suru; (: to date, price etc) 縛り付ける shibáritsukerù

tier [ti:r] *n* (of stadium etc) 列 rétsù; (of cake) 層 số

tie up vt (parcel) ...にひもを掛ける ...ni himó wò kakérù; (dog, boat) つなぐ tsunagu; (prisoner) 縛る shibárù; (arrangements) 整える totónoerù

to be tied up (busy) 忙しい isógashiì

tiger [tai'gəːr] n トラ torá

tight [tait] adj (firm: rope) ぴんと張った pín tò hattá; (scarce: money) 少ない sukúnaì; (narrow: shoes, clothes) きつい kitsúì; (bend) 急な kyū́ na; (strict: security, budget, schedule) 厳しい kibíshiì; (inf: drunk) 酔っ払った yoppárattà

♦adv (hold, squeeze, shut) 堅く katákú

tighten [tait'ən] vt (rope, screw) 締める shimérù; (grip) 固くする katáku suru; (security) 厳しくする kibíshikù suru

♦vi (grip) 固くなる katáku narù; (rope) 締る shimárù

tightfisted [tait'fis'tid] adj けちな kéchi na

tightly [tait'li:] adv (grasp) 固く katákú

tightrope [tait'roup] n 綱渡りの綱 tsunáwatàri no tsuná

tights [taits] npl タイツ táĩtsu

tile [tail] n (on roof) かわら kawára; (on floor, wall) タイル táĩru

tiled [taild] adj (roof) かわらぶきの kawárabuki no; (floor, wall) タイル張りの tafrubari no

till [til] n (in shop etc) レジの引出し réjì no hikídashi

♦vt (land: cultivate) 耕す tagáyasù

♦prep, conj = **until**

tiller [til'əːr] n (NAUT) だ柄 dahéi, チラー chírá

tilt [tilt] vt 傾ける katámukerù

♦vi 傾く katámukù

timber [tim'bəːr] n (material) 材木 zaímoku; (trees) 材木用の木 zaímokuyò no kí

time [taim] n (gen) 時間 jíkàn; (epoch: often pl) 時代 jidái; (by clock) 時刻 jíkòku; (moment) 瞬間 shuñkan; (occasion) 回 kái; (MUS) テンポ téñpo

♦vt (measure time of: race, boiling an egg etc) ...の時間を計る ...no jíkàn wo hakárù; (fix moment for: visit etc) ...の時期を選ぶ ...no jíkì wo erábù; (remark

etc) ...のタイミングを合せる ...no taímingu wo awáserù

a long time 長い間 nagái aidà

for the time being 取りあえず toríaezù

4 at a time 4つずつ yottsú zùtsu

from time to time 時々 tokídoki

at times 時には tokí ni wà

in time (soon enough) 間に合って ma ní attè; (after some time) やがて yagáte; (MUS) ...のリズムに合せて ...no rízùmu ni awásetè

in a week's time 1週間で isshū́kàn de

in no time 直ぐに súgù ni

any time いつでも ítsù de mo

on time 間に合って ma ní attè

5 times 5 5かける5 gó kakerù gó

what time is it? 何時ですか náñji desu ká

to have a good time 楽しむ tanóshimù

time bomb n 時限爆弾 jigénbakùdan

time lag n 遅れ okúre

timeless [taim'lis] adj 普遍的な fuhénteki na

time limit n 期限 kígen

timely [taim'li:] adj (arrival, reminder) 時宜を得た jígì wo étà, 丁度いい時の chódo ii tokì no, タイムリーな táĩmurī na

time off n 休暇 kyū́ka

timer [tai'məːr] n (time switch) タイムスイッチ taímusuitchì; (in cooking) タイマー táĩmā

time scale (BRIT) n 期間 kíkàn

time-share [taim'jeːr] n リゾート施設の共同使用権 rizótoshisètsu no kyódoshiyōken

time switch n タイムスイッチ taímusuitchì, タイマー taimā

timetable [taim'teibəl] n (RAIL etc) 時刻表 jikókuhyò; (SCOL etc) 時間割 jikánwari

time zone n 時間帯 jikántai

timid [tim'id] adj (shy) 気が小さい ki gá chiìsai; (easily frightened) 臆病な okúbyò na

timing [tai'miŋ] n (SPORT) タイミング taímingu

the timing of his resignation 彼の辞

退のタイミング kárè no jíttai no taímin-gu

timpani [tim'pəni:] *npl* ティンパニー tínpanī

tin [tin] *n* (material) すず súzù; (*also:* **tin plate**) ブリキ buríki; (container: biscuit tin etc) 箱 hakó; (: *BRIT*: can) 缶 kán

tinfoil [tin'fɔil] *n* ホイル hóiru

tinge [tindʒ] *n* (of color) 薄い色合い usúi i-róaì; (of feeling) 気味 kimí
◆*vt*: **tinged with** (color) ...の色合いを帯びた ...no iróaì wo óbìta; (feeling) ...の気味を帯びた ...no kimí wo óbìta

tingle [tiŋ'gəl] *vi* (person, arms etc) ぴりぴりする bíríbiri suru

tinker [tiŋk'ə:r]: **to tinker with** *vt fus* いじくる ijíkurù

tinned [tind] (*BRIT*) *adj* (food, salmon, peas) 缶詰の kañzumè no

tin opener [-ou'pənə:r] (*BRIT*) *n* 缶切り kañkirì

tinsel [tin'səl] *n* ティンセル tíñseru

tint [tint] *n* (color) 色合い iróaì; (for hair) 染毛剤 señmōzai

tinted [tin'tid] *adj* (hair) 染めた sómeta; (spectacles, glass) 色付きの irótsuki no

tiny [tai'ni:] *adj* 小さな chíisa na

tip [tip] *n* (end: of paintbrush etc) 先端 señtan; (gratuity) チップ chíppù; (*BRIT*: for rubbish) ごみ捨て場 gomí suteba; (advice) 助言 jogén
◆*vt* (waiter) ...にチップをあげる ...ni chíppù wo agérù; (tilt) 傾ける katámukerù; (overturn: *also:* **tip over**) 引っ繰り返す hikkúrikaesù; (empty: *also:* **tip out**) 空ける akérù

tip-off [tip'ɔ:f] *n* (hint) 内報 naíhō

tipped [tipt] (*BRIT*) *adj* (cigarette) フィルター付きの firútātsuki no

Tipp-Ex [tip'eks] (® *BRIT*) *n* 修正ペン shūseipeñ ◇白い修正液の出るフェルトペン shirói shūseieki no derù ferútopeñ

tipsy [tip'si:] (*inf*) *adj* 酔っ払った yoppárattà

tiptoe [tip'tou] *n*: **on tiptoe** つま先立って tsumásakidattè

tiptop [tip'tɑ:p] *adj*: **in tiptop condition** 状態が最高で jōtai gà saíkō dè

tire [taiə:r'] *n* (*BRIT* **tyre**) タイヤ táiya
◆*vt* (make tired) 疲れさせる tsukáresaserù
◆*vi* (become tired) 疲れる tsukárerù; (become wearied) うんざりする uñzarí suru

tired [taiə:rd'] *adj* (person, voice) 疲れた tsukáretà
to be tired of something ...にうんざりしている ...ni uñzarí shité irù

tireless [taiə:r'lis] *adj* (worker) 疲れを知らない tsukáre wò shiránaì; (efforts) たゆまない tayúmanaì

tire pressure *n* タイヤの空気圧 táiya no kūkiatsu

tiresome [taiə:r'səm] *adj* (person, thing) うんざりさせる uñzarí saserù

tiring [taiə:r'iŋ] *adj* 疲れさせる tsukáresaserù

tissue [tiʃ'u:] *n* (ANAT, BIO) 組織 sóshìki; (paper handkerchief) ティッシュ tísshù

tissue paper *n* ティッシュペーパー tisshúpēpā

tit [tit] *n* (bird) シジュウカラ shijúkàra
to give tit for tat しっぺ返しする shippégaèshi suru

titbit [tit'bit] = **tidbit**

titillate [tit'əleit] *vt* 刺激する shigéki suru ◇特に性的描写などについて言う tókù ni seíteki byósha nádò ni tsúte iú

title [tait'əl] *n* (of book, play etc) 題 dáì; (personal rank etc) 肩書 katágaki; (BOXING etc) タイトル táìtoru

title deed *n* (LAW) 権利証書 keñrishósho

title role *n* 主役 shuyáku

titter [tit'ə:r] *vi* くすくす笑う kusúkusu waraù

TM [ti:em'] *abbr* = **trademark**

KEYWORD
---

to [tu:] *prep* **1** (direction) ...へ ...é
to go to France/London/school/the station フランス〔ロンドン, 学校, 駅〕へ行く furánsu(róñdon, gakkố, ékì)e i-kù
to go to Claude's/the doctor's クロー

ドの家〔医者〕へ行く kurŏdò no iê〔ishá〕e ikù

the road to Edinburgh エジンバラへの道 ejínbara ê nò michí

to the left/right 左〔右〕へ hidári〔migî〕e

2 (as far as) ...まで ...mádè

from here to London ここからロンドンまで kokŏ karà rôndon madè

to count to 10 10まで数える jû madè kazŏerù

from 40 to 50 people 40ないし50人の人 yônjù nâishi gojûnìn no hitô

3 (with expressions of time): *a quarter to 5* 5時15分前 gójì jûgofùn máè

it's twenty to 3 3時20分です sánji nijúppuñ máè desu

4 (for, of) ...の ...no

the key to the front door 玄関のかぎ génkan no kagí

she is secretary to the director 彼女は所長の秘書です kánòjo wa shochô nò hishô desù

a letter to his wife 妻への手紙 tsúmà e no tegámi

5 (expressing indirect object) ...に ...ni

to give something to someone ...に...を与える ...ni ...wò atáerù

to talk to someone ...に話す ...ni hanásù

I sold it to a friend 友達にそれを売りました tomódachi nì soré wò urímashìta

to cause damage to something ...に損害を与える ...ni sofigai wò atáerù

to be a danger to someone/something ...を危険にさらす ...wò kikén nì sarásù

to carry out repairs to something ...を修理する ...wò shûrì suru

you've done something to your hair あなたは髪型を変えましたね anátà wa kamígata wò kaêmashìta nê

6 (in relation to) ...に対して ...ni táìshite

A is to B as C is to D A対Bの関係はC対Dの関係に等しい A tâî B no kañkei wà C tâî D no kañkei nì hitóshiì

3 goals to 2 スコアは3対2 sukôâ wa sañ tâî ní

30 miles to the gallon ガソリン1ガロンで30マイル走れる gasôrin ichígarôn de sañjùmaîru hashírerù

7 (purpose, result): *to come to someone's aid* ...を助けに来る ...wò tasúke nì kúrù

to sentence someone to death ...に死刑の宣告を下す ...ni shikéi nò señkoku wò kudásù

to my surprise 驚いた事に odŏroita kotô ni

◆*with vb* **1** (simple infinitive): *to go/eat* 行く〔食べる〕事 ikú〔tabérù〕kotò

2 (following another verb): *to want to do* ...したい ...shitái

to try to do ...をしようとする ...wò shiyô tò suru

to start to do ...をし始める ...wò shihájimerù

3 (with vb omitted): *I don't want to* それをしたくない soré wò shitákùnai

you ought to あなたはそうすべきです anátà wa sô sùbeki desu

4 (purpose, result) ...するために ...surú tamè ni, ...する様に ...surú yò ni, ...しに ...shí nì

I did it to help you あなたを助け様と思ってそれをしました anátà wo tasúke yò to omóttè soré wò shimáshìta

he came to see you 彼はあなたに会いに来ました kárè wa anátà ni áî ni kimáshìta

I went there to meet him 彼に会おうとしてあそこへ行きました kárè ni aô tò shite asóko e ikimashìta

5 (equivalent to relative clause): *I have things to do* 色々とする事があります iróiro tò suru kotò ga arímasù

he has a lot to lose if ... ...が起れば、彼は大損をするだろう ...gà okórèba, kárè wa ôzòn wo suru darô

the main thing is to try 一番大切なのは努力です ichíban taîsetsu ná no wà dóryòku desu

6 (after adjective etc): *ready to go* 行く準備ができた ikú juñbi ga dékìta

too old/young to ... ...するのに年を取り過ぎている〔若過ぎる〕...surú no nì to-

shī wǒ torísugite irù(wakásugirù)
it's too heavy to lift 重くて持ち上げられ
ません omókùte mochíageraremaseǹ

♦*adv: push/pull the door to* ドアを閉
める dóàwo shimérù ◇ぴったり閉めない
場合に使う pittárì shiménài baái nì tsukáù

toad [toud] *n* ヒキガエル hikígaèru

toadstool [toud'stu:l] *n* キノコ kínòko

toast [toust] *n* (CULIN) トースト tōsuto;
(drink, speech) 乾杯 kaǹpai

♦*vt* (CULIN: bread etc) 焼く yákù;
(drink to) ...のために乾杯する ...no tamé
nì kaǹpai suru

toaster [tous'tə:r] *n* トースター tōsutā

tobacco [təbæk'ou] *n* タバコ tabákò

tobacconist [təbæk'ənist] *n* タバコ売り
tabákoùri

tobacconist's (shop) [təbæk'ənists-] *n*
タバコ屋 tabákoya

toboggan [təba:g'ən] *n* (*also* child's) ト
ボガン tobógaǹ

today [tədei'] *adv* (*also fig*) 今日 (は) kyō
(wà)

♦*n* 今日 kyō; (*fig*) 現在 geǹzai

toddler [ta:d'lə:r] *n* 幼児 yṓjì

to-do [tədu:'] *n* (fuss) 騒ぎ sáwàgi

toe [tou] *n* (of foot) 足 指 ashíyùbi; (of
shoe, sock) つま先 tsumásaki

♦*vt: to toe the line* (*fig*) 服従する fukújū suru

toenail [tou'neil] *n* 足のつめ ashí no tsu-
mè

toffee [tɔːf'iː] *n* = **taffy**

toffee apple (BRIT) *n* タフィー衣のり
んご tafígoromo no riǹgo

toga [tou'gə] *n* トーガ tōga

together [tu:geð'ə:r] *adv* (to/with each
other) 一緒に ísshò ni; (at same time) 同
時に dṓjì ni

together with ...と一緒に ...to ísshò ni

toil [tɔil] *n* 労苦 rōkù

♦*vi* あくせく働く ákùseku határakù

toilet [tɔi'lit] *n* (apparatus) 便器 béǹki,
トイレ tōìre; (room with this apparatus)
便所 beǹjo, お手洗い o-téarài, トイレ tōìre

toilet bag (for woman) 化粧バッグ ke-
shōbaggù; (for man) 洗面バッグ seǹmen-
baggù

toilet paper *n* トイレットペーパー tof-
rettopēpā

toiletries [tɔi'litri:z] *npl* 化粧品 keshṓhìn

toilet roll *n* トイレットペーパーのロー
ル toírettopēpā no rṓru

toilet soap *n* 化粧石けん keshṓsekkèn

toilet water *n* 化粧水 keshṓsùi

token [tou'kən] *n* (sign, souvenir) 印 shirúshi; (substitute coin) コイン kóìn

♦*adj* (strike, payment etc) 名目の meí-
moku no

book/record/gift token (BRIT) 商品
券 shṓhìnken

Tokyo [tou'ki:jou] *n* 東京 tṓkyō

told [tould] *pt, pp of* **tell**

tolerable [ta:l'ə:rəbəl] *adj* (bearable) 我
慢できる gámàn dekírù; (fairly good) ま
あまあの mâma no

tolerance [ta:l'ə:rəns] *n* (patience) 寛容
kaǹ-yō; (TECH) 耐久力 taíkyūr* yoku

tolerant [ta:l'ə:rənt] *adj: tolerant (of)*
(...に) 耐えられる (...ni) taérarerù

tolerate [ta:l'ə:reit] *vt* (pain, noise, injustice) 我慢する gámàn suru

toll [toul] *n* (of casualties, deaths) 数 kázù; (tax, charge) 料金 ryṓkin

♦*vi* (bell) 鳴る narú

tomato [təmei'tou] (*pl* **tomatoes**) *n* トマ
ト tómàto

tomb [tu:m] *n* 墓 haká

tomboy [ta:m'bɔi] *n* お転婆 o-téǹba

tombstone [tu:m'stoun] *n* 墓石 haká-ishi

tomcat [ta:m'kæt] *n* 雄ネコ osúneko

tomorrow [təmɔːr'ou] *adv* (*also fig*) 明
日 asú, あした ashíta

♦*n* (*also fig*) 明日 asu, あした ashíta

the day after tomorrow あさって a-
sáttè

tomorrow morning あしたの朝 ashíta
nò ásà

ton [tʌn] *n* トン tóǹ ◇BRIT = 1016 kg;
US = 907 kg

tons of (*inf*) ものすごく沢山の monósu-
gòku takúsan no

tone [toun] *n* (of voice) 調子 chṓshi; (of

instrument) 音色 ne-íro; (of color) 色調 shikíchō

♦*vi* (colors: also: **tone in**) 合う áu

tone-deaf [toun'def] *adj* 音痴の ōnchi no

tone down *vt* (color, criticism, demands) 和らげる yawáragerù; (sound) 小さくする chíisakù suru

tone up *vt* (muscles) 強くする tsúyòku suru

tongs [tɔŋz] *npl* (also: **coal tongs**) 炭ばさみ sumíbasàmi; (curling tongs) 髪ごて kamígote

tongue [tʌŋ] *n* (ANAT) 舌 shitá; (CULIN) タン táñ; (language) 言語 géñgo

tongue in cheek (speak, say) からかって karákattè

tongue-tied [tʌŋ'taid] *adj* (*fig*) ものも言えない monó mò iénaì

tongue-twister [tʌŋ'twistə:r] *n* 早口言葉 hayákuchi kotobà

tonic [tɑn'ik] *n* (MED, *also fig*) 強壮剤 kyōsōzai; (*also*: **tonic water**) トニックウォーター toníkkuuòtā

tonight [tənait'] *adv* (this evening) 今日の夕方 kyō no yūgata; (this night) 今夜 kóñ-ya

♦*n* (this evening) 今日の夕方 kyō no yūgata; (this night) 今夜 kóñ-ya

tonnage [tʌn'idʒ] *n* (NAUT) トン数 toñsū

tonsil [tɑn'səl] *n* へんとうせん heñtōsen

tonsillitis [tɑnsəlai'tis] *n* へんとうせん炎 heñtōsen-èn

too [tu:] *adv* (excessively) あまりに...過ぎる amári nì ...sugírù; (*also*) ...も (また) ...mo (matá)

too much adv あまり沢山で amári takusañ de

♦*adj* あまり沢山の amári takusañ no

too many adv あまり沢山の amári takusañ no

♦*pron* あまり沢山 amári takusañ

took [tuk] *pt of* **take**

tool [tu:l] *n* 道具 dōgu

tool box *n* 道具箱 dōgubàko

toot [tu:t] *n* (of horn) ぶーぶー pūpū; (of whistle) ぴーぴー pīpī

♦*vi* (with car-horn) クラクションを鳴らす kurákùshon wo narásù

tooth [tu:θ] (*pl* **teeth**) *n* (ANAT, TECH) 歯 há

toothache [tu:θ'eik] *n* 歯の痛み há nò itámi, 歯痛 shitsū

toothbrush [tu:θ'brʌʃ] *n* 歯ブラシ habúràshi

toothpaste [tu:θ'peist] *n* 歯磨き hamigaki

toothpick [tu:θ'pik] *n* つまようじ tsumáyòji

top [tɑp] *n* (of mountain, tree, head, ladder) 天辺 teppéñ; (page) 頭 atáma; (of cupboard, table, box) ...の上 ...no ué; (of list etc) 筆頭 hittō; (lid: of box, jar, bottle) ふた futá; (blouse etc) トップ tóppù; (toy) こま kómà

♦*adj* (highest: shelf, step) 一番上の ichíban ue no; (: marks) 最高の saíkō no; (in rank: salesman etc) ぴかーの piká-ichí no

♦*vt* (be first in: poll, vote, list) ...の首位に立つ ...no shúì ni tátsù; (exceed: estimate etc) 越える koérù

on top of (above) ...の上に ...no ué nì; (in addition to) ...に加えて ...ni kuwáetè

from top to bottom 上から下まで ué karà shitá madè

top floor *n* 最上階 saíjōkai

top hat *n* シルクハット shirúkuhattò

top-heavy [tɑp'hevi:] *adj* (object) 不安定な fuáñtei na; (administration) 幹部の多過ぎる káñbu no ōsugìrù

topic [tɑp'ik] *n* 話題 wadái

topical [tɑp'ikəl] *adj* 時事問題の jijímoñdai no

topless [tɑp'lis] *adj* (bather, waitress, swimsuit) トップレスの tóppùresu no

top-level [tɑp'lev'əl] *adj* (talks, decision) 首脳の shunō no

topmost [tɑp'moust] *adj* (branch etc) 一番上の ichíban ue no

top off (*US*) *vt* = **top up**

topple [tɑp'əl] *vt* (government, leader) 倒す taósù

♦*vi* (person, object) 倒れる taórerù

top-secret [tɑp'si:'krit] *adj* 極秘の go-

kúhi no

topsy-turvy [ta:p'si:tər'vi:] *adj* (world) はちゃめちゃの háchàmecha no
♦*adv* (fall, land etc) 逆様に sakásama ni

top up *vt* (bottle etc) 一杯にする ippái ni surú

torch [tɔ:rtʃ] *n* (with flame) たいまつ tái-matsu; (*BRIT*: electric) 懐中電とう kaí-chūdeǹtō

tore [tɔ:r] *pt of* **tear**

torment [*n* tɔ:r'ment *vb* tɔ:rment'] *n* 苦しみ kurúshimì
♦*vt* (subj: feelings, guilt etc) 苦しませる kurúshimaserù, 悩ませる nayámaserù; (*fig*: annoy: subj: person) いじめる ijímerù

torn [tɔ:rn] *pp of* **tear**

tornado [tɔ:rnei'dou] (*pl* **tornadoes**) *n* 竜巻 tatsúmaki

torpedo [tɔ:rpi:'dou] (*pl* **torpedoes**) *n* 魚雷 gyorái

torrent [tɔ:r'ənt] *n* (flood) 急流 kyúryū; (*fig*) 奔流 hoñryū

torrential [tɔ:ren'tʃəl] *adj* (rain) 土砂降りの doshábùri no

torrid [tɔ:r'id] *adj* (sun) しゃく熱の sha-kúnetsu no; (love affair) 情熱的な jōnet-suteki na

torso [tɔ:r'sou] *n* 胴 dō

tortoise [tɔ:r'təs] *n* カメ kámè

tortoiseshell [tɔ:r'təʃel] *adj* べっ甲の bekkō no

tortuous [tɔ:r'tʃu:əs] *adj* (path) 曲りくねった magárikunettà; (argument) 回りくどい mawárikudoì; (mind) 邪悪な jaáku na

torture [tɔ:r'tʃə:r] *n* (*also fig*) 拷問 gṓmon
♦*vt* (*also fig*) 拷問にかける gṓmon nì kakérù

Tory [tɔ:r'i:] (*BRIT*) *adj* 保守党の hoshú-tō no
♦*n* 保守党員 hoshútòin

toss [tɔ:s] *vt* (throw) 投げる nagérù; (one's head) 振る furú

to toss a coin コインをトスする kóìn wo tósù suru

to toss up for something コインをトスして...を決める kóìn wo tósù shité ...wò

kimérù

to toss and turn (in bed) ころげ回る korógemawarù

tot [ta:t] *n* (*BRIT*: drink) おちょこ一杯 ochókò íppai; (child) 小さい子供 chiísaì kodómo

total [tout'əl] *adj* (complete: number, workforce etc) 全体の zeñtai no; (: failure, wreck etc) 完全な kañzen na
♦*n* 合計 gókei
♦*vt* (add up: numbers, objects) 合計する gókei suru; (add up to: X dollars/pounds) 合計は...になる gókei wà ...ni nárù

totalitarian [toutæliter'i:ən] *adj* 全体主義の zeñtaishùgi no

totally [tou'təli:] *adv* (agree, write off, unprepared) 全く mattáku

totter [ta:t'ə:r] *vi* (person) よろめく yo-rómekù

touch [tʌtʃ] *n* (sense of touch) 触覚 shokk-káku; (contact) 触る事 sawáru kotó
♦*vt* (with hand, foot) ...に触る ...ni sawá-rù; (tamper with) いじる ijiru; (make contact with) ...に接触する ...ni sesshóku suru; (emotionally) 感動させる kañdō sa-serù

a touch of (*fig*: frost etc) 少しばかり sukóshi bakàri

to get in touch with someone ...に連絡する ...ni reñraku suru

to lose touch (friends) ...との連絡が途絶える ...tó nò reñraku gà todáerù

touch-and-go [tʌtʃ'æŋgou'] *adj* 危ない abúnai

touchdown [tʌtʃ'daun] *n* (of rocket, plane: on land) 着陸 chakúriku; (: on water) 着水 chakúsui; (US FOOTBALL) タッチダウン tatchídaùn

touched [tʌtʃt] *adj* (moved) 感動した kañ-dō shita

touching [tʌtʃ'iŋ] *adj* 感動的な kañdōte-ki na

touchline [tʌtʃ'lain] *n* (SPORT) サイドライン saídoraìn

touch on *vt fus* (topic) ...に触れる ...ni furérù

touch up *vt* (paint) 修正する shúsei suru

touchy [tʌtʃiː] *adj* (person) 気難しい ki-múzukashii

tough [tʌf] *adj* (strong, hard-wearing: material) 丈夫な jóbu na; (meat) 固い katái; (person: physically) 頑丈な gañjō na; (: mentally) 神経が太い shiñkei gà futóì; (difficult: task, problem, way of life) 難しい muzúkashiì; (firm: stance, negotiations, policies) 譲らない yuzúranaì

toughen [tʌfˈən] *vt* (someone's character) 強くする tsúyòku suru; (glass etc) 強化する kyóka suru

toupée [tuːpeiˈ] *n* かつら katsúra ◇男性のはげを隠す小さな物を指す dañsei no hagè wo kakúsù chíisa na monò wo sásù

tour [tuːr] *n* (journey) 旅行 ryokō; (*also*: **package tour**) ツアー tsúā; (of town, factory, museum) 見学 keñgaku; (by pop group etc) 巡業 juñgyō
　♦*vt* (country, city, factory etc) 観光旅行する kañkōryokō suru; (city) 見物する keñbutsu suru; (factory etc) 見学する keñgaku suru

tourism [tuːrˈizəm] *n* (business) 観光観光 kañkō

tourist [tuːrˈist] *n* 観光客 kañkōkyaku
　♦*cpd* (attractions etc) 観光の kañkō no

tourist class (on ship, plane) ツーリストクラス tsúrisutokuràsu

tourist office *n* 観光案内所 kañkōannaisho

tournament [tuːrˈnəmənt] *n* トーナメント tónamento

tousled [tauˈzəld] *adj* (hair) 乱れた midáretà

tout [taut] *vi*: **to tout for business** (business) 御用聞きする goyókìki suru
　♦*n* (*also*: **ticket tout**) だふ屋 dafúyà

tow [tou] *vt* (vehicle, caravan, trailer) 引く hikú, けん引する keñ-in suru
　「**in** (US) **or** (BRIT) **on tow**」(AUT) けん引中 keñ-iñchū

toward(s) [tɔːrd(z)] *prep* (direction) …の方へ …no hố è; (attitude) …に対して …ni táìshite; (purpose) …に向かって …ni mukátte; (in time) …のちょっと前に …no chóttò máè ni

towel [tauˈəl] *n* (hand/bath towel) タオル táòru

towelling [tauˈəliŋ] *n* (fabric) タオル地 taóruji

towel rack (*BRIT*: **towel rail**) *n* タオル掛け taórukàke

tower [tauˈəːr] *n* 塔 tố

tower block (*BRIT*) *n* 高層ビル kốsōbirù

towering [tauˈəːriŋ] *adj* (buildings, trees, cliffs) 高くそびえる tákàku sobférù; (figure) 体の大きな karáda nò ốkì na

town [taun] *n* 町 machí
　to go to town 町に出掛ける machí nì dekákerù; (*fig*: on something) 思い切りやる omóikiri yarù, 派手にやる hadé nì yárù

town center *n* 町の中心部 machí nò chúshìñbu

town council *n* 町議会 chốgikài

town hall *n* 町役場 machíyakùba

town plan *n* 町の道路地図 machí nò dốrochizù

town planning *n* 開発計画 kaíhatsuke-ikàku

towrope [touˈroup] *n* けん引用ロープ keñ-in-yō rốpù

tow truck (*US*) *n* (breakdown lorry) レッカー車 rekkáshà

toxic [tɑːkˈsik] *adj* (fumes, waste etc) 有毒の yúdoku no

toy [tɔi] *n* おもちゃ omóchà

toyshop [tɔiˈʃɑːp] *n* おもちゃ屋 omócha-yà

toy with *vt fus* (object, food) いじくり回す ijíkurimawasù; (idea) …しようかなと考えてみる …shiyố kà na to kañgaete mirù

trace [treis] *n* (sign) 跡 átò; (small amount) 微量 biryō
　♦*vt* (draw) トレースする torésù suru; (follow) 追跡する tsuíseki suru; (locate) 見付ける mitsúkerù

tracing paper [treiˈsiŋ-] *n* トレーシングペーパー toréshingupèpā

track [træk] *n* (mark) 跡 átò; (path: *gen*) 道 michí; (: of bullet etc) 弾道 dáñdō; (: of suspect, animal) 足跡 ashífatò; (RAIL) 線路 sēñro; (on tape, record: *also* SPORT)

トラック torákkù
♦vt (follow: animal, person) 追跡する tsuíseki suru

to keep track of ...を監視する ...wo kañshi suru

track down vt (prey) 追詰める oítsumerù; (something lost) 見付ける mitsúkerù

tracksuit [træk'su:t] n トレーニングウエア torḗningu ueà

tract [trækt] n (GEO) 地帯 chitái; (pamphlet) 論文 roñbun

traction [træk'ʃən] n (power) けん引力 keñ-íñryoku; (MED): *in traction* けん引療法中 keñ-iñryōhōchū

tractor [træk'tə:r] n トラクター torákutā

trade [treid] n (activity) 貿易 bốeki; (skill) 技術 gíjùtsu; (job) 職業 shokúgyò
♦vi (do business) 商売する shốbai suru
♦vt (exchange): *to trade something (for something)* (...と)...を交換する (...to)...wò kốkan suru

trade fair n トレードフェアー torḗdofeà

trade in vt (old car etc) 下取に出す shitádori nì dásù

trademark [treid'ma:rk] n 商標 shốhyō

trade name n 商品名 shōhíñmei

trader [trei'də:r] n 貿易業者 bốekigyồsha

tradesman [treidz'mən] (pl **tradesmen**) n 商人 shốnin

trade union n 労働組合 rốdōkumìai

trade unionist [-ju:n'jənist] n 労働組合員 rốdōkumiaiìn

tradition [trədiʃ'ən] n 伝統 deñtō

traditional [trədiʃ'ənəl] adj (dress, costume, meal) 伝統的な deñtōteki na

traffic [træf'ik] n (movement: of people, vehicles) 往来 ốrai; (: of drugs etc) 売買 báibai; (air traffic, road traffic etc) 交通 kốtsū
♦vi: *to traffic in* (liquor, drugs) 売買する báibai suru

traffic circle (US) n ロータリー rồtarī

traffic jam n 交通渋滞 kốtsūjùtai

traffic lights npl 信号(機) shíñgō(kì)

traffic warden n 違反駐車取締官 ihán-

chūsa toríshimarikàn

tragedy [trædʒ'idi:] n 悲劇 higéki

tragic [trædʒ'ik] adj (death, consequences) 悲劇的な higékiteki na; (play, novel etc) 悲劇の higéki no

trail [treil] n (path) 小道 kốmichi; (track) 足跡 ashíatò; (of smoke, dust) 尾 ố
♦vt (drag) 後に引く átò ni hikú; (follow: person, animal) 追跡する tsuíseki suru
♦vi (hang loosely) 後ろに垂れる ushíro nì tarérù; (in game, contest) 負けている makéte irù

trail behind vi (lag) 遅れる okúrerù

trailer [trei'lə:r] n (AUT) トレーラー torḗrà; (US: caravan) キャンピングカー kyañpingukầ; (CINEMA) 予告編 yokốkuheñ

trailer truck (US) n トレーラートラック torḗrātorakkù

train [trein] n (RAIL) 列車 resshá; (underground train) 地下鉄 chikátetsu; (of dress) トレイン toréìn
♦vt (educate: mind) 教育する kyốiku suru; (teach skills to: apprentice, doctor, dog etc) 訓練する kuñren suru; (athlete) 鍛える kitáerù; (point: camera, hose, gun etc): *to train on* 向ける mukérù
♦vi (learn a skill) 訓練を受ける kuñren wò ukérù; (SPORT) トレーニングする torḗniñgu suru

one's train of thought 考えの流れ kañgaè no nagáre

trained [treind] adj (worker, teacher) 技術が確かな gíjùtsu ga táshika na; (animal) 訓練された kuñren saretà

trainee [treini:'] n (apprentice: hairdresser etc) 見習 mínàrai; (teacher etc) 実習生 jisshűsei

trainer [trei'nə:r] n (SPORT: coach) コーチ kồchi; (: shoe) スニーカー suníkầ; (of animals) 訓練師 kuñreñshi

training [trei'niŋ] n (for occupation) 訓練 kúñren; (SPORT) トレーニング torḗniñgu

in training トレーニング中 torḗningu-chū

training college n (gen) 職業大学 shokúgyōdaigàku; (for teachers) 教育大学

kyồikudaigàku

training shoes npl スニーカー sunˊikầ

traipse [treips] vi 足を棒にして歩き回る
ashˊi wồ bồ ni shitề arˊukimawarˊu

trait [treit] n 特徴 tokúchō

traitor [treiˈtɔːr] n 裏切者 urágirimồno

tram [træm] (BRIT) n (also: **tramcar**)
路面電車 roméndeñsha

tramp [træmp] n (person) ルンペン rúñpen; (inf: pej: woman) 浮気女 uwắkioñ-
na
◆vi どしんどしん歩く doshˊiñdoshin arˊu-
kˊu

trample [træmˈpəl] vt: **to trample**
(underfoot) 踏み付ける fumˊitsukerˊu

trampoline [træmpəliːnˈ] n トランポリ
ン toráñporin

trance [træns] n (gen) こん睡状態 koñsu-
ijồtai; (fig) ぼう然とした状態 bồzen to
shità jồtai

tranquil [træŋˈkwil] adj (place, old age)
平穏な heˊon na; (sleep) 静かな shˊizùka
na

tranquillity [træŋkwilˈitiː] n 平静さ hef-
seisà

tranquillizer [træŋˈkwəlaizəːr] n (MED)
鎮静剤 chiñseˊizai

transact [trænsæktˈ] vt: **to transact**
business 取引する toríhˊiki suru

transaction [trænsækˈʃən] n (piece of
business) 取引 torˊihˊiki

transatlantic [trænsətlænˈtik] adj (trade,
phone-call etc) 英米間の eˊbeikàn no

transcend [trænsendˈ] vt 越える koéru

transcript [trænˈskript] n (of tape
recording etc) 記録文書 kiróku buñsho

transfer [trænsˈfəːr] n (moving: of
employees etc) 異動 idồ; (: of money) 振
替 furˊikaề; (POL: of power) 引継ぎ hikˊi-
tsugi; (SPORT) トレード torếdồ; (picture, design) 写し絵 utsˊushiề
◆vt (move: employees) 転任させる teñnin
saserˊu; (: money) 振替える furˊikaerˊu;
(: power) 譲る yuzˊurù

to transfer the charges (BRIT: TEL)
コレクトコールにする korˊekutokồru ni
suru

transform [trænsfɔːrmˈ] vt 変化させる

hếñka saserˊu

transformation [trænsfəːrmeiˈʃən] n 変
化 hếñka

transfusion [trænsfjuːˈʒən] n (also:
blood transfusion) 輸血 yukétsu

transient [trænˈʃənt] adj 一時的な ichˊiji-
teki na

transistor [trænzistəːr] n (ELEC) トラ
ンジスタ toráñjisùta; (also: **transistor**
radio) トランジスタラジオ toráñjisuta
rajˊio

transit [trænˈsit] n: **in transit** (people,
things) 通過中の tsˊukachˊu no

transition [trænziˈʃən] n 移行 ikồ

transitional [trænziˈʃənəl] adj (period,
stage) 移行の ikồ no

transitive [trænˈsətiv] adj (LING):
transitive verb 他動詞 tadồshˊi

transit lounge n (at airport etc) トラン
ジットラウンジ toráñjitto raừnji

transitory [trænˈsitɔːriː] adj つかの間の
tsukˊá no mà nồ

translate [trænzleitˈ] vt (word, book
etc) 翻訳する hoñ-yaku suru

translation [trænzleiˈʃən] n (act/result
of translating) 訳 yákù

translator [trænzleitəːr] n 訳者 yákù-
sha

transmission [trænzmiˈʃən] n (of information, disease) 伝達 deñtatsu; (TV:
broadcasting, program broadcast) 放送
hồsō; (AUT) トランスミッション toráñ-
sumisshồn

transmit [trænzmitˈ] vt (message, signal, disease) 伝達する deñtatsu suru

transmitter [trænzmitˈəːr] n (piece of
equipment) トランスミッタ toráñsumit-
tầ

transparency [trænsperˈənsiː] n (of
glass etc) 透明度 tồmeˊdo; (PHOT: slide)
スライド surˊaido

transparent [trænsperˈənt] adj (see-
through) 透明の tồmei no

transpire [trænspaiəːrˈ] vi (turn out) 明
らかになる akˊiràka ni nárù; (happen) 起
る okˊórù

transplant [vb trænzplænˈtˈ n trænzˈ-
plænˈt] vt (seedlings: also: MED: organ)

移植する ishóku suru
◆n (MED) 移植 ishóku

transport [n trænsˈpɔːrt vb trænsˈpɔːrt] n (moving people, goods) 輸送 yusó; (also: **road/rail transport** etc) 輸送機関 yusókikàn; (car) 車 kurúma
◆vt (carry) 輸送する yusó suru

transportation [trænspərrteiˈʃən] n (transport) 輸送 yusó; (means of transport) 輸送機関 yusókikàn

transport café (BRIT) n トラック運転手向きのレストラン torákkuuntenshu mukí no resútoraǹ

transvestite [trænsvesˈtait] n 女装趣味の男性 josóshùmi no dańsei

trap [træp] n (snare, trick) わな wánà; (carriage) 軽馬車 keíbashà
◆vt (animal) わなで捕える wánà de toraérù; (person: trick) わなにかける wánà ni kakérù; (: confine: in bad marriage, burning building): **to be trapped** 逃げられなくなっている nigérarenakù natté irù

trap door n 落し戸 otóshidò

trapeze [træpiːzˈ] n 空中ぶらんこ kúchūburankò

trappings [træpˈiŋz] npl 飾り kazári

trash [træʃ] n (rubbish: also pej) ごみ gomí; (: nonsense) でたらめ detárame

trash can (US) n ごみ入れ gomírè

trauma [trɔːˈmə] n 衝撃 shógeki, ショック shókkù

traumatic [trɔːmætˈik] adj 衝撃的な shógekiteki na

travel [trævˈəl] n (traveling) 旅行 ryokó
◆vi (person) 旅行する ryokó suru; (news, sound) 伝わる tsutáwarù; (wine etc): **to travel well/badly** 運搬に耐えられる〔耐えられない〕uńpan ni taérarerù〔taérarenaì〕
◆vt (distance) 旅行する ryokó suru

travel agency n 旅行代理店 ryokódairitèn

travel agent n 旅行業者 ryokógyòsha

traveler [trævˈələr] (BRIT **traveller**) n 旅行者 ryokóshà

traveler's check [trævˈələrz-] (BRIT **traveller's cheque**) n トラベラーズチェ

ック toráberāzuchekkù

traveling [trævˈəliŋ] (BRIT **travelling**) n 旅行 ryokó

travels [trævˈəlz] npl (journeys) 旅行 ryokó

travel sickness n 乗物酔い norímonoyoì

travesty [trævˈisti:] n パロディー páròdī

trawler [trɔːˈləːr] n トロール漁船 toróru-gyòsen

tray [trei] n (for carrying) お盆 o-bón; (on desk) デスクトレー desúkutorè

treacherous [tretʃˈəːrəs] adj (person, look) 裏切り者の urágirimòno no; (ground, tide) 危険な kikén na

treachery [tretʃˈəːri:] n 裏切り urágirì

treacle [triːˈkəl] n 糖みつ tómitsu

tread [tred] n (step) 歩調 hochó; (sound) 足音 ashíotò; (of stair) 踏面 fumízùra; (of tire) トレッド toréddò
◆vi (pt **trod**, pp **trodden**) 歩く arúkù

tread on vt fus 踏む fumú

treason [triːˈzən] n 反逆罪 hańgyakuzài

treasure [treʒˈəːr] n (gold, jewels etc) 宝物 takáramono; (person) 重宝な人 chóhò nà hitó
◆vt (value: object) 重宝する chóhò suru; (: friendship) 大事にしている daíji nì shité irù; (: memory, thought) 心に銘記する kokórò ni méìki suru

treasurer [treʒˈəːrəːr] n 会計 kaíkei

treasures [treʒˈəːrz] npl (art treasures etc) 貴重品 kichóhìn

treasury [treʒˈəːriː] n: (US) **the Treasury Department**, (BRIT) **the Treasury** 大蔵省 ókurashò

treat [triːt] n (present) 贈物 okúrimono
◆vt (handle, regard: person, object) 扱う atsúkaù; (MED: patient, illness) 治療する chiryó suru; (TECH: coat) 処理する shórì suru
to treat someone to something ...に...をおごる ...ni ...wo ogórù

treatment [triːtˈmənt] n (attention, handling) 扱い方 atsúkaikata; (MED) 治療 chiryó

treaty [triːˈtiː] n 協定 kyótei

treble [trebˈəl] adj 3倍の sańbai no;

(MUS) 高音部の kōonbu no
♦vt 3倍にする sañbai nǐ suru
♦vi 3倍になる sañbai ni narǔ

treble clef n (MUS) 高音部記号 kōonbu-kigō

tree [tri:] n 木 kǐ

tree trunk n 木の幹 kǐ nò mǐkǐ

trek [trek] n (long difficult journey: on foot) 徒歩旅行 tohǒryokǒ; (: by car) 自動車旅行 jidǒsharyokǒ; (tiring walk) 苦しい道のり kurǔshiǐ michǐnori

trellis [trel'is] n (for climbing plants) 棚 tanǎ

tremble [trem'bəl] vi (voice, body, trees: with fear, cold etc) 震える furǔerǔ; (ground) 揺れる yurěrǔ

tremendous [trimen'dəs] adj (enormous: amount etc) ばく大な bakúdai na; (excellent: success, holiday, view etc) 素晴らしい subárashiǐ

tremor [trem'ər] n (trembling: of excitement, fear: in voice) 震え furǔě; (also: **earth tremor**) 地震 jishín

trench [trentʃ] n (channel) 溝 mizǒ; (for defense) ざんごう zañgoǔ

trend [trend] n (tendency) 傾向 keǐkǒ; (of events) 動向 dǒkō; (fashion) トレンド torěndo

trendy [tren'di:] adj (idea, person, clothes) トレンディな torěndi na

trepidation [trepidei'ʃən] n (apprehension) 不安 fuán

trespass [tres'pæs] vi: **to trespass on** (private property) ...に不法侵入する ...ni fuhǒshiñnyū suru
「**no trespassing**」立入禁止 tachǐirikiñshi

trestle [tres'əl] n (support for table etc) うま umǎ

trial [trail] n (LAW) 裁判 saǐban; (test: of machine etc) テスト tésùto
on trial (LAW) 裁判に掛けられて saǐban ni kakěrareté
by trial and error 試行錯誤で shikǒsakùgo de

trial period n テスト期間 tesúto kikàn

trials [trailz] npl (unpleasant experiences) 試練 shǐrèn

triangle [trai'æŋgəl] n (MATH) 三角 sáñkaku; (MUS) トライアングル toráiañguru

triangular [traiæŋ'gjələr] adj 三角形の sañkakkèi no

tribal [trai'bəl] adj (warrior, warfare, dance) 種族の shúzòku no

tribe [traib] n 種族 shúzòku

tribesman [traibz'mən] (pl **tribesmen**) n 種族の男性 shúzòku no dañsei

tribulations [tribjəlei'ʃənz] npl 苦労 kúrǒ, 苦難 kúnàn

tribunal [traibju:'nəl] n 審判委員会 shiñpan iíñkai

tributary [trib'jəteːri:] n 支流 shiryǔ

tribute [trib'ju:t] n (compliment) ほめの言葉 homě no kotobà
to pay tribute to ...をほめる ...wò homěrù

trice [trais] n: **in a trice** あっという間に áttò iú ma nǐ

trick [trik] n (magic trick) 手品 tějìna; (prank, joke) いたずら itázura; (skill, knack) こつ kotsú; (CARDS) トリック toríkkù
♦vt (deceive) だます damásù
to play a trick on someone ...にいたずらをする ...ni itázura wò suru
that should do the trick これでいいはずだ korě de iǐ hazú dà

trickery [trik'əːriː] n 計略 keíryaku

trickle [trik'əl] n (of water etc) 滴り shitátari
♦vi (water, rain etc) 滴る shitátarù

tricky [trik'iː] adj (job, problem, business) 厄介な yákkài na

tricycle [trai'sikəl] n 三輪車 sañriñsha

trifle [trai'fəl] n (small detail) ささいな事 sásài na kotǒ; (CULIN) トライフル toráìfuru ◊カステラにゼリー、フルーツ、プリンなどのせたデザート kasútera nǐ zěrǐ, furǔtsù, púrìn nádò wo nosětà dezátò
♦adv: **a trifle long** ちょっと長い chóttò nagáì

trifling [traif'liŋ] adj (detail, matter) ささいな sásài na

trigger [trig'əːr] n (of gun) 引金 hikǐ-

gane

trigger off vt (reaction, riot) ...の引金となる ...no hikígane to nárù

trigonometry [trigənɑːˈmɛtriː] n 三角法 sankakuhō

trill [tril] vi (birds) さえずる saézurù

trim [trim] adj (house, garden) 手入れの行届いた teíre nò ikítodoità; (figure) すらっとした suráttò shitá

♦n (haircut etc) 刈る事 karú kotò; (on car) 飾り kazári

♦vt (cut: hair, beard) 刈る karú; (decorate): to trim (with) (...で) 飾る (...de) kazárù; (NAUT: a sail) 調節する chōsetsu suru

trimmings [ˈtrimiŋz] npl (CULIN) お決りの付け合せ o-kímàri no tsukéawase

trinket [ˈtriŋkit] n (ornament) 安い置物 yasúî okímono; (piece of jewellery) 安い装身具 yasúî sōshìngu

trio [ˈtriːou] n (gen) 三つ組 mitsúgumi; (MUS) トリオ tōrìo

trip [trip] n (journey) 旅行 ryokō; (outing) 遠足 ensoku; (stumble) つまずき tsumázuki

♦vi (stumble) つまずく tsumázukù; (go lightly) 軽快に歩く keíkai nì arúkù

on a trip 旅行中で ryokōchū de

tripe [traip] n (CULIN) トライプ toráîpu ◇ウシ、ブタなどの胃の料理 ushí, butá nadò no i no ryōri; (pej: rubbish) 下らない物 kudaranai mono ◇特に人の発言や文書について言う tōkù ni hitó nò hatsúgen yà búnsho ni tsúîte iú

triple [ˈtripəl] adj (ice cream, somersault etc) トリプルの torípùru no

triplets [ˈtriplits] npl 三つ子 mitsúgo

triplicate [ˈtripləkit] n: in triplicate 三通で santsū de

tripod [ˈtraipɑːd] n 三脚 sankyaku

trip up vi (stumble) つまずく tsumázukù

♦vt (person) つまずかせる tsumázukaserù

trite [trait] adj 陳腐な chínpu na

triumph [ˈtraiəmf] n (satisfaction) 大満足 daímanzoku; (great achievement) 輝かしい勝利 kagáyakashiî shōrì

♦vi: to triumph (over) (...に) 打勝つ (...ni) uchíkatsù

triumphant [traiˈʌmfənt] adj (team, wave, return) 意気揚々とした íkîyōyō to shitá

trivia [ˈtriviːə] npl 詰まらない事 tsumáranai kotò

trivial [ˈtriviːəl] adj (unimportant) 詰まらない tsumáranaî; (commonplace) 平凡な heíbon na

trod [trɑːd] pt of tread

trodden [ˈtrɑːdən] pp of tread

trolley [ˈtrɑːliː] n (for luggage, shopping, also in supermarkets) 手車 tegúruma; (table on wheels) ワゴン wágòn; (also: trolley bus) トロリーバス torōrîbasu

trombone [trɑːmˈboun] n トロンボーン toronbōn

troop [truːp] n (of people, monkeys etc) 群れ muré

troop in/out vi ぞろぞろと入って来る (出て行く) zórðzoro to haítte kurù (détè iku)

trooping the color [ˈtruːpiŋ-] (BRIT) n (ceremony) 軍旗敬礼の分列行進 kunkikeírei no bunretsu kōshin

troops [truːps] npl (MIL) 兵隊 heítai

trophy [ˈtroufiː] n トロフィー tōrðfî

tropic [ˈtrɑːpik] n 回帰線 kaíkisen

the tropics 熱帯地方 nettái chihō

tropical [ˈtrɑːpikəl] adj (rain forest etc) 熱帯 (地方) の nettái(chihō) no

trot [trɑːt] n (fast pace) 小走り kobáshîri; (of horse) 速足 hayáàshi, トロット torôttò

♦vi (horse) トロットで駆ける torôttò de kakérù; (person) 小走りで行く kobáshîri de ikú

on the trot (BRIT: fig) 立続けに tatétsuzuke ni

trouble [ˈtrʌbəl] n (difficulty) 困難 konnan; (worry) 心配 shinpai; (bother, effort) 苦労 kúrò; (unrest) トラブル toráburù; (MED): heart etc trouble ...病 ...byō

♦vt (worry) ...に心配を掛ける ...ni shinpai wò kakérù; (person: disturb) 面倒をかける meído wo kakérù

♦*vi*: *to trouble to do something* わざ わざ...する wázawaza ...suru

to be in trouble (gen) 困っている ko-mátte irù; (ship, climber etc) 危険にあっ ている kikén ni atte irù

it's no trouble! 迷惑ではありませんか ら meíwaku de wa arímàsen kará

what's the trouble? (with broken tele-vision etc) どうなっていますか dô natté imasù ká; (doctor to patient) いかがです か ikága desù ká

troubled [trʌ́b'əld] *adj* (person, country, life, era) 不安な fuáñ na

troublemaker [trʌ́b'əlmeikə:r] *n* トラブ ルを起す常習犯 toráburu wo okósù jó-shūhaǹ; (child) 問題児 moñdaìji

troubles [trʌ́b'əlz] *npl* (personal, POL etc) 問題 moñdai

troubleshooter [trʌ́b'əlʃu:tə:r] *n* (in con-flict) 調停人 chôteiniǹ

troublesome [trʌ́b'əlsəm] *adj* (child, cough etc) 厄介な yákkài na

trough [trɔːf] *n* (*also*: **drinking trough**) 水入れ mizúirè; (feeding trough) えさ入 れ esá-irè; (depression) 谷間 taníma

troupe [tru:p] *n* (of actors, singers, dancers) 団 dáñ

trousers [trau'zə:rz] *npl* ズボン zubóñ

short trousers 半ズボン hañzubòn

trousseau [tru:'sou] (*pl* **trousseaux** *or* **trousseaus**) *n* 嫁入り道具 yomé-iri dògu

trout [traut] *n inv* マス masu

trowel [trau'əl] *n* (garden tool) 移植ごて ishókugòte; (builder's tool) こて koté

truant [tru:'ənt] (*BRIT*) *n*: *to play tru-ant* 学校をサボる gakkô wo sabórù

truce [tru:s] *n* 休戦 kyūsen

truck [trʌk] *n* (*US*) トラック torákkù; (*RAIL*) 台車 daíshà

truck driver *n* トラック運転手 torákku unteñshu

truck farm (*US*) *n* 野菜農園 yasáinòen

trudge [trʌdʒ] *vi* (*also*: **trudge along**) と ぼとぼ歩く tóbòtobo arúkù

true [tru:] *adj* (real: motive) 本当の hoñtô no; (accurate: likeness) 正確な seíkaku na; (genuine: love) 本物の hoñmono no; (faithful: friend) 忠実な chûjitsu na

to come true (dreams, predictions) 実現 される jitsúgen sarerù

truffle [trʌ́f'əl] *n* (fungus) トリュフ tó-ryùfu; (sweet) トラッフル toráffùru ◇菓 子の一種 káshì no ísshù

truly [tru:'li:] *adv* (really) 本当に hoñtô ni; (truthfully) 真実に shíñjitsu ni; (faith-fully): *yours truly* (in letter) 敬具 keígu

trump [trʌmp] *n* (*also*: **trump card**: *also fig*) 切札 kirífùda

trumped-up [trʌmpt'ʌp'] *adj* (charge, pretext) でっち上げた detchíagetà

trumpet [trʌm'pit] *n* トランペット toráñ-petto

truncheon [trʌn'tʃən] *n* 警棒 keíbō

trundle [trʌn'dəl] *vt* (push chair etc) ご ろごろ動かす górògoro ugókasù

♦*vi*: *to trundle along* (vehicle) 重そう に動く omósò ni ugókù; (person) ゆっく り行く yukkûrí ikú

trunk [trʌŋk] *n* (of tree, person) 幹 míkì; (of person) 胴 dô; (of elephant) 鼻 haná; (case) トランク toráñku; (*US*: AUT) ト ランク toráñku

trunks [trʌŋks] *npl* (*also*: **swimming trunks**) 水泳パンツ suíei paǹtsu

truss [trʌs] *n* (MED) ヘルニアバンド he-rúnia baǹdo

truss (up) *vt* (CULIN) 縛る shibárù

trust [trʌst] *n* (faith) 信用 shíñ-yō; (responsibility) 責任 sekínin; (LAW) 信 託 shiñtaku

♦*vt* (rely on, have faith in) 信用する shíñ-yō suru; (hope) きっと...だろうね kittô ...dárô né; (entrust): *to trust something to someone* ...を...に任せる ...wo ...ni makáserù

to take something on trust (advice, information) 証拠なしで...を信じる shô-ko nashî de ...wo shiñjirù

trusted [trʌs'tid] *adj* (friend, servant) 信 用された shiñ-yō saretà

trustee [trʌsti:'] *n* (LAW) 受託者 jutáku-shà; (of school etc) 理事 ríji

trustful/trusting [trʌst'fəl/trʌs'tiŋ] *adj* (person, nature, smile) 信用する shiñ-yō suru

trustworthy [trʌst'wə:rði:] *adj* (person,

report) 信用できる shíń-yō dekirù

truth [tru:θ] *n* (true fact) 真実 shíñjitsu; (universal principle) 真理 shíñri

truthful [tru:θˈfəl] *adj* (person, answer) 正直な shōjìki na

try [trai] *n* (attempt) 努力 dóryòku; (RUGBY) トライ torái

♦*vt* (attempt) やってみる yatté mirù; (test: something new: *also*: **try out**) 試す tamésù; (LAW: person) 裁判にかける sáiban ni kakérù; (strain: patience) ぎりぎりまで追込む girígiri madè oíkomù

♦*vi* (make effort, attempt) 努力する dóryòku suru

to have a try やってみる yatté mirù

to try to do something (seek) ...をしようとうする ...wo shíyō to suru

trying [traiˈiŋ] *adj* (person) 気難しい kimúzukashiì; (experience) 苦しい kurúshiì

try on *vt* (dress, hat, shoes) 試着する shicháku suru

tsar [zɑːr] *n* ロシア皇帝 roshía kōtei

T-shirt [tiːˈʃəːrt] *n* Tシャツ tíshatsu

T-square [tiːˈskwəːr] *n* T定規 tíjōgi

tub [tʌb] *n* (container: shallow) たらい tarái; (: deeper) おけ ókè; (bath) 湯舟 yúbùne

tuba [tuːˈbə] *n* チューバ chūba

tubby [tʌbˈiː] *adj* 太った futóttà

tube [tuːb] *n* (pipe) 管 kúdà; (container, in tire) チューブ chūbu; (BRIT: underground) 地下鉄 chikátetsu

tuberculosis [tuːbəːrkjəlouˈsis] *n* 結核 kekkáku

tube station (BRIT) *n* 地下鉄の駅 chikátetsu nò ékì

tubular [tuːˈbjələːr] *adj* (furniture, metal) 管状の kañjō no; (furniture) パイプ製の paípusei no

TUC [tiːjuːsiːˈ] *n abbr* (BRIT: = Trades Union Congress) 英国労働組合会議 eíkoku rōdōkumiai kaígi

tuck [tʌk] *vt* (put) 押込む oshíkomù

tuck away *vt* (money) 仕舞い込む shimáikomù; (building): *to be tucked away* 隠れている kakúrete irù

tuck in *vt* (clothing) 押込む oshíkomù;

(child) 毛布にくるんで寝かせる mốfù ni kurúnde nekáserù

tuck shop (BRIT) *n* 売店 baíten ◇学校内でお菓子などを売る売店を指す gakkố-naì de o-káshi nadò wo urú baíten wò sásù

tuck up *vt* (invalid, child) 毛布にくるんで寝かせる mốfù ni kurúñde nekáserù

Tuesday [tuːzˈdei] *n* 火曜日 kayốbì

tuft [tʌft] *n* (of hair, grass etc) 一房 hitófùsa

tug [tʌg] *n* (ship) タグボート tagúbòto

♦*vt* 引っ張る hippárù

tug-of-war [tagˈəvwɔːrˈ] *n* (SPORT) 綱引き tsunáhiki; (fig) 競り合い seríaì ◇二者間の競り合いを指す nishákàn no seríaì wo sásù

tuition [tuːiʃˈən] *n* (BRIT) 教授 kyốju; (: private tuition) 個人教授 kojíñkyòju; (US: school fees) 授業料 jugyốryò

tulip [tuːˈlip] *n* チューリップ chūrippu

tumble [tʌmˈbəl] *n* (fall) 転ぶ事 koróbu kotò

♦*vi* (fall: person) 転ぶ koróbù; (water) 落ちる ochírù

to tumble to something (inf) ...に気が付く ...ni ki gá tsukù

tumbledown [tʌmˈbəldaun] *adj* (building) 荒れ果てた aréhatetà

tumble dryer (BRIT) *n* 乾燥機 kañsòki

tumbler [tʌmˈbləːr] *n* (glass) コップ koppú

tummy [tʌmˈiː] (inf) *n* (belly, stomach) おなか onákà

tumor [tuːˈməːr] (BRIT **tumour**) *n* しゅよう shuyố

tumult [tuːˈməlt] *n* 大騒ぎ ốsawàgi

tumultuous [tuːmʌlˈtʃuːəs] *adj* (welcome, applause etc) にぎやかな nigíyàka na

tuna [tuːˈnə] *n inv* (also: **tuna fish**) マグロ maguro; (in can, sandwich) ツナ tsúnà

tune [tuːn] *n* (melody) 旋律 señritsu

♦*vt* (MUS) 調律する chốritsu suru; (RADIO, TV) 合せる awáserù; (AUT) チューンアップする chūn-appù suru

to be in/out of tune (instrument, singer)

調子が合って〔外れて〕いる chōshi gà atte 〔hazúrete〕irù

to be in/out of tune with (fig) ...と気が合っている〔いない〕 ...to ki ga atte irù 〔inái〕

tuneful [tuːnˈfəl] adj (music) 旋律のきれいな seńritsu nò kírèi na

tuner [tuːˈnəːr] n: **piano tuner** 調律師 chōritsushì

tune in vi (RADIO, TV): **to tune in (to)** (...を) 聞く (...wo) kikú

tune up vi (musician, orchestra) 調子を合せる chōshi wò awáserù

tunic [tuːˈnik] n チュニック chuníkkù

Tunisia [tuːniːˈʒə] n チュニジア chuníjìa

tunnel [tʌnˈəl] n (passage) トンネル tońneru; (in mine) 坑道 kódō
♦vi トンネルを掘る tońneru wo hórù

turban [təːrˈbən] n ターバン tábàn

turbine [təːrˈbain] n タービン tábìn

turbulence [təːrˈbjələns] n (AVIAT) 乱気流 rańkiryū

turbulent [təːrˈbjələnt] adj (water) 荒れ狂う arékuruù; (fig: career) 起伏の多い kífùku no ōî

tureen [tariːnˈ] n スープ鉢 sūpubàchi, チューリン chúrìn

turf [təːrf] n (grass) 芝生 shibáfu; (clod) 芝土 shibátsuchi
♦vt (area) 芝生を敷く shibáfu wò shikú

turf out (inf) vt (person) 追出す oídasù

turgid [təːrˈdʒid] adj (speech) 仰々しい gyōgyōshiì

Turk [təːrk] n トルコ人 torúkojìn

Turkey [təːrˈkiː] n トルコ tórùko

turkey [təːrˈkiː] n (bird, meat) 七面鳥 shichímenchò, ターキー tákì

Turkish [təːrˈkiʃ] adj トルコの tórùko no; (LING) トルコ語の torúkogò no
♦n (LING) トルコ語 torúkogò

Turkish bath n トルコ風呂 torúkobùro

turmoil [təːrˈmoil] n 混乱 kóńran

in turmoil 混乱して kóńran shitè

turn [təːrn] n (change) 変化 hêńka; (in road) カーブ kábu; (tendency: of mind, events) 傾向 keíkō; (performance) 出し物 dashímòno; (chance) 番 báń; (MED) 発作 hossá

♦vt (handle, key) 回す mawásù; (collar, page) めくる mekúrù; (steak) 裏返す urágaesù; (change): **to turn something into** ...を...に変える ...wo ...ni kaérù

♦vi (object) 回る mawárù; (person: look back) 振向く furímukù; (reverse direction: in car) Uターンする yútàn suru; (: wind) 向きが変る múkì ga kawárù; (milk) 悪くなる wárùku nárù; (become) なる nárù

a good turn 親切 shíñsetsu

it gave me quite a turn ああ, 怖かった, kowákattà

「**no left turn**」 (AUT) 左折禁止 sasétsukiñshi

it's your turn あなたの番です anáta nò báñ desu

in turn 次々と tsugítsugi tò

to take turns (at) 交替で (...を) する kótai dè (...wo) suru

turn away vi 顔をそむける kaó wò somúkerù
♦vt (applicants) 門前払いする mońzenbarài suru

turn back vi 引返す hikíkaesù
♦vt (person, vehicle) 引返させる hikíkaesaserù; (clock) 遅らせる okúraserù

turn down vt (refuse: request) 断る kotówarù; (reduce: heating) 弱くする yówàku suru; (fold: bedclothes) 折返す oríkaesù

turn in vi (inf: go to bed) 寝る nerú
♦vt (fold) 折込む oríkomù

turning [təːrˈniŋ] n (in road) 曲り角 magárikadò

turning point n (fig) 変り目 kawárimè

turnip [təːrˈnip] n カブ kábù

turn off vi (from road) 横道に入る yokómichi nì háìru
♦vt (light, radio etc) 消す kesú; (tap) ...の水を止める ...no mizú wò tomérù; (engine) 止める tomérù

turn on vt (light, radio etc) つける tsukérù; (tap) ...の水を出す ...no mizú wò dásù; (engine) かける kakérù

turn out vt (light, gas) 消す kesú; (produce) 作る tsukúrù
♦vi (voters) 出る dérù

to turn out to be (prove to be) 結局...で あると分かる kekkyóku ...de árù to wakaru

turnout [təːrnˈaut] *n* (of voters etc) 人出 hitódè

turn over *vi* (person) 寝返りを打つ negáeri wò utsù

♦*vt* (object) 引っ繰り返す hikkúrikaesu; (page) めくる mekúrù

turnover [təːrnˈouvəːr] *n* (COMM: amount of money) 売上高 uríagedàka; (: of goods) 回転率 kaíteñritsu; (: of staff) 異動率 idóritsu

turnpike [təːrnˈpaik] (*US*) *n* 有料道路 yúryōdòro

turn round *vi* (person) 振り向く furímukù; (vehicle) Uターンする yútàn suru; (rotate) 回転する kaíten suru

turnstile [təːrnˈstail] *n* ターンスタイル tánsutaìru

turntable [təːrnˈteibəl] *n* (on record player) ターンテーブル tántèburu

turn up *vi* (person) 現れる aráwarerù; (lost object) 見付かる mitsúkarù

♦*vt* (collar) 立てる tatérù; (radio, stereo etc) ...のボリュームを上げる ...no boryúmu wò agérù; (heater) 強くする tsúyòku suru

turn-up [təːrnˈʌp] (*BRIT*) *n* (on trousers) 折返し oríkaeshi

turpentine [təːrˈpəntain] *n* (*also*: **turps**) テレピン油 te-rébiñ-yu

turquoise [təːrˈkɔiz] *n* (stone) トルコ石 torúkoìshi

♦*adj* (color) 青みどりの aómidòri no

turret [təːrˈit] *n* (on building) 小塔 shótō; (on tank) 旋回砲塔 señkaihòtō

turtle [təːrˈtəl] *n* カメ kámè

turtleneck (sweater) [təːrˈtəlnek-] *n* タートルネック tátorunekkù

tusk [tʌsk] *n* きば kíbà

tussle [tʌsˈəl] *n* (fight, scuffle) 取っ組み 合い tokkúmiài

tutor [tuːˈtəːr] *n* (SCOL) チューター chūtā; (private tutor) 家庭教師 katéikyòshi

tutorial [tuːtɔːrˈiːəl] *n* (SCOL) 討論授業 tóronjugyò

tuxedo [tʌksiːˈdou] (*US*) *n* タキシード ta-

kíshìdo

TV [tiːviː] *n abbr* = **television**

twang [twæŋ] *n* (of instrument) びゅん という音 byún to iú otò; (of voice) 鼻声 hanágoè

tweed [twiːd] *n* ツィード tsuídò

tweezers [twiːˈzəːrz] *npl* ピンセット píñsetto

twelfth [twelfθ] *num* 第十二の dái júni no

twelve [twelv] *num* 十二 (の) júni (no)

at twelve (o'clock) (midday) 正午に shógò ni; (midnight) 零時に reiji ni

twentieth [twenˈtiːiθ] *num* 第二十の dái níjù no

twenty [twenˈtiː] *num* 二十 (の) níjù (no)

twice [twais] *adv* 2回 nikái

twice as much ...の二倍 ...no nibái

twiddle [twidˈəl] *vt* いじくる ijíkurù

♦*vi*: *to twiddle (with) something* ...を いじくる ...wo ijíkurù

to twiddle one's thumbs (*fig*) 手をこま ねく té wò kománeku

twig [twig] *n* 小枝 koéda

♦*vi* (*inf*: realize) 気が付く ki gá tsukù

twilight [twaiˈlait] *n* 夕暮 yúgure

twin [twin] *adj* (sister, brother) 双子の futágo no; (towers, beds etc) 対の tsuí no, ツインの tsuíñ no

♦*n* 双子の一人 futágo nò hitórì

♦*vt* (towns etc) 姉妹都市にする shimáitoshi ni suru

twin-bedded room [twinˈbedid-] *n* ツイ ンルーム tsuínrùmu

twine [twain] *n* ひも himó

♦*vi* (plant) 巻付く makítsukù

twinge [twindʒ] *n* (of pain) うずき uzúki; (of conscience) かしゃく kashÁku; (of regret) 苦しみ kurúshimì

twinkle [twiŋˈkəl] *vi* (star, light, eyes) き らめく kirámekù

twirl [twəːrl] *vt* くるくる回す kúrùkuru mawásù

♦*vi* くるくる回る kúrùkuru mawárù

twist [twist] *n* (action) ひねり hinéri; (in road, coil, flex) 曲り magári; (in story) ひねり hinéri

◆*vt* (turn) ひねる hinérù; (injure: ankle etc) ねんざする neñza suru; (weave) より合さる yoríawasarù; (roll around) 巻付ける makítsukerù; (*fig*: meaning, words) 曲げる magérù

◆*vi* (road, river) 曲りくねる magáriku-nerù

twit [twit] (*inf*) *n* ばか bákà

twitch [twitʃ] *n* (pull) ぐいと引く事 guí tò hikú kotò; (nervous) 引きつり hikítsuri

◆*vi* (muscle, body) 引きつる hikítsurù

two [tu:] *num* 二（の）ní (no), 二つ（の）futátsù (no)

to put two and two together (*fig*) あれこれを総合してなぞを解く arékòre wo sōgō shitè nazó wò tókù

two-door [tu:'dɔ:r] *adj* (AUT) ツードアの tsúdoa no

two-faced [tu:'feist] (*pej*) *adj* (person) 二枚舌の nimáïjita no

twofold [tu:'fould] *adv*: *to increase twofold* 倍になる bai ni narù

two-piece (suit) [tu:'pi:s-] *n* ツーピースの服 tsúpìsu no fukú

two-piece (swimsuit) *n* ツーピースの水着 tsúpìsu no mizúgi

twosome [tu:'səm] *n* (people) 二人組 futárigùmi

two-way [tu:'wei'] *adj*: *two-way traffic* 両方向交通 ryóhōkōkōtsū

tycoon [taiku:n'] *n*: *(business) tycoon* 大物実業家 ómonojitsugyōka

type [taip] *n* (category, model, example) 種類 shúrùi; (TYP) 活字 katsúji

◆*vt* (letter etc) タイプする táïpu suru

type-cast [taip'kæst] *adj* (actor) はまり役の hamáriyaku no

typeface [taip'feis] *n* 書体 shotái

typescript [taip'skript] *n* タイプライターで打った原稿 taípuraìta de úttà geñkō

typewriter [taip'raitəːr] *n* タイプライター taípuraìta

typewritten [taip'ritən] *adj* タイプライターで打った taípuraìta de úttà

typhoid [tai'fɔid] *n* 腸チフス chóchifùsu

typhoon [taifu:n'] *n* 台風 taífù

typical [tip'ikəl] *adj* 典型的な teñkeiteki na

typify [tip'əfai] *vt* ...の典型的な例である ...no teñkeiteki nà reí de arù

typing [tai'piŋ] *n* タイプライターを打つ事 taípuraìta wo útsù kotó

typist [tai'pist] *n* タイピスト taípisùto

tyranny [tiːr'əni:] *n* 暴政 bōsei

tyrant [tai'rənt] *n* 暴君 bōkun

tyre [taiəːr] (*BRIT*) *n* = **tire**

tzar [zɑːr] *n* = **tsar**

U

U-bend [ju:'bend] *n* (in pipe) トラップ toráppù

ubiquitous [ju:bik'witəs] *adj* いたる所にある itáru tokoro nì aru

udder [ʌd'əːr] *n* 乳房 chibùsa ◇ ウシ、ヤギなどについて言う ushí, yagí nado ni tsuite iú

UFO [ju:efou'] *n abbr* (= *unidentified flying object*) 未確認飛行物体 mikákunin hikōbuttài, ユーフォー yūfō

Uganda [ju:gæn'də] *n* ウガンダ ugáñda

ugh [ʌ] *excl* おえっ oét

ugliness [ʌg'liːnis] *n* 醜さ miníkusà

ugly [ʌg'li:] *adj* (person, dress etc) 醜い miníkuî; (dangerous: situation) 物騒な bussō nà

UK [ju:'kei'] *n abbr* = **United Kingdom**

ulcer [ʌl'səːr] *n* かいよう kaíyō

Ulster [ʌl'stəːr] *n* アルスター arùsutá

ulterior [ʌltiːr'i:əːr] *adj*: *ulterior motive* 下心 shitágokòro

ultimate [ʌl'təmit] *adj* (final: aim, destination, result) 最後の saígo no; (greatest: insult, deterrent, authority) 最大の saídai no

ultimately [ʌl'təmitli:] *adv* (in the end) やがて yagáte; (basically) 根本的に koñponteki ni

ultimatum [ʌltimei'təm] *n* 最後通ちょう saígotsùchō

ultrasound [ʌl'trəsaund] *n* (MED) 超音波 chóònpa

ultraviolet [ʌltrəvai'əlit] *adj* (rays, light) 紫外線の shigáisen no

umbilical cord [ʌmbil'ikəl-] *n* へその緒 hesó no o

umbrella [ʌmbrel'ə] *n* (for rain) 傘 kasà, 雨傘 ámágasà; (for sun) 日傘 higása, パラソル paràsoru

umpire [ʌm'paiə:r] *n* (TENNIS, CRICKET) 審判 shinpan, アンパイア añpaìa

◆*vt* (game) ...のアンパイアをする ...no añpaìa wo suru

umpteen [ʌmp'ti:n] *adj* うんと沢山の uñto takusan no

umpteenth [ʌmp'ti:nθ] *adj*: *for the umpteenth time* 何回目か分からないが nañkaime kà wakáranài ga

UN [ju:'en'] *n abbr* = **United Nations**

unable [ʌnei'bəl] *adj*: *to be unable to do something* ...する事ができない ...surú koto gà dekínai

unaccompanied [ʌnəkʌm'pəni:d] *adj* (child, woman) 同伴者のいない dóhañsha ni inai; (luggage) 別送の bessó no; (song) 無伴奏の mubáñsō no

unaccountably [ʌnəkaunt'əbli:] *adv* 妙に myó ní

unaccustomed [ʌnəkʌs'təmd] *adj*: *to be unaccustomed to* (public speaking, Western clothes etc) ...になれていない ...ni naréte inai

unanimous [ju:næn'əməs] *adj* (vote) 満場一致の mañjóitchi no; (people) 全員同意の zeñ-indòi no

unanimously [ju:næn'əməsli:] *adv* (vote) 満場一致で mañjóitchi de

unarmed [ʌnɑ:rmd'] *adj* 武器を持たない búkì wo motánaì, 丸腰の marúgoshi no *unarmed combat* 武器を使わない武術 búkì wo tsukáwanaì bújutsu

unashamed [ʌnəʃeimd'] *adj* (greed) 恥知らずの hajíshiràzu no; (pleasure) 人目をはばからない hitóme wo habákaranaì

unassuming [ʌnəsu:'miŋ] *adj* (person, manner) 気取らない kidóranai

unattached [ʌnətætʃt'] *adj* (person) 独身の dokúshin no; (part etc) 遊んでいる a-sónde iru

unattended [ʌnəten'did] *adj* (car, luggage, child) ほったらかしの hottáraka-

shi no

unattractive [ʌnətræk'tiv] *adj* (person, character) いやな iyá na; (building, appearance, idea) 魅力のない miryóku no nai

unauthorized [ʌnɔ:θ'ə:raizd] *adj* (visit, use, version) 無許可の mukyókà no

unavoidable [ʌnəvɔi'dəbəl] *adj* (delay) 避けられない sakérarenaì

unaware [ʌnəwe:r'] *adj*: *to be unaware of* ...に気が付いていない ...ni ki gá tsuìte inai

unawares [ʌnəwe:rz'] *adv* (catch, take) 不意に fuì ni

unbalanced [ʌnbæl'ənst] *adj* (report) 偏った katáyottà; (mentally) 狂った kurúttà

unbearable [ʌnbe:r'əbəl] *adj* (heat, pain) 耐えられない taérarenaì; (person) 我慢できない程いやな gamàn dekínai hodo iyá na

unbeatable [ʌnbi:'təbəl] *adj* (team) 無敵の mutéki no; (quality) 最高の saíkō no; (price) 最高に安い saíkō ni yasúì

unbeknown(st) [ʌnbinoun(st)'] *adv*: *unbeknown(st) to me/Peter* 私(ピーター)に気付かれずに watákushi(pītā)ni kizúkarezù ni

unbelievable [ʌnbili:'vəbəl] *adj* 信じられない shiñjirarenaì

unbend [ʌnbend'] (*pt, pp* **bent**) *vi* (relax) くつろぐ kutsúrogù

◆*vt* (wire) 真っ直ぐにする massúgù ni suru

unbiased [ʌnbai'əst] *adj* (person, report) 公正な kóseì na

unborn [ʌnbɔ:rn'] *adj* (child, young) おなかの中の onáka no nakà no

unbreakable [ʌnbrei'kəbəl] *adj* (glassware, crockery etc) 割れない warénaì; (other objects) 壊れない kowárenaì

unbroken [ʌnbrou'kən] *adj* (seal) 開けてない akéte naì; (silence, series) 続く tsuzúku; (record) 破られていない yabúrarète inai; (spirit) くじけない kujíkenaì

unbutton [ʌnbʌt'ən] *vt* ...のボタンを外す ...no botán wo hazúsu

uncalled-for [ʌnkɔ:ld'fɔ:r] *adj* (remark)

余計な yokéi na; (rudeness etc) いわれの
ない iwáre no nai

uncanny [ʌnkǽnɪ:] adj (silence, resemblance, knack) 不気味な bukími na

unceasing [ʌnsíːsɪŋ] adj 引っ切り無しの
hikkírinashì no

unceremonious [ʌnseːrəmouˈniːəs] adj
(abrupt, rude) ぶしつけな bushítsuke na

uncertain [ʌnsəːrˈtən] adj (hesitant:
voice, steps) 自信のない jishín no nai;
(unsure) 不確実な fukákùjitsu na

uncertainty [ʌnsəːrˈtənti:] n (not knowing) 不確実さ fukákùjitsusa; (also pl:
doubts) 疑問 gimón

unchanged [ʌntʃéindʒd'] adj (condition)
変っていない kawátte inai

unchecked [ʌntʃékt'] adv (grow, continue) 無制限に muséigen ni

uncivilized [ʌnsívˈilaizd] adj (gen: country, people) 未開の mikái no; (fig: behavior, hour etc) 野蛮な yabán na

uncle [ʌŋˈkəl] n おじ ojí

uncomfortable [ʌnkʌ́mfˈtəbəl] adj (physically, also furniture) 使い心地の悪い
tsukáigokochi no warúî; (uneasy) 不安な
fuán na; (unpleasant: situation, fact) 厄
介な yakkài na

uncommon [ʌnkɑːmˈən] adj (rare, unusual) 珍しい mezúrashiî

uncompromising [ʌnkɑːmˈprəmaiziŋ]
adj (person, belief) 融通の利かない yúzu
no kikánai

unconcerned [ʌnkənsəːrnd'] adj (indifferent) 関心がない kañshin ga naí; (not
worried) 平気な heíki na

unconditional [ʌnkəndiʃˈənəl] adj 無条
件の mujókèn no

unconscious [ʌnkɑːnˈtʃəs] adj (in faint,
also MED) 意識不明の ishíkifumei no;
(unaware): **unconscious of** ...に気が付
かない ...ni kí ga tsukanaî

◆n: **the unconscious** 潜在意識 señzai-
shìki

unconsciously [ʌnkɑːnˈtʃəsli:] adv (unawares) 無意識に muíshiki ni

uncontrollable [ʌnkəntrouˈləbəl] adj
(child, animal) 手に負えない te nî oénai;
(temper) 抑制のきかない yokúsei no ki-

kánai; (laughter) やめられない yaméra-
renái

unconventional [ʌnkənvenˈtʃənəl] adj
型破りの katáyabùri no

uncouth [ʌnkuːθ'] adj 無様な buzáma na

uncover [ʌnkʌˈəːr] vt (take lid, veil etc
off) ...の覆いを取る ...no ōí wo torú;
(plot, secret) 発見する hakkén suru

undecided [ʌndisaiˈdid] adj (person) 決定
していない kettéi shite inai; (question)
未決定の mikettéi no

undeniable [ʌndinaiˈəbəl] adj (fact, evidence) 否定できない hitéi dekínai

under [ʌnˈdəːr] prep (beneath) ...の下に
...no shitá ni; (in age, price: less than)
...以下に ...ikà ni; (according to: law,
agreement etc) ...によって ...ni yottè;
(someone's leadership) ...のもとに ...no
motô ni

◆adv (go, fly etc) ...の下に〔で〕...no shitá
ni(de)

under there あそこの下に〔で〕asóko
no shitá ni(de)

under repair 修理中 shūríchū

under... prefix 下の... shitá no...

under-age [ʌndəːreidʒ'] adj (person,
drinking) 未成年の miséinen no

undercarriage [ʌndəːrkæˈridʒ] (BRIT)
n (AVIAT) 着陸装置 chakúrikusochi

undercharge [ʌnˈdəːrtʃɑːrdʒ] vt ...から正
当な料金を取らない ...kara séitō na ryō-
kìn wo toránai

underclothes [ʌnˈdəːrklouz] npl 下着
shitági

undercoat [ʌnˈdəːrkout] n (paint) 下塗り
shitánuri

undercover [ʌndəːrkʌˈvəːr] adj (work,
agent) 秘密の himítsu no

undercurrent [ʌnˈdəːrkəˈrənt] n (fig: of
feeling) 底流 teíryū

undercut [ʌnˈdəːrkʌt] (pt, pp **undercut**)
vt (person, prices) ...より低い値段で物を
売る ...yorí hikúî nedán de monô wo urú

underdog [ʌnˈdəːrdɔg] n 弱者 jakùsha

underdone [ʌnˈdəːrdʌn'] adj (CULIN) 生
焼けの namáyake no

underestimate [ʌndəːresˈtəmeit] vt
(person, thing) 見くびる mikúbiru

underexposed [ʌndə:rikspouzd'] *adj* (PHOT) 露出不足の roshútsubusoku no

underfed [ʌndə:rfed'] *adj* (person, animal) 栄養不足の efyōbusòku no

underfoot [ʌndə:rfut'] *adv* (crush, trample) 脚の下に〔で〕ashí no shitá ni(de)

undergo [ʌndə:rgou'] (*pt* **underwent** *pp* **undergone**) *vt* (test, operation, treatment) 受ける ukérù

to undergo change 変る kawárù

undergraduate [ʌndə:rgrædʒ'u:it] *n* 学部の学生 gakúbu no gakúsei

underground [ʌn'də:rgraund] *n* (*BRIT*: railway) 地下鉄 chikátetsu; (POL) 地下組織 chikásoshiki

♦*adj* (car park) 地下の chiká no; (newspaper, activities) 潜りの mogúrì no

♦*adv* (work) 潜りで mogúrì de; (*fig*): *to go underground* 地下に潜る chiká ni mogúrù

undergrowth [ʌn'də:rgrouθ] *n* 下生え shitábae

underhand [ʌndə:rhænd] *adj* (*fig*) ずるい zurúi

underhanded [ʌndə:rhæn'did] *adj* = **underhand**

underlie [ʌndə:rlai'] (*pt* **underlay** *pp* **underlain**) *vt* (*fig*: be basis of) ...の根底になっている ...no kontéi ni nattè iru

underline [ʌn'də:rlain] *vt* 下線する kasén suru, ...にアンダーラインを引く ...ni afídārain wo hikú; (*fig*) 強調する kyōchō suru

underling [ʌn'də:rliŋ] (*pej*) *n* 手下 teshítā

undermine [ʌndə:rmain'] *vt* (confidence) 失わせる ushínawaseru; (authority) 弱める yowámerù

underneath [ʌndə:rni:θ'] *adv* 下に〔で〕shitá ni(de)

♦*prep* ...の下に〔で〕...no shitá ni(de)

underpaid [ʌndə:rpeid'] *adj* 安給料の yasúkyūryò no

underpants [ʌn'də:rpænts] *npl* パンツ pañtsu

underpass [ʌn'də:rpæs] (*BRIT*) *n* 地下道 chikádō

underprivileged [ʌndə:rpriv'əlidʒd] *adj* (country, race, family) 恵まれない megúmarenai

underrate [ʌndə:reit'] *vt* (person, power etc) 見くびる mikúbirù; (size) 見誤る miáyamarù

undershirt [ʌn'də:rʃə:rt] (*US*) *n* アンダーシャツ afídāshatsù

undershorts [ʌn'də:rʃɔːrts] (*US*) *npl* パンツ pañtsu

underside [ʌn'də:rsaid] *n* (of object) 下側 shitágawa; (of animal) おなか onáka

underskirt [ʌn'də:rskə:rt] (*BRIT*) *n* アンダースカート afídāsukàtō

understand [ʌndə:rstænd'] (*pt*, *pp* **understood**) *vt* 分かる wakárù, 理解する rikái suru

♦*vi* (believe): *I understand that* ...だそうですね ...da sōdesù ne, ...だと聞いていますが ...da tò kiíte imasu gà

understandable [ʌndə:rstæn'dəbəl] *adj* (behavior, reaction, mistake) 理解できる rikái dekírù

understanding [ʌndə:rstæn'diŋ] *adj* (kind) 思いやりのある omóiyari no aru

♦*n* (gen) 理解 rikái; (agreement) 合意 gōi

understatement [ʌndə:rsteit'mənt] *n* (of quality) 控え目な表現 hikáeme na hyōgen

that's an understatement! それは控え目過ぎるよ sore wa hikáemesugírù yo

understood [ʌndə:rstud'] *pt*, *pp* *of* **understand**

♦*adj* (agreed) 合意された gōi sareta; (implied) 暗黙の afímoku no

understudy [ʌn'də:rstʌdi:] *n* (actor, actress) 代役 daíyaku

undertake [ʌndə:rteik'] (*pt* **undertook** *pp* **undertaken**) *vt* (task) 引受ける hikíukerù

to undertake to do something ...する事を約束する ...surú koto wo yakúsoku suru

undertaker [ʌn'də:rteikə:r] *n* 葬儀屋 sōgiyà

undertaking [ʌn'də:rteikiŋ] *n* (job) 事業 jigyō; (promise) 約束 yakúsoku

undertone [ʌn'də:rtoun] *n*: *in an undertone* 小声 kogóe

underwater [ʌn'də:rwɔ:t'ər] *adv* (use) 水中に〔で〕suíchū ni〔de〕; (swim) 水中に 潜って suíchū ni mogútte
♦*adj* (exploration) 水中の suíchū no; (camera etc) 潜水用の sénsuiyō no

underwear [ʌn'də:rwe:r] *n* 下着 shítagi

underworld [ʌn'də:rwə:rld] *n* (of crime) 暗黒街 añkokugai

underwriter [ʌn'də:raitər] *n* (INSUR-ANCE) 保険業者 hokéngyōshà

undesirable [ʌndizaiə:r'əbəl] *adj* (person, thing) 好ましくない konómashikunai

undies [ʌn'di:z] (*inf*) *npl* 下着 shítagi ◊ 女性用を指す joséiyō wo sasù

undisputed [ʌndispju:'tid] *adj* (fact) 否定 できない hitéi dekinaì; (champion etc) 断 トツの dañtotsu no

undo [ʌndu:'] (*pt* **undid** *pp* **undone**) *vt* (unfasten) 外す hazúsu; (spoil) 台無しに する daínashi ni suru

undoing [ʌndu:'iŋ] *n* 破滅 hamétsu

undoubted [ʌndau'tid] *adj* 疑う余地のな い utágau yochì no naì

undoubtedly [ʌndau'tidli:] *adv* 疑う余地 なく utágau yochì naku

undress [ʌndres'] *vi* 服を脱ぐ fukú wo nugù

undue [ʌndu:'] *adj* (excessive) 余分な yobún na

undulating [ʌn'dʒəleitiŋ] *adj* (country-side, hills) 起伏の多い kifúku no ōì

unduly [ʌndu:'li:] *adv* (excessively) 余分 に yobún ni

unearth [ʌnə:rθ'] *vt* (skeleton etc) 発掘 する hakkútsu suru; (*fig*: secrets etc) 発 見する hakkén suru

unearthly [ʌnə:rθ'li:] *adj* (hour) とんで もない toñde mo naì

uneasy [ʌni:'zi:] *adj* (person: not com-fortable) 窮屈な kyūkútsu na; (: worried: *also* feeling) 不安な fuán na; (peace, truce) 不安定な fuáñtei na

uneconomic(al) [ʌni:kənə:m'ik(əl)] *adj* 不経済な fukéīzai na

uneducated [ʌnedʒʹuːkeitid] *adj* (person) 教育のない kyóiku no nai

unemployed [ʌnemplɔid'] *adj* (worker) 失業中の shitsúgyōchū no
♦*npl*: **the unemployed** 失業者 shitsú-gyōshà ◊ 総称 sōshō

unemployment [ʌnemplɔi'mənt] *n* 失業 shitsúgyō

unending [ʌnen'diŋ] *adj* 果てし無い ha-téshi naì

unerring [ʌnə:r'iŋ] *adj* (instinct etc) 確実 な kakújitsu na

uneven [ʌni:'vən] *adj* (not regular: teeth) 不ぞろいの fuzórōi no; (performance) む らのある murá no aru; (road etc) 凸凹の dekóboko no

unexpected [ʌnikspek'tid] *adj* (arrival) 不意の fuí no; (success etc) 思い掛けない omóigakenaì, 意外な igái na

unexpectedly [ʌnikspek'tidli:] *adv* (ar-rive) 不意に fuí ni; (succeed) 意外に igái ni

unfailing [ʌnfei'liŋ] *adj* (support, energy) 尽きる事のない tsukíru koto no naì

unfair [ʌnfe:r'] *adj*: **unfair (to)** (...に 対して) 不当な (...ni taishite) futó na

unfaithful [ʌnfeiθ'fəl] *adj* (lover, spouse) 浮気な uwáki na

unfamiliar [ʌnfəmil'jə:r] *adj* (place, per-son, subject) 知らない shiránai
to be unfamiliar with ...を知らない ...wo shiránai

unfashionable [ʌnfæʃ'ənəbəl] *adj* (clothes, ideas, place) はやらない hayá-ranaì

unfasten [ʌnfæs'ən] *vt* (undo) 外す hazú-su; (open) 開ける akéru

unfavorable [ʌnfei'və:rəbəl] (*BRIT* **un-favourable**) *adj* (circumstances, weather) 良くない yokúnai; (opinion, report) 批判的な hihánteki na

unfeeling [ʌnfi:'liŋ] *adj* 冷たい tsumétai, 冷酷な reíkoku na

unfinished [ʌnfin'iʃt] *adj* (incomplete) 未 完成の mikáñsei no

unfit [ʌnfit'] *adj* (physically) 運動不足の uñdōbusoku no; (incompetent): **unfit (for)** (...に) 不向きな (...ni) fumúki na
to be unfit for work 仕事に不向きであ る shigóto ni fumúki de aru

unfold [ʌnfould'] vt (sheets, map) 広げる hirógeru

♦vi (situation) 展開する teñkai suru

unforeseen [ʌnfɔ:rsi:n'] adj (circumstances etc) 予期しなかった yoki shinákatta, 思い掛けない omóigakenaī

unforgettable [ʌnfə:rget'əbəl] adj 忘れられない wasúrerarenaī

unforgivable [ʌnfə:rgiv'əbəl] adj 許せない yurúsenaī

unfortunate [ʌnfɔ:r't'ənit] adj (poor) 哀れな awáre na; (event) 不幸な fukó na; (remark) まずい mazúi

unfortunately [ʌnfɔ:r't'ənitli:] adv 残念ながら zañneññagara

unfounded [ʌnfaun'did] adj (criticism, fears) 根拠のない koñkyo no nái

unfriendly [ʌnfrend'li:] adj (person, behavior, remark) 不親切な fushíñsetsu na

ungainly [ʌngein'li:] adj ぎこちない gikóchinaī

ungodly [ʌngɑ:d'li:] adj (hour) とんでもない toñdemonaī

ungrateful [ʌngreit'fəl] adj (person) 恩知らずの oñshirázu no

unhappiness [ʌnhæp'i:nis] n 不幸せ fushíawàse, 不幸 fukó

unhappy [ʌnhæp'i:] adj (sad) 悲しい kanáshii; (unfortunate) 不幸な fukó na; (childhood) 恵まれない megúmarenaī; (dissatisfied): **unhappy about/with** (arrangements etc) ...に不満がある ...ni fumán ga aru

unharmed [ʌnhɑ:rmd'] adj 無事な bují na

unhealthy [ʌnhel'θi:] adj (person) 病弱な byójaku na; (place) 健康に悪い keñkō-ni warúī; (fig: interest) 不健全な fukéñzen na

unheard-of [ʌnhə:rd'əv] adj (shocking) 前代未聞の zeñdaimimon no; (unknown) 知られていない shirárete inaī

unhurt [ʌnhə:rt'] adj 無事な bují na

unidentified [ʌnaiden'təfaid] adj 未確定の mikákutei no ¶ see also **UFO**

uniform [ju:'nəfɔ:rm] n 制服 seífuku, ユニフォーム yunífōmu

♦adj (length, width etc) 一定の ittéi no

uniformity [ju:nəfɔ:r'miti:] n 均一性 kiñitsusei

unify [ju:'nəfai] vt 統一する tóītsu suru

unilateral [ju:nəlæt'ə:rəl] adj (disarmament etc) 一方的な ippóteki na

uninhabited [ʌninhæb'itid] adj (island etc) 無人の mujín no; (house) 空き家になっている akíya ni nattè iru

unintentional [ʌninten'tʃənəl] adj 意図的でない itóteki de naī

union [ju:n'jən] n (joining) 合併 gappéi; (grouping) 連合 reñgō; (also: **trade union**) 組合 kumíai

♦cpd (activities, leader etc) 組合の kumíai no

Union Jack n 英国国旗 eíkokukòkki, ユニオンジャック yuníoñjakkù

unique [ju:ni:k'] adj 独特な dokútoku na, ユニークな yuníkù na

unisex [ju:'niseks] adj (clothes, hairdresser etc) ユニセックスの yunísekkusu no

unison [ju:'nisən] n: **in unison** (say) 一同に ichídō ni; (sing) 同音で dóon de, ユニゾンで yunízon de

unit [ju:'nit] n (single whole, also measurement) 単位 tañ-i; (section: of furniture etc) ユニット yunítto; (team, squad) 班 hàn

kitchen unit 台所用ユニット daídokoroyō yunítto

unite [ju:nait'] vt (join: gen) 一緒にする isshò ni suru, 一つにする hitótsù ni suru; (: country, party) 結束させる kessokusaseru

♦vi 一緒になる isshò ni naru, 一つになる hitótsù ni naru

united [ju:nai'tid] adj (gen) 一緒になった isshò ni natta, 一つになった hitótsù ni natta; (effort) 団結した dañketsu shita

United Kingdom n 英国 eíkoku

United Nations (Organization) n 国連 kokúren

United States (of America) n (アメリカ) 合衆国 (amérika)gasshúkoku

unit trust (BRIT) n ユニット型投資信託 yuníttogata tóshishiñtaku

unity [ju:'niti:] *n* 一致 itchí

universal [ju:nəvə:r'səl] *adj* 普遍的な fuhénteki na

universe [ju:'nəvə:rs] *n* 宇宙 uchū

university [ju:nəvə:r'siti:] *n* 大学 daígaku

unjust [ʌndʒʌst'] *adj* 不当な futō na

unkempt [ʌnkempt'] *adj* (appearance) だらしのない daráshi no naī; (hair, beard) もじゃもじゃの mojámoja no

unkind [ʌnkaind'] *adj* (person, behavior, comment etc) 不親切な fushínsetsu na

unknown [ʌnnoun'] *adj* 知られていない shiráretè inái

unlawful [ʌnlɔ:'fəl] *adj* (act, activity) 非合法な higōhō na

unleash [ʌnli:ʃ'] *vt* (fig: feeling, forces etc) 爆発させる bakúhatsu saseru

unless [ʌnles'] *conj* ...しなければ(でなければ) ...shínakereba(dénakereba)
unless he comes 彼が来なければ karè ga konákereba

unlike [ʌnlaik'] *adj* (not alike) 似ていない nitē inái; (not like) 違った chigátta
♦*prep* (different from) ...と違って ...to chigátte

unlikely [ʌnlaik'li:] *adj* (not likely) ありそうもない arísò mo naī; (unexpected: combination etc) 驚くべき odórokubeki

unlimited [ʌnlim'itid] *adj* (travel, wine etc) 無制限の musêîgen no

unlisted [ʌnlis'tid] (*BRIT* ex-directory) *adj* (ex-directory) 電話帳に載っていない deñwachò ni nottè inaí

unload [ʌnloud'] *vt* (box, car etc) ...の積荷を降ろす ...no tsumíni wo orósù

unlock [ʌnlɑ:k'] *vt* ...のかぎを開ける ...no kagí wo akéru

unlucky [ʌnlʌk'i:] *adj* (person) 運の悪い uñ no warúî; (object, number) 縁起の悪い eñgi no warúî
to be unlucky (person) 運が悪い uñ ga warúî

unmarried [ʌnmær'i:d] *adj* (person) 独身の dokúshin no; (mother) 未婚の mikón no

unmask [ʌnmæsk'] *vt* (reveal: thief etc) ...の正体を暴く ...no shōtai wo abákù

unmistakable [ʌnmistei'kəbəl] *adj* (voice, sound, person) 間違え様のない machígaeyō no naī

unmitigated [ʌnmit'əgeitid] *adj* (disaster etc) 紛れもない magíre mò naí

unnatural [ʌnnætʃ'ə:rəl] *adj* 不自然な fushízen na

unnecessary [ʌnnes'ise:ri:] *adj* 不必要な fuhítsuyō na

unnoticed [ʌnnou'tist] *adj*: (to go/pass)
unnoticed 気付かれない kizúkàrenai

UNO [u:'nou] *n abbr* = **United Nations Organization**

unobtainable [ʌnəbtei'nəbəl] *adj* (item) 手に入らない te nì haíranài; (TEL): *this number is unobtainable* この電話番号は現在使用されていません konó deñwabangò wa geñzai shiyō sarete imásen

unobtrusive [ʌnəbtru:'siv] *adj* (person) 遠慮がちな eñryogachi na; (thing) 目立たない medátanaî

unofficial [ʌnəfiʃ'əl] *adj* (news) 公表されていない kőhyō sarete inaî; (strike) 公認されていない kőnin sarete inaî

unorthodox [ʌnɔ:r'θədɑ:ks] *adj* (treatment) 通常でない tsūjō de nai; (REL) 正統でない seítō de nai

unpack [ʌnpæk'] *vi* 荷物の中身を出して片付ける nimótsu no nakámi wo dashîte katázukerù
♦*vt* (suitcase etc) ...の中身を出して片付ける ...no nakamî wo dashîte katázukerù

unpalatable [ʌnpæl'ətəbəl] *adj* (meal) まずい mazúî; (truth) 不愉快な fuyúkai na

unparalleled [ʌnpær'əleld] *adj* (unequalled) 前代未聞の zeñdaimimon no

unpleasant [ʌnplez'ənt] *adj* (disagreeable: thing) やな iyá na; (: person, manner) 不愉快な fuyúkai na

unplug [ʌnplʌg'] *vt* (iron, TV etc) ...のプラグを抜く ...no purágu wo nukú

unpopular [ʌnpɑ:p'jələ:r] *adj* (person, decision etc) 不評の fuhyō no

unprecedented [ʌnpres'identid] *adj* 前代未聞の zeñdaimimon no

unpredictable [ʌnpridik'təbəl] *adj*

(weather, reaction) 予測できない yosóku dekínaì; (person): *he is unpredictable* 彼のする事は予測できない karè no suru koto wa yosóku dekínai

unprofessional [ʌnprəfeʃˈənəl] *adj* (attitude, conduct) 職業倫理に反する shokúgyōriñri ni hañ suru

unqualified [ʌnkwɑːlˈəfaid] *adj* (teacher, nurse etc) 資格のない shikáku no nai; (complete: disaster) 全くの mattáku no, 大...daì...; (: success) 完全な kañzen na, 大...daì...

unquestionably [ʌnkwesˈtʃənəbliː] *adv* 疑いもなく utágai mò naku

unravel [ʌnrævˈəl] *vt* (ball of string) ほぐす hogúsù; (mystery) 解明する kaímei suru

unreal [ʌnriːlˈ] *adj* (not real) 偽の nisé no; (extraordinary) うその様な usò no yō na

unrealistic [ʌnriːəlisˈtik] *adj* (person, project) 非現実的な higéñjitsuteki na

unreasonable [ʌnriːzˈənəbəl] *adj* (person, attitude) 不合理な fugṓri na; (demand) 不当な futṓ na; (length of time) 非常識な hijṓshìki na

unrelated [ʌnrileiˈtid] *adj* (incident) 関係のない kañkei no naì, 無関係な mukáñkei na; (family) 親族でない shiñzoku de naì

unrelenting [ʌnrilenˈtiŋ] *adj* 執念深い shūnenbukai

unreliable [ʌnrilaiˈəbəl] *adj* (person, firm) 信頼できない shiñrai dekinaì; (machine, watch, method) 当てにならない até ni naranaì

unremitting [ʌnrimitˈiŋ] *adj* (efforts, attempts) 絶間ない taéma naì

unreservedly [ʌnrizəːrˈvidliː] *adv* 心から kokórò kara

unrest [ʌnrestˈ] *n* (social, political, industrial etc) 不安 fuán

unroll [ʌnroulˈ] *vt* 広げる hirógeru

unruly [ʌnruːˈliː] *adj* (child, behavior) 素直でない sunáo de nai, 手に負えない te nî oénaì; (hair) もじゃもじゃの mojámoja no

unsafe [ʌnseifˈ] *adj* (in danger) 危険にさ

らされた kinkén ni sarásareta; (journey, machine, bridge etc) 危険な kikén na, 危ない abúnai

unsaid [ʌnsedˈ] *adj*: *to leave something unsaid* ...を言わないでおく ...wo iwánaide okù

unsatisfactory [ʌnsætisfækˈtəːriː] *adj* (progress, work, results) 不満足な fumáñzoku na

unsavory [ʌnseiˈvəːriː] (*BRIT* **unsavoury**) *adj* (*fig*: person, place) いかがわしい ikágawashiì

unscathed [ʌnskeiðdˈ] *adj* 無傷の mukízu no

unscrew [ʌnskruːˈ] *vt* (bottletop etc) ねじって開ける nejítte akéru; (sign, mirror etc) ...のねじを抜く ...no nejî wo nukú

unscrupulous [ʌnskruːpˈjələs] *adj* (person, behavior) 悪徳... akútoku...

unsettled [ʌnsetˈəld] *adj* (person) 落付かない ochítsukanài; (weather) 変りやすい kawáriyasuì

unshaven [ʌnʃeiˈvən] *adj* 不精ひげの bushṓhìge no

unsightly [ʌnsaitˈliː] *adj* (mark, building etc) 醜い miníkuì, 目障りな mezáwàri na

unskilled [ʌnskildˈ] *adj* (work, worker) 未熟練の mijúkuren no

unspeakable [ʌnspiːˈkəbəl] *adj* (indescribable) 言語に絶する geñgo ni zéssuru, 想像を絶する sṓzō wo zéssurù; (awful) ひどい hidṓì

unstable [ʌnsteiˈbəl] *adj* (piece of furniture) ぐらぐらする gurágura suru; (government) 不安定な fuáñtei na; (mentally) 情緒不安定な jṓchofuáñtei na

unsteady [ʌnstedˈiː] *adj* (step, legs) ふらふらする furáfura suru; (hands, voice) 震える furúeru; (ladder) ぐらぐらする gurágura suru

unstuck [ʌnstʌkˈ] *adj*: *to come unstuck* (label etc) 取れてしまう torête shimaù; (*fig*: plan, idea etc) 失敗する shippái suru

unsuccessful [ʌnsəksesˈfəl] *adj* (attempt) 失敗した shippái shita; (writer) 成功しない seíkō shinaì, 売れない urénaì; (proposal) 採用されなかった saíyō sarènakatta

to be unsuccessful (in attempting something) 失敗する shippai suru; (application) 採用されない saíyō sarènai

unsuccessfully [ʌnsəksesˈfəliː] adv (try) 成功せずに seíkō sezu ni

unsuitable [ʌnsuːˈtəbəl] adj (inconvenient: time, moment) 不適当な futékìto na; (inappropriate: clothes) 場違いの bachígaì no; (: person) 不適当な futékìto na

unsure [ʌnʃuːr] adj (uncertain) 不確実な fukákùjitsu na

unsure about ...について確信できない ...ni tsuíte kakúshin dekinaì

to be unsure of oneself 自信がない jishín ga nai

unsuspecting [ʌnsəspekˈtiŋ] adj 気付いていない kizúite inai

unsympathetic [ʌnsimpəθetˈik] adj (showing little understanding) 同情しない dōjō shinai; (unlikeable) いやな iyá na

untapped [ʌntæptˈ] adj (resources) 未開発の mikáihatsu no

unthinkable [ʌnθiŋkˈəbəl] adj 考えられない kañgaerarenaì

untidy [ʌntaiˈdiː] adj (room) 散らかった chírakatta; (person, appearance) だらしない daráshi nai

untie [ʌntaiˈ] vt (knot, parcel, ribbon) ほどく hodókù; (prisoner) ...の縄をほどく ...no nawá wo hodókù; (parcel, dog) ...のひもをほどく ...no himó wo hodókù

until [ʌntilˈ] prep ...まで ...madè

◆conj ...するまで ...suru madè

until he comes 彼が来るまで karè ga kurù made

until now 今まで imámadè

until then その時まで sonó toki madè

untimely [ʌntaimˈliː] adj (inopportune: moment, arrival) 時機の悪い jikì no warúì

an untimely death 早死に hayájini, 若死に wakájini

untold [ʌntouldˈ] adj (story) 明かされていない akásarete inai; (joy, suffering, wealth) 想像を絶する sōzō wo zessúru

untoward [ʌntɔːrdˈ] adj 困った komáttà

unused [ʌnjuːzdˈ] adj (not used: clothes, portion etc) 未使用の mishíyō no

unusual [ʌnjuːˈʒuːəl] adj (strange) 変った kawátta; (rare) 珍しい mezúrashiì; (exceptional, distinctive) 並外れた namíhazureta

unveil [ʌnveilˈ] vt (statue) ...の除幕式を行う ...no jomákushìki wo okónau

unwanted [ʌnwɔːnˈtid] adj (clothing etc) 不要の fuyō no; (child, pregnancy) 望まれなかった nozómarenakatta

unwavering [ʌnweiˈvəriŋ] adj (faith) 揺るぎ無い yurúginaì; (gaze) じっとした jittō shita

unwelcome [ʌnwelˈkəm] adj (guest) 歓迎されない kañgeisarenaì; (news) 悪い warúì

unwell [ʌnwelˈ] adj: *to feel unwell* 気分が悪い kibún ga warúì

to be unwell 病気である byōki de aru

unwieldy [ʌnwiːlˈdiː] adj (object, system) 大きくて扱いにくい ōkìkute atsúkainikuì

unwilling [ʌnwilˈiŋ] adj: *to be unwilling to do something* ...するのをいやがっている ...surú no wo iyagatte iru

unwillingly [ʌnwilˈiŋliː] adv いやがって iyágatte

unwind [ʌnwaindˈ] (pt, pp **unwound**) vt (undo) ほどく hodókù

◆vi (relax) くつろぐ kutsúrogù

unwise [ʌnwaizˈ] adj (person) 思慮の足りない shiryō no tarínai; (decision) 浅はかな asáhàka na

unwitting [ʌnwitˈiŋ] adj (victim, accomplice) 気付かない kizúkànai

unworkable [ʌnwəːrˈkəbəl] adj (plan) 実行不可能な jikkōfukanō nà

unworthy [ʌnwəːrˈðiː] adj ...の値打がない ...no neúchi ga naì

unwrap [ʌnræpˈ] vt 開ける akéru

unwritten [ʌnritˈən] adj (law) 慣習の kañshū no; (agreement) 口頭での kōtō de no

---

KEYWORD

up [ʌp] prep: *to go up something* ...を登る ...wo nobóru

to be up something ...の上に（登って）いる ...no ué ni nobotte iru

he went up the stairs/the hill 彼は階段(坂)を登った karè wa kaídan(sakà) wo nobótta

the cat was up a tree ネコは木の上にいた nekò wa ki nò ué ni ita

we walked/climbed up the hill 私たちは丘を登った watákushitachi wa okà wo nobótta

they live further up the street 彼らはこの道をもう少し行った所に住んでいます karèra wa konó michi wo mó sukoshi ittá tokoro ni suǹde imasu

go up that road and turn left この道を交差点まで行って左に曲って下さい konó michi wo kōsaten màde itte hidári ni magátte kudásaì

♦*adv* 1 (upwards, higher) 上に〔で，へ〕 ué ni〔de, e〕

up in the sky/the mountains 空〔山の上〕に sorà〔yamá no ué〕ni

put it at bit higher up もう少し高い所に置いて下さい mó sukoshì takáì tokoro ni oìte kudásaì

up there あの上に anó ue ni

what's the cat doing up there? ネコは何であの上にいるのかしら nekò wa naǹde anó ue nì irú no kashira

up above 上の方に〔で〕 ué no hō nì〔de〕

there's a village and up above, on the hill, a monastery 村があって，その上の丘に修道院がある murá ga atte, sonó ue no okà ni shūdòin ga aru

2: *to be up* (out of bed) 起きている okíte iru; (prices, level) 上がっている agátte iru; (building) 建ててある tatète aru, 立っている tattè iru; (tent) 張ってある hatté aru

3: *up to* (as far as) ...まで ...madè

I've read up to p.60 私は60ページまで読みました watákushi wa rokújupēji madè yomímashita

the water came up to his knees 水深は彼のひざまでだった suíshin wa karè no hizá made datta

up to now 今〔これ〕まで imà〔korè〕madè

I can spend up to $10 10ドルまで使えます jūdòru made tsukáemasu

4: *to be up to* (depending on) ...の責任である ...no sekínin de aru, ...次第である ...shidái de aru

it's up to you あなた次第です anàta shidái desu

it's not up to me to decide 決めるのは私の責任ではない kiméru no wa watákushi no sekínin de wa naì

5: *to be up to* (equal to) ...に合う ...ni aù

he's not up to it (job, task etc) 彼にはその仕事は無理です karè ni wa sonó shigoto wa murì desu

his work is not up to the required standard 彼の仕事は基準に合いません karè no shigóto wa kijún ni aìmasen

6: *to be up to* (inf: be doing) やっている yatté iru

what is he up to? (showing disapproval, suspicion) あいつは何をやらかしているんだろうね aítsu wa naǹi wo yarákashite irún darō ne

♦*n: ups and downs* (in life, career) 浮き沈み ukíshizumi

we all have our ups and downs だれだっていい時と悪い時があります darè datte iì toki to warúì toki ga arimasu yo

his life had its ups and downs, but he died happy 彼の人生には浮き沈みが多かったが，死ぬ時は幸せだった karè no jiǹsei ni wa ukíshizumi ga ōkattà ga, shinú toki wa shiáwase datta

upbringing [ʌp'briŋiŋ] *n* 養育 yōiku

update [ʌpdeit'] *vt* (records, information) 更新する kōshin suru

upgrade [ʌp'greid'] *vt* (improve: house) 改築する kaíchiku suru; (job) 格上げする kakúage suru; (employee) 昇格させる shōkaku saseru

upheaval [ʌphiːvəl] *n* 変動 heǹdō

uphill [adj ʌp'hil adv ʌp'hil'] *adj* (climb) 上りの nobóri no; (fig: task) 困難な koǹnan na

♦*adv: to go uphill* 坂を上る sakà wo nobóru

uphold [ʌphould'] (*pt, pp* upheld) *vt* (law, principle, decision) 守る mamórù

upholstery [ʌphoul'stəriː] *n* いすに張っ

た生地 isú ni hattá kijí

upkeep [ʌpˈkiːp] *n* (maintenance) 維持 ijí

upon [əpɑːn] *prep* ...の上に〔で〕...no ué ni 〔de〕

upper [ʌpˈəːr] *adj* 上の方の ué no hō nò
♦*n* (of shoe) 甲皮 kôhi

upper-class [ʌpˈəːrklæs] *adj* (families, accent) 上流の jōryū no

upper hand *n*: **to have the upper hand** 優勢である yū́sei de aru

uppermost [ʌpˈəːrmoust] *adj* 一番上の i-chíban ué no
what was uppermost in my mind 私が真っ先に考えたのは watákushi ga massákí ni kañgaèta no wa

upright [ʌpˈrait] *adj* (straight) 直立のchokúritsu no; (vertical) 垂直の suíchoku no; (*fig*: honest) 正直な shōjiki na

uprising [ʌpˈraiziŋ] *n* 反乱 hañran

uproar [ʌpˈrɔːr] *n* (protests, shouts) 大騒ぎ ṓsawàgi

uproot [ʌpruːˈt] *vt* (tree) 根こそぎにする nekōsogi ni suru; (*fig*: family) 故郷から追出す kokyō kara oídasù

upset [*n* ʌpˈset *vb* ʌpsetˈ] (*pt, pp* **upset**) *n* (to plan etc) 失敗 shippái
♦*vt* (knock over: glass etc) 倒す taósu; (routine, plan) 台無しにする daínashi ni suru; (person: offend, make unhappy) 動転させる dṓten saseru
♦*adj* (unhappy) 動転した dṓten shita
to have an upset stomach 胃の具合が悪い i no gúai ga warúi

upshot [ʌpˈʃɑːt] *n* 結果 kekká

upside down [ʌpˈsaid-] *adv* (hang, hold) 逆様に〔で〕sakásama ni〔de〕
to turn a place upside down (*fig*) 家中を引っかき回す iejū wo híkkakímawasu

upstairs [ʌpˈsteːrz] *adv* (be) 2階に〔で〕nikái ni〔de〕; (go) 2階へ nikái e
♦*adj* (window, room) 2階の nikái no
♦*n* 2階 nikái

upstart [ʌpˈstɑːrt] *n* 横柄な奴 ṓhei na yatsú

upstream [ʌpˈstriːm] *adv* 川上に〔で、へ〕kawákami ni〔de, e〕, 上流に〔で、へ〕jṓryū ni〔de, e〕

uptake [ʌpˈteik] *n*: **to be quick/slow on**

the uptake 物分かりがいい〔悪い〕monówakàri ga íi〔warui〕

uptight [ʌpˈtait] *adj* ぴりぴりした pirí-piri shita

up-to-date [ʌpˈtədeitˈ] *adj* (most recent: information) 最新の saíshin no; (person) 最新の情報に通じている saíshin no jṓhō ni tsújíte irù

upturn [ʌpˈtəːrn] *n* (in luck) 好転 kṓten; (COMM: in market) 上向き uwámuki

upward [ʌpˈwəːrd] *adj* (movement, glance) 上への ué e no

upwards [ʌpˈwəːrdz] *adv* (move, glance) 上の方へ ué no hō è; (more than): *upward(s) of* ...以上の ...íjō no

uranium [jureiˈniːəm] *n* ウラン uràn, ウラニウム urániumù

urban [əːrˈbən] *adj* 都会の tokái no

urbane [əːrbeinˈ] *adj* 上品な jōhin na

urchin [əːrˈtʃin] *n* (child) がき gakí; (waif) 浮浪児 furṓjì

urge [əːrdʒ] *n* (need, desire) 衝動 shṓdō
♦*vt*: *to urge someone to do something* ...する様に...を説得する ...surú yō ni ...wo settóku suru

urgency [əːrˈdʒənsiː] *n* (importance) 緊急性 kíñkyūseî; (of tone) 緊迫した調子 kiñpaku shita chṓshi

urgent [əːrˈdʒənt] *adj* (need, message) 緊急な kíñkyū na; (voice) 切迫した seppáku shita

urinal [juːrˈənəl] *n* 小便器 shṓbeñki

urinate [juːrˈəneit] *vi* 小便をする shṓbeñ wo suru

urine [juːrˈin] *n* 尿 nyṓ, 小便 shṓbeñ

urn [əːrn] *n* (container) 骨つぼ kotsútsubo; (*also*: **coffee/tea urn**) 大型コーヒー〔紅茶〕メーカー ōgátakōhī́〔kṓcha〕mèká

Uruguay [juːˈrəgwei] *n* ウルグアイ urúguai

us [ʌs] *pron* 私たちを〔に〕watákushitachi wo〔ni〕¶ *see also* **me**

US(A) [juːˈesˈ(eiˈ)] *n abbr* = **United States (of America)**

usage [juːˈsidʒ] *n* (LING) 慣用 kañyō

use [*n* juːs *vb* juːz] *n* (using) 使用 shíyō; (usefulness, purpose) 役に立つ事 yakú ni tatsu koto 利益 ríeki

♦vt (object, tool, phrase etc) 使う tsukáu, 用いる mochíirù, 使用する shíyō suru
in use 使用中 shíyōchū
out of use 廃れて sutáretè
to be of use 役に立つ yakú ni tatsu
it's no use (not useful) 使えません tsukáemasen; (pointless) 役に立ちません yakú ni tachimasen, 無意味です muímì desu
she used to do it 前は彼女はそれをする習慣でした maè wa kanòjo wa soré wo suru shūkan deshita
to be used to ...に慣れている ...ni naréte iru

used [ju:zd] *adj* (object) 使われた tsukáwareta; (car) 中古の chūkò no

useful [ju:s'fəl] *adj* 役に立つ yakú ni tatsu, 有益な yúeki na, 便利な beñri na

usefulness [ju:s'fəlnis] *n* 実用性 jitsúyōsei

useless [ju:s'lis] *adj* (unusable) 使えない tsukáenai, 役に立たない yakú ni tatanai; (pointless) 無意味な muímì na, 無駄な mudá na; (person: hopeless) 能無しの nṓnashi no, 役に立たない yakú ni tatanai

user [ju:'zə:r] *n* 使用者 shiyōsha

user-friendly [ju:'zə:rfrend'li:] *adj* (computer) 使いやすい tsukáiyasuì, ユーザーフレンドリーな yū́záfuréndorī na

use up *vt* 全部使ってしまう zeñbu tsukátte shimaù, 使い尽す tsukáitsukusù

usher [ʌʃ'ə:r] *n* (at wedding) 案内係 añnaigakàri

usherette [ʌʃəret'] *n* (in cinema) 女性案内係 joséi añnaigakàri

USSR [ju:esesar'] *n*: *the USSR* ソ連 soRèn

usual [ju:'ʒuəl] *adj* (time, place etc) いつもの itsùmo no
as usual いつもの様に itsùmo no yō ni

usually [ju:'ʒuːəli:] *adv* 普通は futsū́ wa

usurp [ju:sə:rp'] *vt* (title, position) 強奪する gōdatsu suru

utensil [ju:ten'səl] *n* 用具 yōgu
kitchen utensils 台所用具 daídokoro yōgu

uterus [ju:'tə:rəs] *n* 子宮 shikyū́

utility [ju:til'iti:] *n* (usefulness) 有用性 yúyōsei, 実用性 jitsúyōsei; (*also*: **public utility**) 公益事業 kōekijigyō

utility room *n* 洗濯部屋 señtakubeya

utilize [ju:'təlaiz] *vt* (object) 利用する riyṓ suru, 使う tsukáu

utmost [ʌt'moust] *adj* 最大の saídai no
♦*n*: *to do one's utmost* 全力を尽す zeñryoku wo tsukusù

utter [ʌt'ə:r] *adj* (total: amazement, fool, waste, rubbish) 全くの mattáku no
♦*vt* (sounds) 出す dasù, 発する hassúru; (words) 口に出す kuchí ni dasù, 言う iù

utterance [ʌt'ə:rəns] *n* 発言 hatsúgen, 言葉 kotóba

utterly [ʌt'ə:rli:] *adv* 全く mattáku

U-turn [ju:'tə:rn] *n* Uターン yū́tāñ

V

v. *abbr* = **verse; versus; volt;** (= **vide**)
...を見よ ...wo mìyo

vacancy [vei'kənsi:] *n* (*BRIT*: job) 欠員 ketsúin; (room) 空き部屋 akíbeya

vacant [vei'kənt] *adj* (room, seat, toilet) 空いている aíte iru; (look, expression) うつろの utsúro no

vacant lot (*US*) *n* 空き地 akíchi

vacate [vei'keit] *vt* (house, one's seat) 空ける akéru; (job) 辞める yaméru

vacation [veikei'ʃən] *n* (*esp US*: holiday) 休暇 kyū́ka; (SCOL) 夏休み natsúyasùmi

vaccinate [væk'səneit] *vt*: *to vaccinate someone (against something)* ...に (...の) 予防注射をする ...ni (...no) yobóchūshà wo suru

vaccine [væksin:'] *n* ワクチン wakúchin

vacuum [væk'ju:m] *n* (empty space) 真空 shiñkū

vacuum cleaner *n* (真空) 掃除機 (shiñkū)sṓjikì

vacuum-packed [væk'ju:mpækt'] *adj* 真空パックの shiñkūpakkù no

vagabond [væg'əba:nd] *n* 浮浪者 furṓshà, ルンペン ruñpen

vagina [vədʒai'nə] *n* ちつ chitsú

vagrant [vei'grənt] *n* 浮浪者 furṓshà, ルンペン ruñpen

vague [veig] *adj* (blurred: memory, outline) ぼんやりした bofi-yarī to shita; (uncertain: look, idea, instructions) 漠然とした bakúzen to shita; (person: not precise) 不正確な fuseíkaku na; (: evasive) 煮え切らない niékiranài

vaguely [veig'li:] *adv* (not clearly) ぼんやりとして bofi-yarī to shite; (without certainty) 漠然と bakúzen to, 不正確に fuseíkaku ni; (evasively) あいまいに aímai ni

vain [vein] *adj* (conceited) うぬぼれた unúboreta; (useless: attempt, action) 無駄な mudá na

in vain 何のかいもなく naň no kaí mo nakù

valentine [væl'əntain] *n* (*also*: **valentine card**) バレンタインカード baréntaiňkàdo; (person) バレンタインデーの恋人 baréntaiňdè no koíbito

valet [væl'ei'] *n* 召使い meshítsukài

valiant [væl'jənt] *adj* (attempt, effort) 勇敢な yūkan na

valid [væl'id] *adj* (ticket, document) 有効な yūkō na; (argument, reason) 妥当な datṓ na

validity [vəlid'iti:] *n* (of ticket, document) 有効性 yūkōseì; (of argument, reason) 妥当性 datṓseì

valley [væl'i:] *n* 谷(間) taní(ma)

valor [væl'ə:r] (*BRIT* **valour**) *n* 勇ましさ isámashisà

valuable [væl'ju:əbəl] *adj* (jewel etc) 高価な kōka na; (time, help, advice) 貴重な kichō na

valuables [væl'ju:əbəlz] *npl* (jewellery etc) 貴重品 kichṓhin

valuation [væljuːei'ʃən] *n* (worth: of house etc) 価値 kachī; (judgment of quality) 評価 hyōka

value [væl'ju:] *n* (financial worth) 価値 kachī, 価格 kakáku; (importance, usefulness) 価値 kachī

♦*vt* (fix price or worth of) ...に値を付ける ...ni ne wó tsukérù; (appreciate) 大切にする taísetsu ni suru, 重宝する chōhō suru

values [væl'ju:z] *npl* (principles, beliefs)

価値観 kachíkañ

value added tax [-æd'id-] (*BRIT*) *n* 付加価値税 fukákachizèi

valued [væl'ju:d] *adj* (appreciated: customer, advice) 大切な taísetsu na

valve [vælv] *n* 弁 beñ, バルブ barúbu

vampire [væm'paiə:r] *n* 吸血鬼 kyúketsùki

van [væn] *n* (AUT) バン bañ

vandal [væn'dəl] *n* 心無い破壊者 kokóronaì hakáisha

vandalism [væn'dəlizəm] *n* 破壊行動 hakáikōdō

vandalize [væn'dəlaiz] *vt* 破壊する hakái suru

vanguard [væn'gɑ:rd] *n* (*fig*): *in the vanguard of* ...の先端に立って ...no señtan ni tattè

vanilla [vənil'ə] *n* バニラ banîra

vanilla ice cream *n* バニラアイスクリーム banîra aísukurīmu

vanish [væn'iʃ] *vi* (disappear suddenly) 見えなくなる miénàku narù, 消える kiéru

vanity [væn'iti:] *n* (of person: unreasonable pride) 虚栄心 kyoéishiñ

vantage point [væn'tidʒ-] *n* (lookout place) 観察点 kañsatsuten; (viewpoint) 有利な立場 yūri na tachíba

vapor [vei'pə:r] (*BRIT* **vapour**) *n* (gas) 気体 kitái; (mist, steam) 蒸気 jṓki

variable [ve:r'i:əbəl] *adj* (likely to change: mood, quality, weather) 変りやすい kawáriyasuì; (able to be changed: temperature, height, speed) 調節できる chṓsetsu dekírù

variance [ve:r'i:əns] *n*: *to be at variance (with)* (people) (...と) 仲たがいしている (...to) nakátagài shitè iru; (facts) (...と) 矛盾している (...to) mujúnshitè iru

variation [ve:ri:ei'ʃən] *n* (change in level, amount, quantity) 変化 heňka, 変動 heñdō; (different form: of plot, musical theme etc) 変形 heňkei

varicose [vær'əkous] *adj*: *varicose veins* 拡張蛇行静脈 kakúchōdakōjōmyaku

varied [veːr'iːd] *adj* (diverse: opinions, reasons) 様々な sámàzama na; (full of changes: career) 多彩な tasái na

variety [vərai'əti:] *n* (degree of choice, diversity) 変化 heñka, バラエティー baráètī; (varied collection, quantity) 様々な物 sámàzama na mono; (type) 種類 shurùi

variety show *n* バラエティーショー baráetīshò

various [veːr'iːəs] *adj* 色々な iróiro na

varnish [vɑːr'niʃ] *n* (product applied to surface) ニス nisù
◆*vt* (apply varnish to: wood, piece of furniture etc) ...にニスを塗る ...ni nisù wo nuru; (: nails) ...にマニキュアをする ...ni maníkyua wo suru
nail varnish マニキュア maníkyua

vary [veːr'iː] *vt* (make changes to: routine, diet) 変える kaéru
◆*vi* (be different: sizes, colors) ...が色々ある ...ga iróiro aru; (become different): *to vary with* (weather, season etc) ...によって変る ...ni yótte kawáru

vase [veis] *n* 花瓶 kabín

Vaseline [væs'əliːn] ® *n* ワセリン wasérin

vast [væst] *adj* (wide: area, knowledge) 広い hiróì; (enormous: expense etc) ばく大な bakúdai na

VAT [væt] *n abbr* = **value added tax**

vat [væt] *n* 大おけ óokè

Vatican [væt'ikən] *n*: *the Vatican* (palace) バチカン宮殿 bachíkan kyūdeñ; (authority) ローマ法王庁 rōma hōōchō

vault [vɔːlt] *n* (of roof) 丸天井 marúteñjō; (tomb) 地下納骨堂 chikánōkotsudō; (in bank) 金庫室 kiñkoshitsú
◆*vt* (*also*: **vault over**) 飛越える tobíkoerù

vaunted [vɔːn'tid] *adj*: *much-vaunted* ご自慢の go-jíman no

VCR [viːsiːɑːr'] *n abbr* = **video cassette recorder**

VD [viːdiː'] *n abbr* = **venereal disease**

VDU [viːdiːjuː'] *n abbr* = **visual display unit**

veal [viːl] *n* 子ウシ肉 koúshiniku

veer [viːr] *vi* (vehicle, wind) 急に向きを変える kyū ni mukí wo kaéru

vegetable [vedʒ'təbəl] *n* (BOT) 植物 shokúbùtsu; (edible plant) 野菜 yasái
◆*adj* (oil etc) 植物性の shokúbutsusei no

vegetarian [vedʒiteːr'iːən] *n* 菜食主義者 saíshokushugishà
◆*adj* (diet etc) 菜食主義の saíshokushugi no

vegetate [vedʒ'iteit] *vi* 無為に暮す muì ni kurásu

vegetation [vedʒiteiʃən] *n* (plants) 植物 shokúbùtsu ◇総称 sóshō

vehement [viː'əmənt] *adj* (strong: attack, passions, denial) 猛烈な móretsu na

vehicle [viː'ikəl] *n* (machine) 車 kurúma; (*fig*: means of expressing) 手段 shudàn

veil [veil] *n* ベール bēru

veiled [veild] *adj* (*fig*: threat) 隠された kakúsaretà

vein [vein] *n* (ANAT) 静脈 jōmyaku; (of ore etc) 脈 myakú
vein of a leaf 葉脈 yōmyaku

velocity [vəlɑːs'iti:] *n* 速度 sokùdo

velvet [vel'vit] *n* ビロード biródo, ベルベット berúbetto
◆*adj* ビロードの biródo no, ベルベットの berúbettō no

vendetta [vendet'ə] *n* 復しゅう fukúshū

vending machine [ven'diŋ-] *n* 自動販売機 jidōhanbaiki

vendor [ven'dəːr] *n* (of house, land) 売手 urìte; (of cigarettes, beer etc) 売子 urìko

veneer [vəniːr'] *n* (on furniture) 化粧張り keshôbari; (*fig*: of person, place) 虚飾 kyoshóku

venereal [vəniːr'iːəl] *adj*: *venereal disease* 性病 seíbyō

Venetian blind [vəniː'ʃən-] *n* ベネシャンブラインド benéshanburaindò

Venezuela [venizwei'lə] *n* ベネズエラ benézuèra

vengeance [ven'dʒəns] *n* (revenge) 復しゅう fukúshū
with a vengeance (*fig*: to a greater extent) 驚く程 odórokù hodo

venison [ven'isən] *n* シカ肉 shikániku

venom [ven'əm] n (of snake, insect) 毒
dokú; (bitterness, anger) 悪意 ákui

venomous [ven'əməs] adj (poisonous:
snake, insect) 毒... dokú...; (full of bitterness: look, stare) 敵意に満ちた tekíi ni
michíta

vent [vent] n (also: **air vent**) 通気孔 tsú-
kikō; (in jacket) ベンツ beńtsu
♦vt (fig: feelings, anger) ぶちまける bu-
chímakeru

ventilate [ven'təleit] vt (room, building)
換気する káńki suru

ventilation [ventəlei'ʃən] n 換気 káńki

ventilator [ven'təleitər] n (TECH) 換気
装置 kańkisōchi, ベンチレーター beńchi-
rētà; (MED) 人工呼吸器 jińkōkokyūkì,
レスピレタ resúpiretà

ventriloquist [ventril'əkwist] n 腹話術
師 fukúwajùtsushi

venture [ven'tʃər] n (risky undertaking)
冒険 bōken
♦vt (opinion) おずおず言う ozùozu iú
♦vi (dare to go) おずおず行く ozùozu i-
kú
business venture 投機 tōki

venue [ven'ju:] n (place fixed for something) 開催地 kaísaichi

veranda(h) [væræn'də] n ベランダ beráń-
da

verb [və:rb] n 動詞 dóshi

verbal [və:r'bəl] adj (spoken: skills etc)
言葉の kotóba no; (: translation etc) 口頭
の kōtō no; (of a verb) 動詞の dóshi no

verbatim [və:rbei'tim] adj 言葉通りの
kotóbadòri no
♦adv 言葉通りに kotóbadòri ni

verbose [və:rbous'] adj (person) 口数の多
い kuchíkazu no ōì; (speech, report etc)
冗長な jôchō na

verdict [və:r'dikt] n (LAW) 判決 hańke-
tsu; (fig: opinion) 判断 hańdan

verge [və:rdʒ] n (BRIT: of road) 路肩 rokáta
「**soft verges**」(BRIT: AUT) 路肩軟弱
rokáta nanjaku
**to be on the verge of doing some-
thing** ...する所である ...surú tokoro dè
arù

verge on vt fus ...同然である ...dôzen de
arù

verify [ve:r'əfai] vt (confirm, check) 確
認する kakúnin suru

veritable [ve:r'itəbəl] adj (reinforcer: =
real) 全くの mattáku no

vermin [və:r'min] npl (animals) 害獣 gaí-
jū; (fleas, lice etc) 害虫 gaíchū

vermouth [və:rmu:θ'] n ベルモット be-
rúmottò

vernacular [və:rnæk'jələr] n (language)
その土地の言葉 sonó tochi no kotóba

versatile [və:r'sətəl] adj (person) 多才の
tasái no; (substance, machine, tool etc)
使い道の多い tsukáimichi no ōì

verse [və:rs] n (poetry) 詩 shi; (one part
of a poem: also in bible) 節 setsù

versed [və:rst] adj: **(well-)versed in**
...に詳しい ...ni kuwáshii

version [və:r'ʒən] n (form: of design,
production) 型 katá; (: of book, play etc)
...版...bań; (account: of events, accident
etc) 説明 setsúmei

versus [və:r'səs] prep ...対... ...tai ...

vertebra [və:r'təbrə] (pl **vertebrae**) n せ
きつい sekítsùi

vertebrae [və:r'təbrei] npl of **vertebra**

vertebrate [və:r'təbreit] n せきつい動物
sekítsuidōbutsu

vertical [və:r'tikəl] adj 垂直の suíchoku
no

vertigo [və:r'təgou] n めまい memáì

verve [və:rv] n (vivacity) 気迫 kiháku

very [ve:r'i:] adv (+ adjective, adverb) と
ても totémo, 大変 taíhen, 非常に hijō ni
♦adj: **it's the very book he'd told me
about** 彼が話していたのは正にその本だ
karè ga hanáshite ita no wà masà ni
sonó hon dà
the very last 正に最後の masà ni saígo
no
at the very least 少なくとも sukunà-
kutomo
very much 大変 taíhen

vessel [ves'əl] n (NAUT) 船 funè; (container) 容器 yōki see **blood**

vest [vest] n (US: waistcoat) チョッキ
chókki; (BRIT) アンダーシャツ añdā-

shatsù

vested interests [ves'tid-] *npl* 自分の利益 jibún no rièki, 私利 shirì

vestige [ves'tidʒ] *n* 残り nokóri

vet [vet] (*BRIT*) *n abbr* = **veterinary surgeon**
♦*vt* (examine: candidate) 調べる shirábe-rù

veteran [vet'ə:rən] *n* (of war) ...戦争で戦った人 ...seńsō de tatákatta hito; (former soldier) 退役軍人 taíekigunjin; (old hand) ベテラン betéran

veterinarian [vetə:rəne:r'i:ən] (*US*) *n* 獣医 jūí

veterinary [vet'ə:rəne:ri:] *adj* (practice, care etc) 獣医の jūí no

veterinary surgeon (*BRIT*) *n* = **veterinarian**

veto [vi:'tou] (*pl* **vetoes**) *n* (right to forbid) 拒否権 kyohíken; (act of forbidding) 拒否権の行使 kyohíken no kōshí
♦*vt* ...に拒否権を行使する ...ni kyohíken wo kōshí suru

vex [veks] *vt* (irritate, upset) 怒らせる o-kóraserù

vexed [vekst] *adj* (question) 厄介な yakkài na

via [vai'ə] *prep* (through, by way of) ...を経て ...wo hetè, ...経由 ...keíyu

viable [vai'əbəl] *adj* (project) 実行可能な jikkôkanō na; (company) 存立できる soństsu dekirù

viaduct [vai'ədʌkt] *n* 陸橋 rikkyó

vibrant [vai'brənt] *adj* (lively) 力強い chikárazuyoì; (bright) 生き生きした ikíkì shita; (full of emotion: voice) 感情のこもった kańjō no komótta

vibrate [vai'breit] *vi* (house, machine etc) 振動する shińdō suru

vibration [vaibrei'ʃən] *n* 振動 shińdō

vicar [vik'ə:r] *n* 主任司祭 shuńínshisaì

vicarage [vik'ə:ridʒ] *n* 司祭館 shisáikaǹ

vicarious [vaike:r'i:əs] *adj* (pleasure) 他人の身になって感じる tanín no mi ní nattè kańjirù

vice [vais] *n* (moral fault) 悪徳 akútoku; (TECH) 万力 mańriki

vice- [vais] *prefix* 副... fukú...

vice-president [vais'prez'idənt] *n* (*US POL*) 副大統領 fukúdaitōryð

vice squad *n* 風俗犯罪取締班 fūzokuhań-zai toríshimarihaǹ

vice versa [vais'və:r'sə] *adv* 逆の場合も同じ gyakú no baái mo onáji

vicinity [visin'əti:] *n* (area): *in the vicinity (of)* (...の) 近所に (...no) kiń-jo ni

vicious [viʃ'əs] *adj* (violent: attack, blow) 猛烈な mõretsu na; (cruel: words, look) 残酷な zańkoku na; (horse, dog) どう猛な dõmō na

vicious circle *n* 悪循環 akújuǹkan

victim [vik'tim] *n* (person, animal, business) 犠牲者 giséìsha

victimize [vik'təmaiz] *vt* (strikers etc) 食い物にする kuímono nì suru

victor [vik'tə:r] *n* 勝利者 shōrìsha

Victorian [viktour'i:ən] *adj* ヴィクトリア朝の bikútoriachō no

victorious [viktɔ:r'i:əs] *adj* (triumphant: team, shout) 勝ち誇る kachíhokoru

victory [vik'tə:ri:] *n* 勝利 shōrì

video [vid'i:ou] *cpd* ビデオの bideo no
♦*n* (video film) ビデオ bídeo, ビデオ映画 bídeo eíga; (*also*: **video cassette**) ビデオカセット bidéokasettð; (*also*: **video cassette recorder**) ビデオテープレコーダー bídeo tēpúrekōdà, VTR buitíaru

video tape *n* ビデオテープ bidéotēpù

vie [vai] *vi*: *to vie (with someone)(for something)* (...のために) (...と) 競り合う (...no tamé ni) (...to) seríaù

Vienna [vi:en'ə] *n* ウィーン uíǹ

Vietnam [vi:etnɑ:m'] *n* ベトナム betónamu

Vietnamese [vi:etnɑ:mi:z'] *adj* ベトナムの betónamu no; (*LING*) ベトナム語の betónamugð no
♦*n inv* (person) ベトナム人 betónamujìn; (*LING*) ベトナム語 betónamugð

view [vju:] *n* (sight) 景色 keshíki; (outlook) 見方 mikáta; (opinion) 意見 ikén
♦*vt* (look at: *also fig*) 見る mirù
on view (in museum etc) 展示中 teñjichū
in full view (of) (...の) 見ている前で (...no) mitè iru maè de

in view of the weather こういう天気だから kō fu teñki da karā

in view of the fact that ...だという事を考えて ...da tō iu koto wo kañgaetè

in my view 私の考えでは watákushi no kañgae de wà

viewer [vju:'ə:r] *n* (person) 見る人 mirù hito

viewfinder [vju:'faində:r] *n* ファインダー faiñdā

viewpoint [vju:'pɔint] *n* (attitude) 考え方 kañgaekata, 見地 keñchi; (place) 観察する地点 kañsatsu suru chitèn

vigil [vidʒ'əl] *n* 不寝番 fushíñban

vigilance [vidʒ'ələns] *n* 用心 yōjin

vigilant [vidʒ'ələnt] *adj* 用心する yōjin suru

vigor [vig'ə:r] (*BRIT* **vigour**) *n* (energy: of person, campaign) 力強さ chikárazuyosà

vigorous [vig'ə:rəs] *adj* (full of energy: person) 元気のいい geñki no iì; (: action, campaign) 強力な kyōryoku na; (: plant) よく茂った yokù shigéttà

vile [vail] *adj* (evil: action) 下劣な gerétsu na; (: language) 下品な gehiñ na; (: unpleasant: smell, weather, food, temper) ひどい hidoì

villa [vil'ə] *n* (country house) 別荘 bessō; (suburban house) 郊外の屋敷 kōgài no yashikí

village [vil'idʒ] *n* 村 murá

villager [vil'idʒə:r] *n* 村民 soñmiñ

villain [vil'in] *n* (scoundrel) 悪党 akútō; (in novel) 悪役 akúyaku; (*BRIT*: criminal) 犯人 hañnin

vindicate [vin'dikeit] *vt* (person: free from blame) ...の正しさを立証する ...no tadashìsa wo risshōsuru; (action: justify) ...が正当である事を立証する ...ga seítō de arù koto wo risshō suru

vindictive [vindik'tiv] *adj* (person) 執念深い shúnenbukaì; (action etc) 復しゅう心による fukúshūshìn ni yoru

vine [vain] *n* (climbing plant) ツル tsurù; (grapevine) ブドウの木 budō no ki

vinegar [vin'əgə:r] *n* 酢 su

vineyard [vin'jə:rd] *n* ブドウ園 budóen

vintage [vin'tidʒ] *n* (year) ブドウ収穫年 budō shūkakuneñ

♦*cpd* (classic: comedy, performance etc) 典型的な teñkeiteki na

vintage car *n* クラシックカー kurashìkku kā

vintage wine *n* 当り年のワイン atáridoshi no waiñ

vinyl [vai'nil] *n* ビニール binírù

viola [vi:ou'lə] *n* (MUS) ビオラ biòra

violate [vai'əleit] *vt* (agreement, peace) 破る yaburù; (graveyard) 汚す kegasù

violation [vaiəlei'ʃən] *n* (of agreement etc) 違反 iháñ

violence [vai'ələns] *n* (brutality) 暴力 bōryòku; (strength) 乱暴 rañbō

violent [vai'ələnt] *adj* (brutal: behavior) 暴力の bōryòku no, 乱暴な rañbō na; (intense: debate, criticism) 猛烈な mōrétsu na

a violent death 変死 heñshi

violet [vai'əlit] *adj* 紫色の murásakiiro no

♦*n* (color) 紫 murasàki; (plant) スミレ sumíre

violin [vaiəlin'] *n* バイオリン baíorin

violinist [vaiəlin'ist] *n* バイオリン奏者 baíorinsōsha, バイオリニスト baíorinisuto

VIP [vi:aipi:'] *n abbr* (= *very important person*) 要人 yōjìn, 貴賓 kihíñ, ブイアイピー buíaipī, ビップ bippù

viper [vai'pə:r] *n* クサリヘビ kusárihebì

virgin [və:r'dʒin] *n* (person) 処女 shojò, バージン bājìn

♦*adj* (snow, forest etc) 処女... shojò...

virginity [və:rdʒin'əti:] *n* (of person) 処女 shojò

Virgo [və:r'gou] *n* (sign) 乙女座 otomèza

virile [vir'əl] *adj* 男らしい otókorashiì

virility [vəril'əti:] *n* (sexual power) 性的能力 seítekinōryòku; (*fig*: masculine qualities) 男らしさ otókorashisà

virtually [və:r'tʃu:əli:] *adv* (almost) 事実上 jijítsujō

virtue [və:r'tʃu:] *n* (moral correctness) 徳 tokú, 徳行 tokkō; (good quality) 美徳 bítoku; (advantage) 利点 ritén, 長所 chō-

shò

by virtue of ...である事で ... de arù kotò de

virtuosi [vəːrtʃuːou'zi:] *npl of* **virtuoso**

virtuoso [vəːrtʃuːou'zou] (*pl* **virtuosos**
or **virtuosi**) *n* 名人 meíjin

virtuous [vəːr'tʃuːəs] *adj* (displaying virtue) 良心的な ryōshínteki na, 高潔な kō-
kétsu na, 敬けんな keíken na

virulent [vir'jələnt] *adj* (disease) 悪性の
akúsei no 危険な kiken na; (actions, feelings) 憎悪に満ちた zōō ni michíta

virus [vai'rəs] *n* ウイルス uírusu

visa [vi:'zə] *n* 査証 sashō、ビザ bìzà

vis-à-vis [vi:zɑːvi:'] *prep* (compared to)
...と比べて ...to kurábete; (in regard to)
...に関して ...ni kañ shite

viscose [vis'kouz] *n* ビスコース人絹 bisú-
kōsùjiñkeñ、ビスコースレーヨン bisúkō-
sùrēyòn

viscous [vis'kəs] *adj* ねばねばした nebà-
neba shita

visibility [vizəbil'əti:] *n* 視界 shikái

visible [viz'əbəl] *adj* (able to be seen or
recognized: *also fig*) 目に見える me nì
mierù

vision [viʒ'ən] *n* (sight: ability) 視力 shi-
ryòku; (: sense) 視覚 shikáku; (foresight)
ビジョン bijòn; (in dream) 幻影 geñ-ei

visit [viz'it] *n* (to person, place) 訪問 hômon
♦*vt* (person: *US also*: visit with) 訪問す
る hômon suru, 訪ねる tazúnerù, ...の所
へ遊びに行く ...no tokóro e asóbi ni ikú;
(place) 訪問する hômon suru, 訪ねる tazúnerù

visiting hours [viz'itiŋ-] *npl* (in hospital etc) 面会時間 meñkaijikan

visitor [viz'itəːr] *n* (person visiting, in-
vited) 客 kyakú; (tourist) 観光客 kañkō-
kyàku

visor [vai'zəːr] *n* (of helmet etc) 面 meñ;
(of cap etc) ひさし hisáshi; (AUT: *also*:
sun visor) ひよけ hiyóke

vista [vis'tə] *n* (view) 景色 keshíki

visual [viʒ'uːəl] *adj* (arts etc) 視覚の shikáku no

visual aid *n* 視覚教材 shikákukyōzai

visual display unit *n* モニター monîtā,
ディスプレー disúpurē

visualize [viʒ'uːəlaiz] *vt* (picture, imagine) 想像する sôzō suru

vital [vait'əl] *adj* (essential, important,
crucial) 重要な jûyō na; (full of life: person) 活発な kappátsu na; (necessary for
life: organ) 生命に必要な seímei ni hitsúyō na

vitality [vaitæl'iti:] *n* (liveliness) 元気
geñki

vitally [vai'təli:] *adv*: ***vitally important*** 極めて重要な jûyō na

vital statistics *npl* (of population) 人口
動態統計 jiñkōdōtaitōkei; (*inf*: woman's
measurements) スリーサイズ surísaizù

vitamin [vai'təmin] *n* ビタミン bitámin

vivacious [vivei'ʃəs] *adj* にぎやかな nigi-
yàka na

vivid [viv'id] *adj* (clear: description,
memory) 鮮明な seímei na; (bright:
color, light) 鮮やかな azáyaka na; (imagination) はつらつとした hatsúratsu to
shitá

vividly [viv'idli:] *adv* (describe) 目に見え
る様に me nì mierù yō ni; (remember) は
っきりと hakkírì to

vivisection [vivisek'ʃən] *n* 生体解剖 seí-
taikaibō

V-neck [vi:'nek] *n* (*also*: **V-neck
jumper/pullover**) V ネックセーター buí-
nekkusētā

vocabulary [voukæb'jələːri:] *n* (words
known) 語い goî

vocal [vou'kəl] *adj* (of the voice) 声の ko-
è no; (articulate) はっきり物を言う hak-
kírì monó wo iú

vocal c(h)ords *npl* 声帯 seítai

vocation [voukei'ʃən] *n* (calling) 使命感
shimèikan; (chosen career) 職業 shoku-
gyò

vocational [voukei'ʃənəl] *adj* (training
etc) 職業の shokugyō no

vociferous [vousif'əːrəs] *adj* (protesters,
demands) やかましい yakámashii、しつ
こい shitsúkoî

vodka [vɑd'kə] *n* ウォッカ uókkà

vogue [voug] *n* 流行 ryūkô

in vogue 流行して ryūkṓ shite

voice [vɔis] *n* (of person) 声 koè
♦*vt* (opinion) 表明する hyṓmei suru

void [vɔid] *n* (emptiness) 空虚 kūkyò;
(hole) 穴 aná, 空間 kū́kan
♦*adj* (invalid) 無効の mukṓ no; (empty):
void of ...が全くない ...ga mattáku naì

volatile [vɑ:l'ətəl] *adj* (liable to change:
situation) 不安定な fuáñtei na; (: person)
気まぐれな kimágure na; (: liquid) 揮発
性の kihátsusei no

volcanic [vɑ:lkæn'ik] *adj* (eruption) 火山
の kazáñ no; (rock etc) 火山性の kazáñ-
sei no

volcano [vɑ:lkei'nou] (*pl* **volcanoes**) *n* 火
山 kazáñ

volition [voulíʃ'ən] *n*: *of one's own
volition* 自発的に jihátsuteki ni, 自由意
志で jiyū́ishì de

volley [vɑ:l'i:] *n* (of stones etc) 一斉に投
げられる... isséi ni nagérareru ...; (of
questions etc) 連発 reñpatsu; (TENNIS
etc) ボレー borè
a volley of gunfire 一斉射撃 isséishagèki

volleyball [vɑ:l'i:bɔ:l] *n* バレーボール ba-
rḗbōrù

volt [voult] *n* ボルト borúto

voltage [voul'tidʒ] *n* 電圧 deñ-atsu

voluble [vɑ:l'jəbəl] *adj* (person) 口達者な
kuchídasshà na; (speech etc) 流ちょうな
ryūchṓ na

volume [vɑ:l'ju:m] *n* (space) 容積 yōsèki;
(amount) 容量 yōryṓ; (book) 本 hoñ;
(sound level) 音量 oñryō, ボリューム bo-
ryū́mu
Volume 2 第2巻 daíníkan

voluminous [vəlu:'minəs] *adj* (clothes)
だぶだぶの dabúdabu no; (correspon-
dence, notes) 大量の taíryō no, 多数のta-
sū́ no

voluntarily [vɑ:lənter:r'ili:] *adv* (willingly) 自発的に jihátsuteki ni, 自由意志で ji-
yū́ishì de

voluntary [vɑ:l'ənter:i:] *adj* (willing,
done willingly: exile, redundancy) 自発
的な jihátsuteki na, 自由意志による jiyū́-
ishì ni yoru; (unpaid: work, worker) 奉仕

の hṓshī no

volunteer [vɑ:lənti:r'] *n* (unpaid helper)
奉仕者 hōshísha, ボランティア borántìa;
(to army etc) 志願者 shigánshà
♦*vt* (information) 自発的に言う jihátsuteki ni iú, 提供する teñkyō suru
♦*vi* (for army etc) ...への入隊を志願する
...e no nyū́tai wo shigán suru
to volunteer to do ...しようと申出る
...shiyṓ to mōshíderu

voluptuous [vəlʌp'tʃʊəs] *adj* (movement, body, feeling) 官能的な kañnōteki
na, 色っぽい iróppoi

vomit [vɑ:m'it] *n* 吐いた物 haíta monó,
反吐 hedð
♦*vt* 吐く hakù
♦*vi* 吐く hakù

vote [vout] *n* (method of choosing) 票決
hyṓketsu; (indication of choice, opinion)
投票 tṓhyō; (votes cast) 投票数 tṓhyōsū;
(*also*: **right to vote**) 投票権 tṓhyōkèn
♦*vt* (elect): *to be voted chairman etc*
座長に選出される zachṓ ni señshutsu sarèru; (propose): *to vote that* ...という事
を提案する ...to iú koto wo teñan suru
♦*vi* (in election etc) 投票する tṓhyō suru
vote of thanks 感謝決議 kañshaketsu-
gì

voter [vou'tə:r] *n* (person voting) 投票者
tṓhyōshà; (person with right to vote) 有
権者 yū́kenshà

voting [vou'tiŋ] *n* 投票 tṓhyō

vouch for [vautʃ-] *vt fus* (person, quality etc) 保証する hoshṓ suru

voucher [vau'tʃə:r] *n* (for meal: *also*:
luncheon voucher) 食券 shokkèn; (with
petrol, cigarettes etc) クーポン kū́poñ;
(*also*: **gift voucher**) ギフト券 gifútokeñ

vow [vau] *n* 誓い chikái
♦*vt*: *to vow to do/that* ...する事[...だと
いう事]を誓う ...surú koto[...da to iú
koto]wo chikáu

vowel [vau'əl] *n* 母音 boíñ

voyage [vɔi'idʒ] *n* (journey: by ship,
spacecraft) 旅 tabí, 旅行 ryokō

V-sign [vi:'sain] (*BRIT*) *n* Vサイン buí-
sain ◇手の甲を相手に向けると軽べつの
サイン；手のひらを向けると勝利のサイ

ン té no kō wo aíte ni mukéru to keíbetsu no saín; te nó hirá wo mukéru to shōrí no saín

vulgar [vʌl'gəːr] *adj* (rude: remarks, gestures, graffiti) 下品な gehín na; (in bad taste: decor, ostentation) 野暮な yabò na

vulgarity [vʌlgær'iti:] *n* (rudeness) 下品な言葉 gehín na kotóba; (ostentation) 野暮ったい事 yabôttaì kotó

vulnerable [vʌl'nəːrəbəl] *adj* (person, position) やられやすい yaráreyasuï, 無防備な mubôbì na

vulture [vʌl'tʃəːr] *n* ハゲタカ hagétaka

W

wad [wɑːd] *n* (of cotton wool, paper) 塊 katámari; (of banknotes etc) 束 tabà

waddle [wɑːd'əl] *vi* (duck, baby) よちよち歩く yochíyochi arúkù; (fat person) よたよた歩く yotáyota arúkù

wade [weid] *vi*: *to wade through* (water) ...の中を歩いて通る ...no nakà wo arúite tōrù; (*fig*: a book) 苦労して読む kurō shité yomù

wafer [wei'fəːr] *n* (biscuit) ウエハース uéhàsu

waffle [wɑː'fəl] *n* (CULIN) ワッフル waffùru; (empty talk) 下らない話 kudáranai hanáshi

♦*vi* (in speech, writing) 下らない話をする kudáranai hanáshi wo surù

waft [wæft] *vt* (sound, scent) 漂わせる tadayowaseru

♦*vi* (sound, scent) 漂う tadáyou

wag [wæg] *vt* (tail, finger) 振る furù

♦*vi*: *the dog's tail was wagging* イヌはしっぽを振っていた inú wà shippó wo futté ità

wage [weidʒ] *n* (*also*: **wages**) 賃金 chiñgin, 給料 kyūryō

♦*vt*: *to wage war* 戦争をする señsō wo suru

wage earner [-əːr'nəːr] *n* 賃金労働者 chiñginrōdōshà

wage packet *n* 給料袋 kyúryòbukùro

wager [wei'dʒəːr] *n* かけ kaké

waggle [wæg'əl] *vt* (hips) 振る furù; (eyebrows etc) ぴくぴくさせる píkùpiku saséru

wag(g)on [wæg'ən] *n* (*also*: **horse-drawn wag(g)on**) 荷馬車 nibáshà; (*BRIT*: RAIL) 貨車 kashá

wail [weil] *n* (of person) 泣き声 nakígoè; (of siren etc) うなり unári

♦*vi* (person) 泣き声をあげる nakígoè wo agérù; (siren) うなる unarù

waist [weist] *n* (ANAT, *also* of clothing) ウエスト uésùto

waistcoat [weist'kout] (*BRIT*) *n* チョッキ chókki, ベスト besùto

waistline [weist'lain] *n* (of body) 胴回り dōmawàri, ウエスト uésùto; (of garment) ウエストライン uésùtoraìn

wait [weit] *n* (interval) 待ち時間 machí jikan

♦*vi* 待つ matsù

to lie in wait for ...を待伏せする ...wo machíbuse suru

I can't wait to (*fig*) 早く...したい hayáku ...shitái

to wait for someone/something ...を待つ ...wo matsu

wait behind *vi* 居残って待つ inokotte matsù

waiter [wei'təːr] *n* (in restaurant etc) 給仕 kyūjì, ウエーター uétā, ボーイ bóì

waiting [wei'tiŋ] *n*: *"no waiting"* (*BRIT*: AUT) 停車禁止 teísha kiñshi

waiting list *n* 順番待ちの名簿 juñbanmachi no meíbo

waiting room *n* (in surgery, railway station) 待合室 machíaìshitsu

wait on *vt fus* (people in restaurant) ...に給仕する ...ni kyūjì suru

waitress [wei'tris] *n* ウエートレス uétòresu

waive [weiv] *vt* (rule) 適用するのをやめる tekíyō suru no wò yaméru; (rights etc) 放棄する hōkî suru

wake [weik] (*pt* **woke** *or* **waked**, *pp* **woken** *or* **waked**) *vt* (*also*: **wake up**) 起す okósù

♦*vi* (*also*: **wake up**) 目が覚める me gá samérù

♦*n* (for dead person) 通夜 tsuyà, tsúya; (NAUT) 航跡 kōseki

waken [wei'kən] *vt, vi* = **wake**

Wales [weilz] *n* ウェールズ uērùzu

the Prince of Wales プリンスオブウェールズ purīnsu obu uērùzu

walk [wɔːk] *n* (hike) ハイキング haīkingu; (shorter) 散歩 sańpo; (gait) 歩調 hochō; (in park, along coast etc) 散歩道 sańpomichi, 遊歩道 yūhodō

♦*vi* (go on foot) 歩く arúkù; (for pleasure, exercise) 散歩する sańpo suru

♦*vt* (distance) 歩く arúkù; (dog) 散歩に連れて行く sańpo ni tsuréte ikú

10 minutes' walk from here ここから徒歩で10分の所に kokó karà tohò do juppùn no tokóro ni

people from all walks of life あらゆる身分の人々 aráyurù mibùn no hitóbìto

walker [wɔːk'əːr] *n* (person) ハイカー haíkā

walkie-talkie [wɔːk'iːtɔː'kiː] *n* トランシーバー toránshībā

walking [wɔː'kiŋ] *n* ハイキング haíkingu

walking shoes *npl* 散歩靴 sańpogutsu

walking stick *n* ステッキ sutékkì

walk out *vi* (audience) 出て行く detè ikú; (workers) ストライキをする sutóraìki wo suru

walkout [wɔːk'aut] *n* (of workers) ストライキ sutóraìki

walk out on (*inf*) *vt fus* (family etc) 見捨てる misúteru

walkover [wɔːk'ouvəːr] (*inf*) *n* (competition, exam etc) 朝飯前 asámeshimaè

walkway [wɔːk'wei] *n* 連絡通路 reńrakutsūrò

wall [wɔːl] *n* (gen) 壁 kabé; (city wall etc) 城壁 jōheki

walled [wɔːld] *adj* (city) 城壁に囲まれた jōheki ni kakómareta; (garden) 塀をめぐらした heī wo megúrashita

wallet [wɑː'lit] *n* 札入れ satsúire, 財布 saífu

wallflower [wɔːl'flauəːr] *n* ニオイアラセイトウ niōiaraseitō

to be a wallflower (*fig*) だれもダンスの相手になってくれない darè mo dańsu no aíte ni nattè kurénai, 壁の花である kabé no hana de arù

wallop [wɑː'ləp] (*inf*) *vt* ぶん殴る buńnaguru

wallow [wɑː'lou] *vi* (animal: in mud, water) ころげ回る korógemawarù; (person: in sentiment, guilt) ふける fukérù

wallpaper [wɔːl'peipəːr] *n* 壁紙 kabégami

♦*vt* (room) ...に壁紙を張る ...ni kabégami wo harú

wally [wei'liː] (*BRIT: inf*) *n* ばか bakà

walnut [wɔːl'nʌt] *n* (nut) クルミ kurúmi; (*also:* **walnut tree**) クルミの木 kurúmi no ki; (wood) クルミ材 kurúmizaì

walrus [wɔːl'rəs] (*pl* **walrus** *or* **walruses**) *n* セイウチ seíuchì

waltz [wɔːlts] *n* (dance, MUS) 円舞曲 eńbukyòku, ワルツ warùtsu

♦*vi* (dancers) ワルツを踊る warùtsu wo odóru

wan [wɑːn] *adj* (person, complexion) 青白い aójiroi; (smile) 悲しげな kanáshigenà

wand [wɑːnd] *n* (*also:* **magic wand**) 魔法の棒 mahō no bō

wander [wɑːn'dəːr] *vi* (person) ぶらぶら歩く buràbura arúkù; (attention) 散漫になる sańman ni narù; (mind, thoughts: here and there) さまよう samáyoù; (: to specific topic) 漂う tadáyoù

♦*vt* (the streets, the hills etc) ...をぶらぶら歩く ...wo buràbura arúkù

wane [wein] *vi* (moon) 欠ける kakérù; (enthusiasm, influence etc) 減る herú

wangle [wæŋ'gəl] (*inf*) *vt* うまい具合に獲得する umái guái ni kakútoku suru

want [wɑːnt] *vt* (wish for) 望む nozómu, ...が欲しい ...ga hoshiì; (need, require) ...が必要である ...ga hitsúyō de arù

♦*n*: *for want of* ...がないので ...ga naì no de

to want to do ...したい ...shitái

to want someone to do something ...に...してもらいたい ...ni ...shité moraitaì

wanted [wɑːnt'id] *adj* (criminal etc) 指名手配中の shiméitehàichū no

「*wanted*」(in advertisements) 求む mo-
tómù

wanting [wɑːntiŋ] *adj*: **to be found
wanting** 期待を裏切る kítái wo urágírù

wanton [wɑːntən] *adj* (gratuitous) 理由
のない riyǔ no naî; (promiscuous) 浮気な
uwáki na

wants [wɑːnts] *npl* (needs) 必要とする物
hitsúyǒ to suru monó, ニーズ nízù

war [wɔːr] *n* 戦争 sefísō

to make war (on) (*also fig*) …と戦う
…to tatákau

ward [wɔːrd] *n* (in hospital) 病棟 byótō;
(POL) 区 ku; (LAW: child: *also*: **ward of
court**) 被後見人 hikǒkennin

warden [wɔːrdən] *n* (of park, game
reserve, youth hostel) 管理人 kafírinîn;
(of prison etc) 所長 shochǒ; (*BRIT*: *also*:
traffic warden) 交通監視官 kōtsǔkan-
shikaǹ

warder [wɔːrdəːr] *n* (*BRIT*) 看守 kaǹ-
shu

ward off *vt* (attack, enemy) 食止める
kuítomeru; (danger, illness) 防ぐ fuségù

wardrobe [wɔːrdroub] *n* (for clothes) 洋
服だんす yǒfukudaǹsu; (collection of
clothes) 衣装 ishǒ; (CINEMA, THEA-
TER) 衣装部屋 ishóbeya

warehouse [weːrhaus] *n* 倉庫 sōkò

wares [weːrz] *npl* 商品 shǒhin, 売り物 urímono

warfare [wɔːrfeːr] *n* 戦争 sefísō

warhead [wɔːrhed] *n* 弾頭 dańtō

warily [weːrili:] *adv* 用心深く yǒjínbu-
kakù

warlike [wɔːrlaik] *adj* (nation) 好戦的な
kǒsenteki na; (appearance) 武装した bu-
sǒshita

warm [wɔːrm] *adj* (meal, soup, day,
clothes etc) 暖かい atátakaî; (thanks) 心
からの kokóro kara no; (applause, welcome) 熱烈な netsúretsu na; (person,
heart) 優しい yasáshii, 温情のある ofíjō
no arù

it's warm (just right) 暖かい atátakaî;
(too warm) 暑い atsúî

I'm warm 暑い atsúî

warm water ぬるま湯 murúmayù

warm-hearted [wɔːrmhɑːrtid] *adj* 心
の優しい kokóro no yasáshii

warmly [wɔːrmliː] *adv* (applaud, welcome) 熱烈に netsúretsu ni

to dress warmly 厚着する atsúgi suru

warmth [wɔːrmθ] *n* (heat) 暖かさ atáta-
kasa; (friendliness) 温かみ atátakami

warm up *vi* (person, room, soup, etc) 暖
まる atátamarù; (weather) 暖かくなる a-
tátakaku narù; (athlete) 準備運動をする
juńbiuǹdō wo suru, ウォーミングアップ
する uǒminguappù suru

♦*vt* (hands etc) 暖める atátamerù;
(engine) 暖気運転する daǹkiuńten suru

warn [wɔːrn] *vt* (advise): **to warn someone of/that** …に…があると[…だと]警
告する …ni …ga arù to […da to]kefíkoku
suru

to warn someone not to do …に…しな
いよう警告する …ni …shinái yō kefíkoku
suru

warning [wɔːrniŋ] *n* 警告 kefíkoku

warning light *n* 警告灯 kefíkokutō

warning triangle *n* (AUT) 停止表示板
teíshihyǒjibaǹ

warp [wɔːrp] *vi* (wood etc) ゆがむ yugámu

♦*vt* (*fig*: character) ゆがめる yugámerù

warrant [wɔːrənt] *n* (voucher) 証明書
shǒmeîsho; (LAW: for arrest) 逮捕状 taî-
hojō; (: search warrant) 捜索令状 sǒsa-
kureijō

warranty [wɔːrənti:] *n* (guarantee) 保証
hoshǒ

warren [wɔːrən] *n* (*also*: **rabbit warren**)
ウサギ小屋 uságigoya; (*fig*: of passages,
streets) 迷路 meîro

warrior [wɔːriːər] *n* 戦士 seǹshi

Warsaw [wɔːrsɔː] *n* ワルシャワ warú-
shawa

warship [wɔːrʃip] *n* 軍艦 guńkan

wart [wɔːrt] *n* いぼ ibô

wartime [wɔːrtaim] *n*: **in wartime** 戦
時中 seǹjichū

wary [weːriː] *adj* 用心深い yǒjinbukaî

was [wʌz] *pt of* be

wash [wɔːʃ] *vt* (gen) 洗う aráu; (clothes
etc) 洗濯する seǹtaku suru

♦*vi* (person) 手を洗う te wò aráu; (sea etc): *to wash over/against something* ...に打寄せる ...ni uchíyoseru, ...を洗う ...wo aráu

♦*n* (clothes etc) 洗濯物 señtakumono; (washing program) 洗い arái; (of ship) 航跡の波 kōseki no namî

to have a wash 手を洗う te wò aráu

to give something a wash ...を洗う ...wo aráu

washable [wɔːˈʃəbəl] *adj* 洗濯できる señtaku dekirù

wash away *vt* (stain) 洗い落す araiotosu; (subj: flood, river etc) 流す nagasu

washbasin [wɔːˈʃbeisin] (*US also:* **washbowl**) *n* 洗面器 señmeñki

washcloth [wɔːˈʃklɔːθ] (*US*) *n* (face cloth) フェースタオル fēsutaorù

washer [wɔːˈʃəːr] *n* (TECH: metal) 座金 zagáne, ワッシャー wasshā; (machine) 洗濯機 señtakuki

washing [wɔːˈʃiŋ] *n* (dirty, clean) 洗濯物 señtakumono

washing machine *n* 洗濯機 señtakuki

washing powder (*BRIT*) *n* 洗剤 señzai

washing-up [wɔːˈʃiŋʌpˈ] (*BRIT*) *n* (action) 皿洗い saráaraì; (dirty dishes) 汚れた皿 yogóretà sará

washing-up liquid (*BRIT*) *n* 台所用洗剤 daídokoroyō senzai

wash off *vi* 洗い落される aráiotosáreru

wash-out [wɔːˈʃaut] (*inf*) *n* (failed event) 失敗 shippai

washroom [wɔːˈʃruːm] (*US*) *n* お手洗い o-téaraì

wash up *vi* (*US*) 手を洗う te wò aráu; (*BRIT*) 皿洗いをする saráarài wo suru

wasn't [wʌzˈənt] = **was not**

wasp [wɑːsp] *n* アシナガバチ ashínagabàchi ◇スズメバチなど肉食性のハチの総称 suzúmebàchi nado nikúshokuseī no hachi no sōshō

wastage [weisˈtidʒ] *n* (amount wasted, loss) 浪費 rōhi

natural wastage 自然消耗 shizénshōmō

waste [weist] *n* (act of wasting: life, money, energy, time) 浪費 rōhi; (rubbish)

廃棄物 haíkibutsu; (*also:* **household waste**) ごみ gomî

♦*adj* (material) 廃棄の haíki no; (left over) 残り物の nokórimono no; (land) 荒れた aréta

♦*vt* (time, life, money, energy) 浪費する rōhi suru; (opportunity) 失う ushínau, 逃す nogásu

to lay waste (destroy: area, town) 破壊する hakái suru

waste away *vi* 衰弱する suíjaku suru

waste disposal unit (*BRIT*) *n* ディスポーザー disúpōzā

wasteful [weistˈfəl] *adj* (person) 無駄使いの多い mudázukai no ōî; (process) 不経済な fukéīzai na

waste ground (*BRIT*) *n* 空き地 akíchi

wastepaper basket [weistˈpeipəːr-] *n* くずかご kuzúkàgo

waste pipe *n* 排水管 haísuīkan

wastes [weists] *npl* (area of land) 荒れ野 aréno

watch [wɑːtʃ] *n* (*also:* **wristwatch**) 腕時計 udédokèi; (act of watching) 見張り mihári; (vigilance) 警戒 keíkai; (group of guards: MIL, NAUT) 番兵 bañpei; (NAUT: spell of duty) 当直 tōchoku, ワッチ watchì

♦*vt* (look at: people, objects, TV etc) 見る míru; (spy on, guard) 見張る miháru; (be careful of) ...に気を付ける ...ni ki wò tsukerù

♦*vi* (look) 見る míru; (keep guard) 見張る miháru

watchdog [wɑːtʃˈdɔːg] *n* (dog) 番犬 bañken; (*fig*) 監視者 kañshisha, お目付け役 o-métsukeyaku

watchful [wɑːtʃˈfəl] *adj* 注意深い chúibukaì

watchmaker [wɑːtʃˈmeikəːr] *n* 時計屋 tokéiya

watchman [wɑːtʃˈmən] (*pl* **watchmen**) *n*
see **night**

watch out *vi* 気を付ける ki wó tsukerù, 注意する chūi suru

watch out! 危ない！ abúnai!

watch strap *n* 腕時計のバンド udédokèi no bañdo

water [wɔːˈtər] *n* (cold) 水 mizú; (hot) (お) 湯 (o)yú

◆*vt* (plant) ...に水をやる ...ni mizú wo yarú

◆*vi* (eyes) 涙が出る namída ga derù; (mouth) よだれが出る yodáre ga derù

in British waters 英国領海に〔で〕 eíkokuryōkai ni〔de〕

water cannon *n* 放水砲 hōsuihō

water closet (*BRIT*) *n* トイレ toíre

watercolor [wɔːˈtərkʌlər] *n* (picture) 水彩画 suísaiga

watercress [wɔːˈtərkres] *n* クレソン kuréson

water down *vt* (milk etc) 水で薄める mizú de usúmeru; (fig: story) 和らげる yawáragerù

waterfall [wɔːˈtərfɔːl] *n* 滝 takí

water heater *n* 湯沸器 yuwákashikì

watering can [wɔːˈtəriŋ-] *n* じょうろ jōrō

water level *n* 水位 suíi

water lily *n* スイレン suíren

waterline [wɔːˈtərlain] *n* (NAUT) 喫水線 kissuísen

waterlogged [wɔːˈtərlɔːgd] *adj* (ground) 水浸しの mizúbitashi no

water main *n* 水道本管 suídōhonkaǹ

watermelon [wɔːˈtərmelən] *n* スイカ suíka

waterproof [wɔːˈtərpruːf] *adj* (trousers, jacket etc) 防水の bōsui no

watershed [wɔːˈtərʃed] *n* (GEO: natural boundary) 分水界 buńsuikaì; (: high ridge) 分水嶺 buńsuirei; (fig) 分岐点 buńkitèn

water-skiing [wɔːˈtərskiːiŋ] *n* 水上スキー suíjōsukī

watertight [wɔːˈtərtait] *adj* (seal) 水密の suímitsu no

waterway [wɔːˈtərwei] *n* 水路 suíro

waterworks [wɔːˈtərwəːrks] *n* (building) 浄水場 jōsuijō

watery [wɔːˈtəriː] *adj* (coffee) 水っぽい mizúppoì; (eyes) 涙ぐんだ namídagundà

watt [wɑːt] *n* ワット wattò

wave [weiv] *n* (of hand) 一振り hitófuri; (on water) 波 namí; (RADIO) 電波 deñpɛ; (in hair) ウェーブ uébù; (*fig*: surge) 高まり takámarì, 急増 kyūzō

◆*vi* (signal) 手を振る te wò furù; (branches, grass) 揺れる yuréru; (flag) なびく nabíkù

◆*vt* (hand, flag, handkerchief) 振る furù; (gun, stick) 振回す furímawasù

wavelength [weivˈleŋkθ] *n* (RADIO) 波長 hachō

on the same wavelength (*fig*) 気が合って ki gà attè

waver [weiˈvər] *vi* (voice) 震える furúeru; (love) 揺らぐ yurágu; (person) 動揺する dōyō suru

his gaze did not waver 彼は目を反らさなかった kárè wa mé wò sorásanakattà

wavy [weiˈviː] *adj* (line) くねくねした kunékune shita; (hair) ウェーブのある uébù no aru

wax [wæks] *n* (polish, for skis) ワックス wakkùsu; (*also*: **earwax**) 耳あか mimíakà

◆*vt* (floor, car, skis) ...にワックスを掛ける ...ni wakkùsu wo kakérù

◆*vi* (moon) 満ちる michírù

waxworks [wæksˈwəːrks] *npl* (models) ろう人形 rōníǹgyō

◆*n* (place) ろう人形館 rōníǹgyōkan

way [wei] *n* (route) ...へ行く道 ...e ikú michí; (path) 道 michí; (access) 出入口 deíriguchi; (distance) 距離 kyórì; (direction) 方向 hōkō; (manner, method) 方法 hōhō; (habit) 習慣 shūkan

which way? - this way どちらへ？-こちらへ dochìra é ? -kochíra e

on the way (en route) 途中で tochū de

to be on one's way 今向かっている imà mukátte irù, 今途中である imà tochū de arù

to be in the way (*also fig*) 邪魔である jamá de arù

to go out of one's way to do something わざわざ...する wazàwaza ...suru

under way (project etc) 進行中で shiñkōchū de

to lose one's way 道に迷う michí ni mayóù

in a way ある意味では arù imì de wa

in some ways ある面では arù men de wa

no way! (*inf*) 絶対に駄目だ zettái ni damé dà

by the way ... ところで tokórð dè

「*way in*」(*BRIT*) 入口 iríguchi

「*way out*」(*BRIT*) 出口 degùchi

the way back 帰路 kirò

「*give way*」(*BRIT*: *AUT*) 進路譲れ shiñro yuzúre

waylay [weilei'] (*pt*, *pp* **waylaid**) *vt* 待伏せする machíbuse suru

wayward [wei'wərd] *adj* (behavior, child) わがままな wagamáma na

W.C. [dʌb'əlju:si:'] (*BRIT*) *n* トイレ toìre

we [wi:] *pl pron* 私たちが〔が〕watákushitàchi wa〔ga〕

weak [wi:k] *adj* (*gen*) 弱い yowáì; (dollar, pound) 安い yasúì; (excuse) 下手なhetá nà; (argument) 説得力のない settőkuryoku no naì; (tea) 薄い usúi

weaken [wi:'kən] *vi* (person, resolve) 弱る yowárù; (health) 衰える otóroerù; (influence, power) 劣る otóru

♦*vt* (person, government) 弱くする yowákù suru

weakling [wi:k'liŋ] *n* (physically) 虚弱児 kyojákuji; (morally) 骨無し honénashi

weakness [wi:k'nis] *n* (frailty) 弱さ yowàsa; (fault) 弱点 jakúteñ

*to have a weakness for ...*に目がない ...ni me gà naì

wealth [welθ] *n* (money, resources) 富 tomí, 財産 zaísan; (of details, knowledge etc) 豊富な hốfu_na

wealthy [wel'θi:] *adj* (person, family, country) 裕福な yūfùku na

wean [wi:n] *vt* (baby) 離乳させる rinyū saséru

weapon [wep'ən] *n* 武器 bukî

wear [we:r] *n* (use) 使用 shiyő; (damage through use) 消耗 shőmò; (clothing): *sportswear* スポーツウェア supőtsùuea

♦*vb* (*pt* **wore**, *pp* **worn**)

♦*vt* (shirt, blouse, dress etc) 着る kirú; (hat etc) かぶる kabúrù; (shoes, pants, skirt etc) はく hakù; (gloves etc) はめる

haméru; (make-up) つける tsukérù; (damage: through use) 使い古す tsukáifurusù

♦*vi* (last) 使用に耐える shiyő ni taéru; (rub through etc: carpet, shoes, jeans) すり減る suríheru

babywear 幼児ウェア yōjìuea

evening wear イブニングウェア ibúningu ueà

wear and tear *n* 消耗 shőmò

wear away *vt* すり減らす suríherasu

♦*vi* (inscription etc) すり減って消える suríhette kiéru

wear down *vt* (heels) すり減らす suríherasu; (person, strength) 弱くする yowákù suru, 弱らせる yowáraserù

wear off *vi* (pain etc) なくなる nakúnaru

wear out *vt* (shoes, clothing) 使い古す tsukáifurusù; (person) すっかり疲れさせる sukkári tsukáresaséru; (strength) なくす nakúsu

weary [wi:'ri:] *adj* (tired) 疲れ果てた tsukárehatetà; (dispirited) がっかりした gakkári shita

♦*vi*: *to weary of* ...に飽きる ...ni akíru

weasel [wi:'zəl] *n* イタチ itáchi

weather [weð'ə:r] *n* 天気 teñki, 天候 teñkō

♦*vt* (storm, crisis) 乗切る noríkirù

under the weather (*fig*: ill) 気分が悪い kibùn ga warúi

weather-beaten [weð'ə:rbi:tən] *adj* (face, skin, building, stone) 風雪に鍛えられた fűsetsu ni kitáeraretà

weathercock [weð'ə:rkɑ:k] *n* 風見鶏 kazámidòri

weather forecast *n* 天気予報 teñkiyohồ

weatherman [weð'ə:rmæn] (*pl* **weathermen**) *n* 天気予報係 teñkiyohōgakarì

weather vane [-vein] *n* = **weathercock**

weave [wi:v] (*pt* **wove**, *pp* **woven**) *vt* (cloth) 織る orù; (basket) 編む amù

weaver [wi:'və:r] *n* 機織職人 hatáorishokunin

weaving [wi:'viŋ] *n* (craft) 機織 hatáori

web [web] n (also: **spiderweb**) クモの巣 kumó no su; (on duck's foot) 水かき mizúkaki; (network, also fig) 網 amí

we'd [wi:d] = we had; we would

wed [wed] (pt, pp **wedded**) vt (marry) ...と結婚する ...to kekkón suru
♦vi 結婚する kekkón suru

wedding [wed'iŋ] n 結婚式 kekkónshiki
silver/golden wedding (anniversary) 銀〔金〕婚式 gíñ(kíñ)kónshiki

wedding day n (day of the wedding) 結婚の日 kekkón no hi; (US: anniversary) 結婚記念日 kekkón kinéñbi

wedding dress n 花嫁衣裳 hanáyome ishô, ウエディングドレス uédingudorèsu

wedding present n 結婚祝い kekkón iwaí

wedding ring n 結婚指輪 kekkón yubíwa

wedge [wedʒ] n (of wood etc) くさび kusábi; (of cake) 一切れ hitókire
♦vt (jam with a wedge) くさびで留める kusábi dè toméru; (pack tightly: of people, animals) 押込む oshíkomù

Wednesday [wenz'dei] n 水曜日 suíyōbì

wee [wi:] (SCOTTISH) adj 小さい chíísaì

weed [wi:d] n 雑草 zassó
♦vt (garden) ...の草むしりをする ...no kusámushirì wo suru

weedkiller [wi:d'kilər] n 除草剤 josózai

weedy [wi:'di:] adj (man) 柔そうな yawásō na

week [wi:k] n 週間 shúkan
a week today/on Friday 来週の今日〔金曜日〕raíshū no kyô(kíñ-yōbì)

weekday [wi:k'dei] n (gen, COMM) 平日 heíjitsu, ウイークデー uíkùdē

weekend [wi:k'end] n 週末 shūmátsu, ウイークエンド uíkuèndo

weekly [wi:k'li:] adv (deliver etc) 毎週 maíshū
♦adj (newspaper) 週刊の shúkan no; (payment) 週払いの shúbarai no; (visit etc) 毎週の maíshū no
♦n (magazine) 週刊誌 shúkanshi; (newspaper) 週刊新聞 shúkanshíñbun

weep [wi:p] (pt, pp **wept**) vi (person) 泣く naku

weeping willow [wi:'piŋ-] n シダレヤナギ shídareyanàgi

weigh [wei] vt ...の重さを計る ...no omósa wo hakáru
♦vi ...の重さは...である ...no omósa wa ...de arù
to weigh anchor いかりを揚げる ikári wo agéru

weigh down vt (person, pack animal etc) ...の重さで動きが遅くなる ...no omósa de ugóki ga osóku narù; (fig: with worry): **to be weighed down** ...で沈み込む ...de shizúmikomu

weight [weit] n (metal object) 重り omóri; (heaviness) 重さ omósa
to lose/put on weight 体重が減る〔増える〕taíjū ga herú(fueru)

weighting [wei'tiŋ] (BRIT) n (allowance) 地域手当 chíìkiteatè

weightlifter [weit'liftər] n 重量挙げ選手 jūryóage señshu

weighty [wei'ti:] adj (heavy) 重い omói; (important: matters) 重大な júdai na

weigh up vt (person, offer, risk) 評価する hyóka suru

weir [wi:r] n せき sekí

weird [wi:rd] adj 奇妙な kimyó na

welcome [wel'kəm] adj (visitor, suggestion, change) 歓迎すべき kangeisubeki; (news) うれしい ureshii
♦n 歓迎 kañgei
♦vt (visitor, delegation, suggestion, change) 歓迎する kañgei suru; (be glad of: news) うれしく思う uréshìku omóù
thank you - you're welcome! どうも有難う - どういたしまして dōmò arígàtò - dō.itáshimashitè

weld [weld] n 溶接 yósetsu
♦vt 溶接する yósetsu suru

welfare [wel'fe:r] n (well-being) 幸福 kófuku, 福祉 fukúshì; (social aid) 生活保護 seíkatsuhogò

welfare state n 福祉国家 fukúshikokkà

welfare work n 福祉事業 fukúshijigyò

well [wel] n (for water) 井戸 idò; (also: oil well) 油井 yuséi

◆*adv* (to a high standard, thoroughly: *also* for emphasis with adv, adj or prep phrase) よく yokù

◆*adj: to be well* (person: in good health) 元気である geñkì de árù

◆*excl* そう, ねえ sō, nē

as well (in addition) も mo

as well as (in addition to) …の外に …no hoká ni

well done! よくやった yokù yattá

get well soon! 早く治ります様に hayàku naórimasu yō nì, お大事に o-dáiji ni

to do well (person) 順調である juñchō de árù; (business) 繁盛する hañjō suru

we'll [wi:l] = **we will; we shall**

well-behaved [welbiheivd'] *adj* (child, dog) 行儀の良い gyōgi no yoí

well-being [wel'bi:'iŋ] *n* 幸福 kōfuku, 福祉 fukúshi

well-built [wel'bilt'] *adj* (person) 体格の良い taîkaku no yoí

well-deserved [wel'dizə:rvd'] *adj* (success, prize) 努力相応の doryòkusōō no

well-dressed [wel'drest'] *adj* 身なりの良い minári no yoí

well-heeled [wel'hi:ld'] (*inf*) *adj* (wealthy) 金持の kanémochì no

wellingtons [wel'iŋtənz] *npl* (*also: **wellington boots**) ゴム長靴 gomúnagagutsu

well-known [wel'noun'] *adj* (famous: person, place) 有名な yūmei na

well-mannered [wel'mæn'ə:rd] *adj* 礼儀正しい reîgitádashiì

well-meaning [wel'mi:'niŋ] *adj* (person) 善意の zeñ-i no; (offer etc) 善意に基づく zeñ-i ni motózukù

well-off [wel'ɔ:f'] *adj* (rich) 金持の kanémochì no

well-read [wel'red'] *adj* 博学の hakúgaku no

well-to-do [wel'tədu:'] *adj* 金持の kanémochì no

well up *vi* (tears) こみ上げる komíageru

well-wisher [wel'wiʃə:r] *n* (friends, admirers) 支持者 shijìsha, ファン faň

Welsh [welʃ] *adj* ウェールズの uéruzu no; (LING) ウェールズ語の uéruzugo no

◆*n* (LING) ウェールズ語 uéruzugo

Welsh *npl: the Welsh* ウェールズ人 uéruzujin

Welshman/woman [welʃ'mən/wumən] (*pl **Welshmen/women**) *n* ウェールズ人の男性〔女性〕 uéruzujin no dañsei〔joséi〕

Welsh rarebit [-re:r'bit] *n* チーズトースト chīzùtōsùto

went [went] *pt of* **go**

wept [wept] *pt, pp of* **weep**

we're [wi:r] = **we are**

were [wə:r] *pt of* **be**

weren't [wə:r'ənt] = **were not**

west [west] *n* (direction) 西 nishí; (part of country) 西部 seîbu

◆*adj* (wing, coast, side) 西の nishí no, 西側の nishígawa no

◆*adv* (to/towards the west) 西へ nishí e

west wind 西風 nishíkaze

West *n: the West* (POL: US plus western Europe) 西洋 seîyō

West Country *n: the West Country* (BRIT) 西部地方 seîbuchihō

westerly [wes'tə:rli:] *adj* (point) 西寄りの nishíyori no; (wind) 西からの nishí kara no

western [wes'tə:rn] *adj* (of the west) 西の nishí no; (POL: of the West) 西洋の seîyō no

◆*n* (CINEMA) 西部劇 seîbugeki

West Germany *n* 西ドイツ nishídoitsu

West Indian *adj* 西インド諸島の nishíindoshotō nò

◆*n* 西インド諸島の人 nishíindoshotō no hitó

West Indies [-in'di:z] *npl* 西インド諸島 nishíindoshotō

westward(s) [west'wə:rd(z)] *adv* 西へ nishí e

wet [wet] *adj* (damp) 湿った shimétta; (wet through) ぬれた nuréta; (rainy: weather, day) 雨模様の amémòyō no

◆*n* (BRIT: POL) 穏健派の人 onkénha no hitó

to get wet (person, hair, clothes) ぬれる nuréru

「*wet paint*」ペンキ塗立て peñki nurítate

to be a wet blanket (fig) 座を白けさせ

る za wò shirákesaseru

wet suit n ウェットスーツ uéttōsūtsu

we've [wi:v] = **we have**

whack [wæk] vt たたく tatákù

whale [weil] n (ZOOL) クジラ kujíra

wharf [wɔ:rf] (pl **wharves**) n 岸壁 gañpeki

wharves [wɔ:rvz] npl of **wharf**

KEYWORD

what [wʌt] adj 1 (in direct/indirect questions) 何の náñ no, 何... nánì...

what size is it? サイズは幾つですか sáīzu wa íkùtsu desu ká

what color is it? 何色ですか nánì iro desu ká

what shape is it? 形はどうなっていますか katáchi wà dṓ nattè imásù ká

what books do you need? どんな本がいりますか dóñna hóñ ga irímasù ká

he asked me what books I needed 私にはどんな本がいるかと彼は聞いていました watákushi ni wà dóñna hóñ ga irú kà to kárè wa kíìte imáshìta

2 (in exclamations) 何て... náñte...

what a mess! 何て有様だ náñte arísama dà

what a fool I am! 私は何てばかだ watákushi wà náñte bákà da

♦pron 1 (interrogative) 何 nánì, 何 náñ

what are you doing? 何をしていますか nánì wo shité imasù ká

what is happening? どうなっていますか dō nattè imásù ká

what's in there? その中に何が入っていますか sonó nakà ni nánì ga háìtte imasu ká

what is it? - it's a tool 何ですか-道具です náñ desu ká - dṓgu desu

what are you talking about? 何の話ですか náñ no hanáshì desu ká

what is it called? これは何と言いますか kórè wa náñ to iímasù ká

what about me? 私はどうすればいいんですか watákushi wà dṓ surèba íñ desu ká

what about doing ...? ...しませんか ...shimáseñ ká

2 (relative): **is that what happened?** 事件は今話した通りですか jíkèn wa ímà hanáshìta tōri desu ká

I saw what you did/was on the table あなたのした事〔テーブルにあった物〕を見ました anátà no shitá kotò〔tébùru ni attá monò〕wo mimáshìta

he asked me what she had said 彼は彼女の言った事を私に尋ねた kárè wa kánòjo no ittá kotò wo watákushi nì tazúnetà

tell me what you're thinking about 今何を考えているか教えて下さい ímà nánì wo kañgaete irù ká oshíète kudasai

what you say is wrong あなたの言っている事は間違っています anátà no itté iru kotò wà machígattè imásù

♦excl (disbelieving) 何 nánì

what, no coffee! 何，コーヒーがないんだって？ nánì, kṓhì gà naíñ dattè?

I've crashed the car - what! 車をぶつけてしまった−何？ kurúma wò butsúkete shimattà - nanî?

---

whatever [wʌtev'əːr] adj: **whatever book** どんな本でも dóñna hoñ de mo

♦pron: **do whatever is necessary/you want** 何でも必要〔好き〕な事をしなさい nañ de mo hitsúyō〔sukí〕na koto wò shinásai

whatever happens 何が起っても naní ga okótte mo

no reason whatever/whatsoever 全く理由がない mattáku riyū ga nai

nothing whatever 全く何もない mattáku nanì mo nai

whatsoever [wʌtsouev'əːr] adj = **whatever**

wheat [wi:t] n 小麦 komúgi

wheedle [wi:d'əl] vt: **to wheedle someone into doing something** ...を口車に乗せて...させる ...wo kuchíguruma ni noséte ...sasèru

to wheedle something out of someone 口車に乗せて...を...からだまし取る kuchíguruma ni noséte ...wo ...karà damáshitorù

wheel [wi:l] n (of vehicle etc) 車 kurúma,

車輪 sharín, ホイール hoíru; (*also:* **steering wheel**) ハンドル handoru; (NAUT) だ輪 darín

◆*vt* (pram etc) 押す osú

◆*vi* (birds) 旋回する senkai suru; (*also:* **wheel round**: person) 急に向き直る kyū ní mukínaorù

wheelbarrow [wi:l'bærou] *n* 一輪車 i-chírīnsha, ネコ車 nekóguruma

wheelchair [wi:l'tʃe:r] *n* 車いす kurúma-isù

wheel clamp *n* (AUT) ◇違反駐車の自動車車輪に付けて走れなくする金具 ihánchūsha no jidóshàsharin ni tsukéte hashírenaku surù kanágu

wheeze [wi:z] *vi* (person) ぜいぜいいう zeízei iú

KEYWORD

when [wen] *adv* いつ ítsù

when did it happen? いつ起ったんですか ítsù okóttan desù ká

I know when it happened いつ起ったかはちゃんと分かっています ítsù okótta kà wa chánto wakátté imásù

when are you going to Italy? イタリアにはいつ行きますか itárìa ni wa ítsù ikímasù ká

when will you be back? いつ帰って来ますか ítsù kaétte kimasù ká

◆*conj* **1** (at, during, after the time that) ...する時 ...surú tokì, ...すると ...surú tò, ...したら ...shitárà, ...してから ...shité karà

she was reading when I came in 私が部屋に入った時彼女は本を読んでいました watákushi gà heyá nì háìtta toki kánòjo wa hón wo yónde imáshìta

when you've read it, tell me what you think これを読んだらご意見を聞かせて下さい kóre wo yóndara go-íkèn wo kikásete kudasaì

be careful when you cross the road 道路を横断する時には気を付けてね dóro wo ódàn suru tokì ni wa kí wò tsukéte né

that was when I needed you あなたにいて欲しかったのはその時ですよ aná-

---

tà ni ité hoshikattà no wa sonó tokì desu yó

2: (*on, at which*): *on the day when I met him* 彼に会った日は kárè ni áttà hí wà

one day when it was raining 雨が降っていたある日 áme ga futté ità árù hí

3 (whereas): *you said I was wrong when in fact I was right* あなたは私が間違っていると言いましたが、事実は間違っていませんでした anátà wa watákushi gà machígatte irù to iímashita gà, jíjitsu wa machígatte imásen deshìta

why did you buy that when you can't afford it? 金の余裕がないのになぜあれを買ったんですか kané nò yoyū gà náì no ni náze aré wò kattán desu ká

whenever [wenev'ə:r] *adv* いつか itsù ka

◆*conj* (any time) ...するといつも ...surù to itsùmo...; (every time that) ...する度に ...surù tabì ni

where [we:r] *adv* (place, direction) どこ (に, で) dokò (ni, de)

◆*conj* ...の所に〔で〕 ...no tokóro ni〔de〕

this is where ... これは...する所です kóre wa ... surù tokoro desu

whereabouts [we:r'əbauts] *adv* どの辺に donò hen ni

◆*n*: *nobody knows his whereabouts* 彼の居場所は不明だ karè no ibásho wa fuméi da

whereas [we:ræz'] *conj* ...であるのに対して ...de arù no ni taìshite

whereby [we:rbai'] *pron* それによって soré ni yotté

whereupon [we:rəpɑ:n'] *conj* すると surú to

wherever [we:rev'ə:r] *conj* (no matter where) どこに〔で〕...しても dokò ni〔de〕...shite mo; (not knowing where) どこに...か知らないが dokò ni ...ká shiranai ga

◆*adv* (interrogative: surprise) 一体全体どこに〔で〕 ittái zentai dokò ni〔de〕

wherewithal [we:r'wiθɔ:l] *n* 金 kané

whet [wet] *vt* (appetite) そそる sosóru

whether [weð'ə:r] *conj* ...かどうか ...ka dō kà

I don't know whether to accept or not 引受けるべきかどうかは分からない hikíukerubeki kà dő kà wa wakáranài

whether you go or not 行くにしても行かないにしても ikú nì shité mò ikánai nì shité mò

it's doubtful whether he will come 彼はたぶん来ないだろう karè wa tabùn konài darő

KEYWORD
---

which [wɪtʃ] *adj* **1** (interrogative: direct, indirect) どの dőnò, どちらの dóchìra no

which picture do you want? どちらの絵がいいんですか dóchìra no é gà iíñ desu ká

which books are yours? あなたの本はどれとどれですか anátà no hőñ wa dőrè to dőrè desu ká

tell me which picture/books you want どの絵(本)が欲しいか言って下さい dőnò é(hőñ)gà hoshíì kà itté kudasaì

which one? どれ dőrè

which one do you want? どれが欲しいんですか dőrè ga hoshíìñ desu ká

which one of you did it? あなたたちのだれがやったんですか anátà tachi no dárè ga yattáñ desu ká

2: *in which case* その場合 sonő baầi

the train may be late, in which case don't wait up 列車が遅れるかもしれないが, その場合先に寝て下さい résshà ga okúreru ka mò shirénaì ga, sonő baầi sakí ni neté kudasaì

by which time その時 sonő tokí

we got there at 8 pm, by which time the cinema was full 映画館に着いたのは夜の8時でしたが, もう満席になっていました eígakàn ni tsúìta no wa yőrùno hachíjì deshita ga, mő mañseki ni natté imashìta

◆*pron* **1** (interrogative) どれ dőrè

which (of these) are yours? どれとどれがあなたの物ですか dőrè to dőrè ga anátà no monő desù ká

which of you are coming? あなたたちのだれとだれが一緒に来てくれますか a-nátàtachi no dárè to dárè ga ísshò ni

kité kuremasù ká

here are the books/files - tell me which you want 本(ファイル)はこれだけありますが, どれとどれが欲しいんですか hőñ(fáìru)wa koré dakè arímasù ga, dőrè to dőrè ga hoshíìñ desu ká

I don't mind which どれでもいいんですよ dőrè de mo iíñ desu yő

2 (relative): *the apple (which) you ate/which is on the table* あなたの食べた(テーブルにある)りんご anátà no tábèta (tèburu ni árù)ríñgo

the meeting (which) we attended 私たちが出席した会議 watákushitàchi ga shusséki shità kấigi

the chair on which you are sitting あなたが座っているいす anátà ga suwát-te irù ísú

the book of which you spoke あなたが話していた本 anátà ga hanáshite ità hőñ

he said he knew, which is true/I feared 彼は知っていると言ったが, その通りでした(私の心配していた通りでした) kárè wa shitté irù to ittá gà, sonő tőri deshita(watákushi nő shiñpai shite ita tőri deshita)

after which その後 sonő atő

---

whichever [wɪtʃevˈəːr] *adj*: *take whichever book you prefer* どれでもいいから好きな本を取って下さい dőré de mo iì kara sukí nà hon wo tottě kudasai

whichever book you take あなたがどの本を取っても anátà ga dőñ hon wo tottě mo

whiff [wɪf] *n* (of perfume, gasoline, smoke) ちょっと...のにおいがすること chottő ...no niőì ga suru koto

while [waɪl] *n* (period of time) 間 aída

◆*conj* (at the same time as) ...する間 ...surú aida; (as long as) ...する限りは ...surú kagìri wa; (although) ...するにもかかわらず ...surú nì mo kakáwarazù

for a while しばらくの間 shibáràku no aída

while away *vt* (time) つぶす tsubúsu

whim [wɪm] *n* 気まぐれ kimágure

whimper [wim'pə:r] n (cry, moan) 哀れっぽい泣き声 awáreppoì nakígoè
♦vi (child, animal) 哀れっぽいなき声を出す awáreppoì nakígoè wo dasù

whimsical [wim'zikəl] adj (person) 気まぐれな kimágure na; (poem) 奇抜な kibátsu na; (look, smile) 変な heñ na

whine [wain] n (of pain) 哀れっぽいなき声 awáreppoì nakígoè; (of engine, siren) うなり unári
♦vi (person, animal) 哀れっぽいなき声を出す awáreppoì nakígoè wo dasù; (engine, siren) うなる unárù; (fig: complain) 愚痴をこぼす guchí wo kobósù

whip [wip] n (lash, riding whip) むち muchì; (POL) 院内幹事 iñnaikañji
♦vt (person, animal) むち打つ muchíutsù; (cream, eggs) 泡立てる awádaterù, ホイップする hoíppù suru; (move quickly): **to whip something out/off** さっと取出す〔はずす，脱ぐ〕sattò torídasu (hazúsu, nugú)

whipped cream [wipt-] n ホイップクリーム hoíppukurīmù

whip-round [wip'raund] (BRIT) n 募金 bokín

whirl [wə:rl] vt (arms, sword etc) 振回す furímawasù
♦vi (dancers) ぐるぐる回る gurùguru mawáru; (leaves, water etc) 渦巻く uzúmakù

whirlpool [wə:rl'pu:l] n 渦巻 uzúmàki

whirlwind [wə:rl'wind] n 竜巻 tatsúmaki

whir(r) [wə:r] vi (motor etc) うなり unári

whisk [wisk] n (CULIN) 泡立て器 awádatekì
♦vt (cream, eggs) 泡立てる awádaterù
to whisk someone away/off ...を素早く連去る ...wo subáyakù tsurésarù

whiskers [wis'kə:rz] npl (of animal, man) ひげ higé

whiskey [wis'ki:] (BRIT **whisky**) n ウイスキー uísukì

whisper [wis'pə:r] n (low voice) ささやき sasáyaki
♦vi ささやく sasáyakù

♦vt ささやく sasáyakù

whist [wist] (BRIT) n ホイスト hoísuto

whistle [wis'əl] n (sound) 口笛 kuchíbue; (object) 笛 fué
♦vi (person) 口笛を吹く kuchíbue wo fukù; (bird) ぴーぴーさえずる pīpī saézurù; (bullet) ひゅーとうなる hyū to unárù; (kettle) ぴゅーと鳴る pyū to narú

white [wait] adj (color) 白い shiróì; (pale: person, face) 青白い aójiroì; (with fear) 青ざめた aózameta
♦n (color) 白 shiró; (person) 白人 hakújin; (of egg) 白身 shirómì

white coffee (BRIT) n ミルク入りコーヒー mirúkuirikōhī

white-collar worker [wait'kɑ:l'ə:r-] n サラリーマン sarárīman, ホワイトカラー howáitokarā

white elephant n (fig) 無用の長物 muyố no chōbutsu

white lie n 方便のうそ hōben no usó

white paper n (POL) 白書 hakúsho

whitewash [wait'wɑ:ʃ] n (paint) のろ norò◇石灰，白亜，のりを水に混ぜた塗料 sekkài, hakùa, norí wo mizú ni mazèta toryô
♦vt (building) ...にのろを塗る ...ni norò wo nurú; (fig: happening, career, reputation) ...の表面を繕う ...no hyômeñ wo tsukúroù

whiting [wai'tiŋ] n inv (fish) タラ tarà

Whitsun [wit'sən] n 聖霊降臨節 seírei-kōriñsetsu

whittle [wit'əl] vt: **to whittle away, whittle down** (costs: reduce) 減らす herásu

whizz(z) [wiz] vi: **to whizz past/by** (person, vehicle etc) ぴゅーんと通り過ぎる byūn to tốrisugirù

whiz(z) kid (inf) n 天才 teñsai

KEYWORD

who [hu:] pron **1** (interrogative) だれ dárè, どなた dónàta
who is it?, who's there? だれですか dárè desu ká
who are you looking for? だれを捜しているんですか dárè wo sagáshite irúñ

desu ká

I told her who I was 彼女に名乗りました kánòjo ni nanórimashìta

I told her who was coming to the party パーティの出席予定者を彼女に知らせました pāti no shussékiyoteìsha wo kánòjo ni shírasemashìta

who did you see? だれを見ましたか dárè wo mimáshìta ká

2 (relative): *my cousin who lives in New York* ニューヨークに住んでいるいとこ nyúyòku ni súnde iru itókò

the man/woman who spoke to me 私に話しかけた男性〔女性〕watákushi nì hanáshikaketà dañsei〔joséi〕

those who can swim 泳げる人たち oyŏgerù hitótàchi

whodunit [huːdʌnˈit] (*inf*) *n* 探偵小説 tañteishōsetsu

whole [houl] *adj* (entire) 全体の zeñtai no; (not broken) 無傷の mukìzu no
♦*n* (entire unit) 全体 zeñtai; (all): *the whole of* 全体の zeñtai no
the whole of the town 町全体 machízeñtai
on the whole, as a whole 全体として zeñtai toshite

whole food(s) [houlˈfuːd(z)] *n(pl)* 無加工の食べ物 mukákò no tabémonò

wholehearted [houlˈhɑːrˈtid] *adj* (agreement etc) 心からの kokóro kàra no

wholemeal [houlˈmiːl] *adj* (bread, flour) 全粒の zeñryū no, 全麦の zeñbaku no

wholesale [houlˈseil] *n* (business) 卸 oróshi, 卸売 oróshiuri
♦*adj* (price) 卸の oróshi nð; (destruction) 大規模の daíkibò no
♦*adv* (buy, sell) 卸で oróshi dè

wholesaler [houlˈseilə:r] *n* 問屋 toñ-ya

wholesome [houlˈsəm] *adj* (food, climate) 健康に良い keñkō ni yoì; (person) 健全な keñzen na

wholewheat [houlˈwiːt] *adj* = **wholemeal**

wholly [houˈliː] *adv* (completely) 完全に kañzen ni

whom [huːm] *pron* 1 (interrogative) だれを dárè wo, どなたを dónàta wo
whom did you see? だれを見ましたか dárè wo mimáshìta ká
to whom did you give it? だれに渡しましたか dárè ni watáshimashìta ká
tell me from whom you received it だれに〔から〕それを教えて下さい dárè ni〔kárà〕soré wò morátta kà wo oshíete kudasaì

2 (relative): *the man whom I saw/to whom I spoke* 私が見た〔話し掛けた〕男性 watákushi gà mítà〔hanáshikaketà〕dañsei

the lady with whom I was talking 私と話していた女性 watákushi tò hanáshite itã joséi

whooping cough [wuːˈpiŋ-] *n* 百日ぜき hyakúnichizèki

whore [hɔːr] (*inf: pej*) *n* 売女 baíta

whose [huːz] *adj* 1 (possessive: interrogative) だれの dárè no, どなたの dónàta no
whose book is this?, whose is this book? これはだれの本ですか koré wà dárè no hòñ desu ká
whose pencil have you taken? だれの鉛筆を持って来たんですか dárè no eñpitsu wò motté kitañ desu ká
whose daughter are you? あなたはどなたの娘さんですか anátà wa dónàta no musúme-sañ desu ká
I don't know whose it is だれの物か私には分かりません dárè no monó kà watákushi ni wà wakárimaseñ

2 (possessive: relative): *the man whose son you rescued* あなたが助けた子供の父親 anátà ga tasúketa kodomò no chichíoya

the girl whose sister you were speaking to あなたと話していた女性の妹 anátà to hanáshite itã joséi no imótò

the woman whose car was stolen 車を盗まれた女性 kurúma wð nusúmaretà

joséi

♦*pron* だれの物 dárè no monó, どなたの
物 dónàta no monó

whose is this? これはだれのですか kórè wa dárè no desu ká

I know whose it is だれの物か知って
います dárè no monó kà shitté imasù

whose are these? これらはだれの物で
すか korérà wa dárè no monó desù ká

KEYWORD

why [wai] *adv* なぜ názè, どうして dóshìte

why is he always late? どうして彼は
いつも遅刻するのですか dóshìte kárè
wa ítsùmo chikóku suru nò desu ká

why don't you come too? あなたも来
ませんか anátà mo kimásen ká

I'm not coming - why not? 私は行き
ません－どうしてですか watákushi wà i-
kímasen - dóshìte desu ká

fancy a drink? - why not? 一杯やろ
うか－いいね íppai yaró ká - íi né

why not do it now? 今すぐやりません
か ímà súgù yarímasen ka

♦*conj* なぜ názè, どうして dóshìte

I wonder why he said that どうして
そんな事を言ったのかしら dóshìte sofina
kotò wo ittá nò kashira

the reason why 理由 riyú

that's not (the reason) why I'm here
私が来たのはそのためじゃありません
watákushi gà kitá no wà sonó tamè ja
arímasen

♦*excl* (expressing surprise, shock,
annoyance etc) ◇日本語では表現しない
場合が多い nihóngo de wà hyógen shinaì
baái gà óì

why, it's you! おや，あなたでしたか
oyá, anátà deshita ka

*why, that's impossible/quite unac-
ceptable!* そんな事はできません〔認めら
れません〕sofina kotò wà dekímasen
[mitómeraremasen]

*I don't understand - why, it's obvi-
ous!* 訳が分かりません－ばかでも分かる
事だよ wákè ga wakárimasen - bákà de

mo wakárù kotó dà yó

---

whyever [waiev'ə:r] *adv* 一体 なぜ ittai
názè

wicked [wik'id] *adj* (crime, man, witch)
極悪の gokúaku no; (smile) 意地悪そうな
ijíwarusō nà

wickerwork [wik'ə:rwə:rk] *adj* (basket,
chair etc) 籐編みの tóami no, 枝編みの
edáami no

♦*n* (objects) 籐編み細工品 tóamizaikuhin,
枝編み細工品 edáamizaikuhin

wicket [wik'it] *n* (CRICKET: stumps) 三
柱門 sañchūmón, ウイケット uíkètto; (:
grass area) ピッチ pitchì

◇2つのウイケット間のグランド futátsu
nò uíkettokàn no gurándo

wide [waid] *adj* (gen) 広い hiróì; (grin) 楽
しげな tanóshìge na

♦*adv*: *to open wide* (window etc) 広く開
ける hiróku akéru

to shoot wide ねらいを外す nerái wo
hazúsu

wide-angle lens [waid'æŋ'gəl-] *n* 広角
レンズ kōkaku reñzu

wide-awake [waid'əweik'] *adj* すっかり
目が覚めた sukkárì me gà samèta

widely [waid'li:] *adv* (gen) 広く hiróku;
(differing) 甚だしく hanáhadashiku

widen [wai'dən] *vt* (road, river, experience) 広くする hiróku suru, 広げる hiró-
geru

♦*vi* (road, river, gap) 広くなる hiróku
narù, 広がる hirógaru

wide open *adj* (window, eyes, mouth) 大
きく開けた ōkìku akéta

widespread [waidspred'] *adj* (belief etc)
はびこった habíkottà

widow [wid'ou] *n* 未亡人 mibójìn, 後家
goké

widowed [wid'oud] *adj* (mother, father)
やもめになった yamóme ni nattà

widower [wid'ouə:r] *n* 男やもめ otóko-
yamóme

width [widθ] *n* (distance) 広さ hirósa; (of
cloth) 幅 habá

wield [wi:ld] *vt* (sword, power) 振るう furúu

wife [waif] (pl **wives**) n (gen) 妻 tsumà; (one's own) 家内 kanài; (someone else's) 奥さん okùsan

wig [wig] n かつら katsúra

wiggle [wig'əl] vt (hips) くねらす kunérasù; (ears etc) ぴくぴく動かす pikùpiku ugókasù

wild [waild] adj (animal, plant) 野生の yaséi no; (rough: land) 荒れ果てた aréhatèta; (: weather, sea) 荒れ狂う arékuruù; (person, behavior, applause) 興奮した kófun shita; (idea) 突飛な toppí na; (guess) 当てずっぽうの atézuppō no

wilderness [wil'dərnis] n 荒野 kōya, 原野 geñ-ya, 未開地 mikáichì

wild-goose chase [waild'guːs'-] n (fig) 無駄な捜索 mudá na sōsaku

wildlife [waild'laif] n (animals) 野生動物 yaséidōbùtsu

wildly [waild'li:] adv (behave) 狂った様に kurúttà yō ni; (applaud) 熱狂的に nekkyóteki ni; (hit) めくら滅法に mekúramèppō ni; (guess) 当てずっぽうに atézuppō ni; (happy) 最高に saíkō ni

wilds [waildz] npl 荒野 kōya, 原野 geñ-ya, 未開地 mikáichì

wilful [wil'fəl] (US also: **willful**) adj (obstinate: child, character) わがままな wagámamà na; (deliberate: action, disregard etc) 故意の koì no

KEYWORD

will [wil] (vt: pt, pp **willed**) aux vb 1 (forming future tense): **I will finish it tomorrow** 明日終ります ashíta owárimasù

I will have finished it by tomorrow 明日にでもなれば終るでしょう asú ni dè mo nárèba owárù deshō

will you do it? - yes I will/no I won't やりますか - はい、やります〔いいえ、やりません〕yarímasù ká - háì, yarímasù〔ifè, yarímaseň〕

when will you finish it? いつ終りますか ítsù owárimasù ká

2 (in conjectures, predictions): **he will/he'll be there by now** 彼はもう着いているでしょう kárè wa mó tsúite irú de-

shō

that will be the postman 郵便屋さんでしょう yúbinya-san deshō

this medicine will help you この薬なら効くでしょう konó kusuri narà kikú deshō

this medicine won't help you この薬は何の役にも立ちません konó kusuri wà nañ no yakú ni mò tachímaseň

3 (in commands, requests, offers): **will you be quiet!** 黙りなさい damárinasaì

will you come? 来てくれますか kitè kuremasù ká

will you help me? 手伝ってくれますか tetsúdattè kurémasù ká

will you have a cup of tea? お茶をいかがですか o-chá wò ikága desù ká

I won't put up with it! 我慢できませんgámàn dekímaseň

♦vt: **to will someone to do something** 意志の力で...に...をさせようとする íshì no chikára dè ...ni ...wò saséyō tò suru

he willed himself to go on 彼は精神力だけで続けようとした kárè wa seíshin-ryòku dakè dè tsuzúkeyò to shita

♦n (volition) 意志 íshì; (testament) 遺言 yuígon

---

willful [wil'fəl] (US) adj = **wilful**

willing [wil'iŋ] adj (with goodwill) 進んで...する susúnde ...surù; (enthusiastic) 熱心な nesshìn na

he's willing to do it 彼はそれを引き受けてくれるそうです karè wa soré wo hikúkète kureru sō dèsu

willingly [wil'iŋli:] adv 進んで susúnde

willingness [wil'iŋnis] n 好意 kōì

willow [wil'ou] n ヤナギ yanági

willpower [wil'pauər] n 精神力 seíshiñ-ryoku

willy-nilly [wil'i:nil'i:] adv 否応なしに i-yáō nashì ni

wilt [wilt] vi (flower, plant) 枯れる karéru

wily [wai'li:] adj (fox, move, person) ずる賢い zurúgashikoì

win [win] n (in sports etc) 勝利 shōrì, 勝ち kachí

♦vb (pt, pp **won**)

♦vt (game, competition) ...で 勝 つ ...de katsù; (election) ...で当選する ...de tōsen suru; (obtain: prize, medal) もらう moráu, 受ける ukérù; (money) 当てる atérù; (support, popularity) 獲得する kakútoku suru

♦vi 勝つ katsù

wince [wins] vi 顔がこわばる kaó ga ko-wábaru

winch [wintʃ] n ウインチ uínchi

wind[1] [wind] n (air) 風 kazé; (MED) 呼吸 kokyú; (breath) 息 ikí

♦vt (take breath away from) ...の息を切らせる ...no ikí wo kiráserù

wind[2] [waind] (pt, pp **wound**) vt (roll: thread, rope) 巻く makú; (wrap: bandage) 巻き付ける makítsukerù; (clock, toy) ...のぜんまいを巻く ...no zeńmai wo makú

♦vi (road, river) 曲りくねる magárikunerù

windfall [wind'fɔːl] n (money) 棚ぼた tanábota

winding [wain'diŋ] adj (road) 曲りくねった magárikunettà; (staircase) らせん状の rasénjō no

wind instrument n (MUS) 管楽器 kaṅgakki

windmill [wind'mil] n 風車 kazáguruma

window [win'dou] n 窓 madò

window box n ウインドーボックス uíndōbokkùsu

window cleaner n (person) 窓ふき職人 madófukishokùnin

window envelope n 窓付き封筒 madótsukifūtò

window ledge n 窓下枠 madóshitawàku

window pane n 窓ガラス madógarasu

window-shopping [win'douʃɑːpiŋ] n ウインドーショッピング uíndoshoppìngu

windowsill [win'dousil] n 窓下枠 madóshitawàku

windpipe [wind'paip] n 気管 kikán

windscreen [wind'skriːn] (BRIT) n = **windshield**

windshield [wind'ʃiːld] (US) n フロント

ガラス furóntogaràsu, ウインドシールド uíndoshīrùdo

windshield washer n ウインドシールドワシャー uíndoshirudowashã

windshield wiper [-waip'əːr] n ワイパー waîpā

windswept [wind'swept] adj (place) 吹きさらしの fukísarashi no; (person) 風で髪が乱れた kazé de kamí gà midáréta

wind up vt (clock, toy) ...のぜんまいを巻く ...no zeńmai wo makú; (debate) 終りにする owári ni suru

windy [win'diː] adj (weather, day) 風の強い kazé no tsuyoì

it's windy 風が強い kazé ga tsuyoì

wine [wain] n ブドウ酒 budóshu, ワイン waîn

wine bar n ワインバー waînbā

wine cellar n ワインの地下貯蔵庫 waîn no chikáchozōkò

wine glass n ワイングラス waíngurasù

wine list n ワインリスト waînrisùto

wine merchant n ワイン商 waínshō

wine waiter n ソムリエ somúrie

wing [wiŋ] n (of bird, insect, plane) 羽根 hané, 翼 tsubása; (of building) 翼 yokú; (BRIT: AUT) フェンダー feńdā

winger [wiŋ'əːr] n (SPORT) ウイング uíngu

wings [wiŋz] npl (THEATER) そで sodé

wink [wiŋk] n (of eye) ウインク uíŋku

♦vi (with eye) ウインクする uíŋku suru; (light etc) 瞬く matátakù

winner [win'əːr] n (of prize, race, competition) 勝者 shōshà

winning [win'iŋ] adj (team, competitor, entry) 勝った kattà; (shot, goal) 決勝の kesshō no; (smile) 愛敬たっぷりの aíkyō tappúrì no

winnings [win'iŋz] npl 賞金 shōkin

win over vt (person: persuade) 味方にする mikáta ni suru

win round (BRIT) vt = **win over**

winter [win'təːr] n (season) 冬 fuyú

in winter 冬には fuyú ni wa

winter sports npl ウインタースポーツ uíntasupōtsù

wintry [win'triː] adj (weather, day) 冬ら

しい fuyúrashiì

wipe [waip] *n*: *to give something a wipe* ...をふく ...wo fukú
♦*vt* (rub) ふく fukú; (erase: tape) 消す kesú

wipe off *vt* (remove) ふき取る fukítorù

wipe out *vt* (debt) 完済する kańsai suru; (memory) 忘れる wasúreru; (destroy: city, population) 滅ぼす horóbosù

wipe up *vt* (mess) ふき取る fukítorù

wire [wai'ə:r] *n* (metal etc) 針金 harígane; (ELEC) 電線 deńsen; (telegram) 電報 deńpō
♦*vt* (house) ...の配線工事をする ...no haísenkōji wo suru; (*also*: **wire up**: electrical fitting) 取付ける torítsukerù; (person: telegram) ...に電報を打つ ...ni deńpō wo utsù

wireless [wai'ə:rlis] (*BRIT*) *n* ラジオ rajìo

wiring [waiə:r'iŋ] *n* (ELEC) 配線 haísen

wiry [waiə:r'i:] *adj* (person) やせで強じんな yasé de kyōjin na; (hair) こわい kowáì

wisdom [wiz'dəm] *n* (of person) 知恵 chié; (of action, remark) 適切さ tekísetsusa

wisdom tooth *n* 親知らず oyáshirazù

wise [waiz] *adj* (person, action, remark) 賢い kashíkoì, 賢明な keńmei na

...wise *suffix*: *timewise* / *moneywise etc* 時間〔金銭〕的に jikán(kińsen)teki ni

wisecrack [waiz'kræk] *n* 皮肉な冗談 hiníku na jōdañ

wish [wiʃ] *n* (desire) 望み nozómi, 希望 kibō; (specific) 望みの物 nozómi no mono
♦*vt* (want) 望む nozómù, 希望する kibō suru
best wishes (for birthday, etc) おめでとう omédetō
with best wishes (in letter) お体をお大事に o-kárada wo o-dáiji ni
to wish someone goodbye ...に別れのあいさつを言う ...ni wakáre no aísatsu wo iu, ...にさよならを言う ...ni sayónarà wo iu
he wished me well 彼は「成功を祈る」と言いました karè wa 「seíkō wo inorù」to iímashìta

to wish to do ...したいと思う ...shitaí to omóù

to wish someone to do something ...に...してもらいたいと思う ...ni ...shité moraitaí to omóù

to wish for ...が欲しいと思う ...ga hoshíì to omóù

wishful [wiʃ'fəl] *adj*: *it's wishful thinking* その考えは甘い sonó kangaè wa amáì, それは有り得ない事だ soré wa aríenài kotó dà

wishy-washy [wiʃ'i:wɑ:ʃi:] (*inf*) *adj* (color) 薄い usúì; (ideas, person) 迫力のない hakúryoku no naì

wisp [wisp] *n* (of grass, hair) 小さな束 chìsana tabà; (of smoke) 一筋 hitósùji

wistful [wist'fəl] *adj* (look, smile) 残念そうな zańnensō na

wit [wit] *n* (wittiness) ユーモア yūmòa, ウイット uíttò; (intelligence: *also*: **wits**) 知恵 chié; (person) ウイットのある人 uíttò no aru hito

witch [witʃ] *n* 魔女 majò

witchcraft [witʃ'kræft] *n* 魔術 majùtsu

witch-hunt [witʃ'hʌnt] *n* (*fig*) 魔女狩り majógari

KEYWORD

with [wiθ] *prep* **1** (accompanying, in the company of) ...と ...to, ...と一緒に ...to ísshò ni

I was with him 私は彼と一緒にいました watákushi wà kárè to ísshò ni ímáshìtà

we stayed with friends 私たちは友達の家に泊りました watákushitàchi wa tomódachi nò ié nì tomárimashìta

we'll take the children with us 子供たちを一緒に連れて行きます kodómotàchi wo ísshò ni tsuréte ikimasù

mix the sugar with the eggs 砂糖を卵に混ぜて下さい satő wò tamágo nì mázète kudásaì

I'll be with you in a minute 直ぐ行きますからお待ち下さい súgù ikímasu karà o-máchi kudásaì

I'm with you (I understand) 分かります wakárimasù

to be with it (*inf*: up-to-date) 現代的である geñdaiteki de arù; (: alert) 抜け目がない nukéme gà náí

2 (descriptive): *a room with a view* 見晴らしのいい部屋 mihárashi nò íi heyá
the man with the grey hat/blue eyes 灰色の帽子をかぶった〔青い目の〕男 haíiro nò bóshi wò kabútta〔aóí mé nò〕otòko

3 (indicating manner, means, cause):
with tears in her eyes 目に涙を浮かべながら mé nì námìda wo ukábènagara
to walk with a stick つえをついて歩く tsúé wo tsuíte arùkú
red with anger 怒りで顔を真っ赤にして ikári dè kaó wò makká ni shitè
to shake with fear 恐怖で震える kyófu dè furúerù
to fill something with water ...を水で一杯にする ...wò mizú dè ippái nì suru
you can open the door with this key このかぎでドアを開けられます konó kagí dè dóa wo akéraremasù

withdraw [wiðdrɔː'] (*pt* **withdrew** *pp* **withdrawn**) *vt* (object) 取出す torídasu; (offer, remark) 取消す toríkesu, 撤回する tekkái suru
♦*vi* (troops) 撤退する tettái suru; (person) 下がる sagárù
to withdraw money (from the bank) 金を引出す kané wo hikidasù

withdrawal [wiðdrɔː'əl] *n* (of offer, remark) 撤回 tekkái; (of troops) 撤退 tettái; (of services) 停止 teíshi; (of participation) 取りやめる事 toríyameru koto; (of money) 引出し hikídashi

withdrawal symptoms *n* (MED) 禁断症状 kiñdanshōjō

withdrawn [wiðdrɔːn'] *adj* (person) 引っ込みがちな hikkómigachi na

wither [wiðˈəːr] *vi* (plant) 枯れる karéru

withhold [wiθhould'] (*pt*, *pp* **withheld**) *vt* (tax etc) 源泉徴収する geñsenchōshū suru; (permission) 拒む kobámù; (information) 隠す kakúsù

within [wiðin'] *prep* (inside: referring to place, time, distance) ...以内に〔で〕...inái ni〔de〕
♦*adv* (inside) 中の nakà no
within reach (of) (...に) 手が届く所に〔で〕 (...ni) tê gà todókù tokoro ni〔de〕
within sight of (...が) 見える所に〔で〕 (...ga) miérù tokoro ni〔de〕
within the week 今週中に koñshūchū ni
within a mile of ...の1マイル以内に ...no ichímairu inái ni

without [wiðaut'] *prep* ...なしで ...nashì de
without a coat コートなしで kótò nashì de
without speaking 何も言わないで naní mo iwanàìde
to go without something ...なしで済ます ...nashì de sumásù

withstand [wiθstænd'] (*pt*, *pp* **withstood**) *vt* (winds, attack, pressure) ...に耐える ...ni taérù

witness [wit'nis] *n* (person who sees) 目撃者 mokúgekishà; (person who countersigns document: *also* LAW) 証人 shónin
♦*vt* (event) 見る mirù, 目撃する mokúgeki suru; (document) 保証人として...にサインする hoshónin toshite ...ni saín suru
to bear witness to (*fig*: offer proof of) ...を証明する ...wo shómei suru

witness stand (*BRIT* **witness box**) *n* 証人席 shóniñseki

witticism [wit'əsizəm] *n* (remark) 冗談 jódañ

witty [wit'i:] *adj* (person) ウイットのある uíttò no arù; (remark etc) おどけた odókketa

wives [waivz] *npl of* **wife**

wizard [wiz'əːrd] *n* 魔法使い mahótsukài

wk *abbr* = **week**

wobble [wɑːb'əl] *vi* (legs) よろめく yorómekù; (chair) ぐらぐらする guràgura suru; (jelly) ぷるぷるする purùpuru suru

woe [wou] *n* 悲しみ kanáshimi

woke [wouk] *pt of* **wake**

woken [wou'kən] *pp of* **wake**

wolf [wulf] (*pl* **wolves**) *n* オオカミ ókami

wolves [wulvz] *npl of* **wolf**

woman [wum'ən] (*pl* **women**) *n* 女 oñna, 女性 joséi

woman doctor *n* 女医 joí

womanly [wum'ənli:] *adj* (virtues etc) 女性らしい joséirashii

womb [wu:m] *n* (ANAT) 子宮 shikyú

women [wim'ən] *pl of* **woman**

women's lib [wim'ənzlib'] (*inf*) *n* ウーマンリブ ūmanribù

won [wʌn] *pt, pp of* **win**

wonder [wʌn'də:r] *n* (miracle) 不思議 fushígi; (feeling) 驚異 kyōī

♦*vi*: **to wonder whether/why** ...かしら 〔なぜ...かしら〕と思う ...ka shira 〔nazè ...ka shira〕to omóù

to wonder at (marvel at) ...に驚く ...ni odórokù

to wonder about ...の事を考える ...no kotó wò kangáeru

it's no wonder (that) ... (という事) は不思議ではない ... (to iú koto) wà fushígi de wà naī

wonderful [wʌn'də:rfəl] *adj* (excellent) 素晴らしい subárashiī; (miraculous) 不思議な fushígi na

wonderfully [wʌn'də:rfəli:] *adv* (excellently) 素晴らしく subárashikù; (miraculously) 不思議に fushígi ni

won't [wount] = **will not**

woo [wu:] *vt* (woman) ...に言い寄る ...ni iíyorù; (audience etc) ...にこびる ...ni kobírù

wood [wud] *n* (timber) 木材 mokúzai, 木 ki; (forest) 森 morí, 林 hayáshi, 木立 kodáchi

wood carving *n* (act, object) 木彫 kibóri

wooded [wud'id] *adj* (slopes, area) 木の茂った kí nò shigétta

wooden [wud'ən] *adj* (object) 木でできた kí dè dekita, 木製の mokúsei no; (house) 木造の mokúzō no; (*fig*: performance, actor) でくの坊の様な dekúnobō no yō nà

woodpecker [wud'pekə:r] *n* キツツキ kitsútsukī

woodwind [wud'wind] *npl* (MUS) 木管楽器 mokkángakkī

woodwork [wud'wə:rk] *n* (skill) 木材工芸 mokúzaikōgèi

woodworm [wud'wə:rm] *n* キクイムシ kikúimùshi

wool [wul] *n* (material, yarn) 毛糸 keíto, ウール ūrū

to pull the wool over someone's eyes (*fig*) ...をだます ...wo damásù

woolen [wul'ən] (*BRIT* **woollen**) *adj* (socks, hat etc) 毛糸の keíto no, ウールの ūrù no

the woolen industry 羊毛加工業界 yómōkakōgyōkài

woolens [wul'ənz] *npl* 毛糸衣類 keítoirùi

wooly [wul'i:] (*BRIT* **woolly**) *adj* (socks, hat etc) 毛糸の keíto no, ウールの ūrù no; (*fig*: ideas) 取留めのない torítome no naī; (person) 考え方のはっきりしない kañgaekatà no hakkírì shináì

word [wə:rd] *n* (unit of language: written, spoken) 語 go, 単語 tañgo, 言葉 kotóba; (promise) 約束 yakúsoku; (news) 知らせ shiráse, ニュース nyūsù

♦*vt* (letter, message) ...の言回しを選ぶ ...no iímawashi wo erábù

in other words 言替えると iíkaerù to

to break/keep one's word 約束を破る 〔守る〕 yakúsoku wo yabúrù〔mamórù〕

to have words with someone ...と口げんかをする ...to kuchígeñka wo suru

wording [wə:r'diŋ] *n* (of message, contract etc) 言回し iímawashi

word processing *n* ワードプロセシング wádopuroseshìngu

word processor [-pra'sesə:r] *n* ワープロ wápuro

wore [wɔ:r] *pt of* **wear**

work [wə:rk] *n* (*gen*) 仕事 shigóto; (job) 職 shokú; (ART, LITERATURE) 作品 sakúhin

♦*vi* (person: labor) 働く határaku; (mechanism) 動く ugókù; (be successful: medicine etc) 効く kikú

♦*vt* (clay, wood etc) 加工する kakō suru; (land) 耕す tagáyasù; (mine) 採掘する saíkutsu suru; (machine) 動かす ugókasù; (cause: effect) もたらす motárasù; (: miracle) 行う okónau

to be out of work 失業中である shitsúgyōchū de arù

to work loose (part) 緩む yurúmù; (knot) 解ける tokérù

workable [wəːr'kəbəl] *adj* (solution) 実行可能な jikkṓkanō na

workaholic [wəːrkəhɔːl'ik] *n* 仕事中毒の人 shigótochūdòku no hito, ワーカホリック wākahorîkku

worker [wəːr'kəːr] *n* 労働者 rṓdōshà

workforce [wəːk'fɔːrs] *n* 労働人口 rōdōjinkṓ

working class [wəːr'kiŋ-] *n* 労働者階級 rōdōshakaìkyū

working-class [wəːr'kiŋklæs] *adj* 労働者階級の rōdōshakaìkyū no

working order *n*: *in working order* ちゃんと動く状態で chanto ugokù jōtai de

workman [wəːrk'mən] (*pl* **workmen**) *n* 作業員 sagyṓin

workmanship [wəːrk'mənʃip] *n* (skill) 腕前 udémae

work on *vt fus* (task) ...に取組む ...ni toríkumu; (person: influence) 説得する settóku suru; (principle) ...に基づく ...ni motōzukù

work out *vi* (plans etc) うまくいく umáku ikù
♦*vt* (problem) 解決する kaíketsu suru; (plan) 作る tsukúrù
it works out at $100 100ドルになる hyakúdòru ni narù

works [wəːrks] *n* (BRIT: factory) 工場 kōjō
♦*npl* (of clock, machine) 機構 kikṓ

worksheet [wəːrk'ʃiːt] *n* ワークシート wākushītò

workshop [wəːrk'ʃɑːp] *n* (at home, in factory) 作業場 sagyōjṓ; (practical session) ワークショップ wākushoppù

work station *n* ワークステーション wākusutēshòn

work-to-rule [wəːrk'təruːl'] (BRIT) *n* 順法闘争 juňpōtōsō

work up *vt*: *to get worked up* 怒る okórù

world [wəːrld] *n* 世界 sekái

♦*cpd* (champion) 世界... sekái...; (power, war) 国際的... kokúsaiteki..., 国際... kokúsai...

to think the world of someone (fig: admire) ...を高く評価する ...wo takáku suru; (: love) ...が大好きである ...ga daîsuki de arù

worldly [wəːrld'liː] *adj* (not spiritual) 世俗的な sezőkuteki na; (knowledgeable) 世才にたけた sesái ni takéta

worldwide [wəːrld'waid'] *adj* 世界的な sekáiteki na

worm [wəːrm] *n* (also: **earthworm**) ミミズ mimízu

worn [wɔːrn] *pp of* **wear**
♦*adj* (carpet) 使い古した tsukáifurushità; (shoe) 履き古した hakífurushità

worn-out [wɔːrn'aut'] *adj* (object) 使い古した tsukáifurushità; (person) へとへとに疲れた hetóheto ni tsukáretà

worried [wəːr'iːd] *adj* (anxious) 心配している shiñpai shite irù

worry [wəːr'iː] *n* (anxiety) 心配 shínpai
♦*vt* (person) 心配させる shiñpai saserù
♦*vi* (person) 心配する shiñpai surù

worrying [wəːr'iːiŋ] *adj* 心配な shínpai na

worse [wəːrs] *adj* 更に悪い sarà ni wáruî
♦*adv* 更に悪く sarà ni warúku
♦*n* 更に悪い事 sarà ni warúî koto
a change for the worse 悪化 akká

worsen [wəːr'sən] *vt* 悪くする warúku suru
♦*vi* 悪くなる warúku naru

worse off *adj* (financially) 収入が減った shūnyū ga hettá; (fig): *you'll be worse off this way* そんな事は得策ではない sofina koto wa tokúsaku de wa naî

worship [wəːr'ʃip] *n* (act) 礼拝 reíhai
♦*vt* (god) 礼拝する reíhai suru; (person, thing) 崇拝する sūhài suru
Your Worship (BRIT: to mayor, judge) 閣下 kakká

worst [wəːrst] *adj* 最悪の saíaku no
♦*adv* 最もひどく mottōmo hidőku
♦*n* 最悪 saíaku
at worst 最悪の場合 saíaku no baái

worth [wəːrθ] *n* (value) 価値 kachî

◆*adj*: *to be worth $100* 価格は100ドルである kakáku wa hyakúdoru de arù

it's worth it やる価値がある yarú kachì ga aru

to be worth one's while (to do) (...する事は) ...のためになる (...surú koto wa) ...no tamé ni naru

worthless [wəːrθ'lis] *adj* (person, thing) 価値のない kachí no nai

worthwhile [wəːrθ'wail'] *adj* (activity, cause) ためになる tamé ni naru

worthy [wəːr'ði:] *adj* (person) 尊敬すべき soñkeisubeki; (motive) 良い yoì

worthy of ...にふさわしい ...ni fusáwashiì

KEYWORD

would [wud] *aux vb* **1** (conditional tense): *if you asked him he would do it* 彼にお願いすればやってくれるでしょう kárè ni o-négai surébà yatté kureru deshŏ

if you had asked him he would have done it 彼に頼めばやってくれた事でしょう kárè ni tanómebà yatté kuretá kotó deshŏ

2 (in offers, invitations, requests): *would you like a biscuit?* ビスケットはいかがですか bisúkettð wa ikágà desu ká

would you ask him to come in? 彼に入ってもらって下さい kárè ni háitte morátte kudasaì

would you open the window please? 窓を開けてくれますか mádò wo akéte kuremasù ká

3 (in indirect speech): *I said I would do it* 私はやってあげると約束しました watákushi wà yatté agerù to yakúsoku shimashìta

he asked me if I would go with him 一緒に行ってくれと彼に頼まれました isshó ní itté kurè to kárè ni tanómaremashìta

4 (emphatic): *it WOULD have to snow today!* 今日に限って雪が降るなんてなあ kyŏ nì kagíttè yukí gà fúrù náñte ná

you WOULD say that, wouldn't you! あんたの言いそうな事だ áñta no iísŏ na kotó dà

5 (insistence): *she wouldn't behave* あの子はどうしても言う事を聞いてくれない anŏ kò wa dŏ shite mò iú kotó wo kiíte kurenaì

6 (conjecture): *it would have been midnight* だとすれば夜中の12時という事になりますdà tò surébà yonáka nð jǔnijì to iú kotó ni narímasù

it would seem so そうらしいね sŏ rashiì né

7 (indicating habit): *he would go there on Mondays* 彼は毎週月曜日にそこへ行く事にしていました kárè wa maíshū getsúyòbi ni sokó è ikú kotó ni shité imashìta

he would spend every day on the beach 彼は毎日浜でごろごろしていました kárè wa maínichi hamá dè górðgoro shite imáshìta

---

would-be [wud'biː'] (*pej*) *adj* ...志望の ...shibŏ no

wouldn't [wud'ənt] = **would not**

wound[1] [waund] *pt, pp of* **wind**

wound[2] [wuːnd] *n* 傷 kizú

◆*vt* ...に傷を負わせる ...ni kizú wo owáseru, 負傷させる fushŏ saséru

wove [wouv] *pt of* **weave**

woven [wou'vən] *pp of* **weave**

wrangle [ræŋ'gəl] *n* 口論 kŏron

wrap [ræp] *n* (stole) 肩掛 katakake, ストール sutŏrù; (cape) マント mañto, ケープ kēpù

◆*vt* (cover) 包む tsutsúmù; (pack: *also*: **wrap up**) こん包する koñpŏ suru; (wind: tape etc) 巻付ける makítsukerù

wrapper [ræp'əːr] *n* (on chocolate) 包み tsutsúmi; (*BRIT*: of book) カバー kabā

wrapping paper [ræp'iŋ-] *n* (brown) クラフト紙 kuráfùtoshi; (fancy) 包み紙 tsutsúmigàmi

wrath [ræθ] *n* 怒り ikári

wreak [riːk] *vt* (havoc) もたらす motárasù

to wreak vengeance on ...に復しゅうす

る ...ni fukúshū suru

wreath [ri:θ] n (funeral wreath) 花輪 ha-náwa

wreck [rek] n (vehicle) 残がい zańgai; (ship) 難破船 nańpasen; (pej: person) 変り果てた人 kawárihatetà hitó
♦vt (car etc) めちゃめちゃに壊す mechámecha ni kowásù; (fig: chances) 台無しにする daínashi ni surù

wreckage [rek'idʒ] n (of car, plane, ship, building) 残がい zańgai

wren [ren] n (ZOOL) ミソサザイ misósazài

wrench [rentʃ] n (TECH: adjustable) スパナ supánà; (: fixed size) レンチ reńchi; (tug) ひねり hinéri; (fig) 心痛 shíntsū
♦vt (twist) ひねる hinérù
to wrench something from someone ...から...をねじり取る ...kara ...wo nejíritorù

wrestle [res'əl] vi: **to wrestle (with someone)** (fight) (...と) 格闘する (...to) kakútō suru; (for sport) (...と) レスリングする (...to) resúringu suru
to wrestle with (fig) ...と取組む ...to toríkumu, ...と戦う ...to tatákau

wrestler [res'lər] n レスラー resúrā

wrestling [res'liŋ] n レスリング resúringu

wretched [retʃ'id] adj (poor, unhappy) 不幸な fukṓ na; (inf: very bad) どうしようもない dṓ shiyṓ mo nai

wriggle [rig'əl] vi (also: **wriggle about**: person, fish, snake etc) うねうねする unèune suru

wring [riŋ] (pt, pp **wrung**) vt (wet clothes) 絞る shibórù; (hands) もむ momú; (bird's neck) ひねる hinérù; (fig): **to wring something out of someone** ...に...を吐かせる ...ni ...wo hákaserù

wrinkle [riŋ'kəl] n (on skin, paper etc) しわ shiwá
♦vt (nose, forehead etc) ...にしわを寄せる ...ni shiwá wo yoséru
♦vi (skin, paint etc) しわになる shiwá ni naru

wrist [rist] n 手首 tekùbi

wristwatch [rist'wɑ:tʃ] n 腕時計 udédo-

kèi

writ [rit] n 令状 reíjō

write [rait] (pt **wrote**, pp **written**) vt 書く kakù
♦vi 書く kakù
to write to someone ...に手紙を書く ...ni tegámi wo kakù

write down vt 書く kakù, 書留める kakítomeru

write off vt (debt) 帳消しにする chṓkeshi ni suru; (plan, project) 取りやめる toríyameru

write-off [rait'ɔ:f] n 修理不可能な物 shūrífukánṓ na mono

writer [rai'tər] n (author) 著者 choshà; (professional) 作家 sakkà; (person who writes) 書手 kakíte

write up vt (report, minutes etc) 詳しく書く kuwáshikù kakù

writhe [raið] vi 身もだえする mimódàe suru

writing [rai'tiŋ] n (words written) 文字 mojì, 文章 buńshō; (handwriting) 筆跡 hisséki; (of author) 作品 sakúhin, 作風 sakúfū; (activity) 書物 kakímono
in writing 書面で shomén de

writing paper n 便せん bińsen

written [rit'ən] pp of **write**

wrong [rɔ:ŋ] adj (bad) 良くない yokúnai; (incorrect: number, address etc) 間違った machígatta; (not suitable) 不適当な futékitō na; (reverse: side of material) 裏側の urágawa no; (unfair) 不正な fuséi na
♦adv 間違って machígatte, 誤って ayámattè
♦n (injustice) 不正 fuséi
♦vt (treat unfairly) ...に悪い事をする ...ni warúi koto wo surù
you are wrong to do it それは不正な事です sore wa fuséi na koto desù
you are wrong about that, you've got it wrong それは違います soré wa chigáimasù
to be in the wrong 間違っている machígattè iru
what's wrong? どうしましたか dṓ shimáshita ká

to go wrong (person) 間違う machígaù; (plan) 失敗する shippái suru; (machine) 狂う kurúú

wrongful [rɔːŋ'fəl] *adj* (imprisonment, dismissal) 不当な futó na

wrongly [rɔːŋ'liː] *adv* 間違って machígattè

wrote [rout] *pt of* **write**

wrought [rɔːt] *adj*: *wrought iron* 練鉄 reñtetsu

wrung [rʌŋ] *pt, pp of* **wring**

wry [rai] *adj* (smile, humor, expression) 皮肉っぽい hiníkuppoì

wt. *abbr* = **weight**

X

Xmas [eks'mis] *n abbr* = **Christmas**

X-ray [eks'rei] *n* (ray) エックス線 ekkúsusen; (photo) レントゲン写真 reñtogeñshashin

♦*vt* ...のレントゲンを撮る ...no reñtogeñ wo torù

xylophone [zai'ləfoun] *n* 木琴 mokkíñ

Y

yacht [jɑːt] *n* ヨット yottò

yachting [jɑːt'iŋ] *n* ヨット遊び yottóasobi

yachtsman [jɑːts'mən] (*pl* **yachtsmen**) *n* ヨット乗り yottónori

Yank [jæŋk] (*pej*) *n* ヤンキー yañkī

Yankee [jæŋk'iː] (*pej*) *n* = **Yank**

yap [jæp] *vi* (dog) きゃんきゃんほえる kyañkyan hoérù

yard [jɑːrd] *n* (of house etc) 庭 niwá; (measure) ヤード yādò

yardstick [jɑːrd'stik] *n* (*fig*) 尺度 shakúdò

yarn [jɑːrn] *n* (thread) 毛糸 keíto; (tale) ほら話 horábanashi

yawn [jɔːn] *n* あくび akúbi

♦*vi* あくびする akúbi suru

yawning [jɔːn'iŋ] *adj* (gap) 大きな ōkína

yd. *abbr* = **yard(s)**

yeah [je] (*inf*) *adv* はい haì

year [jiːr] *n* 年 neñ, toshí, 1年 ichínèn

to be 8 years old 8才である hassái de aru

an eight-year-old child 8才の子供 hassái no kodómo

yearly [jiːr'liː] *adj* 毎年の maínen no, maítoshi no

♦*adv* 毎年 maínen, maítoshi

yearn [jəːrn] *vi*: *to yearn for something* ...を切に望む ...wo setsù ni nozómu

to yearn to do ...をしたいと切に望む ...wo shitái to setsù ni nozómu

yeast [jiːst] *n* 酵母 kōbò, イースト īsùto

yell [jel] *n* 叫び sakébi

♦*vi* 叫ぶ sakébù

yellow [jel'ou] *adj* 黄色い kiíroi

yelp [jelp] *n* (of animal) キャンと鳴く事 kyañ to nakú koto; (of person) 悲鳴 himéi

♦*vi* (animal) きゃんと鳴く kyañ to nakú; (person) 悲鳴を上げる himéi wò agérù

yeoman [jou'mən] (*pl* **yeomen**) *n*: *yeoman of the guard* 国王の親衛隊員 kokúō no shiñ-eitaiiñ

yes [jes] *adv* はい haì

♦*n* はいという返事 haì to iú henji

to say/answer yes 承諾する shōdaku suru

yesterday [jes'təːrdei] *adv* 昨日 kinó, sakújìtsu

♦*n* 昨日 kinó, sakújìtsu

yesterday morning/evening 昨日の朝〔夕方〕 kinó no asà〔yūgata〕

all day yesterday 昨日一日 kinó ichínichi

yet [jet] *adv* まだ madà; (already) もう mó

♦*conj* がしかし ga shikáshì

it is not finished yet まだできていない madà dekíte inái

the best yet これまでの物で最も良い物 koré madè no mono dè mottómo yoì mono

as yet まだ madà

yew [juː] *n* (tree) イチイ ichíi

Yiddish [jid'iʃ] *n* イディッシュ語 idīsshu-

go

yield [ji:ld] n (AGR) 収穫 shūkaku; (COMM) 収益 shūeki
♦vt (surrender: control, responsibility) 譲る yuzúru; (produce: results, profit) もたらす motárasu
♦vi (surrender) 譲る yuzúru; (US: AUT) 道を譲る michí wo yuzúru

YMCA [waiemsi:ei'] n abbr (= Young Men's Christian Association) キリスト教青年会 kirísutokyōseínenkai, ワイエムシーエー waíemushiē

yog(h)ourt [jou'gər] n ヨーグルト yōgurúto

yog(h)urt [jou'gər] n = **yog(h)ourt**

yoke [jouk] n (of oxen) くびき kubíki; (fig) 重荷 omóni

yolk [jouk] n 卵黄 rañ-ō, 黄身 kimí

KEYWORD

you [ju:] pron 1 (subj: sing) あなたは〔が〕anátá wa〔ga〕; (: pl) あなたたちは〔が〕anátátàchi wa〔ga〕

you are very kind あなたはとても親切ですね anátá wa totémo shíñsetsu desu ne, ご親切に有難うございます go-shíñsetsu ni arígàtō gozáimasù

you Japanese enjoy your food あなたたち日本人は食べるのが好きですね anátatàchi nihóñjìn wa tabérù no ga sukí desù né

you and I will go あなたと私が行く事になっています anátá to watákushi gà ikú kotò ni natté imasù

2 (obj: direct, indirect: sing) あなたを〔に〕anátá wo〔ni〕; (: : pl) あなたたちを〔に〕anátátàchi wo〔ni〕

I know you 私はあなたを知っています watákushi wà anátá wo shitté imasù

I gave it to you 私はそれをあなたに渡しました watákushi wà soré wò anátá ni watáshimashìta

3 (stressed): **I told YOU to do it** やれというのはあなたに言ったんですよ yaré tò iú no wà anátá ni ittá ñ desu yó

4 (after prep, in comparisons)

it's for you あなたのためです anátá no tamé desù

can I come with you? 一緒に行っていいですか isshó nì itté fì desu ká

she's younger than you 彼女はあなたより若いです kánòjo wa anátà yori wakáî desu

5 (impersonal: one)

fresh air does you good 新鮮な空気は健康にいい shiñsen nà kūkí wa keñkō ni íi

you never know どうなるか分かりませんね dố narù ka wakárimaseñ né

you can't do that! それはいけません soré wà ikémaseñ

---

you'd [ju:d] = you had; you would

you'll [ju:l] = you will; you shall

young [jʌŋ] adj (person, animal, plant) 若い wakái
♦npl (of animal) 子 ko; (people): **the young** 若者 wakámono

younger [jʌŋ'gə:r] adj (brother etc) 年下の toshíshita no

youngster [jʌŋ'stə:r] n 子供 kodómo

your [ju:r] adj (singular) あなたの anáta no; (plural) あなたたちの anátatàchi no ¶ see also **my**

you're [ju:r] = you are

yours [ju:rz] pron (singular) あなたの物 anáta no mono; (plural) あなたたちの物 anátátàchi no mono ¶ see also **mine**; **faithfully**; **sincerely**

yourself [ju:rself'] pron あなた自身 anáta jishìn ¶ see also **oneself**

yourselves [ju:rselvz'] pl pron あなたたち自身 anátatàchi jishìn ¶ see also **oneself**

youth [ju:θ] n (young days) 若い時分 wakái jibun; (young man: pl **youths**) 少年 shốnen

youth club n 青少年クラブ seíshōnen kuràbu

youthful [ju:θ'fəl] adj (person) 若い wakáî; (looks) 若々しい wakáwakashiî; (air, enthusiasm) 若者独特の wakámono-dokútoku no

youth hostel n ユースホステル yūsúhosùteru

Youth Training (BRIT) 職業訓練 sho-

kúgyōkunreǹ ◇失業青少年のためのもの
shitsúgyōseishōnen no tamé no monó

you've [ju:v] = **you have**

Yugoslav [ju:'gouslɑːv] *adj* ユーゴスラ
ビアの yúgosurabía no
♦*n* ユーゴスラビア人 yúgosurabiajin

Yugoslavia [ju:'gouslɑː'vi:ə] *n* ユーゴス
ラビア yúgosurabía

yuppie [jʌp'i:] (*inf*) *n* ヤッピー yappī
♦*adj* ヤッピーの yappī no

YWCA [waidʌbəlju:siei'] *n abbr* (=
Young Women's Christian Association)
キリスト教女子青年会 kirísutokyōjoshī-
seínenkai, ワイダブリューシーエー waí-
daburyūshīē

Z

Zambia [zæm'bi:ə] *n* ザンビア zaǹbia

zany [zei'ni:] *adj* (ideas, sense of humor)
ばかげた bakágeta

zap [zæp] *vt* (COMPUT: delete) 削除する
sakújo suru

zeal [zi:l] *n* (enthusiasm) 熱情 netsújō;
(*also*: **religious zeal**) 狂信 kyōshín

zealous [zel'əs] *adj* 熱狂的な nekkyóteki
na

zebra [zi:'brə] *n* シマウマ shimáuma

zebra crossing (*BRIT*) *n* 横断歩道 ōdán-
hodō

zenith [zi:'niθ] *n* 頂点 chōtèn

zero [zi:'rou] *n* 零点 reīten, ゼロ zerð

zest [zest] *n* (for life) 熱意 netsùi; (of
orange) 皮 kawá

zigzag [zig'zæg] *n* ジグザグ jigùzagu
♦*vi* ジグザグに動く jigùzagu ni ugókù

Zimbabwe [zimbɑː'bwei] *n* ジンバブウエ
jiǹbabùe

zinc [ziŋk] *n* 亜鉛 aèn

zip [zip] *n* (*also*: **zip fastener**) = **zipper**
♦*vt* (*also*: **zip up**) = **zipper**

zip code (*US*) *n* 郵便番号 yúbinbaǹgō

zipper [zip'ə:r] (*US*) *n* チャック chakkù,
ジッパー jippā, ファスナー fasùnā
♦*vt* (*also*: **zipper up**) ...のチャックを締め
る ...no chakkù wo shimérù

zodiac [zou'di:æk] *n* 十二宮図 jūníkyūzu

zombie [zɑ:m'bi:] *n* (*fig*): *like a zombie*
ロボットの様に〔な〕robóttò no yồ ni
〔na〕

zone [zoun] *n* (area, *also* MIL) 地帯 chitái

zoo [zu:] *n* 動物園 dóbutsùen

zoologist [zoua:l'ədʒist] *n* 動物学者 dồ-
butsugakùsha

zoology [zoua:l'ədʒi:] *n* 動物学 dóbutsu-
gàku

zoom [zu:m] *vi*: *to zoom past* 猛スピー
ドで通り過ぎる mốsupído de tōrísugiru

zoom lens *n* ズームレンズ zúmureǹzu

zucchini [zu:ki:'ni:] (*US*) *n inv* ズッキー
ニ zukkīnì

SUPPLEMENT

NUMBERS

Cardinal numbers:

1	一	ichi	11	十一	jūichi	21	二十一	nijūichi
2	二	ni	12	十二	jūni	22	二十二	nijūni
3	三	san	13	十三	jūsan		etc	
4	四	yon/shi	14	十四	jūyon/jūshi	30	三十	sanjū
5	五	go	15	十五	jūgo	40	四十	yonjū
6	六	roku	16	十六	jūroku	50	五十	gojū
7	七	nana/shichi	17	十七	jūnana/jūshichi	60	六十	rokujū
8	八	hachi	18	十八	jūhachi	70	七十	nanajū/shichijū
9	九	ku/kyū	19	十九	jūku/jūkyū	80	八十	hachijū
10	十	jū	20	二十	nijū	90	九十	kyūjū

Note: the alternative forms given for 4, 7, 9 etc are not necessarily interchangeable. The choice is determined by usage.

100	百	hyaku	1,000	千 sen, 一千 issen	10,000	一万	ichiman
200	二百	nihyaku	2,000	二千 nisen	20,000	二万	niman
300	三百	sanbyaku	3,000	三千 sanzen		etc	
400	四百	yonhyaku	4,000	四千 yonsen			
500	五百	gohyaku	5,000	五千 gosen			
600	六百	roppyaku	6,000	六千 rokusen			
700	七百	nanahyaku	7,000	七千 nanasen			
800	八百	happyaku	8,000	八千 hassen			
900	九百	kyūhyaku	9,000	九千 kyūsen			

Alternate set of numbers:

These are used often for counting, particularly for counting things without "counters" (see below), and for expressing the age of children.

1	一つ	hitotsu	6	六つ	muttsu
2	二つ	futatsu	7	七つ	nanatsu
3	三つ	mittsu	8	八つ	yattsu
4	四つ	yottsu	9	九つ	kokonotsu
5	五つ	itsutsu	10	十	tō

Ordinal numbers:

"The first," "the second" etc are expressed by the formula 第 x 番目 *dai x banme*, where x is the cardinal number and *dai, banme* or *me* can be variously omitted. Thus "the third" can be expressed by any of the following:

第三番目　daisanbanme

三番目　sanbanme

三番　sanban

第三　daisan

The alternate cardinal numbers from 1 to 9 can also be made into ordinal numbers by the addition of 目 *me* alone: "the third" = 三つ目 *mittsume*.

Days of the month:

The days of the month are written straightforwardly by a cardinal number plus the character for day 日. But the reading is not straightforward and needs to be learned.

一日	tsuitachi	七日	nanoka
二日	futsuka	八日	yōka
三日	mikka	九日	kokonoka
四日	yokka	十日	tōka
五日	itsuka	二十日	hatsuka
六日	muika		

Days 11 to 19 and 21 to 31 are expressed straightforwardly by a cardinal number + *nichi*. Thus the 18th day of the month is *jūhachinichi*.

Fractions:

In Japanese you express fractions by the formula y分のx *y bun no x*, where y is the DENOMINATOR, not the numerator. In other words, in Japanese you say the denominator first, then the numerator, thus:

1/2　二分の一　nibun no ichi

2/3　三分の二　sanbun no ni

3/4　四分の三　yonbun no san

Counters:

As in English we often say "2 *head* of cattle", "a *bunch* of grapes", "a *flock* of geese", Japanese uses counters for almost all everyday things, including people. There are many counters, some common, some exotic (like using the same counter for "rabbit" as you would for "bird"). Here is a list of counters you will need for your daily life.

counter:	used for:
人 nin	people
名 mei	people (interchangeable with *nin* except in set phrases)
匹 hiki	animals in general, except birds
頭 tō	relatively large animals
羽 wa	birds
個 ko	3-dimensional, relatively rounded objects: balls, stones, apples, cups
枚 mai	thin, flat things: pieces of paper, computer disks, handkerchiefs, blankets, dishes
本 hon	long things: pencils, ropes, sticks
冊 satsu	books and things bound like books: notebooks, diaries
台 dai	cars, trucks, bicycles, large machines
足 soku	shoes, socks etc that come in matched pairs
歳 sai	age of living things in years
杯 hai	containers full of something: cupful, glassful, spoonful

Like the use in English of "an" instead of "a" before words that begin with a vowel, Japanese makes pronunciation changes depending on the last syllable of the cardinal number and the first letter of a counter. Here are the most important.

1. Counters beginning with "h"

    一本, 一匹 ippon, ippiki
    二本, 二匹 nihon, nihiki
    三本, 三匹 sanbon, sanbiki
    四本, 四匹 yonhon, yonhiki
    五本, 五匹 gohon, gohiki
    六本, 六匹 roppon, roppiki
    七本, 七匹 nanahon, nanahiki
    八本, 八匹 happon, happiki
    九本, 九匹 kyūhon, kyūhiki
    十本, 十匹 juppon, juppiki

2. Counters beginning with unvoiced consonants (k, s, t, ch) double the consonant after the numbers 1 and 10.

    一個, 一歳 ikko, issai
    十個, 十歳 jukko, jussai

3. "k" also doubles after 6.

    六個 rokko

4. The voiced consonants g, z, d, m, n, r, w generally do not change.

5. The counter 人 *nin* for persons has an atypical pronunciation for 1 and 2.

一人 hitori

二人 futari

6. The counter 歳 *sai* for age has an atypical pronunciation for 20 years of age.

二十歳 hatachi

DEMONSTRATIVES

Japanese demonstratives begin with 4 prefixes: *ko-*, *so-*, *a-*, and *do-*. *Ko-* expresses nearness to the speaker; *so-* expresses distance from the speaker but nearness to the listener; *a-* expresses distance from both speaker and listener; and *do-* forms interrogatives.

kō	like this	sō	like that	aa	like that	dō	how ?
kono	this	sono	that	ano	that	dono	which ?
kore	this (one)	sore	that (one)	are	that (one)	dore	which (one) ?
koko		soko		asoko		doko	
kotchi	here	sotchi	there	atchi	there	dotchi	where ?
kochira		sochira		achira		dochira	
konna	such a	sonna	such a	anna	such a	donna	what kind of ?

UNDERSTANDING JAPANESE

Japanese has certain characteristics not always found in the European family of languages. This shows up in particular in the way the subject of the sentence is expressed (or unexpressed, as we shall see), and in the numerous particles which take the place of declensions, prepositions, auxiliaries etc in Western languages. Although it may take years to learn to use these characteristics like a native, being aware of their existance can serve as a shortcut to a fuller understanding of Japanese.

1. The hidden subject

Consider the following sentence. It is the opening line to Yasunari Kawabata's Nobel Prize-winning "Snow Country".

国境の長いトンネルを抜けると雪国であった。kokkyō no nagai tonneru wo nukeru to yukiguni de atta.

My translation would be:

"When your train emerged from the long tunnel beneath the border, you suddenly found yourself in the snow-bound countryside."

Notice that there is no "train" or "your" or "you" expressed in the original.

Japanese prefers not to express words that are apparent from the context or the choice of expression. This happens most frequently with the grammatical subject of the sentence, not only in literature, but especially in daily conversation.

A: どちらへお出かけですか dochira e o-dekake desu ka

B: 郵便局へ手紙を出しに行きます yūbinkyoku e tegami wo dashi ni ikimasu

Here there is no need for an *anata wa* in A or a *watashi wa* in B. The choice of words (the polite *dochira* with *o-...*) contains the "you" in A, and makes an "I" in B's answer superfluous.

In Japanese the verbal part of the sentence is the most important, and normally comes at the end. In a long sentence the listener has to wait till the end of the sentence in order to grasp the meaning. In English, the grammatical subject is the most important part, and is expressed at the beginning of the sentence, and auxiliary information about the subject is imparted gradually. This makes for great clarity of meaning, whereas Japanese sentences can often produce ambiguities. But this is a product of the Japanese culture, where reticence is considered virtue and outspokenness vice.

2. Particles

Japanese uses particles to make clear the relationship among words in a sentence. English frequently relies on position of words in the sentence for this. In a simple example, the meaning of A below is reversed if you reverse the position of the words, as in B.

A. John hit Sue.

B. Sue hit John.

On the other hand, consider the following example and its literal Japanese translation.

She gave me a book.

彼女は私に1冊の本をくれました.

kanojo *wa* watashi *ni* issatsu *no* hon *wo* kuremashita.

This is a standard translation. But the following are also possible, in context, without changing the meaning.

watashi *ni* kanojo *wa* issatsu *no* hon *wo* kuremashita.

issatsu *no* hon *wo* kanojo *wa* watashi *ni* kuremashita.

kuremashita, kanojo *wa* watashi *ni* issatsu *no* hon *wo*.

In other words, the particles make the meaning clear without regard to the position of the various sentence elements, even when the position is somewhat unnatural. On the other hand, if you confuse the particles, your speech becomes unintelligible. To say that someone's train of thought is illogical or contradictory, the Japanese

have an old metaphor.

てにをはが合わない. te-ni-wo-ha ga awanai.

Literally, "his particles are all mixed up." This underscores the correct use of particles, even for a native speaker of Japanese.

The Japanese classify their particles as follows.

Case particles: Added to nouns and pronouns, they indicate relation to other words in the sentence: no, ga, wo, ni, e, to, yori, kara, de.

Adverbial particles: They are added to nouns, pronouns, and adverbs and restrict the meaning of the verbal parts of the sentence : sae, made, bakari, dake, hodo, kurai, nado, nanka, nante, yara, zo, ka, zutsu.

Modifying particles: They add their own meaning to the word they follow and also modify the verbal parts of the sentence: wa, mo, koso, demo (also written "de mo"), shika, datte.

Sentence particles: They conclude a sentence and indicate interrogation, exclamation, emotion, prohibition etc: ka, kai, kashira, na, zo, ze, tomo (to mo), tte, no, ne, sa, ya, yo.

Parenthetical particles: They are placed at the end of phrases and clauses and are used to adjust sentence rhythm or to express emotion, emphasis etc: na, ne, sa.

Connecting particles: They are appended to various verbal phrases and clauses to indicate their connection with what follows: ba, to, te mo (de mo), keredo (keredomo), ga, no ni, no de, kara, shi, te (de), nagara.

The following illustrate typical Japanese usage of the more important particles. The translations given show one way, but not necessarily the only way, of expressing the concept in English.

a. Case particles

§ の **no**: indicates possession, location etc

父の本　chichi no hon "my father's book" —possession

海の風　umi no kaze "a sea breeze" —location

大学の教授　daigaku no kyōju "a university professor" —affiliation

紫の花　murasaki no hana "a purple flower" —attribute

小説家の川端氏　shōsetsuka no kawabatashi "Mr. Kawabata the novelist" —apposition

§ が **ga**: follows nouns or pronouns

私が行きます　watashi ga ikimasu "I will go." —indicates subject

メロンが好きだ　meron ga suki da "I like melons." —indicates object of desire, ability, likes and dislikes etc

それがね，本当なんだよ　sore ga ne, hontō nan da yo "The thing is, the story is

true." —attached to a demonstrative like a connecting particle

§ **を wo:** follows nouns or pronouns

本を読む   hon wo yomu "to read a book" —indicates object of an action verb

歩道を歩く   hodō wo aruku "to walk on the sidewalk" —indicates location with a verb of movement

この半年を堪え忍んだ   kono hantoshi wo taeshinonda "I have suffered in silence for the past 6 months." —indicates duration of an action

朝9時に家を出る   asa kuji ni ie wo deru "to leave the house at 9 o'clock" —indicates the place where an action commences

§ **に ni:** indicates the person or thing to which an action extends

朝5時に起床する   asa goji ni kishō suru "to get up at 5 a. m." —indicates time

空に虹が出る   sora ni niji ga deru "A rainbow appears in the sky." —indicates place

仕事に熱中する   shigoto ni netchū suru "to concentrate on one's work" —indicates the object of an action

会社にたどりつく   kaisha ni tadoritsuku "to reach one's office" —indicates destination or direction

悪夢にうなされる   akumu ni unasareru "to be tormented by a nightmare" —indicates cause

1週間に2日はお休み   isshūkan ni futsuka wa o-yasumi "We have 2 days a week off." —indicates ratio, proportion etc

犬に吠えられる   inu ni hoerareru "to be barked at by a dog" —indicates the agent of an action

大人になる   otona ni naru "to become an adult" —indicates the result of change

ぴかぴかに光る   pikapika ni hikaru "to shine brightly" —indicates manner

§ **へ e:**

西へ進む   nishi e susumu "to advance toward the west" —indicates the direction of an action

君への思い   kimi e no omoi "my longing for you" —indicates the object of an action

学校へ着く   gakkō e tsuku "to arrive at school" —indicates destination

兄がすぐそこへ来ています   ani ga sugu soko e kite imasu "My brother is right near here." —indicates location of an action

§ **と to:**

友人と話す   yūjin to hanasu "to talk with friends" —expresses the idea of "with"

以前と同じやり方   izen to onaji yarikata "the same manner as before" —indicates a term of comparison

政治家となる　seijika to naru "to become a politician" —indicates the result of change

開催地は山梨と決定した　kaisaichi wa Yamanashi to kettei shita "We decided to hold the meeting in Yamanashi." —indicates the content of an action or state

延々と続く　en-en to tsuzuku "to go on endlessly" —indicates the manner of an action or state

§ より yori:

父より背が高い　chichi yori se ga takai "I am taller than my father." —indicates a term of comparison

5時より前に帰る　goji yori mae ni kaeru "to be back before 5" —indicates a limit

§ から kara: used after nouns and pronouns, and indicates point of departure, or cause

明日から夏休み　myōnichi kara natsuyasumi "Summer vacation starts tomorrow." —indicates a spatial or temporal point of departure

窓から西日が差す　mado kara nishibi ga sasu "The western sun shines in through the window." —expresses the idea of "passing through"

何から何までお世話になりました　nani kara nani made o-sewa ni narimashita "You took wonderful care of me." —indicates extent

母から聞いた話　haha kara kiita hanashi "something I heard from my mother" —indicates a source

ビールは麦から作る　bīru wa mugi kara tsukuru "Beer is made from grain." —indicates constituent materials etc

§ で de:

プールで泳ぐ　pūru de oyogu "to swim in the pool" —indicates the location of an action.

ペンで書く　pen de kaku "to write with a pen" —indicates instrument, means, material etc

病気で死ぬ　byōki de shinu "to die from a sickness" —indicates cause, reason, motive

b. Adverbial particles

§ まで made: used after nouns and pronouns, and connects them with verbal parts or other particles

東京から北海道まで旅する　tōkyō kara hokkaidō made tabi suru "to travel from Tōkyō to Hokkaidō" —indicates the outer limits of an action in space or time

あくまで計画を実行する　aku made keikaku wo jikkō suru "to push a plan through to the finish" —expresses final extent of an action

§ だけ dake: expresses the limits of something

２人だけで話したい　futari dake de hanashitai "I want to talk to you alone." —indicates a limit

あれだけ食べたら満腹です　are dake tabetara manpuku desu "I'm full after eating all that." —expresses the idea of "that much"

§ ほど hodo: used after various noun and verb forms

後５枚ほど必要です　ato gomai hodo hitsuyō desu "I need about 5 more sheets of paper." —expresses an approximation of number or quantity

かわいそうなほどしょんぼりしている　kawaisō na hodo shonbori shite iru "He's looking so depressed I can't help feeling sorry for him." —expresses an action or state resulting from some characteristic

悪い奴ほど手が白い　warui yatsu hodo te ga shiroi "The evilest men have the whitest hands." —indicates 2 items, the second of which changes in direct proportion to change in the first

c. Modifying particles

§ は wa: used after many kinds of words. The original use was to single out one item of a group.

勉強はもう済んだ　benkyō wa mō sunda "I have finished my homework." —here singles out one item from a group of things to do

象は鼻が長い　zō wa hana ga nagai "The elephant has a long trunk." —singles out an item of subject matter about which some information is given

行きはよいよい、帰りは恐い　iki wa yoi yoi, kaeri wa kowai "Going is easy, but getting back is the problem." —expresses 2 or more contrasting judgments

君とは絶交だ　kimi to wa zekkō da "I want nothing more to do with you." —indicates emphasis

◇**Note:** in modern Japanese, wa is frequently used to express a word that corresponds to the grammatical subject of a sentence in English.

§ も mo: used after many kinds of words

花も実もある男　hana mo mi mo aru otoko "a man in both looks and deeds" —coordinates 2 or more concepts

料理もろくにできない　ryōri mo roku ni dekinai "She can't even cook properly." —singles out one among many other implied concepts

兄も病気になった　ani mo byōki ni natta "My older brother got sick too." —expresses the concept of "also"

そして誰もいなくなった　soshite dare mo inakunatta "And then there was no

one." —used with a negative to express the idea of "nothing, no one"

§ しか **shika:**

生き残ったのは1人しかいない　ikinokotta no wa hitori shika inai "Only one person was left alive." —used with a negative to express the idea of "only"

d. Sentence particles

§ か **ka:** expresses a variety of questions

君はだれですか　kimi wa dare desu ka "Who are you?"

本当に行くのか　hontō ni iku no ka "Are you really going?"

散歩に行きませんか　sanpo ni ikimasen ka "How about going for a walk?"

こんなことができないのか　konna koto ga dekinai no ka "Can't you even do something as simple as this?"

そうか，失敗だったのか　sō ka, shippai datta no ka "Oh, so it ended in failure, eh?"

§ ね **ne:** used at the end of a sentence

まあ，きれいな花ね　maa, kirei na hana ne "Oh, look at the pretty flower!" —expresses an exclamation

この本は君のですね　kono hon wa kimi no desu ne "This is your book, right?" —expresses a tag question

遅れてごめんなさいね　okurete gomen nasai ne "Do forgive me for being late." —expresses a request for the listener's understanding, sympathy, agreement etc

e. Parenthetical particles

§ ね **ne:** appended to words or phrases as a transition word, or to adjust sentence rhythm etc

そうですね，考えておきましょう　sō desu ne, kangaete okimashō "Well, let me think about it."

私ね，その秘密知っているの　watashi ne, sono himitsu shitte iru no "Listen, I know the secret behind that."

f. Connecting particles

§ ば **ba**

雨が降れば，旅行は中止　ame ga fureba, ryokō wa chūshi "If it rains, the trip is off." —expresses a possible condition

消息筋によれば，また株価が下がるらしい　shōsokusuji ni yoreba, mata kabuka ga sagaru rashii "According to a knowledgeable source, stock prices are going to fall again." —indicates the basis for a statement

日が沈めば夜になる　hi ga shizumeba yoru ni naru "Night comes when the sun sets." —expresses an invariable cause and effect relationship

5年前を思えば、随分楽になった　gonen mae wo omoeba, zuibun raku ni natta "Compared with 5 years ago, I am quite well off now." —indicates a past time for comparison with the present

§ と to: used after the present tense form of verbs

庭へ出ると、桜が咲いていた　niwa e deru to, sakura ga saite ita "When you went into the garden, you could see the cherry trees in bloom." —joins two contemporaneous actions

本を置くと、すぐ出て行った　hon wo oku to, sugu dete itta "He put down the book and left the room." —joins two successive actions

話が始まると、静かになった　hanashi ga hajimaru to, shizuka ni natta "When the lecture began, the audience became silent and listened." —expresses the beginning or cause etc of an action

はっきり言うと、それは失敗です　hakkiri iu to, sore wa shippai desu "Frankly, it's a failure." —expresses a preamble to what follows

§ ても te mo (with certain verbal forms it becomes でも de mo): used to express permission etc

果物なら食べてもいいですよ　kudamono nara tabete mo ii desu yo "Fruit is all right for you to eat."

§ けれども keredomo: used after verbs and -ii adjectives

貧しいけれども、心は豊かだった　mazushii keredomo, kokoro wa yutaka datta "He was poor materially, but rich in spirit." —expresses some sort of contrast

勝手な言い分ですけれども、帰らせて下さい　katte na iibun desu keredomo, kaerasete kudasai "I'm sorry to do so at this point, but I really must leave." —joins a preamble to the main point of the sentence

レコード持ってきたけれども、聞いてみる　rekōdo motte kita keredomo, kiite miru? "I brought a record along. Do you want to hear it?" —simply joins two clauses

§ が ga: used after verbs and -ii adjectives

ご存知のことと思いますが、一応説明します　go-zonji no koto to omoimasu ga, ichiō setsumei shimasu "I'm sure you are already familiar with the problem, but I'll run through it briefly for you anyway." —joins a preamble to the main part of the sentence

驚いて振り向いたが、もはやだれの姿もなかった　odoroite furimuita ga, mohaya dare no sugata mo nakatta "In surprise I wheeled around to look back, but whoever it was had already disappeared." —expresses a temporal relationship between two clauses

見かけは悪いが，たいへん親切な男　mikake wa warui ga, taihen shinsetsu na otoko "He doesn't look it, but he's really a very kind man." —expresses contrast

§ のに **no ni:** expresses dissatisfaction, unexpectedness etc

待っていたのに，来なかった　matte ita no ni, konakatta "I waited and waited, but he didn't come."

§ ので **no de:** expresses cause, reason, basis etc

分からないので，質問しました wakaranai no de, shitsumon shimashita "I didn't understand, so I asked."

§ から **kara**

暑いから，のどが渇いた　atsui kara, nodo ga kawaita "It was hot, and I became very thirsty." —expresses cause, reason, basis etc

決心したからには，やり通そう　kesshin shita kara ni wa, yaritōsō "We have made the decision, so let's see it through to the end." —expresses the notion of "having done such and such, it follows that..."

DAILY JAPANESE

Here we present a selection of very typical and idiomatic Japanese words and phrases. These examples occur with a high frequency in daily life in Japan. The English translations given in boldface provide an idea of the meaning, but are not absolute. A number of translations are possible, depending on the context, tone of voice, person speaking or spoken to, etc.

Some words occur in the examples which have no English equivalent, or are unintelligible to a person unfamiliar with Japan. Foreigners living in Japan often prefer to use these as loan words in conversation, rather than resorting to some clumsy translation. Such words are marked with an asterisk (*) in the translation, and are explained in a short glossary at the end of the section.

1. Indispensable words

私　watashi **I**

(Note: slightly formal: 私 watakushi; familiar: male: 僕 boku; female: あたし atashi; very familiar/rough/vulgar, usually male: おれ ore)

あなた anata **you**

(Note: familiar/affectionate: 君 kimi; very familiar/rough/vulgar: お前 omae; rough/vulgar: てめえ temē; insulting: きさま kisama)

彼　kare **he**

彼女　kanojo **she**

はい　hai **yes**

いいえ　iie **no**

どうぞ　dōzo **please**

ありがとう（ございます）arigatō (gozaimasu) **Thank you.**

どういたしまして　dō itashimashite **You're welcome./Don't mention it.**

いいえ、結構です　iie, kekkō desu **No, thank you.**

すみません　sumimasen **excuse me/pardon me/I'm sorry**

2. Greetings

General

お早うございます　o-hayō gozaimasu **Good morning.**

今日は　konnichi wa **Good morning./Good afternoon./Hello.** (said from about 10 a. m. to early evening)

今晩は　konban wa **Good evening.**

お休みなさい　o-yasumi nasai **Good night.**

ご機嫌いかがですか　go-kigen ikaga desu ka **How are you?** (very formal)

お元気ですか　o-genki desu ka **How are you?** (less formal)

ありがとう。とても元気です　arigatō. totemo genki desu **I'm fine, thank you.**

よいお天気ですね　yoi o-tenki desu ne **Nice weather, isn't it?**

今日は寒いですね　kyō wa samui desu ne **It's cold today, isn't it?**

さようなら　sayōnara **Goodbye.**

行って参ります　itte mairimasu (no English equivalent; said when leaving for a destination with the intention of returning)

行っていらっしゃい　itte irasshai (no English equivalent; said in response to the above)

ただ今　tadaima **I'm home./I'm back.**

お帰りなさい　o-kaeri nasai **Welcome home./Welcome back.** (said in response to the above, but the order may also be reversed)

Visiting

ごめん下さい　gomen kudasai **Hello./Anybody home?**

いらっしゃいませ　irasshaimase **Welcome.**

おじゃまします　o-jama shimasu (no English equivalent ; said when entering a place)

どうぞこちらへ　dōzo kochira e **This way, please.**

ちょっとお待ち下さい　chotto o-machi kudasai **One moment, please.**

お掛け下さい　o-kake kudasai **Have a seat.**

お目にかかれてうれしいです　o-me ni kakarete ureshii desu **Pleased to meet you.**

長いことおじゃまいたしました　nagai koto o-jama itashimashita **Thank you for your time.**

この辺で失礼いたします　kono hen de shitsurei itashimasu **I'll be going now.**

明日またお会いしましょう　myōnichi mata o-ai shimashō **See you again tomorrow.**

Meals

お上がり下さい　o-agari kudasai **Help yourself** (literally, "please eat")

いただきます　itadakimasu (no English equivalent; said when beginning to eat or drink)

ごちそうさまでした　gochisōsama deshita **I enjoyed the meal./Thanks for the meal.**

3. Introducing oneself

私は日本人（オーストラリア人）です　watashi wa nihonjin (ōsutorariajin) desu **I am Japanese/Australian.**

名前は鈴木花子です　namae wa suzuki hanako desu **My name is Hanako Suzuki.**

私は学生です　watashi wa gakusei desu **I am a university student.**

京都からきました　kyōto kara kimashita **I come from Kyoto.**

22才です　nijūnissai desu **I am 22 years old.**

兄が2人妹が1人います　ani ga futari imōto ga hitori imasu **I have 2 older brothers and a younger sister.**

父は建築家です　chichi wa kenchikuka desu **My father is an architect.**

私は外国に行ったことがありません　watashi wa gaikoku ni itta koto ga arimasen **I have never been to a foreign country.**

私は少ししか英語を話せません　watashi wa sukoshi shika eigo wo hanasemasen **I can only speak a little English.**

趣味は音楽鑑賞です　shumi wa ongaku kanshō desu **My favorite pastime is listening to music.**

．．．が好きではありません　...ga suki de wa arimasen **I don't like ....**

私は水泳が得意です　watashi wa suiei ga tokui desu **I am a good swimmer.**

．．．が苦手です　...ga nigate desu **I am not very good at....**

4. Questions and requests

これは何ですか　kore wa nan desu ka **What is this?**

あの人はだれですか　ano hito wa dare desu ka **Who is that ?**

いつですか　itsu desu ka **When (is it etc) ?**

どこから来ましたか　doko kara kimashita ka **Where did you come from/where are you from ?**

どうなりましたか　dō narimashita ka **What happened/what is the matter ?**

どのぐらい遠いですか　donogurai tōi desu ka **How far (away) is it ?**

いくらですか　ikura desu ka **How much is it ?**

何をしているのですか　nani wo shite iru no desu ka **What are you doing ?**

何がほしいのですか　nani ga hoshii no desu ka **What do you want ?**

... がありますか　...ga arimasu ka **Is there a .../do you have ... ?**

... を持っていますか　...wo motte imasu ka **Do you have a ... ?**

これをいただいてもよろしいですか　kore wo itadaite mo yoroshii desu ka **May I have this ?**

... がほしい　...ga hoshii **I want a ....**

... がほしくない　...ga hoshikunai **I don't want ....**

... を取って下さい　...wo totte kudasai **Take ....**

5. Manners

ごめんなさい　gomen nasai **I'm sorry./Pardon me./Forgive me.**

失礼します　shitsurei shimasu **Excuse me./pardon me.**

すみません　sumimasen **Excuse me.** (used to get attention when seeking information, calling a waiter etc)

お手数掛けてすみません　o-tesū kakete sumimasen **I'm sorry to trouble you like this.**

よろしくお願いします　yoroshiku o-negai shimasu (no English equivalent; rather like a very formal "please")

ご迷惑でしょうか　go-meiwaku deshō ka **Is it too much trouble ?**

心配いりません　shinpai irimasen **Don't worry.**

かまいません　kamaimasen **It doesn't matter.**

よろしいんですよ　yoroshiin desu yo **That's all right.**

何とおっしゃいましたか　nan to osshaimashita ka **What did you say ?**

もう一度言って下さい　mō ichido itte kudasai **Please say that again.**

ゆっくり話して下さい　yukkuri hanashite kudasai **Please speak slowly.**

急いでいます　isoide imasu **I'm in a hurry.**

用意ができています　yōi ga dekite imasu **I'm ready.**

ちょっとお待ち下さい　chotto o-machi kudasai **Just a moment, please.**

6. Conveying information

私はあの少年を知っています　watashi wa ano shōnen wo shitte imasu **I know that boy.**

その人を知りません　sono hito wo shirimasen **I never heard of him/her.**

はっきりとは分かりません　hakkiri to wa wakarimasen **I really don't know for certain.**

覚えています　oboete imasu **(Yes,) I remember.**

忘れました　wasuremashita **I forgot.**

私はとても怒っています　watashi wa totemo okotte imasu **I am very angry.**

私はたいへん不愉快です　watashi wa taihen fuyukai desu **I am very upset.**

気分は最高です　kibun wa saikō desu **I feel great.**

とても幸せです　totemo shiawase desu **I feel very happy.**

残念です　zannen desu **That's too bad.**

家族と／が離ればなれで寂しい　kazoku to／ga hanarebanare de sabishii **I miss my family.**

それは正しいと思います　sore wa tadashii to omoimasu **That's correct.**

あなたは間違っています　anata wa machigatte imasu **You're mistaken.**

あなたの言う通りです　anata no iu tōri desu **It's as you say.**

一生懸命に働きます　isshōkenmei ni hatarakimasu **I'm going to work hard.**

7. Eating out

a. getting seats

私はとても空腹です　watashi wa totemo kūfuku desu **I'm very hungry.**

私はのどが渇きました　watashi wa nodo ga kawakimashita **I'm thirsty.**

食事に行きましょう　shokuji ni ikimashō **Let's go someplace to eat.**

安い店を紹介してくれませんか　yasui mise wo shōkai shite kuremasen ka **Do you know some inexpensive place ?**

角のてんぷら屋がおいしいと評判です　kado no tenpuraya ga oishii to hyōban desu **They say the tempura* place on the corner is pretty good.**

1時にテーブルを予約して下さい　ichiji ni tēburu wo yoyaku shite kudasai **Reserve a table for one o'clock, will you please ?**

3人連れですが，空いているテーブルありますか　sanninzure desu ga, aite iru tēburu arimasu ka **Do you have a table for 3 ?**

満席です　manseki desu **Sorry, we're all filled up.**

昼時はどこも混んでいます　hirudoki wa doko mo konde imasu **At noontime everywhere you go it's crowded.**

禁煙席にお願いします　kin-enseki ni o-negai shimasu **We want a non-smoking**

table, please.

b. ordering

メニューを見せていただけますか　menyū wo misete itadakemasu ka **Can we see a menu, please?**

定食はありますか　teishoku wa arimasu ka **Do you have set meals?**

本日のおすすめ料理は何ですか　honjitsu no o-susume ryōri wa nan desu ka **What's today's specialty?**

この地方の名物は何ですか　kono chihō no meibutsu wa nan desu ka **What's the local specialty?**

何を食べたいですか　nani wo tabetai desu ka **What do you feel like eating?**

これは何の料理ですか　kore wa nan no ryōri desu ka **What is this?**

... を食べて見ませんか　...wo tabete mimasen ka **How about trying the ...?**

私は... にしたい　watashi wa ...ni shitai **I want the ....**

私は魚が大好きです　watashi wa sakana ga daisuki desu **I just love fish.**

私は肉は嫌いです　watashi wa niku wa kirai desu **I hate meat.**

私はピーマンは食べられません　watashi wa pīman wa taberaremasen **I can't eat green peppers.**

おいしいです　oishii desu **It's delicious.**

これはまずい　kore wa mazui **It tastes awful.**

もう少しパンを下さい　mō sukoshi pan wo kudasai **Can we have some more bread, please?**

ご飯のおかわりを下さい　gohan no o-kawari wo kudasai **Another bowl of rice, please.**

塩を取って下さい　shio wo totte kudasai **Please pass the salt.**

スープがまだきていません　sūpu ga mada kite imasen **We didn't get our soup yet.**

味が薄い　aji ga usui **This needs more seasoning.**

辛すぎます　karasugimasu **It's too salty.**

おなかがいっぱいになりました　onaka ga ippai ni narimashita **I'm full.**

c. drinks

飲物は何になさいますか　nomimono wa nani ni nasaimasu ka **What will you have to drink?**

生ビールを下さい　namabīru wo kudasai **We'll have draft beer.**

ブランディーはありますか　burandī wa arimasu ka **Do you have any brandy?**

ミルクティーを２つ下さい　mirukutī wo futatsu kudasai **Two teas with milk,**

please.

ダイエットをしているので砂糖はいりません　daietto wo shite iru no de satō wa irimasen **I'm on a diet, so no sugar, please.**

コーヒーのおかわりを下さい　kōhī no o-kawari wo kudasai **More coffee, please.**

水をもういっぱい下さい　mizu wo mō ippai kudasai **More water, please.**

このお茶は少し熱い　kono o-cha wa sukoshi atsui **This tea is too hot.**

d. paying

勘定をお願いします　kanjō wo o-negai shimasu **Can I have the bill, please?**

伝票を調べて下さい。間違っていると思います　denpyō wo shirabete kudasai. machigatte iru to omoimasu **Check this bill, will you? I think there's a mistake on it.**

サラダは取っていません　sarada wa totte imasen **I didn't order any salad.**

伝票を別々にしてくれませんか　denpyō wo betsubetsu ni shite kuremasen ka **Will you give us separate bills, please ?**

e. restaurant words

レストラン　resutoran **restaurant**

軽食　keishoku **light lunches**

メニュー　menyū **menu**

勘定(書)　kanjō(gaki) **bill/check**

化粧室　keshōshitsu **restroom(s)**

ウエイトレス　ueitoresu **waitress**

ウエイター　ueitā **waiter**

板前　itamae **cook**

茶碗(茶)　chawan **rice bowl/teacup (for Japanese tea)**

湯呑み　yunomi **teacup (for Japanese tea)**

カップ　kappu **cup/teacup/coffee cup (with handle)**

箸(茶)　hashi **chopsticks**

つまようじ　tsumayōji **toothpick**

灰皿　haizara **ashtray**

たばこ　tabako **cigarette**

日本酒　nihonshu **sake***

銚子(茶)／とっくり　chōshi*/tokkuri* **(no English equivalent; see glossary)**

熱燗(茶)　atsukan **hot sake**

水　mizu **water**

ミルク　miruku **milk**

砂糖　satō **sugar**

紅茶　kōcha **tea**

日本茶　nihoncha **Japanese tea**

塩　shio **salt**

こしょう　koshō **pepper**

芥子(からし)　karashi **mustard**

油　abura **oil**

酢　su **vinegar**

正油(しょうゆ)　shōyu **soy sauce**

どんぶり　donburi **bowl**

味噌(みそ)　miso **miso***

わさび　wasabi **wasabi***

f. some Japanese dishes

すき焼き　sukiyaki　beef cooked at table with green onions, tofu, and leafy vegetables

寿司(すし)　sushi　cooked rice seasoned with vinegar and served in various forms with a topping of fish, shellfish, and vegetables

てんぷら　tenpura　fish, shellfish, and vegetables coated with batter and fried in deep fat

天丼(てんどん)　tendon　a bowl of rice topped with tempura* dipped in broth

豆腐　tōfu　white soya-bean curd with a soft, cheeselike consistency

梅干　umeboshi　ume* pickled with salt and a pungent seasoning

刺身　sashimi　fish and shellfish sliced and eaten raw with soy sauce and wasabi*

納豆　nattō　fermented soy beans

うどん　udon　wheat-flour noodles

そば　soba　buckwheat noodles

味噌(みそ)汁　misoshiru　soup flavored with miso

お握(にぎ)り　o-nigiri　rice compacted into a ball or other shape for carrying on outings, to work etc

餅(もち)　mochi　glutinous rice steamed, pounded into a paste, shaped into patties, and allowed to harden

赤飯　sekihan　glutinous rice steamed with red beans

たくあん　takuan　radish pickled in salt and rice bran

お好み焼き　okonomiyaki　a sort of hotcake made from wheat flour batter to which have been added various vegetables and other ingredients and fried on a hot plate

ところてん　tokoroten　　a jelly made from a species of seaweed and eaten as a refreshing dish in summer

おでん　oden　　various fish and vegetable preparations stewed in a light broth

ようかん　yōkan　　a jellied confection made from highly sweetened beans

雑煮　zōni　　a soup with vegetables, fish, and meat to which mochi are added: a traditional New Year's dish

おせち　o-sechi　　an assortment of New Year's dishes prepared several days beforehand from ingredients that will not spoil; the idea is to give the womenfolk a degree of respite from the drudgery of kitchen work on the greatest feast of the year

煎餅(芯)　senbei　　fried crackers made from rice flour

Shopping
a. going out

私は帽子が買いたい　watashi wa bōshi ga kaitai　**I need a new hat.**

どのお店が一番よいですか　dono o-mise ga ichiban yoi desu ka　**Do you know a good store?**

駅のそばの果物屋は安いので有名です　eki no soba no kudamonoya wa yasui no de yūmei desu　**The fruit store near the station is known for its low prices.**

デパートで今セールをやっています　depāto de ima sēru wo yatte imasu　**They're having a sale at the department store today.**

一緒に買い物に行きましょう　issho ni kaimono ni ikimashō　**How about coming shopping with me?**

... はどこで買えますか　...wa doko de kaemasu ka　**Where can you buy a ...?**

一番近い本屋はどこですか　ichiban chikai hon-ya wa doko desu ka　**Where's the closest bookstore?**

靴売場はどこですか　kutsu uriba wa doko desu ka　**Where is the shoe department?**

b. picking things out

店員さん、これを見せて下さい　ten-insan, kore wo misete kudasai　**Excuse me, Miss, could you let me examine this item?**

... を売っていますか　...wo utte imasu ka　**Do you sell ... here?**

... を買いたいのです　...wo kaitai no desu　**I'm looking for ....**

こちらはいかがでしょう　kochira wa ikaga deshou　**How about this one?**

何色がよろしいのですか　nani-iro ga yoroshii no desu ka　**What color would you like?**

きれいな色ですね　kirei na iro desu ne **That's a pretty color, isn't it ?**

これが気に入りました　kore ga ki ni irimashita **I like this one.**

あちらの方が好きです　achira no hō ga suki desu **I like that one.**

この色はあまり好きではありません　kono iro wa amari suki de wa arimasen **I don't like this color.**

別な色のものがありますか　betsu na iro no mono ga arimasu ka **Do you have this in a different color ?**

別の品物を見せて下さい　betsu no shinamono wo misete kudasai **Show me something else.**

もっと安いものはありませんか　motto yasui mono wa arimasen ka **Do you have something cheaper ?**

予算は1万円です　yosan wa ichiman en desu **My spending limit is 10,000 yen.**

予算の枠内で買いたいのです　yosan no wakunai de kaitai no desu **I don't want to go over my limit.**

サイズはいくらですか　saizu wa ikura desu ka **What size do you take ?**

これはどのサイズですか　kore wa dono saizu desu ka **What size is this ?**

サイズ... を下さい　saizu... wo kudasai **Give me a size ....**

もっと大きいものがありますか　motto ōkii mono ga arimasu ka **Do you have something bigger ?**

大きすぎる　ōkisugiru **It's too big.**

高すぎる　takasugiru **It's too expensive.**

c. *in various stores*
clothing and shoes

セーターを見せて下さい　sētā wo misete kudasai **Show me some sweaters.**

ウインドーにあるのが好きです　uindō ni aru no ga suki desu **I like the one in the window.**

その着物は実に豪華ですね　sono kimono wa jitsu ni gōka desu ne **That kimono is really gorgeous.**

残念ながら着物は1人で着られません　zannennagara kimono wa hitori de kiraremasen **It's unfortunate, but a kimono is hard to put on by oneself.**

黒い絹の手袋がほしい　kuroi kinu no tebukuro ga hoshii **I want a pair of black silk gloves.**

試着していいですか　shichaku shite ii desu ka **Can I try it on ?**

胸まわりは... です　munemawari wa ...desu **My bust/chest measures ....**

ウエストは... です　uesuto wa ...desu **My waist measures ....**

襟(衿)のサイズは... です　eri no saizu wa ...desu **My collar size is....**

この色は今年の流行です　kono iro wa kotoshi no ryūkō desu **This color is in fashion this year.**

このスタイルは好きではありません　kono sutairu wa suki de wa arimasen **I don't like this style.**

コート売り場はどこですか　kōto uriba wa doko desu ka **Where do you sell coats?**

このネクタイは実におしゃれです　kono nekutai wa jitsu ni o-share desu **This necktie is really stylish.**

靴下を2足ほしい　kutsushita wo nisoko hoshii **I want 2 pairs of socks.**

ビーチサンダルがほしい　bīchisandaru ga hoshii **I want a pair of beach sandals.**

このかかとは高すぎる　kono kakato wa takasugiru **The heels are too high.**

food and drink

パンを1個下さい　pan wo ikko kudasai **One loaf of bread, please.**

冷凍食品コーナーはどこですか　reitōshokuhin kōnā wa doko desu ka **Where are the frozen foods?**

… を1キロ下さい　...wo ichikiro kudasai **Give me one kilo of ....**

牛乳を1瓶下さい　gyūnyū wo hitobin kudasai **Give me a bottle of milk.**

それは新鮮ですか　sore wa shinsen desu ka **Is that fresh?**

これは古くなっている　kore wa furuku natte iru **This isn't fresh any more.**

賞味期間を過ぎている　shōmikikan wo sugite iru **The date on this has expired.**

これは悪くなっている　kore wa waruku natte iru **This has gone bad.**

medicines

ばんそうこうを下さい　bansōkō wo kudasai **I'd like a roll of adhesive tape.**

バンドエイドを下さい　bandoeido wo kudasai **Give me a box of Band-Aids®.**

日焼け止めの薬ありますか　hiyakedome no kusuri arimasu ka **Have you got something to prevent sunburn?**

消化不良にきく薬を下さい　shōkafuryō ni kiku kusuri wo kudasai **Give me something for indigestion, please.**

のどが痛みます。トローチを下さい　nodo ga itamimasu. torōchi wo kudasai **I have a sore throat; give me a box of cough drops.**

虫刺されにきく薬をくれませんか　mushisasare ni kiku kusuri wo kuremasen ka **Can you give me something for insect bites?**

総合ビタミン剤を下さい　sōgōbitaminzai wo kudasai **I want a bottle of vitamin tablets.**

この処方箋(ｾﾝ)を調合していただけますか　kono shohōsen wo chōgō shite itada-

kemasu ka **Can I have this prescription filled, please ?**

小さな救急箱はありますか　chiisana kyūkyūbako wa arimasu ka **Do you have a small first-aid kit ?**

アスピリンを1瓶下さい　asupirin wo hitobin kudasai **Give me a bottle of aspirin, please.**

newspapers, books, stationery

英字新聞は売っていますか　eijishinbun wa utte imasu ka **Do you carry English-language newspapers ?**

市街地図はありますか　shigaichizu wa arimasu ka **Do you have a city map ?**

... 著の本がありますか　...cho no hon ga arimasu ka **Do you have any books by ... ?**

ノートを2冊とボールペンを1本下さい　nōto wo nisatsu to bōrupen wo ippon kudasai **Two notebooks and a ballpoint, please.**

横書きの便せんはありますか　yokogaki no binsen wa arimasu ka **Have you got letter paper for writing left to right ?**

d. paying for things

これはいくらですか　kore wa ikura desu ka **How much is this ?**

全部でいくらになりますか　zenbu de ikura ni narimasu ka **How much all together ?**

勘定をお願いします　kanjō wo o-negai shimasu **Can I have the bill, please ?**

アメリカの通貨で売ってくれますか　amerika no tsūka de utte kuremasu ka **Can I pay in American money ?**

トラベラーズチェックで受けてくれますか　toraberāzuchekku de ukete kuremasu ka **Will you take traveler's checks ?**

少し高いですね　sukoshi takai desu ne **That's rather expensive, isn't it ?**

割引きしてくれますか　waribiki shite kuremasu ka **Can you give me a discount ?**

ここのレジは混んでいます　koko no reji wa konde imasu **The line at this checkout counter is too long.**

レシートをいただけますか　reshīto wo itadakemasu ka **Can I have a receipt ?**

おつりが間違っています　o-tsuri ga machigatte imasu **You gave me the wrong change.**

e. complaints

責任者に会いたい　sekininsha ni aitai **I want to speak to your superior.**

昨日これを買いました　sakujitsu kore wo kaimashita **I bought this yesterday.**

これは汚れている（破れている，壊れている，ひびが入っている，不良品だ）　kore wa yogorete iru (yaburete iru, kowarete iru, hibi ga haitte iru, furyōhin da) **This is stained (torn, broken, cracked, defective).**

この本には落丁があります　kono hon ni wa rakuchō ga arimasu **This book has pages missing.**

この薬は全く効果がありません　kono kusuri wa mattaku kōka ga arimasen **This medicine doesn't have any effect at all.**

店員の態度が悪い　ten-in no taido ga warui **I don't like your clerk's manners.**

これを取り替えて下さいませんか　kore wo torikaete kudasaimasen ka **Can I exchange this, please?**

お金を払い戻して下さいませんか　o-kane wo haraimodoshite kudasaimasen ka **Can I have my money back, please?**

f. repairing and mending

時計が壊れてしまいました　tokei ga kowarete shimaimashita **My watch is broken.**

修理できますか　shūri dekimasu ka **Can it be fixed?**

これを直して下さい　kore wo naoshite kudasai **Can you fix this?**

残念ながらそれはもはや修理できません　zannennagara sore wa mohaya shūri dekimasen **I'm sorry, but it's beyond repair.**

靴のかかとを新しいのとつけ替えていただけますか　kutsu no kakato wo atarashii no to tsukekaete itadakemasu ka **Can you put new heels on these shoes?**

待っている間にやってくれますか　matte iru aida ni yatte kuremasu ka **Can you do it while I wait?**

いつできますか　itsu dekimasu ka **How soon can you have it done?**

どのぐらい時間がかかりますか　dono gurai jikan ga kakarimasu ka **How long will it take?**

このジャケットのシミは抜けないでしょうか　kono jaketto no shimi wa nukenai deshō ka **Can you remove the stain on this jacket?**

このズボンのすそがほつれているので繕っていただけますか　kono zubon no suso ga hotsurete iru no de tsukurotte itadakemasu ka **The cuffs on these pants are worn. Can you mend them?**

... の具合が悪いのでみていただけますか　...no guai ga warui no de mite itadakemasu ka **The ... is out of order. Could you have a look at it, please?**

できるだけ早く直していただきたい　dekiru dake hayaku naoshite itadakitai **I want**

this fixed as soon as possible.

費用はいくらですか　hiyō wa ikura desu ka **How much will it cost ?**

9. Postal and Telephone Service
a. the post office

一番近い郵便局はどこですか　ichiban chikai yūbinkyoku wa doko desu ka **Where is the nearest post office ?**

郵便局は何時まで開いていますか　yūbinkyoku wa nanji made aite imasu ka **What time does the post office close ?**

ポストはどこにありますか　posuto wa doko ni arimasu ka **Do you know where there's a mailbox ?**

ちょうど記念切手を売り出しているところです　chōdo kinenkitte wo uridashite iru tokoro desu **They have just issued a new commemorative stamp.**

カナダまで葉書はいくらですか　kanada made hagaki wa ikura desu ka **How much is a postcard to Canada ?**

アメリカまで航空便はいくらですか　amerika made kōkūbin wa ikura desu ka **How much is an air mail letter to America ?**

イギリスまで船便ではいくらですか　igirisu made funabin de wa ikura desu ka **How much is surface mail to Britain ?**

この小包をお願いします　kono kozutsumi wo o-negai shimasu **I want to mail this package.**

この手紙を速達で送りたい　kono tegami wo sokutatsu de okuritai **I want to send this letter by express mail.**

この手紙を書留にしたい　kono tegami wo kakitome ni shitai **I want to send this letter by registered mail.**

官製葉書を10枚下さい　kanseihagaki wo jūmai kudasai **Ten government postcards*, please.**

大体何日頃届きますか　daitai nannichi goro todokimasu ka **Do you know how many days it will take to get there ?**

b. telephones and telegrams

一番近い電話ボックスはどこですか　ichiban chikai denwabokkusu wa doko desu ka **Where is the nearest telephone booth ?**

電話を掛けたい　denwa wo kaketai **I want to make a phone call.**

オーストラリアに電話したい　ōsutoraria ni denwa shitai **I want to make a phone call to Australia.**

小銭が不足しています．テレフォンカードをお持ちですか　kozeni ga fusoku shite

imasu. terefonkādo wo o-mochi desu ka **I don't have enough small change. Do you have a telephone card ?**

コレクトコールにしたい　korekutokōru ni shitai **I want to make a collect call.**

もしもし… さんですか　moshimoshi …san desu ka **Hello. Is this Mr. … ?**

どちら様ですか　dochirasama desu ka **Who is this calling, please ?**

内線… 番をお願いします　naisen …ban wo o-negai shimasu **Give me extension …, please.**

そのままお待ち下さい　sono mama o-machi kudasai **Please hold the line a moment.**

… はただ今外出中です　…wa tadaima gaishutsuchū desu **… is out at the moment.**

… はいつお戻りですか　…wa itsu o-modori desu ka **When will … be back ?**

伝言をお願いできますか　dengon wo o-negai dekimasu ka **Will you take a message, please ?**

… より電話があったと彼に伝えて下さい　…yori denwa ga atta to kare ni tsutaete kudasai **Please tell him that … called.**

後ほどお電話します　nochihodo o-denwa shimasu **I'll call again later.**

私に電話するように伝えて下さい　watashi ni denwa suru yō ni tsutaete kudasai **Please tell him to call me.**

話し中です　hanashichū desu **The line is busy.**

電話番号が間違っています　denwabangō ga machigatte imasu **You have the wrong number.**

留守番電話にメッセージが入っています　rusubandenwa ni messēji ga haitte imasu **There's a message on the answering machine.**

電報を打ちたい　denpō wo uchitai **I want to send a telegram.**

1語あたりいくらですか　ichigo atari ikura desu ka **How much is it for each word ?**

祝電(弔電)を打ちたい　shukuden (chōden) wo uchitai **I want to send a telegram of congratulation 〔condolence〕.**

10. Transport

a. trains

駅はどこにありますか　eki wa doko ni arimasu ka **Where is the train station ?**

新幹線のホームはどこですか　shinkansen no hōmu wa doko desu ka **Where are the shinkansen* tracks ?**

切符は自動発券機で買えます　kippu wa jidōhakkenki de kaemasu **You can buy your ticket at the automatic ticket machine.**

新幹線の座席指定はこの用紙に必要事項を記入します shinkansen no zaseki shitei wa kono yōshi ni hitsuyōjikō wo kinyū shimasu **You have to fill out this form to get a reserved seat on the shinkansen*.**

9：30分発京都行きの特急に乗りたいのですが kujisanjippunhatsu kyōtoyuki no tokkyū ni noritai no desu ga **I want a ticket on the 9:30 special express to Kyōto, please.**

禁煙席を希望します kin-enseki wo kibō shimasu **If possible I want a nonsmoking seat.**

往復の切符を買いたい ōfuku no kippu wo kaitai **I want a round-trip ticket.**

寝台車を予約したい shindaisha wo yoyaku shitai **I want to reserve a berth on a sleeping car.**

寝台車はいくらですか shindaisha wa ikura desu ka **How much does a sleeping car ticket cost?**

急行列車ですか，それとも普通列車ですか kyūkōressha desu ka, soretomo futsūresssha desu ka **Do you want the express train or the local train?**

この電車は...へ行きますか kono densha wa ..e ikimasu ka **Does this train go to ...?**

もっと早くでる列車はありますか motto hayaku deru ressha wa arimasu ka **Isn't there an earlier train?**

この列車には食堂車がありますか kono ressha ni wa shokudōsha ga arimasu ka **Is there a dining car on this train?**

...まで片道3枚下さい ...made katamichi sanmai kudasai **Three one-way tickets to ..., please.**

この切符は何日間有効ですか kono kippu wa nannichikan yūkō desu ka **How long is this ticket valid?**

この列車は何時に発車しますか kono ressha wa nanji ni hassha shimasu ka **What time does this train leave?**

... 行きの列車は何番ホームから発車しますか ...yuki no ressha wa nanban hōmu kara hassha shimasu ka **Where do I get the train for ...?**

... には何時に到着しますか ...ni wa nanji ni tōchaku shimasu ka **What time does the train get to ...?**

... からの列車は何時に到着しますか ...kara no ressha wa nanji ni tōchaku shimasu ka **What time does the train from ... get in?**

この列車は...に停まりますか kono ressha wa .. ni tomarimasu ka **Does this train stop at ...?**

この列車は遅れていますか kono ressha wa okurete imasu ka **Is this train running late?**

指定券を持っています　shiteiken wo motte imasu **I have a reservation.**

車掌が検札に来ました　shashō ga kensatsu ni kimashita **The conductor is here to check the tickets.**

この席は空いていますか　kono seki wa aite imasu ka **Is this seat taken ?** (literally, "Is this seat open ?")

どこで乗換えですか　doko de norikae desu ka **Where do I transfer ?**

時刻表はどこにありますか　jikokuhyō wa doko ni arimasu ka **Where is the time-table ?**

近ごろは自動改札が増えました　chikagoro wa jidōkaisatsu ga fuemashita **Nowadays you see more and more automatic wickets.**

b. buses

バス停はどこですか　basutei wa doko desu ka **Where is the bus stop ?**

... 行きのバスの発着所はどこですか　...yuki no basu no hatchakujo wa doko desu ka **Where do I get the bus for ... ?**

このバスは... に停まりますか　kono basu wa ...ni tomarimasu ka **Does this bus stop at ... ?**

... までどのぐらい時間がかかりますか　...made dono gurai jikan ga kakarimasu ka **How long does it take to get to ... ?**

定期観光バスに乗りたい　teiki kankōbasu ni noritai **I want to ride a scheduled sightseeing bus.**

そのバスは何時に... に着きますか　sono basu wa nanji ni ...ni tsukimasu ka **What time does the bus reach ... ?**

そのバスは何時に発車しますか　sono basu wa nanji ni hassha shimasu ka **What time does the bus leave ?**

このバスはどのぐらいの間隔で出ていますか　kono basu wa donogurai no kankaku de dete imasu ka **How often does this bus leave ?**

次のバスは何時ですか　tsugi no basu wa nanji desu ka **What time is the next bus ?**

... の近くを通りますか　...no chikaku wo tōrimasu ka **Does the bus pass near ... ?**

... 行きのバスはどれですか　...yuki no basu wa dore desu ka **Which is the bus for ... ?**

... まで行きたい　...made ikitai **I want to go to ....**

どこで降りたらいいでしょうか　doko de oritara ii deshō ka **Where should I get off ?**

最終バスは出てしまいましたか　saishūbasu wa dete shimaimashita ka **Has the last**

bus already left ?

c. taxis

タクシー乗り場はどこですか　takushīnoriba wa doko desu ka **Where is the taxi stand ?**

空車が来ました　kūsha ga kimashita **Here comes an empty taxi.**

… ホテルまで行って下さい　...hoteru made itte kudasai **Take me to the ... Hotel.**

遅れているので少し急いでくれませんか　okurete iru no de sukoshi isoide kuremasen ka **I'm late, so could you go a little faster ?**

ここで止って下さい　koko de tomatte kudasai **Stop here, please.**

待っていて下さい　matte ite kudasai **Wait for me, please.**

名所旧跡がみたい　meishokyūseki ga mitai **I want to go sightseeing.**

そこは遠いですか　soko wa tōi desu ka **Is it very far from here ?**

… までどのぐらいの時間ですか　...made dono gurai no jikan desu ka **How long does it take to get there ?**

いくらですか　ikura desu ka **How much is it ?**

d. airplanes

航空会社の営業所はどこにありますか　kōkūgaisha no eigyōsho wa doko ni arimasu ka **Where is the airline office ?**

日曜日の午後の便で... まで3席予約したい　nichiyōbi no gogo no bin de ...made sanseki yoyaku shitai **I want 3 tickets to ... on the Sunday afternoon flight.**

金曜日に... までの便がありますか　kinyōbi ni ...made no bin ga arimasu ka **Is there a flight to ... on Friday ?**

その便は何時に発ちますか　sono bin wa nanji ni tachimasu ka **What time does that flight leave ?**

その便は何時に到着しますか　sono bin wa nanji ni tōchaku shimasu ka **What time does that flight arrive ?**

… の予約をキャンセルして下さい　...no yoyaku wo kyanseru shite kudasai **Please cancel my reservation for ...**

予約を変更したい　yoyaku wo henkō shitai **I want to change my reservation.**

次の便は何時ですか　tsugi no bin wa nanji desu ka **When is the next flight ?**

市内から空港までのバスがありますか　shinai kara kūkō made no basu ga arimasu ka **Is there a bus from the city center to the airport ?**

e. boats

その船は何時に出航ですか　sono fune wa nanji ni shukkō desu ka **What time does the boat leave ?**

次の出航は何時ですか　tsugi no shukkō wa nanji desu ka **When does the next boat leave ?**

その船はどこに入港ですか　sono fune wa doko ni nyūkō desu ka **What stops does the boat make ?**

その船は... に寄港しますか　sono fune wa ...ni kikō shimasu ka **Does the boat stop at ... ?**

... まで船便がありますか　...made funabin ga arimasu ka **Is there a boat to ... ?**

この船でどのぐらい時間がかかりますか　kono fune de dono gurai jikan ga kakarimasu ka **How much time does this boat take to get there ?**

一人用船室を予約できますか　hitoriyō senshitsu wo yoyaku dekimasu ka **Can I reserve a single stateroom ?**

部屋にはいくつ寝台がありますか　heya ni wa ikutsu shindai ga arimasu ka **How many beds are there in the stateroom ?**

いつ入港しますか　itsu nyūkō shimasu ka **When will we reach port ?**

何時に乗船しなければなりませんか　nanji ni jōsen shinakereba narimasen ka **By what time do we have to be on board ?**

港にどのぐらい停泊しますか　minato ni dono gurai teihaku shimasu ka **How long will the boat stay in port ?**

f. cars

運転免許証を持っています　unten menkyoshō wo motte imasu **I have a driver's license.**

友人とドライブに出かけましょう　yūjin to doraibu ni dekakemashō **Let's go for a drive with some friends.**

いい車ですね. 自家用車ですか　ii kuruma desu ne. jikayōsha desu ka **Nice car. Is it yours ?**

いいえ. レンタカーです　iie. rentakā desu **No, it's rented.**

どこで車を借りられますか　doko de kuruma wo kariraremasu ka **Where can I rent a car ?**

レンタカーは1時間いくらですか　rentakā wa ichijikan ikura desu ka **What's the fee per hour to rent this car ?**

一番近いガソリンスタンドはどこですか　ichiban chikai gasorinsutando wa doko desu ka **Where is the nearest gas station ?**

満タンにして下さい　mantan ni shite kudasai **Fill it up, please.**

ガソリン，リッターあたりいくらですか　gasorin, rittā atari ikura desu ka **How much is gasoline per liter ?**

洗車して下さい　sensha shite kudasai **Wash the car, please.**

道路地図はありますか　dōrochizu wa arimasu ka **Do you have a road map ?**

駐車場はどこですか　chūshajō wa doko desu ka **Where is the parking lot ?**

ここは駐車禁止ですか　koko wa chūsha kinshi desu ka **Is this a no parking zone ?**

今どこでしょうか　ima doko deshō ka **Where are we now ?**

地図で示して下さい　chizu de shimeshite kudasai **Show me on the map.**

次のドライブインで昼食にしましょう　tsugi no doraibuin de chūshoku ni shimashō **Let's have lunch at the next drive-in.**

… にはどう行けばいいですか　...ni wa dō ikeba ii desu ka **How do you get to … ?**

… はどこにありますか　...wa doko ni arimasu ka **Where is … ?**

… への自動車道にはどう行けばいいですか　...e no jidōshadō ni wa dō ikeba ii desu ka **How do you get to the expressway for … ?**

… へはどの道を行けば一番いいですか　...e wa dono michi wo ikeba ichiban ii desu ka **What's the best road to … ?**

… までどのぐらいの距離がありますか　...made dono gurai no kyori ga arimasu ka **How far is it to … ?**

… に夕刻までには着くのでしょうか　...ni yūkoku made ni wa tsuku no deshō ka **Will we reach … by evening ?**

高速道路は混んでいます　kōsokudōro wa konde imasu **The expressway is clogged with heavy traffic.**

渋滞に巻き込まれました　jūtai ni makikomaremashita **I got caught in heavy traffic.**

抜け道がありますか　nukemichi ga arimasu ka **Is there a back road to get around the traffic ?**

このまま5キロほどまっすぐ行って下さい　kono mama 5 kiro hodo massugu itte kudasai **Go straight along this road for 5 kilometers.**

次の信号を右に曲って下さい　tsugi no shingō wo migi ni magatte kudasai **Turn right at the next signal.**

車の鍵（ぎ）をなくさないように　kuruma no kagi wo nakusanai yō ni **Don't lose your car keys.**

　　　some road signs

右側通行　migigawa tsūkō **keep right**

一方通行道路　ippōtsūkōdōro **one way**

迂回　ukai **detour**

駐車禁止　chūsha kinshi **no parking**

追い越し禁止　oikoshi kinshi **no passing**

進入禁止　shinnyū kinshi **no entry**

前方道路工事中　zenpō dōro kōjichū **construction ahead**

11. Hotels

安くてよいホテルを紹介して下さい　yasukute yoi hoteru wo shōkai shite kudasai **Can you tell me the name of a hotel that is good and also cheap?**

今夜部屋はありますか　kon-ya heya wa arimasu ka **Do you have a vacancy for tonight?**

2人で泊まれる部屋がありますか　futari de tomareru heya ga arimasu ka **Do you have a room for two?**

シングルの部屋を3室予約します　shinguru no heya wo sanshitsu yoyaku shimasu **I would like to reserve 3 single rooms.**

その部屋は何階にありますか　sono heya wa nangai ni arimasu ka **What floor is that room on?**

2階の部屋は空いていますか　nikai no heya wa aite imasu ka **Do you have a room on the second floor?**

この部屋にします　kono heya ni shimasu **I'll take this room.**

別の部屋がありませんか　betsu no heya ga arimasen ka **Don't you have some other room?**

ツインしかありません　tsuin shika arimasen **We only have a twin room.**

空き室はこれだけです　akishitsu wa kore dake desu **This is the only vacancy we have.**

和室の部屋はありますか　washitsu no heya wa arimasu ka **Do you have a Japanese-style room?**

この部屋は1泊いくらですか　kono heya wa ippaku ikura desu ka **What's the rate for this room?**

もっと安い部屋はありませんか　motto yasui heya wa arimasen ka **Don't you have something cheaper?**

明朝7:30分に起して下さい　myōchō shichiji sanjuppun ni okoshite kudasai **Please wake me up at 7:30 tomorrow morning.**

私の部屋にはタオルがありません　watashi no heya ni wa taoru ga arimasen **There are no towels in my room.**

シーツが汚れています　shītsu ga yogorete imasu **The sheets are dirty.**

トイレの水が流れません　toire no mizu ga nagaremasen **The toilet won't flush.**

シャワーの出がよくありません　shawā no de ga yoku arimasen **There's no pressure in the shower.**

窓が空きません．開けて下さい　mado ga akimasen. akete kudasai **I can't get the window open. Please open it.**

暑すぎます　atsusugimasu **It's too hot in here.**

暖房を強くできますか　danbō wo tsuyoku dekimasu ka **Can you turn up the heat?**

冷房がきいていません　reibō ga kiite imasen **The air conditioning isn't working.**

鍵(ぎ)を下さい　kagi wo kudasai **Give me my key, please.**

私宛のメッセージがありますか　watashi ate no messēji ga arimasu ka **Are there any messages for me?**

この洋服を洗濯してほしい　kono yōfuku wo sentaku shite hoshii **I want to get this dress cleaned.**

このスーツにアイロンを掛けてほしい　kono sūtsu ni airon wo kakete hoshii **I want to get this suit pressed.**

明日の午前中までにできますか　myōnichi no gozenchū made ni dekimasu ka **Can you have it done by tomorrow morning?**

食堂はどこですか　shokudō wa doko desu ka **Where is the dining room?**

明後日の朝立ちます　asatte no asa tachimasu **I'll be leaving the day after tomorrow in the morning.**

勘定書きを用意してくれますか　kanjōgaki wo yōi shite kuremasu ka **Will you get my bill ready, please?**

荷物を下におろしていただけますか　nimotsu wo shita ni oroshite itadakemasu ka **Can you have my luggage taken downstairs, please?**

10時にタクシーを1台呼んでいただけますか　jūji ni takushī wo ichidai yonde itadakemasu ka **Will you call me a taxi for 10 o'clock, please?**

お世話になりました　o-sewa ni narimashita **I enjoyed my stay.**

12. Leisure time

a. sightseeing

名所旧跡を見物しましょう　meishokyūseki wo kenbutsu shimashō **Let's go sightseeing.**

ガイドブックを持ってきましたか　gaidobukku wo motte kimashita ka **Did you bring the guidebook?**

当地の見所は何ですか　tōchi no midokoro wa nan desu ka **What is there to see**

around here ?

この建物は何ですか　kono tatemono wa nan desu ka **What is this building ?**

いつ建てられましたか　itsu tateraremashita ka **When was it built ?**

誰(%)が建てましたか　dare ga tatemashita ka **Who built it ?**

このお寺は何と言いますか　kono o-tera wa nan to iimasu ka **What's the name of this temple ?**

これは美術館ですか　kore wa bijutsukan desu ka **Is this an art museum ?**

... は何時に開きますか　...wa nanji ni akimasu ka **What time does ... open ?**

何曜日が休館ですか　nanyōbi ga kyūkan desu ka **What days is it closed on ?**

入場料はいくらですか　nyūjōryō wa ikura desu ka **How much is the entrance fee ?**

切符はどこで買えますか　kippu wa doko de kaemasu ka **Where do they sell the tickets ?**

カメラを持ってきましたか　kamera wo motte kimashita ka **Did you bring your camera ?**

写真をとって下さい　shashin wo totte kudasai **Take a picture of that.**

写真をとってもいいですか　shashin wo totte mo ii desu ka **Is it all right to take pictures ?**

撮影は禁止です　satsuei wa kinshi desu **Picture-taking is forbidden.**

ガイドさんについて行って下さい　gaidosan ni tsuite itte kudasai **Follow the guide.**

ガイドは英語を話せますか　gaido wa eigo wo hanasemasu ka **Can the guide speak English ?**

ガイドはいりません　gaido wa irimasen **I don't need a guide.**

少し足をのばしてみましょう　sukoshi ashi wo nobashite mimashō **Let's walk on a little further.**

城に行くのはどのバスですか　shiro ni iku no wa dono basu desu ka **Which is the bus that goes to the castle ?**

... に行く道はこれですか　...ni iku michi wa kore desu ka **Is this the road that goes to ... ?**

... に行くにはどう行ったらよいですか　...ni iku ni wa dō ittara yoi desu ka **How can I get to ... ?**

歩いて行けますか　aruite ikemasu ka **Is it close enough to walk ?**

当地の名物料理は何ですか　tōchi no meibutsuryōri wa nan desu ka **What kind of cooking is this place known for ?**

有名なお店を教えて下さい　yūmei na o-mise wo oshiete kudasai **Can you tell me the names of important stores in this area ?**

土産には何を買ったらいいですか　miyage ni wa nani wo kattara ii desu ka **What kind of souvenirs should I buy to take home with me ?**

民芸品のお店を紹介して下さい　mingeihin no o-mise wo shōkai shite kudasai **Can you direct me to a place that sells folk art ?**

b. sports

プロ野球の観戦に行きたい　puroyakyū no kansen ni ikitai **I want to go to a professional baseball game.**

一番安い席はいくらですか　ichiban yasui seki wa ikura desu ka **How much is the cheapest ticket ?**

何時に始まりますか　nanji ni hajimarimasu ka **What time does the game start ?**

テニスをやりたい　tenisu wo yaritai **I want to play tennis.**

この海岸で泳げますか　kono kaigan de oyogemasu ka **Can you swim at this beach ?**

水泳禁止です　suiei kinshi desu **It's a no swimming zone.**

私は美容のためにヨガとエアロビクスをやっています　watashi wa biyō no tame ni yoga to earobikusu wo yatte imasu **I do yoga and aerobics for beauty care.**

相撲は日本の国技です　sumō wa nippon no kokugi desu **Sumo is the Japanese national sport.**

兄は柔道5段剣道2段です　ani wa jūdō godan kendō nidan desu **My older brother holds a fifth dan in judo and a second dan in kendo.**

釣りに行きませんか　tsuri ni ikimasen ka **Would you like to go fishing with me ?**

ボートを借りられますか　bōto wo kariraremasu ka **Can we rent a boat ?**

なかなかゴルフの腕前が上がりません　nakanaka gorufu no udemae ga agarimasen **I don't seem to make any progress at golf.**

私はマリンスポーツが得意です　watashi wa marin supōtsu ga tokui desu **I specialize in marine sports.**

運動し過ぎて体じゅうの筋肉が痛い　undō shisugite karadajū no kinniku ga itai **I exercised too hard, and all my muscles are sore.**

子供とキャッチボールをします　kodomo to kyatchibōru wo shimasu **I play catch with my son.**

家族と一緒にアウトドアスポーツを楽しみました　kazoku to issho ni autodoa spōtsu wo tanoshimimashita **I had fun playing outdoors with my family.**

c. events

映画館で何かおもしろいものをやっていますか　eigakan de nanika omoshiroi mono

wo yatte imasu ka **Is there some good movie playing at the theater now ?**

コンサートがありますか　konsāto ga arimasu ka **Are there any concerts scheduled ?**

… デパートで生け花展があります　…depāto de ikebanaten ga arimasu **There is an ikebana* exhibition at the … Department Store.**

… ホールで明晩オペラがあります　…hōru de myōban opera ga arimasu **There is an opera tomorrow night at the … Hall.**

S席のチケットを2枚ほしい　esu-seki no chiketto wo nimai hoshii **I want 2 S tickets*, please.**

来週の火曜日の席を予約したい　raishū no kayōbi no seki wo yoyaku shitai **I want a reserved seat for next Tuesday.**

前売り券は明日から売り出します　maeuriken wa myōnichi kara uridashimasu **Advance tickets go on sale tomorrow.**

開演は何時ですか　kaien wa nanji desu ka **What time does the play start ?**

演目は何ですか　enmoku wa nan desu ka **What's the title of the play ?**

指揮者は誰ですか　shikisha wa dare desu ka **Who is the conductor ?**

配役を教えて下さい　haiyaku wo oshiete kudasai **Tell me the names of the actors.**

プログラムを2部下さい　puroguramu wo nibu kudasai **Two programs, please.**

日本の古典芸能に関心がありますか　nippon no kotengeinō ni kanshin ga arimasu ka **Do you have any interest in classical Japanese theater ?**

歌舞伎は見たことがありますか　kabuki wa mita koto ga arimasu ka **Have you ever been to see Kabuki* ?**

能はまだ一度も見たことがありません　nō wa mada ichido mo mita koto ga arimasen **I have never seen a Noh* play.**

13. Sickness and Accidents

a. sickness

病院へ行きたいのですが，どこがいいでしょうか　byōin e ikitai no desu ga, doko ga ii deshō ka **I want to get medical attention. Can you recommend a good hospital ?**

お医者さんを呼んで下さい　o-ishasan wo yonde kudasai **Please call a doctor.**

救急車を呼んで下さい　kyūkyūsha wo yonde kudasai **Please call an ambulance.**

私は病気です　watashi wa byōki desu **I am sick.**

とても気分が悪い　totemo kibun ga warui **I feel terrible.**

吐き気がする　hakike ga suru **I feel nauseated.**

頭ががんがん痛い　atama ga gangan itai **I have a splitting headache.**

視力が急に落ちた　shiryoku ga kyū ni ochita **My eyesight has gotten bad all of a sudden.**

耳なりがひどいのです　miminari ga hidoi no desu **I have a terrible ringing in my ears.**

虫歯が痛くてたまりません　mushiba ga itakute tamarimasen **I have a terrible toothache.**

歯医者さんへ行かなければなりませんか　haishasan e ikanakereba narimasen ka **Do you need to see a dentist?**

食あたりをしたようです　shokuatari wo shita yō desu **I must've eaten something that didn't agree with me.**

胃をこわしました　i wo kowashimashita **I've got an upset stomach.**

消化不良を起こしました　shōkafuryō wo okoshimashita **I've got indigestion.**

風邪をひきました　kaze wo hikimashita **I have a cold.**

息苦しい　ikigurushii **I have trouble breathing.**

目まいがする　memai ga suru **I feel dizzy.**

私はずっと糖尿病を煩っています　watashi wa zutto tōnyōbyō wo wazuratte imasu **I have had diabetes for a long time.**

全く食欲がありません　mattaku shokuyoku ga arimasen **I have no appetite.**

熟睡できません　jukusui dekimasen **I have trouble sleeping.**

寒気がします　samuke ga shimasu **I'm getting chills.**

咳(½)が止まりません　seki ga tomarimasen **I can't stop coughing.**

持病の...が悪化したようです　jibyō no ...ga akka shita yō desu **His chronic ... has gotten worse.**

足首を捻挫(½^)した　ashikubi wo nenza shita **I sprained my ankle.**

右腕を骨折した　migiude wo kossetsu shita **I broke my right arm.**

やけどをした　yakedo wo shita **I burnt myself.**

切り傷をした　kirikizu wo shita **I cut myself.**

いつからそんな状態ですか　itsu kara sonna jōtai desu ka **How long have you been like this?**

昨日からこんな状態です　sakujitsu kara konna jōtai desu **I've been like this since yesterday.**

どこが痛いですか　doko ga itai desu ka **Where do you hurt?**

寝ていないといけませんか　nete inai to ikemasen ka **Do I absolutely have to stay in bed?**

絶対安静が必要です　zettai ansei ga hitsuyō desu **You need absolute rest.**

口を開けなさい　kuchi wo akenasai **Open your mouth.**

舌を出しなさい　shita wo dashinasai **Stick out your tongue.**

横になりなさい　yoko ni narinasai **Lie down.**

息を吸いなさい〔吐きなさい〕iki wo suinasai 〔hakinasai〕**Breathe in 〔out〕.**

薬局にこの処方箋 (ﾊﾞ) を持って行きなさい　yakkyoku ni kono shohōsen wo motte ikinasai **Take this prescription to a pharmacy.**

1日に3回これを飲んで下さい　ichinichi ni sankai kore wo nonde kudasai **Take this 3 times a day.**

注射しましょう　chūsha shimashō **I'll give you an injection.**

袖(ﾃﾞ)をまくりなさい　sode wo makuri nasai **Roll up your sleeve.**

少し気分がよくなりました　sukoshi kibun ga yoku narimashita **I feel a little better now.**

おかげさまですっかり元気になりました　o-kagesama de sukkari genki ni narimashita **Thanks to you, I am completely cured.**

b. accidents and disasters

交番はどこですか　kōban wa doko desu ka **Is there a police box* around here ?**

警察を呼んで下さい　keisatsu wo yonde kudasai **Call the police.**

大至急110番して下さい　daishikyū hyakutōban shite kudasai **Quick, dial 110.**

領事館に知らせて下さい　ryōjikan ni shirasete kudasai **Please inform my consulate.**

私のカバンが盗まれました　watashi no kaban ga nusumaremashita **My briefcase has been stolen.**

財布をすられました　saifu wo suraremashita **A pickpocket stole my wallet.**

パスポートがなくなりました　pasupōto ga nakunarimashita **My passport is missing.**

交通事故にあいました　kōtsūjiko ni aimashita **I have had a traffic accident.**

... に車をぶつけました　...ni kuruma wo butsukemashita **I crashed my car into a ....**

駅の階段から落ちました　eki no kaidan kara ochimashita **I fell down the stairs in the station.**

雪道で滑りました　yukimichi de suberimashita **I slipped on the snowy street.**

大けがをしました．救急車を呼んで下さい　ōkega wo shimashita. kyūkyūsha wo yonde kudasai **I am badly hurt. Please call an ambulance.**

重傷です．そっと担架に乗せて下さい　jūshō desu. sotto tanka ni nosete kudasai **He is badly hurt. Go easy when you put him on the stretcher.**

意識を失っています．大丈夫でしょうか　ishiki wo ushinatte imasu. daijōbu deshō ka **She's unconscious. Will she be okay ?**

火事だ！火事だ！　kaji da! kaji da! **Fire! Fire!**

消火器はどこですか　shōkaki wa doko desu ka **Where's the fire extinguisher?**

今朝の地震にはびっくりしました　kesa no jishin ni wa bikkuri shimashita **The earthquake this morning was frightening.**

台風の大雨で床下浸水になりました　taifū no ōame de yukashita shinsui ni narimashita **The heavy rains of the typhoon flooded my house almost up to floor level.**

家の前の川が反乱しました　ie no mae no kawa ga hanran shimashita **The river in front of my house overflowed its banks.**

...が行方不明です　...ga yukuefumei desu **...is missing.**

山で遭難しました．救助隊を呼んで下さい　yama de sōnan shimashita. kyūjotai wo yonde kudasai **We've had a bad accident on the mountain. Please call out the rescue squad.**

仕事の現場で事故にあいました　shigoto no genba de jiko ni aimashita **He had an accident at the construction site.**

補償はどうなるのでしょうか　hoshō wa dō naru no deshō ka **What does he have to do to get compensation?**

14. At the office

新入社員の... です．よろしく　shinnyūshain no ...desu. yoroshiku **I have just joined the company and my name is .... I am happy to meet you.**

今日からアルバイトをする事になった... です　kyō kara arubaito wo suru koto ni natta ...desu **My name is ... and I have started today as a part-timer here.**

会社の中を案内しましょうか　kaisha no naka wo annai shimashō ka **Shall I show you around the place?**

名刺をいただけませんか　meishi wo itadakemasen ka **Could I have your card, please?**

私のデスクはどこですか　watashi no desuku wa doko desu ka **Which is my desk?**

初めに何をしたらいいですか　hajime ni nani wo shitara ii desu ka **What's the first thing I need to do?**

この小包を出してきて下さい　kono kozutsumi wo dashite kite kudasai **Go mail this package, will you?**

会議室はどこですか　kaigishitsu wa doko desu ka **Where is the conference room?**

会議を始めます　kaigi wo hajimemasu **The meeting will now come to order.**

食事に行きます　shokuji ni ikimasu **I'm going out to lunch.**

毎日忙しい　mainichi isogashii **Every day is a busy one for me.**

残業をしなければなりません　zangyō wo shinakereba narimasen **I have to work overtime today.**

お先に失礼します　o-saki ni shitsurei shimasu (no English equivalent; said when going home ahead of one's colleagues)

お疲れさまでした　o-tsukaresama deshita (no English equivalent; said as a polite goodbye in response to the above)

忙しくていやになります　isogashikute iya ni narimasu **I'm so busy it isn't funny.**

昨日も終電で帰ったのです　kinō mo shūden de kaetta no desu **Yesterday also I worked till it was time for the last train.**

ストレスがたまっています　sutoresu ga tamatte imasu **I'm all stressed out.**

ファックスは今使っています　fakkusu wa ima tsukatte imasu **The fax machine is busy now.**

コンピュータ通信ができる人はだれですか　konpyūtatsūshin ga dekiru hito wa dare desu ka **Is there someone here who knows how to send electronic mail ?**

コピーをして下さい　kopī wo shite kudasai **Make me a copy of this, please.**

ワープロを打って下さい　wāpuro wo utte kudasai **Type this out on the word processor, will you ?**

ファックスを送って下さい　fakkusu wo okutte kudasai **Fax this out, will you please ?**

これ，すぐお願いできますか　kore, sugu o-negai dekimasu ka **Can you handle this right away, please ?**

今，ちょっと忙しいんだけど　ima, chotto isogashiin da kedo **Sorry, I'm terribly busy right now.**

この件，すぐに調べて下さい　kono ken, sugu ni shirabete kudasai **Will you look into this right away, please ?**

これから課長と打ち合わせです　kore kara kachō to uchiawase desu **I've got a meeting with the manager now.**

出張で大阪へ行ってきました　shutchō de ōsaka e itte kimashita **I just got back from Osaka on a business trip.**

もうじき人事異動があります　mō jiki jinjiidō ga arimasu **There's going to be some personnel changes soon.**

根回しがうまくいっていません　nemawashi ga umaku itte imasen **The prearrangements* aren't going well.**

忘年会はだれが幹事ですか　bōnenkai wa dare ga kanji desu ka **Who's in charge of the bonenkai* ?**

二次会はどこに決まりましたか　nijikai wa doko ni kimarimashita ka **Where are**

you going for the nijikai* ?

彼は企画部のベテランです　kare wa kikakubu no beteran desu **He's a veteran employee of the planning department.**

この資料に目を通して下さい　kono shiryō ni me wo tōshite kudasai **I want you to read through this material, would you ?**

このパソコンの操作を教えて下さい　kono pasokon no sōsa wo oshiete kudasai **Can you show me how to run this computer ?**

... さんを応接室へお通し下さい　...san wo ōsetsushitsu e o-tōshi kudasai **Show ... to the reception room, please.**

帰りにいっぱい飲みませんか　kaeri ni ippai nomimasen ka **How about a drink on the way home ?**

もういっぱいいかがですか　mō ippai ikaga desu ka **Have another drink ?**

ちょっと酔ったからタクシーで帰ります　chotto yotta kara takushī de kaerimasu **I'm drunk, so I'll take a taxi home.**

仕事にやっと慣れました　shigoto ni yatto naremashita **I've finally gotten used to my work.**

昇進おめでとうございます　shōshin omedetō gozaimasu **Congratulations on your promotion.**

... についてご意見を聞かせて下さい　...ni tsuite go-iken wo kikasete kudasai **We'd like to hear your opinion on this matter.**

会社を辞めることにしました　kaisha wo yameru koto ni shimashita **I have decided to leave the company.**

転職することに決めました　tenshoku suru koto ni kimemashita **I have decided to look for a new job.**

15. Calendar events

a. January

日本のお正月は初めてです　nihon no o-shōgatsu wa hajimete desu **This is my first experience of the New Year's celebration in Japan.**

明けましておめでとうございます　akemashite omdetō gozaimasu **Happy New Year !**

初詣(ﾃ)では人がいっぱいでした　hatsumōde wa hito ga ippai deshita **The temples and shrines were crowded with people out for the first prayers of the year.**

みんなで百人一首をやりませんか　minna de hyakuninisshu wo yarimasen ka **How about all of us playing hyakunin-isshu* ?**

雑煮とお節料理を召し上がれ　zōni to o-sechiryōri wo meshiagare **Help yourself to**

the zoni* and New Year's dishes.

年賀状がたくさん来ました　nengajō ga takusan kimashita **I received a whole lot of New Year's cards.**

b. February

2月3日は節分です　nigatsu mikka wa setsubun desu **February 3 is the setsubun* festivity.**

冬が終わって新春を迎える日です　fuyu ga owatte shinshun wo mukaeru hi desu **It is the day for celebrating the end of winter and the advent of spring.**

豆まきをして家の中に福を呼び込みます　mamemaki wo shite ie no naka ni fuku wo yobikomimasu **People throw beans and invoke happiness on their households.**

バレンタインデーは憂鬱(⅔)です　barentaindē wa yūutsu desu **I hate Valentine's Day.**

どうしてチョコレート売り場に女性が殺到するのか不思議です　dōshite chokorēto uriba ni josei ga sattō suru no ka fushigi desu **I never cease to wonder at all those women and girls crowding the chocolate candy counters.**

c. March

3月3日は桃の節句です　sangatsu mikka wa momo no sekku desu **March 3 is the peach blossom festival.**

女の子のいる家ではお雛(½)様を飾ります　onna no ko no iru ie de wa o-hinasama wo kazarimasu **In households with female children they set up a display of dolls.**

そろそろお花見のシーズンですね　sorosoro o-hanami no shīzun desu ne **It's about time for the cherry blossom season.**

桜の花が満開になりました　sakura no hana ga mankai ni narimashita **The cherry trees are in full blossom.**

卒業式帰りの女子大生をよく見かけます　sotsugyōshikigaeri no joshigakusei wo yoku mikakemasu **A conspicuous sight is women university students returning from their graduation ceremony.**

d. April

エープリルフールで以前ひどいいたずらをされました　ēpurirufūru de izen hidoi itazura wo saremashita **I once had a terrible prank played on me on April Fools' Day.**

新入生がお母さんの手に引かれて学校へ行きます　shinnyūsei ga o-kaasan no te ni

hikarete gakkō e ikimasu **Little children walk hand in hand with their mothers to their first day of school.**

会社も新しい社員が入って活気に満ちています　kaisha mo atarashii shain ga haitte kakki ni michite imasu **Companies are busy welcoming their new employees.**

e. May

5月5日は端午の節句です　gogatsu itsuka wa tango no sekku desu **May 5 is the Boys' Festival.**

男の子のいる家では鯉(こい)のぼりを飾ります　otoko no ko no iru ie de wa koinobori wo kazarimasu **Households with male children fly big cloth carps on a pole.**

まちにまったゴールデンウイークの到来　machi ni matta gōruden-uīku no tōrai **Now comes the long-awaited Golden Week*.**

今年は何連休ですか　kotoshi wa nanrenkyū desu ka **How many days off will we have this year?**

どこへ行っても混んでいるから家でゴロゴロします　doko e itte mo konde iru kara ie de gorogoro shimasu **Everywhere you go it will be crowded, so I'm just going to lie around at home.**

f. June

梅雨に入りました　tsuyu ni hairimashita **The rainy season has started.**

毎日雨ばかりでうっとうしいですね　mainichi ame bakari de uttōshii desu ne **Isn't it dreary, all this rain day in and day out?**

g. July

7月7日は七夕です　shichigatsu nanoka wa tanabata desu **July 7 is the Star Festival.**

何か星に願いをかけましょうか　nanika hoshi ni negai wo kakemashō ka **Shall we pray to the stars for something?**

ようやく梅雨が上がり暑さがきびしくなりました　yōyaku tsuyu ga agari atsusa ga kibishikunarimashita **The rainy season has ended and the heat has become oppressive.**

土用の丑(うし)の日には夏ばて防止にウナギを食べる習慣です　doyō no ushi no hi ni wa natsubate bōshi ni unagi wo taberu shūkan desu **On the day of the Ox in the dog days of summer, people customarily eat eel so as not to succumb to the heat.**

夏休みの計画は立てましたか　natsuyasumi no keikaku wa tatemashita ka **Have you made your plans for the summer vacation ?**

h. August

海水浴に行きませんか　kaisuiyoku ni ikimasen ka **Do you care to go to the beach with me ?**

お盆の帰省ラッシュのピークはいつですか　o-bon no kisei rasshu no pīku wa itsu desu ka **When is the back-to-the-country rush going to reach its peak during this o-bon* ?**

盆踊りを見に行きましょう　bon-odori wo mi ni ikimashō **Let's go watch the bon-odori*.**

花火大会があります　hanabi taikai ga arimasu **There is going to be a fireworks display.**

金魚すくいはなかなか難しい　kingyōsukui wa nakanaka muzukashii **It's hard to catch goldfish with these paper nets.**

i. September

新学期が始まります　shingakki ga hajimarimasu **The new school term starts.**

今夜は仲秋の名月です　kon-ya wa chūshū no meigetsu desu **This is the night of the harvest moon.**

今年は台風が多いです　kotoshi wa taifū ga ōi desu **There are a lot of typhoons this year.**

j. October

あちこちで運動会があります　achikochi de undōkai ga arimasu **Many schools are having Field Day.**

芸術の秋です、美術館を散策します　geijutsu no aki desu. bijutsukan wo sansaku shimasu **Autumn is the season for art. I like to visit art museums at this time.**

食欲の秋です、また焼き芋(ﾟ)を買ってしまった　shokuyoku no aki desu. mata yaki-imo wo katte shimatta **The autumn air stimulates the appetite. I bought some roasted sweet potatoes again.**

公園の樹々が見事に紅葉しています　kōen no kigi ga migoto ni kōyō shite imasu **The trees in the park are beautiful in their autumn colors.**

k. November

だんだん寒くなってきました　dandan samuku natte kimashita **It is gradually**

getting colder.

あちこちの大学で学園祭が催されます　achikochi no daigaku de gakuensai ga moyōsaremasu **Many universities are holding their school festival.**

l. December

師走は何となく気ぜわしい月です　shiwasu wa nan to naku kizewashii tsuki desu **Somehow December always makes me feel restless.**

クリスマスのプレゼントはもう買いましたか　kurisumasu no purezento wa mō kaimashita ka **Have you finished your Christmas shopping?**

クリスマスイブは誰(だれ)と過ごしますか　kurisumasuibu wa dare to sugoshimasu ka **Who are you going to spend Christmas Eve with?**

年賀状はもう書きましたか　nengajō wa mō kakimashita ka **Have you written your New Year's cards yet?**

忘年会が続いて少し胃がもたれました　bōnenkai ga tsuzuite sukoshi i ga motaremashita **I have been to so many year-end parties that my stomach feels queasy.**

m. Japanese public holidays

Jan. 1 元旦 gantan **New Year's Day**
Jan. 15 成人の日 seijin no hi **Coming-of-Age Day**
Feb. 11 建国記念日 kenkoku kinenbi **National Foundation Day**
March 20 春分の日 shunbun no hi **Spring Equinox**
April 29 緑の日 midori no hi **Nature Day**
May 3 憲法記念日 kenpō kinenbi **Constitution Day**
May 4 国民の休日 kokumin to kyūjitsu **Citizens' Day**
May 5 子供の日 kodomo no hi **Children's Day**
Sept. 15 敬老の日 keirō no hi **Senior Citizens' Day**
Sept 23 秋分の日 shunbun no hi **Autumn Equinox**
Oct. 10 体育の日 taiiku no hi **Sports Day**
Nov. 3 文化の日 bunka no hi **Culture Day**
Nov. 23 勤労感謝の日 kinrō kansha no hi **Labor Day**
Dec. 23 天皇誕生日 tennō tanjōbi **The Emperor's Birthday**
振替休日 furikae kyūjitsu **substitute holiday***

16. Dates and Times

日 hi/nichi **day**
朝 asa **morning**

昼 hiru **noon/daytime**
夕方 yūgata **evening**
夜 yoru **night**
午前 gozen **morning** (from daybreak to noon)
正午 shōgo **12 noon**
午後 gogo **afternoon**
真夜中 mayonaka **midnight**
今朝 kesa **this morning**
午前中 gozenchū **during the morning**
深夜 shin-ya **late at night**
今日 kyō **today**
昨日 kinō/sakujitsu **yesterday**
明日 ashita/asu/myōnichi **tomorrow**
明後日 asatte/myōgonichi **the day after tomorrow**
一昨日 ototoi/issakujitsu **the day before yesterday**
週 shū **week**
今週 konshū **this week**
先週 senshū **last week**
来週 raishū **next week**
日曜日 nichiyōbi **Sunday**
月曜日 getsuyōbi **Monday**
火曜日 kayōbi **Tuesday**
水曜日 suiyōbi **Wednesday**
木曜日 mokuyōbi **Thursday**
金曜日 kin-yōbi **Friday**
土曜日 doyōbi **Saturday**
月 tsuki/getsu **month**
今月 kongetsu **this month**
先月 sengetsu **last month**
来月 raigetsu **next month**
1 月 ichigatsu **January**
2 月 nigatsu **February**
3 月 sangatsu **March**
4 月 shigatsu **April**
5 月 gogatsu **May**
6 月 rokugatsu **June**
7 月 shichigatsu **July**

8月 hachigatsu **August**

9月 kugatsu **September**

10月 jūgatsu **October**

11月 jūichigatsu **November**

12月 jūnigatsu **December**

年 nen/toshi **year**

今年 kotoshi/konnen **this year**

去年 kyonen **last year**

昨年 sakunen **last year**

来年 rainen **next year**

西暦 seireki **Western calendar year**

1993年 senkyūhyakukyūjūsannen **nineteen ninety-three**

年号 nengō **Japanese calendar year name**

平成5年 heisei gonen **the fifth year of Heisei (= 1993)**

季節 kisetsu **season**

四季 shiki **the four seasons**

春 haru **spring**

夏 natsu **summer**

秋 aki **autumn/fall**

冬 fuyu **winter**

閏年 uruudoshi **leap year**

今日は何日ですか kyō wa nannichi desu ka **What's today's date?**

3月3日です sangatsu mikka desu **It's March (the) third.**

今日は何曜日ですか kyō wa nan-yōbi desu ka **What day of the week is it today?**

水曜日です suiyōbi desu **It's Wednesday.**

今年は何年ですか kotoshi wa nannen desu ka **What year is it?**

1993年です senkyūhyakukyūjūsannen desu **It's nineteen ninety-three.**

今何時ですか ima nanji desu ka **What time is it?**

8時15分です hachiji jūgofun desu **It's eight fifteen.**

10時15分前です jūji jūgofun mae desu **It's fifteen to ten.**

いつ来ましたか itsu kimashita ka **When did you get here?**

お昼過ぎです o-hirusugi desu **A little after noon.**

GLOSSARY

bon-odori: A community dance held on certain evenings around the time of the o-bon festival.

bonenkai: A traditional party held at the end of the year by various work and social groups to bring the year to a happy end.

choshi: A tokkuri (see below) full of sake (see below).

Golden Week: Seven or more days, usually beginning April 29, during which 4 national holidays and 1 or 2 weekends occur.

government postcards: Postcards issued by the government on which the postage has been prepaid, so that no further postage is necessary; said in contrast to picture postcards etc which require a postage stamp.

hyakunin-isshu: A card game played at New Year's.

ikebana: The Japanese art of flower arranging.

Kabuki: A form of classical Japanese drama based on popular legends, with male actors in both male and female roles.

miso: Fermented bean paste.

nijikai: An informal drinking party taking place after a more formal party or banquet.

Noh: A form of classical Japanese drama based on religious or mythical themes and featuring very stylized dancing.

o-bon: The festival of the dead, held to commemorate one's ancestors. It is marked in modern times by a great exodus from the cities as people return to their ancestral homes in the country for the celebration. In most regions it is held on August 13, 14, and 15.

police box: A small local police station manned by 2 or more policemen 24 hours a day. It usually consists of a small office with toilet and sleeping facilities. In the cities there may be one every several hundred meters, depending on the population density.

prearrangements: Also called by their Japanese name, *nemawashi*, such arrangements usually consist of informal, often secret meetings with individual members of some decision-making committee etc to argue one's case before the full committee meets.

S tickets: Tickets to the S seats, i.e., the best reserved seats in the house in a

theater or concert hall.

sake: A kind of wine made from fermented rice and often drunk hot.

setsubun: A festivity where people throw beans toward the outside of their houses to ward off devils.

shinkansen: The Japanese name for the so-called "bullet trains" that run at great speeds on wide, elevated tracks.

substitute holiday: The name given to a Monday observed as a holiday following a national holiday that fell on a Sunday.

tempura: Fish, shellfish, and vegetables dipped in batter and fried in deep fat. Spelled with an *n* in romaji, but with an *m* as an English loan word.

tokkuri: A small bottle for heating sake (see above).

ume: A green, very sour relative of the plum, used for various kinds of pickles and flavorings. Its tree, also called ume, is also cultivated for its beautiful white, pink, or red blossoms, which open in very early spring.

wasabi: A kind of horseradish, cultivated in cold mountain streams, and used as a pungent spice.

zoni: A broth containing vegetables and mochi (see page 605) and eaten at New Year's.